ENCYCLOPEDIA OF INTERNATIONAL DEVELOPMENT

International development is now a major global activity and the focus of the rapidly growing academic discipline of development studies. The *Encyclopedia of International Development* provides definitions and discussions of the key concepts, controversies, and actors associated with international development for a readership of development workers, teachers and students. With 600 entries, ranging in length from shorter factual studies to more in-depth essays, a comprehensive system of cross references and a full index, it is the most definitive guide to international development yet published.

Development is more than a simple increase in a country's wealth and living conditions. It also implies increasing people's choices and freedoms; it is change that is inclusive and empowering. Development theory and practice has important applications to questions of economic growth, trade, governance, education, health care, gender rights and environmental protection, and it involves issues such as international aid, peacekeeping, famine relief, and strategies against HIV/AIDS. The *Encyclopedia* treats these topics and many more, and provides critical analyses of important actors within development such as the United Nations and World Bank, non-governmental organizations and corporations.

Contributors to this volume reflect the multidisciplinary and international nature of the subject. They come from social science disciplines such as economics, international studies, political science and anthropology, and from specialties such as medicine. This encyclopedia will provide crucial information for universities, students and professional organizations involved with international development, or those interested in related topics such as international studies or other studies of social and economic change today.

Tim Forsyth is Senior Lecturer at the Development Studies Institute, London School of Economics, UK.

ENCYCLOPEDIA OF INTERNATIONAL DEVELOPMENT

Edited by Tim Forsyth

Routledge
Taylor & Francis Group

LONDON AND NEW YORK

First published 2005
by Routledge
2 Park Square, Milton Park, Abingdon, Oxon OX14 4RN

Simultaneously published in the USA and Canada
by Routledge
270 Madison Ave, New York, NY 10016

Routledge is an imprint of the Taylor & Francis Group

© 2005 Routledge

Typeset in Goudy and Optima by Newgen Imaging Systems (P) Ltd, India

Printed and bound in Great Britain by
TJ International Ltd, Padstow, Cornwall

British Library Cataloguing in Publication Data
A catalogue record for this book is available from the British Library

Library of Congress Cataloging in Publication Data
A catalog record for this title has been requested

ISBN 0–415–25342–X

Contents

Editorial team

General editor

Tim Forsyth
London School of Economics, UK

Consultant editors

Bina Agarwal
University of Delhi, India

Barbara Harriss-White
University of Oxford, UK

Mahmood Mamdani
Columbia University, USA

Christine Obbo
Center of African Studies,
University of London, UK

Gabriel Palma
Cambridge University, UK

James Scott
Yale University, USA

Judith Tendler
Massachusetts Institute of Technology, USA

Robert Hunter Wade
London School of Economics, UK

List of contributors

W. Neil Adger
University of East Anglia, UK

Bina Agarwal
University of Delhi, India

Oscar Alfranca
Catalunya Polytechnic University,
Barcelona, Spain

Tim Allen
London School of Economics, UK

P. B. Anand
University of Bradford, UK

Leonora C. Angeles
University of British Columbia, Canada

Vibha Arora
University of Oxford, UK

B. Mak Arvin
Trent University, Canada

Richard M. Auty
University of Lancaster, UK

Prerna Banati
University of Cambridge, UK

Jayanta Bandyopadhyay
Indian Institute of Management, India

Imelda Bates
Liverpool School of Tropical Medicine, UK

Simon Batterbury
University of Melbourne, Australia

Pinar Bilgin
Bilkent University, Turkey

Michael Blakemore
University of Durham, UK

Urmilla Bob
University of Durban-Westville, South Africa

Pablo Shiladitya Bose
York University, Toronto, Canada

Deborah Fahy Bryceson
University of Leiden, The Netherlands

John Cameron
University of East Anglia, UK

Edward R. Carr
University of South Carolina, USA

José Esteban Castro
University of Oxford, UK

Erlet Cater
University of Reading, UK

Sanjoy Chakravorty
Temple University, USA

Sylvia Chant
London School of Economics, UK

Graham Chapman
University of Lancaster, UK

Ipsita Chatterjee
Jawaharlal Nehru University, India

Dawn Chatty
University of Oxford, UK

Peter Chua
San Jose State University, USA

Michele Clara
United Nations Industrial Development
Organisation

Matthew Clarke
Victoria University, Australia

Ernestina Coast
London School of Economics, UK

Dennis Conway
Indiana University, USA

Paul Cook
University of Manchester, UK

Bill Cooke
University of Manchester Institute of
Science and Technology, UK

Stuart Corbridge
University of Miami, USA and London
School of Economics, UK

Julie Cupples
University of Canterbury, New Zealand

Parviz Dabir-Alai
Richmond – The American University in
London, UK

William A. Dando
Indiana State University, USA

Tine Davids
University of Nijmegen, The Netherlands

Claudio O. Delang
National University of Singapore

Julie A. Dercle
California State University, Northridge, USA

Robert J. Dickey
Gyeongju University, South Korea

Felipe Krause Dornelles
Secretariat of Culture, Brasilia, Brazil

Mafalda Duarte
Ministry of Education, Mozambique

Marlène Elias
University of California – Los Angeles, USA

Frank Ellis
University of East Anglia, UK

Helen Elsey
School of Nursing and Midwifery,
University of Southampton, UK

Salvatore Engel-Di Mauro
University of Wisconsin-Stevens Point, USA

James Evans
University of Birmingham, UK

Doug Feremenga
University of California, Irvine, USA

Tim Forsyth
London School of Economics, UK

Chris Garforth
University of Reading, UK

Des Gasper
Institute of Social Studies,
The Hague, The Netherlands

Michael Goldman
University of Minnesota, USA

Markus Goldstein
London School of Economics, UK

Seamus Grimes
National University of Ireland, Galway, Eire

Mark Hampton
University of Kent, UK

Ellen R. Hansen
Emporia State University, Kansas, USA

John Harriss
London School of Economics, UK

Barbara Harriss-White
University of Oxford, UK

Elaine Hartwick
Framingham State College, Massachusetts, USA

Paul Harvey
Overseas Development Institute, London, UK

Terence Hay-Edie
United Nations Development Programme, UK

Tassilo Herrschel
University of Westminster, UK

Nik Heynen
Indiana University, USA

Paul Hoebink
Nijmegen Catholic University, The Netherlands

William R. Horne
York University, Canada

Ulli Huber
University of Liverpool, UK

David Hulme
University of Manchester, UK

I. Niklas Hultin
University of Pennsylvania, USA

Sardar M. N. Islam
Victoria University, Melbourne, Australia

John A. Jackson
Trinity College, Ireland

Rhys Jenkins
University of East Anglia, UK

Craig Johnson
University of Guelph, Canada

Susie Jolly
Institute of Development Studies, UK

Gareth A. Jones
London School of Economics, UK

Uma S. Kambhampati
University of Reading, UK

Cristóbal Kay
Institute of Social Studies,
The Hague, The Netherlands

Peter Kellett
University of Newcastle Upon Tyne, UK

Jane Kim
New School University, New York, USA

Paul Kingsbury
University of Kentucky, USA

Colin Kirkpatrick
Institute for Development Policy and
Management, University of Manchester, UK

Tom Kompas
Australian National University, Australia

Uma Kothari
University of Manchester, UK

Jonathan Krueger
United Nations Institute for Training and
Research (UNITAR), Switzerland

Rachel Simon Kumar
University of Auckland, New Zealand

Anne T. Kuriakose
University of Wisconsin-Madison, USA

Takayoshi Kusago
United Nations Development Programme
(UNDP), Bangkok, Thailand

Claire Lahovary
Institut Universitaire de Hautes Etudes
Internationales, Switzerland

David Land
University of Bristol, UK

Alex Law
University of Abertay, Dundee, UK

Melissa Leach
Institute of Development Studies, UK

Les Levidow
Open University, UK

David Lewis
London School of Economics, UK

Tania Murray Li
Dalhousie University, Canada

Michael Lipton
University of Sussex, UK

Catherine Lloyd
University of Oxford, UK

Peter Lloyd-Sherlock
University of East Anglia, UK

Robyn Lui
Griffith University, Australia

Fergus Lyon
Middlesex University, UK

Joanna Macrae
Overseas Development Institute, UK

A M Mannion
University of Reading, UK

Robin Mansell
Londons School of Economics, UK

Anthony Marcus
University of Melbourne, Australia

Letícia Junqueira Marteleto
Cedeplar, Brazil

Patricia M. Martin
Dartmouth College, USA

Emma E. Mawdsley
University of Birkbeck College,
University of London, UK

Peter Mayell
University of Canterbury, New Zealand

Kathleen McAffee
Yale University, USA

William D. McCourt
University of Manchester, UK

Cathy McIlwaine
Queen Mary, University of London, UK

Philip D. McMichael
Cornell Universiy, USA

Konstantinos A. Melachroinos
Queen Mary, University of London, UK

Joseph Mensah
York University, Toronto, Canada

Clare Mills
University of Newcastle, UK

William B. T. Mock
John Marshall Law School, Chicago, USA

Janet Henshall Momsen
University of California at Davis, USA

Vadi Moodley
University of Durban-Westville, South Africa

Karen Moore
University of Manchester, UK

Peter Muennig
Sophie Davis Medical School at
City University of New York, USA

Tanja R. Müller
University of Wageningen, The Netherlands

Warwick E. Murray
Victoria University of Wellington, New Zealand

S Mansoob Murshed
Institute of Social Studies, The Netherlands

Nici Nelson
Goldsmiths College, University of London, UK

Lorraine Nencel
University of Amsterdam, The Netherlands

Edward Newman
United Nations University, Tokyo, Japan

Lenore Newman
York University, Canada

Olga Nieuwenhuys
University of Amsterdam, The Netherlands

Celestine Nyamu-Musembi
Institute of Development Studies, UK

Christine Obbo
Centre for African Studies,
University of London, UK

Dele Ogunseitan
University of California at Irvine, USA

Philip Anthony O'Hara
Curtin University, Perth, Australia

Paul Okojie
Manchester Metropolitan University, UK

Gunnar Olesen
University of Roskilde, Denmark

Kathleen O'Reilly
University of Illinois at Urbana-Champagne, USA

Moses A. Osiro
Kenyatta University, Nairobi, Kenya

Jouni Paavola
University of East Anglia, UK

Firooza Pavri
Emporia State University, Kansas, USA

Richard Peet
Clark University, USA

Richard Perkins
University of Plymouth, UK

Shama Perveen
Indian Institute of Management, India

Pauline E. Peters
Harvard University, USA

Elizabeth Petersen
Australian National University,
Australia

Phillip Petersen
Queensland Medical Laboratory and Queensland
University of Technology, Australia

Ugo Pica Ciamarra
University of Rome, Italy

Aaron Z. Pitluck
University of Wisconsin-Madison, USA

Marcus Power
University of Bristol, UK

Fahim Quadir
York University, Canada

Christopher J. Rees
University of Manchester, UK

Simon Reid-Henry
University of Cambridge, UK

Joe Remenyi
Deakin University, Australia

Marieke Riethof
University of Amsterdam, The Netherlands

Mònica Rivera Escrich
Autonomous University of Barcelona, Spain

Peter T. Robbins
Cranfield University, UK

Dianne Rocheleau
Clark University, USA

Dennis Rodgers
London School of Economics, UK

Pauline Rose
University of Sussex, UK

Benedetta Rossi
London School of Economics, UK

Donna D. Rubinoff
University of Colorado-Boulder, USA

Mesbah-us-Saleheen
Jahangirnagar University, Bangladesh

Ton Salman
Vrije Universiteit, The Netherlands

Emma Samman
University of Oxford, UK

Rickie Sanders
Temple University, Philadelphia, USA

Matteo Scaramella
Abaton S.R.L., Italy

Kathrin Schreckenberg
Overseas Development Insitute, UK

Frans J. Schuurman
University of Nijmegen, Netherlands

Wendy Shaw
Southern Illinois University Edwardsville, USA

J. T. W. Sherval
Lothian NHS Board, Edinburgh, UK

David Simon
Royal Holloway, University of London, UK

Ajay Ranjan Singh
University of Delhi, India

Ronald Skeldon
University of Sussex, UK

Leslie Sklair
London School of Economics, UK

Wynet Smith
University of Cambridge, UK

Amara Soonthorndhada
Institute for Population and Social Research, Mahidol University, Bangkok

Jorge Mario Soto Romero
Monterrey Institute of Technology, Mexico City

Aidan Southall
University of Wisconsin-Madison, USA

Paul Spicker
Robert Gordon University, UK

Bertel S. Squire
Liverpool School of Tropical Medicine, UK

Michael J. Starr
Southern Illinois University, USA

Alison Stenning
University of Newcastle, UK

Michael Stocking
University of East Anglia, UK

Donovan Storey
Massey University, New Zealand

Jørn Støvring
University of Roskilde, Denmark

Celina Su
Massachusetts Institute of Technology, USA

Chikako Takeshita
Virginia Tech, USA

Sally Theobald
Liverpool School of Tropical Medicine, UK

John Thoburn
University of East Anglia, UK

Jim Thomas
London School of Economics, UK

Richard M. J. Thurston
Saint Peter's College, NJ, USA

Rachel Tolhurst
Liverpool School for Tropical Medicine

Emma Tomalin
University of Leeds, UK

John Toye
Oxford University, UK

Michael Tribe
University of Bradford, UK

Jeff Turner
Independent Transport Consultant, UK

Sarah Turner
McGill University, Montreal, Canada

Jon D. Unruh
Indiana University, USA

Jan Kees van Donge
Institute of Social Studies, The Hague,
The Netherlands

Francien van Driel
University of Nijmegen, The Netherlands

Paul van Lindert
Utrecht University, The Netherlands

Peter Vandergeest
York University, Canada

Rob Vos
Institute of Social Studies,
The Hague, The Netherlands

Dinesh Vyas
Selly Oak Hospital,
University of Birmingham, UK

Robert Hunter Wade
London School of Economics, UK

Andrew Warren
University College London, UK

Andrew Watterson
University of Stirling, Scotland, UK

Michael Watts
University of California,
Berkeley, USA

Howard White
Institute of Development Studies/World Bank

Jo Woodman
University of Cambridge, UK

Alan Williams
Massey University, New Zealand

Andrew B. Wyatt
University of Sydney, Australia

Ben Wisner
Oberlin College, USA

Henry Wai-chung Yeung
National University of Singapore

Tzen Wong
International Red Cross Federation, Switzerland

Bin Zhou
Southern Illinois University Edwardsville, USA

Introduction

International development is best understood as the production of social change that creates conditions where more and more people can achieve their human potential. It is now a major worldwide activity and the focus of the growing academic discipline of development studies. This encyclopedia presents a summary of the key concepts, controversies, and actors associated with international development for a readership of policymakers, development workers, teachers and students worldwide. The volume contains 600 entries written by more than 200 authors, at a length of nearly half a million words. It is the most definitive guide to international development yet published.

For many people, development mostly refers to reducing poverty and improving living conditions in poor countries. But "development" is much more than this. Development implies increasing people's choices, and respecting their ability to choose, within diverse processes of social and economic change. It is change that is inclusive and empowering. Development is usually associated with topics such as economic growth, governance, education, food production, urban management, and healthcare, especially in developing countries. More dramatically, development also includes peacekeeping, aid, famine relief, fighting HIV/AIDS, and environmental protection. But "development" cannot be reduced to any one of these activities, and comprises complex, inter-connected engagement with economic, political, and social structures. Similarly, development is not restricted to the so-called developing world, but involves richer (and postsocialist) countries too, and is affected by global systems of trade and governance. For these reasons, academic development studies are manifestly multidisciplinary, and contain a variety of approaches. Contributors to this volume come from different social science disciplines such as economics and political science, and from specialties such as medicine.

"Development," then, is a fundamentally contested concept. Much debate has concerned the means and measurement of development. During most of the twentieth century, formal development practice sought to modernize economies by investing in industry and infrastructure, and measured "development" through the index of gross national product per capita. This approach, however, has been criticized for overlooking questions of income distribution, the negative impacts of large development projects on environment and marginalized people, and for failing to indicate the longer-term causes of chronic poverty (Arndt, 1981). By contrast, newer approaches of social or human development emphasize factors such as education, health and the creation of livelihoods for poor people. The United Nations' Human Development Index combines economic wealth with life expectancy and adult literacy. The Gender Empowerment Measure is broader still, by considering political empowerment and equality of opportunities. These approaches begin to recognize the diversity of experiences of development between social divisions including women and men, young and old, people with differing disability, or different ethnicities, classes or caste.

A similar tension is in the definition of development objectives. Critics have suggested that development reflects its roots in Western projects of colonialism and hegemony (Cowen and Shenton, 1996). Some have even called development, "anthropology's evil twin" because, in mirror image to anthropology, it threatens to destroy locality, autonomy, and tradition in developing societies in the name of "progress" (Ferguson, 1997). Today, there are broader definitions of what constitutes "progress," with more attention given to the right of local determination, and the qualities of indigenous knowledge and diverse perspectives on socio-economic life. Nonetheless, the right to development through social, political, and economic change has been acknowledged in the 1948 Universal Declaration of Human Rights and later statements. Various approaches of equitable or people-centered development now seek to encourage bottom-up and locally determined means of assistance. Participatory development invites people targeted or affected by development to participate in defining its objectives and methods.

Despite these trends, development is still controversial, and often associated with imbalances in world trade and power. According to many critics, the structural adjustment programs coordinated by the International Monetary Fund in response to the debt crisis of the 1980s have actually reversed development objectives by increasing poverty and inequality. The World Bank has been criticized for funding large-scale dams and road projects that have damaged environments and people's livelihoods. Trade liberalization and economic globalization, as conducted through the World Trade Organization, are also blamed for empowering powerful countries and transnational corporations at the expense of smaller producers. In response, the World Bank and other organizations have adopted various reforms and new initiatives to address world poverty. But radical critics – such as the World Social Forum – point out that the balance of power remains strongly in favor of richer nations. When the World Bank was established in 1944, the USA alone held nearly 30 percent of its total voting rights. Today, the "Big Five" countries (the USA, UK, Germany, France, and Japan) still control approximately 38 percent of the vote. Moreover, 46 African countries have together only 5 percent of the vote and typically only two of the Bank's 24 Executive Directors.

This encyclopedia summarizes these concerns, but also contains optimistic accounts of development. Development has had many successes.

Agrarian reform and the green revolution – despite some criticisms – have increased food production in many countries. Primary health care and education have helped reduce infant and maternal mortality and increase prospects in various locations. Civil society and non-governmental organizations provide new opportunities for governance. Opportunities for democracy and state reform are widely increasing. Businesses are now actively involved in development via corporate social responsibility and the United Nations' Global Compact. There is growing global dialogue on human rights. Yet, despite these steps, development remains beset with challenges. In 2001, the United Nations called upon richer countries to donate US$7-10 billion per year to combat HIV/AIDS, but this amount has not been reached, and the topic remains a low priority with many donors. Some analysts say global poverty and inequality are growing, not decreasing. Development also faces challenges from changing attitudes to war, security, and international law. There is a need to engage with new concepts and approaches to development critically, to avoid adopting meaningless "buzzwords."

Today, international development is largely defined by the United Nations' Millennium Development Goals, which identify priorities concerning poverty, education, gender equality, HIV/AIDS, the rights of children, healthcare, environmental protection, and cooperative governance. Yet, development will always be broader than these specific concerns. In the words of Nobel-Prize winning economist, Amartya Sen (1999:3), "development requires the removal of major sources of unfreedom: poverty as well as tyranny, poor economic opportunities as well as systematic social deprivation, neglect of public facilities as well as intolerance or activity of repressive states." Increasing public awareness and debate about these challenges are the first steps towards addressing them. This encyclopedia aims to assist in these processes.

References

Arndt, H. (1981) "Economic Development: A Semantic History," *Economic Development and Cultural Change* 29: 457–66.

Cowen, M. and Shenton, R. (1996) *Doctrines of Development*, London and New York: Routledge. See chapter 1: "The Invention of Development."

Ferguson, J. (1997) "Anthropology and Its Evil Twin," pp. 150–75 in Cooper, F. and Packard, R. (eds) *International Development and the Social Sciences: Essays on the History and Politics of Knowledge*, Berkeley CA: University of California Press.

Sen, A. (1999) *Development as Freedom*, Oxford: Oxford University Press.

Note on entries

This encyclopedia contains 600 entries on diverse topics of development. Readers wishing a fast introduction to the subject are advised to turn to the general entries on **economic development**, **participatory development**, and **sociology of development** as starting points before turning to more specific topics.

The encyclopedia entries were selected by the editors to reflect the most important themes in international development. The entries are intended to summarize conceptual debates, rather than present statistical summaries of problems. Readers seeking up-to-date statistical information should access World Bank and United Nations websites as initial sources of information.

Food and Agriculture Organization statistical databases: http://apps.fao.org/

United Nations statistics and databases: http://www.un.org/databases/index.html

United Nations Development Programme Human Development Reports: http://hdr.undp.org/reports/

World Bank data and statistics: http://www.worldbank.org/data/

World Bank World Development Reports: http://econ.worldbank.org/wdr/

The encyclopedia also does not aim to be an inventory or glossary of development organizations, including non-governmental organizations, although many United Nations specialized agencies, international organizations and multilateral development banks are described because they represent important development debates. There is, unfortunately, insufficient space to list all United Nations agencies, or to mention all important development non-governmental organizations.

The words used to define "development" and "developing countries" are also controversial. This encyclopedia uses the terms, "developed" and "developing" countries in general to refer to the usual distinction made between richer and poorer countries. These terms are used in preference to "Third World" or "North" and "South" (see fuller discussion in the entry, **underdevelopment versus LDC versus Third World**). It is, of course, acknowledged that rich and poor people exist in most countries, and that the causes of poverty are not just explained just by national factors.

Acknowledgments

I would like to thank the editorial advisory panel, and especially Bina Agarwal, Christine Obbo and Barbara Harriss-White, for selecting entries and recruiting writers, and for encouragement throughout the project. Some authors who contributed significantly include Leonora Angeles, Stuart Corbridge, Des Gasper, John Harriss, Tania Li, Phil McMichael, Dele Ogunseitan, Paul Okojie, Paul Spicker, Sally Theobald, John Thoburn, Michael Watts, Howard White and Henry Wai-chung Yeung. My colleagues, Tim Allen, Markus Goldstein and Dennis Rodgers deserve special mention for assistance at various stages of the volume. At Routledge, I would like to thank Stephanie Rodgers and Aileen Harvey who helped steer the book to completion.

Tim Forsyth
London, 2004

A

AARHUS CONVENTION *see* Right to Information Movement

absolute versus relative poverty

The distinction between "absolute" and "relative" concepts of **poverty** refers to whether poverty is measured in terms of specified and normative levels (absolute), or in terms of indices that show how one person's poverty or wealth is related to other people (relative). The dominant concept of poverty in developing countries has been an "absolute" one, based in normative standards related to basic physical needs. Absolute poverty has been described "in terms of some absolute level of minimum needs, below which people are regarded as being poor, for purpose of social and government concern, and which does not change over time" (OECD, 1976:63). Minimum needs are typically defined in terms of biological subsistence, such as calorific intake (see **nutrition**). Such measurements have been used in the past as an indication of when governments or aid agencies may start to intervene to reduce poverty (see also **poverty line**). By contrast, studies of poverty in developed societies have tended to use relative concepts of poverty. Some writers understand this in terms of **inequality**: for example, researchers from the **European Union** have identified poverty as "economic distance" from the mainstream, or average expectancies in a society. Townsend (1979:915) has defined relative poverty as "the absence or inadequacy of those diets, amenities, standards, services and activities which are common or customary in society." The distinction between absolute and relative concepts is questionable, and studies in developing countries have increasingly pointed to the social and relational elements in poverty.

See also: basic needs; indicators of development; measuring development; poverty; poverty line; participatory poverty assessment (PPA); poverty measurement

Further reading

OECD (1976) *Public Expenditure on Income Maintenance Programmes*, Paris: OECD.
Townsend, P. (1979) *Poverty in the United Kingdom*, Harmondsworth: Penguin.

PAUL SPICKER

accountability

Accountability is a political and ethical concept that requires decision-makers to be held responsible, either institutionally or personally, for their decisions to those affected by them. As these parties must know about the decisions, accountability relates to and depends upon the information flow that **transparency** provides. Accountability usually is triggered when an official acts contrary to authority, abuses discretion, or simply makes bad judgments. The exercise of accountability oversight may come from a supervisor, media, watchdog

non-governmental organizations (NGOs), or the public working through politics.

Accountability is commonly applied to the administration of the public sector, but increasingly refers to private-sector businesses. It may be differentiated from command-and-control forms of regulation because it considers actions already taken, whereas control forms of regulation are exercised before action. Accountability may be categorized as vertical (owed to those hierarchically above the decision-maker), horizontal (owed to peer groups), or downward (owed to those subject to the decision-maker's authority).

Development theorists have argued that a lack of political accountability may contribute towards autocracy, authoritarianism and a failed rule of law within governments. A lack of economic accountability may also encourage **corruption**, and the failure of market **institutions**. Administrative bureaucracies that develop where civil institutions and markets are weak tend to institutionalize information in ways that protect officials from risk. Such issues are common in nations lacking well-developed public structures, strong **media** and effective NGO activity. Accepting the principles of accountability helps to break this culture of protection and secrecy, and allows society to influence policy options more freely.

Accountability may operate within a nations formal political systems such as elections or party caucuses or public outcry, if it reminds political leaders of electoral mandates and vulnerability. Legislative investigations, such as the Watergate hearings in the USA in 1974, or legal proceedings, where executive officials are judged for actions exceeding authority, provide other approaches. A sound judicial system is thus fundamental to accountability, provided it has resources adequate to its workload, the poor have decent access, and it reports case decisions. Transparent legislative procedures, including open hearings where the committee or legislative work actually occurs, are essential to legislative accountability at election time.

Articles 19 to 25 of the **Universal Declaration of Human Rights (1948)** sets forth principles of **governance** under which rulers and officials are to be responsive to the needs of the ruled and should be held accountable for them. Accountability can

enhance citizens' understanding and acceptance of the role played by government, the constraints under which it operates, and its legitimacy. Thus, accountability is an asset, not a burden, to enlightened governance.

Accountability can also arise from the oversight exercised by powerful non-state actors, including NGOs like Amnesty International, the World Wildlife Fund and Transparency International, who themselves also have accountability to their own supporters. Some other theorists have proposed that global financial markets also present a form of accountability by making organizations and governments responsive to the sometimes-punishing reality of capital flows.

See also: governance; law; participatory development; transparency

Further reading

Kopits, G. and Craig, J. (1998) *Transparency in Government Operations*, Washington: IMF Occasional Paper 158.

Pillai, P., Pharmy, A., Neoh, K. and Thiruchelvam, K. (eds) (1995) *Managing Trust: Transparency, Accountability and Ethics in Malaysia*, Kuala Lampur: ISIS Malaysia/Goethe Institut.

WILLIAM B. T. MOCK

actor-oriented approaches to development

Actor-oriented approaches were developed in opposition to structuralist and culturalist interpretations of social and **economic development**. They are characterized by an emphasis on social actors and agency; the notions of strategy and negotiation; and a methodological and theoretical focus on interfaces between different realities and "worlds of knowledge." They have been advocated most notably and persistently by Norman Long and colleagues at the University of Wageningen in the Netherlands, but other authors, primarily sociologists and anthropologists of development, have adopted similar or related approaches.

Actor-oriented approaches began to take shape in the mid-1980s. Rejecting structural determinist explanations of "underdevelopment" (see **dependency theory; underdevelopment versus less developed country (LDC) versus Third World**), they support a social constructionist approach grounded in methodological empiricism and "theory from below." This entails deconstructing the notion of intervention to imply not simply the implementation of a plan of action (a unidirectional process), but an ongoing, socially constructed, negotiated process. Hence, understanding and/or evaluating development interventions (programs, projects, policies, etc.) requires paying attention to the meanings they acquire for all the parties involved, and examining how they are constantly reinterpreted and manipulated by differently positioned persons and groups. Two guiding metaphors employed to suggest that development interventions exist as dynamic encounters between different interests and perspectives are "arenas" (of negotiation and/or contestation) and "interfaces" (between different social worlds or logics). Social actors contribute to the production of their social world by engaging in it and unfolding their envisaged trajectories in relation to particular events and institutions. This type of social constructionism is coupled to an emphasis on agency, which is seen, following Giddens, as dependent on the capability of actors to make a difference to a pre-existing state of affairs. Actor-oriented contributions highlight the strategies that actors unfold to develop their own idiosyncratic "projects in the Project." This usually involves attempts to enrol others in one's project and form networks of support in order to improve one's bargaining position. While recognizing hierarchy, actor-oriented analyses tend to emphasize the enabling nature of structure and thereby challenge totalizing interpretations of development as a (hegemonic) discourse (see **power and discourse**). They argue that even the most subordinated actors are capable to exercise some kind of power within the room for maneuver available to them. If in theory this position is defensible, actor-oriented contributions have been criticized for providing over-optimistic accounts of how development works. They run the risk of equating agency with power and understating the

constraints imposed upon marginal actors by the hierarchical structures in which they are integrated, sometimes against their will and without their consent. Actor-oriented authors have responded to this criticism by providing illustrations of how apparently powerless actors are constantly manipulating and turning to their own ends processes that are more or less imposed on them. They have also been criticized for paying too little attention to the structural characteristics of action and for reducing social arenas to the sum of individual strategies (methodological individualism). These charges have been convincingly resisted by various authors, who have argued that their writings present actors and their social and material environments as mutually constituted, and that the use of micro-studies does not necessarily imply individualist and/or reductionist assumptions. A case in point of the combination of micro-history and individual strategies with a concern for broader structural and policy frameworks is Arce and Long's study of peasant-bureaucrat relations following the establishment of the Mexican Food Program in the Peasant Community of La Lobera in Mexico (Arce and Long, 1993).

Methodologically, actor oriented approaches are grounded in anthropological fieldwork and empirical social research methods, including, *inter alia*, the use of extended case studies; social network analysis; **livelihoods** analysis; life histories, career histories, and actors' accounts of social events; discourse analysis; and *ad hoc* developed methods such as the rapid collective enquiry for the identification of conflicts and strategic groups, known as ECRIS (see Bierschenk and Olivier de Sardan, 1997).

Although the work of Norman Long and Wageningen-based researchers has acquired an almost paradigmatic status in this field, different authors have adapted actor-oriented approaches to their specific research focus and theoretical inclinations. In particular, a francophone pole of researchers affiliated with the Euro-African Association for the Anthropology of Social Change and Development (APAD) has produced a corpus of empirical studies of development which stands in opposition to discursive and populist approaches, and shares many theoretical and methodological assumptions with those advanced by the Wageningen group. Other authors have consistently advocated actor-oriented approaches, emphasizing a concern with local history; studying development projects as arenas of negotiation; and unraveling the strategies of different categories of actors (see Elwert and Bierschenk, 1988). Actor-oriented approaches have provided and continue to provide relevant contributions to the study of the social dynamics of development contexts, primarily by increasing the base of in-depth, empirical analyses of the interaction between development rationales and local-level perceptions and strategies.

See also: power and discourse; sociology of development

Further reading

Arce, A. and Long, N. (1993) "Bridging Two Worlds: An Ethnography of Bureaucrat-Peasant Relations in Western Mexico," pp. 179–208 in Hobart, M. (ed.) *An Anthropological Critique of Development: The Growth of Ignorance*, London: Routledge.

Bierschenk, B. and Olivier de Sardan, O. (1997) "ECRIS: Rapid Collective Enquiry for the Identification of Conflicts and Strategic Groups," *Human Organization* 56:2 238–44.

Elwert, G. and Bierschenk, T. (1988) "Development Aid as an Intervention in Dynamic Systems," *Sociologia Ruralis* 28:2–3 99–112.

Long, N. (2001) *Development Sociology: Actor Perspectives*, London: Routledge.

BENEDETTA ROSSI

adjustment with a human face

Adjustment with a Human Face was a book published by the **United Nations Children's Fund (UNICEF)** in 1987. It argued that countries undertaking **structural adjustment** programs could and ought to take measures to protect the needs of their most vulnerable citizens – namely **children** and women from the poorest families – and that the international **community** should assist them in doing so.

In the three decades following World War II, child welfare improved markedly in many poor parts of the world. However, it began to falter in the 1970s and deteriorate markedly in the 1980s, with the onset of global recession and the **debt** crisis. The effects were especially severe in Africa, Latin America, and the Middle East. As a result, many countries enacted anti-inflation measures and **structural adjustment** programs, which involved wide-scale macro-economic restructuring. The immediate effect was often a protracted decline in national output, with deleterious consequences for the poor in particular, who faced a loss of income and the direct negative effects of certain policies. While many causes of decline were international, the adjustment policies adopted were often seen to worsen the situation.

At the same time, this upheaval notwithstanding, some countries managed to protect their most vulnerable citizens through carefully targeted policies focusing on basic **health, education, nutrition**, and **employment** generation. Drawing on UNICEF and developing country experience, researchers amassed a range of evidence to show that the plight of poor children particularly need not inevitably worsen during adjustment. Botswana, the Republic of Korea, and Zimbabwe were singled out for having more successfully combined adjustment with **poverty** alleviation and nutritional protection. The book sought to determine what could be learnt from the adjustment experiences of ten countries (presented in full in a second volume).

The authors of the book argued that adjustment was still needed to restore growth, but that adjustment alone was insufficient to safeguard vulnerable groups. Consequently, there was a need to appropriate macro-, meso- (i.e. governmental) and micro-level policies and agendas to support small-scale producers and low-income activities; improve the equity and efficiency of social services; implement compensatory public works and nutritional support; and monitor social indicators such as the nutritional status of children.

Finally, the authors urged that the international **community** should make the global economic environment more friendly to poor countries, and that it should create mechanisms to compensate them for adverse global shocks, and that it give financial support to those implementing "human face" policies.

This research stressed that the human implications of the reforms were integral to the process of macroeconomic adjustment. Its findings have been extremely influential in shaping the ways in which developing countries have implemented structural reforms, and the international financial **community** has supported them, particularly in ensuring that they do not overlook the basic needs of vulnerable groups during the process, and that they provide targeted assistance to protect them.

See also: children; growth versus holism; nutrition; structural adjustment; vulnerability

Further reading

Cornia, G., Jolly, R. and Stewart, F. (eds) (1987) *Adjustment with a Human Face: Protecting the Vulnerable and Promoting Growth*, Oxford: Oxford University Press.

EMMA SAMMAN

advocacy coalitions

Advocacy coalitions are composed of groups and individuals working together to promote a particular cause or set of causes. Target audiences for these advocacy efforts include policy and decision-makers, specific segments of the population, and the public. Advocacy coalitions are often associated with organizations committed to **social justice** or social change goals. However, many public and private sector institutions also participate in advocacy coalitions. Examples include intra- and international governmental bodies, as when agencies at municipal, regional and federal levels jointly advocate particular positions, or when different national authorities coordinate their efforts to pursue specific policies. They may also include industry lobby groups and cooperative initiatives. This expansive definition of advocacy coalitions builds on the similarities in tactics one finds in such efforts across a range of actors, whether in the public, private or **non-governmental organizations (NGOs)** sectors.

Broadly speaking, the purpose of advocacy coalitions is for participants to work collaboratively with others to achieve commonly defined objectives. The idea is to pool resources that are often in limited supply, to share a knowledge and experience base drawn from a variety of contexts, and to form a unified front against common opponents. It is a strategy that, though attractive to governments and business interests, is particularly well suited to social justice and **grassroots organizations**. A prominent example of an advocacy coalition within **civil society** is Jubilee 2000, a campaign aimed at **debt relief** for the developing world which counts among its constituent members Christian charities and churches, social justice advocates, anti-poverty activists, and even popular culture icons.

Participating in an advocacy coalition affords a locally based or single issue-oriented social justice struggle much greater relative strength than embarking upon an advocacy campaign on its own. Advocacy coalitions offer the ability for local groups to learn from the experience of others, to mobilize effectively and respond quickly to emerging situations, and to achieve greater public exposure for the goal being pursued. Being part of an advocacy coalition also allows local concerns to connect to global issues, which operate and must be addressed at multiple levels simultaneously.

Advocacy coalitions are not without their drawbacks, however. One of the primary problems is that of maintaining coherence and cohesion across a wide range of interests and motivations amongst the coalitions' members. While broad objectives may be similar for participants, the end goals are rarely identical. Cracks in the constitution of advocacy coalitions can be seen most prominently in terms of **race and racism**, **gender**, class, and **ethnicity/identity**. For advocacy coalitions active in the field of international development, these differences often coalesce in what is known as the North-South divide, with North-based environmental and social justice organizations often accused of self-interested and insufficiently self-reflective agendas by their South-based counterparts.

See also: governance; grassroots activism; non-governmental organizations (NGOs); social movements

Further reading

Fenger, M. and Klok, P. (2001) "Interdependency, Beliefs, and Coalition Behavior: A Contribution to the Advocacy Coalition Framework," *Policy Sciences* 34:2 157–70.

Keck, M. and Sikkink, K. (1998) *Activists Beyond Borders: Advocacy Networks in International Politics*, Ithaca NY: Cornell University Press.

PABLO SHILADITYA BOSE

African Development Bank (ADB)

The African Development Bank (ADB), founded in 1964, is the leading multilateral development bank in Africa. Its shareholders include 53 regional members and 24 non-regional members. The Bank provides loans, equity investments, and technical assistance to its members. The bank itself runs on a non-concessional basis (i.e. it operates like a commercial bank); the concessional needs of its regional members are addressed through the African Development Fund (ADF), established in 1972 with funds from the Bank and thirteen non-regional members, and the Nigerian Trust Fund (NTF), established in 1976 with funds from the government of Nigeria. The ADB, ADF, and NTF constitute the ADB Group. The Bank's authority resides in its Board of Governors, which issues general directives, elects the president, admits new members, and makes amendment to existing agreements. The Bank is headquartered in Abidjan, with field offices in Cairo, Libreville, Abuja, and Addis Ababa.

See also: multilateral development banks (MDBs)

JOSEPH MENSAH

African Union

The African Union is an organization seeking greater economic integration and political agreement within the states of Africa. It was originally founded as the Organization of African Unity (OAU) in 1963 in Addis Ababa, with just thirty-two members. Its initial Charter urged unity and solidarity of African States; coordination and cooperation for a better life for African peoples; a defense of sovereignty, territorial integrity and independence; an eradication of all forms of colonialism (see **colonialism, history of; colonialism, impacts of**) from Africa; and a promotion of international cooperation, especially in regard to the **Universal Declaration of Human Rights (1948)**. Some important topics addressed by the OAU have included **decolonization**, opposition against racial discrimination in South Africa (under **apartheid**) or in the old Rhodesia (now Zimbabwe), championing African **culture** and politics, and **peacekeeping**. In Durban in 2002, the OAU was replaced by the African Union, with fifty-three member states, and a structure similar to the **European Union** (EU), including an Assembly, an Executive Council, a Commission, and a Court of Justice. However, unlike the EU, the African Union has not significantly reduced trade barriers between member states, and has comparatively little power.

See also: African Development Bank (ADB); Common Market for Eastern and Southern Africa (COMESA); economic federalization; peacekeeping; Southern African Development Community (SADC)

TIM FORSYTH

ageing

Ageing is usually defined as an increase in the percentage of a **population** aged sixty-five years or older. It is long established in developed countries and is now occurring throughout the world. There is often a tendency to see ageing as a threat to the future. Instead, it is one of the great achievements of the past century, albeit with a range of social, economic, political and cultural challenges. Ageing both affects and is influenced by wider processes of development and transformation. The quality of life of elderly populations is conditioned by their capacity to manage opportunities and risks associated with rapid and complex change.

Despite the emphasis upon the age of sixty-five, there is no universally accepted definition of what constitutes old age. Definitions may vary according to chronology; key biological processes and physical appearances; important life events (such as retirement or some other form of disengagement); or social roles (grandparenthood or ceremonial duties). Since old age can cover a span of over three decades, most cultures distinguish between the "old old" and "young old," and it is usually more meaningful to think in terms of a gradual change, rather than a sharp cut-off between adulthood and later life.

Developed countries tend to have older population structures: older people make up more of the total national population than in developing countries. In absolute terms, however, the majority of the world's population aged sixty or over has lived in developing countries since the early 1980s. By 2030, it is estimated that developing countries may have nearly three times as many people aged sixty or more than developed countries. Indeed, these figures may understate the ageing gap, as old age may effectively set in before the age of sixty in many poor countries.

Population ageing is usually associated with the final stage of the **demographic transition**, which involves sustained falls in **fertility** and hence smaller numbers of younger age groups. The timing and intensity of the demographic transition vary. In most of the South, demographic transition has been much more abrupt than in established industrialized economies. It took about a century for the proportion of elders in Western Europe to double. In many developing countries, including India, China and Brazil, this is expected to occur in less than twenty years.

There is mounting concern about the possible impacts of population ageing on economic performance. Some of this may be based on over-generalized notions of old age dependency. The economic contribution of some older people may be understated, and there may be ways to promote participation (see **participatory development**) through policies such as lifelong training and access to credit. In many countries, a combination of economic necessity, changing social attitudes, and the improving **health** profiles of elders, may weaken the link between ageing and a shrinking workforce. Richer countries may be able to sustain the total size of their workforces by attracting large influxes of replacement **migration**.

Much of the debate about ageing and development draws on the view that the middle years of the life course are characterized by high savings rates, and that later life sees a de-accumulation of assets. It is argued that population ageing will therefore lead to a reduction in aggregate savings rates. This view would appear to be borne out by international comparisons. However, micro-economic research has challenged this, observing that many elders continue to save, albeit at a lower rate than previously. One reason for this may be that sustaining the size of future bequests increases the likelihood that younger family members will take an interest in their well-being.

Another conventional wisdom is that ageing holds back development because investment is lost to the mounting costs of social provision. Again, this process is not inevitable, and will be heavily influenced by the ways in which people experience later life. The costs of supporting an elderly population with high levels of protracted chronic disease (see **disease eradication; disease, social constructions of**) and general dependence will be greater than that for a healthy, active population. There are other problems with demographic determinism: for example, the USA spends twice as much of its economic output on health care as the UK does, but contains a similar proportion of elders. Instead, the gap is mainly due to inefficiencies in the US private health insurance market. This suggests that the impact of ageing on social spending is mediated by the ways in which the social sectors are structured. In poorer countries, the social sectors currently fail to meet the basic needs of many people, old and young. In these cases, it is meaningless to project the impact of population ageing on expenditure based on the experiences of other countries.

Debates about public policy for older people have often derived from the experiences of the developed countries of the North, and have been dominated by controversies about **pensions** reform. Yet, in many low-income countries a major challenge is how to factor older people into public policy for the first time. One key area for change in low-income countries might be factoring older people into **primary health care** programs, through targeted interventions.

Older people are a varied group, living in very different circumstances. However, a number of generalizations are possible. Older people tend to be less involved in salaried economic activity. They are exposed to age-related risks, such as physical decline and some kinds of chronic disease. They are exposed to the stereotypes and prejudices of society: and these may become self-fulfilling. These common issues justify the emerging interest among academics and policy-makers into ageing as a global phenomenon. But they do not justify the portrayal of older people as a special interest group, who interests are separate from, and possibly in conflict with, those of other age groups. Older people do not live in isolation, and so their welfare in intimately bound in with that of society as a whole.

See also: pensions; population; welfare state

Further reading

Lloyd-Sherlock, P. (ed.) (2004) *Living Longer: Ageing, Development, and Social Protection*, London: Zed.

PETER LLOYD-SHERLOCK

Agenda 21

Agenda 21 is a broad action plan adopted at the 1992 **Rio Summit** to promote environmentally sound and **sustainable development** in all countries of the world. Agenda 21 was signed on 13 June 1992 by over one hundred heads of state representing 98 percent of the world's population. Agenda 21 is not legally binding; it is a flexible guide towards the achievement of a sustainable world.

Agenda 21 is divided into six themes composed of sub-areas with specified action plans. The first theme, quality of life, addresses areas such as limiting **poverty**, changing consumption patterns, **population** control, and ensuring the availability of adequate **health** care. The second theme, efficient use of **natural resources**, focuses on land use

planning, **water management** and conservation, energy resources (see **energy policy**), **food** production, forest management, and the protection of **biodiversity**. The third theme, protection of the global commons, discusses management of the atmosphere and the oceans. The fourth theme, management of human settlements, considers urban issues and the provision of adequate **housing**. The fifth theme, **waste management**, focuses on the classification and disposal of chemical, solid, and radioactive wastes. The final theme, sustainable **economic growth**, discusses **trade**, development, and **technology transfer**.

Agenda 21 has been criticized for not including strong positions on transport (see **transport policy**), energy issues, and **tourism**. The action plan has also been criticized for being too focused on increasing trade. Agenda 21 stresses that removing distortions in international trade is essential and that environmental concerns should not restrain trade – positions criticized by many anti-**globalization** groups.

The success of Agenda 21 has been mixed. The action plan has been successful at linking **environment** and **poverty**, and many local working groups have been formed that include the multiple stakeholders such as youth, **indigenous people**, scientists, and farmers called for in the plan. The **Commission on Sustainable Development (CSD)**, which is charged with monitoring the progress of Agenda 21's implementation, has reported positive developments in the areas of controlling population growth, increasing **food** production, and improving local environments. However, they also report an increase in inequity, increasing **water** scarcity, and extensive loss of agricultural land. Implementation in the European countries has been more successful than in other regions.

The action plan's mixed success can be attributed to a lack of commitment of funding for the initiatives in the plan. Every action in Agenda 21 included a projected cost; but no source of funding was secured at the time of signing.

The CSD continues to monitor the implementation of Agenda 21, and follow-up meetings, Rio +5 and Rio +10, were held in 1997 in New York and in 2002 in Johannesburg. In 2002 the **United Nations** General Assembly called the progress of Agenda 21's implementation extremely disappointing, and at Johannesburg a plan was developed to speed the implementation of Agenda 21.

See also: environment; sustainable development; Rio Summit

Further reading

Sitarz, D. (ed.) (1994) *Agenda 21: The Earth Summit Strategy to Save Our Planet*, Boulder CO: EarthPress.

LENORE NEWMAN

agrarian reform

Agrarian reform refers to the variety of supportive measures governments may introduce to make **land reform** more effective in enhancing **rural development**. The term agrarian reform is commonly used as a synonym of land reform. However, it is useful to define **land reform** generally as actions that redistribute land ownership, or redefine the terms of land ownership, usually to enhance access of rural poor to land (see **rural poverty**). Agrarian reform, on the other hand, refers to actions that complement land reform such as the supply of adequate credit (see **micro-credit and micro-finance**), technical assistance, marketing facilities and other supportive measures to the reform sector farm enterprises.

The need for agrarian reform – as an addition to land reform – became clear when many land reforms failed to live up to their original expectations and were characterized as "broken promises" by Thiesenhusen (1995), among others. Evaluations of land reforms revealed that in many countries, far less land was redistributed and far fewer peasants and rural workers had benefitted from this process than had been anticipated (Ramachandran and Swaminathan, 2003). Furthermore, the reform sector (the new farms arising from the expropriations) were not performing as well as it was desired and often even faced major economic problems, particularly in the case of collective tenure arrangements (see **communes, collectives and cooperatives; collectivization**). The analysis

revealed that one major reason for this poor performance was the lack of government supportive measures. Some classic examples of agrarian reform include the creation of credit facilities (see example of the **Grameen Bank (GB)**); rural agricultural extension offices (see **agriculture**); and coordinated marketing for rural products.

See also: agriculture; collectivization; land reform; land rights; micro-credit and micro-finance; rural development; rural poverty; villages

Further reading

Ramachandran, V. and Swaminathan, M. (eds) (2003) *Agrarian Studies: Essays on Agrarian Relations in Less-Developed Countries*, London: Zed.

Thiesenhusen, W. (1989) *Searching for Agrarian Reform in Latin America*, Boston MA: Unwin Hyman.

Thiesenhusen, W. (1995) *Broken Promises: Agrarian Reform and the Latin American Campesino*, Boulder CO: Westview.

CRISTÓBAL KAY

agrarian transformation

Agrarian transformations are major historical shifts in production systems, economic exchange and social relations within **agriculture**, which are often catalyzed by climatic, demographic, political or economic shocks. Tracing agrarian transformations entails an understanding of the changing nature of agrarian agents, their scales of operation and allocation of productive effort between own subsistence and commercial exchange and their land, labor and capital usage.

A schematic juxtapositioning of different agricultural production systems illustrates the dynamic upheavals in agriculture through history. Ancient agrarian civilizations of the Middle East and Far East, associated with the large river basins of the Nile, Tigris and Euphrates, the Ganges, and the Yangtze, tended towards capital investment in **irrigation** organized through a centralized state authority (see **state and state reform**) affording the state a strong position for the appropriation and distribution of peasant producers' surpluses (see **peasantry**). Asian agrarian civilizations are generally considered more technologically advanced than the more diffuse agrarian feudal estates of Europe during the Middle Ages.

Historians widely argue that the drastic population decline arising from repeated plague infections in Europe during the thirteenth and fourteenth centuries undermined agricultural labor control within feudal estates providing economic and political space for the operation of smallholder peasant family agrarian production units responsive to urban commercial demand agricultural products. The fifteenth and sixteenth centuries witnessed the sudden decline in many indigenous self-sufficient rural populations in Latin America as a result of European colonialism (see **colonialism, history of; colonialism, impacts of**), and the subsequent formation of large landed agrarian properties using tenant labor alongside subsistence-based **peasantry**.

In Asia, invading European colonial powers during the seventeenth and eighteenth centuries tended to collaborate with local rulers, sharing taxation powers and pushing agrarian output towards the demands of the international market. These power-sharing exercises tended towards the excessive accumulation of wealth in a view at the expense of growing rural impoverishment and landlessness.

In Sub-Saharan Africa, a sparsely populated continent adversely affected by centuries of slave trading (see **slavery**), colonial powers during the nineteenth and early twentieth century were more apt to implement labor and taxation policies that fostered small peasant household production units, albeit many lacked sufficient labor due to the practice of male **circular migration** labor policies to colonial mines and plantations.

By the mid-twentieth century, European colonialism started to unravel under pressures from **nationalism**. Post-independence nationalist governments, especially in Sub-Saharan Africa, tended to favor small-scale peasant household production units often seeking to bolster their land and labor resources with subsidized improved agricultural inputs to boost yields, thereby encouraging agricultural surpluses that could be marketed. Western donor agencies avidly sought to lend their support with rural **aid** directed primarily at raising living standards and agricultural output of peasant families as a way of eradicating **poverty** and encouraging broad-based national **economic development**.

However, the economic shock of the oil crises of the 1970s marked a turning point in smallholder farming units' fortunes worldwide, particularly in the least developed countries. The small commercial surpluses of peasant producers dispersed in scattered settlements throughout the countryside engendered high transport costs that rose precipitously after the oil crises. Their lower labor costs arising from the use of family labor did not outweigh the increasing transport expense. Peasants' commercial output lost market competitiveness relative to large-scale **agribusiness**es that were streamlining their marketing channels and investing heavily in new production techniques and biotechnology (see **biotechnology and resistance**) to attain ever larger agricultural yields. Increasingly, small-scale producers defensively diversified into non-agricultural income-earning pursuits, while generally retaining food production for home consumption as a subsistence fallback to guard against the risks of their new commercial enterprises. At the outset of the twenty-first century, the world's long history of agrarian transformations seemed destined to be superseded by agro-industrial transformation with the interests of large **transnational corporations (TNCs)** dominating commercial agricultural production and marketing.

See also: agriculture; agrarian reform; rural development

Further reading

Bryceson, D., Kay, C. and Mooij, J. (2000) *Disappearing Peasantries: Rural Labour in Africa, Asia and Latin America*, London: Intermediate Technology Publications.

Diamond, J. (1998) *Guns, Germs and Steel: A Short History of Everybody for the Last 13,000 Years*, London: Vintage.

DEBORAH FAHY BRYCESON

agribusiness

The term agribusiness originated in the 1950s in the context of the post-World War II rise of largely US transnational agro-**food** industries and the **industrialization** of **agriculture** more generally. Coined by Harvard Business School policy wonks, it referred to the "sum of all operations involved in the manufacture and distribution of farm supplies; production operations on the farm; storage; processing and distribution of farm commodities and items made from them" (Davis and Goldberg, 1957:3). In effect, this statement was a sort of commodity-chain approach (see also **commodification; value chains**) to agriculture at a moment when many elements from the point of production to consumption were being integrated by agro-food companies with a global reach. Agribusiness has come to refer to global agro-food systems increasing dominated by vertically integrated and vertically coordinated forms of transnational capital (the French term "la complex agro-alimentaire" better captures this character of modern agriculture (Allaire and Boyer, 1995). **Transnational corporations (TNCs)** like Cargill, Nestlé or Tysons are exemplary cases of agribusiness as they control key nodes and flows within single or multiple agro-food commodity systems. Agribusiness is not, however, always concerned with the direct control over the point of production through vertically integrated plantations or corporate estates. Indeed, the proliferation of contract farming in which exporters or processes sub-contact to small growers indicates how concerned agribusinesses are to control upstream activities where value and quality are added. The onset of agro-biotechnology including genetically modified organisms (see **genetically modified organisms (GMOs)**), coupled with **intellectual property rights (IPRs)** over seed and **livestock** has meant that agribusiness is being shaped on the one hand by the huge life science industries (such as Monsanto and Novartis), and on the other by a shift from "appropriation" (control of land based activities) to "substitution" (the production of agro-foods and fibers through increasingly artificial and non-land based practices, e.g. synthetic sugars). Transnational agriculture has proliferated in the context of the breakdown of what Harriet Friedmann (1993)

has called the "international food regime" of the post-1945 period. **Aid** and **trade** in food was tightly regulated through inter-state arrangements and the disposal of national surpluses. **Neo-liberalism** and the shift from **aid** to **"free trade,"** and the assault by the **World Trade Organization/General Agreement on Tariffs and Trade (WTO/GATT)** on agricultural **tariffs**, has meant that the global agro-food system has been radically privatized and dominated by global agribusinesses, some of the most of aggressive being the fastfood companies (McDonalds) and the chemical-pharmaceutical industries. It is nonetheless the case that while developing countries have been under enormous pressure to reduce agricultural trade tariffs, the agribusinesses in the USA and Western Europe have benefitted from enormous subsidies.

See also: agriculture; biotechnology and resistance; Cartagena Protocol on Biosafety; contract farming; food; genetically modified organisms (GMOs); transnational corporations (TNCs); World Trade Organization/General Agreement on Tariffs and Trade (WTO/GATT)

Further reading

Allaire, G. and Boyer, R. (1995) *La Grande Transformation*, Paris: INRA.
Davis, J. and Goldberg. R. (1957) *A Concept of Agribusiness*, Cambridge MA: Harvard Business School.
Friedmann, H. (1993) "The Political Economy of Food," *New Left Review* 197: 29–57.

MICHAEL WATTS

agricultural involution

The concept of agricultural involution has been used in a variety of rural and urban contexts to denote a particular variety of non-evolutionary, non-revolutionary change. Clifford Geertz (1963) coined the term agricultural involution to refer to the process whereby Javanese farmers during the Dutch colonial period reacted to population pressures by increasing labor inputs rather than by adopting new more efficient technologies. In so doing they were able to keep agricultural output per capita constant, but relations of production, rather than changing into more productive ones, were endlessly elaborated becoming more complex and **labor-intensive**, while the accompanying social and economic structures were kept rigid. The endless sharing of access to land and opportunities for wage work resulted in "shared **poverty**" in the agricultural areas, and a dual economy made up of an agricultural sector impoverished by involution, and a more dynamic industrial sector. There is some doubt of whether Geertz was correct in his description of the Javanese economy, but his notion of agricultural involution, and the associated idea of shared poverty, remain important in research on agrarian change in Indonesia and elsewhere.

See also: agriculture; agrarian reform; rural "depressor"; rural development

Further reading

Geertz, Clifford (1963) *Agricultural Involution: The Process of Ecological Change in Indonesia*, Berkeley and Los Angeles: University of California Press.

CLAUDIO O. DELANG

agriculture

Agriculture refers to the formal cultivation of crops and plants, usually for **food** production, and plays a key role in development, at local, national and international levels. It provides an important part of the **livelihoods** of a large proportion of the world's **population**. Changes in the structure of agriculture and in the contribution of agriculture to the national economy are used as indicators of the level of **economic development**. Farming systems are diverse and dynamic rather than traditional and slow to change. Evidence of harmful environmental and health impacts from intensive farming have prompted new directions in agricultural research and development activity (see **environment**). There are institutional barriers at international level to trade in agricultural products, which raise questions over the ability of

countries to maximize the potential of agriculture within their development strategies.

Agriculture is variously portrayed in development theory. Some writers see it as a residual economic activity, engaging people who are not employed in sectors which are driving the economy forward. For others, it plays a more dynamic role by releasing labor for expanding industries, earning foreign exchange to fund investment in imported capital goods and producing raw materials for industrial processing and manufacture (see **industrialization**). Some assert that it can be a driving force for development in its own right. Others point out that countries can develop without a significant agriculture sector, Singapore being a case in point.

These contrasting positions are reflected in differences in policy towards agriculture. Some governments have ruthlessly exploited agriculture, keeping prices down in the interests of urban consumers and manufacturing industries, and using marketing boards to divert export earnings into non-agricultural investments. Others have seen a thriving agriculture as a way of alleviating **rural poverty** and capturing the potential benefits of **globalization** and international trade. What is common to all theoretical and policy positions is that as **economic development** takes place, agriculture accounts for a declining proportion of **gross domestic product (GDP)** and **employment**.

Differences between theorists and between government policies are mirrored at the household level. For some households, farming is their main source of livelihood and they are continually seeking to improve the return they gain from it. For others, it is a residual activity, providing a basic level of subsistence in hard times and a base for the elderly and young children while other household members earn a living in other activities. Nor is agriculture only a rural activity. **Livestock** keeping and vegetable production are common in urban and peri-urban areas where they pose particular problems and opportunities (see **urban agriculture**).

From a **dependency theory** perspective, commentators argue that a development trajectory based initially on agriculture was forced on countries by the nature of their contact and relationships with developed countries. Political, military and commercial power were used to establish systems of production which served the interests of industrializing countries in Europe. trade in agricultural products continues to be overlaid by unequal relationships: it faces some of the highest tariff and non-tariff barriers imposed by developed countries to protect their own farmers and processing industries (see **tariffs; protectionism**). Barriers are particularly high for more highly processed – and therefore more valuable – products. This makes it difficult for developing countries to take the logical step of concentrating on increasing the value added to agricultural products before they are exported.

Development within the agricultural sector is often portrayed as a progression from subsistence-based systems, where the farm is producing food for the family, through initial engagement with the market, to a fully commercial agriculture in which all or most of the production is sold. For the national economy, this is an essential feature of development, supporting the growth of urban areas and non-agricultural sectors. In the case of Uganda's Plan for Modernization of Agriculture it is the model which guides development **planning**. For the farming household, total reliance on the market brings opportunities for improved standards of living but also new forms of **vulnerability**. Prices of agricultural products are very sensitive to changes in production. A bigger than usual harvest – locally or globally – can lead to a sharp fall in prices and therefore in farm incomes. Similarly, long-term increases in production through improved technology and management can lead to a long-term fall in prices if demand is not increasing at least as fast. Farmers then have to produce even more in order to maintain incomes.

Farming systems are very diverse, reflecting differences in environmental and socio-economic conditions. They are also very dynamic. Agriculture in developing countries is often portrayed as traditional, with farmers reluctant or unable to change to new enterprises and technologies. History tells us this is nonsense. Globally and locally, systems are continually changing in response to pressures, opportunities and new ideas. Products that are now firmly associated with particular countries are in fact relatively recent introductions, from the potato in Europe to maize in Africa (see also **green revolution**).

Until the late nineteenth century, most technical change came from farmers – from local observations and experiments, as well as from ideas brought by travelers or traders from farmers in other places. These processes are still at work, but they are less visible than the large infrastructure now devoted to formal agricultural research in both the public and the commercial sectors. The **Consultative Group on International Agricultural Research (CGIAR)** funds and oversees the work of fifteen international research centers across the world and most countries have their own government funded research institutes. Research by multi-national biotechnology (see **biotechnology and resistance**) companies is increasing rapidly, as the new techniques for genetic manipulation (see **genetically modified organisms (GMOs)**) offer opportunities for capturing the returns on investment through **intellectual property rights (IPRs)**. But there remains tremendous innovation potential among farmers. Current farming systems have come about – and continue to evolve – through local innovation and through adaptation of ideas from further afield. Recent developments in agricultural research methods, such as farming systems research and participatory plant breeding, try to bring together the creative potential of farmers and scientists. On the other hand, proponents of research into **genetically modified organisms (GMOs)** argue that these offer the only way of securing the doubling of agricultural production that will be needed in the next fifty years. They suggest that a second **green revolution** can be achieved by developing crop varieties and animals which are resistant to pests and diseases and which use light, water and nutrients more efficiently. Others caution that the spread of GMOs will reduce **biodiversity** and the genetic variation on which the future vitality of agriculture depends.

There are recurrent debates on the ability of agriculture, at a global scale, to feed the world's increasing **population** given the finite physical resource base on which it depends. The *Limits to Growth* **report (1972)** rekindled the debate in the 1970s. These views have so far been countered by empirical data showing that global per capita food production has risen rather than fallen in the past hundred years. Theorists like Ester Boserup have argued that it is changes in the balance between population and land area which drive changes in agricultural technology and systems, from **shifting cultivation** in virgin forest, through bush fallow systems, to intensive cultivation of permanent plots.

Whatever the merits of these arguments about future global production, its distribution does cause concern. Surplus food production in developed countries leads to the maintenance of barriers to food imports from developing countries (see **European Union; World Trade Organization/General Agreement on Tariffs and Trade (WTO/GATT)**). It also encourages subsidized dumping of surpluses on the world market and their diversion to food aid which can undermine local food production and marketing in developing countries.

The effectiveness of policies and projects in agriculture has suffered in the past from conventional perceptions about farming from developed countries. These see farmers as men, and farming as a full time activity undertaken by family units who own their land. The reality is much more complex. In many countries, women are responsible for most of the work and much of the farm decision-making (see **rural development**). In others there is a clear **gender division of labor**. In some rural societies, it is common for women and men within the household to manage separate plots. In others, looking after **livestock** is the responsibility of women. Projects that provide credit only to men as the notional "head of household," or promote "men's" enterprises, can seriously damage the interests of women. In other cases, men have taken over activities that have in the past been carried out by women when development projects have created a market for what had previously been largely a subsistence enterprise. Increasing attention is now given to **gender** issues in agricultural development and project planning.

Because agricultural production uses land as its basic resource, land tenure arrangements have a big impact on farming systems and on the distribution of the economic benefits from farming. Large estates concentrate the benefits in the hands of a few landholding families or companies, while thriving smallholder agriculture can spread the benefits more widely. The design of agricultural development policy and projects must take prevailing systems of land tenure into account.

As agriculture intensifies, its impact on the environment increases (see **environment; sustainable livelihoods**). This potentially damages the ability of the physical resources of soil and water to continue to support production at current levels (see **soil erosion and soil fertility**). Many **irrigation** systems are affected by the deposition of salts which can eventually make crop production impossible unless corrective action is taken. Continued cultivation on soils that have inherently low levels of essential plant nutrients leads to declines in fertility (see **shifting cultivation**). Compensating through applying mineral **fertilizers** may not be an economically viable option for many small-scale farmers. Regular cultivation of farmland can stimulate soil erosion through the action of wind and rain. There are also concerns about the impact of agriculture on health of producers and consumers. Excessive or indiscriminate use of **agrochemicals** (or fertilizers) to control the pests (weeds, insects, diseases) which accompany intensification already causes thousands of deaths each year among those who apply them. In urban and peri-urban areas, use of industrial and domestic effluent to irrigate vegetables for the urban market is a major **health** hazard.

These concerns have led to greater emphasis on the long-term sustainability of agricultural production. The focus of research effort in the public sector has shifted from increasing **productivity** to systems that maximize the use and recycling of local physical resources and do minimum damage to the environment. These include **rainwater harvesting** and improved management of recycled biomass in the form of animal manures and composted crop residues. Research with farmers into locally effective strategies for managing pests has led to reductions in the reliance on **agrochemicals**. This re-orientation of research has led many scientists to a new respect for the **local knowledge** which underpins most farming systems.

An issue for development planners in national governments and international development agencies in the late 1990s was whether agriculture could provide the basis for **poverty** alleviation. Research suggests that it can do so for some people, but for the majority of the rural poor, moving out of poverty will entail moving out of farming or at least moving some of their human resources into higher-earning non-agricultural activities. A critical question at the start of the twenty-first century was how far the opportunities from **globalization** will spread. Niche markets for high-value products, such as off-season vegetables and flowers, can be supplied more easily by well capitalized entrepreneurs who can invest in systems to comply with stringent food safety, quality and quantity requirements of markets in developed countries. While governments can act to create a supportive infrastructure and policy environment for smallholder production, much depends on whether international institutions and agreements such as WTO/GATT and **trade-related aspects of intellectual property rights (TRIPS)** work in, or at least not against, the interests of developing countries.

See also: agribusiness; agrarian reform; agrarian transformation; agrochemicals; dryland agriculture; Consultative Group on International Agricultural Research (CGIAR); collectivization; commodification; contract farming; environment; food; food security; green revolution; intermediate classes; land reform; land rights; peasantry; rural development; rural poverty; shifting cultivation; sustainable livelihoods; urban agriculture; urban bias; World Trade Organization/General Agreement on Tariffs and Trade (WTO/GATT)

Further reading

Boserup, E. (1968) *The Conditions of Agricultural Growth: The Economics of Agrarian Change under Population Pressure*, London: Allen and Unwin (republished 1993, Earthscan Publications; London).

Ellis, F. (1993, 2nd edn) *Peasant Economics: Farm Households and Agrarian Development*, Cambridge; Cambridge University Press.

IFAD (2001) *Rural Poverty Report 2001: The Challenge of Ending Rural Poverty*, Oxford: Oxford University Press.

Pretty, J. (1995) *Regenerating Agriculture: Policies and Practices for Sustainability and Self-reliance*, London: Earthscan.

Upton, M. (1996) *The Economics of Tropical Farming Systems*, Cambridge: Cambridge University Press.

CHRIS GARFORTH

agrochemicals

Agrochemicals are various types of chemicals used to improve agricultural production. They operate in two key ways: by improving the nutrient availability for crops; or by reducing losses caused by the consumption of environmental resources and/or crops or animals by competitors such as weeds, diseases and parasites. Agrochemicals comprise inorganic **fertilizers**, crop protection chemicals and animal health products. Inorganic fertilizers replace traditional animal manures by enhancing the availability of nutrients such as nitrogen and phosphorus. Crop protection chemicals are synthetic organic chemicals, including several which mimic naturally occurring compounds, which are herbicides and pesticides. There are many types of herbicides, which operate over a broad spectrum: i.e. they kill all plants, or are selective by killing target plants. Pesticides are designed to kill target insects, fungi, nematodes, molluscs and aphids. Animal health chemicals reduce the adverse impact of bacteria, fungi and insects on farm animals, thus improving animal productivity. Agrochemical production is a global business, having intensified and diversified since the 1940s as agricultural **industrialization** has occurred.

See also: agriculture; fertilizers

A. M. MANNION

agroecology

Agroecology is a set of principles and practices that combine ecological science and **local knowledge** to enhance the productivity, sustainability and social benefits of **agriculture**, especially but not exclusively for resource-poor farmers. It approaches farms as dynamic systems "embedded within complex ecologies" (Levins and Vandermeer, 1990) that co-evolve with human communities. Agroecology is carried out by locally based and internationally linked networks of farmers, scientists and **non-governmental organizations (NGOs)** who see it as an alternative to conventional agricultural technologies designed for large-scale farms in temperate climates.

Agroecology responds to the agronomic inefficiencies and social failures of conventional agriculture. Such problems include a heavy dependence on purchased, external inputs (see **agrochemicals**); **vulnerability** of genetically uniform fields to pests and diseases; increased crop losses despite rising pesticide use; soil erosion (see **soil erosion and soil fertility**) and **salinization**; toxic **pollution**; eutrophication; high consumption of energy (see **energy policy**) and non-renewable resources; and the failure of biotechnology to solve productivity and pest problems (see **biotechnology and resistance**). Social failures include increased control of **food**-producing resources by a shrinking number of **agribusiness** enterprises, and the **displacement** of farmers and disintegration of rural society.

Agroecologists analyze agroecosystems in terms of their composition in three dimensions (not just the field) and their dynamics over time (not just one harvest cycle). They study nutrient and energy flow and interactions among organisms (soil biota, pests, beneficial insects, other animals and plants) at a range of spatial and temporal scales. They aim to reduce costs and waste by maintaining more closed systems than in conventional farming and to reduce risk by increasing the stability, resilience and self-regulating capacities of agroecosystems.

Agroecology takes account of "externalities" – the environmental, economic, and social costs that are generated by industrial-farm enterprises but born by the wider ecology and society – and attempts to transform these into net benefits. It promotes crop variety (see **intercropping**) and genetic diversity in food systems, includes domesticated animals and permanent crops in production cycles, and encourages wild species. Indeed, complex agroecosystems often support greater **biodiversity** than **monocultures** or even undisturbed forests.

Agroecology is multidisciplinary, drawing upon **population**, **community**, and landscape ecology, agronomy, entomology, and social sciences such as geography, anthropology, rural sociology, and **political ecology**. For some, although not all, practitioners agroecology is as much a political as a technological project: a means toward greater equity, **empowerment** and local control over food sources and supplies (see **food security**) and a space for multiple, alternative **developments**.

Agroecological principles can be generalized, but ecosystems, communities, and agroecological practices are necessarily place-specific. Agroecology therefore requires collaborative research and experimentation with farmers and other experts and continuing inputs of local intelligence. Although not yet applied and evaluated systematically across regions, agroecology has achieved substantial increases in production in many localities.

See also: agriculture; agroforestry; deep ecology; environment; food; political ecology; sustainable development; sustainable livelihoods

Further reading

Altieri, M. (1987) *Agroecology: The Scientific Basis of Alternative Agriculture*, Boulder CO: Westview Press.

Levins R. and Vandermeer J. (1990) "The Agroecosystem Embedded in a Complex Ecological Community," in Carroll, R., Vandermeer, J. and Rosset, P. (eds) *Agroecology*, New York: Wiley.

Uphoff, N. (ed.) (2002) *Agroecological Innovations: Increasing Food Production with Participatory Development*, London: Earthscan.

KATHLEEN MCAFFEE

agroforestry

Agroforestry may be defined generally as an economically viable land-use system that integrates **agriculture** and forest land uses. There are, however, many hundreds of forms of agroforestry within diverse cultures and contexts around the world. Two general characteristics may be identified. First, agroforestry includes the deliberate association of trees and shrubs with crops, pastures,

livestock, and other forms of agricultural production. Second, it aims to increase and diversify the total production of a given area of land by establishing identifiable ecological and economic interactions between woody plants and other components of the production system. Because of these characteristics, agroforestry also aims to provide various service functions, such as increasing soil organic matter and nutrient levels, and reducing runoff and soil loss. These services can increase the productivity of agricultural fields beyond what occurs in fields without trees, as well as provide synergistic aspects of production that result from having these mixes of land uses.

Agroforestry systems can be readily adapted to highly variable site conditions, and present potential savings to **labor-intensive** farming that commonly typify most traditional farming systems. Examples of agroforestry systems include: silvo-pastoral arrangements involving fodder producing trees; fruit tree systems providing **food** and income; **fuelwood** systems for areas depending on wood for cooking; timber (see **logging/timber trade**) in a wide variety of arrangements; shelter-belt agroforestry providing beneficial biophysical enhancements involving soil and crops; or indeed, any combinations of these. The adoption of agroforestry can result, over time, in decreases in labor, capital and resource use costs, and increases in yield because of greater physical output, and in the concentration of capital and labor costs into the same area. Agroforestry is often most effective in land commonly considered marginal for agriculture, such as **drylands**, stony, steep land, or where there is low soil fertility (see **soil erosion and soil fertility**), high agricultural risk or **unemployment**.

Much successful agroforestry depends, however, on the establishment of effective land tenure systems. Such systems are crucial in making a transition from current land uses to agroforestry, and may be equally diverse as agroforestry itself. Agroforestry tree tenure issues in the developing world must begin with departure from the "fixture presumption" common to Western law: the presumption that a tree belongs to the owner of the land on which it is a fixture. Some other cultures share this presumption, but many do not. The owner of the land is frequently different from the person who planted trees, and the person who receives the produce from the tree. It is important to acknowledge the diversity of access and tenure arrangements.

Indeed, much development intervention using agroforestry attempts to operate within local land tenure arrangements, rather than replace these. Acknowledging such local practices helps make agroforestry an **appropriate technology** for local development, tailored for local circumstances. It is worth noting, however, that much national legislated land ownership and customary tenure systems very frequently do not agree in developing countries. Many rural groups recognize individual or family ownership of land and/or trees based on occupancy and use, but governments can ignore traditional tenure systems and regard such areas as part of the public domain.

Agroforestry has also been highlighted for its potential environmental benefits. Much research has linked agroforestry to decreases in rates of deforestation in nearby natural forests by providing households with woody biomass needs that would have otherwise come from forest; for enhancing soil fertility; and for contributing to local **sustainable livelihoods**. Agroforestry has also been highlighted as an approach that has the potential to sequester a significant amount of atmospheric carbon at the global level, and hence mitigating anthropogenic **climate change**.

See also: agriculture; Consultative Group on International Agricultural Research (CGIAR); community forestry; deforestation; environment; deforestation; non-timber forest products (NTFPs); silviculture; soil erosion and soil fertility; sustainable livelihoods

Further reading

MacDicken, K. and Vergara, N. (eds) (1990) *Agroforestry: Classification and Management*, New York: John Wiley.

Nair, P. (ed.) (1989) *Agroforestry Systems in the Tropics*, London: Kluwer.

Unruh, J. and Lefebvre, P. (1995) "A Spatial Database Approach for Estimating Areas

Suitable for Agroforestry in Africa," *Agroforestry Systems* 32: 81–96.

JON D. UNRUH

aid

The Development Assistance Committee (DAC) of the **Organization for Economic Cooperation and Development (OECD)** defines "aid" as flows to developing countries and multilateral institutions from official agencies that satisfy two criteria. First, it is primarily intended for development purposes (ruling out both military aid and export credits). Second, it is highly concessional, meaning a grant element of at least 25 percent (see below). Aid flows comprise the largest part of official capital flows to developing countries. Other flows (as defined by DAC) include private commercial flows, and grants from **non-governmental organizations (NGOs)**.

The DAC maintains a two-part list of "eligible recipients" for aid. Flows meeting the above criteria to countries on Part I of the list are called *official development assistance* (ODA), and those to countries on Part II, *official aid* (OA). A further category, *official development finance* (ODF), comprises bilateral ODA (see **bilateral aid agencies**), multilateral receipts, and non-trade related official flows. Other official flows (OOF) are official transactions for which the main objective is not development, or if it is, the funds are insufficiently concessional to qualify as ODA/OA.

Trends in aid volume

In nominal terms, aid increased in nearly every year until the early 1990s, when it peaked at US$62.7 billion in 1992. In the next four years, the total fell by US$15 billion, dropping to US$47.9 billion in 1997, recovering slightly and erratically in the following years. These trends are more muted, but still present, for real aid, for which the increase in the 1980s was quite marked, though it has since fluctuated quite substantially with no evident trend.

The trend in aid's share of donor income deteriorated in the 1990s. The average for the whole period is well under one half of one percent: aid is a tiny share of donor income. Having fallen from the 1960s, this average fluctuated between 0.30 and 0.35 percent for two decades, but then fell to its present level of just 0.20 percent. There is a **United Nations** target, adopted by all DAC members other than the USA and Switzerland, that aid should be 0.7 percent of **gross national product (GNP)** (see **Pearson Commission**). But that target is further away than ever from being met.

The fall in aid has been a general phenomenon. Most donors are now contributing less aid – as a percentage of GNP – than in the 1990s. Eleven donors recorded a substantial decline (a fall of more than 0.1 percent of GNP), and five others a small fall. The largest falls have been amongst both good performers, such as Norway and Sweden, but also poor performers, most notably the USA (from 0.21 percent in 1991 to 0.08 percent in 1997, recovered to 0.10 percent by 2000). Only one country, the UK, has experienced no change, in fact being a story of a decline from the mid-1990s, reversed in just the last two years. Four countries have implemented increasing aid ratios: a very substantial one in the case of Luxembourg, and in the case of Denmark bringing it up to the position of "top-ranking donor."

The aid infrastructure and types of aid

About two thirds of aid is bilateral, flowing from the donor government direct to the recipient country (see **bilateral aid agencies**). The bulk of bilateral aid flows are through each country's aid agency such as the UK's Department of International Development (DFID) and the United States Agency for International Development (USAID). Multilateral aid is routed through international bodies, such as the various parts of the UN, the **World Bank** and the regional development banks (e.g. the **African Development Bank (ADB)**). The share of multilateral aid has been rising over time, from around 20 percent at the start of the 1970s, to over a quarter by the end of that decade, and further to its current share of one third. The rising share in the 1970s was accounted for by the growth of the **World Bank** and the **International Monetary Fund (IMF)**, which grew further with the start of the **debt crisis** in the early 1980s. The growing multilateral share is also explained by the growth of the **European Union**'s aid program, which has taken funds that would otherwise have been spent through European bilateral aid budgets.

Aid also comes through **non-governmental organizations (NGOs)** such as Oxfam and CARE. Monies these groups raise from the public to fund their activities does not qualify as ODA, and does not appear in the aid data. These private flows are small compared to official flows, accounting for around 4 percent of developing country receipts compared to the 40–50 percent coming from ODA. But much NGO activity is financed by official agencies. About 1.5 percent of ODA is direct support to NGOs for the latter's own programs. In addition, official agencies have increasingly used NGOs as implementing agencies for their projects.

Most aid is project aid. The donor and recipient agree to spend the funds for a particular project, such as road building, supplies for schools or institutional development for the Ministry of Finance. Program aid is funds not linked to a specific project, making resources freely available to the government budget. Previously designated as import support, program aid is today called budget support (also known as **sector-wide approaches (SWAps)**). **Debt relief** can also be seen as a type of program aid. Technical assistance is expatriate experts or training courses for local staff.

The allocation of aid

In 1973, just over half of all aid went to low-income countries. Nearly a fifth went to high and upper middle-income countries – but this fell to 5 percent by 1990. The share to low-income countries rose to around 70 percent for bilateral donors and 80 percent for multilateral aid. But in the 1990s, the share of low-income countries has fallen back by around 10 percent, the amount going to lower middle-income countries rising by a similar amount. This trend is partly explained by aid recipients graduating from the low-income country category. But it also reflects increased aid to European countries. For example, the Federal Republic of Yugoslavia and Bosnia-Herzegovina are now among the top recipients of aid from Norway, Sweden and Switzerland, whereas they did not feature ten years ago. A result has been a declining share of aid for Sub-Saharan Africa. In real terms, aid per person to Africa has fallen considerably since the region has been getting a falling share of a declining aid budget.

Analysis of why aid goes from particular donors to specific recipients reveals a number of patterns. First, there is a small country bias, whereby smaller countries get more aid per person than do larger ones. Second, models distinguish measures of recipient need (such as low income, poor social indicators and macroeconomic deficits) from donor interest (commercial and political relations). For bilateral donors the latter factors play a large role in explaining aid allocation, whereas for multilateral agencies recipient need dominates. For ex-colonial powers, their former colonies are particularly favored. However, the overall pattern of aid is generally progressive: more goes to poorer countries. The extent of this progressiveness varies. A historical exception has been the USA, which has given a very large share of its aid to Israel (which is no longer a Part I country).

The terms and conditions of aid

The grant equivalent of a loan is the face value of the loan minus the present value of repayments. The grant element is the grant equivalent divided by the loan's face value. There has been a historical trend toward improved terms of aid. Rising concessionality has historically been associated with a rising grant share. By 1989–90, the aid of six bilateral donors was entirely grant finance and so had a grant element of 100 percent, and another six donors had a grant element of close to 100 percent (five over 99 percent and the USA at 98.3 percent). Since then, there have been continued increases in the grant element of DAC ODA from improvements in the terms of the remaining donors.

The conditions attached to aid are called aid tying, which has various meanings. The most common refers to the practice of linking aid to the procurement of goods and services from the donor country. Many donors have made considerable progress with untying. By 2000, over 90 percent of aid was untied for seven donors, and over

80 percent for over five more. In that year, the UK announced an end to tied aid. In every case, these figures represent a considerable move toward untying compared to the situation in 1980. However, the case of the UK notwithstanding, this does not mean that untying is here to stay. The values attained in 2000 are *not* a peak for nearly all countries. The reversal has been greatest amongst northern European donors (Austria, Norway, Finland, Denmark and Germany), which saw big increases in untying in the first part of 1990s which have since been partially reversed.

Aid tying has also been taken to mean (1) linking the use of aid to particular projects, and (2) making aid conditional on implementing agreed policy changes. The bulk of aid has always had, and continues to have, its intended use specified by the donor. Program aid usually has policy conditions.

Changes in aid management

Aid has traditionally been project aid. A large part of project budgets are taken with technical assistance. Program aid is around 10 percent of total ODA. This proportion has fallen since the 1970s, since US **food aid** was largely program aid with the funds raised from the sale of the **food** available to the recipient government to use as it wished. But food aid has fallen from 15 percent in the 1970s to less than 5 percent today. During the 1980s financial program, aid became more important and was increasingly linked to policy change (see **structural adjustment**). By the 1990s, most bilateral donors were also giving program aid linked to policy reform. The scope of these reforms has spread over time, from macro stabilization to market liberalization and then onto the allocation of government spending. Since the late 1990s, the conditions relate explicitly to the recipient's **poverty** reduction strategy. In addition, **governance** has become an established part of **conditionality**.

Despite the use of conditionality, the donor **community** emphasizes ownership and partnership. Aid should finance activities planned in full collaboration with the recipient government and the intended beneficiaries. Various trends manifest these sentiments, such as the increased focus on **participatory development** and the emergence of

sector-wide approaches (SWAps), in which donor funds are provided in an overall strategic framework led by government. The apparent contradiction between partnership and conditionality (see **partnerships**) is side-stepped by use of selectivity, focusing aid relationships on countries whose governments are genuinely committed to reform. However, this approach raises problems such as detecting commitment and deciding what are the "right policies" in the first place. Aid effectiveness has always been questioned, and it is not clear to what extent these changes in aid management will increase that effectiveness.

See also: aid effectiveness and aid evaluation; bilateral aid agencies; charities; debt relief; emergency assistance; food aid; Live Aid/Band Aid; Pearson Commission; sector-wide approaches (SWAps)

Further reading

Burnell, P. (1997) *Foreign Aid in a Changing World*, Maidenhead: Open University Press (McGraw-Hill).

DAC (OECD) *Development Co-operation Report*, Paris: OECD. Published annually.

German, T. and Randell, J. (eds) (2002) *Reality of Aid*, London: Earthscan.

Raffer, K. and Singer, H. (1999) *The Foreign Aid Business: Economic Assistance and Development Co-operation*, Cheltenham: Edward Elgar.

Tarp, F. and Hjertholm, P. (ed.) (2000) *Foreign Aid and Development*, London: Routledge.

White, H. (2002) "Long-Run Trends and Recent Developments in Official Assistance from Developing Countries," *WIDER Discussion Paper 2002/106*, Helsinki: WIDER.

HOWARD WHITE

aid effectiveness and aid evaluation

Aid effectiveness can be assessed either at the project level, through evaluations, or at the macroeconomic level using econometric approaches or case studies. Donor agency project evaluations find that the majority of **aid** projects are successful, although there remain areas of concern such as reaching the poorest, **gender** differentials, and impacts on **environment**. Assessment at the macroeconomic level is more contentious. A dominant view in this literature has been that aid does not increase **economic growth**, with a recent variant being that it will only do so if the policy environment is right. However, others argue for a more positive view of aid's impact.

Project evaluations

The **World Bank** reports that just over 80 percent of its projects perform satisfactorily. This figure is based on reviews of completed projects by the organization's evaluation department. Other agencies report similar figures. What do these numbers mean?

Evaluation is a post-project review of project performance. In the 1970s, evaluation was dominated by the economic methodology of **cost-benefit analysis (CBA)**. But, partly because of a sectoral shift of aid into the social sectors, and partly because of a broadening of objectives to issues such as participation and gender equality, evaluations during the 1980s became less focused on a formal statement of costs and benefits and more on the process behind the project. Process evaluation is important for understanding why projects work or not, but may provide little information on the welfare impact of the intervention.

However, producing firm evidence of welfare impact has proved problematic, usually because the rigorous data requirements of a baseline survey and a good control group (i.e. a similar population which does not benefit from the project) are not addressed in project design. Even where there is a control group, the results can be biased by unobservable differences between the beneficiary and control populations. Randomized project design – implementing the project amongst a random sample of potential beneficiaries – overcomes these problems, but is not applicable for a great many projects for both practical and political reasons.

But overall assessments of agency performance are not based on these in-depth studies. The number of projects subject to a full-scale evaluation is very limited in comparison to the total number of projects being financed. So project ratings are generally based on a more superficial assessment of whether a project met its objectives, largely based on observing if activities were implemented or not. Where **welfare indicators** are available, data are not usually available to address the issue of attribution, that is being able to attribute observed changes to the project intervention.

However, the evidence supports the argument that projects achieve at least their intermediate objectives, though there are important reservations. Historically some projects have supported interventions that had adverse effects on both many people and the **environment**, such as large **dams**. Support to such activities has been greatly reduced and more effort made to listen directly to intended beneficiaries. A second important caveat is that whilst some aid undoubtedly benefits the poor, much of it does not, especially the very poor (see **chronic poverty**).

Failure to benefit the poor results in large part from the fact that most aid is not directly intended to help them. For example the UK's Department for International Development (DFID) distinguishes three different approaches to helping the poor: enabling (policy issues); inclusive (projects benefitting both poor and non-poor); and focused (targeted at the poor). The majority of activities supported fall into the first two categories. Looking across all donors, it is estimated that only around 10–15 percent of aid directly helps the poor. There are good reasons for aid that indirectly supports **poverty** reduction, such as by **capacity building** for a sound economic and legal framework (see **law**). But if the vast majority of aid is at best indirectly supporting poverty reduction, then it is to be expected that the observed impact of aid on poverty will be slight.

Macroeconomic perspectives

In the 1960s, aid's macroeconomic impact was framed in the context of the two-gap model, in which aid supplements domestic savings to increase investment and export earnings to pay for imports. According to this model, aid necessarily increases **economic growth**, but econometric studies showed this was not so. Some high aid recipients had very poor growth performance, whilst other countries had grown rapidly without aid. This finding was explained by the savings displacement hypothesis. Higher aid resulted in lower savings and so a less than one-for-one increase in investment, as had been predicted by the two-gap model. Later analysis argued that public savings were particularly affected in this way, as recipient governments reduced taxes when receiving aid. It was also argued that aid can have "**Dutch disease**" effects, causing an appreciation of the real exchange rate (see **exchange rates**), and so a reduction in imports, meaning that aid is a less than one-to-one increment to export earnings.

Rather than model these channels affecting aid's impact on growth, most studies are econometric analyses of the aid-growth relationship. Using this approach, the **World Bank** (1998) report *Assessing Aid* argued that aid would only increase growth if the policy environment was right, meaning that the country was pursuing **structural adjustment** policies. These findings have led to support for selectivity, allocating most aid to those countries' good policies. But academic critics argue that aid-growth regressions started showing positive coefficients in the 1990s. This finding does not depend on policy stance: academic studies show that the interactive term, on which the World Bank's argument depends, is not significant in many model specifications. An alternative approach consists of case studies, which support the view that aid has beneficial impacts at the macro level and facilitates policy reform's beneficial effects rather than *vice versa*.

See also: aid; food aid; cost-benefit analysis (CBA); indicators of development; measuring development; project appraisal; sector-wide approaches (SWAps); welfare indicators

Further reading

Mosley, P. (1986) *Overseas Aid: Its Defence and Reform*, Brighton: Harvester Wheatsheaf.
Tarp, F. and Hjertholm, P. (ed.) (2000) *Foreign Aid and Development*, London: Routledge.

White, H. and Dijkstra, G. (2002) *Programme Aid and Development: Beyond Conditionality*, London: Routledge.
World Bank (1998) *Assessing Aid: What Works, What Doesn't and Why?*, Washington DC: World Bank.

HOWARD WHITE

AIDS *see* HIV/AIDS (definition and treatment); HIV/AIDS (policy issues)

amniocentesis (sex-selection)

Amniocentesis is the removal of amniotic fluid through a needle inserted into the maternal uterus, from which various fetal abnormalities and the sex of the fetus can be identified. Amongst some cultural groups and regions, the technique has been used to selectively abort females. The practice has become increasingly prevalent in China in the context of the one child policy and strong son preference; while in the north Indian state of Haryana, mobile amniocentesis clinics used to carry the slogan "Pay 500 rupees now and save 50,000 rupees later" (referring to the cost of dowry). Often upwardly mobile higher-class households are the worst offenders. Although sex-selective amniocentesis is now illegal in India, it is widely practiced with little enforcement of the law. Sex-selective amniocentesis is one factor contributing to the many millions of "missing" women in the world, with **gender** discrimination now possible from before birth.

See also: fertility; infant and child mortality; population

EMMA E. MAWDSLEY

ANTI-DEVELOPMENT CRITICISMS *see* postmodernism and postdevelopment

anti-politics

The term "anti-politics" refers to the deliberate restriction of development decisions within bureaucracies or development agencies as a means of reducing political debate or **transparency** about how decisions are made (see **politics**). It is an influential part of the "anti" or "post-development" debate (see **postmodernism and postdevelopment**), which question the inherent politics in the project of development.

Anti-politics entered development discourse through a path-breaking and widely cited book by James Ferguson (1990) entitled *The Anti-Politics Machine: "Development," Depoliticization, and Bureaucratic Power in Lesotho*. The study offers a critical analysis of the institutional logic of planned development, including its characteristic forms of knowledge, its practices and its effects. Its influence on academic debate may be considered to be greater than on development practice, perhaps because the implications of Ferguson's argument touch the very core of the development enterprise and require that its premises be radically rethought.

For Ferguson, the anti-politics of development has two components. First, development discourse consistently reposes political issues concerning resource access, power and **inequality** as technical problems amenable to technical solutions. In his example, development "experts" characterized rural Lesotho as a "traditional subsistence peasant society" in which rapid **population** growth, land pressure, deteriorating soil and declining agricultural yields were causing a **food** crisis, **poverty** and outmigration. Proposed solutions focused on soils, seeds, credit, **livestock** improvement, market access and other technical matters. What institutionalized development discourse precluded, according to Ferguson, was a historically grounded, political economic analysis of the emergence of Lesotho as a labor reserve for South African gold mines; the undermining of **agriculture** by the annexation of productive farmland; and the role of cattle not as an economic enterprise but as a social place-holder for migrants who would return home old or sick after decades of absence. These are not the kinds of problems the development apparatus is designed to explore or resolve, and it misrecognizes them in order to proffer its customary repertoire of technical fixes.

The second component of anti-politics concerns the expansion of bureaucratic state power. Ferguson argues that "development" problems requiring technical solutions serve as a point of entry for services that "serve to govern," bringing the state (see **state and state reform**) apparatus closer to peoples' lives and tying them up in new rules, procedures and forms of surveillance. This "preeminently political operation" is not planned but occurs rather as a consistent "side effect" of development interventions. Even projects that fail to meet their technical goals create new bureaucratic pathways and facilities such as roads and administrative offices.

The concept of anti-politics draws researchers' attention to development discourse and its lacunae, and to the (often unintended) effects of development interventions. For development practitioners the implications of Ferguson's argument are far reaching: diligent efforts to improve development projects, learning from mistakes in order to reduce "failure" and enhance success merely oil the "anti-politics machine." They cannot solve underlying problems and may exacerbate them by strengthening the position of rapacious **elites** and authoritarian regimes (see **authoritarianism**). Ferguson argues that technical "development" interventions cannot improve peoples' lives: the fundamental problems can only be solved through political mobilization. His critics respond that technical interventions can help to reduce poverty, and "development," despite its flaws, is still an important vehicle for doing good. Some point to participatory methods and **community**-based initiatives as remedies, but it can be argued that these, too, have anti-political effects.

See also: accountability; governmentality; democracy; narratives of development; politics; postmodernism and postdevelopment; power and discourse; transparency

Further reading

Cooper, F. and Packard, R. (1997) "Introduction," pp. 1–41 in Cooper, F. and Pakard, R. (eds) *International Development and the Social Sciences*, Berkeley: University of California Press.

Ferguson, J. (1990) *The Anti-Politics Machine: "Development," Depoliticization, and Bureaucratic*

Power in Lesotho, St Paul: University of Minnesota Press.
Fisher, W. (1997) "Doing Good? The Politics and Antipolitics of NGO Practices," *Annual Review of Anthropology* 26: 439–64.

TANIA MURRAY LI

apartheid

Apartheid was a system of racial segregation unique to the Republic of South Africa that lasted throughout most of the twentieth century. The word, "apartheid" literally means "apartness" in Afrikaans. The purpose of apartheid was separation of racial groups at different levels: Whites (of European ancestry) from non-Whites, non-Whites from each other; and among the indigenous African populations, one group from another on the basis of tribal affiliation. Non-Whites were made up of Africans (who constitute about 75 percent of the total **population**), Coloureds (people of mixed descent) and Asians (mainly of Indian ancestry). The Department of Home Affairs (a government bureau) was responsible for the classification of South Africans into different racial groups.

The 1913 Land Act, the 1936 Native Land and Trust Act, the 1952 Native Law Amendment Act and later amendments aimed to create a cheap, rural African labor force. The 1913 Land Act delimited specific areas for Black occupation and established the framework for segregation and later apartheid. The birth of apartheid policies in 1948, which was the extension of colonial practices by a Nationalist Government dominated by Afrikaans-speaking Whites, lead to the institutionalization of racial discrimination in South Africa that consolidated White domination and extended statutory racial separation.

The Population Registration Act and the Group Areas Act legislated in 1950 were central to forced removals in the urban areas that saw Africans as "temporary sojourners" in the cities and which ensured that past their useful working life they returned to the rural reserves. The Group Areas Act ensured urban segregation based on the specified population groups defined by the Population Registration Act. People residing in an area designated for a population group other than their own were forced to leave. Thus, the Group Areas Act promoted total segregation, the elimination of competition for space and resources, and the minimization of social contacts between the different racial groups. Other aspects of apartheid laws affecting social life included the prohibition of marriage between non-Whites and Whites; racially segregated facilities and social service provision; and the endorsement of White-only jobs. Also, several Acts (such as the Public Safety Act passed in 1953) were enacted to empower the government to declare stringent states of emergency and repress anti-apartheid protests and movements.

Another major component of apartheid's separate development policy was the Bantu Authorities Act passed in 1951, which established the foundation for ethnic government in African reserves, known as Homelands or Bantustans. These Homelands were independent states to which each African was assigned by the government according to their ethnic/tribal origin. All political rights, including voting, held by Africans were restricted to the designated Homeland. Only Africans with permits were allowed to reside in restricted areas demarcated for Whites. Such permits generally did not include the spouse or family of a permit holder. All Blacks were required to carry "passbooks" which contained fingerprints, photo and information on access to non-Black areas. Furthermore, Africans living in the Homelands needed passports to enter South Africa, making them foreigners in their own country. This system of encouraging predominantly male cyclical **migration** contributed to the break-up of family life among many Africans.

Both internal and external pressures were exerted on the South African government to repeal its apartheid laws. Some of the international pressures included socio-economic and political sanctions and restrictions. Together with domestic opposition and struggles, these pressures led to the eventual demise of apartheid's legal basis in 1990.

See also: authoritarianism; ethnicity/identity; politics; race and racism; state and state reform

Further reading

Deegan, H. (2000) *The Politics of the New South Africa: Apartheid and After*, London: Longman.

Worden, N. and Lee, K. (eds) (2000) *The Making of Modern South Africa*, Oxford: Blackwell.

URMILLA BOB

appropriate technology

Appropriate technology (AT) is technology that is designed with the needs, values, and capabilities of the user in mind. As such, AT can mean many things to many people, partly because by definition it involves the idea that a technology "appropriate" to one set of circumstances is not necessarily appropriate for another. Usually AT refers to technologies and processes that are appropriate to the resources and needs of low-income communities, and therefore have the following characteristics: simple to apply; not **capital intensive**; not energy intensive; use local resources and labor; and nurture the environment and human health.

See also: intermediate technology; technological capability; technology policy; technology transfer

CLAUDIO O. DELANG

AQUACULTURE *see* fisheries

Arab League

The Arab League, or the League of Arab States, is a voluntary association of countries whose people mainly speak Arabic. Its aims are to strengthen ties between members and coordinate policies. The League was formed in 1945 by seven states: Egypt, Iraq, Lebanon, Saudi Arabia, Syria, Transjordan (Jordan since 1950), and Yemen. It now has twenty-two members, including the Palestine Liberation Organization (admitted in 1976). Egypt was excluded as a member in 1979 after it signed a peace treaty with Israel, and the League's headquarters was moved from Cairo to Tunis.

Diplomatic ties with Egypt were renewed in 1987, and in 1989, Egypt was readmitted as a member and the headquarters returned to Cairo. The League is dissimilar to the international unions such as the **European Union** because the League does not aim for any significant level of regional integration, and the organization does not influence laws of individual states. The League's charter focuses instead on commercial relations, communications, **health** and cultural affairs. The League's charter also forbids members from using force against each other. The League was influential in limiting the Lebanese civil wars of 1954, and in creating the Joint Arab Economic Action Charter, which set out principles for economic activities.

See also: economic federalization

TIM FORSYTH

arms sales and controls

Arms sales and controls are relevant to development because of their influence on the incidence of **war** and **violence**; the international politics of **security**; and their impact on government spending. There is a growing tendency to classify arms into three categories: nuclear, chemical/biological, and conventional. The commonly heard name of Weapons of Mass Destruction (WMD) may include nuclear, chemical and biological weapons capable of killing many people at one time.

Efforts to control nuclear proliferation since the **Cold War** are directed in two directions: first, restricting the number of states (see **state and state reform**) having a nuclear capacity; and, second, limiting the size and strength of those nuclear arsenals. The USA, Russia, China, France and the UK are nuclear powers; India and Pakistan joined this group during the late 1990s. Other states suspected of developing nuclear capacity include Iran, Israel, North Korea and Algeria. Iraq's nuclear program was halted and dismantled after the 1991 Gulf War.

During the Iran-Iraq war of the 1980s, chemical weapons were used and Iraq also used poison gas against its Kurdish minority in 1988. Since the attacks against the USA on 11 September 2001, fear of terrorist activity has grown and there are concerns about the use of chemical and/or biological weapons from groups such as Al Qaeda. As the component materials of such weapons have commercial uses, however, it is difficult to implement controls and monitor activity effectively.

By contrast, conventional weapons are widespread. By the late 1990s, weapons production was in excess of states' defense procurement and this, coupled with sales of surplus weapons by states in need of hard currency, has led to a glut of weaponry for sale. **Oxfam** (2001) estimates around 500 million small arms alone in circulation. The prevalence of arms sales to differing factions in civil **wars**, or to oppressive states (see **authoritarianism**) are crucial contributory factors to **famine**, and the emergence of short-term **food** shortages and movements of **refugees** may result from the conflicts that occur partly because of the supply of arms from abroad. **Landmines** used in conflicts such as in Cambodia and Vietnam have claimed thousands of innocent lives years after the formal end of conflict. Classically, some governments in developed countries would face political pressure at home by being tempted to make arms sales to governments overseas, and hence support the domestic arms industries, while also being criticized for allowing the spread of weapons.

Treaties and conventions, both bilateral and multilateral, have been used to control arms transfers and limit stocks of WMD and conventional weapons. The 1968 Nuclear Non-Proliferation Treaty was revised in 1995 and almost all states are signatories. The problem of landmines is the subject of the Ottawa Treaty of 1999. A number of **non-governmental organizations (NGOs)**, such as Campaign Against the Arms Trade, campaign for states to adopt international agreements on arms sales and controls which can then be used as a basis for measuring compliance.

The United Nations' Register of Conventional Weapons was created to promote **transparency** on arms transfers and holdings, being a voluntary disclosure procedure in which states register their annual sales and acquisitions. The Register only has information about imports and exports and does not include acquisition from domestic producers. Furthermore, there has been little participation, particularly by states from the Middle East (see **United Nations**).

States have traditionally been the purchasers of weapons but, since the end of the Cold War, other groups have found it easier to buy arms. Despite export controls, the market for arms has become more open, in part because of overcapacity. Also, until export controls are universally adopted and applied, the potential for unrestricted sales remains.

See also: complex emergencies; famine; landmines; military and security; post-conflict violence; torture; war

Further reading

Oxfam (2001) *Up In Arms: Controlling the International Trade in Small Arms*, Oxford: Oxfam.

Stockholm International Peace Research Institute (annual publication) *SIPRI Yearbook: Armaments, Disarmaments and International Security*, Oxford: Oxford University Press.

CLARE MILLS

ASEAN *see* Association of Southeast Asian Nations (ASEAN)

Asian crises

In the second half of 1997 and throughout 1998, most Asian economies were struggling to contain their worst-ever economic crisis. The crisis came just about four years after the **World Bank** praised the spectacular **economic development** in East Asia as a "miracle." In July 1997, Thailand became the first casualty of the crisis when its finance minister declared that its fixed foreign exchange regime (see **exchange rates**) could no longer be maintained. In the ensuring months, the currencies of most Asian economies fell drastically in their value against the US dollar. What started as currency speculation in Thailand spread rapidly throughout Asia to bring down the foreign exchange regimes of Indonesia and South Korea. All three economies subsequently turned to the

International Monetary Fund (IMF) for financial assistance. Other Asian economies witnessed the downward dwindling of their currencies, stock markets and real estate prices within a very short period. By the end of 1997, most Asian economies suffered from severe interruptions to their industrial production and domestic consumption and economic recessions followed.

Like the Great Depression in the 1930s, different explanations have been offered to unravel the complex origins of the Asian economic crisis. On the one hand, neo-liberal market followers (see **neoliberalism**) have argued fiercely that for decades Asian governments have engaged in an interventionist form of **economic development** that disables the market mechanism. This so-called "crony **capitalism**" perspective seeks to explain the origins of the crisis in relation to government interventions that breed cronies through personal favors of powerful politicians and increase the likelihood of "moral hazard" – a term used by such economists as Paul Krugman to describe the fact that governments in developing economies often bail out failed businesses by favored cronies. As a result of these government interventions, so the argument goes, most cronies in Asian economies engaged in excessive borrowing of foreign debts denominated in US dollars that in turn put tremendous pressures on domestic currencies and eventually triggered the currency speculation and the financial crisis.

Defenders of the **developmental state** in Asia, however, have counteracted the neo-liberal argument by asserting the fact that government interventions had already existed throughout the three decades preceding the crisis and, yet, the crisis broke out only in 1997. They have argued that government interventions cannot be the cause of the crisis. Instead, the global financial architecture and the unhelpful prescriptions of the IMF have been blamed. Robert Wade – a highly vocal proponent in this genre of explanation – put the blame what he calls the "Wall Street-Treasury-IMF complex" (also see **Washington consensus**) that sought relentlessly to expand their corporate and political interests throughout the world by forcing Asian economies to liberalize prematurely their financial markets (e.g. full capital account convertibility). This process greatly increased the **vulnerability** of Asian financial markets and

exchange regimes to speculations by global investors. Jeffrey Sachs, another highly visible figure from Harvard, pointed the finger at the ways in which the IMF prescriptions in the form of **structural adjustment** programs had aggravated the situation and deepened the crisis. Whatever perspective one takes, it is clear that the crisis has enormous impacts on the life of ordinary citizens in most Asian economies.

See also: contagion effect; economic development; exchange rates; international economic order; International Monetary Fund (IMF); neoliberalism; stock markets; Washington consensus

Further reading

Chang, H., Palma, G. and Whittaker, D. (eds) (2001) *Financial Liberalization and the Asian Crisis*, New York: Palgrave.

Radelet, S. and Sachs, J. (1998) "The East Asian Financial Crisis: Diagnosis, Remedies, Prospects," *Brookings Papers on Economic Activity* 1: 1–90.

Wade, R. and Veneroso, F. (1998) "The Asian Crisis: The High Debt Model Versus the Wall Street-Treasury-IMF Complex," *New Left Review* 228: 3–23.

HENRY WAI-CHUNG YEUNG

Asian Development Bank (ADB)

The Asian Development Bank (ADB) is a multilateral development finance institution with a pledge to reduce **poverty** in Asia and the Pacific. It aims to help improve the quality of people's lives by providing loans and technical assistance for development activities in countries in the region. Its charter calls on ADB to favor small, vulnerable economies, while encouraging regional and subregional cooperation. The ADB was established in 1966 with 31 member countries. By 2003, this had risen to 61 members, mostly from the region, with the ADB headquarters located in Manila, Philippines. The ADB maintains close working relationships with other **international organizations and associations** such as the **World Bank**,

International Monetary Fund (IMF), and the **United Nations**, yet remains independent from them. The President of ADB is elected by a Board of Governors, ADB's highest policy-making body, which meets annually and is composed of one representative from each member country.

See also: multilateral development banks (MDBs)

SARAH TURNER

Association of Southeast Asian Nations (ASEAN)

The Association of Southeast Asian Nations (ASEAN) was established on 8 August 1967 in Bangkok by five original member countries: Indonesia, Malaysia, Philippines, Singapore, and Thailand. Brunei Darussalam was to join in 1984, Vietnam in 1995, Laos and Myanmar in 1997, and Cambodia in 1999. The aims of ASEAN, spelt out in the ASEAN Declaration, are to accelerate **economic growth**, social progress and cultural development in the region, and to promote peace and stability. The highest decision-making body within ASEAN is the Meeting of the ASEAN Heads of State and Government, held on an annual basis. The Secretary-General of ASEAN, mandated to initiate, advise, coordinate, and implement ASEAN activities, is appointed on merit and serves a five-year term. In 1994, ASEAN established the ASEAN Regional Forum drawing together twenty-three countries to maintain peace and stability in the region and to promote regional development and prosperity.

See also: economic federalization

SARAH TURNER

asylum seeking

An asylum seeker is an individual who crosses an internationally recognized border and makes an application to be granted refugee status. The words "asylum" and "refugee" (see **refugees**) are often used interchangeably, but have different outcomes.

A refugee may be an individual who has experienced **displacement** or who has been forced to leave their usual site of residence. An asylum seeker, however, can only apply for refugee status in a country that is signatory to the 1951 United Nations Convention on the Status of Refugees (and its 1967 Protocol). If the person's application is accepted under the terms of the Refugee Convention, the person becomes a refugee. Whereas a refugee can apply for refugee status prior to arrival, the asylum seeker has to be physically present in the country where asylum is being sought.

Asylum seekers and host governments have different obligations under the 1951 Convention. Seekers have to show that the application is based on a well-founded fear of persecution under the conditions set out in the Convention. State (see **state and state reform**) parties to the Convention are also committed to certain rules when considering asylum applications. The most important rule is *non-foulement*, meaning not returning a person to a country or place where the person's life would be in danger or at risk. This rule has acquired the principle of customary **international law** and hence is applicable to non-state parties to the Refugee Convention. When a person's refugee status is recognized, there is an entitlement under the Convention to a travel document and protection against discrimination on grounds of race (see **race and racism**), **religion** or country of origin. The person is also entitled to other rights concerning **education**, **employment**, state benefits and **health** care.

There is considerable variation between states in how asylum applications are processed. In general, illegal entry into a country should not be used by a state party to the Convention as a reason for not considering the merits of the asylum application. In some countries, all asylum seekers are held in detention while their applications are processed. The detention of asylum-seekers is controversial and one which is discouraged by the **United Nations High Commissioner for Refugees (UNHCR)**. Most states use detention in certain circumstances, most commonly where states seek to protect national **security** and public order, or where asylum-seekers arrive without documentation and time is needed to establish their identity.

Under the Convention, certain categories of people need not be afforded international protection. These categories include people who have committed certain types of **crime** specified in the Convention, including crimes against peace, war crimes, crimes against humanity, or serious non-political crimes outside the country of refuge. Crimes committed in the country of refuge are the subject of **domestic law**, though some may give cause for removal.

See also: citizenship; displacement; international law; international migration; refugees; stateless people

Further reading

Tuitt, P. (1996) *False Images: The Law's Construction of the Refugee*, London, Pluto.

US Committee for Refugees (ed.) (2003) *World Refugee Survey 2003: An Annual Assessment of Conditions Affecting Refugees, Asylum Seekers, and Internally Displaced Persons*, Washington DC: US Committee for Refugees. http://www.refugees.org/

PAUL OKOJIE

ATOMIC ENERGY *see* nuclear energy

authoritarianism

Authoritarianism applies to a broad range of non-democratic forms of government, from brutally oppressive regimes, personal dictatorships and one-party systems, to varieties of oligarchic forms of institutionalized, or "soft" authoritarianism. All share an effective lack of popular political participation or participatory **governance**. As a form of government, authoritarianism is inherently unstable and requires any or all of the following to support it: a charismatic and politically adept leader; a monopolization of the routes to power; control of such key institutions as the military (see **military and security; politics**) and the support of **elites**. The decline of authoritarianism, whether initiated internally as in the case of Brazil, or

through gradual change and compromise, as in the case of South Africa, often ushers in a process of democratization (see **democracy**). As with colonialism however (see **colonialism, history of; colonialism, impacts of**, the profound reach of authoritarianism into all parts of a country's social and political life, which likely includes structural changes to the constitution, the politicization of key institutions, and a restructuring of social relations, leaves a powerful legacy that continues to shape life in the post-authoritarian society.

Importantly, authoritarianism differs from "totalitarianism," famously characterized by Friedrich and Brzezinski (1965) as involving a totalist ideology; a single party committed to this ideology; and having control of the **media**, armed forces and institutions and therefore involving a planned economy. While totalitarianism was used specifically to delineate forms of governance within states allied to the former Soviet Union in the context of the **Cold War**, authoritarianism covers many different geographical settings. In all these settings, however, modern authoritarianism has characteristically been instantiated after the breakdown of traditional legitimacy. Definitions therefore tend to exclude the exercise of monarchical power as a more traditional form of governance.

Given this wide variation between different instances of modern authoritarianism, there have been many attempts to categorize "types" of authoritarian regimes. Linz (2000:54), for example, distinguishes between "the degree or type of limited political pluralism," and "the degree to which such regimes are based on political apathy and demobilization of the population or limited and controlled mobilizations." On this basis, there are five ideal types: bureaucratic-military authoritarian regimes; organic statism (institutionalized forms of authoritarianism); mobilizational authoritarian regimes in post-democratic societies; post-independence mobilizational authoritarian regimes; and post-totalitarian regimes. Huntington (1991) (see also **clash of civilizations**) more simply divides authoritarianism into three varieties: cases where the party monopolizes power and access to power must be through the party organs (such as the Soviet Union); military regimes that exercise power on an institutional basis (such as Peron's

Argentina); or personal dictatorships (such as Franco's Spain). Such characterizations fail to account for many experiences, however. Malaysia, for example, or Batista's Cuba (1952–9), can be better characterized as "authoritarian populist," with the formal institutions of democracy in place but tight media control and voter interference. It is more useful, therefore, to establish how authoritarianism operates as a particular arrangement of **politics**, and how this arrangement is socially constructed.

An instructive example of the relationship between authoritarianism and development is found in Latin America, where authoritarianism has dominated much of the continent's post-independence history. Based on this experience, O'Donnell (1973) characterized a number of Latin American non-democratic regimes as "Bureaucratic Authoritarian." Unlike the above characterizations, O'Donnell's model sought to link authoritarian forms of governance with their social and economic contexts. O'Donnell's thesis sparked a renewed wave of interest on what has come to be called the "new" authoritarianism, and while this characterization has subsequently been critiqued for implying an overly strong causal relationship between political economy and regime type, the attention it has drawn to the institutional structuring of authoritarianism remains pertinent.

There are at least four ways in which the form and function of authoritarianism intersects with the political economy of domestic and international modes of production, and the social and cultural milieu in which such relations may be constituted: institutions, ideology and identity, nationalism, and resistance. First, while authoritarianism usually involves a charismatic and politically adept leader, such individuals also rely crucially on the support of key **institutions**, such as the military and the church, which may have to become politicized in order to remain socially relevant. Second, authoritarian regimes invariably sanction a particular form of cultural identity that serves to support the official state ideology as well as the formation of an apparatus of political and cultural control. Third, authoritarianism therefore often has an important relationship to **nationalism**, which can provide the cohesive material required to fill the vacuum of popular consensus.

The role of nationalism is particularly important in mobilizational authoritarian regimes such as Cuba under Castro. Finally, authoritarianism also begs the question of resistance and how transitions to more egalitarian forms of governance might take place. An authoritarian regime may be undermined internally or externally by a decline in the ruling power's support base, for example by the death of a leader, or through poor economic performance. Most usually, such changes lead to processes of democratization.

As with the experience of the transition from colonialism to **postcolonialism**, authoritarianism continues to affect post-authoritarian societies and therefore has a lasting impact on the development policies of many developing nations, from the poorest to the most dynamic. As a result, post-authoritarian democracies are noted for being particularly fragile. Authoritarianism therefore poses highly specific developmental challenges that must be taken in to account long after the formal collapse of an authoritarian regime.

See also: apartheid; democracy; elites; governance; military and security; politics

Further reading

Friedrich, C. and Brzezinski, Z. (1965) *Totalitarian Dictatorship and Autocracy*, Cambridge MA: Harvard University Press.

Huntington, S. (1991) *The Third Wave: Democratization in the late Twentieth Century*, London: University of Oklahoma Press.

Linz, J. (2000) *Totalitarian and Authoritarian Regimes*, London: Lynne Rienner.

Munro-Kua, A. (1996) *Authoritarian Populism in Malaysia*, London: Macmillan.

O'Donnell, G. (1973) *Modernization and Bureaucratic Authoritarianism: Studies in South American Politics*, Berkeley: University of California Press.

SIMON REID-HENRY

auto industry

The auto industry specializes in the manufacture and assembly of passenger cars. Since the late nineteenth century it has played a key role in global economic development, not least because the auto industry is a major source of employment, value-added and technological learning. Even today, it remains the world's largest manufacturing industry.

Automobile production is predominantly located in Europe, North America and Japan, reflecting the industry's market-oriented character. Yet, the majority of recent growth in production capacity has taken place in a number of **newly industrialized economies (NIEs)** in Asia, Eastern Europe and Latin America. In part, this can be explained by the emergence of a handful of indigenous volume manufacturers, such as Hyundai, Proton and Tata (see **transnational corporations (TNCs) from developing economies**). Of far greater significance, however, have been the activities of large, transnational vehicle manufacturers headquartered in industrialized countries. Particularly since the early 1990s corporations such as Ford, Fiat and Toyota have invested heavily in creating and/or expanding production capacity in so-called "emerging markets."

One of the principal motives for these investments has been to establish a presence in local markets. Consumer demand for automobiles in developed countries has more or less stagnated. Exploiting market growth in rapidly industrializing economies, therefore, has become an important strategy for global majors such as General Motors (GM) and Nissan. What is more, by increasing production and sales of similar models across a larger number of countries, expansion into emerging markets has allowed vehicle manufacturers to secure economies of scale. Typically, this has gone hand-in-hand with a broader trend towards "commonalization," whereby firms share principal components between several markets in which they operate.

Most of the early plants established by **transnational corporations (TNCs)** in developing countries were little more than stand-alone, assembly operations. More recently, vehicle manufacturers have sought to integrate their foreign operations into regional networks, where they perform specialist functions as part of a spatial division of labor. An oft-cited example here is the regional integration of Japanese and US owned plants in Mexico into their wider North American production systems. This approach permits economies of scale by concentrating production in particular facilities and, moreover, for manufacturers to organize production systems in a way that best exploits the specific advantages of different locations.

Aside from shifts in the geography of production, one of the most far-reaching changes in the auto industry over the past decade has been the relationship between outside suppliers and vehicle manufacturers. Until recently, a large share of the components that go into making a car were purchased from numerous small-scale firms, manufacturing parts according to designs supplied by auto producers. Driven by the requirements of flexibility and cost competitiveness, auto manufacturers are increasingly sourcing components, sub-assemblies and entire modules from a smaller number of companies. The result has been the emergence of large, increasingly transnational "tier-one" suppliers, who not only take on greater responsibility for product development, but also the management and coordination of component supply chains comprising second- and third-tier suppliers.

See also: export-led growth; Fordism versus Toyotaism; iron and steel; transnational corporations (TNCs); transnational corporations (TNCs) from developing economies

Further reading

Dicken, P. (2003) *Global shift: Reshaping the Global Economic Map in the 21st Century*, London: Sage.
Humphrey, J., Lecler, Y. and Salerno, S. (2000) *Global Strategies and Local Realities: The Auto Industry in Emerging Markets*, New York: St Martin's Press.

RICHARD PERKINS AND
KONSTANTINOS A. MELACHROINOS

B

BABYMILK *see* corporate social responsibility (CSR); nutrition

BALANCE OF PAYMENTS *see* trade; World Trade Organization/General Agreement on Tariffs and Trade (WTO/GATT)

BAMAKO INITIATIVE *see* United Nations Children's Fund (UNICEF)

Bandung conference (1955)

The 1955 Bandung Conference in Indonesia was a meeting between representatives of twenty-nine African and Asian nations, with the aim of promoting economic and cultural cooperation (see **South-South cooperation**), opposing colonialism (see **colonialism, history of; colonialism, impacts of**), and urging neutrality between East and West during the **Cold War**. The meeting was organized by Indonesia, Myanmar (Burma), Sri Lanka, India and Pakistan. The meeting is seen to be the inspiration for the **non-aligned movement** in 1961, and eventually the **Group of 77 (G-77)**. Some notable speakers included Dr Mohammed Natsir, former prime minister of Indonesia and at the time head of Indonesia's largest political party, Masjumi, who called for "Pan-Islam" as a socialist and Islamic alternative to communism. Gamal Abdel Nasser of Egypt also laid the foundations for both Pan-Arabism and Pan-Africanism, and denounced the **United Nations** and the West for complicity in the **displacement** of the Palestinians from their homeland. Lebanese, Algerian,

Tunisian and Moroccan delegates denounced French colonialism at the conference. China used the event to strengthen friendly relations with other Asian nations. Not invited to the conference were South Africa, Israel, Taiwan, South Korea, and North Korea.

See also: Cold War; Group of 77 (G-77); non-aligned movement; South-South cooperation

TIM FORSYTH

Basel Convention on hazardous waste

The Basel Convention on the Control of Transboundary Movements of Hazardous Wastes and their Disposal was adopted in 1989 and entered into force on 5 May 1992, under the auspices of the **United Nations** Environment Programme (UNEP). The main objectives of the Basel Convention are: transboundary movements of **hazardous waste**s should be reduced to a minimum consistent with their environmentally sound management; hazardous wastes should be treated and disposed of as close as possible to their source of generation; and hazardous waste generation should be reduced and minimized at source. In order to achieve these objectives, the Convention aims to control the transboundary movement of hazardous wastes; monitor and prevent illegal traffic; provide assistance for the environmentally sound management of hazardous wastes; promote cooperation between parties in this field; and develop technical guidelines for the management of hazardous wastes. As of July 2004, the Convention had 162 parties.

See also: environment; hazardous waste; trade

JONATHAN KRUEGER

basic needs

A "basic needs" approach to development focuses on providing access to the minimum income or items necessary to ensure the continuation of healthy life. Early social research on **poverty** sought to identify the idea of poverty with the concept of subsistence, understood as the minimum income necessary to ensure basic physical efficiency, such as **food**, fuel (see **energy policy**) and shelter (see **housing**). The idea of "basic needs" was extended in the 1970s to include a broader range of minimum needs. Basic needs were said to include not only the minimum needed to support a household's private consumption, but also a infrastructure of essential public and social services, such as **drinking water**, **education** and **primary health care**. The effect of including communal activities placed basic needs in the context of **social development**. The International Fund for Agricultural Development uses a Basic Needs Index to refer to social development, including access to education and **health**. The factors taken into account include adult literacy (see **illiteracy**); primary school enrolment; **population** for each doctor; **infant and child**

mortality; access to health (see **primary health care**); access to safe water; and **sanitation**.

Needs are generally defined in the context of the society in which they occur. Even if needs are basic and universal, the processes through which they are recognized and met are necessarily social ones. The needs for food, clothing or shelter are determined only in part by physical circumstances; they also depend on the norms and standards that apply in different societies. Homelessness, for example, depends not only on access to housing, but on the alternatives to housing: squatting (see **squatters**) is permitted in some societies, and not in others. Moreover, some needs are relational. Educational attainment, for example, is essential to achieve the resources and opportunities that other people have, but levels of educational attainment depend on the levels of education elsewhere in society. (Literacy ceases to be a key indicator in a society where the test is possession of a high school diploma.) This means that the tests for basic needs shift as societies change.

The purpose of arguments about "basic needs" has been to extend the narrow focus on "absolute poverty" to include some of the social concepts favored by advocates of "relative poverty" (see **absolute versus relative poverty**). However, there are conceptual problems with the approach. Although the idea of basic extends a minimalist concept of subsistence, it does so only on a restricted basis. Some needs, like education and health, are treated as "basic;" others, like **security**, transport (see **transport policy**), or political **empowerment** are not. This seems arbitrary. A common approach to defining poverty is the

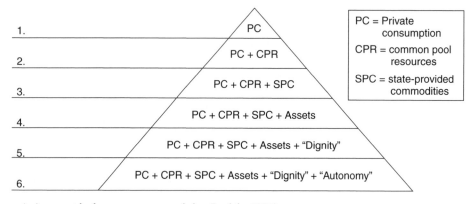

Figure 1 A pyramid of poverty concepts (after Baulch, 1996).

"poverty pyramid" (Baulch, 1996), which shows a variety of means of defining poverty according to diversifying the criteria from simple measurements of income, to concepts including social **empowerment**, **citizenship**, and support networks. See Figure 1. There are further problems in using the concept of basic needs for **poverty measurement**. Boltvinik (1998) argues, based on applications made in Latin America, that the numbers of people in poverty, and the severity of problems, appear to vary directly with the number and type of basic needs that are included in the assessment.

See also: absolute versus relative poverty; chronic poverty; human rights; measuring development; poverty; participatory poverty assessment (PPA); poverty measurement

Further reading

Baulch, B. (1996) "The New Poverty Agenda: A Disputed Consensus," *IDS Bulletin* 27:1 1–10.

Boltvinik, J. (1998) *Poverty in Latin America*, UNDP SEPED Series on Poverty Reduction, New York: UNDP. http://www.undp.org/poverty/publications/pov_red/Poverty_in_Latin_America.pdf

Drakakis Smith, D. (1997) "Third World Cities: Sustainable Urban Development III – Basic Needs and Human Rights," *Urban Studies* 34: 5–6 797–824.

Townsend, P. (1993) *The International Analysis of Poverty*, Hemel Hempstead: Harvester Wheatsheaf.

PAUL SPICKER

big push

The notion of the big push goes back to the work of Rosenstein-Rodan in 1943 concerning the **industrialization** of the relatively backward Eastern Europe. The term emphasizes the multisectoral nature of the economy and the links between different sectors. The concept argues that full industrialization may only take place when there is sufficient demand for traditional forms of manufacturing to be replaced by more efficient, highly industrialized forms of production. The "big push" refers to the efforts by the state both to invest in industrialization, and educate and encourage citizens to buy products, and become involved in assisting industrialization.

Murphy, Shleifer and Vishny (1989) present a modern version of this theory that acknowledges the creation of demand, but also includes coordination problems between various sectors in the economy; the role of intermediate inputs (services); and the possibility of multiple outcomes (or equilibria). The economy can come to a rest at a variety of points between an underdevelopment trap and full-fledged industrialization.

Other analysts have proposed two further distinctions. First, more attention should be given to **human capital** (or labor) as a means of generating growth; and second that a distinction must be made between a non-traded sector in the economy (purely for domestic consumption); a traded-good sector (e.g. manufacturing); and a purely exportable natural resource (see **natural resources**) or mineral sector. Human capital accumulation, in the form of an externality or indirect effect, takes place because of traded goods/manufacturing production only. Temporary rises in the price of exportable minerals – or so-called "resource booms" – retard the growth of the economy because it discourages or crowds out production in the traded sector. The stock of human capital is diminished as **employment** in tradable declines; this in turn hampers future production of all goods, and hence **economic growth**.

To illustrate this, Sachs and Warner (1999) examined a case where increasing returns to scale is permitted in either one of the two sectors of the economy (traded or non-traded), but not in both. They found that overall returns were increased when a range of intermediate inputs were made, which could then be employed in final production. They then questioned whether resource booms contribute towards big-push type industrialization, and found that they unambiguously expand the non-tradable sector, while at the same time shrinking the traded sector. If the expanding (non-traded) sector uses these intermediate inputs, it may contribute to a successful big push. However, if the traded sector uses the intermediate inputs, big-pushes are less likely.

See also: developmental state economic development; industrialization; modernization theory; natural resources; stages of economic growth

Further reading

Murphy, K., Shleifer, A. and Vishny, R. (1989) "Industrialization and the Big Push," *Journal of Political Economy* 97: 1003–26.

Sachs, J. and Warner, A. (1999) "The Big Push, Natural Resource Booms and Growth," *Journal of Development Economics* 59: 43–76.

S. MANSOOB MURSHED

bilateral aid agencies

Bilateral aid agencies are the official government organizations that coordinate Official Development Assistance (ODA), or **aid**, on behalf of donor countries in collaboration with host countries. About 70 percent of ODA is bilateral. Agencies can be ministries, but also local governments or executive agencies of donor states. In the 1990s, bilateral aid amounted to between US$35 and US$41 billion net. There are major differences between the donors. The largest donors in absolute terms are the USA ($11 billion in 2001) and Japan ($9.8 billion). The smallest donors of the OECD-countries are Greece, Luxemburg and New Zealand. Luxemburg though belongs to the largest donors (with Denmark, Norway, the Netherlands and Sweden) in relative terms. These five donors are the only ones to have reached the **United Nations** target (adopted in October 1970 on advice of the **Pearson Commission**) of 0.7 percent of **gross national product (GNP)**. Small donors (in relative terms) often have to spend a large part of their budget on multilateral aid (i.e. aid coordinated by more than one country), due to obligatory contributions. Large donors (in relative terms) often spend a large proportion of their budget through **non-governmental organizations (NGOs)**.

There are several motives for bilateral aid. Development assistance is not only determined by humanitarian motives such as compassion for victims of **famine** (see **humanitarianism**), or visions of a more equitable world; it is also determined by political, economic and environmental motives (see **conditionality**). Behind the political/strategic motive is the idea to bring or keep aid-recipients in the donor's sphere of influence or in its (military) alliances. Under this motive, aid can also be used to gain influence or, in its softest form, to make friends all over the globe. Politico-strategic motives obviously play a prominent role in the aid programs from the superpowers, but they can also play a role in the aid policy of smaller nations at times. The political/strategic motive is best reflected in donors' choices of aid-receiving countries.

A second motive is economic/commercial, especially relating to the expansion of trade or export markets from the donor country, or safeguarding the supply of raw materials for the donor. Aid can also be used to establish shipping or air treaties. In addition, aid can be applied to help reduce the impacts of downturns in cyclical economies when used to combat recession by providing goods and services from severely hit industrial sectors (for example transport (see **transport policy**), **iron and steel**, ship yards). Most donors have specific programs to promote investments from their national firms in developing countries, often organized via special financing corporations via mechanisms such as investment guarantees or pilot projects. The existence of this economic motive can be most easily identified by analyzing the back flow of aid, or the percentage of aid spent in the donor country itself on goods and services delivered to the aid recipients. This figure is not officially reported. Sometimes this motivation for aid can also be indicated by the types of aid program initiated within specific types of country.

The third determinant of aid programs is ethical/humanitarian. Various ethical considerations may be relevant here. The Christian commandment to "love thy neighbor," (see **Christianity; religion**) or socio-democratic or socialist solidarity with the poor and the oppressed are common motivations. In particular, Christian Democrat and Social Democrat Parties in the **European Union** are the bearers of these ideas, dubbed "humane internationalism" by some authors and seen as connected to the Rhineland-model of economic development.

A fourth motive is environmental. The rise of transboundary environmental problems and international environmental agreements (see **environment; Basel Convention on hazardous waste; climate change**) prompt some donors to invest in schemes of international **technology transfer** or environmental assistance.

In the 1990s, the question of **refugees** became a fifth determinant of ODA. Growing numbers of refugees, and governments' fear of receiving asylum seekers (see **asylum seeking**) in European and North American countries, began to influence aid to reduce the flow of refugees. In the early 1990s, this trend was seen in a shift of aid from Western European countries to countries of Eastern and Central Europe (see **postsocialism; shock therapy**). Haiti has also become more prominent in USA aid. The decision of the 1995 European Summit in Cannes to enter a major Mediterranean cooperation program reflected the desire to manage the flow of refugees, and to help stabilize domestic politics in partner countries.

The value given to different motives for aid is influenced more by the power relations in the donor countries themselves than by international relations, or socio-economic developments in the aid-receiving countries. The ideologies and socio-economic influence of various agents within the donor country (such as diplomats, international firms, NGOs, churches) will shape the regulation of the aid program.

There are also questions of how different bilateral aid agencies are organized. Some countries such as the UK have a minister for International Development with a specific government department. Others countries, such as the Netherlands and Denmark, have a minister and a directorate for international cooperation within the ministry of foreign affairs. Sweden and Norway have a minister, a directorate for international cooperation within the ministry of foreign affairs and an executing agency to implement the program. The Southern European countries generally have a secretary of state for international cooperation and an implementing agency, but aid is disbursed via several ministries, chiefly including the ministry of finance or the ministry of economic affairs and

finance. In the USA, there is no cabinet post for development cooperation. The National Security Council and State Department take all important policy decisions. USAID (the United States Agency for International Development) is the implementing agency, although this organization carries relatively less power than some of the European departments.

Since the 1970s, most bilateral aid agencies have evaluated their work. The Northern European and Anglophone countries are most open in their evaluation policy (see **accountability; transparency**). Different aid programs can be evaluated on various grounds. But critics agree generally that, if largely the donor's interests determine aid, then major failures can be found easily.

See also: aid; aid effectiveness and aid evaluation; accountability; conditionality; emergency assistance; European Union; food aid; humanitarianism

Further reading

Cox, A., Healy, J., Hoebink, P. and Voipio, T. (2000) *European Development Cooperation and the Poor*, London: Macmillan.

Hoebink, P. and Stokke, O. (eds) (2004) *Perspectives on European Development Cooperation*, London: Frank Cass.

Ruttan, V. (1996) *United States Development Assistance Policy: The Domestic Politics of Foreign Economic Aid*, Baltimore: Johns Hopkins University Press.

Stokke, O. (ed.) (1989) *Western Middle Powers and Global Poverty*, Uppsala: Scandinavian Institute of African Studies.

PAUL HOEBINK

biodiversity

The word biodiversity is a contraction of "biological diversity," meaning the variety of life on Earth, ranging from genes and bacteria to ecosystems and landscapes. On one hand, biodiversity has stimulated attempts to measure and conserve landscapes around the world. On the other, it has been written off as a buzzword, and a biological form of modern-day imperialism.

Concern about the accelerating loss of global species and **habitats** was voiced throughout the late 1970s. In the 1980s, conservation biology emerged as a discipline that explicitly addressed the conservation of biological diversity. While the exact number of species being lost was unknown, it was generally accepted that human-induced (rather than natural or background) extinctions were occurring, due to the increasingly visible destruction of natural habitats on a global scale. The **deforestation** of equatorial regions (the Earth's most biodiverse habitats) was the major cause for concern. By 1989, rainforests were reduced to 55 percent of their maximum extent during the Holocene era (i.e. 10,000 years ago to present), with annual rates of loss doubling between 1979 and 1989, to as much as 2 percent a year. Similarly, extinctions of plant species, although limited, were unprecedented in the geological record.

In response, the US National Academy for Science organized a forum for leading conservation biologists on biological diversity in Washington in 1986, coining the word "biodiversity" for its title. The forum attracted a huge amount of scientific and popular attention, and Edward Wilson, a leading evolutionary biologist and one of *Time* magazine's twenty-five most influential Americans in 1996, edited the forum's proceedings that appeared in 1989 under the title *Biodiversity*. In it, the world's leading biologists set out a comprehensive case for biodiversity conservation, arguing that great losses have already occurred, which will have drastic consequences if they continue unchecked. They suggest that the human race has an obligation to conserve biodiversity on moral grounds (as our living companions), economic grounds (for the potential benefits to agriculture, medicine and industry), and survivalist grounds (because the atmosphere, soils, food chains and so forth that we depend upon are maintained by ecosystems of diverse species).

The forum provided a springboard for further negotiations at the Rio **Earth Summit (1992) (United Nations Conference on Environment and Development)**, and the presentation of the **Convention on Biological Diversity (CBD)**, which received 168 signatures during the year following the summit. The CBD constitutes a legally binding agreement between signatories to protect their biodiversity, defined in Article Two as the "variability among living organisms from all sources including, *inter alia*, terrestrial, marine and other aquatic ecosystems and the ecological complexes of which they are part; this includes diversity within species, between species and of ecosystems." This definition was intentionally inclusive, reflecting the global dimensions of ecological change. However, its inclusiveness raised questions about how best to conceptualize, measure and conserve biodiversity.

Biodiversity can be conceived of ecologically, organismally, and genetically, with each comprising a series of scaled elements (Gaston and Spicer, 1998). Ecological diversity covers biomes, bioregions, landscapes, ecosystems, habitats, niches and populations; genetic diversity includes genes, chromosomes, populations and individuals; while organismal diversity covers the taxonomic divisions of kingdoms, phyla, families, genera, and species. However, some of these terms are more easily defined than others. While genetic material such as chromosomes form discrete units that are readily identifiable, ecological concepts like populations defy clear definition in either spatial or temporal terms. Furthermore, exact definitions of elements such as species, habitats and ecosystems do not exist. Habitats and ecosystems are as much conceptual tools as observable units in reality, while species can be defined variously by evolutionary lineage, morphological similarity, biological compatibility and so forth.

Each criterion produces different classifications, which affect how biodiversity is measured and conserved. Discerning the absolute biodiversity of an area is impossible, because theoretically there are an infinite number of potential measures. Accordingly, surrogates are adopted as being representative of overall diversity. Species richness is the most commonly used surrogate measure, because large numbers of species indicate genetic, organismal and ecological diversity. Furthermore, large amounts of data already exist about the distribution of species, as they are relatively easy to measure compared to, say, chromosomes or landscapes.

However, while approximately 1.4 million species have been given scientific names, global taxonomy remains in an elementary state, and this figure represents little more than a scratch on the surface of overall species diversity. The best estimates of evolutionary biologists place the number of tropical insect species alone at between 10 and 80 million, and the number of species on the planet is not known even to the order of magnitude (current knowledge places it at between 10 and 100 million). As a result, the exact rate of biodiversity loss is unknown (according to the World Conservation Monitoring Center, estimates vary between 1 and 11 percent per year since 1975), and the amount of biodiversity already lost is a matter of speculation, as opposed to scientific fact.

Similarly, the actual effects of biodiversity loss upon ecosystem processes are not fully known, and a number of potential relationships exist. Biodiversity conservation assumes that stable ecosystems are typified by increasing diversity, and that a reduction in species diversity will cause a corresponding reduction in ecosystem productivity. However, species can also act like rivets holding an ecosystem together, and while some are expendable with little effect, the loss or removal of others can be catastrophic. Along similar lines, the redundant species hypothesis suggests that some species reduction may have little effect, as many functions are performed by more than one species. Nonequilibrium concepts have gained ground in ecology over the 1990s (see **environment**), with competition displacement theories arguing that because ecosystems become ossified under hyperstable conditions, low-level disturbance may actually maintain or increase species diversity by displacing dominant species, creating new niches and introducing new competitors.

While the term's flexibility has lent it popular and political appeal, the considerable uncertainties surrounding its definition and measurement of biodiversity have led some to criticize its scientific credentials. Perhaps because of this, the CBD has applied the **precautionary principle** to conservation, focusing upon the creation of proactive policies across a range of political and economic activities that extend well beyond the realm of science. Article One of the CBD states that its objectives are to conserve biological diversity, and to pursue "the fair and equitable sharing of the benefits arising out of the utilization of genetic resources." The policy framework for conserving biodiversity consists of a hierarchy of species and habitat action plans drawn up at the national, regional and local levels. These action plans are now being implemented in signatory countries, and translate the global aims of the CBD into local actions designed to effect change across the political, economic and social arenas, in accordance with the **Agenda 21** blueprint. However, the emphasis of the CBD upon conserving biodiversity through the utilization of genetic resources has provoked controversy.

The CBD emphasized the need for a legal, political and economic framework for patenting and trading genetic material (see **intellectual property rights (IPRs)**). This aspect of biodiversity has serious developmental implications, because the vast majority of the world's remaining biodiversity (both known and unknown) is concentrated in developing countries (due to the latitudinal rule, whereby biodiversity increases towards the equator). By creating a market for biodiversity, **transnational corporations (TNCs)** from richer developed countries are able to procure environmental resources through **bioprospecting**, at the expense of **indigenous peoples**. Organisms from the developing world can be patented as **biomedicines** and biotechnologies (see **biotechnology and resistance**), and marketed in the West with no benefit accruing to the country of its origin, while agricultural plants can be patented, modified and then sold back to economically disadvantaged farmers at a profit.

These practices constitute a form of **biopiracy**, or biological imperialism, with many commentators claiming that the CBD represents a form of green developmentalism, extending existing global economic and political inequalities into the ecological sphere. While the USA did not sign the CBD, claiming that there was insufficient provision for genetic resource patenting and trading, these debates are increasingly implicated in political and popular disputes over global **terms of trade**.

See also: Cartagena protocol on Biosafety; Convention on Biological Diversity (CBD);

deforestation; biopiracy; bioprospecting; environment; sustainable development

Further reading

Gaston, K. and Spicer, J. (1998) *Biodiversity*, Oxford: Blackwell.

McAffee, K. (1999) "Selling Nature to Save It? Biodiversity and Green Developmentalism," *Environment and Planning D: Society and Space*, 17: 133–54.

Takacs, D. (1996) *The Idea of Biodiversity: Philosophies of Paradise*, Baltimore: Johns Hopkins University Press.

Wilson, E. (1992) *The Diversity of Life*, London: Penguin.

JAMES EVANS

BIOGAS *see* renewable energy

biomedicine

Biomedicine is concerned with alleviating human suffering, **disease eradication**, and countering **mortality**, as commonly practiced in hospitals worldwide. Biomedicine is based on the conception of the body being a complex biological machine. Practices involve a diagnosis and treatment of patient's symptoms (both in mental and physical health), within settings that implement professional rules of conduct and international health policy guidelines. However, cross-cultural studies clearly demonstrate that biomedicine is not objective or universal as claimed, and they acknowledge the hegemonic character of biomedicine and its foundations in Western knowledge. For instance, disease is perceived as a biologically defined symptom of abnormality in the body, however the social construction of disease (see **disease, social constructions of**) establishes the subjectivity involved therein. A very political critique of biomedicine had emerged in the 1960s, and it involved the recognition of the linkages between **health** and development, and **health and poverty**. These simultaneously recognized the

diversity and efficacy of **indigenous medicine** as alternatives.

See also: disease eradication; disease, social constructions of; health; health and poverty; indigenous medicine; nutrition; pharmaceuticals

Further reading

Good, B. (1994) *Medicine, Rationality, and Experience: An Anthropological Perspective*, Cambridge: Cambridge University Press.

VIBHA ARORA

biopiracy

Biopiracy is an expression used to denounce **bioprospecting**. The term "biopiracy" articulates the perspective that **transnational corporations (TNCs)** and research institutions are "stealing" or "plundering" genetic material found in biodiverse regions in the developing world and leaving source countries and communities (see **community**) without benefits (see **biodiversity** and **Convention on Biological Diversity (CBD)**). Patents taken out in industrialized countries on plant resources traditionally used for food and medicine such as basmati rice, turmeric, and the neem tree in South Asia; and Ayahuasca, Cunani, and Tipir in the Amazons have been accused of biopiracy. Bioprospecting projects carried out without proper informed consent of the local inhabitants, traditional healers, and source country government or without a mutual agreement on equitable benefit sharing have also been strongly resisted as biopiracy. The movements to prevent biopiracy, led by **non-governmental organizations (NGOs)**, developing country governments, **indigenous people**, and traditional healers around the globe, have succeeded in revoking patents, halting bioprospecting projects, and installing strict research protocols for bioprospectors.

See also: biotechnology and resistance; biodiversity; bioprospecting; Convention on Biological Diversity (CBD)

CHIKAKO TAKESHITA

bioprospecting

Bioprospecting is a contraction of **biodiversity** prospecting, and refers to the endeavor to discover valuable chemical compounds and genetic material for pharmaceutical, agricultural, and industrial use from biological resources found in biodiverse regions. Proponents present bioprospecting as a desirable project that returns economic compensation to developing nations for providing biological resources and generates incentives to conserve biodiversity as a reservoir of genetic resources. Critics, however, regard bioprospecting as an exploitation of developing country resources or **biopiracy**. One of the first showcase bioprospecting projects is the 1991 agreement between Costa Rica's National Biodiversity Institute (INBio) and the pharmaceutical company Merck and Co., in which part of the commission paid by Merck to INBio for biological samples was allocated specifically to nature conservation efforts. The largest public initiative on bioprospecting is known as the International Cooperative Diversity Group funded by US government agencies and conducted by multiple institutions from the US and host developing countries.

See also: biodiversity; biopiracy; Convention on Biological Diversity (CBD); environment

CHIKAKO TAKESHITA

biotechnology and resistance

Biotechnology usually refers to modern biological techniques, especially genetic engineering, and their products. Agricultural biotechnology now almost exclusively refers to **genetically modified organisms (GMOs)**. In popular debates, however, it is sometimes used to refer to the entire human history of biological intervention – including such practices as yoghurt fermentation, beer brewing, and bread-making. In that vein, a widespread definition of biotechnology may be "any technique that uses living organisms (or parts of organisms) to make or modify products, to improve plants or animals, or to develop microorganisms for specific uses." A more apt definition, however, may also acknowledge the recent commercial impetus behind biotechnology: "the application of organisms, biological systems or biological processes to manufacturing and service industries."

Many genetically modified (GM) products in **agriculture** entered commercial cultivation during the 1990s, mainly in North America, Canada and Argentina. Long before **commercialization** began, the entire technological trajectory provoked a wide-ranging debate, and GM products have not always been seen as legitimate or socially acceptable. According to supporters, GM crops offer essential tools for environmentally-friendly products, greater productivity and the means to increase **food** production, especially in developing countries; therefore society faces the risk of foregoing these benefits. According to critics, however, biotechnology will aggravate the problems of intensive **monoculture**, as well as imposing new hazards; therefore the technology poses the risk of precluding beneficial alternatives.

The controversy has been further fuelled by the decisions of the USA and EU that patents can be authorised for genes inserted into GM crops. Patent-holders can charge farmers royalties (or sue them) for re-sowing seeds; indeed, they have sought to extend such controls to some traditional varieties (such as basmati rice or the neem tree in India) which produce substances similar to GM ones. For advocates of greater patent rights, "**biopiracy**" means violations of those rights, and hence rights are essential for protecting the investment in "biological inventions." For opponents of these rights, however, the patents themselves are seen as biopiracy, because they privatize mere discoveries and common resources, while deterring potentially beneficial innovations.

GM crops have become a focus for the wider debate over **sustainable development**. Proponents within industry have promoted GM crops as "high-input sustainable agriculture," offering chances to increase food production, decrease agrochemical usage (see **agrochemicals**), and preserve soil fertility (see **soil erosion and soil fertility**). Such actions also use less energy, help protect habitats, and make previously marginal environments (such as **drylands** or areas affected by **salinization**) more productive. Furthermore, proponents of GM crops point out the apparently degrading impacts of existing agricultural techniques especially through the use of **agrochemicals**.

Critics, however, argue that world hunger and environmental degradation do not result from the existence of marginal land or inefficient agriculture, but from other causes such as unjust forms of land use, maldistribution of food, and **war** disrupting cultivation. Environmentalists have also feared that **genetically modified organisms (GMOs)** may impact negatively on native flora and fauna via so-called "gene flow," or the transfer of GMO DNA via the spread of pollen. Similarly, GM crops that are herbicide or disease resistant may become persistent weeds if their seeds spread to unwanted locations. Local **biodiversity** may also be affected by the impacts of toxins within GMOs on non-target insect species, or by the need to use extra amounts of herbicide against GMOs when they are seen as weeds.

In recent years, more and more land has been converted from staple food crops to cash crops such as bulk commodities used as animal feed. Under pressures of **structural adjustment** policies, imposed by the **International Monetary Fund (IMF)** and **World Bank**, many developing countries have changed land use to ehance exports, including "higher-yield" seeds which have frequently remained vulnerable to pests or **drought**, and have reduced agricultural subsidies – thus allowing cheap imports to undermine their own production systems (see **green revolution**). GM seeds are consequently seen by some critics to assist the movement towards cultivating high-volume export crops, and hence exacerbate rather than alleviate problems of food sovereignty. For example, critics have claimed that the famous "Golden Rice" – a GM variety promising to overcome children's deficiency of vitamin A – is addressing a problem that emerged only since the adoption of industrialized agriculture, and the replacement of previous multi-cropping methods. Critics also point out that industrialized **agriculture**, including GM cropping, may extend the area of land under monoculture, and cheapen weed control, and hence undermine both **biodiversity** and **livelihoods** in places where weeds were formerly controlled by hand.

In Mexico, maize yields have been increased by using green revolution-type "modern varieties"

with more purchased inputs. Moreover, under the **North American Free Trade Agreement (NAFTA)**, Mexico must accept imports of US maize which generally sells at lower prices, thanks to more favorable conditions and export-credit subsidies. Together, these developments threaten traditional methods of maize cultivation, including such practices as crop rotations, which help to control pests. An estimated 2.5 million households still cultivate maize on small-scale, low-input, rainfed farms. Market competition increases the pressures on peasants to abandon agriculture or else adopt intensive methods in order to survive economically. Critics claim GM crops embody such methods and thus threatens their livelihoods.

It is not surprising, then, that GM crops have encountered much resistance worldwide. When the transnational corporation, Monsanto (see **transnational corporations (TNCs)**), started shipping GM soya beans from the USA to Europe, European **non-governmental organizations (NGOs)** began catalyzing mass opposition against GM food. GM products were turned into a symbol of corporate control over the agro-food chain and its further **industrialization**. Public protest had diverse sources – for example, many French farmers counterposed their own skills in less-intensive cultivation methods; Italian smallholders regarded GM crops as a threat to local specialty crops; and British nature conservationists argued that broad-spectrum herbicides could harm wildlife habitats near farmland.

In response to the protest, European supermarket chains decided to exclude GM grain from their own-brand products. This commercial blockage, coinciding with greater scientific debate over agro-environmental hazards (see **science and technology**), led to more stringent regulation and long delays in decisions on further products. This situation also opened up opportunities for more extensive cultivation methods.

Several countries of the South also developed opposition movements against GM crops in the late 1990s. Long before then, some Indian farmers' organizations had been campaigning against hybrid seeds as a threat to farmers' control over their livelihoods. They opposed Monsanto's GM insecticidal cotton as a further step towards privatizing seeds; farmers in Andhra Pradesh symbolically "cremated" field trials. They also counterposed alternative means for farmers to improve seeds, to control pests and to remain independent of agrochemicals.

When the Brazilian government sought to approve commercial cultivation of Monsanto's herbicide-tolerant GM soya in the late 1990s, this was blocked by a broad coalition. Opponents include farmers who regarded GM crops as contrary to sustainable agriculture, as well as those seeking to preserve non-GM grain markets in Europe. A prime mover there has been the landless movement, Movimento de Trabalhadores Sem Terra, especially in Rio Grande del Sur. On occupied land they initially imitated chemical-intensive methods but have begun shifting to organic methods of cultivation. In all these ways, resistance to GM crops makes links with alternative agricultural models for sustainable development (see **agroecology**).

See also: agriculture; agrochemicals; Cartagena Protocol on Biosafety; environment; genetically modified organisms (GMOs); green revolution; science and technology; World Trade Organization/General Agreement on Tariffs and Trade (WTO/GATT)

Further reading

Kloppenburg, J. (1988) *First the Seed: The Political Economy of Plant Biotechnology, 1492–2000,* Cambridge: Cambridge University Press.

Lappé, M. and Bailey, B. (1999) *Against the Grain: the Genetic ransformation of Global Agriculture,* London: Earthscan.

Levidow, L. and Carr, S. (eds) (2000) "Precautionary Regulation: GM Crops in the European Union," special issue, *Journal of Risk Research* 3:3 187–285.

Parrott, N. and Marsden, T. (2002) *The Real Green Revolution: Organic and Agroecological Farming in the South,* London: Greenpeace.

Pimbert, M. and Wakeford, T. (2002) *Prajateerpu: A Citizens Jury/Scenario Workshop on Food and Farming Futures for Andhra Pradesh, India,* London: IIED.

LES LEVIDOW

BIRTH CONTROL *see* family planning

BIRTH RATE *see* fertility

boreholes

Boreholes are deep wells sunk with small diameter drills to tap underground sources of water for use by people, **livestock** and **agriculture**. They are lined, and require a pump to bring up the water. They are sometimes referred to as "bores." The advantages of boreholes are to supply water to areas with few surface water sources, thus allowing settlement, livestock raising, and agriculture in areas where they would not have been possible. The disadvantages include: overcrowding of cattle, compacting soils, and degradation around boreholes in semi-arid and arid areas; disruptive changes in seasonal patterns of herding and associated conflict between groups; excessive draw-down from underground sources of water, leading to diminished supply of water in boreholes and other wells, and problems of **salinization**.

See also: agriculture; desertification; drinking water; drylands; irrigation; livestock; water management

PAULINE E. PETERS

BOTTOM-UP DEVELOPMENT *see* participatory development; people-centered development

brain drain

A brain drain is said to occur when skilled and educated people migrate to more developed areas and the resultant loss is seen as being detrimental to the development prospects of countries or areas of origin. Such a situation may apply where the supply of the educated is small, and the economy is stagnant in origin areas. Where economies are more dynamic, as in parts of East Asia, the loss of the educated may have little impact on overall development and the later return of even relatively small numbers with enhanced skills and ideas is a contributory factor in promoting economic, social and political development. Consequently, brain gains and brain exchanges are critical in fostering development and, globally, are as important as brain drains. Even where the latter do occur, they can be offset by **remittances** sent back to home areas.

See also: education; human capital; international migration

RONALD SKELDON

Brandt Commission

The Brandt Commission (or Independent Commission on International Development Issues) was established in 1977 to "present recommendations which could improve the climate for further deliberations on North-South relations." Chaired by Willy Brandt, the former West German Chancellor, it produced the books *North-South: A Programme for Survival* (1980) and *Common Crisis* (1983). Their central theme was interdependence - the mutual international economic and political benefits of development and growth in developing countries. The reports therefore proposed greater financial and **technology transfer**s from the richer nations. Few would object to the sentiments expressed by the Commission, and some argue that it initiated positive changes and became a useful tool for those challenging world **inequality**. However, critics argue that the Brandt Commission had no powers to promote the implementation of its recommendations, and that it was merely a gesture in order to help neutralize the **Organization of Petroleum Exporting Countries (OPEC)** – and led demands for a new **international economic order**.

See also: inequality; inequality and poverty, world trends; international economic order; technology transfer

EMMA E. MAWDSLEY

Bretton Woods

Forty-four nations, led by the USA and Great Britain, met at Bretton Woods, New Hampshire between 1 and 22 July 1944 to discuss economic plans for the post-war peace. In reaction to the anarchy of the inter-war period, governments sought to secure world peace and prosperity through international economic cooperation. While the form in which this was proposed was based on neo-classical economic principles of a world market, in which capital and goods would move freely, it also encompassed Keynesian notions of regulation by global **institutions** in the interest of greater stability and predictability. Member governments signed a series of agreements that culminated in two regulatory institutions: the **International Monetary Fund (IMF)** and the International Bank for Reconstruction and Development, later known as the **World Bank**; The IMF dealt with **exchange rates** and balance of payments problems, while the IBRD at first gave loans for the reconstruction of Western Europe, and later switched focus toward developing countries in the South. The term "Bretton Woods" often refers to the entire system of institutions, agreements and regulations that governed the emerging global economy of the second half of the twentieth century.

See also: International Monetary Fund (IMF); neo-liberalism; World Bank; world economic conference (London, 1933)

Further reading

Scammel, W. (1973) *International Monetary Policy: Bretton Woods and After*, London: Macmillan.
Van Dormael, A. (1978) *Bretton Woods: Birth of a Monetary System*, New York: Holmes and Meier.

RICHARD PEET

brown environmental agenda

The "brown" environmental agenda refers to environmental problems associated with urban or industrial locations such as **pollution**, poor **sanitation**, and **waste management**. The term is used in contrast to the "green" environmental agenda, which describes environmental problems associated with vegetation and wildlife such as **biodiversity** and **deforestation**. The brown environmental agenda is also closely linked to debates in environmental health (see **environment and health**).

There is a consensus that "brown" environmental problems have received inadequate attention. According to **United Nations** statistics, 90 percent of global **population** growth occurs in cities, and by 2025, the urban population will be 5.2 billion, of which 77 percent will live in developing countries (see **urbanization; urban development**). **Mega-cities** such as Lagos, Mexico City, Shanghai and Cairo are set to contain tens of millions of people by 2010. This rapid growth has been associated with a variety of environmental health problems. In 1994, at least 220 million people still lacked a source of **drinking water** near their homes. There are some 1.8 billion episodes of diarrheal illness annually, causing the deaths of some three million (**World Health Organization (WHO)**, 1999). Pollution of both air and water is a growing problem within cities and factories, as the result of rapid urban growth and **industrialization**. One common hazard is indoor air pollution, caused by burning of dirty fuel, which is often not measured in macro-indications of air pollution at the city or national scale, and is often inhaled by the most vulnerable in society, including the very young and the very old.

Some analysts have proposed that the lack of attention to the brown agenda is because many environmental problems of cities and industrial districts (see **industrial district model**) are relatively new and hence poorly understood. Others have argued that the lack of attention reflects the class-based nature of environmentalism, and that much environmental concern (in the developed world at least) emerged contemporaneously with middle-class urban **elites**, who emphasized green concerns such as threats to wilderness and wildlife. This latter concern is added to by the general focus, to date, of environmental policy from **international organizations and associations** and international environmental **non-governmental organizations (NGOs)** on green issues during the 1970s and 1980s. Such organizations may also form alliances with elites in developing countries, who may also share these concerns, or even be industrialists, and hence may resist regulation of factories. The people most affected by brown environmental problems tend to be among the poorest inhabitants of developing countries, such as shanty town dwellers (see **shantytowns**), migrant workers, and **street children**, and therefore have little direct influence on the direction of environmental policy. Consequently, the important attention to the "green" agenda may not be matched by an equally powerful lobbying for the "brown" environmental agenda.

Analysts believe environmental problems in cities undergo two main stages over time. First, hazards include pathogens from human waste or bacteria- and insect-borne infections such as dysentery and cholera caused by poor **sanitation**, overcrowding and inadequate **water management** (see **water-borne diseases**). The second stage includes hazards resulting from **industrialization** and technological advancement, such as traffic fumes, heavy metal poisoning (such as from lead and cadmium), or threats inside factories such as solvent poisoning (solvents are highly toxic fluids used for cleaning, and if inhaled in sufficient quantity can kill within seconds). The World Health Organization estimated in the late 1990s that suspended particulate matter from vehicles and others sources in Mexico City contributes to 6,400 deaths each year, and unhealthy blood lead levels in 29 percent of all children. **World Bank** figures estimate that if particulate levels alone were reduced to WHO guidelines, between 300,000 and 700,000 premature deaths per year could be avoided globally.

Yet, the threat from such risks are also affected by institutional factors that increase **vulnerability** among **population**s such as **education** or the availability of **primary health care** and ambulances. For example, one major cause of infant mortality (see **infant and child mortality**) in developing countries is scalding from hot water. Better emergency care would radically decrease this number. Risks are also experienced disproportionately between social groups: many electronics factories employ a majority of women, for example (see **gender and industrialization**). Indoor air pollution may affect women and **children** more as mothers tending children often spend more time indoors. Some optimists have suggested that environmental problems in cities will decline over time as the result of increasing wealth leading to greater provision of infrastructure, transport (see **transport policy**), health care and regulations (see, for example, the arguments associated with the **Kuznets curve**). Yet, critics have suggested that attention to the institutional factors underlying **vulnerability** suggest that optimistic predictions about pollution overlook how risks are distributed socially, and hence that the elimination of hazards can only occur if social vulnerability is addressed first.

The incidence of brown environmental problems also changes over space as cities grow and become more developed. As pollution grows, many authorities are tempted to transport waste elsewhere by physically moving it in containers, waste pipelines, or by using high stack chimneys that can spread pollution in the atmosphere. Acid rain in Germany and New England, for example, has been blamed in part on industrial emissions in Britain. Waste dumps are often again based in land inhabited by poor and politically powerless people. Local authorities often lack the infrastructure, training or funding to collect all urban and industrial waste created under rapid **urbanization**, leading to such inadequate and dangerous dumping (see **waste management**). Other spatially related implications of the brown agenda include the emergence of **pollution havens** (or locations in developing countries that attract polluting industries because of comparatively less stringent environmental regulations and lower costs), and the international trade in **hazardous waste**.

International responses to brown environmental problems are increasing. The **Basel Convention on hazardous waste** of 1989 provided the first international restrictions on the transport of **hazardous waste**. The **United Nations** created a Sustainable Cities program in 1990, and the Habitat II conference (UN Second Conference on Human Settlements) in 1996 (see **Habitat I and II**) highlighted environmental problems. Some analysts are also optimistic that economic globalization – or increasing investment in developing countries by **transnational corporations (TNCs)** – will also decrease environmental problems. TNCs have often proved stricter than local manufacturers in implementing international standards, or may introduce new technologies that reduce certain forms of **pollution**, such as photovoltaic energy

sources. Critics, however, have suggested that the success of these ventures depend on the measurement of hazards. Measurement of greenhouse gas emissions from factories may enable factories to adhere to some international standards, but it may not benefit local populations if the factories also emit water-borne waste that is not measured, or if **shantytowns** develop around factories with poor **sanitation** or health care. The **World Summit on Sustainable Development (Johannesburg, 2002)** also sought to address brown environmental problems such as **sanitation** and **water management**, yet set no formal targets. The WSSD also discussed the provision of environmental infrastructures through **public-private partnerships**, which has worried some environmentalists as this may mean depending on companies who – at other times – may also be responsible for pollution.

See also: environment; Habitat I and II; hazardous waste; environment and health; Kuznets curve; pollution; pollution havens; sanitation; shantytowns; sustainable development; transport policy; urban development; urbanization; vulnerability; waste management; water-borne diseases; water management

Further reading

See the journal *Environment and Urbanization*.

Carley, M., Jenkins, P. and Smith, H. (2001) *Urban Development and Civil Society: The Role of Communities in Sustainable Cities*, London: Earthscan.

Hardoy, J., Mitlin, D. and Satterthwaite, D. (2001) *Environmental Problems in an Urbanizing World*, London: Earthscan.

McGranahan, G. and Murray, F. (2003) *Air Pollution and Health in Rapidly Developing Countries*, London: Earthscan.

Satterthwaite, D. (1997) "Environmental Transformations in Cities as They Get Larger, Wealthier and Better Managed," *The Geographical Journal* 163:2 216–24.

Satterthwaite, D. (ed.) (1999) *The Earthscan Reader in Sustainable Cities*, London: Earthscan.

TIM FORSYTH

Brundtland Commission

The World Commission on Environment and Development, more commonly known as the Brundtland Commission after its chair Gro Harlem Brundtland, the former Norwegian prime minister, was established in 1983 on the recommendations of the United Nations General Assembly (UNGAS) and charged with outlining a new agenda for development in the twenty-first century. This body was put together in response to the development and environmental crises of the latter part of the twentieth century, and asked to provide a broad policy framework to strengthen the ability of international political and economic **institutions** to promote development worldwide. The commission included development and environment experts, politicians and civil servants from twenty-one countries, over half of whom were from developing nations. After three years of work, the commission produced its now famous report, *Our Common Future*, which brought the term **sustainable development** to the forefront of the global environmental agenda.

See also: environment; sustainable development

Further reading

World Commission on Environment and Development (1987) *Our Common Future*, New York: United Nations.

FIROOZA PAVRI

Bucharest world population conference (1974)

The United Nations World Population Conference was the first major international meeting to discuss **population** growth, and produced an important division between states that sought to control population growth by direct intervention in **fertility** trends, and those who urged longer-term **poverty** alleviation and **education** because "development is the best contraceptive." At the conference, the USA delegation (headed by Casper Weinberger, who later became President

Reagan's Defense Secretary), proposed a "World Population Plan of Action," which urged population control on the grounds of environmental protection, **food** security, and **maternal mortality**. Many developing countries, however, opposed this plan, alleging it violated the sovereignty of developing states, infringed civil and religious rights, and would hinder **economic development**. The conference eventually adopted the World Population Programme of Action, which recognized that "all couples and individuals have the basic right to decide freely and responsibly the number and spacing of their children and to have the information, education and means to do so." Later conferences on population, such as Mexico 1984, and Cairo 1994 (see **Cairo conference on population and development**), urged the achievement of holistic development objectives and **reproductive rights** as well as contraceptives (**family planning**), thus recognizing that questions of population are best addressed by understanding individuals' (especially mothers') circumstances and rights, rather than through state directives (see **state and state reform**) without attention to the contexts in which individuals make decisions.

See also: Cairo conference on population and development; family planning; population; reproductive rights

TIM FORSYTH

build-operate-transfer (BOT) projects

Build-operate-transfer (BOT) projects are popular variants of **public-private partnerships** to deliver infrastructure facilities. They gained favor in the early 1980s in developing countries as a way to mobilize private investment into infrastructure sectors that remain under public ownership for political or structural reasons. Sometimes called a policy "soft option," they are a form of privatization that avoids politically controversial or impossible privatization of a whole public sector, enterprise or utility. Other variants include build-transfer-operate (BTO) and rehabilitate-operate-transfer (ROT). In some countries, the politically less palatable term build-own-operate-transfer (BOOT), which explicitly indicates a **property rights** relation is used instead of BOT.

BOT involves the private developer financing, building and operating an infrastructure facility for a concessionary period of between 10 and 30 years. During the concession period, the developer is given the right of ownership, charging users a fee for its product at a rate high enough to repay debt and to generate internal rates of return of up to 20–30 percent in high-risk developing countries. At the end of the concession period, the facility is transferred to government ownership at no cost to the government. Common BOT infrastructure projects include power stations (see **electrification and power-sector reform**), water treatment plants (see **water management; sanitation**), roads, railways, seaports, and airports. Less common are social infrastructure such as **housing** projects, **education** facilities, and hospitals.

In the developing world, the proponents of BOT include the international financial institutions (IFIs) and the BOT industry comprising international financiers and banks, large engineering corporations and consultants with specialist expertise on the complexities of BOT. Proponents argue that the approach brings private sector efficiency to public infrastructure provision. Under competitive tenders, which are not always the case, creative solutions to financing and technology result. Ostensibly, BOT also allows the **public sector** to transfer risks to the party best able to manage that risk. For example, in BOT projects the risk of construction cost and time overruns are assumed by the constructor. Ultimately, proponents hold that BOT allows governments to avoid greater levels of public debt in the provision of infrastructure.

However, critics hold that BOT projects contain significant, sometimes hidden, costs and risks for sponsor governments. Infrastructure projects involve large sunk costs that restrict developers' ability to move equity out of investments. The result is that both developers and financiers seek a range of onerous guarantees from the sponsor governments, leaving the latter with the bulk of the risks. Governments have provided guarantees on fuel supply, power and water off-take, and protec-tion against foreign exchange movements. Governments providing such guarantees take on contingent liabilities that, in most cases, are not accounted for. These are potential liabilities with significant negative implications not only for national budgets, but also for intergenerational equity. For example, the 1997–8 **Asian crises** left the governments of Indonesia and the Philippines bearing the costs of power purchase guarantees denominated in US dollars for power which it could not sell as power market demand collapsed. The devaluation of their currencies escalated these costs and public power utilities such as the Philippines National Power Corporation have incurred unsustainable **debt**, forcing the government to sell off the Corporation in a bid to stem the losses.

An important category of risk in developing countries is sovereign or political risk. In the late 1990s, in order to catalyze greater levels of private investment and to protect developers and financiers against these risks, IFIs such as the **World Bank** began to provide subsidized guarantees called Partial Risk Guarantees (PRGs) in International Development Association countries considered by international credit rating agencies and financiers to have poorly developed regulatory and legal systems and less than transparent decision-making processes. However, critics argue that PRGs may in fact create a moral hazard by allowing governments to avoid the establishment of legal and regulatory systems that foster investor confidence under normal circumstances. Furthermore, BOT projects have reduced **transparency** and public oversight in comparison to publicly funded and built infrastructure because of the frequent claims by private-sector developers to commercial-in-confidence negotiations and concession contracts including government guarantees.

See also: electrification and power-sector reform; privatization and liberalization; public-private partnerships; public management; public sector; water management

Further reading

Handley, P. (1997) "A Critical View of the Build-Operate-Transfer Privatisation Process in Asia," *Asian Journal of Public Administration* 19:2 203–43.

Levy, S. (1996) *Build, Operate, Transfer: Paving the way for Tomorrow's Infrastructure*, New York: Wiley.

Wyatt, A. (2002) "The Privatisation of Public Infrastructure in Transitional Southeast Asian Economies: The Case of Build-Own-Operate-Transfer Projects in Vietnam and Laos," in Sargeson, S. (ed.) *Collective Goods, Collective Futures in Asia*, London: Routledge.

ANDREW B. WYATT

BUREAUCRACY *see* public management; public sector; state and state reform

Butler's model of tourism development

Butler's model of **tourism** development is a model that hypothesizes the development of tourist areas using an S curve, two axes of time and number of tourists. The model proposes five stages to tourism development over time and space: First, an *exploration stage* with few visitors and no tourism facilities. Second, an *involvement stage* with the establishment of facilities, and greater interaction between locals and increasing numbers of visitors. Third, a *development stage* of more control exerted by external organizations that impact on the area's physical appearance. Fourth, a *consolidation stage* when the rate of increase in tourist arrivals declines and influential economic franchises prompt opposition from locals. Fifth, a *stagnation stage* occurs during peak visitation, and when capacity levels are reached or exceeded causing environmental and/or socio-economic problems. Finally, tourist areas face four potential outcomes ranging from *rejuvenation* if they can overhaul or reinvent existing attraction(s) to *decline* if they cannot compete with newer attractions elsewhere. The model has been widely quoted in literature about tourism development, although academics and policy-makers have been keen to seek ways to avoid the prediction of tourism decline.

See also: ecotourism; tourism

Further reading

Butler, R. (1980) "The Concept of a Tourist-area Cycle of Evolution and Implications for Management," *The Canadian Geographer* 24: 5–12.

PAUL KINGSBURY

C

Cairo conference on population and development

The Cairo conference is the popular name given to the **United Nations** International Conference on Population and Development (ICPD) held 5–13 September 1994 in Cairo, Egypt. At the conference, delegates from 179 states, plus some **non-governmental organizations (NGOs)** and United Nations agencies gathered to negotiate an action plan on **population** for the next twenty years. The Cairo conference had a broad agenda on developmental issues, and considered the interconnectedness of population, **poverty**, **gender**, patterns of production and consumption (see **indicators of development**), and **environment**. The ratification of the ICPD Program of Action marked a turning point in the history of population studies, bringing reproductive health (see **reproductive rights**) and women's rights to the forefront of debate. The resulting 115-page conference statement emphasized the linkages between population and development and focused on meeting the needs of individual women and men rather than on achieving demographic targets.

See also: population

LETÍCIA JUNQUEIRA MARTELETO

capability approach

The capability approach consists of the concepts and framework developed by the Nobel Prize winning economist Amartya Sen for discussing well-being and **human development**. The approach underlies the United Nations Development Programme's work on human development (see also **Human Development Index (HDI)**). "Capability" refers to the range of valued life-options (including life-paths over time) that a given person can attain. The accompanying approach by the philosopher Martha Nussbaum uses the title "capabilities approach" since it emphasizes human skills and abilities and the priority of having a specific set of abilities and life-options.

A key theme in Sen's approach is that in addition to the types of information that are discussed in conventional **welfare economics** (notably: income, consumption, preference fulfillment, utility/satisfaction) various other types are important in normative discussions about **well-being**. In particular, the capability approach refers also to valued **functionings** and the capabilities to achieve those functionings (the "beings and doings" that constitute life-options). It refers to functionings because resource inputs, preference fulfillment and felt satisfaction are identified as unreliable proxies for the actual content of people's lives. The emphasis on capability reflects a belief that people should be able to achieve things of importance, and yet be free to pursue any or none of these, according to their wishes. Narrow versions of the capability approach add only these two categories (capability and functionings), or even consider them only; and the narrowest version considers capability alone, as in the slogan "development is the enlargement of the range of human choices" (see **freedom versus choice**).

Table 1 Different approaches to capability

Different concepts of capability, and alternative labels	An undeveloped human potential, skill, capacity	A developed human potential, skill, capacity	An attainable (set of) functioning(s), given a person's skills and the external conditions	A priority for attainable (and/or achieved) functioning
Sen's label		Capability (*de facto* usage)	Capability	Basic capability (occasional usage)
Nussbaum's label	Basic capability; innate	Internal capability	Combined capability (earlier: external capability)	Central capability, or (occasional usage) basic capability
Alternative label	P-capability (P for potential)	S-capability (S for skill)	O-capability, or option (O for option)	Priority capability/Basic need or basic right

Broad versions, including Sen's own work, acknowledge many other normatively relevant aspects.

The emphasis on capability may be described as liberal, but Sen goes beyond pure liberalism by insisting that priority capabilities and functionings are those which "people have *reason* to value." He holds further that in public prioritization, these reasons must be publicly shared and debated, and he leaves the listing of priority capabilities or functionings to these public procedures. In practice, all his policy work tacitly assumes a standard set of development priority areas, and of minimum levels to be achieved in them (e.g. literacy (see **illiteracy**), for the priority capability of understanding). Nussbaum, in contrast, presents an explicit priority list of relatively broadly stated capabilities, proposed as of universal relevance and comparable to universal **human rights**. The list needs to be interpreted and elaborated in particular contexts, but would set some limits to the operation of power in each context.

The capability and capabilities approaches offer one type of intellectual basis for human rights and for systematic answers to "rights to what?" human rights language provides appropriately strong terms for trying to ensure basic entitlements for people, and to convey that a person both has a right to a priority capability, *and* a right not to use that capability.

Sen adopted the term "capability" for a person's set of attainable life-paths, seen as a measure of the person's "positive freedom." This opportunity-oriented concept of capability differs from a more common everyday usage, of a capability as a skill or aptitude. Nussbaum helpfully distinguishes different meanings of capability, although other labels might be clearer than those she chose, as indicated in Table 1.

See also: capacity building; ethics; freedom versus choice; functionings; human development; human rights; technological capability; well-being

Further reading

Alkire, S. (2002) *Valuing Freedoms: Sen's Capability Approach and Poverty Reduction*, Oxford: Oxford University Press.

Crocker, D. (1995) "Functioning and Capability: The Foundations of Sen's and Nussbaum's Development Ethic," pp. 153–198 in Nussbaum, M. and Glover, J. (eds) *Women, Culture and Development – a study of human capabilities*, Oxford: Clarendon.

Nussbaum, M. and Sen, A. (eds) (1993) *The Quality of Life*, Oxford: Clarendon.

UNDP (2000) *Human Development Report 2000: Human Rights and Human Development*, New York: Oxford University Press.

DES GASPER

capacity building

Capacity building encompasses a variety of strategies that improve the effectiveness, efficiency and responsiveness of various development agents. Initially, it was used to refer to the upgrading of government and **public sector** institutions. More recently, the term has also included strengthening local organizational capacities of intermediary **non-governmental organizations (NGOs)**, service providers, **community**-based organizations (CBOs), and development **aid** recipients. When referring to the local organizational capacity of CBOs and aid recipients, the term connotes reinforcing the ability of people to trust one another, mobilize resources, resolve conflicts, and work together on common problems (see also **social capital**). Capacity building is about enabling people to rediscover their strengths and limitations, and empowering them to take control of their lives and develop their fullest potential. The **United Nations Development Programme (UNDP)**, for example, defines capacity building as "the process by which individuals, organizations, institutions and societies develop abilities (individually and collectively) to perform functions, solve problems and set and achieve objectives" (UNDP, 1997:3). Hence, capacity building is seen as closely related to the concepts of **civil society**, local participation (see **participatory development**), **empowerment**, good **governance**, and **social capital**.

Some development experts prefer the term capacity development or capacity enhancement instead of capacity building, suggesting that the challenge is one of strengthening existing capacities rather than creating new ones. More generally, development practitioners tend to use capacity development, capacity building and capacity enhancement interchangeably when tasks may include supporting, reforming, or creating activities that result in better governance and organizational abilities. Others, however, view capacity building to occur more at the meso- (institutional) and micro- (project) levels, while capacity development implies changes at the macro-level systems and structures of **institutions** and **environment**s. Capacity building and capacity development therefore emphasize complex learning (see **social learning**); long-term

changes in human behavior, attitudes, values and relationships; adaptation and organizational change at all levels of society to support systemic sustainable improvement and meet new development challenges. They are generally seen as forms of **people-centered development** and tailored to the needs of recipient countries or organizations to plan and manage their own affairs, rather than serve the agenda of external donor agencies.

Widespread interest in capacity building grew out of neo-liberal economic reforms (see **neo-liberalism**) and discourse of **sustainable development** during the 1980s, and the post-**Washington consensus** in the 1990s that accompanied public discontent with dominant approaches to development aid. The historical origins of the term, however, are deeper and reflect a complex synthesis of management, political and economic approaches. They can be traced historically to the 1950s and 1960s emphasis on nation-, state- and institution-building (see **state and state reform; institutions**) that accompanied the **decolonization** period. In the late 1960s and early 1970s, development practitioners realized that **institutions** were falling short of expected performance. The idea of **development management** emerged in the late 1970s to stress the government's and state sector's developmental responsibilities, especially towards the poor. In the early 1980s, the concept of institutional development was resurrected to show concern for the broader activities and contributions of the private sector and NGOs to development efforts (see **public-private partnerships**). International organizations such as the **World Bank**, **bilateral aid agencies** under the **Organization for Economic Cooperation and Development (OECD)**-DAC and the **United Nations Development Programme (UNDP)** since the 1990s have pushed for "capacity development" and/or "capacity building" as a new orientation in development assistance linked to the concept of good **governance**, and aiming to increase **accountability** of aid.

Capacity building, however, has had its critics. Some observers have claimed the term is used too universally and rhetorically, and hence is all encompassing, a slogan empty of meaning, and thus analytically and practically useless. Others reject some assumptions as patronizing: e.g. that the capacities of the poor, local NGOs and developing countries in general have yet to be built or developed. Capacity building also raises a number of questions about what exactly governments and the **public sector** should be responsible for, *vis-à-vis* the private sector, NGOs and CBOs. For example, whose capacities are to be built, which capacities, where and at what level, who will develop them, and how? Consequently, proponents of capacity building often find themselves needing to define the term. Other organizations (e.g. World Neighbors, 2000) produce guidebooks, indicators, measurements, and training manuals on capacity building using **participatory development** approaches.

See also: aid; civil society; empowerment; institutions; participatory development; public-private partnerships; social capital; social learning

Further reading

Grindle, M. (ed.) (1997) *Getting Good Government: Capacity Building in the Public Sectors of Developing Countries*, Cambridge MA: Harvard Institute for International Development.

Maconick, R. and Morgan, P. (1999) *Capacity-building Supported by the United Nations: Some Evaluations and Some Lessons*, New York: United Nations.

Smillie, I. (2001) *Patronage or Partnership: Local Capacity Building in Humanitarian Crises*, Bloomfield CT: Kumarian Press.

UNDP (1997) *Capacity Development*, Technical Advisory Paper 2. New York: United Nations Development Programme.

World Neighbors (2000) *From the Roots Up: Strengthening Organizational Capacity Through Guided Self-Assessment*, Oklahoma: World Neighbors.

LEONORA C. ANGELES

capital flight

Capital flight commonly refers to the outflow of private funds from a country on a scale that negatively impacts on the vitality and stability of its national financial market. In broader terms, capital flight may also describe any outflow of wealth-producing resources (i.e. capital) that is sufficiently large to detrimentally affect a country's rate of **economic growth** and development.

Much research on capital flight has tended to focus on developing countries, especially following the 1980s **debt** crisis. But capital flight has also occurred in developed countries, and hence is not necessarily associated with general levels of **economic development**. A fuller and more correct understanding of capital flight in its financial form associates it with investors' perceptions of domestic economic, political, and social conditions which lead them to remove their capital to more financially attractive foreign markets. Usually, such destinations are "safe havens" for capital where they are promised low or zero taxation on their investment earning (see **offshore finance; fiscal and monetary policy**).

Not surprisingly, capital flight is most frequent when **exchange rates** are unstable and a country's currency undergoes devaluation, the two conditions combining to reduce returns on investment. If investors, both domestic and foreign, perceive that their investments in a country's economy will earn them less than they get elsewhere, they will remove those investments to more profitable and stable foreign markets. It is because developing countries tend to be more prone to experiencing periods of economic and financial instability that can arise from a broad variety of domestic and international economic, political, and social conditions that capital flight looms as a greater problem for them than for developed countries.

There are many economic, political, and social consequences arising to a country from capital flight. The most noteworthy of these is a decline in tax revenue, which can severely constrain the financial resources that a government has available for the implementation of policies needed to address the domestic conditions which gave rise to the capital flight in the first place.

Even the mere threat of capital flight can be used to pressure a government to adopt taxation polices more conducive to the interests of large investors (such as consumption or sales taxes), and reduce its reliance on taxes on interest and profits for fear of losing substantial amounts of investment capital. Indeed, this threat of moving investments has been used extensively by **transnational corporations**

(TNCs). The adoption of such policies, particularly in developing countries, may not be consistent with the overall long-term welfare of the national economy and the bulk of the people.

See also: Asian crises; capital markets; computable general equilibrium (CGE) models; contagion effect; debt; fiscal and monetary policy; offshore finance; stock markets; transnational corporations (TNCs)

Further reading

Lessard, D. and Williamson, J. (1987) *Capital Flight and Third World Debt*, Washington DC: Institute for International Economics.
Martin, H-P. and Schumann, H. (1996) *The Global Trap*, London: Zed.

RICHARD M. J. THURSTON

capital intensive

The term, capital intensive, refers to industries, technologies or sectors that – when compared with others – use relatively higher proportions of capital inputs than labor in production. Existing levels of skills and technology, the cost of labor (often unskilled), and overall macroeconomic performance (which determines cost capital) generally influence capital-intensive production. In most developing countries, access to foreign exchange is critical in securing imports of capital goods. Many countries pursuing **export-led growth** depend on agricultural exports as the main source of foreign exchange. However, poor **terms of trade** and unstable commodity prices in world markets pose significant risks to this strategy. Collateral incentives for industrial development such as subsidies for imports of machinery and equipment, **exchange rates** regulations, **import substitution** strategies and **technology transfer** via **foreign direct investment** also significantly contribute to capital-intensive production processes.

See also: industrialization; labor-intensive

MOSES A. OSIRO

capital markets

Capital markets are markets where long-term **debt** (maturity of one year or longer) and equity instruments are traded. Specific instruments include stocks, mortgages, corporate bonds, central and local government bonds, government agency securities, and consumer and commercial bank loans.

Capital markets constitute one of the basic components of the financial system. Another component is money markets where short-term debt instruments are traded. Distinctions in debt finance can be made between primary and secondary markets. The primary market creates new securities. Through public issues, a group (or a syndicate) of investment banks purchases (or underwrites) a new issue of bonds from a borrower and resells it to investors at large. New securities can also be issued through private placements where new issues are sold to a small number of investors. The difference is that issues in the public issue market are subject to more stringent scrutiny through registration and sale-regulations than in the private placement market. In secondary markets, existing securities are traded. The secondary market itself is divided into auction and over-the-counter markets. In auction markets, securities prices are set by competitive bidding of a large number of traders acting on behalf of buyers and sellers. The most common auction markets are organized stock exchanges, each of which uses a physical location as the trading floor. Over-the-counter markets do not have a central trading floor. Instead, they operate through a computer or telephone network of securities brokers and dealers that matches buyers and sellers. A distinction can also be made between direct and indirect finance. In direct finance, securities such as bonds and stocks are normally held directly by investors. Funds can also be transferred to the final users through financial intermediaries such as banks, leading to indirect finance or financial intermediation. Finally, according to how settlement is made, there are cash markets and derivatives markets. In cash markets, securities are traded for immediate settlement and cash transfer. In derivatives markets, trades are made now, but settlements and cash transfers are made later.

Although the financial press pays great attention to national capital markets, sub-national markets do exist. A clear example is within the banking markets of the USA. During the nineteenth century, the "free banking movement" and subsequent national banking movement significantly lowered barrier to entry in banking, resulting in the mushrooming of local **community**-based banks. Many states subsequently banned branch banking outright, which was further reinforced by federal banking legislation. Locally based banking existed well into the 1970s. Since then, many states gave banks a greater freedom to forge integrated banking until the late 1990s when federal legislation legalized nationwide banking institutions. However, up until the early twenty-first century, metropolitan areas were still treated as bank markets for antitrust purposes, and banking institutions were required by law to issue mortgages and small business loans in local markets where they obtain their funds.

Local and regional capital markets notwithstanding, national capital markets have long transferred funds to large corporations from wealthy individuals, and increasingly, from institutional investors such as pension funds and insurance companies. Many national economies have a dominant stock market (see **stock markets**) that trades shares, and serves as a symbol of the country's financial center and, through shares prices, the indicator of their financial health. Development of national capital markets has led to the rise of powerful investment banks and securities trading firms, which, along with capital markets, are seen by many as a symbol of Western **capitalism**. In many instances, financial intermediaries are active in both local and national capital markets as they hold both locally based assets and national securities. Many large banks also have subsidiaries in investment banking. The late twentieth century saw major changes in the intermediate finance market, where mortgages and even commercial loans are repackaged and sold as securities in secondary markets. Such securitization increases the liquidity of the mortgage markets and bank lending, and enables mortgage and bank lending to tap the national market for funds. Amid volatile and fluctuating interest rates, the late twentieth century witnessed the rise of derivatives markets where contracts tied to some underlying securities are traded to hedge against potential loss or gain advantage brought on by uncertainties. Unlike goods and services, where prices mostly undergo gradual changes, financial markets are strongly influenced by expectations and uncertainty. The regulations of financial markets by government or by trade organizations become inevitable to ensure information **transparency**, liquidity, and stability.

The international dimension has been an important component from the earliest days of capital markets. Cross-border foreign bond lending, equity investing, and banking began as early as the seventeenth century in Europe. Between 1870 and 1914, capital flows from industrialized Western European countries led by the UK were financed by expanding colonialism (see **colonialism, history of; colonialism, impacts of**). London emerged as dominant international financial center. Since the 1920s, the USA has become a major world financer. Wars and the Great Depression caused cross-border capital flows to dwindle. Between 1945 and the early 1970s, nations instituted capital controls and cross-border capital flows were limited to official lending, trade finance, and **foreign direct investment**. Euromoney and Eurobonds (or **offshore finance**, since credits are denominated in currencies other than those of host countries) rose to meet the need for private international finance. Over-borrowing and sudden changes in international macroeconomic conditions led to the **debt** crisis of many developing countries in the 1980s. Many countries dismantled their capital controls in the last quarter of the twentieth century, leading to an explosive growth of international finance. However, these developments were overshadowed by the Mexican "Peso Crisis" in 1994–5, the Asian financial crisis in 1997, and Russian default on their government bonds in 1998. Regulation of international capital markets to ensure information **transparency**, liquidity, and stability is still a major issue facing the world financial **community**.

See also: contagion effect; fiscal and monetary policy; inflation and its effects; multilateral development banks (MDBs); offshore finance

Further reading

Butler, K. (2000) *Multinational Finance*, Cincinnati: South-Western College Publishing.

Levich, R. (2001) *International Financial Markets: Prices and Policies*, Boston MA: McGraw Hill.

Mishkin F. (1997) *The Economics of Money, Banking, and Financial Markets*, New York: Addison-Wesley.

BIN ZHOU

capitalism

Capitalism is the mother lode of "development." As such, capitalism has four significant dynamics. First, capitalism has always involved a world-scale political economy. Second, the colonial division of labor originating in the expansion of European states into the non-European world generated a global political-economic hierarchy forcing colonial subjects to specialize in primary goods production for European industries and consumers ("underdevelopment"). Third, the decolonization movements across the nineteenth and twentieth centuries successfully deployed the capitalist discourse of rights against their European masters. And fourth, the twentieth-century postcolonial order derived from the political and technological relations of capitalism, whereby postcolonial states (see **state and state reform**) sought to reduce the effect of the colonial division of labor through **industrialization** and economic nationalism, known at the time as "development" (see **colonialism, history of; colonialism, impacts of**).

Debates about the origins of capitalism remain unresolved, since the definition of capitalism is a matter of interpretation. Adam Smith associated capitalism with exchange, arguing that this was a natural propensity of humans, maturing in the eighteenth century. Max Weber viewed capitalism as a **culture** of rationality, understood in terms of individual and institutional practices, and stemming from the sixteenth-century protestant rebellion (see **Protestant work ethic**). Karl Marx viewed capitalism as a form of social organization, presaged in the European mercantile empires and their commodity-producing slave labor forces (**slavery**), and maturing in the nineteenth century as machine production spawned a wage labor force in Europe. For Marx, the key to the rise of capitalism was the transformation of property relations, whereby peasant land was expropriated through state-sanctioned enclosures by increasingly commercial landlords, and an urban bourgeoisie emerged at the expense of the traditional craftsman/apprentice relationship.

Central to the debates on the rise of capitalism is the transition from feudalism to capitalism, involving the transformation of feudal relations of fealty and bonded labor, into capitalist relations governed by the cash nexus, where access to material livelihood (see **livelihoods**) depends upon labor and commodity markets. Interpretations as to what triggered the transformation divide between emphases on market expansion or on the transformation of the labor relation. The former argues that markets eroded the traditional order, fostering the circulation of goods and money, the rise of a consequential merchant capitalist class, and a general **commercialization** of material life. The latter position argues that feudalism only disappeared when serf labor yielded to wage labor, as a consequence of peasant resistance to super-exploitation by their financially pressed feudal masters, and the substitution over time of hired labor in increasingly commercial landed relations.

World systems theory, championed by Immanuel Wallerstein, sought to transcend this debate by arguing that capitalism originated in the formation of a world economy in the sixteenth century (also see the related debate of **dependency theory**). Expanding markets were structured by global relations of production, related hierarchically to a division of labor comprising wage labor in the European core, sharecropping in the Eastern European semi-periphery, and slave and bonded labor in the Americas, as periphery. Unlike Marx, who argued that the *differentia specifica* of capitalism was wage labor, Wallerstein argued that the secret of capitalism lay in the inability of one state to monopolize trading profits deriving from the **international division of labor**. This inability led to cycles of rivalry and hegemony as the political expression of an interstate system in which states and their firms create, and compete for, markets. With this definition of capitalism, which does not distinguish wage labor as the key form of labor under capitalism, Wallerstein has been identified with the neo-Smithian emphasis on markets. This binarist debate regarding the definition of capitalism offers one-sided interpretations that lose sight of the methodological question of how to view capitalism as a historical social form that includes a mutual conditioning of circulation and production spheres. Machine production, based in wage labor, could not have arisen without substantial markets for both inputs (labor and raw materials) and outputs (commodities), and vice-versa.

Further, there is an important political dimension to capitalism, which concerns its organization of global markets. As Marx and Karl Polanyi remind us, markets are profoundly political **institutions**. The emergence of modern, bureaucratic states coincided with, and conditioned, the rise of a capitalist world economy. Initially, early modern states sponsored a world market built on mercantilist principles, by capturing existing long-distance trading networks through alliances with merchants. States came to depend on financial resources from merchants, as merchants in turn came to depend on state protection of their commercial activity. Commercial policy institutionalized the monopolizing tendencies of merchant capital, as a means of enlarging national wealth. This policy suited the division of the world among competing colonial empires. And it laid the foundations of industry by building national markets and intensifying the commercial plunder of the colonies. Marx viewed slave labor as the pedestal of wage labor. With the rise of industrial capital in the nineteenth century, states competed increasingly through an informal empire of **free trade** imposed by the British state through its naval, commercial, and financial supremacy.

Industrial capitalism depended on the subordination of wage labor to machine production, through the application of a technical division of labor in the production process. Traditional craft skills became redundant as machine production fragmented the labor process, assigning workers specialized tasks that devalued the individual laborer at the same time as it recombined those specializations as social labor overall. This was the source of the immense **productivity** of modern industry, and its boundless demand for inputs from a world market increasingly organized by the railway, the steamship, and the telegraph. As Marx noted, whereas manufacture simply concentrated artisans in one place, modern industry revolutionized production, exchange, and consumption relations.

In an exemplary account, Sidney Mintz documents the expansion of sugar production by slaves for the emerging industrial proletariat in nineteenth-century England. Once a luxury item, sugar became a strategic commodity for the working class, since its consumption satisfied caloric needs in an impoverished diet while it allowed a cultural identification with consumption habits associated with the aristocracy. In the construction of this consumer identity, the consumption relation involved identification with both empire and social hierarchy, mediated by the market. Twentieth-century corporate capitalism has refined this relation through advertising strategies involving subliminal associations with status, sex and global power.

The story of sugar is a trace not only on the integral role of colonialism (see **colonialism, history of; colonialism, impacts of**) in the rise of industrial capitalism, but also on the importance of the consumption relation as a dynamic integral to the realization of capitalist profits. Certainly, in the nineteenth century, the basic goal was reproduction of the work force, and sugar was vital as a fuel. But the fact of a working population needing to purchase its material needs in the market, and the infinite potential for profit through a market culture of consumption would not be lost on today's social observer. In the nineteenth century, capitalists sought to expand profits by reducing labor costs, through **deskilling** in the workplace and through access to cheap inputs and wage goods. Accordingly, labor organized in Europe and the USA to establish its rights in the workplace and to a living wage. The power of organized labor underwrote a rising demand for social rights in the state, and Western states responded eventually by elaborating welfare systems in the mid-twentieth century (see **welfare economics; welfare state**). Meanwhile, the Fordist model of accumulation, deriving from Henry Ford's strategy of paying his workers enough to allow them to purchase automobiles, incorporated consumption as central to profitability. Both of these adjustments by states (see **state and state reform**) and capital would undergird a resurgent capitalism in the era of American hegemony.

In the USA, the post-World War II era was marked by an explosion and endless differentiation of consumer goods, nurtured by new patterns of suburbanization and increasingly sophisticated forms of consumer credit. As part of the construction of US hegemony, this form of consumer capitalism was universalized and became the model of development to the world, even though emulation of the American consumer remains confined to roughly 20 percent of the world's **population**.

The American model of capitalism arose in the wake of a world depression in the 1930s marked by political extremism and intense economic **nationalism**, marking the unraveling of the British-centered world market. The American model, based in a domestic agro-industrial dynamic of "inner-directed" capitalist expansion, contrasted with the "outer-directed" form of capitalism associated with the British "workshop of the world" model. The US model, of a coherent national economy, informed the understanding of the framework of post-World War II development. Through the institutional complex of **Bretton Woods** (see **World Bank; International Monetary Fund (IMF)**) and the **United Nations**, American new dealism was writ large in the world via an international project of development. These institutions complemented US financial disbursements to redistribute liquidity and subsidize the infrastructures of development. The development project targeted new, postcolonial states, as the US sought access to their raw materials and markets, and sought to incorporate them within the empire of free world capitalism ranged against the empires of communism in Europe and East Asia. While development was represented as a national goal, each national case served to stabilize and extend capitalism, and US power, via international **organizations and associations**, both private (**transnational corporations (TNCs)**) and public (**Bretton Woods** institutions, foreign **aid** programs). As corporations extended their reach, so a global unregulated (stateless) money market formed, which eventually undermined the Bretton Woods order, based as it was on the international reserve role of the American dollar. Subsequent global deregulation

of financial markets and heightened capital mobility has reduced the regulatory powers of all states and nurtured the "virtual" or "networked" corporation that operates globally through flexible, strategic alliances facilitated by informational technologies.

Arguably, development was an ideological representation of a power relation elaborated as a hegemonic project for American capitalism. Some have argued that while the rhetoric of development was universal, its goal was never more than to benefit a relatively small segment of the world's population, known as the "fast world" and inhabiting all countries (including now ex-communist Eastern Europe), but concentrated in the North. The management of the **debt crisis** of the 1980s and beyond is a measure of this, since indebted states have been instructed to adhere to **International Monetary Fund (IMF)/World Bank** conditions (of austerity, **privatization and liberalization**) in order to obtain funds to service their **debt** (see **conditionality**). Sharply reduced wages and increased exports have not only destabilized southern working and rural **population**s, but through the global market, labor in developed countries has been progressively demobilized by cheap labor competition from offshore.

Liberalization was universalized, in 1994, in the institution of the **World Trade Organization/General Agreement on Tariffs and Trade (WTO/GATT)**, arguably a surrogate for the USA in prosecuting a **free trade** regime to open commodity and financial markets. This is the **globalization** project: an increasingly contested attempt to impose market rule across the world, largely by dismantling public capacities built up during the developmentalist era, but also by opening new frontiers of capitalist ownership in genetic materials and services (**health**, **education**, infrastructures like water, transport (see **transport policy**), banking, etc). The incorporation of labor forces from developing countries into world capitalism, via **export processing zones (EPZs)**, sweatshops, and in-migration to factories and harvest circuits in developed countries, accelerated since the implementation of the debt regime. Labor forces find themselves in competitive relation with one another as capital scours the world to source its labor and raw material inputs.

Under these conditions, development has become increasingly a private matter, an exclusionary ethic based on rhetoric of "**comparative advantage**," where labor rights (see **labor rights and standards**) evaporate and communities (see **community**) are compelled to compete for access to the global economy with no guarantee of enduring success. In becoming truly global, through such abstraction of place, dismissal of public protections and **casualization of work**, capitalism has reverted to a predatory form. Arguably, the contradictions of capitalism are clearer now than ever, including, but broadening beyond the capital/labor relation identified by Marx as the principal contradiction. The measure of this is the global counter-movement, constituting an array of labor, peasant, environmental, consumer, indigenous, feminist, gay, and other social justice movements represented in the **World Social Forum (WSF)**.

See also: debt crisis; dependency theory; globalization; International Monetary Fund (IMF); international economic order; marginalization; Marxism; neo-liberalism; peasantry; primitive accumulation; terms of trade; trade; transnational capitalist class (TCC); World Bank; World Social Forum (WSF); world systems theory

Further reading

Arrighi, G. (1994) *The Long Twentieth Century. Money, Power and the Origins of Our Time*, London: Verso.

Hilton, R. (1976) *The Transition from Feudalism to Capitalism*, London: Verso.

Marx, K. and Engels, F. (1967) *The Communist Manifesto*, Harmondsworth: Penguin.

Mintz, S. (1986) *Sweetness and Power: The Place of Sugar in Modern History*, New York: Penguin.

Polanyi, K. (1957) *The Great Transformation. The Political and Economic Origins of Our Time*, Boston MA: Beacon.

Tomich, D. (1987) *Slavery in the Circuit of Sugar. Martinique and the World Economy, 1830–1848*, Baltimore: Johns Hopkins University Press.

Wallerstein, I. (1974) *The Modern World System. Vol. 1. Capitalist Agriculture and the Origins of the European World-Economy in the Sixteenth Century*, New York: Academic Press.

PHILIP D. MCMICHAEL

carrying capacity

Carrying capacity is the maximum population of a species that can be supported indefinitely in a defined habitat allowing for seasonal and random changes without damaging that habitat's ecosystem. The concept of carrying capacity (K) originates in biology. It is not a constant, as carrying capacity can change over the long term; the carrying capacity of a species will rise for example if that species develops the ability to utilize a new **food** source, and it will fall if that species causes permanent environmental degradation. External effects such as **climate change** may affect a carrying capacity beneficially or adversely.

Applying the concept of carrying capacity to human **population** is both common and problematic. Human populations can raise their carrying capacity dramatically through innovation and through the appropriation of resources from other species. Human populations can change an area's carrying capacity in a number of ways, including **deforestation** and **agriculture**. Human populations also trade, and are thus not dependent on their immediate geographical area in the same way as other species. Estimates of the Earth's carrying capacity with respect to human population vary wildly; many of the deep ecologists (see **deep ecology**) argue for a maximum **population** of no more than a few hundred million, and many neo-liberal economists feel our power to innovate renders human carrying capacity so large as to be meaningless.

Thomas Robert Malthus is often credited as a key early writer on the concept of human carrying capacity, largely due to his 1798 work, *An Essay on the Principle of Population*. He believed human populations would always rise to their carrying capacity and would overrun their ability to innovate due to their high rate of reproduction (see **Malthusian demography**). In the twentieth century, those who caution against **population growth**, such as Garret Hardin and Paul Ehrlich, mirror his arguments. Their arguments focus heavily on population growth in the developing world, and largely ignore consumption rates in the developed countries, or the political debates concerning technological innovations (see **population**).

Adjusting human carrying capacity calculations to account for trade can alleviate the bias against developing nations present in most discussions of human carrying capacity. Developed by Mathis Wackernagel and William Rees, the ecological footprint model considers human settlements independent of geographical location. Instead, settlements are seen in terms of resource and waste flows, regardless of where those flows originate. The ecological footprint measures the land needed to provide a **community**'s needs in the categories of **food** production, **housing**, transport (see **transport policy**), consumer goods, and services. This total "footprint" is compared to the population's share of the total available land on Earth, or Earthshare. If a **community**'s footprint is equal to its Earthshare, it is at its carrying capacity. By calculating ecological footprints instead of geographical carrying capacities, one finds that the residents of the developed countries are using the bulk of the Earth's resources, even though they represent a minority of the world's population. Critics of the ecological footprint concept, however, argue that it places too much emphasis on the presumed physical limits of land or ecosystems, and insufficient attention onto the ability or requirement for people to avoid reaching such limits.

See also: environment; Malthusian demography; natural resources; overpopulation; population; trade

Further reading

Wackernagel, M. and Rees, W. (1996) *Our Ecological Footprint*, Gabriola Island, Canada: New Society.

LENORE NEWMAN

Cartagena Protocol on Biosafety

The Cartagena Protocol on Biosafety is an international agreement seeking to govern transboundary shipments of living modified organisms (LMOs), including **genetically modified organisms (GMOs)**. It was finalized at Cartagena in Colombia in 2000. The protocol followed a decision at the 1995 Conference of Parties to the **Convention on Biological Diversity (CBD)** to develop a protocol on biosafety, in order to regulate movements on any LMOs or GMOs that may have adverse effects on **biodiversity**.

A variety of political actors campaigned in favor of a protocol. Sustained pressure came from an international network of **non-governmental organizations (NGOs)** such as the Third World Network, which mobilized their own experts to raise uncertainties about the safety of GMOs. In the late 1990s, stronger support came from the Like-Minded Group. This group represented developing countries that would face decisions about permitting imports of GM grain or seeds, and sought to establish legal guidelines for restricting imports, especially in countries with poorly developed regulatory systems. Public protests in Europe also added strength to the campaign for an effective protocol on GMOs.

A protocol on biosafety, however, was initially opposed by the Global Industry Coalition, an alliance of countries seeking to export genetically modified (GM) grain. These countries later became known as the Miami Group (including the USA, Argentina, Australia, Canada, Chile, Uruguay). The **European Union** (EU) also led efforts to promote voluntary guidelines, widely seen as an attempt to avert a statutory protocol.

Eventually European public protest against GM crops led the EU to support more stringent regulation there and an international protocol, thus overcoming resistance by the Miami Group. The main impacts of the Cartagena Protocol are to guarantee "advance informed agreement" (AIA) about LMOs and GMOs through risk-assessment information from the exporting to the importing country. It also requires that each grain shipment be labeled according to any GM varieties which it may contain. These rules are to be implemented systematically through the Biotechnology Clearing

House. AIA was intended to implement the broader principle of prior informed consent.

Despite opposition from the Miami Group, the Protocol adopted the **precautionary principle** by allowing member states to block imports of GM products if they believe it may pose risks to biodiversity or human health. Going beyond biophysical risk, the Protocol also allows them to cite socio-economic reasons for blocking such products. The latter criteria were demanded by developing countries, which anticipated that economic competition could lead GM crops to displace traditional varieties or entire crops.

The success of the Protocol, however, may depend on **capacity building** to implement the Protocol, especially in developing countries. Unlike many international agreements, the Cartagena Protocol includes measures to develop national capacity for making expert judgments and enforcing the Protocol rules on certification of shipments. Such measures involve private-sector funding and expert assistance from countries which export GM products – factors designed either to facilitate trade, or to strengthen the ability of host countries to restrict GM imports.

A further distinctive element of the Cartagena Protocol is the statement that environmental and trade agreements are "mutually supportive." This statement is contrary to proposals that the Protocol should be subordinate to the 1994 WTO agreement, which requires member states to provide scientific evidence to justify any blockages on imports. The relationship between the two treaties remains contentious and fluid. At the "Rio + 10" conference in 2002, the US government proposed that the Protocol be made subordinate to the WTO (see **World Trade Organization/General Agreement on Tariffs and Trade (WTO/GATT)**), though this proposal was rejected. But ultimately, the practical role of the Protocol will depend less upon legal interpretation than upon power relations – for example, how effectively the WTO may request countries to accept GM imports; indirect pressures such as **International Monetary Fund (IMF)** loans; and public protests in each country.

See also: biotechnology and resistance; biodiversity; Convention on Biological Diversity (CBD); environmental movements; genetically modified organisms (GMOs)

Further reading

Bail, C., Falkner, R. and Marquard, H. (eds) (2002) *The Cartagena Protocol on Biosafety: Reconciling Trade in Biotechnology with Environment and Development?* London: Earthscan.
CBD (2000) *Cartagena Protocol on Biosafety*, Convention on Biodiversity, United Nations Environment Program: http://www.biodiv.org/biosafety/protocol.asp
Russell, A. and Vogler, J. (2000) *The International Politics of Biotechnology: Investigating Global Futures*, Manchester: Manchester University Press.

LES LEVIDOW

cartels

A cartel is a group of agents – such as businesses or countries – that coordinate their decisions in order to maximize total joint benefits. The joint agreements associated with cartels reduce the uncertainty that arises from a mutual interdependence. The operation of a cartel typically involves a group of producers restricting total output in order to inflate price. Prior to this, the cartel needs to determine each member's share of the total output, which determines individual profits. However, at the output level that maximizes joint profits, each member has an incentive to increase unilaterally its output if it believes that others will keep theirs fixed. This makes cartels unstable, especially in the long run. While collusion among firms is illegal in most Western countries, price-fixing international cartels do exist. An example is the **Organization of Petroleum Exporting Countries (OPEC)** oil cartel, which has brought prosperity to its members. However, developing-country importers of oil have been among the hardest hit by OPEC's price-fixing arrangements.

See also: London Club; Organization of Petroleum Exporting Countries (OPEC); Paris Club

B. MAK ARVIN

caste

The *jati* (caste) system, which evolved during the vedic period (*c.*1500–500 BCE) of Hinduism, refers to the endogamous social groups comprising contemporary and vedic Hindu society and the rules of behavior that govern interaction between these groups. The more familiar term "caste" used to refer to this system actually derives from the Portuguese word *casta*, which roughly translates into breed. The social anthropologist Hutton (1977) suggests that early Portuguese traders probably used the word first in the mid-1500s to describe the segregation rules, codes of conduct, and more generally, the social interactions of people they encountered in Goa, India.

The origins of the caste system are difficult to pinpoint with certainty, yet ancient vedic texts provide insights. For many Hindus, the Veda is akin to a text of revelation, and includes writings of great import that form the very foundations of Hinduism. The Veda comprises several categories of texts, of which the Rg Veda, the earliest collection of books, provides historians with the most detailed account of vedic society, its structure and functioning, its organization, its ritual practices, and indeed the caste system.

It is in the Vedas that the concept of *varna*, roughly translating into category, class, or the universal order of things, is made clear. Some scholars have argued that *varna* and caste are virtually indistinguishable, while others offer a more sophisticated theoretical explanation for the relationship between *varna* and caste. According to them, *varna* provides the historical and ideological foundation of the caste system, which only emerges in later vedic society. Ancient texts suggest that vedic society was hierarchically divided into four major *varnas*, including the *Brahmans* (priests, or alternatively, those that taught the Veda), *Ksatriya* (warriors or nobles), *Vaisya* (commoners) and *Sudra* (serfs, menial laborers, or artisans). This system assumed definitive qualities, traits, and powers inherent in each *varna*. Early writings considered inter-marriage between the *varnas* to have eventually produced individual castes, and as such, scholars suggest that the numerous contemporary castes are in fact reducible to one of the four aforementioned *varnas*. *Varna* could thus be conceptualized as a systematizing framework by which numerous locally distinct castes identify themselves and others.

The *Manu Smriti*, a text of laws from the late vedic period, identified the customs, duties and obligations that governed interaction between caste groups. An individual's caste was considered absolute, ascribed at birth and governed by the notion of *dharma*, or an individual's duty to family and society. *Dharma* provided the functional and occupational distinctions that set different castes apart. This organizational system also ascribed individual castes with grades of purity, with *Brahmans* considered the most pure and moving down from there. Moreover, strict purification rituals, marital restrictions and food taboos were also a matter of caste association.

It is in *Manu Smriti* that we also learn of groups referred to, in general parlance, as untouchables. Manu considers these groups to be products of inter-caste marriages, and especially 'undesirable' unions between *Sudra* women and other caste groups. Untouchables were ostracized from vedic society and their proximity was considered polluting to higher castes. They were prohibited from partaking in high caste ritual traditions and generally considered outcasts beyond the four-tier *varna* system. This group, whose contemporaries call themselves *dalits* (or sometimes, "unscheduled castes") and form a very large proportion of India's population today, were made to live on the outskirts of villages, unable to mingle with mainstream society and relegated to occupations like leather working or the disposing of dead animals.

Like all social institutions, the caste system as practiced in contemporary Hindu society has evolved through time. It is not practiced with strict adherence across all parts of India, rather one finds considerable spatial variation. In urban India, the caste system still prescribes to the ritual traditions and practices outlined in the ancient texts, but adherence to rules of inter-caste association are more flexible. While rituals gain special meaning during symbolically important events in an individual's life, like an initiation ceremony or marriage, urban Hindus are very unlikely to adhere to notions of caste purity when associating with other individuals in society, whatever their caste affiliation. Furthermore, caste-defined occupational associations blur in urban contexts. For example, it is entirely reasonable to expect a *dalit* to become a doctor or politician today. While caste might not govern all aspects of social interaction anymore, individuals are still acutely aware of their caste identity and history and take pride in caste loyalty.

The interplay of caste and society in rural India tends to vary quite significantly from that observed in urban regions. One might say more generally that regions furthest removed from modern influences observe stricter adherence to caste-based traditions and associations. For instance, in theory, the practice of untouchability was outlawed during British rule, yet cases of discrimination against lower castes still occur across parts of India today. Since independence, the Indian state has set up an extensive educational and vocational system to provide opportunities for *dalits* and similar other groups, and has likewise ensured their political representation. Finally, while caste is distinctively Indian in origin, social scientists also often use it to describe inflexible social class barriers in other contexts.

See also: religion; social exclusion

Further reading

Flood, G. (1996) *An Introduction to Hinduism*, Cambridge: Cambridge University Press.

Hutton, J. (1977) *Caste in India – Its Nature, Function, and Origins*, New Delhi: Oxford University Press.

Inden, R. (1990) *Imagining India*, Oxford: Blackwell.

Smith, B. (1994) *Classifying the Universe: The Ancient Indian Varna System and the Origins of Caste*, Oxford: Oxford University Press.

FIROOZA PAVRI

casualization of work

Casualization of work refers to the process in which work increasingly takes place in an unregulated setting and a growing number of jobs differs from the typical situation of full-time work, protection by labor legislation, permanent employment contracts and guaranteed **job security**. The casualization of work consists of two processes: the informalization of work, and the flexibilization of work and **labor markets**.

First, the growth of the informal economy (see **urban informal sector**), in which workers are not protected by formal labor legislation, indicates that the working hours, wage levels, job security and the right to collective bargaining of a large proportion of the population in developing countries are not regulated. Second, flexibilization of work and labor markets refers to the adjustment of labor legislation in order to accommodate or promote forms of work and employment that differ from the typical **employment** situation. Flexibilization can include a range of measures, but a general distinction can be made between flexibilization of work and flexibilization of labor markets. Flexibilization of work is intended to allow companies to adapt to adverse economic circumstances and includes the following measures: the outsourcing of services or parts of the production process, and the variation of weekly or daily working hours and shifts. Other measures are the introduction of functional flexibility (variation in job assignments) and wage flexibility (wage level variation according to productivity and performance). Flexibilization of labor markets refers to a process in which mobility of workers in the labor market, both geographical and between different types of jobs, is stimulated in order to facilitate economic recovery in difficult times. This process often implies the deregulation of labor legislation in order to make it easier to dismiss employees and to vary the number of employees companies hire in response to economic circumstances by increasing the number of part-time and fixed-term employment contracts.

The causes of the casualization of work can be found in short-term and long-term responses to economic crisis in developing countries. Entry in the informal labor market is often a survival strategy when formal employment opportunities are not available. The formal and informal sectors become more similar as flexibilization and deregulation of work and labor markets create a gray area between the formal and the informal labor market. On the one hand, economic crisis contributes to the erosion of labor rights (see **labor rights and standards**) in the formal sector, and on the other hand, the lack of full-time **employment** opportunities in the formal sector implies that individuals and families move between the formal and informal sector or work simultaneously in both sectors. Labor reforms in developing countries (usually consisting of deregulation and the introduction of flexible employment forms in labor legislation) are part of economic reform and adjustment programs, in which facilitating the reduction of labor costs is considered as a key to **economic development**.

See also: flexible specialization; Fordism versus Toyotaism; International Labor Organization (ILO); job security; labor markets; labor rights and standards; trade unions; urban informal sector

Further reading

Lavalette, M. and Kennedy, J. (1996) "Casual Lives? The Social Effects of Work Casualization and the Lock Out on the Liverpool Docks," *Critical Social Policy* 16:3 95–107.

MARIEKE RIETHOF

CEDAW *see* Convention on the Elimination of All Forms of Discrimination Against Women (CEDAW)

charities

Charities are a specific type of non-governmental organization (see **non-governmental organizations (NGOs)**), and thus form part of the **voluntary sector** and subsequently part of **civil society**. Charities are NGOs that are registered with the government and so conform to one or more of the legal understandings of a charitable purpose. This status usually entitles charities to various tax-related benefits, and increases their access to monies that non-registered organizations might be excluded from. While charities are both forms of non-profit organizations and NGOs, these

terms are not synonymous. The legally binding nature of charitable status means that charities are likely to be restricted by the government in the type of activities they can undertake. Usually charitable status also implies that activities have to "apolitical," which may be paradoxical when anything in the public interest has some kind of political impact, and may be controversial when it depends on different people's definitions of what is political. Charities exist at every scale – local, regional, national, and international – and in most countries. Overseas charities are those that have a registered head office in one country but deliver (at least some of) their charitable aims elsewhere.

See also: aid; civil society; non-governmental organizations (NGOs); voluntary sector

DAVID LAND

child labor

Child labor refers to the exploitation of **children** through work. Child labor is widely seen as a corollary to **poverty**, though little is known about precise causes. Definitions and statistics are a matter of debate among players in the debate. International **media** attention to the issue was prompted at he beginning of the 1990s by threatened US boycotts against products from developing countries (see **corporate social responsibility (CSR)**). The WTO refusal (see **World Trade Organization/General Agreement on Tariffs and Trade (WTO/GATT)**) in 1996 to adopt core-labor standards has resulted in a strong presence of **non-governmental organizations (NGOs)** in the field.

Profound dissimilarities in labor conditions between industrial and developing countries makes a precise definition of child labor difficult. A basic definition is that child labor is work that is exploitative and detrimental to the development of children below the age of fifteen. This definition excludes the performance of light work after school and work that does not put excessive physical or psychological strain on a child. Exploitation may not only occur in **employment** but also when children are not formally employed, as when they work in **agriculture**, in rural industries, in the **urban informal sector** or in domestic work. This is the case with an estimated 90 percent of today's working children. The **International Labor Organization (ILO)** estimates that there are 250 million children aged 5–14 at work in the mid-1990s, of which 120 million are working full-time. Of the 250 million, 153 are in Asia, 80 million in Africa and 18 million in Latin America (ILO 1996). Only 5 percent of these children are in the manufacturing export sector.

The causes of child labor are complex, but are linked to the lack of affordable **education** and child welfare services, poor labor conditions of adult workers (see **labor rights and standards**) and international competition among developing countries' exporters. **Culture**, political indifference towards the fate of the poor, and parental ignorance have been cited as causes as well. The case of the Indian state of Kerala, with its remarkable low incidence of officially registered child labor in spite of widespread **poverty**, is often mentioned in support of the view that child exploitation is more a matter of political choices than of poor material conditions.

Given the informal character of child labor, statistics are notoriously unreliable and may vary according to whether one takes a restrictive or an inclusive stance. Restrictive estimates count only those who are part of the full-time labor force or focus on those who work in the most exploitative conditions. Inclusive estimates may add to this number children (mainly girls) between 5 and 14 who are out of school, those who live in conditions of extreme deprivation such as abandoned or refugee (see **refugees**) children, or, alternatively, give more weight to children's own experience of work. Statistics are linked to political positions in the debate. They range from advocates of an immediate ban (abolitionists), gradual abolition through protective measures (protectionists), and emancipation through work (liberationists or protagonists). To prove that governments can solve the problem, abolitionists adopt a restrictive count. NGOs are typically protectionist if not liberationist, and find justification in inclusive counts.

Child labor has gained international profile in connection with the 1980s liberalization of markets, pursued in view of the **comparative advantage** of exchanging **labor-intensive** goods with **capital intensive** ones. From the onset, US exporters and **trade unions** have sought to prevent international competition from threatening US jobs and markets. Respect of international **labor rights and standards**, including the prohibition of using **slavery**, **forced labor** or child labor in exports, formed the backdrop of heated debates leading to the formation of the WTO (see **World Trade Organization/General Agreement on Tariffs and Trade (WTO/GATT)**). In 1994, the USA threatened to pass Senator Tom Harkin's Bill, which sought to boycott goods made with child labor. Bangladeshi garment manufacturers dismissed about 50,000 working girls in response. The issue gained **media** attention when the **United Nations Children's Fund (UNICEF)** produced data showing that many of the girls, who had protested vehemently losing their jobs, had landed in **child prostitution**.

The WTO Singapore ministerial meeting (1996) decided to refer the issue of child labor to the **International Labor Organization (ILO)**. The ILO adopted Convention 182 on the Worst Forms of Child Labor in 1999. Convention 182 mentions **slavery**, forced labor, **debt** bondage, prostitution (see **prostitution/sex work**), participation in armed conflict and drug trafficking as areas of priority action. Though ILO's Convention 138 (1973) on the minimum age for **employment** remains in force, it should be noted that it has not been ratified by the largest Asian economies (notably India and China). Critics have commented that, as the ILO, in contrast to the WTO, cannot impose economic sanctions, child labor has *de facto* been accepted as part of the reality of developing countries for many years to come.

Governmental intervention in developing countries is limited to legislation and the implementation of special programs, often in collaboration with ILO-IPEC (International Program for the Elimination of Child Labor) and NGOs. Both IPEC and NGOs place primary emphasis on children who are greatest at risk, such as children in bondage, **child soldiers** or sexually exploited children and expect a great deal from **civil society**. IPEC receives important contributions from industrial countries and works mainly through

NGOs. The typical package includes micro-credits (see **micro-credit and micro-finance**), non-formal **education** or training in children's rights advocacy.

Today's approaches to child labor depart significantly from earlier visions of children as objects of (state) welfare and stress children's agency instead. Some NGOs have challenged anti-child labor legislation and organized children in **trade unions**. Bal Mazdoor (New Delhi) had to fight its right to register as a trade union in the Indian Supreme Court. But even those who take an abolitionist stance can hardly do without children's participation as became apparent during the Global March against Child Labor (1998) leading up to the ILO meeting that discussed draft Convention 182. Though recognizing children's agency is an important step towards addressing the issue, there is a serious danger of dumping the responsibility for what should primarily be a concern of the state (see **state and state reform**) and of society in general, on the frail shoulders of working children.

See also: adjustment with a human face; child prostitution; child soldiers; children; International Labor Organization (ILO); coping strategies; United Nations Convention on the Rights of the Child (1989)

Further reading

Boyden, J., Ling, B. and Myers, W. (1998) *What Works for Working Children*, Florence: UNICEF.

ILO (1996) *Child Labor: Targeting the Intolerable*, Geneva: ILO.

Nieuwenhuys, O. (1994) *Children's Lifeworlds, Gender Welfare and Labor in the Developing World*, London: Routledge.

Schlemmer, B. (ed.) (2000) *The Exploited Child*, London: Zed.

OLGA NIEUWENHUYS

child prostitution

Child prostitution refers to the involvement of children in **prostitution/sex work**. Few topics within international development are associated

with such general condemnation. One of the first international **non-governmental organizations (NGOs)** working against commercial sexual exploitation of children (or CSEC) is ECPAT (End Child Prostitution in Asian Tourism). This NGO was initially established to stop child prostitution in Asian tourism (see also **sex tourism**). It has since grown into a global network that defines all forms of CSEC as a fundamental violation of children's **human rights**. Like other NGOs fighting for children's rights, the programs and policies they stipulate are based on international treaties such as the **United Nations Convention on the Rights of the Child (1989)** (see **children**).

Despite the unequivocal agreement regarding the seriousness of child prostitution, there is still insufficient research conducted on the subject. A hiatus exists in many areas, including the consequences of prostitution for children's health (see **health**). There are also some misleading generalizations, or myths, concerning who participates in child prostitution. It is commonly assumed that there is a strong relationship between **sex tourism** and child prostitution. Yet research has shown that many clients are non-tourists. For example, Ennew et al. (1996) note that despite the international attention to **sex tourism** in Thailand and Cambodia, male nationals of these countries use child prostitutes' services regularly. There is a need to conduct more research on the diversity of clients of child prostitution. Similarly, it is important to acknowledge that child prostitution occurs in many countries (including developed countries), and not just those in Asia, or those with reputations for sex tourism.

Research has also questioned the numbers of **children** involved in child prostitution: much popular discussion and reporting has used rough estimates instead of detailed research. There are few reliable statistics, and there are problems in defining a universal category of a "child." Age and gender are essential markers in creating differences in the experiences of children. The experiences of a child prostitute aged seven cannot be compared to a child prostitute of seventeen. **United Nations** treaties define a child as a human being under the age of eighteen. But many national laws concerning permissible ages for factors such as marriage, work and criminal responsibility can conflict with this universal definition, and consequently make the implementation of international standards difficult (see **youth violence**).

A further criticism is the need to contextualize children's experience of prostitution within their own lives and social and cultural norms. To accomplish this, it is important to listen to children's own voices and agency within the analysis and description of child prostitution. Sometimes, such research has indicated that child prostitutes do not always experience what they do as victimization. In Thailand, children's participation in prostitution has contributed to constructing an identity of a dutiful offspring rather than a victim of exploitation. Australian young people living on the streets never defined their "sex for favors" as prostitution. They were uncomfortable with the term and claimed that only "other kids" did this, and not themselves. The ability for children to define themselves and their actions in this way is a demonstration of their agency. As a result of this kind of research, analysts suggest that programs aimed at prevention, rehabilitation and reintegration of child prostitutes will have difficulty succeeding if children's voices – as controversial as they may seem – are not listened to and reflected in their policy and strategic decisions (see **participatory development**).

See also: children; prostitution/sex work; sex tourism; slavery; United Nations Convention on the Rights of the Child (1989)

Further reading

ECPAT (End Child Prostitution in Asian Tourism) http://www.ecpat.net/eng/index.asp

Ennew, J., Gopal, K., Heeran, J. and Montgomery, H. (1996) *Children and Prostitution. How Can We Measure and Monitor The Commercial Sexual Exploitation of Children?* Literature Review and Annotated Bibliography (website): http://child-abuse.com/childhouse/childwatch/cwi/projects/indicators/prostitution/index.html

Montgomery H. (2001) *Modern Babylon? Prostituting Children in Thailand*, Oxford: Berghahn.

LORRAINE NENCEL

child soldiers

A child soldier is a boy or girl under the age of eighteen who is compulsorily or voluntarily recruited or otherwise used in hostilities by armed forces, paramilitaries, civil defense units or other armed groups. Child soldiers are estimated at 300,000 in the early 2000s. Half of them are in Africa, particularly Sierra Leone, Liberia, Uganda, Angola, Mozambique, Somalia and Congo. Reasons for the phenomenon are demographic, political and socio-economic. Demographically, areas with young populations such as Africa, where more than half the people are under eighteen, are more likely to involve youngsters in armed conflict than countries with proportionally less youngsters in the populations. Politically, developing world areas have become more unstable in the aftermath of the new international order emerging in the 1990s (see **Cold War**). Struggle over **natural resources** (diamonds, gold, oil and narcotics) and global trade in light weaponry are reasons for militia's demand for young combatants. Instability has also triggered both military and humanitarian intervention in the name of universal moral values that override claims to national sovereignty (see **humanitarianism**). Intervention is justified on the ground of international legal instruments such as ILO-Convention 182 (1999) that mentions the forced involvement of **children** in armed conflict (art. 3) as one of the worst forms of **child labor**. The Optional Protocol to the **United Nations Convention on the Rights of the Child (1989)** on the involvement of children in armed conflict (2002) also prohibits the use of children by armed groups other than governmental forces (art. 4).

There are three main socio-economic reasons for children joining armed forces: forced recruitment, often through abduction; legal recruitment in government armies; and voluntary participation as a way to secure **food**, protection and **employment**. It is worth noting that many analysts consider the notion of voluntary recruitment is problematic because factors influencing participation are often beyond the control of children. In war-torn areas, militia may take over the role of destroyed families or provide opportunities for training and **livelihoods**, offering young people a chance to make their way in the world. Debates revolve around the question whether "child soldiers" are victims. The use of a universal definition of "child soldiers" would deform contextual realities and experiences. Some critics see the images produced in the discourse on child soldiers as a form of political justification for intervention in **complex emergencies** that are both local and international in character (see **right of intervention**). Youngsters would also actively engage in armed struggle to negotiate their identity based on age, **gender**, status or opportunities. **Non-governmental organizations (NGOs)** seek to achieve reintegration through reunification with families, psycho-social treatment, schooling and professional training. The interventions tend to be most effective in individual cases, but leave the wider political and socio-economic context untouched.

See also: child labor; children; complex emergencies; humanitarianism; law of armed conflict (LAC); Geneva Conventions; right of intervention; United Nations Convention on the Rights of the Child (1989); war; youth violence

Further reading

Machel G. (2000) *The Impact of Armed Conflict on Children: A Critical Review of Progress Made, Obstacles Encountered in Increasing Protection for War-affected Children*, Winnipeg: Government of Canada.

Peters, K. and Richards, P. (1998) "'Why We Fight': Voices of Youth Combatants in Sierra Leone," *Africa* 68:2 183–210.

OLGA NIEUWENHUYS

children

The topic of children and development is probably best thought of as a series of on-going debates about the relationship between children and the development process. Children have held a prominent position in development policy discourse throughout the twentieth century, principally as the targets of **education** and **health** programs and measures to prohibit **child labor**. Such actions

are provided a moral imperative by images of children in **poverty**, at **war** (see **child soldiers**), dying from disease or victims of abuse (see **child prostitution**) that adorn campaign posters and the physical presence of one "exceptional" child at international summits. Yet, despite improvements to children's lives, there was growing concern during the 1980s that 600 million children continued to live in poverty and children remained especially vulnerable to conflict, economic crisis or environmental disaster (see **vulnerability**). Despite the best of intentions, it was clear that development "for children" had left "something missing" (Edwards, 1996:814), and a debate ensued to identify the missing elements and how they might fit into more holistic development frameworks.

During these debates, three related challenges were posted to the view that development had been "for children." The first challenge was to the prevailing attitudes that children were passive recipients of development and their engagement in any activity that went against an idealized vision of childhood was deviant. These attitudes had legitimated a long-standing regime of child protection, for example through the 1919 ILO Convention on the Minimum Age for Admission of Children to Industrial Employment, and the Forced Labor Convention of 1930 (White, 1994; see **International Labor Organization (ILO)**). Research had shown for some time that large numbers of children, perhaps as many as 200–250 million worldwide, were an important and sometimes the principal source of income in a household. Researchers now argued that the "problem" of **child labor** was not that children worked *per se*, but the conditions of such work. Studies pointed to the low **productivity** of long hours for little remuneration, the difficulties of balancing the pressures of school, the lack of social connectedness gained through leisure, and possible health problems later in life (Boyden *et al.*, 1998). While evidence suggested that childhood poverty was a strong predictor of poverty through the lifecourse, very few existing policies appeared to enable children to strengthen their capabilities (see **capability approach**) or empower them to negotiate better conditions (Harper, Marcus and Moore, 2003).

A second challenge concerned the conceptualization of children as the subjects of rights rather than as objects (see **human rights; rights-based approaches to development**). Advocacy that children's rights should be akin to human rights had gathered momentum following the International Year of the Child in 1979, and by 1986 had prompted the United Nations Commission for Human Rights to draft a **United Nations Convention on the Rights of the Child (1989)** that was adopted by the UN General Assembly on 20 November 1989. The Convention recognized the "right of every child to a standard of living adequate for the child's physical, mental, spiritual, moral and social development" as well as to "rest and leisure, to engage in play and recreational activities appropriate to the age of the child" (Articles 27 and 31). The Convention set out the obligations of the state (see **state and state reform**) to provide children with free compulsory **education**, **health** care, legal representation (see **law**) and freedom of speech. Henceforth, such rights would be indivisible according to a child's physical ability, ethnicity (see **ethnicity/identity**), **religion** or **gender**. In order to ensure that these rights were mainstreamed into a child-centered development, a World Summit on Children in 1990 in New York adopted a clear list of practical priorities codified as the Declaration on the Survival, Protection and Development of Children and a Plan of Action.

A third challenge was posted to the political complacency that considered it unnecessary to seek the views of children or to afford youth-led organizations credibility during research or policy discussion (Edwards, 1996:814). As exemplified clearly by some measures within **structural adjustment** programs, the lack of voice had allowed adults to make decisions inappropriate to the needs of children. If children were to be taken seriously as social actors with rights, then the Victorian stance that "children should be seen and not heard" had to change. Indeed, Article 12 of the Convention committed governments to assure all children the right to express views freely on "all matters affecting the child" and a number of innovative ideas for children's councils and use of the **media** were initiated or given greater prominence.

By the 1990s, optimists might argue that children had moved from being targets of development to be considered actors within development, a position that was legitimated as a matter of legal responsibility rather than moral imperative. They might also point to a rejuvenated **United Nations Children's Fund (UNICEF)** as perhaps the only UN agency with credibility among governments and the public, a shift of operations from reactive to more preventative interventions, a battery of new laws, and an increasing number of professional NGOs. Yet, the debates concerning children and development are far from over.

One frustration is whether the emphasis put on institutional reform has been appropriate to mainstream child-centered development. Superficially, institutional reforms appear to have recorded some impressive results. The government of India, for example, amended constitutional articles 83 and 93 in 1997 and 2001 to make a compulsory and quality **education** a fundamental right of the child and set out to improve the representation of children with a new Juvenile Justice Act (2000) and a Children's Code (2001). In 1994, the government established a National Authority for the Elimination of Child Labor, and in 1996 signed the Rawalpindi Resolution on Children that committed India to eliminate exploitative and hazardous forms of child labor by 2005 and all other forms of child labor by 2010. But, some question whether these new laws, agencies and protocols have delivered real change. On education, only about 29 percent of India's children between ages five and fourteen are in school compared to 81 percent in Indonesia, school drop-out and **gender** inequality in education have persisted, and new forms of hazardous child labor have emerged. The links between childhood **poverty** and poverty through the life-course have been shown to be highly complex and beyond the scope of institutional reform alone to change (Harper *et al.*, 2003).

A second concern focuses on the "universalism" of the child rights agenda. As Pupavac (2001) has argued, extending rights to children served as an integrative symbol of society at a time when other moral (and political) orders seemed in doubt. Yet, critics have argued that the rights discourse is predicated upon a West-centric bias that may appear to reaffirm the cultural grounding of what is best or normal (White, 2002). The Convention, for example, conceptualizes child-parent relations as one of rights-responsibilities, when in some **culture**s children hold responsibilities to parents that may manifest as forms of domestic work regarded as unacceptable by Western standards. This cultural bias has been particularly problematic for NGOs that are charged with both being culturally sensitive and adopting a rights-based approach (see **rights-based approaches to development**) that threatens to draw them into social contexts in which they feel ethically unwilling to venture. More cynically, some NGOs have expressed concerns that the rights-based approach has lacked a systematic map of service planning, and that its covert objective was to provide some donors with excuses for not funding certain projects. In countries such as Ghana, NGOs promote advocacy even though many lack experience "on the ground" or a research base to underpin their arguments.

A third concern is how and why, having recognized children as the holders of human rights, children are denied full **citizenship** through extension into political rights. Is the lack of self-determination a means to ensure the legitimacy of adults exercising rights in the "best interests" of children or as "resources allow"? Do agencies distrust child participation for fear that children might not express views that serve their best interests or complicate existing agendas? A foretaste of a "rights within constraints" position was already present during the drafting of the Convention that took place without the participation of children, and many countries ratified the Convention again without consultation. Indeed, by 2003, only one NGO that I interviewed in Ghana claimed to have been consulted on the new Plan for Action required following the 2002 UN General Assembly Special Session on Children (UNGASS). This session stated: "We must respect [young peoples'] right to express themselves and to participate in all matters affecting them, in accordance to their age and maturity." Yet, the trend toward greater participation at UNGASS was symbolic at best. Of the 7,000 participants from 117 countries, there were only 600 children in attendance, mostly invited by the 1,700 NGOs to launch videos, books or make speeches at side-discussions. To critics, the record of child-led development remains miserable.

Finally, awkward questions are being asked of development organizations that appear not to have fully embraced child-first and rights-based approaches to development. According to Ennew (1996), UNICEF manipulated the World Summit of 1990 to recast rights as a prosaic list of its long-standing "goals." More recently, UNICEF's framework of activities for the twenty-first century identified just five priorities – completion of quality primary **education**, promotion of integrated childhood development, safeguards against disease and **disability**, stopping the spread of HIV/AIDS (see **HIV/AIDS (definition and treatment); HIV/AIDS (policy issues)**), and, growing up free from **violence**, exploitation, abuse and discrimination. Critics claim this is "business as usual" which, apart from the absence of rights, ignores horizontal linkages across interventions, the importance of creating enabling environments involving non-child agents, and makes no specific mention of **child labor**. Meanwhile, some believe that the ILO has toughened its prohibitive stance toward child labor. In launching the International Program on the Elimination of Child Labor and Convention 182 on Worst Forms of Child Labor (1999), ILO was supported by many observers who believed that a proactive rights agenda might be inappropriate to address the most hazardous working conditions. But, in A Future without Child Labor (2002), the ILO seems to raise the number of children it considers to be "toiling in the worst forms" of labor that must be eliminated immediately from an oft-cited 8–20 million (out of a total of 200 million children working) to 180 million. Yet, there is limited evidence that prohibition works, or that children forced out of work return to school or, if consulted, how many of these children would prefer a right to work under improved conditions (Boyden et al., 1998).

There was a lot of momentum for progress built up by the Convention on the Rights of the Child, the 1990 World Summit, some national reforms, and exciting research agendas. But the overwhelming sensation was that the UNGASS in 2002 was disappointing. Reanimating the debate along positive lines will require many changes, but two points might be for policy makers to be aware that childhood is not a demographic category but a social relation, and for researchers to demonstrate how extending rights can be linked to **poverty** reduction.

See also: child labor; child prostitution; child soldiers; education; human rights; poverty; rights-based approaches to development; United Nations Children's Education Fund (UNICEF); United Nations Convention on the Rights of the Child (1989); youth violence

Further reading

Anti-Slavery International http://www.antislavery.org

Child Rights Information Network http://www.crin.org

Global Movement for Children http://www.gmfc.org

Boyden, J., Ling, B. and Myers, W. (1998) *What Works for Working Children?*, New York: UNICEF.

Edwards, M. (1996) "New Approaches to Children and Development: Introduction and Overview," *Journal of International Development* 8:6 813–27.

Ennew, J. (1996) "The Child Business: Comments on the Management of International Policies for Children," *Journal of International Development* 8:6 849–58.

Harper, C., Marcus, R. and Moore, K. (2003) "Enduring Poverty and the Conditions of Childhood: Lifecourse and Intergenerational Poverty Transmissions," *World Development* 31:3 535–54.

Pupavac, V. (2001) "Misanthropy without Borders: The International Children's Rights Regime," *Disasters* 25:2 95–112.

Save the Children: http://www.savethechildren.org

UNICEF http://www.unicef.org

White, B. (1994) "Children, Work and 'Child Labour': Changing Response to the Employment of Children," *Development and Change* 25:4, 849–78.

White, S. (2002) "Being, Becoming and Relationship: Conceptual Challenges of a Child Rights Approach in Development," *Journal of International Development* 14: 1095–104.

GARETH A. JONES

Chipko movement

The Chipko Andolan (Embrace the Tree) movement is a local **environment**al movement in India that has come to represent both grassroots resistance (see **grassroots activism; grassroots development; grassroots organizations**) to environmental degradation, and the diverse political meanings that are contained within environmental movements. The movement has its geographical origin in the present Himalayan state of Uttaranchal in India. In April 1973, some villagers in this region spontaneously demonstrated against and stopped the felling of ash trees by a sports goods company in the Mandal forests. In course of time, this token victory of the marginalized village people over the politically powerful contractor system evolved into a resistance movement against the contract system of felling. The movement got its name from the idea that if needed, the village people would protect the forests from felling, by embracing the trees (and hence inspiring the term "tree hugging"). Yet, such direct non-violent actions were resorted to in only very few instances.

The mountain communities (see **community**) in this Himalayan region have traditionally depended on the forests for their fuel, fodder and other domestic biomass needs. To meet the growing demand for timber (see **logging/timber trade**) in the markets in the plains, a system of felling by government appointed contractors was introduced. This new system allowed the contractors from the plains to make huge profits from the mountain forests, to which the local people had very little access. The mountain communities, facing an acute problem with increasing **population** and declining forest resources, saw the contract system as an unjust exploitation of the forests that should belong to them. The emergence of the movement as a protest against the felling of Himalayan forests by the contractors from the plains, is expressed precisely in the words of Raturi, the folk-poet of the movement:

> Embrace the trees in the forests
> And save them from being felled!
> Do not let the treasure of our mountains
> Be looted away to the plains!!

Among the activists of the movement were both the Marxists and Gandhians who had established good organizational network in this region. The movement took a new and ecological turn in 1977, when, in recognition of the wider ecological significance of the Himalayan forests, a section of the Chipko activists decided to oppose all tree-felling activities in the region. In this phase of the movement, the Gandhian activists under the coordination of Sarla Devi, the noted European disciple of Mahatma Gandhi, played a crucial role.

Thus, from 1977 the movement addressed a newer and more complex contradiction between short-term economic advantages of commercial felling of the trees and the long-term ecological advantages of conserving the Himalayan forests. This transcendence to the ecological level also made Chipko an inspiration for environmentalists all over the world. This later form of the movement did not enjoy a big support in the local context of Uttaranchal because it was described by many to be against the economic advancement (see **economic development**) of the mountain communities. Others have also alleged that Chipko became absorbed into wider regional politics of defining Uttaranchal province (Rangan, 2000). However, the environmental phase of Chipko has made a significant contribution to the evolution of environmental consciousness in India and globally.

See also: deforestation; environmental movements; grassroots activism; grassroots development; logging/timber trade; mountain development

Further reading

Bandyopadhyay, J. (1999) "Chipko Movement: Of Floated Myths and Flouted Realities," *Economic and Political Weekly* 34:15 10–16.

Guha, R. (1989) *The Unquiet Woods*, Delhi: Oxford University Press.

Rangan, H. (2000) *Of Myths and Movements: Rewriting Chipko into Himalayan History*, London: Verso.

JAYANTA BANDYOPADHYAY

Christianity

Christianity is linked to much past and present development theory and practices. It is also controversial: believing Christians see the Christian faith as a valuable and dynamic enhancement of **livelihoods** and **well-being**. Critics of Christianity (or other forms of **religion** as development) see it as cultural imperialism, and closely associated with colonialism (see **colonialism, history of; colonialism, impacts of**). Many others see Christianity in less emotive terms, but acknowledge its diverse influences on development.

Christianity initially came from Judaism, and developed under the Roman empire. The Romans resisted Christianity at first, but – starting with the Emperor Constantine in the fourth century AD – the Roman empire formally supported Christianity, leading to the establishment of the papacy in the Vatican, and the first formal construction at the Vatican by a pope started in AD 501. The Roman empire also allowed Christian bishops to hold subjects of the Roman empire as slaves. Christianity was then communicated to other regions by monks and nuns; Ethiopia was contacted before northwestern Europe and Russia. The establishment of empires, particularly by Portugal and Spain in South America, also spread Christianity, with missionaries frequently following merchants. By the late fifteenth century, Franciscan missionaries had established a church in the kingdom of Kongo, plus other churches existed on the West African coasts, the south coast of China (Macao), and in Indonesia. The basilica of Bom Jesus in Goa, India (completed 1622) contains the relics of St Francis Xavier, who was given the task of spreading Christianity in eastern Portuguese colonies in 1541. The first English church in India was completed in Madras (Chennai) in 1680.

Much discussion of Christianity and development has focused on the role of missionaries, although these were (and are) not restricted to the Christian faith. Islam as a religion rose during the seventh century AD. Initial Christian missionaries were Roman Catholics. Protestant missionaries become more prevalent in the eighteenth and nineteenth centuries, and, unlike the Catholics, were notable for their general opposition to **slavery** (Hansen and Twaddle, 2002:2). The opposition to slavery was, in part, linked to the political stances of countries espousing Protestantism: in Britain (a protestant country), Adam Smith had written that free labor was more likely to be profitable than unfree (or slave) labor. Britain was the first country to ban slave-trading (in 1807) leading to an eventual ban on slave holdings (in 1833). The sociologist Max Weber also described the influence of Christianity in early **capitalism** in Britain through the **Protestant work ethic**, which influenced entrepreneurs' commitment to assiduous profit making. Different colonists espoused different religions: the British were Anglican; the Danish Lutheran; the Dutch Presbyterian or Reformed Church; and the French, Spanish and Portuguese were Roman Catholic. By 1914, the number of North American missionaries equaled British missionaries.

Missionaries claimed that proselytization (or the attempt to convert people) brought various benefits. Conversion to Christianity usually implied also learning to read the Bible, and this in turn created greater employability, or leadership skills among class leaders. Contact with missionaries also formed one of the key ways to relate to the colonizing powers, and hence converted people had greater ability to become **elites**. Some converted slaves returned as missionaries to Africa. The Berlin Act of 1885, and 1919 Convention signed at St Germain-en-Laye established rules for European activities in colonial territories, and these included instructions not to differentiate or inhibit missionaries from different faiths (including Muslims), and not to damage pre-Christian shrines. Many missionaries were supported by colonial states because they performed tasks – such as **education** – that were beyond state capacity (see **state and state reform**). For example, in Uganda, the British provided funds for the voluntary associations of the British Anglican Church Missionary Society and the French Roman Catholic White Fathers.

There are, of course, many examples to claim either positive or negative impacts resulting from Christianity's involvement with development. Critics like to point out that simply converting people to a different religion, or promising them "life after death" did little for materially for people, and frequently made life worse by replacing old cultural systems with new and uncontextualized practices. The US Student Volunteer Movement for Foreign Missions was described as culturally imperialist for urging, in 1888, "the evangelization of the world in this generation" (Hansen and Twaddle, 2002:12). In 1949, all missionaries were expelled from China following the communist revolution.

Some current criticisms claim the church is politically conservative, and fails to act on important pressing needs. The Roman Catholic church, for example, is widely criticized for refusing to endorse **family planning**, and for the statement by Pope John Paul II in 2003 that condoms do not protect against HIV/AIDS (a statement challenged by most medical officials) (see **HIV/AIDS (definition and treatment); HIV/AIDS (policy issues)**). The resistance of the Roman Catholic Church to the ordination of women priests has also been criticized for further upholding traditional approaches to **gender**. The Protestant Anglican church has also experienced controversy. In 2003, the opposition of many African Anglican bishops to the ordination of an openly gay bishop in the USA split the Anglican church into those who supported or resisted his ordination (see **same-sex sexualities**). Yet, Christianity has also proven to be a powerful force for local **empowerment** in **civil society** in various societies. In Latin America, the concept of **liberation theology** is an approach to empowering poor people based predominantly through the Catholic church. In Poland in the 1980s, the Catholic church formed a powerful social rallying point against the Soviet-dominated state.

One current example of Christianity and development at work is in the NGO Christian Aid (see **non-governmental organizations (NGOs)**), which was established by churches in the UK and Ireland in 1945, and aims to address the causes of **poverty** and **inequality**. The Christian Aid slogan "we believe in life before death" demonstrates the desire to focus on material and political needs (in a spiritual and ethical context) rather than simply on religious conversion. CAFOD (Catholic Agency for Overseas Development) is another Christian NGO, founded in England and Wales in 1962, fighting the immediate manifestations of poverty without overtly seeking to proselytize.

See also: colonialism, history of; colonialism, impacts of; culture; ethics; religion; slavery

Further reading

CAFOD website: http://www.cafod.org.uk/

Christian Aid website: http://www.christian-aid.org.uk

Dunch, R. (2002) "Beyond Cultural Imperialism: Cultural Theory, Christian Missions, and Global Modernity," *History and Theory* 41: 30–325.

Hansen, H. and Twaddle, M. (2002) *Christian Missionaries and the State in the Third World*, Oxford: James Currey/Athens OH: Ohio University Press.

Harris, P. (1991) "Cultural Imperialism and American Protestant Missions: Collaboration and Dependency in Mid-nineteenth-century China," *Pacific Historical Review* 60:3 309–38.

TIM FORSYTH

chronic poverty

Chronic poverty may be distinguished from the general concept of **poverty** because of its extended duration. The exact length of time that needs to elapse is, as with the level chosen for a **poverty line**, somewhat arbitrary. Intuitively, the chronically poor are those who remain poor for all or much of their lives, pass on poverty to subsequent generations, or die a preventable poverty-related death. The chronically poor are likely to require a different set of poverty reduction interventions to improve their situation than policies targeted at the transitory poor. Many of the chronically poor will also be the extreme poor (i.e. far below a given poverty line), but the available evidence of overlap is limited and mixed.

Chronic poverty is a facet of *poverty dynamics* rather than *poverty trends*, and as such, its analysis requires household-level panel data. For example, consider the approximate 20 percent decline in Uganda's aggregate national poverty rate from 1992 to 1999 (poverty trend). This does not imply, as is often assumed, that 20 percent of individuals or households that were permanently poor have moved out of poverty, nor that all households have

become 20 percent richer. In fact, this aggregate poverty trend masks important poverty dynamics: about 19 percent of households were poor in both years (the chronically poor), and while almost 30 percent of households moved out of poverty, another 10 percent moved in (the transitory poor).

Absolute, money-metric poverty lines have generally been used for the measurement and analysis of chronic poverty. It has been argued, however, that using multidimensional indicators of deprivation may more accurately represent the persistence of poverty.

There are two main approaches to the conceptualization and measurement of chronic poverty (see also **poverty measurement; participatory poverty assessment (PPA)**). Both provide valuable insights. The *spells approach*, used above in the Ugandan example, focuses on transitions in and out of poverty. In this case, the chronically poor are generally defined as those that have been poor in every, or almost every, time period (wave). Between the chronically poor and the never-poor lie the *transitory poor* – those who move in and out of poverty. The *components approach* to chronic poverty considers the mean income etc. over all waves, and generally produces higher estimates of chronic poverty.

The chronically poor are not a homogenous group – people are trapped in poverty for a range of often overlapping reasons. Some live in spatial **poverty trap**s, including remote rural areas, urban slums (see **housing; shantytowns**), and regions experiencing prolonged violent conflict (see **complex emergencies**). Others are chronically poor based on their position within households, communities (see **community**), and countries. Those who are chronically poor based on discrimination include marginalized ethnic, religious or **caste** groups, including **indigenous people** and nomadic peoples; migrant, stigmatized and bonded laborers (see **labor migration; slavery**); **refugees** and **internally displaced persons**; people with disabilities (see **disability**); people with ill-health (see **health and poverty**), especially HIV/AIDS (see **HIV/AIDS (definition and treatment); HIV/AIDS (policy issues)**); and, to different extents, women and girls (see **male bias**). Those whose chronic poverty is related to household composition and life-cycle position include: **children**; older people (see **ageing**); widows; households headed by older people, disabled people, children and, in certain cases, women (see **women-headed households**).

It has been estimated that at the beginning of the twenty-first century there were between 275 and 400 million absolutely chronically poor people. South Asia has the highest number of chronically poor people, while Sub-Saharan Africa, particularly West and Central Africa, have the highest prevalence of chronic poverty. The fastest growth rates of chronic poverty are found in Central Asia and Russia. There are smaller pockets of absolute and relative chronic poverty around the world.

See also: gender and poverty; health and poverty; participatory poverty assessment (PPA); poverty; poverty line; poverty measurement; poverty trap; rural poverty; urban poverty

Further reading

Chronic Poverty Research Center (2004) *Chronic Poverty Report 2004*, University of Manchester: CPRC. http://www.chronicpoverty.org

Hulme, D. and Shepherd, A. (eds) (2003) "Chronic Poverty and Development Policy," *World Development* 31:3, special issue.

KAREN MOORE AND DAVID HULME

circular migration

Circular migration, or circulation, has been commonly conceived as "a great variety of movements, usually short-term, repetitive, or cyclical in nature, but all having in common the lack of any declared intention of a permanent or long-lasting change of residence" (Zelinsky, 1971:225–6). It may be associated with, for example, the periodic **migration** of villagers to cities during agricultural growing seasons in order to find temporary waged **employment** before returning to villages at harvest time. Over time, the circuits adopted in rural societies have been strengthened or modified by a variety of internally- and externally-generated changes, but they have endured, and even become

more complex and spatially extensive. One principle of circulation, in both customary and contemporary forms, is a territorial separation of obligations, activities and goods, in which the security of a "home-place" is matched with a wider field of opportunities and associated risks at more distant locations. Another is that, irrespective of the length of time away, a continuing attachment to the home **community** is manifest in the cross-flow of communication and the return flow of **remittances** (see Chapman and Prothero 1985).

See also: migration; remittances; rural-urban migration; urbanization

Further reading

Chapman, M. and Prothero, R. (eds) (1985) *Circulation in Population Movement: Substance and Concepts from the Melanesian Case*, New York: Routledge.

Zelinsky, W. (1971) "The Hypothesis of the Mobility Transition," *The Geographical Review*, 61: 219–49.

DENNIS CONWAY

citizenship

Citizenship refers to the formal rights and duties governing the interactions between individuals belonging to a political **community**. Traditionally, citizenship encompasses civil rights, which include the right to own property and have access to fair judicial procedures in a court of justice, and political rights, namely the right to elect and be elected for government positions.

Following World War II, with the development of **welfare state**s in Western Europe and universal access to **education** and **health** care, some authors argued for a similar provision of social rights of citizenship, although no consensus was reached. Since the late 1960s, the emergence of **new social movements** struggling over ethnic, gender, environmental, and sexual rights, have fuelled further changes in the traditional meanings of citizenship, while the processes of **economic**

federalization and mass **migration** have prompted radical redefinitions of citizenship rights in most developed countries. Formally, the granting of citizenship rights operates as a double-sided process of inclusion and exclusion of individuals in and from a given political community (see **social integration; social exclusion**). In practice, however, the system is also internally exclusive regarding the quality of citizenship actually enjoyed by different categories of people within the same **community**, which is captured by the use of qualifiers such as first-, second- and even third-class citizens. This has been conceptualized as the distinction between formal and substantive citizenship.

Strictly speaking, the modern concept of citizenship is bound up with the nation-state as it developed in Western Europe since the Renaissance and later in the independent British American colonies, and is generally included in democratic systems of government based on the exercise of individual rights, **freedom of association**, and political participation. The historical specificity of Western experience, however, implies that concepts of citizenship should not be extended uncritically to non-Western societies. Indeed, even Western concepts of citizenship are diverse. For instance, much discussion about social rights of citizenship is rooted in well-established European liberal principles about equality, communitarianism, and mutual responsibility, or in republican ideals of citizen participation. But in the USA, political culture has generally been less hospitable to the notion of social rights. Here, the classic components of social citizenship, such as the provision of essential services and welfare benefits, do not imply the meaning of equal respect and enhanced membership of the community, but rather are perceived as impediments to the achievement of full community membership. However, even within the European context, the traditions associated with the notion of social citizenship have combined in different ways with striking differences across different countries. The contrast is even more prominent when we consider the development of systems of citizenship in the non-Western world, where this has been often the uneven product of conquest, imitation, assimilation, and syncretistic recreation of European ideas and traditions.

Geographical, cultural-historic and political cleavages are, however, not the most important factors in determining the meaning of citizenship, as they change over time within the same political community. First, peaceful or violent changes in political regimes frequently mean the loss of citizenship rights for large parts of a given territorial community, as often happens to the increasing numbers of **refugees** and **internally displaced persons** caused by civil wars, economic crises, and **natural disasters**. Second, sectors of the **population** which are excluded from enjoying full community membership struggle for widening and deepening the content of citizenship rights, and securing both formal and substantive access to them (e.g. women's struggles to gain access to equal civil and political rights).

In this context, the impact of **globalization** has exposed the limits of traditional citizenship systems, while at the same time has highlighted the need for expanding the content and deepening the actual exercise of citizenship rights at the local level. Global processes such as the unregulated financial operations of **capital markets** are beyond citizen control even in the most developed countries, as is the development of technologies that allow the genetic modification and creation of living organisms by scientists (see **genetically modified organisms (GMOs)**). These processes are challenging the capacity of traditional systems of **governance** based on political **accountability**, market regulation, and citizen participation. At the same time, however, it is widely recognized that achieving success in the actual implementation of policies agreed at the global level requires the **empowerment** and active participation of the stakeholders through community and citizen involvement at the local level. This is particularly the case with development policies such as those aimed at enhancing the quality of life of people in developing countries, for instance by ensuring the entitlement to basic services such as safe **drinking water** supply and **sanitation**. Although formal rights such as the right to work, to good health or to water can be bestowed on people and become formalized in citizenship charters, in practice these formal rights do not guarantee people the sustained entitlement to these goods and services. Closing the gap between formal and substantive citizenship is still one the crucial challenges for achieving **sustainable development**.

See also: asylum seeking; civil society; democracy; human rights; refugees; rights-based approaches to development; social exclusion; social integration; Universal Declaration of Human Rights (1948)

Further reading

Lister, R. (1997) *Citizenship: Feminist Perspectives*, Basingstoke: Macmillan.

Marshall, T. (1949 [1992]) "Citizenship and Social Class," pp. 3–51 in Marshall, T. and Bottomore, T. (eds) *Citizenship and Social Class*, London and Concord MA: Pluto.

van Steenbergen, B. (1994) *The Condition of Citizenship*, London: Sage.

JOSÉ ESTEBAN CASTRO

CIVIL SERVICE *see* public management; public sector

civil society

Since the end of the **Cold War**, the concept of civil society has become an influential one among development agencies, researchers and practitioners. Despite many different understandings of the term, "civil society" is broadly understood as the institutional space between state (see **state and state reform**), market and household in which citizens try to organize and represent their interests. Civil society is usually conceived as being situated beyond the household, and writers such as Putnam (1993) – whose work on the related issue of **social capital** has recently been influential – argue that an essential component of civil society is made up of the horizontal, solidaristic groups or associations which cross-cut vertical ties of kinship and patronage. **Non-governmental organizations (NGOs)** have come to be seen as one form of civil society organization – alongside **trade unions**, religious groups, **community**-based organizations,

activist networks, media agencies, professional associations and others. Liberal understandings of civil society as balancing state and market have underpinned growing donor support to NGOs in pursuit of **governance** and "socially responsible capitalism" agendas. By contrast, radical interpretations of civil society have formed the basis for contesting dominant ideologies and the imagining and enactment of alternative development paradigms (see **postmodernism and postdevelopment**). The concept of civil society has multiple attractions – as a normative ideal, as an analytical tool, or simply as a way to refer to an empirical reality. This multidimensionality is a key factor in its rise to prominence. The concept of civil society is increasingly seen as "useful to think with" because it may support analysis which can help to make sense of political and social change. But it may also be regarded as "useful to act with" as a focal point for organizing, and accordingly has been taken up with enthusiasm by activists and policy-makers.

The idea of civil society has diverse philosophical roots. The Scottish enlightenment thinker Adam Ferguson saw civil society as a socially desirable alternative both to the state of nature and the heightened individualism of emergent **capitalism**, while a moral core resided within a society increasingly organized around commercial relations. The German philosopher G. W. F. Hegel argued that self-organized civil society in the form of private associations might contribute to social integration but also need to be balanced and ordered by the state, otherwise it would become self-interested and would not contribute to the common good. Both understandings contributed to the early evolution of the concept of civil society. Later, the work of Alexis de Tocqueville has been used to support arguments "in favor of" civil society, bringing a keener normative edge and a narrower organizational focus. De Tocqueville's positive account of nineteenth-century associationalism (i.e. the existence of associations) in the USA stressed volunteerism, community spirit and independent associational life as protections against the domination of society by the state, and indeed as a counterbalance that helped to keep the state accountable and effective (see **accountability**). This approach to civil society – and elements of those that preceded it – tended to emphasize the role of civil society as one in which some kind of equilibrium was created in relation to the state and the market. The neo-Tocquevillian position can now be seen in current debates in the USA and other Western countries, such as that generated by Putnam's work, that the level of associationalism within a society can be associated with positive values of trust and cooperation.

Civil society ideas have become influential in relation to efforts by development policy-makers during the past decade to promote democratic **institutions** and market reforms in developing countries, forming part of the so-called "good governance" agenda made popular by the **World Bank** and other donors such as the UK Department for International Development (DFID) during the early 1990s (see **governance**). It was proposed that international development assistance (or **aid**) could help build a virtuous circle between state, economy and civil society that would balance growth, equity and stability. Development donor support for the emergence and strengthening of NGOs has formed a central part of this approach, where civil society was seen as having the potential to contribute to the emergence of more competitive market economies, better-managed states with the capacity to enable mixed provision of services, and improved citizen participation in public decision-making (see **democracy; participatory development**). The growth of interest in civil society during the past decade has been clearly linked to the global dominance of ideologies of **neo-liberalism**, which envisage a reduced role for the state and privatized forms of services delivery through flexible combinations of governmental, non-governmental and private institutional actors (see **partnerships; public-private partnerships**). Within this framework, there was a tendency among many development agencies to think of "civil society" and "NGOs" as almost synonymous, resulting in increased funding to the NGO sectors in both developed and developing countries.

The result has been a tendency among development donors and other agencies to view civil society predominantly as a normative concept, and to seek the "building" of civil society through narrow programs of financial and organizational support to NGOs. Such NGOs may at best show limited levels of **accountability** and effectiveness, while at worst they may simply be passive instruments for the implementation of donor programs which detracts from rather than contributing to **state and state reform** agendas. There is perhaps now a growing recognition by donors that NGOs by themselves do not constitute solutions to development problems, and that civil society itself amounts to more than this narrow organizational realm. The new attention being given to civil society may focus useful attention on **human rights**, citizen action and **institutions**.

Can these types of programs contribute to the more political, dynamic aspects of civil society, or do such initiatives remain neutralized by the forces that act to maintain Ferguson's (1990) "anti-politics machine"? (i.e. the imposition of development agendas without active debate about their origin or purpose; see **anti-politics; governmentality**). A pessimistic view argues that bilateral donors who support the strengthening of civil society continue to "mistake **governance** for politics" (Jenkins, 2001). It is argued here that aid donors seek to build only an apolitical "sanitized" version of civil society, which excludes organizations and individuals engaged in struggles for political power and influence and which may be critical of neo-liberal orthodoxy. However, the efforts of donor-assisted civil society actors to develop more autonomous "room for maneuver" should not automatically be ruled out. For example, the struggle in Mozambique to recognize collective **land rights** in the development of the 1997 Land Law, and the subsequent civic movement in support of the rights which it enshrines, has involved a pragmatic combination of mobilization and advocacy work by local NGOs, international NGOs and some donors (Kanji et al., 2002) (see **advocacy coalitions**).

While neo-liberal development policy was turning to civil society as part of its program for de-centering the state as the key development actor, a different strand of civil society thinking, which placed politics at its center, had gained influence elsewhere in the world. This version was influenced by Antonio Gramsci, who argued that civil society is the arena, separate from state and market, in which ideological hegemony is contested (see **politics; weapons of the weak**). This view implies that civil society contains a wide range of different organizations and ideologies that both challenge and uphold the existing order. These ideas were influential in the context the analysis and enactment of resistance to totalitarian regimes in Eastern Europe and Latin America from the 1970s onwards (see **authoritarianism**). Gramscian ideas about civil society can also be linked to the growing area of social science research on **new social movements** which seek to challenge and transform structures and identities.

Arguments have been made for a more politicized use of the civil society concept, and one that is sensitive to history and difference. For example, Blaney and Pasha (1993) argue that understanding civil society must include the analysis of both "structure" and "process" to avoid it being represented as static and ahistorical. This means linking the analysis of civil society more closely with the capitalist **international division of labor** and avoiding any simple conflation of "society" and civil society. It also means rejecting a crudely normative view of civil society by accepting the idea that civil society in reality contains a wide range of diverse values, ideologies and intentions. Keane (1998) has elaborated on the phenomenon of "uncivil society" in which organized groups of citizens may threaten the identities and rights of other groups.

Webster and Engberg-Pedersen (2002) reject the generalized, apolitical view of civil society in favor of a Gramscian perspective that explores the contested political space in which different groups, organizations, and individuals each seek to influence public policy. An example is the case of Adivasi women's silkworm cooperatives in West Bengal, India through which marginalized women have gained greater voice in **community** forest management policy and practice (see **Joint Forest Management (JFM)**). The broader concept of civil society also allows for the analysis of the connections between the local and global dimensions of political struggle. For example, Mamdani (1996) shows how it can reveal the dangers of a simplified binary opposition between state and civil society in Africa in the light of colonial histories of exclusion and the increasing importance of horizontal transnational identities and linkages.

Two differing civil society traditions can therefore usefully be distinguished, the liberal and the radical. It is the neo-Tocquevillian organizational view of civil society that has strongly influenced mainstream development agencies during the past decade (Davis and McGregor, 2000). The transition of the concept of civil society from the theoretical terrain of political science to the development policy sphere has not been a straightforward one. While the concept may be useful for the purposes of analysis, for policy-makers its practical value is far less clear. There are four main reasons for this. The first is that different understandings of the term exist, and this makes it difficult to agree precise policy purposes. The second is that since the concept of civil society is primarily a theoretical construct, it may not lend itself in any straightforward way to a practical policy-level application. Third, the concept of civil society is arguably historically specific to particular time(s) and place(s) and may be sensitive to differences of history, culture and economy. Finally, a key problem with the concept is that it is not always clear within the research literature or within political discourse whether what is being referred to is a discussion of civil society as an analytical concept, or as an actually existing social form. This latter point is a difficulty that muddles much of the policy-level debate on the importance of civil society.

With these problems in mind, it is useful to hold on to Van Rooy's (1998) characterization of the usefulness of the concept of civil society in terms of an "analytical hat-stand" on which can be placed a whole range of ideas about politics, organization, **citizenship**, activism and self-help. There is a rich ongoing debate about the organizational, historical, political and cultural dimensions of civil society, which continues to mean different things to different kinds of people. Nevertheless, analysis of the concept of civil society and its empirical manifestations is potentially revealing of relationships between concepts, ideologies and development policy and, perhaps, aspects of development practice.

See also: advocacy coalitions; charities; grassroots activism; governance; new social movements; non-governmental organizations (NGOs); partnerships; politics; public-private partnerships; social capital; state and state reform; trade unions; voluntary sector

Further reading

Blaney, D. and Pasha, M. (1993) "Civil Society and Democracy in the Third World: Ambiguities and Historical Possibilities," *Studies in Comparative International Development* 28:1 3–24.

Davis, P. and McGregor, J. (2000) "Civil Society, International Donors and Poverty in Bangladesh," *Commonwealth and Comparative Politics* 38:1 47–64.

Ferguson, J. (1990) *The Anti-Politics Machine: Development, "Depoliticization" and Bureaucratic Power in Lesotho*, Minneapolis: University of Minnesota Press.

Howell, J. and Pearce, J. (2001) *Civil Society and Development: A Critical Exploration*, London: Lynne Rienner.

Jenkins, R. (2001) "Mistaking 'Governance' for 'Politics': Foreign Aid, Democracy and the Construction of Civil Society," in Kaviraj, S. and Khilnani, S. (eds) (2001) *Civil Society: History and Possibilities*, Cambridge: Cambridge University Press.

Kanji, N., Braga, C. and Mitullah, W. (2002) *Promoting Land Rights in Mozambique and Kenya: How Do NGOs Make a Difference?*, London: Department for International Development.

Keane, J. (1998) *Civil Society: Old Images, New Visions*, Cambridge: Polity.

Mamdani, M. (1996) *Citizen and Subject: Contemporary Africa and the Legacy of Late Colonialism*, Princeton: Princeton University Press.

Putnam, R. (1993) *Making Democracy Work: Civic Traditions in Modern Italy*, Princeton: Princeton University Press.

Van Rooy, A. (1998) *Civil Society and the Aid Industry*, London: Earthscan.

Webster, N. and Engberg-Pedersen, L. (eds) (2002) *In the Name of the Poor: Contesting Political Space for Poverty Reduction*, London: Zed.

DAVID LEWIS

clash of civilizations

The "Clash of Civilizations" is an argument advanced by Harvard professor Samuel P. Huntington in the 1990s, which asserts that future world politics will be dominated by conflict between different civilizations and **cultures**, rather than between different nationalities, social classes, or rich and poor. The argument has strong supporters and opponents. The argument is attractive to some social scientists because it urges the continued strength of local culture in the face of **globalization**. Yet, critics say that the argument adopts a highly simplistic and functional approach to culture that avoids the diversity and contextual nature of political feeling in different countries, the positive role of multiculturalism within other countries, and the complex connections between culture, identity, and livelihood (see **livelihoods**) in different regions of the world. Many observers claim the concept gained credence at a time when political tensions were high following the 1991 and 2003 Gulf Wars and 2001 attacks on the USA, and may have contributed to a rather simplistic vision of "us" versus "them" that may have added to, rather than reduced, tensions. Indeed, the argument has been attractive to some politicians in the USA who have wished to promote an isolationist agenda in international politics.

See also: culture; globalization; globalization and culture; Orientalism; race and racism; security

Further reading

Huntington, S. (1996) *The Clash of Civilizations and the Remaking of World Order*, New York: Simon and Schuster.

TIM FORSYTH

CLASS *see* elites; intermediate classes; sociology of development; transnational capitalist class

Clean Development Mechanism (CDM)

The Clean Development Mechanism (CDM) was created in 1997 as part of the Kyoto Protocol to the United Nations Framework Convention on Climate Change (UNFCCC) (see **climate change;**

Earth Summit (1992) (United Nations Conference on Environment and Development)). The CDM is a means for countries that need to reduce greenhouse gas emissions (the so-called Annex I countries) to achieve some of these reductions by investing in climate-friendly activities in non-Annex I countries (which are usually taken to mean developing countries). The CDM is therefore one of three flexible mechanisms of climate change mitigation, in which countries may achieve their commitments to reduce emissions by cooperating with or investing in other countries. The other flexible mechanisms are Emissions Trading, and Joint Implementation. The CDM, however, is the only flexible mechanism that specifically includes non-Annex I countries, and hence is one of the most direct ways that **climate change** policy affects developing countries. Investments under the CDM are meant to include actions that are additional to business-as-usual scenarios that deliberately take actions to mitigate climate change. For example, investment may include upgrading a coal-fired power station to natural gas; disseminating **renewable energy** technologies; or planting trees that can sequester carbon dioxide. The net reductions in greenhouse gases may then be certified and count against the emissions of the investing country, or the certificate may be sold to a further country or company seeking to achieve greenhouse gas reductions.

The CDM, however, has a variety of controversies. Flexible mechanisms in general have been opposed by many developing countries because they are seen as ways for Annex I countries to avoid taking responsibility for reducing greenhouse gas emissions at home. The original framework for the CDM came from a 1997 Brazilian proposal for a "Clean Development Fund," through which Annex I countries would be *penalized* if they failed to meet their commitments. But this proposal was adapted at the Kyoto Summit into a *mechanism* by which Annex I countries could *achieve* their targets, and left no formal method for penalizing non-performers. There are also worries about the nature of investment under flexible mechanisms. A precursor to the CDM was so-called Activities Implemented Jointly (AIJ), which was established as a pilot phase for Joint Implementation at the First Conference of the

Parties (COP1) to the UNFCCC at Berlin in 1995. AIJ was criticized by many developing countries, however, for providing projects that were relatively low-cost and whose climate impacts were difficult to monitor, such as reforestation and forest protection, rather than addressing some of the more costly and trenchant problems of development such as upgrading industrial infrastructure and technology. Some observers – such as the Uruguay-based non-governmental organization, the World Rainforest Movement – also alleged that **plantation forestry** climate projects had exaggerated ecological benefits, risked **biodiversity** loss, and threatened to produce local social and political impacts such as **displacement** of local farmers. The establishment of baselines – or the ability to indicate how far CDM projects have actually provided additional greenhouse gas-mitigation – is particularly problematic. Partly as a result of these kinds of criticisms, the Kyoto Protocol limited Joint Implementation to just Annex I countries, and used text for the CDM that deliberately avoided "sinks" (i.e. carbon sequestration through land use and forestry projects), as a means to indicate that the CDM should be used for **sustainable development** in general, including possibly industrial **technology transfer**.

Following Kyoto, however, controversies continued. Many investing countries insisted on the continued use of "sinks" for CDM projects, and this was either welcomed or strongly opposed by a variety of non-Annex I countries. Costa Rica in particular was pro-sinks. China, Brazil, India and Thailand, however, were against the use of sinks, or land-use based projects. The controversy reached its height at COP6 in The Hague in 2000, when – during uncertainties about the USA presidential elections – delegates failed to reach agreement of the role of sinks-based projects in any of the flexible mechanisms. Then, following the withdrawal of the USA from the Kyoto process in March 2001, a follow-up COP6-bis meeting was held at Bonn in July 2001, where remaining delegates did reach agreement. The details of the agreements were then clarified in Marrakesh, Morocco, in October 2001. The so-called Marrakesh Accords addressed various aspects of the UNFCCC, but concerning the CDM, it established an "Adaptation Fund" to help capacity building for long-term technology transfer in developing countries, financed by a level of 2 percent of all proceeds under the CDM. The Accords limited participation in the CDM only to those countries who have ratified Kyoto (and hence providing an incentive for ratification). They also placed caps on the amount of sinks-based projects to be included in each country's activities, and various definitions of the type of project and sink to be encouraged. For example, the total contribution of reforestation and afforestation projects by individual countries was capped at 1 percent of their total target.

Proponents claimed the Marrakesh Accords have transformed the CDM into a workable and dynamic mechanism that can harness private-sector investment, and help break through long-term barriers to technology transfer. Critics argued the Adaptation Fund would repel investment by acting as a tax on projects, and that there was still too great an uncertainty about different technologies and projects that could be allowed or disallowed. Most fundamentally, while the CDM inevitably will accelerate certain types of investment in developing countries, its influence in mitigating climate change compared with reductions of emissions in developed (Annex I) countries will always be small.

See also: capacity building; climate change; deforestation; environment; Global Environment Facility (GEF); renewable energy; technology transfer

Further reading

Forsyth, T. (1999) "Flexible Mechanisms of Climate Technology Transfer," *Journal of Environment and Development* 8:3 238–57.

Grubb, M., Brack, D. and Vrolijk, C. (1999) *The Kyoto Protocol: A Guide and Assessment*, London: Earthscan and the Royal Institute of International Affairs.

UNDP CDM Connect (information about CDM): http://www.cdm-connect.org/

UNFCCC website: http://unfccc.int/

Vrolijk, C. (2002) "A New Interpretation of the Kyoto Protocol: Outcomes from The Hague, Bonn, and Marrakesh," *Royal Institute of International Affairs*, Sustainable Development Program Briefing Paper no. 1, April 2002, London: RIIA. http://www.riia.org

TIM FORSYTH

climate change

"Climate change" or so-called "global warming" refers to the anthropogenically induced raising of climatic temperatures by increased concentration of atmospheric greenhouse gases such as carbon dioxide or methane. It is usually associated with burning fossil fuels such as oil and coal, the burning of forests or grassland, the decomposition of organic material, or the removal of carbon-sequestering vegetation (such as by **deforestation**). There are also diverse non-anthropogenic causes of climate change, which also have complex and long-term causes. Many people in developed countries see climate change as the world's most pressing environmental problem, but in developing countries more localized problems such as declining soil fertility, unclean **drinking water**, and **pollution** are commonly seen as more urgent. In part, this reflects a lack of awareness about climate change in developing countries, but some critics see climate change in hostile terms as the concern only of richer countries, or a potential ploy to restrict **industrialization** in developing countries. Climate change is complex and diverse in both biophysical and political terms, and may relate to developing countries in terms of its causes, impacts, and concerning the formulation and implementation of policies.

Assessing causes of climate change has been controversial. In 1991, the Washington DC-based think tank, World Resources Institute (WRI), famously published a report that allocated national responsibilities for greenhouse gas emissions, giving substantial weight to **deforestation** and predicted methane releases from wet rice and **livestock**, and placing Brazil, India and China among the top six emitting countries (Hammond *et al.*, 1991). The Indian non-governmental organization, Center for Science and Environment (CSE) (see **non-governmental organizations (NGOs)**) criticized the report for overlooking per capita emissions; using simplistic estimates of deforestation and methane emissions (e.g. the report estimated global wet-rice methane emissions based on Italian figures); and for equating emissions caused by land clearance for **poverty**-alleviation or **food** production with high-consumption lifestyles in developed countries (Agarwal and Narain, 1991). Today, it is believed that 80–85 percent of greenhouse gas emissions come from fossil fuels, with land-use changes (including deforestation) accounting for the remainder, and that per capita carbon usage is approximately six tons per year in the USA, but some 0.5 tons per year in India and China. Moreover, some developing countries have highlighted the role of historic industrialization in producing greenhouse gases, which exist in the atmosphere for many years. In 1997, the Brazilian government controversially proposed that emissions reductions targets should be linked to the years in which different countries underwent the industrial revolution (placing developed countries at the top of the list). In the same year, the US Senate voted 95–0 against signing any climate change-treaty that did not include the participation of developing countries.

Impacts of climate change are also highly debated. Some scenarios predict that extreme impacts of climate change such as **droughts**, storms and sea-level rises are more likely to occur in developing countries (or **small island developing states (SIDS)**) and will add to existing problems such as forest fires or **desertification**. Such scenarios are questioned, however, by worst-case scenarios that warn of major Northern climatic freezing if climate change redirects the Gulf Stream. Moreover, critics point out that the emphasis of global climate models on analyzing changes at the atmospheric level (such as the residence time and photochemical reactivity of greenhouse gases) do not necessarily assist in explaining the local risks experienced by diverse social groups in locations where environmental change, including non-anthropogenic climate change, is already well known. Furthermore, social and political analysis proposes that any predictions

of biophysical impacts of climate change have to be tempered by analysis of the role of social **vulnerability** in determining who is at risk, and of various adaptation practices including **trade**, **resource tenure** and state (see **state and state reform**) capacity that reduce risks. Consequently, the prediction of climate change impacts should also consider the evolution of climate change adaptation strategies. Some critics also point out that climate change may bring positive benefits, although these views are controversial.

The political response to climate change has been dominated by scientific assessments produced by the Intergovernmental Panel on Climate Change (IPCC), and the negotiations concerning the United Nations Framework Convention on Climate Change (UNFCCC) signed at the Rio **Earth Summit (1992) (United Nations Conference on Environment and Development)**. Differences between developed and developing countries were represented by the creation of two categories: Annex I countries (who were expected to adopt quantified targets for reducing emissions), and non-Annex I countries (mostly developing countries, which did not yet have specified targets). Targets were finally agreed at the third conference of the parties to the UNFCCC at Kyoto in 1997, but were limited at just an average of 5.2 percent reduction for Annex I countries below 1990 emission levels, compared to the initial recommendation of the IPCC that emissions be cut by 60 percent. (1990 was chosen partly because of the year of the first IPCC assessment, and because many countries claimed to attain "economic maturity" then, when rises in **gross national product (GNP)** were not linked to increases in energy use (see **energy policy**)). Many developing countries were concerned that climate change policies would restrict **industrialization**, and insisted that signing the UNFCCC should be accompanied by enhanced **technology transfer**, financial assistance to developing countries, and a guaranteed right to development (see **right to development**).

There are several post-Kyoto political concerns for developing countries. First, the Kyoto Protocol allowed Annex I countries to achieve some of their emissions targets through the so-called "flexible mechanisms" of emissions trading (buying and selling certificates of emissions reductions), joint implementation (climate-friendly investment in other Annex I countries), and the **Clean Development Mechanism (CDM)** (climate-friendly investment in non-Annex I countries). But many developing countries opposed flexible mechanisms because they reduce pressure on Annex I countries to reduce emissions at source, and their impacts on climate are notoriously difficult to measure. Furthermore, they may only attract investment in the most profitable ventures, leading costlier tasks to governments, and may encourage investments in allegedly ineffective or politically unpopular projects in developing countries (see **Clean Development Mechanism (CDM)** for fuller discussion). "Sinks" projects – or carbon sequestration via land use and forestry – are particularly controversial as they may (in worst-case scenarios) displace poor farmers, add little to industrial **technology transfer**, and may even increase **vulnerability** if they reduce **resource tenure** and industrialization. Second, little progress in technology transfer has been achieved, mainly because most environmental technology is privately owned, and there are few incentives to pass technology to developing countries. Third, the Kyoto process remains politically fragile, especially after the unilateral withdrawal of the USA under President George W. Bush in 2001, and uncertainty concerning the ratification of Russia (which is necessary to create the necessary quorum of members, and to allow much emissions trading to occur). There is a need for greater coordination between host governments and investors to create greater incentives for basing energy systems on **renewable energy**, and for building local **governance** mechanisms that can ensure technologies are appropriate for local users and do not undermine the competitiveness of locally manufactured products. Some analysts propose that the system of "contraction and convergence" – whereby each country adopts carbon quotas on an equal per capita basis – is the most equitable long-term political approach to climate change policy.

Despite the great rhetoric about climate change, it has to be remembered that its potential impacts are highly uncertain, and that – although it is extremely likely that humans have influenced climate – non-anthropogenic factors may have

greater impacts. It is possible that the weather phenomenon, *El Niño*, is associated with anthropogenic climate change, but this is not proven. Environmentalists insist that it is wise to adopt the **precautionary principle** concerning climate change, and to err on the side of caution. An alternative view is to ask how far climate change should dominate environmental policies in developing countries when there are other pressing concerns, or when some climate policies may increase local vulnerability. One possible compromise is to ensure that climate policies both mitigate greenhouse gas concentrations and increase local adaptation capacities in developing countries. But, to date, much international discussion at climate change negotiations have focused on seeking the cheapest means of sequestration or reducing greenhouse gas emissions, rather than on reducing vulnerability or increasing adaptation in developing countries.

See also: Clean Development Mechanism (CDM); Earth Summit (1992) (United Nations Conference on Environment and Development); electrification and power-sector reform; energy policy; environment; renewable energy; small island developing states (SIDS); technology transfer; vulnerability

Further reading

Agarwal, A. and Narain, S. (1991) *Global Warming in an Unequal World*, New Delhi: Center for Science and Environment.

Grubb, M., Brack, D. and Vrolijk, C. (1999) *The Kyoto Protocol, A Guide and Assessment*, London: Earthscan and the Royal Institute of International Affairs.

Hammond, A., Rodenburg, E. and Moomaw, W. (1991) "Calculating National Accountability for Climate Change," *Environment* 33:1 11–15, 33–5.

IPCC (Intergovernmental Panel on Climate Change) (2001) *Third Assessment Report of the IPCC: Summary for Policymakers: Climate Change 2001: Impacts, Adaptation and Vulnerability*, http://www.ipcc.ch

Lohmann, L. (2001) *Democracy or Carbocracy? Intellectual Corruption and the Future of the Climate Debate*, Briefing number 24, The Corner House, Sturminster Newton, UK. http://www.thecornerhouse.org.uk

Rayner, S. and Malone, E. (eds) *Human Choice and Climate Change* (5 vols), Columbus: Battelle Press.

Tiempo: web-based journal focusing on climate change and developing countries: http://www.cru.uea.ac.uk/tiempo/

UNFCCC website: http://www.unfccc.int/

TIM FORSYTH

Club of Rome

The Club of Rome is a global non-governmental, non-profit group composed of scientists, economists, business leaders, and members of government. The group's mission is to foster solutions to global political, social, economic, and environmental problems. It was founded by British scientist Alex King and Italian industrialist Aurelio Peccei, and its first meeting (involving some forty people) occurred in Rome, Italy, in 1967. Formally incorporated in 1970, the Club of Rome holds annual global meetings and supports local initiatives through national chapters. The Club of Rome has sponsored many studies but is best known for funding the **Limits to Growth report (1972)**, which predicted a rapid depletion of world resources resulting from uncontrolled **population** growth. Critics of the Club of Rome argue that its research is overly pessimistic, relies heavily on interventionist solutions, and suffers from an elitist bias.

See also: *Limits to Growth* report (1972)

LENORE NEWMAN

clustering

Clustering refers the tendency of enterprises operating in the same industrial sector, especially **small and medium enterprises (SMEs)**, to be located in close proximity with one another. This tendency is widespread: SME clusters have been observed in a large number of countries (both in developed and developing ones) and industrial sectors. Evidence now exists for clusters that house from a few dozen to several hundreds *core units* (enterprises directly involved in the production for which the cluster is known) and an equivalent number of *ancillary units* (such as the providers of semi-manufactured inputs to core units, or business development services). Within these contexts, whole production processes are undertaken, albeit fragmented among a large number of legally independent business units.

Geographical agglomeration helps SMEs overcome the constraints resulting from their size, improve their capacity to compete, and promote technological development (see **technological capability; technology policy**). Clustering can result in localized external economies as firms enjoy the opportunity to specialize through a very fine local division of labor. Proximity also facilitates joint action between firms and through local **institutions** (see **joint venture; public-private partnerships**). Schmitz (1995) captures these advantages with the notion of *collective efficiency*, and he differentiates between the *passively* acquired benefits that arise from specialized agglomeration – of skills, inputs and knowledge – and the *actively* generated gains that stem from conscious collaboration among cluster stakeholders.

SME clusters are an important topic of study for development economists. On the one hand, the collective efficiency that SMEs can achieve through clustering is at the core of a specific path to sustainable **industrialization**. Many SME clusters have nowadays reached a leading role in global market niches because of their production flexibility, continuous innovation and decentralized decision-making (Markusen, 1996).

On the other hand, peculiar development strategies are required to support "under-performing" clusters. Especially in developing countries, many clusters are yet to achieve the benefits of collective efficiency: cooperation among firms is accidental or inexistent; entrepreneurs do not share business information; collective action is unheard of; trust among stakeholders is low. In an environment of latent conflicts and cutthroat competition, SMEs are locked in a cycle of stagnation and **poverty**. Under such settings, external interventions to increase the extent of networking among stakeholders, to rebuild depleted **social capital**, and to foster broad-based local **governance** mechanisms have succeeded in bringing about collective efficiency (UNIDO, 2001). Having thus strengthened the sources of their competitiveness, SME clusters in developing countries can hope to participate in global **value chains** on much better terms.

See also: economic development; free trade zones (FTZs); industrial district model; industrialization; small and medium enterprises (SMEs); value chains

Further reading

Markusen, A. (1996) "Sticky Places in Slippery Space: A Typology of Industrial Districts," *Economic Geography* 72: 293–313.

Nadvi, K. and Schmitz, H. (1999) "Clustering and Industrialization: Special Issue," *World Development* 27:9.

Schmitz, H. (1995) "Collective Efficiency: Growth Path for Small-scale Industry," *Journal of Development Studies* 31:4 529–66.

UNIDO, 2001, *Development of Clusters and Networks of SMEs: The UNIDO Programme*, Vienna: UNIDO.

MICHELE CLARA

coherence

The concept of coherence refers to the deliberate management of different policies to ensure that they support, rather than undermine, each other's objectives. The term has been used increasingly since the 1990s. Coherence can be defined either narrowly or broadly. A narrow definition would be that objectives of policy in a particular field may not be undermined or obstructed by actions or activities in this field. This mainly involves here incoherence between the different objectives and/or instruments of development policy. A wide definition would be that objectives of policy in a particular field may not be undermined or obstructed by actions or activities of government in that field or in other policy fields. This broader definition of fields refers to development policy and, in theory, all parts of policy-making, but the most common incoherences could be found in trade, **agriculture**, **human rights** and arms trade policies (see **arms sales and controls**).

Despite these efforts to achieve coherence, incoherences do occur. One cause for incoherences may be the need for governments try and find optimal – if contradictory – solutions to the demands placed on them by wide-ranging pressure groups and constituencies. Second, governments are rarely unitary wholes, but also consist of large numbers of departments, **institutions** and corporations. Central government cannot always keep a grip on the policy of all these different bodies. Third, it is difficult to evaluate all end results of policies because of the diverse factors and parties involved in initial policy decisions, or the reactions of different groups to policies. Finally, administrators and politicians often take decisions to remedy short-term negative effects at the expense of optimal policy in the long term.

The concept of coherence gained influence during the 1990s largely because of the work of the Development Assistance Committee (DAC) of the **Organization for Economic Cooperation and Development (OECD)** and the 1992 Treaty of Maastricht (see **European Union**). The DAC (and **International Monetary Fund (IMF)** and **World Bank**) emphasized economic liberalization the means to promote development. It criticized **protectionism** and specific policies of its member states. In particular, the DAC criticized the agricultural policies of the **European Union** and the USA for their ability to undermine other policies that sought to assist developing countries. Coherence also became important under the Treaty of Maastricht when several member states of the European Union and some European NGOs tried to influence the debate on European trade, **fisheries** and **agriculture**, by showing how these policies are hurting the interests of developing countries. In part, this was an old debate, because the European Common Agricultural Policy had been criticized since the end of the 1960s for its negative effects on developing countries. The debate in Europe gained impetus though through the legal backing in the European Constitution. As a result, some Departments for

International Development created "coherence bureaus" which have to deal on coherence issues with aligning ministries. The European Commission by the mid-2000s, had still not installed concrete procedures or instruments for coherence.

See also: aid; European Union; politics; state and state reform; sector-wide approaches (SWAps)

Further reading

Hoebink, P. (1999) "Coherence and Development Policy: The Case of the European Union," pp. 323–45 in Forster, J. and Stokke, O. (eds) *Policy Coherence in Development Co-operation*, London: Frank Cass.

PAUL HOEBINK

Cold War

The Cold War refers to the period of diplomatic hostility that developed between the USA, the USSR, and their allies after World War II. It concerned the world geo-political order constructed after 1945. Over the next four decades, both superpowers would struggle over the contours of global political space in a way that produced a tripartite division of the globe into a First World of "advanced" capitalist states; a Second World of communist states and a "Third World" of "developing" countries (see **underdevelopment versus less developed country (LDC) versus Third World**). Russia, under leader Josef Stalin, felt it had a right to govern the Eastern European nations that it had occupied during the war, believing that they could be used to buffer and extend the borders of Russia itself through the creation of a communist empire or sphere of influence in Eastern and Central Europe. The USSR built a huge military-industrial complex to support and protect its ideology but with far less resources and wealth than the capitalist West. The Soviet state was able nonetheless to sponsor a selection of radical states (if only for a short period) as in Egypt, Vietnam, Cuba, Angola, Mozambique and North Korea.

In 1945, with its leading competitors in ruins, the USA was a powerful state on the global political stage, one that aimed to build a post-war global capitalist empire. In an important speech of 1947, President Truman talked of a global struggle between freedom and totalitarianism and of a universal choice between alternative and competing "ways of life." Truman had thus created a black and white map of international politics, with good versus evil, **capitalism** versus communism, the West versus the East, America versus the Soviet Union. In emphasizing (some might say exaggerating) the Soviet threat, the US state (see **state and state reform**) effectively transformed itself into a crusading interventionist power dedicated to promoting an open world economy and safeguarding the free enterprise system. Peoples and states considered a threat to the USA (including many radical social **revolution**s) were freely attacked, involving interventions in Iran (1953) Guatemala (1956) and Chile (1973), which overthrew democratically elected governments. During the Cold War, the USA was also entangled in an assortment of costly military engagements in countries such as Korea and Vietnam, all deemed as necessary to the strategy of containing the global communist "threat."

The militarization of the US state continued and intensified under Ronald Reagan's administration of 1980–8, involving the CIA and other covert organizations in the sponsorship of counter-revolutionary movements as in Afghanistan, Angola and Nicaragua. Indeed, for some, the beginning of the end of the Cold War lies with this escalating intensity of militarization and in Mikhail Gorbachev's reaction to it in the USSR. In many ways, Gorbachev was anti-militarist, pushing for arms reductions and refusing to intervene to save the communist dictatorships in Eastern Europe in 1989. The fall of the Berlin Wall in 1989 was heralded in Europe as representing the collapse of East/West polarities, but in global terms, the consequences of the Cold War continue to unfold. Particularly in the so-called space of the "Third World" (or developing countries), the implications of a new post-Cold War "world order" have arguably only just begun to ripple out.

See also: international economic order; military and security; politics; postsocialism; revolution

Further reading

Berger, M. (2001) "The Post-Cold War Predicament: A Conclusion," *Third World Quarterly*, 22: 61079–85.

Frank, A. (1997) "The Cold War and Me," *Bulletin of Concerned Asian Scholars*, 29: 4.

MARCUS POWER

collectivization

Collectivization refers to the variety of experiences and practices associated with efforts, in post-revolutionary settings, to transform private **agriculture**, typically dominated by peasant or landed **elites**, into a "socialized' or collectively controlled form of production. The early socialist theoreticians (Marx, Lenin and Luxemburg among them) had no ready-made model of what such a collectivized agrarian economy might look like, at least beyond the idea of nationalizing land. Marx himself even seemed to prevaricate on whether the pre-revolutionary Russian *mir* might provide the incubus for a Bolshevik collective agriculture. While the idea of a collective refers, in theory, to a form of self-governing farm organization in which the state (see **state and state reform**) ultimately retains land ownership (see also **communes, collectives and cooperatives; land rights**), the historical record of actually-existing socialisms has thrown up myriad forms of collective. The Russian *kolkhoz* and the Chinese commune were organizationally different and indeed emerged from very different sorts of revolutionary settings. Most forms of socialist agriculture rested, in the name of collectivization, on the twin pillars of state farms (in effect state-owned estates employing "socialist workers") and collectives. The latter were to emerge from agrarian realities dominated in most settings at by highly differentiated peasant communities (see **community; peasantry**). The political question turned on how the imperatives of centralized planning put to the service of rapid **industrialization** were to be made compatible with the eradication of private property in a setting in which millions of peasants were deeply entrenched in a moral economy of extra-economic coercion. In Russia after 1917, as in many post-revolutionary settings, this political question was an object of ferocious debate in which Marxists, agrarian populists such as Alexandre Chayanov, and academics were centrally involved. The debate was of course cut short in Russia and resolved by a forced collectivization from above in the 1930s, the costs of which, in human, ecological and resource terms, were enormous.

The Chinese case is different, emerging from a different pre-revolutionary trajectory in which a communist party constructed and depended upon in some measure peasant cadres. Here the Chinese commune emerged from a period of land reform and peasant mobilization characterized by little of the anti-kulak violence of the Russian example. The Maoist commune, while certainly not a model of agrarian **democracy**, nonetheless had a very different organizational character and its achievements, social and economic, were much more profound than the Soviet kolkhoz. In both cases, however the collectives were directly subject to the will of the party state and to the imposition of direct production quotas (often with devastating consequences, as the Russian and Chinese famines of the 1930s and 1950s respectively reveal). In both cases too, "peasants" retained some control over small private plots, which were often lifelines in periods of hardship. What passes as collectivization reveals similar institutional and organizational differences in other socialist cases such as Hungary (generally regarded as quite successful), Cuba or Ethiopia. In a number of developing world socialisms, the collectivization abolished neither private property nor the peasantry. In Tanzania and Ethiopia, collectivization took the forms of an authoritarian "villagization" by the state and entailed forced settlement. The collectives rarely functioned as communes and were held together as collectives by various forms of marketing cooperatives. By the 1990s, virtually all of these efforts at agrarian collectivization had foundered in the sense that even the robust communist states such as Vietnam and China had commenced a process of "decollectivization," in which in the first instance incentives were given for household over collective production, and subsequently the collective land base itself was privatized (through auction, direct redistribution and other mechanisms). In effect, this produced in rapid succession quite literally millions of peasant producers, a sort of agrarian question in reverse.

See also: agrarian reform; communes, collectives and cooperatives; land reform; land rights; Marxism; peasantry; rural development; villages

Further reading

Huang, P. (1990) *The Peasant Family and Rural Development in the Yangtze Delta*, Stanford: Stanford University Press.

Lampland, M. (1995) *The Object of Labor*, Chicago: University of Chicago Press.

Szelenyi, I. (ed.) (1998) *Privatising the Land*, London: Routledge.

MICHAEL WATTS

colonialism, history of

Colonialism (see also **colonialism, impacts of**) is the establishment and maintenance of rule, for an extended period, by a sovereign power over a subordinate and alien people that is separate from the ruling power. Colonialism is frequently associated with "colonization," namely, the physical settlement of people (settlers) from the imperial center in the colonial periphery (for example the ancient Greek colonies, or British settlers in the Kenyan White Highlands). Characteristic features of the colonial situation include political and legal domination over an alien society, relations of economic and political dependence, a reorientation of the colonial political economy toward imperial economic interests and needs, and institutionalized racial and cultural inequalities (Fanon, 1963) (see **inequality; race and racism**).

Colonialism is a variant of imperialism, the latter understood as unequal territorial relationships among states based on subordination and domination, associated with particular expressions of industrial **capitalism** such as financial monopolies and transnational capital flows. As a form of territorial expansion, colonialism is one expression of uneven development within a developing global capitalist system and of changing international divisions of labor (see **international division of labor**) (Barratt-Brown, 1974).

In the modern period (since 1870), "colonialism" has been employed as a general description of the state of subjection of non-European societies through specific forms of European, American, and Japanese imperial expansion, organization and rule (Fieldhouse, 1981). Colonialism, and anti-colonial struggles, have been fundamental forces in the making of what, until recently, was termed the "Third World" and in the shaping of a distinctively modern global system (see **world systems theory; dependency theory**).

The age of colonialism began in the fifteenth century with the European expansion in Africa, Asia, and the New World. Spearheaded by Spain and Portugal, and subsequently by other Western European powers such as the Low Countries and England, colonialism emerged in the wake of violent conquest and settlement after a period of extensive exploration. The most ambitious colonial project was established under Spanish auspices in the New World and involved complex forms of direct and indirect rule and administration, Spanish settlement through land and labor grants (the *encomienda* and the *repartimiento* system), and new forms of economic exploitation (plantations and haciendas, and **labor-intensive** intensive mining for bullion). This first phase of colonialism was driven in some ways by what Eric Wolf (1982) called "the search for bullion" and other forms of wealth (spices, ivory, and slaves), but the origins of European expansion are complex, rooted in growing European mercantile competition, religious and ideological impulses, and regional political developments associated with the crisis of European feudalism.

Colonialism was framed by limited **technological capability** (the colonies were often geographically distant from the imperial center and hence relatively autonomous) and by the social power and impulses of a particular mode of production (late feudalism). Although early colonialism is often seen as "mercantile" in nature, promoted by European states through merchant houses and chartered companies, its impact around the globe far exceeded the sphere of trade or exchange. For example, millions of people were forcibly taken from Africa to work in **slavery** on plantations in the Caribbean and the US South while mining and ranching enterprises linked the New World into new circuits of international trade in mass commodities (Stravrianos, 1981).

Colonialism as a moment of an emerging global system in the sixteenth century grew from the soil of European feudalism and lasted for three centuries. It was disrupted in the eighteenth century by the rapid advance of industrial capitalism in England, France, and Germany and ushered in a second phase of colonialism, much shorter in duration and rooted in an expansionary world capitalism. The century between 1820 and World War I saw the growth of a modern colonial order backed by complete European hegemony over world trade, finance, and shipping and by new forms of political and military authority sustained by technology, applied science, and informatics (the telegraph and so on).

Between 1870 and 1918, the colonial powers added and average of 240,000 square miles each year to their possessions; between 1875 and 1915 one quarter of the globe's land surface was distributed or redistributed as colonies among half a dozen states (Hobsbawm, 1987). Britain, France, and Germany increased their colonies by 4 million, 3.5 million, and 1 million square miles respectively; Belgium and Italy, and the USA and Japan each increased their holdings by roughly 1 million and 100,000 square miles respectively. This phase of "classical imperialism" was no longer cast in terms of laissez-faire and mercantilism, but represented a new phase of capitalist development and of interimperial rivalry.

Modern colonialism

Modern colonialism can be classified according to the timing and the manner in which alien territories were incorporated and subjugated, usually through violent conquest and plunder, into a world system (Hobsbawm, 1987; Kay, 1978). More precisely, variations in colonial experience arise from specific combinations of: the form of capitalist political economy at specific moments in world time; distinctive forms of colonial state (see **state and state reform**) (understood as a cultural as much as a political project), and their interests served; and the diversity of pre-colonial societies upon which European domination was differentially imposed. Insofar as colonizer and colonized are geographically separated, all colonialisms must confront the critical questions of how the

colonies are to be administered, financed, and made profitable.

Colonial states were central to the establishment of conditions under which revenue could be raised (i.e. taxation, customs), labor regimes (based on various forms of free or servile labor) instituted to promote commodity production, and political alliances sealed to maintain the fiction of local participation and yet ensure (an often fragile) imperial hegemony.

In its late nineteenth- and early twentieth-century guises, colonialism assumed a variety of forms. One useful typology employs the coordinates of forms of commodity production, labor regime, and political rule (Hicks, 1969). In the case of Africa, there were three distinctive forms (Amin 1973). (1) Settler colonies, such as Kenya and Mozambique, in which direct rule by a settler class was associated with plantation-based export-commodity production, including such products as cotton, tea, coffee, and sugar. (2) Trade or trading post economies, such as Nigeria and Senegal, that were characterized by indirect rule through local ruling classes (Native Authorities) who acted as colonial bureaucrats, and peasant-based production of export commodities, such as palm oil and peanuts. (3) Mine concessions in places like South Africa or Zaire, where transnational capital dominated the national economy and migrant labor was recruited, often by direct compulsion in the first instance, from spatially segregated "native reserves" for work in the mines that overdetermined the shape of the local political economy.

Western **education** and missionaries introduced as a means of training lower-order civil servants and as the civilizing arm of the colonial state, had contradictory consequences. The first-generation anti-colonial, nationalist leaders were often products of the civil service (clerks, teachers) and mission schools who continued their education beyond the limits set by their colonial teachers. In the period after 1945, the rise of anti-colonial movements in the colonies, and the economic crises within an aging imperial system, both contributed to the rapid process of **decolonization**. The colonial system was found to be expensive by the imperial powers and increasingly ungovernable. Colonialism was politically and ideologically discredited by emergent nationalist movements, which were often actively supported by the socialist bloc.

Independence from colonial rule came quickly in the post-war period, though white settler colonies were especially resistant to any notion of indigenous rule. Independence was only achieved in such cases through organized insurrection, such as the Mau Mau in Kenya, or through a long guerilla wars of liberation, as in Mozambique. There is a general sense throughout much of the developing world that decolonization has not resulted in meaningful economic or political independence. The persistence of primary-export production and of dependent political **elites** linked to former colonial powers suggests that colonialism has been transformed into "perpetual **neocolonialism**."

Efforts to explain the origins and timing, and the character and consequences, of modern colonialism have produced a vast literature. Colonialism has been seen as a benign force of economic modernization (see **modernization theory**) and social advancement (the so-called *mission civilatrice*) ensuring law and order, private property and contract, basic infrastructure, and modern politicolegal institutions (Bauer, 1976) (see **law**). It has also been posited within various traditions of Marxism and neo-Marxism as an instrument of wholesale destruction, dependency (see **dependency theory**), and systematic exploitation, producing "distorted" economies, socio-psychological disorientation, and massive **poverty** and neocolonial dependency (Rodney, 1972; Baran, 1957; Frank, 1967) (see **Marxism; dependency theory**). Some lines of neo-Marxist thinking have posited that colonial **capitalism** was "progressive," acting as a powerful engine of social change (Warren, 1980); other Marxist work has argued that colonialism was not progressive enough, provoking Kay's (1975) famous remark that what the developing world needed was *more* not less exploitation. Equally, controversial research has posited a distinctive colonial mode of production. What is clear, however, is that the shift from informal "spheres of influence" to formal colonial rule in the nineteenth century was rooted in a new phase of capitalist transformation (sometimes called the "second" industrial revolution) in which

inter-capitalist rivalry and the growth of transnational forms of industrial and finance capital promoted a search for raw materials, new markets, and new investment opportunities. Anthropological research has in general not contributed to grand theories of colonialism, it has effectively focused on the particular cultural representations of non-European "Others," (see **Orientalism**) and the ideologies and practices (**missionaries**, travelers, scientists) associated with the colonial apparatuses in different localities (Taussig, 1987; Comaroff and Comaroff, 1992).

See also: capitalism; colonialism, impacts of; decolonization; dependency theory; indigenous people; Marxism; missionaries; Orientalism; postcolonialism; slavery; world systems theory; United Nations Declaration on the Granting of Independence to Colonial Countries and Peoples, Res. 1514 (XV) 1960

Further reading

Amin, S. (1973) *Neo-colonialism in West Africa* [*Afrique de l'Ouest bloquée*, Paris, 1971], Harmondsworth: Penguin.

Baran, P. (1957) *The Political Economy of Growth*, New York: Monthly Review.

Bauer, P. (1976) *Dissent on Development*, Cambridge MA: Harvard University Press.

Comaroff, J. and Comaroff, J. (1992) *Ethnography and the Historical Imagination*, Boulder: Westview.

Fanon, F. (1963) *The Wretched of the Earth* [*Damnés de la terre*, Paris, 1961]. New York: Grove.

Fieldhouse, David (1981) *Colonialism 1870–1945: An Introduction*, London: Weidenfeld and Nicolson.

Frank, A-G. (1967) *Capitalism and Underdevelopment in Latin America: Historical Studies of Chile and Brazil*, New York: Monthly Review.

Hicks, J. (1969) *A Theory of Economic History*, Oxford: Clarendon.

Hobsbawm, E. (1987) *Age of Empire, 1875–1914*, New York: Pantheon.

Kay, G. (1975) *Development and Underdevelopment: A Marxist Analysis*, London: Macmillan.

Rodney, W. (1972) *How Europe Developed Africa*, London: Bogle.

Taussig, M. (1987) *Shamanism, Colonialism, and the Wild Man: A Study in Terror and Healing*, Chicago: University of Chicago Press.

MICHAEL WATTS

colonialism, impacts of

The evolution of colonial empires (see also **colonialism, history of**) has had fundamental impacts on a variety of developmental concerns. Empire was founded on the violent assertion of sovereignty, one party's capacity to subjugate another. But during the nineteenth century it came to be sustained and, to varying degrees, justified by the ability of colonial regimes to bring "improvement" to native lives and profitable management to nature's bounty, the so-called dual mandate enunciated in the 1920s by Lord Frederick Lugard. Improvement was, however, an ambivalent endeavor. Empire was founded on the assertion of a fundamental, racialized difference between colonizer and colonized (see **race and racism**). It was difference that justified coercion, including coercive improvement. Colonial authorities assumed the role of "trustees" with the right and obligation to intervene to develop the capacities of subjects deemed both different and deficient. Yet, difference was also the subject of imperial nostalgia, a desire to retain authentic otherness. A similar ambivalence besets contemporary development agendas, in which trustees balance the will to improve with the desire to preserve **community**, custom and **indigenous knowledge**.

Imperial sovereignty and the role of trustee

Sovereignty, the basis upon which colonial rule was established, is predicated upon violence. Achille Mbembe (2001) emphasizes the violence by which peoples were conquered, territories were bounded, the prerogatives of rule were declared, commands were issued, laws were imposed, and sovereign authority was displayed and justified. In the name of Empire, private sovereign powers were granted to individuals and companies, and later to colonial officials, including the right to wage **war**, levy taxes, monopolize **trade**, issue orders and decrees, and exclude or expel populations – powers, that is, over matters of life and death. There was, Mbembe reminds us, no colonial contract, no set of obligations corresponding to the sovereign powers assumed, no rights of protection. "Arbitrariness and intrinsic unconditionality," he argues, were the "distinctive feature of colonial sovereignty."

Colonial sovereignty justified domination, plunder, exploitation, expulsion, **genocide**, and appropriation of resources, practices pushed to the limit in settler colonies, to devastating effect. But in many colonial situations, there was a gradual shift towards pacification, as war evolved into policing, and military reconnaissance into strategies for managing relations between rulers and ruled. **Villages**, for example, became sites where representatives of the sovereign could meet their subjects, and data was collected as a basis for taxation. Often they were relocated for ease of access and surveillance, and enmeshed in administrative grids.

To create imperial order at a micro level, disciplinary techniques and expertise were assembled from diverse sources. Some were imported from the metropole, others were devised in colonial situations which became social laboratories for experimentation. There was a sense in which, from a racialized, colonizers' perspective, the entire colonial **population** could be regarded as deviant, in need of the kinds of discipline reserved in Europe for children, criminals and the insane. But beyond discipline, the **security** of colonial regimes, their long-term viability, was increasingly seen to require what Foucault called a "governmental rationality," one that operated on the ensemble of territory and population to balance diverse projects and goals, including the survival of native populations, the interests of settlers, missionaries and profiteers, and the concerns of politicians and keepers of the home-country treasury, where support for colonial ventures was not guaranteed.

The linking of imperial order to projects of improvement has a particular historical trajectory. Rulers have not always espoused the intention to develop or improve the condition of their populations. This was not the practice of European sovereigns, as Foucault argues, until the emergence of governmental rationality in the eighteenth century. Similarly, pre-colonial traditions in Asia sustained a popular presumption that rulers are responsible for their people, but the forms taken by this responsibility were mainly ritual and charismatic. In his article "India's Development Regime" (1992:266), David Ludden observes that in India there was no ancient cultural injunction that rulers "remove the curse of **poverty**," "prevent vested interests inimical to society from growing," or "plan and coordinate social advance." In Southeast Asia, sovereigns were not dedicated to improvement; arguably, the Han Empire in China was more involved in projects to develop the capacities of the population as a whole.

Some authors have argued that in Europe, the concept of development before the eighteenth century was predominantly cyclical: civilizations, dynasties and social formations would rise and fall, just as an organism lives and dies. The eighteenth century ushered in a new idea of progress as a "linear unfolding of the universal potential for human improvement." Understood initially in terms of God's purpose, such progress was later understood in secular terms, as a process subject to human design and direction. Debates then focused on the role of government in removing constraints to the unfolding of human potential, harnessing benefits for the public good (including the maintenance of the state apparatus (see **state and state reform**)) and addressing the destructive side-effects of progress.

Observers could not fail to notice that **capitalism** routinely produced not only growth and prosperity, but also surplus populations, poverty, dislocation, destruction and decay. Addressing these negative effects required a series of interventions, ongoing management and adjustment, so that idle populations could be set to work, revolutions averted, and resources optimally deployed. Such interventions came to be understood as the responsibility of the state as "trustee." **Trusteeship**, "the intent which is expressed, by one source of agency, to develop the capacities of another," requires judgment about what is optimal and what is deficient, a judgment backed by science and new techniques of measurement, as well as qualitative concerns such as social harmony or authenticity (Cowen and Shenton, 1996:446). Trusteeship is also backed by the coercive power characteristic of sovereignty: the power not only to educate or encourage but to impose particular versions of "improvement" upon another.

Assuming the role of trustees, colonial governments became "development regimes," institutionalized configurations that comprised, in Ludden's definition, (1) ruling powers that claim progress as a goal, (2) a "people" whose conditions must be improved, (3) an ideology of science that controls principles and techniques to effect and measure progress, and (4) self-declared, enlightened leaders who would use state power for development and compete for power with claims of their ability to effect progress. From the nineteenth century onwards it was not sufficient for imperial trading companies such as the British East India Company to reap monopolistic profits. Instead, past systems of resource control had to be replaced by new policies and social orders designed by enlightened rulers to benefit people in ways that acknowledged the problems of the past. The colonial balance sheet had to include both company profits and native welfare, as new rulers defined themselves in contrast to – and as an improvement over – the old. Thus, the negative impact of oppressive, indigenous rulers had to be demonstrated; the under-utilized potential of plants, soils, and **livestock** investigated and reported by appropriate scientific experts; and the results tabulated in standardized form for purposes of comparability.

Techniques and measures

Colonial claims of improvement required quantification and the standardization of measures permitting comparison between sectors, locations or **populations** and the identification of development deficits. **Villages**, for example, now became the focus of efforts to improve households and bodies, fields and homes, often in the name of hygiene and public **health**.

Data about the conditions of populations both legitimated colonial rule and framed the contours of dissent. Debates among colonial officials focused on whether or not improvement according to defined indices had been optimized.

Absorbing the problematic of intentional development and the attendant techniques and practices, post-independence regimes did not reject improvement. In India, Ludden argues, nationalists aspired to do everything the colonial powers had done, but do more and do it better, removing the curse of **poverty** and uplifting the masses through **planning**, coordination, and state control of key resources and industries. Strikingly, the African National Congress, a radical critic of development while opposing South Africa's **apartheid** regime, rapidly adopted the cause of "development" once in charge. As Nicholas Thomas (1994) observes, "**postcolonialism** is distinguished, not by a clean leap into another discourse, but by its critical reaccentuation of colonial and anti-colonial languages," doctrines of development and **trusteeship** prominent among them.

Tensions of empire

The legitimacy of colonial projects of improvement was never self-evident. As Cooper and Stoler (1997) describe, criteria and rationales were continuously debated among colonial officials, in missionary and charitable organizations, and in the parliaments, committees and newspapers of the home countries. For missionaries, the benefits of conversion to **Christianity** were clear enough. Moreover there was a sense in which, lingering racism aside, a Christian convert became like oneself, a person to be judged, ultimately, by the same God. Contradicting this notion of latent sameness was the assumption of permanent, ineffable, hierarchical difference. Colonial subjects might be improved, but they would never be white. Indeed "improved" subjects, educated natives, made colonial authorities and settlers very nervous. One response to this tension was imperial nostalgia: the desire to maintain or recreate in the colonies the innocent life, the perfect village, the pristine landscape. Another response was deferral, the argument that colonized people might indeed share a common destiny as liberal, modern, rights-bearing subjects, but they were chronically immature and thus effectively ignored.

The tensions of empire and dilemmas of improvement were worked out differently across time and space. In Sri Lanka, the Colebrooke-Cameron Reforms of c.1832 aimed to restrict the absolute and autocratic control exercised by the British governor, now seen to stultify enterprise, in favor of liberal freedoms. The reforms encouraged a free press; removed mercantilist monopolies on key commodities; promoted the development of private property, market relations and capitalist **agriculture**; and instituted a jury-based system of justice, reducing bribery and intimidation (see **corruption; law**). Together these reforms were to inculcate a new social order of duty and achievement. Reform, by setting the natives on the path to improvement, would forestall revolution and secure colonial rule.

Half a century later, in West Africa, British colonial authorities faced with rebellion and disorder took an entirely different, and decidedly unliberal approach. As Michael Adas explains, they set out to (re)establish indirect rule and restore "traditional cultures," hoping to arrest and reverse the chaos and decimation that had resulted from centuries of slave trade (see **slavery**), mercantile concessions, misguided colonial policies, market penetration, and the disruptive effect of colonial conquest itself. The argument for custom included the view that the proper place of colonial subjects was in the countryside, not in the cities and towns where detribalized, Westernized natives were beginning to make new and "unnatural" demands. Rather than taming savages, the nineteenth-century project, colonial rule was to consist in the enlightened supervision of native authorities now recognized to be capable of (limited) self-administration. Nicholas Thomas outlines a similar move to reinvigorate cultural difference in Oceania, where British aristocrats doubling as colonial administrators reasserted the value of fixed hierarchies and paternalist protection. Practical concerns about administrative costs and the need for order and stability meshed with concerns about cultural sensitivity and social justice enunciated by missionaries and anthropologists, and with a broad public sentiment in Britain seeking to preserve in the colonies that which had been lost at home in the transition to urbanism, industrialism and **democracy**.

The late colonial assemblage of indirect rule drew on a racialized, evolutionary logic proposing that colonial societies should not be forced to follow an alien path, but should develop along their own lines, at their own pace under the guidance of their own chiefs. This perspective had its critics: some colonial officials continued to favor rapid modernization. The debate was resolved in Sub-Saharan Africa and elsewhere by the variants on the bifurcation Mahmood Mamdani (1996) describes, in which urban citizens were governed as individuals through a system of rights and freedoms, and rural subjects were governed as culture-bound communities (see **community**) by the sovereign authority of native chiefs. Both formations were equally the product of colonial intervention, and they highlight imperial ambivalence about development.

See also: Christianity; colonialism, history of; decolonization; indigenous people; law; missionaries; neocolonialism; Orientalism; postcolonialism; race and racism; slavery; United Nations Declaration on the Granting of Independence to Colonial Countries and Peoples, Res. 1514 (XV) 1960

Further reading

Adas, M. (1995) "The Reconstruction of 'Tradition' and the Defense of the Colonial Order: British West Africa in the Early Twentieth Century," pp. 291–307 in Schneider, J. and Rapp, R. (eds) *Articulating Hidden Histories: Exploring the Influence of Eric R. Wolf*, Berkeley: University of California Press.

Cooper, F. and Stoler, L. (eds) (1992) *Tensions of Empire: Colonial Cultures in a Bourgeois World*, Berkeley: University of California Press.

Drayton, R. (2000) *Nature's Government: Science, Imperial Britain, and the 'Improvement' of the World*, New Haven: Yale University Press.

Foucault, M. (1991) "Governmentality," in Burchell, G., Godon, C. and Miller, P. (eds) *The Foucault Effect: Studies in Governmentality*, Chicago: University of Chicago Press.

Ludden, D. (1992) "India's Development Regime," pp. 247–88 in Dirks, N. (ed.) *Colonialism and Culture*, Ann Arbor: University of Michigan Press.

Mamdani, M. (1996) *Citizen and Subject*, Princeton: Princeton University Press.

Mbembe, A. (2001) *On the Post Colony*, Berkeley: University of California Press.

Pels, P. (1997) "The Anthropology of Colonialism: Culture, History, and the Emergence of Western Governmentality," *Annual Review of Anthropology* 26: 163–83.

Thomas, N. (1994) *Colonialism's Culture*, Princeton, Princeton University Press.

TANIA MURRAY LI

COMESA *see* Common Market for Eastern and Southern Africa (COMESA)

commercialization

Commercialization describes the process whereby people's production and consumption activities are obtained through purchase and sale. Selling and buying are mediated through forms of money and through markets. By being exchanged through markets, goods and services are converted into commodities (see **commodification**). A frequent synonym of commerce is trade. The economic historian John Hicks (1969:25) identified the "rise of the market" and "specialization [of] trade" as the beginning of economic transformation. The reigning theory of modernization (see **modernization theory**) in the early years of development studies posited commercialization as the first stage in the process of development (see also **primitive accumulation**).

Current writing depends far less on ideas of **stages of economic growth**. Moreover, the neat dichotomy of "subsistence" versus "commercialized production" has been heavily criticized in light of studies showing that most rural families combine strategies, and often there is a positive correlation between the degree of subsistence and of commercialization (families most able to provide all or most of their **food** are also those who produce most cash crops). Thus, researchers use a relative measure: the degree of commercialization is the proportion of product sold and of consumption needs purchased.

An extended connotation of commercialization refers beyond trade to profit-making and thence, to different attitudes and incentives. Karl Polanyi, in *The Great Transformation* (1957 [1944]:41–2) for example, posited that a transformation from an agricultural society to a market system

> implies a change in the motive of action on the part of the members of society: for the motive of subsistence that of gain must be substituted. All transactions are turned into money transactions.... All incomes must derive from the sale of something or other.

The degree to which commercialized exchanges entail a shift towards "gain," self-interest, and rational action is a question that has engaged theorists from Weber and Marx to contemporary writers such as Parry and Bloch (1989). Marx focused not on commercialization but on **commodification**, arguing (in *Capital*, Book One, 1867) that, in commodity production, the basic relation between men "assumes, in their eyes, the fantastic form of a relation between things" (see **Marxism**). His ideas about commodity fetishism continue to inform some writers' analyses of processes of commercialization, especially, perhaps, with reference to the rise of consumerism.

Often, the terms commercialization and commodification are associated, respectively, with "liberal" and Marxist approaches and reflect differences in theoretical premises. Sometimes, the contrast is reduced to a beneficial image for commercialization Thus, on one hand, trade expansionists may argue that "commerce may go freely forth leading civilization with one hand, and peace with the other, to render mankind happier, wiser, better" (as British prime minister Lord Palmerston reportedly said in 1842). But on the other hand, commodification may have negative connotations implying exploitation and alienation. Such caricatures have been rejected by authors from a range of theoretical positions who see commodities as purveyors of self-definition and struggle as well as of alienation; who find commercial expansion may result in either political emancipation or oppression; and who reject a "binary opposition between capitalist and non-capitalist economies" (Bernal, 1994:806).

See also: commodification; modernization theory; peasantry; petty commodity production; primitive accumulation; rural development; trade

Further reading

Bernal, V. (1994) "Peasants, Capitalism, and (Ir)rationality," *American Ethnologist* 21:4 792–810.

Hicks, J. (1969) *A Theory of Economic History*, Oxford, Clarendon Press.

Grabowski, R. (1995) "Commercialization, Non-agricultural Production, Agricultural Innovation, and Economic Development," *Journal of Developing Areas* 30:1 41–61.

Parry, J. and Bloch, M. (eds) (1989) *Money and the Morality of Exchange*, Cambridge: University of Cambridge Press.

Polanyi, K. (1957 [1944]) *The Great Transformation: The Political and Economic Origins of Our Time*, Boston MA: Beacon Press.

PAULINE E. PETERS

Commission on Sustainable Development (CSD)

The United Nations Commission on Sustainable Development (CSD) was created in 1992 following the adoption of a comprehensive plan for achieving sustainable development in all countries known as **Agenda 21** by the **Earth Summit (1992) (United Nations Conference on Environment and Development)** held in Rio de Janeiro, Brazil. As a functional body of the **United Nations** Economic and Social Council (ECOSOC), it is mandated to monitor progress in the implementation of Agenda 21 and promote international cooperation and rationalization of inter-governmental decision-making capacity for integrating environment and development issues at all levels. It therefore engages input from a broad spectrum of interests, including **civil society** organizations, multilateral financial institutions, regional economic blocs, and private sector and industry representatives in its deliberations. It is composed of fifty-three representatives from UN member states elected by ECOSOC for three-year terms, and representatives from UN agencies.

See also: Agenda 21; Earth Summit (1992) (United Nations Conference on Environment and Development); sustainable development; United Nations

MOSES A. OSIRO

commodification

Commodification is the process by which objects (commodities) are produced for the purpose of exchange. Since no person is an island, commodification occurs in all societies. It is only in societies with extensive divisions of labor, however, that commodification comes to dominate the conduct of social life. In capitalist societies, furthermore, labor becomes a commodity to be bought and sold. Marxists maintain that labor produces more in a given time period than is returned to it by the employer. The difference between labor and labor power (the latter being the payment made for labor as a commodity) is the source of surplus value and profit.

Commodification is an integral part of most processes of development. The transition from peasant **agriculture** to farming seemingly implies as much. The classic "middle-peasant" household is held to be a self-contained or even "subsistence" unit, which provides its own unpaid labor to produce goods and services that are mainly consumed by household members. When goods or services are exchanged with other peasant households, it might be for other goods and services. This is a form of commodification, but without the intermediation of money. Farming more often connotes the production of goods for sale, including to supermarkets in richer countries. (In practice, the distinction is not always well founded, for many "peasants" work in **contract farming** for **agribusiness** companies, and produce high-value crops that are funneled into commodity chains or filieres).

For some commentators, the process of turning objects into exchange items is unexceptional. Others will maintain that the pricing of all objects makes for more efficient investment decisions. On the political left, however, commodification is rarely treated so kindly. Not only is it taken to conceal an important non-equivalence (labor versus labor power), but the process itself is said to disguise the "real" relationships that exist between human beings. Social relations appear as "things," and the pervasiveness of money encourages a form of "commodity fetishism." Money becomes an end in itself, and its magical powers are sometimes resisted by peasants who object to the suggestion that "real" work is done by money-changers. Michael Taussig's (1983) account of the devil and commodity fetishism in the Cauca valley of southern Colombia powerfully illustrates this point. Freud's suggestion that money is to adults what excrement is to **children**, also draws attention to the "dirtiness" of money (which needs to be laundered), and to the "inauthentic" nature of societies that worship the commodification of everything (including sports and childhood).

Jean Baudrillard (1988) has argued that hyper-modernity can be defined as a state in which the consumption of the images and signs associated with commodities becomes as important as the consumption of the commodities "themselves." To the extent that this argument is morally charged (and it needn't be: it could pose simply as a description), it sits easily with political movements that seek the de-commodification of social life. Postdevelopment might be seen in this light (see **postmodernism and postdevelopment**). More often, though, social and economic groups in poorer countries will seek to challenge the terms under which commodities are exchanged. At issue here is the fairness of commodification – as discussed under the concept of **fair trade** campaigns and some **peasant movements**.

See also: agribusiness; capitalism; commercialization; Marxism; petty commodity production

Further reading

Baudrillard, J. (1988) *Jean Baudrillard: Selected Writings*, Cambridge: Polity Press.

Burke, T. (1996) *Lifebuoy Men, Lux Women: Commodification, Consumption, and Cleanliness in*

Modern Zimbabwe, Durham NC: Duke University Press.

Taussig, M. (1983) *The Devil and Commodity Fetishism in Latin America*, Chapel Hill: University of North Carolina Press.

STUART CORBRIDGE

common heritage of humankind

"Common heritage of humankind" refers to terrestrial biological reserves that are seen to have global significance, and consequently may require international regulation of the actions of specific nation-states who may see them as their own **natural resources**. The term was originally used in debates concerning the **United Nations Convention on the Law of the Sea (UNCLOS)**, and has been used in different contexts since. Although national sovereignty over natural resources is a basic principle of **international law**, in 1983 the **Food and Agriculture Organization (FAO)** adopted the non-binding International Undertaking on Plant Genetic Resources (IUPGR). The IUPGR treated all plant germplasm as a common heritage, including commercial breeding lines and the folk varieties of traditional farmers. Disputes later qualified its application by excluding intellectual property right-protected varieties (see **intellectual property rights (IPRs)**) and by introducing the concept of farmers' rights. However, "gene-rich" countries of the South remained concerned about losing control over their genetic resources (see **biodiversity; biopiracy**). So when the **Convention on Biological Diversity (CBD)** was adopted in 1992, the principle was rejected in place of national sovereignty in harmony with the CBD. In December 2001, IUPGR was converted into a legally binding treaty.

See also: Convention on Biological Diversity (CBD); intellectual property rights (IPRs); United Nations Convention on the Law of the Sea (UNCLOS); United Nations Education, Scientific and Cultural Organization (UNESCO)

TERENCE HAY-EDIE

Common Market for Eastern and Southern Africa (COMESA)

The COMESA represents an ambitious attempt to promote economic integration in the eastern part of Africa, embracing more than twenty countries stretching from Sudan to Lesotho. Originally established as the Preferential Trade Area for Eastern and Southern Africa (PTA) in 1981, as part of the Lagos Plan of Action to reduce African states' external dependence on developed countries by fostering closer economic ties on the continent, its relaunch with the more ambitious common market agenda occurred in 1994. This reflected progress toward the original objectives; the need to adapt to post-**Cold War** geo-economic changes; South Africa's re-emergence from **apartheid** isolation; and rivalry with the **Southern African Development Community (SADC)**. Actual progress since 1994 has been poor, owing to internal divisions, undue overlap with the SADC, and – crucially – concerns that the largest economies, especially Kenya and Zimbabwe, have benefitted disproportionately, and even at the expense of weaker countries.

See also: economic federalization; Economic Community of West African States (ECOWAS); Southern African Development Community (SADC)

DAVID SIMON

common pool resources

Common pool resources are resources whose size, mobility and complexity make it difficult – although not impossible – to prevent individuals from using them and whose use can deplete the number and quality of benefits the resource can provide. Under these circumstances, the high costs of exclusion and the "subtractability" of the resource can create ideal conditions for a "tragedy of the commons," in which the (personal) benefits of resource extraction outweigh the (social) costs of exercising restraint. Classic examples of common pool resources would include aquifers, coastal and inshore **fisheries**, open fields, forests, and the atmosphere (see **environment; natural resources**).

Whether common pool resources will in fact fall prey to the tragedy of the commons depends to a large degree on the existence of **institutions** or rules governing access, utilization, management, exclusion, ownership and transfer of ownership. Rules, it is argued, eliminate the open-access dilemma by increasing predictability, restricting access and encouraging conservation. The efficiency of these rules, however, depends upon the "institutional arrangements" (the system of monitoring and sanctioning) that encourage individuals to comply with collective rules.

A critical distinction relates to the way in which the resource is managed, and the ways in which rights (of access, withdrawal, ownership, etc.) are allocated. In private property regimes, rights, duties and decisions about how the resource will be used are generally in the hands of a single individual (see **property rights**). In common property regimes, such rights are conferred to a **community** of individuals, whose members are granted rights of access, withdrawal, management, and other types of decision. Scholars of common property have argued that groups of individuals will act collectively to manage and conserve common pool resources when they possess, first, a clear idea about what is being managed; second, a means of determining who is entitled to use the resource; and third, a mechanism for excluding "non-members," and ensuring that members follow the rules. The logic here is that individuals will be more likely to conserve a resource when they believe they will reap the long-term benefits of conservation and restraint. Common property, it is argued, provides this assurance by restricting otherwise open-access resources to a group that agrees to abide by rules regulating membership and resource utilization.

Such findings have important bearing on the ways in which environmental problems are now understood, and on the solutions that are devised to address these problems. First, they challenge the notion that the only way of resolving the tragedy of the commons is to institute systems of private property or to implement draconian measures. Second, they highlight the importance of indigenous

systems of resource conservation and husbandry (see **indigenous knowledge**). Finally, they make a strong case against over-centralized resource management regimes. However, a problem that is well recognized in the common property literature is that common property regimes often co-exist with competing systems of (state and private) property, which can undermine the ability of communities (see **community**) to manage and conserve common pool resources. Moreover, states (see **state and state reform**) are not necessarily disinterested parties in this process.

See also: community-based natural resource management (CBNRM); environment; environmental entitlements; deforestation; fisheries; gender and property rights; institutions and environment; natural resources; property rights; resource tenure

Further reading

Baland, J-M. and Platteau, J-P. (1996) *Halting Degradation of Natural Resources: Is There a Role for Rural Communities?* Oxford: Clarendon Press for the FAO.

Ostrom, E. (1990) *Governing the Commons: The Evolution of Institutions for Collective Action,* Cambridge: Cambridge University Press.

CRAIG JOHNSON

Commonwealth

A commonwealth is another name for an independent state, or grouping of states (see **state and state reform**). In international development, the term usually refers to the organization formerly known as the British Commonwealth of Nations, which is the voluntary association formed in 1931 to provide links between nations of the British Empire, before and after **decolonization**, plus Mozambique, which has no historical colonial ties to Britain. Much overt colonial administration in the organization was changed after the independence of India in 1947, when the name was simplified to "Commonwealth," and allegiance to the British monarch was dropped from its statute (although the monarch remains the nominal head). The Commonwealth has no constitution or charter, but heads of governments meet every two years to discuss common interests. It includes some 1.5 billion people, including fifty-three states (following the departure of Zimbabwe in 2003), and – unlike many other international groupings – each member is afforded equal status. Themes addressed by the Commonwealth include **human rights**, **governance**, and **trade**, and occasionally members place pressure on specific governments. A Commonwealth Ministerial Action Group was established in 1955 to impose sanctions, or even suspension, on governments that violate Commonwealth principles. Nigeria was suspended in 1995 after its military regime executed writer Ken Saro-Wiwa and other activists; Fiji in 2000 after its elected government was overthrown; and Zimbabwe in 2002 following allegedly unfair elections (leading eventually to Zimbabwe's resignation from the Commonwealth in 2003). South Africa withdrew from the Commonwealth in 1961 following its criticisms of **apartheid**, but re-entered in 1994. Critics claim the Commonwealth is a largely rhetorical and ineffective organization that is too closely associated with countries' pasts rather than their futures. But the continued willingness of countries to be members – if only for rhetorical purposes and the existence of some benefits such as technical assistance – suggest the association has many advantages.

See also: African Union; apartheid; colonialism, history of; Common Market for Eastern and Southern Africa (COMESA); decolonization; economic federalization

TIM FORSYTH

communes, collectives and cooperatives

Communes, collectives and cooperatives all refer to local **institutions** that involve the coming-together of people for shared benefits, most commonly for political representation or for shared economic production. The concept of sharing the talent and the property of individuals in a **community** began within primitive societies. Survival dictated that all members of a group, tribe, or clan work and defend what they had as a concertive unit. Goals and aspirations of individual members were subordinate to that of the group and that of the collective will. All shared in aspects of hunting, gathering, and later food-growing activities, and all received that which was required to survive according to their needs. As humans increased in numbers and as they advanced technologically and socially, the basic community concept was modified to include not only defense and survival but also promotion of group or local interests. Eventually groups of organized people bonded together, and their expanded community became the smallest districts of **local government**s, i.e. communes in France, Italy, and Switzerland, and townships in the USA.

In Western European society, the concept of the commune was expanded in the 1800s to include any visionary system of political or social perfection. European philosophers and thinkers such as Comte de Saint-Simon, Robert Owen, Charles Fourier, and Pierre Joseph Proudhon sought means to cure the evils of exploitive **capitalism**, divisive individualism, **poverty**, and hunger by means of some form of communal society that would inhibit unearned wealth but retain some private ownership. Other socio-economic thinkers and writers advocated establishment of communal societies and nations in which everyone would be equal and no one owned private property. Concomitantly, there was a deliberate attempt among various Christian sects to revive the structure of the first Christian community established in Jerusalem during the first century (Acts 2–4) (see **Christianity**). Modern communes, collectives and cooperatives have their antecedents in the basic concepts, the model developed, and the writings of those who wished to create an ideal society.

A modern collective is composed of individuals bound together by political, religious, or social principles of centralized decision-making and group control of all means of production. Activities of a collective are designed to enhance the whole collective, not individual members. They are characterized by uniformity of actions in response to a threat, an opportunity, or a group goal. Collectives have been organized in all aspects of human socio-economic and political activities. In the twentieth century, the collective farms found in many nations of the world have a great impact upon individuals and societies (see **collectivization; peasantry**). The government-owned and government-planned collective farms of China, nations of the former Soviet Union, and Central Europe can trace their heritage back to the earlier experimental idealistic communities (see **community**) in Western Europe and North America.

Whereas collectives are essentially rural entities, cooperatives are both rural and urban organizations. Cooperatives are primarily business enterprises, jointly owned by their members and operated without profit for the benefit of the membership. There are many types of cooperatives – marketing, consumer, producer, and service, for example. Some sell goods produced by the membership, some buy goods to resell to members, some furnish loans or provide apartments, and some perform services (financial, medical care, telephone, and electricity). A common set of goals and objectives links communes, collectives and cooperatives. They were established essentially as means for like-minded individuals to pool their talents and resources, share in the fruits of their labor, and create a safe social environment without antagonistic competition and interpersonal strife.

See also: collectivization; community; decentralization; land reform; land rights; local government; rural development; social capital; villages

Further reading

Meurs, M. (2001) *The Evolution of Agrarian Institutions: A Comparative Study of Post-socialist Hungary and Bulgaria*, Ann Arbor: University of Michigan Press.

Esmann, M. and Uphoff, N. (1993) *Local Organizations: Intermediaries in Rural Development*, Ithaca NY: Cornell University Press.

WILLIAM A. DANDO

COMMUNISM see Cold War; communes, collectives and cooperatives; collectivization; Marxism; postsocialism

community

Community has come to characterize a wide range of groups whose members share a sense of identity, specific interests, values and a role definition with respect to others. In a general sense a village, a neighborhood, a club, or **trade unions** – and many other groupings of people – can be called a community (see **ethnicity/identity; social capital**). Conceptually, community has also been used to examine the challenges to local solidarity apparently posed by new and invasive social and political changes, such as the growth of the modern state (see **state and state reform**), heterogeneous city life, and economic and cultural **globalization**.

Historically, the word "community" has often indicated a sense of idealized togetherness. In 1887, the sociologist F. J. Tonnies distinguished between community (*gemeinschaft*) and society (*gesellschaft*). A community was maintained by traditional rules and a universal sense of solidarity, whereas in society, solidarity depended upon deliberately formulated contractual prescriptions (see **sociology of development; social exclusion**). These concepts were elaborated in the 1920s and 1930s by the Chicago sociologists who contrasted rural (community) and urban (society) solidarities. Community also implied a territorial base for people, **institutions** and activities. In rural areas, they argued, people lived together because of kinship and symbiotic interdependence of interests. In cities, however, people were emancipated from the personal claims and expectations of others because human relationships were fragmented.

Community was also associated with norms of social organization. Small peasant **villages** were characterized as "closed corporate communities" with four basic organizing principles: property, culture, equality and religious ritual. Unity was maintained by strict conformity to norms that defined the identity of members and the territorial boundaries. Universal participation in religious and festive rituals was everyone's collective duty. Financial costs were usually addressed by community members who could most afford to do so. In principle, these actions redistributed wealth, restored economic equality, and minimized the consequences of envy. The family was the largest solidarity kin group within the community and each stood on equal footing with other families. The household was the basic unit of residence and production. In principle again, people had equal access to land, pastures and forests, although often there were rules and exclusions.

These early approaches to community were largely based on European or North American experience. In the 1950s and 1960s, scholars focused on the emerging solidarities among African migrants in mining towns and segregated colonial cities. Africans organized ethnic associations based on assumptions of common area of origin, shared language and culture. Participation in recreation activities and mutual assistance in times of illness and bereavement provided migrants with a sense of personal and collective urban belonging and attachment. These were constructed urban communities.

In the 1970s and 1980s, however, scholars began to question the analytical relevance of assumptions about the spatial locality of communities, especially in post-material societies. Following rapid physical and professional mobility and communication systems, community became a "structure of feelings," "imagined," and "symbolic constructs" (Anderson, 1985). Imagined communities were conceptualized as the effective loyalties invested in **nationalism**, which originated in the sixteenth century with the invention of the printing press. The mass publication of books and pamphlets, especially in vernacular languages, led readers to feel a shared commonality even without meeting face-to-face. The intelligentsia, through the educational system, the administrative structures and other **institutions** manipulated the reading public to think of themselves as belonging and sharing solidarity with others in communities of nations (see **elites**). This conception of solidarity created the sentiments of nationalism that in part drove men to wars on behalf of people they did not know. Critics of imagined communities focused on the process through which abstract categories of elite (see **elites**) propaganda

are translated into expressions of social solidarity that may encourage people to undertake such actions as willingly fight wars (see **media**). Critics argued that community building implied communicating messages that readers understood as their own reality, and hence the creation of so-called "cultural intimacy" (see **culture**). Other studies suggested that communities were symbolic constructions based on the meanings people attribute to their community and membership of it. Community represented the intersection between culture, place, intricate social relationships, and collective identity. It became the symbolic framework for conceptualizing and articulating differences. A community, with or without structural boundaries, is real if it is perceived as a meaningful resource and a representation of identity.

The concept of an imagined community is based on the assumption that people's identities are detached from actual social relations. Community had become much more than locality because it could be extended to virtually any form of collective consciousness. However, even in the postmodern world of complex relationships, people still connect through shared experiences. This has led scholars to refocus on how and where experiences are grounded. For example, the concept of "neighborhood" refers to an actual situated spatial form that provides the context for interaction. In neighborhoods, intimate interactions occur through specialized, and often overlapping, roles that help people avoid the tensions inherent in the previous face-to-face co-existence of smaller-scale societies. The conventions of intimate interaction are maintained without revealing too much personal knowledge to others (see **social exclusion**). Computerization and satellite communications have provided means and bases for numerous virtual communities whose connection is not based on place and physical interaction, but on knowledge of shared experiences of pain and struggles.

The word "community" remains controversial. Much debate concerning so-called community, or **grassroots development** has been criticized for romanticizing rural societies, and for imploding the social divisions and injustices that may exist even within agreements reached by consensus (also see **community-based natural resource management (CBNRM); local knowledge**). The word "community" may still be used to denote a sense of togetherness that is not shared by all, and which may be promoted in order to serve political interests. Scholars need to acknowledge that there are many extended social categories with possibilities of community, and that individuals should have the right to resist and opt out of norms and expectations of particular social groups. Many of the discussions of the uncritical use of the word "community" are similar to criticisms of "**social capital**."

People join groups to overcome social isolation. They develop social relations as they share experiences and places, and create a sense of shared belonging. Communities, whether imagined or symbolic, are grounded as reality through the actual lived experiences and practices which take different manifestations. The dynamics of the community depend on individual perceptions and interests of members who are the "stakeholders in a cultural inventory."

See also: community-based natural resource management (CBNRM); community forestry; grassroots development; people-centered development; social capital; social integration

Further reading

Amit, V. (2000) (ed.) *Realizing Community*, London and New York: Routledge.

Anderson, B. (1985) *Imagined Communities: Reflections on the Origin and Spread of Nationalism*, London and New York: Verso.

Cohen A. (1985) *The Symbolic Construction of Community*, London and New York: Tavistock.

Herzfeld, M. (1997) *Cultural Intimacy: Social Poetics in the Nation State*, New York and London: Routledge.

Writh, L. (1938) "Urbanism as a Way of Life," *American Journal of Sociology* 144: 1–24.

CHRISTINE OBBO

community forestry

Community forestry is tree production initiated through locally organized groups that can be either governmental or non-governmental in origin. It has been an essential component in local development for many decades. In most cases, community forestry takes place on common land. Again, however these common tracts can be land with historical ties to local **villages**, or can be state owned (see **state and state reform**). Community forestry includes the harvesting of forest products for a wide range of uses, including fuel, building materials, food, fodder, grazing, commodity production and other raw materials (see **deforestation; non-timber forest products (NTFPs); pastoralism**). The word "**community**" implies a sense of devolved **governance** over forest resources, or the local determination of how forests are used (see **community-based natural resource management (CBNRM)**).

Community forestry is impeded most by two contradictory factors. First, non-**community** interests may erode control over community resources. Second, resources may be used in a unsustainable manner and are thus depleted (see **natural resources; sustainable development**). These two issues often overlap within the same scenario. A better understanding the complexities inherent to **common pool resources (CPRs)** is necessary to understand the problems that can arise within community forestry. Some states and environmentalists have consequently argued that the fullest protection of forests can only be achieved by a rejection of community forestry, and reliance instead on strong state bureaucracies such as a forestry department. Against this, critics have suggested that centralized bureaucracies may not necessarily protect forests successfully; that local people may possess the knowledge and motivation to protect forests; and that some policies enforced by centralized bureaucracies may actually impede local access to forests, and hence restrict **livelihoods** (also see **sustainable livelihoods**).

Proponents of community forestry usually point to its local benefits in providing livelihoods for local people. Critics of community forestry, however, have questioned how far community forestry may contribute to widespread **deforestation** across the world. In particular, attention has fallen on countries such as Brazil and Indonesia where there are both large forest areas, plus large rural **population**s who use community forestry. Some crucial elements of this debate include how far systems of community forestry may be established by new migrants to rural areas who do not have long-term experience of local forests (see **migration**), and how far community forestry may be supported by systems of land tenure, which may encourage settlers to adopt long-term conservation practices. In some cases, community forestry may be similar to forms of **shifting cultivation**, which some critics claim unnecessarily damages forests. Establishing systems of training and mutual help between settlers and local offices of state forestry departments may be the best way to achieve "co-management," or shared responsibility for achieving community forestry. In many countries, such as Thailand, attempts to control deforestation in general through logging bans are now being reconsidered through new legislation seeking to establish, who, where, and for which purposes forests may be used by local people. State forestry departments often resist such steps because they fear losing administrative power because of such devolution (see **state and state reform**).

A further important element of the debate about community forestry is the revision in underlying understandings of forests and forest degradation. Much international debate about forest conservation has been dominated by notions of environmental fragility, and the need to protect dwindling **biodiversity**. Yet, new thinking in ecology has stressed the continued existence of disturbance in forest areas – such as by fires – and the role of social norms in establishing what is seen to be normal in forests (see **environment**). Proponents of community forestry have argued that devolving **governance** of forests to local **institutions** may both enhance livelihoods and reduce the influence of current dominant discourses about forest management, and hence aid the reduction of **poverty**.

See also: agroforestry; common pool resources; community; community-based natural resource management (CBNRM); deforestation; institutions and environment; Joint Forest Management (JFM); logging/timber trade; non-timber forest products (NTFPs); shifting cultivation

Further reading

FAO (1978) *Forestry for Local Development*, Rome: FAO.

Gibson, C., McKean, M. and Ostrom, E. (2000) *People and Forests: Communities, Institutions and Governance*, Cambridge MA: MIT Press.

NIK HEYNEN

community-based natural resource management (CBNRM)

Community-based natural resource management (CBNRM) refers to the management and conservation of **natural resources** such as water, forest products and soils by groups of local users. While the term can describe spontaneous environment-focused **community** action, it is more often applied to an increasingly popular set of approaches with external support by development agencies.

International consensus in the wake of the **Earth Summit (1992) (United Nations Conference on Environment and Development)** (Rio Conference) and its **Agenda 21**, presaged earlier by the **Brundtland Commission** and others, suggested that the implementation of **sustainable development** should be based on local-level solutions derived from community initiatives. Approaches to address **deforestation, desertification, soil erosion and soil fertility**, wildlife depletion and **water management** now strongly advocate a combination of government **decentralization**, devolution to local communities (see **community**) of responsibility for **common pool resources**, and community participation. Such approaches, now strongly evident in the policies and programs of national governments, donor agencies and **non-governmental organizations (NGOs)**, rarely give communities full autonomy but argue instead for "co-management" partnerships and an appropriate sharing of responsibilities between national and **local government**s, civic organizations, and local communities.

Many advantages are claimed for CBNRM. It can enhance the efficiency and effectiveness of **natural resources** management and conservation, especially where governments lack sufficient personnel and resources to ensure this. It can allow natural resource management to build on **local knowledge** and finely-tuned practical skills in dealing with local ecologies. It can build on established local institutional arrangements that have proved effective in protecting and sustainably managing soils, trees and water. It can link environmental protection to **poverty** reduction and **sustainable livelihoods** by ensuring that local users benefit form their resources, and it can enhance community **empowerment** and **participatory development**. CBNRM is frequently justified by arguments that effective "traditional" natural resource management once prevailed, but has been compromised by **commercialization**, poverty and **overpopulation**. The task is thus to reinstate, rebuild or build new community-based institutions to bring society and **environment** back into harmony. While projects and programs vary, this frequently takes the form of establishing "user groups" or "user associations" to oversee natural resource management. Project procedures frequently include establishing resource maps, inventories and management plans; committees to manage and designate funds arising from resource exploitation; and a degree of state surveillance to ensure that procedures are adhered to.

In practice, however, the implementation of CBNRM has often fallen short of expectations. A number of reasons have been identified, including a tendency (despite rhetoric to the contrary) for local resource users to be treated as passive recipients of project activities; a tendency for local users to receive inadequate shares of resource revenues; a tendency for projects to be too short-term in nature and over-reliant on external expertise; and a lack of clear criteria by which to judge success in meeting conservation or resource management goals. Conflicts have emerged over how resources should be managed, and even what the goals of management should be. Others suggest that while **elites** have benefitted, the interests of certain social groups, such as women, migrants and the poor, have been consistently marginalized. There are many instances where local resource users express anxiety at CBNRM activities, fearing their complex management procedures, plans and committees to presage alienation of their **property rights** in favor of external agents.

Critics have identified a more fundamental set of flawed assumptions underlying CBNRM that help to explain these implementation problems. Among these are, first, that the assumption, implicit or explicit, of a distinct local community of resource users frequently does not hold. Approaches commonly focus on the people of a local administrative unit, cultural or ethnic group, or local area, seeing these as relatively homogeneous. It is thus seen as relatively straightforward to establish a group or committee to represent "community" interests, and for this to engage in consensus building and agreement with outside agencies in establishing natural resource management plans. In practice, though, "communities" are not static, bounded, homogeneous entities, but socially differentiated and diverse, cross-cut by differences and dynamics around gender, **caste**, wealth, age, origins, occupation, and other aspects of social identity, and different people may have very different priorities in the use of **natural resources**. Second, CBNRM approaches commonly assume a distinct, and relatively stable, local environment or set of natural resources. Yet, environments are in practice highly dynamic, with many interacting factors of climate, ecology and human influence, unintentional as well as intentional, shaping resource availability over time. Complex, flexible local knowledge and institutional arrangements may effectively have adapted to and worked with these social and ecological dynamics and uncertainties. CBNRM approaches that override these, imposing more static, single-goal user associations may thus miss their mark.

At the extreme, some commentators have used these and other critiques to argue for a return to state-based natural resource management or for handing responsibility over to NGOs or the private sector. However, they are generally outvoiced by the mass of consensus in favor of CBNRM, where such critiques could be used to improve its practice.

See also: common pool resources; community; community forestry; environment; environmental entitlements; institutions and environment; feminist political ecology; gender, environment and development; natural resources; participatory development; political ecology; resource tenure; shifting cultivation

Further reading

Agrawal, A. and Gibson, C. (1999) "Enchantment and Disenchantment: The Role of Community in Natural Resource Conservation," *World Development* 27:4 629–49.

Baland, J.-M. and Platteau, J.-P. (1996) *Halting Degradation of Natural Resources: Is there a Role for Rural Communities?* Oxford: Clarendon Press for FAO.

Guijt, I. and Shah, M. (1997) *The Myth of Community*, London: IT Publications.

Leach, M., Mearns, R. and Scoones, I. (eds) (1997) "Community-based Sustainable Development: Consensus or Conflict?" Special issue of *IDS Bulletin* 28: 4.

Li, T. (1996) "Images of Community: Discourse and Strategy in Property Relations," *Development and Change* 27: 501–27.

Western, D., Wright, M. and Strum, S. (eds) (1994) *Natural Connections: Perspectives in Community-based Conservation*, Washington DC: Island Press.

MELISSA LEACH

comparative advantage

Comparative advantage is a position of better competitiveness of one trading party over another. In economic theory, the term provides the strongest explanation for international trade and the fundamental economic rationale for the **World Trade Organization/General Agreement on Tariffs and Trade (WTO/GATT)** system. As first proposed by Scottish economist David Ricardo in 1817, the theory of comparative advantage states that two nations will trade even when one nation is absolutely better at producing goods, so long as each nation is relatively better at producing some goods than others. If each nation shifts production into those goods, and exports excess production, these countries will generate wealth from trade, provided trade costs are not excessive. Extrapolated broadly, nations will export products for which they have a relative abundance of factor endowments and import products for which they have a relative scarcity. According to the Coase Theorem, the issue of the increased wealth generated by trade based upon comparative advantage is analytically distinct from the issue of how to divide that wealth.

See also: terms of trade; trade

WILLIAM B. T. MOCK

COMPETITIVENESS *see* comparative advantage; productivity; technology policy

complex emergencies

The term complex emergencies is used to describe what is seen as a new type of post-**Cold War** humanitarian crisis, and which usually refers to the breakdown of political authority in a country or region, requiring the intervention of various groups to provide assistance and sometimes **peacekeeping**. The term came into increasingly common usage in the early 1990s, having emerged with regard to Africa in the late 1980s. Of course, humanitarian emergencies were never simple, but the term was partly intended to distinguish humanitarian response in situations of **war** from a response to **natural disasters**. It was also intended to suggest the complex and multi-causal nature of post-Cold War conflicts.

In 1994, the **United Nations** (UN) defined a complex emergency as, "a major humanitarian crisis of a multi-causal nature that requires a system-wide response. Commonly a long-term combination of political, conflict and peace-keeping factors is also involved" (United Nations, 1994). Another commonly used definition is that of the Inter-Agency Standing Committee (1994): "a humanitarian crisis in a country, region or society where there is a total or considerable breakdown of authority resulting from internal or external conflict and which requires an international response that goes beyond the mandate or capacity of any single agency." In this definition, a complex emergency may be distinguished from other shocks (such as natural disasters) because of the complexity of their causes. This simple explanation, of complex emergencies as crises with multiple causes, has been criticized on two main grounds. First, natural disasters are rarely in practice simple or mono-causal. Second, the definition ignores the essentially political aspects of complex emergencies (see Duffield, 1994). Indeed, some critics have defined complex emergencies according to particular characteristics common in past Cold War conflicts, and have used the term "complex political emergencies" (CPEs).

Many important events were known as complex emergencies during the 1990s. In Somalia, 1991–2, some 300,000 people died of starvation and famine-related diseases because of fighting between rival clans following the ouster of ex-dictator Siad Barre in 1991. The civil strife led to an intervention by the UN, including troops from the USA, but these soldiers were withdrawn after about sixty were killed. The UN still maintains a presence. The southern Sudan experienced **famine** in the late 1980s because of **drought** and civil war. Operation Lifeline Sudan (OLS) was established in April 1989 as a consortium of two UN agencies – the **United Nations Children's Fund (UNICEF)** and the World Food Program – as well as more than thirty-five **non-governmental organizations (NGOs)**. OLS negotiated with the Government of Sudan and the Sudan People's Liberation Movement/Army (SPLM/A) to deliver humanitarian assistance to all civilians in need, regardless of their location. The African Great Lakes Crisis in 1994-5 is another example. The Great Lakes region – comprised roughly of Uganda, Western Tanzania, Rwanda, Burundi, and the northeastern part of Democratic Republic of the Congo – experienced widespread **violence** with the annihilation of up to 850,000 Tutsi people in Rwanda. Other examples include the persecution and migration of the Iraqi Kurds in northern Iraq in 1992 after the end of the 1991 Gulf War; the disintegration and conflict in former Yugoslavia during the 1990s (including alleged **genocide** of ethnic Albanians in Kosovo); and the status of Angola throughout the 1990s because of civil **war**.

Increasingly, analysts acknowledge some common features within definitions of complex emergencies. Complex emergencies have a political causality. The competition for power and scarce resources is the central dynamic in social conflict. They are often highly protracted, and characterized by periods of fragile peace and renewed conflict. The state (see **state and state reform**) is frequently incapacitated and complex emergencies are highly destructive of **civil society** and **social capital**. Civilian populations in complex emergencies are frequently the target of military strategies and assistance is likely to be highly politicized and risks being caught up in the dynamics of war (see **humanitarianism**). Complex emergencies have groups that benefit from ongoing conflict (winners) as well as people that suffer (losers) and powerful groups may have vested interests in continued conflict. They often have political economies that help to sustain the warring parties and that include asset transfer. They often operate within and across state boundaries.

A further explanation for the use of the term complex emergency was that it derived from the widening range of options available to international agencies in responding to humanitarian crises after the end of the Cold War. It was not that **war** had become more complex, but that the response to them was increasingly complex. Indeed, the response to crises may place intergovernmental organizations in positions of new power if they choose to intervene on the ground, and involve diverse and powerful resources to assist (see Slim and Penrose in Macrae and Zwi, 1994:194).

The emergence of the term complex emergencies must therefore also be seen in the context of a number of linked trends in the provision of humanitarian relief. The end of the Cold War increased the ability of the international **community** to act in humanitarian emergencies, as the UN was no longer paralyzed by vetoes on both sides of the East-West divide. This resulted in increased access for traditional humanitarian agencies to provide humanitarian relief in war zones, and not just to **refugees** at their margins. It also resulted in an increase in UN-sanctioned military engagement in crises. The publication of the UN Secretary General's *An Agenda for Peace* in 1992 distilled the growing consensus that international political, economic and military assets could and should be deployed in order to promote peace and stability (Boutros-Ghali, 1992). The early 1990s also saw a huge increase in emergency relief expenditure, because of this increased access.

Complex emergencies may therefore be seen as multi-causal emergencies, with a particular set of complex features focusing on the political economy of wars, and as emergencies that require a more complex response, including different aspects of the international response system. Yet, some important questions remain. Is it possible to have complex emergencies that do not include war or conflict? Possible examples of complex emergencies that are not conflict based might be Zimbabwe in 2002 (where the government of Robert Mugabe instigated forced redistribution of land tenure and other repressive actions), and North Korea through the 1990s (where the government came under increasing international pressure to adopt international standards of **transparency** and **governance**). A second question is whether the term complex emergency should now be applied to all wars. For example, was the US-UK invasion of Iraq in 2003 a complex emergency?

See also: aid; emergency assistance; ethnic cleansing; famine; genocide; humanitarianism; Médecins Sans Frontières (MSF); peacekeeping; post-conflict rehabilitation; post-conflict violence; Red Cross and Red Crescent; right of intervention; United Nations; war

Further reading

Boutros-Ghali, B. (1992) *An Agenda for Peace: Preventive Diplomacy, Peace-making and Peace-keeping*, Report of the Secretary General pursuant to the statement adopted by the Summit meeting of the Security Council on 31 January 1992, United Nations, New York.

Duffield, M. (1994) "Complex Emergencies and the Crisis of Developmentalism," Special issue of *IDS Bulletin* 25: 4.

Macrae, J. and Leader, N. (2000) *Shifting Sands: The Search for "Coherence" between Political and Humanitarian Responses to Complex Emergencies*,

Humanitarian Policy Group Report 8, Overseas Development Institute, London.

Macrae, J. and Zwi, A. (eds) (1994) *War and Hunger: Rethinking International Responses to Complex Emergencies*, London and New Jersey: Zed.

United Nations (1994) *Strengthening of the Coordination of Humanitarian Emergency Assistance of the United Nations*, Report of the Secretary General A/48/536, New York: United Nations.

PAUL HARVEY

computable general equilibrium (CGE) models

Computable general equilibrium models (or CGEs) are statistical economic models that provide a powerful tool for the quantitative analysis of the economy-wide effects of development policies. Policy-makers are commonly interested in the effects of particular policies, such as trade reforms, a change in taxes or the structure of government expenditures, on the welfare of various socio-economic groups and on economic performance in general (see **fiscal and monetary policy; trade**). If the effects of policies are limited to specific economic sectors or commodity markets, a partial analysis may be sufficient. However, when one may expect substantial indirect effects on other markets or other groups, an economy-wide analysis will be needed. Trade reform is a typical example of this. Reduction of **tariffs** and other restrictions on trade will affect the previously protected production sectors, which now have to compete with cheapened imports, but at the same time relative prices and thus the incentive structure (see **incentive structures**) in the economy will change. The latter will induce resources (capital, labor) to shift to more profitable ventures and there will be effects on the trade balance and the government budget affecting other parts of the economy. This calls for models that can capture the interaction between various commodity markets and various economic agents. CGEs are well suited for this purpose and can specify well-defined rules for the economic behavior of agents, technical feasibility of production and resource constraints. The capacity to specify various socio-economic groups, such as different groups of workers or household groups, makes CGEs also suitable instruments to analyze the impact of economic policies on **income distribution** and **poverty**.

A CGE generally works by: (a) specifying various actors in the economy (institutional actors such as firms, households, government, and rest of the world; and factors of production, such as labor groups and owners of capital); (b) describing the economic behavior of those actors (utility maximization of consumers, profit maximization of firms); (c) specifying the institutional and nature structure of markets (competitive markets for goods and factors of production); and (d) solving for the equilibrium values of all endogenous variables. Theoretical general equilibrium analysis originally focused on assumptions of competitive equilibrium with all markets clearing smoothly (and instantaneously) in response to changing relative prices. Such assumptions would be very different from most real world conditions and particularly so in developing countries. Applied CGEs have shown to be capable of dropping several of these limiting assumptions, introducing price rigidities, government interventions in markets, imperfect competition, quantity rationing (such as credit rationing in financial markets), and so on. This way, this type of model has become increasingly useful for development policy analysis. Also, CGEs now often are dynamic, both in the sense of a sequence of temporary equilibriums linked by asset accumulation and inter-temporally optimizing agents with perfect or imperfect foresight, enabling the user to address issues of intergenerational distribution of welfare.

CGEs integrate micro-and macro-level analysis within a consistent framework. The basic accounting consistency of a typical CGE is given by a Social Accounting Matrix (SAM), which identifies the supply and demand balances for all commodities and budget constraints (incomes and outlays) for all agents. The SAM is in essence a matrix representation of the national accounts, but adds the desired detail for production and input-output relations, labor and other factor markets, and transactions among representative households and with other agents in the system. The SAM

thus provides a static picture of the structure of the economy and the interrelations that exist in terms of production, consumption, trade, **income distribution**, and asset accumulation. It typically also provides a large number of the parameter values for a CGE and the base year solution of the model is "calibrated" such as to reproduce the structure of the economy as represented by the SAM.

Another critical feature, as well as a source of controversy, of CGEs for development policy analysis is how the macroeconomic equilibrium is established. In the basic, neo-classical formulation the savings-investment balance is assured by imposing Walras' law, which states that the sum of the excess demand (or supply) for all commodities must equal zero. Investment decisions are not separately modeled and savings decisions "drive" the level of investment in the economy. CGE models in this formulation essentially are only concerned with relative price effects and related resource allocation in the long run. Disturbances in nominal macro balances (say a fiscal deficit that cannot be financed or the monetary effect of capital inflows) play no role. Alternative specifications have been proposed to this type of "macro closure," by specifying an independent investment function, for instance, and letting Keynesian **multiplier effect**s or **income distribution** shifts lead to the required adjustment in aggregate savings such as to establish the required macroeconomic equilibrium (see **fiscal and monetary policy**). If this condition is imposed on an economy where nominal wages are fixed through institutional wage setting, the macro equilibrating variable will be the aggregate price level (see **inflation and its effects**) which will cause real wages to fall following an exogenous increase in, say, public investment. This will induce firms to expand labor demand and increase output, leading to higher income and savings.

This more explicit treatment of macroeconomic adjustment has made CGEs also more useful to analyze questions of **structural adjustment** and the effects of related reform policies on income distribution. The theoretical adequacy of introducing short-run adjustment in monetary aggregates to subsequently analyze the effect of policy or exogenous shocks over the medium run, is subject to some controversy and could make policy-makers prefer a more conventional macroeconometric model if the main interest is in the short-run effects. The drawback is then a lack of detail at the sector level and in the distribution effects. In sum, CGEs have now proved to be useful to tackle a wide range of development policy issues ranging from tax and trade reforms to changes in price subsidies, exchange-rate policies (see **exchange rates**), financial sector reforms and **International Monetary Fund (IMF)** and **World Bank** stabilization and structural adjustment programs. Of course, CGE modeling results remain in the eye of the beholder, being nothing more than stylized representations of the economy as defined by the model builder.

See also: economic development; fiscal and monetary policy; inflation and its effects; structural adjustment

Further reading

Bourguignon, F., da Silva, L. and Stern, N. (eds) (2003) *Tool Kit: Techniques and Tools for Evaluating the Poverty Impact of Economic Policies*, Washington DC: World Bank (in particular, chs 13 and 14).

Gunning, J. and Keyzer, M. (1995) "Applied General Equilibrium Models for Policy Analysis," pp. 2025–107 in Behrman, J. and Srinivasan, T. (eds) *Handbook of Development Economics*, Volume 3A, Amsterdam: North-Holland.

Robinson, S. (1988) "Multi-sectoral models," pp. 885–948 in Chenery, B. and Srinivasan, T. (eds) *Handbook of Development Economics*, Volume 2, Amsterdam: North-Holland.

Taylor, L. (ed.) (1990) *Socially Relevant Policy Analysis. Structuralist Computable General Equilibrium Models for the Developing World*, Cambridge MA: MIT Press.

ROB VOS

conditionality

Conditionality refers to the imposition of terms on recipient countries for the loans and other financial or technical assistance that they receive from the **World Bank** and **International Monetary Fund (IMF)** and **bilateral aid agencies** of the **Organization for Economic Cooperation and Development (OECD)** countries. Simply put, a country seeking assistance from these institutional actors is obliged to make certain internal changes (or, in the terminology of the World Bank and IMF, **structural adjustment**s) as the "conditions" for the receiving of that assistance.

The World Bank and IMF are financial institutions, and capitalist financial institutions make loans under a calculated expectation that the loan recipients will be able to repay those loans, with interest, in a specified period of time (see **debt**). What distinguishes the conditionality of World Bank and IMF loans and other forms of assistance from the calculated expectations of private financial institutions is that while the calculated expectations of the latter are limited to assessments of a borrower's financial capacity to repay, World Bank and IMF conditionality is based on ensuring the recipient country's capacity to repay. In pursuit of that goal, the conditionality requirements of these institutions and borrowing countries are more broad-based and extensive than merely agreements about financial terms. By imposing complex matrices of conditionality, the World Bank and the IMF often require sovereign borrowers to make profound changes to their macroeconomic, legal, and institutional frameworks to comply with World Bank and IMF conditionality before any financing is made available to them.

The specific structural changes to be made by a sovereign borrower under World Bank and IMF conditionality are determined on a case-by-case basis and the elements of conditionality imposed on borrowing countries by the two institutions have changed over the years of their existence in response to changing global economic, financial, and political conditions. Nevertheless, there has developed a consistent conditionality orthodoxy premised on the interest of the rich member countries in maintaining a neo-liberal (see **neoliberalism**) **international economic order** and consistent with that interest, global market conditions that they perceive as favorable. The interest of the rich member countries, in particular that of the USA, is expressed through the voting and organizational structures of the World Bank and IMF.

The conditionality of the World Bank and IMF have become more complex and, critics have argued, more intrusive. In the period since the collapse of the centrally planned economies of the communist bloc countries (also referred to as the post-**Cold War** era), both the World Bank and IMF have shown greater concern with the issue of **governance**. This is made clear in a new set of IMF guidelines promulgated in 1997 by its Board of Directors (which is dominated in terms of voting power by rich member countries). These guidelines legitimize the evaluation of a recipient country's ability to implement reforms by the IMF, and hence has led to new conditionality "issues" such as levels of military spending, government **corruption**, **democracy** and government legitimacy, and "crony **capitalism**." Hence, conforming to World Bank and IMF conditionality may require borrowing countries to make substantial and potentially domestically unpopular political and social policy changes. Because evaluation is now undertaken only by the IMF and World Bank, the borrowing government has no choice but to conform – even though, technically, the World Bank's charter forbids it from entering into political judgments and intervention (see also **structural adjustment**).

Critics argue that the World Bank and IMF cannot act independently or apolitically in how they set conditions on loans and technical assistance. Critics point out that the IMF and World Bank were established by the leading capitalist countries (notably, the USA and the UK) following World War II (see **Bretton Woods**), and were designed to promote the stability of global capitalism as a way to avoid the calamitous economic **nationalism** of the 1930s. Some say it is not erroneous to conclude that to a significant extent, both the World Bank and the IMF function as vehicles for the international economic and political agendas of the leading capitalist countries, especially those of the USA.

See also: aid; aid effectiveness and aid evaluation; adjustment with a human face; Bretton Woods; coherence; debt; European Union; International Monetary Fund (IMF); neo-liberalism; sector-wide approaches (SWAps); Washington consensus; World Bank

Further reading

Ascher, W. (1983) "New Development Approaches and the Adaptability of International Agencies: The Case of the World Bank," *International Organization* 37:3 415–39.

Biersteker, T. (1990) "Reducing the Role of the State in the Economy: A Conceptual Exploration of IMF and World Bank Prescriptions," *International Studies Quarterly* 34:4 477–92.

Collier, P. and Gunning P. (1999) "The IMF's Role in Structural Adjustment," *Economic Journal* 109: 634–51.

Darrow, M. (2003) *Between Light and Shadow: The World Bank, the International Monetary Fund and International Human Rights Law*, Portland, Oregon: Hart Publishing.

RICHARD M. J. THURSTON

conflict management

Conflict management is an umbrella term for a range of techniques employed by protagonists and/or third parties to transform a conflict in order to mitigate the destructive consequences of **violence** and **war**. Because conflict management is usually employed after a dispute escalates to violence and the conflict continues, it is not normally targeted at producing a lasting resolution. Instead, conflict management is intended to minimize the effects of certain aspects of a conflict, especially on civilian **population**s. Thus, conflict management may be distinguished from dispute settlement (the elimination of differences between parties before a dispute escalates into violence through legal processes such as negotiation, mediation, and arbitration), and from conflict resolution (the post-violence settlement of a disagreement through changes to the relationship between protagonists that overcome the sources of the disagreement). Conflict management, instead, is commonly applied *after* the opportunity for pre-violence settlement and *before* the conditions for post-conflict resolution are propitious (Burgess and Burgess, 1997).

Conflict management is predominantly practiced by states and inter-state organizations that are not party to but have an interest in a particular conflict. These entities are able to exert significant political, military, and economic pressure on the protagonists in an attempt to alleviate human suffering (see **humanitarianism**). Consequently, there are numerous mechanisms along the conflict management spectrum ranging from political encouragement to military coercion. This spectrum begins with diplomatic peacemaking aimed at, *inter alia*, obtaining a ceasefire, guaranteeing the protection of non-combatants, securing access for an international observer operation, and facilitating the provision of humanitarian relief to civilians. The initial Vance-Owen and later Holbrooke initiatives in the former Yugoslavia during the 1990s are examples of peacemaking as a conflict management technique.

Next, **peacekeeping** operations, such as the original Australian and New Zealand mission to East Timor in 1999, are used to separate the protagonists and stabilize the conflict zone, observe ceasefires and breaches thereof, protect vulnerable civilians, and provide time and space for conflict resolution efforts to develop. Peacekeeping is also a vital part of peace-building, which seeks to foster confidence between opposing parties through the facilitation of **civil society**, infrastructure (re)construction, refugee repatriation (see **refugees**), de-militarization, democratization and **economic development**. As discussed under **peacekeeping**, the most successful example of a peace-building operation was the 1992–3 United Nations' Transitional Authority in Cambodia.

Finally, at the military end of the spectrum, peace-enforcement is used as a last resort to establish the conditions for other conflict management (or resolution) techniques when the protagonists are unwilling for these to proceed. Peace-enforcement therefore contains some paradoxes through its use of military power. It employs further violence to redress major breaches of international peace and security (e.g. the 1991 Gulf War to reverse Iraq's invasion of Kuwait). It minimizes the scale of **war** by enforcing economic and military sanctions (e.g. the trade and arms embargo on Bosnia and Croatia during the disintegration of Yugoslavia). It protects civilians from further **violence** (e.g., NATO's air war against Serbia to protect the Albanian minority in Kosovo), and/or enables the delivery of humanitarian relief to civilians within conflict zones (e.g. the "safe havens" and "no-fly-zones" enforced over southern and northern Iraq to protect the Shi'ites and Kurds after the 1991 Gulf War).

Since the end of the **Cold War**, however, states and inter-state organizations have increasingly retreated from involvement in conflict management, especially from complex intra-state ethnic "new wars" in **weak states**. This state and inter-state withdrawal is primarily a consequence of this transformation in contemporary violence and their disastrous (non)interventions during the 1990s, such as in Somalia, Rwanda, and Bosnia. Consequently, over the last decade states and inter-state organizations have increasingly turned to the non-governmental development community to fill this void. This **community**, premised as it is on the moral legitimacy of neutrality and impartiality, has a predisposed interest in the conflict management potential of programs that target the safety and **well-being** of civilians; thus conflict management is a growing area of operation within development contexts. Rigby's (2001) review of this expansion identifies two broad types of such development agencies: non-governmental humanitarian agencies (NGHAs) work *in* conflict zones to provide **emergency assistance** to civilians while conflict transformation agencies (CTAs) work *on* the conflicts themselves to decrease levels of violence.

However, post-Cold War changes in violence and war have presented NGHAs and CTAs with several dilemmas. Again, Rigby's review is useful here, identifying six common problems faced by these organizations. First, in conflicts where an armed group has a vested interest in the violence continuing, such groups can manipulate NGHAs (by preventing supplies and personnel reaching the enemy, taking responsibility for relief "protection," or "diverting" relief supplies for military purposes), thus perpetuating the conflict. Second, the need to protect **aid** convoys, delivery, and staff has necessitated an ever-closer association between NGHAs and military peacekeepers, which can jeopardize the NGHA's supposed political neutrality and therefore operations. Third, with the risk of perpetuating the violence and the neutrality of NGHAs under scrutiny, humanitarian assistance is undermined as a conflict management technique.

Fourth, the shift of humanitarian assistance provision to NGHAs and CTAs means that these organizations are often in competition with each other for donor funding and consequently need to publicize their activities and success. This has the detrimental effect of forcing them to shift their resources to the latest high-profile conflict before its current operation is complete. Fifth, as labor employers in conflict zones, NGHAs and CTAs may exacerbate an original source of the conflict by favoring a higher-skilled section of the population and thus distort local wage rates and **employment** access. Finally, Rigby notes that while NGHAs and CTAs are good at identifying these and other practical problems, they are much less adept at actually overcoming them. This last problem will require significant attention if the non-governmental development **community** is to make a more meaningful and less problematic contribution to conflict management.

See also: complex emergencies; emergency assistance; Geneva Conventions; genocide; humanitarianism; law of armed conflict (LAC); peacekeeping; post-conflict violence; violence; war

Further reading

Burgess, H. and Burgess, G. (1997) *Encyclopedia of Conflict Resolution*, Santa Barbara: ABC-CLIO.

Rigby, A. (2001) "Humanitarian Assistance and Conflict Management: The View from the Non-governmental Sector," *International Affairs* 77:4 957–66.

PETER MAYELL

CONSTITUTION *see* law

Consultative Group on International Agricultural Research (CGIAR)

The Consultative Group on International Agricultural Research (CGIAR) is the world's most extensive network of scientific research establishments seeking to increase world production of **food** through **agriculture**. It was created in 1971 under the sponsorship of the **World Bank**; **Food and Agriculture Organization (FAO)**; **United Nations Development Programme (UNDP)**; and the International Fund for Agricultural Development of the United Nations (IFAD), and with the agreement of eighteen governments of developed countries. CGIAR initially comprised four existing international centers established by the Ford and Rockefeller Foundations: the International Rice Research Institute (IRRI) at Los Baños, Philippines (founded 1960); the International Wheat and Maize Improvement Center (CIMMYT, Mexico City, 1966); International Institute of Tropical Agriculture (IITA, Ibadan, Nigeria, 1967); and the International Center for Tropical Agriculture (CIAT, Cali, Columbia, 1967). By 2004, membership had grown to fifty-eight governments (including twenty from developing countries), and the number of centers to fifteen (see website for full details of members).

The initial objective of CGIAR was the "increase the pile of rice" (or food in general) in developing countries that faced **famine**, with particular emphasis on cereals. CGIAR was particularly involved in the **green revolution**, which introduced new agricultural technologies and high-yielding varieties of seeds to developing countries. There is little doubt that the CGIAR has assisted greatly in increasing production of food staples, but it has sometimes been criticized for overlooking social and economic implications of new agricultural technologies, and especially for causing environmental degradation, genetic erosion (see **biodiversity**), displacement of small farmers and lack of accountability in its research agenda and management. In later decades, the CGIAR responded to criticisms by focusing on making agricultural technologies more sustainable and with greater attention to **poverty** alleviation and well-being. Between 1994 and 2000, the CGIAR chairman Ismail Serageldin initiated a renewal program, involving diversification from **food** production alone to include **agroforestry, fisheries**, and social sustainability of technologies within smallholders. Furthermore, the program sought greater research and use of biotechnology (see **biotechnology and resistance**) within agriculture. These reforms, however, have encouraged further criticism: from farmers and campaigners opposed to **genetically modified organisms (GMOs)**, or from critics who claim that the CGIAR's general approach still depends too closely upon introducing new approaches without acknowledging existing expertise within smallholder farmers or the political impacts of replacing historic agriculture. Such criticisms have been made, for example, concerning the CGIAR's "Alternatives to Slash and Burn" program, founded in 1994, whose very name suggests that **shifting cultivation** needs to be reformed, and that expertise exists primarily within the CGIAR. Some critics of the CGIAR argue that the network's scientific expertise should be complemented with a still more holistic approach to understanding the political and socio-economic contexts of agricultural technologies, and to increasing poor people's participation in shaping them.

See also: agriculture; biotechnology and resistance; food; green revolution; science and technology; shifting cultivation

Further reading

CGIAR website: http://www.cgiar.org/
Manicad, G. and Lehmann, V. (1997) "CGIAR: Evaluation and New Directions," *Biotechnology and Development Monitor* 33: 1217.

TIM FORSYTH

contagion effect

The term contagion effect (also known as financial contagion) refers to a phenomenon that can only occur because there are increasingly close ties between domestic and financial systems of countries and the **international economic order**. Put simply, when investors decide to flee a national market out of concern about the volatility of the market, the result can be the creation of economic crises not only in the country from which they are fleeing but also in other countries that previously were thought to be financially sound (see also **capital flight**).

The most extensive examination of the contagion effect has been in relation to the East Asian financial crises of 1997–8 (see **Asian crises**). When East Asian economies began collapsing, this led investors to sell off their assets not only in those economies, but also assets in Russia, which led to a decline in stock prices there and a weakening of the Russian currency (see **stock markets; exchange rates**). The financial downturn in Russia then precipitated a similar downturn in Brazil and, though less pronounced, elsewhere in Latin America.

Precisely why the contagion effect does not have a similar impact on different countries (for example, in the East Asian financial crisis, while South Korea suffered severe economic and financial downturns, Taiwan emerged from the crisis relatively unscathed) has been the subject of considerable study. Though there are varying views on the financial specifics of the transmission of contagion, the general thesis that seems to have emerged emphasizes the dependence of a country's economy on investment, in particular on portfolio investment. Those countries whose economies are more dependent on portfolio investment are more susceptible to the contagion effect than are less dependent countries.

Portfolio investment which is more short-term and speculative in character than **foreign direct investment** tends to concentrate in financial domains where returns on investment are perceived to be high and quickly realized (e.g. in real estate in a country experiencing rapid **economic growth**). However, portfolio investment also tends to be very skittish, and when an investment fails to perform as anticipated, the investors may be led to sell off their most speculative assets in an effort to minimize their losses.

Therefore, the contagion effect does not refer to a phenomenon of one national economy's collapse causing another's collapse. Rather, it refers to speculative investors seeking to minimize the investment losses they suffer in one country by selling off their portfolio investments in other countries. Consequently, a financial crisis in a country heavily dependent on foreign portfolio investment can spread, because of the increasingly numerous and deep financial links characterizing **globalization**, to other similarly dependent countries through the actions of domestic and foreign investors.

See also: Asian crises; fiscal and monetary policy; globalization; International Monetary Fund (IMF); inflation and its effects; international economic order; stock markets

Further reading

Baig, T. and Goldfajn, I. (1998) "Financial Market contagion in the Asian Crisis," *IMF Working Paper WP/98/155*, Washington DC: International Monetary Fund.

Berg, A. and Sachs, J. (1988) "The Debt Crisis: Structural Explanations of Country Performance," *Journal of Development Economics* 29:3 271–306.

Scharfstein, D. and Stein, J. (1990) "Herd Behavior and Investment," *American Economic Review* 80: 465–79.

RICHARD M. J. THURSTON

CONTRACEPTION *see* family planning

contract farming

Contract farming, sometimes referred to as outgrower production or nucleus estate systems, is a widespread form of organizing agricultural production in the advanced capitalist states, and increasingly over the last three decades in the developing world (see **agriculture**). Contract farming can be simply defined as arrangements between a grower (a peasant, a family farm, a large commercial farm) and a private or public firm (an exporter, a processor, a shipper) in which

non-transferable contracts specify one, and typically more, conditions of marketing and production. In more technical language, contract farming is a form of vertical coordination between growers and buyer-processors that directly shapes the production conditions through the contractual specification of market obligations (volume, time and quality of delivery), the provision of specific inputs, and direct exercise over the point of production (i.e. a division of labor between the contractor and the contractee). There are a variety of institutional and organizational conditions under which contracts are put into effect. In parts of the developing world, export crops such as palm oil, tea and coffee are grown through contracts between peasant producers (often "middle" peasants with access to resources such as land and capital – see **peasantry**) and nucleus estates in which peasants contractors complement plantation production (see **plantation forestry**) typically owned by **state-owned enterprises (SOEs)** or private **agribusiness transnational corporations (TNCs)**. Sugar production in Kenya and palm oil in Malaysia are two such examples. Contract production is exceptionally widespread in US **agriculture** and represents the dominant mode of organization in key sectors like chickens, hogs and fresh fruits and vegetables. In the poultry sector dominated by the southern states (like Akansas, Georgia and North Carolina), the so-called integrators (billion-dollar enterprises such as Purdue and Tysons) provide day-old young chicks to thousands of contract growers who must be facilities to precise specification and adhere to strict nutrient and health regimes during the 6–8 week growth period. The poultry case highlights clearly the centrality of the autonomy of the growers themselves and the extent to which they are subordinated, not through the market but through the company, to highly regimented conditions. In effect, contract growers can be seen as instances of what Lenin called "propertied laborers:" that is to say owners of the means of production but in some way fundamentally "unfree." The origins of contract framing extends back at least to the sorts of colonial schemes associated with British cotton production in the Sudan (Gezira) and the Japanese sugar schemes in Taiwan. But the growth and proliferation of flexible production schemes (**flexible specialization**) under the aegis of agribusiness in the last thirty years raises important questions as regards the parallels between the contemporary forms of restructuring of global agriculture, and the debates over post-Fordist manufacturing and the rise of subcontracting in advanced manufacturing systems (see **Fordism versus Toyotaism**).

See also: agriculture; agribusiness; food; peasantry; transnational corporations (TNCs)

Further reading

Boyd, W. and Watts, M. (1997) "Agroindustrial Just-in-Time," in Goodman, D. and Watts, M. (eds) *Globalising Food*, London: Routledge.

Little, P. and Watts, M. (1994) (eds) *Living Under Contract*, Madison: University of Wisconsin Press.

MICHAEL WATTS

Convention on Biological Diversity (CBD)

The Convention on Biological Diversity (CBD) was first signed at the **Earth Summit (1992) (United Nations Conference on Environment and Development)** (June) and entered into force in December 1993. It calls for participant countries to promote the conservation of **biodiversity**; sustainable use of its components; and equitable sharing of benefits from the use of genetic resources. The Convention formally recognizes sovereign rights of nations to their biological resources. Under the Convention, users of genetic material are mandated to provide equitable share of the benefits to parties providing the genetic material and indigenous knowledge of natural resources that contributed to the generation of commercial profit. As of December 2003, 188 countries are parties to the Convention. The **Cartagena Protocol on Biosafety** was added in January 2000, as a means of regulating the international shipment of modified living organisms. The Convention is governed by regular Conference of the Parties, which are attended by all governments that have ratified the treaty.

See also: biodiversity; biopiracy; bioprospecting; Cartagena Protocol on Biosafety; Earth Summit (1992) (United Nations Conference on Environment and Development); environment; genetically modified organisms (GMOs)

Further reading

Convention on Biological Diversity (CBD) website: http://www.biodiv.org/

CHIKAKO TAKESHITA

Convention on the Elimination of All Forms of Discrimination Against Women (CEDAW)

The Convention on the Elimination of All Forms of Discrimination Against Women (CEDAW) is an international bill of women's rights and a pioneer treaty that addresses equality issues pertaining to the position and status of women in society. It was drafted by the United Nations Commission on the Status of Women, adopted by the **United Nations** General Assembly in 1979, came into force in 1981, and by 1991 had been ratified by over 101 states. CEDAW is overseen by a committee consisting of twenty-three experts, which reviews the documentation and actions of member states. A further group, the Women's Rights Action Watch, an international consortium of scholars and activists, monitors and maintains pressure on governments to abide by the provisions of CEDAW. The treaty's provisions include subjects already discussed in earlier treaties on **slavery, migrant trafficking**, nationality, **education** and **employment**; as well as new issues. The Plans for Action presented at the 1985 and 1995 conferences to mark the UN Decade for Women, however, show that inequality persists in old and new forms; and that progress is slow and incremental.

See also: gender; international law; United Nations World Conferences on Women

Further reading

Fraser, A. (1987) *The UN Decade for Women: Documents and Dialogue*, Boulder: Westview.

CHRISTINE OBBO

convergence

Convergence, or "catch-up," is the process whereby per capita income tends to grow faster in poorer rather than richer economies of a given group of regions or countries. A more even geographical distribution of income per person emerges over time, as the lagging economies of the group expand more rapidly than their advanced counterparts. From an empirical viewpoint, convergence is neither a continuous nor an automatic process. Furthermore, it does not necessarily lead to the eradication of spatial inequalities, although it reduces them. The duration, intensity and the forms that convergence may take depend heavily on the triggering mechanisms.

Diminishing returns to scale can be an important source of convergence. According to this law of economics, **productivity** (and *ceteris paribus* income per capita) growth becomes slower as the availability of capital per worker in an economy increases (see **capital intensive**). This entails that under certain conditions economic expansion can be less rapid in areas that are rich in capital and faster in poorer places where capital investment initially can be more productive. In particular, convergence is likely to occur when both the advanced and the lagging economies under examination are heading towards the same steady state target (the point at which the economy expands along a balanced growth path). This stage happens when the economies in question share some similar attributes, such as technology levels, investment and **population growth rate (PGR)**. In contrast, the emergence of convergence across economies that have different steady states depends on the distance of each individual economy from its own steady state. Economies that are well below their steady state will expand faster than economies that are nearer to it, while economies that are well above their steady state will tend to grow at a slower pace.

Technology transfer provides another convergence mechanism. The adoption of innovations that have been developed elsewhere can accelerate **economic growth** in poorer countries. By not having to bear the research and development costs, lagging states have a chance, at least theoretically, to benefit more from the efforts of the technological leaders. In practice, the impact of this mechanism is subject not only to the ability of backward economies to absorb and adapt new technologies to their specific needs, but also to the costs associated with innovative activity. For instance, if the costs of producing new technologies are declining with the accumulation of technical knowledge then convergence is an implausible outcome.

Finally, structural change is another cause of convergence. The productive structure of developing economies is usually dominated by sectors, such as **agriculture**, that are characterized by low productivity. As these economies expand, capital and labor are transferred from agriculture to higher productivity industries. This shift of resources raises the aggregate productivity of developing economies further, giving them an advantage in relation to the advanced economies.

See also: economic development; economic growth; inequality; inequality and poverty, world trends; technology policy

Further reading

de la Fuente, A. (2000) "Convergence across Countries and Regions: Theory and Empirics," *European Investment Bank Papers* 5:2 25–45.
Jones, C. (1998) *Introduction to Economic Growth*, New York: Norton.

KONSTANTINOS A. MELACHROINOS

COPENHAGEN SUMMIT FOR SOCIAL DEVELOPMENT *see* social development

coping strategies

Survival or coping strategies are specific approaches by households and communities (see **community**) to managing crises of **food security**, conflict (**war**), or natural disaster (see **natural disasters**). Coping strategies generally involve a sequence of decisions by those affected that identify phased stages of response in order to mitigate the effects of a progressively worsening situations involving food security or personal or livelihood security (see **livelihoods**). Such strategies focus on obtaining the necessary **food** and personal **security** necessary for survival. However, strategies that maximize this security at the household level are in many cases different from those at the **community** level. Household coping strategies can follow an economically rational logic amenable to donor intervention. But frequently strategies that operate at the community level can appear less logical, due to an orientation toward saving a way of life, as opposed to saving lives. Such a focus has influence on the household level, and can frustrate attempts by the donors or **aid** workers to understand the reasons for decisions by communities.

See also: complex emergencies; early warning systems; safety nets against poverty

JON D. UNRUH

corporate social responsibility (CSR)

Corporate social responsibility (CSR) refers to the active involvement of businesses in socially aware activities, or the reduction of potential negative impacts of business activities on workforces and environments. CSR is a growing trend in development policy and has been encouraged by the **United Nations** in its **Global Compact**, and under the growing debate about **partnerships** in development policy. It was also discussed at the **World Summit on Sustainable Development (Johannesburg, 2002)**. Yet, many observers treat CSR with mistrust, not least because many companies see it as an unwanted interference with business. The free-market economist Milton Friedman famously once stated that CSR begins and ends with maximizing profits. Some companies, and especially **transnational corporations (TNCs)**, have also become infamous for allegedly

irresponsible behavior. Nestlé, for example, gained notoriety in the 1970s for promoting powdered babymilk (and hence discouraging breastfeeding) in regions of Africa where it was mixed with unsafe water, and where incomes might have been better used. Nestlé added to this controversy in 2002 when it insisted on receiving US$6 million compensation from the government of Ethiopia (a poor country that has experienced **famine**) for the **nationalization** of a Nestlé-owned company in 1975 (following protests, Nestlé said they would use some of this payment for famine relief). Nike also attracted adverse publicity when it was revealed in 1992 that its annual profits outreached US$180 million and had spent some US$20 million on its advertising campaign employing basketball player Michael Jordan, but paid workers in Indonesia just 90 US cents a day (or US$270 a year) (Kemp, 2001:11).

Of course, not all companies deserve nor receive bad publicity. Some individual companies, such as the UK's Burroughs Wellcome, have for decades actively supported charitable work. International CSR initiative started in 1976 with the ILO World Employment Conference on Basic Needs, which urged "good citizenship" for companies; and the publication in the same year of the **Organization for Economic Cooperation and Development (OECD)** Guidelines for Multinational Enterprises (updated since). During the 1980s, new networks of businesses and business leaders emerged on CSR, such as the UN Global Sullivan Principles, or the 1986 roundtable meeting in Caux, Switzerland. The World Business Council for Sustainable Development was established in 1991. In 1999 the UN issued its **Global Compact**, which set out nine principles for companies to "give **globalization** a human face" including the protection of **human rights**, upholding the **freedom of association**, avoidance of forced and **child labor**, and enhancing **technology transfer** and environmental protection. The 2000 Lisbon meeting of the **European Union** was the first occasion when heads of government formally acknowledged a social agenda of business and established a new Global Reporting Initiative for CSR activities. Socially responsible investment funds are another aspect of CSR. The first "ethical" investment trust in the UK was launched in 1984.

Critics, however, have alleged that CSR may only have limited impacts, or that voluntary or self-regulating initiatives in industry are chiefly designed to avoid attracting more bad publicity or draconian command-and-control regulation from the state (see **state and state reform**). One common criticism is that actions such as the "Monsanto pledge" – a statement by that company in the early 1990s to reduce air emission within a specific period – were mainly designed to direct attention away from the company's other impacts, and to create an image that the company was acting responsibly. Some critics call self-regulation "greenwash," because they have little impact on long-term impacts, and aim instead to make businesses look good. CSR is also difficult to define, and its perceived value may differ between industries. The ice-cream manufacturer, Ben and Jerry's, for example, has a positive reputation for CSR, but perhaps it is easier to introduce in luxury goods such as ice cream (where consumers may also experience guilt when buying), unlike more mundane objects such as rubber washers, where comparatively fewer customers care how the product was made. CSR may therefore only add value to selective products. Pharmaceutical activities are also difficult to define in terms of CSR, as some companies both save human lives and experiment on animals. There may also be general disagreement about what constitutes "environmental" or "ethical" properties. For example, the first advertising posters for ethical investment funds in the UK in the 1980s featured pictures of nuclear power plants alongside trees and flowers because they have less air pollution than coal-fired plants, even though many environmentalists consider **nuclear energy** unacceptable.

There is, however, some evidence and examples to show CSR as successful. Research in the Philippines (Standing, 1992) revealed that companies who adopted CSR practices such as non-discriminatory recruitment, regular employment for the majority of workers, protected working conditions and worker participation in production processes experienced no disproportionately higher costs than other companies, nor did such practices curtail **employment** growth. The Levi Strauss company, in the 1990s, after learning that a subcontractor in Bangladesh had employed children

under fourteen years, built a school and bought uniforms and books for these workers. The Body Shop International developed guidelines for community trade partnerships in 1994. Rio Tinto helped launch a Global Mining Initiative in 1999 to reduce impacts of mining. The Polo Ralph Lauren Corporation in 2000 launched a scheme for staff to volunteer for good causes. Such schemes, of course, may be considered to help business, or prevent criticisms of companies, but they are considered good examples of CSR.

Much discussion currently concerns establishing transparent and transferable guidelines for CSR and for measuring the success of CSR (e.g. see **triple bottom line**; or websites below). But for many critics, the crucial questions are who evaluates CSR; and whether the objectives of CSR are established voluntarily by companies (which may be insufficient), by the state (see **state and state reform**) (which may be unpopular with the companies), or in consultation with **civil society** (which may carry greatest developmental impacts). Allowing diverse and independent formulation and evaluation of CSR will lead to the most effective development results.

See also: accountability; corruption; ethics; fair trade; partnerships; public-private partnerships; transnational corporations (TNCs); transparency; triple bottom line

Further reading

Baby Milk Action: an organization seeking to reduce infant mortality and corporate social responsibility in baby feeding: http://www.babymilkaction.org/

Ethical Investment Research Service: http://www.eiris.org/

FTSE4Good: an index of ethical companies in the UK stock market: http://www.ftse.com/ftse4good/

Hopkins, M. (1999) *The Planetary Bargain: Corporate Social Responsibility Comes of Age*, Basingstoke: Macmillan.

Kemp, M. (2001) *Corporate Social Responsibility in Indonesia: Quixotic Dream or Confident Expectation?* Geneva: UNRISD.

OECD (2001) *Corporate Social Responsibility: Partners for Progress*, Paris: OECD.

Rugmark: an organization seeking to end child labor in rug production: http://www.rugmark.org/

Standing, G. (1992) "Identifying the 'Human Resource Enterprise:' A South East Asian Example," *International Labour Review* 131:3 281–95.

World Business Council for Sustainable Development: http:/www.wbcsd.ch/

TIM FORSYTH

corruption

Corruption usually refers to dishonesty or bribe-taking by people in authority, but its meaning and definition varies between places and contexts. It is the flouting of rules by willing partners, with consequent loss of **accountability**. Unlike fraud, all the parties to corrupt practices must share a guilty knowledge of the corruption. They can be said to be in breach of the moral compass by which such transactions are normally judged. Corruption has contributed to the collapse of national economies and banking systems in some countries, examples being the Democratic Republic of the Congo under Mobutu Sese Seko (1960–97) and Russia under the regime of Boris Yeltsin (1991–9). Corruption can contribute to the high cost of commodity prices; destroy markets, currencies and investments. In some cases, it can be a cause of the violent overthrow of governments.

Corruption affects countries in different ways; the scandals that engulfed Enron and WorldCom during 2002 were in billions of dollars, estimated by some to be greater than the **gross national product (GNP)** of many countries (see also **corporate social responsibility (CSR)**). Corruption can be the progeny of other crimes such as drug trafficking (see **drugs**), **migrant trafficking**, organized **crime** and, in some cases, trade in dangerous weaponry.

There are shades of corruption. What is regarded as standard practice in one country may be unacceptable in another. The nature of corruption is constantly changing. While in some developing countries kleptocracy (or the use of political power

to misuse public funds for personal gain) is common, in certain parts of developed economies, the major cause of concern is corporate corruption (see **transnational corporations (TNCs)**). Corporate corruption may include schemes where shareholder value is devalued by the nature of stock options unrelated to the long-term performance of the corporate organizations.

Cultural relativism in the identification of corrupt practices makes it all the more difficult to find an all-embracing definition. Most definitions therefore, tend to describe the essential characteristics of corruption, rather than list practices. Some analysts have proposed that corruption may be differentiated between public and private sectors. This is not entirely a helpful distinction, as corruption occurs in all spheres of life. Corruption, however, may be transnational if it involves acts such as **money laundering**, drugs or migrant trafficking. These crimes have grown in scale due to advances in modern **information technology**. In advance fee fraud, for example, the fraudsters are able to solicit funds usually through the **Internet** by falsely promising to share a large sum of money with the unsuspecting or gullible victim if a certain amount was sent to the initiator in advance.

Although a corrupt practice can be a crime in both **domestic law** and **international law**, it is not always easy to prosecute the perpetrators where the crime originates in one jurisdiction and is completed in another. Furthermore, for some years, the Foreign Corrupt Practices Act (1977) of the USA was the only national legislation that sanctioned firms for offering bribes abroad. To address corruption, a number of initiatives are still developed at bilateral and international levels. The non-governmental organization, Transparency International (launched in 1994) (see **non-governmental organizations (NGOs)**) publishes an annual index on the level of corruption in different countries. The Council of Europe, the **European Union** and the African Union have all passed conventions for combating corruption. Networks for monitoring corruption have been established in Latin America, Central and Eastern Europe, and Central Asia. The Inter-American Convention Against Convention was opened for ratification in 1996. The International Chamber of

Commerce adopted its own rules and regulations about corruption in 1996. In 1999, the **Organization for Economic Cooperation and Development (OECD)** passed the OECD Convention on the Bribery of Foreign Public Officials, which is the first legally binding international instrument that aims to curb the behaviour of corrupt **transnational corporations (TNCs)** operating overseas.

See also: accountability; corporate social responsibility (CSR); crime; drugs; ethics; money laundering; offshore finance; rent seeking; transnational corporations (TNCs); transparency

Further reading

Gabriel, L. and Stapenhurst, R. (eds) (2001) *The Role of Bilateral Donors in Fighting Corruption*, Washington DC: World Bank.
Gilmore, W. (1999) *Dirty Money: The Evolution of Money Laundering Countermeasures*, Strasbourg: Council of Europe.
Transparency International website: http://www.transparency.org/

PAUL OKOJIE

cost-benefit analysis (CBA)

Cost-benefit analysis (CBA) is an economic technique for evaluating the cumulative effects of both the positive and negative implications of any development decision. It is used to assist planning and decision-making. It was originally developed in the 1960s in response to widening demands on the state (see **state and state reform**) plus growing confidence in a mixed economy with widespread market prices; electronic data processing capacity; and a shortage of investible savings and international purchasing power. It became popular again in the 1990s largely because of growing concern at the impacts of development projects on the natural environment, and to a lesser extent distributional concerns.

The apparent advantage of CBA techniques – as developed in much development economics – is that it allowed economists to appraise any development activities comparatively, and against an international standard. The CBA process involved a chain of activities that link state activities to development outcomes. Such activities include, for example, a numeric system to give standards for comparison; valuation of activities in terms of shadow prices; valuation of time through discounting; and the use of economic evaluation methods such as Net Present Values, Benefit/Cost ratios, or internal rates of return in order to rank decision-making criteria. The method gave systematic insights into choice of techniques and distributional weights and compensation for welfare losses.

The basic model of CBA used in development economics builds on a technique used in financial analysis by commercial enterprises to appraise or evaluate an investment activity for private profitability. It accepts market prices (including interest on borrowing), pays the taxes it cannot avoid (or evade), and welcomes any subsidies. If it can displace costs onto other economic agents (such as other producers, consumers, government, or neighbors) it will. The result of this analysis is – in effect – to find financial profitability for the enterprise as a single institution, rather than society as a whole. Neo-liberal economists have claimed that this kind of analysis is both necessary and sufficient for **project appraisal** (see **neo-liberalism**).

Proponents of CBA have argued that it provides a flexible and easily transferable technique that produces a simple summary of the net advantages and disadvantages of a proposed investment or decision. Furthermore, CBA can claim to capture market failures such as externalities, public goods (see **global public goods**), imperfect competition, civil society activism, and institutional conventions on pricing resources such as labor. These factors are generally difficult to analyze using neoclassical, market-based, analysis.

Critics of CBA, however, have argued that CBA reduces to money values, culturally valuable objects that cannot be simply described or transferred between cultures and contexts. CBA may therefore suppress the contested nature of many development projects by giving the appearance of a uniform, technically closed evaluation. (For example, some decisions concerning the location of **dams**, and subsequent **displacement** of people have used CBA controversially, often by **international organizations and associations** such as the **World Bank**). More specifically, economist critics have argued that CBA has concentrated on state interventions such as regulations, taxes and subsidies at regional, national and international levels. Yet, such actions have been generally reduced in recent years following **structural adjustment**, and the desire to remove government interventions in the marketplace. Therefore, original CBA concerns have been qualitatively and quantitatively reduced in their effects on **public sector** decision-making.

Moreover, some economists have questioned the accuracy of data used to conduct CBA, which further undermines its apparent objectivity and accuracy. According to some critics, the attempts to use CBA as a means of evaluating projects is effectively a means of enacting "politics by other means" by hiding the social influences on how data and analysis have been framed, and trying to legitimize decisions through presenting CBA as an apparently neutral science.

See also: computable general equilibrium (CGE) models; anti-politics; indicators of development; measuring development; project appraisal

Further reading

Cameron, J. (2001) *Notes on CBA and Worked Examples of Rural Development Projects on Excel Spreadsheets*, Norwich: University of East Anglia. http://www.uea.ac.uk/dev/publink/cameron/cba.shtml

Heal, G. (1997) *Valuing Our Future: Cost-Benefit Analysis and Sustainability*, ODS Discussion Paper, UNDP: New York.

Lohmann, L. (1998) *Whose Voice Is Speaking? How Opinion Polls and Cost-Benefit Analysis Synthesize New "Publics,"* Briefing Paper 7, The Corner House, Sturminster Newton, UK: The Corner House. http://www.thecornerhouse.org.uk

JOHN CAMERON

crime

Crime is not a new concern in the field of development theory or practice. There has long existed something of an orthodoxy within development studies that high levels of crime are an inevitable corollary of development, conceived in terms of modernization (see **modernization theory**; see also **violence**). Crime from this perspective is seen as a consequence of social upheavals resulting from **industrialization** and **urbanization** that have traditionally been equated with modernization. Social organization and behavior are altered, traditional **institutions** affected, and individual alienation and anomie spread at the margins of society, leading to crime. At the same time, this perspective also assumes that as developing societies modernize and stabilize, levels of crime will decline, and patterns of criminal behavior will change (with violent, personal crimes giving way to more impersonal and less brutal forms of crime linked to property theft, for example).

The experience of the developing world in the last quarter of the twentieth century has undermined this perspective. Global crime rates increased vertiginously between 1975 and 2000, particularly in Latin America and Sub-Saharan Africa, where in some countries crime has arguably become the dominant feature of social life. As a result, the phenomenon of crime is increasingly seen not so much as an inevitable – and temporary – consequence of the development process occurring at the margins of society, but rather as a critical obstacle to the realization of development objectives, and even a potential cause of underdevelopment. In many developing societies, questions of crime are now increasingly attracting attention away from traditional issues associated with development policy determination such as **economic growth**, for example, particularly as the devastating societal consequences of the phenomenon become clear.

The costs of crime vary from direct costs such as the physical and psychological damage and loss suffered by victims to more indirect economic, social, and political costs. Economically, for example, crime can negatively affect physical capital (see **capitalism**), in ways that range from minor acts of vandalism such as the painting of graffiti to the wholesale destruction of infra-structure, for example. The widespread presence of crime can also disrupt entitlement structures (see **food security; poverty**), the operation of markets (see **capital markets**), and can lead to weak investor confidence, both directly, through injury and loss of life, but also indirectly, through the diversion of scarce resources which could otherwise be devoted to the creation of **human capital** toward criminal justice and incarceration. Crime can also be an important strain on the social fabric. Insecurity can lead to norms of trust and reciprocity being replaced by a Hobbesian "war of all against all," as local **community** links deteriorate, hampering collective action and cooperation. Moral and referential frameworks dissolve, rendering the transactions of social agents unpredictable. High levels of criminal violence – particularly organized crime – can also constitute a fundamental challenge to the state (see **state and state reform**), defying its mono-poly over the use of **violence**.

At the same time, crime is not a unitary phe-nomenon, but has a wide range of possible mani-festations, from street-level pick-pocketing to mafia-style organized criminality to non-violent corruption. These all have different ramifications and can be related to development in distinct ways. In particular, rather than being the result of development, crime is often seen as a response to underdevelopment. From this perspective, crime is seen as being intimately connected to phenomena such as **poverty**, **inequality**, and **unemploy-ment**. Similarly, certain forms of criminal activity have been associated with the lack of **governance** structures or alternatively with the existence of oppressive governance structures. Seen in this way, crime amounts less to a dysfunctional social form or an epiphenomenon of modernization (see **modernization theory**) than a logical adaptation to adverse – even dysfunctional – structural cir-cumstances. The relationship of crime to devel-opment obviously become highly complex from such a perspective, but at the same time the focus is squarely shifted away from looking at the mere manifestation of crime to exploring its causes, consequences, and dynamics. This analysis allows us to explore what crime means from a develop-mental perspective in a global context, where it is on the rise and becoming one of the dominant features of social life in an increasing number of developing societies.

See also: corruption; money laundering; social capital; structural violence; violence; youth violence

Further reading

McIllwaine, C. (1999) "Geography and Develop-ment: Crime and Violence as Development Issues," *Progress in Human Geography* 23:3 453–63.

Rogers, J. (1989) "Theories of Crime and Devel-opment: An Historical Perspective," *Journal of Development Studies* 25: 314–28.

DENNIS RODGERS

cultural heritage

Cultural heritage – as recognized by international conventions – refers to tangible manifestations of **culture**, both moveable and immoveable, as well as intangible cultural expressions such as music, art, literature and the performing arts. The 1921 Treaty of Sèvres first examined the trade in archaeological objects in the Middle East, followed in the 1960s by a wider concern by many newly independent countries to restitute their national heritage. The **United Nations Education, Scientific and Cultural Organization (UNES-CO)**'s "Hague Convention" of 1970 affirmed the free circulation of cultural property, but outlawed pillaging and strives to assign proof of origin to regulate the international trade in moveable cul-tural objects (paintings, ceramics, sculptures) between source and importing countries. The **World Heritage Convention (UNESCO 1972)** protects immoveable cultural heritage, namely monuments, groups of buildings, and sites as the combined works of nature and human beings.

See also: common heritage of humankind; culture; tourism; World Heritage Convention (UNESCO 1972)

TERENCE HAY-EDIE

CULTURAL IMPERIALISM *see* colonialism, impacts of; culture; ethnocentricism; neocolonialism; postcolonialism; postmodernism and postdevelopment

cultural relativism

Cultural relativism is the belief that all cultural practices and moral views can be seen as worthy, even when they are seen as unacceptable by many observers. It is both a cultural and political stance, based on the desire to question the dominance of any absolute point of view no matter how seemingly natural it may seem to those who hold it. In some ways, cultural relativism champions the ability for different cultures' values and practices to be respected for what they are, and hence reverse the trend during the nineteenth century when colonial powers ranked peoples according to racist evolutionary narratives of their progress toward (European) civilization. But cultural relativism may also be a controversial stance: the **Universal Declaration of Human Rights (1948)**, drawn up by the **United Nations** after the horrors of World War II, set out to institutionalize an international moral standard where none had previously existed. Cultural relativism, in its purest form, would oppose such international codes of "rights" and "wrongs."

In the context of debates on development and **human rights**, relativizng arguments for and against specific cultural forms appear most often in connection with taboo practices. These are behavioral traits which Mary Douglas describes as potentially "revolting" to other cultures – such as **female genital mutilation**, infanticide, cannibalism or peculiar eating habits (i.e. eating cats or dogs); but are also extended to more widespread concerns over **child labor**, concepts of the individual, **gender**, and attitudes toward **ageing**.

East Asian countries, notably, have invoked a culturally relativist position to resist what they see to be Western individualistic concepts of society, unsuited to Confucianist or patriarchal values. Political scientist Samuel Huntington extends this argument to include sweeping "civilizational blocks," based on religious and cultural fault lines,

labeled as "Sinic," "Buddhist," "Latin American," and (most notoriously) "Islamic," which he predicted would come into increasing conflict with the libertarian or degenerate moral values of the West (see **clash of civilizations**). Nonetheless, relativism is seldom boundless, as certain types of behavior such as incest are universally condemned.

According to the social anthropologist Claude Lévi-Strauss, "the barbarian is first and foremost the man who believes in barbarism." He elaborates the structuralist principle that **ethnocentricism**, the bias towards one's own group, is a common ideological attitude, inherent to all human collective life. He reports that South American Indians, like the invading *conquistadors*, considered that only their in-group could fully incarnate humanity – indeed, just as the Spanish investigated whether "natives" could have a soul, these same Amerindians drowned white people to distinguish them as either humans or spirits.

In this light, humanity – as it comes to be culturally perceived – is neither universal nor automatic, but conditioned by geographical and historical discontinuities. Viveiros de Castro (1998) argues that by the standards of cultural relativism in the 1960s, "savages" were once deemed ethnocentric, and thereby very human; yet by the 1990s "**indigenous people**s" were recast within the principles of ecology and "cosmocentric" by their rejection of the Cartesian divide between nature and culture. "Now we have to recognize how *in*human *we* are for opposing humans to animals in a way they never did," he observes. Bruno Latour, like other relativist sociologists, abandons altogether any dichotomy that separates modern from traditional, humanity from animality, in favor of a pervasive social universe composed of humans, non-humans, hybrids and cyborgs.

See also: clash of civilizations; culture; ethnocentricism; female genital mutilation; indigenous people; Universal Declaration of Human Rights (1948)

Further reading

Douglas, M. (1966) *Purity and Danger*, London: Routledge and Kegan Paul.

Viveiros de Castro, E. (1998) "Cosmological Deixis and Amerindian Perspectivism," *Journal of the Royal Anthropological Institute*, 4:3 469–88.

TERENCE HAY-EDIE

culture

The relationship between culture and development is important, but difficult to conceptualize because culture can mean different things to different people. Two main approaches to culture exist: the first sees culture as a tangible resource, such as a particular kind of knowledge, an art form, a geographical location, or an activity. Such culture resides in social forms including literature, films, sculptures, paintings, historical monuments, etc. The second sees culture as shared values, beliefs, habits of thought and behavior prevalent in a group, **community** or society, and which provide templates for how people act and make sense of their lives. This second approach to culture has at least two further strands: the "primordialist," which sees culture as an age-old and quasi-immutable fundamental property of humans, and the "relational," which sees culture as more fluid and dynamic, linked to a less rigid concept of identity and being.

Until recently, theorists have given more attention to economics than culture within development studies. Culture was generally viewed as "residual factors" in explaining development, or relevant only to **economic development** activities such as **tourism**. During the 1990s, culture became seen as more important than this, and as either instrumentally or intrinsically important to development. An instrumental approach sees culture as having functions external to itself, and hence may either promote or hinder development. The intrinsic view considers culture as inevitably deeply embedded within the development process.

Perhaps the most famous example of the instrumentalist conceptualization of culture is in Max Weber's famous work on *The Protestant Ethic and the Spirit of Capitalism* (1904–5) (see **Protestant work ethic**). According to Weber, the economic conditions determining European **capitalism** in the sevententh century were embedded in behavior patterns linked to Protestantism, which he saw as a cultural form. Weber argued that the transformation of modern European capitalism from pre-existing mercantile operations required the regular reproduction of capital, involving its continued investment and reinvestment for the sake of economic efficiency (or, simply, the accumulation of wealth for its own sake). For Weber, this was the essence of the spirit of capitalism, and he argued that it derived from Protestantism and especially the notion of pre-destination, or the belief that only some human beings were to be saved from damnation and that no-one could change this. As a result, individuals tended to assume they were among the chosen, and demonstrated their status by combining wealth accumulation with frugal life-styles. Of course, this religious element of European capitalism was influential for only a short period, but its consequences became institutionalized.

Weber's general line of argument has been adopted by numerous scholars, particularly to link the **newly industrialized economies (NIEs)** of East Asia with Confucianism. But instrumental approaches to culture and development have also portrayed culture as an obstacle to development. Perhaps most famously, Oscar Lewis' 1960s concept of the "**culture of poverty**" argued that a mixture of economic, social and socio-psychological factors among Puerto Rican and Mexican communities (see **community**) could be passed on between generations, keeping the poor in **poverty**. Lewis' proposals were widely criticized for "blaming the poor" for their poverty, and critics urged more attention should be placed on structural factors such as **unemployment**, lack of **education**, and **social exclusion**, rather than culture. In many ways, though, what is perhaps most important to consider is the destructive interplay between structural and cultural factors. It is never just cultural factors, nor just structural factors that can explain situations, but the combination of both. Indeed, the "culture of poverty" argument may ultimately be a materialist rather than a cultural theory, as it emphasizes primarily the material circumstances of poverty, which are then mediated by cultural factors.

The relationship between material and cultural worlds has been contested more widely in development studies and all social sciences in the so-called "economism" versus "culturalism" debate. Put simply, "economism" refers to the belief in the primacy of material things in determining human behavior, whereas "culturalism" sees ideas or beliefs as basic motivators. The debate was well illustrated by the famous "Worsley-Fortes controversy" between two anthropologists (see Sahlins, 1976). In 1956, Peter Worsley, at the start of his career, applied a Marxist critique (see **Marxism**) to the work of the established anthropologist Meyer Fortes on the Tallensi people of Ghana. Fortes had used orthodox anthropological analysis of kinship, lineage and ritual. Worsley reinterpreted these in terms of Marxist thinking, most notably asserting that cultural practices were simply epiphenomena (or products of) material factors. For example, where Fortes had argued that cooperative farming relations between Tallensi fathers and sons were fundamentally culturally-determined, Worsley claimed that other factors – such as access to family farms – were more important. Hence, sons rejecting their fathers' authority would mean cutting themselves off from their means of production. Later work by Sahlins (1976) pointed out that while such material relationships do exist, they arguably exist secondarily to the initial relationship of father and son; economic factors are influential but do not *necessarily* determine the *logic* of things. The fact that father and son cooperate is determined by the specificities of the Tallensi kinship system such as its patrilineal nature, for example, or in other words cultural factors.

Ultimately, the "Worsley-Fortes controversy" demonstrated that "cultural" factors should not be considered in isolation from economic or political factors. Hence, it is probably unhelpful to discuss culture and development as if they were separate phenomena. From this perspective, culture has to be seen as something that is more than instrumental: it is intrinsically linked to the goals and objectives of development. This intrinsic relationship is shown by two further current approaches to culture and development.

The first approach sees culture as a desirable end in itself, or which enriches individuals and their life quality. The **United Nations Education, Scientific and Cultural Organization (UNESCO)**, for example, has developed the **common heritage of humankind** approach, which seeks to protect geographical and physical sites and features that have been identified as special (examples include the ruins of Angkor in Cambodia, or the limestone scenery of Halong Bay in Vietnam) (see also **World Heritage Convention (UNESCO 1972)**). Another, epistemologically similar approach is the **World Bank**'s "Culture and Poverty" approach, which sees culture as a potential asset for poor people to mitigate **poverty**, such as through norms of generalized reciprocity, and so on (see **safety nets against poverty; social capital**). Both conceptions of culture see the phenomenon as rather static, however, and ultimately limited to something that can be instrumentally used.

A different approach to culture as intrinsically important sees culture as central to development because it mediates all human experience. This is a more open-ended approach to culture, and allows greater diversity in how culture is defined and expressed. Yet, it states that culture ultimately determines the content of what constitutes "development," and effectively becomes the "meta-structure" for the human condition. This view is at the heart of the culturalist critique of development, which has portrayed development as a culturally determined discourse (see **antipolitics; ethnocentrism; postmodernism and postdevelopment**). Development theory, in particular, is considered a Eurocentric discourse, fundamentally rooted in the rise of the West and the history of **capitalism**, and championing a linear view of history, **stages of economic growth**, and the acceptance of current claims about freedom, justice, and equality without criticism. Some postdevelopment writers such as Arturo Escobar (1995) have denounced the whole concept of "development" as a fiction, and urged the reanalysis of the world based on the primacy of culture.

Treating culture as meaningful, however, should not imply adopting a new form of "culturalism," as Escobar is sometimes accused of promoting. While the cultural dimension of the world cannot be excluded or underestimated, it is important to consider *both* cultural and material approaches to development. Attempting to determine which one is more important than the other, or else trying to separate culture from history, politics, or economics, are futile exercises, as social reality must be considered holistically. This of course makes thinking about development much more difficult, but it is preferable to acknowledge, or indeed rejoice in, complexity than to deny it.

See also: common heritage of humankind; cultural heritage; cultural relativism; culture of poverty; globalization and culture; International Covenant on Economic, Social and Cultural Rights; Protestant work ethic; Orientalism; religion; social capital; World Heritage Convention (UNESCO 1972)

Further reading

Carranza Valdés, J. (2002) "Culture and Development: Some Considerations for Debate," *Latin American Perspectives* (Issue 125) 29:4 31–46.

Escobar, A. (1995) *Encountering Development*, Princeton: Princeton University Press.

Mehmet. O. (1995) *Westernising the Third World*, London: Routledge.

Sahlins, M. (1976) *Culture and Practical Reason*, Chicago: University of Chicago Press.

Worsley, P. (1999) "Culture and Development Theory," in Skelton, T. and Allen, T. (eds) *Culture and Global Change*, London: Routledge.

UNESCO Programme for Culture: http://www.unesco.org/culture/index.htm

UNESCO World Commission on Culture and Development: http://www.unesco.org/culture_and_development/wccd/wccd.html

UNRISD Culture and Development research project: http://www.unrisd.org/engindex/research/resrec.htm#Culture

World Bank Culture and Poverty initiative: http://www.worldbank.org/poverty/culture/

DENNIS RODGERS

culture of poverty

The idea of a "culture of poverty" was developed by Oscar Lewis based on anthropological work with Mexican and Puerto Rican communities (see **community**) in their own countries and in US cities in the 1960s. Lewis argued that **poverty** led to a sub-cultural adaptation in the behavior and patterns of life of poor people. The main features of the culture of poverty included personality traits – marginality, dependence, **authoritarianism** and a lack of impulse control – and differences in family life, including mother-centered families, limited emotional bonding and sexual promiscuity.

Lewis's model has been heavily criticized for misunderstanding of the nature of cultural adaptations, overgeneralization, and a tendency to sensationalism. The argument that the culture of poverty reinforced the transmission of poverty between generations has been exploded by empirical research: there is no persistent intergenerational pattern in developed countries. Nevertheless, Lewis's model was highly influential in the development of the USA's "War on Poverty" since the 1960s, and is still reflected in concepts such as the "underclass" that aim to explain where poverty is experienced most.

See also: culture; limited good; marginalization; poverty; poverty trap

Further reading

Lewis, O. (1965) *Five Families: Case Studies in the Culture of Poverty*, New York: New American Library.

PAUL SPICKER

D

dams

Dams are barriers to the flow of rivers and streams constructed by human beings with the purpose of storing the flow for subsequent diversion and utilization. The history of human civilizations has an undeniable link with the ever-increasing degree of human-induced interventions in the natural watercourses. The early great civilizations flourished along major rivers such as the Tigris-Euphrates, Nile, and Indus. Over the past millennia, dams have played an immense role in the alterations of river flows. Starting from providing large water storage for municipal/industrial supplies and **irrigation**, dams have also been built for protection against floods and promotion of navigation. The earliest evidence of dam building comes from the river Nile in Egypt, where a masonry structure, about 15 meters high, was built to protect the ancient city of Memphis from flooding, reportedly in 2900 BC.

With the emergence of modern societies and the availability of new construction technologies based on cement and steel, dams became larger. The generation of electricity (see **electrification and power-sector reform**) also became an important function of dams. The Hoover dam, built in 1935 in the USA with a height of 221 meters, is identified as the origin of a worldwide trend in the construction of large dams. During the three or four decades following the commissioning of the Hoover dam, this technology for **water management** found extensive use all over the world. By the end of the twentieth century, over 45,000 large dams (the International Commission of Large Dams has defined large dams as those with a height of more

than 15m) in more than 140 countries had been built to meet the growing water and energy needs. The five countries topping the list in terms of the number of large dams built – by the end of the twentieth century – are China (22,000), USA (6,390), India (4,291), Japan (2,675) and Spain (1,196). Some of these dams are of gigantic size, the largest being the Nurek dam (300m in height) in Tajikistan. An estimated global investment of about US$2 trillion has gone in the construction of dams in the last century. Today, dams are the sole source of water for about 35 percent of irrigated land in the world. Dams generate about 19 percent of the total electricity generated in the world (see **renewable energy; electrification and power-sector reform**).

Undoubtedly, dams have played a significant economic role in the last century. Yet, increasingly, critics have pointed to the social and environmental impacts of large dams. Key social impacts include large scale and involuntary **displacement**, technocratic insensitivity in the rehabilitation process, huge cost overrun, and **debt**. Physical impacts include fragmentation of the integrity of river basins, drying up of rivers downstream from dams, reduced productivity of areas below dams, and danger to the **biodiversity** of the flood plains or the delta ecosystems. It is estimated that about 40–80 million people worldwide have experienced displacement through dam projects. The two most populated countries in the world, China and India, have taken leading roles in dam construction, accentuating the problem of displacement. Indeed, the various proposed or existing dams on the Narmada River in the central Indian states of Madhya Pradesh, Maharashtra, and Gujarat continue to be a source of international activism; and the Three Gorges dam on the Yangtze River in central China may displace some 1.9 million people and create a reservoir 350 miles long.

Concern about these impacts started to undermine the unquestioned global acceptability of dams as a tool for socio-economic advancement, and a reconsideration from major donors such as the **World Bank**. Some ecologically minded engineers also started to have doubt the ultimate efficacy of dams. Against this background of the global debate on dams, the **World Commission on Dams (WCD)** was created in 1997.

The publication of the Report of the World Commission on Dams in 2000 marked a watershed in understanding dams. The report reflected both positive and negative impacts of dams and provided a more comprehensive framework for decision-making on future dams. Ecologically informed engineers have frequently recommended decommissioning large dams. Dam projects in the future will have to pass through comprehensive assessment processes that allow only exceptionally useful dam projects.

See also: energy policy; environment; environmental movements; water management; World Bank; World Commission on Dams (WCD)

Further reading

Bandyopadhyay, J., Mallik, B., Mandal, M. and Perveen, S. (2002) "Dams and Development," *Economic and Political Weekly* 37:4 4108–12.

World Commission on Dams (2000) *Dams and Development: A New Framework for Decision Making*, London: Earthscan.

JAYANTA BANDYOPADHYAY AND SHAMA PERVEEN

DEATH RATE *see* mortality

debt

Within a development context, debt refers to the money owed to Western banks and multilateral creditor institutions such as the **International Monetary Fund (IMF)** by developing countries. While debt is often associated with developing countries, the biggest borrowers in international financial markets in the twentieth century have been the richer industrialized countries. However, a number of countries, particularly in Latin America and Sub-Saharan Africa, accumulated significant debts in the 1970s. The two increases in oil prices in 1973 and 1979 led to rising fuel import bills in many parts of the world. The profits from these price increases, the so-called **Organization of Petroleum Exporting Countries (OPEC)** "petrodollars," were deposited in Western banks. Anxious to avert a global economic recession, the banks were keen to recycle these petrodollars and so they were lent to a number of developing countries, most of who were suffering from balance of payments shortfalls. The banks were aggressive in their lending and the governments of many developing countries, believing that the interest rates offered would not be subject to change, were eager to borrow. This massive inflow of petrodollars has been called the "dance of the millions." At the time the money was initially lent, borrowing seemed sustainable as interest rates were low and in many cases even negative in real terms, and commodity prices were rising. The situation changed by the end of the 1970s when the industrialized countries were experiencing a deep economic slump and runaway inflation (see **inflation and its effects**) which led governments in the UK, USA and elsewhere to implement restrictive monetary policies (see **fiscal and monetary policy**). These were the conditions which led to the Third World debt and the beginning of the **debt crisis** in the early 1980s.

The amount of debt owed varies from country to country and continent to continent. Latin America's debt is owed primarily to private **institutions** and multilateral organizations. While absolute debt burdens are highest in Brazil and Mexico, per capita rates are highest in Nicaragua and Honduras. Africa's creditors are mostly states (see **state and state reform**) and multilateral organizations, and the bulk of the debt is concentrated in Sub-Saharan Africa. While debt burdens in Asia are comparatively much lower owing to a number of economic and political factors, a number of Asian countries including North

Korea, Indonesia and the Philippines have considerable debt burdens. The high levels of foreign debt, and the flow of capital from the developing to developed countries which debt service entails, are seen by many commentators as representing one of the most challenging obstacles to development.

See also: debt crisis; debt relief; fiscal and monetary policy; Heavily Indebted Poor Countries (HIPC) initiative; London Club; Paris Club; structural adjustment

Further reading

Corbridge, S. (1993) *Debt and Development*, Oxford: Blackwell.
George, S. (1988) *A Fate Worst than Debt*, London: Penguin.

JULIE CUPPLES

debt crisis

The 1980s debt crisis was one of the most significant events in international development in recent decades, and was triggered when a number of developing countries defaulted on loans made by international banks. The crisis emerged in August 1982 when Mexico announced that it had run out of foreign exchange reserves and could no longer afford to service its foreign debt. This is seen as the beginning of what is referred to in Latin America as the "lost decade" given the hardship and **poverty** it provoked for millions of people.

The debt crisis has its origins in the lending by commercial banks in the 1970s of **Organization of Petroleum Exporting Countries (OPEC)** "petrodollars" after the first oil-price shock in 1973, when the price of oil was increased fivefold. Banks were eager to lend, and developing countries, especially in Latin America, were eager to borrow. Major UK and US banks such as Midland and Citicorp led the way and many others followed. Many of the funds were lent to military governments and dictatorships, and were often not used to finance development in a productive or responsible way. Rather they were largely used to prop up a failing economic model, purchase arms or fund huge white elephant projects such as dysfunctional power plants, steel plants which never opened or ecologically destructive **dams**. Many funds also found their way back into US banks through **capital flight**, ending up in overseas assets and bank accounts (see **offshore finance**).

Despite the unproductive ways in which loans were used, borrowing only became unsustainable when conservative world leaders such as Ronald Reagan in the US and Margaret Thatcher in the UK began to implement restrictive monetary policies after 1979 in an attempt to address the stagflation afflicting their economies (see **inflation and its effects; fiscal and monetary policy**). These policies led to massive increases in global interest rates at a time when commodity prices were falling and prices of manufactured goods were rising. Together, these changes had disastrous consequences for many developing countries that suddenly found that the gap between export revenue and debt service had widened. The world recession provoked by the second oil crisis in 1979 reduced demand for both commodities and manufactured goods from the developing world, which meant countries had to meet higher interest payments as their export earnings were falling. The situation was also made worse because in the 1980s the US administration maintained a huge trade deficit and an overvalued dollar, which kept global interest rates high and exacerbated the **debt crisis** in developing countries. Real interest rates rose from -7 percent in 1980 to 21 percent in 1982. This meant that between 1980 and 1985, debt service payments experienced a massive rise while non-oil primary commodity export earnings fell. The reduction in the foreign exchange base that this created forced debtor countries to continue to borrow more capital in order to finance their interest payments.

The Mexican default sent Western bankers into panic and the initial reaction was to save the commercial banks that had lent money. The banks discovered that they had lent more than 100 percent of their capital to governments in the developing world. Many feared that Mexico's default would be repeated in other countries and would lead to a rush on the banks and the collapse of the international financial system. From the bankers' point of view, the most important objective was to keep the interest payments flowing and prevent debts going bad. However, most bankers felt at the time that this was a short-term liquidity problem, and that payments of principal could be rescheduled but would eventually be repaid. An emergency financial rescue package of public and private money was put together by the US Treasury and the **International Monetary Fund (IMF)** was appointed as the overall debt crisis manager. The banks were forced to contribute to the package by the IMF.

In the wake of the Mexican default, the IMF worked hard to prevent governments declaring a moratorium on debt service payments. Mexico was bailed out by the banks, which then adopted a bilateral approach to negotiations to prevent the formation of a debtors' cartel (see **cartels**). Across the developing world, banks and creditor governments entered into lengthy negotiations to reschedule loans. As debt/service ratios (total payments of interest plus principal calculated as a percentage of a country's exports) increased, rescheduling of both official (**Paris Club**) debts, and debts to the commercial banks, became widespread. **structural adjustment** loans were granted by the IMF and the **World Bank** to enable them to meet their debt service obligations to commercial banks. Consequently, the debt crisis has paradoxically been managed by extending credit, a practice that has increased the total debt burdens of many debtor countries but has saved the banks from financial collapse. As a result, most new loans are used to pay interest on old debts, which had the effect of converting the countries of the South into net exporters of capital to the North. US$178 billion was transferred from debtor countries to the creditor countries between 1984 and 1990, and the total debt burden of developing countries rose from $785 billion at the start of the debt crisis to $1.5 trillion in 1993.

The debt crisis marked the end of import substitution industrialization (ISI) (see **import substitution; industrialization**) and paved the way for led to a profound restructuring of developing economies in the form of economic stabilization and **structural adjustment** policies led by the IMF. These policies, which have had devastating social consequences, were designed specifically to keep interest payments flowing to creditors by cutting spending, promoting exports and liberalizing trade.

Structural adjustment policies have been central to the global response to the debt crisis. Both the IMF and the World Bank have played key roles in the development and implementation of these policies and in the provision of new loans.

Critics of the management of the debt crisis have pointed out how the burden of the debt has been borne by those who did not borrow it, given that it has fallen onto the poorest sectors of the population, leading to increased **poverty**, long-term **unemployment** and **malnutrition**. Debt servicing in many of the most indebted countries has often outstripped spending on social services such as **health** and **education** and has swallowed up export revenues. The outcome of the debt crisis has been devastating for ordinary people in debtor countries across the developing world. Latin America and Sub-Saharan Africa were the most negatively affected regions, experiencing massive falls in real per capita incomes and living standards. Campaigners across the world, concerned by the harm caused by the debt crisis and the way in which it has intensified **poverty**, have called for the repudiation of the debt. Many commentators have stressed that because of high global interest rates, unequal **terms of trade** and **capital flight**, the debt has been paid many times over. However, most debtor governments have been reluctant to stop interest payments as defaulting countries would risk losing access to future loans from the World Bank and the IMF. Countries like Brazil and Peru, which did attempt this in the 1980s, did not anticipate the loss of trade credit which forced them to cut imports and grow even faster. A number of Latin American countries did, however, form the Cartagena group in response to the ways in which both **Paris Club** (official debt) and **London Club** (commercial debt) creditors tended to negotiate in groups, while debtor countries were expected to negotiate individually. So, the threat of a collective default continued to loom over the financial system throughout the 1980s.

There have been a number of initiatives aimed at reducing the debt burdens of individual countries. While some individual countries have been able to negotiate debt reductions (as did Nicaragua under the government of Violeta Chamorro in 1995–6), most "solutions" have involved an extension of credit as described above. US Treasury Secretaries, James Baker and Nicolas Brady, both devised plans to bring about debt reduction, which met with limited success. The Baker Plan implemented in 1985 was aimed primarily at preventing the formation of a debtors' cartel (see **cartels**) and focused on providing new lending for developing countries by pushing through structural adjustment packages and emphasizing market **conditionality**. In this period, commercial lenders reduced their debt stock, which was largely shifted to the multilateral financial institutions.

By the end of the 1980s, it had become clear that the debt was not a short-term liquidity problem and that many loans could and would never be repaid. The Brady Plan, adopted in 1989 by the incoming George Bush (senior) administration, attempted to encourage banks to voluntarily reduce debts by providing enhancements to the value of reduced debts. Moderate debt reductions were achieved under the Brady Plan through debt-equity swaps (where a company can buy a country's debt at a lower face value and receive its total value in local currency to invest in local business or to buy newly privatized industries, thus converting commercial debt into investment); debt for bonds (where commercial banks are able to swap their existing loans for more secure and publicly guaranteed bonds at a lower face value than the existing debt); or debt buy-backs (where a debtor country can buy back part of its own debt at a discount). As was the case with its predecessor, the debt reduction achieved under the Brady Plan came at the price of an increase in official lending and continued to be conditional on economic reforms. A further plan involved **debt for nature swaps**, in which debtor countries would guarantee protection of nature reserves in return for debt reduction.

There was a sense in the 1990s that the debt crisis was over. However, the total debt burden of developing countries was substantially greater at the end of the 1990s than it was at the time of the debt crisis. Debt continues to have devastating social consequences across the developing world, with interest payments swallowing up export revenue and national governments forced to divert resources away from social spending to keep up with interest payments. In the late 1990s, Latin American governments were still paying 30 percent of export earnings to service debts and Latin America owed about 45 percent of its combined **gross domestic product (GDP)** to foreign creditors. The debt is now more diverse, which means there is unlikely to be a repeat of the 1980s crisis. However, the question of external debt returned to the global political agenda at the end of the 1990s with the highly prominent and global Jubilee 2000 movement which put considerable political pressure on the (then) G7 leaders to cancel the unpayable debts of the developing countries by the year 2000. Although 100 percent cancellation of the debt was not achieved by this date and many countries have little hope of debt cancellation, the urgent need for debt reduction has been highlighted and the movement continues to monitor and analyze the latest debt relief initiatives such as **Heavily Indebted Poor Countries (HIPC) initiative**.

See also: adjustment with a human face; debt; debt relief; debt-for-nature swaps; Heavily Indebted Poor Countries (HIPC) initiative; International Monetary Fund (IMF); London Club; multilateral development banks (MDBs); neoliberalism; Paris Club; structural adjustment; World Bank

Further reading

Adams, P. (1991) *Odious Debts: Loose Lending, Corruption, and the Third World's Environmental Legacy*, London and Toronto: Earthscan.

Bretton Woods Project: A critical information service about the IMF and World Bank. http://www.brettonwoodsproject.org/

Corbridge, S. (1993) *Debt and Development*, Oxford: Blackwell.

George, S. (1988) *A Fate Worst than Debt*, London: Penguin.

Green, D. (1995) *The Silent Revolution*, London: Latin America Bureau.

Potter, G. (2000) *Deeper than Debt: Economic Globalisation and the Poor*, London: Latin America Bureau.

Roddick, J. (1988) *Dance of the Millions: Latin America and the Debt Crisis*, London: Latin America Bureau.

Woodward, D. (1992) *Debt, Adjustment and Poverty in Developing Countries: National and International Dimensions of Debt and Adjustment*, London: Pinter and Save the Children.

JULIE CUPPLES

debt for nature swaps

Debt for nature swaps refer to the exchange of international **debt** in return for commitments to protect lands with high **biodiversity** in developing countries. During the 1980s, overexposed commercial banks began selling developing countries' high-risk debt at a heavily discounted rate. The resulting secondary debt market allowed for conversion into assets (debt-for-equity swaps), or claims on debtor country's exports. In 1984, conservation organizations such as the World Wildlife Fund and Conservation International pioneered debt for nature swaps (DFNs) in Bolivia, Ecuador and Costa Rica. Although no two DFNs are ever identical, the basic structure for most swaps has been for discounted debt to be purchased through donor funds (typically at 10–30 percent of its theoretical face value), and converted at an agreed "redemption price" into local currency, or long-term bonds, for environmental activities. Despite an apparent win-win situation, problems encountered with DFNs are the complexity of negotiating each settlement; local fears that land has been "sold" to foreign creditors; an arbitrary correspondence of debt relative to the size of protected spaces; and the tiny total proportion of poor countries' debt impacted.

See also: biodiversity; debt; debt crisis; environment

TERENCE HAY-EDIE

debt relief

Debt relief refers to the various means by which states (see **state and state reform**) and **international organizations and associations** have sought to reduce the burden of **debt** experienced by many developing countries. The increased supply of international capital, stemming from the combination of petrodollars and a lax regulatory environment for international lending, led to escalating external debt of many developing countries during the 1970s, especially as many countries borrowed more money to pay existing debts. But in August 1982, Mexico announced that it could not pay its debt. This event marked the onset of the debt crisis, as international banks became wary of lending to other developing countries, undermining their ability to repay existing debts.

With the debt crisis came various forms of debt relief. Debt relief should not be confused with debt reduction. Debt rescheduling need not mean a reduction in repayments. For example, you owe me $100, which you cannot afford to pay. So I say, "okay, don't pay me now, but give me $110 next month instead. ... And another $20 as my rescheduling fee." Debt relief in the 1980s was usually of this sort, rescheduling repayments whilst increasing the debt, and adding a rescheduling fee on top of that.

A further cost of debt relief is that the creditors expect policy reform to enhance the country's capacity to service future payments. These reforms are a condition for participating in **Paris Club** and **London Club** meetings in which official and private debt, respectively, are rescheduled. Simply put, the requirement is to increase exports and reduce imports, so that there is more foreign exchange to pay debt. Devaluation serves both these ends, but the simplest way to reduce imports is to reduce spending, i.e. contract the economy. The earliest "stabilization programs" were often very contractionary, so that the country's **population** suffered as a result of the policies undertaken to service the debt. Criticisms of these costs led to calls for "adjustment with growth," supposedly embodied in the 1985 Baker Plan. Since that time the combination of **International Monetary Fund (IMF)** stabilization and **World Bank** structural adjustment programs (see **structural adjustment**) are rarely contractionary by design, though whether they are the appropriate policies to bring about sustained growth (which is what their advocates claim) has been much disputed.

There are arguments for and against calls to drop the debt, i.e. debt reduction. Arguments against are that debt forgiveness encourages other borrowers to default and raises the cost of credit to countries that do repay. The arguments in favor are based on the social cost of debt repayments (displacing social spending on schools and clinics, etc.), and that the original debt was used to benefit a small elite (see **elites**) no longer in power rather than the mass of the **population** who bears the cost of repayment. The latter argument is called the "odious debt" doctrine. Finally there is an argument appealing to fairness – all countries, and certainly the Western banks, benefitted from the expansion of international lending in the 1970s, so that they should also bear some of the costs of the problems caused by that debt.

Debt relief has evolved over time to become more generous. The package to Mexico in 1982 comprised non-concessional loans mostly from the US government, IMF and World Bank. Similar operations followed to other countries, becoming formalized in the 1985 Baker Plan. Part of the rationale of the plan was to get private banks to put new money (that is, over and above the value of the country's debt service obligations) to restore growth. However, private sector participation was low, so that the multilaterals, notably the World Bank and IMF, took a larger share, building up a problem of growing debt to these organizations. In low-income countries, multilateral organizations anyhow accounted for a large share of external debt.

By the end of the 1980s, the crisis in the most severely indebted countries was considered to be over. This view refers to those middle-income countries responsible for the bulk of the debt, such as Mexico and Brazil. Subsequent events have shown that stability was far from ensured. In terms of country-level indicators, such as the debt service ratio (the proportion of export earnings swallowed up in debt payments) many low-income countries were still saddled with a substantial and growing debt problem at the beginning of the 1990s. These began to be addressed by the Toronto (1988) and Trinidad (1990) terms adopted by the Paris Club, which began the write down of official debt. The Brady Plan of 1989 included the reduction of private debt, financing debt buyback schemes in which banks received a fraction (less than 10 percent) of the face value of the debt. The IMF and World Bank continued to resist the idea that their debt should be reduced, so that Western governments took over paying these obligations through

a mechanism called the Fifth Dimension. However, political pressure, including the influential Jubilee 2000 campaign, resulted in the adoption of the **Heavily Indebted Poor Countries (HIPC) initiative** in 1996. Further campaigning resulted in the Enhanced HIPC in 1999, which provided deeper debt relief, and linked the provision of that relief to the **poverty** reduction efforts of the borrower government.

Although campaigns such as Jubilee 2000 take some credit for the improved terms of debt relief, political economy has also played a role. When the debt crisis began in 1982, the US financial system was at risk from the reckless overexposure of key US banks to a small number of highly indebted countries. If one of these countries had defaulted the US could have experienced a financial crisis throwing the economy into depression. The US government thus had a strong interest in the resolution of the crisis, and did so in a way that put the main costs on developing countries, banks often receiving back more rather than less money as a result. By 1989, the risk was gone, the debt having been largely shifted to multilateral banks and laying in low-income countries. The IMF and World Bank wanted their own loans to be repaid. First, this was ensured by shifting the burden to the taxpayers of Western countries through Fifth Dimension. This inequitable system was not providing sufficient relief for countries to attain sustained growth paths, so the need for deeper relief was finally accepted. However, although more generous that what had been hitherto available, Enhanced HIPC far from drops the debt. A substantial burden remains for countries that successfully "complete" HIPC, especially as they are required to take more IMF and World Bank loans as part of their participation in the program.

See also: adjustment with a human face; debt; debt crisis; Heavily Indebted Poor Countries (HIPC) initiative; International Monetary Fund (IMF); multilateral development banks (MDBs); structural adjustment; World Bank

Further reading

Oxfam (2001) *Debt Relief: Still Failing the Poor*, Oxford: Oxfam. http://www.oxfamamerica.org/news/art557.html

World Bank HIPC website: http://www.worldbank.
org/hipc

HOWARD WHITE

decent work deficit

Decent work means productive work in which
rights are protected, which generates an adequate
income, with adequate social protection. It also
means sufficient work, in the sense that all should
have full access to income-earning opportunities.
The first Report of the Director-General of the
International Labor Organization (ILO), Juan
Somavia, in March 1999 proposed that the primary
goal for the ILO should be securing decent work for
women and men everywhere. This led to a budgetary reorganization of the ILO from involvement
in thirty-nine major programs to a concentration
on four strategic objectives: fundamental principles
and rights at work; **employment**; social protection; and social dialog. Rather than setting up a
single definition of decent work as a target for
improvement, the 1999 Report suggested a relative
concept, as "all societies have a notion of decent
work, but the quality of employment can mean
many different things" (p. 4).

The term decent work deficit refers to how far
individuals or groups are in deficit from the relevant concept of decent work and the causes of the
deficit. For example, women in many developing
countries are in deficit in relation to basic labor
rights (see **labor rights and standards**) because of
sexual discrimination and a concentration in low
wage jobs (see **gender division of labor**). Job
segregation affects their freedom of choice of
employment, leading to a deficit here. A high
proportion is self-employed or works in domestic
service and generally does not receive social protection. As they generally do not belong to **trade
unions**, they are also likely to be excluded from
participation in social dialog. An analysis of
the nature of the deficit can help to formulate the
necessary policies to reduce it.

There have been a number of reports and publications on decent work deficit since 1999, but it
is still too early to judge whether the concept is
inspirational rather than operational. Furthermore,
it is not clear whether this approach will lead to a
significant improvement in the ILO's attempts to
focus on and solve problems in **labor markets**. As
with all ILO initiatives, much depends on the
willingness of the members of the tripartite structure to implement the necessary policies.

See also: employment; International Labor Organization (ILO); labor markets; labor rights and
standards; livelihoods; unemployment

Further reading

ILO (1999) *Decent Work*, Geneva: International
Labor Office.
ILO (2001) *Reducing the Decent Work Deficit: a
Global Challenge*, Geneva: International Labor
Office.
Thomas, J. (2002) *Decent Work in the Informal
Sector: Latin America*, Geneva: International
Labor Office, Employment Sector Paper No.
2002/12.

JIM THOMAS

decentralization

Decentralization involves the transfer of power
(decision-making and implementation) and
resources (financial and juridical) from a central
government to lower levels of the politico-
administrative system and/or to non-state organizations. Several types of decentralization arise
because the degree, the content and the receiving
actor of this transfer can in practice differ significantly. In general, four types of decentralization
are distinguished.

First, deconcentration refers to the transfer of
power and resources from central government
to local branches of the central bureaucratic
apparatus. This involves just the spatial displacement of power but does not affect the degree of
centralization in the politico-administrative system. Shifting the physical location of central
government institutions and parliament to a different city is an example of deconcentration (as in
Chile, from Santiago to Valparaiso). This form of

decentralization is also known as administrative decentralization.

Second, delegation is the transfer of specific tasks to **local government** institutions or semi-autonomous organizations, which have been created specifically for these tasks, but which remain accountable to the central government. Sometimes delegation is also known as functional decentralization. The creation of a parastatal organization specifically for activities related to nuclear research programs or large infrastructural projects are examples of delegation.

Third, devolution, also known as democratic or fiscal decentralization, is decentralization in its most commonly understood appearance. Compared to deconcentration and delegation, it covers a much broader and more intensive transfer of power and resources to regional or local political authorities. Whereas in the first two forms of decentralization there is still an upward-oriented **accountability**, in the case of devolution there is a downward-oriented accountability.

Fourth, privatization (see **privatization and liberalization**) is the transfer of the responsibility for the delivery of specific services to the private sector. Actually, this form of decentralization is more commonly understood as deregulation. As such, it is the ultimate form of decentralization, as all power is transferred from the state (see **state and state reform**) to non-state actors, but, at the same time, it no longer involves the transfer of resources.

The idea of decentralization is not new as such. Already in colonial times, especially under regimes of indirect rule, the colonial powers relied on decentralization to control their empires. After the **decolonization** period of the 1960s, however, and specifically from the beginning of the 1990s onwards, decentralization is considered to be an important strategy towards democratization (see **democracy**). The decentralization discourse is based on two principles, which are not *per se* naturally compatible, i.e. efficiency and equity. It is assumed that decentralization improves efficiency on the basis that the central bureaucratic apparatus has grown too large (one of the characteristics of urban primacy in many developing countries), or that it lacks coordination between the various departments, is riddled with **corruption** and does

not dispose of enough information from the districts and **municipalities** to come up with an adequate policy which matches local demand and supply of public goods. This matter of inefficiency is especially at stake when the state is behaving as an economic entrepreneur (see **state-owned enterprises (SOEs)**).

Equity is being served by decentralization because it is supposed to bring the policy into closer contact with the poor, who have hitherto been excluded from adequate participation in decision-making procedures. The international development **community** (from the **World Bank** to **non-governmental organizations (NGOs)**) have adopted decentralization as one of the pillars of democratization and good **governance** in developing countries. Since the mid-1980s, decentralization in its various forms has been introduced by states which had very different political regimes (from military dictatorships to multi-party democracies) and undoubtedly also had very different strategic reasons to be interested in decentralization. It is often pointed out in decentralization literature that, paradoxically, decentralization needs a strong government to be implemented at all. When the transfer of power and resources affects the power balance (as it should) then some elite groups (see **elites**) will not support this policy change. It needs a strong state to counteract protests, which might emerge.

Various contentious issues influence the outcome of decentralization in terms of efficiency and equity. Local governments often complain that they are being given new responsibilities but not the accompanying resources necessary to be able to truly take on these responsibilities. This is especially problematic when it concerns important services like **education** and **health** care. Rich communities (see **community**) might be able to increase their own budget because they have a sufficient local tax base. Poor communities, though, lack this possibility and remain dependent upon central government funds, which are not enough or arrive too late to guarantee an efficient service delivery. Another problem is that these new responsibilities for local government presuppose the existence of a minimum degree of professionalism in the local government apparatus. This is only true, if at all, for the richer communities. Also, there is no guarantee that the poor and excluded are in fact able to hold local government accountable. Institutionalized channels for effective participation, and reliable **account-ability** mechanisms seldom form part of the decentralization package. As such, it could lead to a situation where decentralization works more in favor of local **elites** instead of enhancing equity. A final contentious issue is whether decentralization is not counter-productive for countries that historically have not known a phase of nation-building and are characterized by serious disparities in terms of regional growth, religious affiliation and/or ethnicity (see **ethnicity/identity**). Does decentralization exacerbate these problems or can it live up to its promises? The available empirical evidence is not conclusive enough to provide a definitive answer.

See also: accountability; civil society; community; local government; municipalities; new public management (NPM); politics; privatization and liberalization; public management; public sector; state and state reform

Further reading

Crook, R. and Sverrisson, A. (2001) *Decentralization and Poverty-Alleviation in Developing Countries: A Comparative Analysis or, Is West Bengal Unique?*, Brighton: IDS Working Paper 130.

van Oosterhout, F. (2002) *Moving Targets. Towards Monitoring Democratic Decentralization*, Amsterdam: Royal Tropical Institute.

Nickson, R. (1995) *Local Government in Latin America*, Boulder: Lynn Rienner.

Ribot, J. (2002) *African Decentralization. Local Actors, Powers and Accountability*, Geneva: UNRISD (Democracy, Governance and Human Rights: paper 8).

FRANS J. SCHUURMAN

Declaration on Fundamental Principles and Rights at Work

The *Declaration on Fundamental Principles and Rights at Work* was adopted by the International Labor Conference of the **International Labor**

Organization (ILO) in June 1998. It maintains that all member states (see **state and state reform**) of the ILO have an obligation arising from their membership to the organization to respect, promote and realize fundamental principles and rights at work. These four principles and rights stem from eight fundamental conventions of the ILO and regard (1) **freedom of association** and the effective recognition of the right to collective bargaining; (2) the elimination of all forms of forced or compulsory labor; (3) the abolition of **child labor**; and (4) the elimination of discrimination in respect of **employment** and occupation. As well as identifying clearly what the core labor standards are, the Declaration provides a twofold follow-up mechanism, the aim of which is to help the implementation of the four fundamental principles and rights at work in all member states. The Declaration is considered one of the most important developments in **labor rights and standards**.

See also: child labor; freedom of association; International Labor Organization (ILO); labor rights and standards; slavery; trade unions

Further reading

Langille, B. (1999) "The ILO and the New Economy: Recent Developments," *International Journal of Comparative Labor Law and Industrial Relations* 15: 229–57.

CLAIRE LAHOVARY

decolonization

Decolonization is the term used to describe the end of a period of empire (or colonialism: see **colonialism, history of; colonialism, impacts of**), and the emergence of new, locally determined forms of government and **governance**. The process of decolonization does not simply occur at the point when an imperial power formally leaves a colony, but can influence events long after the point of transition. "Decolonization" usually refers to the political process of transition, and overlaps with the similar term, **postcolonialism**, which generally refers to the cultural legacy of empire on identity and discourses.

Between 1800 and 1878, European rule, including former colonies in North and South America, increased from 35 percent to 67 percent of the earth's land surface, adding another 18 percent between 1875 and 1914, the period of "formal colonialism." In the last three decades of the nineteenth century, European states thus added 10 million square miles of territory and 150 million people to their areas of control, an area commonly referred to as one fifth of the earth's land surface and one tenth of its people. Decolonization is in many ways a process of recognizing that the time to depart is overdue and (perhaps) that one should never have been there in the first place. This realization (and the responses it led to in many former imperial powers) took many forms: Portugal's departure from Africa, for example, was more akin to mass deportation and was in many ways an entirely different psychological experience to those of many other European imperial powers.

Decolonization is partly about working through and coming to terms with the cultural, social, political and economic legacies of colonial power relations. Abdou Maliq Simone (1998) has explored the legacies of colonialism for African cities and the social spaces of urban areas, arguing that they were not designed with African "rhythms and sensibilities" in mind but they have been transformed as physical and cultural spaces through the process of decolonization.

Decolonization has often started with the acknowledgment that colonial states and bureaucracies were constructed directly from a program of colonial conquest. The colonial state was thus coercive and centralized since its power ultimately depended on force, control and subordination. Each state set up the administration and infrastructure needed to rule the colonies at minimal cost to the empire, and all were charged with exploiting the resources of their colonies and attempting to "civilize" their colonial subjects in their own image. During the move to decolonization, however, many anti-colonial nationalists (especially in Africa) identified the capture of state power as a primary objective. Nationalists believed that what was wrong with the colonial state was its mission (colonialism) not its bureaucracy. The

idea was that if you changed the ideology then the machinery of the colonial state could still be used for nationalist ends (e.g. development). But in many postcolonial states, this machinery and infrastructure has been inherited from colonial states but has not always been fully transformed.

Decolonization is thus partly about a recognition that the colonial state rested on force for its legitimacy, a legitimacy which was thus highly superficial with the colonial state creating political communities (see **community**), defining the rules of the game, defining the boundaries of the community and creating power structures to dominate it (also see **power and discourse; postcolonialism**). The colonial state was also the dominant economic actor, creating a currency, levying taxes, introducing crops, developing markets, controlling labor and production. Postcolonial states have thus had to create new methods of garnering legitimacy because independence changed the notion of state legitimacy and created new principles of **accountability**.

The legitimacy of the postcolonial state has depended in part on the perception of the nationalists as the embodiment of the (newly independent) nation and of its values. Independence also changed the relations between the individual and the state (see **state and state reform**). On one hand, all legal, racial and political restrictions were swept away to ensure that the state belonged to everyone. But on the other hand, it acquired new obligations *vis-à-vis* its new citizens. Whilst the colonial state could call on the imperial government for resources and support, postcolonial states have much less capacity to mobilize resources on such a scale.

The cultural legacies of colonialism (see **colonialism, history of; colonialism, impacts of**) also bequeathed deep social and cultural divisions in many societies. In the process of decolonization "development" became an over-arching objective for many nationalist movements and the independent states they tried to form. It is important however to avoid the argument that because colonization was "bad" then decolonization must automatically be "good," just as we need to avoid seeing development itself in such simplistic ways. What is clear, however, is that contemporary development theory and practice needs to be "decolonized" given the important legacies of imperial assumptions and mindsets in framing global development thinking today. Following the work of a group of Indian historians known as the "Subaltern Studies Group," it has been argued that the project of decolonization involves the recovery of the lost historical voices of the marginalized, the oppressed and the dominated (see **marginalization**). On the other hand "decolonization" is about mental revolutions, about "decolonizing the mind," about the realization that "we too might have a story to tell." Some critics have argued that European languages need to be replaced with local languages in order for this new **empowerment** to be encouraged fully.

More than eighty nations whose peoples were formerly under colonial rule have joined the **United Nations** as sovereign independent states since it was founded in 1945. The United Nations has played an important role in that historic change and in shaping the interconnections between projects of decolonization and development. Today, there are still sixteen Non-Self-Governing Territories remaining, and the current administering powers include France, New Zealand, the UK and the USA.

See also: colonialism, history of; colonialism, impacts of; neocolonialism; politics; postcolonialism; state and state reform

Further reading

Guha, R. and Spivak, G. (1988) *Selected Subaltern Studies*, Delhi, India: Oxford University Press.
Pieterse, J. and Parekh B. (eds) (1995) *Decolonization of the Imagination: Culture, Knowledge and Power*, New York: St Martin's Press.
Thiongo, N. (1986) *Decolonizing the Mind*, London: Heinemann.
Young, R. (2001) *Postcolonialism: An Historical Introduction*, Blackwell, Oxford.

MARCUS POWER

deep ecology

Deep ecology is a philosophical and political approach to environmentalism that believes in the fragility, equilibrium, and innate value of the biophysical world. The term was coined by the Norwegian philosopher Arne Naess in 1973. Naess considered that mainstream **environmental** movements had tended to concentrate upon the symptoms of the environmental crisis rather than its causes. In lobbying for legal and political solutions to the destruction of the environment, they had achieved little more than applying superficial, temporary remedies to the problem, and environmental devastation was only being postponed. This "shallow ecology" was contrasted with deep ecology that called for a transformation in the way in which humans relate to nature. Deep ecology is opposed to a mechanistic worldview that values the natural world because of the resources it provides to serve human ends. Instead, it insists that all life is interconnected and has equal as well as intrinsic value. This "eco-centric" ethic supports a holistic worldview that challenges anthropocentric attitudes towards nature (see **ethics**).

Deep ecology draws upon earlier movements and traditions including romanticism, Eastern religions, such as Taoism and Buddhism, as well as the writings of individuals such as Henry David Thoreau, Aldo Leopold and Baruch Spinoza (see **religion**). Some observers question, however, the extent to which deep ecology is a consistent body of thought. Its sources are diverse and it is a product of emotive as well as rational thought, with adherents commonly claiming that their belief in deep ecological values is a result of a personal and even quasi-sacred relationship to the Earth. Deep ecology evolved from the experiences of those engaged in environmental direct action, the most prominent manifestation being the *Earth First!* movement that emerged in the early 1980s in the USA, and which became famous for direct intervention by activists at construction sites in threatened areas.

While the action orientation of deep ecology can be seen as a strength, its system of environmental thought has been challenged for being irrational and mystical, as well as implicitly anti-people. Critics perceive that its Malthusian stance on population (see **Malthusian demography**) and its emphasis upon wilderness preservation, work to the disadvantage of the poor in developing countries by blaming **population** growth for environmental destruction and seeking to evict the poor from their lands in an attempt to preserve designated areas of wilderness. Moreover, critics ask, "why should we agree that all life has equal value?" Where deep ecology considers that this idea of biocentric equality reflects a non-anthropocentric attitude towards the natural world, it fails to realize that this ideology is itself the product of human constructions.

See also: biodiversity; ecodevelopment; environment; environmental movements; ethics; *Limits to Growth* report (1972); Malthusian demography

Further reading

Bradford, G. (1989) *How Deep is Deep Ecology?* Hadley MA: Times Change Press.

Devall, B. and G. Sessions (1985) *Deep Ecology: Living as if Nature Mattered*, Salt Lake City: Perguine Smith.

Naess, A. (1973) "The Shallow and the Deep, Long-range Ecology Movement: A Summary," *Inquiry* 16: 95–100.

EMMA TOMALIN

deforestation

Deforestation refers either to total loss of previous tree cover or to the degradation of forest ecosystems. While deforestation is imaged as a devastating problem in many regions, problems of definition, measurement and interpretation have sometimes led to exaggeration and misunderstanding of actual vegetation changes. Deforestation has many inter-related causes and consequences, ecological and socio-economic, operating at various scales.

Forests can be defined as vegetation dominated by trees, without a grassy under-storey, and which has not recently been farmed. They can be temperate or tropical, the latter ranging from humid evergreen (rain forest) and semi-deciduous types to semi-arid "dry forests" such as the *miombo* woodlands of East Africa. The extent and rate of deforestation can appear very differently depending on how it is defined and assessed. For instance, environmentalists and ecologists usually define deforestation broadly, as forest ecosystem degradation through loss of biomass and ecosystem services. Those focusing on economic forestry, by contrast, distinguish forest degradation from true deforestation in which forest is entirely converted to other land uses, or canopy cover reduced below a threshold percentage.

Debate also turns on the baselines from which to assess deforestation. Many national and international statistics portray a massive and relentless loss of "original" forest cover. "Original" is sometimes assumed equivalent to "potential" forest cover, by assuming that where today's climate and soil conditions could support forest, they once did. Alternatively, "original forest" is taken to be the forest believed to have been extant about 8,000 years ago, after the last Ice Age, and "before human disturbance." Disturbance is usually portrayed as accelerating over recent centuries and decades. However, these assumptions are problematic. First, written and oral historical sources describing vegetation and landscapes frequently prove to falsify assumptions of intact forest. In West Africa, for instance, parts of the forest zone assumed to have been forested in the nineteenth century were actually under farmland or savanna then; failure to recognize this has led international agencies to exaggerate twentieth-century deforestation nearly threefold. Second, and more fundamentally, evidence from social and climate history undermines the very concept of an "original" natural forest baseline, showing that there have been episodes of deep climatic deterioration at different times since the pre-agricultural period, in which forests contracted due to climatic, not human influence, and then recovered. Recent perspectives thus question the image of deforestation as a one-way decline in natural vegetation, instead highlighting continuous dynamism involving afforestation and vegetation quality changes as well as forest loss. This suggests the need for historical precision on exactly what vegetation changes have occurred, where and how. Such time series can be constructed by comparing recent remotely-sensed imagery and ground surveys with aerial photographs, and documentary and oral historical sources from earlier periods.

Where deforestation does occur there are many causes. These vary from place to place and interact in specific combinations. It is usual to distinguish between proximate and underlying causes. The main proximate causes are usually taken to be **shifting cultivation**, the expansion of commercial **agriculture**, and logging, especially where logging (see **logging/timber trade**) roads open up entry for farmers to colonize the forest. Underlying causes range from demographic factors, including **population** growth and **migration** into forest areas, to economic factors, including **poverty**, income growth, external indebtedness, interest rates and land market values. Also of key importance are the national and international policies that influence these trends. Agricultural incentive policies, trade policies, timber royalty and concession policies which underprice timber, and tenure policies which give immigrant forest farmers little incentive to conserve resources, have all been identified as hastening deforestation in specific circumstances. Other processes and factors can increase or enrich tree or forest cover, such as certain local land use practices, or population shifts linked to conflict. The causes of forest cover and quality change thus need to be understood in terms of how social, economic and political processes interact with ecological and climatic ones to create specific pathways of vegetation change.

Deforestation is thought to matter because of its range of consequences. Locally, these can include the loss of **non-timber forest products (NTFPs)** (e.g. food, fuel, medicines) important to **sustainable livelihoods**; the reduction of places and opportunities to express cultural and spiritual values, and associated loss of lifestyle, such as for **indigenous people**s; and the loss of important services such as shade, soil protection and the conservation of water sources (see **watershed management**). At the same time, deforestation can be valued by local people, for instance to open up land for farming, reduce crop pest populations, or expel unwanted spirits. Regionally, deforestation has been thought to threaten hydrology and climate, although these links are disputed. Nationally, deforestation many imply loss of timber resources or other **natural capital** important to a country's economy and **sustainable development**. Internationally-felt consequences of deforestation include threats to global **biodiversity** and the loss of carbon sinks important in global

climate change. Because differently-located people and **institutions** feel and value these consequences differently, and because there can be trade-offs between them (e.g. forest biodiversity protection can reduce local access to forest products), whether and how to address deforestation are matters of highly contested social and political choice.

See also: biodiversity; climate change; community forestry; environment; indigenous people; Joint Forest Management (JFM); logging/timber trade; narratives of development; non-timber forest products (NTFPs); shifting cultivation; sustainable development; watershed management

Further reading

Barraclough, S. and Ghimire, K. (eds) (1995) *Forests and Livelihoods: The Social Dynamics of Deforestation in Developing Countries*, Geneva: UNRISD.

Fairhead, J. and Leach, M. (1998) *Reframing Deforestation: Global Analyses and Local Realities – Studies in West Africa*, London: Routledge.

Colchester, M. and Lohmann, L. (eds) (1993) *The Struggle for Land and the Fate of the Forests*, World Rainforest Movement, The Ecologist and Zed.

Rietbergen, S. (ed.) (1994) *The Earthscan Reader in Tropical Forestry*, London: Earthscan.

MELISSA LEACH

democracy

Democracy, in its most general sense, refers to a system of government that is based on, and representative of, the views of the constitutive people. It is usually held up as the most desirable and accountable form of government (see **accountability**). There are, of course, many meanings to the word, and many ways of achieving it. The most common understanding of democracy today is a procedural definition that refers primarily to the formal sphere of politics. Some consider, however, that the meaning of democracy is a site of discursive struggle and reflects the social, theoretical, and political context in which the term is being used. Alternative understandings include, for example, "substantive" and "popular," or "radical" democracy.

The emergence of a procedural definition of democracy can be traced to the work of Joseph Schumpeter's (1942) book, *Capitalism, Socialism and Democracy*. Schumpeter replaced classical definitions of democracy such as "the will of the people" and "the common good" with a notion of "the democratic method." This understanding of democracy posits that for a society to be considered democratic, it should be governed by a particular set of procedures. These include periodic elections with universal suffrage; primary political decision-making carried out by elected officials; rules and procedures that maintain accountability (a rule of law); and freedom of expression and association (see **freedom of association**). While these qualities can be understood as forming a minimalist definition of democracy, they provide clear markers for evaluating whether a society is democratic or not. This definition of formal, procedural democracy also has a close affinity with Robert Dahl's notion of "polyarchy." By defining such a political system as "polyarchy" rather than democracy, Dahl suggests, nonetheless, that such a political system falls short of the democratic ideal of a fully participatory system in which citizens can deliberate about specific issues. This shortfall is linked to the scale of contemporary democracy; deliberation among all citizens with regard to particular issues is not feasible at the nation-state scale.

In contrast to the definitional clarity and hegemonic status of procedural, formal democracy, other interpretations of democracy exist that partially critique procedural, formal democracy as being either insufficient or misguided. These alternative understandings of democracy demonstrate the influence of Marxist, socialist, feminist, and republican approaches to **politics**. There is less consensus about these projects, making it somewhat difficult to construct a precise categorization. Nonetheless, it remains useful to draw some distinctions between these different perspectives on democracy.

In democratic theory, procedural democracy is often contrasted to a "substantive" understanding of democracy. "Substantive" democracy typically places particular emphasis on outcomes such as social and economic equality, fairness, and **social justice**. Certain democratic theorists draw such a distinction with procedural democracy to argue that systemic inequalities (e.g. **gender**, class, race (see **race and racism**)) exist that prevent equal access on the part of all citizens to a system of formal, procedural democracy. In such a situation, formal procedural democracy can reinforce systemic **inequality**, rather providing the means for ameliorating such an order. As a result, substantive outcomes provide an important alternative tool for evaluating democracy.

If definitions of substantive democracy are built around a particular set of outcomes, then often times the state is seen as a key site through which those outcomes can be achieved. By contrast, another set of democratic theories centers on the political qualities and nature of the terrain of **civil society**. These theories are referred to at times as "popular democracy" or "radical democracy." To a large degree this group of theories is concerned with putting the full practice of **citizenship** and citizen **governance** at the center of a democratic project. In this view, citizenship is not necessarily or solely defined as a juridical set of rights or obligations, but instead as active, political engagement. Struggles over what might be considered issues of common concern, the formation of new social and cultural identities, and qualities such as reciprocity, dialog and mutual respect can be considered central to this view of democracy.

There are some general terms that may describe political outcomes in relationship to "radical" or "popular" democracy. They might include "recognition" (of new social subjects or identities) or "redistribution" (of power). These outcomes are linked to democratizing systemic inequalities within society. Yet, many radical democratic theorists emphasize the unfixity of politics, and thus the impossibility of specifying particular outcomes. Such perspectives support the end of hegemonic political projects, including a formal, institutional democratic order, by arguing in favor of multiple overlapping spaces and communities, the boundaries of which would always be in flux. In keeping with this, radical democratic theorists frequently argue in favor of a strong and effective decentralization of power.

A mix of different democratic projects shapes contemporary political landscapes. Indeed, one could argue the relationship between these different democratic projects is unclear and highly contested. In some cases, one form of democracy may lead to another. For example, popular democracy might lead to substantive democracy, or procedural democracy might lead to popular democracy. However, it is also conceivable that a more antagonistic relationship exists between different forms of democracy, where emphasis on one kind of democracy precludes the emphasis and development of another. The uncertain nature of contemporary processes of democratic transition is precisely about which political practices become expanded and heightened, and which become de-emphasized as democracy becomes institutionalized. Processes of **globalization** further exacerbate the uncertainties of contemporary democracy. Reflecting new geographies of power and politics, certain political movements and theories have emphasized sub-national regions and localities as providing sites for effective democratization, while other political movements and theories emphasize the importance of democratic governance at the global scale. These ideas and movements stand in partial contrast to an emphasis on liberal democracy at the nation-state level.

See also: citizenship; civil society; governance; grassroots development; inequality; participatory development; people-centered development; politics; social justice; state and state reform

Further reading

Dahl, R. (1989) *Democracy and its Critics*, New Haven: Yale University Press.

Eschle, C. (2001) *Global Democracy, Social Movements, and Feminism*, Boulder: Westview Press.

Esteva, G. and Prakash, M. (1997) *Grassroots Postmodernism*, London and New York: Zed.

Fraser, N. (1997) *Justice Interruptus, Critical Reflections on the "Postsocialist" Condition*, London and New York: Routledge.

Huber, E., Rueschemeyer, D. and Stephens, J. (1997) "The Paradoxes of Contemporary Democracy: Formal, Participatory and Social Dimensions," *Comparative Politics* 29: 323–342.

Huntington, S. (1991) *The Third Wave: Democratisation in the Late Twentieth Century*, Norman OK: University of Oklahoma Press.

PATRICIA M. MARTIN

demographic transition

The demographic transition is a general model that seeks to explain the gradual transformation of countries from high to low **fertility** and **mortality** levels (see **population**). There are many versions of demographic transition theory but there is some consensus that the demographic transition involves general stages of variation in death and birth rates and population growth. Stage one characterizes most of human history and involves high and relatively equal birth and death rates. The second stage is characterized by declining death rates, especially concentrated in the years of infancy and childhood (see **infant and child mortality**). At this point, fertility remains high, leading to at least moderate population growth. Stage three of the demographic transition entails further declines in mortality and initial sustained declines in fertility. Population growth may become high, as levels of fertility and mortality increasingly deviate. The fourth stage is characterized by the achievement of low mortality in addition to the rapid emergence of low fertility levels. Population growth becomes fairly low or negligible.

The European demographic transition occurred from the late 1800s to the twentieth century, and involved a relatively continuous movement from average fertility levels of five or six children to replacement levels by the end of the 1930s. The high birth and death rates were somewhat stable and meant slow population growth. In the mid-eighteenth century, the death rate dropped due to improvements in **sanitation** and medicine, whereas the birth rate remained high. This dropping death rate but stable birth rate contributed to increasing population growth rates (see **population growth rate (PGR)**). **Children** became an expense and were less able to contribute to family wealth. For this reason, in addition to advances in birth control, birth rates were reduced throughout the twentieth century. Populations of developed countries still grew rapidly but this growth began to slow down. In the late twentieth century, both mortality and fertility levels leveled off at a low rate in developed countries. Some European countries currently have levels of fertility that are well below replacement levels.

Developing countries began the demographic transition much later than developed countries. The transition is much faster in today's developing countries, where improvements in preventive health and medical care have significantly reduced mortality, especially infant mortality, and increased **life expectancy**. In some developing countries, mostly in Africa, fertility and mortality are still high, though declining. A greater range in fertility characterizes much of the world, but fertility declines are spreading throughout the world. The speed with which the mortality transition was achieved among developing countries has had a profound effect on the magnitude of the growth of population during the past few decades (see **demographic trap**).

See also: demographic trap; fertility; infant and child mortality; health; health transition; mortality; population; population growth rate (PGR)

Further reading

Caldwell, J. (1976) "Toward a Restatement of Demographic Transition Theory," *Population and Development Review* 2: 321–366.
Mason, K. (1997) "Explaining Fertility Transitions," *Demography* 34: 454–443.

LETÍCIA JUNQUEIRA MARTELETO

demographic trap

The demographic trap is a term used by demographers to describe the combination of high **fertility** (birth rates) and declining **mortality** (death rates) in developing countries resulting in a period of a high **population growth rate (PGR)**. This coincidence of high fertility and declining mortality is usually considered to be an expected stage of the **demographic transition**, which marks a gradual adjustment from high rates to low rates of both fertility and mortality. But when developing countries are apparently stuck in the stage where fertility remains high, despite falling mortality, this is considered to be the "trap." The existence of the trap is controversial. Some analysts predict that this is temporary, and results from a lack of progress in extending or educating people about **family planning**. Others suggest the trap is a symptom of more serious underdevelopment, reflecting a lack of **education** or local **safety nets against poverty**, or **welfare state**s that result in families continuing to see childbirth as the most effective means of securing incomes in the future.

See also: demographic transition; family planning; fertility; mortality; population

MÒNICA RIVERA ESCRICH

dependency theory

The basic message of dependency theory is that European development has been predicated on the active *under*development of the non-European world. It is related to the wider debate of **world systems theory**, which understands levels of development as a function of the global system, rather than specific circumstances in any one country. Dependency theory began with criticisms by Latin American economists of the universal applicability of classical and neo-classical economics. An appreciation of the different historical contexts and natural situations of developing countries, their different social structures, types of behavior and economies, required taking structural differences among economies into account. Raul Prebisch (1972) saw the world as two distinct areas: a center of economic power in Europe and the United States; and a periphery of weak countries in Latin America, Africa and Asia. Conventional **comparative advantage** theory argued that the exchange of central industrial goods for peripheral agricultural goods was to the periphery's advantage. Prebisch, however, argued that Latin America's peripheral position and primary exports were the basic causes of its lack of progress, specifically because of a long-term decline in the periphery's **terms of trade** (the ratio between the value of exports and the value of imports). The solution for Latin America lay in structural change: **industrialization** using an **import substitution** strategy (i.e. replacing industrial imports with domestic production, under the cover of tariff **protectionism** (see **tariffs**)).

A more radical *dependentista* position was proposed by writers such as Osvaldo Sunkel (1972), Celso Furtado (1963), Fernando H. Cardoso and Enzo Falleto (1979), and Teontonio Dos Santos (1970). For dependency theorists, Europe's development was based on external destruction – brutal conquest, colonial control, and the stripping of non-Western societies of their peoples, resources and surpluses. From historical processes like these came a new global geography of European First World center and non-European "Third World" periphery. The relationship between center and periphery assumed, for the Brazilian geographer Teontonio Dos Santos (1970), the spatial form of dependence, in which some countries (the dominant) achieved self-sustaining **economic growth**, while others (the dominated and dependent) grew only as a reflection of changes in the dominant countries. The incorporation of Latin America into the capitalist world economy, directly through (Spanish and Portuguese) colonial administration, but more subtly through foreign trade, geared the region's economies toward demands from the center. Dependence skewed the region's social structure so that local power was held by a small ruling class (see **elites**), which used the gains derived from exporting for luxury consumption rather than investment; real power was exercised from external centers of command in dominant ("metropolitan") countries (see **urban bias**). Dependence continues into the present through international ownership of the region's most dynamic sectors, transnational corporate control over technology, and payments of royalties, interest and profits to external corporations, banks and development agencies.

Dependency theory was popularized in the English-speaking world through the writings of Andre Gunder Frank. Frank focused on the metropole-satellite (or center-periphery) relations he found typical of Latin America. Drawing on Marxist analyses of the class expropriation of surplus value, especially Baran's (1960) version, which emphasized the potential surplus which could be made available for investment under non-capitalist circumstances, Frank argued that external monopoly resulted in the expropriation (and thus local unavailability) of a significant part of the economic surplus produced in Latin America. The region was actively *under*developed (made less developed) by the expropriation of its surplus product (source of investment capital in Marxist theory). Using a case study of Chile, Frank (1969:7-8) described the pattern of surplus extraction as a massive, geographical system reaching into the most remote corners of the region:

> The monopoly capitalist structure and the surplus expropriation/appropriation contradiction run through the entire Chilean economy, past and present. Indeed, it is this exploitative relation which in chain-like fashion extends the link between the capitalist world and national metropolises to the regional centers (part of whose surplus they appropriate), and from these to local centers, and so on to large landowners or merchants who expropriate surplus from small peasants or tenants, and sometimes even from these latter to landless laborers exploited by them in turn. ... Thus at each point, the international, national, and local capitalist system generates economic development for the few and underdevelopment for the many.

Center and periphery become increasingly polarized as capitalism developed the one, and underdeveloped the other, in a single historical process. In this perspective, only a weaker or lesser degree of metropole-satellite relations allowed the possibility of local development.

From this perspective on underdevelopment, Frank generated specific hypotheses for guiding development theory and policy. The development of national and regional metropolises in the periphery was limited by their dependent status – for example, metropoles such as Sao Paulo, Brazil, or Buenos Aires, Argentina, could only achieve a dependent form of **industrialization**. Real development thus entailed separation and autonomy from the global capitalist system. Similarly, Frank hypothesized that the satellites experienced their greatest development when ties to the center were weakest – historically during wars, geographically in terms of spatial isolation. By extension, regions that had the closest ties to the center in the past were the most underdeveloped in the present – Frank found this confirmed by the "ultra-underdevelopment" of the sugar-exporting region of northeastern Brazil and the mining towns of Bolivia. In summary, underdevelopment in Frank's theory was generated by the same processes that developed the center; in particular, underdevelopment in the periphery resulted from the loss of surplus which was expropriated for investment in the center's development (Frank, 1969; 1979).

Dependency theories enjoyed wide support among critical social theorists and radical development practitioners in the 1960s and 1970s, particularly in Latin America, India and Sub-Saharan Africa. But these theories have also been widely criticized. Indeed, some critics believe dependency theory is so dated it can no longer be taken seriously – one proclaimed dependency theory "is now a theoretical-political memory" (James, 1997:205). A number of writers (e.g. Jackman, 1984) have shown that dependent countries can have economic growth rates higher than non-dependent countries, or more generally that **capitalism** could develop the periphery. Behind this kind of empirical inaccuracy, some critics said, were basic errors in philosophy and methodology. Frank's mistake, in the view of economist Gabriel Palma (1978), lay in the "mechanico-formalistic" structure of his analysis that rendered dependency theory static and unhistorical. Palma was particularly referring to dependency theory's tendency to see the internal structures of developing countries as "mechanically determined" by external relations with developed countries. David Booth (1985) argued that the Marxist **sociology of development** (including dependency theory) had reached an impasse in the 1980s related to generic difficulties in its underlying social theory. The basic problem with Marxist theory, for Booth, was its metatheoretical commitment to demonstrating that events were necessary results of the objective laws of the

teleological unfolding of capitalism. Peter Vandergeest and Frederick Buttell (1988) criticized neo-Marxist theories from a Weberian perspective. Weber had criticized Marx for assuming the theoretical constructs, like mode of production, were empirically valid to the point of being "real," whereas they were actually just "ideal types." Neo-Weberian Marxists instead constructed generalizations from grounded historical work and insisted on a continuing dialog between theory and empirical evidence.

In defense, dependency theory played an important role in the critique of conventional theories – whether the theory of **comparative advantage** in mainstream economics, or **modernization theory** in mainstream developmental sociology. It accounted for the historical experiences of the peoples of peripheral societies by proposing that contact with **capitalism** led to underdevelopment rather than development. For many theorists still, the notion of dependent development more accurately describes the experiences of developing countries than neoliberal economic theory (Hart-Landsberg and Burkett, 1998). While changes in the global capitalist system, such as **industrialization** and **economic growth** in Latin America and East Asia, are said to contradict dependency theory's notion of blocked development in the periphery, these countries continue to be dependent on developed world markets, and the use of external capital (such as bail-outs by the **International Monetary Fund (IMF)** in the East Asian crises of 1997–8 or crises in Brazil and Argentina in 2002–3) might signify a new form of dependence.

See also: Economic Commission for Latin America and the Caribbean (ECLAC); economic development; Marxism; modernization theory; terms of trade; trade; world systems theory

Further reading

Baran, P. (1960) *The Political Economy of Growth*, New York: Monthly Review Press.
Booth, D. (1985) "Marxism Sociology: Interpreting the Impasse," *World Development* 13: 761–87.

Cardoso, F. and Faletto, R. (1979) *Dependency and Development*, Berkeley: University of California Press.

Dos Santos, T. (1970) "The Structure of Dependence," *American Economic Review* 60: 231–6.

Frank, A. G. (1969) *Capitalism and Underdevelopment in Latin America*, New York: Monthly Review Press.

Frank, A. G. (1979) *Dependent Accumulation and Underdevelopment*, New York: Monthly Review Press.

Furtado, C. (1963) *The Economic Growth of Brazil*, Berkeley: University of California Press.

Hart-Landsberg, M. and Burkett, P. (1998) "Contradictions of Capitalist Industrialization in East Asia: A Critique of 'Flying Geese' Theories of Development," *Economic Geography* 74: 87–110.

Jackman, R. (1984) "Dependence on Foreign Investment and Economic Growth in the Third World," pp. 211–23 in Seligson, M. (ed.) *The Gap Between Rich and Poor: Contending Perspectives on the Political Economy of Development*, Boulder: Westview.

James, P. (1997) "Postdependency? The Third World in an Era of Globalism and Late-Capitalism," *Alternatives* 22: 205–26.

Palma, G. (1978) "Dependency: A Formal Theory of Underdevelopment or a Methodology for the Analysis of Concrete Situations of Underdevelopment?" *World Development* 6: 881–924.

Prebisch, R. (1972) *International Economics and Development*, New York: Academic Press.

Sunkel, O. (1972) "Big Business and Dependencia," *Foreign Affairs* 50: 517–31.

Vandergeest, P. and Buttel, F. (1988) "Marx, Weber, and Development Sociology: Beyond the Impasse," *World Development* 16: 683–95.

ELAINE HARTWICK

DEREGULATION *see* privatization and liberalization; state and state reform

desertification

Desertification refers to land degradation in **drylands**, although its causes are highly debated. The term itself dates from the 1940s, but it took the African **drought**s of the late 1960s and 1970s in the western **Sahel**, and attendant widespread **famine**, to stir up a major international response. This included the foundation of the **United Nations** Sahelian Office (now called the Drylands Development Centre) in 1973, and its efforts to relieve suffering from drought, and the United Nations UN Desertification Conference in 1977. By 1994, the **United Nations Convention to Combat Desertification (UNCCD)** had been established, with a focus on desertification as "land degradation in arid, semi-arid and dry sub-humid areas resulting from various factors, including climatic variations and human activities." This includes reduction in quality of resources in and around arid lands, of both anthropogenic and natural provenance.

The history of desertification "narratives" (see **narratives of development**) is more complex than this, and includes many accounts, based on dubious science and sweeping warnings of the imminent demise of dryland environments and societies affected by moving sands, or extreme land degradation. Science influenced the thinking of colonial governments under both capitalist and socialist regimes (see **science and technology**), and the early UN initiatives to tended to blame dryland people for sowing the seeds of their own destruction through over-grazing, over-cultivation, and **salinization** (Thomas and Middleton, 1994). In the 1970s, meager funding was allocated to projects that focused on the physical remediation of soil erosion (many involving massive earthworks or shelter-belts) (see **soil erosion and soil fertility**). Most were top-down, state-led, and unsuccessful. Twenty years later, the addition of "climatic variations" in the CCD definition is more accurate and welcome, but it has not added clarity to a term that is still colored by "scientism" and vagueness (Warren and Ollsen, 2004). The UNCCD itself may have raised the profile of drylands problems worldwide, but despite its ratification into "soft law," it still has too little funding, and risks being caught up in bureaucratic procedures.

A rapidly growing body of scientific research now shows that deserts have expanded and contracted over geological, even recent geological time, without any significant interference from people.

The Sahara did grow in the twentieth century, but only temporarily. Much more alarming is the evidence that it grew very much more substantially in the late Neolithic, about 5,000 years ago (and stayed enlarged), and that there have been many shorter periods of expansion since. The research shows that changes to desert margins have often been sudden (within a decade), as in the North American Midwest and the Western Sahel many times in the Holocene, and in western India at the end of the last glacial period. These were all unforced by human agency. But anthropogenic causation cannot be wholly dismissed: the Aral Sea, and the former Lake Owens in northern California were both deprived of water by diversion, and both are now the origins of unpleasant, even dangerous clouds of wind-blown dust. The vast Diyala plains to the east of Baghdad, and smaller but significant parts of central Asia and the Indian subcontinent have been salinized since large-scale **irrigation** was discovered four millennia ago.

With land degradation such a central part of the present definition of the problem, it is worrying that techniques to assess it all suffer problems of interpretation and their scale-dependency is seldom acknowledged. The scientific and socio-economic task of assessment is huge, and is not made easier by repeated changes in scientific thinking. Following Ellis and Swift's lead (1988), in pastoral regions, few range scientists now believe the earlier damning biophysical assessments of indigenous grazing methods. In agricultural regions, too little effort has gone into the assessment of physical land use changes, particularly soil fertility, on crop and pasture yield. The scientific **community** is still uncertain as to whether changes in land use affect regional climate. Despite the new ideas and data (some of it now well substantiated), it is difficult to escape the conclusion that policy is still founded on a belief in the misbehaviour of indigenous farmers and pastoralists (see **pastoralism**), particularly in the ministries of dryland nations. Hasty judgments are still common, and cloud thinking about the management of environments that are more resilient than once believed, though maybe not as resilient as some now maintain.

Despite this lack of clarity, dryland problems are real. The arid west of the United States and the dry parts of South America suffer water shortages, and some salinization. The dry heart of Australia suffers from periodic droughts, a greater extent of "dryland salinization" than in any other part of the world (perhaps because its ancient land surface has collected salt for many millennia), and some wetland salinization in the Murray-Darling system. The Chinese drylands suffer wind erosion, dune encroachment and salinization (though the battle against these may be being won). The Central Asian deserts, apart from the Aral Sea, and the salinity legacy of ill-designed Soviet irrigation schemes, may also be seeing a revival of vegetation cover in many areas as state-controlled agriculture and **pastoralism** contract. The dry parts of India suffer endemic water shortages, despite major investments in canals and **dams**, and some wind erosion and dune encroachment. The huge irrigation schemes of the Indo-Gangetic plains have suffered a continuous build-up of salinization since they were built nearly two centuries ago.

In the African drylands that lack such irrigation schemes, droughts are a way of life. Plants and animals only survive if they can withstand them. The same is true of most rainfed agricultural and pastoral (and even hunting and gathering) communities, at least until recently. It is true that droughts of the severity of the Sahelian ones of the 1970s and 1980s initiate drastic changes. People diversify away from **agriculture** and pastoralism, as far as they are able. Some migrate to the wetter zones, or to the towns, and some never return. Herd size is diminished. Whole communities and livelihood systems may disappear. But, though some changes are permanent, it is surprising how few years it takes for systems to become re-established even after severe droughts, because dryland society is well adapted to quotidian **vulnerability**. Most indigenous land use systems have developed strategies to cope, painful though they often are. The successful dryland development policies, many now enacted by **non-governmental organizations (NGOs)** and **bilateral aid agencies**, are built around increasing local resilience – helping to diversify livelihood options (see **livelihoods**), providing credit for the purchase of **livestock**, or financing locally appropriate conservation efforts. The science that assists these efforts is becoming more adaptive, and is more focused on understanding coupled human-environmental systems and responses at multiple scales (Reynolds and Stafford-Smith, 2002). Understanding vulnerability and resilience, however, necessarily involves addressing the effects of international trade and subsidy on the **livelihoods** of dryland peoples, and remedying inequity and uncertainty of access to land and resources, and managing complex socio-political emergencies – unfortunately all of these concerns lie beyond the remit of the UNCCD (Marcussen et al., 2002; Toulmin, 2001).

The next chapter in the desertification story has yet to be written, but may be much more somber. People will continue to live in drylands, although a greater percentage of them will be in urban environments. They will be vulnerable now not only to the decadal droughts, but also to the repercussions of anthropogenic **climate change**, brought about by the artificial release of greenhouse gases. But due to current inadequacies in climate modeling, its impacts on dryland temperature, rainfall, and the soil water balance are not at all clear. The extreme and unprecedentedly hot summer of 2003 in Europe and elsewhere in the world brought a very worrying message, although, ironically, the Sahel and other parts of the tropical dry world may not suffer widespread desiccation. In fact, the northern Sahel has seen a revival of vegetation since 1984.

See also: climate change; United Nations Convention to Combat Desertification (UNCCD); drought; drylands; environment; narratives of development; pastoralism; Sahel; salinization; soil erosion and soil fertility; sustainable livelihoods

Further reading

Ellis, J. and Swift, D. (1988) "Stability of African Pastoral Systems: Alternate Paradigms and Implications for Development," *Journal of Range Management* 41:6 450–9.

Marcussen, H., Nygaard, I. and Reenberg, A. (eds) (2002) *Implementing the UN Convention to Combat Desertification (CCD). Past Experiences and Future Challenges.* SEREIN Occasional Paper 14. Copenhagen: Institute of Geography.

Reynolds, J. and Stafford-Smith, D. (eds) (2002) *Global Desertification: Do Humans Cause Deserts?* Berlin: Dahlem University Press.

Toulmin, C. (2001) *Lessons from the Theatre: Should This Be the Final Curtain Call for the Convention to Combat Desertification?* London: International Institute for Environment and Development (available at http://www.iied.org/docs/wssd)

Thomas, D. and Middleton, N. (1994) *Desertification: Exploding the Myth*, Chichester: Wiley.

Tiffen, M. and Mortimore, M. (2002) "Questioning Desertification in Dryland Sub-Saharan Africa," *National Resources Forum* 26:3 218–33.

ANDREW WARREN AND SIMON BATTERBURY

deskilling

Deskilling refers to the removal of control over labor and manufacturing from the hands of workers during the processes of **industrialization** and **capitalism**. It has been a feature of debates within **Marxism**. Karl Marx (1867), while analyzing the nature and evolution of work, hypothesized that there is a tendency for workers to get deskilled under capitalism. While he did not provide a robust definition of skill, his reference point was that of "craft skill." The deskilling thesis argues that the imperatives of accumulation and surplus creation necessitates that workers be deprived of any substantial control over the labor process. Deskilling weakens the use of skill as an instrument of control by labor and ensures a widening supply of workers, thus suppressing wage levels. The transition in work organization under capitalism from cooperation to manufacture to machinofacture (modern manufacturing) has been marked by an increasing division of labor and concomitant loss of skills, first as a collectivity and finally even as individuals. Modern manufacturing finally reduces workers to feeders and minders of machines.

As a counterpoint, Becker (1964) argued that the increasing division of labor – far from leading to deskilling – has created a plethora of specialized skills. Thus, the division of labor creates opportunities for individuals to postpone participation in labor markets and acquire those skills. Expansion of higher education and the rise of white-collar employment is adduced as evidence for this argument.

Reviving Marx's thesis, Braverman (1974) argued that organized knowledge was harnessed to control the uncertainty and variability of the work effort. Work was increasingly fragmented, with tasks being redistributed amongst skilled and semi-skilled workers, there was an increasing separation of conception (mental labor) from execution (manual labor). This allowed management to concentrate knowledge in the top echelons of the hierarchy and use this monopoly to control every step of the labor process. As these principles were applied to wider areas of the occupational structure, the complexities of scale required an expansion of the administrative and office tasks. This explains the rise of white-collar occupations, which, to begin with, required new skills but are also subject to the same tendencies of deskilling in the long run. Hence, the disproportionate rise of low-level clerical staff among these occupations. The increasing mismatch between educational qualifications for recruitment and those necessary for the jobs highlighted the fallacy of attributing the general rise in the years of formal education to a rise in skill requirements.

Much research has focused on the empirical evidence of the rise of new skilled occupations under capitalism as counteracting tendencies to deskilling. It should be appreciated that counter-tendencies, far from negating the tendency, indicate its actual causal movement and dynamic. Also, like other tendencies inherent in capitalism, deskilling cannot be realized in an absolute and all-conquering form.

See also: capitalism; human capital; Marxism

Further reading

Becker, G. (1964) *Human Capital*, New York: Colombia University Press.

Braverman, H. (1974) *Labor and Monopoly Capital*, New York: Monthly Review Press.

Marx, K. (1867), *Capital*, vol. 1, London: Lawrence and Wishart, 1970.

Spencer, D. (2000) "Braverman and the Contribution of Labor Process Analysis to the Critique of Capitalist Production: Twenty Five Years on," *Work, Employment and Society* 14:2 223–43.

AJAY RANJAN SINGH

DEVELOPMENT *see* Introduction; capability approach; economic development; participatory development; sociology of development; well-being

development management

Development management is about how development interventions are planned, implemented, and evaluated. Its focus ranges from relatively micro-level issues of management within specific projects, through middle-range concerns with general project management principles and processes, to, at its broadest, the design and implementation of development policies at the national and trans-national level. Development management can therefore be hard to distinguish from development *per se*; and overlaps with, and draws from related fields, such as generic management, development policy (see **politics**), **public sector** management (see also **public management**), and NGO management (see **non-governmental organizations (NGOs)**).

Development management was called development administration until, roughly speaking, the late 1980s. While there clearly is continuity in ideas, practices and practitioners, notably among those who write and teach about the field, the renaming also reflects an extension of scope. This extension relates both to development management's purposes (its ends), and the managerial methods and organizational mechanisms it proposes (it means). At the start of the twenty-first century, there were however still vestigial uses of the old term, notably in the conflation "development administration and management" (DAM).

Historically, development administration emerged as a field of theory and practice as the post-1945 development era got under way. Its proponents argued that conventional (i.e. developed-world) versions and processes of public administration were not appropriate for "developing" nations, given the factors that differentiated them from the industrialized world. Typically, these factors included a lack of developmental capacity (see **capacity building**), **poverty**, poor communications, and from early on, supposed "cultural" impediments to effective bureaucracy (see **culture**). The consequence was the emergence from the 1960s onwards of administrative practices and ideas designed to meet the identified needs and circumstances of developing countries. This nascent field, although it took the developing world as its subject, was mainly a developed-world phenomenon. The centers of expertise that thrived throughout the development era established themselves in the USA and the UK more than anywhere else.

As the link with public administration suggests, development administration shared the more general assumption that the state (see **state and state reform**) would be the main vehicle of development. Its particular emphasis was the building of the capacity of states to carry out their own development (see **capacity building**). This was classically through the training of policy-makers and bureaucrats; and assistance in the establishment and operation of bureaucracies at state and local levels, with general government and specific technical (e.g. **health**, infrastructure) remits. There was, therefore, an elitist assumption – the capacity to be developed was of the vital few, who would provide an institutional infrastructure that would enable a nation as a whole to benefit. There was also the assumption that foreign **aid** was a prerequisite of effective development administration. Although this was rarely acknowledged at the time, development administration was also therefore different to public administration, as it is generally understood, in that it was about developed world states (see **state and state reform**) and **institutions** intervening in the management of those in the developing world, rather than about how states and institutions manage themselves.

Different accounts from within the field see development administration having different trajectories. There certainly were, from the 1970s right through to the late 1990s, assessments of having been in "crisis," "impasse," or "deadlock." Problems identified were those associated with development more generally at that time, for example whether the state was a suitable vehicle for development, and whether bureaucrats, wanting to maintain their elite/class status (see **elites**) were actually obstructers of development. There was also a debate about the relationship between development administration theorists and practitioners. Did the former actually influence how the latter operated, or was development administration in practice merely a basket of ad-hoc, improvised and borrowed techniques?

This last point, common to almost all varieties of administration and management, continues to be a concern, as does the question of the role of bureaucrats. There is nonetheless an alternative depiction of the evolution of development administration into development management, in which the field is described as adapting to its problems, and embracing new ideas with an open mind. Support for this version was claimed in a reality in which the renamed field thrived, at least institutionally, for example in terms of the numbers writing, researching and studying it. The changes that accompanied the new identity were therefore more a consequence of general changes in ideas about how development should be achieved, rather than any perceived internal crisis of development administration. Of these, the most significant was the shift away from the view that the state was the most appropriate vehicle of development, coupled with the more widespread neo-liberally inspired diminutions of states and extensions of markets (see **state and state reform**). Consequently, development management distanced itself from development administration, and still further from public administration, by claiming to offer more nuanced and pragmatic sets of ideas about how to implement development interventions.

Not surprisingly, the starting point was an increased willingness to engage with private, as well as **public sector**s, and, as it turned out, even more so with NGOs. Besides being a proxy for the newly significant **civil society**, NGOs offered development management another set of organizations through which development could be delivered, and, in more than passing, another subject for development management experts' research and consultancy. It is important to recognize, though, that development management did not abandon the state. The emerging field of institutional development (see **institutions**) characterized the state as providing an important (if not the sole) part of the institutional framework (e.g. law and order) without which all sectors of society would not be able to make their contribution to progress. A concern for the state (see **state and state reform**) remained, therefore, but as part of a broadened development management portfolio.

Along with new sets of organizations, development management incorporated new (to it) managerial approaches, notably those which claimed to facilitate participatory organizational change, and which managed the impact of culture on organizational performance. These were applied in a range of development organizations and **institutions**, and had their roots in workplace applications of action research and group dynamics, and included organization development (OD) and process consultation. Their application had become particularly widespread in the developed world from the 1980s as a means of dealing with the privatizations and **public sector** reforms begun in that era (see **privatization and liberalization**). Many developed world development organizations were subjected to these changed management approaches themselves, but their use in development management was more than just a transfer of ideas (see **new public management (NPM)**). Additionally they appeared to offer, first, means of dealing with the perennial development administration/management concern about the relationship between national and organizational culture management. Second, their emphasis on participatory change resonated with the advocacy and uses of participation elsewhere in development, most famously with participatory appraisal (see **project appraisal**; also see **empowerment**).

Participatory development was itself also incorporated into ideal development management practice, and these development-specific methods in turn became another factor that distinguished development management from public sector management, development administration, and management generically. This incorporation reflected more than a managerial need for techniques that worked in a development context. It was also indicative of change in purpose. Development management, it was argued, was now partly defined by its focus on the elimination of **poverty**, and working with the poor.

Particularly influential in this redefinition of purpose was the work of Alan Thomas. He began by distinguishing between management in a context of **economic development** (i.e. the generic form of management), which he called "management *in* development," and the management of deliberate development interventions ("management *of* development"), that is, development management. He subsequently differentiated further, between the latter general category, and management of development interventions that had an orientation toward progressive social change, which challenged existing inequalities and injustices (see **inequality**). Thomas's normative position was that this progressive "management *for* development" was what good development management should be, but that it would have to incorporate aspects of management *in* and management *of* development (Thomas, 2000).

Thomas was less than optimistic about whether this progressive management *for* development was what was actually happening in practice. In particular, he recognized that there were contested sets of values surrounding the idea of development, which had implications for what it should look like when implemented; and among those most contested were the extent to which development can, and/or should have progressive outcomes. To its credit, development management is now very open that it is largely about the implementation of developed world agendas for and in the developing world. Thomas's particular concern in this light is that those with most power within the development process – that is, developed world donors – not only might not share his ideal progressive orientation, but will actively oppose it. Thomas's message nonetheless was one of hope, that his version of development management, management *for* development, could be achieved.

There are, however, other accounts of development management that see it as inevitably problematic. Development administration and development management have always been open to critiques applied to development more generally, for example from postcolonial or postdevelopment (see **postcolonialism; postmodernism and postdevelopment**) perspectives. But they have also been seen as having their own specific problems. Historically, development administration has been criticized as being complicit in the achievement of Western, particularly US **Cold War** aims. For example, interventions during the Vietnam War were accused of being more about achieving US military goals than achieving development. Having said that, some of its early proponents were quite open about the way in which administrative rationality would achieve the progress that would undercut the alternative vision of material improvement offered by Communism.

Others have continued to point out the extent to which individuals, **institutions** and ideas claimed to have emerged in a new post-1945 development era were actually a carry-over from colonialism (see **colonialism, history of; colonialism, impacts of; empire**). The continuity, from colonial administration through development administration to development management, was seen as indicating that at bottom exploitative colonial/imperial power relationships had never disappeared, but merely taken new forms. The assumption of the word "management" by development management also signaled its subsequent susceptibility to the critique of Critical Management Studies (CMS), which argues that all types of management sustain exploitation and inequality behind a façade of technocratic neutrality. Relevant here are CMS critiques of the participatory change management methods newly adopted by development management, which also apply by extension to development management's adaptations of participatory development. These are claimed to facilitate the cooptation and manipulation of those who would otherwise resist managerial control. Managing culture, that is people's values, attitudes and beliefs, is from this perspective an attempt at ideological conversion, in the case of development management, to a neoliberal worldview often concealed by the a rhetoric of **poverty** reduction.

Ironically, postcolonialist CMS histories of generic participatory change management have also revealed the extent of their debt to colonialism (see **colonialism, history of; colonialism, impacts of**) and imperialism. The case has been made, for

example, that action research was invented as a means of operationalizing the British philosophy of colonial administration known as indirect rule, a means of sustaining colonial power by granting the colonized a limited amount of control. Participatory group practices are also seen as in having a history of having distracted the oppressed from the structural causes of their oppression with the false but seductive potential of group **empowerment**. This method of limiting and managing of resistance, contrary often to the good intentions of its proponents, started off, it is argued, as a means of keeping the lid on African-American anti-racist revolt in the US in the mid-1940s.

Two criticisms apply in turn to these critical analyses of development management. The first is that, whatever their validity, no-one outside the tiny **community** producing them takes any notice; in particular, they have no impact on the work of development managers. The second, relating to this, is that perhaps this is just as well, given that no alternative modes of operating are proposed. Until this happens, the implication of critical analyses is that there should be no engagement at all with development management. Yet, whatever the status of development management is understood to be, and whatever is written about it, development managers do, and will continue to intervene and manage the lives of people.

See also: advocacy coalitions; capacity building; non-governmental organizations (NGOs); public management; public sector; state and state reform

Further reading

See the journal *Public Administration and Development* for up-to-date research and papers concerning development management in public, private and NGO sectors.

Brinkerhoff, D. and Coston, J. (1999) "International Development Management in a Globalized World," *Public Administration Review* 59:4 346–61.

Cooke, B. (2004) "The Managing of the (Third) World," *Organization* 11:5 603–29.

Cooke, B. (2003) "A New Continuity With Colonial Administration: Participation in

Development Management," *Third World Quarterly* 24:1 47–61.

Esman, M. (1991) *Managerial Dimensions of Development, Perspectives and Strategies*, West Hartford CT: Kumarian.

Hirschmann, D. (1999) "Development Management Versus Third World Bureaucracies: A Brief History of Conflicting Interests," *Development and Change* 30: 287–305.

Thomas, A. (2000) "What Makes Good Development Management," in Wallace, T. (ed.) *Development and Management*, Oxford: Oxfam.

BILL COOKE

developmental state

A "developmental state" is a form of state (see **state and state reform**), typically associated with the **newly industrialized economies (NIEs)** of East Asia, that has sought to maximize **industrialization** through shrewd economic and social policy, and careful liaison with local businesses. Woo-Cumings (1999:1, 16) writes:

A developmental state is a shorthand for the seamless web of political, bureaucratic, and managed influences that structures economic life in capitalist northeast Asia ... [it] is not an imperious entity lording it over society but a partner with the business sector in a historical compact of industrial transformation.

Activities of a developmental state include investment in science (see **science and technology**), **technology policy**, and **human capital**, in order to provide competitiveness through building technologies and skills, and by manipulation of import **tariffs**. A developmental state promotes neither centrally planned **state-owned enterprises (SOEs)** nor open free markets. In Japan, for example, the Ministry of Economy, Trade and Industry (METI) (formerly the Ministry of Trade and Industry (MITI)) provides structures for civil servants and business workers to gain mutual work experience. In South Korea, industrial policy was developed through regular consultation with *chaebols*, or local business conglomerates. Much debate has tried to identify rules for future **industrialization** based on the developmental

states of East Asia, although some authors (e.g. Wade, 2000) have argued that it is more important to understand the local context of economy and society rather than to identify supposedly transferable, inflexible rules.

See also: Asian crises; industrialization; newly industrialized economies (NIEs); transnational corporations (TNCs) from developing economies

Further reading

Wade, R. (2000) "Wheels Within Wheels: Rethinking the Asian Crisis and the Asian Model," *Annual Review of Political Science* 3: 85–115.

Woo-Cumings, M. (1999) *The Developmental State*, Ithaca NY: Cornell University Press.

TIM FORSYTH

diaspora

The term "disapora" describes a scattering of people, and has been associated mainly with those who had been expelled from their homeland, such as the Jews. Increasingly, however, diaspora is used interchangeably with **international migration** in certain parts of the current social science literature. The use of diaspora implies that the migrant is a victim, living in exile, and concepts of identity and belonging are of central concern. Diaspora brings to the fore the continuing linkages between origin and destinations, and draws attention to the emergence of transnational communities (see **community**) that may rival the coterminous nation-state. These "ungrounded" communities, in the sense that they have no loyalties to a single territory, raise **security** issues and bring into question the idea of the nation-state based around core sets of values. Diaspora communities may, however, be but a phase on the way toward more integrated multicultural states as **education** and intermarriage tie migrants more closely to destinations.

See also: ethnicity/identity; international migration; refugees

RONALD SKELDON

DIGITAL DIVIDE *see* Internet; information and technology; telecommunications; media

disability

Disability is a taboo in development, if measured by the quantity of resources committed, or by the quality of analysis and information. The condition of being disabled competes with homelessness and destitution for the dubious distinction of being bottom on the list of priorities for development policy and activism in practically all underdeveloped countries – and arguably in all countries.

Medically and sometimes for the purposes of legal claim, disabilities are distinguished by type (visual, aural, locomotor and mental) and by severity. Eligibility to state support (see **state and state reform**), if available at all, is confined to extreme severity in most developing countries. Disabled people are impaired by blindness, deafness, being dumb, by being physically crippled and being mentally handicapped. Impairment forms a continuum from "normal" to a range of kinds, combinations and intensities of disability, many of which are entirely preventable. Impairments restrict what people can be or do and this restriction is what is known as disability. A handicap is the disadvantage to an individual. The **World Health Organization (WHO)** estimates that 5 percent of people are disabled and that some three quarters live in developing countries. But the specificity and universalism of the medical definitions mask a science-based **ethnocentrism**. The medical classification's apparent clarity and focus on the individual is compromised in the real world because here disability is mapped off "ability," and cultures define differently their norms of conformity.

Although work capacity is the most important kind of conformity in developing countries where the economy depends on physical effort, people may be identified as disabled by their appearance (for example, "ugliness," albinism or the absence of – even a functionally unimportant – digit). Impairments recognized as disabling in Western cultures (such as mild to moderate mental

retardation, club foot) are often not treated as disabling. In some developing countries, social deviancy is understood by many educated people as a disability, as is an ascribed and collective condition such as being outcast from the **caste** system. Others are astonished to be told that economically oppressive, socially tyrannical and politically disenfranchising forms of work such as **child labor** and bonded labor are not what is meant by being disabled. Yet, others find (female) infertility or the delayed onset of menarche a disabling impairment. Conditions such as asthma and **tuberculosis**, which are medically classified as "sickness," are experienced as disabling in agrarian economies still based substantially on manual labor. In societies where people do not retire, the onset of old age is defined not so much by the piling up of years but by incapacity for work. A far higher proportion of the population will be affected: one survey in South Indian villages found that between 17 and 30 percent of rural households had one or more members "incapacitated."

A further gloss on disability is the development of a "social" model. Disability "does not simply express a medical condition but a complex system of social restrictions emanating from discrimination" (DFID, 2000:8). It is not so much the impairment, but more the way society responds to it that constitutes disability. Disability is not only a problem for the impaired individual, it is a matter of social attitudes, institutional discrimination and the built and natural environment. Common social attitudes are embarrassment, fear and hostility. Common forms of institutional discrimination include the absence of entitlement to special means to access public goods and services, especially to **food**, **education** and **health** care, lack of all of which may in turn be actively disabling. Common problems with the built environment include physical barriers, lack of warning sounds or signs, and lack of light at night. Common disabling aspects of the environment include iodine deficiency, disease ecology (e.g. polio, leprosy and lathyrism) as well as rutted paths, jutting roots, and the blinding sunlight reflected off flooded fields. All of society, all populations, are implicated in this definition of disability. At their extremes, the medical model of disability ignores all but the individual and focuses on therapeutic technique, while the social model sees the impairment in the eye of the beholder and not in the impaired person at all.

Disability is a probabilistic type of development problem – different from those which are location-, income- or **gender** specific. Just as there are demographic, nutritional and epidemiological transitions (see **health transition; nutrition**) so there is a disability transition. It takes a perverse form in that the proportion of the **population** deprived by disabilities increases with development – from 5 percent in underdeveloped countries to 10 percent in **Organization for Economic Cooperation and Development (OECD)** ones. Causative factors are the decline in disabilities due to **malnutrition** and infectious/contagious disease, and increases in **life expectancy** and survival rates from disabling accidents and diseases. The prevalence of moderate to severe disability increases from 2 percent in infancy to 55 percent in people over eighty. To the extent that development is a socially uneven process, the disability transition will display its full complexity across social classes within a given developing nation. While disabled people are everywhere used as a "reserve army" to define the normal body of a worker, the boundaries of access to the labor market and the scope of being "deserving poor," in developing countries the social and medical needs of those of the wealthy elite (see **elites**) with disabilities take precedence over those of poor disabled people.

That disability causes poverty is incontrovertible. Even in OECD countries and despite formally protective law, the vicious pincer of labor-market exclusion (see **labor markets**) and inadequate social transfers render disabled people among society's poorest. But **poverty** causes disability. The mechanisms include **malnutrition**, inadequate access to preventative and curative medical care, prevalent risks of accident and occupational injury (see **occupational health**). Impairment often comes as a shock to poor households, pitching them into **debt** and downward mobility through immediate loss of income, through the direct costs of care and the costs of future income foregone by those bearing the burden of care.

Throughout the developing world, injuries from **war** or conflict and their aftermath (e.g. **landmines**) disable significant numbers of people – in Afghanistan in the mid-1990s prior to Taleban rule, one estimate was 12 percent of the population. The privileged social status of disabled young male fighters unravels during protracted wars and is replaced by indifference. The burden of care, wear and tear falls upon girls and women and diverts effort from childcare, **agriculture** and animal husbandry. War-disabled young women face crises of un-marriagability.

The routine material and ideological subordination of women makes disabled women multiply handicapped. Women may also be disabled in abuses of their rights: for instance over 100 million girls and women in more than twenty-eight African countries are disabled by **female genital mutilation**. Though children with disabilities may anyway be weeded out, disability-related mortality may be higher among girl children and women than among boys and men. In India, women surviving childhood have a lower incidence of disability. This perverse female "advantage" is not distributed evenly across clinical disabilities: the sex bias for blindness is still anti-female.

The social and economic costs of disability will differ according to class, **gender**, age and ethnic status (see **ethnicity/identity**). When people face disabilities in adulthood they are not necessarily socially stigmatized, but their loss of earnings affects self-esteem. One estimate of the economic loss to a rural region from the direct, indirect and opportunity costs of adult disability alone put it at about 5 percent of production, on a par with estimates of the losses to production due to undernutrition in Asia, considered "huge."

As a form of deprivation, disability is intractably complex. Yet, the concept of "disability" is a crude political label akin to being "black;" and it is very frequently as stigmatizing as being called a "nigger." Development needs to be seen as a liberation from medical and social disabilities and from the systems of technology, reason and value producing them. For disabled people, it has rather a long way to go. On the few occasions when people with disabilities have been asked what they most need, they have asked for treatment, restorative equipment, access to rights and entitlements – not only transfers, education and pensions but also to be allowed the possibility of marriage and sexual fulfillment – mobility, credit, **employment** and

livelihoods. However, the overwhelming majority of people with disabilities in developing countries have had no contact whatsoever with specialized disability professionals. In any case, though many are of high integrity, not all such professionals are free from **corruption** and abusive proclivities.

At the base of the many layers of developmental response are shelters run by local **non-governmental organizations (NGOs)** and segregated institutions sometimes providing training and work – often associated with Christian missionaries or their postcolonial legacies (see **christianity; post-colonialism**). For the "habilitation" of an estimated 20 percent of people with disabilities, there is thought to be no readily available alternative. Yet, only a tiny proportion of that 20 percent are actually living and working in segregated institutions.

Community-based rehabilitation (CBR) is an attempt to provide medical care without removing the disabled person from their locality and with the participation, skills and knowledge of local people. Limited in its impact, necessarily small in scale and vulnerable to outsiders' imposed notions of **community**, it has claims to be cost effective and aspirations to individual and collective **empowerment**: "Nothing about us without us!" Innovative adaptations to CBR for the specially stigmatizing conditions of mental ill health and mental disability are being institutionalized.

Preventive policy has had a selective impact, high in the case of the WHO's lead on polio and UN programs against leprosy and river blindness; but the general state of public health and **sanitation** still leaves much to be desired. Making infrastructure and public transport friendly and not dangerous to disabled people is a development project in its infancy all over the world.

In some countries, disabled people have quota rights to inclusive **education** and to **public sector employment**. In Uganda, seats in parliament and **local government** have been reserved for disabled people, with quotas for women with disabilities. As South Africa is trying to do, these rights need to be made binding and to be extended throughout society. The UN has developed twenty-two comprehensive rights-based guidelines, the observance of which would go a long way to equalize the opportunities of disabled people. Much can be done, but mainstreaming disability is an uphill

struggle. Disability is a development problem in so-called developed countries.

It is society that is disabling as well as people who have disabilities. Development means the social change which weakens the forces disabling people, households and classes. If gender and environment can become intellectual paradigms, why not also disability? Disability raises fundamental questions about human welfare (e.g. rights and **citizenship**, the social and material preconditions for freedom, the exercise of agency and enjoyment, the question of the class-space assumed in the notions of "participation" and "integration," and the definition of health).

Disability, like gender, is a cross-class phenomenon, even if relations of disability manifest themselves differently by class. Like gender, the relations of disability are reinforced by social divisions of labor and by ideologies, which appear natural but are in fact historically constructed and which in practice are remarkably similar to gender-based ideologies of subordination. Like environmental issues, disability has a weak constituency. Like low **caste**, disability is stigmatizing regardless of economic status. Like caste, ethnicity and old age (see **ethnicity/identity; ageing**), disability is a distinct kind of passport to exclusion, intensified with poverty, but cutting across **poverty**. Like poverty, disability entails political remoteness, but the second deprivation cuts across the first.

Response to the experienced indignities of disability requires changes in public **ethics**, but if public ethics were changed and if political institutions came to reflect an intensified social **accountability**, then other vulgar development pathologies such as widespread tax evasion, economic **crime** and political and bureaucratic **corruption** would also be alleviated. If development is self-realization through social agency as well as material improvement, then the condition of people with disabilities is one of its most sensitive indicators.

See also: chronic poverty; health; landmines; primary health care; social exclusion

Further reading

DFID (2000) *Disability, Poverty and Development*, London: DFID.

Erb, S. and Harriss-White, B. (2002) *Outcast from Social Welfare: Adult Disability in Rural South India*, Bangalore: Books for Change.

Russell, M. and Malhotra, R. (2002) "Capitalism and Disability," pp. 211–28 in Panitch. L. and Leys, C. (eds) *A World of Contradictions, Socialist Register*, London: Merlin Press.

United Nations High Commission for Human Rights (2002) *Human Rights and Disability*, Geneva: OHCHR.

BARBARA HARRISS-WHITE

DISCOURSE *see* power and discourse; governmentality; narratives of development; postmodernism and postdevelopment

disease eradication

Disease eradication refers to the permanent reduction to zero of the worldwide incidence of infection caused by a specific agent. On one level, disease eradication appears to be an immense contribution to health care and development. However, some critics see disease eradication as taking desperately needed resources away from basic **health** services.

The eradication of smallpox is the exemplar of the success of this approach. It has been estimated that some 350 million new infections, with 40 million deaths, would have occurred in the past twenty years if it had not been eradicated. This is, however, misleading, since it assumes 1967 incidence rates, and significant reduction in these rates could well have been achieved without an eradication campaign.

The special features of smallpox – its easy diagnosis, the lack of any reservoir or vector outside humans, the immunological simplicity of the virus and the existence of an effective vaccine – must also be borne in mind.

The failure of earlier campaigns should also be examined. Campaigns to eradicate yaws and **malaria** both began about 1955. Both floundered on ignorance of the natural history of the disease. In the case of yaws, the fact of a high prevalence of subclinical infections was not discovered until ten years into the program. With malaria, it proved

possible to interrupt transmission and eliminate the disease only in regions where favorable climatic and human factors existed.

Perhaps an even bigger problem with attempts to eliminate malaria in developing regions was the completely vertical (or "top-down") approach adopted, with a demand for absolutely standardized (and frequently inappropriate) operations and a lack of **community** involvement.

To an extent, these lessons have been learned in the current campaigns to eradicate polio and measles. There is more flexibility in approach, more community involvement and more continuing research into effectiveness of procedures.

These campaigns have apparently been quite effective in eliminating the target diseases from certain regions, but there are grounds for skepticism regarding the reaching of target dates for eradication. In the case of polio, there are pockets which are proving very difficult to reach, especially in areas of civil unrest in Africa, and the virus may be shed for prolonged periods in oral vaccine recipients and has, in some instances, reverted to virulence.

Despite this, some would argue that the campaign to eradicate polio, even if ultimately unsuccessful, would have conferred considerable benefits. First, there is the obvious human and economic benefit of the large reduction in morbidity (rates of ill health) and **mortality** (death rates) that has been obtained.

In addition to this, eradication brings improved and additional advocacy and mobilization of financial and human resources at global, national and local levels and from public and private sources, for both eradication-related activities and basic services. It frequently leads to an expanded role of the private sector in public **health**.

Eradication may strengthen national health policy development, increase **transparency** and broaden the commitment to health. The systematic introduction of targets and indicators and mechanisms for delegating authority to districts may strengthen institutional arrangements. The introduction of performance-based incentive models and the coordination of a strong training component with national plans may provide an ongoing benefit.

Programs set up under eradication campaigns can increase access to, and utilization of, health services. They can establish surveillance as a key tool in disease control. For example, the majority of African countries use resources (including the laboratory specimen transport system) set up for the polio campaign also for surveillance of, and response to, other infectious diseases. Again, polio surveillance systems in Latin America were helpful in determining the scope of cholera outbreaks in the early 1990s, while the global polio laboratory network is a model for global infectious disease laboratory surveillance. Another benefit of the global polio eradication campaign is its role in expanding computer capacity and the development of health information systems in developing countries (see **information technology; Internet**).

Perhaps the greatest benefit has been the increase in enthusiasm for immunization (see **vaccination**) and other public health programs engendered in local and political officials by the success of polio eradication activities. Enthusiasts claim that incidental benefits from the dracunculiasis (Guinea worm) eradication campaign exceed the direct effects from the reduction in cases. They point to improvements in agricultural production, school attendance, infant **nutrition**, care and vaccination, and the establishment of community-based health education, mobilization and surveillance, and claim that the Guinea worm eradication program has probably done more to improve health care in some communities (see **community**) than **primary health care** programs.

On the other hand, eradication campaigns may divert financial and human resources from basic services and from research. They may compromise local decision-making by imposing external priorities, and even result in the establishment of parallel structures. Personnel may be diverted and subjected to uncoordinated in-service training. Routine service delivery may be disrupted.

The best summation might be that eradication and elimination activities can make substantial contributions to sustainable health development, but that such activities must be designed in such way that they provide maximum benefits to national **health** systems. Some experts suggest that, unless elimination is a step on the way to eradication of a disease, very good control is a more appropriate objective. But when eradication or elimination is feasible and an effective use of

health resources, the decision to make the effort may boil down to **social justice**. If my children are protected from having polio, don't I have an obligation to share this with all parents?

See also: health; HIV/AIDS (definition and treatment); HIV/AIDS (policy issues); gender and communicable disease; malaria; pharmaceuticals; primary health care; tuberculosis; vaccination

Further reading

Melgaard, B., Creese, A., Aylward, B., Olive, J.-M., Maher, C., Okwo-Bele, J.-M. and Lee, J. (1999) "Disease Eradication and Health Systems Development," *Morbidity and Mortality Weekly Reports* 48 (SU01): 28–35.

Salisbury, D. (1999) "Report of the Workgroup on Disease Elimination/Eradication and Sustainable Health Development," *Morbidity and Mortality Weekly Reports* 48 (SU01): 92–104.

PHILLIP PETERSEN

disease, social constructions of

The term "social constructions of disease" refers to the complex social processes through which disease, or ill **health**, are experienced and perceived. Such social constructions are vitally important in understanding health problems in developing countries, in treating them, and in working to prevent their recurrence (see **health**).

Disease refers to the usually physical manifestations of abnormality or infection by a pathogen in an individual or host. Many social scientists, however, distinguish between "disease," which is an objective clinical biological phenomenon, and "illness," which includes psychological and social dimensions. The **World Health Organization (WHO)** Charter states that health is not simply the absence of disease but a state of physical, social and psychological **well-being**. The conceptualization of health and illness therefore depends upon the cultural construction of normality. People interpret what they feel in their bodies using culturally constructed filters of allowable levels of complaints for types and severity of symptoms considered salient and important for their age, **gender** and social status. Stoicism, uninhibited crying and ignoring pain are cultural practices of social circumstances. Perceptions of illness influence behavior, including the acceptance of the role of being sick, and the seeking of healers' therapeutic help. The resolution of an illness depends upon the relationship between a person who feels or is informed of being sick in some way and a person who tries to offer some professional diagnostic knowledge and treatment.

The relationship between the patient and the healer can be as important as the delivery of treatment. Medicine can become a mechanism of social control if people are defined as ill in reference to "normality." In many developed countries, disease has become medicalized and illness has become individualized, with the consequence that a patient complaining of a non-diagnosable disease is referred to as "psychosomatic" (imagining themselves to be ill). **Biomedicine** focuses on eliminating biological disease and not on the psychological and social dimensions of illness. Many societies (frequently in developing countries) accommodate other, or "folk" ethnophysical and ethnomedical ways of being ill. Explanatory folk models of illness are used to understand why an illness occurred and to predict its course. The biological consequences of "folk illness" can be severe. For example, in Uganda, many members of the Banganda ethnic group believe malevolent spirits sent by envious or wronged individuals cause the illness of "Mayembe." The symptoms include fevers, wasting delirium or death. Patient testimonials commonly cite sudden events such as the breaking of doors by invisible four-wheel drive vehicles or heavy stones as a symptom of the onset of illness. Some patients describe hearing the surreptitious movement of mice and finding their feet soles gnawed on waking up. Treatment is expensive and impoverishes families. A specialist sends his spirits to hunt down the illness-causing spirits, whose capture may require several sessions. Similarly, "Susto" (soul loss), is a folk illness reported in Latin America. It is believed to result from the unintentional separation of the soul from the body after a frightening event. The symptoms include insomnia, loss of appetite and debility. Mayembe

and Susto are perhaps good examples of the so-called exotic psychiatric illnesses anthropologists call "culture bound syndromes."

Some illnesses acquire powerful symbolic meanings in particular social contexts. These "cultural metaphors" of diseases are often negative and lead to stigma and ostracism. The HIV/AIDS metaphors (see **HIV/AIDS (definition and treatment); HIV/AIDS (policy issues)**) provoked sexual shame in some communities (see **community**) but in others a determination to curb its spread and not allow the homophobes to triumph (see **gender and communicable disease; sexually transmitted diseases (STDs)**). In a few instances, cultural metaphors are neutral or positive. In some Ugandan societies, "mad" people are credited with perceptiveness and truth telling. Understanding local perceptions of disease is crucial to both learning about how people problematize and experience disease, and in finding ways to accelerate treatment methods.

See also: disease eradication; health; indigenous medicine

Further reading

Budd, S. and Sharma, U. (eds) (1994) *The Healing Bond: The Patient-Practitioner Relationship and Therapeutic Responsibility*, London: Routledge.
Rubel, A., O'Nell, C. and Collado, R. (1984) *Susto, a Folk Illness*, Berkeley: University of California Press.
Sontag, S. (1990) *Illness as Metaphor, and AIDS and Its Metaphors*, New York: Doubleday.

CHRISTINE OBBO

displacement

Displacement refers to the physical relocation of people, or separation of people from **livelihoods**, often by the actions of states (see **state and state reform**). It is arguably inherent to all development practice, insofar as development is a process of creative destruction. In practice, attention to the displacement effects of development has often focused on the estimated 10 million people who are physically displaced annually by large development projects, especially by dam construction (see **dams**). Criticisms of displacement-inducing development projects took off during the 1980s, and gained in influence through the 1990s. These criticisms, together with widespread resistance to large projects, have provoked many studies of the benefits of these projects in relation to their displacement impacts, the most prominent of which is the report of the **World Commission on Dams (WCD)** (2002). Other studies have aimed to understand the failures of resettlement, and find ways of better reconstituting lives and livelihoods after displacement (Cernea and McDowell, 2000). Major development organizations like the **World Bank** have responded with policies which set minimum standards with respect to reconstituting livelihoods after **resettlement** in projects which they support. Although attention to development-induced displacement has fallen primarily on large projects, the term displacement is also used to describe the loss of access to livelihood resources due to development policies as well as projects.

The emphasis on project-induced displacement and resettlement is due to the way that these processes are often the fulcrums around which opposition to specific development projects emerge. This emphasis has been reinforced by the way that much academic work on development-induced displacement has emerged from refugee studies, for example, via Oxford University's Refugee Studies Centre in England (see **refugees**). This has contributed to a focus among larger development organizations on the situation of displaced persons, often at the expense of a careful analysis of the causes of displacement. The underlying premise of this approach is that there are times when displacement is inevitable and justified in order to achieve larger goods obtained by development projects. Cernea's arguments that what is crucial in these circumstances is that displacement should be turned into a development opportunity through the reconstitution of livelihoods and communities (see **community**), have been particularly influential in shaping how large development organizations approach the question of displacement.

There is a wide consensus, however, that satisfactory resettlement has almost never been achieved, lending more force to critics for whom widespread displacement and the impoverishment of displaced persons demonstrate that current development practice is fundamentally flawed. What Dwivedi (2002) has labeled the "radical-movementist" approach to development-induced displacement has emerged through the scaling-up of many local struggles around development projects. This scaling-up is achieved by linking specific local struggles to a broader critique of "top down" development planning. This critique has found expression not only in the writing of authors linked to social movements opposing megaprojects, but also in the process leading to the report of the WCD.

One direction taken by this critique has been to reinforce calls for fundamental reform of development organizations and state institutions (Dwivedi, 2002) to increase **accountability**, **transparency**, and **civil society** participation. The WCD, for example, points to the need better **governance** among state (see **state and state reform**) and development institutions. Better governance, it is argued, would go a long way toward both minimizing displacement, and ensuring the appropriate reconstitution of livelihoods and sharing of benefits after displacement.

A broader view on displacement and development begins with the observation that people do not have to be physically evicted from a project site in order to be displaced. Displacement occurs, for example, when people lose access to resources important to their livelihoods, or when these resources are degraded. People can also be considered displaced when their occupations are undermined, for example, when neo-liberal trade policies undermine prices obtained by farmers (see **neo-liberalism; structural adjustment**), or when governments fail to provide basic services to groups living in national parks or reserve forests (see **protected areas**). Even the literature on common property (see **common pool resources**) has made it clear that exclusion is necessary for building effective common property institutions. Indeed, the displacement effects of creating new boundaries around village forests (see **villages**) is one of the major problems plaguing the widespread application of community-based forest management (see **community forestry; community-based natural resource management (CBNRM)**).

This broader understanding of displacement emerges in part from the way resistance to large development projects has enhanced our understanding of the indirect impacts of these projects. For example, the protests against the Pak Mun dam in Thailand has made it clear that the most significant displacement impacts of some dams are not due to the flooding of villages, but the loss of livelihoods caused by the degradation of **fisheries**. The impact on fisheries has since become a major issue in most new dam proposals in Southeast Asia. This in turn has forced changes in how development organizations assess the benefits and costs of large dams (WCD, 2000).

The broader view of displacement goes to the heart of a critique of the development enterprise as based in paternalistic utilitarian principles of reorganizing societies to maximize some kind of overall good. The studies that are proliferating around the displacement effects of development almost all highlight how displaced people seldom share in the benefits of development projects. More importantly, they are seldom consulted, let alone given any say in the major decisions directing development practice. The critique of development-induced displacement has become an important driving force behind efforts to reform development practice.

See also: dams; internally displaced persons; livelihoods; Polonoreste; refugees; transmigration; World Commission on Dams (WCD)

Further reading

Baviskar, A. (1998) *In the Belly of the River: Tribal Conflicts over Development in the Narmada Valley*, Delhi: Oxford University Press.

Cernea, M. and McDowell, C. (eds) (2000) *Risks and Reconstruction: Experiences of Resettlers and Refugees*, Washington DC: World Bank.

Dwivedi, R. (2002) "Models and Methods in Development-Induced Diplacement," *Development and Change* 33:4 709–32.

Feldman, S., Geisler, C. and Silbering, L. (eds) (2003) "Moving Targets," special issue of *International Social Science Journal* 55:1.

World Commission on Dams (2000) *Dams and Development: A New Framework for Decision-Making*, London: Earthscan.

PETER VANDERGEEST

dollarization

Dollarization occurs when residents of a country extensively use the US dollar or another foreign currency alongside or instead of the domestic currency. Dollarization can be unofficial, semi-official, and official. Unofficial dollarization can be legal or illegal, and occurs when people hold much of their financial wealth in foreign assets, even though this foreign currency is not legal tender. Under semiofficial dollarization, foreign currency is legal tender and may even dominate bank deposits, but plays a secondary role to domestic currency in paying wages, taxes, and everyday expenses. Unlike officially dollarized countries, semiofficially dollarized ones retain a domestic central bank or other monetary authority and have the freedom to conduct their own monetary policy. Official dollarization, or full dollarization, occurs when foreign currency has exclusive or predominant status as full legal tender. This is the case, for example, of Panama and Ecuador.

See also: exchange rates; fiscal and monetary policy; inflation and its effects

CLAUDIO O. DELANG

domestic law

Domestic law, often termed "family law," frequently expresses basic cultural values in **human rights**: it consists of the written and unwritten legal bases of proper relationships between spouses, siblings, parents/children, and often, more extended familial and household relationships. In developing countries, there may be competing legal frameworks; these may or may not be officially designated by the government. Tribal, customary, or heritage laws generally predate state (see **state and state reform**) or Western contact with local peoples, are typically unwritten, and are adjudicated and enforced by indigenous village or tribal authorities (see **villages**). These heritage laws are considered by most national governments to have no legal authority, yet they are of great importance to those who live within the minority ethnic communities (see **community**) where such heritage laws continue to be observed. Religious laws, such as the Sharia codes based on the Koran and ancient practices of Islam, often co-exist equal in stature to Western-based civil codes for matters of personal status and relationship, but apply only to those who identify themselves with that faith, or are identified as members of the ethnic group traditionally associated with that faith and who have not adopted another religion (such as **Christianity** or Buddhism). In some multicultural countries, more than one set of religious laws may be recognized; these are interpreted and enforced through religious courts or local practices. Finally there are the civil laws, which are frequently based on the civil codes of Spain, France, or Germany, or civil law derived from the common law tradition of England and the United States: such civil law applies to those outside recognized religious laws, as well as to commercial dealings.

Domestic law can be of great importance to developing nations as a basis for establishing eligibility for continuing financial support from "more advanced" nations, whether through governmental grants or **non-governmental organizations (NGOs)**. Donor nations, including Canada, Australia and the UK, often have explicit requirements for legal protection of women and children as part of their **aid** programs. **Female genital mutilation** is an example of a local cultural practice and heritage law that may conflict with civil laws meant for the protection of women, and continuation of the heritage practice can impact the decision by NGOs to maintain, decrease, or eliminate developmental support based on a "lack of protection for women."

Three international agreements form much of the international standards for assessing the development of local domestic law: the **Universal Declaration of Human Rights (1948)**, the **United Nations Convention on the Rights of the Child (1989)** (CRC), and the **Convention on the Elimination of All Forms of Discrimination Against Women (CEDAW)**. CEDAW provides a universal definition of discrimination against women, rebutting the frequent claim that no clear definition exists. It also calls for action in nearly every field of human endeavor: politics, law, **employment**, **education**, **health** care, commercial transactions and domestic relations; and CRC does similarly for **children**. Despite the fact that every nation but Somalia and the USA have signed the CRC, violations of children's rights, including **child labor**, **street children**, and **child prostitution**, are prevalent in many lands: this is indicative of the problem where treaties may not match civil law, religious law, nor heritage laws and practices. On the other hand, Islamic nations such as Morocco, which have signed CEDAW, have attempted to implement it in such a fashion as to not contradict local Sharia (Muslim religious) laws and cultural practices. Similarly, constitutional enactments proclaiming the equality of all persons are often contradicted in civil statutes, administrative procedures, bureaucratic officialdom, and religious codes, some of which may entrench the status of women as subservient to fathers, brothers, and husbands (see **male bias**).

Issues of domestic law go far beyond the simple right to marry, divorce, adopt children, seek protection from **domestic violence**, and gain emancipation from parents (see **gender and property rights**). Inheritance, filial and ancestral duties such as care and maintenance of elderly parents or orphaned great-nephews; **ageing**; **male bias** and gender-based equality such as the right of women to vote, gain an **education**, enter **employment** and live independently; women's **right to self-determination**, women's property rights (see **gender and property rights**), legal standing upon death of spouse, recognition of **women-headed households**, sex selection (see **sex ratio**) and dowry practices; **family planning** and **reproductive rights**; various other aspects of female **empowerment** and **women's movements**; parental rights; and all other matters of intra-familial discrimination, as well as issues between household servants and their masters, are often incorporated within the topic of domestic law, making this an extremely challenging area for traditional cultures' compliance with the norms of the developed nations. Issues include questions of whether there are legal, social, and administrative mechanisms in place to educate the populace and monitor and enforce implementation of laws, and whether there are appropriate remedies for those who are abused (restitution of lost property, government assistance for those who are unable to return to an earlier lifestyle due to abuse, etc.).

Increasingly, developing nations are establishing "family courts" to remove these issues from the courts of law, and direct attention to finding workable solutions rather than legal answers. Mediation, counseling, and other extra-legal dispute resolution schemes, along with court enforcement mechanisms, are essential in order to generate long-term solutions where traditional cultures clash with modern living. Governmental policies in **family planning** that penalize or reward pregnancies also may be included under the umbrella of domestic law, particularly when freedom of choice is limited due to political or **chronic poverty**, pre-natal care services are withdrawn, or mandatory abortion or sterilization become institutionalized.

See also: child labor; domestic violence; freedom of association; gender and property rights; human rights; international law; labor rights and standards; law; male bias; property rights

Further reading

Asian Development Bank (2002) *Sociolegal Status of Women in Indonesia, Malaysia, Philippines, and Thailand*, Manila: Asian Development Bank. Also at: http://www.adb.org/Documents/Studies/Sociolegal_Status_Women/

World Bank (2001) *World Development Indicators 2001*, Washington DC: World Bank. Extracts available at: http://www.worldbank.org/data/wdi2001/

ROBERT J. DICKEY

domestic violence

Domestic violence can be understood as **violence** perpetrated usually by male intimate partners or other family members against women in the home or elsewhere. It includes physical abuse, sexual violence, psychological and emotional abuse and neglect. Yet, while domestic violence is an endemic and pervasive global problem, it is also context-specific: domestic violence takes different forms in different cultural contexts and is responded to in culturally specific ways. **World Bank** figures in the mid-1990s suggested that between 25 and 50 percent of the world's women have been abused (Heise *et al.*, 1994). In many societies, domestic violence is part of everyday life and tolerated by men, women and the state as part of "normal" **gender** relations. Tolerance of domestic violence is culturally reinforced because of its construction as a private rather than a public issue that falls outside of government responsibility. Women are often socialized into accepting their subordination with respect to men, which means they feel unable to speak out against violence, suffering in silence.

While many see domestic violence as resulting from **poverty** or **unemployment**, it is more fruitful to view domestic violence as lying in the way individual societies socially construct gender relations, depriving women of the political, economic, cultural and sexual resources available to men. In this respect, domestic violence is directly linked to questions of power and gender inequality.

Since the 1990s, however, domestic violence has increasingly been conceptualized as a development issue and a question of both **human rights** and public health (see **health**). Violence against women prevents women from participating in the development process in a number of ways. It restricts or prevents their participation in **labor markets** or in other activities outside the home; curtails their decision-making power within the household; limits their ability to control their **fertility**; leads to loss of self-esteem and results in poor physical, reproductive or mental health. It frequently results in HIV/AIDS and other **sexually transmitted diseases (STDs)** (see **HIV/AIDS (definition and treatment); HIV/AIDS (policy issues)**), unwanted pregnancies and unsafe abortions, and occasionally results in death. The social and economic costs of domestic violence are therefore considerable, preventing women from meeting basic needs or contributing to the national economy. A report by the **Inter-American Development Bank (IADB)** on domestic violence in Nicaragua estimated that 1.6 percent of **gross domestic product (GDP)** is lost as a result of a fall in income of women who are victims of domestic violence, a figure which amounts to US$29.5 million (Morrison *et al.*, 1999). While domestic violence is prevalent in a number of households, cutting across class, age, **education** and ethnicity (see **ethnicity/identity**), low-income or financially dependent women are often much more likely to become victims of domestic violence. Domestic violence also has serious impacts on **children**. Children who witness domestic violence or are themselves abused at home experience a wide range of problems, such as poor physical or mental health or low educational achievement. The intergenerational transmission of violence also means they are more likely to become victims of abuse or abusers in adulthood.

A number of governmental and **non-governmental organizations (NGOs)** have worked to demonstrate the links between domestic violence and development through **education** and training; the provision of support services to victims such as legal aid, advocacy and counseling and through awareness-raising campaigns conducted through the **media** and other forms of political activism (see **women's movements**).

Women's groups across the world have urged the need to recognize the social costs of domestic violence, and a number of **international organizations and associations** now have programs designed to address the question of gender-based violence. The United Nations General Assembly (UNGAS) adopted the Declaration on the Elimination of Violence against Women in 1993, while the Second World Conference on Human Rights held in Vienna that same year conceptualized violence against women and girls as a violation of human rights (see **Convention on the Elimination of All Forms of Discrimination Against Women (CEDAW); United Nations World Conferences on Women; Vienna Declaration (1993)**). As a result, the UN Commission for **human rights** appointed a Special Rapporteur on Violence against Women, to investigate and inform on the extent and form of gender-based violence across the world. Similarly, the Fourth

World Conference on Women, held in Beijing in 1995, highlighted violence against women as an area of significant concern in its Platform for Action. Consequently, many governments around the world have ratified international agreements and conventions aimed at eradicating domestic violence, and have begun to implement legal or constitutional changes aimed at protecting women and children from violence. Some regions have passed their own conventions to tackle the question of domestic violence. These include the Inter-American Convention on the Prevention, Punishment and Eradication of Violence against Women, and the African Convention on Human and People's Rights.

These processes have placed domestic violence firmly on the human rights agenda. However, the everyday normality of domestic violence in many parts of the world, its location in the private sphere, and the collusion of sufferers in perpetuating violence, constitute the most significant barriers to its elimination. Financial, cultural and social constraints mean that much domestic violence is never reported. Many women are forced to remain in abusive relationships because of financial, emotional or cultural reasons. Even when legislation exists, a whole series of cultural and economic barriers often prevent women from accessing the justice system.

Development projects aiming to address domestic violence are fraught with complexity, given that they are disruptive to existing social relations. Attempts to reduce domestic violence through women's **empowerment** are often met with resistance from men and can lead to increases in violence against women. However, despite slow progress in many areas, mobilizations and campaigns conducted by women's groups are successfully challenging the idea that domestic violence is something normal to be tolerated. There is evidence that tolerance of domestic violence is decreasing: it is now reconceptualized as a question of human rights, and legal frameworks designed to address domestic violence are being strengthened both nationally and internationally.

See also: Convention on the Elimination of All Forms of Discrimination Against Women

(CEDAW); domestic law; female genital mutilation; gender; gender and property rights; human rights; law; reproductive rights; United Nations World Conferences on Women; violence; women's movements

Further reading

Carrillo, R. (1992) *Battered Dreams: Violence against Women as an Obstacle to Development*, New York: UNIFEM.

Heise, L., Pitanguy, J. and Germain, A. (1994) *Violence against Women: The Hidden Burden*, World Bank Discussion Paper 225, Washington DC: World Bank.

Morrison, A. and Biehl, L. (eds) (1999) *Too Close to Home: Domestic Violence in the Americas*, Washington DC and Baltimore: Inter-American Development Bank and Johns Hopkins University Press.

UNICEF (2003) *Domestic Violence against Women and Girls*, UNICEF: Florence. http://www.unicef-icdc.org/publications/pdf/digest6e.pdf

JULIE CUPPLES

drinking water

Drinking water is water that is suitable for human consumption. Standards from the **World Health Organization (WHO)** require that drinking water should be free of any organic or inorganic constituents that can have a direct impact on public health. These constituents include pathogenic microorganisms and toxic substances which may occur naturally or be the product of **pollution**. In addition, WHO recommends that drinking water should also have good aesthetic and organoleptic quality (i.e. appearance, taste, and odor), but these parameters are not subject to enforceable regulation. Although WHO recommends a minimum of 150 liters of water per day per household, only 1 liter of safe drinking water is required per day per person, while other needs such as washing and cooking can be met with water of a lower quality.

The key strategy for achieving satisfactory drinking-water quality is the protection of water sources from contamination. Pollution by human and animal excreta can be the vehicle for a wide range of pathogens (bacterial, viral, and protozoan) and parasites responsible for **water-borne diseases**, which continue to be one of the highest causes of morbi-mortality in developing countries. Providing safe drinking water can significantly reduce the risk of disease outbreaks or spread of diseases via other routes. However, complete control of water-related diseases is unfeasible, given that most pathogens can also be transmitted via other routes (e.g. person-to-person).

Pollution by industrial and agricultural effluents also poses significant **health** risks. Heavy metals (e.g. copper, lead, zinc, mercury, cadmium), nutrients (e.g. nitrogen, phosphorus) and other **agrochemicals** (e.g. pesticides, herbicides) in drinking water can have long-term health effects. These substances have a cumulative impact on living organisms, causing acute or chronic toxicity with potentially carcinogenic, mutagenic or teratogenic effects (i.e. can promote cancer, mutations, or malformations of the embryo) given their genotoxic potential (i.e. they can damage human DNA). Also, the use of disinfectants in water treatment generates chemical by-products, some of which are potentially hazardous, although the high rates of infant mortality (see **infant and child mortality**) from infectious diseases in developing countries leave little margin for alternative methods of drinking-water disinfection.

In addition to protecting raw water sources, achieving drinking-water quality requires treatment through different purification methods (e.g. coagulation, flocculation, sedimentation, filtration, and disinfection) during storage and distribution. Unfortunately, quality targets are seldom met in most developing countries, where people collect water directly from raw sources or have to carry water from distribution points away from home and then store water in often-unsanitary conditions in the household. Thus, even when the basic quality procedures are followed in the abstraction, treatment and distribution stages, contamination of the drinking-water supply can also occur owing to inadequate household storage or domestic plumbing systems. For this reason, in addition to **capacity building** and infrastructure development to enhance **water management** standards, ensuring the safety of drinking water requires raising public awareness and providing **education** to promote safe water handling in the household.

See also: boreholes; health; nutrition; pollution; rainwater harvesting; water management

Further reading

World Health Organization (1993, 2nd edn) *Guidelines for Drinking-Water Quality*, Geneva: WHO.

JOSÉ ESTEBAN CASTRO

drought

A drought is generally defined as an extended period of abnormally dry weather (usually a season or more), which results in a significant water deficiency that adversely affects the local **environment**. In such a definition, the "normal" amount of precipitation is usually considered the long-term average (mean) amount of precipitation that the area receives seasonally or yearly. However, many other factors can complicate what may be considered a drought. For example, the timing of the precipitation is often critical (to crop success or seasonal animal **migration**) as is the effectiveness of the precipitation (a few intense storms versus many days of steady rain). In addition, high temperatures, high wind speeds and low humidity increase evaporation rates, which further reduces moisture availability. It must also be remembered that droughts themselves are a normal, reoccurring feature of all climates, although the frequency may vary. For example, droughts in tropical rain forests (such as Brazil in 2002–3) may not recur for decades, while the central plains of the USA experience drought conditions three of every ten years. The drought experienced in the **Sahel** (the area of land immediately south of the Sahara Desert) since the 1970s, however, has been a source of controversy, as some analysts have argued that this period of time is non-cyclical, and may be related to the impacts of land use on rainfall patterns (see **desertification**).

Drought, however, is more than merely a physical phenomenon; it is a human concept as well,

due to the many impacts it has on human endeavors, especially on **agriculture**. For example, many climatological treatments classify drought into three primary types: permanent drought (e.g. arid, desert environments), seasonal drought (e.g. semi-arid or humid areas with distinct dry seasons), and intermittent drought (e.g. areas with highly variable and irregular precipitation) (see **drylands**). Such a classification system is clearly focused on agricultural use, since arid and semi-arid environments are only drought-like to crops with high water needs (as compared with native plants that are well adapted to aridity). Further, such a definition is misleading because even arid environments experience true drought. For example, the Mojave Desert of southern California is classified as an extremely arid environment, receiving on average less than 5 inches (12 centimeters) per year. Yet, from 1998 to 2001, no measurable precipitation fell at any of the recording stations in the western portion of this desert, and these drought conditions adversely affected (quantitatively) both plant and animal species. Similarly, both seasonal and intermittent "drought" types are part of the natural cycle of these **environments**, and should not be considered as droughts until the dry period (precipitation is less than potential evapotranspiration) is abnormally prolonged for the specific environment under consideration.

In contrast, the human conception of drought has also resulted in a number of discipline specific definitions that remain truer to the basic meaning of the word. *Meteorological drought* is usually defined by the degree of dryness and the duration of the dry period as compared with the average amount of precipitation for a specific climatic region (e.g. less than 75 percent of normal, lasting at least one season). *Agricultural drought* typically refers to a reduced amount of soil water that is insufficient to meet the needs of a specific crop. Obviously, the amount of soil water is related to the amount of precipitation, but soils may also store sufficient water to offset short-term reductions in precipitation (see **soil erosion and soil fertility**). In this definition, the duration of the drought conditions may not be as important as the timing of the reduced available moisture (e.g. a critical period in the growing season) to the overall development and yield of the crop. *Hydrologic drought* is generally defined as below-normal amounts of surface or sub-surface water (streams and reservoirs or ground-water). While this type of drought results from a deficiency of precipitation as well, the effects are generally delayed, and may not be measurable for many months. Therefore, reductions in reservoir or groundwater levels generally reflect months (e.g. low winter snow pack) or years of below-average precipitation.

Given the large number of specific definitions of drought, it should come as no surprise that there are a concomitant amount of drought indices used to quantitatively measure and operationally define droughts. These are often as simple as comparing current precipitation amounts to the yearly or seasonal averages, or to some defined threshold (e.g. 75 percent of normal for three months). These types are commonly seen on television newscasts. However, agriculturalists and others use much more specific and predictive measures. One example of this type, used by the United States Department of Agriculture, is the Palmer Drought Severity Index (Palmer, 1965). This is a complex formula which includes current weather data such as precipitation, temperature, evapotranspiration and soil moisture, that are compared with the normal values, including both long-term averages as well as recent (weekly) changes to show trends. This index works best for large regions with uniform topography (such as the central USA) and it is therefore the basis for the production of most of the US drought monitoring maps. In other areas of the world with more varied topography, or where hydrologic concerns are primary, other indices are used, but many are variations of Palmer's original formulation.

It should also be noted that the interaction between drought and human society is not solely one-way. While many human endeavors are adversely affected by drought, these and other human endeavors can also help to increase the severity and frequency of droughts. For example, over-mining of ground water reduces soil moisture (see **boreholes; water management**). Over-grazing and soil compaction increases runoff of rainfall, reducing soil infiltration and overall water availability (see **livestock**). **Deforestation** changes the local microclimate, increasing temperatures and wind speed and decreasing humidity. There-fore, the many definitions of drought that derive

from human conceptions may be ironically appropriate. In the end therefore, though drought can be defined solely by physical criteria, it ulti-mately results from the interaction between these physical aspects of the environments and many of our human endeavors.

See also: boreholes; climate change; desertifica-tion; dryland agriculture; drylands; rainwater harvesting; Sahel; water management

Further reading

Hulme, M. (2001) "Climatic Perspectives on Sahelian Desiccation: 1973–1998," *Global Environmental Change* 11: 19–29.
Palmer, W. (1965) *Meteorological Drought*, Washington DC: Department of Commerce, Research Paper no. 45.

MICHAEL J. STARR

drugs

The term "drugs" refers to any substance that is used to achieve a psychoactive effect, by which is meant a change in perception, mood, behavior or motor function. The term may be distinguished from **pharmaceuticals**, which usually refers to drugs specifically used in **health** care, although many pharmaceutical drugs are also used for their psychoactive effect. Drugs include plant-based substances such as heroin and cocaine, and both licit and illicitly manufactured chemicals such as ecstasy and tranquillizers. Drugs can also be clas-sified by effect, with a basic division between stimulants, such as cocaine and amphetamine, and sedatives such as heroin. While tobacco, a stimu-lant, and alcohol, a sedative, are also psychoactive, they are usually not included in the term drugs. Their harmful and addictive qualities deserve separate consideration.

The United Nations International Drug Control Program, in its *World Drug Report*, has estimated that the annual turnover of the illicit drugs industry in the late 1990s was US$400 billion, approximately equivalent to 8 percent of interna-tional trade (see **crime**). A common mistake is to forget that the drug trade and the attempts at its control are a product of particular circumstances. It has deep roots in colonial history, notably the profitable British trade in Indian opium to China in the nineteenth century, and in the geopolitics of the **Cold War**, where international drug control often came second to wider strategic interests.

International drug control is based on three **United Nations** conventions from 1961, 1971 and 1988. Signatories undertake to introduce domestic legislation in line with the conventions and to cooperate with international efforts at control. The 1988 convention introduced measures aimed at trafficking, **money laundering**, asset seizure and the diversion of chemicals essential in the manufacture of drugs.

The USA has historically been a driving force behind international drug control from the turn of the nineteenth century. Originally declared by US President Richard Nixon, the "war on drugs" was reinvigorated in the early 1990s with the fall of the Berlin wall. Material and technical enforcement assistance is given to the governments of producer countries. A process of certification also exists in which the US President recommends to Congress countries that are deemed to have been involved in the drug trade and therefore should not receive **aid**. The United States Agency for International Development is obliged by law to seek to support programs that will reduce illicit drug crop cultivation.

Classically, a division has been made between producer countries, largely in the developing world, and consumer countries in the developed West. The vast majority of illicit opiate production is in the Golden Crescent (Afghanistan, Pakistan and Iran) and the Golden Triangle of Lao PDR, Myanmar and Thailand. Most cocaine comes from Bolivia, Colombia and Peru. Most of this production is consumed in developed countries.

However, the producer/consumer dichotomy is too simplistic, as it suggests that the harmful effects of mass drug use are only felt in consumer countries. The drug trade is driven by a ready demand for various forms of intoxication in the developed world, where the vast profits are made. So-called producer countries suffer much harm because of this trade, and many point to the need for a reduction in demand to accompany their efforts at supply reduction. The main consequences can be divided into public health issues, ecological damage (see **environment**), economic distortion, demographic shifts, political instability, and international pressure.

Developing countries have seen a general increase in drug consumption and a breakdown of traditional modes of consumption with a switch to ones with more problematic consequences, particularly intravenous injection. In countries such as Thailand, this helped to spread HIV/AIDS (see **HIV/AIDS (definition and treatment); HIV/AIDS (policy issues)**), with over 40 percent of heroin users being positive in the early 1990s. Accompanying the trend toward **urbanization**, consumption of drugs has also increased with amphetamine-type stimulants, such as methamphetamine, now being consumed in most countries and produced in all regions of the world.

Politically, being seen as a producer means a country's problems are always seen in the light of drugs, rather than as arising out of other political, historical and economic pressures. Drugs are often wrongly seen as the cause of problems rather than an effect.

The current strategy pursued by the UN drug control agencies alongside the enforcement of the Conventions is that of alternative development (see **postmodernism and postdevelopment**). This approach developed from previous strategies of crop substitution and **rural development** that were seen to have treated the issue in isolation. Alternative development aims to create an economic and social climate in which households can attain an acceptable standard of living without needing to cultivate illicit drug crops. It is widely argued that this approach is still not sophisticated enough to be successful.

Mansfield (1999) argues that the decision to cultivate at the household level is a survival strategy in the face of restrictions on the use of land due to **population** movement and the degeneration of land quality. **Food security** and the ability to access sources of credit that would not otherwise be available are also key factors in continuing cultivation. While cultivation often occurs in the poorest parts of a country, it is not found to benefit source areas either socially or economically.

Alternative development has also been criticized as being out of step with other development approaches. The Feldafing Declaration emerged from a conference in Germany in January 2002 that aimed to bring key actors together to discuss how control strategies can be brought closer to general development policy, in particular to poverty reduction and the realization of the **Universal Declaration of Human Rights (1948)**. The Feldafing Declaration observes how in the past success has been measured in terms of reduction in illicit drug cultivation rather than in **human development** to no one's long term benefit.

See also: crime; HIV/AIDS (policy issues); money laundering; offshore finance; pharmaceuticals; shifting cultivation

Further reading

Mansfield, D. (1999) "Alternative Development: The Modern Thrust of Supply-side Policy," *Bulletin on Narcotics* 51:1–2 19–44.

McCoy, A. (2003) *The Politics of Heroin*, New York: Lawrence Hill Books.

United Nations International Drug Control Program (1997) *World Drug Report*, Oxford: Oxford University Press.

The Feldafing Declaration: http://www.alternative-development.net

The Transnational Institute: http//:www.tni.org

J. T. W. SHERVAL

DRUGS (MEDICAL) *see* pharmaceuticals

dryland agriculture

Dryland agriculture occurs in the world's **drylands**, namely the arid, semi-arid and sub-humid regions of the tropics and sub-tropics, including desert, dry forest, savanna and grassland environments. Drylands are as extensive as the world's tropical and sub-tropical forests, and just as susceptible to **environment**al change. In the developed world extensive drylands occur in the western and southwestern USA and Australia, though some parts of the Mediterranean basin must also be included. However, the greatest extent of drylands is in the developing world, especially in Africa (see **Sahel**), Asia and South America, which already house millions of people and which are experiencing high rates of **population** growth. Together with the limitations of the physical environment, this provides a major challenge for agricultural improvement and **sustainable development**.

The biggest constraint on agriculture in drylands is water availability (see **water management; boreholes; rainwater harvesting**); even where adequate rainfall occurs its usefulness is diminished by high rates of evaporation. The degree of reliability of rainfall is also important; erratic rainfall precludes cultivation, but a short regular rainy season facilitates rainfed crop production. Similarly, the possibilities for crop production and **livestock** rearing will be improved if water can be made available from wells and canals. Other environmental constraints include direct heat, lack of shade in non-wooded areas, and wind, which can be destructive to crops. Soil characteristics may also limit growth as persistent and/or seasonal aridity can cause high salinity and/or alkalinity to which only a limited range of crops and forage plants are adjusted. A vicious circle may operate because a sparse vegetation cover and relatively extreme conditions for soil flora and fauna result in a poor organic content, and so the water-retention capacity and nutrient content of soils is limited. This in turn inhibits growth. Such conditions impose limits on primary **productivity**, i.e. the production of organic matter per unit area per year, and on biomass, i.e. the amount of above- and below-ground organic matter per unit area. Moreover, primary productivity determines the secondary productivity of animal communities, though the mobility of the latter means that some augmentation of primary productivity can be achieved through migration. This is why many drylands are characterized by migratory herds of large herbivores.

Agriculture, since it comprises primary and secondary productivity, must operate within these same environmental constraints. Crops, animal herds and management practices have to be interwoven to create sustainable production in a demanding environment (see **pastoralism**). Much debate in recent years has questioned how far dryland agriculture or pastoral systems are ecologically fragile or not, or whether they exist within a state of equilibrium or balance that may be upset by agriculture (see Scoones, 1995; Scoones and Wolmer, 2002). Increasingly, analysts are seeing pastoral dryland systems as dynamic, or in a state of non- or multiple-equilibrium, where change may occur within a variety of spatial and temporal scales. Apparent short-term degradation may not indicate the existence of long-term environmental problems, and local pastoralists may adopt diverse means of reacting to shortages (see **sustainable livelihoods; environmental entitlements**).

Nonetheless, dryland agriculture requires careful management of soil conditions. In terms of crop production, drought-resistant species are very important, as are crop types that have an association with nitrogen-fixing bacteria, i.e. legumes such as types of pea and bean, and which benefit the overall productivity of a cropping system by enhancing the supply of a vital nutrient. The success of **intercropping**, which involves a mixture of crops within individual fields, and rotational cropping, which involves a succession of different crops, is improved if legumes are included. Similarly, some types of **agroforestry**, which combines tree crops with ground crops and/or pasture, are suited to drylands. This is because crop and feed legumes can be included while the tree species provide protection for the soil and so reduce erosion; they also produce organic matter which improves nutrient provision and water retention as well as providing shade for understorey crops. Such multicrop systems provide insurance against the complete failure of all crops (see **risk and insurance strategies**), generate fuelwood which is essential in these environments where woody species are limited, and provide a range of products for trade and local consumption. The choice of each crop depends on the characteristics of the particular environment.

Amongst the crops for human consumption which are suited to drylands are the fruit trees tamarind, prickly pear, date, pomegranite, cashew and jujube; cereal grains include maize, sorghum and pearl millet; grain legumes include cowpea, grasspea, pigeon pea, mung bean, mat bean and lablab bean; root crops include white yam, cassava (also known as manioc), and African yam bean; oil plants include sunflower and owala oil. Cereal crops for animal feed include Bermuda grass, pangola grass and Sudan sorghum; feed legumes include mesquite, lucerne Jerusalem thorn, various acacia species, mother of cacao and leucaena. Other crops suited to drylands include sisal, sea-island cotton and agave which are fiber crops, the timber trees mahogany and umbrella thorn, trees that provide wind breaks, including casuarinas, tamarisk and eucalyptus, while lower-growing shrub species for hedging and **fuelwood** include babul acacia, mother of cacao and gumbolimbo; the lablab bean and jack bean provide good ground cover and leucaena, pigeon pea and mother of cacao are valuable in **agroforestry** systems. As this list shows, many species are multipurpose. The possibilities are likely to increase in the future as biotechnology (see **biotechnology and resistance**) facilitates the expression of **drought** and salt resistance in other food and feed crop types. In many drylands, crop production is impossible because of inadequate water, but animals can graze on the natural or semi-natural vegetation communities. By ranging over vast areas, nomadic pastoralists can generate meat, milk and blood protein. The animal herds comprise cattle, sheep, goats and camels, which not only provide a way of life but also represent wealth for their owners. There is some interaction with crop farmers at the "boundary" between the two; the nomads graze their animals on crop residues and the croppers' fields benefit from the animal manure; there is also an exchange of protein for carbohydrate. The nomadic life is, however, being curtailed as a sedentary lifestyle is being encouraged so that people can receive **health** care and **education**.

Incorrectly managed, however, dryland agriculture may contribute to many environmental problems, such as **salinization**, which may be caused particularly through the misuse of **irrigation**. Dryland agriculture has also been linked to **desertification**, although this term, and the presumed role of agriculture, are now seen as problematic because these links overlook diverse non-human causes of dryland desiccation, or the social **vulnerability** that makes different people exposed to **drought** (see Mortimore and Adams, 1999). As with many environmental problems in developing countries, the links between human actions and physical impacts on environment are still being understood, and it is necessary to consider local perceptions of problems, and the vulnerability of different groups to environmental changes, before assuming that dryland agriculture, by itself, is environmentally degrading.

See also: agriculture; agroforestry; desertification; drylands; fuelwood; intercropping; livestock; pastoralism; poverty; Sahel; soil erosion and soil fertility; sustainable livelihoods

Further reading

Ashley, J. (1999) *Food Crops and Drought*, Basingstoke: Macmillan.

Mortimore, M. and Adams, W. (1999) *Working the Sahel: Environment and Society in Northern Nigeria*, London: Routledge.

Saxena, N. (ed.) (2002) *Management of Agricultural Drought: Agronomic and Genetic Options*, Enfield NH: Science Publishers Inc.

Scoones, I. (ed.) (1995) *Living with Uncertainty: New Directions in Pastoral Development in Africa*, London: ITDG Publishing.

Scoones, I. and Wolmer, W. (eds) (2002) *Pathways of Change: Crops, Livestock and Livelihoods in Africa*, Oxford: James Currey.

A. M. MANNION

drylands

Drylands are areas of land whose boundaries are defined by a water deficiency, often classified by the amount of precipitation received per year. For example, areas receiving less than 10 inches (25 centimeters) of precipitation annually are considered arid, while those receiving 10–25 inches (25–60 centimeters) per year are considered semi-arid. However, water availability in an **environment** also depends on evaporation, which in turn is related to temperature. For example, 25 centimeters of precipitation supports a forest in Scandinavia. Therefore, drylands are often classified using a moisture index that includes temperature, potential evapotranspiration and precipitation. An area might then be classified as arid if the precipitation is only 50 percent of the potential evapotranspiration.

Arid and semi-arid environments are characterized by small, sparse vegetation, and are the most common type of habitat on the planet, covering about 30 percent of the earth's surface, mostly between 30 degrees north and south latitude.

See also: boreholes; desertification; drought; dryland agriculture; rainwater harvesting; Sahel; water management

MICHAEL J. STARR

dual economy

The term, "dual economy" was commonly used in the mid-twentieth century to refer to the asymmetries in production and organization systems between the "traditional" (generally rural) sector and "modern" (generally industrial and urban) sectors. The term was first used by Boeke (1953), but was generally associated with W. Arthur Lewis's (1954) model of **economic development** that emphasized conditions of high **labor supply** in rural areas, and hence the incompatibility of orthodox economic models in such zones. Analysts studied the dual economy in order to understand how **economic growth** could be achieved under such conditions, and how changes in either sector could impact on growth and vice-versa (e.g. see **Harris-Todaro model**). Economic models since the late twentieth century tend not to discuss the dual economy because of increasing integration between rural, urban and industrial areas, and the greater penetration of markets.

See also: economic development; Harris-Todaro model; rural development

Further reading

Boeke, J. (1953) *Economics and Economic Policy of Dual Societies as Exemplified by Indonesia*, New York: Institute of Public Relations.

Lewis, W. A. (1954) "Economic Development with Unlimited Supplies of Labour," *Manchester School of Economics and Social Studies* 22: 139–91.

TIM FORSYTH

Dutch disease

Dutch disease refers to the negative impacts on **economic growth** and **industrialization** in an economy after the discovery of **natural resources** raises the value of the country's exchange rate (see **exchange rates**), and hence makes its exports less competitive with other nations. The term was first used in the Netherlands after the discovery of natural gas. The damaging effects of Dutch disease depend on various factors, including how far exchange rates are allowed to change; complementary investment in non-natural resources sectors of the economy; and job creation.

See also: exchange rates; inflation and its effects; natural resources; oil and gas development; resource curse thesis

TIM FORSYTH

E

early warning systems

Early warning systems are designed to alert national governments and the donor community to the potential for complex and acute emergencies (see **complex emergencies; famine; natural disasters**). Such systems provide detailed information on problems that both require a response, but also require significant resource and/or policy change, and therefore time, to deliver a response. Some of the most common early warning systems seek to predict **food** shortage. USAID (United States Agency for International Development) has operated a Famine Early Warning System for some time in select countries in Sub-Saharan Africa, and the **Food and Agriculture Organization (FAO)** has similar warning systems in place in Africa. National governments in some developing countries also have their own food shortage early warning systems, one of the most impressive being that of Ethiopia. Other early warning systems provide information about pending **natural disasters**: **drought**, flooding, hurricanes, volcanic eruptions, etc.

See also: complex emergencies; coping strategies; natural disasters; famine

JON D. UNRUH

Earth Summit (1992) (United Nations Conference on Environment and Development)

The United Nations Conference on Environment and Development (UNCED), also known as the Rio Summit or Earth Summit, was one of the most important international conferences on **environment** and development. It was convened in Rio de Janeiro in June 1992. The conference was proposed by the **United Nations** in 1989 in order to evaluate progress five years on from the Brundtland Report (see **Brundtland Commission**), which had been published in 1987. UNCED's Secretary-General was Maurice Strong, who had chaired the **Stockholm 1972 world conference on environment and development**. Expectations were high, although political divisions became apparent during the five Preparatory Commission meetings (PrepComs). At Rio, 172 nations were represented, 116 by their heads of state (see **state and state reform**). There were around 8,000 delegates, over 3,000 representatives of **non-governmental organizations (NGOs)**, and vast media interest.

UNCED adopted three resolutions: **Agenda 21**, the Rio Principles, and the Statement of Principles of Forest Management. Later, after initial failure to reach consensus at the meeting, the **Convention on Biological Diversity (CBD)** and the Framework Convention on Climate Change were also adopted (see **climate change**). These were indications that governments and other powerful **institutions** were being forced to acknowledge environmental issues, but they shared problematic common assumptions. The tone of the debate was firmly technocentric, growth-centered and managerialist – all characteristic of the "mainstream" **sustainable development** paradigm. Many of the NGOs represented at the "Global Forum" were frustrated by their lack of influence on the debate, and the failure to consider alternative perspectives on environment and development. A second problem concerned the general failure to achieve legally binding conventions, funding for the proposals, or timetables for action. In large part, this failure to make firm decisions related to a third problem, which was the naked pursuit of national interest. This coalesced in profound disagreements between developed and developing countries. Poorer countries accused negotiators from North America and Europe of green imperialism, claiming industrialized countries' newly found environmental concerns threatened the **economic growth** and development of the South. (For example, a proposed Convention on Forests was rejected during the PrepComs largely because it was seen to be unfair to some developing countries). In the meantime, developed countries were deeply unwilling to consider reducing their consumption levels, and none more so than the USA. It has been suggested that one reason behind the USA's uncompromising and often damaging stance at the conference was the unwillingness of President George Bush (Snr) to make environmental promises during an election year.

Overall, the outcome of the Earth Summit was a series of rather bland, non-mandatory, and sometimes-contradictory principles and statements, which tended to reflect the interests of the more powerful actors (governments over NGOs; **elites** over the poor; and North over South). It did represent an important event in the ongoing dialog over what constitutes **sustainable development** and how to achieve it. However, commitment and action continues to lag far behind the rhetoric, and hegemonic groups and **institutions** continue to define the agenda.

See also: biodiversity; Convention on Biological Diversity (CBD); climate change; environment; environmental movements; logging/timber trade; sustainable development; World Summit on Sustainable Development (Johannesburg, 2002)

Further reading

Keating, M. (1994) *The Earth Summit's Agenda for Change: A Plain Language Version of Agenda 21*

and the other Rio Agreements, Geneva: Centre for Our Common Future.

Middleton, N., O'Keefe, P. and Moyo, S. (1993) *The Tears of the Crocodile: From Rio to Reality in the Developing World*, London: Pluto.

EMMA E. MAWDSLEY

EBRD *see* European Bank for Reconstruction and Development (EBRD)

ECLAC *see* Economic Commission for Latin America and the Caribbean (ECLAC)

ecodevelopment

The concept of ecodevelopment was developed in the early 1970s as a visionary alternative to modernization (see **modernization theory**) prior to the genesis of **sustainable development** to promote the sustainable use of local resources to meet locally defined needs. Ecodevelopment is generally attributed to Maurice Strong, the first director of the United Nations Environment Programme (UNEP). Strong was Secretary-General of the **Stockholm 1972 world conference on environment and development** from 1970–2 and of the **Earth Summit (1992) (United Nations Conference on Environment and Development)** or Rio Conference. He developed the concept in the early 1970s in conjunction with Professor Ignacy Sachs as "the marriage of ecology and economics."

The ecodevelopment approach combined **participatory development** with **grassroots activism** and had four central tenets. First, development should be tailored to the scale of ecoregions (homogeneous areas of ecosystem with self-contained human **populations**). Second, resources should be developed and distributed along socially and ecologically efficient and equitable lines, with "solidarity for future generations." Third, a horizontal authority should be established, with effective participation of the population of the ecoregion, to oversee all aspects of development. Finally, there should be efforts at balancing human settlements with human activities, population with **natural resources**.

This radical form of ecodevelopment had philosophical and academic links with the strong **basic needs** approach and was established in direct contrast to top-down modernization (see **modernization theory**). Ecodevelopment emphasized enhancement of indigenous human and natural resources, and a Gandhian philosophy of local self-reliance. It rejected the notion of universal development, favoring locally, socially and environmentally appropriate improvements. These concepts were taken up as guiding principles by the UNEP and the World Conservation Strategy (1980). But with its broad remit, radical philosophy and political naivety, the concept of ecodevelopment failed to gain acceptance or make significant impact. Both Sachs and Strong were involved in the **Brundtland Commission** on Environment and Development and influenced the evolution of sustainable development, a concept which has largely replaced ecodevelopment.

The concept disappeared as an ideal in the 1980s, and re-emerged as a type of practical assistance in the early 1990s with little resemblance to Strong and Sachs's philosophy. The later incarnation, most commonly used in India, aims to provide alternative livelihood options to "wean" villagers away from dependence on natural ecosystems around **protected areas**. The **World Bank** and World Wide Fund for Nature (WWF) champion this form of ecodevelopment that uses **rural development** as a means to **biodiversity** conservation. Ecodevelopment projects in India have been criticized for failing to afford beneficiaries rights of use and access to protected areas and the authority to participate meaningfully in management planning. Conservationists have criticized ecodevelopment for channeling environment funds toward rural development. This new, program-based form of ecodevelopment thus differs fundamentally from the visionary ideal of the 1970s with which it shares a name.

See also: community-based natural resource management (CBNRM); environment; natural resources; sustainable development

Further reading

Glaeser, B. (ed.) (1984) *Ecodevelopment: Concepts, Projects, Strategies*, London: Pergamon Press.

Baviskar, A. (1999) "Participating in Ecodevelopment: The Case of the Great Himalayan National Park," in Jeffery, R. and Sundar, N. (eds) *A New Moral Economy for India's Forests: Discourses of Community and Participation*, London: Sage Publications.

JO WOODMAN

Economic Commission for Latin America and the Caribbean (ECLAC)

The Economic Commission for Latin America (ECLA) was part of the **United Nations** system and was established in 1948 to coordinate **economic development** policies in Latin America. It became ECLAC in 1984 when the Caribbean was incorporated. The organization has two central objectives: first, to increase economic development in Latin America (although this has recently broadened to include **social development**), and second to strengthen economic relations between Latin America and the rest of the world. Its membership is not restricted to the independent nation-states of Latin America and the Caribbean, and members include western hemisphere powers such as the USA, UK, Canada and Spain. Funds come from UN budget and voluntary contributions. ECLAC is an authoritative source of research and analysis about Latin America and the Caribbean, publishing the Annual *Economic and Social Survey of Latin America and the Caribbean*. In 1962, the Institute for Social and Economic Planning was established in Santiago, Chile and today the ECLAC headquarters is located there.

In Spanish, the acronym for ECLAC is CEPAL, leading to the widespread use of the term *cepalismo* to refer to its particular approach(es) to development theory and policy. ECLAC has long had the reputation of a distinctive approach to development theory and policy, and has been fertile ground for the evolution of alternatives to mainstream thinking. This was particularly the case in the late 1940s through to the early 1960s. Building on the earlier thinking of Haya de la Torre, the first director, Raul Prebisch, wrote *El desarollo económico de América Latina y algunos de sus principales problemas* (1949) ("The Economic Development of Latin America and some of Its Principal Problems"). This work was highly influential in the evolution of structuralist approaches to development theory (see **economic development; trade**), which laid the ground for some forms of **dependency theory** in the 1960s, and which became associated with ECLA.

One concept associated with ECLA was the thesis of secular decline. This thesis argued that countries specializing in primary product exports that were reliant on imports of manufactured goods (most nations in Latin America) would experience a long-run decline in the **terms of trade** given that the income elasticity of demand for primary products is lower than that for manufactured products. This countered earlier ideas of neo-classical **modernization theory** that conceptualized "development" as an a-historic trajectory. Given this, an argument for state intervention in order to break out of this asymmetric pattern and promote development from within was established. This entailed the implementation of **import substitution** industrialization (ISI) and regional integration. Many countries in Latin America pursued ISI until the 1980s, and the regional trade organization **Latin American Free Trade Agreement (LAFTA)** grew out of ECLA recommendations in 1961.

From the early days, ECLA analysis exhibited a distributional perspective and saw the promotion of equity as complementary to the alleviation of structural economic problems and promotion of growth. For example, **land reform** was posited as a means of reducing inflationary bottlenecks in the economy whilst simultaneously helping peasants and non-landed rural **populations**. But by the mid-1980s, ISI had been roundly criticized (both from within ECLA and by neo-liberal theorists outside the organization) and the land reform movement had largely died out (although there is something of a revitalization at the present time). Today, ECLAC's stance is more orthodox than in the past, and is seen mainly to work with market forces, rather than seek to resist market forces.

See also: dependency theory; import substitution; Latin American Free Trade Agreement (LAFTA); MERCOSUR; terms of trade

Further reading

Gwynne, R. and Kay, C. (2000) "The Relevance of Structuralist and Dependency Theories in the Neoliberal Period: A Latin American Perspective," *Journal of Developing Societies* 16:1 49–69.
Prebisch, R. (1949) "El desarrollo económico de América Latina y algunos de sus principales problemas," *El Trimestre Económico* 16/3, no.63.

WARWICK E. MURRAY

Economic Community of West African States (ECOWAS)

ECOWAS (the Economic Community of West African States) is one of the major regional economic integration bodies in Africa. It was established in 1975 with a membership of sixteen countries and a potential single market of nearly 215 million people. ECOWAS seeks to eliminate custom duties among its member states; adopt a common external tariff (see **tariffs**) and trade policies toward non-members; remove barriers to the movement of goods, services, and people in the sub-region; and harmonize trade, agricultural, energy, and environmental policies among member states (see **economic federalization**). The ECOWAS treaty permits its members to join other regional and sub-regional associations, as long as such concurrent memberships do not conflict with the spirit and purpose of ECOWAS.

The leading ECOWAS institution is the Authority of Heads of States and Governments, which is made up of all leaders of the member states. Next in importance is the Council of Ministers, which monitors the activities of the organization and makes recommendations to the Authority of Heads of States and Governments. Another important institution is the Executive Secretariat, headed by the Executive Secretary, who performs the main administrative duties of

ECOWAS. Other notable institutions are the Community Parliament; the Economic and Social Council; the Community Court of Justice; and the Fund for Co-operation, Compensation and Development. In addition, ECOWAS has five major Specialized and Technical Commissions, including those of Trade, Customs, Immigration, Monetary and Payments; Transport, Telecommunication, and Energy; Agriculture and Natural Resources; Administration and Finance; and Social and Cultural Affairs. ECOWAS is headquartered in Abuja, Nigeria.

The achievements of ECOWAS to date are quite modest. Yet, given the wide ethno-cultural diversity in West Africa, the mere fact that these sixteen nations have been able to come together is an epic feat. Among other things, ECOWAS has fostered intra-regional cooperation, reduced international conflicts, and helped maintain peace and **security** in West Africa. Perhaps the most important accomplishment of ECOWAS regarding regional peace is the decisive role played by the ECOWAS Cease-Fire Monitoring Group (ECOMOG) in ending the Liberian **war**. ECOWAS has also facilitated the free movement of people within the region and improved transportation and **telecommunications** links between member states. There is a proposal under way to establish an airline company, ECOAIR, to smoothen air travel within West Africa. ECOWAS has also made remarkable advances in the **agriculture** and energy sectors (see **energy policy**), and forged reputable coalitions with **international organizations and associations** such as the Organization of African Unity (OAU), the Economic Commission on Africa (ECA), and the **World Bank**. As with many such regional economic integration bodies in the developing world, grinding **poverty**, limited potential for intra-regional trade, and the prevalence of competing trading blocs continue to undermine the attainment of ECOWAS goals.

See also: Common Market for Eastern and Southern Africa (COMESA); economic federalization; Southern African Development Community (SADC)

Further reading

Asante, S. (1986) *The Political Economy of Regionalism in Africa: A Decade of the Economic Community of West African States (ECOWAS)*, New York: Praeger.

Ezenwe, U. 1983, *ECOWAS and the Economic Integration of West Africa*, London: Hurst.

JOSEPH MENSAH

economic development

Economic development has often been considered the most important element of all development, and refers to the inculcation of growth in productive capacities within countries, frequently through **industrialization** and investment. Increasingly, the focus of development on **economic growth** alone has been challenged by greater attention to aspects of political reform, **civil society**, and **participatory development**, yet economic development still demands attention. Crucially, however, such challenges do not reject the need for economic development, but instead indicate how both economic and social approaches to development need to be integrated.

The early Keynesian influences

The modern problem of economic development was formulated during the war-torn decade of the 1940s. The question posed was: what are the possibilities of government-engineered economic transformation in poor countries? The main thrust of inquiry was thus not to ask how economic development had occurred previously, or to seek past patterns of development. The vision behind the new economics of development was that governments needed guidance from economists on how to make economic development happen differently in future – and, especially, faster.

At that time, the Western liberal democracies (see **democracy**) agreed that the international economy could not go on as it had in the 1930s. The harsh experience of the Great Depression and the failure to prevent the recurrence of world **war** had persuaded them that a better post-war world would have to include new multilateral economic

institutions to promote prosperity and peace. The world, however, was still a very unequal place. Hopes that their colonial masters would lead poorer countries to greater prosperity flickered and died, and newly independent countries in Asia, and later Africa, began to join Latin America in the search for ways to conjure up security and prosperity for themselves.

In 1943, Paul Rosenstein-Rodan had argued that a significant share of the labor force in the poor agricultural economies of east and southeast Europe was in a state of "disguised **unemployment**." This meant that they were in low productivity occupations that added little to either aggregate output or aggregate demand. If world income **inequality** was to be reduced, this agrarian excess **population** either had to engaged in **migration** to find capital to work with (an option not favored), or capital had to be brought in to create more productive and better-paid occupations – through **industrialization**. In this context, Rosenstein-Rodan introduced his "**big push**" concept, that the industrial investment should be large, but diversified across a wide range of **labor-intensive** light wage goods industries, to generate an increased supply that was well matched to the additional demand created by the investment. The induced growth, through higher real wages in industry, would then decrease **poverty**.

Industrialization in this mode was something new. Not driven by technical progress, it was an attempt to apply existing technology in the "international depressed areas." It depended on the engineering of complementary demand, and would therefore not happen – or would not happen anything like as quickly – if left to private-sector initiatives. It had to be planned by the state (see **state and state reform**), and partly funded from international sources. It provided a regional solution, independent of other parts of the international trade system, in order to avoid disrupting the broader **international division of labor**. Here then was a way to engineer a quick forward advance in industrialization, a way correctly described as *dirigiste*.

The Lewis model and its critics

W. Arthur Lewis was the main inspiration for the **United Nations** report on *Measures for the*

Economic Development of Under-Developed Countries (1951). This report also assumes that under-developed countries can draw on an ever-increasing stock of technologies, that the marginal productivity of capital must be higher in under-developed countries because of its scarcity relative to labor, and that gross **underemployment** of labor creates an opportunity to put low-cost labor together with additional capital to produce **labor-intensive** manufactures.

These three assumptions underpin Lewis's model of capitalist accumulation in the long run. "Excess agrarian population" became "surplus labor," to be transferred progressively into industrial **employment** (see also **labor supply**). It is assumed that this transfer can take place without any increase in the industrial real wage, and without any diminution of agricultural production. The transfer continues as long as surplus labor remains in the agricultural sector, because the industry wage rate maintains a fixed premium over the rural wage, and the capitalists in the industrial sector reinvest their profits and thereby expand their demand for labor and their output.

During the labor transfer process, the share of industry in national output, the share of profits in national income and the share of savings and investment in national expenditure all rise markedly. The increasing profit share implies a rise in income **inequality**. These structural changes end as the real wage in industry begins to rise, reducing the incentive for the reinvestment of capital in industry. Income inequality then begins to decrease.

One reaction to the Lewis model was to question the link between capital investment and **economic growth**, which was derived through a fixed incremental capital/output ratio. T. W. Schultz raised the important question of individuals' and families' own investments in what he called **human capital** – a stock of skills that could be used be deployed to earn future income. Another query was about dynamics of **rural-urban migration**. Harris and Todaro (see **Harris-Todaro model**) argued that the rural-urban differential in the real wage would generate an excess supply of job seekers migrating to the towns in search of an urban job. Perhaps the most important reaction was to dispute the negative view of **agriculture** that was implicit in the Lewis model. Was it not both inefficient and inequitable to pour more resources into a sector that was already relatively well endowed with them? Could not agriculture be the starting point for growth?

Practical applications: planning and project appraisal

Development economics had been conceived as a policy science. The practical problem was how to go beyond the development plans of colonialism (see **colonialism, history of; colonialism, impacts of**), which were incoherent lists of possible investment projects. New techniques were borrowed from Keynesian macroeconomics. In particular, a framework for **planning** economic development was provided by the system of national accounts linking the sources and uses of the aggregate product, investment and saving, the government budget and the balance of payments. A complementary tool was the inter-industry input-output table, by which the intermediate demands arising in the course of economic growth could be projected. Using both, planners could calculate in a consistent way the implications of a given **growth rate** for the composition of both final demand and inter-industry demand.

Consistency is a minimum requirement of good planning: the skill in it is to identify correctly the constraints that will bind in the course of growth, and to judge the maximum feasible rate of growth that the country can achieve. This calls for sensitivity to economic facts, such as the elasticity of the **food** supply and latent inflationary pressures, but more importantly to political facts, such as the goals of leaders and popular expectations. Such sensitivity was often lacking in practice.

Making a sensible macroeconomic plan could indicate the appropriate amount of investment in aggregate, but it did not bring coherence to the list of investment projects. What was needed for that was a technique that would rank projects in order of their economic desirability, to be undertaken until the investment budget was exhausted. Previously, development economists had argued the merits of different partial criteria for deciding on project investment. The integration of these various partial criteria within a single procedure of appraisal of net present value was the work of Little and Mirrlees (1974).

A major issue of project appraisal was to measure the true cost of transferring a marginal unit of rural labor to urban **employment**, rather than assuming (with Lewis) that the transfer was costless. At the same time, however, it became clear that the valuation of a project's non-labor inputs and outputs was difficult, owing to many interventions by governments that made actual prices deviate from market-clearing prices. These deviations were called price distortions. The idea of a price distortion made sense only relative to some standard of undistorted prices. Little and Mirrlees proposed "world prices" as their "sheet anchor," though not without meeting some skepticism. The use of world prices as a norm marked a significant shift in economic thinking about development, even though in practice social **cost-benefit analysis (CBA)** techniques were scarcely more successful than macroeconomic **planning**.

Trade regimes, international and national

Ever since the Havana Conference of 1947–8, developing countries had argued that an international trade regime based on rules of reciprocity and non-discrimination was inadequate, in a world of gross inequalities between nations, to support their economic development. Rosenstein-Rodan, Raul Prebisch and other development economists did not advocate autarky, but did envisage growing regional economic cooperation (see **economic federalization**). The GATT (General Agreement on Tariffs and Trade) (see **World Trade Organization/General Agreement on Tariffs and Trade (WTO/GATT)**) disapproved of them, and while it provided a forum in which industrial countries could reduce their **tariffs** on industrial products, it had little to offer countries that had yet to industrialize. The culmination of the developing countries' drive to modify the **institutions** of international trade was their demand for a new **international economic order** (NIEO) in the 1970s. The policy centerpiece of the NIEO was an integrated program of international commodity agreements, to be financed from a new Common Fund.

The policy activism of the developing countries in the international economic arena provoked a tart response from the industrial countries. Their message was that the main obstacles impeding development were internal, not external. The **Organization for Economic Cooperation and Development (OECD)**, representing the industrial countries, funded a series of studies designed to substantiate this thesis. Their analytical key was the measurement of the effective rate of protection, reflecting not just the height of individual **tariffs**, but the overall structure of **protectionism**. The OECD studies revealed the extent of protection in the national trade regimes of selected developing countries. The effective rate of protection of some industries was at times twice as high as the nominal rate, often around 100 percent. This suggested that governments were exploiting **agriculture**, and not just neglecting it, in order to build up uncompetitive industries.

These studies of trade regimes changed the perspective on development in the 1970s. Detailed microeconomic analysis of government policy had been neglected in the earlier grand macroeconomic theories. The new view was that the economy should no longer be treated as closed; foreign **aid** should no longer be assumed automatically to fill any balance of payments gap. Responsibility for the good management of foreign trade was pushed back to developing country governments.

Neo-liberalism: less state, more market

The 1970s witnessed a groundswell of negative views of the performance of the state (see **state and state reform**), not least in developing countries. The growing negativity about the state came from all parts of the ideological compass, and was by no means the monopoly of the political right wing. Analysts began to explain the failure of development policies in terms, not of the conflict between development and other governments' public objectives, but of conflict between development and the state's hidden agenda. The nature of this hidden agenda was explored in a variety of political economy analyses of the nature of the state.

Resurgent **Marxism** in Europe related the hidden agenda of the state to the interests of the capitalist class. Non-Marxist political economy suggested that the state was dominated by an urban coalition, unified by location but cutting across class lines, whose collective interest was the exploitation of the rural hinterland – in short, **urban bias**. However, the form of political economy that won approval from the conservative governments of the US, Germany and the UK in the 1980s was centered on the collusion between the state in developing countries and rent-seeking domestic interest groups.

Based in the Research Department of the **World Bank**, this doctrine animated a policy program of minimizing the role of the state in development and of "getting prices right." Governments were now adjured to divest themselves of **state-owned enterprises (SOEs)** and to liberalize comprehensively – in goods markets, labor markets, financial markets, **capital markets** and foreign trade markets. They were encouraged to concentrate their efforts on law and order, **education** and **health**. This view became codified in what was called the **Washington consensus** on economic policy for developing countries.

Champions of the free price mechanism highlighted and celebrated the **newly industrialized economies (NIEs)** of Asia as examples of the fast growth and good **income distribution** resulting from economic liberalization. This claim now seems increasingly implausible. Despite intercountry differences, the East Asian growth story seems to be about government and businesses coordinating to secure high investment, high saving and reinvestment, and rapid growth of competitive exports in a joint strategy of national development. The debate now centers on whether a similar development strategy could succeed equally well elsewhere.

From structural adjustment to poverty reduction

In the wake of the Latin American **debt** crisis, the industrial countries of the G7 used the **International Monetary Fund (IMF)** and the World Bank to engineer the **structural adjustment** of the economies of developing countries. The shift was profound: instead of industrial countries changing their economic structure to accommodate additional output of the late developers, developing countries had to change their economic structure to accommodate more imports and private investment from the G7 (see **neo-liberalism**).

For countries whose balance of payments gap could no longer be filled by expanding **aid** grants, adjustment meant reducing aggregate demand to equal aggregate supply, plus whatever amount sustainable borrowing could finance. A simple reduction in absorption would, however, typically create an imbalance between the supply of and demand for non-traded goods, so that contraction of demand would have to be accompanied by an exchange rate devaluation (see **exchange rates**). After successful macroeconomic stabilization, the removal of price distortions, plus the shrinkage of the **public sector**, was intended to provide the impulse to resumed growth. The justification and criticism of this type of adjustment policy provided a major debate throughout the 1980s.

In general, the verdict on structural adjustment in the 1980s was that it delivered much less than its advocates had claimed for it. Exports and overall growth grew slightly as a result, while the share of investment to **gross domestic product (GDP)** declined somewhat. Structural adjustment was a very large policy package, since it was composed of stabilization, **privatization and liberalization**, and each of these sub-categories of policy consisted of many different specific actions that, for success, should have been pursued in a coordinated program. Development economists were not well equipped to resolve the practical issue of the sequencing of this package of policies. Subsequent evaluations showed that important sequencing errors were one of the factors that blunted the effectiveness of reforms.

By the end of the 1980s, the effort expended on structural adjustment seemed to have distracted attention from other central issues of development, especially **poverty** reduction. The **World Bank** acknowledged the new interest in poverty reduction in its *World Development Report 1990*, which stressed the need to ensure that growth was **labor-intensive**, and that basic social services were effective. Also in 1990, the **United Nations Development Programme (UNDP)** began its *Human Development Report* series, featuring a statistically questionable but well-intentioned **Human Development Index (HDI)** that was an equal-weight combination of **gross national product (GNP)** figures with **life expectancy** and literacy data (see **illiteracy**).

Re-introducing institutions into economic development

In the 1990s, thinking about economic development became more flexible and more adventurous, even though **neo-liberalism** by no means faded from the scene. Two new strands of thinking about **institutions** and development were particularly noteworthy. Early development economists like Arthur Lewis had stressed the importance of sound institutions in promoting economic development. This tended to be ignored, however, because institutions were not integral to his economic development model. Institutions were taken as a fixed framework within which economic transactions occurred, one that was not itself amenable to or integral to economic analysis.

The **new institutional economics** annulled this analytical divorce between institutions and economics. The key insight was that all economic transactions have a cost. Hence the need to minimize the sum of production and transactions costs, and to choose between transacting at arm's length on the market, or inside an institution – such as a firm, family, cooperative or government agency (see also **new institutional economics**). The possibility of substitution of market for non-market institutions presents a challenge to both to align incentives in ways that reduce transaction costs.

The theory of **social capital** draws in part on the same logic. Networks of personal relationships are useful for economic transactions when people are too poor to support formal institutions. The reputation of others can be learned through personal contacts, and this knowledge used to lower transaction costs, and to facilitate transactions that would not otherwise take place. In such a context, it makes sense to talk about investing in personal relationships, no less than in **education** and **health** care.

Social capital has another aspect, however, that does so clearly belong within the tradition of methodological individualism. Transactions conducted through personal networks are likely to be quite limited, given the amount of networking that any individual can do. A more profound problem, therefore, is specifying the conditions for the creation of a climate of impersonal trust that would improve the working of formal institutions, or permit a much wider expansion of economic activity in countries where formal institutions are still weak. This remains a challenging and controversial area of research, with much potential relevance to the economics of development.

See also: big push; capital markets; developmental state; Dutch disease; employment; fiscal and monetary policy; foreign direct investment; globalization; industrialization; industrialization and trade policy; institutions; international economic order; new institutional economics; privatization and liberalization; resource curse thesis; stages of economic growth; structural adjustment; trade; unemployment

Further reading

Harriss, J., Hunter, I. and Lewis, C. (eds) (1996) *The New Institutional Economics and Third World Development*, London: Routledge.

Lewis, W. (1954) "Economic Development with Unlimited Supplies of Labour," *The Manchester School* 22: 139–91.

Little, I. and Mirrlees, J. (1974) *Project Appraisal and Planning for Developing Countries*, London: Heinemann Educational.

Little, I., Scitovsky, T. and Scott, M. (1970) *Industry and Trade in Some Developing Countries*, Oxford: Oxford University Press.

Mosley, P., Harrigan, J. and Toye, J. (1995 [1991]) *Aid and Power. The World Bank and Policy-based Lending*, 2 vols, London: Routledge.

Rosenstein-Rodan, P. (1943) "Problems of Industrialization in Eastern and South-Eastern Europe," *Economic Journal* 53: 202–11.

JOHN TOYE

economic federalization

Economic federalization refers to the process of international economic integration by which groups of states (see **state and state reform**) increasingly develop arrangements to coordinate (parts of) their national economic realms within a concerted supra-national framework of rules and regulations. More often than not, economic integration starts with preferential trading arrangements between two or more states, which means that **tariffs** on commodities imported from the partners are lower then those on imports from other states. As these partner states commonly are geographically contiguous entities, economic federalization often induces the formation of regional economic blocs.

Various types of economic federalization may be distinguished, ranging from relatively simple forms of trade agreements for one or more (similar) commodities only, to arrangements aiming at **free trade** areas and customs unions, and to increasingly complex patterns of common markets and economic (and monetary) unions. With increasing integration and harmonization of economic policies (see **economic development**), the political autonomy of the partner states will become curtailed.

Cooperation between states in the field of one particular sector will be directed at agreements on the production and trade of some (often strategic) products, such as coal and steel in the European Coal and Steel Community (ECSC) of the 1950s (see **iron and steel**). From this relatively modest scheme of cooperation between six European countries, in 1957 the European Economic Community (EEC) developed.

In free trade areas, all former trade restrictions (e.g. import tariffs and quotas) between the partner states are being removed within an established time frame, aiming at complete trade liberalization for the entire area. With respect to trade with non-participating states, however, each individual member maintains its particular trade policies. The **North American Free Trade Agreement (NAFTA)** of 1994 is a good example of this type of regional integration.

Customs unions also aim at the complete elimination of custom duties between all partner states, but at variance with free trade areas their aim is to establish a common trade policy toward other states as well. The oldest example is the Southern African Customs Union (SACU, 1910). The Andean Pact (1969, revived in 1991) and – in spite of its name – the Central American Common Market (1960, revived in 1993) are also customs unions.

Within a common market, in addition to a common external tariff, the partner states agree upon totally free movement of commodities, labor and capital. The *Mercado Común del Sur* (**MERCOSUR**, 1991) presents an outstanding example of four South American countries that are fully engaged in a dynamic process of transformation from a customs union toward a common market.

The economic union (such as the **European Union**) is the deepest form of regional integration. In addition to internally free factor movements and common external trade policies, the members of an economic union share other policies, both economic and non-economic, and supra-national legislation (and monetary policy) substitutes national decision-making powers.

See also: African Union; Association of Southeast Asian Nations (ASEAN); Common Market for Eastern and Southern Africa (COMESA); European Union; free trade zones (FTZs); Latin American Free Trade Agreement (LAFTA); MERCOSUR; North American Free Trade Agreement (NAFTA); tariffs; trade

Further reading

Dicken, P. (2003) *Global Shift. Reshaping the Global Economic Map in the 21st Century*, London: Sage.
Schiff, M. and Winters, L. (2003) *Regional Integration and Development*, Washington DC: World Bank.

PAUL VAN LINDERT

economic growth

Economic growth is variously described and measured by increases in either real income, **gross domestic product (GDP)**, consumption or the capital stock, usually all expressed in per capita form. It is almost impossible to overstate the importance of economic growth to living standards and their differences throughout the world. The fact that income in North America and Western Europe is at least thirty times greater than many countries in Sub-Saharan Africa is the result of differences in economic growth during the last century. The differences in economic performance in Asia, especially in the comparison of Hong Kong, Taiwan and Singapore to the rest of Asia, depend on differences in economic growth rates in the last few decades.

Modern growth theory in economics has its origins in a famous paper by Robert Solow (1956) and the field as a whole is expertly described and examined in two major textbooks: Jones (1998) at the level of an undergraduate student or general reader and Barro and Sala-i-Martin (1995) at the postgraduate level in economics. The paper by Solow (and the supporting literature) constructs a theory of economic growth for a simple one-sector economy in which the savings and population growth rates (see **population growth rate (PGR)**) are exogenous. The growth rate in steady state is simply equal to the growth in **population** (or exogenous technological change, or some combination), with all variables, including capital and income, growing at the same proportional rate as population. Steady-state differences in per capita income (over time and across countries) are due to variations in savings per capital and the growth in population. Differences in growth rates depend on out-of-steady-state changes in savings and the distance between current and steady state values of the capital-labor ratio (see **capital intensive; labor-intensive**).

Research since has extended the basic Solow model to account for both an endogenous determination of savings rates and growth rates. The former, often using advanced mathematical techniques such as optimal control theory, suggests that the rate of economic growth also depends on the manner in which individual preferences result in a trade-off between current and future consumption. Economies in which individuals have a low preference for consumption smoothing over time will, in response to an increase in the rate of return to savings, save more and generate more rapid increases in the capital stock. This is often been used as part of the explanation for differences in **growth rates** given the same or similar market reforms (as moves toward private **property rights** and more competitive markets) in transitional economies (Che *et al.*, 2001). The latter work, on the endogenous determination of growth rates, focuses instead on more broadly defined determinates of economic growth, with an emphasis on a distinction between physical and **human capital**, or that between the accumulation of machines and physical assets on the one hand and the acquisition of skills, technology and knowledge on the other (see **technology transfer**).

In addition to differences in savings rates (which in any case have never been viewed as the entire story) and skill levels, the most perplexing question is the cause of the enormous differences in economic growth rates, **productivity** and factor accumulation across countries. Many explanations have been offered for the large disparities observed over time and space, including the initial level of capital stocks (physical and human), **poverty traps**, natural resource availability (see **natural resources**), macroeconomic stability, the quality of **institutions**, geography, trade openness and rules over **foreign direct investment**, among others. Increasingly, economists are exploring the ways that public and civic institutions, as well as social mores and norms of behavior, influence economic activity. Such analysis recognizes that economic growth goes beyond factor accumulation (physical and human) and is linked to other economic dimensions, such as social networks and social divergence (Grafton *et al.*, 2003) (see **social capital**).

The idea of social networks supports a number of important stylized facts on economic growth and productivity at an economy-wide level: a common language increases trade; the positive relationship between ethnic and family business groups increases trade flows, and the greater the importance of these ties the more differentiated the product traded; mass communication is strongly and positively correlated with economic growth; ethnolinguistic diversity is negatively associated with economic performance; educational inequality is negatively associated with per capita income;

the existence of agglomeration externalities and geographically localized knowledge; the importance of social networks in the creation of localized spillovers (see **clustering**); the lower the spending on public goods, the greater is the ethnic fragmentation; and the positive association between initial **population** size and population density on economic growth or technological change.

Social divergence and its effect of economic growth blend three key ideas. First, cooperation and group interactions enable economies to use large amounts of specialized knowledge. Second, although knowledge is inherently nonrival, the creation and transfer of tacit knowledge or "know-how" is highly dependent on communication links within social networks and across social networks, represented by "weak ties" between disparate individuals. Third, individuals communicate more easily the greater the similarity between them, and communication and cooperation across social networks is often much more limited than within networks.

Finally, economists have begun to recognize that economic growth is often at the expense of the **environment** or what might be called **natural capital**. Adjustments to growth rates to account for the depletion of natural capital are thus becoming more accepted. Likewise, the idea of sustainability or growth that maintains the natural resource base (see **natural resources**) is emerging as a standard in measures of economic performance.

See also: computable general equilibrium (CGE) models; economic development; gross domestic product (GDP); gross national product (GNP); growth measurement; growth rate; natural capital; poverty trap

Further reading

Barro, R. and Sala-i-Martin, X. (1995) *Economic Growth*, New York: MacGraw-Hill.

Che, T., Kompas, T. and Vousden, N. (2001) "Incentives and Static and Dynamic Gains from Market Reform: Rice Production in Vietnam," *Australian Journal of Agricultural and Resource Economics* 45:4 547–72.

Grafton, R., Kompas, T. and Owen, D. (2003) "Productivity, Factor Accumulation and Social Networks," University of Otago, New Zealand: Otago Discussion Papers.

Jones, C. (1998) *Introduction to Economic Growth*, London: W. W. Norton.

Solow, R. (1956) "A Contribution to the Theory of Economic Growth," *Quarterly Journal of Economics* 70:1 65–94.

TOM KOMPAS

economic risk factors for health

Economic risk factors for health are the most important predictors of a person's **life expectancy** besides **ageing**. Low educational attainment and **poverty** are intertwined factors that lead to a downward cascade of risks that adversely impact health. These include inadequate **nutrition**, poor **housing** conditions, poor **sanitation**, exposure to infectious and toxic agents (see **pollution**), lack of access to **health** care, and dangerous work environments (see **occupational health**). Less tangible risk factors include low social status and inadequate democratic representation.

Over one billion people lack access to safe **drinking water**, over two billion lack access to adequate **waste management**, and about 800 million people go hungry on any given day (**World Health Organization (WHO)**, 2003). In the developing context, infectious diseases are the principal causes of death, and a large proportion of these deaths would be avoidable were access to potable water and **food** readily available. For instance, **children** deficient in Vitamin A may be more than twice as likely to die from measles as their well-nourished counterparts. Diarrhea arises from a lack of access to safe water (see **water management**), and the undernourished are most likely to die from this disease (see **brown environmental agenda; health and poverty**).

While under-nourishment is prevalent worldwide, **famine** typically occurs when market factors drive up the price of food. Likewise, while water treatment infrastructure (see **water management**) is central to preventing **water-borne diseases**, when infrastructure fails or is non-existent, clean water can only be had by those able to afford the timber or fuel required to boil it. Those that cannot afford the **nutrition** to stave off infection or clean water are even less likely to be able to afford antimicrobial medications (see **pharmaceuticals**).

While many developing countries offer some medical services to some of their poor citizens, few provide universal, free, and reliable health care. Countries that provide universal or near universal health care, such as Cuba and Chile, tend to have health outcomes that are comparable to developed nations.

However, it is difficult to disentangle the benefits of health sector investments from other social investments, especially **education**. Educational attainment explains a larger proportion of differences in life expectancy than access to health care in cross-national studies. Countries or states (e.g. Kerala in India) that invest heavily in education, but not health care, tend to have high life expectancy and low infant mortality (see **infant and child mortality**).

Housing policy may also play a role. Poor housing and neighborhood conditions increase risk of infectious exposure. Overcrowding in outer ring urban developments is common, exposing persons indoors to infectious agents, such as **tuberculosis**, and outdoors to soil and water that is contaminated with feces. Perhaps half of the world's population is infected with intestinal parasites, which are acquired by walking barefoot on soil contaminated with feces (WHO, 2003). Runoff from contaminated soil enters water supplies, creating exposure to bacterial agents (e.g. salmonella, shigella, and campylobacter), viral agents (e.g. hepatitis A), and amoebas.

Even in overcrowded housing developments that provide little economic opportunity for families with children, birth rates (see **fertility**) are often higher than average. This takes a large toll on the economic viability of the family unit during early childhood years by reducing the economic **productivity** of parents and producing another mouth to feed. For rural families who expect that the child will contribute economically to the family in the future, high rates of infant mortality usually require a greater number of conceptions, jeopardizing the health of poor women; high infant mortality (see **infant and child**

mortality) usually goes hand-in-hand with high **maternal mortality**.

In some countries, female infants and children are especially susceptible to the effects of poverty. Scarce food is sometimes distributed to male children who have higher earnings potential, and female infants are sometimes killed at birth in the hopes that future pregnancies will bare male children with higher earnings potential (see **amniocentesis (sex-selection)**).

In more developed contexts, such as many South American and Southeast Asian countries, impoverished families are more likely to be exposed to **pollution** and industrial toxins, and impoverished individuals are more likely to have an unsafe work environment (see **brown environmental agenda; occupational health**). Such unsafe work environments span the spectrum of production, from mining (where exposure to toxins and industrial accidents is high) to the manufacture of shoes and garments (where glues, blocked fire escapes, and overcrowding may play significant roles).

The cascade of factors leading from poverty to disease is complex. Pollutants resulting from the process of development increase a person's risk of respiratory infections that would be curable were access to affordable health care available. A lack of access to education leads to lower earnings potential, which in turn leads to increased exposure to toxins, a lack of knowledge regarding how to prevent disease, how to use **family planning**, how to improve housing conditions, and a lower social status. Non-democratic societies deprive persons of representation, which in turn leads to unheard local demands for **employment**, sanitation, education, and famine relief. Low-income members of democratic societies, too, often have less of a voice in demanding such services.

Since these risks are complex and intertwined, it is pragmatic to alleviate the root causes of disease rather than downstream factors. For instance, sustainable income can be thought of as the factor that reduces one's exposure to harmful deprivation, and education can be seen as the universal tool for improving one's chances of earning income. Education improves social status, earnings potential, and tends to reduce risky health behaviors, such as unprotected sex and alcohol consumption. On a macroeconomic level, education may increase productivity and reduce barriers to the creation of viable small businesses (see **micro-enterprises; small and medium enterprises (SMEs)**), even when jobs are scarce. In virtually all instances, money invested in education produces returns for both the individual and the state (see **state and state reform**).

See also: drinking water; health and poverty; brown environmental agenda; water management

Further reading

Sen, A. (1996) *Development as Freedom*, New York: Knopf.
WHO (World Health Organization) website and reports: http://www.who.int/

PETER MUENNIG

ECONOMISM VERSUS CULTURISM DEBATE *see* culture

ECOSOC *see* United Nations

ecotourism

Ecotourism refers to forms of **tourism** that focus specifically upon nature-based, environmentally educative, and sustainably managed activities. The term became used in the 1980s, but nature-based recreation has been popular for centuries. Early definitions of ecotourism emphasized nature-based experience, but with increasing debate over effective management of **natural resources** and **sustainable development**, a plethora of interpretations arose, embracing a wide range of criteria such as **community** involvement and cultural dimensions. Indeed, the term, "sustainable tourism" has also emerged to refer to tourism that is environmentally sensitive, yet which incorporates mainstream mass tourism, as well as specific themes of nature-based tourism. In particular, there is a growing appreciation of the need for symbiotic relationships between different stakeholders. Thus, environmental conservation should result both from and in enhanced local **livelihoods**; continued industry profits; sustained visitor attraction; and revenue for conservation.

There has been growing realization of the contribution that ecotourism can make towards sustainable development in general and of its relevance to **poverty** alleviation. Proponents of ecotourism claim that it offers enhanced prospects for local involvement, both beneficiary and participatory, compared with conventional tourism. There are various ways in which ecotourism can produce local economic benefits and assist with **capacity building** to realize these. The three main avenues of capturing a greater share of ecotourism revenue locally are: revenue sharing; local entrepreneurship and labor; and the sale of tourist merchandise. The emphasis on local involvement in ecotourism offers the opportunity to allow livelihood priorities to influence tourism development. Engagement in ecotourism can help build **social capital** in a number of ways by affecting social networks and community organizations. The most positive impacts occur when ecotourism is set within community-based natural resource management.

Not surprisingly, ecotourism has been endorsed by a wide range of stakeholders, decision-makers, and international agencies, reflected in the UN designation of 2002 as the International Year of Ecotourism. However, this apparent legitimization of ecotourism has drawn criticism from some **non-governmental organizations (NGOs)**, many from developing countries, that highlight the threat of eco-opportunism. There is a concern that ecotourism is being used in many less developed locations as a springboard to develop unsustainable mass tourism. Another frequently voiced criticism of ecotourism is that of Western centricity. Ecotourism is not exempt from center-periphery dominance inherent in the international organization of the tourism industry. Ecotourists originate largely from the more developed countries, consequently their tour, travel and accommodation needs are largely coordinated by firms based there. This has lead to accusations of ecotourism as "eco-colonialism." There are also fundamental problems in addressing cross-cultural differences in the

choices and activities of Western visitors and the burgeoning number of regional and domestic tourists.

Discussions of ecotourism need to acknowledge the wider context. Ecotourism is both shaped by, and shapes the social, cultural, environmental, political and economic milieus in which it is set. It cannot be analyzed in isolation, and it is not a universal panacea for unsustainable resource utilization.

See also: common heritage of humankind; environment; globalization and culture; Orientalism; protected areas; tourism

Further reading

Weaver, D. (ed.) (2001) *The Encyclopedia of Ecotourism*, Wallingford: CABI.

ERLET CATER

ECOWAS *see* Economic Community of West African States (ECOWAS)

education

Education, defined as formal schooling, has become one of the key issues in international development debate. Within this context, the major focus is on primary school enrollment especially for women and girls, which is regarded as a prerequisite for other development targets with the ultimate objective of **poverty** alleviation to succeed. Arguably, an important part of the essence of education is neglected in this narrowly focused international approach.

Education in its wider sense does include areas as diverse as upbringing, schooling (along the lines of a system of primary, secondary, tertiary education), vocational training, adult literacy programs, health training and **nutrition** programs, agricultural training, learning in the home, **community** rites, initiation ceremonies, religious schooling and various forms of non-formal schooling and learning-by-doing experiences. The focus of debates on education and its role in **human development**, however, centers on formal schooling.

Formal schooling

Education in this sense is a quite recent phenomenon. The concept of a system of education including public, basic education for all, and further education theoretically open to all on merit was fully established in the developed world only after World War II. Almost immediately it spread into the developing world, enforced through the process of **decolonization**, and its inclusion in the **Universal Declaration of Human Rights (1948)** as a basic right to formal schooling. It has since become a truly transnational concept, as in many ways the development potential of a given society is regarded as strongly linked to its educational system – part of the successful development of the **newly industrialized economies (NIEs)** is for example explained by the rapid and equitable expansion of educational opportunities.

Looking at the history of formal education since 1945, one speaks of the enrollment explosion, with an unprecedented increase in schooling in many developing countries. At first, this was largely confined to primary education, as the main objective at the time was the provision of fundamental education, with an emphasis on the promotion of practical skills and functional literacy.

By the mid-1950s, the enrollment explosion reached secondary and in the 1970s post-secondary education. Especially in postcolonial Africa, increased rates of enrollment were spectacular: In francophone West-Africa for example, fewer than 150,000 pupils attended primary school in 1949 and about 6,000 went to secondary school. By 1970, ten times more children were in primary and nearly fifty times more in secondary schools. In 1990, these figures reached about four million at primary and more than one million at secondary level.

However impressive the above figures might look, at the beginning of the 1990s education was still an unattainable luxury for large parts of the population in developing countries and for an even larger part of women and girls. This was partly due to the **population growth rate (PGR)**, with

which increases in educational enrollment could never keep up, and partly related to **structural adjustment** programs, which often led governments to cut the budget for education.

Human capital and human capabilities

Underlying the discourse on education and its role in development, different streams of thinking can be distinguished which emphasize different aspects of education and determine different policy approaches. The mainstream approach, propagated by the **World Bank** within the framework of the post-**Washington consensus**, relates education to **human capital** and its optimization. This instrumentalist approach puts the role of formal education in **capacity building** to the forefront. Education allows people to make better use of the resources available in a society.

At the opposite end of the spectrum, and strongly rejecting this instrumentalist approach, is education in the context of Critical Pedagogy, whose main proponent is Brazilian educator Paolo Freire under the concept of **pedagogy of the oppressed**. Freire describes education as a specifically human act of intervening in the world in order to promote change, and is thus linking education to emancipation and regards it as a tool in the fight against any kind of oppression and in the struggle for **social justice**.

A compromise view, which draws on the work of Amartya Sen and has gained momentum since the first publication of the *Human Development Report* in 1990 by the **United Nations Development Programme (UNDP)**, defines education in the context of capabilities and as such is connected to self-development as a basic human right (see **human rights**), to which everybody is entitled. In that sense, education is crucial not only for people to become more efficient in the sphere of production (as they might, for example, be able to find a better job) but equally, and arguably more importantly, adds to people's capabilities (see **capability approach**): they might for example learn to read, to communicate better, participate more fully in communal life. Therewith people's ability to lead a fulfilled life is enhanced and real choices of lifestyle are increased, both of which ultimately contribute to holistic human development.

Education for All (EFA) and the International Development Targets (IDTs)

In 1990, an estimated 100 million children were without access to schools, 60 million of whom were girls; one billion adults were illiterate, two thirds of whom were women. It became obvious that because of the overall increase in schooling, those excluded from any formal education were vulnerable to **marginalization**. At the same time, greater awareness had developed among **bilateral aid agencies** concerning problems of education. Donors acknowledged that it was insufficient to look at education in terms of private economic returns only (**human capital** theory in its narrow sense), but that social returns had to be acknowledged. Various studies showed that the highest social returns to society were achieved by investing in primary education, while the reality in many developing countries showed the major share of the education budget going into academic secondary education, which often led to critical imbalances in society.

In that context, the strategy of Education for All (EFA) was proclaimed. The EFA declaration, signed by the majority of governments in Jomtien, Thailand, in 1990, aims to give basic primary education to children and adults alike and proposes to eradicate **illiteracy** by the year 2000. In the wake of Jomtien, substantial increases in funds to support primary education were pledged, and several countries developed national plans of action to implement the EFA objectives. However, lack of funds and other constraints have led to only minor successes. At the follow-up international gathering, the World Forum on Education for All in Dakar in April 2000, the focus was still on the pledge to achieve basic education for all, now by the year 2015. For Sub-Saharan Africa, where overall absolute enrollment levels in primary schools have actually fallen over the last decade, special initiatives are envisaged to give access to education utmost priority – an example includes **debt relief** in the framework of the **Heavily Indebted Poor Countries (HIPC)**

initiative to free funds for investment into primary education.

Universal primary education (UPE) also occupies a prominent role as one of the seven International Development Targets which have been set in a joint effort to alleviate **poverty** in the new millennium by the **International Monetary Fund (IMF)**, the **Organization for Economic Cooperation and Development (OECD)** the **World Bank** and the **United Nations**. Not only UPE *per se* is envisaged, but a further target envisages the elimination of gender disparities in primary and secondary education by the year 2005. However unrealistic both of these targets might seem, they are seen to be a prerequisite for achieving the other targets of reducing the proportion of people living in extreme **poverty** by half, reducing **infant and child mortality** by two thirds; reducing **maternal mortality** rates by three quarters; and providing reproductive health services for all who need them. UPE has been described as the most productive process of poverty alleviation because it provides people with the tools to change their lives. In this context, educating women and girls is considered to have most overall social benefits.

Female education

The Jomtien declaration for the first time secured an international commitment to educate girls and women. It states as the most urgent priority the ensuring of access to education for girls and women and the removal of every obstacle that hinders their active participation. This statement is in line with one of the most powerful narratives in current development debate, which considers primary education for women and girls as the key to economic and social advancement. Female education will lead to a number of other benefits: Girls who have attended school longer marry later, will have fewer children and will have their children educated. Female literacy has been shown to be the crucial factor for a decline in infant mortality, improved family **nutrition** and lower **population** growth.

This virtuous correlation is achieved because education is seen as raising human and **social capital** at the same time, as it strengthens both the productive and socially reproductive roles of women. Whereas the impact of additional schooling – notably at primary level between six and twelve years of age – on increased private economic returns is only marginally better for women than men in developing countries, educating females generates more substantial social benefits. The underlying assumption here is that female schooling is a basic requirement for other development policies to succeed, and that simultaneously, these policies can be reinforced through female education.

Contemporary issues

Whereas stakeholders and scholars agree that its quality of education is crucial for the development potential of a country, the focus on primary education since the 1990s has been criticized by some as short-sighted. More recently it was acknowledged by the **World Bank**, among others, that in a global economy based on knowledge, technical and higher education is essential for the future national social and **economic development** of any country.

Some scholars and stakeholders alike are critical of the way in which education is perceived as a panacea. They argue that in spite of the emergence of the **capability approach**, **human capital** theory is still the dominant approach which underlines international development policy on education. But due to its instrumentalist nature, the human capital approach does not take account of the many dimensions of the educational process. For example, under the human capital approach, female education is not considered important for enhancing women's own position in society or increasing women's choices in life (as it would be considered under the capability approach), but centers on their role as the nurturers of the family who in turn influence their children. As such, the human capital approach neglects the very essence of education: it is a multidimensional activity strongly related to the development of identity and new forms of personal agency.

See also: capability approach; capacity building; children; human capital; human development; illiteracy; Millennium Development Goals (MDGs); United Nations Education, Sciectific and Cultural Organization (UNESCO)

Further reading

See the journals*International Journal of Educational Development* and *Compare* for research on international and comparative education, and the following websites for further information relating to education and development:

United Nations Educational Scientific and Cultural Organization: http://www.unesco.org/education

World Bank: http://www.worldbank.org/education

Partnership on Sustainable Strategies for Girls' Education: http://www.girlseducation.org

Fine, B. and Rose, P. (2001) "Education and the post-Washington Consensus," pp. 155–81 in Fine, B., Lapavitsas, C. and Pincus, J. (eds) *Development Policy in the Twenty-first Century*, London: Routledge.

Freire, P. (1998) *Pedagogy of Freedom. Ethics, Democracy, and Civic Courage*, Lanham MD: Rowman and Littlefield.

Heward, C. and Bunwaree, S. (eds) (1999) *Gender, Education and Development. Beyond Access to Empowerment*, London: Zed.

United Nations Development Programme (1990) *Human Development Report 1990*, New York: Oxford University Press.

UNESCO (United Nations Education, Scientific and Cultural Organization) (1997) *50 Years for Education*, Paris: UNESCO.

World Bank (1998) *World Development Report 1998/99: Knowledge for Development*, New York: Oxford University Press.

TANJA R. MÜLLER

electrification and power-sector reform

Electrification is the extension of electricity (or power) supplies to new areas or new users. Power-sector reform usually refers to the privatization (see **privatization and liberalization**), deregulation, or modernization (see **modernization theory**) of electricity supply industries. Increasing electricity supply in developing countries is a major factor underlying **industrialization**, **urban**

development and **rural development**, and has implications for **pollution** and **climate change** policy. But even though there are an estimated two billion people worldwide without modern forms of energy (see **energy policy**) such as oil and electricity, these people are among the world's poorest and therefore represent little consumer demand for electrification. Consequently, extending electricity to poor people carries difficult economic and political challenges.

Electricity supply industries (ESIs) comprise three key sectors: generation, transmission, and distribution of electricity. Electricity is usually transmitted through a national grid that is fed by large power stations. Off-grid supplies may come from stand-alone generators, or via mini-grids, which may supply smaller areas such as a village or valley. The term, "electrification" has generally become understood as the process of extending the national grid into rural zones, but it should also include providing electricity via mini-grid or off-grid sources. Each option has important implications: extending the national grid usually implies increasing investment in large power stations often fueled by burning fossil fuels such as coal and natural gas, or by **nuclear energy**. Decentralized (or off-grid) electrification may use diesel generators, or small, **renewable energy** technologies such as photovoltaics or micro-hydro generators. Some **renewable energy** technology such as photovoltaics or wind turbines can also supply national grids.

Before the 1980s, ESIs in Europe and North America were largely **state-owned enterprises (SOEs)** and monopolies. Since then, industries have been reformed largely by the following steps: corporatization (providing commercial incentives to SOEs); unbundling (separating different sectors such as generation and distribution); privatization (selling assets to private companies; see **privatization and liberalization**); deregulation (reducing state control; see **state and state reform**); and competition (allowing different suppliers to compete for customers). These steps were aimed to increase efficiency of production, reduce costs, and increase consumer choice. Such acts, however, are not always transferable to developing countries because many industrializing economies require the construction of new generating and

transmission capacity that was never state-owned. Consequently, much private-sector investment in electricity in developing countries has focused on increasing generating capacity from so-called Independent Power Producers (IPPs) but has not included deregulation or the introduction of retail competition. Furthermore, the use of IPPs has – to date – usually involved increasing generating capacity by the fastest and cheapest (per electricity unit) cost, rather than decentralized electrification or renewable energies.

Many power sectors in developing countries carry a number of entrenched political and economic problems. Much initial capacity dates from colonial times, and may be inefficient and outdated. Transmission efficiency may be low because of pilfering of electricity from lines by unauthorized users. Supply may be notoriously unreliable. In Indonesia, it is estimated that private (backup) generating capacity from diesel generators may be equivalent to 40 percent of installed grid capacity. Electrification to countries containing many islands (such as Indonesia or the Philippines) may be difficult because of the costs of laying lines. In other countries such as Thailand, electrification has been linked to national security objectives by providing means for remote villages to become sedentarized, and hence national grid coverage is higher than in other Asian countries. Large hydroelectric dam projects (see **dams**) have also been claimed to reflect the objectives of a centralized state to control remote regions, or place urban and elite (see **elites**) electricity needs above local requirements of people displaced by such dams. State electricity boards may also be difficult to reform, or resist the creation of new electricity authorities to oversee new investment. Specific agencies to develop decentralized forms of electrification, such as the Indian Renewable Energy Development Agency (IREDA), may be comparatively powerless in relation to other parts of government. **Technological capability** may be low both within the state and in rural areas to accept new electricity-generating technologies. Electricity markets may also be accustomed to government subsidies for electricity, which provide a drain on government resources and hence discourage investment in other aspects of electricity supply or in alternative forms of generation. The

World Bank estimated that in the early 1990s, the average electricity tariff in developing countries was less than four US cents per kilowatt hour, compared with an average cost of ten US cents.

Many countries, however, have achieved levels of successful reform. Thailand has successfully demonstrated energy efficiency through demand-side management (DSM), or the ability to reduce peak-electricity demand and hence the need for overall generating capacity. A "small-producers' program" in Thailand also provides incentives for companies to supply the national grid by practices such as using biomass. In Vietnam, for example, the US organization, Solar Electric Lighting Fund (SELF) achieved a partnership (see **partnerships**) with the Vietnam Women's Union to distribute solar lanterns and photovoltaics in rural areas. The US non-governmental organization, Winrock (see **non-governmental organizations (NGOs)**), has established wind turbines in Eastern Indonesia by constructing distributed utilities, or local means of collecting tariffs for electricity use and providing maintenance. In various countries, the extension of micro-credit to villagers (see **micro-credit and micro-finance**) has allowed them to pay for new renewable technologies such as solar-heating systems, or for the connection charge to grid systems. Experience has shown that overcoming the startup costs of electrification at the local level is an important step to increasing electricity use. Electricity storage however, remains difficult, and many villagers still rely on rechargeable car batteries as the most immediate form of electricity.

Advisers agree that future priorities require electricity prices to reflect costs; that there should be greater enhancement of public funding for electrification (such as the extension of bond markets, or mobilization of national savings); that electricity trading should be allowed between regions and countries; and that new investment in generating capacity should be matched by the establishment of independent and imaginative regulatory authorities. However, it is clear that – despite concerns about **climate change** – much future power generation in developing countries will continue to use coal, which is relatively cheap and plentiful, especially in East Asia, and that **nuclear energy** remains attractive to some countries, especially India and China. Support for

alternative, decentralized forms of electrification may be enhanced if state agencies favoring them can be empowered, and if the indirect benefits of such electrification (such as in mitigating **rural-urban migration**, or enhancing **rural development**) can be demonstrated.

See also: climate change; dams; energy policy; nuclear energy; privatization and liberalization

Further reading

See the journal *Energy Policy*.

Bruggink, J. (1997) "Market Metaphors and Electricity Sector Restructuring: Lessons for Developing Countries," *Pacific and Asian Journal of Energy* 7:2 81–8.

Forsyth, T. (1999) *International Investment and Climate Change: Energy Technologies for Developing Countries*, London: Earthscan and RIIA.

Kozloff, K. (1994) *Rethinking Development Assistance for Renewable Energy*, Washington DC: World Resources Institute.

Turkson, J. (ed.) (2000) *Power Sector Reform in SubSaharan Africa*, Basingstoke: Macmillan.

USAID (1998) *The Environmental Implications of Power Sector Reform in Developing Countries*, Washington DC: USAID.

TIM FORSYTH

elites

The term elite/elites refers to people who by virtue of their high economic, social, political or intellectual position or standing enjoy certain advantages, privileges or power in society. Elites are often seen as a special group of people who tend to excel in their chosen field or profession. From a political economic perspective, elites form part of the larger social class or power structure. Hence, the term "power elite" refers to a small set of individual actors within that power structure who are responsible for organizing and maintaining wider social structures. They shape policies within society, and share formal, direct, or informal access to other elite actors within and outside their spheres of influence (see **politics**).

The concept of elites has a much longer history rooted in nineteenth-century *fin de siècle* social and political theory than in contemporary development theory. Elite theories developed as a direct reaction to theories on **democracy** popularized by liberal and Marxist thinkers in the nineteenth century. At the turn of the twentieth century, two elite theorists, Vilfredo Pareto and Gaetano Mosca, provided some of the earliest conceptualization of elites and elitism. It is said that the best-known theories on elitism came from Italians like Pareto and Mosca perhaps because the disenchantment with mass democratic politics and high hopes of democratic idealists was most severe in Italy in the 1880s. Pareto, in particular, accused Marx of utopianism, as he saw a never-ending struggle for power between groups and classes, one in which even the victory of Marx's proletariat would lead to a new ruling class against which others would also rebel (see **Marxism**).

The anti-democracy, or at least anti-mass, impulse of the *fin de siècle* permeated the writings of many European philosophers, including Friedrich Nietzche, Max Weber, Henri Bergson, Georg Sorel, Gustav LeBon and Sigmund Freud. Max Weber, for example, concludes that the implementation of democracy, paradoxically, only leads to a new kind of elite rule, where "politics is *made by the few.*" Weber's friend Robert Michels called this the "iron law of oligarchy" where the mass political party and other so-called democratic **institutions** are controlled by a small group of insiders or party bosses.

From the perspective of elite theorists, all societies are governed by elites and democracy is only one way of selecting this ruling class, and may not be necessarily the best or most effective way. Formal democracies in North America and Europe, as well as in developing countries, tend to have "invisible governments" and political parties nurtured by the closeness between government and business. How groups of elites relate to the ruling class has been the subject of much theorizing, especially in the USA. C. Wright Mills, for example, examined the existence of a "power elite" in the USA, contributing to a long academic tradition analyzing various perspectives on power and elite-state relations. By the 1980s, the academic debate on power and power elites, at least in the USA, was framed by three general theories – pluralism, institutional elitism, and **Marxism**; three basic methods – positional, decisional, reputational; and three indicators – who sits, who decides, who benefits. Alford and Friedland (1985) had proposed that these three theories, methods and indicators could be synthesized and understood as different levels of analysis instead of mutually exclusive, competing theories.

The academic debate on elites, elitism and state-elite relations has also influenced writings in developing countries as diverse as Mexico, Chile, Brazil, the Philippines, Indonesia, and the communist world. The terms of the debates are also diverse, ranging from (1) the conceptualization of the difference between the so-called "traditional" versus "modern" or "modernizing" elites, hence the question of the continuity, survival or transformation of elites; (2) the strategies of ruling by elites using their overlapping socio-spatial networks of economic, political, military and ideological power (see **military and security**); (3) the relationship between elites or oligarchs, states, and markets or capitals; (4) the relationship between elites, socialism, democracies or other types of **governance**; (5) the contribution of elites to **industrialization** and national development; (6) elite stratification, and their interlocking directorates, or the various types of economic elites and their political alliances, and how and why they decline or survive in the midst of economic change; among others.

Perhaps the first key questions asked by writers on elites in developing countries are whether such power elites exist at all, who are they, how are they selected or recruited, and how have they managed to retain power for so long. Other key questions asked by elite theorists relate to development questions. For example, how elites in the form of the national bourgeoisie contribute to **industrialization** or national development figured prominently in the "mode of production" debate in development theory in the 1970s and 1980s. This question was important in view of determining who are the key agents in improving the forces of production or bringing about industrialization, and in identifying the key actors in political alliances that would bring about change in the nature of the state (see **state and state reform**). Likewise, the understanding of elites, particularly agrarians (landowners or rentiers and agrarian capitalists) and industrial elites, was important in the so-called "agrarian question" or "industrial transition" debate that emerged within development studies in the 1980s and 1990s. This question centers on how agrarians manage to retain their political leadership in an industrializing society, similar to how the Prussian Junkers in the nineteenth century perpetuated their economic and political dominance, by using their state power to protect **agriculture** and minimize competition from the industrial sector. The agrarian question has been reformulated to include experiences of Asian and African countries and understand the role of agriculture and agrarian elites in promoting industrialization where agriculture are not fully dominated by wage labor and where the state is dominated by agrarians who are simultaneously capitalists (Angeles, 1999).

More recently, the discussion of elites and their role in social and political change has re-emerged within development studies in light of its interest in **social capital** theory. The relationship between the so-called "uppers" (read elites) and "lowers" (read non-elites) is critical to the cultivation of horizontal and vertical forms of social capital, or of having "friends in the high places," that could promote **economic growth** and prosperity.

See also: accountability; civil society; democracy; politics; state and state reform

Further reading

Alford, R. and Friedland, R. (1985) *Powers of Theory: Capitalism, the State and Democracy*, Cambridge: Cambridge University Press.

Angeles, L. (1999) "The Political Dimension of the Agrarian Question: Strategies of Resilience and Entrepreneurship of Agrarian Elite Families in a Philippine Province," *Rural Sociology* 64:4 667–92.

Camp, R. (2002) *Mexico's Mandarins: Crafting a Power Elite for the Twenty-First Century*, Berkeley: University of California Press.

Domhoff, G. and Dye, T. (1987) *Power Elites and Organizations*, Beverly Hills: Sage.

Higley, J. and Gunther, R. (eds) (1992) *Elites and Democratic Consolidation in Latin America and Southern Europe*, Cambridge: Cambridge University Press.

LEONORA C. ANGELES

emergency assistance

Emergency assistance refers to the provision of **aid** to populations in need during times of disaster. The term is often used to distinguish emergency assistance from development assistance. It is also often used interchangeably with other terms for the provision of aid in **natural disasters**, notably disaster relief and humanitarian aid (see **humanitarianism**), although there are important nuances in meanings between these terms.

Emergency assistance is generally understood to consist of a limited range of interventions aimed at saving lives, and sometimes **livelihoods**. Types of assistance are often divided into key sectors, that address disaster-affected populations' **basic needs** for **food**, water, shelter, **health** and physical security. For example, the Sphere Handbook, which sets out minimum standards in disaster response, is divided into chapters on water supply and **sanitation**, **nutrition**, **food aid**, shelter and site planning, and health services. However, it is sometimes argued that emergency assistance should take a wider view of the livelihoods of affected populations and consider a broader range of possible interventions than the standard set of basic needs, including for example cash grants or support to **agriculture**.

Emergencies can be categorized in many different ways. Common distinctions include between natural disasters, conflict-based and **complex emergencies**, and between rapid and slow-onset disasters. These distinctions, however, are problematic and the boundaries between them are often blurred. Natural disasters can take place in areas of conflict such as the 2002 volcanic explosion in Goma, or floods in Somalia, and it is also important to understand the complex political economy that underlies **vulnerability** to natural disasters. Similarly, the common statement that disasters may be "man-made" or "natural" overlooks the diverse ways in which physical events and social vulnerability are linked (see **natural disasters**).

The differences in the meaning and use of the terms emergency assistance and humanitarian relief need to be explored. The term humanitarianism comes from a specific tradition of providing assistance in conflicts and comes with a set of widely agreed principles of humanity, neutrality, independence and impartiality (see **Médecins Sans Frontières (MSF); Red Cross and Red Crescent**). It is also understood, within the international disaster response system, to encompass both the provision of assistance to populations in need and the issue of protection for vulnerable civilian populations during conflict. Emergency assistance, by contrast, does not automatically bring with it an association with humanitarian values and principles, does not include the issue of protection and is less associated with conflict. For a few international agencies, protection is explicitly part of their mandate, notably the ICRC (International Red Cross Committee) and the **United Nations High Commissioner for Refugees (UNHCR)**, but protection issues have often been neglected in both the literature on, and the provision of, emergency assistance.

The distinction between development and emergency assistance opens up a series of complex issues. At its simplest, development assistance refers to aid that is provided during situations of normality with the aim of encouraging development; be it reduction of **poverty**, or the enhancement of **economic growth, empowerment**, etc. Emergency assistance, by contrast is aid that is provided at the time of a disaster, with the aim of saving lives and enabling a return of the affected population to a situation of normalcy.

This simple formulation, however, has been much criticized in research on both emergencies and development during the 1980s and 1990s, because it misrepresents the development process, emergency assistance and the links between them.

Development assistance cannot in practice always be neatly separated from emergency assistance. The process of development in developing countries often takes place in areas that are at serious risk of disaster, where conflict is to some extent endemic or where underlying vulnerability is such that development and emergency assistance take place at the same time. For example, Uganda throughout the 1990s and early 2000s, was a country labeled by international donors as a place where development assistance was appropriate but one where a serious conflict in the north of the country was ongoing throughout the period. The increasingly devastating impact of HIV/AIDS in Sub-Saharan and particularly southern Africa (see **HIV/AIDS (definition and treatment); HIV/AIDS (policy issues)**) and the possibility that this will need to be responded to with a combination of emergency and development assistance is another example.

The idea that emergency assistance can be simply described as aiming to return people to some idea of normalcy is also deeply problematic. It has been pointed out that in many disasters there is not a neat linear sequence from development to relief to recovery and back to development (see **complex emergencies; post-conflict rehabilitation**). Emergencies in conflicts have often gone on for decades and the recovery process is often characterized by periods of uneasy peace and continuing low-scale conflict. The situation in many areas of Sub-Saharan Africa, where **chronic poverty** and food insecurity interact with **droughts** or other natural disasters and now with the HIV/AIDS epidemic, also challenges any notion of a neat distinction between emergency and development assistance.

Emergency and development assistance are separated within the architecture of the international aid system. Western donors usually have distinct modalities and instruments for the funding of emergency and development aid. Development aid is generally delivered through states and is associated with building the capacity of the state (see **state and state reform; capacity building**). Emergency assistance, by contrast, is seen as the aid instrument of last resort and is more often used to fund **non-governmental organizations (NGOs)**, the **United Nations** and Red Cross, bypassing governments. Development assistance is often provided with **conditionality**, whereas emergency aid is usually seen to be politically unconditional.

The links, or lack of them, between emergency and development assistance are also debated among academics and aid agencies. On the one hand, there have been calls for emergency assistance to be better integrated with development assistance, a discourse commonly labeled as "linking relief and development." However, this has been criticized as inappropriate in some circumstances, because humanitarian relief should be seen as a separate endeavor in order to protect the principles of neutrality, impartiality and independence. Also, that keeping the political distinction between humanitarian and development aid is crucial to maintaining the integrity and technical efficacy of both forms of aid.

See also: aid; complex emergencies; humanitarianism; Médecins Sans Frontières (MSF); post-conflict rehabilitation; post-conflict violence; natural disasters; Red Cross and Red Crescent; right of intervention

Further reading

Macrae, J. (2002) *The New Humanitarianisms: A Review of Trends in Global Humanitarian Action*, Humanitarian Policy Group Report 11, Overseas Development Institute, London.

Maxwell, S. and Buchanan-Smith, M. (1994) "Linking Relief and Development," Special issue of *IDS Bulletin* 25:4.

The Sphere Project (2000) *Humanitarian Charter and Minimum Standards in Disaster Response*, Oxford: Oxfam.

PAUL HARVEY

EMPIRE *see* colonialism, history of; colonialism, impacts of

Employment

Employment is the engagement of a factor of production in a productive activity. It most commonly refers to the level of labor used in production, or the proportion of a working population that has gainful occupation. Achieving full, or high levels of, employment is consequently a consistent objective of **economic development**, and has important corollary social implications of **well-being**. The British economist John Maynard

Keynes (1883–1946) saw the achievement of full employment by the management of aggregate economic demand as the chief social and economic objective of governments, and his *General Theory of Employment, Interest and Money* (1945) formed the backbone of government for much of the mid-twentieth century (see **fiscal and monetary policy**).

Economic discussions of employment have historically focused on its relationship with **unemployment**. Theorists questioned how far employment (or unemployment) was voluntary or involuntary, and consequently whether there was an equilibrium level of employment within economies. Similar debates linked employment/unemployment with inflation (see **inflation and its effects**). Marx argued that "the reserve army of the unemployed" was in the employers' interests, as they would keep wages low. Economists of the twentieth century used the conceptual Phillips Curve, which proposed an inverse relationship between inflation and unemployment, whereby steps toward full employment would lead to increases in inflation because of rising labor costs, and vice-versa. Such a relationship was based upon the idea of a market in equilibrium because inflation and unemployment would react to each other. But experience since the 1970s has questioned the Phillips curve following so-called "stagflation" (or combined unemployment and inflation) during the 1970s and 1980s, and then periods of relatively low inflation and unemployment in the 1990s.

Debates in development economics have questioned how far developing economies follow the same principles as in developed countries. The economist W. Arthur Lewis (1954) conceptualized developing countries as "dual economies," in which modern, industrialized sectors (often in cities or near coasts) would differ from relatively backward, rural economies where rapid **economic growth** was dissuaded by the lack of formal **labor markets**, and a relative abundance of labor, which may often include **children** and the aged, as well as active adults, and without clearly defined hours or terms of working (see **dual economy**). The result was a relative oversupply of labor (or "unlimited labor") that offered few incentives for wages to be attractive to workers, and hence few economic benefits for those who participated in paid employment. Since these early economic writings, however, rural labor markets have become more regularized and the concept of a dual economy has been largely abandoned. A further early concept relating to employment was the employment multiplier, which was the ratio of employment in secondary industry (i.e. manufacturing) to primary industries (**agriculture** or resource extraction). Governments sought to make the ratio between primary and secondary employment equal as a means of achieving **industrialization**, or as an important stage of economic growth (see **stages of economic growth**). Currently, **United Nations** figures estimate that about 45 percent of the world's workforce is engaged in agriculture: the wealthiest countries typically have less than 5 percent in agriculture while the poorest countries of Africa often have over 80 percent. China and India sit near the mean at about 50 percent.

Many critics, however, have argued that much theoretical economics has paid insufficient attention to the social and political factors underlying employment in developing countries. The continued prevalence of informal economies in both rural and urban areas (see **urban informal sector; micro-enterprises**) represent important areas where employment is partial or sporadic, yet contributes to **livelihoods**. Informal activities are closely linked to **entrepreneurship**, and may supplement paid employment in other activities, or be combined with income from other family or household members. Employment may also be temporary or linked to **circular migration**, where workers migrate (usually) to cities before returning for work (usually agricultural) for specified periods. Such influences on employment depend on social networks and shared duties with other family/household members, rather than on macroeconomic demand. Similarly, some of the constraints on employment/unemployment lie in the development of labor markets, **trade unions**, and **labor rights and standards**. Such new controls on employment influence the terms and quality of employment offered, by the state (see **state and state reform**), local companies, and **transnational corporations (TNCs)**, and may also include defining the employment of women and men on equal terms (see **gender and industrialization**), or

the banning of **child labor** (see also **International Labor Organization (ILO)**).

See also: dual economy; International Labor Organization (ILO); labor markets; labor supply; micro-enterprises; underemployment; unemployment

Further reading

Allen, T. (1998) "From 'Informal Sectors' to 'Real Economies:' Changing Conceptions of Africa's Hidden Livelihoods," *Contemporary Politics* 4:4 357–73.

Lewis, W. A. (1954) "Economic Development with Unlimited Supplies of Labour," *Manchester School of Economics and Social Studies* 22: 139–91.

Sen, A. (1999) *Employment, Technology and Development*, New Delhi: Oxford University Press.

TIM FORSYTH AND WILLIAM R. HORNE

empowerment

The concept of empowerment implies recognizing the need for changes in the distribution of power, and the increase in power for previously disadvantaged groups. The concept of empowerment has been widely used since the mid-1970s, and points to **people-centered development**. Empowerment of the poor, women, **children**, minorities and other identified disadvantaged groups is a common feature within development literature and policies. But the notions of power, and empowerment, are difficult to define and to achieve. Scholars have approached power from a variety of perspectives: from *power over* (considering power as dominance), to *power to* (i.e. enablement), and *power within* (in which power is seen as both enabling and as a competence). In the latter sense, empowerment is considered a complex relational process and is always embedded in local, regional, national and global contexts.

In simple terms, empowerment may be seen as a process of transferring power from powerful actors to powerless people. Here empowerment involves intervention based on interpretation of a certain situation or even changes of the status quo to the extent that power relations are reversed. Empowerment in this sense is defined in terms of objectives that can be reached and targets that can be measured. When the transfer of power is accomplished, empowerment is achieved. For example, this kind of empowerment may be achieved when poor people are allowed access to resources such as credit and land, or even the replacement of a government by a former repressed group.

This simple notion of empowerment, however, may be criticized for its lack of attention to how power operates, or to the complexity of power relations. A different approach to empowerment, therefore, may define power as a complex series of relations between individuals, groups of people, and institutions, etc., that is created and transformed in everyday encounters of actors. Here power is neither a fixed entity nor a substance, but is relational and only exists in its exercise. When adopting this complex definition of power, empowerment generally refers to the undermining of dominant patterns of power relations, toward greater resistance, autonomy and participation in decision-making processes, in which the actors increasingly do so on their own terms (see **participatory development**). In this sense, people are not seen as powerless, but as active agents who can wield and yield power. Empowerment is hence both relational and a process with no ending: it is an ongoing process in which people see themselves as having the capacity and right to act and influence decisions (see **capacity building; rights-based approaches to development**). When the objective of empowerment is to change situations of oppression, **inequality**, **social exclusion** and subordination, analysis also needs to consider the different perspectives on what constitutes these problems. In these circumstances, the meaning of empowerment becomes less clear, and can mean different things for different people. Hence, empowerment is both a concept and a practice, and its meaning changes according to the circumstances and perspectives of different people.

See also: Gender Empowerment Measure (GEM); new social movements; participatory development; power and discourse

Further reading

Parpart, J., Rai, S. and Staudt, K. (eds) (2002) *Rethinking Empowerment: Gender and Development in a Global/Local World*, London: Routledge.
Rowland, J. (1997) *Questioning Empowerment: Working with Women in Honduras*, Oxford: Oxfam.

FRANCIEN VAN DRIEL

end of history

The "end of history" debate refers to a controversial theory proposed in 1989 by Francis Fukuyama that presented the Soviet Union's collapse as the United States' winning of the **Cold War**. Fukuyama argued that the failure of Soviet-style communism and socialism was proof that US-led Western liberal **democracy** and free-market **capitalism** were the highest forms of political and economic organization. Consequently, Fukuyama rendered the pursuit of other alternatives unnecessary. This fundamental proposition implied that history – which Fukuyama read as the struggle between competing forms of politics and economics – had ended. The post-Cold War world would therefore be divided into "post-historical" states that had already achieved democracy and capitalism and the "historical" states still struggling to obtain Fukuyama's utopia. "The End of History" argument was controversial because of its neo-liberal (see **neo-liberalism**) and neo-conservative reading of the Cold War's end and the coming "new world order," which many observers considered to be triumphalistic and exclusive of other possibilities.

See also: Cold War; international economic order; neo-liberalism; revolution

Further reading

Fukuyama, F. (1989) "The End of History?" *The National Interest* 16: 3–18.

PETER MAYELL

endogenous growth theory

The endogenous growth theory presents a model of **economic growth** based on the notion that technological progress results from choices that agents make in order to maximize utility or profit. Responding to economic signals, agents may engage in costly and risky research and development, and in the diffusion of technology (see **technology transfer**). Such activities determine the pace of technological change and the economy's **growth rate**. Growth may go on indefinitely since returns to investment (in research and development, **human capital**, etc.) do not necessarily diminish as the economy develops. Real **gross domestic product (GDP)** per capita can increase as long as agents undertake investment that yields a higher rate of return than their rate of time preference, which influences the rate at which they save. The theory has important implications for developing countries as it draws attention to the importance of promoting and financing literacy (see **illiteracy**), **education**, research, and the spread of ideas.

See also: economic development; economic growth; technology policy

B. MAK ARVIN

energy policy

Energy, like transport (see **transport policy**), is integrally linked to the development process at both high and low levels of income, and is closely linked to other aspects of national and international **security** and **environment** (especially **climate change**). Despite widespread discussion of oil supplies and rapid **economic growth** relating to energy, it is worth remembering that much energy usage for poor people is human or animal-based, and that there are an estimated two billion people worldwide without access to modern forms of energy such as oil or electrification (World Bank, 1996) (see **electrification and power-sector reform**). An estimated one third of energy consumption in developing countries comprises biofuels such as burning **fuelwood**, crop residues and animal dung. These fuels have comparatively low efficiency, present health problems (see **pollution**), and imply investing time in collecting fuels, an activity that can take rural people (and frequently predominantly women) two or three hours a day. **Population** growth in developing countries has led many analysts to suggest that there is now a "fuelwood crisis" especially where **deforestation** is already a problem, such as in Nepal or West Africa, although some have suggested such views overlook the diversity of forest regeneration and fuel sources in rural economies (Leach and Mearns, 1988). Governments and **aid** agencies have responded by encouraging use of cooking stoves that increase fuel efficiency. For example, in Kenya, 80 percent of urban and 10 percent of rural families use the ceramic Jiko Stove, with similar schemes in India and China. The **World Bank** (1996:39) estimated that people with annual incomes of US$300 or less predominantly use fuelwood and dung for cooking, and that people with incomes of US$1,500 or more predominantly adopt modern fuels.

At larger scales, national **economic development** is clearly linked to the availability of inexpensive and reliable energy. Many oil-importing developing countries are greatly affected by changes in oil prices, thus encouraging the use of alternative energy supplies, including coal and even the incineration (or pyrolysis) of municipal solid waste, which have been criticized for environmental reasons (see **climate change; waste management**). Yet in developing countries with energy endowments, such as Gabon (oil) and Algeria (gas), economic development has been affected by impacts on **exchange rates** and inflation (see **inflation and its effects; Dutch disease**), and by an observed tendency to use resources in inefficient ways (see **resource curse thesis**). Indeed, it is estimated that in Nigeria, Africa's largest petroleum exporter, some 80 percent of natural gas associated with oil is flared. The concept of energy intensity is the relationship between energy consumption and **gross domestic product (GDP)**. For **Organization for Economic Cooperation and Development (OECD)** countries, the International Energy Agency (IEA) estimates that energy intensity has been declining at 1.4 percent annually since the early 1970s, but that energy intensity increases for countries undergoing **industrialization**, or where initial levels of energy consumption were low (as in Africa). The IEA estimates that oil production from conventional sources amounted to 40 percent of all energy production in 2000 but will peak in 2030. Oil sources will then remain increasingly within the Middle East, and especially Saudi Arabia, thus making alternate fossil-fuel sources, such as natural gas in Central Asian states, and the pipelines connecting these to users elsewhere, of increasing political and economic importance. Elsewhere, despite **environmental** considerations, coal will remain an important source of fuel. About one quarter of global coal production comes from the Asia-Pacific region and especially China and Indonesia, where the greatest consumers are Japan, South Korea and Taiwan, and other **newly industrialized economies (NIEs)** are growing. So-called "clean-coal" technologies (such as washing coal before combustion) have been proposed as a way to reduce environmental impacts of coal use, although their overall effects remain controversial. For some countries, especially China and India, **nuclear energy** also remains a preferred option for governments.

Renewable energies (see **renewable energy**) present a variety of ways of integrating local development with environmental objectives. Yet, large-scale renewable energy projects such as hydroelectric **dams** and geothermal sites have been criticized for environmental impacts and for ignoring the needs of local people. Many developing countries are already world experts within some renewable energy technologies such as biogas generators, or alcohol-based replacements for gasoline (such as in Brazil). But expanding these to greater involvement in electrification (see **electrification and power-sector reform**) requires investment in new, and competitive forms of technology, at either large scales (e.g. wind farms) or at the level of households and villages (e.g. micro-hydro or solo wind turbines). The **Clean Development Mechanism (CDM)** of the Kyoto Protocol (see **climate change**) offers incentives for companies to invest in new climate-friendly technologies, but these may often imply incurring costs of **technology transfer**, and may even undermine some locally produced technologies in

developing countries. The widespread subsidization of fossil fuels such as diesel and kerosene by many governments was initially seen as a way for states (see **state and state reform**) to assist poor people, but increasingly absorb scarce funds that could be invested in improving other energy infrastructure and discourage investment in alternative sources of energy.

During the 1970s and early 1980s, the **World Bank** was involved mainly in supporting energy and electrification projects (see **electrification and power-sector reform**) that were state-owned. Since the mid-1980s, it has supported privatization (see **privatization and liberalization**) of energy and power sectors, which critics have claimed has underplayed important environmental and developmental objectives. Much rhetoric, for example, has linked privatization to increased energy efficiency. But in the early 1990s, only 1.6 percent of World Bank energy-sector lending was linked to energy efficiency (Tellam, 2000:25). Plus, much investment in electrification has supplied large thermal (fossil-fuel supplied) power stations to centrally controlled grids, rather than introduced decentralized forms of electricity in rural areas. The World Bank has been accused of being "market fixated" because it sees no other ways of promoting rural energy than to privatize energy sectors (Tellam, 2000). Critics propose that privatization needs to be accompanied by incentives and new regulatory structures that direct investment towards the needs of poor people, such as by encouraging investment in decentralized forms of electricity generation. For its part, the World Bank since 1983 has run an Energy Sector Management Assistance Program (ESMAP), and since 1989, the Financing Energy Services for Small-Scale Energy Users (FINESSSE) program that encourages small-scale supplements to grids, and the Asian Alternative Energy Unit (ASTAE), which promotes **renewable energy**. The International Finance Corporation of the World Bank also created the Renewable Energy and Energy Efficiency Fund (REEF) and assisted other programs to address non-conventional energy sources. The Bank, however, attracted criticism in the early 1990s for its involvement in the proposed Narmada Sagar and Sardar Sarovar **dams** in western India, from which the Bank eventually withdrew.

Some critics state that setting firm government targets for energy from renewable or non-conventional use will be the only way to challenge existing trends, or to take **climate change** policy seriously. Yet, achieving such changes in part depends on the growing realization that energy or electricity supply is not simply the domain of the state, but the adoption of more flexible and forms of energy and electrification involving more localized activities by private companies and citizens.

See also: climate change; dams; electrification and power-sector reform; nuclear energy; oil and gas development; Organization of Petroleum Exporting Countries (OPEC); renewable energy; transport policy

Further reading

International Energy Agency: http://www.iea.org/
Leach, G. and Mearns, R. (1988) *Beyond the Fuelwood Crisis*, London: Earthscan.
Tellam, I. (ed.) (2000) *Fuel For Change: World Bank Energy Policy – Rhetoric Versus Reality*, London: Zed.
World Bank (1996) *Rural Energy and Development: Improving Energy Supplies for Two Billion People*, Washington DC: World Bank.
World Bank Energy Program: http://www.worldbank.org/energy/
World Energy Council: http://www.worldenergy.org/

TIM FORSYTH

ENTITLEMENTS AND ENDOWMENTS *see*
famine; food security

entrepreneurship

Entrepreneurship has been defined as a set of behavioral characteristics linked to creating something new, starting a new enterprise, taking initiative, and taking risks, usually through the actions of individual entrepreneurs. Within economics, entrepreneurship is primarily seen as the ways in which entrepreneurs are motivated to influence events around them, cope with risk, and how they are rewarded. Within psychology, models of entrepreneurship focus on the personality traits or characteristics of individuals. Attention within sociology, anthropology and geography has been given to the range of contextual factors that shape the entrepreneur's talents, temperament, resources and opportunities. Within international development, analysts are divided between those who see entrepreneurship as highly varied (and consequently requiring policies that are adapted to the specific contexts of **micro-enterprises**) and those who assume wide-scale changes to economic policy (such as **privatization and liberalization**) will automatically increase entrepreneurship, and hence growth.

The selection of different policies to support entrepreneurship depends on whether entrepreneurs choose to make investments and take risks, or if they are pushed into entrepreneurship as a survival mechanism. The former often have more education and established networks with similar businesses, while the latter are more likely to be in the **urban informal sector** and involved in **street-trading in urban areas**. There are a wide range of **public sector** policies to encourage entrepreneurship and enterprise development including **education** programs, training, advice, and **micro-credit and micro-finance**.

While some people use the term entrepreneurship synonymously with self-**employment**, business ownership or creating new ventures, others make a distinction between these general categories and those individuals who take on more risks and have to find ways of mobilizing resources. An element of entrepreneurship is the ability to mobilize resources to building networks and relationships. These networks differ between places, cultures and sectors with particular concentrations of certain types of **social capital** found within clusters (see **clustering**) of interrelated businesses. For example, a study by Fadahunsi and Rosa (2000) found that entrepreneurship in Nigeria involved coping with uncertainty and particular types of harassment. Cross-border trading entrepreneurs were found to be using a range of sub-contracting relationships to pass on risk, and were moving freely between the informal and formal sectors (see **urban informal sector**). As an enterprise grows, it was found to be moving into the formal sector, while keeping many of its informal links. These trusting relationships are also found by Lyon (2000) with entrepreneur traders building dense networks of trusting relationships in order to access credit and get information from their farmer suppliers and their buyers. Entrepreneurs with very few resources or support can find innovative ways of sustaining their enterprises using relationships and trust. The building of these relationships is based on cultural norms of how business is done. Attempts to promote entrepreneurship therefore need to recognize how it differs between cultures rather than taking a simplistic ethnocentric notion of what constitutes entrepreneurial behavior based on European or North American models.

Elements of entrepreneurship can also be found within larger organizations (intrapreneurship) and within the not-for-profit sector (social entrepreneurship – see **communes, collectives and cooperatives; new social movements; voluntary sector**), while others have emphasized entrepreneurship as a property of networks or localities. It should also be noted that entrepreneurship and entrepreneurial behavior can be used to the detriment of certain groups such as through restricting access to markets, **cartels**, illegality and protection rackets.

See also: clustering; economic development; informal sector; micro-credit and micro-finance; micro-enterprises; small and medium enterprises (SMEs); street-trading in urban areas; urban informal sector

Further reading

Fadahunsi, A. and Rosa, P. (2002) "Entrepreneurship and Illegality: Some Field Lessons from Nigeria," *Journal of Business Venturing* 17:5 397–429.

Lyon, F. (2000) "Trust, Networks and Norms: The Creation of Social Capital in Agricultural Economies in Ghana," *World Development* 28:4 663–82.

Swedberg, R. (2000) *The Social Science View of Entrepreneurship*, Oxford: Oxford University Press.

FERGUS LYON

environment

Debates about environment and development consider questions of environmental conservation, **natural resources**, and environmental health in developing countries, and the relationship of developing countries to global environmental problems and agreements. There are many themes within environment and development. The so-called "green" agenda considers themes such as **deforestation, biodiversity** and wildlife conservation. The **brown environmental agenda** looks at largely urban and industrial problems such as **pollution** and **sanitation**. Other themes include **gender, environment and development; environment and health; natural disasters**, and **political ecology**. Much recent debate has focused on "**sustainable development**" as an umbrella term for development that protects the environment, but this term is criticized for being vague, and for overlooking complex political problems in achieving uniform perceptions of environmental quality, especially between rich and poor, or developed and developing countries.

Much debate about environment and development presents a stark image of crisis, in which **industrialization**, modernization (see **modernization theory**), and **population** growth cause serious damage to fragile ecosystems such as **deforestation, desertification**, damage to marine ecosystems, and anthropogenic **climate change**. Sometimes this image is challenged by a small group of optimists who deny these factors cause environmental damage. Both views, however, should be viewed critically and with reference to the biophysical complexity underlying environmental change; the social complexity with which environmental problems are perceived by diverse social groups; and the uncertainty in both our physical and social knowledge of environmental problems. Increasingly, debates in environment and development do not ask simply whether environmental problems "do" or "do not" exist in general – there is no doubt that development is imbued with a variety of deep environmental concerns. But instead, analysts ask *which* of many concerns should be addressed; *who* is involved (or not involved) in identifying or solving them; and *how far* proposed solutions may actually address (or even add to) concerns experienced by poor people.

Resources and population

Much environment and development debate has linked population to resource depletion and environmental degradation, although many now see this link as simplistic. Many early discussions of environment and development suggested immanent crisis. Rachel Carson's (1962) influential book, *Silent Spring* described the damaging impacts of the pesticide DDT. Paul Ehrlich's (1968) *The Population Bomb* urged **population** controls. The *Limits to Growth* **report (1972)** by the **Club of Rome** used a computer model to predict the rapid depletion of **natural resources** at current rates of consumption. These books had a generally Malthusian tone (see **Malthusian demography; carrying capacity**), which assumed the fragility or fixity of ecological or resource-production systems, and consequently predicted that continued economic and population growth would lead to economic and social declines. Such concerns have often been adopted by later on **environmental** security, regarding the likelihood of **wars** or **violence** resulting from competition for scarce resources.

A variety of analysts, however, have criticized Malthusian notions for overlooking how market demand may influence scarcity of resources, or the development of technology to limit resource use or find substitute resources (see **technology policy**). So-called "technological optimists" – frequently influenced by the writings of Ester Boserup (1965)– proposed instead that limits to growth (see *Limits to Growth* **report (1972)**) are only temporary, and are controlled by the degree to which technological progress can avoid scarcity, or how far different socio-economic trends may dictate which resources are currently used. Hence, the optimists suggested, the Stone Age did not end because of a shortage of stone. Or, as the saying goes, "resources are not: they become." (A current example may include declining demand in copper for wire because of innovations in fiberoptics). Such arguments have been used to explain why many of the crises predicted during the 1960s and early 1970s failed to materialize. Similarly, these arguments claim **population** growth itself need not be problematic if the access to technology, and the means to avoid environmental degradation, are available.

Yet, while such arguments have obviously applied to the richer economies, many political economists suggested that such technological adaptation was not possible in some poorer countries, and that the supply of resources and technology is controlled by international political economy. Consequently, certain countries, under certain political scenarios, may still experience significant limits to growth, and these were illustrated through crises such as **famine**. These arguments consequently alleged that political factors underlying limits to growth were more important than natural limits, and hence international **aid** should be increased. Other, more ecologist, critics claimed that natural limits still exist, but they have yet to be experienced fully.

Poverty and environment

A similar theme has been the alleged association of **poverty** and environmental degradation. At the **Stockholm 1972 world conference on environment and development**, the Indian Prime Minister, Indira Gandhi, famously stated that poverty was the world's greatest environmental threat. This was later reflected in theorizing about environment, and particularly the so-called $I = PAT$ equation, which stated that environmental impacts (I) were a function of population (P), affluence (or poverty) (A), and technology (T), and which still underlies much environmental explanation and assessment today. In the **Brundtland Commission** of the 1980s (which went on to define the concept of **sustainable development**), poverty was described as both a cause and effect of environmental degradation, and that many poor people were caught in a "downward spiral" of environmentally degrading practices because they had no alternative but to degrade resources in order to survive. For many, the relationship of poverty and environment was summarized by Hardin's (1968) notion of *The Tragedy of the Commons*, which described how uncontrolled access to common access resources would lead to collapse (see **common pool resources; institutions and environment**).

These statements, too, have been criticized. Much anthropological or local research in developing countries has indicated that poor people frequently conserve resources more efficiently than commonly thought (e.g. see **deforestation**). New approaches to poverty show that entitlements to land and resources are more important indications of poverty than monetary wealth alone, and that these are controlled by social and political factors involving, for example, **gender, caste**, or other means of **social exclusion** (see **food security**). Furthermore, once these entitlements are in place, there is greater ability to form **institutions** (or norms of shared behavior) to protect resources. Hence, environmental protection in poor countries may depend more upon securing the ability of poor people to farm or collect resources sustainably (through mechanisms such as **resource tenure**, or access to technologies) than in preventing their access to resources. For this reason, the simple $I = PAT$ equation has been criticized for overlooking the political access to resources, or the ability for poor people to form protective **institutions** (see **community-based natural resource management (CBNRM); environmental entitlements; gender and property rights; institutions and environment; sustainable livelihoods**).

Challenging environmental assumptions

Partly because of these preceding debates, a growing theme of environment and development is to question the basis upon which policy-makers have explained environment degradation in the past, and how far these are either accurate or useful. In particular, statements of universal causality (such as "population growth must cause environmental decline") are being questioned, and instead the contexts in which either biophysical changes or environmental problems are experienced, are seen to be more important. For example, Tiffen and Mortimore (1994) analyzed alleged environmental decline in Kenya, and concluded that "more people" may indeed mean "less erosion" because local people had been able to adopt soil-conservation measures and economic

diversification, resulting in the avoidance of environmental breakdown for most inhabitants. (Similar findings questioning the applicability of the $I = PAT$ equation have been replicated in many other studies: e.g. see **deforestation; desertification; mountain development; shifting cultivation; watershed management**).

These studies in part reflect the need to acknowledge the influence of **institutions** and **community-based natural resource management (CBNRM)** mentioned above. More fundamentally, however, these findings have inspired discussions of the politically and culturally situated nature of ecological science itself. Critical studies of ecological science have criticized many of the basic "laws" underlying much orthodox environmental explanation for overlooking the importance of local contexts where such "laws" were constructed, or where they are applied. For example, the so-called Universal Soil-Loss Equation (USLE), was developed in response to the undoubtedly serious problems of erosion encountered in the USA during the 1930s' Dust Bowl phenomenon, and has been used by many development agencies in addressing erosion worldwide. But experience has suggested the equation is not "universal" either because it insufficiently acknowledges the local diversity of **agriculture** and slope management; or because the equation assumes *erosion* to be the primary concern of farmers, when in fact the underlying problem of declining soil *fertility* may be caused by various means (see **soil erosion and soil fertility**). The problems with this scientific generalization is that it fails to acknowledge the assumptions about environmental problems made by modelers, and it proposes solutions that do not necessarily acknowledge local perceptions of problems or of environmental changes. Similar questions have also been posed of other commonly heard generalizations (or narratives; see **narratives of development**) of **deforestation, dryland agriculture, pastoralism**, etc. (Leach and Mearns, 1996; Forsyth, 2003).

A further trend is the acknowledgement of so-called "non-equilibrium" or non-linear ecology, which acknowledges the role of diversity in ecological change over time and space scales, and the difficulty of achieving comprehensive explanations of such changes based on limited observations from selected viewpoints (Adams, 2001). In turn, these studies question how different states of ecological stability are seen to be "normal" in biophysical terms, or as socially acceptable by different social groups. For example, the "myths" of "nature in balance" or that the US landscape was "pristine" before the arrival of Columbus have been claimed to be romantic visions of how nature is meant to be, rather than a full understanding of dynamic ecological change. More controversially, such debates also question whether current ecological changes such as forest fires or forms of **shifting cultivation** are as damaging as commonly claimed in the media because ecosystems have experienced such disturbances in the past, and current **biodiversity** reflects such changes. It is important to note that such debates are not intended to legitimize destructive practices, but instead to highlight that land-use policies based on equilibrium (or "balance of nature") ecology may not address underlying biophysical changes, and impose unnecessary restrictions on how people (especially smallholders) use land. Accordingly, some analysts of environment and development consider that descriptions of environmental problems discussed in annual documents such as *The State of the World* reports published by Worldwatch Institute (whom many believe to be influenced by Malthusian and equilibrium approaches) need to be considered in context concerning how they create problems, and for whom. Many modelers of global environmental change, however, insist that it is possible to go too far, and forget that rates of global change are unprecedented, and that with increasing anthropogenic **climate change** and its potential link with *El Niño* (with associated impacts on both rich and poor), human influences on land cover should be both measured and controlled.

Local and global governance

The growing debate about the nature and complexity of environmental change, however, has to be matched by developments in governing such change. Environmental politics generally have sought to represent the findings of environmental science (see **science and technology**) at the level of legislation and government policy (see also **political ecology**). Much concern has also rightly highlighted that international agreements are the only way to limit transboundary environmental problems such as long-range **pollution** and climate change. But the popular phrase to "think global, act local" has been criticized recently for downplaying the controversies about how "global" environmental problems such as climate change are experienced similarly worldwide, or how far people agree on solutions.

The first major international conference on environment, at Stockholm in 1972 (see **Stockholm 1972 world conference on environment and development**) witnessed clashes between, for example, the USA (who favored a ban on whaling, but resisted restrictions on petrochemicals), and India (who urged attention to **poverty**, and who feared environmentalism might mean anti-developmentalism). The **Earth Summit (1992) (United Nations Conference on Environment and Development)** in Rio reiterated the right to development (see **right to development**), and provided the first legally binding conventions on **biodiversity** and **climate change**. But developing countries (especially Brazil and Malaysia) rejected a proposed convention on forests before the meeting because it was seen to restrict their right to govern their own resources. Moreover, many proposals for addressing climate change suggested that **deforestation** should be seen on a par with industrial or domestic emissions, which, critics alleged, overlooked questions of international justice, or imposed Western visions of nature upon the South (see **climate change**). At later negotiations, such as at Kyoto (1997) and afterwards, many developing countries (although not all) disagreed with projects aiming to address climate change by investing in carbon "sinks" (e.g. through **plantation forestry**) in developing countries, and instead urged greater **technology transfer** or **leapfrogging** for industrial development (see **Clean Development Mechanism (CDM)**). Yet, many observers still believe developed countries are dragging their feet on climate change or **biodiversity**. At Rio, President George Bush (Snr) notoriously commented that the American lifestyle was not for negotiation. In 2001, President George Bush (Jnr) unilaterally withdrew the USA from the Kyoto protocol. These positions reflected skepticism by conservative US governments about international agreements they could not control, and an unwillingness to consider policies that constrained corporate profitability.

Since Rio, **civil society** has been encouraged in both the formulation and implementation of environmental policy, including both the role of **environment**al movements and **community-based natural resource management (CBNRM)**. On one hand, **decentralization** of policy is important to avoid some environmental excesses of state-led (see **state and state reform**) development (e.g. **Polonoreste; transmigration**); to provide capacity where the state has no influence; to acknowledge **local knowledge** or **indigenous knowledge**; and to harness business investment for environmental purposes. On the other hand, some have claimed that over-reliance on "communities" exaggerates the benefit of local knowledge; or overlooks either the differences contained within communities (see **community**), and how wider politics may romanticize or commodify **indigenous peoples** in ways that represent outsiders', rather than local people's interests. This has also been claimed for ecofeminism (see **feminism and ecology; feminist political ecology**); and for some movements, for example the **Chipko movement** – although this is by no means a rule. Increasingly, co-management between communities, the state, and national and international **non-governmental organizations (NGOs)** – rather than reliance on single actors alone – is considered effective **governance**.

Similarly, many agree with the statement of Maurice Strong, when chairing Rio, that "the environment is not going to be saved by environmentalists: environmentalists do not hold the levers of economic power." At the **World Summit on Sustainable Development (Johannesburg, 2002)**, the **United Nations** called for new **partnerships** between international business and other actors in environmental policy. **Corporate social responsibility (CSR)** is escalating as an arena of environment and development policy. Skeptics, however, question how far such partnerships may actually regulate industry. Opposition to **globalization**, the WTO (see **World Trade Organization/General Agreement on Tariffs and Trade (WTO/GATT)**) and **World Bank**, or proposals such as the **Multilateral Agreement on Investment (MAI)** are now common forms of international environmentalism.

Environment and development remains a diverse and contested theme. Many analysts agree that the initial crisis narratives (see **narratives of development**) typified by the *Limits to Growth* report **(1972)** and associated writings, overlooked crucial questions of **governance**, **resource tenure**, and access to technology, or the capacity of people of create **sustainable livelihoods** when these factors exist. But many critics also suggest that underlying trends in consumption, exploitative development of **natural resources**, and under-representation of poor and vulnerable people, mean that environmental problems remain fundamentally unchallenged.

See also: Agenda 21; brown environmental agenda; climate change; community-based natural resource management (CBNRM); deforestation; desertification; Earth Summit (1992) (United Nations Conference on Environment and Development); environment and health; environmental entitlements; environmental movements; environmental security; feminism and ecology; feminist political ecology; gender, environment and development; institutions and environment; *Limits to Growth* report (1972); natural resources; political ecology; pollution; resource tenure; shifting cultivation; soil erosion and soil fertility; sustainable development; sustainable livelihoods; water management

Further reading

Adams, W. (2001, 2nd edn) *Green Development: Environment and Sustainability in the South*, London: Routledge.

Boserup, E. (1965) *The Conditions of Agricultural Growth: The Economics of Agriculture under Population Pressure*, London and New York: Allen and Unwin.

Carson, R. (1962) *Silent Spring*, Boston MA: Houghton Mifflin.

Ehrlich, P. (1968) *The Population Bomb*, San Francisco: Sierra Club.

Forsyth, T. (2003) *Critical Political Ecology: The Politics of Environmental Science*, London: Routledge.

Hardin, G. (1968) "The Tragedy of the Commons," *Science* 162: 1243–8.

Meadows, D., Meadows, D., Randers, J. and Behrens III, W. (1972) *The Limits to Growth: A Report for the Club of Rome's Project on the Predicament of Mankind*, New York: University Books.

Leach, M. and Mearns, R. (eds) (1996) *The Lie of the Land: Challenging Received Wisdom on the African Environment*, Oxford: James Currey.

Tiffen, M. and Mortimore, M. (1994) *More People, Less Erosion? Environmental Recovery in Kenya*, Chichester: John Wiley.

Worldwatch Institute (annual publication) *State of the World*, Washington DC: Worldwatch.

TIM FORSYTH

environment and health

The analysis of environment and health seeks to establish links between environmental surroundings and human health. It is sometimes seen to be part of the "**brown environmental agenda**." Human conceptions of the links between environment and health are rooted in early miasmal theories of the origin of disease. Thus, the determinants of pestilence and illness were thought to be associated with decomposing animal and vegetable remains, swamps, and polluted air. Scientific discoveries regarding the contribution of microorganisms to pathogenesis deposed the rather vague miasma conjecture, as it became clear that careful management of the environmental conditions that control the proliferation of pathogens could reduce human infections and the spread of disease. The link between environment and health has since been recognized to encompass a variety of physical causative agents of disease, including all classes of pathogens, toxic chemicals, electromagnetic radiation, noise levels, dust particles, and natural disasters. However, the geographical distribution of these environmental threats is uneven across the globe. Naturally occurring pathogens tend to dominate environmental health concerns in poorer countries, whereas chemical pollutants of industrial origin tend to dominate concerns in developed countries.

Environmental health science, the field of investigation that studies the link between environment and health has adopted a broad definition of "**environment**" rather than narrower definitions that focus only on physical environmental compartments such as water, air, soil, and **food**. Consequently, the structure and integrity of social environments are recognized as important contributors to disease burden, inasmuch as poor social conditions breed poverty, and are therefore inextricably linked to inadequate physical environmental conditions that are otherwise necessary to support good public health.

Despite the great strides have been made in controlling human diseases associated with polluted environments, the first comprehensive assessment of the global burden of disease conducted by the **World Health Organization (WHO)** indicated that diseases associated with poor environmental quality continue to exert a huge burden on human health and welfare. For example, more than 10 million childhood deaths occur annually due to preventable environmental diseases such as diarrhea from water-borne pathogens including cholera (see **water-borne diseases**), and acute respiratory infections from both indoor and outdoor air pollutants (see **infant and child mortality; pollution**). Environmental vector-borne diseases such as **malaria** claim up to 3 million deaths every year, with many more disabled for long periods. Most of the casualties in these categories are in developing countries, but environmental threats to human health also abound in developed countries. More than 80 million residents of the USA are routinely exposed to levels of air pollutants that can produce severe health impairment through protracted periods of exposure.

The inherent differences in the variety of local environmental threats to health are well recognized. Attempts to understand these differences have contributed substantially to the agenda of various international health agencies that are engaged with reducing the burden of human disease attributed to environmental factors. However, a new category of environmental threat is emerging that is global in dimension, and as such, has implications for all geographical regions of the world. Changes in the global environment, including thinning of the ozone layer, **climate change**, and declining **biodiversity** are expected to have considerable impacts on all regions, but integrated assessments of such impacts are currently premature.

The projection of local health impacts of global environmental change is difficult because the phenomena of global environmental change are expected to interact with varying levels of **vulnerability** in the health sectors of different countries, and this interaction will doubtlessly produce different outcomes for public health. Improvements in this direction will require greater depth of coverage, as well as increased spatial and temporal resolution of technologies such as satellites that are used to monitor environmental change. Innovations in study design strategies employed in environmental and social epidemiology are also needed to accommodate remote populations that are likely to be vulnerable to **epidemics** stimulated and sustained by environmental factors.

Much of the effort that is currently dedicated to the improvement of environmental health aims to increase herd immunity through large-scale **vaccination**s, a strategy which proved to be successful in the global initiative to eradicate smallpox (see **disease eradication**). However, other strategies including appropriate environmental impact assessments of development projects must be coordinated with vaccinations in order to achieve sustainable environmental health, particularly in developing countries. For example, several economic and rural development projects, such as the construction of **dams** for hydroelectric power and water supply, have led to disasters in environmental health, either through the inadvertent proliferation of habitats suitable for disease vectors such as mosquitoes, or through the creation of new flood zones that provoke local epidemics of water-borne gastroenteritis.

Similarly, current discussions of strategies to mitigate global **climate change** have focused on carbon dioxide emissions. This focus has unfortunately polarized the debate along the lines of developed countries against developing countries. Common ground may be reached by focusing on certain co-benefits of mitigation for the environmental health sector, particularly through the elimination of toxic lead (Pb) from fossil fuels used in developing countries. Global reduction of fossil fuel consumption will also benefit environmental health in all countries through the reduction of public exposure to other toxicants including mercury, tropospheric ozone, and suspended particulate matter. Yet, the **vulnerability** of different people to such changes at the atmospheric level may also be influenced by local concerns such as **livelihoods**, **nutrition**, etc., and hence environment and health is not simply about understanding the biophysical causes of hazards, but in understanding how different people may be affected and protected.

See also: brown environmental agenda; disease eradication; disease, social constructions of; epidemics; environment; health; health and poverty; malaria; sanitation; vaccination; vulnerability; water-borne diseases; World Health Organization (WHO)

Further reading

Murray, C. and Lopez, A. (eds) (1996) *The Global Burden of Disease*, Cambridge MA: Harvard University Press.

World Resources Institute; United Nations Environment Program; United Nations Development Programme; World Bank (1998) *Environmental Change and Human Health*, New York: Oxford University Press.

DELE OGUNSEITAN

environmental entitlements

Environmental entitlements are an analytical approach to understanding people-environment relations. It illuminates the ways in which different people value, access and control environmental resources and services, using these to maintain or enhance their **well-being**, and the role of **institutions** in these processes (see **institutions and environment**).

Environmental problems are frequently understood in terms of mismatches between populations and resource availability, shaped perhaps by choice of technology or by **poverty**. However, such formulations obscure critical questions of socially differentiated resource value and access: for instance who sees which components of variable, dynamic ecologies as resources at different times; how they gain access to and control over these, and how natural resource use (see **natural resources**) by different social actors in turn transforms different components of the environment.

An analytical approach to address such questions draws on and extends the notions of entitlements and endowments originally developed by Amartya Sen to draw attention to the analogous issue of command over **food** (see explanation in **food security**). Complementing other related approaches such as **sustainable livelihoods** analysis, the approach helps track how particular components of the environment contribute to the **well-being** of socially differentiated people. The distribution, quality and quantity of environmental goods and services are explained in terms of the interface between biophysical ecological dynamics and human actions. Environmental goods and services become endowments for particular people through processes of "mapping," where endowments refer to *the rights and resources that people have*, such as land, labor or skills. Endowments may, in turn, be transformed into environmental entitlements, which refer to *alternative sets of benefits derived from environmental goods and services over which people have legitimate effective command and which are instrumental in achieving well-being.* Environmental entitlements may include any or all of the following: direct uses in the form of commodities, such as **food**, water or fuel; the market value of such resources, or of rights to them; and the benefits derived from environmental services, such as **pollution** sinks or the properties of the hydrological cycle. Entitlements in turn enhance people's capabilities (see **capability approach**), which are *what people can do or be with their entitlements*. To take a very simple example, command over fuel resources – derived from rights over

trees – gives warmth or the ability to cook, and so contributes to well-being.

The environmental entitlements approach explains access to, and control over resources as structured by **institutions**, understood as regularized patterns of behavior between individuals and groups in society. These may be formal (e.g. a statutory tenure regime) or informal (e.g. customary norms regarding labor use). Institutions at multiple scale levels – local, national, international – may interact to shape the benefits people derive from environmental goods and services and the ways they manage them, and thus the trajectories of livelihood-environment relations over time.

See also: capability approach; common pool resources; community forestry; environment; feminist political ecology; gender and property rights; institutions and environment; land rights; natural resources; political ecology; property rights; resource tenure; well-being

Further reading

Leach, M., Mearns, R. and Scoones, I. (1999) "Environmental Entitlements: Dynamics and Institutions in Community-based Natural Resource Management," *World Development* 27:2 225–47.

Leach, M., Mearns, R. and Scoones, I. (eds) (1997) "Community-Based Sustainable Development: Consensus or Conflict?" Special issue of *IDS Bulletin* 28:4.

MELISSA LEACH

environmental movements

Environmental movements are social movements or political campaigns that highlight environmental problems. They are often attributed with introducing environmentalism as a political concern to national and international arenas. Environmental movements, however, are highly varied, and do not always share similar views. Furthermore, some social theorists have argued that environmentalism, or environmental movements, are frequently inspired by political concerns not necessarily related to environmental change, and that the environmental message of different movements needs to be understood within wider social and political contexts (see **environment; political ecology**).

Much disagreement about environmental movements results from different approaches to explaining their origin. One school of thought sees movements inspired by new and worrying results of environmental science about the state of the world, which are then communicated through alliances of scientists and activists to the policy arena (see **science and technology**). This was claimed, for example, concerning the emergence of the ozone hole or anthropogenic **climate change** as topics of international environmental concern. But another approach sees environmental movements (and environmentalism) as linked to broader social changes that influence, first, which aspects of environmental change are considered worrying, and second, how these are communicated. For example, many social theorists see environmentalism as a classic "new" social movement (see **new social movements**) of the 1960s associated with a "post-industrial" concern about modernization's impacts on society and nature (see **modernization theory**), and the desire to highlight new identity-based politics such as feminism and racial rights. As such, "new" social movements could be distinguished from "old" social movements based on classic oppositions between the social classes of industrial societies, and therefore represent global concerns on behalf of all society, rather than specific groups.

Critics, however, have questioned whether environmental movements can be so inclusive. Some historians of environmentalism have linked the emergence of "wilderness" conservation (or the "green" agenda), such as by the US Sierra Club, with rises in **industrialization** and **urbanization**, and hence not necessarily shared by all groups. Some Marxist critics in the 1970s alleged that mainstream environmentalism was essentially bourgeois, and indeed should be challenged by a "red" or "redgreen" agenda focusing on **livelihoods** rather than conservation for its own sake. A further concern is how far environmental movements in developing countries can also "speak for themselves," or be shaped by outside interests or even alliances with non-governmental organizations (NGOs) or middle classes who are sometimes internationally educated (see also **advocacy coalitions; solidarity campaigns**). Much debate about the Chipko antideforestation movement in India, for example (see **Chipko movement**), has been claimed to have falsely represented local people as in-tune with Western notions of protecting nature, when many local activists were actually resisting either illegal activity or state controls (see **state and state reform**) that restricted **livelihoods**. Other campaigns, such as the resistance to **dams** on the Narmada river in western India may similarly have become dominated by a general opposition to inflexibility from the state, or the influence of the **World Bank** in general, rather than the promotion of poor people's livelihoods *per se*. Many smaller movements, represented under the concept of **weapons of the weak**, may legitimately be called environmental because they involve uses of **natural resources**, but they are often not called environmental in international debates because they do not coincide with current political campaigns from more powerful activists.

Consequently, some authors (e.g. Guha and Martinez-Alier, 1997; Escobar, 1998) have argued for a new "environmentalism of the poor," or greater attention to how wider political trends shape what is considered to be environmental in developing countries. But environmentalism remains an important political force, especially in the opposition to **globalization** or the proposed **Multilateral Agreement on Investment (MAI)** at WTO meetings (see **World Trade Organization/General Agreement on Tariffs and Trade (WTO/GATT); World Social Forum (WSF)**).

See also: Chipko movement; dams; environment; new social movements; political ecology; World Social Forum (WSF)

Further reading

Escobar, A. (1998) "Whose Knowledge, Whose Nature? Biodiversity, Conservation, and the Political Ecology of Social Movements," *Journal of Political Ecology*, 5, 53–82.

Guha, R. and Martinez-Allier, J. (1997) *Varieties of Environmentalism*, London: Earthscan.

Peet, R. and Watts, M. (2004, 2nd edn) *Liberation Ecologies: Environment, Development and Social Movements*, London: Routledge.

TIM FORSYTH

environmental security

Environmental security is, in its most general sense, a concern with human **vulnerability** to natural resource (see **natural resources**) scarcity created by human and/or natural processes. This concept has been most greatly developed in political science and geopolitics literatures, which focus on the potential connections between resource scarcity and conflict. Development intervenes in this conceptualization by bringing to the fore links between scarcity and broader economic and political processes that produce underdevelopment. Despite this intervention, the use of environmental security in development studies does not often reference the more detailed work conducted in political science and geopolitics, resulting in distinct uses of this term in each literature.

Natural resource scarcity arose as a **security** issue in the political science and geopolitics literature across the 1980s as traditional, state-centered security threats declined (see **state and state reform**) and the awareness of environmental change and its impacts grew. This created a narrowly focused environmental security that links natural resource scarcity to conflict around the world in an effort to predict and control such conflicts. For example, the increasing demand for water resources in the Middle East has frequently been predicted to be the origin of future armed conflict. Similarly, anthropogenic **climate change** has also been described as the source of future resource depletion, leading to **international migration** and **refugees**, and even **war** (e.g. Homer-Dixon and Blitt, 1998).

This kind of prediction, however, has been criticized by social and political scholars who claim that they rarely conduct nuanced examinations of the causes of scarcity, or attention to how various scarcities filter through particular social contexts to set the stage for demographic, economic and resource pressures that can develop into conflict that threatens national boundaries and state **institutions** (e.g. Barnett, 2001; Peluso and Watts, 2001).

Development's use of environmental security diverges from that of the above literatures in that it explores the causes of scarcity. While the use of environmental security in the political science/geopolitics literature brings to the surface issues of environmental degradation, **environment and health**, and the safety and certainty of those living in developing countries when addressing resource scarcity, in much of the existing literature the idea of **vulnerability** is underdeveloped. A close consideration of vulnerability in the context of environmental change and resource scarcity brings to the fore issues of underdevelopment, where **poverty** is a key generator of insecurity. Further, local underdevelopment can only be understood in the context of larger environmental, economic and political processes, relating seemingly local scarcity issues to a global frame. From the development perspective, the road to environmental security must pass through economic (see **economic development**) and **social development** focused on developing resilience to economic and environmental change. In this manner a nuanced use of the term environmental security, which includes a measured definition of **vulnerability** that is to be mitigated, may become coterminous with the goals of **sustainable development**.

See also: environment; food security; human security; natural disasters; natural resources; security; vulnerability

Further reading

Barnett, J. (2001) *The Meaning of Environmental Security: Ecological Politics and Policy in the New Security Era*, London: Zed.

Homer-Dixon, T. F. and Blitt, J. (1998) *Ecoviolence: Links Among Environment, Population and Security*, Lanham MD: Rowman and Littlefield.

Peluso, N. and Watts, M. (eds) (2001) *Violent Environments*, Ithaca NY: Cornell University Press.

EDWARD R. CARR

epidemics

An epidemic is defined as the prevalence of disease within a **community** group during a particular time, which is the result of a causative agent that is usually present in the affected area. The term "epidemic" comes from the Greek: *epi* meaning "upon" or "close to" and *demos* meaning "people." The word has been used in English medical literature since the early seventeenth century to mean an unusually high incidence of disease. The number of cases required to define an epidemic depends on the infectious agent, size and type of **population** exposed, experience with the disease and time and place of occurrence. The term "endemic" refers to the usual presence of the disease in a population in a given geographic space. This can offer an idea of the "background" incidence of a disease and provide a benchmark against which epidemic conditions can be identified. However, criteria for the identification of an epidemic as relative to the background "normal" incidence in the population can be complicated, and analysts frequently use sophisticated modeling techniques.

While epidemics can describe both infectious and chronic diseases, the term is ordinarily used to describe diseases of a communicable nature (see also **gender and communicable disease**). Two main types of communicable disease epidemic exist: the propagated epidemic, which is spread through chain transmission (such as measles); and the common-vehicle epidemic (such as cholera), which is spread from the dissemination of a causative agent, often from a shared medium.

Epidemics are described graphically as epidemic curves, usually depicted with a time-based x-axis and a measure of cases on the y-axis. The typical curve follows an S-shaped pattern, rising slowly and gradually. At a certain point in the epidemic, a critical number of people are infected, causing mass acceleration of disease spread. The epidemic spreads through the susceptible population until it is saturated and most people are infected. The end of the curve flattens out when either recovery takes place or deaths outnumber new infections. Varying determinants of disease prevalence, such as incubation distributions and modes of transmission, determine the shape of an epidemic curve.

The "Black Death" probably remains the most remarkable example of the influence of epidemic disease. The bubonic plague killed 20 million people, a quarter of the population of fourteenth-century Western Europe, within ten years. The cause of the bubonic plague was a bacterial disease carried by fleas that fed on rats. The rat host is killed by the flea, which at that point begins to look for food and jumps to a human host if one is available.

See also: disease eradication; gender and communicable disease; health; HIV/AIDS (definition and treatment); HIV/AIDS (policy issues); mortality; primary health care; sexually transmitted diseases (STDs)

Further reading

Cliff, A., Haggett, P. and Smallman-Raynor, M. (1998) *Deciphering Global Epidemics*, Cambridge: Cambridge University Press.
Rothman, K. (2002) *Epidemiology: An Introduction*, Boston MA: Boston University Press.

PRERNA BANATI

EPIDEMIOLOGY/EPIDEMIOLOGICAL TRANSITION *see* health; health transition

equitable development

Equitable development refers to development that aims to provide opportunities and **social justice** to people who are disadvantaged in society, and who may have fewer chances to benefit from large-scale development projects (see **marginalization; poverty**). Conventional large-scale programs and projects in pursuit of modernization (see **modernization theory**) often proved highly inequitable in practice. Particular categories of people and place, particularly urban-based (but also some rural) **elites** and middle classes, benefitted disproportionately from the new facilities and services (see **sociology of development**). Conversely, poor, landless people and the **peasantry** often gained little or actually lost out, especially if they suffered dispossession or displacement during project implementation, since compensation would be inadequate or non-existent. Disillusionment with conventional approaches mounted from the late 1960s onwards, spawning a plethora of different critiques and approaches from various intellectual and political traditions. However, the normative concern that development should be more equitable represents a common strand. Equitability is generally more achievable in small- than in large-scale interventions, especially through participatory and bottom-up development (see **participatory development**) with the objective of **empowerment**. Current approaches to sustainable and alternative development (see **sustainable development; postmodernism and postdevelopment**) also now generally recognize the reduction of **poverty** and **inequality** as essential corollaries.

See also: empowerment; inequality; people-centered development; postmodernism and postdevelopment

DAVID SIMON

ethics

Debates concerning ethics and development refer to questions of right and wrong in the formulation, purpose, and implementation of development (also see **social justice; human development**). Underlying this debate has been some form of moral reasoning and a shared concern with improving the lot of humanity. Most concern within ethics and development has been placed at the global **inequality** in **income distribution** and **poverty** (see **inequality and poverty, world trends**). Yet, a further concern (commonly voiced from **postmodernism and postdevelopment**) is the alleged inability of development methodologies to reverse poverty. More critically still, some

allege the continued existence of the formal "development industry" itself, despite such apparent failures, is also an ethical issue (see also **culture; anti-politics; World Bank**).

Different development methodologies have explained inequality and poverty in alternative ways. The dominant model of development, relying largely upon economics, has focused primarily on improving economic performance in terms of competitiveness and **productivity**. Development and restructuring are elements of an economic system, which is constantly in a state of flux, involving an on-going search for higher levels of profitability through the exploitation of resources and business opportunities in optimal locations. An alternative approach, reliant largely on political economy, has focused instead on the regional dimension, or unevenness, of development, which is seen to result inevitably from the spatial functioning of **capitalism**. Some political economists acknowledge that the market is the best mechanism to realize human desires with a maximum of freedom and a minimum of constraint. Others, however, such as Corbridge (1998) have argued that political economic approaches should develop ethical and moral criticism of development, in order to acknowledge the impact of **economic growth** on factors such as **life expectancy**, as well as simply in terms of **economic development**. Hence, an ethical approach to development studies might focus on who benefits or loses from the development process, and how inequalities may be reduced. Moreover, this approach proposes a refocusing of debates concerning **Marxism** to consider the ethical and distributional aspects of development, rather than on the scientific or explanatory logic within Marxism concerning the origins of economic growth.

Accordingly, much debate about development ethics has reconsidered the role of orthodox, growth-oriented development theory. Some have argued that the concept has outlived its usefulness, or is too closely linked to the extension of Western consumer values to the rest of the world. Wolfgang Sachs (1992:104) described the development process as "an ahistorical and delocalized universalism of European origins," which substituted the term "underdevelopment" for "savages," and which has replaced reason with economic performance as the key criterion of progress. Corbridge (1998) and others, however, are concerned about the "amoral politics of indifference" which can characterize the position of anti-developmentalists (see **postmodernism and postdevelopment**), because they pay little attention to the real dilemmas of development and fail to spell out the consequences of the actions or inactions that they propose.

Some scholars have argued that we must move beyond our own frameworks in order to understand "other" societies and explain what they do from their perspective (see **postmodernism and postdevelopment**). A further means of introducing a more ethical focus to development is to adopt a minimalist, or gradual approach of integrating **social justice** with **economic growth**. Friedmann (1992), for example, criticized market-led accumulation models of development in Latin America because they failed to include the majority of citizens in its benefits. He called for an alternative form of development with the concept of "human flourishing" as a primary objective, which asks the fundamental question of what it means to be human, and what empowers individuals and communities (see **community**) to achieve their full capacity (see **capability approach; functionings**). Friedmann pointed to the **Universal Declaration of Human Rights (1948)** as a basis for integrating social justice with **economic development**. The implications for **human rights** have been further developed in later UN documents such as the 1966 **International Covenant on Economic, Social and Cultural Rights**. While Friedmann acknowledged that much of this thinking has its roots in the Judeo-Christian tradition, other traditions including Confucianism, Gandhiism and Islamic radicalism have also rejected Western development models driven by relentless competition. The establishment of universal "rights," however, may prove problematic in other cultural settings (see **cultural relativism**).

The scholars attributed with establishing the new discipline of development ethics are L. J. Lebret, and his student Denis Goulet. Goulet (1991) warned ethicists of the need to deal with pragmatic constraints of planners while evaluating competing policy proposals. He argued that development policy should acknowledge the need to "be more" rather than "have more" (see **well-being; freedom versus choice**). A key dimension of this approach is solidarity, by which development is geared toward benefitting all by focusing on the common good. In Goulet's view, development that accentuated inequalities (see **inequality**) was "illusory antidevelopment." Instead, development should acknowledge the values of traditions such as religious **institutions, local knowledge**, and extended family networks (see **joint families**): such traditions represent useful solidarities. Friedmann (1992), however, argued that we should be careful about overemphasizing the role of communities (see **community**), as they tend to see situations from their own perspective, and instead there should be a greater role for the state in promoting **social justice** (see **state and state reform**).

Other scholars have applied debates in moral philosophy to development, but this has proven difficult because of the need to understand what it means to be human. For example, it is difficult to propose universal **basic needs** or **human rights** on one hand, and identify what is possible or acceptable at the local level on the other. One major task, therefore, is to establish some minimalist conception of living standards that are universally acceptable. Corbridge (1998) argues in favor of "minimalist universalism" based on the principle that the lives of other people are inextricably linked to our own, and therefore they have a right to call on our resources.

The influence of an ethical approach to development has been evident in major policy documents for some years. The 1994 UNDP *Human Development Report* argued for a global ethic based on "sustainable human development." By adopting **people-centered development**, this concept is more inclusive than **sustainable development**, and states that it is unacceptable to perpetuate the inequities of today for future generations. The underlying philosophy of this concept rejects the pursuit of material **well-being** alone, or the classification of people as **human capital**, and instead argues for development based on "the universalism of life claims."

Questions about the ethics of "development" itself continue (see **culture; postmodernism and postdevelopment**). In particular, the use of development expertise to reduce public negotiation over the objectives and processes of development have been described as **anti-politics**, and campaigners accordingly call for greater **accountability** and **transparency** in development and increasingly within the private sector (see **corporate social responsibility (CSR); corruption; World Bank; World Trade Organization/General Agreement on Tariffs and Trade (WTO/GATT)**). Consequently, ethical questions for development include both philosophical dimensions of defining its objectives, but also shorter-term issues of management and **governance** within the practices called development.

See also: anti-politics; capability approach; Christianity; corporate social responsibility (CSR); corruption; culture; economic development; freedom versus choice; functionings; growth versus holism; human rights; inequality; inequality and poverty, world trends; Marxism; people-centered development; postmodernism and post-development; religion; rights-based approaches to development; social justice; well-being

Further reading

Corbridge, S. (1998) "Development Ethics: Distance, Difference, Plausibility," *Ethics, Place and Environment* 1:1 35–54.

Friedmann, J. (1992) *Empowerment: The Politics of Alternative Development*, Oxford: Blackwell.

Goulet, D. (1991) "On Authentic Social Development: Concepts, Content, and Criteria," pp. 3–23 in Williams, O. and Houck, J. (eds) *The Making of an Economic Vision*, Lanham MD: University Press of America.

Sachs, W. (1992) "One World," in Sachs, W. (ed.) *The Development Dictionary: A Guide to Knowledge as Power*, London: Zed Books.

Smith, D. (2000) *Moral Geographies: Ethics in a World of Difference*, Edinburgh: Edinburgh University Press.

UNDP (1994) *Human Development Report 1994*, Oxford: Oxford University Press.

SEAMUS GRIMES

ethnic cleansing

Ethnic cleansing is a euphemism initially coined in the early 1990s to describe (or rather obscure) the **genocide** perpetrated by Serb forces against Croats and Muslims in Croatia and Bosnia-Herzegovina in order to establish a "greater Serbia" as Yugoslavia disintegrated. "Ethnic cleansing" was the extreme outcome of the ethnic **nationalism** that tore apart the federal Yugoslavia and involved mass murder, forced deportations, **torture**, rape, the destruction of homes and villages, and general terror tactics to purge the Serb-dominated areas of the "polluting" presence of non-Serb minorities. One of the worst incidents occurred in the Bosnian town of Srebrenica in July 1995, when Serb forces killed 8,000 Muslims. Although initially used to describe Serb treatment of Croats and Muslims, the latter also engaged in "ethnic cleansing" against the former at various times during the Yugoslav wars. Thereafter, the euphemism entered common usage to describe/obscure similar practices in other conflicts, e.g. Rwanda and Kosovo.

See also: complex emergencies; ethnicity/identity; genocide; race and racism; post-conflict rehabilitation

PETER MAYELL

ethnicity/identity

Ethnicity has replaced "race" (see **race and racism**) as a term in general academic and official usage. However, its precise meaning varies widely. Early anthropological and sociological researchers used ethnicity to refer to essential group attributes like biology, language or **cultural heritage** that ethnic groups were presumed to possess in common. More recently, usage tends to understand ethnicity in much looser terms, focusing on how boundaries between ethnic groups are constructed, maintained and challenged. This shift in part reflects unease over violent conflicts between groups based on notions of ethnic purity as in "**ethnic cleansing**," but also to promote more positive conceptions of ethnic minorities in multicultural countries.

A key shift occurred in the 1960s in the analysis of **indigenous people** in terms of ethnicity rather than "tribe." British anthropologist Max Gluckman's 1930s study of the interaction of Zulus and Europeans in Africa began to point to the ways that boundaries between colonial and other people were maintained to produce separate "communities" (see **community**). Gluckman influenced later studies such as Clyde Mitchell's *The Kalela Dance* (1956), where rural-based "tribal" rituals and identities were replicated in urban settings by migrant laborers, and Abner Cohen's *Custom and Politics in Urban Africa* (1969). Cohen adopted the newly fashionable term "ethnicity" from US sociology (see **sociology of development**) to account for the distinctive identity and economic self-interest of Hausa migrants to the Nigerian city of Ibadan. A strong sense of ethnic identity emerged out of the need for mutual trust among Ibadan Hausa to maintain control over the trade in kola nuts and cattle. Such ethnic instrumentalism has been criticized for neglecting the meanings that group members themselves hold about their ethnic identity.

Around the same time as Cohen's work, the Norwegian anthropologist Frederick Barth advanced the view that the substantive content of ethnic group identity and practices is much less important than the ways in which the idea of ethnic distinctiveness is reproduced. In *Ethnic Groups and Boundaries* (1969), Barth moved away from colonialist concerns with the minutiae of "tribal" affiliation to focus instead on the more or less permanent boundary markers between ethnic groups. As Thomas Erickson (2002:1) more recently put it, "Ethnicity is essentially an aspect of a relationship, not a property of a group."

There are clear differences in approaches to ethnicity between "primordialist" and "modernist" perspectives (see also **culture**). The former argues that ethnic belonging is rooted deep in the past; the latter suggests it is a creation of the modern period. Primoridialism is derived from J. G. Herder's Romantic idea of a *Volk*, a nationalist fiction about ethnic origins in blood and soil, which notoriously became an ideological organizing principle for Nazi policies of racial supremacy. For the Soviet anthropologist Yulian

Bromley, a general "*ethnos*" prevails throughout history and becomes manifest in a more specific "*ethnikos*," under specific economic and political conditions. Bromley stipulates the enduring basis of the *ethnos* as residing in a historically formed community of people characterized by common, relatively stable cultural features, certain distinctive psychological traits, and the consciousness of their unity as distinguished from other similar communities (see **community**). Barth also took a broadly "primordialist" approach that sees new group members inherit ancient traditions and lines of descent.

In contrast, "modernists" like Nathan Glazer and Daniel P. Moynihan in the USA claim that ethnicity is a product of specifically modern conditions and that the "new word" ethnicity "reflects a new reality." In their collection, *The Invention of Tradition* (1983), Eric Hobsbawm and Terence Ranger catalog the creation of a specifically modernist sense of ethnicity and **nationalism** for binding **population**s into a shared group identity. Few today accept the notion of an enduring structure of ethnicity prevailing all the way through history from the earliest hunter-gatherer societies to global **capitalism**. The attribution of ethnic categories became a useful vehicle for Europeans organizing colonial labor along a hierarchy of occupational functions. As such, ethnic identities emerge only with the rise of an imperialist political economy (see **colonialism, history of; colonialism, impacts of**). In Rwanda and Burundi, for example, complex and fluid relationships between Tutsis, Hutus and Twas became rigid ethnic identities under German and Belgian colonial administrations. While pre-colonial Rwanda was no pre-modern bucolic idyll, it lacked the defined ethnic rivalries that erupted into the **genocide** violence of 1994, when one million people were massacred in one hundred days.

Ethnicities can also emerge where no previous identity, culture, religion or ancestry was claimed, sometimes with disastrous consequences as in the case of the **ethnic cleansing** of Bosnian Muslims in 1992. Before the **war**, "ethnic Muslims" in Bosnia-Herzegovina identified with either Croat or Serbian culture. Muslim ethnicity solidified into a shared defensive identity only after they faced violent persecution because of a common Islamic identity.

Thomas Ericksen (2002) distinguishes four contexts out of which ethnic identity typically arises. First, among urban minorities like traders or migrant labor; second, among minority "stateless" nations like the Kurds in Turkey, Iraq and Iran; third, among multi-ethnic populations found typically in **postcolonialism** settings; fourth, among indigenous minorities dispossessed by colonial occupation, as in the **indigenous people**s of the Americas. To Erickson's typology Steve Fenton (1999) adds a fifth category, that of post-**slavery** minorities, such as the "black" Afro-Caribbeans or Afro-Americans.

Many approaches tend to be silent over the ethnic identity of dominant, majority or powerful groups in Western societies. These are simply deemed "white" local, regional or national cultures without any specific claim to ethnic identity. Here the politics of multiculturalism tends to be reduced to seeing "others" in terms of exotic cultures, which ought to be tolerated or respected as radically different from the dominant "host" culture. This claim has been resisted by "universalists" who argue that differences are socially acquired and are not inherent or "natural." Therefore, other cultural practices can be learned and, ultimately, ethnic identity threatens the ideal of a universal humanity.

See also: community; culture; ethnic cleansing; empire; genocide; indigenous people; nationalism; race and racism; sociology of development

Further reading

See the journal *Ethnicities* for current research on ethnicity and related areas such as identity politics, multiculturalism and nationalism.

Davidson, N. (1999) "The Trouble with Ethnicity," *International Socialism* 84: 1–32.

Erickson, T. (2002) *Ethnicity and Nationalism: Anthropological Perspectives*, London: Pluto Press.

Fenton, S. (1999) *Ethnicity: Racism, Class and Culture*, London: Macmillan.

Hobsbawm, E., Verdery, K. and Fox, R. (1992) "Ethnicity and Nationalism in Europe today," *Anthropology Today* 8:1 3–15.

Hutchison, J. and Smith, A. (eds) (1996) *Ethnicity*, Oxford: Oxford University Press.

ALEX LAW

ethnocentrism

Ethnocentrism refers to the tendency to view the world in ways that reflect one's cultural background alone, rather than acknowledging the diverse ranges of alternatives that may exist given different backgrounds. The term suggests that one's ethnicity (see **ethnicity/identity**) is the most crucial aspect in creating this bias in perception, but increasingly the term is used simply to refer to a lack of self-awareness in perceptions that may result from a variety of influences, such as nationhood, class-background, or even cultures within organizations. Most importantly, ethnocentrism describes the tendency to privilege one's own background – often unwittingly – and to see it as dominant and in some senses superior.

Within development debates, a common example of ethnocentrism has been Eurocentrism, which refers to the universalization of European and Western forms of knowledge, cultures, and practices. Through the construction and representation of other people in other places as non-European, Europe and the West become inscribed as the norm. Thus, non-European societies become framed by the West, precluding the possibility of other social, cultural, political and economic frameworks being founded on anything other than the principles provided by European discourses. Eurocentric narratives are manifest in a variety ways that include a selective and glorified history of European science, progress and humanism.

Postcolonial (see **postcolonialism**) and postmodern theorists have problematized this universalism and begun a process of de-centering the West. Attempts have been made to challenge Eurocentrism through an examination of the power relations reinforced through the approaches, language and activities promoted by development theorists and practitioners, and by presenting other non-European narratives.

See also: colonialism, impacts of; culture; Orientalism; postcolonialism; power and discourse

Further reading

Mehmet, O. (1999) *Westernizing the Third World: The Eurocentricity of Economic Development Theories*, London: Routledge.

UMA KOTHARI

EUROCENTRISM *see* ethnocentricism

European Bank for Reconstruction and Development (EBRD)

The EBRD (European Bank for Reconstruction and Development) was established in 1991 to build market economies and democracies in the former Soviet Union and its east-central European satellites, funded by subscriptions from twenty-four European states, the USA, Canada, Japan and two **international organizations and associations** (the European Commission and the European Investment Bank). Between 1991 and 2003, the EBRD has invested €21.6 billion, primarily in the development of finance, infrastructure and small- and medium-sized enterprises (see **small and medium enterprises (SMEs)**); it lends mainly to private enterprise. Alongside its investment activities, the EBRD's influence rests on its annual publication of Transition Reports which track the performance of individual countries in achieving "progress in transition" on a scale from 1 to 4+. Despite a stated commitment to **transparency, accountability** and **sustainable development**, organizations such as CEE Bankwatch have criticized the EBRD for its weak safeguard policies and its involvement in a number of problematic projects, allegedly causing negative impacts on local people (see **shock therapy**), or holding meetings in locations such as Uzbekistan with poor **human rights** records. Critics have also criticized the large amounts spent on outfitting its London headquarters, high salaries for staff (some say up to 10 percent of its funds), and the large losses of money in Russia's 1998 financial crash because of poor judgment.

See also: International Monetary Fund (IMF); World Bank; postsocialism; shock therapy; Washington consensus

Further reading

CEE Bankwatch: a network of non-governmental organizations monitoring activities of international financial institutes in Central and Eastern Europe: http://www.bankwatch.org/
EBRD website: http://www.ebrd.com/

ALISON STENNING

European Union

The European Union (EU) is the most important international donor of **aid**, and is a key actor in shaping international discussions on the purpose and implementation of aid and development discourse. Together with its member states, it provides approximately half of all official development assistance (ODA or aid) to developing countries, and spends about 10 percent of this amount on itself. The EU is also the most important trading partner for developing countries. The EU is the biggest importer of goods from developing countries with 42 percent of total EU imports, representing €432 billion of **trade** in 2000.

The EU is probably the only state or inter-state entity (see **state and state reform**) whose constitution contains a specific paragraph for development cooperation. This paragraph in the Treaties of Maastricht (1992) and Amsterdam (1997) – the treaties that sought to establish some commonality of policy for European member states – stands under the sign of the three C's: complementarity, coordination and **coherence**. This so-called Triple C is part of Title XVII of the Treaty of Maastricht (Title XX of the Treaty of Amsterdam). In the Title the main goals of the EU's development cooperation are given: to contribute to sustainable economic and **social development** as well as to the war against **poverty**, but also the consolidation of **democracy** and the rule of law (see **law**). In Article 177, complementarity is stressed; and in Article 180, the Community and the Member States promise to coordinate their efforts. Article

178 is the "**coherence** Article," in which the Community and the Member States state that they shall take account of the goals of development cooperation in all the policies they pursue that may effect developing countries. In November 2000, the European Council and the European Commission came with a new combined statement that placed poverty reduction even more prominently as an official goal of European development assistance.

Recipients of aid

European development cooperation began with the foundation of the European Community itself, under the 1957 Treaty of Rome. Development cooperation initially had three elements: it was part of the price that Germany had to pay for its reintegration in the **community** of European states; it was directed at the colonies and overseas territories of a small number of member states ("associationism"); and trade issues were included from the beginning. The Convention of Yaoundé (initially signed in 1963), and its successor the Convention of Lomé (1975) were for a long time the cornerstone of European development cooperation. It included the supply of financial aid to the associates via the European Development Fund (EDF), financed outside the general European Budget. The geographical scope changed dramatically in 1975, when twenty-one Commonwealth countries plus five other countries were added to the list. It also meant looking at it from a per capita perspective that the aid flow to the so-called ACP countries (Africa, Caribbean, Pacific) decreased clearly. Over the years, the position of ACP countries in the total aid flow from the European Community has been weakened, and during the 1980s and 1990s was replaced in prominence by Mediterranean and Eastern European countries.

The Lomé Convention has been praised for combining aid and trade, seeking additionality of aid above existing trade flows, and for establishing supposed political and economic neutrality and joint management of its aid funds. Critics, however, suggest that concepts of "joint management" and "partnership" are probably overstated when actual decision-making in Brussels is analyzed. The tendency to centralize decision-making in Brussels

has become stronger over time. This could probably best be shown in the negotiations on the extension of the Convention of Lomé, finally to become the Convention of Cotonou (2000). The European Commission, supported by the member states, dominated negotiations on topics such as the implementation of a more results-based aid allocation and the change in trade preferences.

European relationships have also affected the Mediterranean and north-African regions. The so-called "New Mediterranean Policy" initiated in 1989 after the Second Enlargement of the Union. The policy aims to address problems of youth **unemployment**, growing **poverty** and **asylum seeking** and **international migration**. European **protectionism** *vis-à-vis* the Mediterranean countries (in particular with regard to agricultural products and **textiles**) changed little, but aid flows did grow slowly. The European summits with Mediterranean countries in 1995 (Cannes in June, and Barcelona in December) are described as "watersheds" because they started to consider topics of common security, peace and stability for the region. The fear of upcoming Muslim fundamentalism, especially in Algeria, however, forced the EU to take a new stance toward the southern Mediterranean countries, and slowed the development of a proposed **free trade** zone in the region.

Relations with Asian and Latin American (non-ACP) countries also grew slowly, and resulted in the so-called Asia-Latin America Program. At the bilateral level, the EU has a full association agreement with Mexico and Chile, establishing free trade. EC cooperation programs with the developing countries of Asia have grown moderately in recent years.

There are also three other regional programs: PHARE (the Poland and Hungary Aid for the Restructuring of Economies) was originally created to assist Poland and Hungary in 1989. It was later expanded to the ten candidate countries for EU entry. Some Balkan countries also received aid from this program. As of 2001, the CARDS program (Community Assistance to Reconstruction, Development and Stability in the Balkans) provides financial assistance to the Western Balkans. The TACIS (Technical Assistance to the Commonwealth of Independent States) provides assistance to the republics of the former Soviet Union.

Themes of aid

Apart from these regional programs, EU aid also adopts thematic budget-lines. The most important of these is humanitarian aid through its Humanitarian Aid Office (ECHO). A second important budget-line is that for **food aid** and **food security**. Since the European Community gave its first food aid in 1967, the EU was criticized for apparently using food aid as a means to export surplus production. This program has changed dramatically with a clear emphasis on food security now.

The EU has a pyramid of **trade** preferences for developing countries. At the top of this pyramid, at least for developing countries, should be participants of the Yaoundé and Lomé Conventions, but their position at the top of this preference system has been continuously eroded by other trade agreements that the EU concluded with other countries or groups of countries. The erosion deepened because the trade preferences were bound to the Common Agricultural Policy, and because of the fact that also other international agreements on trade, like the Multifiber Arrangement and its predecessors, became progressively directed against the exemption of trade restrictions (see **tariffs**). A step to bring EU trade policy more in line with its development goals was presented in February 2001 with the "Everything but Arms" amendment to the EU's Generalized Scheme of Preferences (GSP). The European Union approved this so-called groundbreaking proposal to eliminate quotas and duties on all products except arms from the forty-eight least developed countries (LDCs). One should keep in mind that the member states of the European Union have no trade element in their development policies on its own, since all access is regulated through the central administration in Brussels through the Common Market mechanisms.

Organization and decision-making

The EU decision-making process is very complex, and especially for ODA. There is a large gap between policy-making at the one side and policy implementation at the other side. The conduct of external relations is shared between three Directorates General (DGs): External Relations, Development, and Trade. Relations with the ACP countries are the primary responsibility of the DG Development, although other DGs are relevant such as the DG for Trade; ECHO, which ensures emergency **aid** to the ACP. Other DGs include the DG for Fisheries, which negotiates fishing agreements with the ACP, or the DG for Agriculture, which holds the food aid portfolio. The DG for External Relations is responsible for the ALA and Mediterranean Programs as well as some of the assistance to the Balkans. The Council of Ministers is the decision-making body of the EU. The work of the Council is prepared by the Presidency of the EU (which rotates on a six-monthly basis) and the General Secretariat of the Council. This arrangement also holds for the Development Council. Various Council working groups deal with developing countries.

Weaknesses in the Commission management were found by a series of evaluations that revealed staffing problems and administrative and policy constraints imposed on the Commission. Staffing problems are partly caused by the low numbers of staff that the Commission can employ. There is a clear shortage of in-house specialists. Policy formulation expanded the agenda and thus the administrative burden. Enhanced administrative and financial controls extended this burden. In May 2000, the Commission adopted a *Reform of the Management of External Assistance* that established the EuropeAid Co-operation Office and devolved many responsibilities to delegations in developing countries.

See also: aid; bilateral aid agencies; coherence; economic federalization

Further reading

Beraud, P., Perrault, J-L. and Sy, O. (eds) (1999) *Géo-économie de la Coopération Européenne – De Yaoundé à Barcelone*, Paris: Maisonneuve et Larose.

Cox, A. and Chapman, J. (1999) *The European Community External Cooperation Programmes:*

Policies, Management and Distribution, London: Overseas Development Institute.

Grilli, E. (1993) The European Community and the Developing Countries, Cambridge: Cambridge University Press.

PAUL HOEBINK

exchange rates

Exchange rates refer to the prices of a currency measured in other currencies. There are two ways to quote the exchange rate of a currency. The price quotation system quotes the amount of domestic currency per unit of foreign currency. The volume quotation system quotes the amount of foreign currency per unit of domestic currency. For example, if the UK were the home country, the exchange rate for the pound against American dollars might be, say, 0.63 pounds per dollar under the price quotation system, and 1.59 dollars per pound under the volume quotation system. An increase in price of a currency is called appreciation. Otherwise it is called depreciation. If these price changes are engineered by government actions, they are called revaluation and devaluation respectively.

The definition given above is called the nominal exchange rate. The alternative is real exchange rate or the **terms of trade**, which is the price of commodities in one country measured by commodities in another country. One example of real exchange rate is the relative price such as a car equivalent in value to five color televisions. **Trade** theorists use a real exchange rate calculated as the ratio of prices of export commodities to prices of import commodities. International macro-economists use a real exchange as the ratio of price levels between countries, which gives the exchange rate between baskets of commodities and services in different countries. Numerically, real exchange rate is the nominal exchange rate multiplied by the ratio of price levels in two countries. Depreciation of a country's currency makes its goods cheaper to foreigners. The same amount of goods can exchange for less foreign goods. This is called deterioration of the country's terms of trade.

Exchange rates between major currencies can be directly quoted from foreign exchange markets since parties more likely trade one major currency for another. For exchange rates between two less frequently traded currencies, a cross exchange rate can be calculated by using the exchange rate of the each minor currency with a major currency. For example, if the exchange rate of the South African rand is 11.9 rand per British pound, and the exchange rate of the Indian rupee is 74.8 rupee per pound, a cross exchange rate can be calculated as 6.3 rupees per rand. In exchange markets, traders scrutinize the exchange rates at different exchange centers and spot any opportunity to make a profit by purchasing one currency at a lower rate at one location and selling at a higher rate at another. This is called arbitrage. Continuous arbitrage leads to a negligible price differential among foreign exchange centers. Similarly, arbitrage results in a negligible difference between direct exchange rate and indirect or cross exchange rate.

So far, exchange rates have been defined between pair-wise currencies. To illustrate the exchange rate between one currency and a group of other currencies, the effective exchange rate is used. This is the weighted sum of one country's exchange rates with a group of other countries. Weights are usually the country's trade shares with this group of countries.

The spot exchange rate is the price at which currencies are traded for immediate settlement. Forward exchange rate is the price at which currencies are traded for settlement on a future day (one month, three months . . . but seldom beyond a year). Use of forward exchange rate protects foreign currency users against unexpected changes in future spot exchange rates.

The systems that set exchange rates are called exchange regimes. A fixed exchange rate regime refers to the system where a country fixes the ratio at which the domestic currency exchanges for foreign currencies. To this end, the monetary authorities of the country stand ready to buy or sell foreign exchange reserves in order to maintain the predetermined exchange rate. A fixed exchange rate regime eliminates exchange rate uncertainty and gives a measure of price stability. Countries facing rampant inflation (see **inflation and its effects**) may choose to link (or peg) their currencies to a major currency (or a basket of major currencies, called a currency board) to make its own currency more credible. The drawback is that the country loses control of its money supply and needs to maintain sufficient exchange reserves. A perceived exchange reserves shortage brought on by balance of payment disturbances may cause anticipation of a possible domestic currency devaluation, which may trigger an exodus of foreign investors or even a currency crisis. The world was on fixed exchange rates from 1870 to 1914 in form of the **gold standard**, and from 1945 to the early 1970s under the **Bretton Woods** system. In a floating exchange rate regime, the exchange rate of a currency constantly adjusts depending on the market for this currency. The system allows a country to control its money supply but at the expense of foreign exchange certainty. Major economies have been on a floating regime since the early 1970s. In practice, governments still intervene in exchange markets in order to correct exchange rates that are considered undesirable. This is called managed floating.

Different theories have been put forth to explain exchange rate determination. The classical theory of purchasing power parity and its modern incarnation, the monetary approach, state that in a very long run, nominal exchange rates and price levels adjust to maintain unchanged real exchange rates. The portfolio approach determines exchange rates that help equilibrate money holding, net capital flow and current account balance. The asset approach explains the short run exchange rates based on interest parity condition, where interest rate differential between domestic and foreign assets equals the difference between spot and forward exchange rates. While these mainstream theories view exchange rate adjustments as a price system to achieve efficient resource allocation, many have emphasized the speculative nature of portfolio investment and the resultant misalignment during the post-Bretton Woods era.

See also: Asian crises; Bretton Woods; economic development; fiscal and monetary policy; gold standard; multilateral development banks (MDBs); trade

Further reading

Deprez, J. and Harvey, J. (1999) *Foundations of International Economics: Post Keynesian Perspectives*, London: Routledge.

Krugman, P. and Obstfeld, M. (1997) *International Economics: Theory and Policy*, New York: Addison-Wesley.

Mankiw, N. (2003) *Macroeconomics*, New York: Worth.

BIN ZHOU

export processing zones (EPZs)

Export processing zones (EPZs) are designated areas of a country, usually near a port, which aim to attract **foreign direct investment** by giving exporters special privileges. They are often physically fenced off from the rest of the country, though this is less common now than in the past. EPZs have been used to "kick-start" manufacturing exports by a wide range of developing countries since the 1970s (see **export-led growth; industrialization**). They are similar to **free trade zones (FTZs)**, although free trade zones *per se* may often not attract exporters alone, and may be located in sites away from ports.

The key incentive offered by EPZs to exporters is the right to import inputs (such as fabrics for garments) without paying import duty (**tariffs**) and with a minimum of bureaucratic formalities. Zones also attract direct foreign investment by offering incentives such as tax holidays on profits, and good infrastructural facilities, sometimes subsidized. Some zones restrict **trade unions**' activity.

EPZs are used in economies where the domestic market is protected from import competition by tariffs or other trade restrictions. Thus, EPZs allow exporters more of a free trade setting than ordinary domestic firms. However, in order to develop exports it is also important for a country to have a realistic exchange rate, macroeconomic stability, and other aspects of a good investment "climate" such as the absence of **corruption**.

EPZs are one of a number of export promoting devices used to develop exports of manufactures. Take the case of Indonesia, which in the late 1980s and early 1990s successively developed exports of **textiles** and garments, footwear, and electronics products, having previously depended on oil exports. Indonesia used EPZs, but also allowed some exporters outside the zones to be designated as bonded factories (with the right to import inputs duty free), or to be offered facilities giving the right to import inputs duty free for export or to claim refunds ("drawbacks") on import duty paid. EPZs and these other facilities were run by different agencies, which competed for foreign investment. In the event, Indonesia's EPZs faced difficulties in the form of labor shortages and a perception that corrupt payments were necessary to operate successfully, and many exporting firms preferred to locate outside the zones.

A problem associated with manufactured exports from EPZs is that – by the very nature of the zones – the *net* foreign exchange receipts from exports are much less than the *gross* receipts, because of the importance of imported inputs. While importing intermediate products frees exporters from the supply constraints of the domestic economy, in the long run exporting countries hope linkages (between investors and indigenous companies) will develop as exporters increasingly buy inputs from domestic suppliers (see **joint venture**). This is more likely to happen the more industrially developed is the economy in question, and a higher level of development may facilitate **technology transfer** from EPZ firms to domestic firms.

See also: export-led growth; free trade zones (FTZs); gender and industrialization; industrial district model; industrialization; joint venture; tariffs

Further reading

Madani, D. (1998) *A Review of the Role and Impact of Export Processing Zones*, Washington DC: World Bank. http://econ.worldbank.org/docs/965.pdf

Thoburn, J. (2001) "Becoming an Exporter of Manufactures: The Case of Indonesia," pp. 97–119 in Morrissey, O. and Tribe, M. (eds) *Economic Policy and Manufacturing Performance*

in Developing Countries, Cheltenham: Edward Elgar.

JOHN THOBURN

export-led growth

Export-led growth represents a situation where a country's growth follows from its ability to export. It has become an oft-recommended policy prescription for developing countries since the 1980s, when the so-called **newly industrialized economies (NIEs)** of East Asia were seen to benefit from export-oriented **industrialization**. Export-led growth is usually seen in opposition to industrialization via **import substitution**, which was more common in the 1950s and 1960s.

The key question facing developing countries in this context is "exporting what?" Though many developing countries are in a position to export primary products, few have grown from such exports (the exceptions being the oil-exporting economies of the Middle East, see **Organization of Petroleum Exporting Countries (OPEC)**). Primary product exports face many disadvantages including unstable or even secularly declining prices, extreme dependence on world market conditions and a vulnerability to substitution by cheaper synthetic products. The alternative strategy – the export of manufactured products – is also often termed export-oriented industrialization. It is, however, limited by the non-existence of manufacturing in many of these economies and the international uncompetitiveness of the manufacturing firms that do exist. These issues have been central to the development debate over the last five decades.

Why might exports be expected to increase **growth rates**? Trade provides a vent for the surplus output produced by a country and is especially important in the case of perishable products like fish and mineral resources. In the manufacturing sector, **trade** is useful if minimum efficient scale is greater than domestic absorptive capacity. Production for export markets also allows capacity to be more utilized and technological improvements to be undertaken. The **multiplier effects** for foreign trade are generally high and, for efficient economies, can lead to almost indefinite growth.

Export activities also have higher factor productivities than non-export activities because competition encourages innovativeness, adaptability and efficient management. In addition, there are "the indirect effects of exports operating through changes in incomes and costs" i.e. the spillover effects (Balassa, 1978). These occur through the development of efficient and internationally competitive management, the introduction of improved techniques, training of higher quality labor, a steadier flow of inputs, etc. Finally, the increased efficiency of the exporting sector has benefits for the domestic sectors with which it has linkages. The exporting sector also provides much-needed foreign exchange and helps the trade balance. The export-growth relationship, however, is complicated by the possibility of a positive feedback effect from growth back to exports, creating a virtuous circle. Recent studies attempting to test this two-way causality show mixed results.

In this context, the operative question is not whether exports lead to growth because the experience of the East Asian economies indicates that they do, but instead to whether exports are necessary or sufficient for growth, and whether manufactured exports from developing countries can continue to expand. This concern was articulated in a well known paper by Cline (1982), which asked whether the East Asian Miracle can be generalized. There are two sources of concern. First, if all developing countries shift toward export promotion, would there be sufficient demand to absorb the increased output? Second, would Western markets remain open to such imports?

In answer to the first question, it is argued that import-penetration rates into high-income markets for individual products remain below 15–20 percent, even though the share of exports from developing countries has been increasing (Pomfret, 1997:102). Second, the potential for trade between developing countries remains largely untapped. Third, not all developing countries would produce the same goods and there are many niches still to be occupied. Thus, false eyelashes and wigs, which were amongst Hong Kong's leading exports, provided the territory with a niche from which it could market other fashion products. Many developing countries today export "non-traditional" products such as

flowers (Zimbabwe), wine (Chile) and horticultural products (Chile and Costa Rica), although demand for these goods depends upon good economic conditions in Europe and North America. Fourth, not all developing countries are at the same stage of development. Therefore, they will be producing different goods at different stages and need not compete directly with each other. Thus, when South Korea moved out of light manufactures, the second tier of Asian Tigers started to manufacture them.

In response to the second question, the fear of **protectionism** in many developed countries has been articulated by a number of writers. Bello (1992) cites a number of examples to illustrate the "demise of **free trade**" in the USA when competition from the Far East became threatening. Examples include the USA revoking the tariff-free entry (see **tariffs**) of selected imports from NIEs under the Generalized System of Preferences; quota restrictions on Korean textile and steel imports; the forced appreciation of the Korean won and Taiwanese dollar; the aggressive drive for lower tariff barriers and other restraints on US products in the Korean market; and the increased difficulty of making unauthorized **technology transfer** to NIEs. Despite these measures, Bhagwati (1988) argued that US protectionism has not been disastrous because many American companies invest abroad and expect to import their output back into the USA.

The export-led growth strategy gained ground in the 1980s through liberalization and **structural adjustment** programs worldwide (see **neoliberalism**). Today, however, it is increasingly criticized for overlooking broader developmental goals. The strategy simply assumes that exports lead to growth, which will **trickle down** to the development of the majority. In the absence of well developed linkages between the export sectors and the domestic economy, any development that takes place will be, spatially and sectorally, limited. Finally, the question of how manufacturing exports are to be encouraged remains open. The East Asian experience highlights the importance of **import substitution** in developing the manufacturing sector, and indicates that most developing countries cannot rely exclusively either on export promotion or import substitution.

See also: developmental state; export processing zones (EPZs); import substitution; industrialization; industrialization and trade policy; late industrialization; leapfrogging; newly industrialized economies (NIEs); protectionism; tariffs; technological capability; trade; transnational corporations (TNCs) from developing economies

Further reading

Balassa, B. (1978) "Exports and Economic Growth," *Journal of Development Economics* 5:2 181–9.

Bello, W. (1992) "Export-led Development in East Asia: A Flawed Model," *Trocaire Development Review*, pp. 11–27, reprinted in Ayres, R. (ed.) (1995) *Development Studies*, Greenwich: Greenwich University Press.

Bhagwati, J. (1988) *Protectionism*, Cambridge MA: MIT Press.

Cline, W. (1982) "Can the East-Asian Model of Development be Generalized?," *World Development* 10:2 81–90.

Pomfret, R. (1997) *Development Economics*, London: Prentice-Hall.

UMA S. KAMBHAMPATI

F

FACTOR ENDOWMENTS *see* terms of trade; comparative advantage; capital intensive; labor-intensive

fair trade

Fair trade refers to trading activities that seek to provide maximum value to producers in developing countries. It is often associated with the slogan, "trade not aid," which was first launched at the UN Conference on Trade and Development (UNCTAD), held in 1964 following the access to independence of many African countries. It was proposed by African delegates, to support the idea that development comes from financial independence more than from **aid**; it represented an evolution of the "fair trade" concept, which originated in the 1940s in the USA, mainly from **nongovernmental organizations (NGOs)**, as an alternative and more equitable form of trade between developed countries and their colonies. A great diffusion to this concept was given in the late 1950s by an **Oxfam** project called "Helping by Selling" based on a more direct exchange between developing-world producers and consumers in developing countries. Fair trade has over time slightly changed its meaning, stressing the need to fight **protectionism**, or the need to reform consumers' culture, or of achieving more equitable **terms of trade**. In general, fair trade can be defined as an effort to move toward an equal exchange between developing and developed countries (see **equitable development**).

The main requests of developing countries under the common definition of "trade not aid," put forth in a number of UNCTAD conferences, are: better deal for raw commodities, improved access to Western markets, with a lower level of subsidy of their internal production, some form of control on **transnational corporations (TNCs)**, changes in the international monetary system, **debt relief**, and more aid.

However, the only largely used commodity that experienced a significant cost increase was oil in the years following the 1973 crisis (see **Organization of Petroleum Exporting Countries (OPEC)**). At that moment, all developed nations acknowledged the right of developing countries to a greater share of the wealth created by trade, but no positive action has been taken since; on the contrary, poor countries have particularly suffered from the rising price of oil.

The slogan "trade not aid," has more recently been turned by **World Bank** officials into "trade and aid." The World Bank and the **International Monetary Fund (IMF)** continue imposing binding **conditionality** to developing countries to access their loans, compelling them to open their markets very rapidly, regardless of the consequences on the vulnerable groups of those countries, and without paying due attention to the problems posed to exporting countries by the low and unstable prices of commodities.

On the other side, developed countries keep practicing, in one form or another, trade protection against developing countries. Furthermore, through the WTO (see **World Trade Organization/ General Agreement on Tariffs and Trade**

(WTO/GATT)) they support a system of rules on intellectual property (see **intellectual property rights (IPRs)**), investments and services, imposing huge costs on developing countries (see **trade**).

Moreover, developing countries also suffer from the disparity in negotiation capacity that keeps developing countries excluded from the mechanisms shaping new rules for world trade. The dramatic issue of the cost of anti-HIV drugs (see **HIV/ AIDS (definition and treatment); HIV/AIDS (policy issues)**), tied to their IPRs, is a hot indicator of the importance of trade regulations for development at the beginning of the third millennium (see **pharmaceuticals; World Trade Organization/General Agreement on Tariffs and Trade (WTO/GATT)**).

See also: corporate social responsibility (CSR); equitable development; protectionism; terms of trade; trade; value chains; World Trade Organization/General Agreement on Tariffs and Trade (WTO/GATT)

Further reading

Littrell, M. and Dickson, M. (1999) *Social Responsibility in the Global Market: Fair Trade of Cultural Products*, Thousand Oaks CA: Sage.

MATTEO SCARAMELLA

family planning

Modern family planning refers to the range of state (see **state and state reform**), household and **civil society** practices that regulate social processes involving **fertility**, conception, birth, reproductive health and post-natal household care. Often through state-led incentives, these practices seek either to increase or decrease the number of **children**. China's one-child policy provides an example of a state seeking to limit **population** growth while Italy's and Singapore's pro-natal policies exemplify states seeking to increase their population.

The best family planning practices in developing countries have sought to manage safely the timing, spacing and total number of children while providing accessible, non-coercive, sustainable and economically viable health care to women, mothers and children. At the other extreme, many poor women in developing countries experience family planning as population control and as intimidating, disempowering and not economically sensible, particularly those who have received unsafe abortions or involuntary sterilizations.

Providing birth control options and services is a major aspect of family planning activities. These options and services range from "natural" methods (withdrawal, calendar), hormonal contraceptives (pill, implant, injections), mechanical contraceptives (male condom, female condom, diaphragm, intra-uterine device), and permanent surgical procedures (vasectomy and sterilization). Support services include the testing for pregnancy, HIV antibodies and **sexually transmitted diseases (STDs)**. The popularity of family planning options differs geographically. For instance, Indian women have primarily received sterilization while South African women have generally opted for oral contraceptives and injections.

International family planning emerged in the 1950s as part of development projects with the national goals of fostering economic growth through state-managed and household-centered reduction in fertility rates. Donor agencies in developed countries (such as United States Agency for International Development) and private voluntary organizations (such as the International Planned Parenthood Federation and Marie Stopes International) led the implementation of early programs in developing countries, and assisted in development national population policies and family planning programs. By the 1990s, national family planning programs as state-led activities were beginning to be phased out. In East Asia and parts of Southeast Asia, the reduction in these programs is occurring due to a decline in **fertility** rates. Elsewhere, programs continue to exist on a smaller scale as the result of limited success in controlling population growth and of attempts to privatize reproductive health services to overcome state fiscal crisis.

Perspectives vary among those who shape, implement, and live through family planning policies and programs in developing countries. Debates among the various perspectives continue over how to achieve significant gains in women's **empowerment, gender** justice, greater male responsibility, household and communal autonomy, commitment to sexual rights (see **reproductive rights**), equitable reproductive health economics and access to safe contraceptives and abortion services.

The modernization (see **modernization theory**) perspective on family planning has dominated international development policy and practice. This perspective maintains that efficient state-led family planning eradicates poverty and promotes **economic growth** and social **well-being** by reducing the fertility rates of poor women. Initiatives proposed during the **Bucharest world population conference (1974)** exemplify the attempts to link **overpopulation** with increased **poverty** and the call for state-led development strategies (see **Malthusian demography**). Modernization technicians also argue that their family planning programs would result in smaller families, overcome religious opposition, enhance maternal and child health and relieve pressures on social services and employment opportunities.

This perspective views the family planning crisis as one of structural inefficiency of resource allocation at the communal, national and international levels. It seeks to reform – or establish where needed – local and national **primary health care** infrastructures in order to achieve its goals of declining fertility rates. In the 1970s and 1980s, the reforms include attempts, for instance, to standardize (using criteria developed by donors) the quality and delivery of modern contraceptive supplies and to use educational techniques to increase contraceptive demand. In effect, these reforms dramatically realigned and decentralized public health systems in aid-recipient countries to satisfy donors. In the 1990s with the arrival of **neo-liberalism** and **structural adjustment**, reformers took new structural initiatives. The rise of public-private family planning initiatives moves health care systems away from sole control of public **health** agencies in developing countries to increased private-sector management of reproductive health programs. For instance, donors in developed countries have been seeking ways to get for-profit entities to privatize and commercialize the public-health promotion of family planning in developing countries.

Some critics, however, have claimed modern contraceptives have limited women's autonomy and **empowerment**. For instance, these critics provided evidence that many early clinical trials on contraceptive pills, sterilization injections and hormonal contraceptives did not get adequate informed consent from women who participated. Other commentators demonstrated, in some cases, how increased reliance on family planning has resulted in increased male dominance and decreased educational opportunities for young women (see **male bias**).

Sustained criticism of the modernizers' perspective came from the reproductive health perspective. This perspective challenges the assertion that uncontrolled sexual activities of poor women and their higher fertility rates directly cause widespread **poverty** (see the 1994 **Cairo conference on population and development**). Instead, the reproductive health perspective argues that birth control options should promote women's equity and empowerment, liberating them from male dominance, family constraints and repressive moral norms, and offer greater reproductive health. This perspective shifts the discourse from **overpopulation** and family planning to **reproductive rights** and reproductive health programs.

These modern and reproductive health perspectives nevertheless hold a heterosexist bias with their distinct constructions of heterosexuality that give primacy to reproductive functions within the family (see **same-sex sexualities; sexualities**).

See also: fertility; gender; gender and communicable disease; health; HIV/AIDS (policy issues); infant and child mortality; maternal mortality; population; reproductive rights; sexualities; sexually transmitted diseases (STDs)

Further reading

Bandarage, A. (1997) *Women, Population and Global Crisis: A Political-Economic Analysis*, London: Zed.

Caldwell, J., Phillips, J. F. and Barkat-e-Khuda (2002) "The Future of Family Planning Programs," *Studies In Family Planning* 33:1 1–10.

Chua, P. (2003) "Condoms and Pedagogy: Changing Global Knowledge Practices," pp. 124–8 in Bhavnani, K.-K., Foran, J. and Kurian, P. (eds) *Feminist Futures: Re-Imagining Women, Culture, and Development*, London: Zed.

Hartmann, B. (1995) *Reproductive Rights and Wrongs*, Boston MA: South End Press.

International Planned Parenthood Foundation: http://www.ippf.org/

Marie Stopes International: http://www.mariestopes.org.uk/

Russell, A., Sobo, E. and Thompson, M. (eds) (2000) *Contraception Across Cultures: Technologies, Choices, Constraints*, London: Berg.

PETER CHUA

famine

Famine refers to a relatively sudden event involving mass mortalities from starvation within a short period. Famine is typically distinguished from chronic hunger, understood as epidemic nutritional deprivation (see **nutrition; malnutrition**) on a persistent basis (as opposed to seasonal hunger, for example). Definitions of famine are fraught with danger because (1) cultural, as opposed to biological, definitions of starvation vary around diverse, locally defined norms, and (2) deaths from starvation are frequently impossible to distinguish from those from disease.

Nearly all societies have periodically suffered from the consequences of famine. The earliest recorded famine, which occurred in ancient Egypt, dates to 4000 BC; famine conditions currently exist (1998) in Sudan and North Korea (1999). The dynamics and characteristics of mass starvation in modern times have similar structural properties, however; typically such famines involve sharp price increases for staple foodstuffs, decapitalization of household assets, gathering of wild **foods**, borrowing and begging, petty crime and occasionally food riots, and out-migration. According to the Hunger Program at Brown University, the trend in famine casualties has been downward since 1945, but in the late 1980s states with a combined **population** of 200 million failed to prevent famine within their national borders. Hunger, and famine in particular, is intolerable in the modern world, however, because it is unnecessary and unwarranted (Sen and Dreze, 1989).

Famine causation has often been linked to **natural disasters**, population growth and **war** producing a reduction in **food** supply (see **Malthusian demography**). But some major famines (for example, Bengal in 1943) were not preceded by a significant decline in food production or absolute availability and in some cases have been associated with food export. Recent analyses, most notably the work of Amartya Sen (1981) have focused on access to and control over food resources – sometimes called the *food availability decline hypothesis*. Sen (1981) approaches hunger, and most especially how hunger and food insecurity (see **food security**) on certain parts of the map can degenerate into famine (in his view "simultaneous" mass mortality due to starvation), from an indisputably microeconomic vantage point. Sen begins with the individual endowment which is mapped into a bundle of entitlements, the latter understood as "the set of alternative commodity bundles that a person can command" (1981:46) through various *legal* channels of acquirement open to someone of his/her position. Such entitlement bundles confer particular capabilities that ultimately underline **well-being**. The basic unit of analysis is the individual person, his/her endowment, and his/her entitlement arrangements, though there is considerable ambiguity and slippage in Sen's analysis over the aggregation of such individuals into social assemblages such as households or communities or classes. Sen's theory turns on what Fine (1997:624) properly calls the "micro (-economic) capability for survival," and on the means by which such individual capabilities fail, producing as a consequence "excess" individual deaths through generalized individual entitlement failure. In Sen's (1981) language, famine as a short-term event characterized by acute deprivation of staple foodstuffs occurs because "the entitlement set does not include any commodity bundle with enough food."

Central to Sen's account of why famine occurs is the process of transforming endowments into entitlements, so-called E-mapping. The sorts of entitlements which Sen details are rewards to labor, production, inheritance or asset transfer, and state provisioning (transfers) typically through social security and food relief policies (i.e. anti-famine policies of which the Indian Famine Codes are customarily seen as a model). Insofar as an individual's entitlement set is the consequence of E-mapping on the endowment set, entitlements can only change through transformations in the endowment or E-mapping. Famine occurs through a collapse or adverse change in endowment or E-mapping or both (Sen, 1981). Entitlement, in contrast to other theories, "draws our attention to such variables as ownership patterns, **unemployment**, relative prices, wage-price rations, and so on" (Sen, 1993:30).

Deploying entitlement in this way, Sen is able to show how famines may occur without a decline in food availability and how entitlements attached to individuals through a generalization of the exchange economy – through markets – may shift in complex ways among differing classes, occupational groups and sections of the population. In Bengal in 1943, the events of the war years displaced entitlements of certain occupational classes with devastating consequences (over 2.5 million died in 1943–4). Food did not move into famine-stricken Wollo in Ethiopia in 1973 because food prices were not in general higher in Wollo despite starvation, since purchasing power of the local population of peasants and workers had fallen with food output decline. Conversely, a famine "*need not* necessarily occur even when there is a decline of food availability" (Sen, 1993:36–7). Famines can then be seen to have differing dynamics: what he calls "boom" and "slump" famines expressing the conditions under which entitlements may fail. Sen is concerned to demonstrate that food supply is not unimportant. The entitlements themselves are influenced *inter alia* by the food system through changes in direct ownership or through contributing to food prices rises (Sen, 1993:37). The real danger resides in concentrating exclusively on food production and availability, which can often lull governments into soporific complacency, what Sen calls "Malthusian optimism:"

Focusing attention on the Malthusian variable of food output per head, the food situation has often appeared to be comfortable even when there have been good economic grounds for expecting terrible troubles for particular occupational groups.

(1984:524)

Sen was of course addressing developing-world conditions, but the insight that E-mapping can change in a way in which hunger and even famine may occur amidst plenty, has a particular resonance in a number of postsocialist and advanced capitalist states. A concern with entitlement failure in market circumstances leads Sen (see Dreze and Sen, 1989) to emphasize public action through entitlement *protection* (state funded famine protection through food for work or public food distribution) *and promotion* (a public social security net) (see **safety nets against poverty; welfare state**).

The power of Sen's analysis derives in my view from the fact that it sees the poor and the economically marginal in terms of a set of endowments, and the mapping – a complex and largely unexplored term in Sen's corpus – by which they gain command over food. It situates hunger, then, on a landscape, irreducibly social, of the capabilities (see **capability approach**) that individuals, and potentially classes, may mobilize. By examining mapping as an active and transformative process – how the capacity to labor, or access to land can generate an entitlement – it dislodges a concern with output *per se* and focuses on access to and control over food. It offers a *proximate* sort of causal analysis predicated on what immediate or conjunctural forces might shift such forms of access and control, and permits a social mapping of such shifts to understand *who* dies or starves (say artisanal craftsmen versus peasants) and *why*. Entitlements – the central mechanism in his intellectual architecture – are individually assigned in virtue of a largely unexamined endowment, and are legally derived from state law (ownership, **property rights**, contract). Entitlements necessitate making legitimate claims, that is to say, rights resting on the foundations of power (opportunity or actual command) and law (legitimacy and protection).

Running across Sen's scholarship on entitlements are a number of unresolved tensions, a number of which it needs to be said, *contra* his critics, he is acutely sensitive to. One way to reflect upon these tensions is to acknowledge what famines are in practice – a reality that has been immeasurably deepened by the work of geographers (and anthropologists) working on food systems (see Gore, 1993; Watts, 1983). Famines have in fact a complex internal architecture, which is to say that the E-mapping is much more complex and dynamic (involving all manner of social, cultural, institutional, and collective actions beyond the entitlements discussed by Sen). E-mapping is a rather passive term for the multiplicity – and the creativity – of coping and adaptive strategies pursued by peasants or petty commodity producers (see **petty commodity production**) prior to and during a food crisis. In addition, famines must be located historically in terms of the structural tendencies within the political economy, and the crisis proneness of systems of provisioning: proximate causes (Sen's strength) must be distinguished from longer-term secular dynamics. A famine is inseparable from the historical processes and tendencies that may, quite literally, manufacture it. And not least, as one recent report of famine puts it, "the study of famine must integrate institutional, political, market, production spheres at both macro and micro levels" (von Braun, 1999:73).

It is the relation between the entitlements of the individual and the social group – how are individual (micro) entitlements aggregated for example to account for (macro) class dynamics? – and between the existence of endowments and their social determination which are undeveloped in Sen's corpus. It is not simply that Sen, for example, ignores the role of **war** in famine genesis – clearly the fundamental cause of famine in much of postcolonial Africa – but that he simply assumes that war displaces production-based entitlements which cause food shortage and famine. But as de Waal (1997) and Keen (1994) have shown, war is often about the political construction of markets. In a similar vein, Sen does not, as Nolan (1993) imputes, ignore socialist famine in China, but instead attributes it to policy failures during the famine years without providing an account of how a theory of the state and socialist political economy (a Kornai-like theory of shortage) might provide the reference point for individual entitlements. The social, historical and structural character of famine is not reducible to individual entitlements any more than the proximate causes of individual

entitlement changes have anything to say about the fact that "the exchange entitlements faced by a person depend, *naturally*, on his position in the economic class structure as well as the modes of production in the country" (1981:4, emphasis added). In Sen's practice, however, the socioeconomic are, as Fine (1997:638) says, "necessarily filtered through the analytical framework provided by the microeconomics of entitlements."

In sum, mass **poverty** results from long-term changes in entitlements associated with social production and distribution mechanisms; famines arise from short-term changes in these same mechanisms. Famine and endemic deprivation correspond to two forms of public action to eradicate them: famine policy requires entitlement protection ensuring that it does not collapse among vulnerable groups (i.e. landless laborers, women) (see **vulnerability**). Chronic hunger demands entitlement promotion to expand the command people have over **basic needs** (Sen and Dreze, 1989). Since 1945, India has implemented a successful anti-famine policy yet conspicuously failed to eradicate endemic deprivation; China, conversely, has overcome the hunger problem but failed to prevent massive famine in the 1950s. Africa has witnessed a catastrophic growth in the incidence of both mass starvation and chronic hunger (de Waal, 1997).

The role of state policy (see **state and state reform**) and of humanitarian **aid** (see **humanitarianism**) figures centrally in discussion of famine and famine causation. While the public sphere is key in understanding how and why the right to food is and the right to not be hungry are made effective, the recent history of famine shows clearly how the state can use famine and humanitarian aid for explicitly political purposes. The case against Stalin and the Ukrainian famine is clear in this regard, and the catastrophic Chinese famine of the late 1950s is a compelling instance of how inept state policies to achieve rapid **industrialization** backfired, but also how an authoritarian state ignored famine signals and colluded in the deaths of 20 million people (Becker, 1997) (see **authoritarianism; collectivization**). Sen (1981) has argued that famines rarely occur in societies in which there is freedom of the press (and in which states are therefore held to be accountable in some way). Humanitarian assistance has also been an object of critique insofar as it itself becomes politicized (and rendered as a business), and often fails to be more than a short-term palliative (rather than assisting in rehabilitation and reconstruction of famine-devastated communities (see **community**) (de Waal, 1997).

See also: aid; complex emergencies; emergency assistance; food; food aid; food security; humanitarianism; land reform; malnutrition; nutrition; war

Further reading

Becker, J. (1997) *Hungry Ghosts: China's Secret Famine*, London: John Murray.

de Waal, A. (1997) *Famine Crimes*, London: Heinemann.

Fine, B. (1997) "Entitlement Failure?" *Development and Change* 28: 617–47.

Gore, C. (1993) "Entitlement Relations and 'Unruly' Social Practices," *Journal of Development Studies* 29: 429–60.

Keen, D. (1994) *The Benefits of Famine*, Princeton: Princeton University Press.

Nolan, P. (1993) "The Causation and Prevention of Famines," *Journal of Peasant Studies* 21: 1–28.

Sen, A. (1981) *Poverty and Famines*, Oxford: Clarendon Press.

Sen, A. (1984) *Resources, Values and Development*, Oxford: Blackwell.

Sen, A. (1993) "The Causation and Prevention of Famines: A Reply," *Journal of Peasant Studies* 21: 29–40.

Sen, A. and Dreze, J. (1989) *Hunger and Public Action*, Oxford: Clarendon Press.

Von Braun, J., Teklu, T. and Webb, P. (1999), *Famine in Africa: Causes, Responses, and Prevention*, Baltimore: Johns Hopkins University Press.

Watts, M. (1983) *Silent Violence: Food, Famine and Peasantry in Northern Nigeria*, Berkeley: University of California Press.

MICHAEL WATTS

FAO *see* Food and Agriculture Organization (FAO)

female genital mutilation

Female genital mutilation (FGM) is also referred to as female genital cutting or female circumcision, and refers to all procedures involving partial or total removal of external female genitalia or other injury to female genital organs. Up to 140 million girls and women have undergone FGM, with a further two million girls at risk each year.

The most extreme form of FGM, referred to as infibulation or pharaonic circumcision, involves excision of part or all of the external genitalia and stitching or narrowing of the vaginal opening, and is estimated to account for 15 percent of FGM worldwide. The most common form of FGM, accounting for up to 80 percent of all cases, involves excision of the clitoris and the labia minora. The type of FGM practiced is a function of a wide range of factors, including age, ethnicity (see **ethnicity/identity**), place of residence (urban or rural), **religion** and reason for the procedure. The circumstances under which FGM is carried out varies greatly between locations, and reflects differences in both cultural and socio-economic context. The medicalization of FGM has increasingly been reported among urban populations.

FGM is practiced extensively in Africa and among selected communities (see **community**) in Asia. Increasingly, cases of FGM are being reported in North America and Europe among immigrant communities from populations where FGM is practiced. Women and girls have occasionally been recognized as **refugees** on the grounds that they would be at risk of FGM, although the numbers involved are very small.

The reasons given for practicing FGM often include broad headings such as custom, tradition, **religion** and **culture**. More specifically, aspects of female **sexualities** might be cited, including the attenuation of sexual desire among women and girls to maintain virginity and/or fidelity. Gender identity, including initiation to adulthood, might be associated with FGM. The linkage of FGM with reproduction is common, including beliefs about child development and survival. Reasons of hygiene and esthetics are included, for example, if external female genitalia are considered dirty or unsightly. Frequently, the reasons are many and overlapping and operate at a variety of scales, from the individual to the household to the society and maintenance of social or cultural cohesion.

The consequences of FGM vary according to the type of procedure performed, and reliable data on the impact of FGM are difficult to collect. Health consequences include: **mortality**, pain, hemorrhage, infection, discomfort, development of scar tissue, cysts and abscesses, increased risk of HIV transmission (see **HIV/AIDS (definition and treatment); HIV/AIDS (policy issues)**), obstructed labor, shock, trauma, sexual dysfunction and painful intercourse.

The eradication of FGM is enshrined within the international **human rights** agenda, placing FGM within a broader context of **violence** against women. This is a recent development because it was considered that eradication risked being perceived as cultural **imperialism**. FGM is now on the global agenda and universally condemned, although implementation of laws and policies for individual countries remains at a low level.

See also: cultural relativism; domestic violence; gender; health; sexualities

Further reading

Toubia, N. (2000) *Female Genital Mutilation: A Human Rights Analysis*, London: Zed.

ERNESTINA COAST

FEMINISM *see* gender; feminism and ecology; feminist political ecology; women's movements

feminism and ecology

Debates about feminism and ecology refer to a relatively broad line of academic inquiry emerging in the 1960s and 1970s that examines links between feminist and ecological concerns. The emergence of this literature can be traced back to the rise of **new social movements** during the 1960s, including both **women's movements** and **environment**al movements. Simultaneously, writers in North America and Europe identified

parallels between the domination of nature and the domination of women within the context of value dualisms (for example, nature/culture; men/women) emerging from Western patriarchal frameworks. Their arguments identified numerous systems of patriarchy harking back to early classical Greek philosophy, Western Enlightenment thinking and the scientific revolution, and processes of colonialism (see **colonialism, history of; colonialism, impacts of**) as key contributors to historical and contemporary dominations of nature and women. They further suggested that environmentalism and feminism could gain by joining forces to replace current structures of domination by egalitarian and ecologically sustainable alternatives. This perspective has spawned recent cross-disciplinary work in ecofeminism, **feminist political ecology**, feminist environmentalism, **gender**, **environment**, radical environmentalism and **deep ecology**, among others.

Today, many disciplines such as geography, environmental history, environmental economics, feminist studies, sociology and philosophy, among others, apply the feminism and ecology framework. Using a feminist perspective, these fields provide their own unique insights to environmental investigations in philosophical or day-to-day practical concerns. Research includes women's relationships and interactions with nature; how these might differ from men; and how women might contribute to addressing ecological problems.

For example, ecofeminists have written much about the links between the domination of women and the environment. The term ecofeminism was first introduced by French feminist writer Francoise d'Eaubonne in 1984. Today, a wide range of views from liberal, to socialist, to radical encompass ecofeminist writing. A good deal of this research ascribes women with an intimate connection with nature and a superior ability to care for the environment. Part of this argument comes from the fact that in many contexts, women are more knowledgeable about **natural resources** such as **food** and water because they are more involved in their provision within households. Another, more rhetorical, argument suggests there is an actual biological connection between women and nature that makes women more acutely aware of nature and her workings. Regardless of the argument used, ecofeminists suggest that environmental destruction can pose special problems for women. They suggest that such problems are both an outcome of the patriarchal quest to dominate nature, plus they sever women's ties to nature and make them more vulnerable to the consequences of environmental destruction. While these contributions are welcomed as providing new insights to environmental issues, they are also often criticized for insufficiently identifying the materially and empirically grounded connections between women and nature.

In response to these criticisms, other perspectives and most notably, the literature from debates in **gender, environment and development** has looked instead at the material realities that impinge on women's everyday interactions with the environment. For instance, these studies concentrate on documenting how environmental degradation can have particularly adverse impacts on the lives of women. Such investigations are also particularly interested in redressing the failures of ill conceived, top-down environmental policies and programs that ignore contextually based gendered rights to the environment and often end up further perpetuating the very problems they aim to alleviate. Likewise, research in **feminist political ecology** engages feminist and ecological concerns by directing attention to gendered knowledge, rights and responsibilities as they pertain to environment.

Many perspectives arising from feminism and ecology have impacted upon mainstream international environment and development organizations by emphasizing women's participation in environmental projects in the developing world, and women's **empowerment** through access and control over water, forests, and other **natural resources** (see **environmental entitlements; gender and property rights**). In this context, we see the more practical merging of feminist and ecological concerns. Not only are women empowered by such policies, but they might also become better guardians of the environment because of the stake and responsibilities now conferred upon them. Promoting women's participation must, however, be undertaken with care to not further burden women with new responsibilities (see **women in development (WID) versus gender and development (GAD)**). Undoubtedly, when applied with appropriate cultural sensitivity, the feminism and ecology approach can have some very useful practical outcomes that further both feminist and environmental agendas.

See also: deep ecology; feminist political ecology; gender, environment and development; women in development (WID) versus gender and development (GAD); Women's Environment and Development Organization (WEDO); World Women's Congress for a Healthy Planet (1991); World Women's Planet (1992)

Further reading

Agarwal, B. (1998) "Environmental Management, Equity and Ecofeminism: Debating India's Experience," *The Journal of Peasant Studies* 25:4 55–95.

Braidott, R, Charkiewicz, E., Hausler, S. and Wieringa, S. (eds) (1994) *Women, the Environment and Sustainable Development: Toward a Theoretical Synthesis*, London: Zed.

Diamond, I. (1994) *Fertile Ground: Women, Earth and the Limits of Control*, Boston MA: Beacon.

Merchant, C. (1980) *The Death of Nature: Women, Ecology, and the Scientific Revolution*, San Francisco: Harper and Row.

Seager, J. (1993) *Earth Follies: Coming to Feminist Terms with the Global Environmental Crisis*, New York: Routledge.

FIROOZA PAVRI

feminist political ecology

Feminist political ecology (FPE) is a specific approach to **political ecology** that treats gender as a critical variable in shaping environmental quality and resource access and control, interacting with class, **caste**, race (see **race and racism**), **culture**, and ethnicity (see **ethnicity/identity**). Together these multiple elements of identity shape processes of ecological change, the struggles of men and women to achieve ecologically **sustainable livelihoods**, and the prospects of any **community** for socially just economic and environmental futures. This relatively new field – developed in the

1990s – incorporates feminist critiques of **sustainable development** and feminist visions of alternative approaches to **gender, environment and development**. It is inspired by, and seeks to join, existing strands of feminist debate such as ecofeminism (the recognition of women's distinct environmental knowledge), and the respect for other species and shared environments from environmentalist feminists (see **feminism and ecology**). Other themes include socialist feminism (the critique of development's impact on women); and the complex identities and multiple possibilities envisioned by poststructural feminism (Haraway, 1991) (see **postmodernism and postdevelopment**). FPE brings a feminist perspective to political ecology and environmental justice, rather than simply adding women to existing theory and practice. FPE also acknowledges the positive, as well as negative aspects of power in development (see **power and discourse**), allowing for recognition of *power-with* (solidarity), as well as *power-over* (coercion) and *power-against* (resistance). FPE acknowledges the multiple and complex identities, and the often unpredictable workings of coalition politics and hybrid cultures, as keys to understanding social and environmental changes.

Research within FPE generally assumes that gender and environment are socially constructed. The approach addresses the intersection of gender and environment through the lens of several recurrent themes: gendered knowledge and science; gendered property, space and landscapes; gendered labor and **livelihoods**; gendered environmental decision-making; and gendered political organizations and activities (mainstream and opposition organizations, as well as resistance movements) (see **gender and property rights; women's movements**). FPE may include local as well as global analysis, spanning rural and urban environments in both developed and developing countries, and both industrial and agrarian settings. Examples of FPE work include: women's leadership in opposition to the selective siting of a sewage treatment facility in West Harlem, New York City; gendered construction and protection of biodiversity in home gardens controlled primarily by women in the Dominican Republic; and gendered knowledge, landscapes and organizations responding to **drought** and **famine** in Kenya. Other work has considered conflicts in gendered control of cash and resources in Gambian garden and reforestation projects; women's roles in forest protection and reforestation in the Himalayas; women's participation in European **environmental movements** to combat **pollution** from industrial waste sites; and gender politics of resistance to **dams** in India, Austria, and Southeast Asia.

See also: environment; feminism and ecology; gender and property rights; gender, environment and development; political ecology; postmodernism and postdevelopment; power and discourse; sustainable livelihoods

Further reading

Haraway, D. (1991) *Simians, Cyborgs, and Women: The Reinvention of Nature*, London and New York: Routledge.

Rocheleau, D., Thomas-Slayter, B. and Wangani, E. (eds) (1996) *Feminist Political Ecology: Global Issues and Local Experiences*, London and New York: Routledge.

Seager, J. (2003) "Review Essay: Rachel Carson Died of Breast Cancer: The Coming of Age of Feminist Environmentalism," *Signs*, 28: 945–72.

DIANNE ROCHELEAU

fertility

The term fertility generally refers to the numerous aspects of human reproduction that lead to live births. Several measures of fertility relate to development. The most common measure is the crude birth rate (CBR). CBR refers to the number of live births in one year per 1,000 of the total **population**. CBR varies between approximately 8 and 55 for countries worldwide. Total fertility rate (TFR) is another measure of fertility, and refers to the average number of children a woman is likely to have during her lifetime. For example, a world TFR of 2.9 means that, on average, a woman will have 2.9 children during her life. General fertility rate (GFR) refers to the number of live births per

1,000 women of childbearing age (15–49) during a one-year period. The impact of fertility on population growth and size is related to attendant **mortality** rates.

See also: mortality; population; population growth rate (PGR)

WENDY SHAW

fertilizers

Fertilizers are human-made soil additions that are rich in essential nutrients for plant growth. Such amendments aim to raise overall soil fertility (see **soil erosion and soil fertility**) or to counteract an absence or paucity of specific nutrients. Elements and compounds dispersed through fertilizer application enter biogeochemical cycles and alter the nutrient cycling processes of ecosystems. Examples range from nitrate accumulation in groundwater beyond cycling capacity through the application of fertilizer nitrate to the cumulative effects of long-term manuring on topsoil organic matter content.

There can be both inorganic and organic forms of fertilizer. Inorganic fertilizers, along with synthetic organic compounds (biocides, growth-controlling compounds) and industrial wastes (organic and inorganic), comprise the manufactured chemicals that have been increasingly introduced into **agriculture** since the middle of the nineteenth century. They are compounds intended to enhance crop yield by releasing additional amounts of plant nutrients, such as nitrogen and phosphorus, which typically occur as ions in soils without human intervention. Such chemicals are also incorporated into soils that are less fertile relative to the cropping system desired to compensate for a dearth in certain plant nutrients. The main advantages of using inorganic fertilizers lie in the ease of field application (less overall mass due to its concentrated form) and greater control over the accuracy of nutrient content.

Organic fertilizers are derived from the decomposition of biogenic materials, such as plant and animal tissues, secretions, and excretions. Part of the **indigenous knowledge** base of many social formations, they are increasingly reconsidered as complementary amendments in mainstream, industrialized farming as a result of environmental problems wrought by an excessive use of inorganic forms, especially since the 1950s, and the **waste management** problems created through industrial production and **urbanization**. Organic fertilizers entail a more diluted addition of nutrients using biogenic wastes and thereby mimic an ecosystemic cycling of nutrients. Aside from the difficulty of transport (see **transport policy**) resulting from their sheer bulk, organic fertilizers exhibit high variability in nutrient content and composition, making it difficult to control for the level of nutrient concentration desired for a cropping system. The main advantage of organic fertilizers is their characteristically high organic matter content, an essential component of soil systems, and the slow-release of nutrients, which reduces such impacts as the leaching of nitrates into groundwater.

Economic processes in a social formation play a pivotal role in the development and ecological consequences of soil amendment systems. The reliance on inorganic fertilizers is characteristic of market-based societies (including the former Soviet system, which relied on international trade with liberal democracies), where the intensity of soil nutrient extraction and long-distance translocation through crop harvesting and sale is so high that it requires large quantities of nutrient additions in order to prevent the rapid exhaustion of soil nutrient supplies. In contrast, many non-market forms of **agriculture** typically feature the recycling of organic wastes into the soil and thereby largely replace the nutrients mined through crop harvest and consumption.

See also: agriculture; agrochemicals; green revolution; irrigation; pollution; soil erosion and soil fertility

Further reading

Tisdale, S. (1999, 6th edn) *Soil fertility and Fertilizers: an Introduction to Nutrient Management*, Upper Saddle River NJ: Prentice Hall.

SALVATORE ENGEL-DI MAURO

FINANCE see capital markets; fiscal and monetary policy; International Monetary Fund (IMF); inflation and its effects; international economic order; micro-credit and micro-finance ; multilateral development banks (MDBs); stock markets; World Bank

fiscal and monetary policy

Fiscal and monetary policies affect the economy by altering aggregate demand, and are referred to as policies of demand management. Monetary policy is conducted by the central banking authority and involves altering the supply of money in the economy. Fiscal policy entails the use of the government's budget to influence total spending in the economy. These policies are used to attain economic stability, i.e. dampen fluctuations in output and attain low levels of inflation (see **inflation and its effects**) and **unemployment**. They have also been used to foster **economic development**, especially in developing countries.

Fiscal policy uses the instruments of government expenditure (on administration, defense, health services, etc.), transfer payments (welfare benefits, **unemployment** compensation, etc.) and taxes to affect total expenditure in the economy. Changes in government expenditure have a direct impact on total expenditure; transfers and taxes have an indirect influence through consumption expenditure. An increase in government spending and transfers has a positive impact on output, while taxes have a dampening effect. The final impact of these instruments on output and hence income is normally a multiple of the magnitude of the initial change (**multiplier effect**). As the tax multiplier is less than the government spending multiplier an interesting possibility arises: An overall increase in income can be attained by an increase in government spending and taxes by an equal magnitude (balanced budget multiplier). Falling income because of a fall in private expenditure (consumption and investment) can be checked by appropriate fiscal policy, and is an example of discretionary fiscal policy. A combination of an increase in government expenditure and tax cuts worth $700 billion between 1983 and 1988

resulted in a period of economic expansion lasting till 1991 for the US economy. On the other hand, tax collection and transfer payments rise and fall with income and output in the economy, acting as automatic stabilizers. For example, the impact of a fall in private expenditure on output is dampened by the rise of unemployment and other welfare benefits. This is the non-discretionary aspect of fiscal policy.

Critics argue that expansionary fiscal policy can crowd out investment through an increase in the rate of interest in the economy. This can happen in two ways. Increasing income leads to an increase in the demand for money and hence the rate of interest; alternatively, government expenditure financed by market borrowings can also lead to an increase in the rate of interest. Further, as there are time lags involved in the implementation of government projects, expansionary fiscal policies may not be the best tool to smoothen short-term fluctuations in output.

Instruments of monetary policy are best understood by keeping in mind that bank deposits comprise the bulk of money in developed economies. The modern banking system is a fractional reserve system – i.e. a certain part of deposits is held as reserves by the banks and the rest is available for lending. Deposits lent out create further deposits, thus creating money (i.e. deposits) by a multiple of itself. One instrument of monetary policy is the required reserve ratio, which sets a minimum fraction of deposit liabilities to be held by banks on reserve, either as cash in their vaults or deposits at the central bank. The discount rate – the interest charged by the central bank to provide reserve deposits directly or by rediscounting or purchasing financial assets held by banks – is another instrument of monetary policy. Any change in the discount rate alters the cost of borrowed reserves. The selling and buying of government securities by the central bank by debiting and crediting (respectively) the reserves of the buyer's and the seller's bank held by it (the banks in turn debit and credit the buyer's and seller's accounts) is another instrument of monetary policy and is referred to as open market operations and affects the non-borrowed reserves. Given total reserves, the required reserve ratio sets an upper limit on the amount of deposits that can be created. Through these instruments, the central bank can alter the supply of money in the economy. In any given situation, this affects demand and hence output, income and **employment** in the economy. For example an increase in money supply by bringing about a fall in the rate of interest may trigger off an increase in investment expenditure and hence output and income. But critics argue that changes in the supply of money do not affect any variable (e.g. output, income, etc.) in real terms, especially in the long run.

Despite an enduring controversy between monetarists and fiscalists, these policies are often used in tandem. This is not merely because the authorities administering these policies are aware of each other's actions. Each affects the other, especially through the government's budget deficit (net tax revenues minus expenditure). If it is financed through borrowings, it can lead to an increase in the rate of interest with implications for the monetary sector. On the other hand, if deficits get monetized (thus increasing the supply of money) they have a direct impact on monetary policy.

As mentioned earlier, these policies can also play a role in economic development by influencing the financing and the pattern of investment. Fiscal measures to decrease government consumption (e.g. defense expenditure) and private consumption (through a system of progressive taxation on income and wealth) can result in an increase in savings, thus helping the financing of investment. Import tariffs and tax concessions encourage import substitution and channelize investment in core sectors respectively. Further development banks (industrial and agricultural) by subsidized lending have also been used to funnel investment in specific industrial and agricultural activities.

See also: economic development; employment; income distribution; inflation and its effects; state and state reform; unemployment

Further reading

Biswas, R. (ed.) (2002) *International Tax Competition: Globalization and Fiscal Sovereignty*, London: Commonwealth Secretariat.

Blinder, A. and Solow, R. (1974) "Analytical Foundations of Fiscal Policy," in Blinder, A. (ed.) *The Economics of Public Finance*, Washington DC: Brookings Institution.

Eshag, E. (1983) *Fiscal and Monetary Policies and Problems in Developing countries*, Cambridge: Cambridge University Press.

AJAY RANJAN SINGH

fisheries

Fisheries, or fishing industries, are important sources of **food**, **employment** and revenue for many countries. While aquaculture production is increasing, inland and offshore capture production is steady, reflecting the status of world fish stocks. Approximately half of all fish stocks are fully exploited and a further quarter is over-exploited, depleted or recovering. As a result, global management objectives, especially in developed countries, no longer focus on development of the resource alone, but also focus on conservation of the resource. However, it is debatable whether management improvements will outpace the increasing pressures on the resource (see **natural resources**).

Annual capture fisheries and aquaculture production remains at approximately 120 million metric tons (statistics from FAO, 2000), although supply fluctuates due to the changing state of fisheries resources, the economic climate and environmental conditions. Total capture production accounts for three quarters of this production (90 percent from offshore and 10 percent from inland fish resources). Aquaculture production accounts for the remaining quarter of production. Capture fisheries production increased by approximately 6 percent per year during the 1950s to 1970s and 2 percent per year during the 1980s. No increase in capture production has been experienced since the early 1990s. In contrast, aquaculture production has shown the opposite tendency. Starting from insignificant production in 1950, aquaculture production grew about 5 percent per year to the late 1960s, by about 8 percent during the 1970s and 1980s, and by about 10 percent since 1990. China is the world's largest fishing nation, accounting for approximately 32 percent of world production. Other major fishing producers are Japan, India, the United States, the Russian Federation and Indonesia.

Total capture production is no longer increasing due to the status of world fish stocks. Apart from the Southeast Atlantic, the Southwest Pacific and the Western Central Pacific (which have shown positive trends in catches in the late 1990s), all the world's major fishing areas are showing minor changes or declines in offshore capture landings. Approximately 25–27 percent of fisheries resources are under- or moderately exploited, and this percentage is declining slowly due to increases in fishing effort. Forty-seven to 50 percent of fisheries resources are fully exploited with fishing effort having reached (or being very close to) the maximum sustainable yield. This proportion of fully exploited fisheries has been stable through time. Twenty-four to 28 percent of fish resource is over-exploited, depleted or recovering stock, and this percentage is increasing slowly through time. These fish stocks will decline unless swift remedial action is taken in managing the resource.

The fisheries literature is replete with examples of failed fisheries management as reflected in the status of stocks. In general terms, management has improved greatly in the 1980s and 1990s; however, it is debatable whether these improvements will outpace the increasing pressures on the resource. Management objectives in most countries have moved from being development-focused only, to focus also on conservation of the resource. Most developed countries are faced with fully or over-exploited stocks, so their management objectives concentrate on stock rebuilding and capacity reduction. In contrast, developing country objectives are more focused on enhancing and diversifying fisheries rather than limiting fishing effort. Their underlying concern is the relatively important role fisheries play for **employment** and **food security** for their people.

As a common-property resource (see **common pool resources**), strong **governance** of fisheries is required to prevent the resource from being over-exploited. The interests of the fishers, who are motivated by private profit, and the interests of the global **community**, which seeks to prevent dissipation of the resource, are in conflict. The negotiation of the **United Nations Convention on the Law of the Sea (UNCLOS)** in 1982 (which was not ratified until 1994) gave resource-adjacent countries state-**property rights** and responsibility for resource use within the sea area 200 miles from their coastline, an area termed the exclusive economic zone. The Convention contributed much to the allocation of property rights to world fish stocks, given that 90 percent of world offshore capture production is taken within the exclusive economic zones of national jurisdiction (mainly due to the higher productivity of the coast and shelf areas). However, the open seas are still subject to the problems of "open-access" associated with common-property resources (see **common pool resources**).

The way in which control is placed over resource use is actively debated in the fisheries literature. Controls can be placed over fishing effort either through input controls (i.e. gear restrictions, closed areas and closed seasons) or output controls (i.e. individual tradable quotas, limits on size or conditions of fish landed, and limits on entry). Input controls are relatively simple to enforce; however, the economic efficiency of operators is reduced and effort creep (through changes in unregulated inputs) is difficult to contain. Output controls do not suffer the inefficiency costs of input controls, but they have other shortcomings such as the risk of over-capitalization, relatively large enforcement costs and the encouragement of exploitative behavior. Individual tradable quotas are growing in popularity as an effort control, and have been successfully implemented in many countries, often in conjunction with other control measures.

See also: common pool resources; community-based natural resource management (CBNRM); dams; environment; food; Global Environment Facility (GEF); institutions and environment; natural resources; United Nations Convention on the Law of the Sea (UNCLOS)

Further reading

FAO (Food and Agriculture Organization) (2000) *The State of World Fisheries and Aquaculture*, Rome: FAO. Published every two years and

available from website: http://www.fao.org/sof/
sofia/

Gordon, H. (1954) "The Economic Theory of a Common-property Resource: The Fishery," *The Journal of Political Economy* 62:2 124–42.

Petersen, E. (2002) "Institutional Structures of Fishery Management: The Fortuna in the South Pacific," pp. 187–220 in Garnaut, R. (ed.) *Resource Management in Asia Pacific Developing Countries*, Canberra: Asia Pacific Press.

Tietenberg, T. (2000) *Environmental and Natural Resource Economics*, New York: Addison-Wesley (ch. 13).

ELIZABETH PETERSEN

flexible specialization

Flexible specialization is an approach to industrial development that emphasizes diversity and specialization of production rather than mass production. The concept was originally proposed by Piore and Sabel (1984), who argued that Fordist mass production (see **Fordism versus Toyotaism**) would be followed by a regime based upon flexible specialization. This new regime would incorporate a return to craft production, albeit via the application of computer technology. Since then, flexible specialization has been used in various ways, as a general theoretical model of industrial change, as well as a specific model of the organization of production.

At the macro level, the term has been related to an examination of the move away from mass production systems to more diversified systems, vital aspects being flexibility and innovation. At the micro level, flexible specialization has been used to explore an innovative and flexible style of industrial organization incorporating skilled workers using general-purpose machinery, able to respond to changing market demands. An extension of this flexibility to the inter-firm level allows for the "discovery of dense webs of inter-firm linkages [that] outdate analyses which focus on the enterprise as an isolated unit" (Rasmussen *et al.*, 1992:2). For this reason, flexible specialization can be used to explain linkages among firms of equal status, as well as those involved in vertical subcontracting arrangements.

Flexible specialization relies on a number of key defining variables. These include a broadly trained workforce which can undertake a number of production tasks; an emphasis on the virtues of craftspersonship; flexible and informal management; general or multi-purpose machinery; just-in-time delivery systems of inputs; and designs and varied products which respond to an increasingly specialized and fragmented market, in turn leading to the pursuit of niche rather than mass markets.

Due to the broad variety of industrial organization the flexible specialization term attempts to address, it has been argued that further disaggregation is required when analyzing small firms. Various features facilitate the integration of small enterprises and therefore make flexible specialization successful. These involve the establishment of networks, clusters (see **clustering**) and linkages, and other forms of interaction and interdependence. Firms must strike a balance between competition and cooperation in areas such as design, innovation and the introduction of new technology, and a form of integration that allows small enterprises to enjoy "collective efficiency" – economies of agglomeration – unobtainable by individual firms.

More recently, there has been a growth of literature focusing specifically on the applicability of flexible specialization to small enterprises in developing country contexts. However, the application of flexible specialization in this realm has been subject to a range of criticisms, including a fundamental concern regarding the use of a model based on "Western" economic rationale, in non-Western circumstances (Turner, 2003).

See also: clustering; Fordism versus Toyotaism; industrialization; small and medium enterprises (SMEs)

Further reading

Piore, M. and Sabel, C. (1984) *The Second Industrial Divide: Possibilities for Prosperity*, New York: Basic Books.

Rasmussen, J., Schmitz H. and van Dijk, M. (eds)
(1992) "Flexible Specialization: A New View on
Small Industry?" Special issue of *IDS Bulletin*
23: 3.

Turner, S. (2003) *Indonesia's Small Entrepreneurs*,
London: Routledge Curzon.

SARAH TURNER

food

Food embodies both nutritional qualities and social
relationships. The social relations of food have
always included a global dimension. For example,
in the "Columbian exchange," Christopher
Columbus introduced wheat to the New World,
returning to Europe with American maize and the
Andean potato. Through the European colonial
circuit, the potato traveled to Africa and India. In
this way, potatoes and chilies, deriving originally
from the New World, have imparted a world-historical dimension to what is now staple Indian
food. Similarly, the pasta and tomato sauce of
global Italian cuisine originated in the Columbian
exchange. In pre-Columbian times, sugar was
transported from Polynesia to Asia, to the Mediterranean, and thence, via Columbus, to the West
Indies. And recently, East Asian soya has come to
supply expanding global needs for cooking oil and
protein for **livestock** and vegetarians alike.

While cuisines may be "local," "global," or some
combination, the "**globalization**" of local diets
may have been incorporated or imposed, depending
on historical circumstances. Traders may introduce
new foods into local diets and/or **agriculture**s.
Alternatively, one of colonialism's enduring legacies has been to impose agri-export monocultures,
to provision metropolitan industries or consumer
markets elsewhere. And this pattern of reorganization of world agriculture has deepened in recent
years under the neo-liberal project of global
development (see **neo-liberalism**). Because export
monoculture is increasingly dominant, but
unsustainable in its assault on rural communities
(see **community**) and **biodiversity**, and its consumption of chemicals and fossil fuels, eating
locally has assumed growing significance as a social
and ecological necessity.

Monoculture defines modern industrial agriculture, extending to the contemporary crop
development industry as biotechnologists develop
miracle seeds and livestock forms. Monoculture
has its origins in colonial history, in the plantations of the New World and the pervasive beef
culture (see **colonialism, history of**). The introduction of European cattle to the New World
anticipated an **agribusiness** complex that now
links specialized soy producers, feedcorn farmers,
and lot-fed cattle across the world. The global
cattle complex embodies a series of commodity
chains binding the world into an animal protein
dependency that imposes monocultures on local
ecologies, competing with the consumption of food
staples like wheat, rice and beans. Beef followed
the lead of sugar, a formerly aristocratic food whose
modern availability to the emerging European
proletariat was sourced globally from slave plantations (see **slavery**). In the nineteenth century,
beef moved down the social scale from the aristocracy to the swelling urban classes who dined
"up" the food chain, consuming North American
beef financed by British investors. With the advent
of mass consumption in the mid-twentieth century,
the beef industry divided between lot-fed high-
value beefsteak, and grass-fed, cheaper, lean hamburger beef for the global fast-food industry. Thus,
beef represents modernity, and its social hierarchy
of class-based diets.

Class, cultural and imperial relations have
shaped the political history of diets. Rising affluence is symbolized by rising animal protein consumption, emulating the Western diet. Modernity
is identified in moving up the food chain hierarchy
(from starch, to grain, to animal protein and
vegetables). Historically represented as nutritional
improvement, the food chain hierarchy is also a
political construct, with beef as the archetype of
political and corporate legitimacy. A recent
example of this is **World Bank** sponsorship of
China's domestic "livestock revolution" (see also
white revolution (milk)) and previous export
strategies encouraged by development agencies in
Central America to develop an offshore source of
hamburger meat for US consumers. International
trade policies and corporate investments sustain
such a food chain hierarchy through market relations that source a global supply of affluent foods.

As wealthy global consumers "dine up" on beef and shrimp, local peasants and fishermen, displaced by cattle pastures, shrimp farms and deteriorating coastal lands and mangroves, "descend" the food chain, depending on low-protein starchy diets.

The inequalities of globalization are manifest in the international food order. The affluent one fifth of the world's **population** stimulates a growing and highly visible trade in foodstuffs including exotic, high-value and all-seasonal foods supplied through global sourcing. This global class relationship deepens the international food order through affluent sourcing and compensatory food dependency. In the 1990s, half of the foreign exchange of the **Food and Agriculture Organization (FAO)**'s eighty-eight low-income food deficit countries went to food imports – flowing in the opposite direction to agri-exports expanding to service foreign **debt**. There is a considerable discrepancy between globalization's affluent image and experience, and the reality of hunger and **malnutrition** – a discrepancy that, perversely, drives the politics of globalization.

Food and biotechnology (see **biotechnology and resistance**) corporations derive their legitimacy from representing global hunger, and the promise of transgenic crops, as the twenty-first century challenge. The crop development industry is positioning itself in the developing world to inherit the commercial momentum triggered by the **green revolution**. Crop development corporations represent transgenic crops as a solution to the negative effects of green revolution **monoculture** (plant disease, soil depletion and pest infestation), and are busy acquiring local seed companies to obtain control over a possible future of transgenic cropping. The full implementation of this corporate project threatens to destabilize the world's remaining 3 billion farmers, intensify environmental jeopardy (with the growing threat of biological, on top of chemical, **pollution**), and reduce global **biodiversity** to agro-industrial monocultures, increasing the **vulnerability** of crops and livestock to disease. Meanwhile growing numbers of small farmers, environmentalists and consumers contest this undemocratic and unsustainable project of corporate globalization (see **environmental movements**). Most notably, the transnational farmers' rights movement, *Via*

Campesina (the largest chapter of which is the Brazilian landless-workers' movement) has organized its opposition around the redefinition of **food security** as "food sovereignty."

Food **commodification** is a key component in the rise and reproduction of capitalist culture and the ideology of "development." **Capitalism**'s singular logic not only undermines non-capitalist food cultures, but adulterates distinctive capitalist food cultures via "McDonaldization," incubating serious **epidemics** of diet-related cancers, obesity and unforeseen health risks. There is now a discernible reaction against McDonaldization, reflected in declining market fortunes of that corporation. There is also a "global epidemic of **malnutrition**," (see **epidemics**) in which the 1.2 billion underfed are matched by the 1.2 billion overfed, expressing the intensification of global food inequity. In this context, food's staple, cultural, and bio-physical qualities position it as a central site of resistance to the project of corporate globalization.

Within the globalization project, **agribusiness** has targeted the WTO (see **World Trade Organization/General Agreement on Tariffs and Trade (WTO/GATT)**) to institutionalize transnational rights to source food and food inputs, to prospect for genetic patents (see **genetically modified organisms (GMOs)**), and to gain access to local and national food markets. The trade-related intellectual property rights (see **trade-related aspects of intellectual property rights (TRIPS)**) protocol empowers corporations to patent genetic materials such as seed germplasm, potentially endangering the rights of farmers to plant their crops on the grounds of patent infringement. This expropriation of genetic resources developed by peasants, forest dwellers and local communities (see **community**) over centuries of cultural experimentation is termed "**biopiracy:**" exemplified in the patenting of Indian basmati rice by the US company Rice Tec, which sells "Kasmati" rice and "Texmati" rice as authentic basmati. Patenting intensifies an already monopolized global seed industry. The significance of the TRIPS is that **intellectual property rights (IPRs)** on gene patenting privilege governments and corporations as legal entities, and disempower communities and farmers whose rights over traditional knowledge go unrecognized.

Food security has been redefined, via the WTO regime, as the reduction of barriers to agricultural trade, privileging agro-exporting regions as global "breadbaskets," and global **agribusiness**es as instruments of regional "**comparative advantage**." Under this regime, Mexico's 2.5 million rainfed maize farms are forced to compete, via a **productivity** differential of 2–3 tons per hectare compared with 7.5 tons per hectare, with Midwestern American corn farms. Should the **North American Free Trade Agreement (NAFTA)** be fully implemented by 2008, it is estimated that corn imports may rise 200 percent and swamp over two thirds of Mexican maize production. The additional casualty here is the local **biodiversity** that complements export crops, but is invisibilized in the monocultural language of comparative advantage. Displaced maize farmers (especially women) find their way either to the new *agromaquilas* in Mexico, or to North American orchards or plantations, where what they may earn in a week in Mexico they earn in a day in the USA. Either way they enter global circuits, producing food for (socially) distant consumers under the control largely of **transnational corporations (TNCs)**.

The project of corporate globalization of the food system is contradictory. First, market liberalization centralizes the power of food corporations via their control over global sourcing and trade relations. But, since not all nations are equal, and food cultures differ, such global power has to contend with sovereignty questions, which routinely paralyze international **institutions** like the WTO. Second, biotech/food corporation clusters may claim solutions to world hunger, but their genetically modified (GM) (see **genetically modified organisms (GMOs)**) food products (milk, soybeans, animal feed, canola, sugar beets, corn and potatoes) often profit the chemical industry before feeding hungry people. Third, since corporate agriculture is premised on the reduction of biodiversity, the corporate development of transgenic technology (including the monopoly of genetically-altered seeds) threatens human, environmental and **community** sustainability. In addition, many countries eschew the introduction of transgenic crops that would compromise their trade relations, and could contaminate centers of crop diversity through gene drift from transgenic plants to landraces (gene-complexes with multiple forms of resistance to disease), especially following the contamination of maize landraces in Mexico. Fourth, global corporate foods promote a "**nutrition** transition" involving a declining consumption of cereals and legumes and a rising consumption of meat and dairy fats, salt and sugars, including exposure to the diseases of affluence (especially obesity, diabetes and heart failure) associated with processed foods (see **health transition**). Fifth, the market regime favors multilateral bodies such as the northern/corporate-dominated Codex Alimentarius Commission, which compromises the ability of national institutions to adjudicate questions of food contamination by pesticide and hormone residues, chemical additives and genetically engineered foods. And sixth, environmentalist, consumer, farmer, and **fair trade** movements, providing an array of alternatives in the production and consumption of food, offer a growing resistance to market rule (see **environmental movements**).

Food safety and food sovereignty has inspired a broadening counter-movement across the world since the 1990s. In developed countries, food labeling is on the political agenda, as a protection against GM foods. French farmers attacked a storage facility owned by Novartis, destroying 30 tons of transgenic corn seed, when the French government allowed planting of GM corn (see **biotechnology and resistance**). Such opposition underlies the **European Union**'s current resistance to US attempts to open Europe up to trade in GM foods via WTO rules. In Bangalore, the 10-million strong Karnataka Farmers Union challenged Cargill's attempts to patent germplasm and burned Monsanto's GM crops, giving life to other grassroots organizations in this struggle. Sustainable agricultures crop up across the world. In Madhya Pradesh, the Centre for Conservation of Traditional Farming Systems uses traditional methods to cultivate unirrigated wheat varieties, reversing the **green revolution** and the socially and environmentally unsustainable impact of high-input agriculture – modeling small farming and subsistence agriculture as the alternative to big-dam-based irrigated agriculture (see **dams; irrigation**). The Brazilian landless-workers movement (MST), in a massive bid for food sovereignty, has settled 400,000 families on more than 15 million acres of land seized by takeovers since the mid-1980s. The confiscation of uncultivated private property is legitimized by the 1988 Brazilian constitution. The MST offers an alternative to globalized corporate agriculture, focusing on producing staple foods for the excluded majority of Brazilians. Elsewhere, the Andean PRATEC group is recovering traditional Andean peasant practices and reclaiming food as culture.

Meanwhile, **fair trade** has blossomed as a method of transcending abuses in the **free trade** system, rendering more visible the conditions of production of globally traded commodities in order to establish just prices, democratic producer and farm labor associations, environmentally sound practices, healthy consumption and direct understanding between producers and consumers of their respective needs. Fair trade exchanges have an annual market value of US$400 million, and the market for fair trade products (organic products such as coffee, bananas, cocoa, honey, tea, orange juice – representing about 60 percent of the fair trade market) expands at between 10–25 percent a year. Three fair trade labels, Transfair, Max Havelaar, and Fairtrade Mark, broke into European markets in the late 1980s, and are now united under the umbrella NGO, Fairtrade Labeling Organizations International (FLO), which harmonizes different standards and organizes a single fair trade market (in the absence of national regulations). FLO aims to "raise awareness among consumers of the negative effects on producers of international trade so that they exercise their purchasing power positively." Above world market prices are guaranteed. In Costa Rica, for instance, a cooperative, Coopetrabasur, achieved Fairtrade registration to supply bananas, eliminating herbicide use, reducing chemical **fertilizers**, building democratic union procedures, raising wages and establishing a "social premium" set aside for community projects such as **housing** improvement, electrification (see **electrification and power-sector reform**), and environmental monitoring. Current attempts to reconstitute the WTO as the Fair Trade Organization testifies to the political significance of food.

In sum, food security, sovereignty and safety, and environmental movements express the crisis of the corporate project of global development. Their point is that the corporate logic is culturally reductive and unsustainable, and food may be the strongest litmus test of this. Certainly, cuisines evolve across time and space, but pharma-food is beginning to reconstitute what some term the Fast World. An intense dialectic is playing out between the abstraction of corporate foods (origin, form and content), and the intimacy of the Slow Food movement, and of fresh and organic food that expresses both locality and sustainability. For the majority of the world's population, food is not just an item of consumption, it is a way of life, with deep material and symbolic power. This fact underlies the growing resistance to the commodification of food.

See also: agriculture; capitalism; environment; environmental movements; fair trade; famine; food security; free trade; globalization; health; malnutrition; nutrition; sustainable development

Further reading

Barndt, D. (2002) *Tangled Routes: Women, Work and Globalization on the Tomato Trail*, Lanham MD: Rowman and Littlefield.

Friedmann, H. (1993) "The Political Economy of Food: A Global Crisis," *New Left Review* 197: 27–59.

Lappé, F. M. and Lappé, A. (2002) *Hope's Edge*, New York: Tarcher/Putnam.

Magdoff, F., Foster, J. and Buttel, F. (eds) (2000) *Hungry for Profit: The Agribusiness Threat to Farmers, Livelihoods*, New York: Monthly Review Press.

Mintz, S. (1986) *Sweetness and Power: The Place of Sugar in Modern History*, New York: Vintage.

Pistorius, R. and van Wijk, J. (1999) *The Exploitation of Plant Genetic Information: Political Strategies in Crop Development*, Oxfordshire: CABI Publishing.

Rifkin, J. (1992) *Beyond Beef: The Rise and Fall of the Cattle Culture*, New York: Penguin.

PHILIP D. McMICHAEL

food aid

Food aid is commodity **aid** used to support food assistance and general development actions in aid-eligible countries. It is commonly distinguished into three main forms: program food aid, relief or emergency food aid, and project food aid. Relief food aid and project food aid constitute targeted food aid. Low-Income Food-Deficit Countries (LIFDCs) and Least Developed Countries (LDCs) are classified as priority recipients of food aid. Food aid has been, and continues to be, one of the most controversial types of aid, alternatively defined as the product of humanitarian altruism (see **humanitarianism**), or as part of the foreign policy of donor countries for the imposition of political and economic agendas (see **conditionality**).

Program food aid is usually supplied as a resource transfer for balance of payment and/or budgetary support objectives. It is provided as a grant or a loan, mainly on a bilateral basis. It is not targeted to specific beneficiary groups, but sold on the market of the recipient country. Relief (or emergency) food aid is targeted and freely distributed to victims of natural or man-made disasters (see **emergency assistance**). Project food aid is targeted and distributed to support specific development objectives. Examples of project food aid are food-for-work and food-for-**education**. It is always supplied on a grant basis.

The **World Food Programme (WFP)** is distributor of virtually all multilateral food aid. Food aid procurement follows three main patterns: "direct transfers" include food aid originating from the donor country; "local purchases" are procured by donors in a developing country for use as food aid in the same country; and "triangular transactions" are purchases in one developing country for use as food aid in another developing country. It has been remarked that food aid involves a larger economy than the declared price of food given by donors. "Food aid commodity chains" include services of transportation, distribution, packaging and storing, banking transactions and administrative tasks that principally benefit institutions linked to the donor country.

Food aid has been criticized as a means of getting rid of price-depressing surpluses produced by protected farm sectors in donor countries; for depressing prices and reducing the incentives to expand output among farmers in recipient countries (see **European Union**); and for establishing a demand for commodities that are not produced locally, or inducing consumer preference for higher-quality imported cereals. It has been intensely politically motivated, and/or has been used as a leverage to acquire access to local materials. Food aid is often poorly targeted, benefitting the politically powerful, the easily accessible, and the already better off.

The **International Covenant on Economic, Social and Cultural Rights** of 1996 recognizes a universal right to food, and the importance of international cooperation toward the achievement of the objectives of the 1996 Rome Declaration on World Food Security and the World Food Summit Plan of Action. Since the second half of the 1990s, the **United Nations** System has made steps to redefine food aid not as a mere commodity, but as a fundamental human right (see **human rights**) inextricably related to the **right to development**.

See also: agriculture; aid; aid effectiveness and aid evaluation; early warning systems; emergency assistance; food; food security; malnutrition; targeting; World Food Programme

Further reading

Clay, E. and Stokke, O. (eds) (2000) *Food Aid and Human Security*, London: Frank Cass.

United Nations (2003) *Report Submitted by the Special Rapporteur on the Right to Food, Jean Ziegler, in Accordance with Commission on Human Rights resolution 2002/25*, Economic and Social Council, Commission on Human Rights, New York: United Nations.

BENEDETTA ROSSI

Food and Agriculture Organization (FAO)

The Food and Agriculture Organization (FAO) was established in 1945 as part of the newly formed **United Nations**. It was created following discussions involving forty-four governments in 1943, with the stated mandate "to raise levels of **nutrition** and standards of living, to improve agricultural productivity, and to better the condition of rural populations."

The main activities of the FAO focus on **agriculture**, forestry, **fisheries** and **rural development**, with the key objective of achieving **sustainable development** and **food security**. In 2002, the FAO had 183 country members, and one member organization (the **European Union**). Members meet biennially, where they oversee work programs, budgets, and the election of the Director General. It also elects a council of forty-nine member nations, with an independent chairperson, as a provisional governing body with each member nation elected for a three-year period.

The FAO has eight departments: Administration and Finance, Agriculture, Economic and Social, Fisheries, Forestry, General Affairs and Information, Sustainable Development, and Technical Cooperation. The headquarters are in Rome, with many regional and country offices which employ almost 4,000 staff overall. FAO activity comprises the regular program and the field program. Member countries finance the former, which includes support for fieldwork, advice on policy and planning for governments, and development projects. The field program involves the execution of development strategies, especially through joint projects with national governments and other agencies such as foundations and **charities**. Most finance for this derives from national trust funds, with contributions from the United Nations Development Programme and FAO itself. In recent years, expenditure for the Field program has been less than for the regular program. In 1994, a major restructuring program of the FAO was implemented to cut costs and decentralize operations. Since 1999, a *Strategic Framework* has been in operation to provide a structure for FAO's activities until 2015.

In practical terms, FAO provides development assistance, often involving technical inputs to field projects with emphasis on holistic approaches to integrate environmental, cultural and economic factors. FAO also plays an important role as a repository of information. This includes data on a variety of factors related to agriculture, **food**, fisheries, forestry and population trends (see **population**), collected on a national and regional basis. Inaugurated in 1986 as AGROSTAT, these statistics are now available as FAOSTAT. Such statistics and their analysis are invaluable for researchers, government and **non-governmental organizations (NGOs)** for decision-making for project implementation, training and education, and finance. Specialist technical, legal and administrative expertise is made available to governments for **rural development**, the mitigation of **poverty** and enhancing **food security**. Moreover, FAO acts a catalyst for development opportunities through its role as an independent forum for formal and informal discussion. It contributes to the formulation of international standards, conventions and agreements and facilitates meetings and international conferences, including two *World Food Summits* in 1996 and 2002.

Critics of the FAO have alleged that much money has been spent on bureaucratically controlled enterprises, or on the excessive use of technocentric solutions to problems such as **malaria** or agricultural **productivity**, rather than on understanding the local **vulnerability** of farmers, or the political influences on food security. The role of the FAO in the **green revolution** was criticized for emphasizing new high-yielding seeds, rather than acknowledging the socio-economic factors necessary for the update of such seeds. Supporters of the FAO, however, acknowledge that the organization needs to become more flexible in localities, but point to the organization's achievements over the years.

See also: agriculture; fisheries; food; food security; green revolution; United Nations

Further reading

Food and Agriculture Organization (FAO) http://www.fao.org
FAOSTAT: http://apps.fao.org/

A. M. MANNION

food security

Food security refers to the diverse means by which individuals or states (see **state and state reform**) can secure access to **food**. **Poverty** and hunger are very much part of the landscape of the twenty-first century. According to **United Nations** statistics, in the period since 1980, **economic growth** in fifteen countries has brought rapidly rising incomes to 1.5 billion people, yet one person in three still lives in poverty and basic social services are unavailable to more than 1 billion people. Nowhere is this privation more vivid and pronounced than along **gender** lines. Of the 1.3 billion people in poverty, 70 percent are women. Between 1965 and 1988 the number of rural women living below the **poverty line** increased by 47 percent; the corresponding figure for men was less than 30 percent. One measure of poverty is the extent to which individuals are able to secure sufficient food to conduct a healthy and active life. By the conventional measure of hunger, namely the **Food and Agriculture Organization (FAO)**'s definition of household food security (HFS), "physical and economic access to adequate food for all household members, without undue risk of losing such access" (FAO, 1996:50), millions of people are not household food secure. In 1990–2, 840 million consumed so little food relative to requirements that they suffered caloric undernourishment (which often leads to anthropometric deficiency and risk of damaged **human development**) (FAO 1996). Yet, in 1990–2 global food consumption provided 2,720 dietary calories per person, which would have been sufficient if distributed in proportion to requirements.

In global terms, then, food consumption is so unequal that caloric undernourishment is serious. It is true that the proportion of malnourished people has fallen greatly (more in the past fifty years than in the previous 3,000 according to Michael Lipton (2000) but hunger and undernourishment remains endemic in some regions (notably Sub-Saharan Africa and South Asia). Paradoxically, there is much evidence to suggest growing hunger in some of the North Atlantic economies and within a number of postsocialist societies. According to the International Food Policy Research Institute (IFPRI), agricultural production fell by 30 percent in Russia between 1989 and 1994 and hunger is increasingly common. In California (a place seemingly obsessed by eating less and by losing weight), the reform of "welfare as we know it," has produced 8.4 million who are "food insecure." In 1994, 1.5 million families in the UK could not afford to feed their children an 1876 workhouse diet.

A conventional way to think about food security is in terms of output or gross availability. Food security decreases accordingly as food availability declines. **Famines**, an extreme case of food insecurity, are a function of a massive collapse of food availability, a sort of Malthusian event (see **Malthusian demography**). In contrast to the Malthusian and demographic approach in which food insecurity arises as food output is incapable of keeping up with **population** growth, Amartya Sen (1981) approaches hunger, and most especially how hunger and food insecurity can degenerate into famine, from a micro-economic vantage point and entitlements. Sen is able to show how gross food insecurity may occur without a decline in food availability, and how entitlements attached to individuals through a generalization of the exchange economy – through markets – may shift in complex ways among differing classes, occupational groups and sections of the population. The real danger resides in concentrating exclusively on food production and availability, which can often lull governments into soporific complacency, what Sen calls "Malthusian optimism:" "Focusing attention on the Malthusian variable of food output per head, the food situation has often appeared to be comfortable even when there have been good economic grounds for expecting terrible troubles for particular occupational groups" (Sen, 1981:524).

Sen begins with the individual endowment, which is mapped into a bundle of entitlements, the latter understood as "the set of alternative commodity bundles that a person can command" (1981:46) using various *legal* channels of acquirement open to someone of his/her position. Such entitlement bundles confer particular capabilities (see **capability approach**) that ultimately underline **well-being**. The basic unit of analysis is the individual person, his/her endowment, and his/her entitlement arrangements, though there is considerable ambiguity and slippage in Sen's analysis over the aggregation of such individuals into social assemblages such as households or communities or classes. Sen's theory turns on what Fine (1997:624) properly calls the "micro (-economic) capability for survival," and on the means by which such individual capabilities fail, producing as a consequence "excess" individual deaths through generalized individual entitlement failure, or increased food insecurity through inadequate or risky entitlements. According to Sen, famine as a short-term event characterized by acute deprivation of staple foodstuffs and food insecurity occurs because the entitlement set does not include any commodity bundle with enough food. Conversely, food security presupposes an entitlement set capably and reliably, in the event of various short- and medium term crises and perturbations.

Central to Sen's account of why food insecurity exists is the process of transforming endowments into entitlements, so-called E-mapping. The sorts of entitlements which Sen details are rewards to labor, production, inheritance or asset transfer, and state provisioning (transfers) typically through social security and food relief policies (i.e. anti-famine policies of which the Indian Famine Codes are customarily seen as a model, see Dreze and Sen, 1990). Insofar as an individual's entitlement set is the consequence of E-mapping on the endowment set, entitlements can only change through transformations in the endowment or E-mapping (see Osmani, 1995:256). Hunger and shortage occurs through a collapse or adverse change in endowment or E-mapping or both (Sen, 1981). Entitlement, in contrast to other theories, "draws our attention to such variables as ownership patterns, unemployment, relative prices, wage-price rations, and so on" (1993:30).

Sen situates hunger, then, on a landscape, irreducibly social, of the capabilities that individuals, and potentially classes, may mobilize. By examining mapping as an active and transformative process – how the capacity to labor, or access to land can generate an entitlement – it dislodges a concern with output *per se* and focuses on access to and control over food. It offers a *proximate* sort of causal analysis predicated on what immediate or conjunctural forces might shift such forms of access and control, and permits a social mapping of such shifts to understand *who* dies or starves (say artisanal craftsmen versus peasants) and *why*. Entitlements – the central mechanism in his intellectual architecture – are individually assigned in virtue of a largely unexamined endowment, and are legally derived from state **law** (ownership, **property rights**, contract). Entitlements necessitate making legitimate claims, that is to say, rights resting on the foundations of power (opportunity or actual command) and law (legitimacy and protection). A concern with entitlement failure in market circumstances leads Sen (see Drèze and Sen, 1990) to emphasize public action through entitlement *protection* (state-funded famine protection through food for work or public food distribution) *and promotion* (a public social security net).

Sen's concern with entitlements, and these related to the capabilities of individuals, can be extended to better grasp the conditions under which people become food secure. To begin with entitlements themselves, geographer Charles Gore has noted that "command over food depends upon something more than legal rights" (1993:433). Extended entitlements, for example, might include *socially determined entitlements* (a moral economy, indigenous security institutions), *non-legal entitlements* (food riots, demonstrations, theft) and *non-entitlement transfers* (charity). This highlights a rather different way of thinking about E-mapping. First, entitlements are socially constructed (not just individually conferred); they are forms of social process and a type of representation. Second, like all forms of representation, entitlements are complex congeries of cultural, institutional and political practice which are unstable: that is to say, they are both constituted and reproduced through conflict, negotiation and struggle. Entitlements are, then, political and social achievements which are customarily fought over in the course of modernization (in this sense one can think about the means by which entitlements enter the political arena in the course of the differing routes to modernity). And third, social entitlements confirm Sen's unelaborated observation that the relations between people and food must be grasped as a "*network* of entitlement *relations*" (1981:159, emphasis added). Food security or famine proneness are the products of historically specific *networks of social entitlements*.

To map such networks as a basis for food security, however, requires a theory of entitlements themselves. What are the sources of the entitlements, beyond the fact that they grow in the soil of endowments? Using the work of de Gaay Fortman (1990), one can conceive of a simple mapping along four dimensions:

Institutions: affiliation to semi-autonomous, rule-making entities in which social networks and positionality determine whether, and what sorts of, entitlements are available.

Direct access: direct access to forms of legally derived access that turn on property and contract (in Sen's work, ownership and **property rights**, exchange of labor).

State: forms of instrumental state law (in Sen, social welfare) which identify need and categories of the poor and which in turn are rooted in citizenship rights as a bedrock of the modern nation-state.

Global legal order: forms of humanitarian assistance grounded in **human rights** discourse and general principles of freedom, equality and solidarity for all people as embodied in the **Universal Declaration of Human Rights (1948)**.

The strength, depth and density of the entitlements in each of the four realms will of course vary, and this differing patterning of entitlements shapes what one might call the architecture of the "food security system." Put simply, the geometry of the network for a rural worker in Kerala in South India will look very different from a northern Nigerian peasant. In the former, a regulated agrarian labor market (see **labor markets**) and forms of institutionalized bargaining between state (see **state and state reform**) and landlords provides a wage sensitive to price increases. There is additionally a credible and relatively accountable public distribution system that operates effectively in rural areas, plus a number of regional and local civic institutions which provide credit, food for work and other assistance. For the Nigerian peasant, state-derived entitlements are almost non-existent; direct access to land is compromised by small holdings incapable of providing self-sufficiency in staple foods; and local food security turns, in some degree, on his/her positionality with respect to local forms of support through lineages, extended families, village redistributive offices, Islamic alms, and the village moral economy (Watts, 1983).

Endowment embraces not simply assets (land, labor) but **citizenship** (the right to state support), *local group membership* (civic identity in village or **community** association), and *universal* **human rights**. The E-mapping then refers to the actual transformative process by which assets, **citizenship**, and other claims are rendered into effective (i.e. meaningful) entitlement bundles. Put differently, actual state support depends on **accountability** and **transparency** (what Sen, 1999, simply refers to as **democracy**). A functioning moral economy rests upon the forms of **governance** – what others have called **social capital** – within self-organizing heterarchies; humanitarian assistance depends upon the commitment of states and, as de Waal (1997) shows, on the politics and accountability of relief agencies.

These four broad categories of entitlement (and their differing social endowments represent what de Waal (1997) calls "an anti famine political contract" (or a "food security contract"). This contract is both a functional configuration of entitlements to provide food security and also a political achievement. The shape of the contract will change over time, and as a function of the dynamics of the political economy, forms of political action, and so on. **Structural adjustment** in Africa and the growing privatization (see **privatization and liberalization**) of the humanitarian industry for example, has reduced an already minimal set of state-based entitlements (see **state and state reform**), and radically reconfigured the space of humanitarian **aid** (de Waal, 1997). The network of social entitlements and the food contract it represents delimits a field or social space of field food security, or put differently it defines a "space of **vulnerability**" (Watts and Bohle, 1993). Vulnerability is here understood as the risks of exposure and the limited capacities to respond to shocks or crises that precipitate entitlement or E-mapping changes. The network of entitlements is more or less inclusive, more or less robust, more or less reliable, and so on. In light of particular perturbations – a **drought**, an economic recession, price fluctuations, **unemployment**, and so on – one can begin to think about those who are structurally vulnerable in relation to the extant networks of entitlements.

One of the great strengths of Sen's approach to food security is that its entitlements are part of a larger architecture of thinking about development as a state of **well-being** and choice or freedom (see **freedom versus choice**). In his language, the capability of a person reflects the "alternative combinations of functioning the person achieve and from which he or she can choose one collection" (1999:3) (see **functionings**). Functionings represent parts of the state of a person and especially those things that a person can do or be in leading a life. In seeing **poverty** or hunger as a failure of capabilities (see **capability approach**) – rather than insufficient income, or inadequate primary goods as in the Rawlsian sense of **social justice** – Sen shows how the freedom to lead different types of life is a reflected in the person's capabilities (see Sen, 1999).

See also: aid; agriculture; capability approach; emergency assistance; famine; food; food aid; functionings; gender and property rights; nutrition; property rights; rural development; targeting; vulnerability; World Food Programme

Further reading

De Gaay Fortman, B. (1990) *Entitlement and Development*, Working Paper Series #87, The Hague: Institute of Social Studies.

de Waal, A. (1997) *Famine Crimes*, London: International African Institute.

Drèze, J. and Sen, A. (1990) *Hunger and Public Action*, Oxford: Clarendon Press.

FAO (1996) *Sixth World Food Survey*, Rome: FAO.

Fine, B. (1997) "Entitlement Failure?" *Development and Change* 28: 617–47.

Gore, C. (1993) "Entitlement Relations and 'Unruly' Social Practices," *Journal of Development Studies* 29: 429–60.

Lipton, M. (2000) "Food and Nutrition Security: Why Food Production Matters," pp. 199–242 in FAO (ed.) *State of Food and Agriculture*, Rome: FAO.

Osmani, S. (1995) "The Entitlement Approach to Famine," pp. 254–94 in Basu, K. *et al.* (eds) *Choice, Welfare and Development*, Oxford: Clarendon Press.

Sen, A. (1981) *Poverty and Famines*, Oxford: Clarendon Press.

Sen, A. (1999) *Development as Freedom*, New York: Knopf.

Watts, M. and Bohle, H. (1993) "The Space of Vulnerability," *Progress in Human Geography* 17: 43–67.

Watts, M. (1983) *Silent Violence*, Berkeley: University of California Press.

MICHAEL WATTS

FORCED LABOR see child labor; ILO Declaration on Fundamental Principles and Rights at Work; labor rights and standards; slavery

Fordism versus Toyotaism

Fordism is the production system that changed the world during the past century. It was named after industrialist Henry Ford, in whose automobile plant it was first developed (see **auto industry**). The main characteristics of the system were the standardization of products and parts, the fragmentation of tasks, the introduction of special-purpose machine tools, and perhaps more important the re-organization of the production process around the assembly line. The machinery was arranged in a sequence of the production stages, with the output flowing from one stage to another through a moving conveyor belt. This layout minimized the time wasted in transferring parts on the shop floor and unnecessary workers' movements. The workers in particular were allocated single tasks, which they had to repeat at regular intervals following the pace of the machines. Their skills and personal control over their work were reduced in the process; however, the speed and consequently the capacity of production were increased spectacularly. Higher production volumes and the achievement of economies of scale slashed production costs and hence retail prices. The subsequent adoption of Fordism by other sectors made accessible a long list of standardized consumer goods to many people.

Although efficient, the success of Fordism depended on mass consumption. The system needed stable and growing markets that would absorb the vast quantities of produced goods. Thus, a particular mode of regulation (a system linking production to consumption) also named Fordism emerged, ensuring that large segments of Western societies had enough resources to buy the goods. The **welfare state**, strong **trade unions** that guaranteed minimum wages and credit-based consumerism were some of its key aspects. In the early 1970s, the crisis of these elements led to the downturn of Fordism. The demand for consumer goods declined, as household ownership of car and electrical appliances increased in developed countries. The shrinking of the welfare state and the slow growth of wages reduced consumer income, while the production system itself had difficulties in meeting the new consumer preferences for differentiated products of higher quality.

Consequently, since the late 1970s some alternative production systems have arisen, one of which is Toyotaism. This system was developed in Toyota car plants and involves the use of highly flexible machinery operated by multi-skilled workers, which enables the mass production of many differentiated goods. Quality enhancement and the reduction of buffer stocks of parts and finished products (just-in-time production) are important elements of the system, which are achieved by engaging workers in the production management, forming very close relationships with suppliers and applying the latest information technology. The minimization of production errors and the easy switch of machinery and personnel between products are significant sources of cost reduction. The overall system forms an intelligent organization that receives the market signs and responds quickly to changing consumer tastes.

See also: auto industry; flexible specialization; industrialization; productivity; small and medium enterprises (SMEs); transnational corporations (TNCs); transnational corporations (TNCs) from developing economies

Further reading

Boyer, R. and Durand, J. (1997) *After Fordism*, London: Macmillan Press.

Shiomi, H. and Wada, K. (eds) (1995) *Fordism Transformed: The Development of Production Methods in the Automobile Industry*, Oxford: Oxford University Press.

KONSTANTINOS A. MELACHROINOS

foreign direct investment

Foreign direct investment (FDI) is investment by foreign individuals, firms and governments into generally industrial activities in another country where the investor acquires *control* over the firm in which it invests. It can be differentiated from forms of indirect investment, such as portfolio investment, which may include the purchase of shares in companies on stock exchanges (see **stock markets**) without achieving control. Frequently, FDI implies establishing factories or similar manufacturing units in the territory of another country, and hence contributes to **industrialization**.

For empirical purposes, an investor's control over a firm is defined in terms of the acquisition of a minimum percentage share holding in the foreign subsidiary. The **Organization for Economic Cooperation and Development (OECD)**, for example, recommends a share holding of 10 percent as sufficient to define a transaction as involving FDI, but different countries have adopted different cut-off points.

FDI is a major feature of contemporary international economic relations. Over the past half century, FDI has outstripped the growth of both world production and international trade. In 2001, the total global stock of FDI came to US$6,846 billion, of which almost a third was in developing countries. Today attracting foreign investment is seen as a key strategy to promote **economic development**, although critics point to the pitfalls of heavy reliance on foreign capital. This is not surprising, since FDI now accounts for 60 percent of all resources flows to developing countries, and is ten times as large as bilateral official development assistance.

The bulk of FDI comes from a small group of advanced industrial countries. In recent years some **newly industrialized economies (NIEs)** have also started to invest overseas, becoming significant investors particularly in East and Southeast Asia (also see **transnational corporations (TNCs) from developing economies**). Most FDI also goes to advanced industrial countries, with the USA as the leading host country. The share of FDI going to developing countries increased significantly in the 1990s, reaching a peak of around 40 percent of total flows, but has fallen back again since the **Asian crises** of 1997–8.

Among developing countries, there has been a very marked concentration of FDI in a small number of countries, with about ten economies accounting for two thirds of the stock of investment. These have tended to be primarily the newly industrializing countries of Asia and Latin America. Consequently, most developing countries, accounting for the bulk of the world's **population**, have received only a very limited share of total FDI.

Until the mid-twentieth century, FDI in developing countries was concentrated in the primary sector with large-scale investments in mining, oil (see **oil and gas development**) and plantations (see **plantation forestry**). With **import substitution** from the 1950s onwards, the emphasis shifted to the manufacturing sector. More recently, there has been a further shift with an increasing share going into services.

FDI was originally thought of simply as an international capital flow, and analyzed as an extension of international trade theory. By the 1960s, however, it was clear that FDI consisted of much more than just capital, and generally involved a "package" of assets and intermediate products, such as capital, technology, management skills, access to markets, and **entrepreneurship**. As a result, FDI came to be included under the theory of the firm and industrial organization (see also **new institutional economics**). The attempts to analyze foreign investment from this perspective led to various theories concerning **transnational corporations (TNCs)**. These theories broke new ground in recognizing the specific institutional form within which most FDI took place.

Firms are influenced by a variety of economic and political factors in deciding where to invest overseas. Empirical studies have identified a number of major determinants. Firms tend to invest in countries with large or rapidly growing markets and high income levels. They also tend to prefer to invest in countries with well-developed infrastructure. Interestingly, a less significant factor determining investment is the level of labor cost in a country. Political factors that are regarded as important are the level of political instability or political risk that would tend to deter investment.

Despite the high incidence of tax and other fiscal incentives given to foreign investors by governments, there is little evidence to suggest that these are important determinants of FDI. It is possible that countries that are least attractive to foreign investors tend to resort most extensively to such incentives, but that these incentives are insufficient to offset perceived disadvantages of investment. The impact of trade liberalization and greater access for FDI are still debated. **protectionism** acts as an incentive for certain kinds of investment that seek to serve the domestic market (**import substitution**), whereas it may be a disincentive to investment for **export-led growth**.

FDI impacts on recipient countries in various ways. A crucial question is whether FDI is additional to, or a substitute for, domestic investment. On the assumption that FDI adds to domestic resources, then it can be seen to fill a number of gaps in host economies. First, it can help bridge a resource gap between a desired level of investment and locally available savings. Second, it can help close a foreign exchange gap where a country suffers from balance of payments pressures. Third, it may provide additional tax revenues to hard-pressed governments facing fiscal deficits (see **fiscal and monetary policy**). It can provide additional managerial and technical skills where these are in short supply. Finally, there may be important "spillovers" to local firms who benefit from the presence of foreign firms, for example because of an increased pool of skilled workers.

Many of the concerns about FDI reflect a fear that it is often a substitute for domestic investment and hence may displace local firms and crowd out domestic entrepreneurship. These fears are particularly acute because the bulk of FDI is undertaken by TNCs which often have substantial market power. Other concerns are for the long-term balance of payments effects of FDI when profit remittances begin to outweigh new capital inflows. Finally, there is also a fear that a high level of dependence on FDI will lead to a loss of national sovereignty.

See also: auto industry; economic development; export-led growth; industrialization; industrialization and trade policy; iron and steel; Multilateral Agreement on Investment (MAI); newly industrialized economies (NIEs); protectionism; small and medium enterprises (SMEs); technological capability; technology transfer; textiles; transnational corporations (TNCs); transnational corporations (TNCs) from developing economies

Further reading

Chen, J-R. (ed.) (2000) *Foreign Direct Investment*, Basingstoke: Macmillan.
Dicken, P. (2003) *Global Shift: Reshaping the Global Economic Map in the 21st Century*, 4th edn, London: Sage, ch. 2.
UNCTAD (various years) *World Investment Report*, Geneva: United Nations.
Woodward, D. (2001) *The next Crisis? Direct and Equity Investment in Developing Countries*, London: Zed.

RHYS JENKINS

Fourth World

The Fourth World refers to the poorest, the most disadvantaged and socially excluded (see **social exclusion**) individuals in developed countries. This **poverty** is mainly concentrated in urban areas, and refers to people who are becoming increasingly marginalized, or who live in **chronic poverty**. They are called "Fourth World" to indicate that they are poor, but not in the "Third World" (see **underdevelopment versus less developed country (LDC) versus Third World**). Fourth World people experience deep-seated poverty not simply because they lack money, but because they do not have access to health care or other cultural, personal and social resources (see **safety nets against poverty**). Some

analysts claim this group also increasingly comprise urban migrants or **street children**, who may not have immediate access to local state resources (see **state and state reform**), **employment**, political representation, and similar support mechanisms.

See also: chronic poverty; marginalization; street children

MÒNICA RIVERA ESCRICH

free trade

Free trade is **trade** based upon market forces and **comparative advantage** alone, rather than with government-imposed barriers or incentives that would distort these patterns. Such government interventions would include **tariffs**, quotas, export subsidies, currency manipulations, preferential government purchasing patterns, and a great number of other financial and trade devices banned or otherwise regulated by the **World Trade Organization/General Agreement on Tariffs and Trade (WTO/GATT)**, the **International Monetary Fund (IMF)**, and other intergovernmental organizations operating to advance the broad **Washington consensus**. The advantages of free trade are widely recognized to be greater overall global wealth, concentrated in the nations freeing their trading, **transparency** and increased development. Disadvantages involve possible inequity of redistribution of the increased wealth, along with alleged disadvantages for labor, environmental standards and **human rights**.

Comparative advantage demonstrates that if nations specialize their production in products where they have large factor endowments, they can generate increased wealth, provided they also trade their excess production to countries which produce the products they desire but do not produce enough of to meet local demand. This principle works so long as the costs of trading are lower than the added value generated by national specialization of production, and only to the extent that the added value exceeds the trading costs. In essence, nations seek to capture some of the benefit of trade for themselves, from private traders or from other national governments, by imposing burdens on the trading system, aware that trade will continue at least up to the point that the trading costs equal the gains from specialization. In the 1930s, this effort at unilateral national capture of trade's benefits, led by the USA and the Smoot-Hawley Tariff Act, resulted in global cycles of imitation and retaliation known as the "beggar thy neighbor" period in international trade. Largely because of experience with this period of rampant **protectionism**, free trade has been a cornerstone of the international financial consensus since World War II.

Ironically, it is hard to say the same within any given country over that same period, thanks to the politics of trade. Although both theory and practice illustrate that lowering trade barriers will generally help the country lowering the barriers, much as clearing rocks from a harbor will benefit the country whose harbor is cleared, trade negotiations generally have to be sold as concessions granted in order to gain lowered barriers overseas – a reversal of economic reality. The reason is not hard to trace: those who will benefit from lowering an import barrier are usually a large, diffuse group receiving small individual benefits who will not be politically organized. In contrast, those who will be hurt already know it, will suffer clear injury and will lobby hard against the trade concession. Unless countered by import-consuming industries, import-averse lobbying will often sway politicians, to the cost of the consuming public (see **import substitution**).

Although free trade promises to generate greater wealth overall for those nations engaging in it, the Coase Theorem makes clear that there is no guarantee that such wealth will necessarily be distributed in an equal or equitable fashion. Indeed, the issue of distribution is analytically distinct from the issue of increased wealth: how the pie is cut is different from how the pie grows. This has produced a repeated challenge to the major trading nations, who have received most of the increased wealth from the freeing of world trade since the founding of GATT in 1947 (see **World Trade Organization/General Agreement on Tariffs and Trade (WTO/GATT)**).

Most arguments against free trade concern the impacts of trade beyond simple generation of broad growth. GATT Dispute Settlement Panel decisions in the Turtle-Dolphin and Shrimp-Turtle cases convinced many people that free trade is inherently counter-environmental. Severely abusive conditions in some developing country factories serving the interests of **transnational corporations (TNCs)** (or supplying such TNCs) have enraged those concerned about **human rights**. Lower-wage workers in developed nations find job losses threatening, even if they have prospects of retraining. Other people are concerned about loss of local economic and democratic sovereignty to foreign economic influence. Large protests by loose associations of those who oppose **globalization** in general, and free trade in particular, have become regular features at meetings of the **World Bank**, the IMF, the WTO, and the finance ministers of the major industrialized nations.

Thus, free trade is generally opposed both by those who dislike globalization for one or another reason and by those who actively favor **protectionism**. The interests of both groups converge in seeking to raise barriers against imported goods, through high tariffs, strict quotas and imposition of strong remedies against foreign trade practices viewed as unfair or threatening. Proponents of managed or strategic trade also advocate other actions contrary to free trade: export promotion; maintenance of special **exchange rates** for trade transactions; currency devaluation to encourage exports and discourage imports; setting of product standards to favor local producers; announcement of government procurement contract opportunities after awards to local companies; long delays in processing customs paperwork; requirements for using national carriers; and insurance companies during all import transactions.

Domestic politics, opportunities for **corruption** and other forms of wealth-capture, and the mixed commitment of leading trading nations to free trade policies, particularly in **agriculture** and textiles trade, are common explanations for the fact that few developing nations have embraced free trade policies as part of an overall development strategy. Those doing so have generally enjoyed stronger growth than countries that have protected their markets and adopted such policies as **import substitution**, which, by imposing external constraints upon product choices, is another form of deviation from free trade principles.

See also: globalization; most favored nation (MFN) status; Multilateral Agreement on Investment (MAI); protectionism; tariffs; trade; terms of trade; World Trade Organization/General Agreement on Tariffs and Trade (WTO/GATT)

Further reading

Baneth, J. (1993) "*Fortress Europe*" *and Other Myths about Trade: Policies toward Merchandise Imports in the EC and Other Major Industrial Economies (and what They Mean for Developing Countries)*, Washington DC: World Bank.

Bhagwati, J. (1988) *Protectionism*, Cambridge MA: MIT Press.

Bhagwati, J. (1991) *The World Trading System at Risk*, Princeton: Princeton University Press.

Hufbauer, G. and Elliott, K. (1994) *Measuring the Costs of Protectionism in the United States*, Washington DC: Institute for International Economics.

Krugman, P. (1987) "Is Free Trade Passé?," *Journal of Economic Perspectives* 1:2 131–44.

WILLIAM B. T. MOCK

free trade zones (FTZs)

Free trade zones (FTZs) are industrial areas that have preferential customs **tariffs** and commercial codes with the aim of attracting trade and investment. FTZs are found mostly in developing countries with relatively large domestic markets such as China and Brazil. They may be distinguished from **export processing zones (EPZs)** because EPZs produce goods solely sold for foreign markets.

FTZs (along with EPZs) have expanded rapidly across the globe over the last three decades after the Shannon Free Zone was established in Ireland in 1959. The exact numbers of employees in FTZs are not known but the **International Labor Organization (ILO)** in 1998 estimated that 28 million people (including 18 million in China's Special Economic Zones) were employed in about 850 zones around the world, and the number is ever growing.

FTZs have been backed by new growth theorists who have pointed out there exist some positive externalities from FTZs such as **technology transfer, human capital** development and **employment** for the host countries. These views are different from neo-classical economists, who have seen FTZs as sub-optimal to total trade liberalization.

Worldwide experience has indicated some important implications of FTZs for macro-economy, **labor markets**, working conditions, and social aspects of **industrialization**. First, the type of products found mostly in FTZs is assembly-type industries of electronics, clothing and **textiles** industries and resource-based industries. Second, economic growth through FTZs has been evidenced in some countries, especially in East and Southeast Asian countries (Singapore, Malaysia, Indonesia and the Philippines). However, experience in many other countries has surprisingly indicated that FTZs do not always make the host country economy more dynamic and prosperous. Third, many studies have criticized working conditions in FTZs, and especially the exploitative treatment of women factory workers (see **gender and industrialization**). Health problems include social repercussions (for example mass hysteria), occupational and industrial diseases (such as eyesight problems in the electronics industry or back pain in many assembly-type works) and those relating to the lack of health and safety standards in the factories (see **labor rights and standards; occupational health**). Fourth, wage levels show mixed results. In some countries (e.g. Thailand and Sri Lanka), the formal wages in FTZs are higher than outside the zones, while in others (e.g. Taiwan and Mauritius) they are lower. Lately, the impact of FTZs has been reflected from **human rights** perspectives as well. Some argue that FTZs violate basic labor conditions by banning **trade unions**.

See also: export processing zones (EPZs); industrial district model; industrialization; tariffs; trade

Further reading

ILO (1998) *Labour and Social Issues Relating to Export Processing Zones*, Geneva: ILO.

Kusago, T. and Tzannatos, Z. (1998) *Export Processing Zones: A Review in Need of Update*, Social Protection Group, Working Paper no. 98–2, Washington DC: World Bank.

TAKAYOSHI KUSAGO

freedom of association

Freedom of association is the right to join, form, and withdraw membership from groups or associations without interference from the state (see **state and state reform**) or other bodies such as companies. The formation of associations is usually conducted in relation to trade union, or similar activities of collective bargaining with employers, or in the context of the formation of political or community groups such as **non-governmental organizations (NGOs)**. The right to freedom of association was recognized as a fundamental human right (see **human rights**) under the **International Labor Organization (ILO)** constitution, and two conventions, the Freedom of Association and Protection of the Right to Organize Convention, 1948 (no. 87), and the Right to Organize and Collective Bargaining Convention, 1949 (no. 98), which together defined rights of collective bargaining. The formal right of freedom of association, however, may not always result in the formation of associations or **trade unions** because of informal practices such as **gender** discrimination, **casualization of work**, or other practices that may make individuals reluctant or disempowered from making associations.

See also: human rights; International Labor Organization (ILO); Declaration on Fundamental Principles and Rights at Work; labor rights and standards; trade unions

TIM FORSYTH

freedom versus choice

The distinction between "freedom," and "choice" is an important aspect of development theory and **ethics** and development, referring to the ability of individuals to express their will. The concept of freedom generally refers to an absence of coercion or restrain from controls. The concept of choice calls for a realization of goals through available alternatives, by exercising choice. Choice and freedom are associated through the notion of individuals being free to exercise their choice in a positive sense.

Choice is a by-product of civilization. The Stone-Age dweller, with an evolving cognitive faculty, had limited freedom depending on his ability to fashion stone implements to his or her advantage. With civilization progressing, social preference progressed from a cave to successfully more advanced forms of accommodation. Therefore, an expansion of choice does empower individuals leading to an enhancement of freedom. In fact, Amartya Sen (1999) in *Development as Freedom* emphasizes the widening of the development agenda beyond the narrow scope of per capita income and **gross national product (GNP)** to include expansion of people's choices amounting to greater freedom. He recommends the eradication of "unfreedoms" like **illiteracy** and **poverty**, resulting in greater freedom, feeding further individual and societal development. In this perspective, freedom is a means for development and is positively correlated with choice.

In contrast to this view, some have argued that choices are accompanied by a social cost that impinges on freedom. With the opening up of developing economies, **rural-urban migration** has occurred, as migrants have sought to increase their available choices of **livelihoods**. This trend, however, has not enhanced their freedom. Being ill informed about opportunities and weak in bargaining, they become casualties of subcontracting, low wages, crowding into slums (see **housing; shantytowns**). Increase in choice therefore is often neutral to and negatively correlated with freedom, unless the nature and availability of alternatives are well advertised. **Education** must exist to facilitate informed choices. Again, irrespective of choice expansion, freedom may not expand unless the most preferred option is available. The range of choices is actually narrower than one may believe, as internal constraints like moral self-policing can shrink freedom further.

The exercise of choices is also never without political and economic underpinning. To have unlimited options in the market place is a myth. The buyer is restrained by his/her purchasing power, the prevalent pattern of consumption, and the haphazard power play of **institutions**. Consequently, negative and positive aspects of freedom get linked in a capitalist market where the issue of freedom gets suffused with maximization of satisfaction. If the state (see **state and state reform**) controls resource distribution through rigid hierarchical bureaucratic body, then choices also get managed and the quest for freedom becomes a project of achieving piecemeal policies hedged between bureaucratic bottlenecks. Choice may therefore continue to compete with freedom until a condition of "social choice" – the integration of multiple preferences into political decision-making – is fully achieved.

See also: capability approach; ethics; functionings; well-being

Further reading

Sen, A. (1999) *Development as Freedom*, New Delhi: Oxford University Press.

IPSITA CHATTERJEE

fuelwood

Fuelwood is any woody vegetation that can be used directly as a source of fuel or to produce charcoal (a more concentrated source of carbon than wood) (see also **energy policy**). Since the ancestors of modern humans domesticated fire 2 million years ago, such material has been a major source of fuel. Even today, more wood is used for fuel than for any other purpose. Globally, the **Food and Agriculture Organization (FAO)** (2003) estimates that fuelwood production was 1,784 million cubic meters in 2000, representing an increase of about 6 percent since 1990 and about 30 percent since 1970. Thus the requirement for fuelwood is increasing rather than decreasing, a surprising trend in an industrializing world that is fossil-fuel dependent. Currently fuelwood accounts for about five percent of global energy consumption (see **energy policy**). Moreover, it is predicted that fuelwood consumption will increase by an estimated 30 percent by 2010. Fuelwood is used mainly for domestic heating and cooking in developing countries, especially in Africa, Asia and Latin America. FAO data show that the major fuelwood consumers are China, India, Indonesia, Brazil and Nigeria, which together use around 50 percent of annual production. In some countries, fuelwood supplements other energy sources, whilst in others, generally the poorest countries such as those in Sub-Sahara, it is almost the only energy source (see **energy policy**). As many as 2 billion people, from a global **population** of 6 billion, rely wholly or in large part on fuelwood. In many cases, fuelwood acquisition is the responsibility of women and children, who often expend considerable effort to collect adequate supplies from a wide area. Moreover, the health of many people is adversely affected by fuelwood use indoors because of the particulates and chemicals such as carbon monoxide, nitrogen oxides and polyaromatic hydrocarbons produced on burning (see **pollution; brown environmental agenda**).

Fuelwood collection is often cited as a major cause of forest loss (see **deforestation**). Clearly, it represents a significant use of biomass resources, though with considerable variation in intensity spatially. Some areas such as the **Sahel** have been alleged to experience a "fuelwood crisis," especially in drought-prone regions where the rate of tree growth and hence the capacity to renew the resource is limited. Resulting wood shortages threaten existing woodlands and have been considered to contribute to **desertification**; they also cause hardship to people who often have to scour large areas for an adequate supply or who are forced to use meager incomes to buy wood in local markets. Yet, the uniform existence of a fuelwood crisis has also been questioned, and shown in some locations to be based on a poor understanding of actual rates of deforestation, and of the local dynamics of resource conservation (see Leach and Mearns, 1988) (see **environment; deforestation**).

The problem of fuelwood availability and the need to conserve forests is recognized in many countries, with the result that designated woodlots grown specifically for fuelwood have been created, employing quick-growing species and active management such as coppicing (see **community forestry; silviculture**). Another approach involves a form of **intercropping** known as **agroforestry** whereby trees, especially fruit or oil producers, and crop production or pasture are combined. Not only does this type of agricultural system generate a variety of crops, but the trees also supply fuelwood. Moreover, the adoption of high-efficiency stoves can reduce the volume of wood required.

See also: agroforestry; community forestry; deforestation; dryland agriculture; energy policy; environment; intercropping; Joint Forest Management (JFM); non-timber forest products (NTFPs); plantation forestry

Further reading

Leach, G. and Mearns, R. (1988) *Beyond the Fuelwood Crisis*, London: Earthscan.

Leach, M. and Mearns, R. (eds) (1996) *The Lie of the Land: Challenging Received Wisdom on the African Environment*, Oxford: James Currey.

A. M. MANNION

functionings

Functionings is a philosophical concept designed to help understand the meanings of "**well-being**" and "development" in greater depth. Functionings are the "doings and beings" in a life, as opposed to the inputs (such as income, commodities and other resources) to such doings and beings, or the feelings generated by doings and beings. Even if feelings are included as one sort of being, a focus on functionings makes us look more widely than only at people's feelings, and more deeply than by considering only inputs.

The focus on functionings is justified because, first, inputs are not reliable proxies for the contents of a life. Input-output relationships vary greatly according to users' skills and needs (e.g. old people and people with disabilities (see **disability**) typically "convert" inputs into functionings far less "productively"), and according to the particular conditions of time and place (e.g. great expense is required to live safely in insecure environments). Second,

feelings are also unreliable proxies, due to "framing effects" (feelings depend on what one is used to, expects, and perceives) and "adaptive preference" (preferences often adjust to rationalize what one has). So, two traditional levels of attention in **welfare economics** and orthodox economic policy analysis – command over resources (income), and feelings of pleasure or satisfaction ("utility") – are insufficient for assessing human well-being. We must look also at the intermediate zone of functionings, and the nature of functionings at diverse sub-levels. This leads us to a multidimensional perspective on well-being and **human development**.

The language of "functionings" entered development studies from the work of the Indian economist-philosopher Amartya Sen and the American ethicist Martha Nussbaum. Nussbaum has shown its antecedents in Aristotle's attention to the detailed distinctive contents of people's activity. Current work brings in contributions from psychology, health sciences, transportation studies, social planning and similar fields (see **ethics**).

The concept of functionings is broad and requires subdivision. If pleasure/utility is included as a functioning, we should distinguish different types of feeling, and also clearly distinguish these from the various non-feelings aspects of a person's life (such as physical health, longevity, mobility, participation). We can then consider for each of these non-feelings aspects what are the associated inputs and feelings, and examine the ratios and correlations (or lack of them) between inputs, non-feeling functionings, and feelings. Research shows enormous variations in the ratios and some remarkable absences of correlation.

The term capability (see **capability approach**) concerns the ability to achieve a certain functioning or functionings; so Nussbaum refers to "functional capabilities," meaning capabilities to function. Sen and Nussbaum give normative priority to capabilities: people should have certain capabilities but also the freedom to use them or not (see **freedom versus choice**). This distinction may suit discussion of policy for informed, competent and responsible adults, but functionings can have normative priority in some other contexts (e.g. when ensuring public **health** and primary **education**). Nussbaum proposes a universal list of priority functional capabilities, which is intended to be acceptable to people with diverse philosophies. The usefulness of the concepts of functioning and capability does not depend on acceptance of her list.

See also: capability approach; ethics; freedom versus choice; measuring development; well-being

Further reading

Nussbaum, M. (1999) *Sex and Social Justice*, New York: Oxford University Press.
Nussbaum, M. and Sen, A. (eds) (1993) *The Quality of Life*, Oxford: Clarendon.

DES GASPER

G

G-7 (GROUP OF 7)/G-8 (GROUP OF 8) *see* international economic order

GATT *see* World Trade Organization/General Agreement on Tariffs and Trade (WTO/GATT)

GDP *see* gross domestic product (GDP)

gender

Debates about gender and development consider the different roles played by women and men in social and economic relations, and the differential impact of the development process on women and men. The after-effects of colonialism (see **colonialism, history of; colonialism, impacts of**), and the peripheral location of developing countries and economies in transition (see **postsocialism**) in today's globalizing world, may exacerbate the effects of discrimination on women. The role of **capitalism**, leading to the modernization (see **modernization theory**) and restructuring of subsistence and centrally planned economies, often increases gender-based disadvantages. The modern sector takes over many of the economic activities, such as **food** processing and making of clothes, which had long been the means by which women supported themselves and their families. But by relieving them of these time-consuming chores it gives them the freedom to find other, perhaps better, sources of earned income and for girls to go to school (see **education**). Yet, a majority of the

better-paid jobs involving new technology go to men, but male income is less likely to be spent on the family. Overall, a lack of gender equality reduces development effectiveness.

Gender inequalities also contribute to **poverty**. Male **population mobility** is higher than female, both between places and between jobs, and more women are being left alone to support children (see **women-headed households**). In some countries, especially in the Middle East, South Asia and Latin America, women cannot do paid work or travel without their husband's or father's written permission. There is growing evidence that several aspects of gender relations such as the **gender division of labor**; disparities between men and women in power and resources; and gender biases in rights and entitlements (see **male bias**), both limit and undermine economic growth. Women are often excluded from rights in property such as land, and are generally unable to access knowledge of improved agricultural methods (see **gender and property rights**). Understanding how socio-economic change both impoverishes people, and affects existing gender relations at the household level, is crucial to the success or failure of development policies.

Definitions

"Men" and "women" may be seen simply as sexual categories based on biophysical attributes. An analysis of gender, on the other hand, considers the social meanings attributed to these categories and their implications for both parties, and society in general. A further level of analysis, sexuality and development (see **sexualities**), may consider the socially constructed sexual identities of both male and female, and indeed, **same-sex sexualities**, with social, economic, and political implications.

Gender *relations* (the socially constructed form of relations between women and men) have been interrogated in terms of the way development policies change the balance of power between women and men. Gender *roles* (the household tasks and types of employment socially assigned to women and men) are not fixed or globally consistent, and indeed become more flexible with the changes brought about by **economic development**. Everywhere gender is crosscut by differences in class, race (see **race and racism**), ethnicity (see **ethnicity/identity**), **religion** and age (see **ageing; sociology of development**). Feminists have often seen women as socially constituted as a homogeneous group based on shared oppression. But in order to understand gender relations we must interpret them within specific societies and through historical and political practices, not *a priori* on gender alone. Different places and societies have different gender systems, and it is necessary to be cognizant of this heterogeneity within a certain global homogeneity of gender roles. At the same time, we need to be aware of different voices and to give them agency (see **participatory development; postmodernism and postdevelopment**).

The roles of men and women in different places show great variation: most clerks in Martinique are women but this is not so in Chennai, just as women make up the vast majority of domestic servants in Lima but not in Lagos. In every country, the jobs done predominantly by women are the least well paid and have the lowest status (see **employment**). In the countries of East and Central Europe, Russia and China, where most jobs were open to men and women under communism, the transition to **capitalism** has led to increased **unemployment**, especially for women, except in Hungary, where the particular character of gendered **education** and employment resulted in more men's jobs being lost (see **postsocialism**). The loss of **employment** for men has resulted in alcoholism, **violence** and higher male **mortality** rates. In most parts of the world, the gender gap in political representation has become smaller, but in the former USSR and its satellite countries in Eastern and Central Europe, there has been a rapid decline in average female representation in parliament (see **politics**).

Women's organizations, and the various **United Nations World Conferences on Women** in Mexico City, Copenhagen, Nairobi and Beijing over the last three decades, have put gender issues firmly on the development agenda, but **economic growth** and modernization (see **modernization theory**) is not gender-neutral. The experiences of different states (see **state and state reform**) and regions show that economic prosperity helps gender equality but some gender gaps are resistant to change. Rapid growth, as in the East Asian countries, has led to a narrowing of the gender differences in wages and education, but **inequality** in political representation remains. Sudden economic change, such as **structural adjustment** programs or the post-**Cold War** transition in Eastern Europe, creates new gender differences.

Gender equality does not necessarily mean equal numbers of men and women or girls and boys in all activities, nor does it mean treating them in the same way. It means equality of opportunity and a society in which women and men are able to lead equally fulfilling lives. The aim of gender equality recognizes that men and women often have different needs and priorities, face different constraints and have different aspirations. Above all, the absence of gender equality means a huge loss of human potential and has costs for both men and women and for development. Investments in **human capital**, especially girls and women's education and health, and investments in physical capital such as access to financial capital and formal sector **employment** for women, can lead to greater gender equality.

In 1946, the **United Nations** set up the Commission on the Status of Women. It was to have two basic functions: to "prepare recommendations and reports to the Economic and Social Council on promoting women's rights in political, economic, civil, social and educational fields;" and to make recommendations on "urgent problems requiring immediate attention in the field of women's rights" (United Nations, 1996:13) (see **rights-based approaches to development**). Today, it is clear that progress toward gender equality in most parts of the world is considerably less than that which was hoped for. However, disparities between women in different countries are greater than those between men and women in any one country. At the beginning of the new millennium, **life expectancy** at birth for women varies from 82 years in Hong Kong to 38 in Zambia, while male life expectancy is lower, ranging from 37 years in Angola and Zambia to 77 in Hong Kong, the same as in Sweden (Population Reference Bureau (PRB), 2002). Globally, only 69 percent of women but 83 percent of men over fifteen years of age are literate (PRB, 2002; see **illiteracy**). The proportion of illiterates in the female population varies from 92 percent in Niger to less than 1 percent in Barbados and Tajikistan, but in some countries such as Lesotho, Jamaica, Uruguay, Qatar and the United Arab Emirates a higher proportion of women than men are literate (PRB, 2002). Even within individual countries, women are not a homogeneous group but can be differentiated by class, race (see **race and racism**), ethnicity (see **ethnicity/identity**), **religion** and life stage. The **elites** and the young are more likely to be educated everywhere, increasing the generational gap. The range on most socio-economic measures is wider for women than for men and is greatest among developing countries.

The **empowerment** of women and the promotion of gender equality is one of the eight internationally agreed **Millennium Development Goals (MDGs)**. There is much evidence from comparisons at national and sub-national scales that societies that discriminate on the basis of gender pay a price in more **poverty**, slower growth, and a lower quality of life, while gender equality enhances development. For example, it has been estimated that increasing the education and access to inputs of female farmers relative to male farmers in Kenya would raise yields by as much as one fifth. Literate mothers have better fed children who are more likely to attend school. Yet, in no country in the developing world do women enjoy equality with men in terms of political, legal, social and economic rights (see **human rights**). In general, women in Eastern Europe have the greatest equality of rights, but this has declined in the last decade. The lowest equality of rights is found in South Asia, Sub-Saharan Africa, the Middle East

and North Africa. There are no global comparative data on rights more recent than 1990, but there is some evidence that equality of rights has improved since the 1995 Fourth World Conference on Women held in Beijing (see **United Nations World Conferences on Women**). The **Convention on the Elimination of All Forms of Discrimination Against Women (CEDAW)** was established in 1979 and came into force in 1981 after it had been ratified by twenty countries (UNIFEM, 2000). By 1996, 152 countries had become party to the Convention, but by the early 2000s the USA had still not ratified it. Unfortunately, ratification of CEDAW does not necessarily lead to an immediate reduction in gender discrimination, but it does enforce regular reporting on progress.

Prior to 1970, when Ester Boserup published her landmark book on women and development (Boserup, 1970), it was thought that the development process affected men and women in the same way (see **women in development (WID) versus gender and development (GAD)**). When it became apparent that **economic development** did not automatically eradicate **poverty** through **trickle down** effects, the problems of distribution and equality of benefits to the various segments of the **population** became of major importance in development theory. Research on women in developing countries challenged the most fundamental assumptions of international development, added a gender dimension to the study of the development process, and demanded a new theoretical approach.

It soon became clear that a focus on women alone was inadequate and that a gender view was needed. Women and men are affected differently by economic change and development and thus an active public policy is needed to intervene in order to close gender gaps. The mission statement of the Beijing Fourth World Conference on Women held in 1995 stated that "A transformed partnership (see **partnerships**) based on equality between women and men is a condition for people-centered **sustainable development**" (United Nations, 1996:652).

The focus on gender in development policies came first from the major national and international **aid** agencies, and governments in developing countries quickly learned that they needed to acknowledge gender in their requests for assistance. Thus at the beginning, developed countries largely imposed the agenda. As **non-governmental organizations (NGOs)** began to play an increasingly important roles in grassroots (see **grassroots organizations**) delivery of aid, their gender policies began to influence local action more directly.

Approaches to gender and development

By the end of the twentieth century, all approaches to development involving a focus on women had been amalgamated into a gender and development (GAD) approach. This approach originated in academic criticism starting in the mid-1970s in the UK. Based on the concept of gender (the socially acquired ideas of masculinity and femininity) and an understanding of gender relations, they analyzed how development reshapes these power relations. Drawing on feminist political activism, gender analysts explicitly see women as agents of change (see **women's movements; feminist political ecology**). They also criticize the WID approach for treating women as a homogeneous category, and they emphasize the important influence of differences of class, age, marital status, **religion** and ethnicity or race on development outcomes. Proponents distinguished between "practical" gender needs, that is items that would improve women's lives within their existing roles, and "strategic" gender needs that seek to increase women's ability to take on new roles and to empower them (Moser, 1993). Gender analysts demanded a commitment to change in the structures of power in national and international agencies (Derbyshire, 2002) as it was realized that discriminatory institutional practices as much as active resistance can block women's advancement. By 1990 WID, GAD and WAD views had largely converged (Rathgeber, 1990) but different approaches to gender and development continued to evolve (see **women in development (WID) versus gender and development (GAD)**).

Mainstreaming Gender Equality: The term "gender Mainstreaming" came into widespread use with the adoption of the Platform for Action at the 1995 UN Fourth World Conference on women

held in Beijing (see **United Nations World Conferences on Women**). The 189 Governments represented in Beijing unanimously affirmed that the advancement of women and the achievement of equality with men are matters of fundamental **human rights** – and therefore a prerequisite for **social justice**. Mainstreaming gender equality tries to ensure that women's as well as men's concerns and experiences are integral to the design, implementation, monitoring and evaluation of all projects so that gender inequality is not perpetuated. It attempts to overcome the common problem of "policy evaporation" as the implementation and impact of development projects fail to reflect policy commitments (Derbyshire, 2002).

Masculinities: The focus on women in much gender and development work has led to a backlash from men (Momsen, 2001). This is especially true when "women only" development projects are successful and so change the local balance of economic power between men and women. It is now realized that in order to improve gender relations, and reduce **domestic violence** against women, men must be brought into the analysis. The study of masculinities and of men as the missing half of Gender and Development is now on the agenda, but is provoking much ambivalence since it has a number of important implications for GAD policies and practice, especially in terms of undermining efforts to help women, as gender equality is still far from being achieved (Cornwall and White, 2000).

Time as a development constraint: Women carry a double or even triple burden of work as they cope with housework, childcare and subsistence **food** production, in addition to an expanding involvement in paid **employment**. Everywhere women work longer hours than men. Rural women are expected to carry out the social reproduction of the household, which includes collecting water and fuel and caring for children and the elderly, as well as housework, unpaid work on family farms and paid work on other farms. They may also process products or make handicrafts for sale. It has been said that female farmers are probably the busiest people in the world. They also undertake social and religious duties at the time of year when there is less demand for their labor on the farm. Overall, in most countries and in both town and country, women have less leisure than men.

Consequently, development projects aimed at women may fail because they do not take into account age, and seasonal and farming system specific labor and time constraints.

Progress: At the beginning of the third millennium most of the world's **population** is living more comfortably than a century before. Women as a group now have a greater voice in both their public and private lives. The spread of education and literacy has opened up new opportunities for many people, and the time-space compression associated with **globalization** is making possible the increasingly rapid and widespread distribution of information and scientific knowledge. Improvements in communications, however, also make us aware that economic development is not always unidirectional and benefits are not equally available (see **information technology; Internet; telecommunications**). No country is entirely free of the gender inequalities that are harmful to development. The gender gap varies both between countries and between regions, but tends to be greater in low-income countries and among poor and minority groups of the **population** (World Bank, 2002).

As the previous UN Director General, Boutros Boutros Ghali, said in 1996: "No true social transformation can occur until every society learns to adopt new values, forging relationships between men and women based on equality, equal responsibility and mutual respect" (United Nations, 1996:73). Although there is formal recognition of women's rights and legal equality, the gender-disaggregated data that are now increasingly available have revealed that women continue to face discrimination. The UN **Gender-related Development Index (GDI)**, and **Gender Empowerment Measure (GEM)** monitor this on a regular basis. Most governments have formally adopted the 1979 **Convention on the Elimination of All Forms of Discrimination Against Women (CEDAW)** but the implementation of the CEDAW principles is far from complete. It is also worth noting that the number of reservations expressed by governments adopting the Convention was the highest for any human rights instrument negotiated under the auspices of the United Nations, indicating the obstacles still faced by women (United Nations, 1996:72).

See also: domestic violence; feminism and ecology; feminist political ecology; gender and communicable disease; gender and property rights; gender, environment and development; male bias; United Nations World Conferences on Women; women in development (WID) versus gender and development (GAD); women's movements

Further reading

Boserup, E. (1970) *Women's Role in Economic Development*, New York: St Martin's Press.

Cornwall, A. and White, S. (2000) "Introduction: Men, Masculinities and Development: Politics, Policies and Practice," *IDS Bulletin* 31:2 1–6.

Derbyshire, H. (2002) *Gender Manual: A Practical guide for Development Policy Makers and Practitioners*, London: DFID.

Momsen, J. (2001) "Backlash: Or How To Snatch Failure from the Jaws of Success in Gender and Development," *Progress in Development Studies* 1:1 51–6.

Moser, C. (1993) *Gender Planning and Development: Theory, Practice and Training*, London and New York: Routledge.

Population Reference Bureau (2002) *Women of Our World*, New York: PRB.

Rathgeber, E. (1990) "WID, WAD, GAD: Trends in Research and Practice," *The Journal of Developing Areas* 24:1 489–502.

UNIFEM (United Nations Development Fund for Women): http://www.unifem.org

United Nations (1996) *The United Nations and the Advancement of Women, 1945–1996*, New York: United Nations.

World Bank (2002) *Integrating Gender into the World Bank's Work: A Strategy for Action*, Washington DC: World Bank.

JANET HENSHALL MOMSEN

gender and communicable disease

Diseases are called communicable or infectious because their spread involves an infected agent that is transmitted between hosts (people or animals) through a variety of mechanisms. Of the 51 million deaths worldwide in 1999 reported by the *World Health Report* (2000), an estimated one third resulted from infectious diseases. The great majority of these deaths occur in low-income countries. In Sub-Saharan Africa in particular, communicable diseases account for a higher percentage of the burden of ill health than in high-income countries. Efforts to address infectious diseases have long been hindered by the failure to take into account the associated social aspects. **Gender** is an often neglected but fundamental dimension of the social aspects of health and illness. Gender analysis is crucial to understanding **vulnerability** to disease, individual and institutional responses, and the burden associated with communicable disease.

Both sex and gender can lead to differences in female and male vulnerability to disease. The extent of these influences varies in different contexts and is often debated. The prevalence of HIV/AIDS by sex and age varies between countries and regions (see **HIV/AIDS (definition and treatment); HIV/AIDS (policy issues)**). However, in many developing countries there is a trend of higher prevalence amongst women than men in younger age groups and vice-versa in older age groups, with infection rates amongst women increasing the fastest. There is increasing evidence that women's gender identity and social and economic position limits their ability to negotiate abstinence or safe sex with partner(s). This is particularly the case with younger women. For example, in Sub-Saharan Africa, the phenomenon of "sugar daddies" who provide material support to young women in **education** in exchange for sex puts young women at risk. Expectations of male promiscuity place pressure on men to seek multiple partners. In addition, the value placed on male sexual pleasure and the way in which gender influences sexuality discourage men from accepting protective measures such as condom use or non-penetrative sex (see **sexualities**). The extent to which there are sex differences in the risk of transmission of HIV is still debated (see **HIV/AIDS (policy issues)**). Similarly there is a debate about how far sex and gender explain the generally higher rate of reported **tuberculosis** cases amongst males.

Gender can also affect responses to communicable disease by individuals, households and the **primary health care** system. For example, one study in India found that whilst more men than women sought care for tuberculosis, the prevalence of the disease was higher amongst women than men in the **community**. A range of studies suggest that individual's ability to seek and complete treatment depends on factors such as their access to financial resources and transport (see **transport policy**), their social mobility, available time, and the stigma associated with the disease (see **disease, social constructions of**). These considerations may lead to differing barriers to care for women, men, girls and boys. For example, in one study in Bangladesh, respondents felt that households generally prioritized tuberculosis treatment for men because, as the main income earners, their health was perceived as most important (see **male bias**). A study in northern Thailand found that health care providers were more likely to diagnose tuberculosis in men than women and that male cases were diagnosed more swiftly. This seems to relate to differences in expected behavior by men and women. Doctors at the hospital studied (in Chiang Rai) felt that females did not clearly explain their symptoms, and often spoke of multiple complaints. The doctors also thought that the quality of sputum might be problematic, as females were considered physically too weak to produce plentiful sputum or that it was culturally unacceptable for them to cough loudly.

Women and men's roles can mean that they are affected differently by communicable disease amongst others in the household and community. For example, because informal **health** care is often seen as women's responsibility, they frequently bear the greatest burden of caring for HIV/AIDS sufferers. Although many communicable disease interventions are targeted at reducing child **mortality** and morbidity, it is adults who are mobilized to participate in these interventions, and their ability to do so is crucially affected by gender. Preventive health interventions that seek to reduce **malaria** in affected areas actively seek out women to ensure that family members, particularly infants and young **children**, are protected from the disease. However, efforts to train mothers in the detection and early intervention of fevers in their children often fail to take into account that women may not control the resources needed to seek anti-malarials or bednets, nor have the decision-making power to act on health education messages alone.

Interventions to address communicable disease need to consider how gender affects **vulnerability** to disease as well as individual and institutional responses. For example, the influence of gender on vulnerability needs to be taken into account in health promotion and prevention campaigns, the burden placed on women needs to be considered in planning support to home-based care, and the accessibility and appropriateness of diagnosis procedures need to be reassessed to ensure equitable provision of care. This means that female and male experiences and priorities need to inform communicable disease policies, and all stages of health interventions from planning to evaluation. To enable this, staff at all levels of the health system need to have the appropriate resources, information, responsibility and training. This requires "gender mainstreaming," which is the process of institutionalizing responsibility for and awareness of gender considerations (see **gender, environment and development; women in development (WID) versus gender and development (GAD)**). Male and female experiences of disease are largely shaped by the social, economic, political and environmental context, and consequently by policies and interventions in these areas. Efforts to address gender **inequality** are therefore necessary across all sectors of society. It is crucial that such interventions are designed with the participation of both women and men, to ensure that their needs and priorities are taken into consideration.

See also: disease, social constructions of; epidemics; family planning; gender; health; HIV/AIDS (definition and treatment); HIV/AIDS (policy issues); primary health care; reproductive rights; sexually transmitted diseases (STDs)

Further reading

Diwan, V., Thorson, A. and Winkvist, A. (1998) *Gender and Tuberculosis*, Göteborg: The Nordic School of Public Health.

Gender and Health Group, Liverpool School of Tropical Medicine (1999) *The Guidelines for the Analysis of Gender and Health*, Liverpool: LSTM. Available at http://www.liv.ac.uk/lstm/gg.html

UNAIDS (1999) *Gender and HIV/AIDS: Taking Stock of Research and Programmes*, Geneva: UNAIDS.

AMARA SOONTHORNDHADA, SALLY THEOBALD AND RACHEL TOLHURST

gender and industrialization

Gender relations influence the manner of **industrialization**, and industrialization may impact differentially on men and women. Industrialization processes, while traditionally associated with men, are deeply embedded with **gender** divisions of labor. With the shift towards **export-led growth** strategies and **globalization** in general since the 1980s, women have been increasingly drawn into factory work. The widespread increase in demand for female workers in export manufacturing in particular, has led to the coining of term the "global feminization of labor." Women now make-up approximately one third of the global manufacturing workforce, with between 70 and 90 percent of workers in **export processing zones (EPZs)** being female (Mehra and Gammage, 1999).

The gender divisions of labor inherent in industrialization processes depend greatly on the type of manufacturing enterprises according to product and product method. Generally, male workers are associated with heavier, technical operations, using **capital intensive** equipment such as the manufacture of **auto industry** products, chemicals, and metallurgical products. Women, on the other hand, tend to be concentrated in labor-intensive sectors, in both "traditional" **textiles**, as well as in the more "modern" electronics industries. In both cases, the reasons for these concentrations depend on deep-seated gender stereotyping, most of which is perceived rather than real.

These patterns also overlap with marked spatial variations in the concentration of these industries. Within the rapidly expanding export manufacturing sector in particular, **transnational corporations (TNCs)** transfer the **labor-intensive** assembly processes to locations where labor costs are lowest and usually within EPZs or **free trade zones (FTZs)** where factories employ a mainly female workforce. This so-called "New **international division of labor**" has been promoted through bilateral and multilateral agreements in a wide range of developing countries, with concentrations on the US-Mexican border and other parts of Central America and the Caribbean (where the factories are known as **maquiladoras**), and in South and Southeast Asia.

The demand for female labor extends beyond cost alone, even though profit maximization is always the underlying motive. Although female workers are cheaper to employ than men, women working in export manufacturing also purportedly possess a range of gender-stereotyped attributes that make them more attractive to employ than men. As well as being cheap, most factory workers are young and single. With few having children, there are negligible maternity benefit costs for employers. Indeed, in some factories, it has been reported that women have to undergo pregnancy tests before securing jobs, and/or that they lose their jobs on becoming pregnant. There are also physiological stereotypes based on women's so-called "nimble fingers;" women are thought to have greater manual dexterity than men, supposedly making the intricate tasks of sewing and assembling circuit boards easier. In turn, this dexterity is enhanced by women's socialization in "feminine" tasks such as needlework.

Also linked with socialization, women are thought to possess greater capacity than men for monotonous assembly-line work. Employers often contend that women make fewer mistakes and have higher productivity than men, again reducing labor costs and increasing profits. In turn, women are thought to be more docile by nature and easier to manage in the workplace. This also means that they will be less likely to form **trade unions**, further reinforced by the limits on women's time through reproductive responsibilities (see **reproductive rights**). The implication is less time and profits lost to labor disputes (see **labor rights and standards**).

Women are also thought to be "naturally disposable," based on the assumption that they will give up work on marriage and/or pregnancy. This may lead to frequent voluntary turnover and the avoidance of redundancy payments, which works in the interests of transnational corporations whose production cycles may fluctuate in response to market demand. Moreover, women are often exhausted, or "burnt out" after a few years of tough working conditions on assembly lines.

Men are also employed according to dubious gendered assumptions. In **capital intensive** manufacturing, as well as some occupations within **labor-intensive** assembly plants, men are deemed to have more physical strength than women. While this may be applicable in a minority of cases, in general, men and women are easily able to conduct the same operations. Also, men are assumed more suited to technical jobs involving the operation of complex machinery. While women invariably do have lower levels of **human capital** than men, this relationship is also spurious.

It is also important to emphasize that the more status and prestige that industrial jobs have, then the greater the likelihood they will be male-dominated. Men are more likely to be employed in senior positions on the factory floor, and if jobs become more capital intensive, then men usually replace female operatives. This process has already occurred in some maquiladoras in Latin America.

A final important gender-differentiated aspect of industrialization is the sub-contracting of labor. This cost-cutting measure usually employs people working in their homes or in small-scale enterprises assembling goods on a piece-rate basis (see also **casualization of work**). The vast majority of these workers are female. Although it allows some women to reconcile reproductive and productive work, it also absolves **transnational corporations (TNCs)** of any responsibilities to pay minimum wages or welfare benefits. This "globalization of flexible labor" is on the increase and is likely to reinforce the continued exploitation of women in industrialization processes throughout the world.

See also: casualization of work; export-led growth; export processing zones (EPZs); free trade zones (FTZs); gender; gender division of labor;

globalization; industrialization; international division of labor; labor rights and standards; male bias; maquiladoras; trade unions; transnational corporations (TNCs)

Further reading

Chant, S. and McIlwaine, C. (1995) "Gender and Export Manufacturing in the Philippines: Continuity or Change in Female Employment? The Case of the Mactan Export Processing Zone," *Gender, Place and Culture* 2:2 147–76.

Elson, D. and Pearson, R. (1981) " 'Nimble Fingers Make Cheap Workers:' An Analysis of Women's Employment in Third World Export Manufacturing," *Feminist Review* 7: 87–107.

Mehra, R. and Gammage, S. (1999) "Trends, Countertrends, and Gaps in Women's Employment," *World Development* 27:3 500–33.

Standing, G. (1999) "Global Feminization through Flexible Labor: A Theme Revisited," *World Development* 27:3 583–602.

CATHY McILWAINE

gender and poverty

Women and men experience **poverty** in different ways. Women are generally perceived to be poorer than men, with nearly three quarters of the world's poor **population** thought to be female. This has led to claims of a "global feminization of poverty" in recent years. This is mainly because women lack the entitlements and endowments (or formal and informal rights of access to resources) enjoyed by men and are more constrained in transforming their labor into income, with women consistently earning less than men (see **food security; gender division of labor**). In turn, women often find it more difficult than men to translate income or earnings into choice, which can help to guard against poverty and **vulnerability** in the long term.

These gender-differentiated experiences of poverty have only been recognized in the last few decades as part of the shift toward broader and less male-centered conceptualizations of poverty (see **male bias**). The roots of this shift in relation to

gender were located within women in development (WID) research in the late 1970s and early 1980s (see **women in development (WID) versus gender and development (GAD)**). This challenged conventional analyses of poverty that assumed that the poor were either male, that men's and women's needs were the same, or that women's needs were subsumed under those of a male household head. While still used, the concept of **poverty line**s were particularly criticized as gender-blind, because, among other reasons, they were constructed using aggregate household survey data which ignore intrahousehold gender inequalities and access to resources, and because they excluded measurements of women's unpaid labor in the home, in subsistence work or in the **urban informal sector** (see **participatory poverty assessment (PPA)**).

Another impetus for recognizing how women and men experience poverty disproportionately emerged from research on the effects of **structural adjustment** programs (SAPs) in the 1980s. Involving widespread cutbacks in state expenditures, **public sector** employment, and **food** subsidies, particularly in urban areas, women bore an unequal burden of coping with SAPs through intensifying their reproductive and productive labor in the form of various types of coping mechanisms. These have involved consumption-minimizing strategies such as reducing the number of meals cooked in a day, as well as income-maximizing such as increasing numbers of women generating informal **employment** or taking on two or three jobs. Although women were increasing their time and other inputs to ensure household survival in the face of increasing poverty, there was little evidence that men were contributing in corresponding ways.

Another key related area of debate on gender and poverty deals with **women-headed households**. These households have been on the increase and become more visible since the implementation of adjustment policies in the 1980s, especially in urban areas. In turn, estimations of poverty began to use the proportion of women-headed households as a proxy for the number of women living in poverty. This assumed relationship has been made on the basis that women-headed households are likely to have fewer wage earners than two-parent units, women tend to be confined to inferior and lower-paying jobs, and because women have greater domestic responsibilities when living on their own with their children.

This link between female-headed households and poverty has been subject to much debate. Although many women-headed households do live in poverty, so do many male-headed households. Moreover, many female-headed units are better off than male-headed ones, especially if they are *de facto* or temporarily headed by a woman receiving **remittances** or other assistance from elsewhere. In addition, female heads of household are free from many constraints experienced by women residing in male-headed units. This relates to material advantages in terms of "secondary poverty," whereby men withhold earnings from female spouses, especially for leisure pursuits, as well as other benefits in terms of freedom from verbal abuse or **domestic violence** for both women and children. Indeed, there are often "tactical trade-offs" to be made: a woman may decide to reduce her household income by leaving her husband or partner, yet by exercising her power and individual agency, she may gain in terms of self-esteem and reduced levels of **vulnerability**. A final danger of associating women with poverty via female household headship is that it cannot be assumed that these families are an outcome of poverty alone: there are other demographic, cultural and institutional factors involved in their formation.

The assumption that the growing numbers of women-headed households are the "poorest of the poor," coupled with women's increasing concentration in low status occupations, often in the **urban informal sector**, has led to claims of a "global feminization of poverty" in the 1990s. Yet, there are dangers with this concept. All too often in the policy domain, the issues of gender and poverty are assumed to be the same. Some commentators, such as Cecile Jackson (1996), have criticized this assumption, and have urged gender to be "rescued from the **poverty trap**" because – first – it cannot be assumed that because the poor are mostly female then by investing in women, poverty will be reduced; and – second – that it is untenable to suggest that poverty reduction will eradicate gender inequalities. It is crucial to recognize instead that living in poverty is a gendered experience rather than a female-only experience, and that women's

subordination is not derived from poverty alone, but from a range of other social, cultural and ideological factors.

See also: children; domestic violence; gender; gender and property rights; poverty; reproductive rights; structural adjustment; urban informal sector; urban poverty; vulnerability; women-headed households; women in development (WID) versus gender and development (GAD)

Further reading

Baden, S. with Milward, K. (1995) *Gender and Poverty*, Bridge Briefings in Development and Gender, Report no. 30, IDS: Brighton. http://www.ids.ac.uk/bridge/

IDS Bulletin (1997) 28:3 " 'Tactics and Trade-offs:' Revisiting the Links between Gender and Poverty" (special issue).

Jackson, C. (1996) "Rescuing Gender from the Poverty Trap," *World Development* 24:3 489–504.

Kabeer, N. (1996) "Agency, Well-being and Inequality: Reflections on the Gender Dimensions of Poverty," *IDS Bulletin* 27:1 11–22.

Development and Change (1999) 30:3 "Gendered Poverty and Well-being" (special issue).

CATHY McILWAINE

gender and property rights

Debates concerning **gender** and **property rights** highlight the differential access of women and men to owning, using, or gaining from property, and the implications of this differential. Effective and equal property rights for women can be seen both as a measure of development and as a means of development. As a key component of women's economic capabilities and as markers of an egalitarian society, they are a constitutive element of development. In their links with the welfare, **empowerment** and **productivity** of millions of women, they are a means of development.

Rights in property can be defined as claims that are legally and socially recognized and enforceable by an external legitimized authority, such as a village-level institution (see **institutions**) or the state (see **state and state reform**). Property access can stem from inheritance, purchase, lease, state transfers, and so on. Rights in property can be of ownership or usufruct, and can provide differing degrees of freedom to use, lease out, mortgage, bequeath, or sell. And rights can be vested in individuals or groups.

We need to distinguish, however, between the legal recognition of a claim and its social recognition, between recognition and enforcement, and between ownership and effective control. Legal ownership, for instance, may come with legal restrictions on disposal, as among the Tamils of Jaffna in Sri Lanka, where a married woman needs her husband's consent to sell land she legally owns. Equally, social barriers can restrict effective control. Women's "independent" rights means rights independent of male ownership and control.

The idea of "command over property" encompasses effective rights and control in both law and practice. In addition, it encompasses control unlinked with formal ownership, and can relate to both private property and public property. For instance, a notable gender **inequality** can lie in men as a gender (even if not all men as individuals) largely controlling wealth-generating public property, as managers in large corporations or heads of bureaucracies. Those with command over property can also perpetuate their existing property advantages by controlling the **institutions** that enact and implement property laws, and the mechanisms of recruitment into bodies that control property. And they can influence institutions that shape ideas about gender, such as the **media**, and **educational** and religious bodies. Who commands property thus has wide ramifications.

Which form of property is important, however, can vary by context. In largely agrarian contexts, arable land is usually the most valued property. It can determine livelihood options (see **livelihoods**), social status and political voice. In urban and industrial settings housing or financial assets gain prominence. In both contexts, however, women's command over *immovable* property, such as land or a house, is especially important.

Effective and independent property rights for women have been emphasized for their potential effects on welfare, efficiency, equality and

empowerment. There are several reasons for expecting positive welfare effects. Research findings from developing countries show that where both spouses earn, women spend a larger part of their earnings on basic household needs than men (Dwyer and Bruce, 1988). The same may be expected from property income. In rural India, children are found more likely to attend school and receive medical attention if the mother has more assets; and the mother's cultivation of a home garden, the output of which she controls, enhances child **nutrition**. In urban Brazil, the effect on child survival probabilities is several times greater when asset incomes accrue to the mother, than to the father (Thomas, 1990). Women with immovable assets are argued to have greater bargaining power, which can lead to more gender-equal allocations even from male incomes. At present, South Asian evidence reveals a persistent **male bias** in household allocations for necessities such as **health** care, **education** and, in some contexts, even **food** (Dreze and Sen, 1995). Women without independent resources are also more vulnerable to **poverty** through desertion, divorce or widowhood. In Bangladesh, elderly widows living as dependents of male relatives face higher **mortality** risks than those who head their own households, and so likely have individual assets (Rahman and Menken, 1996). Where the property is arable land, a woman with a field of her own can grow crops, trees, or fodder. Land also increases her chances of finding wage **employment**, serves as collateral for credit or as a saleable asset in crisis, and provides an asset base for non-farm enterprises. Even a small plot can thus prove critical for diversifying **livelihoods** and reducing poverty.

The potential efficiency benefits are also notable. Recent studies suggest that the incentive effect linked with secure property rights, long recognized as important in motivating farmers to make productivity-enhancing investments, could also be important *within families*. For instance, more secure land rights and control over the produce are noted to enhance the **productivity** of women farmers in parts of Africa (see Elson, 1995, among others). Land titles can also increase output by improving credit access. This may prove critical where women are the principal farmers, say due to male outmigration or widowhood. Moreover, titles can empower women to assert themselves better with agencies providing inputs and extension services.

Gender-equal property rights would also be indicative of a just and progressive society. In addition, they can empower women economically as well as strengthen their ability to challenge social and political gender inequities. Property access is argued to enhance women's "bargaining power" within and outside the household (Agarwal, 1994). Emergent research also shows that owning land or a house can significantly reduce women's risk of marital violence, by serving both as a deterrent to **domestic violence** and providing an exit option should **violence** occur.

Women can access immovable property in three major ways: inheritance, state transfers, and the market. In South Asia, inheritance is the most important since immovable property is largely privatized. Typically inheritance is post-mortem, although in some communities (see **community**) (e.g. in Sri Lanka) pre-mortem transfers occur via dowry. Historically, South Asia's inheritance systems varied considerably by region, religion and type of property. While in most of South Asia inheritance was patrilineal (ancestral property passed through the male line), in southern and eastern South Asia there were also significant pockets of matriliny (ancestral property passed through the female line), as in Meghalaya and Kerala in India, and bilateral inheritance (property passing through and to both sons and daughters) as in Sri Lanka. Indeed, in Sri Lanka bilateral inheritance was the norm among both the majority Sinhalese and the Jaffna Tamils, while the Muslims were largely matrilineal.

In the twentieth century, South Asia's inheritance laws underwent reform, but fell short of full equality, especially on immovable property. In India, for instance, today Parsis and Christians enjoy full gender equality, but laws for Hindus and Muslims continue to be unequal (Agarwal, 1994). In Nepal, the 1853 *Mulki Ain* code still prevails, and despite recent amendments substantial inequalities persist. A daughter, for instance, can inherit her father's property only if she is over thirty-five and unmarried. Regionally, inheritance laws in northern South Asia are more unequal than

in the south, with Sri Lanka and Kerala coming close to equality. These differences broadly overlap with cultural geography. Social norms that allow cross-cousin and in-village marriages, as among most communities of South India and Sri Lanka make for less opposition to daughters' claims in immovable property than the ban on such marriages which characterizes Hindus in Northern South Asia.

Moreover, there is a large gap between **law** and practice. A study for rural India, for instance, found that only 13 percent of women whose fathers owned land inherited any as daughters, and only 51 percent of those whose husbands owned land inherited as widows (Chen, 2000). Regionally, the percentage of daughters inheriting, while small everywhere, was somewhat higher in South India than in North India, where women owning land or a house is extremely rare. In Sri Lanka, by contrast, female land or house owners are not uncommon (Agarwal, 1994).

Several factors underlie the dominant pattern of female disinheritance. One is post-marital residence. Where women marry strangers in distant **villages**, parents tend to disinherit daughters for fear of losing control over immovable property. Many women also forfeit their claims in favor of brothers, whom they see as potential sources of economic and social security in case of marital breakup, in the absence of a state social security system. Where women do not voluntarily give up their claims, male relatives may file court cases, forge wills, and threaten or even use violence. Administratively, many government functionaries share the social biases and fail to implement the law.

Equally, there is a gap between ownership and effective control. Again, marriages in distant villages can obstruct women from claiming or controling their shares in parental property. Obstacles also stem from social restrictions on women's mobility. For arable land, these difficulties are compounded for women seeking to cultivate, due to their limited access to cash and credit for purchasing inputs, and male bias in extension services. Some constraints vary by region. Distant marriages to strangers and female seclusion practices are more common in northern South Asia. But, subtle constraints on women's behavior restricts their public interaction virtually everywhere in South Asia.

State transfers are another source of property (see **state and state reform**). Typically, however, government land reform and **resettlement** schemes allot land or homesteads almost exclusively to males, on the assumption that men are the primary cultivators and breadwinners and women the helpers and dependents. Recent policy shifts in India have led to the granting of joint titles to both spouses. This will reduce gender inequalities (see **inequality**) somewhat, but women can still face difficulties in claiming their shares in case of marital conflict or divorce, or in bequeathing the property as they wish.

A third source of property is through market purchase or lease. This is a limited option, since most women have inadequate financial resources to purchase immovable property; and, for arable land, plots are not always available on sale. Markets therefore cannot compensate for gender inequalities in inheritance or government transfers. They can, however, supplement those means, especially through collective endeavor. In parts of India, for instance, groups of landless women have used state-provided subsidized credit for jointly leasing in or purchasing land and cultivating it collectively (Agarwal, 2003).

Given its potential benefits, scholars and policy advocates have suggested several measures to enhance women's access to immovable property, such as promoting gender-equal inheritance in law and practice; enhancing legal literacy; formulating policies which recognize women as independent claimants in housing and land; providing women farmers with inputs, credit, and information; collecting gender-disaggregated data to monitor shifts in property access; and launching **media** campaigns to change attitudes. Some measures could first be initiated in southern South Asia where circumstances are more conducive.

Other suggestions include forging national and international links between groups with similar goals, and drawing on emerging global support (see **advocacy coalitions; solidarity campaigns**). Equality in property is an important directive in the **Convention on the Elimination of All Forms of Discrimination Against Women (CEDAW)**. The 1996 Habitat II (see **Habitat I and II**) conference in Istanbul also focused centrally on women and land. And the Huairou Commission – a global coalition of grassroots women's organizations (see **grassroots organizations**) stemming from the 1995 World Conference on Women in Beijing (see **United Nations World Conferences on Women**), is planning an international campaign on women's rights in land, property and housing, under the auspices of the UN Center for Human Settlements. All these initiatives portend well for the future.

See also: domestic law; domestic violence; empowerment; gender; housing; inequality; land reform; land rights; male bias; property rights; rural development

Further reading

Agarwal, B. (1994) *A Field of One's Own: Gender and Land Rights in South Asia*, Cambridge: Cambridge University Press.

Agarwal, B. (2003) "Gender and Land Rights Revisited: Exploring New Prospects via the State, Family and Market," *Journal of Agrarian Change* 3:1–2 184–224.

Chen, M. (2000) *Perpetual Mourning: Widowhood in Rural India*, Pittsburg: University of Pennsylvania Press.

Dreze, J. and Sen, A. (1995) *India: Economic Development and Social Opportunity*, Delhi: Oxford University Press.

Dwyer, D. and Bruce, J. (eds) (1988) *A Home Divided: Women and Income Control in the Third World*, Stanford: Stanford University Press.

Elson, D. (1995) "Gender Awareness in Modeling Structural Adjustment," *World Development* 23:11 1851–68.

Rahman, O. and Menken, J. (1990) "The Impact of Marital Status and Living Arrangements on Old Age Female Mortality in Rural Bangladesh," Paper no. 1, Harvard School of Public Health, and Population Studies Center, University of Pennsylvania.

Thomas, D. (1990) "Intra-household Resource Allocation: An Inferential Approach," *Journal of Human Resources* 25:4 635–63.

BINA AGARWAL

gender division of labor

The notion of gender division of labor is an elaboration of the notion of the sexual division of labor. Sexual division of labor refers to the division of labor between the sexes. The dominant image of the sexual division of labor has been for a long time taken for granted both in development theories and policies: women were seen as mothers and housewives – mainly operating in the domestic sphere and confined to domestic labor – whereas men were the income earners, operating in the public sphere. This difference in domestic and public sphere is also referred to as women being confined to the reproductive sphere and men to the productive sphere. This dominant discourse began to be scrutinized in the early 1970s with the so-called second feminist movement. In particular, people began to question whether such divisions of labor between men and women were natural, especially because there was great diversity in labor practices in both developed and developing countries. At this time, no one could really answer why specific types or locations of labor were considered typically male or female. These debates – concerning the divisions of labor in both home and work – became known as the "Domestic Labor Debates." These debates centered around the relative priority of capitalism versus patriarchy and class versus **gender** (see **sociology of development**).

From the mid-1970s, scholars started to abandon analysis based on sexual differences alone, and instead looked at gender. They considered the social constructions of the division of labor from a different angle. Whereas sexual divisions of labor focused on the work achieved by men and women, a gendered division of labor also refers to norms, values, and symbols attached to certain types of labor in both domestic and public spheres. Analysts also questioned the previously rigid distinction between domestic and public spheres because it was clear that men and women could undertake many reproductive and productive tasks in both spheres. It was argued that the definition of both "masculine" and "feminine" was intrinsically linked to social divisions of labor. Normative values about masculinity or femininity were reflected in laws, regulations and the organization

of labor within specific contexts. Consequently, the access of men or women to certain jobs was regulated. Scholars now assess how far different ideas and norms about gender roles influence job opportunities for men and women in different contexts, and consider how far **law** or labor rights (see **labor rights and standards**) may either contribute to these patterns, or be changed in order to achieve a more egalitarian division of labor. In other words, deconstruction of gender discourses has replaced a simple notion of division of labor according to sex.

See also: casualization of work; gender; gender and industrialization; international division of labor; labor migration; labor rights and standards

Further reading

Rai, S. (2002) *Gender and the Political Economy of Development*, Cambridge: Polity.

Young, K., Wolkowitz, C. and McCullagh, R. (eds) (1984) *Of Marriage and the Market: Women's Subordination Internationally and Its Lessons*, London: Routledge.

FRANCIEN VAN DRIEL

Gender Empowerment Measure (GEM)

The Gender Empowerment Measure (GEM) is a statistical indicator of development (see **indicators of development**) focusing on women's opportunities for participation in economic, political and professional arenas. It was first published by the **United Nations** in its 1995 *Human Development Report*. The GEM uses three evenly-weighted country-level variables: per capita income in unadjusted purchasing power parity; percentage of professional, technical, administrative and managerial positions held by women; and percentage of national parliamentary seats occupied by women. The GEM, like the GDI (the Gender-related Development Index), measures a complex set of social relations. A country's rank on the GEM suggests the cultural barriers women may face in gaining access to participation in economic and political decision-making. High or low ranking on the GEM does not depend on a country's economic status, as women in some low-income countries have gained access to positions of political and economic power, and some high-income countries exhibit lower levels of participation by women.

See also: empowerment; gender; Gender-related Development Index (GDI); Human Development Index (HDI); indicators of development; measuring development

ELLEN R. HANSEN

gender, environment and development

The field of gender, environment and development (GED) is best described as a cluster of debates focused on the belief that women's everyday realities and **livelihoods** should form part of the international agenda on **sustainable development**. The roots of this field reach back to two decades of work on "women and development" and "environment and development" that converged during the 1990s (see **gender**). Each theme began in the 1970s as simple add-ons to international development, but evolved over time to more integrative approaches focused more upon *gender* as a social and political phenomenon, and not simply upon women as a target of development work (see **women in development (WID) versus gender and development (GAD)**). GED may be differentiated from ecofeminism (see **feminism and ecology**) by questioning essentialistic links between gender and environmental degradation, and instead seeking to highlight social and political factors in how both gender and **environment** are understood.

The simultaneous introduction of women into the debates about environment, and environment into women and development efforts, was facilitated by the growing participation of women professionals plus **non-governmental organizations (NGOs)** in the several **United Nations** programs and initiatives. Programs within the United Nations Environment Programme (UNEP), the **United Nations Development Programme (UNDP)**, the **Food and Agriculture Organization (FAO)**, and the United Nations Development Fund for Women (UNIFEM) contributed toward this effort. High-profile international initiatives discussed GED, including the UN Decade for Women Conference in Nairobi (1985), the Beijing Fourth World Conference on Women (1995) (see **United Nations World Conferences on Women**); the **Cairo conference on population and development** (1994), and the **Earth Summit (1992) (United Nations Conference on Environment and Development)** and **World Summit on Sustainable Development (Johannesburg, 2002)**. New NGO initiatives such as DAWN (Development Alternatives for Women of a New Era) and the **Women's Environment and Development Organization (WEDO)** have integrated academic and activist research and advocacy. Organizations such as these have linked their efforts on GED to UN initiatives, in both supportive and critical ways.

There are some common themes to GED. First, research and advocacy have sought to highlight the current *invisibility* of women's needs and contributions to resource management, such as in **agriculture**, **water management**, and **community forestry**, including the collection of **non-timber forest products (NTFPs)**. Second, once women's *presence, participation, and interests* were more visible, researchers encouraged sustainable development agencies to integrate women within development plans for the sake of *efficiency, equity, justice, and empowerment*. In contrast, however, some feminist scholars and advocates focused on the need to *protect* women and their worlds from damage by "maldevelopment," including socially and ecologically problematic aspects of **sustainable development**. Feminist critiques of sustainable development decried the uneven discrimination against women in cases of excluding people from parks and reserves; displacement by **dams**; **resource tenure** and **land reform**; and ecological **displacement** through the proliferation of **monoculture** in forestry and agricultural development projects (see Shiva, 1988; also see **environment; political ecology**). A specific group of scholars and activists clustered around the theme of women, population and environment to counter the population-control policies of many agencies that identified women's **fertility** as an environmental problem (Hartmann, 1994, see **Malthusian demography; population**).

One important trend has been the movement within GED from research and advocacy focusing only upon women as subjects or victims of development, toward a more holistic critique of sustainable development from an explicitly feminist perspective. This trend has led to a variety of further debates, including **feminist political ecology**, which adopts a strong but not exclusive focus on gender, informed by feminist critiques of science and post-structural critiques of development. This approach recognizes complexity in both social and ecological spheres, and acknowledges the uneven relations of power embedded in the use, perception and control of **natural resources**. Feminist approaches to GED emphasize the *multiple uses* or values at stake in cases of resource claims and environmental change, and the relations created by, or expressed within, the *multiple actors* involved. Some scholars in this field, especially geographers, analyze the physical and spatial relation of multiple uses and users to *gendered landscapes* and to the distinct, *gendered sciences* that provide authoritative knowledge about land-use practices.

GED has advanced from a focus on gendered labor in production, and gendered interests in technology change and resource allocation, to an interest in gendered knowledge in resource management, gendered space and property, and gendered political participation, organization and decision-making. Cultural politics and **ethnicity/identity** have surfaced increasingly in discussions of gender, **resource tenure** and environmental change. Further new trends are feminist critiques of **human rights, reproductive rights**, and other legal aspects of environment and development policies, and the search for feminist sustainable development alternatives, and alternatives to the development paradigm in general (see **postmodernism and postdevelopment**). Overall, the research and activist communities concerned with GED have increasingly integrated gender within broader feminist approaches in search of viable, just, and humane

ecologies and economies for women and men, and a host of other beings.

See also: environment; feminism and ecology; feminist political ecology; gender; gender and property rights; political ecology; United Nations World Conferences on Women; Women's Environment and Development Organization (WEDO); women in development (WID) versus gender and development (GAD)

Further reading

Braidotti, R., Charkiewicz, E., Haulser, S. and Wieringa, S. (1994) *Women, the Environment and Sustainable Development: Towards a Theoretical Synthesis*, London: Zed.

Hartmann, B. (1994) *Reproductive Rights and Wrongs: The Global Politics of Population Control*, Boston MA: South End Press.

Jackson, C. (1993) "Environmentalism and Gender Interests in the Third World," *Development and Change* 24: 649–77.

Leach, M., Joekes, S. and Green, C. (eds) (1995) "Gender Relations and Environmental Change," special issue of *IDS Bulletin* 26:1.

Shiva, V. (1988) *Staying Alive: Women, Ecology and Development*, London: Zed.

DIANNE ROCHELEAU

Gender-related Development Index (GDI)

The Gender-related Development Index (GDI), first published by the **United Nations** in its 1995 *Human Development Report*, is a gender-disaggregated version of the **Human Development Index (HDI)**, and uses the same country-level variables to measure **gender** disparities in human development. The variables include **life expectancy**; access to **education**, indicated by literacy rates; and adjusted real income, shown by purchasing power parity. Using these variables to look beyond national income level (revealed by **gross domestic product (GDP)** or **gross national product (GNP)**), GDI allows inferences about

income distribution and access to resources in a nation's population. Each variable accounts for one third of the index's value, therefore changes in any one variable may result in a rise or fall in a nation's GDI standing. The GDI indicates that women's situation worldwide has improved dramatically since 1970 by these measures, but that no countries have achieved gender equality.

See also: gender; Gender Empowerment Machine (GEM); indicators of development; measuring development

ELLEN R. HANSEN

GENERALIZED SYSTEM OF PREFERENCES (GSP) see most favored nation (MFN) status; tariffs; trade; World Trade Organization/General Agreement on Tariffs and Trade (WTO/GATT)

genetically modified organisms (GMOs)

Genetically modified organisms (GMOs) are plant or animal species that have been subjected to microbiological practices seeking to enhance or diminish certain properties controlled by the organism's genes, often by integrating its genetic structure with that from another species. The term "genetic engineering" became widespread in the 1970s, when recombinant DNA techniques were first developed to transfer genetic material across bacterial species. The techniques were aimed at engineering microbes to produce therapeutic agents or other valuable substances, and were aimed to operate within contained facilities. During the 1980s, however, public concerns grew about the proposed human health risks of such activity and its products. In response to these concerns, genetic "engineering" was renamed "manipulation," and even more euphemistically renamed as "modification."

By the 1990s, genetically modified organisms (GMOs) encompassed several crop varieties. Most contained agronomic traits, from microbial genes which confer resistance, to broad-spectrum

herbicides or insect pests. Second-generation GM crops contain genes which confer "quality" or "output" traits – different substances which can increase the commercial value of the crop.

Proponents of GMOs have argued that genetic modification results in familiar, predictable products which therefore warrant no special regulation for environmental or health risks. By contrast, critics have claimed that such products are novel, or "inventions," which therefore warrant patent rights. At its most extreme, some critics have called some GMOs "Frankenstein Foods," seeking to highlight the artificial means by which they have been created. Public concerns have also led to immense public protest at GMOs (see **biotechnology and resistance**). Internationally, the **Cartagena Protocol on Biosafety** has sought to regulate the trade and transfer of GMOs.

See also: biotechnology and resistance; Cartagena Protocol on Biosafety; environmental movements; Human Genome Project

LES LEVIDOW

Geneva Conventions

The Geneva Conventions of 1949 aim to give protection to prisoners of **war** and civilians who fall into enemy hands during the course of an armed conflict between two states (see **state and state reform**). The four conventions are the Convention for the Amelioration of the Condition of the Wounded and Sick in Armed Forces in the Field; Convention for the Amelioration of the Condition of Wounded; Sick and Shipwrecked Members of the Armed Forces at Sea; Convention Relative to the Treatment of Prisoners of War; and the Convention Relative to the Protection of Civilian Persons in Time of War. The two Additional Protocols of 1977 increase the level of protection for victims of international armed conflicts, and extend the scope of the conventions to non-international armed conflicts. The Geneva Conventions and their Additional Products form the cornerstone of the **law of armed conflict (LAC)**.

See also: complex emergencies; humanitarianism; landmines; law of armed conflict (LAC); peacekeeping; post-conflict rehabilitation; Red Cross and Red Crescent; torture; war

I. NIKLAS HULTIN

genocide

Genocide is defined as "acts committed with the intent to destroy, in whole or in part, a national, ethnical, racial or religious group, as such..." (Convention on the Prevention and Punishment of the Crime of Genocide, 1948). It is listed by the Rome Statute (1998) of the International Criminal Court as one of the four most serious crimes of concern to the international **community**, and is listed as customary **international law** and hence is required to be resisted by all countries, even if they are not signatory to the 1948 Convention. Examples of attempted genocide include the attempts of Nazi Germany to eradicate the Jews and other minorities such as Gypsies during World War II. The Serbian atrocities against ethnic Albanians in Kosovo, 1998–9, however, was called genocide by critics, but was ruled not to be genocide by the **United Nations** high court (the International Court of Justice) in 2001. Elements of the Genocide Convention have been incorporated into the Rome Statute in an effort by the international community to ensure in future that those who commit genocide are prosecuted and punished by the International Criminal Court based in The Hague. The decisions of the *ad hoc* international criminal tribunals in The Hague and in Rwanda indicate a new commitment to prosecute and punish the perpetrators of genocide.

See also: complex emergencies; human rights; humanitarianism; Red Cross and Red Crescent; right of intervention; United Nations; war

Further reading

Power, S. (2002) *"A Problem from Hell:" America and the Age of Genocide*, London: Flamingo.

PAUL OKOJIE

ghettos

The term "ghetto" is usually confused and often used interchangeably with slum, though there are some distinctions. While slum – or shantytown (see **shantytowns**) – refers to a blighted or depressed area with inadequate **housing** where residents are confined by economic factors, a ghetto refers to a primarily racially or culturally distinct neighborhood in a city which is characterized by unique languages, mannerisms, and even dress, which give the inhabitants a different appearance from the rest of society.

For some, ghetto is a harsh term associated with undesirable elements of society, to be kept at bay, separated in sections by themselves until they can be assimilated into the larger society. Ghettos are therefore "springboards to greater social mobility" (Massey and Denton, 1993). In some countries such as France, ghettos represent a collapse of the rule of law where even the police are unwilling to make arrests or answer calls for help. For some, ghetto refers to the racial and or ethnic makeup of neighborhoods irrespective of class. "Gilded ghettos" sometimes exist where economically well-to-do members of a minority or cultural group may, voluntarily or otherwise, live in relative isolation from the larger society. Yet others believe that there are invisible walls around ghettos, erected by those who have power, both to confine those who have no power and to perpetuate their powerlessness. Others, however, refute this ethnic makeup argument, contending, for example, that in the German, Irish, Italian, Russian, Polish, Swedish, and Czech ghettos in US cities, different nationalities exist to such an extent that no one group is dominant. African-Americans in the USA are perhaps the only ethnic group to have witnessed true "ghettoization." In many developing-world cities such as Bangkok or Jakarta, different neighborhoods may be associated with specific ethnic groups such as Chinese people, but these may not have the negative connotations of a ghetto.

The harshness and segregation of ghettos can be traced back to medieval Europe, where "ghetto" referred to those sections of the city where Jews resided. Jews initially settled in close proximity to each other as a matter of convenience, but by the fifteenth century they were legally segregated into walled, deteriorated, and overcrowded areas of the city where they lived under strictly enforced curfew where non-compliance was punishable by death. Ghettos were also created in Germany between 1939 and 1942, and in Hungary in 1944, with the aim of isolating, controlling and isolating Jews. In the United States, ghettos existed as early as 1820 when freed Negro slaves and low-class Irish immigrants inhabited the Five Points area in New York. Similar areas also existed in Boston and Philadelphia by the middle of the nineteenth century.

See also: diaspora; ethnicity/identity; Habitat I and II; housing; race and racism; shantytowns

Further reading

Collins, W. and Margo, R. (2000) "Residential Segregation and Socioeconomic Outcomes: When Did Ghettos Go Bad?" *Economics Letters* 69: 239–43.

Massey, D. and Denton, N. (1993) *American Apartheid: Segregation and the Making of the Underclass*, Cambridge MA: Harvard University Press.

DOUG FEREMENGA

Gini index

The Gini index is a statistic economists use to calculate **inequality** in **income distribution** (or some other attribute) within a society. Developed by the Italian statistician and demographer Corrado Gini in 1912, it measures the gap between the dispersion of an actual distribution from a hypothesized ideal in which each member of society would receive an amount equal to its share in the population. The actual distribution is represented using a Lorenz curve that ranks incomes in ascending order, and then plots the cumulative percentage of total income received against the population share. Calculated through a simple formula or more complicated integration techniques, the index ranges between zero (complete equality) and one (maximum inequality). The

Gini is much more sensitive to changes in the middle of the distribution than to its ends. One consequence is that countries with very different distributions may produce the same index.

See also: income distribution; indicators of development; inequality; measuring development

EMMA SAMMAN

Global Compact

The Global Compact, launched by the **United Nations** in 2000, is an international initiative to promote corporate adherence to certain standards in **human rights**, labor rights (see **labor rights and standards**), **sustainable development**, and **corporate social responsibility (CSR)**. It is an attempt to moderate some of the negative social effects of **globalization**, relying on the voluntary actions of companies to gain advantage from the market benefits that accrue from an image of CSR (also see **transnational corporations (TNCs); corruption**). Hundreds of companies from all regions of the world, international labor and **civil society** organizations are engaged in the initiative. The Global Compact's principles draw upon the **Universal Declaration of Human Rights (1948)**, the 1998 International Labor Organization's **Declaration on Fundamental Principles and Rights at Work**, and the Rio Declaration on Environment and Development (see **Earth Summit (1992) (United Nations Conference on Environment and Development)**). The nine principles are: in terms of human rights, businesses should support and respect the protection of internationally proclaimed human rights within their sphere of influence, and make sure that they are not complicit in human rights abuses. In terms of labor standards, businesses should uphold the **freedom of association** and the effective recognition of the right to collective bargaining; the elimination of all forms of forced and compulsory labor; the effective abolition of **child labor**; and eliminate discrimination in respect of **employment** and occupation. Regarding the environment, businesses should support a **precautionary principle** approach to environmental challenges;

undertake initiatives to promote greater environmental responsibility; and encourage the development and diffusion of environmentally friendly technologies (see **technology transfer**).

The Global Compact works as a network with the **Office of the United Nations High Commissioner for Human Rights (OHCHR)**; United Nations Environment Program; **International Labor Organization (ILO)**; and **United Nations Development Programme (UNDP)**. The Global Compact involves all the relevant social actors: governments, companies, labor, **civil society** organizations, and the United Nations as the facilitator.

Because the Global Compact is not a regulatory (i.e. coercive) instrument, it does not "police," enforce or measure the behavior or actions of companies. It relies on public **accountability, transparency** and the enlightened self-interest of companies. The non-regulatory nature of the Global Compact has raised debates related to questions of social inequality, distributive justice, CSR and corporate complicity. Skeptics have claimed that the initiative simply gives a stamp of approval – and hence legitimacy – to big business without requiring concrete improvements or enforceable commitments. According to this view, as signatories to international agreements relating to human rights, labor and **environment**, the state (see **state and state reform**) has a responsibility to enact and enforce legislation that should apply to companies registered in or operating in their countries. Why should the United Nations negotiate directly with big business? (see **partnerships**). Companies ultimately behave according the demands of profit maximization; they cannot be expected to effectively regulate themselves.

The contrary view, which supports the Global Compact approach, is that business will always follow the market, that market impulses are always the most effective means of determining corporate behavior (not legislation) and that the market can work in the public interest if there are incentives. John Ruggie, who worked on the Global Compact, describes the initiative as "a learning model for inducing corporate change."

See also: corporate social responsibility (CSR); Millennium Development Goals (MDGs); partnerships; transnational corporations (TNCs); triple bottom line; United Nations

Further reading

Global Compact website: http://www.unglobalcompact.org/

EDWARD NEWMAN

Global Environment Facility (GEF)

The Global Environment Facility (GEF) was established in 1991 as an experimental facility to coordinate international action toward environmentally responsible **economic development**. GEF specializes in organizing and financing international cooperation to solve global environmental problems associated with stratospheric ozone depletion, decline in **biodiversity**, **climate change**, and transboundary water issues (see **water management**). In 2004, GEF was supported by 176 national governments, plus development institutions, scientific communities, and private **non-governmental organizations (NGOs)**. GEF headquarters is located in Washington DC. A Council of representatives from two countries with economies in transition, fourteen developed countries, and sixteen developing countries defines the program agenda of the GEF. GEF Council takes advice from a twelve-member scientific and technical advisory panel whose work is supported by a secretariat at the headquarters of the United Nations Environment Program (UNEP) in Nairobi. GEF, in collaboration with UNEP and the United Nations Development Programme, and the **World Bank** supports individual or group projects that reflect national or regional priorities, and that improve the global environment.

See also: biodiversity; climate change; environment; United Nations

DELE OGUNSEITAN

global public goods

Global public goods (GPGs) are public goods affecting more than one country. Two main characteristics of public goods (or bads) are that they are non-exclusive (i.e. it is difficult or impossible to exclude people from using a good) and non-rivalrous (i.e. one person's consumption does not decrease the amount of good available to others). In the absence of a global government that has tax-raising powers, many GPGs such as control of carbon emissions (see **climate change**), tropical forest conservation (see **protected areas; common heritage of humankind**), require the voluntary cooperation of nations. However, analysts of collective action (see **common pool resources; property rights**) such as Mancur Olson, suggest that collective action depends on who benefits and who bears the costs, and hence are very vulnerable to lack of collective action. Other GPGs, such as the invention of new **pharmaceuticals**, space programs, and lately, controlling "rogue states" (see **state and state reform**) are provided by unilateral actions of nations. The main challenge of providing GPGs is to develop transparent and flexible global **institutions** where the nations that are critically dependent on a GPG are able to influence their provision.

See also: common heritage of humankind; common pool resources; institutions and environment; property rights

Further reading

Sandler, T. (1998) "Global and Regional Public Goods: A Prognosis for Collective Action," *Fiscal Studies* 19:3 221–47.

P. B. ANAND

globalization

Globalization refers to the increasing connectivity between different places in the globe. It is often associated with a sense of increasing world domination by **transnational corporations (TNCs)** or global institutions such as the WTO (see **World Trade Organization/General Agreement on Tariffs and Trade (WTO/GATT)**), and hence, "anti-globalization" may be seen to be a resistance movement that emphasizes locality and diversity against oppressive unification (see **World Social Forum (WSF)**). Yet, the globalization debate is rooted largely within sociological debates that discuss how communications with society have changed in relation to time and space.

Changing relations between time and space

Time and space belong to the innermost dimensions which structure human life. For tens of thousands of years the relationship between time and space was fixed and stable. It took so many days to go to a certain place and the unfriendlier the terrain the more time people had to invest in traveling. Contact was either non-existent or very limited between tribes of hunter-gatherers; for a long time people were locked into their local space. When Homo sapiens settled down and started to till the ground and trade the products which were not consumed, the process of human civilization got on its way. As part of that process, new ways to move around and to communicate with people further away were invented. In fact, it is not uncommon in globalization literature to find references to these historic roots of the current globalization process: globalization as the growing interconnectedness between peoples living on this globe in terms of the exchange and movement of ideas, goods, money and people. It started with the invention of the wheel and it ends where it is nowadays: communication within digital space. Obviously, globalization has not been a steady on-going process; sometimes there was no progress for centuries and the relation between time and space appeared to be fixed and stable as ever. However, the nineteenth century showed in various ways a definite break with the past, and as such is seen by many to be the real beginning of globalization. The train, the automobile, steamships, and telex provided revolutionary new means for transport and communication. The relatively stable relation between time and space was significantly changed and increasingly so in the twentieth century. The current digitalization of the means of communication allows people all over the world to witness the same occurrence at the same moment in time. It seems sometimes as if time has annihilated space, as if space does not matter any more. This idea is reflected in globalization literature by reference to Anthony Giddens's concept of "time-space distanciation" (Giddens, 1984) and David Harvey's "time-space compression" (Harvey, 1989).

The dimensions of globalization

There are many definitions of globalization. A slightly different version from the one above is that globalization is a process, which embodies the emergence of a transnational network of flows of goods, services, finances, ideas and images, and people. The end stadium of this process is called globality and entails an entirely new phase in the spatial organization of economic transactions and social relations. It is important to realize, however, that globalization is a process and that there is discussion as to whether it will ever reach globality. Central in many definitions of globalization is the idea of transnationalism, which literally means "above" or "beyond" nations. While international relations refer to relations between nation-states, from border to border as it were, transnational relations, on the contrary, are flows in a border-less world (with the **Internet** as the common example).

There are economic, political and socio-cultural dimensions of globalization, and, at least in theory, it is not really clear to what extent and how these are interrelated. The reason is that the globalization process in each of these dimensions follows a separate logic. In the "pre-globalization" era (modernity or early-modernity) these dimensions were neatly contained within the confines of the nation-state and as such were tightly interrelated. The emergence of transnational networks in the global era changed that particular time-space framework.

In the *economic domain*, globalization involves the emergence of a global market for goods, money and services. Anyone with a telephone (and enough money) can participate in buying and selling in the global market place. A typical example of this is the fast growth in **Internet** marketing, which went from a turnover of US$2.6 billion in 1996 to US$300 billion in 2002. The increased importance of just a handful of multinational companies in each of the important economic sectors led to a description of globalization as the ultimate form of corporate **capitalism**. Not only goods and services have increasingly become part of a global circulation, but above all the financial flows have increased enormously. From 1979 to 2002 financial flows per day increased from US$79 billion to almost US$2,000 billion. It is understandable that these flows are sometimes seen as the most important characteristic of economic globalization, much more so than the global integration of the production and consumption of material products and services. It is through these financial conduits that economic crises in one part of the world immediately produce shockwaves elsewhere, as the ripple effect of the 1997–8 **Asian crises** have shown (see **contagion effect**). Next to globalization being labeled as corporate capitalism, the fickleness and uncontrollability of the financial flows have led to such labeling as jungle or casino capitalism (see **capital flight; inflation and its effects**).

In the *political domain*, globalization involves the increasing power of supranational political institutions. Essentially this means that the idea of the nation-state as a sovereign political, juridical and military entity is no longer the only guiding principle in international political relations. Supranational bodies not only consist of nation-state representatives, but also **non-governmental organizations (NGOs)** participate in so-called international regimes which monitor, for example, **human rights** situations and the implementation of global environmental treaties. Political globalization will not *per se* lead to a world government but instead to something known also as global **governance**.

In the *cultural domain*, globalization refers to the rise of what is called a global **culture** (see also **globalization and culture**). Exposure to global media and increased flows of international migration has heightened the global exchange of cultural goods (fashion, music, movies, literature, food, etc.) (also see **media**). Culture, in the sense of a set of shared norms and values, used to be contained within the borders of the nation-state.

In the global era, however, the nation-state is no longer the spatial container of cultural expressions. Also the idea of national identity as a point of reference in the process of identity construction of people has lost its hegemonic status and now has to compete with religious, ethnic, gender and regional forms of identity construction. In most cases, these emerging forms of identity construction are not new at all but have been suppressed during the phase of building national political sovereignty. They emerge when central authorities lose their hold over their societies for reasons which are related to global political and economic processes.

The common denominator in this characterization of globalization is the retreat of the nation-state. Globalization essentially implies that the logic and dynamic within the economic, political and socio-cultural dimensions no longer has the nation-state as a spatial frame of reference. This would mean the end of the importance of the nation-state, one which it has held from the beginning of the Westphalian system in 1648. This, however, is contested.

Contentious issues

How are we to define globalization? To what aspects do we specifically look when we say that the world is getting increasingly interconnected? Some emphasize the emergence of a global consciousness, a mutual awareness that the world is one place. Others point to the rise of global markets and the increase in cross-border flows. Sometimes the definition of globalization reflects a subjective value judgment of whether globalization is good or bad which, of course, then leads to tautologies. For example, globalization defined in terms of "global casino capitalism" is a reflection of a negative appreciation of globalization and can undoubtedly be substantiated with empirical data, but as such does not really contribute to a theoretical understanding of the phenomenon.

Is globalization really happening and if so is it a new phenomenon? Here are three positions. The first is that the transnationalization of above all the economy is not only unprecedented but also new in terms of the fast rise of the importance of financial flows. The latter are calculated, as mentioned above, to the amount of US$2,000 billion per day. The second position is that instead of a globalization there is a rationalization of the world economy. There is an economic triad consisting of the **North American Free Trade Agreement (NAFTA)**, the **European Union**, and the major East Asian producers. The third position is that there have been waves of economic globalization before, the first one between 1870 and 1914 (Oman, 1996) with a powerful economic surge of colonialism (see **colonialism, history of; colonialism, impacts of**). The second wave is located in the 1950s and 1960s, with a strong spread of international trade led by (US) **transnational corporations (TNCs)**. So, in fact the present globalization period is supposed to be the third wave with perhaps different characteristics, but as "global wave" a common phenomenon.

When did globalization start? Although this question is directly related to the previous one, it warrants separate attention. In the first paragraph in this contribution on the historic relation between time and space, it was already pointed out that an expansion of human relations over space is an almost constant historic feature in **social development**. So in that sense globalization goes way back, but that does not seem particularly satisfactory from an analytical and theoretical point of view. Indeed, possible alternative starting points for globalization include the first circumnavigations of the earth between 1519 and 1521; the expansion of European capitalism in the sixteenth century; the rapid increase of European investments in overseas infrastructure and international trade in the so-called first globalization wave (1870–1914); the renewed expansion of international trade by transnationals in the post-World War II period; the fall of the Berlin Wall in 1989 and the subsequent "**end of history**" *à la* Fukuyama.

What drives globalization forward? Here we have a choice between technological progress which obeys its own laws, ongoing modernization (see **modernization theory**) which increasingly infuses rationality into the lives of individuals as a global set of norms and values, and, finally, the historic laws of motion of the capitalist mode of production leading to international concentration and centralization. Actually, there is no reason why these variables could not be operating in close interrelationship.

A related debate concerns the issue of whether globalization can be stopped. The answer depends on whether one considers globalization a structure-led process (e.g. driven forward by the laws of capitalism) or an agency-led process (with, for example, multinational companies, the WTO (see **World Trade Organization/General Agreement on Tariffs and Trade (WTO/GATT)**) and the **World Bank** as major players).

Does globalization mean the end of the nation-state? The assumption that the nation-state is losing control *vis-à-vis* global capitalism is at the very heart of the globalization discourse (see **state and state reform**). The neo-liberal characteristics of globalization are responsible for "rolling back the state." On the other hand, however, it is maintained that nation-states might not be the main economic players in the global game as they used to be, but they remain important in political, strategic and military terms.

Does globalization produce convergence? According to the globalization discourse, the world will be a global village *à la* McLuhan, and this end-result is called globality (see **globalization and culture**). There will be a global culture inhabited by cosmopolitan consumers who comfortably from their homes (by digital means) will choose their world leaders. At the same time, there are those who do not see *per se* a contradiction between a borderless capitalism on the one hand and cultural fragmentation on the other hand. In fact, it is pointed out that, for example, the rise of religious fundamentalism is at least in part a reaction to the homogenizing tendencies in globalization. Increasingly popular is the so-called hybridization thesis, which has it that instead of an overwhelming (Western-based) cultural convergence at global level, or a cultural fragmentation, there will be mixed (hybrid) cultural forms where the global meets the local. Alternative terms, which sometimes are used in the same sense, are syncretism and localization (a combination of globalization and localization).

David Held *et al.* (1999) usefully categorized authors with respect to the above-mentioned contentious issues, i.e. the positive and pessimistic globalists, the traditionalists and the transformationalists. In general, the globalists perceive globalization as a substantive process and not only as a theoretical point of view. The positive globalists emphasize the benefits of globalization (in terms of market efficiency, technological progress, cultural pluralism). The pessimistic globalists, however, consider globalization in terms of an asymmetrical power game, which enhances unevenness in the world. The anti-globalization protest movements are examples of pessimistic globalists. They specifically direct their protests against the destabilizing effects of the large uncontrollable transnational financial flows. Traditionalists believe that globalization is, if not a myth, then highly exaggerated. They see the world as less interdependent than in the 1890s. Instead of a global market, traditionalists stress the rise of the three large regional trading blocs in the Americas, Europe and East Asia. The transformationalists, finally, take up a position in the middle. They accept that there are historically unprecedented levels of global interconnectedness, but believe that the role of the state is not ended nor reinforced but restructured; it now has to share the (inter)national political arena with other non-state actors like NGOs and **new social movements**. They emphasize cultural hybridity instead of the emergence of a homogeneous global **culture**.

See also: Asian crises; capitalism; contagion effect; culture; globalization and culture; sociology of development; transnational capitalist class (TCC); transnational corporations (TNCs); World Social Forum (WSF); World Trade Organization/General Agreement on Tariffs and Trade (WTO/GATT)

Further reading

Albrow, M. (1996) *The Global Age: State and Society Beyond Modernity*, Cambridge: Polity.

Giddens, A. (1984) *The Constitution of Society: Outline of the Theory of Structuration*, Cambridge: Polity.

Harvey, D. (1989) *The Condition of Postmodernity: An Enquiry into the Origins of Cultural Change*, Oxford: Blackwell.

Held, D., Goldblatt, D. and Perraton, J. (eds) (1999) *Global Transformations. Politics, Economics and Culture*, Cambridge: Polity.

Hirst, P. and Thompson, G. (1999) *Globalization in Question: The International Economy and the Possibilities of Governance,* Cambridge: Polity.

McMichael, P. (2000) *Development and Social Change: A Global Perspective,* Thousand Oaks CA: Pine Forge.

Oman, C. (1996) *The Policy Challenges of Globalization and Regionalisation,* Paris: OECD Development Center, Policy brief no. 11.

Scholte, J. (2000) *Globalization: A Critical Introduction,* Basingstoke: Palgrave.

FRANS J. SCHUURMAN

globalization and culture

Debates about globalization and culture refer to impacts of increasing connectivity and information flows around the world on topics such as identity and **community** (see **culture; ethnicity/identity**). "Globalization and culture" is therefore slightly different to other discussions of **globalization** that focus on economic investment and industrial relocation around the world. These two forms of globalization, however, are inherently linked and co-evolve.

A crucial feature of debates about globalization and culture is the social impact of modernity, or the adoption of "modern" means of living including **industrialization** and **urbanization** and their impacts on the standardization of life (see **modernization theory; sociology of development**). Sociologists have argued that the difference between the modern and pre-modern epochs is "time-space distanciation" (see Giddens, 1984), which refers to the increasing complex social relations between people that are no longer restricted to the boundaries of face-to-face relations in a specific locality. "Globalization," therefore, is the increasing connectivity, plus complexity, of social relations.

The **international division of labor**, for example, connects people across the world without knowing each other through the jeans they wear, the cars they drive or through the transnational corporation (see **transnational corporations (TNCs)**) they produce for. Electronic and mass **media, tourism, migration, pollution** – or simply

that time can be expressed in compatible time-tables all over the world – create networks of complex connectivity across geographic distances that characterizes modernity as inherently globalizing. Goods, capital, and information **culture** travel through networks of complex connectivity regardless of its local origin. Globalization disconnects culture from a specific locality – a process also known as "deterritorialization" – only to become reterritorialized in another locality or dimension (Appadurai, 1996).

A common debate is whether "deterritorialization" results in a one global culture or not. Nederveen Pieterse (1996) has identified three strands of debate. The first conceptualizes globalization as a unilinear and neo-liberal process of modernization (see **modernization theory; neo-liberalism**). This process creates a world of sameness, or a homogeneous "Coca-Cola culture" of consumerism (or "McDonaldization"). This is the "convergence" paradigm, of which probably Fukuyama and the anti-globalization movement are the most famous proponents (see **end of history**).

The second approach, or "divergence" paradigm, believes globalization results in more – rather than less – diversity. For example, Huntington's **clash of civilizations** thesis predicts greater tension between cultures in the post-**Cold War** period. The third paradigm includes those who think that globalization does not merely result in more sameness or more dichotomies, but produces complex and diverse mixtures of different cultural segments or elements. This is the "creolization" or the "hybridization" paradigm. These authors are convinced of the perseverance of local **culture**s, combining, adapting and transforming different elements, trends and traditions be they old or new, modern or traditional. Some observers believe that globalization contains elements of all three paradigms.

Globalization as a cultural process has a profound impact on ways of living. Whether globalization presents itself in hybrid forms, in a spread of Western-style consumer culture or some degree of fundamentalist militancy, it profoundly interferes with how people give meaning to objects and ideas. Globalization has become a matter of everyday life through increasing – and unstopping – flows of ideas, people, capital, and consumer goods. It alters cultural representations and therefore influences identity building. Identity is no longer solely confined spatially to the borders of local communities (see **community**) or nations (see **ethnicity/ identity**).

Globalization, however, does not imply the end of the nation-state. Social groups coalesce around a variety of circumstances that form the basis of shared identity, most importantly class, **gender**, sexuality, ethnicity, nationhood (see **ethnicity/ identity; sexualities; nationalism**), but also other themes such as rural/urban, age, religion. These themes, and the representations attached to them, are progressively influenced and constructed by elements that do not necessarily originate from the specific locality of such groups. This means that globalization is not a unidirectional process of "one culture going global" – where the "global" acts as an all-encompassing actor that influences local contexts from above. Instead, globalization is a dialectical process in which the local is always informed by the global and the global is always articulated with and situated by the local: a process also called "glocalization." Glocalization implies that every process of globalization is always situated in power relations, calling for the need of always accounting for one's positionality – i.e. self-awareness of how each actor is located within such power relations.

Debates about globalization and culture challenge orthodox ways of linking culture to specific geographical localities. cultures can no longer be seen as discrete bounded entities. To be able to grasp global and local flux requires us to dismiss the idea that the world is a collection of fixed and nameable groups (Geschiere and Meyer, 1998). Identities are not as exclusive, cohesive and fixed as commonly thought, but turn out to be multiple and dynamic. These conclusions challenge historic ways of looking at the world, and especially the dichotomies within Western thinking about the artificially created cultural "other" as suggested within **Orientalism** and **ethnocentrism**. Culture is intrinsic to how we look at the world. This means that culture and development intersect, and that neither can be understood without the other, placing identity politics and cultural differences permanently on the development agenda.

See also: clash of civilizations; community; culture; end of history; ethnicity/identity; ethnocentrism; globalization; information technology; media; Orientalism

Further reading

Appadurai, A. (1996) *Modernity at Large: Cultural Dimensions of Globalization*, Minneapolis: University Press of Minnesota.

Geschiere, P. and Meyer, B. (1998) "Globalization and Identity: Dialectics of Flows and Closures, Introduction," *Development and Change* 29:4 601–15.

Giddens, A. (1984) *The Constitution of Society: Outline of the Theory of Structuration*, Cambridge: Polity Press.

Inda, J. and Rosaldo, R. (eds) (2002) *The Anthropology of Globalization: A Reader*, Oxford: Blackwell.

Nederveen Pieterse, J. (1996) "Globalization and Culture: Three Paradigms," *Economic and Political Weekly* 31:23 1389–93.

Tomlinson, J. (1999) *Globalization and Culture*, Cambridge: Polity Press.

TINE DAVIDS

GNP *see* gross national product (GNP)

gold standard

The gold standard is a form of exchange rate system (see **exchange rates**) where countries fix their currencies to a specified content of gold bullion that is physically held within each country's gold reserves. Currencies and exchange rates are then determined by the ratio of gold content in their currencies, or the so-called mint parity. For example, if the gold content in a pound sterling and a US dollar is 0.005 and 0.0025 ounces of gold respectively, the exchange rate is 2 dollars per pound. If governments fix the exchange rate at a different rate, say 1.5 dollars per pound, anyone could sell dollars for pounds, exchange pounds for gold from Britain, and ship gold to the USA to exchange for more dollars. Gold would flow out of Britain until the country ran out of gold or governments reset the exchange rate at mint parity. The actual exchange rate can diverge from mint parity within certain margins, called gold points, due to the cost of shipping or insuring gold. The gold standard was used as the main means of establishing the value of currency throughout the nineteenth century, but then was gradually abandoned by participating countries because it became difficult for governments to control money supplies and inflation with the gold standard (see **inflation and its effects**). Britain abandoned the gold standard in 1931; the USA abandoned it in 1971. Since 1971, no circulating paper anywhere was redeemable in gold, and the major international currencies became known as "floating," meaning that their value is determined by demand and supply for them on the open markets.

See also: economic development; exchange rates; fiscal and monetary policy; inflation and its effects; trade

BIN ZHOU

governance

Governance refers to an inclusionary means of politics. It can be distinguished from "government" because this refers to an official body – elected or unelected – that conducts policy-making and decision-making. "Governance," however, refers to a process of decision-making that includes bodies more than just "government," and is a process that, ideally, implies willing participation within politics by all citizens (see also **participatory development; politics**).

A consensus seems to be emerging among official aid agencies, key global inter-state organizations, academicians, and development practitioners that the concept of "**economic development**" is inseparably linked with the notion of "political development." Even those global macro-economic institutions that once refused to acknowledge the role of politics in development now claim that economic development cannot succeed without addressing governance. At the heart of this new

understanding of development is the belief that political democratization (see **democracy**) is a necessary condition for economic development (Leftwich, 1993:603). A considerable amount of **aid** is directed toward **democracy** promotion programs designed to enhance movements toward liberal democracy and free markets (Ottaway and Carothers, 2000). All major bilateral and multilateral aid agencies (see **bilateral aid agencies**), including the **World Bank**, **International Monetary Fund (IMF)**, the **United Nations** system, US Agency for International Development (USAID) and Japan International Cooperation Agency (JICA), are now moving away from a traditional focus on "economic development," to a new focus on "good governance" as the instrument for enhancing **human rights**, democracy, **civil society**, and market-oriented economic reforms. While good governance means different things to different organizations, most official aid agencies view it as an essential precondition for sustainable **economic growth** and **social development** (Islam and Morrison, 1995). Interestingly, this new aid paradigm increases opportunities for collaboration between states (see **state and state reform**), **non-governmental organizations (NGOs)**, and global decision-making organizations, and hence to involve non-state actors on more positive terms than in the past. Critics, however, see good governance as a framework for creating a homogeneous world based on the Western, especially the American, model of development (Moore, 1993).

Governance, markets and the World Bank

Throughout the 1980s, the **World Bank** was primarily occupied with **structural adjustment** programs (SAPs), which assumed that a transition to the market would allow developing countries to solve their growing **debt** crisis, and create a market-friendly structure of economic governance. This structure was expected to restore fiscal discipline (see **fiscal and monetary policy**), develop a healthy private sector, and eventually raise standards of living. Many countries, however, were not able to accomplish the macro-economic goals of SAPs. The majority of economies were either not growing or growing much more slowly than anticipated. Hence, instead of reducing debt, pro-market reforms actually contributed to development problems. Even a World Bank report published in the early 1990s admitted that the debt crisis kept growing in the 1980s (World Bank, 1992). **Poverty** levels continued to rise and common people found it increasingly difficult to cope with the contradictions generated by structural adjustment (Oxfam, 1995).

Faced with these problems, the World Bank (1989) published its first major revisionist analysis, *Sub-Saharan Africa: From Crisis to Sustainable Growth*, which highlighted key factors that prevented African nations from implementing successful market-oriented reform programs. Controversially, the document alleged: "a root cause of weak economic performance in the past has been the failure of public **institutions**" (World Bank, 1989:xii). The document rejected the growing criticism of the Bank's reform agendas, but acknowledged the role of public-sector organizations in fighting poverty and the need to strengthen them in order to accomplish successful economic reform. The document concluded that Africa's economic misery resulted from a crisis of governance, and consequently proposed the solution of "good governance." The Bank later defined governance as "the manner in which power is exercised in the management of a country's economic and social resources for development" (World Bank, 1992:3). The lack of good governance, according to the Bank, prevents an enabling environment for sustainable growth, and intensifies people's suffering. Furthermore, the absence of "good governance" has proved to be particularly damaging to the "corrective intervention" role of government. Programs for poverty alleviation and **environment** and development, for example, can be totally undermined by a lack of public **accountability**, **corruption** and the "capture" of public services by **elites**. Funds intended for the poor may be directed to the benefit of special interest groups, and the poor may have inadequate access to legal remedies (World Bank, 1992:10).

For the Bank, "bad governance" refers to a political system, where power is highly centralized, government intervention is excessive, **corruption** is rampant, and civil servants are not skilled enough to meet the demands of the people (see **public management**). Bad governance also means the absence of accountability and **transparency** in public affairs. The system lacks a clearly defined legal framework necessary for the development of a healthy private sector. The Bank therefore called for in an immediate improvement in the structures of **development management** in the troubled economies. These proposals became known as the much-touted "good governance" program of action. The program offers technical and financial assistance to developing nations to create what it calls "an enabling environment for sustainable and equitable growth" (World Bank, 1992:3, 10). This framework is aimed to provide a more productive use of development resources, thereby alleviating poverty in various parts of the world.

The Bank's good governance program has four main elements: public sector management (PSM) (see **public sector; public management**); **accountability**; a legal framework for development; a degree of transparency and information accessibility (see **media; information technology**) (World Bank, 1994:viii). PSM is primarily concerned with the ability of the **public sector** to effectively manage public programs. It identifies three key areas, namely civil service, financial management, and state enterprise sector (see **state and state reform**), where the need for reform is unavoidable. The Bank supports programs that are specifically designed to restructure/reform the civil service in order to make sure that public sector organizations move away from their traditional interventionist role to the creation of an "enabling environment for the private sector" (World Bank, 1994:2). The notion of accountability also aims to redefine the role of the public sector in national economic development. While one of the main purposes of accountability is to hold "public officials responsible for their actions," one key emphasis is on the creation of a space for private-sector organizations, including NGOs, to deliver services to the people (World Bank, 1994:13). The Bank seeks to make public sector organizations more responsive through administrative **decentralization**, legislative and judicial reform, privatization of **state-owned enterprises (SOEs)**, liberalization of **trade**, and tax reform (see **fiscal** and monetary policy; privatization and liberalization).

The Bank has also called for appropriate legal systems (see **law**) that can enable potential investors to assess costs and risks of potential investments. More importantly, legal and regulatory frameworks serve as conflict resolution mechanisms for investors with other actors (World Bank, 1994:23). It is hoped that promoting transparency may also reduce investment risks by reducing **corruption**; allowing investors to access credible information; and keeping the public informed about the way government functions, hence promoting public debate and participation (World Bank, 1992:39).

Contrary to popular belief, therefore, "good governance" does not necessarily promote the concept of democratic governance. Although it's hard to dispute that good governance is essentially a political project, the Bank's agenda seems to be concerned only with issues related to private sector development and economic growth. The non-political mandate of the Bank prevents it from using it as a means to promote liberal democracy and **human rights**. Indeed, the Bank's constitution states that the Bank is a non-political organization. The Articles of Agreement of the Bank state:

> the Bank and its officers shall not interfere in the political affairs of any member; nor shall they be influenced in their decisions by the political character of the member or members concerned. Only economic considerations shall be relevant to their decisions, and these considerations shall be weighed impartially in order to achieve the purposes stated in Article I.

(See Article III, Section 4 (viii) of the IDA Articles of Agreement for The World Bank)

While the Bank's constitution restrains it from interfering with member countries' internal political affairs, a vast majority of donor countries and agencies have already begun to use good governance as a means to export liberal political and social philosophy (Ottaway and Carothers, 2000). In order to support the movements for democracy in the developing world, many **bilateral aid agencies** have already widened the definition of governance by incorporating a variety of political issues, including **civil society**, freedoms of speech, religion and expression, the rule of law and free and fair elections (Islam and Morrison, 1996). The Canadian government, for instance, views good governance as a framework for implementing broader socio-political programs that are designed to give both democracy and development a chance to survive (Schmitz, 1995). Similarly, when providing aid, the US, British, German and Swedish governments are now attaching more importance to undertaking programs that are directly aimed at the promotion of democracy and the strengthening of associational life.

The United Nations and human development

By contrast, the UN system addresses the issue of governance from a somewhat different perspective. Unlike the World Bank and other official aid agencies, the focus of the UN's good governance programs is not so much on the creation of a market economy, but on the attainment of the goals of **human development** and **sustainable development**. The **United Nations Development Programme (UNDP)**, for instance, identifies three main aspects of governance: economic, political, and administrative governance. Economic governance refers to the creation of a political environment in which different actors freely compete with each other to attain the twin goals of economic growth and social development. Similar to the World Bank's approach, UNDP also seeks to redefine the boundaries of public organizations to create healthy market mechanisms. It strongly believes that without making a transition to the market, the developing world may not be able to attain human development. By contrast, political governance implies the construction of a liberal democratic political system. It encourages governments to adopt policies that would allow people to choose their leaders, enable them to protect their civic rights, and hold the decision-makers accountable for all of their actions. Administrative governance, on the other hand, implies the adoption of policies of civil service reform in order to develop an "administrative system that is honest, efficient and responsive to the people" (UNDP, 1997:27).

A central part of UNDP's governance programs is the redefinition of state (see **state and state reform**), the private sector, and **civil society**. All three actors are urged to cooperate to achieve human development. In order to promote competition, the state, for instance, is required to redefine its role in socio-economic development from acting as an entrepreneur to becoming a market facilitator, including steps to decrease its power in the national economy. Despite this major shift in focus, however, the state is expected to continue to play a crucial role in defending individual civic rights, protecting the natural **environment**, and assisting disadvantaged groups in both participating in economic growth and benefitting from it.

Taking advantage of a liberalized economic environment, the private sector will engage itself in improving human conditions by generating **employment**. And for its part, civil society, including a wide variety of non-state organizations as **trade unions**, NGOs, cultural groups, professional associations, and women's groups, would devote itself to the protection and promotion of popular interests. Societal groups will also make efforts to develop alternative institutions for disadvantaged groups so that they can plan and manage human development at the grassroots level (see **grassroots development**) (UNDP, 1997: 14–18).

Many UN governance programs are directed toward restructuring the **public sector**, holding free and fair elections, and training government and civil society leaders. UNDP is currently providing technical assistance for **capacity building** for democracy with well-known regional and global organizations such as the International Institute for Democracy and Electoral Assistance (IDEA) and *Parlamento LatinoAmericano*. It also aims to increase links between donors and the **voluntary sector**.

Participatory governance

The introduction of governance programs signaled a major change in the way aid was delivered. But critics have suggested that the implicit acceptance

of Western notions of democracy and market **capitalism** within concepts of "governance" fail to acknowledge the complex dynamics of poverty in the developing world, or alternative conceptualizations of **social development**. For example, critics have said that "good governance" programs unfairly blames domestic **institutions** and policies for their inability to implement pro-market reform programs, and overlooks structural causes of poverty (see **dependency theory; world systems theory**). There is a need to distribute costs and benefits of market reforms equally, and not to assume that national **structural adjustment** programs impact on all social sectors equally (Oxfam, 1995:6).

Some critics have also suggested that current approaches to governance reflect the dominant liberal perspective of the American model of socio-economic development (Moore, 1993). They claim that, instead of promoting the **ethics** of democracy and **social justice**, governance programs are used to serve the interests of markets. Programs compel governments of the developing world, as Schmitz (1995:68) suggests, "to manage the *prevailing* capitalist political economy of **globalization**, and notably to manage the resulting social tensions in such a way that the lid does not blow off and threaten the entire elite development regime of accumulation and legitimation" (see **elites**). Others view the notion of governance simply as an administrative approach to economic management that hardly focuses on the promotion of democracy in the developing world (Leftwich, 1993).

Critical authors such as these emphasize the need for us to go beyond the discourse of liberal democracy and market capitalism, and instead to consider alternative, and more diverse means of governance, and especially those that consider more structural causes of poverty and **inequality**. Alternatives may create political spaces in which state and civil society groups work together to promote participatory governance (see **participatory development**), and represent the concerns coming from debates in **gender** and development, as well as diverse social differentiation based on factors such as age, **caste**, wealth, class, etc. Strong emphasis will be given to maintaining an autonomous space for civil society, free from co-optation by state or the market. More importantly, participatory governance may allow communities (see **community**) to create accountable and self-determined institutions based on the participation of ordinary citizens in decision-making. This concept of democratic governance is expected to empower ordinary people to determine the course of sustainable human development in the twenty-first century.

See also: civil society; democracy; gender; new social movements; participatory development; people-centered development; politics; Right to Information Movement; social integration; state and state reform; United Nations; World Bank

Further reading

Islam, N. and Morrison, D. (1996) "Introduction: Governance, Democracy and Human Rights," *Canadian Journal of Development Studies* special issue 30: 5–18.

Leftwich, A. (1993) "Governance, Democracy and Development in the Third World," *Third World Quarterly* 14:3 605–24.

Moore, M. (1993) "Declining to Learn from the East? The World Bank on Governance and Development," *IDS Bulletin* 24:1 39–50.

Ottaway, M. and Carothers, T. (eds) (2000) *Funding Virtue: Civil Society Aid and Democracy Promotion*, Washington DC: Carnegie Endowment for International Peace.

Oxfam (1995) *A Case for Reform: Fifty Years of the IMF and World Bank*, Oxford: Oxfam.

Schmitz, G. (1995) "Democratization and Demystification: Deconstructing Governance as Development Paradigm," pp. 54–90 in Moore, D. and Schmitz, G. (eds) *Debating Development Discourse: Institutional and Popular Perspectives*, London: Macmillan.

UNDP (1997) *Reconceptualizing Governance*, New York: UNDP.

World Bank (1989) *Sub-Saharan Africa: From Crisis to Sustainable Growth*, Washington DC: World Bank.

World Bank (1994) *Governance: The World Bank's Experience*, Washington DC: World Bank.

FAHIM QUADIR

governmentality

The notion of governmentality, developed by Michel Foucault, refers to rationalities of government (see **politics; state and state reform**). It is formed by the semantic joining of governing (*gouverner*), and forms of knowledge or modes of thought (*mentalité*). As an analytical concept, it allows an enquiry into how problematics of government are conceptualized and operationalized in particular societies at particular times in history.

In his 1978 and 1979 lectures at the Collège de France in Paris, Foucault used the concept of governmentality to trace a genealogy of the modern state and its techniques of government. These two series of lectures, entitled respectively "Security, Territory and Population" and "The Birth of Biopolitics," apply this framework to the historical reconstruction of the nature of government in Ancient Greece and early Christianity; the police state in sixteenth-century Europe; the origins of Western liberalism in the eighteenth century; and neo-liberal thought in post-war Europe and the USA (see **neo-liberalism**).

The state, according to Foucault, is only one specific institution in which the problem of "how to govern" is codified. He shifts the focus of analysis from the state to government, broadly characterized as "the conduct of conduct." Governmental rationalities inform activities directed toward shaping the conduct of others and of one's self. Government as the "conduct of conduct" encompasses a continuum of practices ranging from the exercise of political sovereignty; to relations within and across various types of social **institutions** (the school, the prison, the army, etc.); to interpersonal relations involving some form of guidance and control (parenting, counseling, teaching, etc.); to "technologies of the self" evident in the ways in which individuals try to conduct their lives by managing their own bodies and persons (diet, body building, training, etc.). This approach emphasizes the continuities across questions of political authority and questions of individual and collective identity. It asks how are people governed, who governs who, and according to which criteria and ethical standards. Governmental rationalities presuppose the establishment of particular forms of knowledge, which are morally colored and imply intervention on human behavior through institutionalized techniques and procedures.

Foucault's 1978 and 1979 lectures reconstruct the historical processes which resulted in the pre-eminence, in the West, of "government" over other expressions and modalities of power such as sovereignty and discipline, which prevailed at earlier moments in European history. The form of governmentality which emerged in Europe in the eighteenth century is characterized by norms and apparatuses which rely on political economy as principal form of knowledge, and have as their target a population, primarily conceived of as living beings (cf. Foucault, 1991:102–3). Modern governmental practices, emanating from a variety of institutions and operating in more or less explicit ways, are increasingly concerned with controlling intimate domains of human life, including sexual and reproductive conduct. They exercise a type of power that Foucault designates as "biopower" in his *History of Sexuality*. Rather than annulling freedom, "biopolitics" attempts to shape the conduct of people precisely insofar as they are free agents, capable of resisting categorization and acting otherwise. Foucault argues that modern governmentality and the modern autonomous individual are mutually constitutive, and that the history of government as the "conduct of conduct" is interwoven with a history of dissenting "counter-conducts." Although the study of governmentality in Foucault's late work has a specific historical anchoring, this concept has been usefully integrated in interdisciplinary and comparative research programs.

See also: anti-politics; governance; narratives of development; politics; power and discourse; state and state reform

Further reading

Foucault, M. (1982) "Afterword: The Subject and Power," pp. 208–28 in Dreyfus, H. and Rabinow, P., *Michel Foucault: Beyond Structuralism and Hermeneutics*, London: Harvester Wheatsheaf.
Foucault, M. (1991) "Governmentality," pp. 87–104 in Burchell, G., Gordon, C. and Miller, P. (eds) *The Foucault Effect: Studies in Governmentality*, London: Harvester Wheatsheaf.

BENEDETTA ROSSI

Grameen Bank (GB)

The Grameen Bank (GB) in Bangladesh is a well-known example of a banking system that prioritizes the needs of the rural poor. The GB began as an action research project undertaken by Mohammed Yunus, a Chittagong University economics professor, in 1976. The aim was to test the hypothesis that if the rural poor (effectively excluded from formal banks due to their lack of collateral and vulnerable to exploitation by traditional money-lenders) were given access to financial resources on reasonable terms and conditions, they would be able to generate productive self-**employment** without external assistance (see **rural poverty**).

An innovative system of collateral-free lending was developed based on tightly structured five-person groups, and the principle of mutual responsibility for the repayment of each individual loan. Peer-group pressure ensures low transaction costs on small loans and high rates of repayment. Early success led to rapid growth, and GB was formally established as a "specialized financial institution" in 1983, with support from the government, public banks and the International Fund for Agricultural Development (IFAD). GB's key focus has been on lending to landless women to finance primarily non-farm activities such as small-scale trading or animal rearing. GB's lending model has been widely acclaimed and replicated by government, private sector and non-governmental agencies, and the Grameen Trust was set up to promote awareness of micro-finance (see **micro-credit and micro-finance**) and **poverty**. GB was one of the co-organizers of the Washington Micro-Finance Summit in 1997 and GB has inspired a micro-finance institution (MFI) "movement." GB has diversified into information and communications technology (ICT) work (see **information technology**), establishing Grameen Communications in 1997.

GB has not been without its critics. Some have argued that the micro-finance approach depoliticizes the structural causes of poverty; that its services exclude the extreme poor (see **chronic poverty**); that it can trap the poor in low **productivity** enterprises (see **poverty trap**); and that its claims for women's **empowerment** hides the fact that loans given to female household members may in practice be controlled by males. Nevertheless, GB is one of the few real "success" stories of **grassroots development** and remains one of Bangladesh's most visible and popular exports.

See also: micro-credit and micro-finance; non-governmental organizations (NGOs); people-centered development; poverty; rural poverty

Further reading

Website: http://www.grameen.com

Goetz, A.-M. and Sen Gupta, R. (1996) "Who Takes the Credit?: Gender, Power and Control over Loan Use in Rural Credit Programmes in Bangladesh," *World Development* 24:1 45–63.

Holcombe, S. (1995) *Managing to Empower: The Grameen Bank's Experience of Poverty Alleviation*, London: Zed Books.

DAVID LEWIS

grassroots activism

Grassroots activism describes the activism conducted by poor people in establishing **grassroots development**, i.e. where development objectives are identified and conducted by local people on their own terms. The idea of grassroots activism is addressed in three bodies of literature. In the first, broader one, the central issue is the plea for bottom-up development (see **participatory development**), born out of criticism of interventionist and centralized visions of development. This approach to grassroots activism is similar to demands for grassroots development itself, and places trust in peoples' capacities to perceive development problems and opportunities, and believes that only transformations carried out and controlled by the beneficiaries are lasting and relevant (see **weapons of the weak**). This approach was criticized in the 1980s and 1990s, however, for alleged naively

overlooking the heterogeneity of communities (see **community**), or naively idolizing grassroots diagnoses of problems and their subsequent remedies (see **local knowledge**).

Second, grassroots activism has been discussed in debates on **new social movements** since the 1960s, which saw social movement as the grassroots' new political protagonism. The movements were seen as harbingers of "new politics" by introducing new, including ethical, concerns in politics based on different classes acting together rather than on old materialist grounds. The state was criticized for its shortcomings in governing, its corruption and its unrepresentative nature (see **state and state reform**). But this critique tended to result in "basismo," which had a propensity to disregard the state's and its institutions' role in the pursuit of development. The subsequent critique of "basismo" focused upon issues such as the questionable suggestion of an independent, parallel system of (self) **governance**, and the tenuous translation of the promotion of grassroots influence in decision-making into social movements' political and developmental solipsism.

Finally, grassroots activism has been discussed in **globalization** debates as a catchphrase relating to new approaches to politics and activism such as transnational **civil society** and "cyberspaced" social activism. Global communication is believed to help counter current political and economic globalization, as it might enhance more effective activism, lobbying and litigation, and facilitate crucial media-interest, to foster goals in the realms of environmental preservation, or **human rights** compliance, and others (see **media**). But the **inequality** of access to these new communications media, and the limits of transnational solidarity, have raised doubts about this idea's feasibility (see **information technology**).

See also: grassroots development; grassroots organizations; liberation theology; new social movements; peasant movements; political ecology; weapons of the weak

Further reading

Community Development Journal, published by Oxford University Press.

Kaufman, M. and Alfonso, H. (eds) (1997) *Community Power and Grassroots Democracy: The Transformation of Social Life*, London: Zed Books.

TON SALMAN

grassroots development

Grassroots development is an approach that challenges top-down, modernization (see **modernization theory**) perspectives to development as well as welfare approaches that view communities (see **community**) and individuals as passive recipients of development. In contrast to these perspectives, grassroots development seeks to empower self-help groups to make their own choices and bring about positive change to improve the quality of their lives in a sustainable way. The concepts "holistic development," "**participatory development**," "community-based development," "**people-centered development**" and "grassroots development" are often used interchangeably.

The grassroots perspective of development centralizes people, who are actual targets of development, as participants, decision-makers and beneficiaries in development processes. Thus, **social capital** (the norms and networks that enable collective action at the local level) is deemed to be the most important resource for **poverty** alleviation. The notion of holistic and **community**-driven development becomes a goal as well as a desirable method for achieving development. Development that has direct and sustainable benefits to those who need it the most – and which results in redistribution of resources and power – depends on the effective organization of poor, landless or marginalized people. This alternative, radical departure from conventional top-down development starts with the problems faced daily by people, their concerns and their experiences. A central aspect is that most developmental problems at the local level are complex and inter-related. Thus, attempts to address any one problem in isolation of other factors leads to only marginal returns or sometimes even worsens a situation.

Many **non-governmental organizations (NGOs)** and governments have realized that the

empowerment of local communities to meet their own needs in a sustainable manner is complex and challenging. Interventions often involve investment or **capacity building** in communities and social groups; responding to development needs and priorities identified by the community; environment protection; **targeting** resources to the poorest; and recognizing the rights of people to make choices and decisions. The role of external agencies is to assist in facilitation, the mobilization of resources and the sharing of information and experiences. In this regard, **education** is a central component of grassroots development and is deemed to play a critical role in empowerment. Effective grassroots development frequently depends on political **decentralization** and a transfer of **accountability** from the state or official development assistance to community-based organizations (CBOs).

Yet, achieving successful grassroots development is difficult because it depends on ensuring a successful transfer of experience, skills and technical know-how to members of the community. Such transfer and empowerment requires careful monitoring of relationships between outsiders and local people in order to ensure that the relationship does not shape the direction of assistance. Furthermore, local **elites** may benefit disproportionately. One main requirement is that external agencies are committed to the agendas and priorities of local communities rather than the budget and political imperatives of the donors. Moreover, communities are highly heterogeneous and are socially differentiated by race, class, **gender**, lineage, ethnicity, etc. (see **race and racism; ethnicity/identity; sociology of development**). Development workers need to acknowledge this diversity, to shape their means of empowerment, and to acknowledge that grassroots development frequently does not mean the discovery of local consensus, but the creation of local means of debate.

See also: community; community-based natural resource management (CBNRM); equitable development; grassroots activism; grassroots organizations; liberation theology; participatory development; people-centered development

Further reading

Fox, A. and Brown, D. (1998) *The Struggle for Accountability: The World Bank, NGOs, and Grassroots*, Cambridge MA: MIT Press.

Momsen, J. (2002) "NGOs, Gender and Indigenous Grassroots Development," *Journal of International Development* 14:6 859–67.

URMILLA BOB

grassroots organizations

Grassroots organizations (GROs) are concerned with association-formation and social mobilization at the local level, drawing upon non-state relationships including **civil society** networks, familial connections, and cultural, religious, and ethnic ties. They are not synonymous with mainstream **non-governmental organizations (NGOs)**, but like NGOs they are an important element of the **new social movements** that emerged during the 1960s and 1970s. Some grassroots organizations resemble neighborhood associations or locally oriented, place-based social movements, and often form in response to specific issues or crises. Examples include citizens' initiatives on **pollution**, safety and **health** concerns, and **community**-based struggles for equity, **social justice**, and especially against environmental racism. In many developing countries, grassroots organizations have included **indigenous peoples**' networks, anti-**dams** campaigns, and **human rights** protection movements. While grassroots organizations often suggest non-hierarchical structures and an embrace of democratic principles, the 1990s has seen the emergence of groups that self-identify as "grassroots" yet function in reality as fronts for corporate and private interests.

See also: community; grassroots activism; grassroots development; new social movements; non-governmental organizations (NGOs); weapons of the weak

PABLO SHILADITYA BOSE

green revolution

The 'green revolution' refers to the impact of **technology transfer** and technology adaptation on tropical and semi-tropical **agriculture** since the late 1950s. Over time, the green revolution has come to be associated with a package of technologies made up of improved seeds commonly referred to as high-yielding varieties, or HYVs, which typically yielded twice the amount of grain to each unit application of fertilizer (see **fertilizers**) and water compared to traditional cultivars for at least the first 70kg of nitrogen fertilizer per hectare. The green revolution also referred to a variety of changed agronomic practices that improved **productivity**, including means of soil preparation, planting depth and density, more intensive weeding practices, and harvesting methods. It also included the introduction of new inputs to agriculture such as **fertilizers** and other **agrochemicals** (e.g. herbicides), **mechanization**, and new means of **water management** (including **irrigation**), which usually added to, or displaced traditional cultivars and crop management with so-called scientific farming methods.

There is little doubt that the green revolution has greatly increased the capacity of the world's farming systems to produce **food**. Consider the data in Table 2.

With the dramatic exception of Africa, developing countries have become more self-reliant in food production since the release of the first HYVs in the early 1960s. In a sense, one can say that Asia has been the biggest winner from the green revolution. Many countries in Asia that were seriously dependent on food imports or **food aid** in the decades prior to 1980 – such as Bangladesh, China, India, Indonesia, Malaysia, Pakistan and the Philippines – have joined the ranks of food exporting nations, reduced their dependence on food aid, or significantly reduced their dependence on food imports. For these reasons, proponents of the green revolution have claimed that it allowed rapid population growth with radically reduced rates of **famine**.

The adoption of green-revolution technologies was also achieved through a network of international agricultural research centers (IARCs) supported by the **World Bank**-based **Consultative**

Table 2 Per capita food production trends 1960–2000

| | Annual average per capita food production (index based on 1989–91 = 100) | | | | | | | |
	1961/5	*1966/70*	*1971/5*	*1976/80*	*1981/5*	*1986/90*	*1991/5*	*1996/00*
Africa Developing countries	109.0	108.7	106.8	99.7	94.6	97.6	100.4	103.8
Asia Developing countries	70.4	72.2	73.4	77.7	87.5	96.4	108.9	124.5
Latin America and Caribbean	83.0	86.4	86.3	93.6	97.0	99.0	103.6	112.9
Developing Countries total	76.8	78.8	79.5	83.3	90.3	97.1	106.8	119.4

Source: FAO (2001). FAOSTATS (online) available from: http://apps.fao.org

Group on International Agricultural Research (**CGIAR**) (see Baum, 1986). Yet, the key actors in bringing the green revolution into being were members of a small group of colleagues from the Rockefeller (George Harrar, Sterling Wortman and Norman Borlaug) and Ford Foundations (Frosty Hill and Lowell Hardin), plus Cornell and Chicago Universities (Ted Schultz and David Hopper). This group launched a scientific research program, first, at the Wheat and Maize Improvement Centre (CIMMYT) in Mexico, and then, at the International Rice Research Institute (IRRI) in the Philippines, based on the hypothesis that superior cultivars could be found or bred if only a sufficient number of field trials and plant crosses could be made. Plant breeders became the lynchpins of the scientific effort to produce HYVs, while agronomists tested the performance of HYVs in farm conditions (see **science and technology**). Hundreds of varieties were tested in strictly managed plots, and varieties with given characteristics selected out and crossed to produce new varieties with preferred characteristics. In a remarkably short time, the research produced superior cultivars that exhibited shorter straw length in the adult plant and a greater leaf area to capture more sunlight. As a result, the HYVs were believed to make more efficient use of sunlight and convert more of their growth potential into grain instead of straw. No attempt was made at this time to select for efficiency of root structure as a key factor bearing on the efficiency of resource use by the plant.

Despite these initial successes, the green revolution has received criticisms for various reasons, although not all criticisms have been borne out. First, the revolution impacted differentially on producers and consumers of food. Farm-gate prices for the major staples of corn, wheat and rice have declined in real terms in every decade since 1950, resulting in threatened income for farmers. As a result, the green revolution may have done a great deal to banish famine and chronic starvation by making food cheaper and more plentiful, but it has done little to reduce **poverty** in farm households (see also **rural poverty**). Yet, by making food cheaper, the green revolution has probably reduced levels of **urban poverty**.

Second, the green revolution has been differential in its impacts. The spread of HYVs has been universal in irrigated cereal cropping. In rainfed agriculture (such as commonly experienced in uplands; see **mountain development**), HYVs have yet to make a major impact.

Third, and more important, there has also been concern that the green revolution would force smallholders off the land because it might empower larger landowners, or those with resources to benefit from the new technologies disproportionately from small landholders. This fear has proven groundless in the case of food crops because the real prices of rice, wheat and corn fell too much to make growing these crops profitable. Instead, increasing landlessness must be explained by the spread of other forces, in particular broadacre livestock farming, industrial crop production (**agribusiness**), and the destruction of millions of acres of tree-crop areas. The spread of urban living has also consumed a lot of land that overtook smallholders occupying land that had been in the low-rent districts but which urban trends transformed into areas with a high opportunity cost for housing and horticulture to serve city markets.

Fourth, other critics have also claimed that the **commercialization** of the green revolution, its links to **globalization**, and the increasing use of Western science and technology (see **science and technology**), especially – increasingly – genetically modified seeds (see **biotechnology and resistance; genetically modified organisms (GMOs)**), lead ultimately to reduced development prospects for poor farmers in developing countries (see Shiva, 1992). As an alternative, such critics have called for greater scientific diversity in approaches to agricultural development, an active role for **local knowledge**, and restrictions on agribusiness and **transnational corporations (TNCs)**.

And fifth, the green revolution has been blamed for being environmentally unsustainable because of its dependence on **irrigation** and inorganic agrochemical use (see **agrochemicals**). The spread of HYVs has narrowed the gene pool that is cultivated, making HYV-based farming more vulnerable to catastrophic losses to pests and pathogens, with the result that farmers using HYVs have also increased their use of chemical agents to control crop losses to disease and insect infestations. Greater use of inorganic fertilizers and other agrochemicals in an irrigation-based farming system, which is the norm when growing HYVs, has also raised the risks associated with toxic chemical build-up in the soil. **Salinization** may occur when salts are brought to the surface by irrigation.

These criticisms are still contested by proponents and opponents of the green revolution. Undoubtedly, the use of green-revolution technologies have increased macro-scale food production in many developing countries. Yet, clearly, **rural development** in general cannot be addressed simply in technological terms, and the social, economic and political contexts of new technologies have to be evaluated before assessing their impacts on people's **livelihoods**. Current research addresses

various relevant themes. The so called "second-generation" problems of the green revolution, such as agrochemical use, have come to dominate the research agendas of most IARCs associated with the **Consultative Group on International Agricultural Research (CGIAR)** system. Other workers in rural development are instead focusing more on the **sustainable livelihoods** and **food security** of poor farmers, in order to ensure that increased technological intervention may provide benefits for the maximum range of people rather than being measured only in terms of increased food production (see Lipton *et al.*, 2002).

See also: agriculture; agrochemicals; agroforestry; biotechnology and resistance; Consultative Group on International Agricultural Research (CGIAR); dryland agriculture; famine; fertilizers; food; food aid; food security; genetically modified organisms (GMOs); irrigation; land tenure; rural development; rural poverty; science and technology

Further reading

Baum, W. (1986) *Partners Against Hunger,* Washington DC: CGIAR.

Consultative Group on International Agricultural Research (CGIAR) website: http://www.cgiar.org/

Das, R. (2002) "The Green Revolution and Poverty: A Theoretical and Empirical Examination of the Relation between Technology and Society," *Geoforum* 33:1 55–72.

Kaosa-ard, M. and Rerkasem, B. (2000) *The Growth and Sustainability of Agriculture in Asia,* Oxford: Oxford University Press.

Lipton, M., Sinha, S. and Blackman, R. (2002) "Reconnecting Agricultural Technology to Human Development," *Journal of Human Development* 3:1 123–52.

Mosley, P. (2005) *Green Revolution in Africa,* London: Routledge.

Pingali, P., Hossain, M. and Geracio, R. (1997) *Asian Rice Bowls: The Returning Crisis,* Oxford: CAB International for CIMMYT and IRRI.

Shiva, V. (1992) *The Violence of the Green Revolution: Third World Agriculture, Ecology and Politics*, London: Zed.

Tripp, R. (2001) "Agricultural Technology Policies for Rural Development," *Development Policy Review* 19:4 479–89.

JOE REMENYI

gross domestic product (GDP)

Gross domestic product (GDP) is the most commonly used measurement of national income. GDP is the total value of final goods and services at market prices (corrected for duplications in fuel, raw materials, and semi-finished products), produced in an economy during a specific period (usually a year). It excludes income earned by domestic residents from overseas investments, but includes income earned in the domestic economy by non-nationals. GDP does not deduct the value of expenditure on capital goods for replacement purposes. As GDP is a measure of what is produced in an economy, it is also a measure of economic activity and is therefore widely used as an indicator of social welfare or **well-being**. The methodology to calculate GDP (and other standard national accounts, such as **gross national product (GNP)**, etc.) was primarily formulated by Simon Kuznets during the 1940s (see **Kuznets curve**). This methodology is now used by nearly all nations. GDP per capita is calculated by dividing GDP by **population**.

See also: gross national product (GNP); gross national product (GNP) per capita; indicators of development; measuring development

MATTHEW CLARKE

gross national product (GNP)

Gross national product (GNP) is a measurement of national income closely related to **gross domestic product (GDP)**. GNP is the total value of final goods and services at market prices (corrected for duplications in fuel, raw materials, and semi-finished products), produced in an economy during a specific period (usually a year) and includes income earned by nationals overseas but it excludes income earned domestically by non-nationals. As with GDP, no allowance is made for the depreciation or consumption of capital used in production. For economies with a high reliance on **foreign direct investment** (such as developing countries), GNP is usually lower than GDP as the latter includes the income earned by this foreign direct investment. For net investing economies, GNP is usually higher than GDP as overseas income is taken into account. The differences between GDP and GNP however are generally not significant. **Gross national product (GNP) per capita** is calculated by dividing GNP by **population**.

See also: gross domestic product (GDP); gross national product (GNP) per capita; indicators of development; measuring development

MATTHEW CLARKE

gross national product (GNP) per capita

One relatively simple form of **poverty measurement**, that has been used extensively by the **World Bank** to rank countries with respect to relative **poverty**, is gross national product (GNP) per capita. This measurement involves dividing a country's GNP by the total **population** to provide a rough measure of average income for that country. Thus, in 1998–9 the World Bank ranked Mozambique as the poorest country with a GNP per capita in constant US$90, and Switzerland as the richest country with a GNP per capita of US$44,320.

GNP per capita is easy to calculate, as data on both GNP and population are available for most countries. However, it suffers from a serious drawback by ignoring **income distribution**, and the more unequal the distribution of income, the more misleading GNP per capita will be as a measure of relative poverty.

Where detailed information is available on the distribution of income, an improvement could be obtained by taking the median income of the population. However, usually only summary data on income distribution are available, giving the proportion of total income going to deciles or quintiles of the population, so that the median income cannot be calculated. In this case, a rough correction can be made that will yield a more representative measure of the income of the poor, by calculating the GNP per capita for the part of the population in the lowest 20 percent of the income distribution. For example, the latest data on Brazil show that the lowest 20 percent of the population only received 2.5 percent of GNP, the second received 5.7 percent, the third 9.9 percent, the fourth 17.7 percent, while the richest fifth quintile received 64.2 percent, giving Brazil the most unequal distribution of income (*World Development Report, 1998–1999*). Given that the GNP of Brazil in 1997, measured was a constant US$1,0199.9 billion, the 2.5 percent going to the poorest 20 percent of the population amounted to US$25.4975 million. The population of Brazil in 1997 was 164 million, so that 20 percent represents 32.8 million Brazilians. Dividing the 2.5 percent of **gross national product (GNP)** that went to the poorest 32.8 million yields a GNP per capita (20 percent poorest) of a constant US$777. This may be compared with the **World Bank**'s figure for GNP per capita in constant US dollars of $6,240.

In a ranking of eighty-six countries by GNP per capita in 1998–9, Brazil appears to be the 33rd richest country. However, when the ranking is carried out using the alternative GNP per capita (20 percent poorest), Brazil drops to 54th place. This position at 54th agrees much more closely than does its GNP per capita ranking of 33rd with its ranking with respect to correlates of poverty, such as (i) the under-five infant mortality rate per 1,000 live births (ranked 50th) (see **infant and child mortality**), (ii) the **maternal mortality** rate per 1,000 live births (55th), (iii) **life expectancy** at birth (56th), (iv) the percentage of the population not expected to reach the age of sixty (58th) and (v) the percentage literacy rate for males (52nd) and females (47th).

Brazil is an extreme case, with its exceptionally unequal distribution of income, but this example illustrates that GNP per capita may not be representative of the average income of a country, and that its use in making comparisons across countries is likely to produce misleading results.

See also: absolute versus relative poverty; gross domestic product (GDP); gross national product (GNP); growth measurement; growth rate; income distribution; inequality; inequality and poverty, world trends; poverty

Further reading

Vaury, O. (2003) "Is GDP a Good Measure of Economic Progress?" *Post-Autistic Economics Review* 20: article 3. http://www.paecon.net

JIM THOMAS

Group of 77 (G-77)

The Group of 77 (G-77) is a coalition of developing countries that frequently takes high-profile negotiating positions in international negotiations on trade, **environment**, or other aspects of development. G-77 was established by the 15 June 1964 "Joint Declaration of the Seventy-Seven Countries," at the close of the first session of the United Nations Conference on Trade and Development in Geneva. Prompted by the **Bandung conference (1955)**, the coalition of developing countries crystallized during the **Cold War** tensions of the 1960–70s, as newly independent nations formed the **non-aligned movement** to eschew the **neocolonialism** of the USSR, the USA and their allies. The first G-77 ministerial meeting was held in Algiers in 1967.

G-77 elaborates and promotes the common interests of its member countries on major international economic and technical issues. It strengthens the joint negotiating capacity of developing nations within the **United Nations**. Despite its name, G-77 claims more than 130 members, divided into five chapters, which make G-77 the largest coalition of developing countries in the UN. G-77 retains its name due to its historic significance.

See also: Bandung conference (1955); international economic order; non-aligned movement; South-South cooperation; United Nations

MARLÈNE ELIAS

growth measurement

Traditional measures of **growth rate**s or **economic growth** focus narrowly on increases in real per capita income, **gross domestic product (GDP)** or the capital stock. Researchers in international **economic development** often broaden these narrow measures to include a wide host of growth indicators, such as nutritional standards (see **nutrition**), infrastructure development (including the number of roads, airports, hospitals and educational facilities), **infant and child mortality**, reductions in tariff barriers or trade openness (see **tariffs**), and computer use and availability (see, for example, **Human Development Index (HDI); indicators of development**). Interest is also usually directed toward changes in total factor productivity (TFP) as a specific combined measure of the contribution of technology, **technology transfer**, market reform, political stability and improved institutional development as sources and measures of economic growth. The point is important since growth can be achieved by merely increasing the amount of available inputs used in production (and hence often degrading the **environment** or the stock of **natural capital**), whereas increases in TFP allow for increases in growth with no or little change in inputs.

There is considerable controversy over making international comparisons in measures of income and growth. The use of market **exchange rates**, for example, to translate incomes into a common currency (from which measures of economic growth are constructed) introduces a "traded sector bias." Since wide variations across countries in the prices of non-traded goods and services are not reflected in the market for foreign exchange, income measures do not reflect purchasing power in each country accurately. They often exaggerate income differentials by ignoring the often-lower cost of living in developing countries, and especially in those that offer less expensive labor-intensive services in the non-traded sector (Dowrick, 2001). It is also the case that the sales of many goods and services in developing countries do not occur in a market context and hence never enter measures of income and growth in the first place, regardless of the use of foreign exchange rates for measurement. Work by economic researchers, and research at the **World Bank** and the **Organization for Economic Cooperation and Development (OECD)**, are attempting to correct for these distortions, obtaining "true measures" of income and growth.

Finally, there is now a growing awareness among economists that measures of growth must account for natural resource use (see **natural resources**), something that has always been excluded from conventional national income accounting. Growth in income that damages the environment or depletes natural resources, for example, necessarily overstates the increase in income and growth that go with development. Attempts to evaluate the loss in **natural capital** through processes of creating income is now a vigorous research program in economics. With this, the concept of sustainable development, or growth that leaves the natural capital stock in place, in some form or another, is now key to our understanding and measurement of growth (see also **sustainable development**).

See also: economic development; economic growth; growth rate; growth versus holism; indicators of development; measuring development; natural capital

Further reading

Dowrick, S. (2001) "True International Income Comparisons: Correcting for Bias in Fixed Price Measures and Exchange Rate Measures," working papers, School of Economics, Australian National University, Canberra.
Landes, D. (1998) *The Wealth and Poverty of Nations*, New York: Norton.

TOM KOMPAS

growth rate

The growth rate, or the rate of **economic growth**, measures the change in per capita values of real **gross domestic product (GDP)**, consumption, or the capital stock. Growth rates are usually constructed in one of two ways. The first is to simply define the difference between the values (say) of real GDP between two periods, divided by the value of GDP in the earliest of these periods. The result is a proportional rate of growth and is typically measured in adjacent periods through time. This value can fluctuate considerably, period by period. The second approach is to define a cumulative growth index, as the change in GDP (in any given period), by dividing real GDP in each year by a base year value, thus set equal to 100. Much like any index number construction, this allows for a defined growth index relative to the base year (that is, so many percentage points larger or smaller than the base year), which is generally less volatile than year-to-year measures of the growth rate. However, it suffers form the fact that all results depend on the choice of the base year. A relatively good year for example, with a high value of GDP, will bias downwards the index for all successive years.

Theoretical explanations for the growth rate or differences in growth rates are far more contentious. Standard neo-classical theory argues that growth rates largely depend (given some parametric change such as an increase in the savings rate) on the distance from the economy's current position to the steady state. The result is driven by an assumption that production exhibits diminishing returns (or output increases but at a decreasing rate) to increases in the capital-labor ratio. This characteristic is often used to explain why countries such as Taiwan, Singapore and Hong Kong have high growth rates relative to the USA. Their initial capital stocks are small (both within country and compared to the USA) relative to their ultimate steady state values, so growth will be faster. This is similar to a common and equally valid argument that claims that starting from a "low base" implies faster percentage growth initially.

More modern or **endogenous growth theory** focuses not just on the distance to steady state as a determinate of the growth rate but also on key model parameters, notably those that determine the willingness to save and the productivity of capital, usually broadly defined to include **human capital** as well as physical capital. A high desire for savings and technological improvements or transfers that increase the marginal product of capital thus increase both the short-term and (unlike in standard neo-classical approaches) the long-run rate of growth. Emphasis on growth without necessarily increasing inputs in production, through the transfer and diffusion of technology, is of first importance in this research.

See also: economic growth; endogenous growth theory; growth measurement; growth versus holism; human capital; technology transfer

Further reading

Aghion, P. and Howitt, P. (1998) *Endogenous Growth Theory*, Cambridge MA: MIT Press.
Jones, C. (1998) *Introduction to Economic Growth*, London: Norton.

TOM KOMPAS

growth versus holism

The growth versus holism debate refers to the relative emphasis that should be placed on **economic growth** *vis-à-vis* additional, and more social, cultural, and political aspects of development. It is arguably one of the most important debates that shape the practice of international development.

Economic growth is the expansion in the aggregate output in an economy over time, commonly measured by **gross national product (GNP)**. GNP when corrected for the effects of inflation (see **inflation and its effects**) (to derive real GNP) and **population** growth gives a measure of the welfare implications of growth known as the real gross national product (GNP) per capita. Nevertheless, **growth measurement**s are imperfect indicators of **well-being** as they are based exclusively on market values, thereby omitting the welfare effects of non-market production. For example, contribution of women's labor to household coping or survival strategies (see **coping**

strategies) in times of crisis, though welfare enhancing is unaccounted for thereby resulting in an exaggeration of the welfare effects of **employment** opportunities outside the household. Similarly, they ignore the negative externalities imposed upon communities (see **community**) whose satisfaction of basic needs is hinged upon collective subsistence on **common pool resources**; ecological destruction engendered by energy (see **energy policy**) and natural resource intensive patterns of industrial and agricultural growth (see **natural resources**) undermines **indigenous peoples**' rights, communities' livelihood security (see **livelihoods**) and aggravates their **marginalization**.

Arguably, patterns of development that are driven by the logic of market-based growth generate many unintended consequences due to their narrow, income-based definition of welfare. The reductionist models of the economic structure and processes which take distribution of income as given and focus exclusively on the interrelated flows of income and product, are inherently biased toward resources and inputs for growth rather than on the quality of growth. In practice, they engender **trickle down** and *laissez faire* policies whose usefulness in **poverty** reduction efforts is often counterproductive.

Consequently, the conceptual and instrumental value of holism is advanced in seeking to remedy such failures of growth. Holism is a concept of well-being that recognizes deprivation as being multidimensional, i.e. consisting of material, political, ecological, psychological and social aspects which in reality are mutually reinforcing and interrelated. Some theorists refer to this phenomenon as the principle of circular causation, or the vicious circle of poverty. This generally means that one aspect of poverty is simultaneously a cause and an effect of the other aspects. Thus, holistic approaches to poverty reduction are based on definitions of poverty that include notions of **social exclusion**, stigma, sustainability, **vulnerability** and powerlessness. These employ measures of well-being that combine income and other measures of human capability (see **capability approach**), e.g. the **Human Development Index (HDI)** developed by the **United Nations Development Programme (UNDP)**. They are therefore of more practical relevance to development practitioners and policy-makers in guiding interventions that enhance opportunities for alleviating poverty of choice and opportunities than economic growth alone.

See also: cost-benefit analysis (CBA); culture; economic growth; growth measurement; growth rate; human development; Human Development Index (HDI); people-centered development; poverty

MOSES A. OSIRO

Habitat I and II

The Habitat I and II conferences provide clear pointers to changing interpretations and policy responses toward **housing**. The first Habitat conference took place in Vancouver in 1976, and proved to be a watershed in influencing housing policy throughout the world. From the 1960s onwards accelerating urban **population** growth, closely linked to increasing **rural-urban migration**, led to the unprecedented growth of **shantytowns** and squatter settlements (see **squatters**) around many of the larger cities in the developing world. At this time, forced evictions and demolitions of informal settlements were commonplace, largely justified by the illegal nature of the settlements, and fears of social unrest and **crime**. However, during the 1970s there was increasing evidence of the innovative approaches developed by the poor to improve their own living environments, and a parallel recognition of the inability of both market-led solutions and **public sector** building programs to provide housing for the urban poor (see **urban development**). The Habitat I conference in 1976 was instrumental in bringing these ideas to world attention, and led to the formation of the United Nations Center for Human Settlements (UNCHS (Habitat)) two years later.

The promotion of "enablement" as opposed to "provision" was effectively an inversion of previous ideas, and proposed an active role for the poor in the provision of their own housing through "aided self-help" including settlement upgrading, core housing and site and service schemes. This endorsement of enabling strategies emphasized "the central role of human resources as an agent for development." It also included recommendations that planners should work more closely with the people and encourage their potential for self-determination; that communities (see **community**) should be involved in the planning, implementation and management of neighborhood schemes; that standards for shelter, infrastructure and services should be based on the needs and priorities of the population; that legislative, institutional and financial measures should be re-orientated to facilitate people's involvement in meeting their own needs for social services; and that public participation is a right, and efforts should be made to expand and strengthen the role of **community**-based organizations.

Habitat II was convened in 1996 in Istanbul to assess progress over the intervening two decades. Again representatives of governments, international agencies and **non-governmental organizations (NGOs)** (more organized and vocal than twenty years earlier) assembled and produced the Habitat Agenda, which reaffirmed a participatory role for the poor, local control and *in-situ* settlement upgrading. Reflecting the **brown environmental agenda** and sustainability concerns of the 1990s (**Agenda 21**), Habitat II placed emphasis on "sustainable human settlements" as well as "shelter for all," and identified the necessity to "explore how human settlement policies can help increase social equity, social integration and social stability" (UNCHS, 1996). The documentation articulated a more inclusive view of urban development to address the role of local government, new principles of environment planning and management and the reduction of **poverty**.

See also: brown environmental agenda; housing; ghettos; shantytowns; squatters; urban development; urbanization

Further reading

Pugh, C. (2000) *Sustainable Cities in Developing Countries: Theory and Practice at the Millennium*, London: Earthscan.

United Nations Center for Human Settlements (Habitat) (1996) *An Urbanizing World: Global Report on Human Settlements 1996*, Oxford: Oxford University Press.

PETER KELLETT

habitats

A habitat is the spatial environment within which a species or organism lives, or in which it could live, because this area contains all the physical and biological characteristics needed for the species' survival. These local surroundings are sometimes referred to as the species' "address," for they supply all the requirements of its home, such as shelter, **food**, water and breeding sites. To be a complete (as opposed to marginal) habitat, the area must supply all the requirements for each life stage of the species (e.g. larvae to adult). Beyond this single species perspective, every **environment** has a broad range of characteristics that can support many species. On this broader scale, habitats are often described by their dominant physical characteristic (e.g. level of aridity) or by their dominant plant type (e.g. oak trees). These larger habitats can then be grouped into habitat types by the similarity of their dominant characteristics (e.g. oak woodlands).

See also: biodiversity; environment

MICHAEL J. STARR

Harris-Todaro model

The Harris-Todaro model describes the link between the expected rural-urban real wage differential and the supply of labor to the urban labor market (see **labor markets**). It represents significant progress in understanding the role of economic incentives underlying decisions for **migration**. The model predicts that the flow of **rural-urban migration** will end once the expected rural-urban wage differential has disappeared. Holding the wage differential to zero, the model predicts an increase in the **migration** flow once job creation rates in urban centers improve. This is due to the chain-migration type processes whereby the would-be migrant relies on news from urban centers as an important part of his efforts in completing his information matrix. The model has been criticized for its neo-classical tendency of ignoring many of the social drivers determining the push and pull effects associated with the migration decision.

See also: labor markets; labor supply; migration; rural-urban migration

PARVIZ DABIR-ALAI

HARROD-DOMAR-KALDOR MODEL *see* Kuznets curve; growth rate; redistribution with growth

hazardous waste

Hazardous wastes are by-products of industrial or household activities that contain substances hazardous to life (see also **brown environmental agenda; pollution**). They range from materials contaminated with dioxins and heavy metals, such as mercury, cadmium or lead, to organic wastes. The waste may take many forms, from barrels of liquid sludge to old computer parts, used batteries or incinerator ash. Industry and mining are the main sources of hazardous wastes in industrialized countries, though small-scale industry, hospitals, military establishments, transport services, and small workshops all contribute to the generation of hazardous wastes in the industrialized and developing worlds.

Improper handling and disposal of hazardous wastes can affect human health and the environment through leakage of toxins into groundwater, soil, waterways, and the atmosphere. Environmental and health effects can be immediate – such as onsite human exposure to toxic chemicals in the waste – or long-term – contaminated waste can leach into groundwater or soil and then into the food chain. Damage caused by hazardous wastes also takes an economic toll, and cleaning up contaminated sites can be costly for local authorities, particularly if they are located in poor communities (see **community**).

Due to widely differing national definitions of hazardous waste, exact figures regarding the amount of hazardous waste generated internationally are not available. Estimates vary from 300–500 million tons per year in the 1990s, with **Organization for Economic Cooperation and Development (OECD)** countries responsible for 80–90 percent of this amount. Additionally, up to 10 percent of hazardous wastes are thought to be traded internationally, with some being sent to developing countries due to cheaper disposal costs and less stringent environmental regulations, thus causing concerns over "toxic colonialism." This trade is partially governed by the United Nations **Basel Convention on hazardous waste**, which considers hazardous wastes to be toxic, poisonous, explosive, corrosive, flammable, eco-toxic, or infectious.

Hazardous wastes are often disposed of by high-temperature incineration, but this is more costly than landfilling or storage and can result in airborne contamination if done improperly (see **waste management**). Hazardous waste landfills should be specially engineered whereby lined cells are capped or somehow isolated in order to prevent leakage and contamination of the surroundings. Other attempts to minimize the negative environmental and human health effects of hazardous waste generation tends to focus on recyling/reuse of the waste (e.g. recuperation of the lead from used lead-acid batteries) and cleaner production techniques (methods of production that prevent **pollution**).

See also: brown environmental agenda; environment and health; nuclear energy; pollution; trade

Further reading

Clapp, J. (2001) *Toxic Exports: The Transfer of Hazardous Wastes from Rich to Poor Countries*, Ithaca NY: Cornell University Press.
Watts, R. (1998) *Hazardous Wastes: Sources, Pathways, Receptors*, New York: John Wiley.

JONATHAN KRUEGER

health

Health is increasingly seen to be a crucial aspect of development. The **United Nations Development Programme (UNDP)** argues annually in the *Human Development Reports* that the real purpose of development is to create an enabling environment for people to enjoy long, *healthy* lives. The logical extension of this argument is that progress toward development objectives can be summarized by changes in composite measures of population health, such as the **Disability** Adjusted Life Years (DALYs) which combines years of life lost due to premature death (**mortality**) with the number of years lived in sub-optimal states of health (morbidity). However, differences in the traditional ways of measuring health and development render this logical interpretation contestable. The widespread recognition of these differences also means that the relationship between health and development is not simple, as it is influenced by several subjective parameters.

In civilized societies, the pursuit of a healthy state of being is considered a fundamental human right (see **human rights**). Although the achievement of perfect health for every citizen is practically impossible, it is the ideal goal of many national and international public health initiatives. Improving health conditions for the majority of the **population** is a more realistic goal, the achievement of which depends on moral, political, and financial commitments of society. Therefore, the provision of infrastructures for basic and advanced health care, and the support of research programs to develop novel curative and preventive health strategies, require a certain level of socio-economic development. Hence, health and development is strongly linked to projects that facilitate the delivery of health care, such as efficient transport (see **transport policy**), urban and regional **planning** that avoids overcrowding, rural clinics and hospitals, clean water (see **water management**) and air, nutritious **food**, psychological counseling centers, **employment** opportunities, and public **education**.

The relationship between health and development is complicated because the definition of both terms invariably includes subjective notions, and because of the absence of reliable linear correspondence between the two sectors in various historical case studies that have been analyzed. Attempts to project specific health characteristics of a population based on development have lacked the robustness required for generalizable principles. The difficulty that arises from the subjective nature of the definitions is particularly challenging under the concept of health advocated by the constitution of the **World Health Organization (WHO)**, that health is a "state of physical, mental, and social well-being and not merely the absence of disease and infirmity." This definition renders certain aspects of health nearly impossible to quantify without risking problems associated with value judgments that are mediated by cross-cultural differences (see **measuring development**).

To some extent, a predictable relationship can be observed between health and development when crude measures of health such as **life expectancy** are compared with crude measures of development such as **gross national product (GNP) per capita**. However, it quickly becomes clear that with increases in **economic development**, gains in one set of disease burden are simply traded for deficits or emergence of a different set of diseases. Moreover, increases in life expectancy provoke questions about the "quality of life" at the end stages of the lifespan. There is also substantial inequity in the distribution of health gains attributable to development in many countries. A measurable portion of the population can be demonstrated to suffer from the "double burden" effect, covering a wide spectrum of diseases from infectious and communicable agents that are typically associated with less developed countries, to chronic diseases that are typically associated with developed countries.

The challenges emanating from disparate conceptual frameworks for health and development prevent broad generalizations about the relationship between the two sectors. The WHO classified these challenges under three broad categories that enable the understanding of health crises in both developed and developing countries. First, there are arrays of hazards associated with the process of development that produce a burden of disease that is different from diseases of the pre-development stages, and which requires different approaches for their control. Second, the cost of managing diseases associated with modernization (see **modernization theory**) in terms of **industrialization**, **urbanization**, and modern medical practice can short-circuit the development process. Third, the required macroeconomic structural adjustments that accompany development pathways may compromise the integrity of health infrastructures in developing countries (see **structural adjustment**). These three categories are certainly interrelated, but each impinges on the linkages between health and development in characteristic ways that contribute to the transition of societies according to demographic and epidemiological patterns, and the nature of environmental risks to health (see **environment and health**).

Development and demographic transition

Despite gains across the world in **family planning** and government-supported limits on the number of **children** per household, there is still a significant correlation between **gross domestic product (GDP)** per capita (GDPPC) and total **fertility** rate. In 1997, Yemen had the highest total fertility rate of 7.6, and the remainder of the top ten countries with the highest fertility rate is located in Sub-Saharan Africa. The average GDPPC for this group of countries is US$214. In comparison, the fertility rate in many wealthy industrialized countries is below the replacement value. For example, in 1997, Italy and Spain each had a total fertility rate of 1.2. However, unlike the top ten list of countries in the high fertility rate group, the group of countries in the low fertility rate group is a mixture of developed countries and countries with economies in transition, such as the Czech Republic, Bulgaria, Romania, and Estonia, with GDPPC in US$ of 5,240; 1,170; 1,410; and 3,360 respectively. In comparison, Japan with a total fertility rate of 1.4 has a GDPPC of US$38,160, and the United States with a total fertility rate of 2.0 has a GDPPC of US$29,080.

The frequency of occurrence of different kinds of health impairments in a population depends on the age distribution (also known as demographic profile or age pyramid) of the society. Thus, a population that is characterized by a large proportion of **children** younger than five years will have a pyramid-shaped demographic profile with a wide base tapering to older age groups. Such populations have a relatively high incidence of perinatal childhood diseases that are communicable and/or preventable with good **nutrition**. Socio-economic development, **urbanization**, and modernization (see **modernization theory**) have been linked to **demographic transition** with a smaller proportion of children and a comparatively larger proportion of older age groups because of lower birth rates and increases in **life expectancy**. Thus, population "**ageing**" is a widely recognized accompaniment of development, which leads to different sets of health concerns.

The pathway between development and demographic transition has been investigated extensively, but many factors contribute unequally to the relationship, and it is difficult to tease apart the various interactions. It is clear, however, that development that mediates progression from an agrarian economy dominated by manual labor to an industrialized state is accompanied by decline in the number of offspring per family (see **agrarian transformation; rural development**). It has also been argued that low **infant and child mortality** rates engendered by investments in health remove the need for child-bearing as a strategy for improving the chances of having familial survivors. In reality, both reasons contribute in different contexts to the impact of development on demographic transition, and consequently on the epidemiological characteristics of a population.

Development and epidemiological transition

The epidemiological, or **health transition** describes the change over time in the distribution of disease burden in a population. The transition typically progresses from communicable diseases such as diarrhea and **malaria** to chronic and lifestyle diseases such as heart disease and cancers. Current understanding of the determinants of epidemiological transition suggests a rather complicated dynamics of disease burden when societies undergo **economic development**. Many developing countries and countries with economies in transition suffer from a double burden of diseases characteristic of underdeveloped and industrialized countries. The traditional focus of health assessment measures on infant **mortality** ratio (IMR) as the key indicator of progress in national health status has marginalized other important components of health that may be more sensitive to development issues. Thus, important aspects of women's health, the quality of life of the elderly, and **occupational health** have only begun to gain visibility, with the emergence of composite measures of disease burden such as DALYs. The widening use of such composite measures, although still controversial in aspects related to different weighting factors assigned to specific diseases, should aid a more realistic appreciation of the interaction between health, epidemiological transition, and sectoral development including **agriculture, education**, mining and manufacturing, construction of public infrastructures, and international **trade**.

Development influences the direction of epidemiological transition in many ways. For example, agricultural development is usually characterized by heavy equipment and chemical-aided farming. Agricultural development contributes important nutritional sufficiency to the health of a population, which marks the embarkation to epidemiological transition through the reduction of infant mortality (see **infant and child mortality**). However, intensive farming is frequently accompanied by increased exposure to low levels of toxic pesticides, which may precipitate increased incidence of chronic late-onset diseases (see **agrochemicals**). Similarly, the rate of injury from **mechanization** in agriculture is increasing in developing and transition countries. Similarly, **industrialization** contributes to epidemiological transition because it fosters **urbanization** and the concentration of health infrastructures in places accessible to large numbers of people. Access to clean water (see **water management**), sewage disposal (**sanitation**), and pest-control are usually promised benefits of industrial development. These benefits contribute substantially to lowering the burden of communicable and infectious diseases. However, the externalized costs of such development for epidemiological transition includes environmental **pollution** and the occurrence of new occupational diseases and psychosocial stress factors that lead to a disproportionately high burden of mental illness.

Development of modernization (see **modernization theory**) infrastructures has also been shown to have detrimental impacts on public health, especially in developing and transition countries where environmental impact assessment studies that are required prior to the implementation of development projects do not adequately address human health concerns. The situation is slowly changing, but only after numerous incidents of widely publicized disasters. For example, increases in the number and frequency of **malaria** and schistosomiasis **epidemics** have been documented following the implementation of **dams** across rivers to provide hydroelectric power supply. Such dams may also produce changes in the hydrological integrity of settled zones, making them vulnerable to **drought**s and floods that impact agricultural productivity, and consequently, health status.

Conversely, well-planned development projects may actually provide unanticipated benefits for public health. In order to fully appreciate such co-benefits, it is important to build local capacity for evaluating development policies, independent of stipulations from the source of funding, prior to the implementation of capital projects. In general, the absence of this local capacity for policy analysis has contributed to less-than-optimal accounting of health benefits for internationally-funded development projects in developing countries. Therefore, the **World Bank** has been criticized for sponsoring development projects that increase health inequities in poor countries. In order to address this problem, the World Bank has established collaboration with the WHO to support a Council on Health Research for Development, with the goal of identifying policy and institutional changes that are needed to support the optimization of health benefits of development projects and vice-versa.

The impact of development policies on health

Changes in approaches to development have significant impacts on health in developing countries. Increasingly, academics and practitioners working in health and development are showing more concern for the impacts of **structural adjustment** and the growing **inequality** both between developed and developing countries, and within developing countries.

National income measured as **gross national product (GNP)** continues to lose favor as the preferred index of development. Therefore, international development agencies have sought replacement indicators such as **unemployment**, proportion of the **population** living below the **poverty line**, and composite measures such as the **Human Development Index (HDI)**. These relatively new indices made it clear that policies for **economic growth** must include strategies for the redistribution of wealth, thereby paving the way for international health agencies to emphasize basic health needs in development plans.

Similarly, proponents of **dependency theory** have urged the WHO to focus on **primary health care** in poor countries in order to provide services as effective as those in affluent industrialized countries. Nations that embraced the socialist development strategies from the 1960s to the end of the **Cold War** in the 1980s, such as Mozambique, Cuba and China, were held up as examples of successful implementation of equitable health care under the dependency approach to **economic development**.

Nevertheless, the convergence of international economic policies toward market-oriented **globalization** in the 1990s undermined the effectiveness of coupled health and development strategies. In order to finance infrastructure development, many developing countries and countries with economies in transition had to follow structural adjustment policies required by international financial agencies. There is near unanimous agreement in the literature on health and development that the austerity measures required by these structural adjustment policies proved detrimental to the standard of living and health care in developing countries. In order to continue servicing **debt** from international agencies, several countries were no longer able to invest in new health services for their growing populations, and already established infrastructures deteriorated rapidly. **International Monetary Fund (IMF)** programs also necessitated currency devaluation and **import substitution**, which affected the availability of pharmaceutical drugs (see **pharmaceuticals**) in developing countries. Stabilization programs also required the reduction of subsidies for sectors that did not contribute directly to the national economy, including health care. Similarly, structural adjustment programs have been criticized for contributing to the problems associated with equitable access to health care within countries, because the programs encouraged the development of market economies at the expense of public expenditure to maintain the access of poor people to **basic needs** for health and **nutrition**.

The Global Forum for Health Research, an international private foundation that is affiliated with the WHO, was established in the mid-1990s to address equity problem in the nexus of health and development. The forum defines the equity problem as the "10/90 gap" where 90 percent of investment in health care is focused on health problems affecting only 10 percent of the population. The "10/90 gap" exists in comparisons across and within countries. In recognition of the challenges facing international development agencies that wish to invest equitably in health, David Gwatkin, the director of the International Health Policy Program of the World Bank, produced a three-tier classification of approaches to improve the health of the poor through international development. The first of these, "an absolute poverty approach," recognizes that 90 percent of the world's 1.3 billion people living below the international poverty line live in Asia and Africa, and international development agencies that endorse this approach should focus their efforts on these regions. But such an approach will limit international investment in the health sectors of Latin America, the Middle East, and Central Europe. A "relative poverty approach" recognizes that poverty exists in every country, and international development agencies may focus on any particular region, but only on the poor within each region (see **absolute versus relative poverty**). The third approach, called the "equality approach," focuses on countries with the most extreme **inequality** in access to health care; for example, Brazil, Nepal, Nicaragua, and South Africa will be prioritized over countries with low health status inequalities including Ghana, Pakistan, and Vietnam.

See also: brown environmental agenda; demographic transition; disability; disease eradication; economic development; economic risk factors for health; environment and health; gender and communicable disease; health and poverty; health transition; HIV/AIDS (definition and treatment); HIV/AIDS (policy issues); Human Development Index (HDI); infant and child mortality; malaria; maternal mortality; measuring development; nutrition; pollution; population; primary health care; reproductive rights; tuberculosis; vaccination; World Health Organization

Further reading

Chen, L., Kleinman, A. and Ware, N. (1994) *Health and Social Change in International Perspective*, Cambridge MA: Harvard University Press.

Commission on Health Research for Development (1990) *Health Research: Essential Link to Equity in Development*, Oxford: Oxford University Press.

Gwatkin, D. (2000) "Health Inequalities and the Health of the Poor: What Do We Know? What Can We Do?" *Bulletin of the World Health Organization* 78:1 3–17.

Phillips, D. and Verhasselt, Y. (eds) (1994) *Health and Development*, London: Routledge.

Ruttan, V. (ed.) (1994) *Health and Sustainable Agricultural Development: Perspectives on Growth and Constraints*, Boulder CO: Westview Press.

Sen, A. (1999) "Health in Development," *Bulletin of the World Health Organization* 77: 619–23.

Weil, D., Alicbusan, A., Wilson, J., Reich, M. and Bradley, D. (1990) *The Impact of Development*

Policies on Health: A Review of the Literature, Geneva: World Health Organization.

World Bank (1993) *Investing in Health: World Development Report, 1993*, Oxford: Oxford University Press.

DELE OGUNSEITAN

health and poverty

Health and **poverty** are closely linked. Poverty increases morbidity (the experience of sub-optimal health) and **mortality** by exposing people to **economic risk factors for health**, such as poor **nutrition**, poor **sanitation**, and unsafe **drinking water**. Likewise, ill health can lead to poverty by diminishing an individual's ability to work or learn productively. This circular relationship between health and wealth is as true for nations as it is for individuals. While industrialized nations are primarily saddled with chronic diseases that affect their citizens late in life (see **health transition**), developing nations face readily preventable illnesses, such as diarrhea, **malaria**, **tuberculosis**, and HIV/AIDS (see **HIV/AIDS (definition and treatment); HIV/AIDS (policy issues)**), which strike productive members of society in the prime of their lives.

The high prevalence of preventable diseases in developing nations stems from governments' inability or unwillingness to devote resources to reducing the risk factors for these diseases. While the wealth of individuals, and the wealth of the society in which they live, are both important determinants of quality and quantity of life, they may be less important than resource allocation and **income distribution** within nations.

An individual's wealth is a major determinant of access to needed services, such as health care and **education**, as well as needed commodities such as **food**, **housing**, and medicines (see **pharmaceuticals**). These resources are available to the wealthy in the poorest of nations. This is underscored by the observation that wealthier members of nations suffering from widespread **drought** and **famine** hardly ever lack food or water (see **water management; food security**). Even when disaster strikes, food, water, and medicine remain on

the market and can nearly always be purchased, albeit at higher than usual prices (Sen, 1993).

Under normal circumstances, higher incomes allow access to education, safe housing, and health care. They are also associated with a safer workplace and social networks that are more secure – factors that help ensure long-term earnings potential. This is true in development contexts as diverse as China and the USA.

The wealth of the nation where individuals live is perhaps less important. Although much of the world's population lives on less than a dollar a day, that dollar may provide access to adequate caloric intake, and even medicines and other essential goods and services so long as that dollar has adequate purchasing power. Nations that prioritize education, clean water, sanitation, sewage, health care, social security, and transportation can provide a relatively high standard of living for their citizens despite widespread poverty (see, for example, Starfield, 1991).

Much of the variation in **life expectancy** from one country to the next may be explained by the mean educational attainment of its members. For this reason, Cuba, an impoverished totalitarian state that provides these services, compares favorably with the USA in terms of infant mortality (see **infant and child mortality**) and life expectancy. Viewed another way, the USA, which is the wealthiest nation on earth, does a poor job of allocating resources; the average American male can expect to live a shorter life than the average Cuban male (WHO, 2002).

These statistics mask great variations in the distribution of health outcomes and social problems within a nation, but these variations, too, appear to be more of a reflection of social resource allocation than absolute poverty. For instance, while persons living in Bangladesh are susceptible to bouts of **famine** and **epidemics** of infectious diseases, persons living in Harlem, New York City, can generally afford housing with electricity, food, and luxury items such as televisions and automobiles. Nonetheless, both groups have similar life expectancies. While factors such as **crime** and illegal **drugs** undoubtedly play a role in determining health outcomes for people in Harlem, the lack of social services and flat or regressive income distribution schemes are perhaps the overriding causal factors leading to these problems in the first place.

In fact, social status appears to be a strong predictor of health outcomes, and this social phenomenon is tightly coupled with government income distribution schemes. While persons in the top 10 percent of income in the developed context should have comparable access to the highest quality of medical care and other needed goods and services, those with more prestigious jobs tend to outlive those below them. Embedded in this notion of equality is the distribution of wealth within a society; countries that have a more equitable distribution of wealth tend to have substantially higher life expectancies than those that do not.

It is not easy to achieve a fair distribution of social resources. Given the constrained budgets of developing nations, rational investments in infrastructure are paramount. For instance, health systems may benefit most from large investments in primary care and preventive medicine rather than expensive tertiary care facilities. Government **corruption** is a major problem in resource allocation; precious resources are often lost to expensive kickback arrangements or outright theft of public funds.

Another overriding factor is the quest for **economic development**. Economic research suggests that per capita growth of **gross domestic product (GDP)** is best achieved by reducing taxation and government expenditures. However, there is a large and growing body of evidence suggesting that the **well-being** of a nation's citizenry is best achieved by increasing progressive taxes and spending on public infrastructure, even if it comes at the expense of robust **economic growth**. Critics of national monetary institutions, such as the **International Monetary Fund (IMF)**, point out that these organizations tend to ignore this research, and instead prioritize economic growth and loan repayments over developing critical infrastructure (see **debt; structural adjustment**). Progressive taxation with investments in education may be the most economical way to achieve both long-term growth in the economy and the health of a population when governments are otherwise unwilling to devote resources to social infrastructure.

See also: absolute versus relative poverty; brown environmental agenda; economic risk factors for health; food security; health; gender and communicable disease; income distribution; poverty; sanitation

Further reading

Kawachi, I. and Kennedy, B. (2002) *The Health of Nations: Why Inequality is Harmful to Your Health*, New York: New Press.

Sen, A. (1993) "The Economics of Life and Death," *Scientific American* 268:5 40–7.

Starfield, B. (1991) "Primary Care and Health: A Cross-national Comparison," *Journal of the American Medical Association* 266: 2268–71.

WHO (2002) *The World Health Report 1999: Reducing Risks, Promoting Healthy Life*, Geneva: WHO.

PETER MUENNIG

health transition

The health transition (sometimes called epidemiological transition) refers to a change over time from a state of high **mortality** in a country, to a state of high morbidity – the experience of illness, or sub-optimal conditions of **health**. The transition is usually also experienced through a decline in communicable diseases such as diarrhea, to chronic or life-style diseases such as heart disease and diabetes, which are associated with richer people and societies. The transition is generally seen to be an indication of various aspects of **economic development**, such as the reduction in **vulnerability** of poor people to communicable disease (see **disease eradication**), and the greater adoption by individuals of measures to protect themselves against infection. Different parts of world are at different stages of health transition depending on development, education and health services. For example, Sri Lanka and the southern Indian state of Kerala enjoy generally good health, partly because of high female literacy rates.

See also: disease eradication; health

DINESH VYAS

Heavily Indebted Poor Countries (HIPC) initiative

The Heavily Indebted Poor Countries (HIPC) initiative was introduced by the **World Bank** and the **International Monetary Fund (IMF)** in 1996, and can be seen as marking a radical departure from previous **debt relief** initiatives. It was promoted as a way of securing a "lasting exit" to the unsustainable **debt** burdens of some of the world's poorest countries. Before HIPC, debtor nations had to negotiate separately with bilateral and multilateral organizations. HIPC facilitates a more comprehensive approach. For the first time, the debts owed to the IMF and the World Bank can be canceled and countries' debt burdens can be reviewed in their totality. To qualify for entry into the scheme, countries must face an "unsustainable debt burden, beyond available debt relief mechanisms" and establish a sound track record in the implementation of **structural adjustment** policies. The HIPC comprises two main stages: the decision point, the point at which debt relief is agreed, and the completion point, the point at which debt relief is provided. A country's debt is considered "unsustainable" if its current value exceeds 150 percent of the value of its exports.

The HIPC initiative was expanded in 1999 to provide debt relief for forty-two of the poorest countries in the world and to allow for some interim relief before the completion point. Participating countries are required to produce a PRSP (Poverty Reduction Strategy Paper) developed in consultation with civil society, demonstrate having made progress in its implementation and then recycle 60 percent of their debt service savings into **poverty** reduction programs.

Debt service is falling in a number of areas and has led to increased spending on **health** and **education**. However, as with traditional debt relief initiatives, campaigners have criticized the HIPC initiative for not going far enough in its provision of debt relief and for subjecting countries to more structural adjustment policies, which are widely seen as increasing hardship and poverty. It is difficult to assess how much debt relief is being achieved under the HIPC because of the time it takes for countries to reach completion point. By 2003, only six countries had reached completion point, although many more were benefitting from some relief. Some critics have also indicated that even at completion point, some countries will still have unsustainable debt burdens. This is partly because the projections for **economic growth** have been wildly optimistic, and because the initiative has not taken sufficient account of the volatility of commodity prices and the impact of HIV/AIDS (see **HIV/AIDS (definition and treatment); HIV/AIDS (policy issues)**) in a number of HIPC countries in Sub-Saharan Africa.

See also: debt; debt crisis; debt relief; International Monetary Fund (IMF); structural adjustment; World Bank

Further reading

Detailed information and research on the HIPC initiative, can be found on the Jubilee website at http://www.jubileeresearch.org/hipc and on the World Bank website at http://www.worldbank.org/hipc

Hanlon, J. (1998) *HIPC Heresies and the Flat Earth Response*, London: Jubilee 2000 Coalition.

JULIE CUPPLES

HIPC *see* Heavily Indebted Poor Countries (HIPC) initiative

HIV/AIDS (definition and treatment)

HIV (human immunodeficiency virus) is a blood-borne retrovirus that leads eventually to AIDS (acquired immunodeficiency syndrome). Together, they are one of the most pressing concerns for **health** and development. By 2000, 18 million people had already died of AIDS-associated illnesses, and an estimated 34.3 million were living with HIV/AIDS. Now in its third decade, the AIDS pandemic threatens global development, health and peace; a cure is still elusive; and existing therapies are experimental and expensive (see **HIV/AIDS (policy issues)**).

AIDS is characterized by a cluster of life-threatening illness, known as opportunistic infections, caused by range of viruses, bacteria, parasites and fungi, which normally live in relative harmony in a healthy body but take advantage and cause infection when the immune system is weakened. The virus is spread, most commonly, by sharing body fluids transmitted during sexual intercourse, intravenous drug use, or blood transfusions. Most viruses produce their main impact in a matter of days or weeks but HIV, which contains more genes than simple retroviruses, is slow acting and most infected people have no symptoms for two to fifteen years.

Infection occurs when HIV attaches its glycoprotein to the protein of the CD4 cell, a white blood cell responsible for the immune system. HIV transcribes its RNA genetic information into the DNA of the CD4 cell, thus starting the process of viral replication. The immune system attempts to neutralize the virus by producing antibodies. The widely used test of HIV infection looks for the presence of these antibodies in the bloodstream. Antibodies take between two weeks to three months (or more) to appear in an infected person who is said to be HIV-positive or seropositive. Depending on the virulence of the HIV strain, an individual's genetic makeup, or the presence of a disease which might accelerate the infection process, the period between infection with HIV and developing AIDS varies between a few years to ten years or more. Infants and young **children** infected with HIV usually die before they are five years old. The advance of HIV disease is indicated by the decline in the CD4 cell count, and the viral load indicates the speed of infection.

The disease manifests itself in several stages. A few weeks following the infection, about 70 percent of people experience mild attacks of fever, sore throat and fever. After five years, a person may develop painless swollen nodes in the neck, armpits and groin. The symptomatic stage of infection is signaled by intense fatigue; persistent fever and cough; profuse sweating at night; skin rashes; mouth ulcers; fungal infections; herpes and shingles. The last stage of HIV infection is usually associated with **tuberculosis**; Kaposi sarcoma

(purple patches of tumor on the skin and internal organs); serious fungal infections such as candida oesophagitis; crypotcoccus meningitis; and parasitic infections such as pneumocytis carinii. Chronic diarrhea and vomiting results in excessive weight loss, hence East Africans call AIDS "Slim." A few patients suffer the final stages in which HIV attacks the brain causing AIDS encyphalopathy, a dementia similar to senility or Alzheimer's disease.

HIV's rapid mutation and replication onto the genetic code of the host cell represents an obstacle to finding a "one fits all" vaccine cure. HIV differs from person to person, and the variations in the viral genetic codes can be as much as 5 percent. Even within one person, HIV reinvents itself into so many versions that the immune system of a clinically diagnosed HIV positive person confronts more than one million viruses. HIV exists in two types: HIV-1 and HIV-2. HIV-2, which is common in West Africa, and has evolved and spread slowly, has remained largely in the **population**s in which it was first diagnosed.

To date, research has indicated that HIV-1 appears most virulent and has ten subtypes. The inter-type variation is 20 to 30 percent, and the genetic differences within subtypes may be as much as 15 percent. Subtypes A, C, D, and E dominate in developing countries. Subtype C, which copies its genome and mutates faster than any other, accounts for half the infections in the world. The transmissibility of subtypes is adapted to specialized cells. Strains of subtype B, which are transmitted through drug injection, binds with blood cells. Subtypes A and E, which are heterosexually transmitted, grow in the langerhans cells which line the cervix, the vagina and the foreskin of the penis.

AIDS still eludes the assiduous efforts of biomedical research despite the tremendous knowledge about it. Within four years of its appearance in 1981, scientists had isolated and established the causal virus, developed a test capable of detecting infection and established the main routes of transmission. Blood screening has curbed the infection through transfusion, needle exchange programs have reduced infection among drug-injecting addicts, but the majority of people continue to be infected through unprotected penetrative sex. Therapies in richer countries have greatly reduced the **mortality** rate of people with HIV – effectively making AIDS a chronic disease. But globally, the majority of people continue to die of treatable opportunistic infections. Of the estimated 40 million (i.e. between 34 and 46 million) people living with HIV/AIDS worldwide in 2003, the **United Nations** estimates that Australia and New Zealand had 12–18,000; Western Europe 520–680,000; Eastern Europe and Central Asia 1.2–1.8 million; and North America 790,000–1.2 million. However, East Asia and Pacific had 700,000–1.3 million; South and Southeast Asia 4.6–5.2 million; North Africa and Middle East 470–730,000; Caribbean 350–590,000; Latin America 1.3–1.9 million; and Sub-Saharan Africa 25–28.2 million. Sub-Saharan Africa is clearly most affected. Public **health** networks are poorly equipped; and medicines countering the effects of HIV/AIDS are too expensive for most people affected (see **HIV/AIDS (policy issues); pharmaceuticals**).

Managing HIV/AIDS is also complicated by the need to complement any vaccine with behavioral changes concerning preventive sexual transmission methods. These methods include intercourse protected by condoms; prompt and effective treatment for conventional **sexually transmitted diseases (STDs)**; abstinence; and mutual fidelity.

Despite concerted global preventive efforts, people continue to be infected. Ninety-five percent of all infections are in developing countries where the pandemic is fueled by **poverty**, social and economic **inequality**, taboos, ignorance, complacency and denial. AIDS cannot be divorced from **human rights** issues. Factors that promote preventive behavior for an individual must be valued and supported by peers, communities (see **community**) and governments. The initial characterization of AIDS as a disease only affecting male homosexuals became an accepted theory in many parts of the world and became a major weapon of denial (see **same-sex sexualities**). Some "dissenting" theorists insist that HIV does not cause AIDS, but that heavy use of certain recreational drugs and poisonous drugs like AZT developed to control HIV exposes people to mutagens and carcinogens (Duesberg, 1990). In 2000, the world scientific community rebuked the "dissenters" by asserting that sound science,

rather than myth, would solve the AIDS crisis. A statement signed by most scientists working on HIV/AIDS was published in the journal *Science*, and issued as the Durban Declaration at the Thirteenth International AIDS Conference. It described the (epidemiological, immunological and viriological) evidence linking HIV and AIDS as "clear cut, exhaustive and unambiguous."

See also: epidemics; gender and communicable disease; health; health and poverty; HIV/AIDS (policy issues); mortality; pharmaceuticals; primary health care; sexualities; sexually transmitted diseases (STDs)

Further reading

Berer, M. (1993) *Women, AIDS: An International Resource Book*, London: Pandora.

Douglas, P. and Pinsky, L. (1996) *The Essential AIDS Fact Book*, New York: Pocket Books.

Duesberg, P. (1990) "AIDS: Non-infectious Deficiencies Caused by Drug Consumption and Other Risk Factors," *Research in Immunology* 141: 5–11.

UNAIDS (Joint United Nations Programme on HIV/AIDS): http://www.unaids.org

CHRISTINE OBBO

HIV/AIDS (policy issues)

The HIV/AIDS pandemic has raised crucial concerns for **health** and development (see **HIV/AIDS (definition and treatment)**), which are yet to be fully recognized or understood. Policy responses have been relatively successful in affluent countries, where they have been implemented in the context of intense lobbying by influential groups and individuals. Awareness campaigns (especially in the 1980s) engendered a fear of infection (and of those infected). Condom use was promoted, and "risk groups" were targeted – notably homosexual men, sex workers and intravenous drug users (who were often provided with free syringes). Places where homosexual men gathered to have sexual intercourse were often closely monitored (sometimes informally by gay activists) or closed down (such as the bath houses in California). There was also the threat of legal action against those who deliberately infected others. At the same time, public concerns about the virus created incentives and secured funding for biomedical therapies to move quickly beyond palliative care for the afflicted. Although a cure or vaccine proved elusive, testing procedures improved and it became possible to prevent transmission through blood transfusions. In addition, early breakthroughs in the development of antiretroviral drugs suggested a potentially effective mode of treatment. The first of these was being marketed in 1986, and by the mid-1990s combinations of antiretrovirals and other drugs were prolonging the lives of HIV-positive people – sometimes indefinitely – and reducing risks of transmission from mothers to their **children**.

Such responses have generally not been replicated in poorer countries (one exception is Brazil where there is a strong domestic lobby). Some of the reasons are obvious: costs of antiretroviral treatment were far too high, and – until **mortality** rates rose dramatically – HIV/AIDS was seen to affect mainly rich countries. In China and India, for example, there is still little appreciation of the scale of the problem. Also, many countries do not have adequate **primary health care** facilities, and HIV has seemed less important than other diseases (like **malaria** and **tuberculosis**), resulting in little domestic pressure on politicians. Thus, the South African government has refused to do anything until very recently, and notoriously has even denied a link between HIV and AIDS.

Much initial work on addressing HIV/AIDS in poorer countries was conducted by international medical agencies such as the **World Health Organization (WHO)**, but these programs have had mixed results partly because of the need to adopt new understandings about modes of transmission. Targeting risk groups proved to be largely ineffective, but so too did encouraging "safe sex" between heterosexual couples, which has requires fundamental and often untenable changes in gender relations. Condoms in particular have been widely rejected, even where it has been possible to supply them consistently. Not only are they considered inconvenient and to reduce sexual pleasure, but they have often been associated with unpopular contraception campaigns, and held to violate religious and moral codes of behavior. Sometimes, they are even believed to cause ill health because their promotion has coincided with numerous (AIDS-related) deaths.

There has also been an acute shortage of international **aid**. Despite formal commitments to funding HIV/AIDS programs under the **Millennium Development Goals (MDGs)** (which include the target of halting and beginning to reverse the spread of HIV/AIDS by 2015), interest has declined in richer countries where the pandemic has been controlled. The **United Nations** launched the Global Fund to fight AIDS, **tuberculosis** and **malaria** in 2001, calling on rich countries to provide US$7–10 billion per year. Richard Feachem, head of the fund, sees this as a bare minimum, but in 2002, raised just $2.2 billion in pledges, some only redeemable in the distant future. The Global Fund is not the only source of aid finance for HIV/AIDS programs, but it is the most important and its failure to secure resources is revealing of donor priorities.

Overall, the situation is bleak. It is therefore scarcely surprising that much has been read into "success stories," such as Thailand. Here, HIV/AIDS policies initially focused on injecting drug users in Bangkok. HIV prevalence rose from 0–30 percent between late 1987 and mid-1988. Prompt needle-replacement and sterilization programs resulted in this figure not exceeding 40 percent. Meanwhile, brothel-based sex workers were another risk group (a 1989 study found 44 percent HIV-positive in one northern city). Following the 1991 military coup, the new army-backed government adopted strict measures. AIDS management shifted from the Health Ministry to Prime Minister's Office and the budget doubled to US$80 million by mid-decade. A "100 percent Condom Program" enforced condom use in all commercial sex establishments and was monitored by **local government** officials, health professionals and police officers. The sexual contacts of infected sex workers and other individuals were traced. Public **education** was enhanced by mass media and by prominent political figures handing out condoms. According to UNAIDS estimates, condom use in brothels grew from 14 to 90 percent 1989–92, and HIV prevalence among army conscripts fell from 4 to 1.9 percent 1993–6.

In Africa, "success stories" are largely absent. The much cited exception is Uganda, where cases of AIDS were diagnosed as early as 1983, and the government of Yoweri Museveni has welcomed research and international aid programs since 1986. During the early 1990s, in the southwestern districts of Masaka and Rakai, adult HIV prevalence rates were found to have declined (by 8.2–7.6 percent in Masaka between 1989 and 1993 and 23.4–20.9 percent in Rakai between 1990 and 1992). Subsequent monitoring here has shown further declines, and rates have also declined among women attending antenatal clinics in other parts of the country. It is, however, not clear what has caused these declines, and to what extent aid-financed behavioral change programs made a difference. Probably public education and **civil society** participation have had some effect, and it is likely that so did the monitoring and informal policing of sexual practices by local councils set up by Museveni's government (some of which occasionally used **violence** against individuals deemed to be acting inappropriately). It is also worth noting that declines in HIV prevalence in Uganda have not been as dramatic as frequently reported (overall prevalence in Uganda never reached the levels now found in southern Africa – possibly because of the low rate of **urbanization**).

Another much discussed African case is Botswana. This is because of its potential as a model for providing treatment. Adult infection rates are an appalling 40 percent, and **life expectancy** has plummeted from over 60 to 44, and is projected to fall to around 30. Advertising campaigns urging behavioral change have proved ineffective, partly because of local antipathy to condoms. Since the late 1990s, however, HIV-positive employees of the diamond industry have received antiretroviral medicines, and the government aims to provide these to the population as a whole (and thereby reduce mother to child transmission, improve the quality of life of those infected, and hopefully change public attitudes towards HIV/AIDS). Botswana has become Africa's first mass-access antiretroviral program, something which has been made possible by declining **pharmaceuticals** costs, the assistance of drug companies, and donors

such as the Gates Foundation. Critics fear, however, that treatments may not address the problem of drug-resistant stains of HIV. Treatments will also not prolong life as effectively as the complex mixture of medicines and care provided to HIV/AIDS patients in rich countries. Moreover, initial results suggest that service delivery and changing attitudes are more difficult than expected. Few people admit to having AIDS, and few people test voluntarily. In 2003, the second year of the program, of the estimated 300,000 HIV-positive people in Botswana, only about 6,000 are receiving antiretroviral therapy.

In conclusion, it is hard to see how the HIV/AIDS pandemic can be controlled, especially when aid commitments are low. Five factors will be influential:

(i) *The degree to which the pandemic slows and begins to decline*

HIV/AIDS, like other diseases, is expected to reach a peak. Some observers hoped that Uganda's declines marked such a peak, but prevalence has increased to much higher levels elsewhere. Peaks will probably occur at different rates in different places (for example, evidence suggests a leveling off among some populations in South Africa).

(ii) *The degree to which HIV/AIDS impacts on the economic growth of affected countries*

The **mortality** and morbidity (ill-health) caused by HIV/AIDS undoubtedly affects individuals and their families. But this may not necessarily affect the national economy. Some economists have even argued that the economic benefits of low **population** growth will counter the negative effects of HIV/AIDS. In 2000, for example, a **World Bank** review of the economic impact of HIV/AIDS in Botswana suggested **gross national product (GNP) per capita** would grow strongly, partly because of diamond exports. It is most likely that economic impacts will vary widely from place to place.

(iii) *The degree to which the pandemic is seen as a threat to the social, economic and political interests of rich countries*

By the late 1990s, the USA described HIV/AIDS as a national **security** issue, and in the UK there have been concerns about the number of people of African origin treated for HIV/AIDS at British hospitals. These fears may lead to the disengagement of countries from HIV/AIDS-affected regions, but this is unlikely to be tenable over time, especially as the pandemic spreads in Asia. It is more likely that affluent populations will place more pressure on their governments to provide more effective global public health.

(iv) *The degree to which bio-medical responses become more effective*

A cure for HIV/AIDS remains a long way off, and current vaccines are expected to provide only limited protection. However, new antiretroviral treatments may be easier to deliver than current treatments. A key challenge will be the degree to which drug and delivery costs is borne by international donors. At present, most developing countries cannot afford to set up delivery programs, even if drugs are donated.

(v) *The degree that concerns about human rights are set aside*

Despite the uncertainties about HIV/AIDS, it is known how to control it, and not just in rich countries. Direct strategies include enforced testing, enforced use of condoms, segregation of those who are positive, and perhaps enforced compliance with antiretroviral regimes. Such acts, however, may infringe civil liberties, and might only be implemented in parts of the world by military force. Such **authoritarianism** has already been used in Thailand, and in Cuba all HIV-positive people were compelled to live in segregated sanatoriums from 1986 until a partial easing of restrictions in the mid-1990s. These strategies provoked criticism but also helped contain HIV/AIDS. Elsewhere, **human rights** of HIV-positive people are privileged over others, which some suggest is counterproductive for public health. If the rates of infection occurring in southern Africa were occurring in a rich country, such as France or Canada, extreme measures would be expected. As rates of HIV infection and AIDS-related **mortality** continue to rise, it is inevitable that some governments with a capacity to act aggressively will do so. More generally, increased use of enforced testing procedures is surely inevitable.

See also: disease eradication; disease, social constructions of; gender and communicable disease; health; health and poverty; HIV/AIDS (definition and treatment); Millennium Development Goals (MDGs); pharmaceuticals; prostitution/sex work; sexually transmitted diseases (STDs)

Further reading

Barnett, T. and Whiteside, A. (2002) *AIDS in the Twenty-first Century: Disease and Globalization*, Basingstoke: Palgrave.

Campbell, C. (2003) *Letting Them Die: Why HIV/AIDS Prevention Programmes Fail*, Oxford: James Currey.

Dyson, T. (2003) "HIV/AIDS and Urbanization," *Population and Development Review* 29:3 427–42.

Ellison, G., Parker, M. and Campbell, C. (eds) (2003) *Learning from HIV and AIDS*, Cambridge: Cambridge University Press.

Heald, S. (2002) "It's Never as Easy as ABC: Understandings of AIDS in Botswana," *African Journal of AIDS Research* 1: 1–11.

United Nations Websites:
http://www.unaids.org/
http://www.un.org/ga/aids/coverage/

TIM ALLEN

housing

Housing is the most visible indicator of income disparities and **poverty**. There is a direct linkage between poverty and substandard housing. Critical housing issues exist in rural areas, but cities contain the most desperate housing conditions. High proportions of the urban poor are excluded from formal private housing and limited public/social housing. Moreover, many public housing budgets have been reduced in recent years, especially because of **structural adjustment** programs. Many urban poor are forced to rely on their own limited resources and in some cases to appropriate state (see **state and state reform**) or private owners' resources such as through squatter settlements (see

squatters) or pirating of water and electricity supplies. The very poorest may indeed have no actual accommodation and are classified as "houseless" (e.g. pavement dwellers) but a much larger group is regarded as "homeless" as their housing conditions are severely substandard.

Four general categories of housing may be identified for the urban poor: inner city slums; slum estates; squatter settlements; and illegal subdivisions. Inner city slums are frequently found in previously prosperous housing areas that have deteriorated, and are typified by overcrowding, low maintenance, high levels of renting, and insecurity of tenure (threat of eviction and redevelopment). Slum estates include both deteriorated public housing estates and housing built by industry for industrial workers (e.g. hostels in South Africa). Slum estates share similar problems to inner-city slums (apart from insecurity of tenure) and conditions in both groups are generally worsening and are rarely upgraded. Squatter settlements where public or private land is illegally occupied are variously labeled around the world: spontaneous settlements, **shantytowns**, self-help settlements, *favelas, bidonvilles,* etc. Illegal subdivisions are settlements where land has been subdivided and sold by its owners against zoning regulations, or without planning permission or infrastructure (e.g. *barrios piratas* in Colombia). Both types of settlements are widespread mainly in so-called "peri-urban" areas on the peripheries of cities.

Until the mid-1970s, informal, illegal and unplanned settlements were generally interpreted negatively as health hazards, threats to social order, or challenges to authority. They were subject either to benign neglect or actively repressive policies of eradication and forced removal (see **displacement; resettlement**). At the same time, state organizations frequently sought to build "low-income" housing projects. These projects were widely criticized at the Habitat I (see **Habitat I and II**) conference in 1976 by critics who urged that the poor should provide their own shelter and that large-scale social housing schemes for the poor were flawed. These criticisms marked a change from the view of the state (see **state and state reform**) as a "provider" to an "enabler," and promoted the notion of "aided self-help" through settlement-upgrading projects and site and service

schemes (where land and infrastructure services are provided and settlers build their own houses). The most articulate proponent of this approach was John Turner, who believed housing should be understood as a process ("housing as a verb"). Turner was one of the first to document how – in positive circumstances – informal settlements are gradually consolidated by their owner-dwellers by activities such as replacing temporary shacks with solidly built houses, and collectively organizing to install infrastructure. In some cases, especially in Latin America, consolidated settlements can become indistinguishable from formal settlements, especially where tenure regularization and upgrading programs are implemented (Kellett, 2002). In contrast, many informal settlements in Kenya are controlled by landlords who rent out rooms in poorly maintained and overcrowded dwellings. In all types of settlement, an increasing proportion of households generates some or all of their income through home-based enterprises (see **urban informal sector; street-trading in urban areas**).

To assist developing global policy responses, UN-Habitat has recently re-adopted the previously pejorative term "slum" as a collective category to identify various kinds of substandard housing. It is recognized that slums are multi-dimensional in nature, and involve some physical characteristics (such as access to physical services) that can be clearly defined, and some social characteristics (such as levels of **poverty**) that are less definable. To overcome this vagueness, a five-point measure to define slums is proposed: inadequate access to safe water and sanitation; poor structural quality; dangerous location; overcrowding; and insecure residential status.

These indicators have been used to compile estimates of the scale of inadequate housing. In 2001, more than 900 million (31.6 percent) of the world's total urban population lived in housing conditions defined as slums. They are unevenly distributed: 43 percent are in developing regions, although 78.2 percent are in the least developed countries. In absolute numbers, most slum dwellers are located in Asia (554 million in 2001), 187 million in Africa and 128 million in Latin America and the Caribbean.

During the 1990s, informal households increased by an estimated 36 percent because slum improvements and formal construction programs failed to keep up with **population** growth. Projections indicate that global numbers of slum dwellers will double to 2 billion within 30 years. Every day the urban population of developing countries increases by more than 170,000 people, requiring an additional 30,000 housing units (see **urbanization**) (UN-Habitat, 2003).

Much debate on housing provision still concerns issues related to "aided self-help," as few alternative paradigms have been proposed. Indeed the move from the "provider" toward the "enabler" paradigm identified in Habitat I was consolidated in the Habitat II conference in Istanbul in 1996, where the ideas developed the Global Shelter Strategy were combined with **Agenda 21** to promote increased participation, local control and in-situ settlement upgrading within the umbrella of greater sustainability. These ideas are reinforced in the most recent of the *Global Reports on Human Settlements* (UN-Habitat, 2003), which argues that policies to address slums must go beyond the physical condition of dwellings and deal with underlying problems of poverty. Acknowledging the recent inclusion of housing as a basic human right (see **human rights**), policies and programs need to support the **livelihoods** of the urban poor by enabling informal sector activities to flourish, link low-income housing development to income generation, and facilitate access to **employment** through transport and settlement location policies (see **transport policy**). In summary, the emphasis should be on reducing poverty, and integrating shelter with transport, **employment**, **health** and **education**.

See also: drinking water; ghettos; Habitat I and II; sanitation; shantytowns; squatters; street-trading in urban areas; urban informal sector; urban development; urban poverty; urbanization

Further reading

Kellett, P. (2002) "The Construction of Home in the Informal City," *Journal of Romance Studies*, 2:3 17–31.
Potter, R. and Lloyd-Evans, S. (1998) *The City in the Developing World*, Harlow: Longman.

Romaya, S. and Rakodi, C. (eds) (2002) *Building Sustainable Urban Settlements: Approaches and Case Studies in the Developing World*, London: ITDG Publishing.
Turner, J. (1976) *Housing by People: Towards Autonomy in Building Environments*, London: Marion Boyars.
UN-Habitat (2003) *Facing the Slum Challenge: Global Report on Human Settlements 2003*, London: Earthscan.

PETER KELLETT

human capital

The term "human capital" was initially coined in 1960 by T. W. Schultz, referring to the notion that people acquire skills and knowledge (assets which are perceived as a form of capital), and that a substantial part of this acquisition is a result of deliberate investment. Increased **productivity** resulting from investment in human capital is perceived to benefit individuals through increased future income, and society as a whole because of improved productivity and larger contributions to national income. Human capital may apply to any form of investment in human beings (including **health** care), but is mostly related to education, and especially an economic approach based on the calculation of costs and benefits (see **cost-benefit analysis (CBA)**). In practice, "human capital" is frequently adopted as a synonym for **education**, which is a misuse of the concept.

A human capital approach implies that it is possible to measure the profitability of, or rate of return on investment in, education. This is achieved by calculating the expected yield in terms of future benefits, compared with the cost of acquiring education. Private rates of return compare all direct and opportunity costs of education (earnings forgone as a result of time spent in school or college) to individuals, with their benefits in terms of increased lifetime earnings. Social rates of return measure the costs and benefits to society as a whole (Woodhall, 1987). Ideally, social rates of return should include societal benefits in terms of higher productivity of educated workers and their contributions to national income (usually proxied by increased lifetime earnings), as well as allowing for non-economic outcomes of education ("externalities") where these are valued by society. Such externalities include, for example, improved health and reduced **fertility**. However, externalities are often not easily quantifiable, so are usually not taken into consideration in the calculations of rates of return to education in practice.

Since the early 1960s, proponents of human capital, notably T. W. Schultz and Gary Becker, have used calculations of rates of return as empirical justification to show that education is a good investment. The notion of human capital rose to prominence in the early 1980s, when George Psacharopoulos was appointed to head the Education Department's Research Unit at the **World Bank**. From the outset, it was made clear that only economic factors should be taken into consideration for World Bank lending in education, and initially the World Bank was cautious about the possibilities of involving itself in education. However, since the 1980s, an emphasis on rates of return to education became increasingly evident within the World Bank, supported in particular by Psacharopoulos's meta-analyses. As a result, investment in primary education was prioritized on the basis that estimates of rates of return to education were highest, and the difference between social and private returns greatest, at that level, particularly for girls (Psacharopoulos, 1994).

It is no coincidence that the World Bank's influence over education via human capital corresponded with the advent of **structural adjustment** programs, since human capital provided the opportunity for the neo-liberal agenda to be applied to education (see **neo-liberalism**). In an era when structural adjustment programs were enforcing cutbacks to government expenditure, calculations of high social returns permitted a view that primary education and health care should be priorities for public expenditure. However, the conflict between the structural adjustment principle of prioritizing public expenditure on social sectors and conditions set for reducing overall government expenditure meant that, in reality, education and health expenditure often suffered. The economic approach to education, encouraged by the notion of human capital, permitted a pricing policy to be rigorously applied to education based

on a supply and demand model. This illustrated that, under certain conditions, excess demand could be met by increasing school fees, including at the primary level where appropriate.

The use of economic rationales for price setting in primary schools was criticized by **United Nations Children's Fund (UNICEF)** under the so-called **adjustment with a human face** debate. The World Bank consequently lessened this approach, but still uses human capital and associated applications of rates of return as an economic rationale for its involvement in education. The notion of human capital has, in fact, become increasingly popularized and liberally adopted, both within as well as outside of economics (see, for example, the **sustainable livelihoods** framework), with attempts to broaden the concept to include consideration of social and cultural aspects of education. Yet, while human capital is still used, there are increasing methodological and empirical criticisms against it. Within the field of economics of education, human capital has been criticized for ignoring the role of education as a "screening" device. It is argued that employers use education to identify individuals with higher innate ability and other desired personal characteristics including motivation and attitudes (attributes which might be related to class, race (see **race and racism**) and **gender**) for example, rather than education purely increasing the productive capacity of individuals as a result of knowledge and skills acquired, as human capital suggests.

By treating educational provision as a stream of costs and benefits, both to individuals and society, social relations within and around education are ignored. In reality, the educational process is heavily embroiled in social structures, relations and processes and their associated conflicts, which are themselves attached to underlying economic and political interests. Moreover, the formation and evolution of both education systems and **labor markets** is historically contingent.

Educationalists criticize human capital for showing no understanding of the educational process. The "black box" of how education is provided remains firmly shut, other than for the labeling of financial costs and benefits. The process of teaching and learning, which transforms inputs into outputs, is outside the scope of human capital.

In addition, human capital focuses on education as a means of individual and collective economic advancement, rather than considering its broader aspects such as a means of social integration. While attempts have been made by human capital proponents to address these broader aspects, and to recognize the importance of market and informational imperfections in the education and **employment** sectors, the reductionism attached to addressing such principles within a human capital framework is incapable of doing justice to the rich complexity of educational systems. The more this occurs, the more human capital theory undermines its own analytical premise with respect to understanding education as an investment measured in terms of costs and benefits.

See also: cost-benefit analysis (CBA); education; employment; labor markets

Further reading

Becker, G. (1964) *Human Capital: A Theoretical and Empirical Analysis with Special Reference to Education*, Chicago: University of Chicago Press.

Fine, B. and Rose, P. (2001) "Education and the post-Washington Consensus," pp. 155–81 in Fine, B., Lapavitsas, C. and Pincus, J. (eds) *Development Policy in the Twenty-first Century: Beyond the post-Washington Consensus*, London: Routledge.

Psacharopoulos, G. (1994) "Returns to Investment in Education: A Global Update," *World Development*, 22:9 1325–43.

Schultz, T. W. (1960) "Capital Formation in Education," *Journal of Political Economy*, 68:6 571–83.

Woodhall, M. (1987) "Human Capital Concepts," pp. 21–4 in Psacharopoulos, G. (ed.) *Economics of Education: Research and Studies*, Oxford: Pergamon.

PAULINE ROSE

human development

"Human development" is a broader and re-focused conception of development, in contrast to development seen centrally as **economic growth** (see also **growth versus holism**). It refers to "development of, by and for people" and to extending the range of favorably valued life-paths that people can choose. The term has been popularized since 1990 by the **United Nations Development Programme (UNDP)**'s Human Development Report Office, which was created by Mahbub ul Haq (1934–98), a Pakistani economist, ex-minister of state and former senior **World Bank** adviser. The concept has been disseminated by the annual global *UNHuman Development Report* (HDR), and widely adopted by national and sub-national governments and other development organizations. It is broader too than a concern only for increase of people's skills ("human resource development," or **human capital**) or the so-called "human sectors," for example **nutrition**, **health**, **education**. Instead, it sees development as the promotion and advance of a broad definition of **well-being**.

The adjective, "human" conveys several messages. First, humans have fundamentally important things in common. Second, these commonalities include fallibility, corruptibility and **vulnerability** (we are "all too human"), but also good potentials, such as concern and caring for others. Third, the approach is people-centered (see **people-centered development**), with development not only for a sub-group of society, or based on the achievement of a numerical target such as **gross national product (GNP)**; equity and participation are important in human development. It rejects "inhuman development," i.e. change which excludes or victimizes many persons, as has often been the case (see **displacement; marginalization**). The conventional emphasis of orthodox economic analysis on economic growth has neglected political questions of **income distribution**; the differing abilities and needs of people; the distribution of expenditure on products and activities, e.g. on **education** or on arms purchases (see **arms sales and controls**); and public goods like peace and security which are not commodities and not primarily dependent on commodities. Many of these items can be achieved by actions by governments of even low-income countries by restructuring public expenditure. But at the same time, the HDRs hold that economic growth is important for long-term progress in **poverty** reduction and human development.

The human development formulation by ul Haq and others draws from diverse intellectual traditions including Aristotle, Adam Smith and Marx. The concept of human development emerged specifically in the 1980s and early 1990s in response to various influences, including negative experience with the extreme focus on monetary variables in programs of **structural adjustment**. The **United Nations Children's Fund (UNICEF)** had argued for **"adjustment with a human face,"** and showed how poverty-reduction schemes can be integrated with, and complement, strategies for economic adjustment and growth. Ul Haq and his collaborators took this much further. They drew on new theories of economic growth which indicate a primary importance of human capital; on the record of dramatic success in East Asian countries which combined sustained rapid growth with increased equity (see **newly industrialized economies (NIEs)**); and on evidence of low or declining quality of life in some rich or fast-growing countries. The group transformed the **basic needs** approach on which ul Haq and many colleagues had worked earlier. Their earlier focus on direct investment and other measures to meet basic material needs had relatively neglected **empowerment** and non-material improvement. (It is worth noting that this was not true for the Basic Human Needs Approach built by thinkers such as Johan Galtung, Rajni Kothari and Manfred Max-Neef.) The concept of human development tries to synthesize these concerns, guided by a philosophical perspective from the Indian Nobel-prize winning economist Amartya Sen, embodied in his **capability approach**.

The resulting conception of development focuses on ends – improvements in the content of people's lives and in their access to benefits – not only on means, and especially not only monetary means. Development is understood as a normative concept, distinct from economic growth or social change. Attention to the content of people's lives leads to a disaggregated approach, looking at **health** and **housing**, work and recreation, and diverse other aspects as seen in the wide-ranging tables of indicators in the HDRs. Human development is defined as covering empowerment (including possession of valued opportunities, and participation), equity, sustainability (see

sustainable development), **community** membership, and physical and economic **security** (HDR, 1996). The human development approach is therefore multidimensional with respect to ends, compared to the traditional focus of development planners on the narrow indicator of GNP. With respect to means, the approach focuses on all available means, without restriction on disciplinary grounds (ul Haq, 1998).

Only part of the conceptualization of "ends" is captured by UNDP's **Human Development Index (HDI)**, which combines (i) the conventional indicator of national per capita income (adjusted to show real purchasing power (see **gross national product (GNP) per capita**); with measures of (ii) basic **education** and (iii) **life expectancy**, and gives equal weights to relative performance in these three areas. Given the presence of per capita income as a large part of the index, overall correlation between the ranking of countries in terms of their HDIs and their per capita incomes is quite high and not surprising. More striking are the many divergences between the rankings, some of them dramatic – even when we use such a simple and incomplete measure of human development as the HDI. The index has highlighted the severe inadequacy of GNP per capita as a measure of progress.

Some commentators find the "human" content of the HDR work too slight, or too dominated by economists' conceptions. The strand of human development theory represented by Martha Nussbaum, an American philosopher and social critic, has a richer and more explicit humanistic content (see **capability approach; functionings; well-being**). Such work looks also at real individuals; emphasizes each person as distinct and deserving respect and concern; and adds the methods of the humanities, such as individual life-stories, reflective essays and the imaginative arts. These methods can deepen both understanding and concern, thus motivate as well as guide attention and action, and help to reach wider audiences.

Human development gives a comprehensive, and hence quite often radical, framework for policy analysis: not only economic, not only social, and not only concerned with human resource development or basic material needs (e.g. see Drèze and Sen, 2002). It highlights **empowerment**: people are declared the key means as well as the key end of development. The framework is radical too in its geographical field of attention. Much more than the **World Bank**'s *World Development Reports*, the HDRs treat the whole world on an equal basis and address the responsibilities of rich countries and the impacts of their policies (see ul Haq, 1998). They have stressed the need for **structural adjustment** in the West, including by opening markets, to promote global social stability rather than belatedly sending expensive and ineffective **peacekeeping** forces to low-income countries that have been excluded from opportunities and become mired in conflict (see **complex emergencies**). The 1994 HDR, for example, argued that rich countries should see development assistance as an investment in their own **human security**, rather than as charity (see **charities**). It proposed "the 20:20 compact" between funders and poor countries: that at least 20 percent of foreign development assistance and 20 percent of low-income country government expenditure should go to priority human development sectors such as **health**. This had rarely happened in the preceding decades, and is still too uncommon.

See also: basic needs; capability approach; economic growth; empowerment; ethics; human capital; Human Development Index (HDI); people-centered development; United Nations; well-being

Further reading

Drèze, J. and Sen, A. (2002) *India: Development and Participation*, Delhi: Oxford University Press.

Gasper, D. (2004) *The Ethics of Development: From Economism to Human Development*, Edinburgh: Edinburgh University Press.

Haq, M. ul (1998, 2nd edn) *Reflections on Human Development*, New York and Delhi: Oxford University Press.

Nussbaum, M. (2000) *Women and Human Development: The Capabilities Approach*, Delhi: Kali for Women, and Cambridge: Cambridge University Press.

Sen, A. (1999) *Development as Freedom*, New York: Oxford University Press.

UNDP (1990-) *Human Development Report* (annual), New York: Oxford University Press.

DES GASPER

Human Development Index (HDI)

The Human Development Index (HDI) is the most influential of global **indicators of development** that are built on the results of **measuring development**. HDI is one of four **United Nations** indicators produced at the nation-state level, the other three being the **Gender-related Development Index (GDI)**, the **Gender Empowerment Measure (GEM)**, and the Human Poverty Index. HDI is a key part of the annual **United Nations Development Programme (UNDP)** *Human Development Report*, and its main objective when introduced was to overcome problems experienced in using previous univariate measures, such as **gross domestic product (GDP)**, which were used as surrogate indicators of development.

The HDI builds on three main areas of information, which are described by UNDP (see http://hdr.undp.org/statistics/default.cfm) as "longevity, knowledge and a decent standard of living," and which are accompanied by UNDP advice that "HDI is a summary, not a comprehensive measure of human development." The UNDP definitions of the three major components are: first, the **life expectancy** index defined as "the number of years a newborn infant would live if prevailing patterns of age-specific mortality rates at the time of birth were to stay the same throughout the child's life." Second, an **education** index based on statistics of adult literacy (aged fifteen and over who can "both read and write a short, simple statement on their everyday life") and **education** enrolment (see **illiteracy**) . The third component is gross domestic product (GDP) per capita (in US dollars).

For each of the components, a minimum and maximum value are set and the position of each country along the value scale is reduced to a value of between zero and 1. For example, with literacy the range is between 0 percent (complete **illiteracy**) to 100 percent (all eligible citizens meeting literacy targets). Minimum **life expectancy** is set to be twenty-five years, and the maximum is eighty-five years. The component parts are used to create the three sub-indicators, which are then averaged. The 2002 index for Bangladesh cites life expectancy as being 0.57, Education as being 0.4, and GDP as 0.46, with the average of the three giving an HDI of 0.478, rank 145 of 173 reported countries. UNDP group the index into three global groupings of low (from Sierre Leone, ranked 173 at 0.275, to 0.499), medium (above low to 0.796), and high (above medium to Norway, ranked 1 at 0.942) development.

The prevailing rationale for HDI is to move away from using economic indices as surrogates of development, to a focus on "outcomes" in terms of the lives of people. Despite its attractions, the index suffers from methodological problems such as a focus on countries, which may result in over-looking trends at sub-national scales (see **measuring development**), and on the time lags between the collection of data and the production of an index. For example, the 2002 HDI was based on data for 2000, and was used in 2003, and hence tends to represent historic trends. The value of all **indicators of development** is limited by the quality of the data used.

See also: human development; indicators of development; measuring development; poverty measurement

Further reading

UNDP (2003) *Human Development Report 2003*, Washington DC: UNDP. http://www.undp.org/hdr2003/

MICHAEL BLAKEMORE

Human Genome Project

The Human Genome Project is a massive scientific venture that had identified all the approximate 30,000 genes in human DNA by 2003. Originating from the US-funded Human Genome Initiative, it became an international project in 1990, with the involvement of the US National Institutes for Health and the UK-based scientific funding charity the Wellcome Trust. Scientific expertise has been contributed by a range of countries, including France, Japan and China, while the financial and organizational scale of the undertaking has led some to draw parallels with the Apollo moon program of the 1960s.

The human genome is our complete set of DNA. All DNA is made up of four physical and chemical components: A, T, C and G nucleotide bases. In humans, these bases are arranged into twenty-four chromosomes (physically separate molecules), which comprise specific series of bases that form hereditary units called genes. Recording genes thus involves a hugely laborious task of determining the sequence of bases that make up DNA. The Human Genome Project has largely been dependent upon technical advances in DNA sequencing technology to allow the approximately three billion base pairs of the human genome to be sequenced.

A multitude of potential benefits has been anticipated. Molecular medicine promises to improve the diagnosis and treatment of disease, detecting predispositions to diseases, and developing gene therapy, and customized drugs based on individual genetic profiles. Microbial genomics promises to protect people from bacterial disease, environmental pollutants and biological and chemical warfare. DNA identification has a multitude of potential uses, including the establishment of family identity or criminal guilt, and biotechnology promises to make our **food** sources more resistant to disease, and more productive (see **biotechnology and resistance**).

However, practically, many of these potential applications are far from becoming reality. The relationship between genes and an individual's physical make-up and functioning is highly complex. Most conditions are triggered and regulated by vast numbers of genes, and it is simply not known how these genes interact. Additionally, a number of ethical reservations exist about the potential uses of the project's findings, related to the wider philosophical implications of genetic determinism (the idea that our genes determine our behavior). Major issues such as genetic privacy (to prevent employers, insurers, schools and so forth, using genetic information to discriminate against individuals), and the use of reproductive technologies to select certain traits in one's **children** (so-called designer babies) remain unresolved.

The regulation of these uses may be threatened by the **commercialization** of the human genome through **intellectual property rights (IPRs)** and patents to specific companies (a core aim of the Human Genome Project). Many fear this will also limit the benefits that may accrue to specific countries, raising questions about whether the genetic material that is common to us all should be in private ownership.

See also: biotechnology and resistance; Cartagena Protocol on Biosafety; ethics; genetically modified organisms (GMOs); health; intellectual property rights (IPRs)

Further reading

Dennis, C., Gallagher, R. and Watson, J. (eds) (2002) *The Human Genome*, New York: Macmillan.

Lewontin, R. (2000) *It Ain't Necessarily So: The Dream of the Human Genome and Other Illusions*, New York: New York Review of Books.

JAMES EVANS

HUMAN POVERTY INDEX *see* poverty measurement

human rights

Human rights are those freedoms and entitlements invested in each person at birth that are universal and inalienable. They are internationally recognized principles, and regarded as fundamental for promoting **well-being**, health and peace (see **freedom versus choice; ethics**). The concept of human rights, however, is both easy to understand, yet complex and abstract to apply. Individuals in different places and at different times have believed in inalienable natural rights belonging to individuals. Ancient Greek and Roman philosophers wrote about ideas that later became formulated as universal principles in the 1789 French Revolution's Declaration of the Rights of Man: "All men are born and equal in rights." This concept was inspired the so-called English **Revolution** of 1688, the American Declaration of

Independence of 1776, and has acted as a cornerstone of Western liberal theory since. The concept, however, is still being elaborated to acknowledge complex modern conditions of global production and trade, **migration** and **epidemics**.

The modern human rights movement began in 1945 with the establishment of the **United Nations** (UN) whose founding Charter affirms "faith in fundamental human rights, in the dignity and worth of the human person, in the equal rights of men and women of nations large and small." The International Bill of Human Rights (IBHR) consists of the following three treaties produced between 1945 and 1976: the **Universal Declaration of Human Rights (1948)** (UDHR, 1948); the **International Covenant on Economic, Social and Cultural Rights** (ICESCR, 1966); and International Covenant on Civil and Political Rights (ICCPR, 1976).

The UDHR sets standards for political and civil rights of national constitutions and legal systems. IBHR covers two sets of rights. First, civil and political rights are regarded as treated as absolute or "non-derogable" because they are regarded as fundamental to human dignity and well-being. These rights include: freedom from discrimination; the right to life; freedom from **torture**, cruel, inhuman or degrading treatment or punishment; freedom from **slavery** and involuntary servitude; freedom from retroactivity for criminal offences; the right to recognition as person before the law; and freedom of thought, conscience and **religion**. These political and civil rights are also known as "negative" rights because they can never be legally limited, restricted or infringed upon by the state (see **state and state reform**) except in very legally compelling exceptional circumstances.

Second, IBHR identifies economic, social and cultural rights. These rights are seen as "positive" because their promotion is "enabling" to basic civil participation, for which states are encouraged to provide support and opportunities. These include: the right to work; to social security; to **education**; the **right to self-determination**; freedom from discrimination; equal pay; equality between men and women (see **gender**); and rights to mental and physical **well-being** (see **disability; health**). UN conventions and declarations highlight the incremental advances in human rights as a global moral force. All UN members pledge themselves to take joint and separate action in cooperation with the UN organizations to achieve universal and fundamental freedoms for all without race, sex, language or religious distinctions.

Other conventions also form milestones in establishing the human rights agenda worldwide. For example, the **United Nations Declaration on the Granting of Independence to Colonial Countries and Peoples, Res. 1514 (XV) 1960**; Elimination of All Forms of Racial Discrimination (1963); the Elimination of Discrimination against Women (1967) (see **Convention on the Elimination of All Forms of Discrimination Against Women (CEDAW)**); and Territorial Asylum (1969). Before these, there were also important earlier conventions on: the Political Rights of Women (1952); Consent to Marriage, Minimum Age for Marriage and Registration of Marriages (1962); Refugees and Stateless Persons (1951); and the European and American conventions on Human Rights. The European Convention on Human Rights was inspired by the UN Charter, and one of its most visible products is the active European Court of Human Rights, a last-resort redress appeal against legal victimization, and one of the most effective rights enforcement agencies in the world. The treatment of the weak and vulnerable is an important indication of value accorded to human rights by society. The declarations on Rights of the Child (1959), the Rights of Mentally Retarded Persons (1971) and the Rights of Disabled Persons (1975) reinforce the right of the weak and vulnerable to fairness and equality (see **disability**).

The **United Nations Declaration on the Right to Development (1986) – Res. 41/128**, stressed the right and duty of states to promote the equitable distribution of resources and benefits to all people. In 1998, the UN Secretary General boosted demands by communities (see **community**) for efficient, effective and equitable use of resources as a right when he launched a broad "rights-based approach to development" (see **rights-based approaches to development**) to refocus development requirements to treat human needs as justice and not charity. Development as a human right must be an extension of existing political and civil rights promoting free and periodic election of leaders; and independent judiciary ensuring due process under law; and freedom of speech and association (see **freedom of association; international law; law**).

In recent decades, the universality of human rights has been challenged by a variety of critics who have asserted that rights are culturally and politically specific; or based on Western liberal theory that may champion individualism (see **cultural relativism; ethnocentrism; postmodernism and postdevelopment**). As such, much debate about human rights may be inapplicable to cultural contexts where communal interests predominate; and may represent a further extension of hegemonic global ideologies by the West. Other critics have been more optimistic, and instead have urged policy-makers to consider which human rights can be considered universal, and which may be seen as culturally grounded.

Some analysts have argued that human rights need to be understood as either group rights or corporation rights. Under group rights, individual stakeholders shape what are defined as rights. Under corporation rights, the moral standing of the group is above the individual. For example, the 1986 African Charter on Cultural and Human Rights (ACHR) uniquely puts **community** rights above individual rights. It was ratified by 41 of the 51 member states of the Organization of African Unity in 1991, despite the hitherto widespread disappointment with the political and development record among the African political and academic elite, who no longer believed that political and economic rights should be sought after economic development had been achieved. Evidence of widespread **poverty**, meaning that very few people enjoy the fundamental economic rights of **food**, shelter, **health** care and basic **education**, suggests that civil and political rights are imperative for the protection of economic rights. The ACHR gives primacy to so-called "second generation" economic rights; is vague over "first generation" political and civil rights; and gives primacy to "third generation" group rights.

The rights of women have also been insufficiently acknowledged by ACHR. The ACHR acknowledges the obligation to honor women's rights under other international human rights conventions. But critics claim that such statements are undermined by the ineffectiveness of the African Human Rights Commission in relation to gender, and the vagueness of plans for the African Human Rights Court. These failings served as a warning to women not to be complacent even in countries with so called "women friendly" regimes.

One of the achievements the 1995 Beijing UN International Conference on Women was the centering of the principle that "women's rights are not special rights but human rights;" and insisting that development, gender and human rights are inseparable issues (see **gender; United Nations World Conferences on Women**). The Beijing Platform for Action may not be binding to governments, but women's continued efforts will make it into a moral force difficult to ignore. Women activists have learned to use UN instruments and forums to increase debate on issues where women's rights still need legal protection. Despite this progress, in many places, women's demands for equal access to education, health, and **employment** are dismissed as subversive.

Violations of human rights have been taking new forms and presenting new challenges to human rights groups. As people in power control how human rights laws are enforced, the development of social movements and identity politics have led to the proliferation of human rights organizations such as Amnesty International, which focuses on the rights of prisoners.

The HIV/AIDS pandemic has focused attention to health as a human right (see **HIV/AIDS (definition and treatment); HIV/AIDS (policy issues)**). Promoting human rights is important for achieving the public health goal of reducing HIV transmission; for lessening the adverse impact of HIV on those affected; and for empowering individuals and communities to respond to HIV/AIDS. Rights to health also demand a working solution the demands of patent protection as stimulation for research and development and getting medicines to poor people (see **pharmaceuticals; trade**).

In the 1994 Paris Declaration concerning AIDS, forty-two political leaders solemnly declared an obligation to use economic, legal and social resources to make the fight against HIV/AIDS a priority, and to act with compassion for and in solidarity with those with HIV or at risk of being infected both within local societies and internationally. Lack of political leadership has led to the mushrooming of organizations and networks that deal with every aspect of the epidemic.

The **United Nations Development Programme (UNDP)** agency has promoted a human rights agenda by using its mandate of human capacity development and **empowerment** to make sustainable local responses to HIV/AIDS. Under UNDP sponsorship, regional networks have grown for people living with AIDS (PLWA), focusing on changing **law** and **ethics**. In Africa, the 1994 Dakar Declaration marked the birth of the African Network on Ethics, Law and HIV. The Declaration covered issues such as mandatory testing, confidentiality, and the use of sensitive language in recognition that "the fundamental value of respect for the human rights, life and human dignity provide the foundation" on which to base shared rights and responsibilities in controlling the HIV/AIDS epidemic.

The Global Network of People Living with HIV/AIDS and the similar network for women, Positively Women, serve as umbrellas for smaller regional and national networks by attracting funding and attention from researchers, drug manufacturers and policy-makers. At the 1998 Eleventh International Conference of PLWA in Poland, Northern PLWA demanded equitable access to therapies by Southern PLWA. In 1997, PLWA asserted their rights in the Chiang Mai Declaration:

> Our status as equal citizens, entitled to the equal enjoyment of human rights, is not altered by our diagnosis, source of infection, race [see **race and racism**], age, gender, sexual orientation or economic situation. Discrimination in access to health information, care and treatment is a violation of those rights.... Without us, there is no prevention, no research, no clinical trials, no care, no treatment

The right to enjoy the benefits of scientific progress movement was born.

In 1998, the UN Commission on Human Rights and the Joint United Nations Programme on HIV/AIDS (UNAIDS) issued the Human Rights and HIV/AIDS International Guidelines, which call for the establishment of participatory, transparent and accountable national frameworks that integrate and coordinate HIV/AIDS and human rights activities into all government policies and pro-grams. The International Council of AIDS Services Organizations is focused on making the Guidelines widely known by distributing and explaining the rights of PLWA and the obligations of the government. In 1998, South Africa Lawyers for Human Rights produced a Charter of Rights on HIV/AIDS, which is now part of the Constitution. They have legally forced the government to make available anti-viral drugs to pregnant women and rape victims.

Human rights demands have mirrored the changing politics of self-determination, power and control; and the international UN guidelines and conventions underscore the need to protect the vulnerable. Yet, as debate about human rights has grown, it is clear that there is a need for a participatory and critical approach to what are considered human rights, and who is allowed to determine what they are (see **human rights indicators**).

See also: ethics; freedom versus choice; HIV/AIDS (policy issues); human rights indicators; International Covenant on Economic, Social and Cultural Rights; law; Office of the United Nations High Commissioner for Human Rights (OHCHR); rights-based approaches to development; United Nations Declaration on the Right to Development (1986) – Res. 41/128; Universal Declaration of Human Rights (1948); Vienna Declaration (1993)

Further reading

Amnesty International: http://www.amnesty.org/
Human Rights Watch Website: http://www.hrw.org/
Ignatieff, M. (2002) "The Rights Stuff," *The New York Review of Books* 13 June, 49:10.
Patterson, D. (2000) "HIV/AIDS, Human Rights and Development," *Development Bulletin* 52: 12–13.
Rabben, L. (2002) *Fierce Legion of Friends: A History of Human Rights Campaigns and Campaigners*, Hyattsville MD: Quixote Center.

Steiner, H. and Alston, P. (2000, 2nd edn) *International Human Rights in Context*, Oxford: Oxford University Press.
UNAIDS (Joint United Nations Programme on HIV/AIDS): http://www.unaids.org
Women in Development (1996) special issue on "Development and Human Rights," 2:1.

CHRISTINE OBBO

human rights indicators

Human rights indicators show how far countries comply with **human rights** obligations. They have been called for to increase **transparency** and monitoring of human rights as a means of measuring **governance**. Some initial indicators exist within the New Economic Partnership for African Development (NEPAD), and under the Human Rights Committee under the International Covenant on Civil and Political Rights (ICCPR) (1966). Proponents of indicators, however, insist that these current approaches are diversified and extended. Some obvious features to be included in indicators are the acceptance and ratification of international human rights treaties, their incorporation into **domestic law**, and enforcement.

See also: domestic law; human rights; indicators of development; measuring development

PAUL OKOJIE

human security

Human security is an approach to development that seeks to secure the welfare and needs of individuals (see also **capability approach; human development; well-being**). Proponents of human security argue that security and development **institutions** and values should be judged according to how far they seek to promote and secure human needs. Thus, human security is often seen in contradistinction to the conventional model of national **security**, which has traditionally been defined as military defense of sovereign territory against "external" military threats (see military and security). Human security argues that for many, or indeed most, people in the world the most tangible threats to security come from internal conflicts (see complex emergencies; violence), preventable disease, forcible displacement, hunger (see famine; food security; malnutrition), pollution, and crime. And for others, a greater threat may come from their own state itself (see state and state reform), rather than from an "external" adversary. Human security focuses upon insecurity *wherever* the threat comes from.

The state remains the central provider of security in ideal circumstances. However, human security suggests that international security – traditionally defined as territorial integrity – does not necessarily guarantee human security. Traditional conceptions of state security are a necessary, but not sufficient, condition of human welfare. Indeed, citizens of states that are "secure," in traditional terms, can also be perilously *insecure* in terms of health, welfare (see welfare economics; welfare indicators; welfare state), human rights and education. Human security aims to redress this asymmetry of attention and resources.

As a concept, human security problematizes the objectives of security and the tools for achieving security. It considers the relationship between development and security, and raises the role of dignity and equity in security. The idea has gained currency in the post-Cold War world as political and intellectual arenas have opened up, and challenges to the state-centric, power-based model of international politics have grown. In addition, globalization is important to this changing context, as it has broadened the unit of analysis in international relations and brought social and economic insecurities to the fore. Finally, normative changes have underpinned, and resulted from, these developments, resulting in strengthened norms relating to human rights. However, it would be wrong to suggest that human security is "new." In fact, it is in some ways a re-labeling of older ideas and arguments, including "comprehensive security" and "societal security." It also owes some roots to the tradition of political liberalism.

In policy terms, human security has been embraced by a number of individual states – notably Canada, Japan and Norway – and a Human Security Network of states to promote human security as a guide to policy. In addition, the United Nations Development Programme (UNDP) has been a pioneer of the concept. At both the theory and policy levels, however, there is disagreement about the scope and focus of human security, leading critics to claim that it is too vague and aims to be too inclusive of all aspects of human rights in unrealistic ways.

See also: capability approach; environmental security; food security; freedom versus choice; human rights; job security; military and security; security; welfare indicators; well-being

Further reading

Commission on Human Security (2003) *Human Security Now: Protecting and Empowering People*, New York: Commission on Human Security.

Newman, E. (2001) "Human Security and Constructivism," *International Studies Perspectives* 2:3 239–51.

EDWARD NEWMAN

humanitarianism

Humanitarianism is a principle adopted by many states, aid donors, and relief workers to provide emergency assistance based on needs and without discrimination. In 1965, the International Red Cross and Red Crescent Movement (see Red Cross and Red Crescent) enunciated seven principles to be used in aid and emergency assistance: humanity, impartiality, neutrality, independence, voluntary service, unity, and universality. The aim of humanitarianism is to focus official development assistance on addressing the most immediate human needs, especially in conflict, but in peacetime too.

Under the Geneva Conventions and the statute of the International Committee of the Red Cross (ICRC), the ICRC enjoys what is called an "exclusive mandate," which allows ICRC personnel to visit and interview those held in detention or place of internment. They can monitor whether those engaged in armed conflicts are observing international humanitarian law. They can help to trace missing families during armed conflict or help those in internment to exchange letters with members of their families. Other aid agencies that observe the principle of neutrality (i.e. non-intervention on different sides of conflicts), are, under the Geneva Conventions, entitled to what is referred to as a "general humanitarian mandate," and which respects their ability to intervene in humanitarian crises (see **right of intervention**).

Humanitarianism raises some important questions. Should those who commit **genocide** and other atrocities receive humanitarian assistance in the same way as their victims? Should levels of assistance be related to the conduct of the combatants? Some critics have argued that humanitarian assistance in conflicts may serve to prolong the conflict. In 1997, for example, the British government used aid to influence the behavior of the side it disapproved of in the civil **war** in Sierra Leone.

A further question is whether humanitarian assistance should continue to be neutral. For some, partisanship by aid workers may both undermine the provision of assistance and cheapen aid work. For the opposing side (often referred to as the "new humanitarians") the politics of the conflict is an objective consideration when organizing humanitarian assistance. They argue that relief workers should bear testimony of the suffering or atrocities caused by combatants. More generally, critics acknowledge that all aid and emergency assistance is rooted within some system of values or political influence between donors and governments. Aid agencies can exert considerable influence on events locally, if not, nationally in the area where they are working, and especially after the collapse of a state (see **state and state reform**). In some cases, the combined resources of the aid agencies can exceed the budget of the collapsed state (see **weak states**). **Accountability** and **transparency** of humanitarian assistance is therefore necessary to maintain trust in the presence of assistance (see also the controversies associated with the **Red Cross and Red Crescent**).

An emerging type of assistance is known as "humanitarian intervention," and involves military intervention by the international community under the aegis of the **United Nations**, frequently for combating suspected genocide and other atrocities. There are strict rules under the UN system for humanitarian intervention (see **peacekeeping**). Force can be used where a country poses a threat to peace and security (Chapter VII of the UN Charter). However, there is no provision under the UN Charter, other than in self-defense, for one country to violate the sovereignty of another country.

Since the end of the **Cold War**, there have been a number of instances where the military (whether under the UN or not) have been drawn into humanitarian intervention (see **military and security**). It means using force to keep the peace and using the same force in emergency relief, and may lead to a confusion of roles. Some observers argue that the military should be confined to providing the technical infrastructure to enable aid agencies to provide relief, rather than provide relief themselves – as happened in Iraq, Kosovo and in Afghanistan. In Afghanistan, the dominant military power was accused of using humanitarian assistance instrumentally in order to achieve a predetermined goal and hence that humanitarian assistance was politicized. Although some are alarmed at this pattern of humanitarian assistance, others see it as an honest reflection of the current development in global politics.

The convergence between humanitarian assistance and militarism is seen by some as the best way of producing a stable political system in the country concerned. This is what is called the "**coherence** agenda." All parties involved in "nation building" act together in the interest of the nation-state. In this way, donors can exert a more critical influence in the use of their resources, and donor countries can shape aid agendas in furtherance of their foreign-policy objectives.

The coherence agenda, however, is controversial. Proponents of humanitarian intervention argue that the nature of war has changed since the end of Cold War, and that the majority of armed conflicts are now within countries, and fought by insurgents who do not always observe the **law of armed conflict (LAC)** and the Geneva Conventions. According to this view, the brutal nature of atrocities committed in armed conflicts calls for a different kind of response, and hence, humanitarian intervention represents a comprehensive way of influencing local politics and achieving peacekeeping.

Opponents of this view point to major ethical questions in the partial use of humanitarian intervention. They doubt if it is possible to confine humanitarian intervention to restoring order and providing emergency relief, and instead suggest that the coherence agenda might compromise the independence and integrity of aid agencies.

See also: aid; complex emergencies; emergency assistance; famine; Médecins San Frontières; natural disasters; peacekeeping; post-conflict rehabilitation; right of intervention; Red Cross/ Red Crescent; war

Further reading

Boutros-Ghali, B. (1992) *Agenda for Peace: Preventive Diplomacy, Peacemaking and Peacekeeping*, New York: United Nations.

Forman, S. and Stewart, P. (eds) (2000) *Good Intentions: Pledges of Aid for Postconflict Recovery*, Boulder: Lynne Reinner.

Galtung, J. (ed.) (1985) *Peace, War, and Defense: Essays in Peace Research, Vol. II*, Copenhagen: Christian Ejlers.

International Committee of the Red Cross: http://www.icrc.org/

International Federation of Red Cross/Red Crescent Societies: http://www.ifrc.org/

Médecins Sans Frontières website: http://www.msf.org

Rieff, D. (2002) *A Bed for the Night: Humanitarianism in Crisis*, Vancouver, WA: Vintage.

PAUL OKOJIE

illiteracy

Illiteracy usually refers to the inability to read or write. In terms of international development, it is also relevant for **human rights, poverty, governance**, and **health**, and is linked to questions of **livelihoods, gender**, and **empowerment**. In 1978, the **United Nations Education, Scientific and Cultural Organization (UNESCO)** stated that, "a person is illiterate who cannot with understanding both read and write a short statement on his [sic] everyday life" (in Limage, 1999:79). But this approach overlooks different needs of literacy in various contexts. Increasingly, analysts now discuss a plurality of forms of literacy, such as *functional literacy* (i.e. the purposes for which literacy is needed); and *post literacy* (i.e. the skills learnt after initial literacy has been achieved).

In 2002, the UK Department for International Development (DFID) proposed that basic skills in reading, writing and numeracy are the "key that unlocks the range of *literacies* that people need in an increasingly globalized world." Different literacies include **media** literacy, map reading, political literacy, economic literacy, legal literacy, computer literacy, and health literacy. The literacies approach recognizes that someone may possess reading and writing skills yet remain illiterate in a given situation because she or he does not possess, for example, computer skills. Illiteracy is therefore defined operationally in terms of demands placed upon a person in a given context.

Advocates of *functional literacy* emphasize that literacy should have a functional value as defined by the specific context of the user. Literacy therefore is not a state to be attained but as a lifelong and incremental process. UNESCO (1978) distinguished between illiteracy and functional illiteracy. A person was defined as functionally illiterate

> who cannot engage in all those activities in which literacy is required for effective functioning of his [sic] group and community and also for enabling him to continue to use his reading, writing and calculation for his own and the community's development.
>
> (In Limage, 1999:79)

The notion of functional literacy highlights the problems with short-term "hit and run" literacy programs that are intended to transform illiterate people into literate people. At the end of such programs (if not during the programs) the newly acquired literacy skills have to be both used and updated as circumstances change. There are now calls for new approaches to *post literacy* (i.e. interventions following initial literacy teaching), which recognize the essential differences between learning literacy skills and using them outside classroom environments.

One key event relating to literacy was the 1990 World Conference on Education For All (WCEFA), at Jomtien, Thailand, which sought international commitment to extending **education. United Nations** agencies such as UNESCO, **United Nations Children's Fund (UNICEF), United Nations Development Programme (UNDP)** and the **World Bank** were active at the conference. It was agreed to halve the 1990 adult illiteracy rates by 2000, with particular emphasis on **gender** disparities. However, at the World Education Forum in Dakar in 2000, the World Bank acknowledged that this target was not reached. Subsequently, the United Nations declared 2003–2012 to be the United Nations Literacy Decade.

In promoting the United Nations Literacy Decade, UNESCO showed that there were about 860 million illiterate adults in the world in 2000; about 70 percent in Sub-Saharan Africa, South and West Asia, and the Arab States and North Africa; about 66 percent were women; plus 100 million children had no access to school. These figures suggest that illiteracy will remain fundamental to international development for many years.

Historically, many nationally focused literacy programs were unsuccessful for various reasons, including shortages of trained teachers, appropriate teaching materials and administrative systems. Increasingly, analysts prefer local literacy initiatives that complement rather than replace national educational initiatives. Tailoring literacy programs to localities can acknowledge the crucial elements of learners' needs and cultural backgrounds such as first language. Literacy programs may also provide child-care and transport (see **transport policy**) facilities to encourage female participation.

The motivation of literacy learners also needs to be considered. Western perspectives may emphasize the literacy as an intrinsic value; but people do not always reap immediate economic benefits from literacy. Some historic teaching by **missionaries** sometimes emphasized the spiritual value of reading the Bible rather than focusing on potential economic benefits of literacy (see also **Christianity; religion**). Literacy clearly helps with vocational skills training, but learners may drop out if literacy is taught before livelihood skills (see **livelihoods**).

Finally, much academic work on illiteracy in developing countries focuses on learners as members of a **community**. Yet, in developed countries illiteracy is often highlighted as a problem encountered by individuals, with issues such as dyslexia, autism and emotional and behavioral difficulties (see **disability**). These differences in approaches need to be considered when extending education from developed to developing countries.

See also: disability; education; human capital

Further reading

DFID (2002) *Improving Livelihoods for the Poor: the Role of Literacy*, London: DFID.

Fordham, P., Holland, D. and Millican, J. (1995) *Adult Literacy: A Handbook for Development Workers*, Oxford: Oxfam/VSO.

Limage, L. (1999) "Literacy Practices and Literacy Policies: Where has UNESCO Been and Where Might it be Going?," *International Journal of Educational Development* 19:1 75–89.

Oxenham, J., Diallo, A. H., Katahoire, A. R., Petkova-Mwangi, A. and Sall, O. (2002) *Skills and Literacy Training for Better Livelihoods: A Review of Approaches and Experiences*, Africa Region Human Development Working Paper Series, Africa Region: World Bank.

World Bank (2000) *Education for All: From Jomtien to Dakar and Beyond*, Washington DC: World Bank.

CHRISTOPHER J. REES

ILO *see* International Labor Organization (ILO)

IMF *see* International Monetary Fund (IMF)

IMPERIALISM *see* colonialism, history of; colonialism, impacts of; Marxism

import substitution

Import substitution refers to the policy objective of reducing dependence on the international economy by protecting new domestic industries. In the 1950s and 1960s, most developing countries pursued import substitution policies believing that rapid **industrialization** would take place as imports would be replaced by expansion of output from protected, domestically replaced goods.

It wasn't until the 1980s that experience presented compelling evidence that import substitution discouraged **export-led growth**, and was associated with foreign exchange shortages and generally retarded **economic development**. By the 1980s and 1990s, most developing countries introduced trade liberalization polices and initiatives for making incentives uniform across exporting and import-competing goods to integrated their economies into the international economic system.

Import substitution policies were borne from a general distrust of markets and a belief that governments could more effectively organize and lead economic activity with regulation and control of private economic activity. This view was shared by most economists in the immediate post-World War II decades, in developed and developing countries alike. The view was partly a legacy of the Great Depression, partly due to the belief that the Soviet Union had succeeded in its development and industrial aspirations through central planning, and partly because of the perceived success of wartime controls. Import substitution advocates argued that new industries would not be able to compete with ones already established in developing countries (see **infant industries; protectionism**). It was widely believed that domestic industries in developing countries should be protected, for four main reasons. First, it was assumed that exports would not grow rapidly enough to meet increasing demands for imports. Second, it was believed that the **comparative advantage** of developing countries would forever lie in primary production and industrialization would not occur if **free trade** policies were adopted. The third reason was to protect infant industries. The fourth was so-called elasticity pessimism.

The infant industry argument supports the protection of a new industry under two circumstances. First, a new industry should be supported if initial costs are high, but in time, the industry would become sufficiently competitive on world markets to experience cost reductions to repay the start-up costs. Second, the infant industry argument is in support of protection of a new industry if it is not initially privately profitable because some of the start-up expenditure leads to **productivity** increases that are not captured by those

undertaking the initial investment (i.e. externality issues).

Elasticity pessimism is a premise that argues that, at least in the case of primary commodities, income elasticity of demand is relatively low and the price elasticity of demand even lower. Hence, an increase in exports would put downward pressure on prices, decreasing prospects for growth in foreign exchange earnings. It was argued that import substitution would provide greater demand for foreign exchange, given the structure of exports during the 1950s and 1960s.

Import substitution policies were implemented through a number of measures, including high levels of **protectionism** once domestic productive capacity was starting in a certain line of activity, and the licensing and ultimate prohibition of imports of particular goods when domestic production capacity was deemed sufficient to supply the domestic market. Furthermore, imports of capital goods and raw materials used in industries were encouraged; **state-owned enterprises (SOEs)** were established; and investments were made directly by the state sector in new manufacturing activities. None of these policies included provision for reducing protection after an initial period, or identification of where dynamic externalities were largest.

Initially, import substitution policies created rapid growth of industrial output. However, in time the policies proved to be import intensive, and export earnings failed to increase as rapidly as did the demand for foreign exchange required to import capital equipment and intermediate goods. Most countries implementing import substitution policies quickly experienced foreign exchange shortages. Moreover, import substitution polices were soon shown to discourage export growth, as producers were given little incentive to expand capacity more rapidly than domestic demand growth, as international prices were much lower than the prices of the sheltered domestic market.

In the early 1970s, empirical evidence of the high costs of import substitution regimes was accumulating. At a similar time, starting first in Taiwan, several East Asian economies began growing rapidly under policies diametrically opposed to those of import substitution. It was generally realized that the rapid growth in demand for imports and the sluggish growth in foreign exchange earnings were not due to the vagaries of the international market, or to weather variations that affected primary production, but rather due to the failure of the import substitution policies. By the 1980s and early 1990s, most developing countries began trade liberalization programs and began introducing policies to make incentives uniform for production across exporting and importing competing goods (mostly through the exchange rate). While the benefits of export-led growth are now widely recognized, the precise mechanisms of causation, and the combination of supporting policies conducive to rapid **economic growth**, are still the subject of analysis and debate.

See also: export-led growth; free trade; industrialization; industrialization and trade policy; infant industries; newly industrialized economies (NIEs); protectionism; trade

Further reading

Bruton, H. (1989) "Import Substitution," pp. 1601–44 in Chenery, H. and Srinivasan, T. (eds) *Handbook of Development Economics Vol II*, Amsterdam: Elsevier Science Publishers.
Bruton, H. (1998) "A Reconsideration of Import Substitution," *Journal of Economic Literature* 36:2 903–36.
Krueger, A. (1995) *Trade Policies and Developing Nations*, Washington DC: Brookings Institution.
Krueger, A. (1997) "Trade Policy and Economic Development: How We Learn," *The American Economic Review* 87:1 1–22.
Perkins, D., Radelet, S., Snodgrass, D., Gillis, M. and Roemer, M. (2001) *Economics of Development*, New York: Norton. See Chapter 18.

ELIZABETH PETERSEN

incentive structures

Incentive structures typically exist in situations that involve delegated choice: one agent is given the responsibility for performing a task in the interest of another, in return for a payment. They may also be present in circumstances where no formal delegation relationship is involved. For instance, a donor country may condition its foreign **aid** on a recipient country's quality of economic management. Alternatively, in the context of insurance (see **risk and insurance strategies**), a plan may be in place so that the insured guards against the risk of an accident. These types of problems necessitate the use of schemes that help align the interests of one party with another. Formally, an incentive structure is a scheme that attempts to influence the action of an agent, by giving it some reward or penalty based on its action. In the presence of asymmetric information, where the action (for example, the effort) or characteristic of the agent is unobservable, the compensation is based on some observable outcome (such as performance) that is influenced by the action or characteristic.

Many incentive structures are observed in **labor markets**, where, in order to motivate workers, firms use tactics that involve both the carrot and the stick. An example, common in many developing countries, is the piece rate system in which workers are paid for each item produced or each task performed. Another system pays workers above-market wages and threatens them with dismissal if they are caught shirking. Fired workers are, of course, effectively disciplined by involuntary **unemployment**. A similar scheme rewards workers with bonuses if they are observed to be working hard whenever they are monitored. In the same vein, commissions and profit sharing are used to provide returns for employees if a desirable outcome is achieved. Deferred compensation can also be used to motivate workers. Here employees are paid less than their marginal product early in their careers and more than their marginal product later on. This incentive structure works as long as the present value of the earnings stream offered to employees is at least equal to alternative streams offered to workers elsewhere in the labor market (see **labor markets**).

Other incentive structures may base rewards, bonuses, or commissions on contests or tournaments among agents or teams of agents (e.g. salespersons). These are particularly useful when it is difficult to determine how hard agents (or teams) are working or what characteristics they possess. When rewards depend on team performance, members of a team have an incentive to help or monitor each other.

Incentive structures also exist in insurance markets where there is often moral hazard (a situation where one agent's unobservable actions can affect the liability of another). Here the optimal contract calls for deductibility provisions or coinsurance.

Incentive structures are especially prevalent in many developing countries where agrarian institutional arrangements exist in the presence of asymmetric information and pervasive risks. In these countries peer monitoring has proved to be an effective means of controlling moral hazard in labor, insurance, and credit markets. The **Grameen Bank (GB)** is a widely noted example.

See also: employment; labor markets; productivity

Further reading

Dixit, A. and Skeath, S. (1999) *Games of Strategy*, New York: Norton.

Salanié, B. (1997) *The Economics of Contracts*, Cambridge MA: MIT Press.

B. MAK ARVIN

income distribution

Income distribution refers to the gaps between rich and poor at a variety of sub-national, national and international scales. It is measured by comparing the proportion of total income going to the richest and poorest sectors of a society. One common technique is the **Gini index**, which is a statistic that measures the gap between the dispersion of an actual distribution from a hypothesized ideal in which each member of society would receive an amount equal to its share in the population. The average income of the richest nations compared to the poorest nations has changed from about 9:1 in 1900 to over 60:1 a century later (Fik, 2000). However, this use of **gross domestic product (GDP)** or **gross national product (GNP) per capita** as a measure of economic **well-being** hides inequalities of income distribution within countries, or between international social classes (see **inequality**). Increasingly, analysts use more holistic indicators of development, such as the **Human Development Index (HDI)**, which include measurements of **education** and **life expectancy**, as well as GDP per capita.

There is much literature to indicate levels of inequality in income distribution (see fuller discussion under **inequality and poverty, world trends**). Within the developing world, some East Asian **newly industrialized economies (NIEs)** have grown rapidly and are approaching the wealth of Europe and North America, but some African countries have actually seen declines in **gross national product (GNP)** in recent decades. Disparities may occur because of various economic, social and political factors. For example, the countries of Latin America have the greatest income disparities. Brazil is probably the nation with the most extreme income distribution. The ratio of the incomes of the top 20 percent of the population to the bottom 20 percent is 32:1. This disparity has been attributed to a land ownership system where less than 2 percent of the farm owners own 65 percent of the agricultural land. The Philippines provides an example of ethnic and religious differences leading to poor income distribution. Citizens of Chinese origin make up less than 1 percent of the population yet they control 30 percent of the top 500 companies, thus concentrating wealth in the hands of a few. Economic disparities between the Muslim south and Christian north underlie ongoing religious conflicts.

See also: Gini index; inequality; inequality and poverty, world trends

Further reading

Birdsall, N. (1998) "Life Is Unfair: Inequality in the World," *Foreign Policy* 111: 76–93.

Fik, T. (2000) *The Geography of Economic Development*, Boston MA: McGraw Hill.

WILLIAM R. HORNE

indicators of development

Indicators are compromises between the ideal of **measuring development** (however "development" is defined) and realities of data availability throughout the world. Indicators are primarily used for informing and influencing **international organizations and associations** and donors of **aid**, although they are sometimes used for developing national strategy and policy within developing countries. Aid provision often is linked to measurable targets (see **conditionality**), particularly where aid is dependent on international comparisons between countries. But is worth noting that the vast disparity between the demographic size and economic performance of countries can mean "the greatest apparent progress towards development targets could be achieved by concentrating resources on small countries which will have a tendency to fall at the extremes in the indicator rankings" (Lievesley, 2001:13). The goal of halving world **poverty** by 2015 (see **Millennium Development Goals (MDGs)**) has broad targets such as universal primary **education**, **empowerment** of women, and reductions in infant mortality (see **infant and child mortality**). Ideally, indicators should provide the basis for rational, evidence-based decision-making, without political influence.

Early indicators of development focused primarily on economic processes, with the measurement of **gross domestic product (GDP)** given pre-eminence in the context of an ideological focus on free markets. The **Human Development Index (HDI)** was developed to provide a broader measure of **life expectancy**, **education** participation, literacy levels (see **illiteracy**), and GDP. Like all indicators of human development, HDI takes a selected range of data to construct a measure, and is an indicator shaped by the particular definition of development being used. Therefore other indicators have been produced, each of which provides a different emphasis on development themes, and each of which is constructed using data that are produced widely within the global statistical system. As such, indicators are surrogate measures of **human development**, because they are not constructed using data specially collected within the objective definition of a measurement of human development. Three further **United Nations Development Programme (UNDP)** indicators illustrate different conceptual emphases.

While HDI measures conditions that may encourage development (longevity of life, literacy, and wealth), the Human Poverty Index (HPI) (UNDP, 2001) seeks to determine whether such prior conditions have had an effect. Data components for HPI include the probability of not living to the age of forty, adult illiteracy rates, access to improved water sources, and childhood **malnutrition** (percentage of **children** aged to five who are underweight). One limitation of using indicators such as the HPI is that many of the poorest countries will not have the statistical capacity to produce all the data that produce the measures. HDI at least uses data that are available from 173 countries, while HPI was produced in 2002 for 88 developing countries, African countries in particular being problematical in data provision – a problem when Africa is identified as being particularly in **debt** (see **Heavily Indebted Poor Countries (HIPC) initiative**).

The **Gender-related Development Index (GDI)** takes the emphasis away from prior conditions and outcomes, to evaluate the extent to which there is equality for women in each country. GDI takes the HDI measure and adjusts it downward for gender equality. In 2002, the GDI was produced for 146 countries, and at the bottom end of the table, there was little difference between HDI and GDI rankings for those African countries that produced data.

The **Gender Empowerment Measure (GEM)** acknowledges that an important basis of the GDI still is economic, notably income as reported via GDP. **Empowerment** does not directly require income, so the GEM measures two further components: levels of female participation in the labor market, and political participation. GEM further illustrates the intersecting problems of data availability and national characteristics. For example, one of the component measures is the percentage of seats in parliament held by women, and so assumes that parliamentary **democracy** exists. Consequently GEM was reported in 2002 for only one (Bangladesh) of the thirty-six "Low Human Development" countries in the HDI rank list, and below rank 116 of 173 HDI countries, Bangladesh alone has a GEM index.

As national and international agencies have placed more emphasis on the role of information communications technologies (ICTs) in development, new indicators have been constructed. The Technology Achievement Index (TAI) assesses "the level of technological progress and capacity of a country to participate in the network age" (Desai et al., 2002). UNDP is developing an index of "e-readiness." The **Food and Agriculture Organization (FAO)** has produced a Food Insecurity Index (FAO, 2000) (see **food security**).

As development theory articulates more complex and multivariate conceptions of development, more demands are placed on official statistical systems, and more secondary and surrogate data are used, often coming from different agencies, with different collection methodologies and collection times and time periods. However, the usage of indicators often ignores "essential metadata" (Lievesley, 2001:12). Comparison over time can be problematic, although like rankings it is frequently used in ignorance of metadata warnings about statistical inconsistencies. Statistically insignificant differences can be overlooked; for example in the 2002 HPI index for Haiti (42.3) and Cambodia (43.4), which is the difference between the rankings of 71 and 76 respectively. A major criticism of the use of indicators is the assumption that rank positions are indicative of significant difference – for example, the difference between ranking 1 and 2 interpreted the same as between 140 and 141.

See also: Gender Empowerment Measure (GEM); Gender-related Development Index (GDI); Gini index; gross domestic product (GDP); gross national product (GNP); Human Development Index (HDI); human rights indicators; measuring development; Paris 21; project appraisal; welfare indicators

Further reading

Desai, M., Fukuda-Parr, S., Johansson, C. and Sagasti, F. (2002) Measuring Technology Achievement of Nations and the Capacity to Participate in the Network Age, IAOS Conference: Official Statistics and the New Economy.

FAO (2000) The State of Food Insecurity in the World 2000, Rome: Food and Agriculture Organization.

Lievesley, D. (2001) "Making a Difference: A Role for the Responsible International Statistician?" The Statistician 50:4 1–38.

UNDP (2001) Human Development Report 2001: Making New Technologies Work for Human Development, New York: UNDP.

MICHAEL BLAKEMORE

indigenous knowledge

The concepts "indigenous knowledge," "traditional knowledge," and "**local knowledge**" are often used to denote a type of knowledge that has evolved within a particular **community** and cultural context, and has been passed on from one generation to another. The focus on indigenous knowledge represents a change from the fixation on Western-based, centralized and technically orientated solutions of past decades, which critics have claimed to have generally failed to improve lives of the world's poor and marginalized. Specifically, the main reasons for paying more attention to indigenous knowledge are that these emerge from the cultural context of the people concerned, and they evolve in close contact with knowledge of specific environmental conditions. Yet, indigenous knowledge is not static and is constantly adapting and changing to new circumstances and opportunities. It is also subject to identification, romanticization, and co-option by outsiders, who may wish to portray it to support other political objectives, or to harness it for profits, such as in **biopiracy**.

See also: grassroots development; local knowledge; Orientalism

URMILLA BOB

indigenous medicine

Indigenous medicine is a generic term for medical practices other than those of **biomedicine**. They range from established medical knowledge systems such as Ayurvedic, Yunani, Tibetan and Chinese systems to herbal medicine and religious healing by a range of practitioners such as indigenous medical doctors, barefoot doctors, religious specialists, and gifted individuals. These diverse indigenous medicine systems are often encoded as a combination of practical, religious, moral or symbolic knowledge.

Indigenous medicine systems offer a broad spectrum of treatments to the sufferer depending on the severity of the perceived illness. Often, medicines (compounds of plant, animal or minerals) are combined with dietary prescriptions, blood-letting, acupuncture, massages, witchcraft, exorcism rituals, prayers, and drama, that restore health. Indigenous medicine allows greater possibility for acknowledging the social constructions of disease (see **disease, social constructions of**) and its expression encodes cultural perceptions of health. Here the performance of healing is not just a cure but also a symbolic transformation. These diverse healing practices are therapeutic, create a curative context for psychosomatic disorders, give cognitive assurance, and enable the expression of individual dissent and feelings in society.

Unlike biomedicine, indigenous medicine sees the individual sufferer not as an isolated suffering system but as a holistic body embedded in a matrix of social relations: it is cosmological. For instance, Tibetan medicine emphasizes the relationship between the body, mind, soul and the social world. Here illness is an expression of disharmony and imbalance between the five elements and the three humors that make the body. The emphasis is on the restoration of humoral equilibrium disturbed by emotions, dietary imbalances, ancestral spirits, angry spirits, and of seasonal variations. On the other hand, healing in shamanism may involve ritual offerings or séances wherein the supernatural spirits responsible for the illness are placated, and animal sacrifices may be performed in conjunction with the recitation of place names or soul flights of the shamans. However, in both systems social and individual health are linked.

The differences between biomedicine and indigenous medicine are sometimes represented as an opposition between the West and the non-West, or between the modern and the traditional. This classification is rather simplistic. The differences between them are in the domains of philosophy, in methods, diversity of practitioners and in the organization of practices. It can be stated

that biomedicine cures while indigenous medicine heals. Sometimes healing performances, though oriented toward a particular individual's suffering at a particular moment in time, are also social healing which address the scars of history and of oppression. In many parts of the world and in the former colonies, biomedical practices were perceived as an expression and extension of hegemonic colonial practices (see **colonialism, history of; colonialism, impacts of**). In such contexts, **indigenous knowledge** and indigenous medicine have emerged as tropes of self-affirmation. In the contemporary period the resurgence of **indigenous people** and indigenous medicine are related and express cultural identities.

The continuing efficacy of these indigenous healers in responding to immediate local health concerns has largely been responsible for their persistance and co-existence with biomedicine. However, an uncritical valorization of indigenous medicine is dangerous, and the therapeutic efficacy of biomedicine cannot be underestimated. Ultimately, people combine diverse medical practices for regaining health.

See also: biomedicine; health; health and poverty; indigenous knowledge; local knowledge; nutrition; pharmaceuticals

Further reading

Laderman, C. and Roseman, M. (eds) (1996) *The Performance of Healing*, Routledge: New York.

VIBHA ARORA

indigenous people

Indigenous people are people who originate or live in locations that have since become colonized or inhabited by other, usually more prominent groups. Indigenous people have long had a tense relationship to development. From the beginning of the conquest of the Americas until the 1960s, indigenous **population**s in the white settler colonies were typically regarded as people chronically lacking in "development" (uncivilized, barbarous, backward). Early in the conquest process, they were sometimes regarded as permanently inferior and incapable of change, an assessment used to justify policies of forced removal or **genocide**. Later, they were subject to cultural assimilation, relocation to reserves and coercive "improvement" that undermined their **health, livelihoods,** families, **institutions,** languages, identities, and much more (see also **ethnicity/identity; culture**).

In the 1970s, intensive lobbying and organizing by indigenous people and their supporters shifted attention to the ways in which indigenous people had been negatively affected by national "development" programs, most significantly by large-scale infrastructure projects such as **dams** and roads, by plantations, mining and forest industries, and by the planned settlement of migrants on their traditional territories. These programs often required forced resettlement of indigenous populations. Resistance to **resettlement** became a focus of protest and political mobilization on site, in national arenas, and in international forums, notably the **United Nations,** where a Working Group on Indigenous People was established in 1982.

In the 1990s, the relationship between indigeneity and development shifted again. Indigenous people were represented, and often represented themselves, as the guardians of **biodiversity** knowledge vital to the planetary future, and exemplars of an alternative model of development that is **community**-based, ecologically friendly, and guided by a distinctive spirituality (see also **community-based natural resource management (CBNRM); ecodevelopment; local knowledge**).

The trajectory of formal international conventions, declarations and policies regarding indigenous people has mirrored these shifts in emphasis. The **International Labor Organization (ILO)**'s 1957 Indigenous and Tribal Populations Convention 107 was assimilationist, designed to facilitate the integration of these "less advanced" groups into the national community. It was replaced in 1989 by ILO Convention 169 on Indigenous and Tribal Peoples, which explicitly notes the damage done to indigenous people in the name of progress, and recognizes

the rights of indigenous people to ownership, possession, and access to their traditional lands

and resources on their lands; prevention of discrimination in the terms, practices, and benefits of employment; government provision of adequate, appropriate health services and educational programs in cooperation and consultation with the people concerned; and support for indigenous language instruction for children.

(ILO, 1989; see also **employment**)

Indicating the shift to an emphasis on the value of indigenous cultures for **sustainable development,** Principle 22 of the Rio Declaration at the **Earth Summit (1992) (United Nations Conference on Environment and Development)** stated that "indigenous people and their communities have a vital role in environmental management and development because of their knowledge and traditional practices." The **Convention on Biological Diversity (CBD)** (formalized in 1993) similarly recognized the role of indigenous people as stewards of nature and knowledge. The United Nations Declaration on the Rights of Indigenous People (1993), still making its way through the UN system, combines the recognition of past damage, the need to recognize indigenous rights, and the contribution of indigenous knowledge, **culture**s and practices to sustainable and **equitable development**.

International development organizations have also undergone a shift in their relationship with indigenous people. The adversarial stance signaled by protests against **World Bank** funded megaprojects was modified in 1982 when the Bank adopted a policy on indigenous and tribal people committing itself to a policy of protection or "do no harm." This policy was revised in 1991 to apply to a wider group, and recognized the right of indigenous people to participate in and benefit from development projects. In 2003 the Bank announced a Global Fund for Indigenous People offering small grants for sustainable development and other culturally-appropriate initiatives proposed by indigenous people's organizations, capacity building for indigenous leaders, and financial support for the UN Permanent Forum on Indigenous Issues. The Bank now expresses its relationship with indigenous people in terms of "partnership" and the need to nurture and build upon indigenous knowledge and capacities – a stance unthinkable two decades before (see **partnerships**). Other development agencies have similar pro-indigenous policies. Nevertheless, damaging megaprojects are still constructed: the damming of India's Narmada river, which displaced hundreds of thousands of tribal people without supplying adequate land for resettlement, is a case in point (see **dams; displacement**).

The definition of indigenous people remains a contentious issue. The ILO 169 definition refers to tribal groups that are distinct from national majorities, or groups present before colonial conquest, who retain some or all of their own social, economic, cultural and political institutions. Given the diversity of conditions and experiences, however, the ILO recognizes that boundaries are hard to draw, and makes "self-identification as indigenous or tribal" a fundamental criterion. This approach corresponds to the dynamism of the indigenous people's movement. Although the term indigenous people was first used in relation to the white settler colonies (such as the Americas, Australia, New Zealand) where it referred to a clearly identifiable group, it has since been adopted by disenfranchised groups in Africa and Asia that have found in the movement a source of inspiration, support, and the possibility of claiming internationally recognized rights. Rather than describe a fixed category of people, the term indigenous has come to signal a process and phenomenon that occurs in struggles that pit localized groups against encompassing states. Therefore, millions of people in Asia and Africa who actually or potentially experience this scenario fall within its compass (Gray, 1995).

Researchers have begun to explore the conjunctures, processes and mechanisms by which identification as indigenous emerges (e.g. Li, 2000). They have also examined the risks associated with the indigenous peoples' movement. One is the risk that exaggerated expectations of indigenous people as "ecologically noble savages" may be disappointed, undermining support for their cause (Baviskar, 1997; Conklin and Graham, 1995). The risk is intensified where legal rights to resources are made contingent on **biodiversity** protection – presumed to be "natural" to natives – in ways that do not recognize their changing aspirations and the market-oriented production regimes in which they are often involved. Disenfranchised groups that no longer have a "special" relation to nature because they have been reduced to a landless, laboring underclass, such as the San of southern Africa, may be overlooked (Sylvain, 2002). People who have migrated away from their ancestral areas, often under duress, may find themselves excluded from rights as "indigenous," and, in the worst-case scenario, subject to expulsion by indigenous groups reasserting exclusive control over their territory. The embedding of rights and identities in a spiritual attachment to an ancestral place, and their protection under **international law**, has furthered the struggles of some of the world's most oppressed people (Muehlebach, 2001).

See also: authoritarianism; displacement; ethnicity/identity; International Covenant on Economic, Social and Cultural Rights; race and racism; resettlement; shifting cultivation; slavery; social justice; transmigration

Further reading

Baviskar, A. (1997) *In the Belly of the River: Tribal Conflicts Over Development in the Narmada Valley*, Oxford and New Delhi: Oxford India Paperbacks.

Conklin, B. and Graham, L. (1995) "The Shifting Middle Ground: Amazonian Indians and Eco-Politics," *American Anthropologist* 97: 695–710.

Gray, A. (1995) "The Indigenous Movement in Asia," pp. 35–58 in Barnes, H., Gray, A. and Kingsbury, B. (eds) *Indigenous Peoples of Asia*, Ann Arbor: The Association for Asian Studies.

Li, T. (2000) "Articulating Indigenous Identity in Indonesia: Resource Politics and the Tribal Slot," *Comparative Studies in Society and History* 42: 149–79.

Muehlebach, A. (2001) " 'Making Place' at the United Nations: Indigenous Cultural Politics at the U.N. Working Group on Indigenous Populations," *Cultural Anthropology* 16: 415–48.

Sylvain, R. (2002) "Land, Water, and Truth: San Identity and Global Indigenism," *American Anthropologist* 104: 1074–85.

TANIA MURRAY LI

industrial district model

Industrial districts are geographic concentrations of **small and medium enterprises (SMEs)** in the same industry which feature networked relations of flexible production within a particular socio-economic community. Industrial districts are a particular form of agglomeration economy wherein firms benefit from external economies (e.g. **clustering** of required inputs for production such as raw material suppliers, and local pooling of specialized labor). Industrial districts also feature joint action on the part of firms, such as the formation of industry associations for marketing, lobbying, joint input purchase or quality certification. Supportive government policies, e.g. on infrastructure, credit, **trade** and logistics support, are considered an important feature of the industrial district model.

The theory of industrial districts was first formulated in 1920 by Alfred Marshall in his *Principles of Economics*, and the concept was extended in the 1970s by Italian theorists writing on the "Third Italy" with its socially-embedded production and strong cultural ties among producers. Since the late 1980s, English-language authors have taken up study of industrial districts. In this literature, the terms "industrial district" and "industrial cluster" are often used interchangeably, although some authors maintain that while clusters are simply geographic agglomerations of firms in the same industry, industrial districts necessarily feature higher-order characteristics of explicit joint action among firms. Cluster studies have since been conducted in countries such as India, Brazil, Pakistan, Kenya and Taiwan in sectors including textiles, footwear, surgical instruments, garments, and electronics.

Industrial districts have been of particular policy interest to local governments around the world as a potential route to regional economic development based on local capabilities and resources. The preponderance of SMEs in industrial districts, and the frequency with which districts are found in **labor-intensive** industries, elicits interest among those seeking to promote pro-poor **sustainable livelihoods**. However, recent examinations of industrial districts have found a diverse range of forms, with hierarchical formations dominated by a few large firms increasingly common. Consequently, there is a new research agenda to determine the **poverty** and social impact of industrial districts. This includes not only examination of income **inequality** and **social exclusion** in trading patterns, but also the nature of skills formation and reproduction in the context of cluster upgrading. With regard to labor and competitiveness, industrial districts, as based on local "tacit knowledge" and **social capital** as well as flexible production methods, are theorized to feature much innovation (and well-remunerated workers whose skill is recognized). Recent research, however, questions both outcomes for workers as well as the potential for innovativeness within tightly sub-contracted production processes. A further critique of industrial district studies comes from value chain theorists (see **value chains**) who argue for locating clusters within larger aspatial markets in order to ascertain global competitiveness and the proportion of value addition retained locally.

See also: clustering; export processing zones (EPZs); free trade zones (FTZs); industrialization; institutions; technology policy; value chains

Further reading

Pyke, F. and Sengenberger, W. (eds) (1992) *Industrial Districts and Local Economic Regeneration*, Geneva: International Institute for Labor Studies.

Schmitz, H. (1999) "Global Competition and Local Cooperation: Success and Failure in the Sinos Valley, Brazil," *World Development* 27:9 1627–50.

ANNE T. KURIAKOSE

INDUSTRIAL POLICY *see* developmental state; industrialization; industrialization and trade policy

industrial standards

Industrial standards are attempts to unify the expected levels of quality and safety for industrial equipment and practices within countries and across international boundaries. They exist to ease commercial transactions and to implement legislation or guidelines concerning environmental and **occupational health** policies. Standards can cover products, services, or materials (both natural and synthetic). Voluntary standards at the international level include the ISO 9000 series on quality and the ISO 14000 series on the environment. While standards are routinely developed, by private-sector systems such as industry associations, that outline norms and guidelines specific to their industries, international and national regulatory standards are also put in place by governments to meet environmental, health and safety objectives. One example is the sanitary and phytosanitary (SPS) measures that cover trade in **food** and agricultural products. Notably, the World Trade Organization (see **World Trade Organization/General Agreement on Tariffs and Trade (WTO/GATT)**) does not come up with industrial standards itself, as this is the role of a number of private and sometimes international bodies, however, it does act as a site for trade dispute settlement between nations, including overstringent application of standards.

Another standard growing in use is the social accountability standard (SA8000) which monitors firms' adherence to **International Labor Organization (ILO)** core labor standards (see **labor rights and standards**). There are other private labeling and certification regimes, including codes of conduct, that address labor and environmental concerns and are negotiated by buyers with suppliers, or as part of an agreed consortium trademark, e.g. Rugmark, which certifies that no **child labor** was used in the production of carpets bearing its seal (see **Corporate Social Responsibility**).

Free trade theorists refer to standards as nontariff barriers (NTBs), the implication being that such regulations hurt free flow of goods and impose harsh costs on developing countries in particular to meet strict export requirements. NTBs are stated to have risen in recent years, particularly among signatories to the GATT (see **World Trade Organization/General Agreement on Tariffs and Trade (WTO/GATT)**), and who have had their tariff rates bound. Countries can put in place domestic standards that have the effect of restricting imports in competing goods, as happens frequently in the agricultural and textile industries where **protectionism** is rampant. Where importing countries have varying standards regimes, exporting firms can face considerable difficulty in obtaining the required testing and licensing, and even packaging requirements, for goods. Overall, however, standards can be said to both enhance trust among transacting parties, as well as promote public welfare in the form of minimum health, safety and environmental guarantees. Further, standards act as an incentive to technological upgrading in both process and product in producer countries. Seen in this light, industrial standards can be considered public goods which exist to protect under-served objectives, including environmental sustainability and public health, which otherwise would likely be the victims of so-called "market failure."

See also: child labor; Corporate Social Responsibility; environment and health; free trade; International Labor Organization (ILO); labor rights and standards; occupational health; protectionism; World Trade Organization/General Agreement on Tariffs and Trade (WTO/GATT)

Further reading

Rotherham, T. (2003) *Implementing Environmental, Health and Safety (EH&S) Standards, and Technical Regulations: The Developing Country Experience*, Winnipeg, Canada: IISD.
Wilson, J. (2002) "Standards, Regulation and Trade," pp. 428–38 in Hoekman, B., Mattoo, A. and English, P. (eds) *Development, Trade and the WTO: A Handbook*, Washington DC: World Bank.

ANNE T. KURIAKOSE

industrialization

Industrialization is often used interchangeably with "**economic growth**" or "development." "Developed countries" are often called "industrialized economies." The term "industrialization," however, specifically refers to a shift toward industrial production by enterprises using labor, capital and raw materials to add value. These units usually employ a number of people and are based on **mechanization**.

Initially, theoretical debates often portrayed industrialization as occurring spontaneously while an economy grows. At very low income levels, a large proportion of income is spent on **food**. As incomes begin to increase, individuals will first spend more on better quality food (and more processed foods) and then will begin to spend on manufactured consumer products (both nondurable and durable). At the same time as demand is shifting toward manufacturing, a number of changes occur on the supply side too. Growing agricultural **productivity** leads to a surplus and an increasing number of people being made redundant in this sector. The excess labor supply is now available for the manufacturing sector. In the final stage of this process, demand for services increases but slows for manufactured products. This is de-industrialization, and a number of advanced countries are in this stage.

This way of explaining industrialization was popular during the 1950s and 1960s, when the so-called dual sector models were introduced by Lewis (1955) and Fei and Ranis (1964). Dual-sector models assume two sectors in an economy – a modern, high productivity sector, and a traditional, low productivity, low wage sector (usually **agriculture**). The low marginal productivity of labor in the agricultural sector implies that withdrawing labor from agriculture is unlikely to decrease productivity (see also **rural development; rural "depressor"**). Dual-sector models continue to play an important conceptual role in the industrialization debate, but have been criticized. For example, many critics believe that the shift toward industry is rarely spontaneous. Instead, it requires investment and some level of government involvement (see **developmental state; industrialization and trade policy**; plus discussion below). In particular, critics have argued that without government intervention, surplus labor from agriculture will simply form a large pool of rural and urban workers in informal activities (see **urban informal sector; street-trading in urban areas**).

Industrialization can be measured by looking at changes in the composition of output and of **employment**. However, where production is **capital intensive**, employment growth in manufacturing will be slower than output growth. Between 1970 and 1993, manufacturing and service industries grew relative to agriculture in most developing countries. During this period, there was also a relative decline or stagnation in manufacturing in medium and high-income economies.

Industrialization has often been seen as necessary for growth and development. But it is unclear if growth is caused by industrialization, or if a shift towards industry causes growth. Much evidence suggests that industrialization can increase the dynamism of an economy. Classical economists like Smith and Ricardo showed how increased specialization or division of labor within manufacturing enhances returns. Manufacturing may also improve *dynamic* returns to scale through learning by doing or technological upgrading (see **technological capability; technology transfer**). Furthermore, the greater linkages between different producers, and the impact (or externalities) that such activities may have on other people and locations, can result in the benefits of manufacturing spreading faster (see **multiplier effect**). Manufacturing provides a market for agricultural produce as well as inputs (like machinery and **fertilizers**) into the agricultural sector. Manufacturing has often been claimed to increase agricultural productivity by absorbing excess agricultural labor or by providing capital goods for agricultural production.

The process of industrialization is also usually accompanied by intra-sectoral shifts. Economies typically begin with production in **labor-intensive**, raw material processing industries like food processing. These industries develop first because they have low capital, technology and skill requirements and a relatively large potential market. They help to increase the value added of primary products by decreasing volume, increasing shelf life and hence decreasing transport costs. Over time, however, growth will involve a shift toward other industries, firstly in consumer goods sectors (where technology and capital requirements remain low), and later in capital intensive and high technology products (see also **technology policy**). Indeed, high-technology products like electronics are now produced in many developing countries, which import and assemble inputs, and export the finished products. This kind of production has been criticized, however, as leading to "shallow industrialization" (Lall, 1996). Some analysts have suggested that deeper forms of industrialization have only occurred in the **newly industrialized economies (NIEs)** of East Asia, and some countries in Latin America.

Industrialization is also accompanied by various social, cultural and political changes, which have diverse additional impacts on development. Usually, there is a change from a relatively rural, subsistence- and often barter-based economy toward an urban, commercial and marketized economy (see **commercialization**). Industrialization is often accompanied by **rural-urban migration** and **urbanization**. Moreover, it is also associated with a rise in factory workforce populations, with attendant new health and environmental risks resulting from **pollution** or hazardous working practices (see **brown environmental agenda; environment; occupational health**). **Trade unions** and other forms of political activism result from these changes. Some analysts have argued that industrialization, and the rise of large cities, may also replace communitarian values with individualism – although this notion has been criticized for being somewhat romantic about pre-industrial life, and for overlooking the coexistence of communitarianism and individualism in both urban and rural locations.

Defining industrial policy

In recent years, academics and policy-makers have challenged the notion that industrialization is spontaneous, and instead stated that it requires careful planning and policy by governments. But what form of policy? One initial approach was to propose that industrialization should proceed through **import substitution**, which aims simultaneously to reduce dependency on imports and enhance investment in domestic (indigenous) industries (see **infant industries**). Some large developing countries such as India and Brazil adopted this approach during the mid-twentieth century, partly using import tariffs or other mechanisms of **protectionism** (see also **big push; stages of economic growth**). Import substitution,

however, later became challenged by the consideration of **export-led growth**, which focused instead on industrialization to manufacture exports, often by increasing **foreign direct investment** (FDI) in indigenous industries, or in foreign-owned industries located in the country (also see **joint venture**). Proponents of export-led growth pointed to the relatively more rapid **economic growth** of the East Asian **newly industrialized economies (NIEs)** such as Taiwan and South Korea as apparent proof of this strategy. During the 1980s, the **World Bank** and **International Monetary Fund (IMF)** argued that the success of the NIEs was based on reducing barriers to **free trade** and FDI (see **neo-liberalism**).

Increasingly, however, these approaches have been criticized. First, the dichotomy between import substitution and export-led growth has been called simplistic, and it has been argued that governments may adopt elements of each at the same time. Second, analysts have shown that the East Asian success was not attributable purely to free markets but also to selective government intervention, which encouraged careful investment in specific sectors (such as high-value products); developed a highly trained indigenous workforce; and formed political coalitions with important groups of indigenous investors (see **developmental state; technology policy**) (Wade, 1990). Indeed, historical analysis has also shown that some of the most ardent proponents of free trade such as the USA have depended upon selective government intervention and protectionism of **infant industries** in the past (Chang, 2002) (see **industrialization and trade policy**). Third, most analysts agree that it is not possible to explain relative economic growth of countries as diverse as India and Taiwan through industrial policies alone, and that questions of **culture**, countries' size, and history remain important too.

Discussions of industrial policy, therefore, depend on deciding when, where, and how far, governments should intervene (see also **leapfrogging**). Some general questions remain. First, which industries should governments identify for indigenous growth? Many developing countries specialize in producing primary products (through **agriculture** and **mineral-led development**).

Hence, one early approach was to add value to these products by developing manufacturing or service industries such as **food** processing. Such industries, however, have limited value and markets. In some countries (especially socialist, or centrally planned economies), industrialization was based on developing heavy industries, or the "commanding heights" of the economy such as **iron and steel**, transport (see **transport policy**) and construction. Mahalanobis (1953), for example, developed a model (for economies closed to imports) where industrial growth was based on expanding the capital and heavy goods sector. In many developing countries, however, this kind of heavy industrialization is not feasible because it is **capital intensive** and requires large domestic markets to be successful.

An alternative to developing capital goods is to focus on consumer goods. Markets for consumer goods are easier to enter because there is usually latent domestic demand for them, and they require less investment than heavy industry. Many Latin American countries opted for consumer goods-based industrialization in the early stages of their **import substitution** policies, but soon experienced problems because they needed to import capital goods, and were constrained by the limits of the domestic market. Early Indian planners rejected this strategy because they feared that consumer goods-based industrialization would highlight the divide between the "haves" and the "have-nots," leading to social and political problems.

A second question is: should production be in small or large units? This question also relates to whether production should be labor-intensive or capital intensive, and has implications for technology used. Schumacher (1973), for example, argued that "small is beautiful" and traced this strategy back to Gandhi and his advocacy of handloom textiles in India (see also **appropriate technology**). This approach to industrialization is **labor-intensive**, and aims to maximize local benefits of production, rather than risk losing autonomy to global economic markets (see **globalization**). Despite the attractions, however, many developing countries use less labor-intensive techniques than their labor and capital endowments would suggest, because capital is often easier to develop and import than skilled labor; governments subsidize

capital investment; **trade unions** increase wages; and low labor **productivity** inflates wage costs per unit of output. Capital intensive industrialization, on the other hand, has proved difficult to achieve because capital intensive technology is costly to develop, and requires to be competitive with existing technology that is frequently owned by **transnational corporations (TNCs)** from more developed countries. Many developing countries have sought **technology transfer** as a way to accelerate industrialization, but this is seen to be costly by investing companies, and a risk to **intellectual property rights (IPRs)**. Moreover, most research and development in capital-rich, labor-scarce Western economies is focused on saving labor, and may not be appropriate for many applications in developing countries.

A third question relates to the regions (or sectors) in which industrialization should be encouraged. The concept of "growth centers" or nodes was popular in the mid-twentieth century (e.g. Hirschmann, 1958), and led to the encouragement of investment in specific locations, often by the establishment of **free trade zones (FTZs)**. Manaus in northern Brazil is one well-known example. Targeted investment was suggested in order to prioritize scarce resources, and to encourage economic growth in less industrialized regions. This approach, however, was criticized for creating bottlenecks in the economy, and hence other analysts (e.g. Nurkse, 1953) proposed balanced growth, which involved spreading resources over a wide range of sectors. This debate has never been resolved with most countries, following the dictates of their resource constraints and political expediency to decide on the sectors to support.

A fourth question relates to the relative contribution made by indigenous and foreign-owned companies. Until the 1980s, many governments – including those in Europe and North America – supported large indigenous companies (or so-called "national champions") as a crucial part of achieving national economic success. Increasingly, however, governments see the success of indigenous companies as less important than the attraction of FDI (however it is owned) within national borders. This development is due partly to the realization of some governments that they cannot, or can no longer, compete in certain industries, so that supporting indigenous companies in these industries may fail in the long term. A further reason is that many TNCs are now so internationally based that they can no longer be seen as national (see also **technology policy**).

Industrialization remains a crucial topic within development policy, but its historic image as the primary route to economic growth and prosperity has been challenged in recent years through studies of **governance** and **inequality**, which indicate that questions of **income distribution**, **sustainable development**, and **labor rights and standards** are also important.

See also: big push; developmental state; foreign direct investment; free trade; gender and industrialization; growth rate; industrial district model; industrial standards; industrialization and trade policy; late industrialization; leapfrogging; natural resources; resource curse thesis; stages of economic growth; technological capability; technology policy; technology transfer; trade

Further reading

Chang, H.-J. (2002) *Kicking Away the Ladder: Development Strategies in Historical Perspective*, London: Anthem.

Fei, J. and Ranis, G. (1964) *Development of the Labor Surplus Economy: Theory and Policy*, Homewood IL: Irwin.

Hirschman, A. (1958) *The Strategy of Economic Development*, New Haven: Yale University Press.

Lall, S. (1996) *Learning from the Asian Tigers: Studies in Technology and Industrial Policy*, Basingstoke: Macmillan.

Lewis, W. (1955) *The Theory of Economic Growth*, London: Allen and Unwin.

Mahalanobis, P. (1953) "Some Observations on the Process of Growth of National Income," *Sankhya* September, 307–12.

Nurkse, R. (1953) "Problems of Capital Formation in Underdeveloped Countries," pp. 13–15 in Meier, G. (ed.) (1989) *Leading Issues in Development*, Oxford: Oxford University Press.

Schumacher, E. (1973) *Small is Beautiful*, London: Blond and Briggs.

Wade, R. (1990) *Governing the Market: Economic Theory and the Role of the State*, Princeton: Princeton University Press.

UMA S. KAMBHAMPATI

industrialization and trade policy

Industrialization and **trade** are intricately linked. The growth of industrialization has been associated with significant increases in international trade. The ability to induce industrialization within one country is dependent on policies governing the import of traded goods and investment.

In the early stages of industrial development, production tended to be concentrated within the textile, **food** processing and building materials sectors. Investing in these sectors offered means to diversify from **agriculture**, and allowed a means to avoid the long-term deterioration of international **terms of trade** for primary product exports. There is a high income elasticity of demand for manufactured goods, meaning that purchase of these goods is buoyant as consumer income increases.

One common policy adopted by governments is to protect indigenous **infant industries** during this early stage of industrialization (see **protectionism**). Germany and the USA are prime examples. The Soviet Union in the 1920s, however, invested chiefly in capital goods production as the basis for **economic growth**. Protecting infant industries and investing in capital goods production were two principles widely adopted by countries emerging from colonialism (see **colonialism, history of; colonialism, impacts of**) in the second half of the twentieth century: for example, India, Pakistan, and a number of Sub-Saharan African countries.

Between 1970 and 2000, a number of East and Southeast Asian countries (the "Asian Tigers"), and some Latin American countries experienced rapid industrialization and growth in trade by adopting outward-oriented development strategies (see **newly industrialized economies (NIEs); export-led growth**). This "East Asian Miracle" has strongly influenced the recommendations of the International Finance Institutions (IFIs) – not without controversy.

Table 3 shows that East Asian and Pacific countries have increased the proportion of manufacturing in GDP from 25 percent to 32 percent over three decades, while this proportion has stagnated or fallen in other world regions. In addition, Table 4 shows that for East Asian and Pacific countries, the proportion of manufactures in total exports has increased from about 32 percent to about 83 percent over the same period. Other regions have experienced similar increases – an aspect of **globalization** – but the success of East Asian countries is notable.

In addition to **protectionism** through tariffs and quotas, some developing countries adopted import and export taxes as a means of raising government revenue as alternatives to income and sales taxes (see **fiscal and monetary policy**). Taxes and quota restrictions on trade discourage both imports and exports, and inhibit "gains from trade." Influential research by the **Organization for Economic Cooperation and Development (OECD)** on industrial development in Latin America, South Asia and Southeast Asia supported these views (Little *et al.*, 1970). Around the same time, the **Asian Development Bank**

(ADB) commissioned Hla Myint to produce a critical review of Southeast Asian industrialization, which also urged the need to abandon forms of protectionism, and instead to adopt an outward-oriented trade policy (**export-led growth**).

From the 1970s, the removal of trade restrictions (i.e. trade liberalization) became a basic principle of economic policy, either spontaneously or as the result of conditionalities imposed by the IFIs as a basis for financial support. This principle is now enshrined in the rules of the World Trade Organization (WTO) – the successor to the General Agreement on Tariffs and Trade (GATT) (see **World Trade Organization/General Agreement on Tariffs and Trade (WTO/GATT)**). The basic reasons for trade liberalization are that (a) taxes and quota restrictions on imports increase the cost of manufactures to consumers, resulting in welfare loss; (b) taxes on exports discourage export earnings and are borne by low-income producers in rural areas; and (c) development of high-cost protected manufacturing reduces opportunities for export diversification. A "strong" version of these arguments is closely related to the views of neo-liberal economists (sometimes referred to as neo-classical) due to their dependence on the economic assumptions associated with "perfect

Table 3 Manufacturing, value added (percent of GDP)

	1970	1980	1990	2000
East Asia and Pacific	24.54	30.55	28.47	31.79
Latin America and Caribbean	26.87	28.47	–	20.98
Middle East & North Africa	–	8.68	12.28	–
South Asia	13.55	15.78	16.71	15.61
Sub-Saharan Africa	16.43	15.97	17.36	14.20

Source: World Bank; World Development Indicators, Washington, 2002.

Table 4 Manufactured exports (percent of merchandise exports)

	1970	1980	1990	2000
East Asia and Pacific	32.09	44.75	68.46	82.74
Latin America and Caribbean	15.85	19.62	33.98	48.46
Middle East and North Africa	4.88	6.14	15.05	14.41
South Asia	48.21	53.76	71.24	–
Sub-Saharan Africa	18.85	12.41	–	36.13

Source: World Bank; World Development Indicators, Washington, 2002.

markets" (see **neo-liberalism**). Structuralist economists, instead, insist that international markets are subject to asymmetric economic power, and are nowhere "perfect." However, a "weaker" version of the arguments against draconian trade protection, and for significant trade liberalization, is accepted by most structuralist economists.

Protectionism became associated with industrialization via **import substitution**, or inward-lookoing development seeking to replace the need to import goods by investing in indigenous industries. Trade liberalization, however, implied the adoption of outward-oriented export-led growth. Protectionism became seen as a basis for economic stagnation.

There have been numerous attempts to improve the access of exports from developing countries' markets in developed countries, the most important of which was the Uruguay Round during the conversion of the GATT into the WTO between 1986 and 1994. However, many economists would still argue that the international economy is biased in favor of the developed countries, in terms of both the basic rules and the application of dispute settlement systems.

Although much of the argument for trade liberalization is unexceptional on economic grounds, the desire to reject protectionism has occasionally oversimplified some arguments. First, there is no logical connection between import substitution and trade protectionism. Most countries have increased their production of domestic substitutes for imports while domestic markets grow. Indeed, where import substitution has occurred without protectionism, domestic production can also lead on to export development. For some products, particularly those with a low-value-to-transport-cost ratio (such as cement, beer and soft drinks), import substitution may develop through natural protection based on high transactions costs.

Second, industrialization strategies do not have to adopt or reject import substitution or export-led growth, but instead can be based on alternatives including resource-based industrialization (based on international market dynamics) and the **basic needs** approach (driven by domestic market opportunities). Many economists would argue that a predominant focus on the international dynamics is unbalanced, and that greater attention to domestic markets is required for a more balanced approach.

Third, the outward-oriented approach linked to trade liberalization has tended to be associated with increased penetration of developing countries by **transnational corporations (TNCs)** based on their control of international markets and of technology. The role of TNCs was highlighted in recent years through the attempt to impose a **Multilateral Agreement on Investment (MAI)**, which would have placed TNCs in a privileged position. Activists have sought to achieve better forms of international **corporate social responsibility** through the United Nations Center for Transnational Corporations (UNCTC) and the United Nations Conference on Trade and Development (UNCTAD).

See also: big push; developmental state; Dutch disease; economic development; export-led growth; import substitution; industrialization; late industrialization; leapfrogging; Multilateral Agreement on Investment (MAI); natural resources; newly industrialized economies (NIEs); protectionism; resource curse thesis; tariffs; technology policy; terms of trade; trade; World Trade Organization/General Agreement on Tariffs and Trade (WTO/GATT)

Further reading

Chenery, H., Behrman, J. and Srinivasan, T. (eds) (1988–95) *Handbook of Development Economics* (4 vols) Amsterdam: North Holland/Elsevier. See particularly ch. 9, "Industrialization and Trade" (H. Pack); and ch. 45, "Trade and Industrial Policy Reform" (D. Rodrik).

Hoekman, B., Mattoo, A. and English, P. (eds) (2002) *Development, Trade, and the WTO: A Handbook*, Washington DC: World Bank.

Krueger, A. (1997) "Trade Policy and Economic Development," *American Economic Review* 87:1 1–22.

Little, I., Scitovsky, T. and Scott, M. (1970) *Industry and Trade in Some Developing Countries*, Oxford: Oxford University Press for the OECD.

Myint, H. (1973) *Southeast Asia's Economy*, Harmondsworth: Penguin Books.

MICHAEL TRIBE

inequality

Inequality – such as in wealth, power, rights and status – forms a common focus of international development work and debate. Most attention is placed on where inequality is associated with social injustice, or where one group's possessions and power have resulted from, or lead to, the disempowerment, or impoverishment of others.

Human societies have suffered from the injustices of inequality throughout the period of written history. Only a few very small scale and now marginalized societies are largely egalitarian. The Athenian civilization, and some other Greeks, were able to practice a phantom kind of equality, in which all male citizens were regarded as free and equal, yet were totally dependent for their way of life on an even larger population of slaves, not recognized as human in the same sense. Surprisingly little attention was paid to equality during the Enlightenment. It was placed in a trilogy at the French Revolution – with liberty and fraternity – but was largely ignored except by François Babeuf's 1836 treatise, *The Conspiracy for Equality*. Marx understood equality in two senses, first in the principle of "from each according to his abilities, to each according to the amount of work performed," and second in the principle of "from each according to his abilities, to each according to his needs." The first became entangled in abstract versions of the labor theory of value and could never be implemented with precision. The second could only be implemented in the higher, communist phase of post-revolutionary society and has never become a reality (see **Marxism**). Inequality of women in society was highlighted in Mary Wollstonecraft's 1792 book, *A Vindication of the Rights of Woman*, and later in John Stuart Mill's *The Subjection of Women* (1869). Many regimes in the past valued inequality positively for its privileges and the gratifying sense of superiority it conferred. Such was the ancient regime until the French Revolution. The emancipation of the serfs in Russia, as in many other countries, was a long and agonizing process involving much **violence** and bloodshed. More stark and blatant was the case of **slavery**. Civil rights in the USA's South were confronted only a century after the formal ending of slavery in the 1861–5 Civil War.

The great paradox of inequality is that since World War II most people strive for equality, yet in the process, inequality grows ever wider, most notoriously between the richest and poorest nations of the world, as well as within the wealthiest nations (see **inequality and poverty, world trends** for statistics). Many observers have believed the creation of the post-war financial institutions of the **World Bank** and **International Monetary Fund (IMF)** were founded to ensure that the capitalist system survived (with attention to the poor adopted only later). Here began the "Development Age," with innumerable organizations and projects all over the world, dedicated to growth and improvement, but with welfare often implied but never a primary aim (see **anti-politics; postmodernism and postdevelopment**). The World Bank's **structural adjustment** programs have been particularly associated with inequality. In Harare (Zimbabwe), one study showed 90 percent of those interviewed felt disadvantaged. Incomes have fallen, jobs lost, prices rocketed, **education** and **health** suffered, personal plans wrecked. Many wanted to know why such disastrous policies had been implemented (Potts, 1999).

This makes accurate knowledge of the situation imperative. World Bank poverty estimates are based on consumption or income data collected through household surveys. Some major factors cannot be officially mentioned. For example, in many counts Nigeria is the richest country in Sub-Saharan Africa, yet its showing in poverty indices is deplorable, largely because of alleged misuse of oil wealth by its governments (see **oil and gas development**). Nigeria's population rose from 71.1 million in 1980 to 123.9 million in 1999. In 1997, Nigeria had 90.8 percent of its people living on less than US$2 a day, (70.7 percent on less than US$1 a day). The highest 10 percent in Nigeria get 40.8 percent of the national income or consumption. The lowest 10 percent get 1.6 percent. Zimbabwe is even more unequal; its highest 10 percent getting 46.9 percent of the country's income or consumption, while the lowest 10 percent get 1.8 percent: its top 10 percent enjoys a bigger share than in any other country. For comparison, the shares of the top 10 percent in the USA and the UK are, respectively, 30.5 percent and 27.3 percent. Moreover, 2.8 billion worldwide live on less than

US$2 a day and 1.2 billion on less than US$1 a day. Six of every 100 infants die in their first year and eight do not reach five (see **infant and child mortality**). Nine boys in 100 and 14 girls in 100 do not attend school. The leading fifteen countries in terms of **gross national product (GNP) per capita** (with rank for total **gross national product (GNP)** in brackets) are as follows: 1: Switzerland (18th); 2: Norway (27th); 3: Japan (2nd); 4: Denmark (23rd); 5: United States (1st); 6: Singapore (36th); 7: Austria (21st); 8: Germany (3rd); 9: Sweden (20th); 10: Belgium (19th); 11: the Netherlands (14th); 12: Finland (30th); 13: Hong Kong (24th); 14: France (4th); 15: United Kingdom (5th). Thus, the countries with the highest GNP per head rank low in total magnitude of GNP. (The figures are from the UNDP *World Development Report, 2001*).

Unjust inequality also occurs with regard to other social groupings, such as **gender**, race (see **race and racism**), **caste**, age, and **sexualities**. Measuring indices of inequality is difficult. The **United Nations** has developed the **Gender-related Development Index (GDI)** and **Gender Empowerment Measure (GEM)** to allow international comparison and a measurement of progress toward ending discrimination. The **Gini index** shows income distribution based on how actual measurements compare with a hypothetical uniform distribution. But experience has shown that reducing inequality has involved attention to the political and historical causes of prolonged injustice, and confronting these, although not always with **violence**. Inequality persists in all countries, but it is worst in the poorest countries.

See also: capitalism; Gini index; income distribution; inequality and poverty, world trends; poverty

Further reading

Potts, D. (1999) "The Impact of Structural Adjustment on Welfare and Livelihood: Assessment by People in Harare, Zimbabwe," in Jones, S. and Nelson, N. (eds) *Urban Poverty in Africa*, London: Intermediate Technology.

Seligson, M. and Passe-Smith, A. (1998, 2nd edn) *Development and Underdevelopment: The Political Economy of Global Inequality*, Boulder: Lynne Rienner.

UNDP (2001) *World Development Report 2000/2001:Poverty in an Unequal World*, New York: UNDP.

AIDAN SOUTHALL

inequality and poverty, world trends

Debates about world trends in **inequality** and **poverty** ask whether **economic growth** has led to a better distribution of wealth and a reduction in poverty. This is an old debate. In the 1870s, the US economist Henry George remarked "the association of poverty with progress is the great enigma of our times." In the early 2000s, it remains so. Average world income has multiplied many times, but life-stunting poverty remains the lot of billions of people. The size of the gap between the income of the "median" household in most developing countries (the household whose income puts it in the middle, with as many households richer as poorer) and the median household in the rich countries of Western Europe, North America and Japan has been widening since the end of World War II, at least.

Many observers, however, now believe the trends are in the right direction. According to Martin Wolf of *The Financial Times*, "Evidence suggests the 1980s and 1990s were decades of declining global inequality and reductions in the proportion of the world's **population** in extreme poverty." James Wolfensohn, president of the **World Bank**, speaking in 2001, remarked: "Over the past 20 years the number of people living on less than US$1 a day has fallen by 200 million, after rising steadily for 200 years." On the other hand, other commentators, often associated with **trade unions** and **non-governmental organizations (NGOs)**, say more or less the opposite. According to Jay Mazur, US union leader, "[G]lobalization has dramatically increased **inequality** between and within nations" (see **globalization**).

Trends in poverty and **income distribution** are politically sensitive, because they are used to judge the worth of different political economies. Proponents of **free trade** (often called "economic globalization") tend to say that poverty and inequality have declined (see **neo-liberalism**). Those who favor more "nationalistic" development strategies aimed at nurturing higher value-added activities within the national borders, and restrictions on flows of funds across national borders (see **import substitution; protectionism**), tend to say the opposite.

According to World Bank figures, the number of people in extreme poverty (the "poverty headcount") declined from 1.4 billion in 1980 to 1.2 billion in 1998. This is good news: it implies that the percentage of the world's population in extreme poverty has fallen from approximately 28 percent to 24 percent. But the Bank does not emphasize that the figures contain a large margin of error. For example, they are based on household surveys (see **measuring development**) of income and expenditure in diverse countries. The available surveys are of widely varying quality, and many do not follow a standard template. Different survey designs yield very different poverty headcounts (see **poverty measurement**). For example, the length of the recall period makes a big difference to the rate of reported expenditure. A recent study in India suggests that a switch from the standard 30-day reporting period to a 7-day reporting period yields such an "increase" in income and expenditure as to lift 175 million people from poverty, a near 50 percent fall. The data for China and India constitutes another source of major error, partly because their governments refused to participate in big crossnational benchmarking exercises, and these countries account for a very large proportion of the world's poor.

Furthermore, the comparison between 1980 and 1998 is problematic because the World Bank introduced a new methodology in the late 1990s, which makes the figures non-comparable. The Bank has recalculated the poverty numbers with the new method only back to 1987. We do not know what the 1980 figure would be with the new method. The Princeton University economist Angus Deaton, who knows as much about world poverty statistics as anyone, claimed "it seems impossible to make statements about changes in world poverty when the ground underneath one's feet is changing in this way [on account of the change in methodology]."

Critics have also suggested that the World Bank's poverty numbers not only carry a large margin of error but also are biased downwards, making the number look lower than it really is. In particular, the Bank's numbers are based on the rather arbitrarily defined "international **poverty line**" of "US$1 per day" (so for each country the number living in extreme poverty is the number with a purchasing-power-parity income of less than US$365 per year expressed in the local currency) (see **poverty line**). Critics have claimed that the level of US$1 per day is not related closely to the income needed to buy sufficient goods and services to escape life-stunting poverty. For example, it is not based on the cost of sufficient calories, micronutrients and shelter for healthy life. Critics have claimed that an international poverty line that reflected the cost of **basic needs** would be much higher than US$1, and therefore the number of people living below it would be higher. For example, a recent study for Latin America shows that national extreme poverty rates, using poverty lines derived from calorific and demographic characteristics, may be more than *twice* as high as those based on the World Bank's US$1 per day line. The World Bank estimates Brazil's extreme poverty rate (using its international poverty line) at 5 percent; the **Economic Commission for Latin America and the Caribbean (ECLAC)**, using a poverty line based on calories and demographic characteristics, estimates the rate at 14 percent. The Bank estimated Bolivia's extreme poverty to be 14 percent, ECLAC estimated 23 percent; for Chile, the figures were 4 and 8 percent; and for Colombia, 11 and 24 percent.

As for **income distribution**, the answer to the question, "What is the trend of world income distribution?" is: "It depends." It depends on which combination out of many plausible combinations of measures and samples we choose. There is no single best combination of measures to indicate world income inequality.

Different combinations of measurements give different weight to the diverse experiences of economic growth in different regions and different income percentiles. World gross domestic product (GDP) has grown about 2 percent faster than world population over the past two decades. The (population-weighted) GDP of developing countries has grown a little faster than that of the high-income countries. Sub-Saharan Africa's economic performance, however, remains poor: its average real income today is below the level of twenty years ago. Latin America's has also been poor; its average income is about the same as twenty years ago. South Asia has fared better than average since the 1990s. China has experienced fast economic growth during the 1980s and 1990s, as has the rest of (non-Japan) East and Southeast Asia (excluding the Asian crises of 1997–8).

Several studies have claimed world income distribution has become less unequal since the 1980s. However, several other studies have concluded the opposite, notwithstanding India's and China's fast growth. There is sufficient evidence of widening inequality to challenge the confident assertion that globalization has caused world income inequality to fall. A quite different source of data strengthens the challenge: namely, data on pay. Inequality of pay within manufacturing was stable or declining from the early 1960s to around 1980–2; then sharply increased from 1980–2 to the present. 1980–2 is a turning point towards greater inequality in manufacturing pay worldwide, coinciding with and perhaps driven by the latest phase of globalization.

See also: chronic poverty; convergence; economic growth; globalization; growth measurement; income distribution; inequality; measuring development; neo-liberalism; participatory poverty assessment (PPA); poverty; poverty measurement; structural adjustment; welfare indicators; World Bank

Further reading

Deaton, A. (2002) "Is World Poverty Falling?" *Finance and Development* 39:2 4–7.

ECLA (2002) *Globalization and Development*, ECLA.

Firebaugh, G. (1999) "Empirics of World Income Inequality," *American Journal of Sociology* 104: 1597–630.

Wade, R. (2004) "Is Globalization Reducing Poverty and Inequality," *World Development* 32:4 567–89.

World Bank (2002) *Globalization, Growth, and Poverty: Building an Inclusive World Economy*, Washington DC: World Bank and Oxford University Press.

ROBERT HUNTER WADE

infant and child mortality

The infant mortality rate (IMR) is the number of children who die before twelve months of age per thousand live births. Child mortality is the proportion dying between the ages of one and five, also expressed per 1,000. These two are combined in under-five mortality. Infant and child mortality are good indicators of social development and critical measures of welfare (see welfare economics; welfare state) in their own right, since child death is one of the worst things that can happen to a family. Accordingly, a two-thirds reduction in infant and under-five mortality is one of the Millennium Development Goals (MDGs).

Mortality levels have been falling in most regions of the world over the past decades (see Table 5). But they remain high, especially in low-income countries mostly in Africa and South Asia, where progress has been slowest and some countries have suffered a set back as HIV/AIDS has increased infant deaths (see HIV/AIDS (definition and treatment); HIV/AIDS (policy issues)).

The reasons behind mortality decline are subject to debate. Some argue that economic growth is the main explanation, in large part because of the higher levels of nutrition which it allows (also see malnutrition). But others point to the importance of public health interventions such as drinking water supply and vaccination. It would be wrong to dichotomize these positions. economic growth is needed to provide a sustainable basis for public interventions, although these can initially be financed by aid. But in order to reduce mortality, the benefits of growth must be translated into health

Table 5 Trends in infant and child mortality

	East Asia and Pacific		Latin America and Caribbean		South Asia		Sub-Saharan Africa		Eastern Europe and Central Asia		High income	
	IMR	CMR	IMR	CMR	IMR	CMR	IMR	CMR	IMR	CMR	IMR	CMR
1960	131	82	105	55	163	91	164	108	n.a.	n.a.	35	10
1980	57	28	61	n.a.	119	69	116	81	41	n.a.	13	3
2000	36	10	29	8	73	25	91	77	20	5	6	2

Note: IMR = infant mortality rate; CMR = child mortality rate; n.a = not available. *Source:* World Bank *World Development Indicators*, CD-Rom, 2003

benefits through efficient public spending on priority activities.

There is, however, agreement that the causes of infant and child death vary. Infant death, especially that in the first month of life, is a function of health services such as antenatal care and attended delivery in sanitary conditions (see **sanitation**). Child death is more strongly related to the general socio-economic environment. As mortality rates fall then the share of infant death in total under-five deaths rises (Table 5), and the share of neo-natal deaths in infant deaths also increases. Hence, as mortality declines the role of health services in achieving further reductions increases.

See also: children; health; health and poverty; HIV/AIDS (policy issues); maternal mortality; Millennium Development Goals (MDGs); mortality

Further reading

Howard, M. and Millard, A. (1997) *Hunger and Shame: Child Malnutrition and Poverty on Mount Kilimanjaro*, London: Routledge.

White, H. (2003) "Reducing Infant and Child Death," in Black, R. and White, H., *Targeting Development: Critical Perspectives on the Millennium Development Goals*, London: Routledge.

HOWARD WHITE

infant industries

Infant industries are business sectors, whether industrial or post-industrial, that – because of commercial youth – are considered relatively vulnerable to economic competition from established foreign enterprises. Such **vulnerability** may be real or perceived, and may arise because of lack of an established customer base or name recognition, or other reasons unrelated to basic product quality, price or other factors. The inherent analogy is that the sector involved will, given care and protection, become a productive adult member of the nation's economy. This is a form of market failure argument. Hence, infant industry claims are arguments for **protectionism**, or relief from foreign competition, and are most likely to gain favor in sectors perceived as nationally prestigious or having potential for spin-off benefits, often scientific or technological. The greatest risk in infant industry protection is creating a permanently dependent industry, rather than a mature global competitor.

See also: industrialization; industrialization and trade policy; protectionism; small and medium enterprises (SMEs); technological capability; transnational corporations (TNCs) from developing economies

WILLIAM B. T. MOCK

inflation and its effects

Inflation refers to an increase in the overall level of prices. The effects of inflation vary depending on the time horizon, severity of inflation, and whether inflation is anticipated. Long and persistent inflation which causes the public to anticipate inflation is termed expected inflation. Inflation causes money to lose value. Real money balances suffer a loss as if being charged an inflation tax. Inflation causes higher nominal interest rates. Households hold less money but make more frequent bank trips to make withdrawals, known as shoe leather costs. As a result of inflation, businesses are forced to update their sale catalogs, menus, and price lists: this is termed menu costs. If prices are slow to be updated this alters a business' relative prices and thus causes inefficient resource use. Inflation distorts taxes in that tax is levied on nominal income and inflation will put people with same real income in higher tax brackets. Non-inflation indexed tax code means higher real tax burdens, known as bracket creep. In addition, the time lag between the time when a tax is levied and the time when it is paid means a loss of the tax measured in commodities. However, mild inflation has the benefit of reducing real costs such as wage levels and material costs, particularly for those businesses where renegotiating wages and resetting costs is highly time-consuming; higher profit margins will stimulate investment and increase **employment**.

Unexpected inflation has the effects of arbitrary wealth redistribution (see **income distribution**). Higher than expected inflation reduces the purchasing power of money received on a fixed income asset, and thus makes debtors better off at the expense of creditors. Lower than expected inflation has the opposite effect, benefitting creditors and making debtors worse off. For the same reason people living on fixed pensions also suffer from unanticipated inflation. Uncertainties due to persistent inflation are the main reason that some long-term **debt** instruments are inflation-indexed, and some pension schemes make periodical adjustments using some form of inflation indicator.

The above problems magnify under hyperinflation, which occurs when the monthly inflation rate reaches over 50 percent. The public minimizes its currency holdings; businesses pay employees frequently; employees spend their money quickly or convert to foreign currencies; households and businesses have great incentives to delay paying taxes; government's tax-collecting ability diminishes. The great uncertainties associated with hyperinflation may force the public to abandon the use of official fiat money and revert to barter.

Within a short time horizon, unexpected inflation due to an increase in aggregate demand, known as demand-pull inflation, has the effect of increasing employment. This contributes to the Philips curve, which describes a negative correlation between inflation rates and **unemployment** rates. However, when inflation is expected, increasing aggregate demand only causes inflation. Unexpected inflation due to higher supply cost, called cost-push inflation, has the effect of lowering employment. Two other notions are related to inflation. *Disinflation* refers to a reduction in the rate of inflation. *Deflation* refers to a reduction in the overall price levels.

See also: Asian crises; computable general equilibrium (CGE) models; contagion effect; debt; economic development; exchange rates; monetary and fiscal policy

Further reading

Hubbard, R. (2000) *Money, the Financial System, and the Economy*, New York: Addison-Wesley.
Mankiw, N. (2003) *Macroeconomics*, New York: Worth.

BIN ZHOU

INFORMAL SECTOR *see* urban informal sector; street-trading in urban areas; micro-enterprises

information technology

Information technology (IT) refers to computer-based equipment and systems which process information in digital form. Their power lies in the high speed with which they can apply routine processing tasks to large amounts of data and their ability to handle and integrate data of different kinds, including text, numerical data, sound and visual images. "IT" is often used synonymously with "information and communication technologies" (ICTs), which refers specifically to the combination of computer and telecommunication technologies for the rapid transfer of digitally processed information. IT includes technology for data acquisition, analysis and storage, and information retrieval, exchange and presentation.

IT affects development in two main ways. Some developing countries have demonstrated a comparative advantage in IT related industries. More generally, IT applications can reduce the cost of many information-intensive processes in development, from planning and project management to **education**, **trade** and **governance**.

Investment in IT manufacturing by transnational companies has been attracted to **newly industrialized economies (NIEs)** by the combination of low wage rates and supportive government polices. Mass production of microprocessors, computers and peripherals is a well-established industrial sector in countries in Southeast Asia. Other countries have found a niche in software development. Another niche, created by a mixture of low labor costs and differences in time zones, has been the processing of large amounts of data for Northern companies between the close of business and start up the next day.

It is on the potential of IT applications, however, that most interest now focuses in development theory and intervention. Many commentators see IT as a breakthrough that will address aspirations currently frustrated by lack of financial or skilled human resources. These range from education for all through multi-media distance learning, to databases of knowledge on CD-ROM or the Internet, to improved governance through universal access to information and services and greater efficiency in the processes of government administration. A UK government policy paper suggested that ICTs "have the potential to help poor people leapfrog some of the traditional barriers to development, by linking them into the global economy, improving their access to knowledge and making government machinery work better" (DFID, 2000). These ideas recognize the crucial importance of information, learning and knowledge in enabling people to benefit from **globalization** and participate fully in development. However, other views suggest that the potential is much less, or at least will only be realized if specific action is taken to address constraints.

First, the research evidence for a dramatic effect of IT is not strong. Research in developed countries shows little association between the spread of IT and **productivity** in the economy, at least in the short to medium term. In developing countries, most attempts to improve governance through IT applications in the late 1990s were not successful. Isolated IT initiatives where there is no infrastructure for maintenance of equipment, or updating of the content of information systems, are not sustainable. Second, there is the "digital divide," the vast gap in access to ICTs between developed and developing countries, and between rich and poor and between urban and rural areas within developing countries. Similar situations persist with communication technologies that have been established for much longer. In 2000, there were eight times as many radios per thousand people in high income compared to low-income countries. For personal computers, the differential was ten times as great.

Third, some commentators challenge the implicit model of information and knowledge in many of the more optimistic suggestions. They argue that knowledge develops through learning, evaluating information and experience, and dialog with others. It is not acquired simply by extracting information from a computer database or the **Internet**. IT applications which are interactive, enable users to carry out tasks which are important to them and facilitate learning have greater potential for development than those which are seen simply as more efficient conduits for delivering information.

There are two main challenges for the effective contribution of IT to development. The first is to build IT systems which assert the validity of, and support the development and exchange of, **local knowledge**. The technology is inherently capable of facilitating the documentation and local exchange of experience, but such applications are rare. Decision support systems for farmers, for example, tend to be built from knowledge and perceptions derived from formal science. Similarly, it is much cheaper to buy multi-media distance learning packages from elsewhere than to invest in the human resources and skills needed to develop locally relevant materials. On the one hand, the widely distributed nature of the technology offers potential for local solutions and innovations. On the other hand, economies of scale and the economic power of IT companies from developed economies encourage the uptake of mass produced software.

The second challenge is to develop infrastructure that provides widespread access to IT systems, thus reducing the digital divide. The private sector is the main source of investment in infrastructure, from countrywide mobile phone and satellite television networks to small cybercafés. Governments and development agencies can fund complementary initiatives to fill gaps in provision. Governments can also establish regulatory frameworks that encourage the private sector to provide services in rural areas. For most potential users in developing countries, access will be through intermediaries: these can include individuals, schools, local resource centers and non-governmental organizations. The sustainability of such mediation is greatest when it is based in an existing organization or relationship rather than in a project-funded resource that is likely to last no longer than the project itself. The **World Summit on the Information Society (WSIS)** represents one of the first international attempts to discuss IT for development.

See also: Internet; measuring development; Paris 21; public management; technology policy; telecommunications; World Summit on the Information Society (WSIS)

Further reading

DFID (2000) *Eliminating World Poverty: Making Globalisation Work for the Poor*, White Paper on International Development, London: HMSO.

Heeks, R. (2001) *Reinventing Government in the Information Age*, London: Routledge.

Heeks, R. (ed.) (2002) "Information and Communication Technologies (ICTs) and Development," *Journal of International Development* 14:1. Special issue.

IICD (2002) Website of the International Institute for Communication and Development: http://www.iicd.org

CHRIS GARFORTH

INFRASTRUCTURE *see* build-operate-transfer (BOT) projects; energy policy; transport policy; auto industry; iron and steel; public-private partnerships

institutions

In the context of development, the word "institutions" is taken to mean the measures people adopt to deal with uncertainty. They are usually defined as the shared rules, norms, and behavior via which people interact and make economic transactions with others and the state (see also **state and state reform; new institutional economics; institutions and environment**). For instance, land titles and copyrights help buyers help safeguard buyers against rival entitlement claims; proper ownership will hold up in the court of **law**. The spectrum of institutions which affect development is quite broad and includes **property rights**, standards such as those adopted by professional organizations, one's informal social networks (see **social capital**), and formal organizations like **trade unions**. Development workers debate about how institutions can contribute most to a country's development and people's **well-being**.

Some analysts focus on how institutions distribute power within a society. A small elite (see **elites**) could manipulate the taxation systems, so that laws are applied to its benefit. Widespread political participation is needed to ensure that elites do not simply exploit institutions to fit their own purposes. By making decision-making processes more predictable and transparent, institutions such as grievance procedures allow communities (see **community**) to empower collective action, gain legitimacy, pool resources, and level the playing field (see **transparency**). Therefore, a challenge of institution-building is to make them sustainable and flexible enough to adapt to changing environments.

Economists are primarily concerned with whether and how institutions can be molded to encourage **economic development**, as entrepreneurs construct new businesses when they anticipate profits. Although current research focuses on which institutions are best, earlier ones questioned whether they were at all beneficial. Modernization theorists (see **modernization theory**) generally viewed social institutions in development as inconsequential or detrimental. It was believed that local norms, kinship systems, and ethnicity-based networks (see **ethnicity/identity**) prevented entrepreneurs from finding the best suppliers and consumers for their products. Neo-liberal economists have traditionally shunned government-led institutions because state (see **state and state reform**) intervention can be used to distort otherwise perfect competition (see also **neo-liberalism; structural adjustment; International Monetary Fund (IMF); World Bank**). Yet, they also admit that only the government can enforce the economic freedoms necessary for **capitalism**, such as the security of private property. In *Capitalism and Freedom*, Milton Friedman (1962) also writes that government not only determines but interprets rules of operation. Thus, the American Civil Rights Act of 1964 made markets more competitive by mandating the admission of all people, regardless of race (see **race and racism**), in private service establishments.

A more recent school of economists, dubbed new institutionalists, have focused on which institutions governments should pursue by exploring how history affects the organization of economic activity across time and among countries (see **new institutional economics**). In *Institutions, Institutional Change, and Economic Performance*, Douglass North (1990) writes of the "persistence" of social landscapes in spite of a total change in the rules: "Japanese culture survived the US occupation after World War II; the post-revolutionary US society remained much as it had been in colonial times." These country studies are examples of path dependence, whereby a norm or institution remains even after a more efficient solution comes along. The most notable example of path dependence is the continued use of the QWERTY English-language keyboard on computers, a layout that was difficult for people to learn but prevented typewriter letter-keys from jamming. North attributes path dependence to factors such as high fixed costs, such as the time it took everyone to learn to type on the QWERTY keyboard, and high transaction costs, such as the money it would take to replace the QWERTY keyboard with a new chosen layout.

In turn, government intervention is geared to streamline such an efficiency framework. Hernando de Soto is another economist who has written extensively on the topic. Specifically, he advocates the formalization of **property rights** as a way of bringing informal markets in developing countries into the formal markets, so that they might be counted in official **gross domestic product (GDP)** and be reinvested in the **community**. He also suggests that **local government**s simplify the process of dealing with government bureaucracies when registering a business, taking out a loan, or paying fines. While new institutionalist economists emphasize institutions as factors in the persistence of disequilibria, they are primarily concerned with the interaction between individual economic agents and the market, not social relations amongst groups of people. In their attempts to explain the divergent growth patterns of countries such as Bangladesh and Japan, their measures of success do not depend on social **inequality** or dislocation, but on economic efficiency.

Other development workers claim that while countries can work towards "good" institutions, formal adoption is not enough. Religious communities could choose to maintain their own courts of law instead of abiding by secular ones. **Corruption**, clientelism, and civil strife could persist as other obstacles to proper implementation of institutions. Many political scientists and sociologists view institutions as products of social interactions, rather than choices made by rational economic agents. Such institutions might shape the very preferences people wish to maximize. Therefore, even if government intervention were to take place, other informal norms might still pervade and subvert the quest for efficiency.

Rather than focusing on the impact of institutions on development, some sociologists emphasize how market forces and economic development can work to harness or disrupt social institutions. For example, workers might be forced to migrate, leaving families and existing social networks of trust and reciprocity (see **labor migration**). These networks might be viewed negatively if they previously limited the number of an entrepreneur's business partners, but they might also be viewed positively, as **social capital**, if they could have been harnessed to initiate joint projects, to form, and to link entrepreneurs to people or organizations with resources and power.

See also: accountability; common pool resources; culture; gender and property rights; governance; institutions and environment; new institutional economics; property rights; social capital; transparency

Further reading

De Soto, H. (1989) *The Other Path: The Economic Answer to Terrorism*, New York: Basic.

Friedman, M. (1962) *Capitalism and Freedom*, Chicago: University of Chicago Press.

Hall, P. and Taylor, R. (1996) "Political Science and the Three New Institutionalisms," *Political Studies* 44:5 936–57.

North, D. (1990) *Institutions, Institutional Change, and Economic Performance*, New York: Cambridge University Press.

Woolcock, M. (1998) "Social Capital and Economic Development: Toward a Theoretical Synthesis and Policy Framework," *Theory and Society* 27:2 151–208.

CELINA SU

institutions and environment

Institutions concerning environment are the rules and shared behavior that control the access of different people to shared resources such as fisheries or forests (see also **institutions; new institutional economics**). Toward the end of the 1980s, scholars of environmental conservation and conflict became increasingly interested in the ways in which institutions – and institutional arrangements – affect collective action to conserve **common pool resources**. At the heart of this scholarship is the notion that institutions and incentives have strong bearing on the ways in which people use, manage and abuse **natural resources**, and that institutional arrangements can have positive impacts on resource use and conservation. Framed in this way, institutions are defined as the formal and informal rules that govern the ways in which people interact with natural resource systems, and with one another.

A common point of departure in this literature is the notion that uncertainty and institutions create incentives through which individuals will organize to regulate common pool resources. Framed in this way, environmental problems are understood as a dilemma of collective action, in which individuals deplete resources because they lack: (1) information about the resource system; (2) information about those with whom they share the resource; and (3) institutions which would regulate the ways in which they use the resource. Starting from the position that information (about resources and resource users) is costly to obtain, institutional theorists contend that institutions *matter* because they reduce the uncertainty that stems from the complexity of natural phenomena and the unpredictable behavior of individuals. Rules, it is argued, eliminate the open-access dilemma by increasing predictability, restricting access and encouraging conservation. The efficiency of these rules, however, depends upon the "institutional arrangements" (the system of monitoring and sanctioning) that encourage individuals to comply with collective rules.

The role that governments can play in the determination and enforcement of institutional arrangements is a matter of some debate. Although they advocate "hard" sanctions such as penalties and fines, institutional theorists tend to favor "softer" arrangements in which rules are followed and collective action is achieved as a by-product of the positive social relations members have enjoyed in the past. Spatial boundaries and temporal restrictions, it is argued, reduce the uncertainty that drives the tragedy of the commons by stipulating terms of exclusion, terms which are (ideally) decided, monitored and enforced by those who use the resource – as opposed to those who manage it from afar.

Conceptual distinctions are often made between formal and informal institutions. Roughly, formal institutions refer to the written rules, laws and codes, which are defined and enforced by national and supra-national states. Informal institutions, by contrast, are the unwritten or "working" rules and sanctions that people use to shape their own behavior (see also **environmental entitlements**). Embracing this distinction, many institutional theorists have argued that informal institutions provide a more lasting and effective way of managing the conservation of natural resource systems. Central to this line of argument is the notion that formal institutions lack the flexibility and contextual knowledge that complex resource management entails. That said, institutional theorists do recognize the fact that informal institutions are often embedded or "nested" within a complex web of formal institutions, which define the legal and normative conditions under which people can implement and use informal institutions and arrangements. Informal institutions will work most effectively, it is argued, when states (see **state and state reform**) and other forms of organizational authority grant resource users the *exclusive* right to manage a resource, without interfering in the day-to-day activities of the institution.

Many institutional theorists share a common methodology, which has its roots in a positivist model of individual decision-making and rational choice (Ostrom, 1990). Drawing upon theories of public goods and the distribution of social cost, this agenda has been centrally concerned with the problem of understanding and *developing principles that would encourage* collective action to conserve common pool resources. Two assumptions are central to this model. One is the notion that social outcomes can be explained in terms of the calculations that individuals (or individual "actors," as the case may be) make about the perceived costs and benefits of future actions (methodological individualism). Another is the notion that individuals are "rule-governed" in this process. A key point made by institutional scholars is the notion that social structure (and the relative distribution of costs and benefits within this structure) will have strong bearing on whether collective action will be pursued, and achieved. Such outcomes are explained not only in terms of individual calculations about future outcomes, but also in terms of the structural incentives created by group attributes, resource attributes, state policies and ecological pressures.

Institutional approaches have been used to understand and address a wide array of domestic and international environmental problems, including localized depletion of forests and **fisheries**, inter-basin conflicts and transfers, and inter- or transnational efforts to manage regional and global environmental problems, such as international water disputes and the emission of greenhouse gases (see **incentive structures**). Because they focus on the incentive structures created by different types of rules, rights and duties, institutional approaches provide an attractive way of explaining social phenomena and of addressing environmental problems. Partly for this reason, they have also become very popular among international donors, governments and **non-governmental organizations (NGOs)**, whose programs frequently require an identifiable point of entry and an objectively verifiable indication of success. Institutions, defined broadly, are thought to provide an important means of meeting both of these ends.

However, the literature is not without its tensions. First, the very definition of institutions is a matter of some debate. Although many scholars accept the notion that institutions represent rules, there are some who argue that institutions can and should be understood in a much broader way, encompassing, for instance, norms, social customs, habits and broad patterns of behavior. Materialistic responses to this line of argument – largely among economists and political scientists – argue that a positivist treatment of institutions requires a more rigorous and narrow definition. Second, a methodological tension exists between a body of scholarship which aims to contribute to an empirically grounded theory of social action, and one whose questions and focus are more firmly rooted in the study of local history and context. Arguments favoring a more positivist approach contend that the institutional literature is too dependent on local case study material, and that a more systematic methodology is required. Such assertions are generally poorly received among those favoring the contextual approach (e.g. Goldman, 1998).

See also: common pool resources; deforestation; environment; environmental entitlements; fisheries; gender and property rights; institutions; new institutional economics; property rights; resource tenure

Further reading

Dietz, T., Dolsak, N., Ostrom, E. and Stern, P. (eds) (2002) *The Drama of the Commons*, Washington DC: National Academy Press.

Goldman, M. (ed.) (1998) *Privatizing Nature: Political Struggles for the Global Commons*, New Jersey: Rutgers University Press.

Haas, P., Keohane, R. and Levy, M. (eds) (1993) *Institutions for the Earth: Sources of Effective International Environmental Protection*, Cambridge MA: MIT Press.

Keohane, R. and Ostrom, E. (eds) (1995) *Local Commons and Global Interdependence: Heterogeneity and Cooperation in Two Domains*, London: Sage.

Ostrom, E. (1990) *Governing the Commons: The Evolution of Institutions for Collective Action*, Cambridge: Cambridge University Press.

CRAIG JOHNSON

intellectual property rights (IPRs)

Intellectual property rights (IPRs) refer to **property rights** in creations of the mind. National legislation varies in its protection of IPR, but multilateral and bilateral initiatives are increasing. The 1994 TRIPS Agreement (see **trade-related aspects of intellectual property rights (TRIPS)**) binds WTO members to minimum standards in intellectual property (IP) protection, with significant implications for development and public welfare (see **World Trade Organization/ General Agreement on Tariffs and Trade (WTO/GATT)**).

A broad spectrum of intangible creations has come within IP protection under distinct historical circumstances. The most commonly known categories of IPRs are patents protecting inventions, and copyright over literary and artistic works. Over the last five centuries, protection has been extended to other categories including trademarks, industrial designs and plant breeders' rights. The TRIPS Agreement also covers other IPRs over such disparate matter as trade secrets, geographical indications, performances, broadcasts and the layout designs of integrated circuits. A **World Intellectual Property Organization (WIPO)** report (April 2002) suggests that IP is a concept broad enough to embrace matter not forming existing categories, as for example the traditional medicinal knowledge or expressions of folklore of **indigenous people**s.

What IPRs can protect does not depend on a layperson's concept of ingenuity, but on legally prescribed conditions and interpretations (e.g. on "originality" for copyright protection). While multilateral agreements stipulate requirements such as "novelty," "inventive step" and "industrial application" for patents, interpretations vary between national courts and patent offices. The differences are especially apparent when new technology challenges both legal jargon and moral sense – for example, in patent claims over the isolation of gene sequences for the human genome (see **Human Genome Project**), or over **genetically modified organisms (GMOs)** such as the cancer-prone Harvard "oncomouse."

IPRs currently protect applications of ideas and information of commercial value (Cornish, 1999). Unlike physical objects, information can be used by an infinite number of persons without diminished use to each. By treating certain forms of information as private property, IP laws enable the rights of owners to prevent others from commercially exploiting the information without authorization. This is usually for a fixed period (exceptions include trademark rights), after which the protected information returns to the "public domain."

Thus, IPRs are essentially "negative" rights. Modern copyright is not so much a right to reproduce one's work (since one can do so anyway) as a right to prevent others from copying or dealing with the work in certain ways. Patent rights go further in preventing others from producing the invention, even if arrived at through independent research. These rights are farther-reaching than copyright, but granted for a shorter term (a minimum twenty years from filing of application under TRIPS). They require registration and are confined to the territory of the granting state.

The term "author's rights" is used instead of "copyright" in some legal systems. While common law justifications for copyright often emphasize the need to economically reward authors for their creative effort, some civil law regimes protect the work as an extension of the author's personality or self. The French tradition of protecting the author's moral rights (e.g. to the integrity and paternity of the work) reflects a view of author's rights as natural rights.

There is a further societal dimension to IPR justifications. The first English statute on copyright included the "encouragement of learning" among its goals. Patents are particularly said to advance **science and technology** by providing economic incentives for innovation, while facilitating the disclosure of technical information from inventions. In exchange for a limited monopoly to exploit their inventions, inventors give up "patent information" which is disclosed for public scrutiny.

It is further said that strong IPR protection will facilitate **technology transfer** to developing countries, for instance by boosting investor's confidence and encouraging technology licensing. In reality, there is little evidence linking patents to domestic research, and particularly to technology transfer. Meanwhile, studies suggest that enterprises in most sectors make limited use of "patent information" for research (European Patent Office, 1994). This could be due to the nature of the information disclosed (e.g. obscure language or lack of contextual information) or issues of access to databases.

Overly strong IP protection may stifle innovation and competition from non-IP owners. For example, an overly broad patent claim may impede downstream research by "follow-on" inventors. Weighing the broader interests of the public against those of IPR-owners requires a delicate balancing act. The fact that most IPRs can usually be assigned or licensed to third parties other than creators or inventors further complicates the equation. In reality, many IPRs are held by companies, **transnational corporations (TNCs)**, and public institutions including universities (see **technology policy**).

In the balancing process, courts make use of exceptions such as "fair use" or "fair dealing" for copyright-protected material, and "experimental use" for patented inventions. The safeguard of "compulsory licensing" also exists to enable supply of the patented good by a third party, where the patent owner has failed to "work" the invention locally, or for other reasons such as public health emergencies.

A state's ability to customize its IP regime to local context and policy goals ultimately depends, nevertheless, on its freedom to decide what to protect and for how long. Multilateral and regional

agreements, as well as bilateral arrangements, may seriously reduce that flexibility. For example, the TRIPS Agreement requires that computer programs be protected as "literary works" under the Berne Convention (1971), which entails a minimum copyright term of "author's life plus 50 years" (this is the same as for novels or Picassos). Since this period extends well beyond the average product life cycle of programs, what is returned eventually to the public domain is of questionable value.

Multilateral agreements on IP protection have appeared since the nineteenth century. They now include various conventions administered by the **World Intellectual Property Organization (WIPO)**, and other organizations including the WTO and the International Union for the Protection of New Varieties of Plants (UPOV). TRIPS is unique among these agreements in providing recourse to the WTO dispute settlement mechanism and binding national IP regimes to the trade interests of member states – a member can ultimately retaliate against another's violation of TRIPS by suspending its obligations under other WTO agreements (e.g. those governing agriculture and textiles). Developing countries are thus under tremendous pressure to strengthen their IP regimes, even though developed countries had much more flexibility in shaping their IP system while in the early stage of **industrialization** (Dutfield, 2003).

Pressures from lobbying industries and foreign partners on states to assimilate tough IP standards existed before – and continue beyond – TRIPS. Alford (1995) traces, for example, how IP protection eclipsed other issues in US foreign relations with China from the mid-1980s. Even as debate continues on the repercussions of TRIPS on developing countries' policy issues including public health, some bilateral arrangements and regional initiatives (e.g. in francophone Africa) have resulted in more stringent protection than that required under TRIPS.

See also: genetically modified organisms (GMOs); property rights; technology transfer; transnational corporations (TNCs); trade-related aspects of intellectual property rights (TRIPS); World Intellectual Property Organization (WIPO);

World Trade Organization/General Agreement on Tariffs and Trade (WTO/GATT)

Further reading

Alford, W. (1995) *To Steal A Book Is An Elegant Offence: Intellectual Property Law in Chinese Civilization*, Stanford: Stanford University Press.

Dutfield, G. (2003) *Intellectual Property Rights And The Life Science Industries: A Twentieth Century History*, Aldershot: Ashgate.

Cornish, W. (1999) *Intellectual Property: Patents, Copyright, Trade Marks and Allied Rights*, London: Sweet and Maxwell.

TZEN WONG

Inter-American Development Bank (IADB)

The Inter-American Development Bank (IADB) is a multinational lending institution dedicated to promoting economic and **social development** (see **economic development**) in Latin America and the Caribbean. Set up in 1959, it is the world's oldest and largest regional development institution, with a membership of more than fifty countries. The Bank provides loans and technical assistance to its members to implement development-oriented projects. For several decades, loans focused on increasing the productive capacity of borrowing countries; however, in the 1990s emphasis shifted to projects associated with social development, **poverty** and **environment**. By 2000, it had distributed more than $85 billion in loans, with annual disbursements exceeding $10 billion. It is funded through member contributions and borrowing on international **capital markets**, with each member receiving voting rights in proportion to its financial contribution. The Bank is headquartered in Washington DC, with offices in each of its member countries, as well as Paris and Tokyo.

See also: multilateral development banks (MDBs)

EMMA SAMMAN

intercropping

Intercropping is the cultivation of two or more crops in alternate rows in the same field. It is often adopted as a means of improving crop **productivity**. Individual crops require specific nutrients and interact with the environment uniquely in relation to light/shade, length of growing season, disease resistance/susceptibility and soil flora and fauna. Consequently, the alternation of crops that complement rather than mimic each other's resource requirements benefits the **environment** and the farmer. Such management is important where costs prohibit the use of artificial **fertilizers** and pesticides. Many intercropping systems combine cereals with legumes because of the latter's association with nitrogen-fixing bacteria, which occupy root nodules. These bacteria fix nitrogen from the atmosphere and produce nitrates, which enter the soil in soluble form and so promote the growth of both crops. Intercropping also inhibits the spread of diseases; the production of two or more crops is less likely to result in total crop loss; and the harvest is versatile for consumption and **trade**.

See also: agriculture; agroforestry; green revolution; shifting cultivation

A. M. MANNION

intermediate classes

Intermediate classes are a grouping of self-employed people and small farmers who occupy a class position between the laboring poor and profit-taking capitalists. The term was first used by Michael Kalecki in 1967. Given the size of this grouping, it might be possible for the intermediate classes to assume power in countries where the agricultural and industrial bourgeoisies are as yet weakly developed. Kalecki pointed to Egypt and Indonesia, but his analysis has since been extended most usefully in India. In such circumstances, the intermediate classes are said to form an intermediate regime.

Small-scale manufacturers, local merchants and small landowners would all be members of the intermediate classes, along with rich and middle-peasants. Kalecki saw the unity of these classes residing in an absence of contradiction between labor and capital, or labor and management, within the unit of production. Members of the intermediate classes make their way by combining rewards from labor and rewards from risk-taking. They generally do not pay wages to family members. Bureaucrats might be considered members of the intermediate classes when a significant part of their real incomes is earned from bribes or commissions (see **corruption**).

Kalecki argued that intermediate regimes would most likely form where incomplete **land reform**s benefitted the middle **peasantry**, where non-alignment (see **non-aligned movement**) allowed the ruling class to access credits from the First and Second worlds, and where the weakness of the domestic bourgeoisie prompted the state to nationalize economic development. As both Jha and Harriss-White have shown, however, in the case of India, **nationalization** did not encourage high rates of **economic growth**. Instead of standing "above" the economy like the **developmental state**s of East Asia, the state in India became a site for the accumulative interests of the country's intermediate classes. These groups competed with one another to benefit from government rents; they also put pressure on politicians to maintain forms of economic management that encouraged the production of scarcity. The scarcities produced by licenses and price controls fostered the proliferation of small-scale and largely unregulated firms that could profit in black markets. The intermediate classes were thus expanded.

Intermediate regime analysis suggests that economic liberalization will proceed slowly in a country like India. Given that perhaps a third of households belong to India's intermediate classes, there will be entrenched political opposition to reforms that threaten a system of licenses and price controls. This has certainly been the case in the countryside, but the pace of India's economic reforms since 1991 highlights certain limitations in the "theory" of intermediate classes. Kalecki's model has little to say about the mechanisms that might ensure solidarities between very diverse groups of actors with no consistent relationship to the means of production. In India, too, the model would seem to underestimate the power of the "big business" class, and the power of that class to work with some members of India's intermediate classes.

See also: nationalization; peasantry; primitive accumulation; rural development; sociology of development

Further reading

Harriss-White, B. (2003) *India Working*, Cambridge: Cambridge University Press.
Jha, P. S. (1980) *The Political Economy of Stagnation*, Delhi: Oxford University Press.
Kalecki, M. (1972) *Essays on the Economic Growth of the Socialist and the Mixed Economy*, London: Unwin.

STUART CORBRIDGE

intermediate technology

Intermediate technology has come to symbolize an approach to development that eschews the obsession with the latest, most sophisticated technology that characterized mainstream modernization theories and strategies (see **modernization theory**), and instead favors more appropriate technologies that can be more readily assimilated. The approach is strongly linked to the question of scale; intermediate and appropriate technologies are generally far smaller in scale, cheaper and less complex than hi-tech equipment and infrastructure.

The German-born British thinker and economist, Fritz Schumacher (1911–77) is generally acknowledged as the father of the intermediate technology movement. His landmark book, *Small is Beautiful* (1973) became a touchstone for concern about the unsustainability of many hi-tech projects and the resultant human alienation. This work proved influential among the various strands of progressive theorizing and planning throughout the 1970s and into the 1980s, in pursuit of more holistic alternative (see **postmodernism and postdevelopment**) and **people-centered development**.

Initially, Schumacher's "small" was taken literally, and debate became unhelpfully polarized between opposite ends of the size spectrum, with "small" and "big" symbolizing not only the technological extremes but also the wider visions of development within which they were embedded. Schumacher's concern was also broader: the obsessive pursuit of profit and progress that engenders ever larger companies, increasingly narrow specialization, environmental destruction and alienating working conditions had to be challenged. He advocated smaller economic units, greater use of local resources, and communal or shared organization and ownership, i.e. development with people at its heart.

Intermediate technology, in his vision, is not synonymous with smallness. Rather, it represents no single form or level of technology, but emphasizes relative simplicity and affordability so that it can be successfully operated, maintained and assimilated by the people it is supposed to benefit without dependence on outside skills and finances. The term has become immortalized in the name of the movement Schumacher founded in 1965 to promote his cause, the Intermediate Technology Development Group (ITDG). Initially focused on the global South and particularly on transport issues (e.g. Hathway, 1985), it has more recently expanded work on technological choices for the UK and elsewhere. Registered as an independent charity, with headquarters in Rugby, UK, and offices and a leading bookshop in London, it now has offices in several developing countries. Their research, design and dissemination activities span transport, energy, and other sectors (see http://www.itdg.org.uk).

Many people today prefer the concept of "appropriate" (rather than "intermediate") technology, seeing it as less restrictive since it allows the selection of whatever technology is most suitable in a particular context and circumstance. This could be anywhere on the scales of size, sophistication and cost. The change seeks to address critiques that always utilizing intermediate (for which read basic) technologies is to condemn developing countries to perpetual second-class status and preclude "catching up" in the way that the **newly industrialized economies (NIEs)** have done, for example.

See also: grassroots development; people-centered development; rainwater harvesting; technology policy; technology transfer

Further reading

Hathway, G. (1985) *Low-cost Vehicles: Options for Moving People and Goods*, London: Intermediate Technology Publications.

Schumacher, E. F. (1973) *Small is Beautiful: A Study of Economics as if People Mattered*, London: Abacus.

DAVID SIMON

internally displaced persons

Internally displaced persons (IDPs) are people forcibly dislocated from home areas or locations of residence, but who do not cross international borders. They can face the same problems as **refugees**, with two additional dilemmas. First, because they have not crossed an international border, they do not qualify for international assistance, even though their circumstances may be similar or more severe. Second, if dislocation has a violent aspect, then – unlike refugees – IDPs do not escape the forces of their dislocation. While dislocation can occur due to **natural disasters**, the vast majority of internal displacement occurs due to conflicts or **war** in the developing world. There has been some international interest in combining IDPs with refugees for purposes of international assistance, but issues of sovereignty generally prevent such a re-categorization.

See also: displacement; migration; refugees

JON D. UNRUH

International Covenant on Economic, Social and Cultural Rights

The International Covenant on Economic, Social and Cultural Rights (1966–76) is a statement of commitment that may be adopted by national governments to affirm the **right to self-determination** of peoples. The Covenant states that people have the right to dispose of their own natural wealth and resources, and that governments should recognize that the inherent dignity of the human person depends on enjoying economic, social and cultural rights, as well as freedom from fear and want. The Covenant derived from the **Universal Declaration of Human Rights (1948)**. It was opened for signature, ratification and accession in December 1966 and entered into force in January 1976. By 2004, forty-two out of the 191 **United Nations** members had not completed ratification, including Cuba, Pakistan and the USA. A Committee on Economic, Social and Cultural Rights was established in 1985 to supervise its implementation. The inclusion of **human rights** dimensions into **poverty** eradication policies is one of its main concerns.

See also: culture; cultural heritage; right to development; right to self-determination; United Nations

MATTEO SCARAMELLA

international division of labor

The international division of labor refers to patterns of **employment** on a global or international scale. The term refers to the common economic concept of "division of labor," which means specialization within **labor markets** to reflect the **comparative advantage** of different individuals or regions. Debates about the international division of labor usually refer to the shift of competitive advantage in **labor-intensive** manufacturing production from the richer **Organization for Economic Cooperation and Development (OECD)** countries to poorer, developing countries. There are two issues here: does this trend represent an opportunity for developing countries, and/or a danger to production (or unskilled) manufacturing sector workers in developed countries?

The international division of labor has been affected by different factors over time. Since World War I, there has been rapid growth in intra-industry **trade** (i.e. trade in different varieties of the same product), compared with the previous reliance on inter-industry trade (i.e. trade between different industries). For example, during the nineteenth century, Britain exported machinery to India, and India exported cotton in return. Nowadays, Germany and Japan increasingly export cars to one another, or **transnational corporations (TNCs)** conduct trade between different units of the same company. Furthermore, industries are increasingly "footloose," meaning that their location is not necessarily fixed to one country or region. Also, different stages of the production of the same commodity may take place in different countries and parts of the world. For example, certain computer components may be produced in Malaysia, others in the Philippines, and the final good may be made in Japan. This means that different countries compete with one another in terms of cost and comparative advantage in producing a thinning slice of the value chain (see **value chains**). This kaleidoscopic comparative advantage implies that the production of a good or its components can shift rapidly between nations. Many Asian countries, for example, have had remarkable success in exporting manufactured goods to developed countries (see **export-led growth; newly industrialized economies (NIEs)**). Developing countries in general, however, still only sell a negligible market share of total manufactured goods consumed in developed nations, and not all developing countries have benefitted from shifting comparative advantages.

Concerning impacts on unskilled or production workers in developed countries, evidence suggests that wages for these workers have declined in the USA and Europe, and their **employment** has declined in other parts of the OECD. Some analysts have suggested that these trends may be explained by the adoption of **capital intensive** labor-saving technologies rather than increased trade with developing countries (e.g. Lawrence and Slaughter, 1993). In general terms too, the share of manufacturing employment tends to decline over time.

See also: brain drain; employment; gender division of labor; labor markets; terms of trade; trade; transnational corporations (TNCs)

Further reading

Krugman, P. (1995) "Growing World Trade: Causes and Consequences," *Brookings Papers in Economic Activity* 1: 327–77.

Lawrence, R. and Slaughter, M. (1993) "International Trade and American Wages in the 1980s: Giant Sucking Sound or Small Hiccup?" *Brookings Papers in Economic Activity, Microeconomics Series* 2: 161–226.

S. MANSOOB MURSHED

international economic order

The term "international economic order" refers to the **institutions** and organizations that govern the functioning of global economic interdependence. These include rules, norms and processes that define the organization and **governance** of international economic actors including sovereign states, the **United Nations** system, **transnational corporations (TNCs)**, multilateral financial and trade organizations, regional economic aggregations, industry and **civil society** representatives. These rules are established to secure certainty and predictability in economic transactions, as well as to enhance international cooperation in realizing common interests and enhanced global welfare.

Initially, the international economic order was perceived to be the particular international **trade** and financial regime established in 1944 at the **Bretton Woods** conference which created the IBRD (International Bank for Reconstruction and Development, also known as the **World Bank**), the **International Monetary Fund (IMF)** and GATT, the General Agreement on Tariffs and Trade – later called the WTO or World Trade Organization (see **World Trade Organization/ General Agreement on Tariffs and Trade (WTO/GATT)**). The ensuing crises and disorder in the global economy in the 1970s and 1980s rendered the meaning of the word "order" (which implies a rationally managed system) somewhat imprecise. The complexity of interrelated and often conflictive interests, together with imbalances of power among actors, often subdued initiatives for transparent **governance**. Consequently, many observers have questioned how the international economic order may benefit poorer countries, through **poverty** alleviation, **social justice**, and equity in international decision-making processes.

The world trading system embodied in WTO rules is based on the free market ideology and envisions free transparent multilateral trading practices among countries. Analysts argue that the design of the world trade regime is not politically neutral; its content reflects the dominance of developed countries' interests. The rules also give disproportionate emphasis on regulation of state interventions in trade (see **state and state reform**) than on the social economic and environmental malignancy of the system. **Protectionism** in developed countries (or subsidies to producers such as farmers) erects barriers against imports from developing countries where – without such interventions – developing countries would enjoy **comparative advantage**, notably in textiles and agricultural products. Agricultural support to farmers within the EU (**European Union**) and USA through subsidies; sector-specific import restrictions; tariff escalation on processed products (see **tariffs**); non-tariff barriers to market access (e.g. stringent sanitary standards, selective application of WTO safeguard measures and arbitrary use of anti-dumping measures) – all undermine the dynamics of **export-led growth** in developing countries.

Similarly, critics have claimed that the **trade-related aspects of intellectual property rights (TRIPS)** agreement designed to protect the patent rights of technological innovators (predominantly TNCs) creates monopoly power on the use of such technologies, and thereby inhibits the dissemination or transfer of technologies (see **technology transfer**). The creation of international rules on trade inevitably reflects the weak negotiating power of many developing countries within organizations such as the WTO.

Foreign direct investment (FDI) is another important element of the international economic order. On one hand, FDI allows flows of investment that contribute to **industrialization**, technology transfer, and **employment**. On the other hand, much FDI is concentrated in a relatively small number of countries: about ten economies in East and Southeast Asia, and Latin America account for two thirds of investment. Moreover, flows of investment are highly related to national policies on protectionism or requirements for external investors to form **joint venture**s with local partners, which host governments see as valuable means to increase the local learning from investment, yet many investors see as unnecessarily costly. Uncontrolled investment by foreign TNCs may reduce the ability for host countries to develop their own internationally competitive firms (see **transnational corporations (TNCs) from developing economies**). The proposed **Multilateral Agreement on Investment (MAI)** was an attempt to centralize policies to restrict or enhance FDI, but was resisted by many developing countries because it was seen to curtail the possibility for controls on FDI by national governments.

Foreign **aid** may similarly influence the international economic order. In the 1960s, debates questioned whether aid contributed to **economic growth**; in the 1970s, discussion shifted towards the effectiveness of aid in contributing to poverty alleviation (see **aid effectiveness and aid evaluation**), and toward policies favoring the **basic needs** approach and **redistribution with growth**. In the 1980s, recognition of the structural constraints to the use of aid saw the emergence of **structural adjustment** policies, and the role as providing support for recipient countries' adjustment processes.

Since the **debt** crisis of 1980s, the international financial community has provided assistance to debtor countries to reduce their debt burden and enhance their capacity for sustained growth. This includes concessional lending from **multilateral development banks (MDBs)**; debt trading; forgiveness by bilateral donors and **debt** rescheduling via the **Paris Club** framework. Structural weaknesses and perceived poor **governance** in low-income countries often ramify mixed success in debt relief interventions. The IMF and World Bank jointly launched the **Heavily Indebted Poor Countries (HIPC) initiative** in 1996 to reduce the external debt burdens of eligible countries, conditional upon undertaking macroeconomic structural and governance reforms. Such countries are required to draw up PRSPs (Poverty Reduction Strategy Papers) in broad consultation with donors and **civil society**. Despite such coordinated initiatives for ensuring aid effectiveness,

self-interest among **bilateral aid agencies** sometimes proves counterproductive. For example aid tying (or **conditionality**) (i.e. requiring aid recipients to use aid to procure goods and services from the donor country, often at a price higher than the market price) hinders **free trade**; consumes foreign exchange (see **exchange rates**) on technology that may not be appropriate to their needs; curtails intra-South trade and protects inefficient industries whose high production cost is passed on to the aid recipients.

For many, the international economic order is best represented by the so-called G7 (or now G8) group of the world's richest nations, that meets regularly to agree on issues of common importance. G8 comprises Canada, France, Germany, Italy, Japan, Russia, the UK, and the USA. The first meeting (excluding Canada and Russia) was in 1975; Canada joined in 1976, and then Russia's participation was formally agreed in 1998.

The international economic order may also be affected by the rise of international alliances between developing countries, such as the **Group of 77 (G-77)**, or the **non-aligned movement** (see also **Bandung conference (1955); South-South cooperation**). The rise of **transnational corporations (TNCs) from developing economies** may also challenge economic hegemony from developed countries.

See also: aid; Bretton Woods; conditionality; debt crisis; foreign direct investment; globalization; international law; Multilateral Agreement on Investment (MAI); neo-liberalism; structural adjustment; terms of trade; trade; transnational corporations (TNCs); transnational corporations (TNCs) from developing economies; world economic conference (London, 1933); World Social Forum (WSF); World Trade Organization/General Agreement on Tariffs and Trade (WTO/GATT)

Further reading

Gilpin, R. (2001) *Global Political Economy: Understanding the International Economic Order*, Princeton: Princeton University Press.

Hirst, P. and Thompson, G. (1999) *Globalization in Question: The International Economy and the Possibilities of Governance*, Cambridge: Polity Press.

Strange, S. (1996) *The Retreat of the State: The Diffusion of Power in the World Economy*, Cambridge: Cambridge University Press.

MOSES A. OSIRO

International Labor Organization (ILO)

The International Labor Organization (ILO) is a **United Nations** (UN) specialized agency working to protect internationally recognized **labor rights and standards**. Founded in 1919 at the Treaty of Versailles, the ILO became the first specialized agency of the UN in 1946. The ILO performs three major functions related to labor and **employment** issues around the world. First, it formulates international labor rights and standards in the form of Conventions and Recommendations which elaborate core labor rights such as **freedom of association**, workers' rights to organize, collective bargaining, abolition of forced labor, and equality of opportunity and treatment. Second, it provides technical assistance to countries in areas such as: vocational training; **employment** policy; labor law and industrial relations; cooperatives; social security; labor statistics; and **occupational health** and safety. Finally, it helps foster independent employers' and workers' organizations including **trade unions**, providing training and advisory services to these as needed.

The ILO is governed through a tripartite structure comprising worker, employer and governmental representatives. As of 2004, the ILO had 177 member states. In recent years the ILO's program interests have spanned four key areas: (i) labor rights and standards, including conventions such as the ILO's **Declaration on Fundamental Principles and Rights at Work** (1998); (ii) employment promotion, including programming on skills formation of workers and development of **small and medium enterprises (SMEs)**; (iii) social protection (including work

on socio-economic security and **decent work deficit**); and (iv) social dialog support for improved tripartite processes.

Critics of the ILO find its focus on international labor **law** and conventions somewhat distant from the day-to-day needs of the world's workers. New developments affecting labor and employment issues include **globalization** trends in the world economy and related phenomena such as the worldwide decline in trade union membership and concurrent rise in enterprise-level labor negotiations, and the growing **casualization of work** and rise of part-time employment. In the face of these, the ILO has had to revise elements of its overall approach to improving outcomes for workers worldwide, by considering workers outside both the union structure and the formal sector. It has in large part been able to do this through national programs of technical assistance, an increased focus on less visible workers such as those in the **urban informal sector**, new use of field-level **partnerships** with **non-governmental organizations (NGOs)**, and the forging of links to broader development initiatives in the UN system, for example in the areas of **gender** and **social development**.

See also: casualization of work; child labor; decent work deficit; Declaration on Fundamental Principles and Rights at Work; freedom of association; labor rights and standards; pensions; trade unions; underemployment; unemployment; welfare state

Further reading

Blanpain, R. and Engels, C. (eds) (2001) *The ILO and the Social Challenges of the 21st Century: The Geneva Lectures*, The Hague: Kluwer Law International.

Weisband, E. (2000) "Discursive Multilateralism: Global Benchmarks, Shame and Learning in the ILO Labor Standards Monitoring Regime," *International Studies Quarterly* 44:4 643–56.

ANNE T. KURIAKOSE

international law

The field of international law and development emerged from a 1970s movement led by developing countries to transform the **international economic order**, largely through legal measures formulated within the United Nations General Assembly (UNGAS). These efforts were generally referred to as the movement for a New International Economic Order (NIEO), and were a bold attempt to establish legal frameworks to address the massive socio-economic **inequality** between industrialized countries and poorer countries (also see **inequality and poverty, world trends**). Debates between the mid-1970s and the late 1980s referred to an emerging "international law of development," and defined this as an instrument for promoting equity in international relations through economic and legal transformation. This definition suggests a general optimism in the ability of law to transform unequal power relations (see **law**).

Five key principles were identified in the field of international development law. First, law sought to uphold economic self-determination and permanent sovereignty over **natural resources** (especially in relation to foreign investors). Second, law should maintain the right for citizens in developing countries to benefit equally from common heritage resources that do not fall within the territory of any state (see **cultural heritage; common heritage of humankind**). Third, law should support solidarity and international cooperation in solving common problems, such as environmental degradation (see **environment**). Fourth, there should be preferential treatment of poor countries in international trade. Fifthly, the **right to development** should be an inalienable human right (see **human rights**).

These principles are embodied in various resolutions and declarations of UNGAS. Examples include the Charter of Economic Rights and Duties of States (1974); the Declaration and Programme of Action on the Establishment of a New International Economic Order (1974); and the **United Nations Declaration on the Right to Development (1986) – Res. 41/128**. However, these resolutions and declarations are not legally binding and have never been translated into binding treaties requiring state parties to undertake precise legal obligations directed toward establishing an equitable international system. Therefore, this "emerging" field has not blossomed into a well-established recognizable field within international law. Rather, it survives through some unresolved debates and the uneven acceptance of some fragments of its key principles.

The principle of permanent sovereignty over natural resources, and the demand for wider latitude in poor countries' regulation of foreign private capital in the interest of public policy was largely unsuccessful. It is now standard for **foreign direct investment** (FDI) contracts to state clearly that the law of the host country shall not apply (see also **Multilateral Agreement on Investment (MAI)**). Since 1986, many investment disputes have been settled by arbitration through the International Center for the Settlement of Investment Disputes (ICSID), set up at the initiative of the **World Bank**, making poor countries' judicial processes irrelevant to FDI. Indeed, critics have claimed that private arrangements such as ICSID disempower national legal policies, and may delegitimize state interventions to shape market relations in favor of public interests.

The right to benefit equally from common heritage resources such as minerals and fossil fuels in deep-sea beds continues to be debated within the sub-field of the **United Nations Convention on the Law of the Sea (UNCLOS)**. The dominant debate has been about balancing the principle of common ownership of resources against incentives for the countries that have the technology to develop them.

Concerning the principle of solidarity and international cooperation, there has been a level of commitment to developing binding international norms on environmental issues such as **climate change** (also see **Basel Convention on hazardous waste; Cartagena Protocol on Biosafety; Convention on Biological Diversity (CBD)**). However, international legal frameworks are often irrelevant to topics of **chronic poverty**, or long-term crises in poor countries that require substantial **aid** and funding. Official development assistance, or aid, is motivated by diverse factors, but definitely not by legal conviction or compulsion.

The demand for preferential **terms of trade** for poor countries rests on the principle that it is disadvantageous to poor countries to insist upon uniform terms of trade when countries are producers of low-value primary commodities. Proponents of a new **international economic order** have sought preferential treatment for poor countries on an unconditional and permanent basis. These demands continue to be expressed through lobbying for "special and differential treatment" (SDT) for poor countries within the WTO (see **World Trade Organization/General Agreement on Tariffs and Trade (WTO/GATT)**). However, progress has been slowed by disagreements between different countries on the principle of applying trading rules selectively, rather than across the board. Some richer countries have sought to make SDT only a temporary measure, or have offered it only as a bargaining chip for concessions in other areas. At other times, the language of SDT has been watered down so that rich countries are simply called upon to make "best efforts" rather than take on precise legal obligations.

The 1986 UN Declaration on the Right to Development (see **right to development**) reiterates every person's right to an adequate standard of living and to full and active participation in economic, social and political development. Besides individual rights, the declaration also promulgates "states' rights" to freely exploit and utilize their **natural resources**; control their own economy; and determine their own path to development. It also calls for the removal of barriers to the realization of the right to development, such as unfavorable terms of trade and the **debt** burden. Rich countries have opposed the right to development, questioning both its conceptual clarity and practicality. As a result, the declaration has never matured into a binding treaty, and since 1987 discussions on its implementation have stagnated in a UN Open-ended Working Group on the Right to Development.

Initiatives to establish a new international economic order, however, have influenced environmental agreements such as the conventions on **climate change** and **biodiversity**. These treaties reiterate the rights of developing countries over their natural resources and territory. They have also responded to developing countries' demands for additional **technology transfer**, and funding on concessional and preferential terms. The bargaining position of developing countries in the negotiations for these treaties was strengthened by the rich countries' obvious concerns about climate change and biodiversity. The **World Bank**-managed **Global Environment Facility (GEF)** was created in 1990 to help disburse the necessary funding. Still, actual transfers under this facility have been small and micro-managed by industrial nations.

As a political project, international law-making in the development arena has been made extremely difficult by the lack of political will of rich countries. Poor countries have largely abandoned their long-running efforts to address global inequality through legislative activism within the **United Nations**, realizing that while their sheer numbers were enough to pass radical resolutions through UNGAS, this does not automatically translate into binding legal obligations. Furthermore, these numbers do not count in the international financial institutions (IFIs) that wield immense economic power. The World Bank and **International Monetary Fund (IMF)** can make decisions irrespective of developing country input, due to rules on weighted voting based on financial contributions. Most important, developing countries have realized that the international economic system is now heavily dominated by **transnational corporations (TNCs)**, which are not always regulated by international legal frameworks. Aiming at rich nations and IFIs is no longer enough as a political strategy.

Conceptually, the experience of the debate about a new international economic order questions whether global inequality can be dealt with by law. Experience so far seems to vindicate the view that state (see **state and state reform**) and corporate interests are all that count. International debt continues to be a major concern. Yet, ongoing deliberations about debt at both bilateral and multilateral levels have proceeded without the pretence of referring to any overarching international legal framework.

See also: domestic law; inequality; inequality and poverty, world trends; international economic order; law; United Nations

Further reading

Bedjaoui, M. (1979) *Toward a New International Economic Order,* Paris: UNESCO and Holmes and Meier.

Bulaji, M. (1993) *Principles of International Development Law,* London: Martinus Nijhoff.

Donnelly, J. (1985) "In Search of the Unicorn: The Jurisprudence and Politics of the Right to Development," pp. 169–206 in Carty, A. (ed.) *Law and Development,* Aldershot: Dartmouth.

Gathii, J. (1999) "The Limits of the *New* International Rule of Law on Good Governance," pp. 207–31 in Okafor, O. and Quashigah, E. (eds) *Legitimate Governance in Africa,* The Hague: Kluwer Law International.

Michalopoulos, C. (2003) "Special and Differential Treatment in Agriculture: Proposals for a Development Round," *IDS Bulletin* 34: 24–37.

Shalakany, A. (2000) "Arbitration and the Third World: A Plea for Reassessing Bias Under the Spectre of Neo-Liberalism," *Harvard International Law Journal* 41: 419–68.

CELESTINE NYAMU-MUSEMBI

international migration

International migration is that component of **migration** that involves a movement across a state border. For many analysts, for example, Castles and Miller (1998), Cohen (1995) and Weiner (1995), international migration *is* migration, with the majority of those who move, that is internal migrants, being considered under **urbanization**. International migration has emerged as one of the most significant political and development issues at the start of the twenty-first century and one that is seen to threaten the integrity of the basic building block of the current world system, the independent nation-state (see **state and state reform**). International migration is a central pillar of **globalization** and profoundly affects both the developed and the developing world,

though in very different ways. Almost half of the **population** growth of the developed world in the 1990s, for example, was due to immigration, and a minimum estimate in 2000 for the number of people outside their country of birth was 175 million.

Despite a marked increase in the number of people living outside their country of birth, that number represented only about 3 percent of the world's population in 2000 and had increased at a rate only marginally greater than that for the global population as a whole (Zlotnik, 2001; United Nations 2002). So, why should such a small proportion of the total population have generated such international concern? First, the absolute numbers represent a minimum estimate of those outside their country of birth. Among the trends in international migration over recent years has been a gradual shift away from migration for permanent settlement toward more temporary forms of admission. It is not that the 175 million in 2000 refer only to permanent settlers (other types of international movers will also be included in that figure) but that other types of entrants have a higher probability of being omitted from official figures. Students, lower-skilled contract laborers and highly skilled workers have become important components of the international migration system. Second, there is a growing clandestine, undocumented or irregular migration, which is notoriously difficult to estimate. The entry of large numbers of undocumented migrants into a country gives the impression that a government has lost control of its own borders, and **migrant trafficking** and human smuggling emerge as major issues. Third, there is the perennial fear of the outsider, with even small numbers of immigrants bringing very different ways of life being seen as a threat to the established traditions of nationals. Xenophobia and racism (see **race and racism**) emerge as political issues. Fourth, there are security concerns, heightened by the destruction of the World Trade Center in September 2001, that some entrants may seek to undermine the stability of host societies.

Changes in the pattern of international migration since the 1960s, rather than the numbers of migrants, lie at the root of the concerns about the movement. International movements to the most developed countries until the 1970s were dominated by peoples from other developed countries, basically migrations from Europe to the Americas and to Australasia. Declining **fertility** (birth rates) in Europe and the emergence of non-discriminatory immigration policies in destination societies saw increasing migration from the developing to the developed world. Western and Southern Europe shifted from being areas of mass emigration to areas of mass immigration, and movements from Latin American and Asian countries came to dominate movements to the USA and Canada. Significant destinations for international migrants have emerged in the developing world itself, and particularly in East and Southeast Asia. Thus, a greater variety of people have been moving in a greater variety of ways than ever before.

Whether the movements from the developing to the developed world represent a failure of development in the South or whether they are more a product of an accelerating demand for labor in the North has been the subject of much debate (see **international division of labor; labor markets**). The causes and consequences of migration are various and complex, and no single outcome can be expected. However, neither policies to stimulate development in origin areas nor aid appear to be effective in stemming the outflows. Quite the reverse: over the short term, development that attempts to link developing areas to a more global economy is likely to accelerate rather than discourage emigration. Those countries that actively seek to promote the interchange of migrants appear to achieve higher levels of **economic growth** than those that do not. Also, **remittances** sent back by migrants to home areas are important sources of foreign exchange at the national level, and of income at local levels. These flows of wealth act to counterbalance the loss of dynamic elements of origin populations through a **brain drain**. Political instability in parts of the developing world, as newly independent governments seek to establish control over heterogeneous populations, has created the conditions for forced migrations. These movements primarily affect neighboring countries, further straining the provision of basic services in already poor parts of the world, but also bringing pressure on the refugee and asylum processes in the developed world (see **refugees; asylum seeking**). The global significance of the

transnational linkages between origins and destinations is captured in the concept of **diaspora**, which in many ways has come to replace the term "international migration." Nevertheless, not all migrants can be seen as victims, living in exile, and many proactive dynamic and entrepreneurial migrants form the demographic foundation for any global economy.

See also: asylum seeking; brain drain; labor migration; migration; refugees; remittances

Further reading

Castles, S. and Miller, M. (eds) (1998, 2nd edn) *The Age of Migration: International Population Movements in the Modern World*, London: Macmillan.

Cohen, R. (ed.) (1995) *The Cambridge Survey of World Migration*, Cambridge: Cambridge University Press.

Skeldon, R. (1997) *Migration and Development: A Global Perspective*, London: Longman.

United Nations (2002) *International Migration Report 2002*, New York: UN Population Division, Department of Economic and Social Affairs.

Weiner, M. (1995) *The Global Migration Crisis: Challenge to States and Human Rights*, New York: HarperCollins.

Zlotnik, H. (2001) "Past Trends in International Migration and Their Implications for Future Prospects" pp. 227–61 in Siddique, M. (ed.) *International Migration into the 21st Century: Essays in Honour of Reginald Appleyard*, Cheltenham: Elgar.

RONALD SKELDON

International Monetary Fund (IMF)

The International Monetary Fund (IMF) was formed at the **Bretton Woods** meetings in 1944 as theoretically situated within the **United Nations** system. However, the IMF has its own Board of Governors, with representatives of all member countries (usually a country's minister of finance or the governor of its central bank) as its highest governing authority. The Board of Governors delegates immediate, day-to-day, decision-making to an Executive Board of twenty-four Executive Directors, with a Managing Director as chairman. The IMF's five biggest shareholders – the USA, Japan, Germany, France, and the UK – along with China, Russia, and Saudi Arabia, have seats on the Board, while other countries are collectively represented by regional directors. The USA, with 17 percent of the total votes, along with a few other countries, has effective control over the institution and its policies. In 2004, the IMF had US$316 billion in total quotas (or SDR216 billion – the SDR, or special drawing right, is an international reserve asset introduced by the IMF in 1969, with a value based on a group of leading world currencies), with further funds available for emergencies. In 2004, 184 countries were members of the IMF.

The IMF focuses on the macroeconomic policies of member governments, including: policies relating to the state budget (see **state and state reform**), the management of money and credit (see **fiscal and monetary policy**), the exchange rate (see **exchange rates**); and the financial policies of governments, including the regulation and supervision of banks and other financial institutions. In addition, the IMF looks at structural policies that affect macroeconomic performance (i.e. the performance of economic aggregates such as national income, total national consumption, investment and the money supply). The IMF monitors the economic policies of member countries and acts as a reserve fund that can be used by countries needing temporary financing mainly to address balance of payments problems. In such emergencies, the IMF gives short-term loans, in part from previously deposited funds, but with the difference that the loans are made in "harder" (more internationally acceptable) currencies than the deposits. To receive these loans countries have to agree to certain conditions, or "conditionalities," (see **conditionality**) that consist of policies that a government has to put into effect to convince the IMF that it will be able to repay the loan within a time span of 1–5 years. Details of the policy program are

spelled out in a "letter of intent" signed by a senior member of the government concerned and the Managing Director of the IMF. The IMF then monitors the government's performance to ensure compliance with the agreement specified in the letter of intent until the loan is repaid or renegotiated (IMF, 1998).

Because of the oil crisis and higher energy prices of the 1970s (see **Organization of Petroleum Exporting Countries (OPEC)**), many developing countries faced balance of payments deficits. To cover these deficits, and to promote development, governments borrowed from recycled "petro-dollars" deposited in New York and London banks. Increasingly, developing countries accrued new **debt** merely to repay interest on the old. By 1982, the aggregate debt of non-oil producing developing countries had risen to $600 billion (de Vries, 1986:183). **Debt crisis** was triggered in August 1982 when Mexico announced that it could no longer make loan payments on time. The formula used by financial institutions to handle the debt crisis was called "rescheduling." During the first phase of the debt crisis, from 1982 to 1985, possible default by developing countries was met by new loans organized by commercial banks, the IMF, and other lenders. Creditor governments formed a committee to deal with **debt relief**, in consultation with the IMF, that was hosted by the French treasury, and known as the "**Paris Club**." Repeated Paris Club re-scheduling of debts led official lenders eventually to recognize that a new approach was needed. Continuing efforts by the USA to find a position adequate for responding to a deteriorating debt situation culminated in a proposal made in October 1985 by James A. Baker III, Secretary of the Treasury between 1985 and 1988 in the Reagan administration, in what came to be known as the "Baker Plan." The idea was that the IMF and the **World Bank** should join forces to increase the amount of loans available from both institutions and the commercial banks. Loans were made conditional on "policy improvements in the macroeconomic framework" under **structural adjustment** programs (SAPs). These followed what many analysts see as a neo-liberal conception of **economic growth**, as with policies aimed at privatization, deregulation of private enterprise, reducing state deficits and increasing the role played by markets (see **privatization and liberalization; state and state reform**). Throughout the 1980s, debtor nations and commercial bank creditors engaged in repeated rounds of rescheduling and restructuring sovereign-nation and private-sector debt. This led broad sectors even of financial and quasi-official opinion toward the recognition that some of the loans would never be repaid. When the (Republican) Bush (Snr) administration assumed office in 1989, the new Secretary of the US Treasury, Nicholas Brady, announced that the only way to address the debt crisis was to encourage banks to begin voluntary debt reduction schemes. Under what became known as the Brady Plan, countries were to implement market-oriented structural adjustment, as with the Baker Plan, but this time in exchange for a reduction of commercial bank debt and, often, new loans from commercial banks and multilateral lending agencies. Behind this flurry of debt rescheduling and relief activity, strong political pressure was exerted by national governments, especially the USA, usually operating in concert with the Paris Club and the IMF. The main concern was preserving the banking system in the face of the possibility of repudiations of hundreds of billions of dollars in unpayable debt. Latin American countries following the free-market policies of structural adjustment have grown at a fraction of the rate they grew at in the 1970s and 1980s, when governments followed more interventionist and protectionist policies. In the late 1990s, and continuing in the early 2000s, many Latin American countries, following IMF-approved stabilization and restructuring programs, became economically depressed – the most serious case being Argentina.

Responding to widespread concern expressed by developed countries, and in concert with the World Bank, the IMF began its **Heavily Indebted Poor Countries (HIPC) initiative** in 1996. The HIPC initiative was intended to manage the debt problems of the most heavily indebted poor countries (originally forty-one countries, mostly in Africa) with total debt of about US$200 billion. By adopting policies judged "sound by the international **community**," debt

relief to the eventual extent of US$60 billion would be granted. As a mere seven countries qualified for assistance in the first three years of the facility's operation, the HIPC initiative was "enhanced" in 1999 to provide interim debt relief, between the decision and completion points that immediately reduced debt service costs. The enhanced facility joined debt relief more obviously with poverty reduction. To qualify for assistance under the HIPC initiative, or to get concessional loans from the IMF or World Bank, countries have to prepare **poverty** reduction strategies with the participation of members of **civil society** (Birdsall and Williamson, 2002). However, a number of studies have critically examined the new initiatives, finding civil society groups unsatisfied with the extent of public involvement, while the strategies still promote economic growth through neo-liberal means without, on the most part, addressing how this growth is redistributed to the poor. Indeed, the core macroeconomic elements of the programs are said to have changed little from the old structural adjustment programs, with continued adherence to privatization, liberalization and a reduced role for the state. As a result, the IMF remains at the center of considerable controversy, with thousands of protestors turning up for every meeting it tries to hold, and a Nobel Prize winning economist calling for its eradication (Stiglitz, 2002).

See also: conditionality; debt; debt crisis; debt relief; fiscal and monetary policy; Heavily Indebted Poor Countries (HIPC) initiative; neo-liberalism; structural adjustment; Washington consensus; World Bank

Further reading

Birdsall, N. and Williamson, J. (2002) *Delivering on Debt Relief: From IMF Gold to a New Aid Architecture*, Washington DC: Center for Global Development.

Bretton Woods Project, A critical information service on the World Bank and IMF: http://www.brettonwoodsproject.org/

de Vries, M. (1986) *The IMF in a Changing World 1945–85*, Washington DC: IMF.

IMF (1998) *What is the International Monetary Fund?* Washington DC: IMF.

Pauly, L. (1997) *Who Elected the Bankers? Surveillence and Control in the World Economy*, Ithaca NY: Cornell University Press.

Peet, R. (2003) *Unholy Trinity: The IMF, World Bank and WTO*, London: Zed.

Stiglitz, J. (2002) *Globalization and its Discontents*, New York: Norton.

RICHARD PEET

international organizations and associations

International organizations and associations take many forms, and are an important part of the local-global dialog in development processes. Though their mandate inherently stretches beyond national borders, international organizations operate at several different scales. International organizations at the level of the world system of nation-states include institutions such as the **United Nations** and its various agencies, the Organization of American States, and the **World Bank**. They can also be seen in private sector organizations including the World Business Council on Sustainable Development and more industry-specific groupings such as the Global Mining Initiative. While ostensibly local in nature, **civil society** networks and **non-governmental organizations (NGOs)** have also become increasingly internationalized, with groups such as the International Rivers Network and the Third World Network advocating **sustainable development** and **social justice** issues across a variety of global situations. Other organizations that are international in scope include religious **charities**, professional and academic associations and **trade unions**.

See also: multilateral development banks (MDBs); non-governmental organizations (NGOs); United Nations; World Bank

PABLO SHILADITYA BOSE

Internet

The Internet is a set of protocols or standards developed in the USA during the 1970s. Supported by the Department of Defense, initially Internetworking was for use by the scientific research **community**. The protocols function to transport packets of digital information from one computer to another.

The global spread of the Internet in the 1990s means that there is a potential for people in developing countries to communicate and exchange information with each other and with those in the industrialized countries very rapidly and at relatively low cost. Many policy-makers and donor agencies have assumed that simple access to the Internet and the use of electronic mail or the World Wide Web will offer a new means to tackle problems of uneven social and **economic development** and **poverty**. The Internet can be used to provide a platform for online services ranging from **health**, **education**, and government to electronic business services. However, effective use of the Internet to address development problems requires that many social, cultural, economic and infrastructure conditions be in place.

Access to the Internet requires a robust and reasonably reliable fixed or mobile **telecommunications** network and a reliable electricity supply to run a computer and software applications. Use of the Internet enables people to access vast stocks of digital information that are available globally, and to create and exchange information about local conditions. However, even where such access is achieved, capabilities ranging from literacy, language facility, **information technology** skills, skills for managing social and technical networks, and educational attainment levels must be developed. This is essential if local or global sources of digital information are to be converted into useful knowledge by Internet users.

Internet applications such as electronic mail, electronic commerce and electronic government require legislative frameworks with respect to privacy protection, commercial practices, electronic payment systems, protection of **intellectual property rights (IPRs)** and many other issues. There are strong pressures from the industrialized countries and from intergovernmental agencies to adopt legislative frameworks that are being implemented in the wealthier countries. However, there are sound reasons for developing countries to develop their own strategies toward the spread of Internet access. Legislative frameworks need to be developed in the light of their economic resources, distinctive **local knowledge** bases and cultural practices, and priorities for improved **governance** and social and **economic development**.

Public-private partnerships are being used to encourage growth in the numbers of Internet subscribers in developing countries and there is a growing number of entrepreneurs who offer Internet access. By 2002, however, in Africa although 1 in 13 people had a television, only 1 in 150 people (a total of 5.5 million) had access to the Internet. Many foresee a growing "digital divide." Public forms of Internet access via kiosks, cybercafes, **community** tele-centers, and other organizations are expanding in developing countries. However, the monthly cost of Internet access is often far in excess of monthly average per capita income. Access is highly skewed in favor of urban areas, and it may be subject to government censorship controls.

National and regional initiatives to promote the use of the Internet to support social and economic development offer opportunities that may enable **civil society** organizations, private-sector firms and governments to take advantage of electronic trading and to strengthen democratic processes. However, growing use of the Internet in developing countries also raises issues of the effects of electronic surveillance, erosion of the taxation base, and reliance on foreign educational and entertainment content. Because the Internet has grown most rapidly in the industrialized countries, the distribution of costs and revenues associated with service supply is slowing the spread of the Internet in many poorer countries. The Internet is one component of a complex digital technology system. Its spread may enable people in developing countries to achieve their social and economic development goals, but the Internet is only a tool for development. The goals of development must shape local and national access to the Internet if it is to be used in ways that are beneficial to the majority of people in developing countries.

See also: information technology; media; telecommunications; World Summit on the Information Society (WSIS)

Further reading

Castells, M. (2001) *The Internet Galaxy: Reflections on the Internet, Business, and Society*, Oxford: Oxford University Press.

Mansell, R. and Wehn, W. (eds) (1998) *Knowledge Societies: Information Technology for Sustainable Development*, published for the United Nations Commission on Science and Technology for Development, Oxford: Oxford University Press.

Naughton, J. (2000) *A Brief History of the Future: From Radio Days to Internet Years in a Lifetime*, New York: The Overlook Press.

Norris, P. (2001) *Digital Divide: Civic Engagement, Information Poverty, and the Internet Worldwide*, Cambridge: Cambridge University Press.

ROBIN MANSELL

intrahousehold allocations

Intrahousehold allocations refer to the differences that occur *within* households concerning the distribution of resources. The concept developed to challenge the sometimes-dominant view that households can be treated *as if* they were acting as an individual or single unit, and hence are the most logical unit for **targeting** policy, as well as the logical unit of consumption and, in many developing country contexts, of production. By default, this idea underlies much of policy made in developing countries today.

This unitary notion of the household has been problematized over time. Work within economics added the notions of bargaining power and a more general collective decision-making process. These concepts raise issues such as the differential impact of targeting men versus women for social policy (see **gender; women-headed households**). These models all assume that households are Pareto efficient in the allocation of resources (i.e. that no one can be made better off without making someone worse off), an assumption that has been questioned theoretically through the development of non-cooperative models, and disproved empirically in a number of developing country settings by different researchers. Inefficient allocation within households may be due to factors that can be either a significant obstacle or opportunity for social policy interventions. Both the collective models and non-cooperative models point to the importance of understanding the household allocation process in order to formulate effective policy. Disciplines outside of economics, such as anthropology or sociology, often provide a richer, albeit less generalizable view of the household through the incorporation of the complex notions of power and **gender** relations (Hart, 1995).

See also: income distribution; joint families; targeting; women-headed households

Further reading

Haddad, L., Hoddinott, J. and Alderman, H. (eds) (1997) *Intrahousehold Resource Allocation in Developing Countries: Models, Methods and Policy*, Baltimore: Johns Hopkins University Press.

Hart, G. (1995) "Gender and Household Dynamics: Recent Theories and Their Implications," in Quibria, M. (ed.) *Critical Issues in Asian Development: Theories, Experiences, and Policies*, Oxford: Oxford University Press.

Strauss, J., Mwabu, G., Beegle, K. and Thomas, D. (2000) "Intrahousehold Allocations: A Review of Theories and Empirical Evidence," *Journal of African Economies* 9:1 83–149.

MARKUS GOLDSTEIN

iron and steel

Iron and steel are highly versatile materials that contain varying proportions of the metallic element iron. According to the International Iron and Steel Institute (IISI) worldwide steel production in 2003 was 965 million tons, and pig iron was 657.3 million tons. The annual value of global steel production is estimated to be over $US200 billion.

The majority of steel is produced through two process routes: the primary (or "integrated") route and secondary (or "minimill") route. Primary producers manufacture iron and steel from basic ingredients – iron ore, coal, etc. – in large integrated facilities comprising coke ovens, blast furnaces and oxygen furnaces. Secondary producers, by contrast, typically operate at smaller scales and use electric arc furnaces to produce steel from scrap and/or iron-bearing substitutes such as directly reduced iron. Historically, the primary processing route has dominated steelmaking. However, since the 1970s it has come under increasing challenge from the secondary one, largely because of the lower capital, operating and environmental costs of minimills. Many analysts predict that the share of steel produced by secondary plants, which currently stands at 34 percent, will rise substantially over coming decades.

Iron and steel play an important role in the development process. They are vital inputs to many basic infrastructural and industrial sectors ranging from construction to heavy engineering. It is for this reason that steel has long been regarded as a strategically significant sector. Beginning in the 1950s, governments in many developing economies actively sought to cultivate an indigenous steel industry, often through a combination of import protection and large public investments in capacity expansion. As a result, the established steel producing nations of Europe and the US have now been joined, and sometimes overtaken, over the past half-century by a number of Asian and Latin American economies. China, for example, now ranks as the world's largest steel producer, accounting for over 20 percent of output; while South Korea, India and Brazil all feature amongst the top ten steel producing countries.

The global iron and steel industry is currently in the middle of a period of far-reaching structural, technological and regulatory change. Many state-owned steel plants have been – or are in the process of being – privatized. Moreover, responding to falling trade barriers, depressed steel prices and heightened competition, steelmakers are vigorously attempting to cut production costs through a combination of plant modernization, restructuring and consolidation. A growing number of firms are also moving away from low-value, commodity steels in favor of high value, premium quality steel products in a bid to improve profitability levels. The long-term implications of these changes for developing countries remain unclear, although they look set to play a growing role in worldwide iron and steel production over coming decades.

See also: auto industry; industrialization; natural resources; privatization and liberalization

Further reading

D'Costa, A. (1999) *The Global Restructuring of the Steel Industry: Innovations, Institutions, and Industrial Change*, New York: Routledge.
IISI (2003) *World Steel in Figures: 2003 Edition*, Brussels: International Iron and Steel Institute (IISI).

RICHARD PERKINS

irrigation

Irrigation simply means the provision of water to plants over and above the amounts naturally available from rainfall and groundwater (see also **agriculture; water management**). Irrigation may allow the production of a crop where none would otherwise be possible, as in desert regions (**dryland agriculture**), or may protect and enhance a crop in the face of a variable natural water supply. Irrigation has been associated with some of the earliest civilizations like that in Mesopotamia (modern Iraq), Lower Egypt and the Indus, which have been termed hydraulic civilizations, showing how social and water control have gone together. Early techniques included the digging of inundation canals through natural levees to capture floods (Indus and Egypt), and myriad devices for lifting water, such as the Persian wheel, powered by animals. Water supply has also been enhanced by digging vertical shafts to the water table (see **boreholes**), and driving tunnels along the water table in *taluses* in arid areas – the *qanat* of the desert edge ranging from Morocco to Pakistan.

Crops are divided into wet irrigated, indicating a high intensity of water use (rice and sugar cane) and dry irrigated, such as cotton and wheat. Rice crops "like their feet in the water and their heads in the sun," so that standing water is required. Standing water also allows the field to be puddled into a fine mud into which young seedlings can be transplanted by hand, for weed suppression during growth, and for the fixation of nitrogen by blue-green algae. To control the water level, *bunds* are built round a field. In many traditional systems a water supply is led to the highest fields in a system, and allowed to flow from field to field from there. Such systems may be associated with a perennial source like a spring, or with a tank (small reservoir), which has trapped water during a rainy season. With dry irrigated crops, the more usual system is to provide water on a rotational basis from field to field as required, perhaps at weekly or ten-day intervals (or even longer).

Traditional systems have been based on flow from rivers, tanks, and wells. Some old systems were large and sophisticated, like the Grand Anicut (barrage) on the Cauvery River in South India, dating from 2,000 years ago, which irrigated much of the Cauvery delta. More commonly, systems have been based on tanks irrigating a thousand or more hectares, and often associated with a village scale of command. Schemes that store water may allow for the growth of a second crop after the rainy season, thereby increasing cropping intensity. Wells might be used at the scale of the individual field or individual farm. From early in the nineteenth century the scale of systems developed in areas of European settlement and European colonization began to grow rapidly. By the latter part of the century schemes in Sudan, India (including modern Pakistan), the Americas and Australia included barrages in rivers as big as the Ganges, main canals hundreds of miles long, and thousands of miles of distributary canals. These schemes worked on the principle of gravity flow. They also had to address numerous technical problems concerning erosion and siltation, such as by attempting to find a mean stable regime of water and sediment flow. In areas of peasant **agriculture**, they also had to address problems of allocation to more than half a million farmers. In north India, for example, irrigation adopted a system of continuous flow through fixed gates for a specified period (*warabandi*); but where farms were larger and more commercial (USA and Australia), variable gates were more often used. In pre-democratic days of colonial administration (see **colonialism, history of; colonialism, impacts of**), some of the larger schemes worked to the extent they did because of the power vested in government authorities. These large schemes also often showed problems with rising water tables, upward movement of water through capillary action, evaporation, and hence **salinization**. One quarter of the land ever irrigated in Pakistan is now too saline for normal agriculture. Rehabilitation is expensive and difficult.

The second half of the twentieth century saw numerous different advances and adaptations. For the first time large-scale storage **dams** using concrete could be built – like the Hoover in the USA and the Bhakra in India – and later huge rock-filled structures like Tarbela on the Indus. Increasingly canals became lined to limit percolation. But the spread of diesel engines and electricity meant that tube wells could be energized. These wells were drilled (at for example 6in (18cm) bore) and lined with a pipe, permeable at the required depth range. Submersible pumps enable water to be drawn from near the surface and from deep aquifers. In many areas of canal irrigation, farmers preferred this new source of ground water because they had control over the timing of delivery, even though it was more expensive energetically. This has led to the conjunctive use of surface and groundwater – sometimes the purpose of the surface system now is to leak to groundwater, in an artificial inland delta. By the end of the twentieth century, large dams were increasingly under question: the benefits were often not as great as supposed, and the social costs of eviction, inundation, and habitat loss often thought to be higher than anticipated. Now the fashion seems to be turning again to schemes in which technology and society work together in sympathetic scale. There is also scope for making existing delivery systems more reliable and less variable, thereby encouraging better use of other inputs. Authority is increasingly "turned over" to **water user associations (WUAs)**. Most of the very large schemes are now emulating this process, so that command systems are replaced by more democratic and open decision-making.

Irrigation has been central to increases in **food** production which have kept the world fed in the twentieth century. It has been central to the **green revolution**. The use of **fertilizers** without assured water can be harmful or simply wasteful. Irrigation will be central to any hopes of feeding the world in the current century, but increasingly water is becoming a scarce commodity, and competition from big cities and industry is intense. Invariably water for agriculture is not properly costed, and urban centers are able to bid more for its use. Some technical responses are to develop very precise delivery systems, like the drip system which place drops of water at each plant individually – used in commercial agriculture in Israel, but the costs are too high for peasant Asia and the maintenance problems too great. Other new ideas include partial root drying, which can halve the water requirements of the crops on which it has so far been tried (e.g. tomatoes), but which has not yet been tried on cereals. Genetic engineering may help develop more drought-resistant crops, and intriguingly in a climate changing CO_2-enhanced atmosphere photosynthesis requires less water anyway (see **climate change; genetically modified organisms (GMOs)**).

See also: agriculture; boreholes; dams; dryland agriculture; rainwater harvesting; salinization; water management

Further reading

Chambers, R. (1988) *Managing Canal Irrigation: Practical Analysis from South Asia*, New Delhi: Oxford University Press and IBH Publishing Co.

Chapman, G. (2002) "Changing Places: The Roles of Science and Social Science in the Development of Large Scale Irrigation in South Asia," in Bradnock, R. and Williams, G. (eds) *South Asia in a Globalising World: A Reconstructed Regional Geography*, London: Pearson.

International Water Management Institute, website: http://www.cgiar.org

Uphoff, N. (1996, 2nd edn) *Learning from Gal Oya: Possibilities for Participatory Development and post-Newtonian Social Science*, Ithaca NY: Cornell University Press, and London: Intermediate Technology.

GRAHAM CHAPMAN

J

job security

Job security presumes that an individual worker has a degree of continuity in **employment**, at least for the duration of a fixed contractual period. Traditionally, it was often assumed that job security was possible in some activities for the entire career of an individual. Empirical evidence on a global scale now challenges this traditional view. The last decades of the twentieth century have experienced an increasing absence of long-term employment in both developed and developing countries. Moreover, there is little evidence that labor surpluses may be absorbed by the growth of a new employment sector. **Agriculture**, manufacturing, and service-based industries are all experiencing technological changes globally that impact on employment. This has been forced in turn by increasing and international market competition.

The root causes of the changes to job security are formally attributed to international **trade** liberalization, increasing market competition, and the free movement of largely private forms of **foreign direct investment** through deregulated banking and financial systems. **Transnational corporations (TNCs)** are the drivers of this trend, which is now seeing the large-scale movement of industrial production into developing countries.

There is little comfort for the recipient states in this activity, since the assumption of lower labor costs informs the strategy. There is also a massive discrepancy in terms of the geography of investment location, with Southeast and East Asia the principle targets, and Africa receiving a relatively small amount.

One theoretical response to these changes has been the popular assumption that the future of employment lies in the knowledge-based industries (see **information technology**). This seems to rest on the assumption that new technology will reduce production costs and increase supply, leading on to a **trickle down** effect, with excess market supply pushing down wages. Lower wage costs will then persuade employers to substitute labor for capital as a saving measure. The assumption then holds that **unemployment** will fall and employment rise, thus leading to some level of job security at the equilibrium.

There are two problems with this assumption. The first is the fact that knowledge-based goods can be produced literally anywhere in the world. This reduces the importance of actual physical location. The second results from the reported movement toward "flatter" organizational structures, based on autonomous work teams, which are horizontally integrated as "lean management" networks.

Individual employees in such firms are constantly updating personal skills for a career that is no longer shaped by external organizational demands. Rather, it is driven by a range of personal choices of income, interest and opportunities, to work anywhere in the world. Of course, underlying all these hypothetical assumptions is the total absence of any notion of job security.

See also: casualization of work; employment; Fordism versus Toyotaism; human security; labor markets; trade unions; underemployment; unemployment

Further reading

Kreuger, A. and Solow, R. (2001) *The Roaring Nineties: Can Full Employment be Sustained?* New York: Century Foundation Press.

Rifkin, J. (1995) *The End of Work*, New York: Putnam.

ALAN WILLIAMS

joint families

Joint families are the combination and extension of nuclear families through co-residence. In contrast to nuclear families, in which a couple and their **children** live separately from the couples' parents, joint families reside together in one dwelling across generations and/or within generations. At their most basic, joint families consist of an individual living with his/her children and the families of these children. Within a joint family, an individual may be spouse, child, parent and sibling, e.g. a young married man who lives with his wife, parents, children, brothers and sisters. Joint families may also consist of siblings and their children who continue to live together as a domestic unit after the death of their parents.

For purposes of social reproduction and economic cooperation, joint families often combine individual efforts for the good of the household. For example, certain members will remain at home to care for dependants, tend to household chores (e.g. cooking, cleaning, provisioning) and perhaps perform home-based, wage-earning work. Other members of the family will be engaged in labor and other activities outside the home (e.g. wage-earning, farming, social service). Joint families have the advantage of a larger pool of labor that can be more flexibly distributed and scheduled than that of nuclear families. In addition, joint families have the ability to provide a safety net for members unable to care for themselves (see **safety nets against poverty**).

While joint families reap the benefits of combined economic cooperation, they do not function as a unified entity. Instead, intrahousehold dynamics are influenced by a diversity of individual interests. Joint families' internal problems often derive from power struggles between members, particularly if family organization is hierarchical. Grown children may struggle with their parents or between themselves for authority and control of labor power, household resources and property. Domestic politics influence not only decisions taken but also negotiations surrounding those decisions. Importantly, such struggles are gendered, and naturalized gender roles often support intrahousehold inequalities (see **intrahousehold allocations**). Outcomes of power struggles between family members are often directly linked to control of resources without it. Women, who frequently work at home, may be at a disadvantage. Furthermore, when wives are outsiders entering joint families, they often carry a heavier work burden (including emotional labor on behalf of members), face more uncertainty due to low status, and exert less control over property and children than original family members.

For the above reasons, joint families are often unstable over time. Upon the death of parents, or in the absence of a central authority as parents age, siblings may divide family property among themselves and move into separate dwellings. Each sibling would then reside separately and perhaps begin to re-establish a joint family with him or herself as the head.

See also: children; food security; intrahousehold allocations; safety nets against poverty; women-headed households

Further reading

Gupta, M. (1999) "Lifeboat Versus Corporate Ethic: Social and Demographic Implications of Stem and Joint Families," *Social Science and Medicine* 49:2 173–84.

KATHLEEN O'REILLY

Joint Forest Management (JFM)

The Joint Forest Management (JFM) policy was first outlined in a 1990 Government of India resolution. It called for a closer working relationship between rural forest user groups and state agencies (see **state and state reform**) charged with managing certain categories of the country's forest reserves. According to the Indian government statistics, JFM projects reportedly cover approximately 10 million hectares of forestland divided amongst approximately 36,000 JFM committees across India. This ostensibly people-centered policy signals a shift from earlier Indian forestry, where resource management decision-making had been almost exclusively dominated by state agencies with little, if any, input from local residents or forest-dependent communities (see **community**).

With JFM, forest protection and management involves jointly defined roles and responsibilities for state forest departments, local **institutions**, and user groups. Thus, in theory, JFM accords rights for specified usufruct forest products, which largely comprise non-commercially valuable **non-timber forest products (NTFPs)**, to Village Forest Institutions (VFIs) or other local **community** groups that enter into agreements with state forest departments. In addition, profit sharing arrangements from the eventual sale of protected timber or other products provide VFIs incentives to continue established relationships.

User groups that comprise VFIs agree to guard JFM sites from illegal encroachment and use by non-members, yet they are accorded neither specific authority nor the means to carry out this protection. Indeed, critics argue that the maze of resolutions and policies, many of which are conflicting and ambiguous and vary from state to state, complicate management. In the absence of broad legal protection, and without explicit and non-contradictory institutional arrangements to protect the rights of VFIs, many have questioned how communities might successfully undertake this challenge. Despite these difficulties, the growing number of success stories from across India clearly indicates the potential of this policy.

Geographically, JFM sites are restricted to what the government designates as degraded forests. These forests generally comprise a crown cover of less than 40 percent, but due to the lack of a specific legal definition for degraded forests, this percentage varies from state to state. What is significant about this restriction is that, in theory,

JFM can then only be implemented across approximately 30 percent of forests across India today. In the original 1990 circular, the Indian government identified the Social Forestry Program under the Forest Department as a possible funding source for raising nurseries, preparing land for planting trees, and long-term protection activities. Due to budgetary limitations, however, JFM programs are observed to rely more heavily on international organizations like the **World Bank** or other private sources. Finally, it is important to recognize that JFM evolved from a resolution and as such faces an uncertain future, easily reversed by new administrative or legal action.

See also: community forestry; community-based natural resource management (CBNRM); deforestation; institutions and environment; non-timber forest products (NTFPs); silviculture

Further reading

Khare, A., Sarin, M., Saxena, N., Palit, S., Bathla, S., Vania, F. and Satyanarayana, M. (2000). *Joint Forest Management: Policy, Practice and Prospects*, London: IIED.

FIROOZA PAVRI

joint venture

A joint venture (JV) is a partnership between two commercial entities undertaken to share risk or expertise, usually in the context of investment. A JV may take a variety of legal forms including partnership, alliance, or licensing of specific assets, that may enable two companies to come together without actually merging into one firm. The purposes of JVs are generally to allow firms to enter new markets or undertake new tasks that they are unable to achieve through their own resources. Many states in developing countries insist that **foreign direct investment** is conducted via JVs with local companies in order to allow domestic firms to learn from international investors, and to encourage **technology transfer**. Many international investors, however, resist JVs with local companies because they represent high transaction costs in terms of lengthy negotiations, controls on investment, and the potential loss of **intellectual property rights (IPRs)**.

See also: foreign direct investment; new institutional economics; small and medium enterprises (SMEs); technology transfer; transnational corporations (TNCs); transnational corporations (TNCs) from developing economies

Further reading

Herzfeld, E. and Wilson, A. (1996, 3rd edn) *Joint Ventures*, Bristol: Jordans.

TIM FORSYTH

JUBILEE DEBT CAMPAIGN *see* debt relief

JUST IN TIME (JIT) *see* flexible specialization; Fordism versus Toyotaism

K

Kuznets curve

The Kuznets curve, also known as the Kuznets hypothesis, suggests that the curve for income **inequality** (see **income distribution**) traces an inverted-U shape through the **economic development** or income growth process. The curve is named after the economist, Simon Kuznets (1901–85). The hypothesis states income **inequality** is low when per capita incomes are low, inequality increases with income up to some indeterminate point, and falls with further income growth. This proposition, first published in 1955, became one of the "stylized facts of development" and one of its most thoroughly researched ideas in the 1970s and early 1980s. However, accumulating studies have shown that there is little empirical evidence of such a curve for income inequality. Instead, the idea of an inverted-U curve through income growth has been adopted by environmental economists and analysts. They argue that a similar temporal relationship between income growth and environmental conditions exists; there are declines in environmental conditions (manifested in higher levels of air and water **pollution**, loss of **biodiversity**, etc.) during income growth from very low incomes, followed by improvements when incomes increase further (see **brown environmental agenda**).

The Kuznets curve of inequality is important for at least two reasons. First, it was the distributional counterpart of the dualistic theories of development that were hegemonic at the time. Kuznets's argument was based on a model of **urbanization**, with population transfers from low-income rural regions to higher-income urban regions. This situation did, and even now does, represent the reality of most developing nations. Second, Kuznets's theory provided (unintended) support for the dominant position which argues that **redistribution with growth** is not possible. This position underlies the savings-driven Harrod-Domar-Kaldor growth models (growth is driven by savings, the rich save more, therefore inequality is a necessary precondition for growth), and the redistribution with "leaky bucket" critique (redistribution is inefficient, expensive, and growth-damaging). The Kuznets hypothesis suggested: "grow now, redistribute later."

Refutations of the Kuznets economic hypothesis have come from different directions. The methodology used by the early supporters of the hypothesis – cross-country inequality regressions – has been called into question, as have the quality and comparability of the income distribution data analyzed. Moreover, with the increasing availability of long-term income distribution data for many developing nations (as in the **United Nations**' WIDER database), it is clear that inequality levels do not follow any discernible universal trend. This has been confirmed by the recent rapid increases in inequality in the UK and the USA and other developed nations.

The environmental Kuznets curve (EKC) was first proposed in 1991, and the empirical evidence on it appears to be contested and inconclusive (Stern, 2004). A reasonable current summary is that the EKC does not apply to all pollutants in all places. Most air pollutants and some water pollutants appear to follow the EKC. The EKC theory continues to be important because, in general, environmental conditions are more amenable to policy intervention than **income distributions**.

See also: brown environmental agenda; economic development; economic growth; income distribution; inequality; pollution; redistribution with growth; sustainable development

Further reading

Fields, G. (2001) *Distribution and Development: A New Look at the Developing World*, Cambridge MA: MIT Press.

Grossman, G. and Krueger, A. (1995) "Economic Growth and the Environment," *Quarterly Journal of Economics* 110: 353–77.

Kuznets, S. (1955) "Economic Growth and Income Inequality," *American Economic Review* 45: 1–28.

Stern, D. (2004) "The Rise and Fall of the Environmental Kuznets Curve," *World Development* 32:8 1419–39.

SANJOY CHAKRAVORTY

L

labor markets

Labor markets are the primary source of **human capital** in the national and international economy. Unlike physical capital, which comprises raw materials, the main characteristic of human capital is the diversity of skills that cannot be separated from the individual endowments of human beings.

This difference between physical and human capital has shaped the history of labor market analysis since the end of the nineteenth century. There have been tensions between approaches that see wages (i.e. the price of labor) as resulting from voluntary exchanges between actors with equal negotiating power, and approaches that note the imbalances of economic power and social class between different actors. The collectivization of workers' interests through **trade unions** are an attempt to redress inequalities between capital and labor.

During the twentieth century, **labor rights and standards** became more common, and were specified by agencies such as the **International Labor Organization (ILO)**. These new rights and standards acknowledged the inequalities in bargaining power and legal status of different negotiators. In a further development, the **Bretton Woods** Agreement of 1944 aimed nominally to sustain full **employment** as a primary social and economic goal during the period of post-war reconstruction.

The period after Bretton Woods has been described by some economists as the golden age of managing demand for labor in Europe and North America (see **economic development**). But for many developing countries, this period coincided with **decolonization**, and periods of economic and political instability that made it difficult to achieve consistent strategies for constructive labor market reform. Indeed, many countries experienced forms of **diaspora** and **brain drain** of educational **elites** to more developed countries.

The so-called golden age of demand management ended in the late 1970s when many developed countries experienced "stagflation" – or the combination of **unemployment** and inflation (see **inflation and its effects**). Keynesian macroeconomics was generally replaced by economic **neo-liberalism** as the ideological underpinning for many government strategies. From a labor-market perspective, it also signaled the increase in individual labor contracts based on a return to the neo-classical concept of wage-price agreements resulting from mutually agreed voluntary exchange. This period has also been associated with the so-called **Washington consensus**, or the reshaping of rules concerning donor **conditionality** and neo-classical economic reforms preferred by the **World Bank** and **International Monetary Fund (IMF)** such as public-sector deregulation; privatization of state owned enterprises (see **privatization and liberalization; state and state reform**); and raising interest rates to counter inflation. Critics claimed these reforms wrongly assumed that they could be implemented using a standard set of procedures in each country.

Recent empirical work on the impacts of reforms to state owned enterprises suggests that cultural factors such as family connections and tribal membership influence post-reform recruitment and training, and consequently may reinforce, rather than reduce inequalities in labor markets (see **inequality**). Studies have also indicated the failure of these reforms to recognize the influence or value of existing tacit knowledge within organizations and labor forces.

The end of the twentieth century has seen a diminution of enthusiasm for neo-classical policy initiatives, and many countries have experienced recession. One result has been a significant increase in labor **migration** especially involving the clandestine and unofficial movements of migrant workers, who are mainly representative of the rural poor in many countries (see **migrant trafficking**).

The introduction of internal market reforms in China during the 1980s by Deng Xiaoping also illustrates the problems of massive labor market readjustment. The abandonment of full employment and pension rights (see **pensions**), together with the privatization of **state owned enterprises** has increased unemployment in the central and northern heartlands, and enhanced **rural-urban migration**. Some analysts predict China will experience a labor surplus of more than 120 million workers, even before accounting for seven to eight million new births each year. Specific countries therefore experience severe challenges for managing labor markets.

See also: casualization of work; employment; International Labor Organization (ILO); job security; labor rights and standards; trade unions; underemployment; unemployment

Further reading

McCourt, W. (2001) "Toward a Strategic Model of Employment Reform in Developing Countries," *The International Journal of Human Resource Management* 12:1 56–74.
Peck, J. (1996) *Work Place: The Social Regulation of Labor Markets*, New York: Guilford.
Rosewarne, S. (1999) "The Globalization and Liberalization of Asian Labor Markets," *The World Economy* 21:7 963–80.
Stiglitz, J. (2002) *Globalization and Its Discontents*, London: Allen Lane.

ALAN WILLIAMS

labor migration

Labor migration is generally understood to be a subset of **international migration** that involves men and women going overseas on contracts to do a specific job of work within a specified period of time. Thus, contract labor migration is implied and the motivation to move is economic. This migration is often associated with the development of the **international division of labor** within a capitalist system. Although the highly skilled are labor migrants and are technically part of the labor migration system, they have generally been seen to form a separate system, with labor migration referring primarily to the less skilled. Labor migration is theoretically temporary in nature in that no permanent settlement is allowed although, in practice, it has often proved to be a precursor of longer-term, even permanent **migration**.

Historically, **slavery** was forced labor migration, and the later system of indentured labor through which tens of thousands of mainly Indians and Chinese were moved within colonies and to the Americas in the nineteenth and early twentieth centuries, creating global **diasporas**, was only less coercive. The great labor migrations of recent times have been those from Mediterranean countries, and later Eastern Europe, to Western Europe and the movements to the oil-rich Gulf States, as well as to Libya and Nigeria, from neighboring countries in the Middle East and Africa, as well as from South, Southeast and East Asia. Perhaps 12 million Asians worked overseas in the 1970s and 1980s, primarily in the Gulf States. Today, there are increasing labor migrations within the Asian region itself. Over time, the participation of women in labor migration has been growing with the demand for domestic workers among the newly rich in Asia and the Middle East. Over time, too, there has been a marked rise in undocumented labor migration.

Two significant characteristics of labor migration can be identified which have particular implications for development. The first is the organization of the movement. Government institutions, private recruiting agencies and employers can all be involved in arranging the transfer of labor from its origin to where it is required, and these create a complex bureaucracy with huge budgets, extracting charges from the migrants at critical points along the way. The second is the significance of the **remittances** sent back by the workers to their families in their home countries. Some US$6.8 billion was remitted by workers from the Philippines in 1999, for example. The exodus of large numbers of workers has also been shown to exert upward pressure on wages in origin areas, further improving economic conditions there.

See also: Harris-Todaro model; International Labor Organization (ILO); international migration; labor markets; labor supply; migrant trafficking; migration; remittances; slavery

Further reading

Papademetriou, G. and Martin, P. (eds) (1991) *The Unsettled Relationship: Labor Migration and Economic Development*, Westport CT: Greenwood Press.

Stalker, P. (1994) *The Work of Strangers: A Survey of International Labor Migration*, Geneva: International Labor Office.

RONALD SKELDON

labor rights and standards

Labor rights and standards ensure certain minimal levels of working conditions, safety, and negotiating power for workers (see also **trade unions; occupational health; freedom of association; job security**). Labor rights and standards also represent a means for states (see **state and state reform**) to enforce national labor legislation and **human development** at a time when state capacity *vis-à-vis* investors is increasingly challenged by the growing power of foreign investors and **transnational corporations (TNCs)**, especially in developing countries.

Despite the potentially significant role of labor legislation in the protection of the rights of working people, there are a number of limits, which are particularly relevant to developing countries. A significant number of working people are not covered by national labor legislation, as they are working in the informal economy (see **urban informal sector; micro-enterprises**). The scale of the informal economy implies that the traditional means of protecting labor rights and standards, through legislation and formal trade unions, is not available for a large number of people in developing countries. Second, although labor legislation in developing countries is often very detailed, it is not always adequately enforced, as states are not able or willing to enforce sections of the labor **law** such as the right to collective bargaining and equal pay. The reasons for the lack of enforcement are complex, but they can be partly attributed to pressures to lower labor costs in order to be competitive in the world economy and partly because states lose the ability to exclusively manage the domestic economy, including labor relations, under pressure of global economic integration (see **state and state reform; industrialization; gender and industrialization**). Third, as economic activity increasingly acquires international dimensions, the effectiveness of trade unions, which are organizations that traditionally negotiated both the enforcement and improvement of national labor legislation, is often limited by national boundaries.

The limits of national-level labor rights and standards have resulted in a call for international campaigns for labor rights and attempts to establish international guarantees of labor rights and standards (see **advocacy coalitions; solidarity campaigns; World Social Forum (WSF)**). The general problem of introducing these forms of international labor **governance** is that it is even more difficult to enforce labor standards at an international level than at a domestic level. At the international level, three main types of agreements on labor rights and standards can be distinguished. The first type concerns the system of principles and rights at work of the **International Labor Organization (ILO)**; the second type concerns the inclusion of labor rights in international or regional trade agreements; and the third type are "codes of conduct" agreed upon by TNCs or other large companies.

First, a number of conventions of the ILO are recognized as "fundamental" labor standards, standards which are considered to be valid for all countries, irrespective of their level of development. The fundamental labor conventions include: **freedom of association** and the right to organize and collective bargaining (Conventions 87 and 98); the abolition of forced labor (Conventions 29 and 105); equality: non-discrimination in **employment** and occupation, and equal remuneration (Conventions 100 and 111); and the elimination of **child labor** (Conventions 138 and 182). The enforcement of ILO conventions is an important problem, on the one hand, because there are no effective sanctions attached to the conventions, and on the other hand, because implementation of the conventions takes place at the level of national governments. Although the ILO regularly monitors the implementation of its conventions, it is not able to apply sanctions if conventions are disregarded. In this respect, the fundamental and other labor standards function as a model for labor relations, rather than a form of global labor legislation. Although there is a general agreement on the importance of the ILO's fundamental labor standards, there is a debate on whether labor rights and standards should be proportional to a country's level of **economic development**. Some argue that a lower level of economic development implies that certain labor rights can be disregarded. For example, child labor is sometimes cited as a phenomenon that is necessary to sustain family income and acceptable as long as it is strictly regulated. In addition, it is sometimes argued that policies to reduce labor costs, often through the flexibilization of **labor markets** (see **casualization of work; flexible specialization; Fordism versus Toyotaism**), are essential for developing countries in order to be competitive in the world market.

Second, international and regional trade treaties and organizations, such as the **North American Free Trade Agreement (NAFTA)**, the **European Union**, and WTO (see **World Trade Organization/General Agreement on Tariffs and Trade (WTO/GATT)**) do include the possibility to attach sanctions to the compliance with international labor standards. The NAFTA treaty includes a labor side agreement which is intended as a dispute settlement mechanism for cross-border labor conflicts. The legislation of social issues, including labor rights and standards, is developed furthest in the **European Union** (EU), although disagreements between the member states have slowed down EU-wide application of the minimum

wage and the regulation of working hours. The WTO is able to apply sanctions to its member states, and the inclusion of labor rights and standards in the WTO is therefore seen as one of the most effective ways to regulate labor issues at a global level. Despite trade union and NGO campaigns (see **non-governmental organizations (NGOs)**) to include labor and environmental standards in the WTO, this has not happened yet.

Third, as regards codes of conduct, the ILO has adopted the "Tripartite Declaration of Principles concerning Multinational Enterprises and Social Policy" (1977), in order to stimulate TNCs to respect fundamental labor standards (see also **corporate social responsibility (CSR)**). Other models for codes of conduct have been established by NGOs and international business associations. Most codes of conduct adopted by TNCs do not only include fundamental labor standards, but also references to the environment, safety at work and **human rights**. These issues are attractive to investors, as they allow investors ways to demonstrate social responsibility in host countries. But this approach is controversial and still growing. For example, it is not yet widely accepted whether investment decisions should consider the record of human rights violations in host countries.

See also: casualization of work; corporate social responsibility (CSR); Declaration on Fundamental Principles and Rights at Work; flexible specialization; freedom of association; Fordism versus Toyotaism; governance; human rights; International Labor Organization (ILO); job security; labor markets; trade unions; transnational corporations (TNCs); urban informal sector

Further reading

Bales, K. (2000) *Disposable People: New Slavery in the Global Economy*, Berkeley: University of California Press.

Hartman, L. and Arnold, D. (eds) (2003) *Rising Above Sweatshops: Innovative Approaches to Global Labor Challenges*, Westport CT: Greenwood Press.

ILO (International Labor Organization) website: http://www.ilo.org/

Mah, J. (1997) "Core Labour Standards and Export Performance in Developing Countries," *World Economy* 20:6 773–85.

Raynauld, A. and Vidal, J.-P. (1998) *Labour Standards and International Competitiveness: A Comparative Analysis of Developing and Industrialized Countries*, London: Edward Elgar.

Singh, A. and Zammit, A. (2000) *The Global Labour Standards Controversy: Critical Issues for Developing Countries*, Geneva: South Center.

MARIEKE RIETHOF

labor supply

Labor supply is an aspect of individual choice where individuals decide whether to work (the "participation decision") and how much to work per unit of time given that participation. A longer-run aspect of labor supply concerns the retirement decision. All these decisions are made given the constraints individuals face, including the compensation they are able to command. These decisions determine how much time individuals leave for leisure and other activities such as home production.

Some of the constraints individuals face (including the wage rate) may be a consequence of their choices (for example, unwillingness to work, or abandoning their **education**). Other constraints may be beyond their control, and because of the conditions faced (for instance, physical **disability**, moral persuasion by family members, lack of education or training due to **poverty**, or discrimination).

A typical labor supply curve is upward sloping, indicating that an individual would work longer hours as the wage rate increases. However, at high wage levels the supply curve may bend backwards if better off workers begin substituting more leisure for work.

In addition to pecuniary returns, other job attributes (flexibility of hours, physical working conditions, etc.) are relevant in analyzing individuals' labor supply decisions. These different dimensions of a job are often related. Thus, in many models of labor supply the wage rate is a function of other job attributes.

In the context of developing economies, the constraints that many individuals face in securing (better paying) jobs are often beyond their control given the deprivations they face. For example, in many poorer developing countries unskilled women are restricted to farm work. In Sub-Saharan Africa subsistence farming is predominantly a female activity (see **gender division of labor**). Similarly, in many parts of Asia a significant number of women are agricultural wage laborers. Women in many developing countries perform largely invisible work at home caring for their families or engaging in home-based production often at meager piece rates.

Another aspect of labor supply in developing countries is that part-time work, multiple jobs, and working for one's own family are more common than in the developed world. In these countries, an individual's labor supply decision is often not taken alone, but in the context of the decision of other family members (see **intrahousehold allocations**).

In the past, some economists thought that development would have a detrimental impact on the labor supply of individuals from developing countries. Their rationale was that as individuals' earnings began to exceed a customary low level, they would take more leisure. These are no longer concerns, as desire for better life styles in a global economy precludes existence of a backward bending labor supply curve.

Since labor supply in developing countries is not a constraint on development, but availability of skilled labor is, improving access to education and adequate training of individuals (especially women) will contribute to these countries' **economic growth**.

See also: employment; gender division of labor; Harris-Todaro model; job security; labor markets; labor migration; unemployment

Further reading

Blundell, R. and MaCurdy, T. (1999) "Labor Supply: A Review of Alternative Approaches," pp. 1559–695 in Ashenfelter, O. and Card, D. (eds) *Handbook of Labor Economics* Volume 3A, Amsterdam: North Holland.

Killingsworth, M. (1983) *Labor Supply*, New York: Cambridge University Press.

B. MAK ARVIN

labor-intensive

The term labor-intensive refers to technologies or industries employing higher proportions of labor relative to capital, or sometimes to skilled labor. It is often used in opposition to the term **capital intensive**. Labor-intensive production is influenced by demand and supply factors in **labor markets**. A country's (or region's) quantitative endowment with labor is determined by its demographic profile (i.e. its **population** structure, growth rates and level of skills) while firms' demand for labor is influenced by existing levels of technology and skills, macroeconomic environment, regulations on industrial relations and the price and supply of other factors of production.

Transnational companies commonly locate labor-intensive operations in developing countries owing to their endowment with abundant cheap labor (see **transnational corporations (TNCs)**). However, increasingly stringent labor laws and regulations due to increased trade union interventions in industrial relations and labor rights enforcement implies high labor costs (see **labor rights and standards**). This induces firms to invest in labor saving technologies with adverse implications for **employment**.

See also: capital intensive; employment; labor markets; labor supply

MOSES A. OSIRO

LAFTA *see* Latin American Free Trade Agreement (LAFTA)

land reform

Land reform usually refers to changes in how land ownership is distributed, recorded and administered. It may occur in both urban and rural contexts, but the term "land reform" is most commonly used in rural areas. Land reform has been a key issue in the economic, social and political development of many countries. Those persons or groups that have control over land and other natural resources are generally also those who have economic, social and political power. A highly unequal land tenure system tends to perpetuate **poverty** and **social exclusion**, and limits the contribution which **agriculture** can make to **economic development** (Sobhan, 1993).

In many developing countries the landlord class used to, or still does, own most of the country's land, and was the dominant class controlling the political system. For example, in Latin America roughly 20 percent of landowners possessed 80 percent of the land. But with the implementation of land reforms, mainly from the 1950s to the 1970s, this situation started to change in some developing countries. How much the situation changes is dependent on a series of factors, including the amount of land that is expropriated, who and how many the beneficiaries are, and whether the changes occur within a capitalist or socialist context. As countries become more developed and the share of agriculture in a country's gross national product declines, so also generally does the power of those who control the land (Ghose, 1983).

There is no universal definition of land reform, as authors tend to include or exclude certain issues in their conceptualization and/or give different emphasis to various aspects of a land reform process. However, a common view is that land reform entails the redistribution of **property rights** over land from usually large landowners to peasants and/or landless rural laborers (see also **land rights; gender and property rights**). Sometimes property rights over water are also redistributed as well as some of the farm's infrastructure. A key actor in this process is the state which implements the redistribution of property rights (see **state and state reform**). Colonization programs would be excluded from this definition as it entails the transfer of state-owned land to the beneficiaries. While the redistribution of public lands to peasant or landless rural workers might accompany land reform programs, the view of many analysts is to exclude them from the definition of land reform as such, so as not to detract from what they consider being the central aspect of a land reform. Many governments have proclaimed the implementation of land reforms when in actual fact they have only carried out colonization projects, hoping thereby to avoid expropriating landlords (Christodoulou, 1990) (see **colonialism, history of; colonialism, impacts of; empire**).

Similarly, under the banner of land reform several governments have only undertaken reforms of landlord-tenant relations by giving more rights to tenants, such as insisting on written contracts, giving greater security of tenure to tenants, regulating and limiting rental payments, and so on. (We are not referring here to capitalist tenants, but to tenants who are rural workers, or to peasants who may own a small piece of land). Although such changes are indeed most welcome and may improve the condition of tenants, they do not lead by themselves to significant changes in the economic, social and political power relationships in the countryside.

The causes of land reforms can differ. In some countries, land reforms have been implemented because of peasant revolts and/or major social revolutions (Ghimire, 2001). For example, peasants played a key role in the Mexican revolution of 1910–17 that led to a major land reform particularly during the populist government of president Cárdenas in the 1930s. In several African countries like Algeria, Kenya and Tanzania land reforms were the outcome of the struggle for independence and **decolonization** after World War II, where peasants were often key participants. Peasants were also actively involved in socialist revolutions in developing countries such as Angola, China, Cuba, Ethiopia and Vietnam.

The more actively peasants and rural workers were involved in these struggles there greater was the likelihood that the process of land reform would result in major expropriations. However, this is not always the case, as occasionally major land reforms were implemented from above by the state without major peasant involvement. Such is the case of the South Korean and Taiwanese land reforms. In these cases the land reform was also much driven by external forces. These countries used to be colonies of Japan. After the defeat of Japan in World War II, the USA was keen that the new governments in South Korea and Taiwan should have the steadfast support of the **peasantry** who were in the majority. Most, if not all, landlords were expropriated and the tenants received

property rights over the piece of land they used to cultivate. The emergence of the **Cold War**, and the fact that South Korea and Taiwan lay next to North Korea and China, whose socialist governments had undertaken radical land reforms, was also a powerful factor for influencing those countries to follow suit, albeit with a different type of land reform (Sobhan, 1993).

Thus, it is useful to distinguish at least between two types of land reform: distributivist or reformist, and collectivist or radical. A distributivist land reform is characterized by the redistribution of property rights to beneficiaries as family farms. It usually takes place within a capitalist system. It is common for landlords to receive some payment as compensation for their expropriated assets, that are usually valued below their market price. Depending on the extent of the land reform, only the less productive landlords might be expropriated and some might be able to retain a part of the landed estate. Beneficiaries tend to be the tenants who already were working on the farm and to a lesser extent other smallholders or agricultural wageworkers, if at all. Furthermore, beneficiaries commonly have to make some payment to the state (or to the landlords) for the land they received. It is very rare for beneficiaries to pay the full value of the land, and the state often condones part of the land debt incurred by beneficiaries. Examples of this type of land reform are those undertaken in Bolivia, Ecuador, Colombia in Latin America; Egypt, Kenya and South Africa in Africa; and South Korea, Taiwan, the Philippines, India and Pakistan in Asia (Ghose, 1983; Christodoulou, 1990).

Meanwhile a collectivist land reform is characterized by the establishment of producer cooperatives (i.e. **communes, collectives and cooperatives**) and/or state farms, and is commonly undertaken by socialist regimes (see **collectivization**). Usually all landlords are expropriated and they hardly receive any compensation due to the revolutionary aims of the new regime. Furthermore, this type of land reform might not only target landlords, i.e. owners of large landed estates, but also capitalist farmers who generally own smaller farms than those of landlords and who work the land much more efficiently using modern technology and employing wage labor rather than tenant labor. Also, expropriated land-lords or capitalist farmers rarely have the right to retain any part of their former property. The ben-eficiaries are not limited to the former tenants but also include rural wage laborers and smallholders. Beneficiaries are normally not required to pay for the land and other assets they may receive as col-lective property. Of course, in the case of the establishment of state farms, beneficiaries should not be required to pay anything, as they do not become owners of the expropriated assets. This type of land reform is thus far more radical than the redistributivist land reform in terms of the greater number of landowners and amount of land that is expropriated, and the wider variety and larger number of beneficiaries. Examples of this type of land reform include those of Cuba, Chile (during the Allende government of 1970–3), Nicaragua (during the Sandinista government from 1979–90) in Latin America; Algeria, Angola, Ethiopia and Mozambique in Africa; and China, North Korea, Vietnam in Asia (Sobhan, 1993).

There are intermediary situations and variations of these two basic types of land reform. For exam-ple, the Peruvian land reform of the military gov-ernments from 1969 to 1980 was of a collectivist kind although it took place within a capitalist context. Similarly, the cases of Tanzania during the presidency of Neyrere with villagization (*ujamaa*) (see **villages**) in the late 1960s, and of Chile during Frei's presidency (1964–70), might be considered hybrid cases, among others.

Land reforms are evolving processes, as the initial land reform might radicalize from a redistributivist to a collectivist kind – as in the case of Chile mentioned above. More recently, in the late 1990s, Zimbabwe's land reform took a new turn with government-sponsored occupation of white-owned farms. Or, more commonly, it might lead to a counter-reform in which the expropriated land is returned partially or fully to the former landowners, as in the cases of Guatemala, Chile and Nicaragua. In Guatemala, the Arbenz government (1951–4) introduced a mild land reform but was overthrown by the military (with CIA involvement) and the land reform was fully reversed. In the case of Chile, the socialist government of Allende was over-thrown by a *coup d'état* and the regime of General Pinochet (1973–89) partially reversed the land

reform by returning all or part of the expropriated farm to about two thirds of the former owners. The remainder of the reform sector or expropriated farms, which had been turned into collectives or state farms, was decollectivized. The land was sub-divided into plots and assigned as family farms to some of the beneficiaries and the remaining bene-ficiaries were expelled. A similar situation hap-pened in the case of Nicaragua after the Sandinistas lost the election in 1990. Some of the expropriated farms were returned fully or partially to their former owners, and the others were subdivided and assigned to the original beneficiaries and the com-batants (labeled the "*contras*" by the Sandinistas) who had fought against the Sandinista government during the civil **war**. Many of the former bene-ficiaries lost their access to the land because of this counter-reform. In the case of Peru, and to a lesser extent in Ethiopia, a process of decollectivization took place by which collectives and state farms were subdivided into family farms and assigned as private property to the beneficiaries.

Most socialist countries in the developing world largely decollectivized their **agriculture**, since col-lectives and state farms were increasingly facing problems of efficiency, incentives for workers, and investment. Governments thus started a process of full or partial decollectivization by a variety of means, which generally did not involve granting private property rights. Thus in post-Mao China and starting in the 1980s, the "household responsibility system" was introduced by which the former peasant members of the collectives were given long-term leases over a piece of land. A similar process took place in Vietnam which the introduction of the market reforms. Even in Cuba, which is one of the more orthodox communist regimes, during the 1990s most state farms were transformed into collective farms (i.e. producer cooperatives). Farm-ing was decentralized to smaller production units (*unidades básicas de producción cooperativa* or UBPC) formed by peasant groups who often were family members, relatives and/or close friends. By forming smaller production units and establishing a clearer link between work effort and income, it was expec-ted that this would create more incentives for the workers and thereby raise **productivity** and output.

In the wake of the **debt** crisis and the imple-mentation of **structural adjustment** programs

(SAPs) during the 1980s in many developing countries, land reform largely disappeared from the agenda as the emphasis was on reducing the role of the state and liberalizing the economy. The emphasis in land policy shifted to land registration and land titling as most peasants lacked clear property rights over the land they were cultivating (Zoomers and van der Haar, 2000). As problems of **poverty**, landlessness and land conflicts persisted in the countryside, the agenda shifted in the 1990s to a new version of land reform as a way of dealing with these problems. This new conception of land reform was spearheaded by the **World Bank** and was referred to as the "market-led" land reform in contrast to the earlier "state-led" land reform. This "market-led" land reform was based on the willing-seller and willing-buyer principle, by which landowners voluntarily could sell their land to smallholders or landless agricultural workers who wished to buy the land. It was also sometimes referred to as the "negotiated" land reform. A government program that received funding and technical support from the World Bank underpinned this whole process. It entailed the creation of an institutional framework for this voluntary transfer of land through the market. This scheme was subsidized by the World Bank and the government. It consisted mainly in providing favorable loans to peasants and rural workers wishing to buy land from those willing to sell it through the scheme. Among the first countries that have undertaken this "market-led" land reform are Brazil, Colombia and South Africa (Borras, 2003). So far, it has had a limited impact and few countries have followed the example of these pioneers (Morales and Putzel, 2001).

See also: agrarian reform; collectivization; communes, collectives and cooperatives; gender and property rights; land rights; peasantry; property rights; rural development; rural poverty; villages

Further reading

Borras, S. (2003) "Questioning Market-led Agrarian Reform: Experiences from Brazil, Colombia and South Africa," *Journal of Agrarian Change* 3:3 1–19.

Christodoulou, D. (1990) *The Unpromised Land: Agrarian Reform and Conflict Worldwide*, London: Zed.

Ghimire, K. (ed.) (2001) *Land Reform and Peasant Livelihoods: The Dynamics of Rural Poverty and Agrarian Reform in Developing Countries*, London: ITDG Publishing.

Ghose, A. (ed.) (1983) *Agrarian Reform in Contemporary Developing Countries*, London: Croom Helm, and New York: St Martin's Press.

Morales, H. and Putzel, J. (eds) (2001) *Power in the Village: Agrarian Reform, Rural Politics, Institutional Change and Globalization*, Quezon City: University of the Philippines Press.

Sobhan, R. (1993) *Agrarian Reform and Social Transformation: Preconditions for Development*, London: Zed.

Zoomers, A. and van der Haar, G. (eds) (2000) *Current Land Policy in Latin America: Regulating Land Tenure Under Neo-liberalism*, Amsterdam: KIT, and Frankfurt: Vervuert Verlag.

CRISTÓBAL KAY

land rights

Land rights are the institutionalized forms of access to, and control over, land, typically understood as a subset of **property rights** in general (see also **gender and property rights**). Insofar as land rights express a relation between a thing and persons, these complex social relationships are usually referred to as Land Tenure. Land rights typically constitute land as property, which involves some jural entity (individuals, households, lineages, communities, corporations, nations, and so on) that has rights and duties over some object (land in this case) against other jural entities. Land rights are, however, always more complex than public (state ownership and transfer) (see **state and state reform**) versus private (a jural person is the owner in which a market system of transfer is implied) for the very good reasons that virtually everywhere complex mixtures of group (or communal) and individual (private) control exist.

Rights over land are customarily divided into: *use rights* (grazing, farming, passage, urban construction, collection and so on); *transfer rights* (movement of ownership or possession through inheritance, gift, sale, pledging, lending and so on); and *administrative rights* (the authority to allocate or withdraw land from use, to tax it, collect tribute, from it, to arbitrate disputes, regulate transfers, entitle it and so on). Rights over land do not necessarily imply ownership (i.e. there can be rights of use or rental). Similarly, communal or collective forms of land management – for example customary land law in Muslim northern Nigeria – may confer substantial "ownership" **security** to some individuals; that is to say there are stable and secure use rights in perpetuity. Fully privatized land rights – *fee simple* – in which rights to sell are not proscribed by laws that assign ultimate ownership to the state or to the powers of **indigenous people**, are far from universal.

Rights are often divided among different units of aggregation that claim different "bundles of rights." Such bundles may be nested or ranked in hierarchies of ownership. But a right of access for one purpose (collecting wood) does not always imply automatic access for another (grazing). Concepts of rights are often rooted in modes of livelihood and their relation to the market (see **livelihoods**). Pastoral communities (see **community**) may have rights to rangeland as a "common property" system: this does not mean open access (*res nullius*) but rather complex lineage or confederal systems of regulation which link land and water rights (*res communes*). Foragers may have rights of use rather than ownership.

Typically, a distinction is made between systems of rights over land rooted in customary or traditional law, and European systems of property law. African systems of law are especially complex and have survived into the postcolonial period (but not without change) as a deliberate artifact of colonial policy to sustain (i.e. not to disrupt radically) local "tribal" or ethnic institutions (Bassett and Crummey, 1993) (see **colonialism, history of**). Customary law allocates bundles of rights; that is so say the identification of some forms of farmland as family or collective confers particular obligations (everyone must work on them) and disposition (by the male head of household). Personal plots may be for individual gain and use. Allocation of land rights in customary conditions may be through the intermediation of village heads or male heads of household. Women therefore may gain (and lose)

access to land rights through marriage. Gender and conjugality are typically important dimensions of land rights allocation in rural African communities, which confirms the fact that land rights are not so much about relations between people and things as between people.

Customary law or traditional land rights are often counterpoised against European notions of property. But it should be remembered that custom is dynamic and flexible and was manipulated by colonial states as much as local peasants and headmen during the colonial period as market and other opportunities arose. Consequently, the history of customary land rights is riven with complex struggles and negotiations over bundles of rights and duties, only some of which reached local courts. In the postcolonial period, growing **commercialization**, land scarcity and efforts at state regulation and registration have further deepened these complex material and symbolic struggles over land rights (Carney and Watts, 1990). The possibility of female exclusion is always present in what passes as the modernization of customary tenure. If customary land rights are dynamic and complex, European property rights – the exercise of perpetual, exclusive and absolute right over land – is also far from a piece: English and French legal traditions differ quite substantially, for example.

In family farm systems under freehold or so-called communal or customary land rights, it is often assumed that there are necessarily problems of access to credit (no collateral confirmed by insecure land rights), tenancy regulation, taxation (inchoate senses of ownership) and fragmentation. Land titles and registration are seen as ways of resolving these problems, by reducing the problems of asymmetric information (knowledge and trust is undermined as sales increase between community and non-community buyers and sellers) and providing an institutional framework to facilitate land sales. Such transfers are assumed to enhance efficiency by transferring land from bad to better farmers and by ensuring credit through collateral. In practice, however, various forms of land titling under state auspices (for example in Kenya) have produced greater land concentration, dispossession, and loss of rights by vulnerable groups (especially women: see **gender and property rights**).

Titling and registration are ways in which rights and duties over land are changed; that is to say they are instances of land or agrarian reform. **Land reform** aims at transforming agrarian structure – that is a system of social relations and a system of land tenure/rights. Land reform can have a multiplicity of forms and implications for land rights, however. In some cases, reform may involve little more than the regularization and stabilization of tenant rights. In others, there may be widespread appropriation of land above specified ceilings, and redistributions of land to landless tenants and semi-proletarians (for example the Land-to-the-Tiller Programs in Taiwan and Kerala). During the twentieth century, most land reforms within **capitalism** – unlike the experience of **collectivization** in the former socialist bloc – were of two broad types: *anti-feudal*, seeking to spur on commercialization and accumulation through a landed elite, a commercial farmer class or peasants (see **elites; intermediate classes; peasantry**); and seeking to create shifts in the dominant rural class from *capitalist landed elites* to *smallholder or peasant operations*, or to amplify the reform sector under one of these groups (de Janvry, 1980). Land reform as a way of transforming land rights can therefore fulfill conservative, liberal, populist or radical political impulses. The collectivization of land rights in the name of socialism has been an object of extraordinary debate, not only over the use and consequences of state **violence**, but also in terms of the lack of incentives within agrarian socialist systems (Medvedev, 1980).

In the wake of the collapse of actually existing socialisms in 1989, and the earlier reforms in China and Eastern Europe in the 1960s and 1970s, one of the most important recent reconfigurations of land rights has been the so-called decollectivization of state farms and communes (see **communes, collectives and cooperatives**). Personal ownership of land in socialist economies was rarely obliterated but the reforms slowly reintroduced various forms of personalized use and *de facto* long-term ownership (for example, ninety-nine tenancy types in Vietnam). Variation within the former socialist bloc has been enormous. In some cases (China), the decollectivization witnessed a remarkably egalitarian redistribution of private property rights in land; in others there have been highly contested forms of land restitution (Nicaragua, Hungary); and in others nothing short of administrative chaos (Russia) as the weakened state is incapable of providing an institutional structure in which land can be sold or redistributed with the possibility of effective use (Kitching, 1998). The experience of the socialist states affirms the complex forms of hybrid rights which emerge in the nature of land privatization (see **privatization and liberalization**), and the complex struggles – the elasticities as Verdery (1993) calls them – of land rights.

Urban land rights, and especially the workings of city property markets, represent another large literature. In many developing world cities, urban land is tightly regulated and is accordingly the source of **corruption** and substantial rents. At the same time, land invasions are common in which **squatters**, if they can resist removal by the state, may be able to *de facto* regularize their claim over waste or state-owned lands. Land markets in North American and European cities have been the object of substantial research (Harvey, 1989), especially in relation to real estate, zoning, redlining and city structure more generally.

See also: collectivization; communes, collectives and cooperatives; domestic law; gender and property rights; institutions; land reform; property rights

Further reading

Bassett, T. and Crummey, J. (eds) (1993) *Land in African Agrarian Systems*, Madison: University of Wisconsin Press.

Carney, J. and Watts, M. (1990) "Disciplining Women?" *Signs* 16:4 651–81.

de Janvry, A. (1980) *The Agrarian Question in Latin America*, Baltimore: Johns Hopkins University Press.

Harvey, D. (1989) *The Urban Experience*, Oxford: Blackwell.

Kitching, G. (1998) "The Revenge of the Peasant," *Journal of Peasant Studies* 26:1 43–81.

Medvedev, R. (1980) *Soviet Agriculture*, New York: Norton.

Verdery, K. (1993) *What Was Socialism and What Comes Next*, Princeton, NJ: Princeton University Press.

MICHAEL WATTS

landlocked developing countries (LLDCs)

Landlocked developing countries (LLDCs) are generally among the poorest of the developing countries. Of the thirty LLDCs, sixteen, including Chad, Central African Republic, and Niger are classified as least developed. Their **poverty** and weak **growth rates** come from the very limited number of commodities they export and the high transport costs involved in exporting these commodities. Their sea-borne **trade** unavoidably depends on transit through other countries, which in most cases have relatively poor transport systems themselves. Additional border crossings and the long distances from major world markets substantially increase the total expenses for transport services, and these high transport costs have become a far more restrictive barrier to trade than **tariffs**. According to UNCTAD (United Nations Conference on Trade and Development) estimates, landlocked developing countries in 1995 spent on average almost twice as much on transport (see **transport policy**) and insurance services than the average for other developing countries, and three times more than the average of developed economies.

See also: chronic poverty; Sahel; transport policy

CLAUDIO O. DELANG

landmines

Landmines are explosive devices buried just below ground and detonated when disturbed or pressured, and have been a common weapon throughout the twentieth century. Although some mines have self-destruct or disarm timers, making them inoperable after a set period, the majority remain active until cleared by explosives specialists or detonated. Landmines are indiscriminate, threatening military and civilians alike; **children** at play have proved particularly vulnerable. People regularly risk their lives venturing into mined territory; often this may be unavoidable if they are to access water or other resources. Land that has been mined cannot be farmed safely until cleared. Aimed at reducing use of landmines, the Convention on the Prohibition of the Use, Stockpiling, Production and Transfer of Antipersonnel Mines and on their Destruction (the Ottawa Treaty) passed into **international law** (see **law of armed conflict (LAC)**) in 1999. Landmine clearance is an alternative approach, rendering mined territory safe.

See also: arms sales and controls; post-conflict rehabilitation; post-conflict violence; war

Further reading

Mines Advisory Group: http://www.mag.org.uk/

CLARE MILLS

late industrialization

Late industrialization refers to the process of **industrialization** at a time when other countries are already industrialized. Although the concept applies to all countries that industrialized after Great Britain (including France, Germany and the United States) it usually alludes to a handful of market economies that started and succeeded in the process during the twentieth century, including Japan, South Korea, India, Turkey, Mexico and Brazil.

Industrializing late is not simply a matter of time, but also includes making up significant differences in investment and technological capacity (see **technological capability**). The later a country starts industrializing, the more distant its goal. Moreover, the industries and firms of previously industrialized countries are already established in the international markets for manufactured commodities, often including the domestic markets of late industrializers, which makes it more difficult for incumbents to compete. Industrializing late is a formidable challenge, and success stories are few.

So, how can countries industrialize late? In the orthodox perspective (embodied in the works of Walt Rostow, Peter Bauer and Jagdish Bhagwati), latecomers have to liberalize their economies and establish the institutional frameworks for markets, therefore facilitating resource allocation, capital accumulation and investment. Industrialization would then "take off" along the path of early movers, and eventually industrial performance would converge with them. In the heterodox perspective (represented by scholars like Alexander Gerschenkron, Raul Prebisch and Alice Amsden) late industrialization entails actively promoting, protecting and directing investments in physical and **human capital**. Competition and upgrading would then become easier for **infant industries**, putting latecomers on a distinct path to "catch up" with the leaders. The controversy also refers to more general debates about the role of the state in industrialization, and the relationship with trade and free markets (see **state and state reform; free trade; trade; industrialization and trade policy; newly industrialized economies (NIEs)**).

Historical evidence suggests that late industrialization requires nurturing, or some form of industrial policy based on institutional arrangements to coordinate capital, labor and government effectively. Once in motion, latecomers can narrow the gaps and advance faster than early movers, at least for some time. This is possible because late industrialization is really a process of learning, of absorbing and eventually improving technology developed and mastered by the industrialized countries (see **technology policy**).

However, in the 1980s and 1990s the road for latecomers became more uncertain, due to economic liberalization and the increased power of **transnational corporations (TNCs)**, which reduced the room for policy maneuvering. Hence, these countries need new strategies to develop the individual, organizational and institutional capabilities required for investment and **technology transfer**. Only then would they be able to change their comparative advantage, going from low wages and **natural resources** to knowledge as the engine of **economic growth**.

See also: developmental state; industrialization; industrialization and trade policy; infant industries; institutions; leapfrogging; newly industrialized economies (NIEs); small and medium enterprises (SMEs); technology policy; transnational corporations (TNCs) from developing economies

Further reading

Amsden, A. (2001) *The Rise of "The Rest": Challenges to the West from Late-Industrializing Economies*, Oxford and New York: Oxford University Press.

Gerschenkron, A. (1962) *Economic Backwardness in Historical Perspective*, Cambridge, MA: Harvard University Press.

JORGE MARIO SOTO ROMERO

Latin American Free Trade Agreement (LAFTA)

The Latin American Free Trade Agreement (LAFTA) is an international agreement to promote intra-regional **free trade** in Latin America. It came into effect on 1 June 1961, created by the Treaty of Montevideo (under the auspices of the United Nations' **Economic Commission for Latin America and the Caribbean (ECLAC)** of 1960. At its inception, eleven nation-states were members of the agreement, comprising the ten independent nation-states of South America plus Mexico. During its first ten years, intra-regional trade increasing significantly. Problems surfaced in the 1970s, however – some countries insisted on continued use of **import substitution** strategies; similarities in the economic structure of members inhibited trade; purchasing power growth remained sluggish; and political mistrust between member states abounded. By 1980, few of its intended reforms had been implemented and only 10 percent of total regional trade took place within the group. In 1991, the Latin America Integration Association grew out of the LAFTA, with the less grandiose agenda of protecting existing trade agreements and promoting sub-regional, especially bilateral, accords.

See also: Economic Commission for Latin America and the Caribbean (ECLAC); economic federalization; free trade zones (FTZs); North American Free Trade Agreement (NAFTA); trade

WARWICK E. MURRAY

law

The topic of law and development refers both to a field of practice and an area of scholarship. As a field of practice, it has its origins and peak in the 1960s, continuing into the late 1970s. In the 1980s, however, the field underwent a time of crisis, with the only growth being in the area of women, law and development (see **gender**). It was only in the post-**Cold War** era that law and development began to make a comeback, albeit much changed since the 1960s. The field of law and development is almost impossible to disentangle from the context of foreign technical assistance to developing countries (see **aid; bilateral aid agencies**) and the policies of international financial institutions (see **international organizations and associations; International Monetary Fund (IMF)**).

As a topic of scholarship, law and development is founded on the optimistic belief that progressive social change can be engineered through the careful deployment of law as an instrument of development. Underlying this view is the Weberian proposition that economic development in developed (or Western) societies came about partly because of "rational legal systems," and therefore the same experience could be replicated in poorer countries by reforming their legal systems. The term, "rational legal system" refers to an ideal type where rules predicated on general concepts are known in advance and applied consistently to all cases. This system is held in contrast to arrangements that react on a case-by-case basis and apply particularistic concepts, such as those drawn from a set of religious or cultural beliefs (see **religion**). Conceptually therefore, the discussion of "law and development" may signal a tacit acceptance of a singular and narrow definition of development as Western modernization (see **modernization theory; ethnocentrism**).

Because of this association between legal reforms and modernization theory, many "law and development" projects of the 1960s and 1970s became synonymous with transplanting Western legal **institutions** to replace indigenous systems that were seen as unsuitable and inefficient. It also meant introducing new laws to regulate activities that did not previously exist, largely in emerging

commercial sectors, such as the regulation of securities; anti-monopoly laws; and privatization of landholding (see **land reform; privatization and liberalization**). The process of transplantation and expansion of formal legal regulation had already begun gradually in many developing countries under colonial rule. Following independence, reforms were seen as crucial to integrate poor countries into international political and economic systems.

The 1960s phase of law and development was primarily a United States initiative, and its main impact was in Latin America, with some projects in Africa. There was little involvement in Asia. Efforts focused on three main activities. The first key action was to provide legal **education** to mold the type of lawyer needed during **decolonization**. This approach was shaped by the belief that, if law could stimulate development and social change, then lawyers had a significant role to play as social engineers. Lawyers were trained to be "omnipotent problem-solvers" and "social engineers," who were able to advise on nation building, **economic development** and diplomacy, rather than simple technicians in the details of law. This view of a lawyer's role was largely informed by the US civil rights movement, and did not necessarily match perceptions of lawyers in developing countries, particularly in Latin America's civil law tradition, where the legislator, rather than the lawyer or judge, occupies center stage.

Under this first activity, legal education projects were mainly funded by the USA, and especially the Ford Foundation and United States Agency for International Development (USAID). Activities included setting up law faculties and legal research centers, introducing US-style case-based law teaching methodology, and establishing systems for public reporting of superior court decisions to make them available both for legal practice and for teaching. A substantial amount of money also went to leading US law schools to set up international legal studies centers, out of which US legal scholars would be sent abroad to teach and set up legal programs, and to bring law teachers from developing countries to the USA for training.

The second key activity, involved building democratic institutions, such as parliaments. This stage did not occur until the late 1960s with the enactment of the 1966 US Foreign Assistance Act.

The third activity lay in harmonizing customary laws based on **culture** or **religion** with formal laws, particularly in the areas of family and property law (see **domestic law**). Most colonial powers had allowed customary laws to operate alongside the imposed formal law, largely for administrative expediency and cooption of existing local **governance** structures (see **local government**). This system raised questions in the run-up to independence: was the continued operation of separate legal systems for different communities consistent with nation-building? What was the best way to achieve unification? Were customary law principles (such as communal ownership and management of land) suitable for a monetary growth-oriented economy?

This third activity was largely undertaken by Britain in its former colonies, but there was some US involvement. Foremost among the projects undertaken was the Restatement of African Law project at the School of Oriental and African Studies (SOAS, London), which produced a series of monographs on specific areas of customary law in selected African communities (see **community**). Such restatement projects have been criticized on three main fronts: First, their methodology was claimed to rely on rapid results rather than painstaking legal-anthropological research. Second, they were allegedly based on partial and biased information (for example, the restatements only drew from the knowledge of men who had served on the customary law tribunals – see **male bias**). Third, critics claimed they led to static and ossified "official" customary law, as some magistrates and judges interpreted the monographs as authoritative, and refused to consider contemporary practice when deciding cases. The issues raised by these criticisms have come to life yet again in post-1990s development practice, as agencies such as the British Department for International Development and the **World Bank** have advocated "**sector-wide approaches (SWAps)**" to reforming law that incorporates both formal and informal institutions.

By the late 1970s, law and development was in decline, both as an intellectual project and as a field of practice. The latter resulted from significant reductions in funding after critics had claimed it had produced little demonstrable impact. As an intellectual project, it failed to grow and influence related disciplines. The instrumentalist problem-solving approach it adopted alienated social scientists. Law and development was seen to be about lawyers doing development, rather than learning about the relationship between law and development and applying this learning to the projects they undertook.

The decline of law and development is attributed to fundamental flaws in its assumptions. First, it was assumed that legal reform had a causal link with development, and that lawyers should be seen as social engineers. These assumptions picture lawyers as well meaning, and state institutions as benign (see **state and state reform**). Instead, many lawyers were **elites** opposed to radical reform, and law can be used instrumentally for cynical and self-interested ends. There are many examples of postcolonial manipulation of constitutions and legislation to consolidate personal rule, perpetuating the crude legalism that characterized colonial administration. Second, it was also assumed that laws and legal institutions could be transplanted into developing countries unproblematically. Many attempts at transfer failed to take root and remained in the books as dead-letter law, or encountered selective rejection or adaptation by postcolonial regimes.

A powerful critique of law and development (as a component of modernization – see **modernization theory**) emerged from the developing world itself during the 1970s, in the form of **dependency theory**. During the 1980s, only two areas of law and development saw any significant activity. One was that of women in development, which is often not discussed at all in standard texts on law and development. The so-called Women, Law and Development movement shared the original belief in a causal link between law and progressive social change. Reforms to improve women's legal status would enable women's fuller participation in development and lead to women's emancipation. But unlike many early approaches to socio-cultural contexts, this movement understood that women's subordination was expressed in embedded social practices as well as in explicit laws and institutions. Their projects therefore focused on changing laws, developing strategies to support women's legal literacy (e.g. through **community**-based paralegals), and raising awareness among communities and officials on how law may reduce women's rights. The 1980s spawned regional networks such as Women, Law and Development in Africa (WILDAF) and other international networks that have continued to grow with successive **United Nations World Conferences on Women** held throughout the 1980s and 1990s.

The second area of law and development that grew during the 1980s was the Access to Justice Movement. Unlike orthodox law and development, this movement focused on both developed and developing countries. It sought to provide legal aid, promote public interest litigation, and provide affordable alternatives to existing legal systems, such as alternative dispute resolution and small claims courts. The movement has suffered setbacks resulting from cutbacks in public spending since the late 1980s.

The post-**Cold War** era has been referred to as a time of "rule of law revival." Rule of law is seen as indispensable to establishing a market economy and democratic rule, which are often referred to as the twin projects of the post-Cold War era. During the 1960s and 1970s, law and development lacked the support of multilateral development agencies such as the World Bank. Now these agencies are key actors in Rule of Law projects, with significant support from scholars supporting the **new institutional economics** and development, who seek to create a suitable legal and institutional environment for the market. Such a suitable legal environment is defined by five criteria: a set of rules known in advance (predictability); that the rules are actually in force; that there are mechanisms for applying rules; that independent bodies can interpret rules in case of conflicts; and that clear procedures exist for amending the rules when necessary.

In the post-Cold War approach to law and development, the state's role is of a facilitator of market transactions by maintaining law and order; guaranteeing **property rights**; and enforcing contracts. There is now more attention to countries in Central and Eastern Europe, as well as China and post-Soviet countries (see **postsocialism**). Multilateral financial institutions, particularly the

World Bank, now play a key role both in funding law and development activities, and attaching Rule of Law **conditionality** to their funding. They are also setting the tone of the discourse by generating a sizeable share of the literature in this field.

Reform of substantive laws has focused on areas considered central to a well functioning economy, such as drafting or rewriting commercial codes, bankruptcy, banking, tax and property laws (including intellectual property – see **intellectual property rights (IPRs)**), laws on corporate governance and freedom of information. The end of the Cold War has also ushered in projects in constitution-making, electoral reform and **human rights** legislation. Funding has also been channeled to **capacity building**, updating court management, computerization of court records, and the training of judges, prosecutors, public defenders, land registrars and police. A much smaller portion of funding has gone to activities seen as "complementary," such as support to **civil society** groups engaged in legal awareness work.

While some of these legal and institutional reforms have originated from requests by the recipient governments, a vast majority of the reforms are tied to **International Monetary Fund (IMF)** and World Bank **conditionality** or to membership in the World Trade Organization (see **World Trade Organization/General Agreement on Tariffs and Trade (WTO/GATT)**). Experiences of hurriedly enacted reforms lacking political support and citizen participation are therefore common. The legal imposition debates of the 1970s are thus revived in this potentially more contentious climate of conditionality and **economic federalization**. Yet critical discussion within the "reforming" countries is muted in comparison to the 1970s, perhaps due to the aura of "efficiency" and "anti-**corruption**" that lends moral urgency and legitimacy to these reforms.

The old and the new strands of law and development may seem, at first, to differ significantly. While the strand of the 1960s–70s explicitly sought to Westernize poor countries' legal systems, the current strand places more value on creating regulatory structures that are consistent with "international best practice." However, "international best practice" is defined primarily by the needs of international investors, and therefore both strands embody an absence of local autonomy and space for poor countries to define their own development and legal institutions.

See also: domestic law; gender and property rights; governance; human rights; international law; politics; property rights; public sector; state and state reform

Further reading

Adelman, S. and Paliwala, A. (1993) *Law and Crisis in the Third World*, London: Hans Zell.

Carothers, T. (1999) *Aiding Democracy Abroad: The Learning Curve*, Washington DC: Carnegie Endowment for International Peace.

Carty, A. (1992) *Law and Development*, Aldershot: Dartmouth.

Faundez, J. (1997) *Good Governance and Law: Legal and Institutional Reform in Developing Countries*, New York: St Martin's Press.

Merryman, J. (1977) "Comparative Law and Social Change: On the Origins, Style, Decline and Revival of the Law and Development Movement," *The American Journal of Comparative Law* 25: 457–83.

Seidman, A., Seidman, R. and Wälde, T. (eds) (1999) *Making Development Work: Legislative Reform for Institutional Transformation and Good Governance*, The Hague: Kluwer Law International.

CELESTINE NYAMU-MUSEMBI

law of armed conflict (LAC)

The law of armed conflict (LAC) seeks to regulate the conduct of warfare and minimize the risk to and suffering of civilians and prisoners of **war**. Its constitutive documents include the Hague Conventions restricting methods of warfare; numerous agreements banning specific weapons; individual countries' regulations for their armed forces; and the **Geneva Conventions** and their Additional Protocols. Modern LAC primarily concerns *jus in bello*, or the law of the conduct of warfare, and is often referred to as international humanitarian law. A second subset of LAC concerns *jus ad bellum*, or the rules governing whether or not a war is just. This second body of rules is largely made obsolete by the blanket prohibition of aggressive war in the **United Nations** Charter.

LAC includes the demand for the protection of medical and religious personnel and facilities, and a proscription against inhumane treatment of prisoners of war (a status which shall not be denied any combatant, except spies and mercenaries). Civilians are to be treated humanely and not subjected to deportation or forced population transfer, and an occupying force is given certain responsibilities, including the provisioning of public order while not imposing a particular political system. LAC furthermore prohibits certain methods of warfare, including the use of some kinds of deception, orders of "no quarter," and some weapons. Unlike most human rights law, LAC is non-derogable: that is, it can never be deviated from in the name of national **security** or for any other reason.

The scope of LAC was significantly expanded by the adoption of the two Additional Protocols to the Geneva Conventions in 1977. The first protocol codified the principles of *distinction* and *proportionality*. The principle of distinction holds that all parties to a conflict must make a distinction between civilian populations and facilities and military targets (with only attacks against the latter being lawful). The principle of proportionality states that an attack on a lawful target is only lawful if excessive civilian loss or damage is not caused. The second protocol advanced the protection of civilians and combatants in non-international armed conflicts such as civil wars. Prior to 1977, the Geneva Conventions applied only to international armed conflicts (save for the minimum standards set forth in Article 3 of the 1949 Geneva Conventions). The scope of LAC remains limited to protracted conflict between a government and an organized force, however, and does not include disturbances such as riots. Other limitations include the ambiguities concerning LAC's applicability to peacekeepers, and how groups such as terrorists are to be treated.

Enforcement of the LAC is traditionally the obligation of the concerned state. The 1990s saw important developments in this regard, however, in the establishment of three tribunals to try war crimes (which include grave breaches of the Geneva Conventions): the *ad-hoc* International Criminal Tribunals for Former Yugoslavia and Rwanda, and the permanent International Criminal Court.

See also: child soldiers; complex emergencies; Geneva Conventions; humanitarianism; international law; military and security; peacekeeping; post-conflict rehabilitation; post-conflict violence; right of intervention; United Nations; violence; war

Further reading

Detter, I. (2000) *The Law of War*, 2nd edn, Cambridge: Cambridge University Press.

I. NIKLAS HULTIN

League of Nations

The League of Nations was established in 1919 from the ruins of World War I to underpin a system of international society, **security** and cooperation amongst states (see **state and state reform**). It is commonly considered to be an initial attempt at creating an organization similar to the current **United Nations**. The League had some early successes in the field of dispute-settlement, and pioneered the development of **international organizations and associations**, the international civil service, and functional cooperation in a number of areas. However, the League is best known for failing to prevent or deal with Japanese, Italian and German aggression during the 1930s, which finally led to World War II. Many organizational weaknesses hampered the League of Nations. Its Covenant allowed members to decide if aggression had been committed and therefore veto action if they did not support it. Furthermore, the League did not have the membership of major states at various times; Japan, Germany, Italy, and the Soviet Union withdrew, while the USA never joined. Nevertheless, the League provided many antecedents for the post-War United Nations.

See also: United Nations; world economic conference (London, 1933)

EDWARD NEWMAN

leapfrogging

Leapfrogging occurs where developing countries bypass the conventional stages of development by moving straight to advanced technology. The opportunity to leapfrog arises out of two factors. First, developing countries are faced with a far greater range of options than their industrialized counterparts in the past, not least because of rapid technological advances over the past half-century. Second, developing countries have yet to install a large share of their production capacity, meaning that they are well placed to adopt leapfrog technologies as an integral part of the development process.

The most commonly cited candidates for leapfrogging-type investments are biotechnologies, information and communication technologies (ICTs), and environmentally sound technologies (ESTs). Examples include skipping over the historic approach of installing centralized, fossil-fueled electricity systems by moving directly to decentralized, renewables-based ones; and bypassing the intermediate stages of development based around heavy industry in favor of high-technology, knowledge-based forms of **industrialization**.

Considerable optimism surrounds the potential benefits of technology leapfrogging. Thus, by adopting leapfrog technologies from an early stage of industrialization, it is often claimed that developing countries will not only be able to accelerate their **economic growth**, but also minimize the environmental impacts of development. No doubt this explains why leapfrogging is frequently portrayed as a "win-win" development strategy ideally suited to the requirements of industrializing economies. Critics have challenged this optimism, however, questioning whether developing countries possess sufficient technological capabilities (see **technological capability**) to incorporate leapfrog technologies directly into their development process.

See also: brown environmental agenda; industrialization; renewable energy; stages of economic growth; technological capability; technology policy; technology transfer

Further reading

Perkins, R. (2003) "Environmental Leapfrogging in Developing Countries: A Critical Assessment and Reconstruction," *Natural Resources Forum* 27: 177–88.

Steinmueller, W. (2001) "ICTs and the Possibilities for Leapfrogging by Developing Countries," *International Labour Review* 140:2 193–210.

RICHARD PERKINS

liberation theology

The concept of liberation theology gained popularity through Gustavo Gutierrez's 1971 book *The Theology of Liberation*, which synthesized a new thinking based on the experiences of the poor being discussed at theological faculties and bible study groups in Latin America over the previous decade. Liberation theology is based on the praxis of the Bible by the poor. It formulates an understanding of the causes of oppression and in light of the Scriptures calls for action to deliver the poor from this oppression. A common summary statement of liberation theology is the *preferential option for the poor*.

Liberation theology is both a Christian (predominately Catholic) theology and a development paradigm. It differs from other development paradigms in that it takes as its starting point the primacy of the oppressed based on biblical experiences of the poor – such as the freeing of the Jewish slaves from Egypt described in the Book of Exodus.

To describe this preferential option for the poor, the concept of liberation was consciously chosen rather than that of development, even though their goals of human betterment may appear to be the same. "Liberation" is more complex than the term "development." Whilst both the concepts of liberation and development result in freedom from oppressive economic, social, and political conditions and enable control of one's own historical destiny, liberation theology is distinct through its focus on emancipation from the structural or social sin that deprives people of life. All development activities therefore are solely aimed at liberating the poor from the oppression of **poverty**.

Liberation theology is often practically expressed through Basic Christian Communities (BCCs). BCCs are **grassroots organizations** acting not only as forums for prayer and reflection, but also for **community** action programs such as improving local infrastructure, providing literacy classes and seed money for micro-credit schemes (see **illiteracy; micro-credit and micro-finance**). BCCs are simultaneously bible reading groups and community-based organizations. They exist in all regions of Latin America and many other parts of the world including Asia and Africa.

Gutierrez is widely considered the foremost liberation theologist. He was ordained a Roman Catholic priest in Peru in 1959. He has also received higher degrees in Belgium and a Ph.D. from the Institut Catholique de Lyon in France. In additional to his pastoral work in Peru, Gutierrez is also a professor of Theology at the Pontifica Universidad Catolica del Peru. Other important liberation theologists include Leonardo Boff, Helder Camero and Juan Segundo. Despite its Catholic origins, liberation theology is strongly criticized by the Vatican as a misrepresentation of the Christian message.

See also: Christianity; grassroots development; religion

Further reading

Boff, L. and Boff, C. (1990) *Introducing Liberation Theology*, New York: Orbis.

Gutierrez, G. (1971) *A Theology of Liberation*, London: SCM Press.

MATTHEW CLARKE

life expectancy

Life expectancy (LE) is an indication of the average number of years an inhabitant of a country may expect to live. Definitions of life expectancy may also be used to assess the effectiveness of specific development strategies or **health** policies in different populations. Various definitions are used. The most widely accepted measure of LE is the "life expectancy at birth," or the average number of years that newborn babies can be expected to live under a given set of regional health conditions. Another calculation of LE focuses on the average expected age at death for people in different age groups. The Disability Adjusted Life Expectancy (DALE) is corrected for the number of years lived with **disability**, and adjusted for the severity of disability by applying relative weighting criteria. LE indices generally reflect distributive qualities of national prosperity, environmental conditions, and public access to high-quality preventive and curative health care. In general, females enjoy higher life expectancies than males, and life expectancy is higher for residents of developed countries than for residents of developing countries.

See also: chronic poverty; health; human development; maternal mortality; mortality; population

DELE OGUNSEITAN

limited good

The concept of limited good refers to the perception of wealth as a finite entity, and hence that one person's gain is made at another person's expense. The term was proposed by the anthropologist George Foster based on research in Mexico. The limited good concept sees economic life is a zero-sum game. If some people are becoming wealthier than others, then there are considerable pressures from leveling mechanisms within society, such as ostentatious spending on fiestas in Latin America. The limited good concept was therefore an obstacle to increasing the productive capacities of individuals.

Foster published his work in the 1960s, and it reflected contemporary modernization theories (see **modernization theory**). The idea was, however, immediately criticized for portraying traditional societies in stereotypical ways. The limited good thesis overlooks dynamism, heterogeneity and rationality in traditional societies. For example, the idea of a limited good can be rational if goods are perceived as actually limited. Yet,

despite criticisms, the concept is still referred to, possibly because it gives insights into social practices that are otherwise difficult to understand, such as the belief that development workers have access to hidden treasure. A recent publication, for instance, found the belief within a Philippine **community** that Japanese development workers had access to hidden gold. Foster was concerned with explaining the envy, jealousy, competition and bitterness he found in the Mexican communities he studied. These emotions are also central in African witchcraft accusations. Access to the wealth of ordinary people by economically successful people through supernatural powers often plays a large role in such accusations. Such beliefs can paralyze economic endeavor in communities. Limited good analysis may also be applied to modern environments, such as to explain the persistence of patron-client relationships in politics: political activity is seen in this context as dividing a limited amount of wealth rather than promoting social change. The idea that the development of rich countries has been at the expense of the underdevelopment of poor countries can also contain the notion of limited good, where the wealth of one is always at the expense of another.

Undoubtedly, the limited good concept can lead to spurious interpretations. It can result in a condescending attitude toward peasant communities. It may overlook how limited goods may be an interpretation of exploitative relationships. If assumed accurate, the limited good idea can easily impose deterministic explanations using predefined assumptions about societies. However, as a heuristic device that is not narrowly applied to peasant communities, it can clarify social practices in development that remain otherwise opaque.

See also: community; peasantry; productivity; rural development

Further reading

Foster, G. (1965) "Peasant Society and the Image of the Limited Good," *American Anthropologist* 67:2 293–315.

JAN KEES VAN DONGE

Limits to Growth report (1972)

The Limits to Growth (Meadows *et al.*, 1972) was a report published as a book in 1972 that predicted the exhaustion of natural resources and subsequent decline in **economic growth** unless radical approaches were adopted to reduce **population** growth and consumption of resources. The cataclysmic arguments of the book introduced the concept of global sustainability to the public and challenged economic theory in an era of post-World War II optimism. The book was the report of the "Project on the Predicament of Mankind" by a then unknown, informally organized think tank of some thirty scientists, educators, economists, humanists, and civil servants from ten countries, called the **Club of Rome**. Its mission was to study systematically the complexity and interdependence of universal social, economic, and environmental variables, called the "world problematique." Given the exponential growth rate of population and capital, when would current trends cause collapse? The report presented a choice. Is it better to promote social change – reduce population through **birth control**, decrease industrial output by shifting consumers away from material goods – or should growth be allowed to continue until naturally limited? Intended to raise the consciousness of the public and policy-makers and thereby avert disaster, *The Limits to Growth* was optimistic in its goal but not in its findings. The global warning issued was held as overly pessimistic and alarmist. The book concluded, "Short of a world effort, today's already explosive gaps and inequalities will continue to grow larger. The outcome can only be disaster" (1972:195). Although it caused a furor, the book nonetheless sold over 12 million copies in thirty-seven languages.

To assist in their study, the Club of Rome engaged a group of computer experts at the Massachusetts Institute of Technology (MIT) to use the data and modeling capabilities available at the time to look at the behaviors and relationships of the world's variables. The MIT team built an admittedly simple model, called World3, that examined five interconnected trends that the Club determined to limit growth: rapid population increase; inadequate agricultural production; accelerating **industrialization**; a deteriorating **environment**; and depletion of non-renewable resources. The study addressed an array of sub-issues further revealing the interdependence of "people, food, investment, depreciation, resources, output." How does maximum population size, given per capita resource use and the increasing need for **food**, affect finite amounts of arable land and available fresh water? What is the cap on industrial production given energy use (see **energy policy**), particularly from fossil fuels? What is the effect of **pollution** levels on **deforestation**, agricultural production, and **life expectancy**? The conclusions offered two possible outcomes. At the present, unchanged **growth rate**, the limits would be reached within the next one hundred years by a "sudden and uncontrollable decline in both population and industrial capacity." Alternatively, global sustainability is possible. But if this outcome is desired, then the sooner measures are taken the greater the chances are for success.

Now, some decades after the publication of *The Limits to Growth*, opinion is divided on its contribution to environmental debate. On one hand, supporters believe it was a useful clarion call about the scarcity of resources and the need to revise growth-inducing policies coupled with increased efficiency in materials and energy used. On the other hand, critics have claimed it clumsily overstated the rates of resource depletion without acknowledging the role of scarcity in inducing innovation or on making new technologies or previously inaccessible reserves of resources economically viable. Furthermore, critics claim the neo-Malthusian (see **Malthusian demography**) overtones of the report highly simplified the politics of scarcity and innovation, and hence overlooked the political means by which certain richer countries or people can avoid reaching limits to growth, whereas poorer countries or people may lack the state capacity (see **state and state reform**) or **technological capability** to do so. A further criticism was that the cataclysmic nature of the book's predictions overstated the nature of the environmental crisis, and hence weakened public support for environmentalism after many of its predictions did not occur. Supporters of the book claim that the "limits" may still be reached – indeed, the 1992 update, *Beyond the*

Limits: Confronting Global Collapse, Envisioning a Sustainable Future, by the same MIT team, argued a more sophisticated, yet still crisis-driven account of pollution and environmental degradation. But despite the continuing debate about the severity of current environmental problems, there is little doubt that the original *Limits to Growth* was highly simplistic in its explanation and prediction of resource scarcity, yet that its sensationalistic appearance in 1972 significantly influenced the perception of environment and global change as potentially catastrophic.

See also: carrying capacity; ecodevelopment; environment; inequality and poverty, world trends; Malthusian demography; natural resources; over-population; population; sustainable development

Further reading

Meadows, D. H., Meadows, D. L., Randers, J. and Behrens III, W. (1972) *The Limits to Growth: A Report for The Club of Rome's Project on the Predicament of Mankind*, New York: Signet.

Meadows, D. H., Meadows, D. L. and Randers, J. (1992) *Beyond the Limits: Confronting Global Collapse, Envisioning a Sustainable Future*, Post Mills VT: Chelsea Green.

JULIE A. DERCLE

Live Aid/Band Aid

Live Aid and Band Aid were activities in the 1980s organized by international pop stars to raise money and bring attention to **famine** in Ethiopia. In October 1984, the British Broadcasting Corporation (BBC) televized shocking pictures of famine at refugee camps in Ethiopia (see **refugees**), which inspired two British rock stars, Bob Geldof and Midge Ure, to recruit other popular British singers and musicians to create a group called "Band Aid" and to record a song about the famine called *Do They Know It's Christmas?/Feed The World*. The song was so successful it later inspired the formation of a similar group in the USA called "USA For Africa," whose single, *We Are The World*, also sold widely. The activities culminated on July 13th

1985 in "Live Aid," which was the world's biggest rock concert, held simultaneously over a 16-hour period in Philadelphia and London, involving some sixty of the world's biggest rock stars performing for free in front of a live and televised audience estimated at nearly 2 billion people worldwide. The Live Aid/Band Aid events were clearly successful in raising consciousness about famine and in suggesting that **aid** need not be left to governments alone (the Band Aid Trust was eventually closed in 1992 after raising in excess of US$144 million from a variety of citizen and institutional sources). Yet, critics also claimed that the activities focused more on the **humanitarianism** of donors than on addressing the more deep-set and political causes of famine resulting from **war**. The activities also coincided with the discussion of a new term, "compassion fatigue" referring to the gradual loss of interest of the public in such topics. Similar attempts at money raising since Live Aid/Band Aid have been less successful.

See also: aid; charities; famine; humanitarianism; media; voluntary sector

TIM FORSYTH

livelihoods

Livelihoods are the capabilities (see **capability approach**), assets and activities required to make a living. What has become known as the livelihoods approach to development studies and policy was first proposed by Robert Chambers in the 1980s. It was later developed by Chambers and Gordon Conway, in particular, and by researchers at the Institute of Development Studies at the University of Sussex. In the 1990s, it was taken up by a number of development agencies, including the UK's Department for International Development. An emphasis on **sustainable livelihoods** is a key part of that agency's approach to development issues.

Everyone has to make a living – in the sense of getting by – but **children** in richer countries do so in different ways than their parents. During childhood, they are improving their capabilities by attending school and enhancing their social and work-related skills. To the extent they earn small amounts of money by running paper rounds, or working in "Saturday jobs," they are contributing to their livelihood in financial terms as well. For the most part, though, their livelihoods, and their entitlements to **food** and accommodation, are secured for them by parents or guardians. Matters are clearly very different in poorer countries. **Child labor** is more common in this context, and some children must consciously strategize about the ways in which they will put together (and hopefully improve) their livelihoods.

A concern for livelihood strategies stands at the heart of *livelihoods analysis* and policy-making. In principle, it is concerned with the individual child or adult, and is properly sensitive to age, **gender**, and other inequalities within a household (see **inequality**). In practice, it recognizes that individuals attempt to shape their livelihoods within wider social units, including households, lineages, clans, **castes**, classes and ethnic groups (see **ethnicity/identity**). In poorer countries, the assumption is that individuals operate within a context of **vulnerability**. People put together multiple livelihood strategies in order to diffuse risk and achieve a range of different goals. These strategies are likely to change over time – they are *dynamic* – and they are unlikely to be achieved in full. Some goals and strategies will clash with one another, and a lack of assets and capabilities will frustrate others. Better off people in richer countries also engage in multiple and conflicting livelihood strategies, but they generally do so against a backdrop of reduced vulnerability. Levels of **social exclusion** and discrimination may be lower, and the available resource base more assured.

Policy-makers now like to address livelihood concerns by **participatory research methods**. Livelihood strategies cannot effectively be strengthened by **non-governmental organizations (NGOs), bilateral aid agencies** or **civil society** groups until the authors of those strategies have defined their aims and concerns. The outcomes of these strategies then depend on a person's ability to access and enhance six sets of assets or "capital." **Human capital** is generally considered to include educational and practical skills, good health and the ability to work. Natural assets (see **natural capital**) consist of those resources and resource flows – including land, water, forests and

biodiversity – that help to secure livelihoods. Physical capital refers to the basic means of production and infrastructure, including transport, shelter and communications. This might be poorly developed in remote rural locations. Financial capital comprises the savings, supplies of credit, **remittances**, **pensions**, entitlements, and so on, available to different persons. **Social capital** refers to the networks and relationships of trust that are built up by membership of groups. Cultural capital refers to those assets that provide people with a sense of identity or self-worth, including feelings of protection, affection and being free.

The livelihoods approach assumes that men, women and children will combine these assets in diverse ways, but almost always with conscious regard for their vulnerability and a desire to make life more secure. Livelihoods are said to become sustainable when individuals can cope with and recover from stresses and shocks in the present and future, while not undermining the natural resource base (see **natural resources; sustainable livelihoods**).

According to DFID, it is precisely the emphasis on the person that distinguishes this approach, and which commends it to policy-makers. "The livelihoods approach puts people at the center of development," and marks an advance upon the area- or sector-based approaches to integrated **rural development** that dominated in the 1970s. This may well be the case, but critics charge that the livelihoods approach to rural development is excessively voluntaristic. By focusing so firmly on the individual and his or her agency, there is a danger that wider and enduring structures of social life (and exclusion) are given insufficient attention. Poorer people can improve their livelihoods only to a limited degree in the face of pervasive discrimination, **corruption** and entrenched inequalities.

See also: capability approach; food security; gender; participatory research methods; rural development; rural poverty; social exclusion; sustainable livelihoods; urban informal sector

Further reading

Bagchi, D., Blaikie, P., Cameron, J., Chatopadhyay, M., Gyawali, N. and Seddon, D.

(1998) "Conceptual and Methodological Challenges in the Study of Livelihood Trajectories: Case-studies in Eastern India and Western Nepal," *Journal of International Development* 10: 453–68.

Carney, D. (ed.) (1998) *Sustainable Rural Livelihoods: What Contribution Can We Make?* London: DFID.

Ellis, F. (2000) *Rural Livelihoods and Diversity in Developing Countries*, Oxford: Oxford University Press.

Francis, E. (2000) *Making a Living: Changing Livelihoods in Rural Africa*, London: Routledge.

STUART CORBRIDGE

livestock

Livestock refers to the rearing and management of animals for meat, milk, eggs, fiber, animal traction and hides. Most of the world's agricultural systems involve some form of livestock. Indeed, these animals often provide a range of products, and this multifunctionality is particularly important for rural people in developing countries (see **rural development; sustainable livelihoods**). All the species involved have been domesticated, i.e. their characteristics have been altered through human intervention and their populations are controled through management. However, only a small proportion of animals on the Earth's surface have been domesticated, a process which occurred in different places and at different times during the last 12,000 years and which is associated with the inception of agricultural systems (see **agrarian transformation**).

The most widely kept livestock are cattle, sheep, goats and pigs, all of which were originally domesticated from their wild ancestors in southwest Asia but which now characterize agricultural systems worldwide. Table 6 gives the approximate numbers of these animals in today's agricultural systems; the large numbers attest to the significance of livestock worldwide as providers of **food** and other commodities and reflect their role in wealth generation through **agriculture** in both developed and developing worlds. Other large species of livestock include asses, buffaloes, horses, mules, camels, deer, yaks, llamas and alpacas; small species include rabbits, guinea pigs and dog (which is reared for human consumption in some Asian countries such as Vietnam) and mink; domesticated birds include chickens, turkeys, geese, ducks and ostriches.

Livestock are important sources of food because they produce protein; a substance required by humans in some abundance and which is not a primary product of cropping systems. Herbivorous animals such as cattle, sheep and goats are ruminants with a complex four-chambered stomach. Grazed material, such as grass and herbs, reaches the first stomach. This is the rumen where the material is stored so that bacteria can decompose the plant material including the complex structural component of cellulose. The material is then regurgitated for further mastication in the mouth before it is swallowed and digested. This capacity is the key to ruminant value in human **nutrition**; it facilitates the production of meat and milk (and sometimes blood) protein from the carbohydrates, cellulose, etc. of forage plants. Similarly, sheep, various goats such as the angora, which produces the much-prized mohair, and the llama, have the capacity to produce useful and valuable fibers from their consumption of forage as well as meat and milk. All of these animals produce hides that can be used for a variety of purposes including footwear, bags, furniture and even tent coverings.

Table 6 Numbers of cattle, sheep, goats and pigs worldwide in 2002

	Cattle	Sheep	Goats	Pigs
Developed world	326,435,260	367,269,662	30,478,896	284,474,665
Developing world	1,034,040,360	676,775,455	716,035,745	654,843,966
Total	1,360,475,620	1,044,045,117	746,514,641	939,318,631

Source: based on FAOSTAT, 2003.

Livestock are reared in intensive or extensive agricultural systems. Intensive systems involve substantial inputs of fossil fuel subsidies in the form of **mechanization** and animal health products (see **energy policy**). The latter include antibiotics, parasiticides and pesticides, which reduce the detrimental impact of pests and diseases. The feed consumed by the animals is also produced in this type of industrialized agricultural system that involves artificial **fertilizers**, mechanization and crop-protection chemicals (see **agrochemicals**). In some circumstances, livestock are grazed extensively and then kept under intensive conditions in feedlots prior to slaughter, or animals are moved in a practice known as transhumance between upland and lowland pastures in alpine regions. The most intensive livestock rearing involves the part or whole confinement of animals in sheds or barns and is a widespread practice of commercial pig and poultry rearing. Such practices also tend to be chemical-intensive. Extensive livestock systems are also varied, ranging from those associated with a sedentary lifestyle to those associated with a nomadic lifestyle. Examples of the latter include the yak-rearing systems of central Asia, which employ a form of transhumance; the reindeer-rearing activities in the Eurasian tundra and boreal zones; and the nomadic pastoralists (see **pastoralism**) who rely mainly on cattle and camels, not only as a source of sustenance but also as a means of trade and as a symbol of social status. Livestock are also kept in small numbers in agricultural systems whose primary objective is crop rather than animal production; these may be shifting or permanent agriculture (see **shifting cultivation**). These animals, mainly poultry, pigs and sometimes cattle, goats, oxen or water buffalo, provide protein as meat, milk or eggs or provide traction for plowing, water wheels, etc.

In general, intensive livestock-producing systems characterize the developed world and occur mainly in temperate environments where pastures are rich and the **carrying capacity**, i.e. the numbers of animals that can be supported per unit area, is relatively high. The exceptions are the extensive ranching systems of the arid and semi-arid regions of Australia and the USA, where carrying capacity is low but where technological inputs are high (see **dryland agriculture**). Lower **productivity** per unit area generally characterizes both the intensive and extensive livestock systems of the developing world, mainly because of a limited, or non-existent, chemical input for both animal health purposes and the control of forage quality. Extensive systems predominate, e.g. the ranching of the South American pampas (grasslands) and the nomadic pastoralism of Sub-Saharan Africa (see **Sahel**). In the driest regions, animal husbandry is the only form of agriculture that is viable because low amounts and erratic patterns of rainfall mean that crop production is not possible (see **drought**). Under these circumstances, animal protein is produced from low quality and often-sparse forage. Nomadic pastoralists do, however, relate to crop farmers. First, in areas and years of higher rainfall the area under crops is increased and range extent is reduced, with the reverse occurring in areas and years of reduced rainfall. Second, pastoralists will seek improved grazing, sometimes on stubble after crop harvesting, to improve animal productivity and to swap animal products for crops, while the crop farmers obtain the benefit of animal manure and animal products.

See also: agrarian transformation; agriculture; dryland agriculture; food; nutrition; pastoralism; white revolution (milk)

Further reading

Gillespie, J. (2002) *Modern Livestock and Poultry Production*, Albany NY: Delmar.

A. M. MANNION

local government

Local government is the apparatus of government at the local level. In many transitional and developing countries, the nature of local administration and local politics is changing rapidly. As a consequence of far-reaching **decentralization** processes, in most of these societies a restructuring is taking place of the **public sector**, leading to a new articulation between the central and the local governments. At the same time, new roles and responsibilities are crystallizing for local governments, **non-governmental organizations (NGOs)**, quasi-NGOs (Quangos), **community-** based organizations (CBOs), the **voluntary sector** and private business interests. In this theatre of national and local **governance**, local governments are rapidly becoming to be recognized as important actors, both in the process of democratic reform and in the local development process.

This recognition of local government is not limited to national states. In the agendas of international development agencies, too, it is pointed out that local governments play a major role in fulfilling the aims and objectives of **sustainable development**. Chapter 28 of **Agenda 21**, the outcome of the 1992 **Earth Summit (1992) (United Nations Conference on Environment and Development)**, is very clear in this respect. As a result of this international agreement, many local governments all over the world have now taken the lead in devising and implementing their own Local Agenda 21. In a similar vein, the Habitat Agenda (outcome of the Habitat II conference at Istanbul, 1996 – see **Habitat I and II**) emphasizes the crucial role of local governments as the "closest partner" in the Habitat process and appeals to the national governments to strengthen local governments. This paradigm shift away from a former central state orientation (see **state and state reform**) toward a new emphasis on **capacity building** for local governments, including their ability to become efficient and effective agents for local development, is also observed in latest **World Bank** policies. In the Cities Alliance program, for instance, **local government asssociations (LGAs)** are fully participating in the Consultative Group and negotiations are being carried out directly with the local authorities of the cities involved.

Because of the waves of democratic reforms in the 1980s and early 1990s, in many developing and transition countries the "new" local government often is less authoritarian and exclusive now than before (see **authoritarianism**). In most of these countries, the reforms have done away with the tradition of appointed mayors who might be tempted to act primarily in the interest of the national president. Under the current conditions

of mayors and councilors being elected, local political autonomy *vis-à-vis* the central state has increased. At the same time, the scope of local authorities to become more inclusive is potentially bigger than under an authoritarian-bureaucratic regime. It also offers enhanced possibilities of establishing multi-sector partnerships for local development, enabling and promoting participation of a wide range of stakeholders (see **public-private partnerships**). **Participatory budgeting** appears to be but one of many innovative approaches which local governments employ respond better to the needs and priorities of their communities and constituencies (see **community**). However, local **elites** may threaten representative, transparent and accountable decision-making (see **transparency; accountability**) if they have personal bonds with individuals of the local bureaucracy. Such practices may easily lead to unethical or **corruption** in local governments.

Even if there is increased political autonomy from the center, this does not mean that decentralization policies have also brought financial autonomy to the local governments. According to the principles of subsidiarity, the various roles and functions of the state at the different tiers of government should be mutually complementary and become decentralized to the lowest administrative level where their implementation is most effective. In many cases of service provision, the locality will be the most appropriate level. In practice, however, the decentralization of responsibilities only occasionally coincides with the new distribution of resources from the central government.

Local governments spend most of their yearly budgets (up to 70–80 percent in some cases) on personnel costs, which is to be attributed to the **labor-intensive** provision of services, facilities and infrastructure in their jurisdiction. Local governments will have their own structural resource base, provided that they are equipped with a competent staff and an adequate set of management tools to levy and to collect local taxes, development fees, user charges, etc. Under certain circumstances, debt financing through, for example, municipal development funds (see **municipalities**) may provide additional means for investment. But for all local governments, transfers from the central government are vital to cover at least the expenses on services provided on behalf of the central government. This is even more important as many local authorities in developing countries lack the necessary revenue-raising capacities.

For the majority of local governments in developing countries, **capacity building** will be one of the most pressing challenges ahead. Each local government needs to devise locally specific policies and to adopt particular regulations and by-laws, through which they may complement and expand what has been established in general terms by the central government. The design and implementation of locally tailored policies demand specific knowledge and skills in the local government apparatus. In many countries, it has become common now for local governments to outsource or privatize the provision, management or maintenance of certain public services. The paradox of this practice is that while it seemingly releases pressure from the local government's administrative apparatus, in general it also implies an additional burden because of the exigencies of regulation and monitoring of such private sector activities.

See also: community; decentralization; municipalities; new public management (NPM); partnerships; politics; public-private partnerships; state and state reform; voluntary sector

Further reading

Gilbert, R., Stevenson, D., Girardet, H. and Stren, R. (1996) *Making Cities Work: The Role of Local Authorities in the Urban Environment*, London: Earthscan.

McCarney, P. (ed.) (1996) *The Changing Nature of Local Government in Developing Countries*, Toronto: University of Toronto/Federation of Canadian Municipalities.

Myers, D. and Dietz, H. (2002) *Capital City Politics in Latin America: Democratization and Empowerment*, Boulder: Lynne Rienner.

Osborne, D. and Gaebler, T. (1993) *Reinventing Government: How the Entrepreneurial Spirit is Transforming the Public Sector*, New York: Penguin.

World Bank (2000) *Cities in Transition: A Strategic View of Urban and Local Government Issues*, Washington DC: World Bank.

PAUL VAN LINDERT

local government associations (LGAs)

Local government associations (LGAs) are national organizations of, and for, **local governments**. Being membership organizations and not an extra tier of government, LGAs' main functions are to strengthen local government institutions and to represent the voice and interests of the local government sector. LGAs lobby and campaign for the recognition of local government concerns, coordinate policy development, and act as intermediary between central and local governments. In addition, they provide relevant information and services to their members, including **capacity building** and training activities. Around the world, some 120 LGAs exist and most are organized in supra-national organizations such as the International Union of Local Authorities (IULA), United Towns Organization (UTO) and the World Association of Major Cities of the World (METROPOLIS).

See also: capacity building; local government; municipalities; public sector

Further reading

International Union of Local Authorities Association Capacity Building website: http://www.iula-acb.org/

PAUL VAN LINDERT

local knowledge

"Local knowledge" refers to knowledge, practices, skills and values that have developed within a specific social system or geographical area. Though often used synonymously with **indigenous**

knowledge, it encompasses the reality that integrating new ideas from outside with their existing stock of knowledge is important to the ability of societies to survive and develop in a changing world. From the early 1980s, development agencies have rediscovered the important contribution that local knowledge can play in development. Two sectors where particular interest is shown are **health** and **agriculture**, in both of which successful local practices are based on detailed knowledge of the local **environment**.

Local knowledge is often contrasted with knowledge derived from formal research in universities, research institutes and commercial companies. In the past, there has been debate between those arguing that local knowledge provides a more appropriate set of ideas and responses to change and opportunity than external science, and those who suggest that changing circumstances require new knowledge that can most efficiently be generated externally (see **science and technology**). This debate is now recognized as sterile: more important is for local development action to benefit from both sources of knowledge.

Local knowledge is not necessarily shared by everyone in the society or area. Its distribution can reflect power relations, including those based on **gender**. Access to particular knowledge may be one way in which groups maintain or assert authority over others, or maintain their own identity. The way in which local knowledge is integrated into development projects and programs can have significant effects on local power structures and gender relations (see **feminism and ecology**).

Nor is local knowledge static. It evolves partly through local experimentation and observation, and partly through integration of ideas from outside. These processes can be enhanced by development intervention. New solutions to health and farming problems have been developed by local people and scientists pooling their knowledge and skills. Farmers with a propensity to innovate and experiment have become the focal point of programs to develop and share new farming practices.

Valuable local knowledge can also be lost. Its development and sharing depend largely on oral rather than written communication. It can also be supplanted by products incorporating knowledge from elsewhere, such as pesticides that are easier to use than locally developed methods of pest control. The **Earth Summit (1992) (United Nations Conference on Environment and Development)** (Rio Conference) highlighted the dangers of losing local knowledge about **biodiversity** and its maintenance. A lot of research now goes into documenting local knowledge so that it can continue to be a resource for future development, and in facilitating its sharing and exchange within and between geographical areas through mass media, exchange visits and the **Internet**. This wider exposure of local knowledge brings the further danger that powerful commercial interests will acquire **intellectual property rights (IPRs)** to techniques and products based on local expertise.

Increasingly, however, social scientists are beginning to acknowledge that the claim for knowledge to be "local" can be politically advantageous for legitimizing claims in disputes, or that the definition of "local" may be politically imposed by people not of that locality. Indeed, "local" knowledge may also be "situated" knowledge, or knowledge or beliefs reproduced within a research network, scientific or development agency, or specific culture that is not spatially delimited (see Jasanoff and Long, 2004). Part of the analysis of local knowledge, therefore, is increasingly an assessment of how, and by whom, such knowledge is deemed "local," and for which political outcomes.

See also: biodiversity; community-based natural resource management (CBNRM); environment; ethnocentricism; grassroots development; indigenous knowledge

Further reading

Jasanoff, S. and Long, M. (eds) (2004) *Earthly Politics: Local and Global in Environmental Governance*, Cambridge MA: MIT Press.

Pottier, J., Bicker, A. and Sillitoe, P. (eds) (2003) *Negotiating Local Knowledge: Power and Identity in Development*, London: Pluto.

Reij, C. and Waters-Bayer, A. (2001) *Farmer Innovation in Africa: A Source of Inspiration for Agricultural Development*, London: Earthscan.

CHRIS GARFORTH

logging/timber trade

Logging and the timber trade are central topics in international debates on forest conservation and development. Logging refers to operations involving the cutting and removal of trees for processing into industrial products. Industrial forest products are generally classed into primary forest products (industrial roundwood or logs, sawnwood, panels, and pulp and paper) and secondary processed products (moldings, doors, and furniture). The timber trade involves the international buying and selling of these products.

Logging operations can involve the complete removal of all trees from a forest area, as often takes place in Canadian and Russian forests, to selective removal of high-value species, the most common practice in tropical moist forests. The scale of commercial logging has increased substantially in recent years. Industrial production of wood increased by 50 percent between 1961 and 1998, with more than 1.5 billion cubic meters of industrial roundwood produced in 2000 according to the **Food and Agriculture Organization (FAO)** (FAOSTAT online at http://www.fao.org). This roundwood was used to produce 424.5 million cubic meters of sawn wood, 150 million cubic meters of wood-based panels, and 175.5 million tons of pulp. This industrial production accounts for about half of total global roundwood production, with **fuelwood** accounting for the other half.

The global trade in timber and other forest products is substantial. Exports of all forest products have increased both in overall terms, and, except for logs, as a portion of total production. In 2001, over 124 million cubic meters of industrial roundwood was exported. The total export value of all forest products was over US$132 billion and the import value was US$140.9 billion (FAOSTAT). Both imports and exports are dominated by developed countries. Plywood exports are an exception, with Indonesia and Malaysia accounting for the majority of exports. Paper and paperboard products account for almost half the total value of trade in forest products. The global tropical timber trade is insignificant compared to the overall timber trade but is important to many forest-rich, developing countries, frequently accounting for a significant portion of their exports. While developing countries are the main exporters of raw tropical timber, some developed countries have a substantial secondary processing industry reliant on tropical timber.

A number of controversial issues surround the logging and timber trade industries. One issue is the growing consolidation of the sector. **Non-governmental organizations (NGOs)** express concern that **transnational corporations (TNCs)** own increasing percentages of concession rights, processing plants and management contracts for activities like logging in many developing countries. Opponents of **free trade** argue that increased trade will negatively impact on forest sustainability, while proponents argue that **protectionism** affects the profitability of the forest industry.

In terms of environmental impacts, an on-going debate focuses upon the role of logging and the timber trade in the loss and degradation of forest ecosystems. While there is no agreement on its contribution to **deforestation**, logging does affect forest quality through **biodiversity** loss and fragmentation. Often rare, valuable species are removed. Roads open previously inaccessible areas, allowing increased **migration**, clearing for **agriculture** and bushmeat hunting. Logging contributes to **climate change** and might under certain circumstances cause soil erosion (see **soil erosion and soil fertility**), flooding, and socio-economic and cultural impacts.

The International Tropical Timber Agreement was signed originally in 1994 to oversee the trade in tropical timber. Within the last decade, international discussions have begun to focus on illegal logging and associated trade activities. ministerial-level meetings were held in Asia in 2001 and in Africa in 2003, and some countries have signed bilateral agreements in an attempt to address the problem of trade of illegally logged timber.

See also: agroforestry; climate change; deforestation; environment; non-timber forest products (NTFPs); plantation forestry; silviculture

Further reading

See http://www.illegal-logging.info for information on illegal logging and associated trade.

Barbier, E., Burgess, J., Bishop, J. and Aylward, B. (1994) *The Economics of the Tropical Timber Trade*, London: Earthscan.

Dudley, N., Jeanrenaud, J.-P. and Sullivan, F. (1996) *Bad Harvest?: The Timber Trade and the Degradation of the World's Forests*, London: Earthscan.

WYNET SMITH

LOMÉ CONVENTION *see* European Union

London Club

The London Club is an informal grouping of commercial banks that meets to agree the rescheduling of commercial **debt** as a means of **debt relief**. It first met in 1976 in response to Zaire's payment problems, meeting more frequently following the **debt crisis** of the early 1980s. Unlike the **Paris Club**, the London Club has no secretariat, so that its procedures are looser. The main principle is that rescheduling agreements must involve all creditors accounting for at least 90 percent of the debtor's exposure, thus overcoming the free rider problem (i.e. it provides incentives for all parties to contribute). While not formally requiring an **International Monetary Fund (IMF)** agreement for eligibility, London Club debt relief is linked to economic reform efforts. A difference with the Paris Club is that relief on interest payments is not provided; rather new money is given together with a Multi-Year Restructuring Agreement (MYRA). Together the Paris and London Clubs can be seen as a creditors' cartel (see **cartels**).

See also: debt; debt relief; International Monetary Fund (IMF); Paris Club

HOWARD WHITE

malaria

Malaria is a potentially fatal mosquito-borne disorder occurring in tropical and sub-tropical regions. Approximately 40 percent of the world's **population** is at risk of malaria. It predominantly affects those living in the poorest countries and causes over 300 million cases of illness and one million deaths every year (see **mortality**). Of these deaths, 90 percent occur in Sub-Saharan Africa, predominantly among young **children** who have not yet developed immunity to malaria. Following an episode of severe malaria, children may require emergency blood transfusion or develop brain damage. In older children and adults, the disease causes fewer deaths but is associated with anemia. Chronic anemia leads to intellectual impairment and reduced productivity, and in pregnant women it is associated with perinatal mortality and low birth weight (see also **maternal mortality**). It is therefore not surprising that malaria slows a nation's **economic growth** by 1.3 percent every year in endemic areas.

Malaria is transmitted to humans by the bite of an infected Anopheles mosquito and infects the liver and blood cells. Symptoms of *Plasmodium falciparum* infection appear 9–14 days after the infected bite. *Plasmodium falciparum* is the most dangerous of the four types of malaria infection, and accounts for almost all malaria deaths.

At the forefront of the fight against malaria is the Roll Back Malaria (RBM) initiative. This is a global partnership (see **partnerships**) founded in 1998 by the **World Health Organization (WHO)**, United Nations Development Programme, the **United Nations Children's Fund (UNICEF)** and the **World Bank**. RBM "seeks to work with governments, other development agencies, **nongovernmental organizations (NGOs)** and private-sector companies to reduce the human and socio-economic costs of malaria." The partnership aims to halve the world's burden of malaria by 2010 by focusing on ensuring prompt access to treatment, promotion of insecticide-treated mosquito nets, improved vector control, prevention and management of malaria in pregnancy, and improving response to malaria epidemics and malaria in **complex emergencies**. It also encourages research into better **pharmaceuticals** and insecticides, and vaccine development (see **vaccination**). RBM's goal was endorsed in Abuja, Nigeria in 2000 at the world's largest ever heads-of-state summit focused on a single health issue.

RBM has had two major successes – it has raised the visibility of a previously neglected disease and it has built up an extensive partnership of agencies with diverse strengths and expertise. However, it has been criticized for not producing a major impact at ground level in the world's poorest countries. Lack of funding has been a major stumbling block, yet the US$1 billion required each year for implementation of RMB should pay for itself in terms of boosting the **gross domestic product (GDP)** of affected countries. Other problems include lack of **transparency** of resource allocation and flow, and inability to get proven effective interventions out where it really matters – in the poorest communities (see **community**) in endemic countries. These criticisms, highlighted through an external review, have been taken seriously by RBM and have resulted in significant organizational and management changes within the partnership.

See also: disease eradication; health; pharmaceuticals; water management; water-borne diseases; World Health Organization (WHO)

Further reading

Roll Back Malaria website: http://www.rbm.who.int

Yamey, G. (2001) "Global Campaign to Eradicate Malaria," *British Medical Journal* 322: 191–2.

IMELDA BATES

male bias

"Male bias" generally refers to ideas, actions and policies that privilege the rights and **well-being** of males over those of females, whether consciously or not (see also **gender**). In the international development literature, the term originally emerged around two particular issues: the invisibility of women within development projects, and gender **inequality** in macro-economic policy (see **gender and industrialization**). "Male bias" was used to indicate that the theories and tools of development are gender-blind, not gender-neutral as often presented. Without an explicit recognition of gender inequalities, development interventions are destined to reinforce them. Alongside the shift from **women in development (WID) versus gender and development (GAD)** approaches, it has become more common to refer to "gender bias." At the same time, the assumption that gender-based discrimination disproportionately affects women and girls remains largely intact. "Male bias" and "gender bias" are now used to identify and expose the unequal position of women and girls in every sphere, from **intrahousehold allocations** of food, to international trade regimes.

Male bias has been experienced in development projects. Robert Chambers (1983) has written of "male bias" as a subset of "person bias" – one of six biases that obstruct outsiders' contact with **rural poverty** and adversely affect project outcomes (see also **urban bias**). Chambers noted that the great majority of development workers, government officials and **poverty** researchers are men, and that it is with other men that they tend to engage. In this way, women are excluded from consultation and participation, and it is the needs and interests of men that inform the design and delivery of development projects. Chambers notes that this occurs in a field dedicated to poverty reduction despite the disproportionate prevalence of poverty among women, particularly widows and (arguably) **women-headed households**.

The past two decades have seen significant improvements in the proportion of women working in development-related fields, and the extent to which women are targeted in development projects (see **targeting**). However, often couched in terms of biology, tradition and **culture**, male bias in development projects remains common. For instance, Hanks *et al.* (1999) identified male bias within the selection process of **Community livestock** workers (CLWs) in Ghana. Although one-third to one-half of the clients of CLWs are women, only about 7 percent of selection groups are gender-balanced, and about 6 percent of selected CLWs are women. Respondents cited social norms surrounding women's independence, mobility and workload, as well as perceptions of their physical strength, as constraints to women's participation in selection and effectiveness as CLWs. While there is no direct discrimination (i.e. rules forbidding women's involvement), women are disproportionately discouraged from participating in selection groups or as CLWs, due to male biases in organizational culture and working environment.

Male bias also affects macro-economic policy. Elson (1995) argued that male bias not only disadvantages women and girls but also undermines the success of the development endeavor as a whole. Building on earlier debates around the invisibility and **marginalization** of women's work, Elson argued that unequal entitlements within the household (see **food security; intrahousehold allocations**), based on socially constructed perceptions of women's roles, lay the foundation for pervasive male bias at every level. The apparent gender-neutrality of economic, social and political structures allows policy-makers and researchers to take male standards as the norm and established gender relations for granted.

Much macro-economic policy – particularly **structural adjustment** – and **labor markets** exhibit gender inequalities. Even without the direct restrictions on women's participation in economic life that continue to exist around the world, markets are far from being level playing fields. Economic models, theories, **institutions** and policies of development, while not intrinsically gendered, become "bearers of gender" via normative gender relations. Equal access to productive resources and economic opportunities cannot emerge on the basis of differential access to social networks, to basic services including **education** and **health**, and, importantly, to mobility and time. Elson (1998) argues that budgeting frameworks, like growth models, are male-biased in several ways. They fail to recognize that women's contribution to the macro-economy is underestimated because of missing and biased markets and incomplete statistics. They ignore the fact that there is an unpaid economy (which has variously been labeled "domestic," "social reproduction," "reproductive") in which women do most of the work of caring for and maintaining the labor force and the social framework or **social capital** (neighborhood networks and **voluntary sector** organizations, formal and informal) – both vital for the paid economy. They do not consider that the parameters of aggregate production, savings, investment, imports and exports in the paid economy may be sensitive to different patterns of gender relations and gender distribution of resources.

Structural adjustment policies developed based on these inaccurate assumptions have been criticized for disproportionately placing the weight of reform on women's shoulders, facilitating the "feminization of poverty." In particular, cuts in public expenditure have been noted to increase the burden on the overwhelmingly female workforce of the care economy.

See also: gender; gender and industrialization; gender and poverty; intrahousehold allocations; urban bias; women in development (WID) versus gender and development (GAD)

Further reading

Chambers, R. (1983) *Rural Development: Putting the Last First*, London: Intermediate Technology.

Elson, D. (ed.) (1995) *Male Bias in the Development Process*, 2nd edn, Manchester: Manchester University Press.

Elson, D. (1998) "Integrating Gender Issues Into National Budgetary Policies and Procedures," *Journal of International Development* 10: 929–41.

Hanks, J., Oakeley, R., Opoku, H., Dasebu, S. and Asaga, J. (1999) *A Critical Analysis of the Selection and Support of Community Livestock Workers in Ghana*, University of Reading Department of Agriculture/Ministry of Food and Agriculture, Ghana.

Jackson, C. and Pearson, R. (eds) (1998) *Feminist Visions of Development: Gender Analysis and Policy*, London: Routledge.

Kabeer, N. (1994) *Reversed Realities: Gender Hierarchies in Development Thought*, London: Verso.

KAREN MOORE

malnutrition

Malnutrition is an anomalous physiological condition characterized by continuous deficiencies, excesses or imbalances in energy, protein and micronutrients intake and/or absorption (see **nutrition**). In developed nations, major symptoms of malnutrition commonly comprise overweight, obesity and diet-related diseases. In developing countries, main manifestations of malnutrition usually include wasting, stunting, or underweight, reduced cognitive ability, poor health status and low productivity. But both types of symptoms may be found in both developed and developing countries, and in recent years, obesity has become more common in many developing countries.

The term "malnutrition" is often used to mean undernutrition, namely the inadequate nutritional status of a population belonging to the poor socio-economic groups of developing countries. The **Food and Agriculture Organization (FAO)** also distinguishes between undernutrition and undernourishment. The latter is when individual nutrient intake falls below an established minimum which is deemed necessary for maintaining an adequate **health** and allowing an adequate level of activity. The former is the outcome of undernourishment, and/or poor absorption and/or poor biological use of nutrients consumed.

There are two major approaches to quantify malnutrition: nutritional intake and anthropometric measures. Measures of nutritional intake estimate the quantity of dietary energy per-capita availability *vis-à-vis* a norm for the lowest acceptable per capita intake of calories. Measures are at the level of individuals, households or countries. Individual intakes are quantified through retrospective, current or prospective reporting of consumption. Household intakes are based on expenditure surveys. Country estimates, such as that of FAO, are based on the number of calories available for human consumption and their distribution across households. The individuals or the households that fail to meet the calorie cut-off point are classified as undernourished. These methods are likely to provide an estimate of the risk of the population or individuals to inadequacy of food, rather than of the actual number of undernourished.

The second approach to quantify malnutrition compares anthropometric characteristics of the individuals or of a representative sample of individuals within a population *vis-à-vis* threshold physiological parameters that indicate inadequate intake or absorption of **food** for a long period of time, or as a result of seasonal fluctuations. These measures reflect the past nutritional history of individuals and are complements to intake measures. The most frequently used anthropometric measures are wasting (low weight for height), stunting (low height for age) and underweight (low weight for age) for **children** in the 0–5 years age group, and body mass index (thinness) and low birth weight (associated with poor nutrition of mothers) for adults. The **World Health Organization (WHO)** continuously updates its Global Database on Child Growth and Malnutrition.

Although the ultimate cause of malnutrition is inadequate food intake and absorption, a multiplicity of socio-economic processes and variables interact to determine the malnutrition problems. Achieving the Millennium Development Goal of eradicating extreme **poverty** and hunger by 2015

(see **Millennium Development Goals (MDGs)**) may thus require a variety of socio-economic policies, such as increasing food availability, enhancing income and entitlements (see **food security**), providing **drinking water**, health services, and improved and widespread **education**.

See also: famine; food; Food and Agriculture Organization (FAO); food security; health; nutrition; poverty; World Health Organization (WHO)

Further reading

Food and Agriculture Organization (2003) *Measurement and Assessment of Food Deprivation and Undernutrition*, Rome: FAO.

Latham, M. C. (1997) *Human Nutrition in the Developing World*, Rome: FAO.

UGO PICA CIAMARRA

Malthusian demography

Malthusian demography refers to approaches to **population** studies influenced by the economist Thomas Malthus (1766–1834). Malthus published anonymously *An Essay on the Principle of Population* in 1798 (First Essay), the objective which was to refute the writings of his Utopian contemporaries, including Condorcet, Godwin and Smith. The First Essay was widely received, and Malthus began work on a revised and much-expanded Second Essay (1803), which discussed how social organization and government influence economic and demographic outcomes.

Malthus is best known for his "Principle of Population," which states that population tends to increase faster than the means of subsistence, unless controlled by "positive" and "preventive" checks. In the absence of such checks, Malthus hypothesized that human populations had the capacity to grow at a geometric rate (1, 2, 4, 8, 16, 32, etc.) and the means of subsistence at an arithmetic rate (1, 2, 3, 4, 5, etc.). Positive checks cause a reduction in the rate of population growth by increasing **mortality** through mechanisms such as **war**, disease and **famine**. Preventive checks (introduced in the Second Essay) reduce the rate of population growth by reducing **fertility** principally because of "moral restraint," including delayed marriage and sexual abstinence. Malthus considered contraception (**family planning**) and abortion to be vices, and not appropriate as positive checks. Malthus drew his conclusions based on a wide range of contemporary data, particularly the rapid rate of population growth in the USA.

Malthus was very influential among nineteenth-century economists. However, events served to confound much of his theorizing, and critics of Malthus highlight his inability to predict the uptake of new technology, particularly agrarian advances, at the time of his writing. Throughout most of the nineteenth and twentieth centuries, per capita income and wage rates increased and fertility declined. For example, fertility had begun to decline in France before 1830. Malthus' hypotheses have been tested extensively using historical data, which demonstrate that the relative effects on population growth of the preventive checks were considerably greater than those of the positive checks.

Malthus has had an enduring influence on many writers and researchers in a wide range of disciplines. In biology, for example, his works influenced Darwin's writing on the theory of evolution and natural selection. Critics of Malthusian approaches are many, and include Marx, Boserup and Julian Simon. A diverse group of twentieth-century researchers have been labeled "neo-Malthusian," linked by a similar pessimistic outlook about the relationship between population and resources. Notable neo-Malthusians include Meadows *et al.* (the authors of the **Limits to Growth report (1972)**), Paul Ehrlich and Anne Ehrlich, Garrett Hardin, Norman Myers, and the Worldwatch Institute. Whichever perspective predominates, Malthus can be credited with developing a simple but powerful theoretical scheme that continues to be debated two centuries after it was first elaborated.

See also: environment; *Limits to Growth* report (1972); overpopulation; population

Further reading

Dupâquier, J., Fauve-Chamoux, A. and Grebenik, E. (eds) (1983) *Malthus Past and Present*, London: Academic Press.

McNicoll, G. (1998) "Malthus for the Twenty-First Century," *Population and Development Review* 24:20: 309–16.

ERNESTINA COAST

maquiladoras

The most common usage of the term "maquiladoras" has been to refer to foreign-owned production units in Mexico taking advantage of lower Mexican labor costs. The more general usage of the term refers to the relocation by foreign companies of one or several of their production facilities to low-cost countries. These factories are relocated to take advantage not only of lower labor costs, but also of the relaxed enforcement of environmental and workplace safety standards and the duty-free importation of production supplies such as raw materials, equipment, machinery, replacement parts, and other items needed for the assembly or manufacture of finished goods. Depending on the legal regime of the country in which it operates, a maquiladora may export its finished product or sell it in the market of the country in which it is located, subject to certain restrictions that vary from country to country.

See also: brown environmental agenda; environment; gender and industrialization; North American Free Trade Agreement (NAFTA); pollution; pollution havens; transnational corporations (TNCs)

RICHARD M. J. THURSTON

marginalization

Marginalization is an umbrella term for processes of impoverishment or disempowerment that make people or specific social groups "at the margin" of mainstream **economic development** or political representation. Marginalized people are therefore commonly the target of much development intervention, although some critics of development have suggested that some interventions have only added to processes of marginalization (see structural adjustment; postmodernism and postdevelopment). Different approaches to development focus on varying means of marginalization. Economists may identify how different countries, regions or firms may become marginalized in global markets and hence less competitive. Marxist analysts (see **Marxism**) propose that marginalization occurs when surplus value is extracted from workers or regions that produce wealth for others (this may also occur internationally, such as argued under **dependency theory**). Other social and political theorists highlight how marginalization may be occurring with **gender, caste**s, race (see **race and racism**), ethnicity (see **ethnicity/identity**), and **disability** (see **social exclusion; sociology of development**). Marginalization may also be based in discourses of development reflecting historic colonial regimes (see **postcolonialism**), **urban bias**, and **male bias**. It is important, however, to avoid assuming that specific groups are always marginalized (see **culture of poverty**), but instead analysts should see the various short- and long-term factors that make specific individuals and social groups marginalized. Some forms of **poverty measurement** may rely on **poverty line**s or people in **poverty trap**s to indicate who are marginalized. Lack of **citizenship** or **asylum seeking** may be further political indicators of marginalization.

See also: asylum seeking; chronic poverty; dependency theory; disability; empowerment; Fourth World; poverty; poverty trap; social exclusion; stateless people; vulnerability

TIM FORSYTH

market socialism

Market socialism can be defined as a theoretical concept and an economic policy model that assumes the public ownership of the majority of land and capital used in larger-scale production, and the minimization of governmental control over productive enterprises. Unearned income (rent, interest, profits) becomes public property evenly distributed among members of the public.

A fundamental aim of market socialism proponents is to reconcile market "efficiency" with "equity."

The argument for market socialism is associated with the work of Oskar Lange, who endeavored in the 1920s to 1930s to devise a socialist equivalent to an idealized perfectly competitive **capitalism**. Such a theoretical position was underpinned by a belief in the allocative efficiency afforded by earned income differentials. This signified the abandonment of the notion of exploitation based on surplus-value extraction in favor of adopting the methodological individualism and subjectivism of neo-classical economics.

Lange's arguments developed from what has been called the "calculation debate," which involved socialists of neo-classical ilk and critics from the Austrian school, such as Hayek and von Mises. The debate revolved about the relative systemic efficiency in accounting for the market price of goods and services in capitalist and socialist systems. Lange envisioned a "Central Planning Board" (CPB) as a principal mechanism to set prices by receiving regular inventory reports from all businesses, harmonizing prices to commodity volume. The CPB would additionally guarantee the efficient allocation of new investment resources by establishing new businesses in sectors earning above-average profits, thereby pre-empting monopolies.

Lange's original ideas have been resuscitated and modified during the 1980s and 1990s to compensate for argumentative weaknesses derived from a reliance on neo-classical assumptions of equilibrium conditions and optimality in the distribution of information, and from an inadequate accounting for incentives and monitoring. Yunker (2001) identifies three market socialist approaches that have been proposed to improve upon Lange's earlier position. The first is Yunker's own position on market socialism, which he names "pragmatic socialism," which would retain capitalist market **institutions**, but establish a revenue redistribution mechanism. Due to the decoupling of enterprise ownership from managerial control in late capitalism, the crucial component, in Yunker's scheme, becomes one of providing a set of incentives for firm managers, rather than owners, to maximize productivity, "efficiency," or innovation rates. Under such a regime, the majority of citizens would not own the instruments of ownership over capital property, except for that pertaining to small-scale enterprise. This would be the case because large-scale property would be publicly owned and returns on property, such as rent, would be redistributed among citizens as dividends.

A second approach to market socialism can be categorized as "service socialism," whereby profit maximization is replaced by output constraints or revenue maximization through state planning, regulation, and incentives (see **state and state reform**). The literature on the **nationalization** of principal industries is frequently associated with this approach, and there are affinities with fractions of the "dependencia" school (related to **dependency theory**). In contrast, a "cooperative socialism" view would entail the governing of enterprises by employees for their own benefit. Despite similarities, this notion departs considerably from Marx's ideas, as employees situated within firms characterized by a high organic composition of capital would obtain more return compared to employees in enterprises based on more **labor-intensive** production methods, thereby maintaining economic **inequality**.

The most notable and controversial contributors to the reformulation of Lange's model have been Roemer and Bardhan. Their version of market socialism would differ from capitalism in five main aspects: the government redistribution of stocks according to birth-right, the nationalization of all banks, the determination of corporate management through the election of delegates from the main lending institutions, the firm's employees, and the stockholders, government investment planning through differential interest rates, and the nationalization (with stock redistribution to the public) of businesses that exceed a certain size or whose founder has died.

Though partially addressing the problems of incentives and monitoring, the Roemer-Bardhan approach exhibits some of the problematic neoclassical assumptions underlying the Lange model, namely Pareto optimality, which ignores distributive justice and innovation issues, and the Walrasian equilibrium framework, which implies fully knowledgeable optimizing market subjects. In the end, all the above market socialist models suffer from the market inefficiencies resulting from individualistic investment decisions, and concentrate merely on notions of distribution and efficiency at the expense of analyzing property relations and the social processes of production and knowledge formation.

See also: capitalism; communes, collectives and cooperatives; Marxism; redistribution with growth; postsocialism

Further reading

Kowalik, T. (1994) *Economic Theory and Market Socialism: Selected Essays of Oskar Lange*, Aldershot: Edward Elgar.

Milonakis, D. (2003) "New Market Socialism: A Case for Rejuvenation or Inspired Alchemy?" *Cambridge Journal of Economics* 27:1 97–121.

Ollman, B. (1998) *Market Socialism: The Debate among Socialists*, New York: Routledge.

Roemer, J. (1994) *A Future for Socialism*, Cambridge MA: Harvard University Press.

Yunker, J. (2001) *On the Political Economy of Market Socialism: Essays and analyses*, Aldershot: Ashgate.

SALVATORE ENGEL-DI MAURO

Marshall Plan

The Marshall Plan, known officially as the European Recovery Program (ERP), was a US plan intended to reconstruct post-World War II European economies while containing communist influence. It takes its name from the speech made by General George Marshall at Harvard in 1947. After approval by Congress in 1948, the USA donated more than US$13 billion between 1948 and 1952 to sixteen Western European countries constituted as OEEC (Organization for European Economic Cooperation). **Aid** was provided through the Plan almost entirely on a grant basis. It is an example of tied aid, as almost three quarters of the goods financed through the Plan came from the USA, consisting mostly of commodity aid (especially **food aid**). Generally acclaimed as a success, the Marshall Plan contributed to the construction of a new international order, and provided a paradigm for aid provision to Southern countries.

See also: aid; European Union; food aid; World Bank

BENEDETTA ROSSI

Marxism

Karl Marx famously wrote very little on the problems of what are now called developing countries. But this has not prevented the emergence of a vibrant and disputatious crop of Marxist writings on development and underdevelopment (see **underdevelopment versus less developed country (LDC) versus Third World**), with scholars and activists from different backgrounds laying claim to the master's "true" legacy. Curiously, this legacy was first seized by a group of neo-Marxists who borrowed more from Lenin than Marx. Their work was challenged in the 1970s by "classical Marxists" who focused on the laws of motion of **capitalism** and the articulation of modes of production. In the 1980s, an impasse was identified in radical development studies, and this prompted a search, in some quarters, for post-Marxian alternatives. The postcolonial turn of the 1990s (see **postcolonialism**) further called into question the "economism" of some Marxist accounts of development, and encouraged the production of texts that combined the undoubted insights of Marxism with those of Max Weber, say, or Michel Foucault.

When Karl Marx wrote on India for the *New York Herald* in 1853 he declared that the ruling classes of Great Britain were intent on turning India into a "reproductive country." They would do this by "gift[ing] her with the means of **irrigation** and of internal communication." This perspective, it would later be argued, was entirely consistent with Marx's understanding of capitalism and its laws of motion. No matter how much Marx reviled capitalism for its **violence** and exploitation, as well as its necessary tendencies to overproduction and instability, he did not accuse it of a lack of dynamism. Capitalism ensured that "all that is solid melts into air," and that production

systems and their accompanying infrastructures would constantly be revolutionized by the bourgeoisie's incessant search for profits. Exploitation, for Marx, occurred at the point of production, rather than between countries or regions.

This perspective was considerably revised in the wake of World War I and Lenin's work on imperialism (see **colonialism, history of; colonialism, impacts of**). Left-wing movements were now faced with the need to explain the behavior of working-class men in the trenches (the apparent appeal of **nationalism**), and, later, with the defense of the Soviet Union against its enemies. Lenin suggested that the era of competitive capitalism that Marx addressed in *Capital* had disappeared. In its place had emerged a system of monopoly capitalism in which bank capitals had merged with industrial capitals, and where the export of capital had acquired exceptional importance. Imperialism, Lenin suggested, represented the highest stage of capitalism (Lenin, 1970). International combines were now forming to share the world economy among themselves, and to complete a territorial division of the world between the major capitalist powers. The Scramble for Africa was one sign of this, and it pointed to a world in which the contradictions of capitalism would be generalized from the workplace to a struggle between nation-states. Not inconveniently, the defense of the Soviet Union in the 1920s and 1930s could then be linked to a wider anti-imperialist struggle. The theory of imperialism resonated with work emerging from India on the "drain of wealth" that was impoverishing South Asia for Great Britain's benefit. Dadabhai Naoroji and R. C. Dutt were prominent exponents of this theory.

What might be called the specialization of Marx was further extended in the 1950s by Paul Baran and Paul Sweezy, two leading lights in the *Monthly Review* school of US Marxism. Baran, in particular, who published *The Political Economy of Growth* in 1957, recognized that it was hard to sell a theory of class conflict and pauperization within the USA, notwithstanding the appalling plight of many black Americans. His critique of capitalism took the form of a moralizing assault upon US consumerism, together with a more serious analysis of what he called the problem of "inadequate investment outlets" in the USA – indeed, in the core areas of capitalism more generally. Baran argued that because "individual firms cannot be expected to function as Santa Claus to their workers and buyers in order to increase mass consumption" (1957:211), it fell to government to maintain fullish **employment** by spending on the military and by shifting investment overseas. Much like Lenin, Baran argued that it was the contradictions of monopoly capitalism that drove capital from its core areas to a periphery that would accept its exports and provide it with cheap imports. "The backward world ... represented the indispensable hinterland of the highly developed capitalist West" (*ibid.*:120).

Baran's work should properly be seen as the first in a long line of neo-Marxist works that brought radical scholars into conflict with the modernization theories of the 1950s and 1960s (see **modernization theory**). Where Bert Hoselitz once said that "if there are developed or 'advanced' countries in the present, they must at some time have been underdeveloped;" Andre Gunder Frank replied that, "the developed countries were never underdeveloped, though they may have been undeveloped" (Frank, 1967) (see **dependency theory**). Frank turned "underdevelopment" into an active verb, and in the process insisted that Latin America had been exploited and impoverished from the time of Cortez and Pizarro, just as Africa had been robbed blind since the time of Rhodes, and India from the time of Clive. More so than Baran, Frank maintained that capitalism had always produced development and underdevelopment as two sides of the same coin; this was not an outcome of monopoly capitalism alone. Frank's model of the "development of underdevelopment" further maintained that there was no possibility of **industrialization** within a capitalist world economy that used its circuits of unequal exchange to transfer wealth and commodities cheaply from the periphery to the core. The periphery could only industrialize at moments of weakness in the core (during wars or depressions), or by de-linking from what Wallerstein would later call the modern world system (Wallerstein, 1979) (see **world systems theory**). Frank pointed to Japan as proof of his theory – Japan had developed because it had not been colonized by the capitalist powers. He also looked to countries like Cuba and China to show the rest of the "Third World" a way out of their misery. The choice, said Frank, echoing Rosa Luxemburg, was between socialism and barbarism.

The strong language and evocative spatial metaphors of Frank's work gave it an undoubted appeal in the 1960s and 1970s, not least at the time of the war in Vietnam. But while his work is often lumped together with the work of other Latin American writers in the *dependencia* school, it is important to note that writers like Osvaldo Sunkel and Fernando Henrique Cardoso rejected the binary "logics" of Frank's brand of neo-Marxism. Cardoso, in particular, preferred to think of "dependency" as a set of conditioning relationships between developed and developing countries. These relationships were undoubtedly asymmetrical, and had been imposed by colonial regimes, but they could be contested and reshaped to some degree. Stronger national bourgeoisies could forge accumulation strategies of their own, and could hope to challenge unfair trading regimes and the powers of **transnational corporations (TNCs)**. The demand for a new **international economic order** in the 1970s spoke to this agenda, as did the strategy of the **Organization of Petroleum Exporting Countries (OPEC)** countries at the time of the oil price rises of 1973–4. In some respects, too, as Gabriel Palma (1978) showed in a justly famous review article, the work of Cardoso had less in common with Frank's work than it did with work carried out by Raul Prebisch and Dudley Seers in the 1950s. That work, and the work of the **Economic Commission for Latin America and the Caribbean (ECLAC)** structuralists more generally, had insisted that poorer countries were damaged by a world trading system which penalized countries producing non-industrial goods. Despite the predictions of **comparative advantage** theory, the income **terms of trade** seemed to move against primary commodities, and this strengthened the case for **import substitution**-type **industrialization**.

The pessimism of Frank's work was further challenged in the 1970s by the work of the Scottish communist Bill Warren. Warren argued that the **decolonization** movements of the 1950s and 1960s had liberated most Southern countries from imperialism, and had set them free to be capitalist. Imperialism was the pioneer of capitalism in the developing world. The proof of this, he said, was to be seen in the extraordinary industrial success stories that could now be seen in semi-peripheral (Greece, Spain, Turkey) and peripheral (South Korea, Taiwan, Malaysia) countries. Furthermore, this was what Marx would have expected. Putting the cat firmly among the pigeons, Warren charged that Frank and his fellow neo-Marxists had led the left down a blind alley of "non-Marxism." Frank's model was logically unsound because it suggested that one and the same cause (capitalism) had different effects (development and under-development) in different parts of the world system (see **world systems theory**). And it was empirically unsound for the reasons just mentioned: in Cardoso's memorable phrase, "history, had prepared a trap for the pessimists."

Warren was roundly abused on the Left before his premature death in 1979. In the 1980s, however, in the wake of an important article by Robert Brenner in the *New Left Review* in 1977, his contribution was taken more seriously. Like Warren, Brenner shifted the debate "back to Marx," and he did so by insisting that the West had developed mainly for "autocentric" reasons. Brenner argued that both Britain and Spain had benefitted from unequal trading relationships with their colonies, but only in Britain did these flows of money and commodities help to fuel an industrial revolution. In Spain, the money was mainly squandered at court and in conspicuous consumption. Feudalism remained the dominant mode of production. In Britain, by contrast, the revenues flowed to a nascent class of capitalists (agrarian and industrial) that had emerged in the wake of the English Revolution and the enclosure movements. They used the revenues to support the further industrialization of the UK, but this development was not dependent on the under-development of Britain's colonies, as Frank had maintained. Britain's relationships with its colonies were also more as Marx had predicted. Wherever capitalism took root there would be **economic growth** and development, as in pockets of the Bombay Presidency. Where it was absent or held back there would be under-development (see **underdevelopment versus less developed country (LDC) versus Third World**).

Brenner's paper appeared at a time when a new generation of radical scholars was returning to Marx to seek fresh insights into "the laws of motion of capitalism." Many of them turned to a group of French structural Marxists (including P. P. Rey and Claude Meillassoux), who argued that the dualistic landscapes of developing countries could be explained by the interaction, or articulation, of pre-capitalist modes of production with small islands of capitalism. To distinguish them-selves from modernization theories, however (see **modernization theory**), and to maintain an edge of pessimism, scholars like Harold Wolpe, writing of **apartheid** South Africa, insisted that there was no reason for the pre-capitalist modes of production to give way in the face of a more dynamic capitalism. It could suit South Africa's ruling capitalist class to maintain and reproduce pre-capitalist regions as sources of cheap labor. The fictional independence of the Bantustans allowed white capitalists to discharge to the black "home-lands" the full costs of the social reproduction of mines labor, including spending on **education** and health care.

The apparent functionalism of this solution would later provoke David Booth (1985) and others to maintain that Marxist development sociology had run out of steam. In Booth's view, Marxism had reached an impasse both theoretically (its economism made it blind to questions of culture, resistance and state formation, for example) and politically (it was hard to see how War-ren's conclusions were so different from those of Walt Rostow, see **stages of economic growth**). Several Marxist writers made a spirited response to this charge, and rightly pointed out that Marxists had produced important work on a vast range of "development" issues. Marxist-inspired scholar-ship had produced key texts on the relative autonomy of the state (Mouzelis, 1978; see **state and state reform**), on the production of **famine**s in the wake of colonialism (Watts, 1983; see **colonialism, history of; colonialism, impacts of**), on the pricing strategies of TNCs (Girvan, 1976), and on the production of environmental problems (Blaikie, 1985), to name just four areas. Others were less defensive and went in search of "post-Marxist" alternatives. In part, these took their cue from the work of Cutler *et al.* (1977) on capitalism's relations of production and their conditions of existence. Instead of thinking of a mode of production as a whole (a "totality"), Cutler *et al.* (1977) suggested that capitalism could profitably be theorized as a complex mix of necessary relationships (capitalism without a system of free waged labor would be a contradiction in terms), and contingent relationships (capitalism could be managed in all manner of ways, as the different histories of "capitalist" countries like the UK, the US and Sweden made clear). This being the case, it made no sense to expect, or look for, a singular model of capitalist development. The precise ways in which capitalism was made flesh in different regions had to do with local traditions, resource endowments and systems of rule.

The recognition of difference that this conclusion pointed toward would later be reinforced by the postcolonial turn, and a fresh assault on what were now called "metanarratives" (grand models of capitalism, modernization or Westernization; see **narratives of development**). Not all Marxists accepted the thrust of this critique, of course, and some have strongly resisted what they see as its more relativizing instincts (see **cultural relativism**). A broadly Marxist outlook has also inspired important recent work on the Indian economy (Harriss-White, 2003), on new conceptions of empire, and on the emergence of a **transnational capitalist class (TCC)** (Sklair, 2001). For the most part, though, at least since the end of the **Cold War**, an earlier faith in socialist development strategies has been diminished. Marxist accounts of development are now more likely to be found as part of a broader oppositional imagination that seeks inspiration also from Gramsci and Gandhi, as well as from Weber and Foucault. Like all vibrant intellectual traditions, Marxism continues to adapt and move on.

See also: capitalism; Cold War; colonialism, history of; colonialism, impacts of; commercialization; commodification; dependency theory; deskilling; Economic Commission for Latin America and the Caribbean (ECLAC); international economic order; marginalization; postcolonialism; postsocialism; revolution; sociology of development; transnational capitalist class (TCC); transnational corporations (TNCs); underdevelopment versus less developed country (LDC) versus Third World; world systems theory

Further reading

Baran, P. (1973 [1957]) *The Political Economy of Growth*, Harmondsworth: Penguin.

Blaikie, P. (1985) *The Political Economy of Soil Erosion*, London: Methuen.

Brenner, R. (1977) "The Origins of Capitalist Development: A Critique of Neo-Smithian Marxism" *New Left Review* 104: 25–92.

Booth, D. (1985) "Marxist Sociology: Interpreting the Impasse," *World Development* 13: 761–87.

Corbridge, S. (1990) "Post-Marxism Studies: Beyond the Impasse," *World Development* 18:5 623–39.

Cutler, A., Hindess, B., Hirst, P. and Hussain, A. (1977) *Marx's Capital and Capitalism Today*, 2 vols, London: Routledge and Kegan Paul.

Frank, A. G. (1967) *Capitalism and Underdevelopment in Latin America*, New York: Monthly Review Press.

Girvan, N. (1976) *Corporate Imperialism*, New York: Monthly Review Press.

Harriss-White, B. (2003) *India Working*, Cambridge: Cambridge University Press.

Lenin, V. I. (1970) *Imperialism: The Highest Stage of Capitalism*, Peking: Foreign Languages Press.

Marx, K. (1976 [1867]) *Capital, Volume 1*, Harmondsworth: Penguin.

Marx, K. and Engels, F. (1967 [1848]) *The Communist Manifesto*, Harmondsworth: Penguin.

Mouzelis, N. (1978) *Modern Greece: Facets of Underdevelopment*, London: Macmillan.

Palma, G. (1978) "Dependency: A Formal Theory of Underdevelopment, or a Methodology for the Analysis of Concrete Situations of Underdevelopment?" *World Development* 6: 881–924.

Sklair, L. (2001) *The Transnational Capitalist Class*, Oxford: Blackwell.

Wallerstein, I. (1974) *The Modern World System*, New York: Academic Press.

Warren, B. (1980) *Imperialism: Pioneer of Capitalism*, London: Verso.

Watts, M. (1983) *Silent Violence: Food, Famine and Peasantry in Northern Nigeria*, Berkeley: University of California Press.

Wolpe, H. (ed.) (1980) *The Articulation of Modes of Production*, London: Routledge and Kegan Paul.

STUART CORBRIDGE

maternal mortality

Maternal mortality refers to death rates among mothers. **United Nations** statistics suggest that more than 50 million women experience poor reproductive health, or illness and **disability** related to pregnancy, and an estimated half million die each year from these reasons. Risks are highest in Sub-Saharan Africa, where they may reach 1-in-16 lifetime risk of dying from maternal causes, compared with 1-in-3,500 risk in North America.

Maternal mortality occurs mainly through lack of reproductive health care, and inadequately spaced births. Immediate causes of death include hemorrhages, infections, hypertension and obstructed labor. Skilled medical staff attend relatively few births. Women may lack money for health care, or may lack permission from male partners. Other factors include distance from health services and multiple demands on women's time. There are also restrictions on advice and treatment before birth (antenatal care). The **World Health Organization (WHO)** estimates that the percentage of women who seek antenatal care is 63 percent in Africa, 65 percent in Asia, and 73 percent in Latin America and the Caribbean, but that national levels may vary greatly: in Nepal an estimated 15 percent of women receive antenatal care.

Maternal mortality is also an indirect cause of **infant and child mortality**. Both have been included in the **Millennium Development Goals (MDGs)**, which aim to reduce the maternal mortality ratio by three quarters between 1990 and 2015. Providing greater **primary health care**, midwives, antibiotics, **nutrition** (especially concerning iodine), and rapid access to emergency obstetrical care are key means of achieving this target. However, addressing maternal mortality also implies increasing the availability and understanding of **family planning** and **reproductive rights**, which in turn also imply empowering the position and **education** of women in many societies, and reducing **poverty**. Allowing greater health care where pregnancies are terminated is also a priority, although frequently this involves engaging with practices that are either suppressed by law or by custom. A recent study (Koblinsky and Campbell, 2003) listed six factors necessary for addressing maternal mortality: the availability of a trained attendant at births who can either assist or refer mothers for help elsewhere; facilities that can provide obstetric care; financing of services (not necessarily reliant on insurance); strong government policies favoring safe motherhood; a functioning referral system for higher levels of medical assistance; and an awareness of how cultural factors may enhance or restrict access to health care in different locations.

See also: amniocentesis (sex-selection); family planning; gender and communicable disease; infant and child mortality; HIV/AIDS (policy issues); Millennium Development Goals (MDGs); nutrition; sexually transmitted diseases (STDs); reproductive rights

Further reading

Koblinsky, M. and Campbell, O. (eds) (2003) *Reducing Maternal Mortality: Case Studies in Development*, Washington DC: World Bank.

MacLean, A. and Neilson, J. (eds) (2002) *Maternal Morbidity and Mortality*, London: RCOG Press.

Regional Prevention of Maternal Mortality Network, A Network of NGOs working to Prevent Maternal Deaths in Sub-Saharan Africa: http://www.rpmm.org/

TIM FORSYTH

measuring development

Measuring development is an important methodological debate concerning the appraisal of development in specific contexts. It is a background to the more specific development of **indicators of development** discussed elsewhere.

Measuring any process inevitably involves reducing it to a series of numbers or geographical units, and assumptions about how these numbers are made. One major assumption is that the definition of development is itself logical. For example, the forms of **capitalism** promulgated by global agencies such as the **International Monetary Fund (IMF)** and **World Bank**, define development more as a production process. As a result, measures conventionally focus on two data groupings: "system variables (e.g. **population**, **gross national product (GNP)** or **gross national product (GNP) per capita**, military expenditure) and aggregate variables based on data about individuals (e.g. literacy level, average **life expectancy**, **employment** level)" (Galtung, 2003; see also **illiteracy**). Neither of these groups makes allowance for **culture** or political system. Indeed, measurements of development often assume away heterogeneity of society, culture, and **politics**.

In most measures, development is "produced" through factors such as economic **productivity** and **economic growth** (per capita **gross domestic product (GDP)**), the extent to which developing countries emulate Western levels of **industrialization**, governmental agency restructuring (see **new public management (NPM)**), the growth of liberal markets, expanding **education**, access to health care, and legislative reform. Such factors can be measured quantitatively. Conversely, development is "consumed" by individual human beings, but factors such as "quality of life," "**community** participation," or "**wellbeing**" are not easily addressed by numerical measurement. Consequently, the measurement of development tends to focus on a diversity of individual measurements that are used to construct an indicator.

Measurement is used in a number of ways. First, it can be a process of checking that something is happening. Second, it can be used to check whether what is happening is what was expected, and that it is progressing at the expected rate, for example through performance management and audit. The measurement of "progress" is itself controversial because it is so broadly defined. Third, it can be used to identify where an entity (typically a country) lies in a league list of other entities. Fourth, it can be used

to check variations within an entity rather than between entities.

For that reason time and space are critical influences in measurement. The usual evaluation period is a calendar year, since this is the administrative reporting time frame of governments (tax years) or UN agencies (calendar years). "Progress" or otherwise is measured as the difference between a measurement made one year with that of a previous year. However, that temporal comparison assumes temporal homogeneity of information, with all nations reporting data for the same dates, something not always possible in advanced nations.

Geography is a critical influence. The global measurement of development is dominantly focused on the country, and UN indicators such as the **Human Development Index (HDI)** report each year on the changes at the level of country. Such a geographical focus suffers from a problem called the "ecological fallacy," which refers to the tendency to give equal statistical weighting to all countries even if they are large like China or small like Togo. Nations with populations of nearing a billion are deemed no more statistically important than those with 5 million or less.

There are further implications arising from the geopolitical focus on the country. First, there is no weight given to the differences within countries, only between them, and some critics of development theory point to significant development challenges in some areas within advanced developed states. Second, there is the impact of small numbers. Countries with small populations will exhibit greater percentage changes in performance than large states, and measures of development therefore need to be sensitive to this and focus not on absolute measures but on standardized indicators.

Third, the country focus suffers from an additional geographical problem of the "modifiable area unit problem" (MAUP). The MAUP describes a condition whereby it is assumed that the geographical unit within which development is measured, is the best geographical unit that can be used. For most measures of development the country is the geographical unit, but it is not the unit that ideally could be used to report measures of components of development such as **health**,

education, productivity, **poverty**, or economic competitiveness.

Measurement, therefore, is not absolute, but is relative, and is specific to the temporal and spatial scales chosen. Resulting measures need to have credibility and authority. Credibility relates more to the methodology in defining and constructing measures and indices. Authority relates to the extent to which measures and indicators influence the development process. Authority largely comes from two sources, governments and the UN/international agency network. Governments of countries remit the collection of statistical measures to their official statistical agencies, and those agencies are formal components of the international official statistical system that includes regional networks (such as the European Union Eurostat agency) and eventually to the United Nations Statistical Office. Individual UN agencies, and the IMF and World Bank, are typical of organizations that produce development measures used in the allocation of political influence and access to capital investment or loans.

Comparability between countries can only be achieved if the measures are "harmonized." Harmonization is a critical statistical process that requires the methodology to be consistent across all collection units, the data collection cycles to be synchronized, and the reporting agency to have authority and credibility. The measures of development used at a global scale are, however, not measures designed specifically for measuring development, but are based mostly on data collected primarily for other reasons – that is the measures make secondary use of statistics. For example, education is an important part of the HDI, but the education data are collected primarily for each country to use in their own policy formulation and for monitoring national trends. The widespread use of secondary data allows measures of development to avoid imposing significant additional costs on countries, thus ensuring that as many as possible provide data. However, all the global measures suffer from a statistical characteristic that international and global measures inevitably mean a loss of thematic and geographical resolution – in essence, few measures go beyond the country, and therefore the ecological fallacy is prevalent.

Comparability introduces an additional tension into measures and indicators. This "naming and shaming" that can arise from the production of league lists, coupled with the success of one particular indicator, the HDI, has "encouraged other agencies to create league tables with their own selection of indicators" (Lievesley, 2001:12). The strong political desire not to be seen as "bottom of the list" further can lead to pressures on the statistical systems of developing nations to "produce" data that paint a suitably optimistic picture.

From an historical perspective, measures have reflected dominant paradigms that are related to the mechanisms that will help deliver development. The 1990s paradigm was that "Regimes that do not at least claim to pursue rapid and sustained **economic growth** (development), popular political participation (**democracy**), and respect for the rights of their citizens (**human rights**) place their national and international legitimacy at risk." It is not just the focus on governmental reform, de-layering legislation, increasing freedoms and human rights, but also the focus on the technologies that are deemed to help the development process. In the late 1990s, **inequality** between rich and poor countries did not just lie in the provisions of human rights, but was also in the areas of **technological capability** and its implications for **information technology**. There are increasing demands to implement governmental reform through e-Government, education through disintermediated learning and flexible and self-programmable skills, and general demands for the creation of an "information society." This is in spite of the fact that many commentators agree that technical advances are taken up faster and exploited more fully by technically developed countries.

The use of information communications technologies (ICTs) (see **information technology**) is the focus of measures promoted early in the twenty-first century, and builds on previous measures of access to conventional land line telephones, with the associated teledensity measures, and the promotion of mobile telecoms. The **United Nations Development Programme (UNDP)** launched a Technology Achievement Index (TAI) in 2001 that aimed to capture how well a country is creating and diffusing technology and building a human skill base – reflecting capacity to participate in the technological innovations of the network age. The TAI is described not as a measure, but as an index based upon a series of indicators, and the indicators themselves are based on diverse measures. UNDP warn that the TAI is a "rough summary – not a comprehensive measure – of a society's technological achievements" (UNDP, 2001), but the caveat itself serves to note the disparity that often arises between the cautionary metadata surrounding measures, and the institutional weight and credibility that is imposed by the measure being produced by UNDP. The index is built from measures at four levels, each of which indicate that measures are still focused on producing, not consuming development.

The TAI covers technology creation (patents, royalties from intellectual property rights), innovation diffusion (assumed to be reflected by access to the **Internet**), old innovation diffusion (access to telephones and electricity), and human skills (education). Other technology-oriented measures include the "networked readiness" index of the World Economic Forum (see **World Social Forum (WSF)**), although the construction of an index for technological advancement noted "only eighty-two countries were considered in our analysis because of limitations in the availability of data from reliable sources. Ranking other countries remains a challenge for the future" (Dutta et al., 2003).

One further emerging global measurement is seen as a surrogate for good **governance**. Yet, again the issues of democratic participation, social and cultural **well-being**, are subjugated to a measure of e-Government readiness, development and performance. As with the governmental re-invention of the 1990s, electronic government is promoted in a framework of "Re-Inventing Good Governance: ICT and Good Governance" (Okot-Uma, 2000). The United Nations Division for Public Economics benchmarked e-Government performance in UN member states, yet again focusing on production (the presence and structure of government websites), rather than consumption of e-Government services by citizens. This is characteristic of most e-Government measures ranging from international agencies to private sector consultants (Booz, 2002). The need to measure the readiness of developing nations to embrace ICTs is hampered by the lack of robust statistics on ICT use, so epitomizing the "Catch-22" situation where developed nations inevitably are better provided to produce the statistics that underpin measures of development.

See also: cost-benefit analysis (CBA); economic growth; growth measurement; growth rate; growth versus holism; indicators of development; information technology; Paris 21; politics; project appraisal

Further reading

Booz (2002) *International e-Economy Benchmarking: The World's Most Effective Policies For The e-Economy*, London: Booz Allen Hamilton.

Dutta, S., Lanvin, B. and Paua, F. (2003) *Global Information Technology Report 2002–2003: Readiness for the Networked World*, World Economic Forum, http://www.weforum.org/

Galtung, J. (2003) "What Did the Experts Predict?" *Futures* 35:2 123–45.

Lievesley, D. (2001) "Making a Difference: A Role for the Responsible International Statistician?" *The Statistician* 50:4 1–38.

Okot-Uma, R. (2000) *Electronic Governance: Reinventing Good Governance*, London: Commonwealth Secretariat. http://www1.worldbank.org/publicsector/egov/Okot-Uma.pdf

Rivers, T. (2003) "Progress and Technology: Their Interdependency," *Technology in Society* 24:4 503–22.

MICHAEL BLAKEMORE

mechanization

Mechanization refers to the application of equipment, tools and machinery as inputs in production processes, using either human draft or motorized power. The role of mechanization in the **economic development** of developing countries exhibits a somewhat sectoral bias as it has tended to be concentrated in specific sectors, notably **agriculture** and **small and medium enterprises (SMEs)**, which are dominated by **labor-intensive** technologies. Mechanization therefore generates the greatest benefits of increased **productivity** in these sectors.

Agricultural mechanization contributes to higher agricultural output through increased productivity of the factors of production employed by farmers, notably land and labor, especially in the activities of seed-bed preparation, sowing, and tillage. Typical machinery may include tractors; water pumping sets; threshers, and reapers. Mechanization also promotes fuller utilization of the modern inputs such as **agrochemicals**, **irrigation** and **fertilizers**. Moreover, it generates economies of large-scale production thereby facilitating increased **commercialization** of production necessary for the development of agro-industries and urban growth. Mechanization can assist in enhancing local **livelihoods** in conjunction with policy measures that ensure equity in the benefits that it can bring. Yet, mechanization may also withdraw **employment** opportunities from some poor and vulnerable people, for whom labor constitutes the asset of last resort for escaping **poverty**.

Mechanization also needs to be understood in terms of the social and economic impacts it can produce. The adoption of new farming methods and limited mechanization during the **green revolution** led to an overall decline in farm prices for **food** staple crops such as wheat and corn. These in turn trigger adjustments in how farming households achieve livelihoods, including diversification of income and new strategies of crop specialization. Ownership of tractors or other pieces of machinery also carries implications of status and wealth, and machines may be owned collectively by **joint families**. The profitability of purchasing machinery depends on the impacts on labor use, and the availability of labor to use it, or hire it from owners. Traditional **caste** roles may be changed by the use or ownership of machinery. If mechanization leads to a reduction of labor inputs, then in principle this may allow children to attend **education**. But **child labor** is often mobilized in production activities during income crises and during peak seasonal demand. **Capital intensive** plantation agriculture involving **monoculture** or **plantation forestry** can create resource management problems owing to deterioration of soil fertility (see **soil erosion and soil fertility**). The replacement of animals by tractors may lead to the decline in supply of animal dung for fertilizers. Increased irrigation (via mechanized water pumps) may increase risks of **salinization**.

The nature of mechanization may be influenced by the nature of export markets, or by government policies. During the green revolution, for example, many developing governments sought to subsidize agricultural mechanization. But such attempts to shape the nature of mechanization frequently failed because the subsidies created short-term market conditions that could not be supported, and because long-term **technology transfer** requires comprehensive attention to the supporting structures for cost recovery, maintenance and training in mechanical technologies.

Demand driven mechanization is often demonstrated by the development and diffusion of intermediate technologies (see **intermediate technology**) especially in the growth of **micro-enterprises** as well as SMEs. These enterprises are characterized by labor-intensive technologies; relatively low capitalization; low level of skills linkage with other sectors of the local economy and adapted to local consumer demand, potentially generating **multiplier effect**s in local economies.

Although NGO interventions in micro-enterprises and SMEs are often project based and so unsustainable in the long term, they are essential in mobilizing local resources and **social capital** necessary for achieving sustainable impact on **well-being**. This calls for a greater role for the private sector in the production and supply of machinery. **Structural adjustment** programs in many developing countries, especially in Africa, accompanied by retrenchment of workers and withdrawal of the state from public investments (see **state and state reform**), provisions of service (e.g. repairs and spares and technical advice) and supply of inputs have generated renewed focus on the role of small enterprises in **economic growth** in general and employment creation in particular. Increased private-sector roles in mechanization require elimination of market distortions to promote competition and profitability. This necessitates developing a policy framework to support financing, infrastructural and human resource development, research and development. Donor interventions could include technical assistance in the development, testing and replication of appropriate technologies, (see **appropriate technology**) provision of grants to finance SMEs, research and support for business development.

See also: capacity building; commercialization; employment; green revolution; irrigation; small and medium enterprises (SMEs)

Further reading

Kaplinsky, R. (1990) *The Economies of Small: Appropriate Technology in a Changing World*, London: Intermediate Technology.

Timmer, C. (1991) "The Role of the State in Agricultural Development," pp. 1–28 in Timmer, C. (ed.) *Agriculture and the State: Growth, Employment and Poverty in Developing Countries*, Ithaca NY: Cornell University Press.

MOSES A. OSIRO

Médecins Sans Frontières (MSF)

Médecins Sans Frontières was established in 1971 by a small group of French doctors, and has developed to become an international humanitarian movement (see **humanitarianism**) with offices in eighteen countries and over 2,500 volunteers working in over eighty countries. MSF is the world's largest independent international medical emergency relief organization (see **emergency assistance**), providing medical help in areas where there is no medical infrastructure or where the existing one cannot withstand the pressure to which it is subjected. MSF frequently collaborates with authorities such as the Ministry of Health to assist people caught in armed conflicts, **natural disasters** such as floods and earthquakes, **epidemics**, and **famines** (see **complex emergencies**). MSF is also involved in less urgent operations, such as the rehabilitation of hospitals and dispensaries, **vaccination** programs, **water management**, and **sanitation** projects, including in areas of chronic instability. Emergency relief programs may also become rehabilitation projects that can run for several years. MSF seeks also to raise awareness of crises, acting as witnesses and speaking out publicly about the plight of the **population**s in danger. MSF won the Nobel Peace Prize in 1999.

See also: complex emergencies; emergency assistance; health; humanitarianism; Red Cross and Red Crescent

Further reading

Allen, T. and Styan, D. (2000) "A Right to Interfere? Bernard Kouchner and the New Humanitarianism," *Journal of International Development* 12: 825–42.

CLAUDIO O. DELANG

media

Debates about media and development consider issues of communication, and the production of communicative materials, such as newspapers, radio and books. Societies which are economically developed and which appear to be politically stable have high levels of communications. The means of communication are often thought of as those moving goods and those transmitting ideas, although the two were almost synonymous until the advent of the telegraph in the early nineteenth century. Even today in developed societies, the marketing of influential newspapers depends upon local rail and road networks. Since the powering of printing presses by steam in the early nineteenth century, the development of mass media in many new forms has been dramatic. In the twentieth century, radio and TV were developed as new mass media. In the USA, both were propelled by the entertainment industry. In Europe, state monopolies (see **state and state reform**) like the BBC regulated the new media more closely. Both can reach illiterate and less-educated sections of the population that did not read "quality" newspapers (see **education; illiteracy**). Hence, the state gave the new media the mission of educating and informing as well as entertaining. In some cases, this became outright propaganda.

The idea of mass media is that of one-to-many transmission – hence the idea of "broadcasting."

Whatever channel is used, be it a newspaper or part of the radio spectrum, it has a limited capacity. Hence, whatever is broadcast has been filtered by a gate-keeper in a position of power. Only in the last decade of the twentieth century has the idea of broadcasting been seriously challenged for the first time by many-to-many transmission in e-mail and the Internet. But at the turn of the century it remained true that 80 percent of the world's **population** had never made a telephone call, and 80 percent of the UK's population (for example) had never sent e-mail.

The media have been seen by many countries – both developed and developing – as essential to the diffusion of new ideas, technologies and values. But the creation of new channel capacity has not been matched by domestic production of content. Hence, by the 1970s there were strident cries from many developing countries for the cessation of the one-way-street of the export of (predominantly American and other Western) cultural values. International news agencies were and are dominated by American and UK companies, which neither the former USSR (Tass) nor the non-aligned (Tanjug) agencies ever remotely threatened. The McBride Commission report of 1980 culminated in the demand within the **United Nations Education, Scientific and Cultural Organization (UNESCO)** for NWICO – a New World Information and Communication Order – that provoked the USA (under Reagan), the UK (under Thatcher) and Singapore (under L. K. Yew) to withdraw from the organization and nearly bankrupt it.

Until the advent of global networks of satellite stations in the 1990s, many developing countries opted for state control of TV and Radio, to forestall the effects of "subversive" elements. As an example, because India's population is fragmented into numerous linguistic and religious groups, the government wished to direct the most powerful media in the process of nation building. Its news broadcasts were dominated by domestic government business with minimal international coverage. When discussion of domestic strife such as the Hindu-Moslem riots in Mumbai could not be avoided, Hindus and Moslems were referred to obliquely as majority and minority communities (see **community**), implicitly within the same

nation state. (Muslims who saw themselves as Indian citizens and equals were disaffected by the use of "minority.") India also experimented with satellite broadcasting for development education in the 1970s, but never promoted this to a national service. Current approaches are more connected to bolstering **civil society** – through participatory video program production on Safer Motherhood in Nepal for example, or indigenous theatre to heighten environmental awareness in Vanuatu. A free press is also thought to be a guardian of democratic values and a promoter of progress. The UK's Department for International Development has funded the BBC to train reporters in post-war Kosovo. Indeed, the role of media and access to media is seen as central to a rights-based approach to development (see **rights-based approaches to development**).

The explosion of new communications technologies, from Xerox machines, which circulated samizdat literature, to PCs, faxes and satellite TV was implicated in the collapse of the Soviet bloc and the end of one-party communist rule (see **postsocialism**). The new technologies empowered resistance to state hegemony (see **state and state reform**). It is not surprising therefore to see that these same technologies with the addition of the Web and CD databases, are also harnessed by other groups to fashion their own forms of resistance. For example, Islamic and Jewish networks can and do reinforce themselves internationally even if traditional values may be challenged domestically. Even many of the satellite broadcasts of **transnational corporations (TNCs)** have had to adapt to the languages and cultural values of regional audiences. The world is still far from a global village, and modernization has not yet proved that it is universally Westernizing (see **modernization theory; globalization and culture**).

The lowering cost of communication, the convergence of media, the evolution of multi-media, and the power of ideas and information, has led some to suggest that it may be possible to leapfrog stages in development (see **leapfrogging**). It may be possible to educate and modernize a rural population, to emancipate women, to provide farmers with better market knowledge and better technical understanding, by means of a small amount of power and some basic information and communications technology (see **information technology**). Though there are many experiments, no one has yet seen a major transformation of a backward rural area based on this model. But there have been other transformations. For example, British Airways data processing is all done in Mumbai, and many insurance companies process their claims in centers in India, because technically proficient labor is cheap and the cost of transmitting even massive quantities of data is small. Bangalore is a hi-tech silicon plateau in India, and a major exporter of software. But there may be factors unique to India – such as the absolute numbers of highly educated people and the use of English – which cannot be easily replicated elsewhere (see **information technology**).

However, just as the economic gap between rich and poor countries has widened over the last few decades, so has the information gap. The wealthy countries which account for 30 percent of the world's population have 80 percent of the world's press circulation, they have one TV for every two people and one radio for every single person – compared with one TV per 30 people and one radio per 7 people in developing countries. In Europe, 12,000 new book titles are published every year – in Africa just 350. Poor countries account for 1 percent of world patents – many of which of course control the development of communications technology.

See also: education; illiteracy; information technology; Internet; globalization and culture; telecommunications

Further reading

Burke, A. (1999) *Communications and Development: a Practical Guide*, London: Social Development Division, DFID.

Chapman, G., Kumar, K., Fraser, C. and Gaber, I. (1997) *Environmentalism and the Mass Media: the North-South Divide*, London: Routledge.

Hamelink, C. (1995) *World Communication: Disempowerment and Self-Empowerment*, London: Zed.

Jensen, K. (ed.) (1998) *News of the World: World Cultures Look at Television News*, London: Routledge.

Mattelart, A. (2000) *Networking the World 1794–2000*, Minneapolis: University of Minnesota Press.

GRAHAM CHAPMAN

mega-cities

A mega-city is defined by the **United Nations** as one which has surpassed a population of 10 million (although other definitions put this figure at 5 million). Mega-cities have become a more significant part of urban landscapes in developing countries over the past three decades. The United Nations estimates that in 2015, eighteen of the world's twenty-one mega-cities will be in the developing world. Asia will have by far the greatest proportion with ten. A more contemporary form of the mega-city is in the growth of "mega urban regions," which transcend rural/urban boundaries and even national borders. There is much debate on the implications of such demographic concentration for development (see **population; urbanization**). While mega-cities may be significant engines of global **economic growth**, they do not necessarily contribute as much to national development (but they do carry significant costs e.g. through their ecological footprints: see **pollution; sustainable development**). Despite their spectacular size, it is important to note that less than 5 percent of the estimated 2.8 billion people living in cities in developing countries in 2015 will live in mega-cities.

See also: brown environmental agenda; circular migration; planning; population; rural-urban migration; urban development; urbanization

DONOVAN STOREY

MERCOSUR

The MERCOSUR (*Mercado Común del Sur*, or Common Market of the Southern Cone) is a sub-regional customs union with headquarters in Montevideo, Uruguay. It was established in 1991 under the Treaty of Asunción with high ambitions for **trade** facilitation. Initially comprising

Argentina, Brazil, Paraguay and Uruguay, the group sought to achieve free movement of goods and services and a customs union with a common external tariff (see **tariffs**) by the end of 1994. To underscore the seriousness of these intentions, in June 1991 there was a 47 percent cut in member countries' tariff rates. During the 1990s, intra-MERCOSUR trade grew considerably (a fivefold increase between 1990 and 1997) and trade barriers were consistently removed. Despite difficulties (disputes over quotas in motor vehicles between Brazil and Argentina in particular and the impacts of the Mexican peso crisis), the common market came in to being on 1 January 1995, and by December a cooperation agreement with the **European Union** was signed. In the eighth summit in August 1995, Bolivia and Chile expressed their interest in joining the group and have both since been admitted as associate members. Talks concerning future expansion, which is likely to draw in Venezuela and Peru first, have begun.

In general, the objectives of the group have been assisted by a large internal market (over 200 million **population** and a total **gross national product (GNP)** of approximately US$500 billion) and, relative to the rest of Latin America, a high per capita purchasing power. It can be argued that the rise of the MERCOSUR, and the particular political-economic conditions existing at the beginning of the 1990s, allowed governments to implement neo-liberal reform by appealing to interest groups who might otherwise demonstrate against the austere policies of **structural adjustment**, by offering the benefits of a larger regional market. In this sense, MERCOSUR has both underpinned and perpetuated the rise of **neo-liberalism** across the region.

Many observers see the MERCOSUR as a leading example of regional integration in the developing world, and one that illustrates the opportunities afforded by open regionalism (Kaltenthaler and Mora, 2002). By 2001, a CET was established between Argentina and Brazil, with the other core members set to implement similar agreements in 2006. However, there are significant asymmetries within the common market – Argentina and Brazil have dominated trade. The MERCOSUR has increased its scope over recent years to include political and social agreements and charters, partly in response to vociferous protest concerning its impacts

on traditional economic sectors and marginalized populations from within member countries.

See also: economic federalization; free trade zones (FTZs); Latin American Free Trade Agreement (LAFTA); North American Free Trade Agreement (NAFTA); trade

Further reading

Calvert, P. (2002) "Attempts at Integration," in Heenan, P. and Monique, M. (eds) *Regional Handbooks of Economic Development: South America*, London: Fitzroy Dearborn.

Kaltenthaler, K. and Mora, F. (2002) "Explaining Latin American Economic Integration: The Case of Mercosur," *Review of International Political Economy* 9:1 72–97.

WARWICK E. MURRAY

MFN *see* most favored nation (MFN) status

micro-credit and micro-finance

Micro-credit and micro-finance operations refer to financial transactions, whether saving or borrowing, carried out on a very small scale. The provision of micro-credit and micro-finance are important responses on the part of many **non-governmental organizations (NGOs)** and some governments to the failure of commercial banks and other formal financial institutions in the formal financial sector (FFS) to meet the financial needs of poor people in most developing countries. Much emphasis in policy discussions has focused on micro-credit; it is argued that a lack of credit limits the scope of individuals and **micro-enterprises** to expand their scale of operation and/or invest in more modern technology. As many developing countries have witnessed a decline in **employment** in large enterprises and the **public sector**, policies to encourage the development of small enterprises, often those in the **urban informal sector**, have been widely encouraged by organizations such as the **World Bank**. However, the need of poor people to save and their ability to do so has also been recognized in many of the most successful micro-finance programs.

The failure of the FFS to provide micro-finance is mainly due to the problem of asymmetric information (see Stiglitz and Weiss, 1981). In other words, FFS institutions have little or no information about potential customers among poor people, as commercial banks generally do not have branches in areas where poor people live. The poor are not their customers, so the banks cannot build up a profile of their creditworthiness and, as they may be living as landless peasants in **rural poverty** or in primitive shacks in **shantytowns**, the poor do not have acceptable collateral to cover bank loans.

A further problem is that the small scale of operation in micro-finance makes it difficult for institutions in the FFS to cover their fixed costs. One solution to this problem is for an intermediate institution (see **institutions**), such as the government or an NGO, to bundle a number of the micro-transactions into a larger and more economical transaction.

One approach to solving the problem of a lack of acceptable collateral is a credit guarantee program, in which the government, Central Bank or an NGO guarantee commercial banks against loss through defaults by poor borrowers. While in principle such programs should work, Levitsky and Prasad (1987) found that in practice the credit guarantee program did not always expand the amount of micro-credit, as the commercial banks used the guarantees to reduce their risks on loans they would have made anyway. However, with careful monitoring of the commercial banks, such schemes do offer the possibility of increasing the quantity of micro-credit.

Other approaches attempt to solve the problem of asymmetric information by helping the banks tap into information on the creditworthiness of individuals that is known to other members of the potential borrower's **community**. For example, village elders or senior members of a poor urban community may be asked to select the borrowers and act as their guarantors. Their knowledge of the members of the community enables them to select suitable, honest, hardworking applicants and, if necessary, their power within the community can enforce the repayment of loans. The most famous

program that taps into local information is the **Grameen Bank (GB)**. The Bank operates by giving a loan to a group of five borrowers who are jointly responsible for the repayment of the loan, but makes group members choose each other and hence taps into the **local knowledge** of potential group members. The only known examples of complete failure of GB programs occurred in cases where the bank staff put the members into arbitrary groups rather than letting the members choose themselves. The Grameen Bank also provides a facility for its members to save, as one of the conditions of membership is to save each period, even if the amount is very small.

In addition to providing loans, many micro-credit programs also provide training as a compulsory part of the program. The topics often include simple bookkeeping and basic stock control, but may include training in new skills and technology. When well done, such training may increase the effectiveness of the loan program.

Many micro-credit programs have been evaluated on a number of criteria, such as whether they charge a rate of interest and achieve a repayment rate that is sufficiently high to make the lending operation viable. Here the Grameen Bank is regarded as a great success, as it charges a high enough rate of interest to cover its major costs and its repayment rates seldom fall below about 97 percent, a figure that greatly exceeds that of the most successful commercial banks. Part of the success of this and other programs depends on the extent to which they can diversify the portfolio of loans to reduce covariate risk. For example, if all the loans in a program are made to peasants in one small area who are growing one particular crop and it is affected by blight, the program will fail, while another that has a portfolio of loans to borrowers working in a range of activities in a number of different geographical regions may avoid covariate risk and succeed.

Attempts to evaluate how much good the loans do the borrowers have been more ambiguous and some have been subject to **male bias**. Many programs have sought to target credit to women among their objectives, but in some cases the criterion chosen to evaluate the success of the program is how much paid employment it generates. A number of studies have shown that these two objectives are inconsistent, as on average more paid employment is generated by lending to men, particularly those involved in small-scale manufacturing, than by lending to women, many of whom work with unpaid members of the family. An evaluation of whether loans to poor women have had a positive effect might need to examine whether the family was better fed or whether the children were able to attend school as a result of the loan.

The poor are not entirely dependent on micro-finance supplied from outside the community, as there are sometimes local sources of credit. First, there are the money-lenders, who are stereotypically seen as usurers who use their monopolistic power to exploit the poor by charging extortionate rates of interest. Research suggests a more complex reality, with money-lenders using their local knowledge to evaluate the appropriate risk premium for different loans. However, severe problems may arise if the borrower cannot repay the loan on time, as the resulting additional interest charges may soon become burdensome, and there have been reports of children being effectively sold into indentured service to pay off the loan (see **children**).

Second, particularly in urban areas, there are pawnshops that are prepared to advance loans based on the collateral supplied by poor borrowers. Transaction costs tend to be low and the loan is available quickly on production of the collateral. Here again the lenders have a reputation of charging high interest rates, but if the borrower cannot repay the loan, while she or he loses the collateral, she or he is not subject to further interest charges.

A popular form of self-help saving and credit program that is found very widely among both rich and poor is rotating savings and credit associations (ROSCAs). In a ROSCA a group is formed and the members agree to pay a fixed amount each period into a "kitty" and then one member is entitled to take the kitty each period until all the members have had it. In some cases, the allocation is based on seniority or by a random draw, but in others it is done through a bidding or discounting system, so that those members who are prepared to wait can earn a return on their contributions. ROSCA groups tend to be relatively small and the members are often neighbors or fellow workers, so they know each other and the risk of default is low.

Credit unions are larger and more formal versions of the ROSCA, often employing paid officials to collect the contributions to the kitty and administer the draw under the supervision of a board appointed by the members. Most credit unions have larger kitties than those produced by most ROSCAs. But the size of credit union tends to decrease information members have about each other or the officials running the program. As a result, default rates are sometimes considerably higher than those of ROSCAs.

As this summary suggests, there are a range of sources of micro-finance and micro-credit in both urban and rural areas, but overall the scale of the provision of micro-finance remains relatively small. Shortage of capital remains a major restraint on the development of many individuals and micro-enterprises, and is likely to remain so for many years to come.

See also: fiscal and monetary policy; Grameen Bank (GB); micro-enterprises; non-governmental organizations (NGOs); people-centered development; poverty; street-trading in urban areas; urban informal sector

Further reading

ACCIÓN International website: http://www. accion.org

Levitsky, J. and Prasad, R. (1987) *Credit Guarantee Schemes for Small and Medium Enterprises*, Washington DC: World Bank.

Stiglitz, J. and Weiss, A. (1981) "Credit Rationing in Markets with Imperfect Information," *American Economic Review* 71:3 393–410.

Thomas, J. (1993) "The Informal Financial Sector: How Does It Operate and Who Are Its Customers?" in Page, S. (ed.) *Monetary Policy in Developing Countries*, London: Routledge.

JIM THOMAS

micro-enterprises

Micro-enterprises are opportunistic economic structures resorted to by poor people for self-employment. They form an essential part of the urban **informal sector** and **street-trading in urban areas**, which offer **employment** and livelihood opportunities (see **livelihoods**) for people outside modern industrial sectors. Micro-enterprises add value to indigenous resources, using small-scale **labor-intensive**, operations under family ownership and management. Typically, people working in micro-enterprises are owner-operators who have acquired skills outside the formal school system. In some circumstances, the owner-operators of micro-enterprises will employ members of their immediate family or other relatives when the need arises. Sometimes micro-enterprises may be transformed to small or medium enterprises (see **small and medium enterprises (SMEs)**).

Micro-enteprises began to be proposed as employment strategies in the late 1960s. One of the best-known strategies was the **International Labor Organization (ILO)** World Employment Program, launched in 1969, which presented an "employment-based" strategy for achieving **basic needs**. Under this program, micro-enterprises were identified as being flexible and opportunistic, and as providing business opportunities that were easy to enter and leave, in keeping with seasonal demand and the availability of alternative employment opportunities in agriculture or urban formal markets. The ILO strategy paper (ILO, 1972) was the first time a public statement highlighted the positive values of the informal sector and micro-enterprises as sources of self-employment, income generation and wealth creation, especially for new entrants to the urban labor force. Yet, micro-enterprises only became important to official development assistance during the 1980s (see Ashe, 1985), and eventually they were applied within debates relating to **micro-credit and micro-finance** (see Remenyi, 1991; Pischke, 1994). Subsequent debates on the gender divisions and management challenges of micro-enterprises have indicated that the micro-finance providers need to become as financially viable as the micro-enterprises they seek to fund (Morduch, 1999). The mobilization and servicing of household savings is also important in facilitating micro-enterprises (Rutherford, 2000).

There is no consensus on the literature that allows for a definitive statement about when a micro-enterprise may become an SME. Some analysts state that the size of an enterprise is less important than its official recognition and legal status. By definition, the informal sector consists of micro-enterprises and livelihood activities that are outside the formal economy regulated by government and counted into official estimates of national income and production. Once an enterprise is officially registered and entered into official statistics, it ceases to be a micro-enterprise. Typically, however, this does not happen before the micro-enterprise has grown significantly beyond reliance on owner-operator status, normally including a more or less permanent workforce of ten or more full-time employees.

See also: entrepreneurship; micro-credit and micro-finance; small and medium enterprises (SMEs); street-trading in urban areas; urban informal sector

Further reading

Ashe, J. (1985) *The PISCES II Experience, Vols 1 and 2: Local Efforts in Microenterprise Development*, Washington DC: USAID.

ILO (1972) *Employment, Incomes and Equality: A Strategy for Increasing Productive Employment in Kenya*, Geneva: ILO.

Morduch, J. (1999) "Microfinance Schism," *World Development* 28:4 617–29.

Pischke, J. von (1994) *Building Sustainable Institutions That Sell Financial Services to Small Enterprises*, Washington DC: Inter-American Development Bank.

Remenyi, J. (1991) *Where Credit Is Due: Income-Generating Programs for the Poor in Developing Countries*, Boulder: Westview Press.

Rutherford, S. (2000) *The Poor and Their Money*, Oxford: Oxford University Press.

JOE REMENYI

migrant trafficking

Migrant trafficking refers to the recruitment and transportation of persons and the facilitation of their illegal entry into a state (see **state and state reform**), often in dangerous or inhumane conditions. Trafficking is a form of undocumented

international migration that often involves elements of coercion, exploitation, and physical and psychological abuse. Organized criminal groups involved in the sex industry (see **prostitution/sex work**), forced labor and other forms of **slavery** often carry out the activity, and the overwhelming majority of those trafficked are women and **children**. Though statistics on migrant trafficking are of varying degrees of reliability, studies by the International Organization for Migration (IOM) have found that the largest number of trafficked persons come from South and Southeast Asia, the former Soviet Union, Eastern Europe, and South America – the majority of whom are sent to the Middle East, Western Europe, North America and Asia. In short, the movement is from poorer to more prosperous countries.

As migrant trafficking is a transnational phenomenon, states, regional organizations and international institutions such as the **United Nations** and the IOM are working together to strengthen crime prevention strategies against the trafficking of humans, and to improve assistance and protection for victims of trafficking. The cooperative effort has resulted in the United Nations Convention against Transnational Organized Crimes, and The Protocol Against the Smuggling of Migrants by Land, Sea and Air and The Protocol to Prevent, Suppress and Punish Trafficking in Persons, Especially Women and Children. Both protocols improve the legal and judicial means to prevent and combat trafficking and enhance information sharing. The Trafficking Protocol expands the scope of protection and support to the victims and witnesses.

But for some states, migrant trafficking is considered primarily as a **crime** that violates their sovereignty and as such they emphasize the importance of strengthening border controls, preventing the use of fraudulent travel documents and prosecuting traffickers rather than the **human rights** needs of the victims. This has raised concern among human rights organizations about the effective of the Protocols in practice. The problem is that the criminalization of irregular **migration** will have negative repercussions on certain groups of vulnerable people. Asylum-seekers (see **asylum seeking**) are particularly at risk because states do not have to permit them to remain in their

territories temporarily or permanently. The implication for the treatment of forced prostitution is also disturbing because the women can be prosecuted as criminals rather than protected as victims.

A comprehensive and effective global anti-trafficking plan needs to ensure that human rights standards are not compromised. The implementation of punitive measures needs to be balanced by robust protection mechanisms. Moreover, an effective action plan must deal with corrupted officials, include a public **education** campaign, and address the conditions such as **poverty** and gender **inequality** that make people vulnerable to traffickers.

See also: asylum seeking; crime; migration; prostitution/sex work; refugees; slavery

Further reading

Gallagher, A. (2001) "Human Rights and the new UN Protocols on Trafficking and Migrant Smuggling: A Preliminary Analysis," *Human Rights Quarterly* 23: 975–1004.

Schloenhardt, A. (2001) "Trafficking in Migrants: Illegal Migration and Organized Crime in Australia and the Asia Pacific Region," *International Journal of the Sociology of Law* 29: 331–78.

ROBYN LUI

migration

Migration is the movement of people, usually involving the relocation of the site of residence. It is both one of the most important consequences of development and one of its most important causes. The creation of new opportunities attracts people; equally, the development of new resources is unlikely to occur without the introduction of a labor force to allow their exploitation. Thus, migration is an integral part of development. The relationship between migration and development is complex and analysts have adopted various means of interpreting it. Many of the difficulties reflect the difficulties of defining migration, and the diversity of **population mobility**. One of the most important forms of migration is that where individuals or families change their usual place of residence: indeed, this is the most common definition of "migration". The term migration, on its own, thus implies a longer-term movement to distinguish it from **circular migration**, or regular and shorter-term movements around a stable or usual place of residence.

The meaning of migration might appear intuitively obvious, but it is difficult to define precisely and measure. Migration is a process that occurs across space and through time, hence the delimitation of units defining "migration" is critical to the number and type of migrants identified through censuses or surveys. The smaller the spatial unit across which a person moves in order to be defined as a "migrant," and the shorter the time period adopted to indicate what a shift in residence should be, the greater the number of migrants captured by the census or survey. For example, the original impression of the immobility of the Indian **population** was derived from the use of the state as the unit of analysis (see **state and state reform**). Once the much smaller district was used, a very different picture emerged. Generally, it has been shown that the majority of migrants move over short distances. Thus, statistics on the volume of migration are entirely the product of the definitions applied, and these vary markedly within a country and from country to country, making direct comparisons problematic. Thus, attempts to relate migration rates to levels of development across countries, and even within country, are virtually impossible to achieve accurately (see **measuring development**).

At the global level, one of the most important spatial units is the independent state and, in the literature, migration is most commonly divided into two main types: **international migration** (the movement between states), and internal migration (the movement within the state). The latter, however, is increasingly referred to as population distribution or redistribution. There are also important linkages between internal and international migrations. For example, the arrival of large numbers of international migrants in a global city such as New York can have an impact on local property and **labor markets** that result in the locally-born moving out of the city. Also, those who leave a country generally do so from the principal cities of that country, and many may have moved internally before later deciding to migrate overseas.

As well as the space and time dimensions, migrants may be classified by their motivation to move. The motivation to move, traditionally, has been divided into forced movements, which produce **refugees** or **internally displaced persons**, and those migrations that are the result of individual choice. In practice, forced and voluntary movements represent endpoints along a continuum rather than two clearly identifiable and separate types of migration. Most voluntary migration is constrained by economic, social and cultural factors to some extent, and a distinction between an "economic migrant" and a "refugee" is sometimes difficult to draw. In so-called voluntary migration, most migrants move for some kind of economic reason and there is a clear economic or developmental foundation to population migration. Given all these caveats, migration is by far the most complex of the three basic demographic variables of **fertility**, **mortality** and migration.

Migration has been a characteristic of all societies in all ages and one of the enduring myths of history has been the immobility of pre-modern populations prior to the industrial revolution. **War**, **famine**, the ambitions of local leaders and demands for labor all contributed to a constant flux of populations. Certainly, some groups moved further and more often than others, and certain periods appear to have been characterized by greater movement than others, but all were marked by migrations. The great migrations have included the movements out of Europe that led to the development of the Americas, the forced **slavery** movements out of Africa, movements to open up new lands, and the movements of Chinese and Indian laborers in the nineteenth century. The historical importance of migration is not to imply that there is nothing new in the patterns of movement seen today. The changing international arena, particularly the emergence of independent states in the developing world and the evolution of modern forms of transportation, have generated new forms of population migration.

Perhaps the greatest of all migrations in terms of numbers of people and implications for development have been those directed toward towns and cities, movements that have been primarily internal to countries (see **rural-urban migration**). Migration is a component of urban growth, along with natural increase and reclassification, and a critical factor behind **urbanization**. Thus, migration has played a key role in facilitating the transformation from rural to urban societies. In 1950, just under 30 percent of the world's population lived in urban areas. By 2000, that proportion had increased to 47.4 percent. Those who move, initially at least, tend to be the younger, the most innovative and the better educated of the communities from which they come (see **community**). Thus, migration has been seen from two starkly different points of view. First, it is the antithesis of development in that it undermines the communities of origin by removing those who are best equipped to improve conditions in rural areas. Second, migration is seen as promoting development by bringing together dynamic populations at central locations in towns and cities. No highly developed society is primarily rural. Benefits to the state may, however, erode development at local levels.

The reality is likely to be more complex than the above two opposing points of view suggest. Family members who find temporary or longer-term work in towns and cities may send money back to their families in the **villages** and hence support increasing rural populations. Conversely, those moving from **rural poverty** may be thrust into situations of **vulnerability** and exploitation in urban areas, neither seeing an improvement in their own quality of life nor making any significant contribution to local or regional economies. Hence, the relationship between migration and development is extremely complex. What can be said with some degree of confidence is that programs to develop rural areas rarely stop or even slow the exodus from the villages. Quite the reverse: **rural development**, by improving levels of **education** and spreading an awareness of opportunities outside the village, often acts to accelerate the exodus. In dynamic economies, it is virtually impossible, and indeed undesirable, to keep people "down on the farm." What is equally clear is that the patterns of migration change over time as levels of development vary and the relationships between them, too, change in a complex matrix of social and economic transformation.

Just as the relationship between migration and development is complex, so, too, is any association between migration and **poverty**. Poverty has often been seen as a root cause of migration but, as outlined above, most migrants have access to some resources and are not from the poorest of the poor. Resources in terms of physical and network capital are required to allow people to move in the first place, and any decision to move is likely to be based more on a feeling of relative deprivation than any absolute measure of poverty. In fact, migration, by allowing people access to sources of income in other areas, can act to alleviate poverty by facilitating wealth transfers from richer to poorer areas. That said, however, in some parts of the world "survival migration" can certainly be found, in which individuals, families and entire groups have to move in order to survive: those fleeing from environmental or political catastrophes, for example. Truly forced migration is likely to affect all groups irrespective of wealth, even if wealthier groups are likely to be able to flee further than poorer groups.

The relationship between migration and **unemployment** is equally complex. Those who move tend not to be the unemployed, and migrants in destination areas usually have lower levels of unemployment than non-migrants. Nevertheless, migrants may persist in moving to areas where overall unemployment is high, such as **mega-cities** in the developing world, where they often engage in occupations that non-migrants are unwilling to undertake. Occupational specialization by area of migrant origin is common, with access to employment controlled by specific migrant networks resulting in highly segmented **labor markets**.

Few truly universal generalizations can be made about migration, but one of these is that the majority of those who move are young adults. Migration thus becomes subject to the supply of young adults that itself is directly a function of fertility (birth rate): where fertility is high, the number of migrants will also be high 15 to 20 years later. Where fertility declines, the number of migrants, too, may eventually decline. The relationship between fertility and development is itself not simple, introducing a further complication into the migration and development equation. In some parts of the world, women have a greater tendency to migrate than men, as in **rural-urban migration** in Latin America, whereas in other parts, Sub-Saharan Africa, for example, men tend to migrate more than women. The generalization can perhaps be made that, over time, the proportion of women tends to increase in most migrant flows, and particularly the proportion of women moving independently of men (see also **gender division of labor**).

Most of the issues involving the relationships between migration and development at the national level may also be seen with respect to discussions of **brain drain** and **remittances** in the context of international migration and the differences between core and peripheral countries (see **international division of labor**).

In view of the complexity of the migration and development interrelationship, it is unlikely that any single overarching theory relating the two can be advanced to provide a truly satisfactory explanation for migration at all levels and in all contexts. Many different approaches have been used in the analysis of migration, ranging from classical economic models based upon migration as the result of an individual decision to maximize income, through to migration which is much more the result of a collective family or household risk minimization strategy (see **risk and insurance strategies**). Neo-Marxist models of labor exploitation have also been prominent in the field, and more recent accounts have tended to focus on the experiences of the migrant as an individual. Again, these shifts in how analysts have approached the topic are to be found in narrower studies of international migration, and reflect broader changes in the social sciences in general.

See also: brain drain; circular migration; displacement; international migration; Harris-Todaro model; labor migration; MIRAB (migration, aid, remittances and bureaucracy); population mobility; refugees; internally displaced persons; remittances; rural-urban migration; transmigration; urbanization

Further reading

Bilsborrow, R. (ed.) (1998) *Migration, Urbanization, and Development: New Directions and Issues*, Norwell MA: Kluwer.

Boyle, P., Halfacree, K. and Robinson, V. (1998) *Exploring Contemporary Migration*, London: Longman.

Skeldon, R. (1990) *Population Mobility in Developing Countries: A Reinterpretation*, London: Belhaven.

Skeldon, R. (1997) *Migration and Development: A Global Perspective*, London: Longman.

United Nations (1998) *Population Distribution and Migration*, New York: UN Department of Economic and Social Affairs, Population Division.

United Nations (1998) *World Population Monitoring 1997: International Migration and Development*, New York: UN Department of Economic and Social Affairs, Population Division.

RONALD SKELDON

military and security

Debates about the military and security, and development refer to the impact of military strategies on development objectives; the roles played by the military in domestic and international politics; and the contribution to other developmental questions such as **economic growth** and **governance**.

The relationship between military expenditure and development is often presented as a "guns versus butter" problem, the assumption being that an increase in investment into the military sector would reduce the resources available for other sectors, thereby hampering economic growth and development. Yet, no conclusive evidence exists to support this view. There are two contrasting views on the relationship between military expenditure and development. One view emphasizes the positive effects of military spending on economic growth rates in developing countries. Evidence indeed suggests that countries with a high military burden may have high rates of growth. Military spending may stimulate the economy by acting as a seed for money for the development of national industries, promoting **technology transfer** and the acquisition of new skills (as with Japan and the newly industrialized countries of East Asia). Furthermore, the military may have a positive influence on the process of development by way of acting as a harbinger of modernization (as with Israel and Turkey in the early years of development) (see **modernization theory; multiplier effect**).

An alternative view proposes that economic growth – such as from military expenditure – does not necessarily foster **economic development**. Furthermore, investment into the military sector may fail to promote indigenous industries. In case of the Arab world, the only military-industrial complex that has developed is a purely mercantile one that links bureaucratic elite (see **elites**) with civilian entrepreneurs who live on arms import commissions. Second, the military establishment, if conservative in nature, may hamper, rather than harbinger, modernization and development. Furthermore, there is always the likelihood that further investment in the military (even when successful in bolstering economic growth) might lead to a decrease in overall **security** by actually triggering security dilemmas. The "peace dividend" (i.e. the reallocation of resources from military to peacetime purposes) may not only permit military expenditures to be transferred to civilian purposes, but also create an atmosphere of security in which investments and foreign economic assistance might grow.

The provision of security receives maximum attention from governments in times of peace as well as war. This attention partly acknowledges the need to provide security for human existence. It also concerns the discursive power of the term "security." When an issue gets labeled as a "security concern," valuable resources are channeled towards it, often without further scrutiny. In the provision of security, the military sector has traditionally been given an important place because resources have been allocated to it at the expense of other socio-economic needs. Governments often legitimize this decision by saying that without security no other human goal can be pursued.

The relationship between military and security was brought to the attention of world opinion by debates on **human security** in the post-Cold War era. human security is understood as a condition in which the material (**food**, shelter, **education** and **health** care) and non-material (human dignity, opportunity to fulfill oneself as a human being)

dimensions of human needs are met. Increasing interest in human security has emerged as a reaction to the decline in the global social indicators of human security, notwithstanding the "peace dividend" created by the end of the **Cold War**. According to the United Nations Human Development Report (1994), although global military spending declined by 3.6 percent per annum between 1987 and 1994, no comparable increase in spending on **human development** was observed. In other words, there has been a lack of genuine commitment by global actors to achieving human security. The **World Bank** and the **International Monetary Fund (IMF)** have attempted to use **conditionality** on lending authority to reduce arms purchases, and increases in human security, but these have not always been successful (see **arms sales and controls**). Indeed, some agencies and their officials have hesitated to raise the sensitive issue of military reform for fear of jeopardizing an otherwise good working relationship with the recipient government. Moreover, the mutual interests and support for each other of military and industrial actors in countries (the so-called military-industrial complex) further hampers efforts for military reform.

The effect of increased military spending on development becomes clearer when viewed through the lenses of the most vulnerable (who are also the least vocal) in society: **children**. Research findings show that countries with high levels of military expenditure also have low levels of child development (measured in terms of the "under-five" mortality rate) (see **children; infant and child mortality**). This is because as defense spending increases, spending on social welfare is usually cut back. Increased military spending may also hamper long-term economic growth, thereby disturbing delicate balances in the country and giving rise to conflict and **war**. Conflict and war, in turn, further exacerbate the difficult condition children find themselves in. Thus, the "guns versus butter" dilemma becomes more acute in the case of child development. As the military sector gains at the expense of the children, what is referred to as the "scissors effect" operates on future economic development. An increase in military expenditure and decrease in spending on child development reinforce each other in hampering economic growth. This, in turn, triggers a new cycle of crisis that may threaten global security.

See also: arms sales and controls; elites; human security; landmines; security; transparency; war

Further reading

Deger, S. (1990) *Military Expenditure: The Political Economy of International Security*, Oxford: Oxford University Press.

Thomas, C. (2000) *Global Governance, Development and Human Security: The Challenge of Poverty and Inequality*, London: Pluto.

UNDP (1994) *Human Development Report 1994: New Dimensions of Human Security*, New York: Cambridge University Press.

PINAR BILGIN

Millennium Development Goals (MDGs)

The Millennium Development Goals (MDGs) are a series of internationally agreed targets of development that form the basis for much international development effort in the twenty-first century. In September 2000, 147 heads of state and government – and 191 nations in total – adopted the Millennium Declaration and the associated MDGs. The MDGs include: (1) *Eradicate poverty and hunger*: reduce the proportion of people living on less than US$1 a day to half the 1990 level by 2015 – from 28.3 percent of all people in low and middle income economies to 14.2 percent. The Goals also call for halving the proportion of people who suffer from hunger between 1990 and 2015. (2) *Achieve universal primary education*: all children everywhere should be able to complete a full course of primary schooling by 2015. (3) *Promote gender equality and empowerment of women*: eliminate gender disparity in primary and secondary education, preferably by 2005, and to all levels of education no later than 2015; (4) *Reduce infant mortality*: reduce by two thirds, between 1990 and 2015, the under-five mortality rate (see **infant and child mortality**). (5) *Improve maternal health*:

reduce by three quarters, between 1990 and 2015, the **maternal mortality** ratio. (6) *Combat HIV/ AIDS, malaria and other diseases*: halt and begin to reverse the spread of HIV/AIDS by 2015, and halt and begin to reverse the incidence of malaria and other major diseases by 2015 (see **HIV/ AIDS (definition and treatment); HIV/AIDS (policy issues)**). (7) *Ensure environmental sustainability*: Integrate the principles of **sustainable development** into country policies and programs and reverse the losses of environmental resources; halve by 2015 the proportion of people without sustainable access to safe **drinking water** and basic **sanitation**; and have achieved by 2020 a significant improvement in the lives of at least 100 million shantytown dwellers (see **shantytowns**). (8) *Develop a global partnership for development* (see **partnerships**): The last goal has various targets: develop further an open, rule-based, predictable, non-discriminatory trading and financial system (such as via commitments to good **governance**, and poverty reduction); address the special needs of the least developed countries (such as tariff and quota-free access for exports (see **tariffs**); **debt** relief and cancellation of official bilateral debt; and more generous official development assistance for countries committed to poverty reduction; address the special needs of landlocked countries (see **landlocked developing countries (LLDCs)**) and **small island developing states (SIDS)**; deal comprehensively with the debt problems of developing countries through national and international measures to make debt sustainable in the long term; develop and implement strategies for decent and productive work for youth; provide access to affordable essential **pharmaceuticals**; and make available the benefits of new technologies, especially information and communications (see **technology transfer**).

Appropriate indicators have been selected to monitor progress on each of the targets (see **indicators of development**). The MDGs incorporate most of the goals and targets set at the global conferences and world summits of the 1990s. MDG monitoring has been taking place at the global and country levels. At the global level, the Secretary-General of the **United Nations** is to report annually to the UN General Assembly on progress towards a subset of the MDGs and to report more comprehensively every five years. At the country level, more than forty national MDG reports (MDGRs) have been produced, which could help in engaging political leaders and top decision-makers, as well as mobilizing **civil society**, communities, the public and **media**.

There are some feasibility questions in the achievement of MDGs by 2015. The 1990s saw improvements in the area of education in Guinea and Malawi; infant mortality in Bangladesh and the Gambia; nutrition in Indonesia, Mexico and Tunisia; and income-poverty in China. On the other hands, there have been some setbacks: the under-5 infant mortality rate increased in Cambodia, Kenya, Malawi and Zambia; the primary school enrolment ratio dropped in Cameroon, Lesotho, Mozambique and Tanzania; gender gaps in primary education widened in Eritrea, Ethiopia and Namibia; **malnutrition** has increased in various countries; access to **drinking water** became more difficult for millions of people. Perhaps most worryingly, despite some success in Thailand and Uganda, HIV/AIDS prevalence rates are at their highest levels.

MDGs have also prompted a critical debate over financing for development. Costing exercises of MDGs have been carried out by donor agencies, and achieving MDGs would require about US$100–120 billion a year. Together, they represent important targets for development practice, but their achievability, or the political will to achieve them, is in doubt.

See also: education; debt relief; drinking water; empowerment; gender; health; HIV/AIDS (policy issues); infant and child mortality; maternal mortality; measuring development; partnerships; poverty; sustainable development; United Nations

Further reading

Black, R. and White, H. (eds) (2003) *Targeting Development: Critical Perspectives on the Millennium Development Goals (MDGs)*, London: Routledge.

Millennium Goals website: http://www.developmentgoals.org/

Vandemoortele, J. (2002) *Are the MDGs Feasible?* New York: UNDP.

TAKAYOSHI KUSAGO

mineral-led development

Mineral-led development refers to the development processes in relation to mining, or the extraction, processing and exporting of minerals. Among the resource-rich countries, the mineral economies (defined as countries that generate more than 10 percent of **gross domestic product (GDP)** and more than 40 percent of exports from mining) have the weakest per capita growth record in recent decades. Yet there is no inherent economic reason why this is so. However, the governments of mineral economies appear to be especially prone to policy failure. Consequently, when increased state intervention (see **state and state reform**) in **economic development** became fashionable during the years 1950–80 the mineral economies were especially vulnerable. The distortions created by misguided domestic policies rendered the economies vulnerable to external shocks that, ironically, were created by the efforts of developing country governments to collude in raising global commodity prices.

Government intervention distorts the economy, and the "point-source" socio-economic linkages of mineral economies increase the scope for such distortion compared with natural resources that generate diffuse socio-economic linkages such as cropland under peasant farming. This is because mining is highly **capital intensive** and employs much foreign capital but only a small, albeit well-paid workforce. This causes final demand linkage (i.e. domestic spending by capital and labor) to be modest. Moreover, productive linkages are limited because mine inputs are usually imported due to their specialized nature, while mineral processing tends to locate at the market. This leaves corporate taxes plus any natural resource rent captured by the government through royalties or special taxation as the dominant linkage. The concentration of mineral rents upon the government increases the risk that they will not be effectively deployed (see **resource curse thesis**). This is because governments are less likely to treat windfall revenues as temporary than private agents such as farmers are, so they tend to spend revenues too quickly and in doing so they distort the economy. In contrast, rents from peasant cash crop exports tend to diffuse across a wider set of economic agents so they are more conducive to economic development.

Yet, a growth collapse is not inevitable for mineral-led development and it is possible to secure sustained rapid **economic growth** from a finite resource. The government of an oil-exporting country needs to invest a sufficient amount from the stream of mineral rents such that when the mineral is exhausted, alternative wealth-generating assets sustain the same income stream as the mineral-rent in perpetuity. There are three basic requirements to maintain the income component of the mineral stream and minimize the adverse impacts of short-run **Dutch disease** effects (or changes in a country's currency following discovery of minerals or **natural resources**). First, sterilize the mineral windfalls. Second, buffer public expenditure from a possible rent collapse. Third, invest a sufficient fraction of the **natural capital** in alternative wealth-producing assets. The implementation of these principles requires appropriate institutional mechanisms that include a capital development fund to manage the allocation of capital between overseas investment, domestic investment and government revenue. In addition, there needs to be a constraint on the rate of domestic absorption in order to mute the strengthening exchange rate (see **exchange rates**) and curb Dutch disease effects that erode the competitiveness of the non-mining tradeables (like farm products) and abort economic diversification. There also needs to be a mineral revenue stabilization fund to smooth fluctuations in government revenue by restricting over-spending during booms and cushioning adjustment to falling rents when the boom collapses. Finally, there must be a project evaluation unit to ensure the efficiency of **public sector** investment. However, the success of these **institutions** depends on the degree of insulation from predatory elements within the government and private sectors.

Unfortunately, few mineral economies engendered developmental political states, so that over-rapid domestic absorption of mineral rents has been the norm. Excess domestic demand causes inflation

(see **inflation and its effects**) and triggers Dutch disease effects that distort the production structure of the economy while expanding social entitlements that are difficult to cut back during a downturn. In this way mineral booms lock in government commitments that prolong high spending levels when revenues falter and trigger macro-economic imbalances, marked by high inflation, that subsequently bring abrupt demand cuts and sharp falls in output and growth. Consequently, mineral booms give an initial boost in income that is followed by a rate of economic growth below the pre-boom average due to Dutch disease effects, so that long-term welfare may be less than if the rents had not been available (Murshed, 2001).

A second set of interventionist policies, the attempt to control primary product prices, exposed the weakened mineral economies to negative trade shocks. The **Organization of Petroleum Exporting Countries (OPEC)** cartel (see **cartels**) inflicted price shocks that triggered growth collapses in most resource-rich economies. Other cartels were no more successful. In 1974–5, Jamaica increased taxes in order to raise the price of bauxite, and persuaded other producers, including Surinam, the Dominican Republic and Guinea, to adopt similar measures. Although the price of bauxite imported into the USA doubled for some years, Caribbean bauxite producers lost market share to Australia and Brazil. Worse, few of the bauxite exporters deployed the windfall rents effectively. There were also cartels in phosphate rock and uranium, which achieved only temporary success in raising prices, but reduced demand in favor of substitutes or other sources of supply.

International commodity agreements (ICAs) differ from cartels in that they are designed to stabilize prices rather than to maximize monopoly profits. Some ICAs were supported by consumer and producer countries because commodity price stability has been regarded as beneficial to both. However, prices are often set at unsupportable levels, and the welfare of both producers and consumers is impaired. For example, the International Tin Agreement provided for a buffer stock plus export quotas for member countries. The buffer stock manager purchased tin between 1982 and 1985 in an effort to defend a price higher than the equilibrium level. By October 1985, the manager's resources for defending the agreed price were exhausted and the world price of tin fell. Although a well-managed buffer stock might reduce price fluctuations, export quotas have never been successful due to smuggling and cheating by member governments.

See also: corruption; Dutch disease; economic development; environment; inflation and its effects; oil and gas development; natural resources; Organization of Petroleum Exporting Countries (OPEC); resource curse thesis

Further reading

Auty, R. and Mikesell, R. (1998) *Sustainable Development in Mineral Economies*, Oxford: Clarendon Press.

Collier, P. and Gunning, J. (1999) (eds) *Trade Shocks in Developing Countries: Africa*, Oxford: Oxford University Press.

Murshed, M. (2001) "Short-Run Models of Contrasting Natural Resource Endowments," pp. 113–25 in Auty, R. (ed.) *Resource Abundance and Economic Development*, Oxford: Oxford University Press.

RICHARD M. AUTY

MIRAB (migration, aid, remittances and bureaucracy)

MIRAB is an acronym for **migration, aid, remittances** and bureaucracy, coined by Victoria University geographers Bertram and Watters (1985), which refers to their "hypothesis" concerning the economic structure and welfare-generating strategies characterizing postcolonial Pacific Island countries, especially those in Polynesia. The authors' original investigation grew out of a desire to explain the fact that Pacific Islanders generally enjoy higher material standards of living than per national income measures would predict and was based on a large empirical data set. Migration, from the islands to former colonial and other powers on the Pacific Rim (predominantly New Zealand, Australia and the USA) establishes

enduring "transnational corporations of kin," through which individuals, acting in a welfare maximizing manner, channel remittances both financially and in-kind. Aid forms a significant proportion of national income, driven (at the time of theorization) by the strategic imperatives of the **Cold War** and the postcolonial "obligations" of former powers. Having inherited relatively large colonial bureaucracies, and given the minimum efficient scale of public service activities, the **public sector** becomes the major **employment** source in these relatively diminutive economies.

The model is applicable in varying degrees to various nation-states in the region (and has been applied less successfully to other island regions). In 1986, Bertram argued that such a system constituted a form of dependent development that was both rational and sustainable. These claims, however, have been questioned as third- and fourth-generation migrants lose physical and psychological ties with their "homelands" (although there is as yet no recorded decline in remittances), and aid from traditional sources declines as the Cold War "geopolitical" comparative advantage of the region has disappeared (although aid from other powers such as China and South Korea – driven by desire for ocean resources – is possibly replacing this). Further problems include the downsizing of public sectors following neo-liberal advice from regional and global development institutions. Within the region itself, MIRAB remains a highly controversial topic (Poirine, 1998), which still frames much development debate at the academic and policy levels.

See also: aid; migration; public sector; remittances; small island developing states (SIDS)

Further reading

Bertram, I. and Watters, R. (1985) "The MIRAB Economy in South Pacific Microstates," *Pacific Viewpoint* 26:3 497–519.

Poirine, B. (1998) "Should We Love or Hate MIRAB?" *Contemporary Pacific* 10:1 65–105.

WARWICK E. MURRAY

MISSIONARIES *see* Christianity; religion

modernization theory

Modernization was the leading sociological theory of development in the 1950s, 1960s and 1970s, and is undergoing a revival in conjunction with neo-liberal theories of development today. The theory derived from structural functionalism, a conceptualization of society and social change elaborated by Talcott Parsons, a leading sociological theorist of the twentieth century (see **sociology of development; social integration**). For Parsons (1966:2), the study of societies was guided by an evolutionary perspective, with humans as integral parts of the organic world, and human culture analyzable in the general framework of the life process. Naturalistic concepts of organic evolution, like variation, selection, adaptation, differentiation and integration, could be applied to questions of societal change. Thus **social development**, like organic evolution, proceeds by variation and differentiation from simple social forms, like hunter-gatherer bands, to progressively more complex forms, like industrial societies (Parsons, 1966:90–110). Drawing on this, modernization theory, according to a leading exponent, looked at societies in terms of how closely they approached the model of modern industrial society (Eisenstadt, 1973b:12–15). Traditional societies were seen as restricted in the environments they could master, whereas modern societies were expansive, able to cope with a wider range of environments and problems. This coping capacity (see **coping strategies**) derived essentially from structural specialization – that is, the degree to which social functions were performed by specialized **institutions**. Additionally, the more thorough the disintegration of traditional elements, the more a society could absorb change and develop the qualitative characteristics of modern societies, like rationality, efficiency and a predilection to liberty – a notion drawn from Max Weber's conception of progressive rationalization. Alex Inkeles and David H. Smith (1974) argued that enlightened, modern humankind was characterized by traits like rationality, scientific thinking and urbanity. A key concept in modernization theory is derived from Karl Deutsch's (1961) term "social mobilization," defined as "the process in which major clusters of old social, economic, and psychological commitments are eroded and broken and people become available for new patterns of socialization and behavior" – this, in turn, depended on exposure to modern life, the **media**, **urbanization**, literacy (see **illiteracy**) and so on. The resulting structural characteristics of modernization were identified by Eisenstadt (1973b:23) as:

> the development of a high extent of differentiation: the development of free resources which are not committed to any fixed, ascriptive groups; the development of wide non–traditional, 'national,' or even super-national group identifications; and the concomitant development, in all major institutional spheres, of specialized roles and of special wider regulative or allocative mechanisms and organization, such as market mechanisms in economic life, voting and party activities in politics, and diverse bureaucratic organizations and mechanisms in most institutional spheres.

More specifically, in the economic sphere modernization meant specialization of economic activities and occupational roles and the growth of markets. In terms of socio–spatial organization modernization meant urbanization, mobility, flexibility and the spread of **education**. In the political sphere, modernization meant the spread of **democracy** and the weakening of traditional **elites**. In the cultural sphere, growing differentiation between the cultural and value systems (e.g. separation of philosophy from religion), secularization, and the emergence of new intelligentsia. These developments were closely related to the expansion of modern communications media and the consumption of **culture** created by elites, all this being manifested as changes in attitudes, especially the emergence of an outlook that stressed individual self–advancement. In general, modern societies were said to become able to absorb change and assure their own continuous growth (see **growth rate**).

The economist Bert Hoselitz (1960) applied these ideas to a reformulation of development theory. For Hoselitz, low levels of **economic development** were associated with low **productivity**, because the division of labor was little developed, and economic objectives focused on the maintenance or strengthening of status relations, rather than production for markets. Traditional societies had low levels of social and geographical mobility. What Hoselitz called "the hard cake of custom" determined the manner, and often the effects, of economic performance. An economically developed society, in contrast, was characterized by a complex division of social labor, a relatively open social structure where **caste** barriers were absent and class barriers surmountable. In developed societies, social roles and gains from economic activity were distributed essentially on the basis of achievement; and innovation, the search for profitable market situations, and the ruthless pursuit of self-interest without regard to the welfare of others, were fully sanctioned (Hoselitz, 1960:60). The main problem for theories of **economic growth** was to determine the mechanisms by which the social structure of an underdeveloped economy could be modernized – that is, altered to take on the features of an economically advanced country. The answer was with entrepreneurs or bureaucrats imbued with modern ideas, and with cities modeled after the urban centers of the West as focal points for the introduction of innovative ideas and new social and economic practices.

Modernization theory saw universal stages of growth lying between traditional and modern and between undeveloped and developed countries, as with Rostow's stages of growth theory (see **stages of economic growth**). Modernization could also be seen as a spatial diffusion process, originating at contact situations, such as port cities, or colonial administration centers, with waves of change cascading down urban hierarchies, and funneling along transport systems. This process could be measured by the spread of modern **institutions**, like schools or medical facilities, and mapped as a "modernization surface." Modernization achieved a leading position in conventional development thinking in the 1960s, when a new set of liberal attitudes toward the developing world were being established: for example these ideas form the basis of the historical understanding of development in Gerald Meier's (1964) influential *Leading Issues in Development Economics*, and aspects of modernization theory can be seen in US president John F. Kennedy's statements on foreign economic policy. The implications of the theory were clear – societies wishing to develop need only copy the already-proven example of the West: "backward

countries" should encourage the diffusion of innovation from the center, should adopt **capitalism**, and should welcome United States **aid**, investment, corporations and policy direction.

Beginning in the late 1950s, but gaining momentum from the mid-1960s on, modernization theory was subjected to increasing political and intellectual criticism. Attacks were launched on all aspects of the theory, from its philosophical base in structural functionalism to the politics of its policy prescriptions. From theorists in the dependency school (e.g. Frank, 1969; see **dependency theory**) the modernization approach to economic and cultural change attributed a history to the developed countries but denied histories to the underdeveloped countries, which were reduced to copying the West. Tamas Szentes (1976) argued that values, institutions or technologies developed in one society often do not fit other cultures, and may actually be dysfunctional for development there – it would be better for developing countries to modify or re-create their own institutions rather than imitate those of the of the West. Because of such criticisms, modernization theory was declared theoretically moribund (Wallerstein, 1979: ch. 7). But this declaration was premature in that modifications have been proposed that would resurrect aspects of modernization theory, for example by critiquing unilinearity and stressing instead multiple paths to development (Roxborough, 1988). While deriving from somewhat different theoretical bases (in classical and neo-classical economics) the neo-liberal idea of copying the institutions and policies of Western countries in order to achieve development is not dissimilar to modernization theory – for example the notion common to both that **industrialization** is crucial to the development process, or the idea of rationalization by self-regulating markets. Hence, theories similar to modernization continue to direct policy in governmental and international agencies (such as the **World Bank**), but theoretical justification now tends to be sought more in neo-classical economics than developmental sociology.

See also: economic growth; dependency theory; industrialization; neo-liberalism; stages of economic growth; trickle down; Truman's Bold New Program (1949); world systems theory

Further reading

Deutsch, K. (1961) "Social Mobilization and Political Development," *American Political Science Review* 60: 463–515.

Eisenstadt, S. N. (1973a) *Tradition, Change and Modernity*, New York: John Wiley.

Eisenstadt, S. N. (1973b) "Social Change and Development," pp. 3–33 in Eisenstadt, S. N. (ed.) *Readings in Social Evolution and Development*, Oxford: Pergamon.

Frank, A. G. (1969) *Latin America: Underdevelopment or Revolution?* New York: Monthly Review Press.

Hoselitz, B. (1960) *Sociological Aspects of Economic Growth*, Glencoe: Free Press.

Inkeles, A. and Smith, D. H. (1974) *Becoming Modern: Individual Change in Six Developing Countries*, Cambridge MA: Harvard University Press.

Meier, G. (1984, 4th edn) *Leading Issues in Development Economics*, New York: Oxford University Press.

Parsons, T. (1966) *Societies: Evolutionary and Comparative Perspectives*, Englewood Cliffs NJ: Prentice–Hall.

Rostow, W. W. (1960) *The Stages of Economic Growth: A Non–Communist Manifesto*, Cambridge: Cambridge University Press.

Roxborough, I. (1988) "Modernization Theory Revisited: A Review Article," *Comparative Studies in Society and History* 30: 753–61.

Wallerstein, I. (1979) *The Capitalist World Economy*, New York: Cambridge University Press.

ELAINE HARTWICK

money laundering

Money laundering is a phrase used to describe financial transactions by criminals designed to conceal the criminal origin of their money (see **crime; offshore finance**). Criminal organizations engaged in drug trafficking, arms dealing and other illicit trades commonly use money laundering. It may also lead to **corruption** among government or bank officials who are bribed by criminals to allow the disguise of money from illegal sources. A number of international initiatives have been developed to control money laundering, including the Revised Forty Recommendations by the Financial Action Task Force (FATF). This organization has also issued guidance for countries to help prevent the use of financial services for terrorist activities. Most countries have cooperated with FATF in its anti-money laundering crusade. Only nine countries have failed to develop measures to FATF's satisfaction.

See also: corruption; crime; offshore finance

Further reading

Stessens, G. (2000) *Money Laundering*, Cambridge: Cambridge University Press.

PAUL OKOJIE

monoculture

Monoculture generally refers to agricultural system(s) where the same crop is grown over several seasons on the same field, without crop rotation. Examples include tree plantations (see **plantation forestry**), intensive farming, and paddy rice cultivation where rice may have been grown over several centuries on the same field. Uniformity of crop is generally sought to facilitate **mechanization** and improve the quality of the harvested product. However, monocultures are blamed for negative social and environmental consequences, including the economic risks associated with growing only one crop, often with unstable prices; soil erosion (see **soil erosion and soil fertility**); high risk of rapid destruction by pests; and modification of the native wildlife (including reduction of **biodiversity**), which could lead to a chain of adverse impacts on the different ecosystems involved. (Indeed, these impacts were claimed to occur during the **green revolution**.) Industrial plantation forestry may also have negative impacts on the hydrological basins, since the fast-growing species of trees commonly used in timber plantations consume large amounts of water, and for the lack of species diversity in such forests, which prevents their use by populations settled close by.

See also: agribusiness; agriculture; biodiversity; plantation forestry

CLAUDIO O. DELANG

mortality

Mortality is a measurement of death rates. The most common measure of mortality is the *crude death rate*, which represents the number of deaths occurring during a particular period (usually a year), per 1,000 people. However, this measure is severely distorted by the age distribution of the **population**. An important measure of *age-specific mortality rates* is the *infant mortality rate*, defined as the number of infants who die before the first birthday per 1,000 live births in a given year (see **infant and child mortality**). This can be broken down into first, the *neonatal mortality rate*, those death occurring in the first four weeks after birth, and second, the *post-neonatal mortality rate*, those deaths that occur between four weeks and one year. Apart from age groups, specific death rates can be calculated to study the causes of death or the mortality patterns of specific segments of the population grouped by sex, race (see **race and racism**), **education**, or other characteristics. For example, the **maternal mortality** rate refers to the number of maternal death per 100,000 women of reproductive age (15–49).

See also: fertility; infant and child mortality; maternal mortality; population

CLAUDIO O. DELANG

most favored nation (MFN) status

MFN, or most favored nation, refers to a **trade** relationship whereby one country grants another country the best trading terms it grants to any third country. It refers to the principle of not discriminating between one's best class of trading partners. Implicit in MFN is that a nation may discriminate against less-favored trading partners who have not received MFN status.

There are two versions of MFN. With conditional MFN, the second country must renegotiate to keep preferential status as third countries gain new concessions. With unconditional MFN, new concessions are granted automatically as third countries negotiate for them. Unconditional MFN is central to the **World Trade Organization/ General Agreement on Tariffs and Trade (WTO/GATT)** system.

Before World War I, conditional MFN was standard in bilateral trade agreements, and prevailing political theory required nations to make reciprocal concessions for trade benefits. This was consistent with the idea that domestic market access was a valuable resource, not to be lightly granted. However, the shifting international patchwork of **tariffs**, quotas, and import procedures made business planning difficult and derogated from the development of trade patterns based upon wealth-generating **comparative advantage**.

By the end of World War II, economic theory and practice had shifted, so that unconditional MFN was embodied as Article I of the GATT and became recognized as one of the most fundamental principles of the post-war global financial infrastructure and of the evolving **Washington consensus**. Unconditional MFN is also embodied in the General Agreement on Trade in Services (GATS) Article II and the **trade-related aspects of intellectual property rights (TRIPS)** Article 4.

MFN status imposes several duties upon the nation according such status. One of these is to accord MFN partners the best generally-available tariff rates on all merchandise imports. Another is to ensure that MFN partners receive import procedures no less favorable than those provided to other trading partners. More generally, to use the language of GATT (1947) Article 1, "any advantage, favor, privilege or immunity granted by any contracting party to any product originating in or destined for any other country shall be accorded immediately and unconditionally to the like product" of other contracting parties. In other applications, the principle is the same, but may be applied to services, investments, or nationals of other countries seeking such advantages, favors, privileges or immunities.

Despite the basic idea that MFN status affords nations all advantages available to any trading partners, there are recognized exceptions. Prime among these are the exceptions for trade preferences for developing countries and regional trade agreements (see **economic federalization**).

MFN should be distinguished from national treatment obligations, which also arise from the GATT and similar international agreements, and with which MFN is sometimes confused. MFN requires a nation to accord the citizens or products of another nation treatment no worse than it accords to those of third nations with respect to specified obligations. In contrast, national treatment requires a nation to extend to designated foreign citizens or products treatment no worse than it accords to its own national citizens or products.

See also: Multilateral Agreement on Investment (MAI); protectionism; tariffs; trade; World Trade Organization/General Agreement on Tariffs and Trade (WTO/GATT)

Further reading

AbuAkeel, A. (1999) "The MFN as It Applies to Service Trade: New Problems for an Old Concept," *Journal of World Trade* 33:4 103–29.

WILLIAM B. T. MOCK

mountain development

Mountainous areas are the subject of a variety of development debates and concerns. Several attempts have been made to develop a clear definition the mountain areas. Considering altitude as the only attribute of a mountain (including hills), cartographic techniques have estimated that 27 percent of the Earth's land surface may be called mountains if the lower cut-off altitude of the mountain areas is taken as 1,000m asl (above sea level). The World Conservation Monitoring Center has estimated that about 22 percent of the Earth's surface, with altitude varying between 300m asl and 2,500m asl, could be taken as

mountains. More than 10 percent of the world's **population** lives in the mountains, while about half of the world's population depends on **natural resources** from mountains, primarily water (see **water management**). In spite of the scenic beauty of mountains, mountain communities (see **community**) often face **food** insecurity. The **Food and Agriculture Organization (FAO)** estimated that about 250–370 million mountain people in developing and former Soviet Union countries are vulnerable to food insecurity (see **food security**).

The vertical formation of the mountain landscape induces certain important characteristics to the mountain environments, namely, structural fragility, micro-climatic mosaic and ecological complexity. These exert serious influences on the selection of sustainable economic activities in mountains. The structural fragility of mountains imposes a great need for the assessment of design of roads, dams and buildings, etc. with respect to slope stability or seismic risk. The micro-climatic mosaic offers the basis for the presence of great biological diversity in mountain areas. Moreover, wise use of the micro-climatic conditions can be profitably made in innovative farming and forestry practices, as much as for **tourism**, etc. The ecological complexity of mountain environments imposes strict requirements for the comprehensive assessment of environmental impacts of economic activities or engineering constructions in such districts, whether small or large. For example, building a large dam (see **dams**) in a seismically active region or setting up a tourist resort in an avalanche-prone area would be environmentally risky propositions. In the case of global **climate change**, mountains are one of the best indicators. Through reduction in their permafrost cover or the upward migration of vegetation types, impacts of climate change can be examined. These prospects and limitations of the mountain environment should be used in the identification of preferable options in mountain development.

As the source of all major rivers, and the sites of reservoirs of a very large part of the globe's biological and cultural diversity, mountain environments have been making significant but largely unrecognized contributions to the advancement of human civilizations and economies for centuries. Over the last few centuries, human economic activities flourished on plains, backed by easier transportation on flat land and along river courses, while mountains, suffering from difficulties in accessibility due to their vertical formation, did not experience much economic transformation. This created the conditions for their rich cultural diversity, as well as for the **marginalization** of mountain communities (see **community**) and economies relative to the surrounding plains. Because of this, many mountain communities are seen as backward when the standard economic criteria for standards of living are applied to mountain districts (see **indigenous people**).

The advent of modernization (see **modernization theory**) and **globalization** and their impact on on mountain environments has resulted in much concern about a coincidence of pressures upon physical and cultural landscapes that are vulnerable to change. In the Himalayas, for example, there was much concern during the 1970s that rapid population growth, coupled with increasing **deforestation** and agricultural intensification would lead to ecological collapse on slopes that were too steep to sustain frequent farming. Much research at a variety of scales has questioned this belief (see also **environment**). At the local level, farmers were shown to adopt local **risk and insurance strategies** that allowed them to minimize **vulnerability** to land failure; or to adopt various techniques of reducing land degradation; or sometimes even using land failures fortuitously to assist in the construction of terraces (see Ives and Messerli, 1989; Ives, 2004). At a larger scale, the human impacts on mountain landscapes are difficult to disentangle from longer-term biophysical processes such as tectonic uplift. More generally, the different observed rates of erosion and either deforestation or reforestation suggested a picture of great uncertainty that could be used by different activists to further different policies about environment (Thompson *et al.*, 1986). Such criticisms imply that mountainous areas should not be seen as necessarily fragile, although this should not be interpreted as the ability to ignore all environmental problems or other dilemmas of poor infrastructure, **education** and other factors that may inhibit the creation of **sustainable livelihoods** in mountains.

Many communities living in the mountains of the developing world, are faced with the challenge of facing and competing with much larger economic activities than the subsistence farming they were so far accustomed to. Into this scenario slowly emerged a global search for new policies and **institutions** for mountain development that would reverse the dual trend of marginalization of mountain communities and unsustainable utilization of their natural resources. At the preparatory stage of the **Earth Summit (1992) (United Nations Conference on Environment and Development)** (Rio Conference) a collective of professionals and academics introduced the "Mountain Agenda," with the objective of achieving a higher priority for mountains on the global environmental agenda. Strongly supported by the Swiss government, this activism led to the introduction of an independent chapter, No. 13, on sustainable mountain development in **Agenda 21**, to be administered by the FAO. The **United Nations** nominated 2002 as the international year of mountains.

See also: Chipko movement; environment; indigenous people; shifting cultivation; water management; watershed management

Further reading

The journal *Mountain Research and Development* specializes in mountain development.

Bandyopadhyay, J. (1992) "From Environmental Conflicts to Sustainable Mountain Transformations," in Ghai, D. and Vivian, J. (eds) *Grassroots Environmental Action: People's Participation in Sustainable Development*, London: Routledge.

Funnel, D. and Parish, R. (2001) *Mountain Environments and Communities*, London: Routledge.

Ives, J. and Messerli, B. (1989) *The Himalayan Dilemma: Reconciling Conservation and Development*, London: Routledge and the United Nations University.

Ives, J. (2004) *Himalayan Perceptions: Environmental Change and the Well-Being of Mountain Peoples*, London and Tokyo: Routledge and the United Nations University.

Thompson, M., Warburton, M. and Hatley, T. (1986) *Uncertainty on a Himalayan Scale: An Institutional Theory of Environmental Perception and a Strategic Framework for the Sustainable Development of the Himalayas*, London: Ethnographica, Milton Ash.

JAYANTA BANDYOPADHYAY

Multilateral Agreement on Investment (MAI)

The Multilateral Agreement on Investment (MAI) was a proposed agreement seeking to establish common trading rules for **Organization for Economic Cooperation and Development (OECD)** member states. A central aspect of the MAI was that signatories should not discriminate against foreign investors compared to nationals ("national treatment"), or between foreign investors from different countries (**most favored nation (MFN) status**, or "most favored nation treatment"). Crucially, the MAI gave investors the right to take governments to an international tribunal in the case of investment disputes and to sue government for damages if they felt that local rules violated the MAI. For this reason, the MAI was seen to be a way to empower transnational companies (see **transnational corporations (TNCs)**) against national governments in international trade.

The MAI began to be negotiated officially among the member states of the OECD in 1995, having been given a mandate by the OECD Ministerial meeting in the previous year. It sought to extend certain features of bilateral investment treaties to all OECD member countries within a multilateral framework. The treaty would be open to accession by non-OECD countries and aimed to provide "a benchmark against which potential investors would assess the openness and legal security offered by countries as investment locations" (OECD). Unlike some other investment liberalization schemes, it covered the pre-establishment as well as the post-establishment phase, and used a very broad definition of investment including intellectual property (see **intellectual property rights (IPRs)**) and portfolio investment as well as **foreign direct investment**.

When news of these proposals leaked out, anti-MAI campaigns sprang up in a number of countries, involving **non-governmental organizations (NGOs)**, consumer organizations, **human rights** groups, **trade unions**, **local governments**, politicians and churches. Critics of the MAI argued that it was being negotiated within an exclusive group of rich countries, and that its provisions took no account of the development needs of the majority of the world's countries. It was also seen as a threat to environmental protection and to workers rights (see **brown environmental agenda; labor rights and standards**). It was seen to be unbalanced by focusing exclusively on investor protection and measures to liberalize international investment, without corresponding obligations on the part of investors. For example, the MAI did not address issues of restrictive business practices on the part of firms. The campaigns were successful in raising public awareness of the dangers associated with the MAI, and helped derail the OECD negotiations. The negotiations collapsed in October 1998 when the French government announced that it would no longer participate, because it conflicted with national sovereignty and the protection of France's cultural industries. Other OECD members also expressed reservations over certain aspects of the proposed agreement.

Following the failure of the negotiations within the OECD, it was suggested that investment issues should come under the purview of the WTO. Many observers believe that the discussions of MAI will continue in the future, and will generate further conflict in international negotiations.

See also: economic development; foreign direct investment; industrialization and trade policy; Organization for Economic Cooperation and Development (OECD); tariffs; trade; World Social Forum; World Trade Organization/General Agreement on Tariffs and Trade (WTO/GATT)

Further reading

Mabey, N. (1999) "Defending the Legacy of Rio: The Civil Society Campaign against the MAI," in Picciotto, S. and Mayne, R. (eds) *Regulating International Business: Beyond Liberalization*, Basingstoke: Macmillan.

Piccioto, S. (1999) "A Critical Assessment of the MAI," in Picciotto, S. and Mayne, R. (eds) *Regulating International Business: Beyond Liberalization*, Basingstoke: Macmillan.

RHYS JENKINS

multilateral development banks (MDBs)

Multilateral development banks (MDBs) are financial institutions owned by the developed and developing countries that provide long-term lending for development. They all have at least some special funds available for lending at concessional rates (in "soft window" facilities) and also special facilities for private sector lending (in some cases managed by specially created agencies). As the largest public source of development financing in the world, they are responsible for setting the development agenda. They have been criticized, however, for causing widespread environmental and social damage with poorly conceived programs; carrying out their activities without the informed participation of affected people; and imposing their decisions on many poor countries. Recognizing their weaknesses, the MDBs are increasingly trying to follow the Comprehensive Development Framework (CDF) principles of country ownership, partnership and results building on Poverty Reduction Strategy Papers, and giving special attention to measuring, monitoring and managing for development results.

See also: African Development Bank (ADB); Asian Development Bank (ADB); Inter-American Development Bank (IADB); international economic order; structural adjustment; World Bank

Further reading

IFIwatchnet: a website monitoring international financial institutions and development banks. http://www.ifiwatchnet.org

MAFALDA DUARTE

multiplier effect

The multiplier is the knock on effect from increased expenditure, usually from government spending. If I receive $100 I will spend some (say 0.7 of it, that is $70) and save the rest. The person receiving the $70 will spend $49 ($= 0.7 \times \$70$); the person receiving the $49 will spend $34.30 ($= 0.7 \times \$49$), and so on. Hence the initial $100 of expenditure creates a total of $333.33 spending. The multiplier is defined as $1/(1-c)$, where c is the amount a person spends out of a $1 increase in income (economists call this the marginal propensity to consume), in our example 0.7, or 70 percent. With $c = 0.7$ the multiplier is 3.33. The theory assumes the economy to be demand constrained, meaning goods can be produced to satisfy higher expenditure. But if there is a supply constraint the additional demand will simply result in inflation (see **inflation and its effects**) with no increase in real expenditure.

See also: economic development; fiscal and monetary policy; inflation and its effects

HOWARD WHITE

municipalities

Municipalities are cities, towns, or districts that enjoy some degree of local self-government. The term also refers to the local governing body, and commonly the most immediate form of **local government** in urban areas. Municipalities are increasingly governed by democratically elected local officials, accountable to both national institutions and their local electors. Their powers can be limited to the delivery of basic services (water, road maintenance, primary **education** and **health**, some social services, etc.) or include land use **planning**, **economic development** promotion, **housing**, physical infrastructure, transport (see **transport policy**) and other services.

Municipalities have become a prominent actor in the development process during the last two decades of the twentieth century, when a significant transfer of powers from central governments to local authorities has taken place. This trend is only partly because of pressure from citizens for local **democracy**. More importantly, the role of national governments has decreased through a general trend toward **globalization**, which has changed the hierarchy of factors influencing the location of **governance** and investment. There is now increasing competition among local governments to attract national and foreign investment (see **foreign direct investment**). Furthermore, the reduction of government expenditure, often following **structural adjustment** programs, has generally increased the powers of municipalities. Consequently, municipalities have undertaken a growing number of tasks and responsibilities without being provided with adequate financial resources to face them, being obliged to find locally the resources they need.

The shift of the role of municipalities from being local administrators to being local governments has had deep implications on the mechanisms of local democracy and on mutual relations among different components of **civil society**. Different kinds of powers have been transferred to municipalities and in different ways. Three types of **decentralization** have been identified: *political*, when a real transfer of decisional powers occurs; *administrative* (sometimes referred to as deconcentration), when only operational tasks are transferred to local offices; and *fiscal*, when local authorities' ability to raise local taxes is established or increased. Increasingly, municipalities operate within the frameworks of **public-private partnerships**.

The new role of municipalities has been recognized by the international **community** first at the **Earth Summit (1992) (United Nations Conference on Environment and Development)** in Rio de Janeiro, and more substantially at the Habitat II (see **Habitat I and II**) conference at Istanbul in 1996. Here, the Habitat Agenda, adopted by 171 governments, clearly advocates decentralization and the strengthening of local authorities and their associations/networks.

Following Habitat II – or during its preparation period – the number of organizations and programs supporting local governments was boosted; among the most important were: UN Advisory Committee of Local Authorities (UNACLA), World Association of Cities and Local Authorities Coordination (WACLAC), Cities Alliance, promoted by the **World Bank**, and a group of programs supporting international cooperation among municipalities funded by the European Commission (Med-Urbs, Asia-Urbs, Tacis City Twinning, Urb-Al, etc.). The role and importance of associations of municipalities has also increased, fostering international cooperation among local governments.

See also: decentralization; Habitat I and II; housing; local government; partnerships; planning; public-private partnerships; public management; public sector; urban development

Further reading

Plummer, J. (2000) *Municipalities and Community Participation: A Sourcebook*, London: Earthscan.

MATTEO SCARAMELLA

NAFTA *see* North American Free Trade Agreement

narratives of development

Development narratives are commonly heard summaries or explanations of development problems that are discussed as though they are true, but which oversimplify and even misrepresent reality. They are also known as "received wisdom," "development blueprints" or "myths," and continue to exist even when there is substantial counter-evidence against the narrative. There are two underlying questions about narratives: how they originate, and how they persist. According to analysts (e.g. Roe, 1991), narratives usually originate from the shaping of initial research on development problems from individuals or organizations with specific agendas (such as colonial scientists, development interventionists or journalists), whose perspectives may differ from people living in regions affected by supposed problems. As a result, certain apparent "facts" in each region are given more importance than others by researchers, who may identify these facts because they highlight their own worldviews, or because they resonate with problems already experienced by the researchers elsewhere, but which do not necessarily exist in the region under consideration. Some examples of narratives include the environmental principle of the "tragedy of the commons," which describes the destruction of open-access resources by overuse, and which has been portrayed as a universal threat, yet which has also been widely criticized as misrepresentative (see **environment**). Other examples include the notion that women may be less corrupt than men because they are household providers, or that land registration leads to increased agricultural **productivity**. There are many others (e.g. see **gender; desertification**).

The persistence of narratives despite the existence of counter-evidence has been explained in various ways. Some analysts have proposed that narratives persist because society will always contain different worldviews that either frame or continue to frame development dilemmas in certain optimistic or pessimistic ways. This has been claimed in particular concerning popular or **media**-based debates, which tend to oversimplify complex issues. Other analysts have proposed that narratives serve political purposes in allowing states or specific organizations to justify a policy despite criticisms. Some critics have further alleged that narratives are self-sustaining because they define development problems in ways that allow **aid** agencies to define both the nature of problems and solutions, and hence allow agencies to demonstrate their own effectiveness in overcoming problems. According to Roe (1991:288), "Development narratives tell scenarios not so much about what should happen as about what will happen according to their tellers – if the events or positions are carried out as described."

Research on development narratives has important implications for development practice, and for the relationship of science and development (see **science and technology**). If narratives exist, then they pose significant criticisms to the ability for development professionals to be self-critical or listen to evidence-based research in different locations. They also indicate a need to understand how knowledge is collected, institutionalized, and legitimized within bureaucracies, and how information about development is controlled by media and other populist forms of communication. Narratives also indicate a need to be more participatory and transparent in collecting information in developing societies, and to avoid imposing predefined visions of problems on other people. A "narrative approach" to development implies that development problems and information are analyzed in terms of storylines, or concerning how, and for whom, development problems and solutions have been defined. Proponents of narrative analysis claim that this approach may explain why so many development problems have been explained through the eyes of outsiders rather than by people living in developing regions.

See also: deforestation; desertification; measuring development; media; participatory development; postmodernism and postdevelopment; science and technology

Further reading

Roe, E. (1991) "Development Narratives, Or Making the Best of Blueprint Development," *World Development* 19:4 287–300.

TIM FORSYTH

nationalism

Nationalism is the individual and collective sense of belonging to a particular nation and the consequent political ideology that demands a nation's **right to self-determination**. Nationalism is commonly considered complex because of its "chameleon-like" character. It can be invoked by various types of groups that perceive themselves as nations, and is consequently used by diverse popular movements across the political spectrum.

In Benedict Anderson's noteworthy 1990 conceptualization, a "nation" is an *imagined* **community** because its members imagine themselves to be part of

a larger political entity based on a variety of factors crucial to group identity. These factors include common ethnicity (see **ethnicity/identity**), **religion**, and language; the long-term occupation of and psychological attachment to a territorial homeland; a shared historical experience; and a unique set of cultural myths, traditions, and pastimes. The nation is an imagined community especially because its members imagine themselves to be linked by a common ethnic *origin* (regardless of whether other indicators may confirm this) and, therefore, by a common *destiny*. This aspect provides the link between nation and nationalism as a political ideology.

An independent nation, imagined by its members as a spatially limited community within which resides an ethnically homogeneous **population** and beyond which are other nations, is consequently imagined as the only legitimate sovereign of itself, its people and territory. Hence, nationalistic discourse holds that a territorially and politically synonymous nation and state (see **state and state reform**), or nation-state, is a necessity for a nation to reach its full social, cultural, economic and political potential. A nation denied this natural independence therefore invokes nationalism as a mass political movement demanding its right to self-determination through the withdrawal of colonial rule (see **decolonization**), military occupation, or secession from or autonomy within an existing state.

Nationalism discourse holds that an individual's national identity is their most important, because ethnicity is the only unchangeable identity and thus transcends all other forms of social, political, and economic affiliations. This essentialism contrasts with the conventional modernist understanding that modernization (see **modernization theory**) produces pervasive cosmopolitan identities which subvert ethnicity and thus circumvent parochial nationalisms. Other forms of identity, such as **gender**, class, sexuality (see **sexualities**), occupation, etc. are meant, with **economic development** and democratization (see **democracy**), to overcome appeals to ethnicity as an essentialist identity and produce a "civic" nationalism.

Nevertheless, a more provincial "ethnic" nationalism, especially amongst **stateless people**, has resisted, even intensified, despite the modernizing forces supposed to dissolve it. Indeed, after the

Cold War a second wave of what Michael Igna-tieff, in his 1993 book *Blood and Belonging*, calls "new nationalisms" tore apart many multi-national states (see **weak states**) through the eruption of ethnic **violence** (see **ethnic cleansing; genocide**) in, for example, Yugoslavia, Chechnya, and Rwanda. Today, the persistence of ethnic nation-alisms in many development contexts (e.g. the Kurds and Palestinians) as well as Western states (e.g. the Basques and Quebecois) demonstrates the contemporary importance of nationalism as a political ideology.

See also: community; ethnicity/identity; geno-cide; politics; right to self-determination; sociology of development

Further reading

Anderson, B. (1990) *Imagined Communities: Reflections on the Origins and Spread of National-ism*, London: Verso.

Ignatieff, M. (1993) *Blood and Belonging: Journeys into the New Nationalism*, New York: Farrar, Straus, and Giroux.

PETER MAYELL

nationalization

Nationalization refers to the forced divestment of foreign-owned assets within a particular state's territory, and is often used interchangeably with expropriation. It is about sovereignty as much as economic policy. Though often understood as an end-point or culmination of events, nationaliza-tion should rather be seen as involving a whole set of legal, technical and managerial processes whereby ownership is transferred through, most usually, bilateral negotiation between the host nation and the investing countries. While it has often been associated with revolutionary transi-tions to socialist governments, most developing nations have at some stage nationalized foreign assets, irrespective of ideology.

Nationalization can take many different forms, but Kobrin (1984) makes a useful distinction between "mass" and "selective" nationalizations.

Mass nationalizations are often occasioned by an ideological shift, itself usually part of a socio-political **revolution**. Fuelled by the growth of **transnational corporations (TNCs)** and the emergence of newly independent nations, selective nationalizations became increasingly prominent during the 1960s and 1970s, and can best be understood as policy instruments aimed at increasing control over particular economic actors, and particularly TNCs. In both cases nationaliza-tion seeks to secure the more fundamental right to actually control any particular economic activity, and it therefore differs strongly from other forms of asset management, such as taxation, which attempts to determine the host nation's share of the profits within an agreed-upon discourse of the rights of economic actors (see **rights-based approaches to development**).

Controversies over nationalization therefore arise precisely through differing interpretations of such rights and responsibilities of states and their economic agents, rendering it a somewhat gray area of **international law**. While capital-exporting countries object on the grounds of diminished income, and therefore question the nationalizing government's right to do so, the expropriating nation holds national development as paramount and points to the responsibilities of the usually richer investor countries. Disputes can involve military action, but a more usual response is regulatory retaliation. Most famously, the US Hickenlooper Amendment to the Foreign Aid Act was passed in 1962. It provided for the cessation of US **aid** to any nation expropriating US-owned property that had not made adequate attempts to compensate. In the event, nationalization may or may not involve compensation, depending on the circumstances, and compensation may be unequal between claimants. For example, while Cuba made efforts to remunerate European countries after its expropriation of land in the early 1960s, it did not remunerate those assets owned by US nationals.

Since the 1970s, poor countries have more often used other forms of regulatory control, such as taxation and foreign exchange controls (see, for example, **tariffs**). Geographically, nationalization is part of broader issues about sovereignty and de-territorialization that are paramount within the global economy. The rapid expansion of new forms of property, such as **intellectual property rights (IPRs)** in the 1990s, has reconfigured the relationship between sovereignty and deterritorialization and occasioned new debates about the issue of nationalization.

See also: intellectual property rights (IPRs); protectionism; state-owned enterprises (SOEs); transnational corporations (TNCs)

Further reading

Andersson, T. (1991) *Multinational Investment in Developing Countries: A Study of Taxation and Nationalization*, London: Routledge.

Kobrin, S. (1984) "Expropriation as an Attempt to Control Foreign Firms in LDCs: Trends from 1960–1979," *International Studies Quarterly* 28: 329–48.

SIMON REID-HENRY

natural capital

The natural capital of a nation is a notional sum of all its **natural resources**. It comprises one of the three main constituents of a nation's wealth (or total capital K), the others being human-made capital and knowledge. Some of these resources are *biotic*, i.e. living organisms, and hence are renewable. Others such as minerals are exhaustible. **Sustainable development** is interpreted as a constraint that capital should not be eroded. For example, a business that eats into its assets is considered unsustainable. Similarly, a nation that erodes its wealth including natural capital can be considered unsustainable. An important question is whether the injunction of not eroding capital applies to the total capital (K) or whether it applies to each constituent of that capital. The answer depends on whether we consider different forms of capital to be compensatory, i.e. a shortfall in one form of capital can be made good by an increase in another form of capital. This is known as substitutability, and in turn gives two interpretations of sustainability. The *strong sustainability* approach considers that natural capital cannot be substituted by human-made capital. This requires us to maintain intact and pass on to future generations not only the total capital but each constituent of that capital. The *weak sustainability* approach considers that sustainability is a "vague and general" obligation to pass on to future generations the overall wealth intact but not a "specific one" to pass on to each constituent. Both of these approaches focus only on the **well-being** of humans (i.e. they are anthropocentric), ignoring the issue of whether the well-being of other beings should also count. Philosophers are divided on whether non-human beings can have an independent moral status, and if so whether this should be limited to sentient beings (those that can feel pain) or apply to all living beings. Others argue that all of nature and its ecosystems should be considered to have a moral standing (**deep ecology**). From that viewpoint, the expression "natural capital" may appear to be far too narrow, reflecting a utilitarian approach to nature. This relates to whether our obligation to preserve nature for future generations is a "selfish" obligation because such natural resources are *instrumental*, i.e. a means to serve certain human ends, or whether it is a broader ethical obligation to preserve nature for its *intrinsic* worth.

Even if we resolve these issues, measuring natural capital can be problematic. Natural capital contains many natural resources and natural features that do not respect political boundaries and **property rights**. A recent approach is to define "critical natural capital" (CNC) as for example the natural capital that is essential for maintaining many important environmental functions (Ekins *et al.*, 2003). For policy, this can be interpreted as a requirement to maintain all CNC intact for future generations and to use efficiency-based decisions for the non-critical natural capital, substitutable by human-made capital. Defining what is critical can be subject to social and political decisions and consensus may not be easy.

See also: environment; natural resources; sustainable development

Further reading

Beckerman, W. (1995) "How Would You Like Your 'Sustainability', Sir? Weak or Strong?

A Reply to My Critics," *Environmental Values* 4: 169–79.

Ekins, P., Folke, C. and de Groot, R. (2003) "Identifying Critical Natural Capital," *Ecological Economics* 44: 159–63.

P. B. ANAND

natural disasters

In the development literature the phrase "natural disaster" is loosely used to refer to a confusing combination of things: extreme natural events such as earthquakes, storms, **droughts**, and floods; the consequences of such events on people, **livelihoods**, the built environment, and **institutions**; efforts to plan for or to reduce these consequences (as in the phrase "natural disaster research"). Not only is this usage ambiguous, but it is misleading on several counts.

There is actually very little about "natural" disasters that is natural. Careful authors distinguish between the trigger event, or hazard, and its consequences. Hazards can be natural events. But the hazard may not directly do harm itself. It may begin a cascade of events: a volcanic eruption that melts snow and ice, causing a rock avalanche that temporarily dams up a river that finally floods a town with mud and other debris (Armero, Colombia, in 1985, killing 23,000 people). In addition, extreme events like earthquakes, high winds, floods, and wild fires often produce secondary technological hazards such as toxicity or explosions as they affect factories, warehouses, pipelines, and other infrastructure. In practice, it is hard to distinguish "natural" from "technological" in such cases.

"Disaster" is usually defined as a disruption or rupture of the normal social order so severe that it requires external assistance. Each year there are many thousands of occurrences of this kind that affect some few dozen or hundreds of households in specific neighborhoods of big cities, in small towns, and in rural places. These events seldom make international news or even the national headlines. They include frequent, small floods in squatter settlements in Mumbai and Manila, landslides in Rio de Janeiro, snowstorms in Central Asia and the Andes, and the cycle of droughts and flood in many parts of Africa, or recurring outbreaks of dengue fever or cholera in Central America.

What is more often discussed both by the media and development studies experts are large-scale events that displace tens of thousands of people, kill hundreds or thousands, do great harm to standing crops and stored **food**, infrastructure, and the built environment. Such disasters call forth large-scale international assistance, and they sometimes cause the legitimacy of governments or their policies to be questioned. Examples include the earthquake in Mexico City in 1985; eruption of Mt Pinatubo in the Philippines in 1991; **famine**s in Sudan and elsewhere in Africa in the 1980s and 1990s; extensive flooding in China in 1998; hurricane Mitch that devastated Honduras and Nicaragua in 1998; another tropical super-cyclone that affected Orissa state in India in 1999; an earthquake in northwest Turkey that killed 30,000 people in 1999; and earthquakes in El Salvador and Gujarat, India, early in 2001.

None of these cases can be considered "natural" or an "an act of God." In all these cases, the extreme event took place in a context of **vulnerability** and exposure that had been produced by patterns of access to resources and information (see **information technology**) in society. Groups of people who are more vulnerable to harm in such events are generally marginal and lack economic and political power. In addition, very long-standing patterns of **urbanization**, land ownership, land use, urban-rural relations, and **governance** determine what is done to prevent loss from extreme events – for example, whether rural **health** centers or schools are built to withstand earthquake and high wind, whether urban building codes are enforced, or whether a low-caste group has access to recovery assistance.

Development studies and disaster studies overlap considerably where both concern themselves with the relationship between social, economic, and political relations during "normal" times and these relations in times of crisis, and also in their pursuit of the root causes of **poverty** and disaster vulnerability, respectively. While development studies has been more concerned with political and economic crisis, and with the question of post-crisis recovery, for example **post-conflict rehabilitation**, disaster researchers work in parallel on the crises created when an extreme natural event impacts a vulnerable **population**. In fact, the connections among these kinds of research are often numerous, as in the case of drought or **livestock** disease that takes place during a civil **war**. This gives rise to what the **United Nations** calls a complex emergency (see **complex emergencies**).

Another connection between development and disaster studies is the growing attention being paid to **local knowledge**, survival and **coping strategies**, capacity for recovery, and resilience in the face of crisis and disruption. The significance of local knowledge and institutions emerged as one of the main findings of the International Decade for Natural Disaster Reduction (IDNDR) (1990–2000). Such localized capacity to withstand and to recover from extreme natural events is a function of the nature of livelihoods, social networks, local knowledge, and connections among localities and between them and higher order systems.

"Routine" or "normal" development programs and projects can do a great deal to build capacity and resilience to the extent that they provide new livelihood options and strengthen old ones, increase social connections, elicit and share local knowledge, and increase the efficiency of **local government**. Ironically, much international assistance following disasters actually undermines capacity by creating dependency and by ignoring local knowledge and organizations. The misuses and contradictions of disaster **aid** have been much discussed (especially in the case of famine relief and **food aid**). They range on a continuum from full blown **corruption** by political **elites** or war lords who seize control of aid flows to milder, though still destructive ways in which aid is used to buy votes, reinforce the position of large landowners and urban landlords, or simply to recreate the status quo before the extreme event. Seldom is aid used in a way that rebuilds physically, socially, and economically in a way that increases resilience to the next shock or crisis. Many **bilateral aid agencies** refer to this ideal situation as making use of a "window of opportunity" provided by the disaster for fundamental changes that would mitigate the impact of future hazard events. While reasonable as an academic idea, such a "relief-development continuum" is hard to achieve in practice.

See also: aid; aid effectiveness and aid evaluation; capacity building; complex emergencies; drought; environment; famine; vulnerability

Further reading

Anderson, M. and Woodrow, P. (1998) *Rising from the Ashes: Development Strategies in Times of Disaster*, Boulder: Lynne Rienner.

Hewitt, K. (1995) "Sustainable Disasters? Perspectives and Powers in the Discourse of Calamity," pp. 115–28 in Crush, J. (ed.) *Power of Development*, London: Routledge.

Oliver-Smith, A. and Hoffman, S. (eds) (1999) *The Angry Earth: Disaster in Anthropological Perspective*, New York: Routledge.

Varley, A. (ed.) (1994) *Disasters, Development and Environment*, Chichester: Wiley.

Wisner, B., Davis, I., Blaikie, P. and Cannon, T. (2004, 2nd edn) *At Risk: Natural Hazards, People's Vulnerability and Disasters*, London: Routledge.

BEN WISNER

natural resources

Natural resources are the endowments of physical items of value for economic production and **industrialization** such as iron ore, coal, **fisheries**, or land necessary for **agriculture**. Over the years, different analysts have claimed that shortages of natural resources might halt **economic growth**, or that an abundant endowment of natural resources retards **economic development**. In fact, nether fear is grounded, provided sound policies are pursued.

Some economists have viewed natural resources as being available in unlimited supply, while others regarded them as a potential constraint on production. In the early nineteenth century, classical economists were concerned that natural resource shortages, particularly in land, constituted a limit to growth in per capita output, and therefore might lead to a Malthusian-type collapse resulting from an inability of resources to maintain current levels of growth (see *Limits to Growth* **report (1972)**; **Malthusian demography**). Yet, a century later, most economists believed society could overcome the Malthusian **population** trap and the law of diminishing returns, so that perpetual economic and social progress is probable, if not assured. The opening up of new territories for agricultural production, the continued discovery of mineral reserves, and rapid technological change supported such optimism.

Most economists came to believe that increased capital and technological progress would prevent natural resources from ever becoming a constraint on world growth. When interest in the economic growth of developing countries increased after World War II and spawned growth models, natural resources played almost no role. Rather, capital was seen as the engine of growth, while technological advance served to increase the **productivity** of capital so that growth could proceed indefinitely. These models suggested that constrained domestic investment kept developing country incomes at low levels. Foreign investment, technical aid and government planning could remove these constraints. Natural resource constraints on growth were ignored because countries could import resource-based products from world markets with revenue from exports of labor-intensive products (see **export-led growth**).

However, rapid increases in non-fuel mineral and petroleum prices in the early 1970s, together with publication of the Club of Rome report, *Limits to Growth* (Meadows *et al.*, 1972), triggered a reassessment of the role of natural resources as a constraint on growth. The *Limits to Growth* **report (1972)** argued that scarcity of minerals and arable land limited growth in the intermediate term, while the degradation of life-supporting environmental resources threatened growth through the long term. The report was widely criticized and its predictions about mineral and land shortages were soon convincingly refuted. However, concern for the sustainability of global economic development strengthened during the 1980s, due to fears about the polluting effect of technology on the environment (see **pollution**).

The growing interest in **sustainable development** also raised the paradox of how a country can achieve sustainable development based on depleting finite resources, like minerals. Conventional economics assumes that substitutes can be found

for minerals either through imports, by substituting an alternative natural resource or by technological substitution. Therefore, it is not necessary to pass the minerals to future generations but instead to ensure that similar (or greater) wealth-generating capacity is passed on. Environmental and natural-resource accounting furnishes a rationale for the management of mineral rents (the surplus after subtracting all costs of production from the revenue). It shows that the government of a mineral economy needs to divide the mineral rents into an income component and a capital component. The latter is the amount that must be invested annually, either domestically or overseas, to maintain the income component of the rent stream in perpetuity. In practical terms, the ratio of the capital component of the rents to the income component (which can be consumed by the present generation) may be low (usually less than 10 percent). It is lower the larger the reserves (longer the life of the mine) and the higher the rate of interest at which the capital component can be invested.

A second recent concern about natural resources and development is how resource abundance affects development. An abundance of natural resources should confer benefits for economic development through an increased capacity to export and earn the foreign exchange with which to import capital goods to build up the economy, and also because the rents increase the capacity to save and invest. Yet, since the 1960s, a counterintuitive relationship has emerged between natural resource abundance and growth in per capita income (Auty, 2001) (see **resource curse thesis**). Data for six categories of natural resource endowment compare economic growth rates both before and after the period of oil shocks (1974–85). They show that during the years 1974–85 all four resource-abundant groups (large, small crop-driven, small ore-exporting and small crop-exporting) experienced a growth collapse. In contrast, both resource-poor groups (large and small countries) sustained growth, and it actually accelerated in the large resource-poor countries. Moreover, growth rates for the post-shock years 1985–97 are inversely related to the share of natural resource rents in **gross domestic product (GDP)**. The mineral-exporting countries had the highest rents and the slowest rate of growth. Within that sub-group the oil-exporters had the highest rents of all and the lowest rate of per capita GDP growth.

Sachs and Warner (1995) confirm the disappointing economic growth of the resource-abundant countries. They link the growth collapses to **Dutch disease** effects arising from mismanaged commodity booms. These effects result when a commodity boom inflates the exchange rate so that the non-boom products loose their viability and contract. As dependence on commodity exports rises, governments tend to intervene to close trade policy and protect domestic manufacturing (see **protectionism**). As the size of the protected sector rises relative to the primary sector, resource-abundant countries require a politically unpopular large devaluation of the exchange rate (see **exchange rates**) to restore competitiveness and thereby sustain economic growth. Interestingly, however, trade policy opens again at higher levels of resource dependence (the trough of the U-shape curve occurs where primary exports reach 33 percent of GDP, with most developing countries below this level). This opening up of trade policy reflects the dominance of that section of the curve by oil-exporters like Saudi Arabia, whose high per capita oil reserves reduced their concern with economic diversification. When oil prices fell, growth collapsed in the absence of alternative earners of foreign exchange to oil.

A recent study (Auty, 2001) identifies two main reasons for the superior performance since the 1973 oil shock of the resource-poor countries compared with the resource-rich countries. The first is the pattern of structural change: resource-poor countries diversify earlier into competitive manufacturing than do resource-rich countries, and in consequence they accumulate all forms of capital (produced, human and social) faster than do resource-rich countries. Resource-rich countries depend for longer on natural resources and experience slower capital accumulation and competitive diversification.

The second important reason for the superior performance of the resource-poor countries is that they are more likely to engender a "developmental" political state (see **developmental state**) whose two defining characteristics are sufficient autonomy to pursue coherent economic policies

and the aim of maximizing social welfare. There are two variants of the developmental state, namely the benevolent autonomous state and the consensual democracy. The former is strongly associated with the resource-poor countries of East Asia. Resource-rich countries tend to engender predatory political states.

Two basic models illustrate how natural resources affect growth. The first is the competitive **industrialization** model, which is strongly associated with the resource-poor countries. The second is the staple trap model that has been associated with the resource-abundant countries since the 1960s. With limited opportunity to expand exports of primary products, resource-poor countries tend to embark on industrialization early. They abandon protectionist policies in favor of a relatively open trade policy. This new policy then triggers an expansion of competitive **labor-intensive** manufacturing, much for export. In principle, the competitive industrialization model contains virtuous interlocking economic and social circles that sustain economic growth that is both rapid and equitable.

The virtuous economic circle exhibits four characteristics. First, early and rapid industrialization accelerates **urbanization**. This speeds the demographic cycle so that the ratio of dependents/worker falls, stimulating saving and raising the rate of investment toward 25 percent of GDP (Bloom and Williamson, 1998). Second, the efficiency of investment is sustained so that per capita GDP can double each decade. Third, labor-intensive manufacturing absorbs surplus rural labor (within a decade after trade policy reform in both South Korea and Taiwan) and causes wage increases that require diversification into competitive heavy industry. This diversification reduces the **vulnerability** of the economy to external shocks. Fourth, the increasing complexity of the economy forces the government to cut back its intervention and to concentrate on providing an enabling environment.

The interlocking virtuous social circle has three features. First, income equality is maintained because the tightening of the labor market (see **labor markets**) removes the drag of surplus rural labor on the wages of the poor. Meanwhile, the upgrading of workforce skills reduces the wage premium on higher skills. Second, the resulting relatively equitable distribution of income together with earlier urbanization and passage through the demographic cycle accelerates **social capital** accumulation, and thereby lowers transaction costs compared with resource-abundant countries. Third, these favorable trends in **human capital** and **social capital** combine to encourage **democracy** that tends to be consensual rather than polarized, so that policy coherence is sustained but the risk of vested interests capturing government policy is reduced.

In contrast, resource-abundant countries rely on primary product exports for longer than resource-poor countries of a similar size, and this delays the process of competitive industrialization. It also breeds predatory governments that extend the delay, with four adverse consequences. First, economic diversification must initially occur into other primary products, and this may be difficult for small resource-rich economies whose natural resource endowment is skewed toward one or two viable commodities. Second, slower industrialization retards urbanization and the demographic cycle so the favorable middle phase of the dependency/worker cycle is delayed and accumulation of produced and human capital is further slowed. Third, surplus rural labor persists and, combined with the slower accumulation of skills, amplifies income inequality and social tensions. Fourth, the beneficial labor-intensive phase of the competitive industrialization model is leapfrogged (see **leapfrogging**) and governments react to pressure to create **employment** by forcing the pace of industrialization with subsidies and protection.

Forced industrialization by **infant industries** protection has three principal flaws. First, it creates discretionary rents that governments deploy with minimal **transparency** so they become a corrupt rent-dispensing mechanism that distorts the economy in an *ad hoc* and cumulative fashion. Second, such industry is **capital intensive** and creates few jobs. Governments respond to growing social tension by providing still more non-productive employment. Yet, further expansion of the protected sector weakens market discipline. Third, protected industry takes decades to mature instead of the five to eight years

considered the maximum if the benefits of supporting infant industry are to compensate for the costs of that support. This imposes increasingly onerous demands on the primary sector for transfers and foreign exchange (see **exchange rates**) that absorb not only the natural resource rents but also the profits and so undermine the primary sector's competitiveness. The efficiency of investment declines steeply and the level of investment flattens and may fall. In this way, the resource-abundant economy becomes locked into a staple trap in which burgeoning slow-maturing industry and bloated public services depend on transfers from a primary sector with waning competitiveness due to diminished incentives, whose share in GDP declines due to structural change.

However, the relationship between the natural resource endowment and the type of political state is not a deterministic one. A handful of resource-abundant countries, including Botswana, Chile, Malaysia and Indonesia, spawned developmental governments. In such cases, the longer reliance on primary products merely postpones competitive industrialization, but does not abort it. The key policy question is, therefore, how to reduce the risk of engendering a predatory political state in resource-abundant countries so that a coherent welfare-maximizing economic policy can be pursued.

See also: common pool resources; community-based natural resource management (CBNRM); developmental state; Dutch disease; environment; industrialization; institutions and environment; *Limits to Growth* report (1972); Malthusian demography; mineral-led development; oil and gas development; rent seeking; resource curse thesis

Further reading

Ascher, W. (1999) *Why Governments Waste Natural Resources*, Baltimore MD: Johns Hopkins University Press.

Auty, R. (ed.) (2001) *Resource Abundance and Economic Development*, Oxford: Oxford University Press.

Bloom, D. and Williamson, J. (1998) "Demographic Transitions and Economic Miracles in Emerging Asia," *The World Bank Economic Review* 12: 419–55.

Meadows, D. H., Meadows, D. L., Randers, J. and Behrens, W. (1972) *The Limits to Growth*, New York: Signet.

Mellor, J. (ed.) (1995) *Agriculture on the Road to Industrialization*, London: Johns Hopkins University Press.

Sachs, J. D. and Warner, A. (1995) "Economic Reform and the Process of Global Integration," *Brookings Papers on Economic Activity* 1: 1–118.

RICHARD M. AUTY

neocolonialism

Neocolonialism is a form of imperialism involving political, economic, or cultural dominance by powerful nation-states (generally taken to mean the G8 and other "core" countries), or the institutions that represent their interests (such as the **World Bank** and the **International Monetary Fund (IMF)**), over economically marginalized nation-states and their socio-economies. This dominance is exerted without the formal territorial and political control that characterizes colonialism (see **colonialism, history of; colonialism, impacts of**) yet results in asymmetric power relations both between and within countries are reminiscent of that arrangement. The economic and political systems of the dominated countries remain closely dependent on external powers, despite their ostensible independence.

Historically, the term is most commonly associated with geo-economic and geo-political change subsequent to World War II. The collapse of the European empires across Asia and Africa in the 1950s and 1960s led to a wave of independence creating many new nation-states (see **decolonization**). Although such countries engaged in postcolonial discourse (see **postcolonialism**), it is argued that the rise of the new **international division of labor**, and the **Bretton Woods** institutions which partly facilitated it, led to economic domination replacing various forms of formal political determination. As such, **transnational corporations (TNCs)** are often argued to be the principal vessels through which such control was extended to the periphery during this period. The global reach of TNCs, particularly from the USA but also from other former colonial powers such as the UK and Germany, expanded rapidly in the post-war period – although the roots of that growth were laid during the colonial period of the late 1800s and early 1900s. The rise of neocolonial relations, then, is associated especially with the post-war period, yet such a condition has certainly been present at other points in history. In Latin America for example, formal political control by the Spanish and the Portuguese following independence of most countries in the early 1800s was replaced by the economic influence of first British and then US firms in particular. Arguably, neocolonial relations need not necessarily be capitalist in form or cause: the relationship of COMECON states to the USSR until the fall of communism has been similarly conceptualized (see **postsocialism**).

In the post-war capitalist world, TNCs are not the only means through which neocolonial relations have been perpetuated. **Aid** to poorer countries, both bilateral and multilateral, has played an important geopolitical and economic role and has become increasingly "conditional" (see **conditionality**). For example, the reconstruction of East Asia partly through the post-war Colombo Plan led by the USA, laid the seeds of subsequent capitalist growth there and was an important instrument in maintaining **Cold War** allegiances. Bodies such as the Central Intelligence Agency (CIA) of the USA have played a major role in regime change in "hostile" countries, particularly in the face of fears concerning the rise of communism in Latin America in the 1970s. Perhaps the most important agents in terms of economic determinism have been the Bretton Woods institutions (principally the World Bank and IMF) and the allied institutions which have grown from it since, notably GATT and later the WTO (see **World Trade Organization/General Agreement on Tariffs and Trade (WTO/GATT)**). The World Bank, for example, formed as a means of stabilizing the world economy following World War II, also assumed an explicit role as a principal agent for the diffusion of capitalism and modernization (see **modernization theory**) from the

West to the periphery. It became particularly influential following the oil-hikes (1973 and 1979) and **debt** crisis of the 1980s, fostering in the era of **structural adjustment**. From the 1980s, loans became increasingly conditional in the adoption of free-market capitalist reforms informed by the theories of **neo-liberalism** and monetarism emanating from the University of Chicago and Milton Friedman in particular (see **fiscal and monetary policy; inflation and its effects**). As such, to varying degrees, neo-liberalism has effectively been forced on the majority of countries in the periphery in places as diverse as Chile, Uganda, and Indonesia. Such reforms further open the doors to international capital and are increasingly protected by the powerful WTO.

Cultural aspects of neocolonialism have also been studied, especially regarding **globalization and culture**. Analysts argue that **media** and other instruments of global capital diffuse cultural norms of the West to the periphery, creating global **commercialization** that perpetuates the illusion of the desirability and inevitably of modernization. There is much debate about the forging of a global **culture**. Human geography, in some areas at least, has been particularly skeptical of the homogenization thesis and has argued that cultural **globalization** increases differentiation and thus asymmetries in cultural and political development. In postdevelopment critiques, development itself has been criticized as a form of neocolonialism that builds on discourses propagated during the colonial period and sustained through a general tendency in Western academia to "Orientalize" "others" in developing countries (see **Orientalism; postmodernism and postdevelopment**). There are growing debates in **postcolonialism** that extend these questions and focus, among other things, on the imperative of "decolonizing the mind." Neocolonialism, then, is not just about circuits of capital but also circuits of ideas and the networks that they create and permeate.

The theories that are most closely associated with neocolonialism are, however, politico-economic in focus and include: **world systems theory**; various core-periphery models developed in structuralism; and dependency analysis (see **dependency theory; economic development; trade**). Many of these ideas have neo-Marxist

overtones in the sense that they theorize the role of foreign capital in perpetuating class conflict on a global scale (see **Marxism; sociology of development; transnational capitalist class (TCC)**). Dependency analysis, for example, talks of the role of the *comprador* bourgeoisie, expanding upon Lenin's ideas concerning colonialism (see **colonialism, history of; colonialism, impacts of**). The "solutions" offered by such perspectives vary. At one extreme, dependency analysis suggests that complete withdrawal from the capitalist economy is required for development. Structuralists and neostructuralists argue that peripheral economies need to restructure the nature of their insertion into wider circuits, particularly through the promotion of endogenous **industrialization** and **land reform**, in order to progress. More radical postdevelopment and postcolonial thinkers argue, given their total rejection of development and the concept of progress, that solutions that tinker at the margins in this way are inherently flawed (see **postcolonialism; postmodernism and postdevelopment**). Further to this, some postmodern-influenced literature has argued that the concept of neocolonialism is too simplistic, class-based, and creates artificial binaries which ignore the complicating influence of multiple axes of identity (see **ethnicity/identity**). The focus of much neocolonialist literature on the nation-state (see **state and state reform**) as the unit of analysis has been similarly criticized. There is certainly a need to re-visit the concept of agency and how this resists and re-configures powerful determining forces. The concept of neocolonialism, however, is generally criticized by neo-liberal thinkers, who argue that global markets and investment have facilitated development, especially in East Asia (see **developmental state; newly industrialized economies (NIEs)**).

While the role of neocolonial relations in Latin America, Asia and Africa is relatively well documented, the case of the Pacific Islands is less well known. Decolonization of the islands began in 1962 (Western Samoa) and continues until today. In those countries that have full independence (for example Fiji, Solomon Islands, Vanuatu), control by foreign capital is growing as countries increasingly embrace neo-liberalism. This is perpetuated by increasing conditionality of aid, which plays a crucial role in a region where per capita grants are among the highest in the world. Regional bodies such as the Pacific Island Forum and the Pacific Community are heavily influenced by the region's major powers, New Zealand and Australia. In 2003, for example, the latter cited the global "War on Terrorism" as the rationale for wanting to extend its military and defense involvement in the region. A number of countries (e.g Niue, Cook Islands, Marshall Islands) practice "self-government in free association" with the former colonial powers, which continue to control foreign and defense policy. Ironically, it is partly because local **population**s were resistant to decolonization that such arrangements exist. This illustrates the contested nature of debates around neocolonialism, especially in societies that have been exposed to discourses of development and colonialism (see **colonialism, history of; colonialism, impacts of**) for generations.

Neocolonialism has been vigorously resisted by various actors in both developed and developing countries. Reactions against neocolonialism include the rise of structuralist and dependency theories in Latin America, the formation of the G-77 (see **Group of 77 (G-77)**) and **non-aligned movement**, Pan-Arab **nationalism**, the anti-globalization movement, and indeed, some current global "terrorist" networks. Neo-liberalism and globalization are likely to perpetuate neocolonial relations, and hence resistance is likely to continue.

See also: conditionality; culture; decolonization; dependency theory; globalization; globalization and culture; neo-liberalism; Orientalism; politics; postcolonialism; postmodernism and postdevelopment; structural adjustment; world systems theory

Further reading

Dicken, P. (1998, 3rd edn) *Global Shift: Transforming the World Economy*, London: Chapman.

Howe, K., Kiste, R. and Lal, B. (1994) *Tides of History: The Pacific Islands in the Twentieth Century*, St Leonards NSW: Allen and Unwin.

Kay, C. (1989) *Latin American Theories of Development and Underdevelopment*, London: Routledge.

Robertson, R. (2002) *The Three Waves of Globalization*, London: Zed.

Timmons Roberts, J. and Hite, A. (2000) *From Modernization To Globalisation*, Oxford: Blackwell.

WARWICK E. MURRAY

neo-liberalism

Neo-liberalism is a system of right-wing, yet not conservative, ideas about political **democracy**, individual freedom and entrepreneurship. For neo-liberals, the main restriction on an inherent tendency for free capitalist economies to grow is market failure resulting from perverse governmental regulation. In neo-liberal thought, governments may usefully provide public goods, such as infrastructure, while macroeconomic (and especially monetary) policy (see **fiscal and monetary policy**) may help to stabilize **economic growth** patterns, but most governments in advanced **welfare state** societies and developing countries alike are said to have gone too far in interfering with the free play of markets. Most societies integrated into the global economy by the last quarter of the twentieth century have seen their economic growth and development policies come under the control of a coherent set of neo-liberal principles (Wade, 1990:270–2).

The economic analysis underlying this system of beliefs derives from a certain reading of the founding texts of classical and neo-classical liberal economics. These texts rest on an early modern, liberal belief, outlined by Adam Smith among others, in the freedom of the self-seeking, yet morally responsible, enlightened individual, disciplined by equally modern **institutions**, principally the market. Smith's *The Wealth of Nations* (first published in 1776) elaborated a theory of competition, specialization, division of labor and **free trade** in contradistinction to the prevailing mercantilist theories that advocated state intervention (see **state and state reform**) particularly into inter-country trading relations.

Twentieth-century neo-liberalism updates these liberal doctrines and pushes them in directions more appropriate to late modernity. The basic liberal (Smithian) notions of free trade and the liberating potential of markets are regarded as proven by the growth (see **growth versus holism**), material abundance and opulence of the West. Yet, the past is remembered not merely as received wisdom, but also through a series of creative re-enactments. Hence a focus in contemporary neo-liberalism on deregulation, free markets and the privatization (see **privatization and liberalization**) of previously state-run enterprises, this time in critical reaction to Keynesianism and social **democracy** rather than liberalism's earlier negative reaction to mercantilism. The classical economic liberalism of the nineteenth century is recalled too within a new domain of geopolitical power relations, marked by market triumphalism stemming from the collapse of the Soviet Union and the apparent ending of all alternatives to market-led, liberal democratic politics (see **end of history**).

The basic beliefs of the neo-liberal school of thought were outlined by the socio-philosopher of economics, Friedrich von Hayek (1984:363–81), as an advocacy of the spontaneous order of the market and an aversion to the coercive powers of government, especially when these operated under the "illusion of social, distributive justice." The conversion of rightist political beliefs into more specific economic theories took place at a number of coordinated centers of influence led by the Chicago School of Political Economy. Initiated by Frank H. Knight, a liberal in the nineteenth-century sense of the term, a believer in individual freedom above all else, and a critic of New Deal (twentieth-century) liberalism, Knight was followed at Chicago by a second generation of liberal revivalists, including Milton Friedman, George Stigler and James Buchanon, who likewise subscribed to self-interested, competitive behavior in economy and polity (Sally, 1998). Of these, the most significant theorist, Milton Friedman, linked neo-liberal attitudes toward society with monetarist theories of economy – i.e. the idea that macroeconomic problems like inflation (see **inflation and its effects**) and indebtedness derive from excessive government spending driving up

the quantity of money circulating in a society. Harry G. Johnson, a critic of Keynesianism, who also taught at the University of Chicago, translated neo-liberal ideas into development economics; neo-liberal development policy basically aims at increasing economic growth through creating competitive markets and encouraging innovative entrepreneurs. The neo-liberal revival in economics was reinforced by anarcho-capitalist notions developed in political science (i.e. the idea that the free market can coordinate all functions of a society currently carried out by the state (see **state and state reform**)) published in works written mainly by Chicago-connected political theorists.

Neo-liberalism moved from the right-wing fringe to a position of recognized convention in 1974 with the awarding of the Nobel Prize in economics to von Hayek at a time of supposed crisis in post-war Keynesianism. Neo-liberal economic policies were imposed by the **International Monetary Fund (IMF)** and the US Treasury Department on a left-leaning Labour government in Britain in the mid-1970s and were eagerly adopted by "supply-siders" in the Reagan and Thatcher governments in the early 1980s. Some of these policies had already been tested in Chile, where General Pinochet was heavily advised by Chicago School economists. The media picked up on these ideas in the early 1980s when neo-liberalism was causally linked with an intensification of **globalization**. Neo-liberal policies were regarded as effective means for underdeveloped countries to join the global economy, despite the contradictory evidence of the East Asian route, led by interventionist, developmental states (Wade, 1990; see **newly industrialized economies (NIEs)**). The **World Bank** began a shift toward neo-liberal positions with the Berg report on development in Sub-Saharan Africa (World Bank, 1981). Subsequent *World Development Reports* in the 1980s generalized and re-theorized these ideas. By the late 1980s, a system of policy recommendations, termed the "**Washington consensus**," dominated a previously social democratic and Keynesian development discourse. Dismissing many of the conclusions previously reached in the (structuralist and Keynesian) development literature, and relying instead on revived classical economic theories, the consensus advocates "prudent macroeconomic policies, outward orientation, and free market **capitalism**" (Williamson, 1990). Following this line, development policy came to consist in withdrawing government intervention in favor of the rationalization of an economy through disciplining by the market led by self-interested individuals efficiently choosing between alternatives in the allocation of resources. In the external sector, neo-liberalism entails the devaluation of currencies, convertible monetary systems, and the removal of restrictions on trade and capital movements (see **capital flight; capital markets**). Internally markets were to be deregulated (including the de-unionizing of **labor markets**), while price subsidies on **food** were to be reduced and then eliminated. Government spending is reduced, and private consumption restricted (by higher prices) so that incomes flow into private investment, stimulating growth. The IMF bases loan conditionalities (the set of conditions on which short-term loans are made; see **conditionality**) on neo-liberal policy prescriptions. The WTO (see **World Trade Organization/General Agreement on Tariffs and Trade (WTO/GATT)**) uses similar principles in reviewing the trade policies of member governments. The World Bank uses neo-liberal ideas to guide its **structural adjustment** policies advocated to developing world governments applying for long-term development loans, although signs of a change toward the advocacy of greater state intervention became increasingly visible as protests mounted against neo-liberalism in the 1990s. Neo-liberalism remains a highly controversial policy issue in development theory and practice (Peet with Hartwick, 1999).

See also: capitalism; conditionality; debt crisis; economic development; free trade; international economic order; International Monetary Fund (IMF); privatization and liberalization; structural adjustment; Washington consensus; World Bank

Further reading

Peet, R. with Hartwick, E. (1999) *Theories of Development*, New York: Guilford.

Sally, R. (1998) *Classical Liberalism and International Economic Order: Studies in Theory and Intellectual History*, London: Routledge.
Smith, A. (1937 [1776]) *The Wealth of Nations*, New York: Modern Library.
von Hayek, F. (1984) *The Essence of Hayek*, C. Nishiyama and K. Leube (eds), Stanford: Hoover Institution.
Wade, R. (1990) *Governing the Market: Economic Theory and the Role of Government in East Asian Industrialization*, Princeton: Princeton University Press.
Williamson, J. (ed.) (1990) *Latin American Adjustment: How Much Has Happened?* Washington DC: Institute for International Economics.
World Bank (1981) *Accelerated Development in Sub-Saharan Africa: An Agenda for Action*, Washington: World Bank.

RICHARD PEET

new institutional economics

The new institutional economics (NIE) is an approach to economic analysis that focuses on the roles of history and **institutions** as complementary to market forces. It differs from neo-classical economics by arguing that the operation of market forces has to be understood in a long-term, path-dependent, and institutional context. Under neo-classical economics, institutions (such as firms or governments) are molded into forms that reflect the operation of markets. Under NIE, institutions have greater autonomy in shaping themselves, and the market.

An important concept associated with NIE is transaction costs – or the costs (financial or non-financial) in enacting change within and between markets and institutions. Transaction costs – such as the costs associated with hiring workers, or making a loan – are usually not predicted under neo-classical economics. Transaction costs can also vary according to factors that are difficult to quantify, such as company culture, or the informal norms associated with dealing with the state (see **state and state reform**) such as **corruption**. Analyses of transaction costs have proved useful in studying the operations of **transnational corporations (TNCs)** when operating in **joint venture**s with other companies, or in the problems of achieving administrative change within companies or bureaucracies.

NIE assumes that more radical changes within institutions can have various high transitional costs to diverse stakeholders. It is also centrally concerned with information deficiency models, including bounded rationality (areas of uncertainty about opportunities and/or their unintended outcomes); public goods (concealed demand and free-rider problems); and moral hazards (ability to cheat others). These models undermine assumptions made under neo-classical analysis about the efficiency, equity and stability of open markets. They also explain the formation and sustainability of institutions as contractual arrangements to reduce transaction and transition costs. As such, these factors have attracted many economists in development studies who have seen NIE as empirically more grounded and realistic than neo-classical economics.

There are, however, some similarities between NIE and neo-classical economics. Some NIE thinking, for example, can be very close to neo-classical economics in its willingness to assume that market price-driven, individual utility-maximizing motivations are both universal and desirable. Such NIE thinking assumes comparative *statics equilibria* models of institutional appropriateness and socio-economic change, and prescribes shifting institutions toward values more compatible with market forces.

Furthermore, critics have argued that much NIE thinking tends to see questions of coercive power and unequal distributions as not institutional relationships, and hence utilizes rather benign, functionalist, games-theory approaches to human competition over resources. Critics suggest that these approaches represent superficial means of understanding power (see **power and discourse**).

On balance, however, interest in NIE has grown among development scholars since the 1990s, largely because of the differing qualities of its two major protagonists. Douglass North is an economic historian who writes on societies in an open, widely accessible, discursive style. Oliver Williamson writes on large organizations as a rigorous economist.

NIE is a valuable addition to understanding institutional issues and development economics. These additional insights can be seen as involving understanding path-dependent change, sovereignty, developmental agency, and **civil society** and **social capital**. In terms of change, much development economics has tended to operate with a model of rapid **economic growth** and/or distributional shifts in which radically changing institutions play a vital role. NIE suggests that institutions have considerable durability and path-dependence, due to high-perceived costs of transition by significant interest groups.

Much development economics has tended to emphasize the sovereign state as the primary institution in terms of decision-making, and has had a very limited view of sovereignty beyond the state. NIE confirms the need for a much broader vision of institutions at all levels of aggregation, each with its own element of constrained autonomy. Closely related to opening up the concept of sovereignty is the evaluation of developmental agency. Much development economics has tended to assume that state institutions are essentially benign, or at least potentially benign, agencies of progress. NIE helps introduce questions about the state. If the state is neither sovereign nor necessarily benign, and market forces are institutionally situated, then **civil society** and **social capital** may have greater roles in explaining resource allocation or in shaping development. NIE complements both economic and political analysis by studying the institutional basis of confidence, or lack of it, in market contracts. NIE contributes to debates about human **well-being** and evaluating welfare through understanding the institutions that allocate resources, and by observing the observed – rather than theorized – roles played by market forces.

See also: civil society; economic development; institutions; joint venture; property rights; social capital

Further reading

Alston, L., Eggertsson, T. and North, D. (eds) (1996) *Empirical Studies in Institutional Change*, Cambridge: Cambridge University Press.

Cameron, J. (2000) "Development Economics, the New Institutional Economics and NGOs," *Third World Quarterly* 21:4 627–35.

Harriss, J., Hunter, J. and Lewis, C. (eds) (1995) *The New Institutional Economics and Third World Development*, London and New York: Routledge.

Williamson, O. (1996) *The Mechanisms of Governance*, Oxford: Oxford University Press.

JOHN CAMERON

new public management (NPM)

New public management (NPM) focuses on changing the ways in which governments are structured organizationally, and how they deliver services to their citizens. NPM has been a feature of advanced developed democracies, and is seen by its supporters (for example the **International Monetary Fund (IMF)**, **World Bank**, United Nations) as being a model form of **governance** for developing nations. It has been a dominant paradigm since the 1990s in nations such as the UK, Australia and New Zealand, and the USA where it formed the basis of the "Re-inventing Government" initiative, with a mantra of making government work better for less money (see **public sector; public-private partnerships; state and state reform**). The theory is that NPM improves the quality of governance through reform of bureaucracy; that it is cost-effective (thus reducing the burden on government funds), and promotes citizen participation in "**civil society**." NPM views citizens as customers of government, "consuming" government services in much the same way as they "consume" commercial products and services. The "customer is king," and expects services of measurable quality and coherence. A large part of NPM depends on defining whether operations of government should be better obtained from private sector companies via processes of privatization (see **privatization and liberalization**) or **public-private partnerships**. Moreover, government staff also tend to be moved to decentralized service functions if they are not central to policy.

Proponents of NPM claim it is a way of reducing costs, and increasing **transparency**. Critics, however, claim NPM is a further way of bypassing the state in ways that may not allow sufficient deliberation about the nature and direction of policies. NPM has encountered logistical problems of moving from current states of governance, and there are financial costs in establishing new structures that may encourage some developing states to seek even more private-sector involvement. Monitoring the implementation of NPM places further demands on **information technology** capability, since this underpins both the assumptions about delivering efficiency gains through technology, and is needed in the monitoring and audit of NPM. As a result, developing nations not only need to re-invent governance, but also need to build and implement sophisticated information cultures and communications and technology infrastructures, and staff them adequately. In so doing, NPM very much assumes that nations will become "modern" as well as becoming citizen-focused. Critics have suggested that information technology has not always delivered cost reductions to developed countries, and hence the attractions to developing countries may be less than thought.

See also: cost-benefit analysis (CBA); decentralization; governance; information technology; local government; public-private partnerships; public sector; state and state reform

Further reading

McLaughlin, K. (2002) "Lesson Drawing From the International Experience of Modernizing Local Governance," *Public Management Review* 4:3 405–10.

Polidano, C. (2001) "Why Civil Service Reforms Fail," *Public Management Review* 3:3 345–61.

MICHAEL BLAKEMORE

new social movements

Social movements are "collective challenges by people with common purposes and solidarity in sustained interaction with **elites**, opponents and authorities" (Tarrow, 1994). During the 1960s and

1970s there emerged in advanced capitalist countries a number of protest groups, which came to be known as new social movements, such as student movements, women's lib, youth movements, the peace and civil rights movements, "squatter" movements (occupying empty office buildings), environmentalist movements, and gay rights movements.

The attempts to theorize the emergence, characteristics, goals and strategies of these movements can be divided into two categories: the resource mobilization theories and the new social movements theories. Specifically the latter approach labeled these social movements as "new." In contradistinction to the old social movements (e.g. **trade unions**), these new social movements (i) have a non-class-based membership; (ii) are not interested in gaining power over the state (see **state and state reform**); (iii) seek to defend non-material needs; (iv) are rather loose networks of contacts; (v) prefer non-institutionalized forms of dialog; and as such (vi) are wary of engaging in alliances with political actors; and (vii) apply unconventional strategies like sit-ins and occupation of buildings.

The two theoretical approaches to the new social movements, the resource mobilization theory and the new social movements theories, came respectively from the USA and from Europe. In the USA, the resource mobilization approach (associated above all with the names of Tilly, and Zald and McCarthy) was a reaction to seeing social movements as an irrational collective reaction from individuals, which could not cope with rapid social change. Also, it questioned theories of relative deprivation, which established a direct link between frustration and collective action. The resource mobilization theory was especially occupied with the question of how social movements managed to combine material and immaterial resources to reach their goals. The assumption was that societies always harbor a level of frustration which is potentially enough to lead to collective action, but that it depends on the availability of resources accessible to would-be protesters and their ability to manipulate these resources whether in fact it would result in collective action. A particular brand of this theoretical approach has become known under the heading of "political

opportunity structure," which emphasizes the rallying potential of openings in (democratizing) political and institutional structures. For example, in many European countries during the 1970s new social movements profited from state subsidies, which were, however, increasingly withdrawn in the next decade as a by-product of emerging **neo-liberalism**. The disappearance of these financial resources was reflected in the downward trends in social movements.

The resource mobilization approach was criticized for various reasons. First, it concentrated on the "how" of collective action but not on the "why." Second, it placed too much attention on the movement as an organization, and neglected the diversity of reasons for individuals to become members. Hence, third, it underestimated the identity, consciousness and ideology-related dimensions of new social movements, which led to – fourth – the acceptance of new social movements as new actors in the mainstream political game and insufficient recognition of new social movements as a "new" praxis redefining the relation between **civil society** and the political domain.

The new social movements theories (associated with authors such as Touraine, Melucci and Castells), which came up in Europe during the 1970s and early 1980s, presented a totally different view. As the resource mobilization theory meant a break with collective behavior theories, the European new social movements theories broke with a Marxist-structuralist emphasis on social classes as the primordial historical agents (see **Marxism**). As Western **capitalism** moved from Fordism to Post-Fordism (represented by changes such as **Fordism versus Toyotaism**, and **flexible specialization**), the insight grew that the labor proletariat could no longer be seen as the only protagonist of social change; an increasing number of people were not even involved in the production process. Thus the European post-structuralist interpretation of new social movements concentrated on these being instances of a new cultural and political praxis in a post-industrial, increasingly complex society. Inspired by Habermas's communicative rationality, these movements were seen as defenders of the "life-world" against the colonizing efforts of the "system." New social movements were sometimes even seen as "cultural laboratories" where new discursive practices (emphasizing such things as identity construction) created "new political spaces."

However, in the course of the 1980s and specifically the 1990s, it became clear that this kind of rhetoric was more a reflection of wishful ideological thinking than a reality. Also, it must be emphasized that neither the resource mobilization theory nor the new social movement approach were adequate reflections of the daily praxis of social movements in developing countries. Social movements in developing countries in the 1970s and 1980s were either forms of protest against military dictatorships and/or formed part of a survival strategy of the (urban) poor (see **urban poverty**). With **globalization** becoming the near hegemonic perspective from the 1990s onwards, the current view on social movements in developed and developing countries alike has changed considerably. Now, above all on a local level, they are considered as important actors in **public-private partnerships** and as such contribute to good **governance**. Another shift in focus concerns the emergence of global social movements, such as the originally French-based ATTAC (an international movement for democratic control of financial markets and their institutions, formed in 1998) or globally organized indigenous movements; these movements have a much more contested character.

See also: advocacy coalitions; civil society; democracy; environmental movements; governance; peasant movements; politics; solidarity campaigns; women's movements

Further reading

Eyerman, R. and Jamison, A. (1991) *Social Movements: A Cognitive Approach*, Cambridge: Polity.

McAdam, D. McCarthy, J. and Zald, M. (eds) (1996) *Comparative Perspectives on Social Movements: Political Opportunities, Mobilizing Structures, and Cultural Framings*, Cambridge: Cambridge University Press.

Melucci, A. (1996) *Challenging Codes: Collective Action in the Information Age*, Cambridge: Cambridge University Press.

Smith, J., Chatfield, C. and Pagnucco, R. (eds) (1997) *Transnational Social Movements and Global Politics: Solidarity Beyond the State*, New York: Syracuse University Press.

Tarrow, S. (1994) *Power in Movement: Social Movements, Collective Action and Politics*, Cambridge: Cambridge University Press.

FRANS J. SCHUURMAN

newly industrialized economies (NIEs)

Newly industrialized economies (NIEs) are countries that have become industrialized since the 1960s. They are sometimes called newly industrialized countries (NICs). The NIEs often refer to such economies as Hong Kong, Taiwan, Singapore and South Korea in East Asia; and Argentina, Brazil and Mexico in Latin America. In general, the NIEs from East Asia and Latin America have followed different pathways to **economic development**. In East Asia, the four NIEs have benefitted significantly from their export-oriented **industrialization**, a form of industrial platform that depends on exports of manufactured goods and foreign exchange earnings to foster domestic economic development (see **export-led growth**). Their counterparts in Latin America, however, have mostly relied on **import substitution** to kick-start their industrialization and economic development processes. Instead of manufacturing for exports, these Latin American NIEs have developed their manufacturing industries to cater to domestic demand that in turn reduces their reliance on imports of foreign goods. Industrialization becomes their solution to excessive reliance on imports of foreign goods that drains foreign exchange and creates inflationary pressures (see **inflation and its effects**).

The economic outcomes of these two contrasting modes of industrialization and economic development are well documented in development studies. Export-led growth has now been widely acknowledged as the successful development model for developing countries. Import substitution, on the other hand, has been discredited as an inward-looking and potentially problematical platform for economic development. Since the 1960s, the export-oriented NIEs have experienced significant **economic growth**, albeit with some unexpected interruptions caused by the oil crisis in the early 1970s and the Asian economic crises in 1997 and 1998 (see **Asian crises**). Hong Kong and Singapore, for example, are now ranked amongst the world's highest per capita income economies. Firms from Taiwan and South Korea are also major players in such strategic high-tech industries as semiconductors, automobiles, electronics, chemicals and so on. By developing their industrial capacity for exports (see also **technological capability**), these NIEs have become deeply articulated into the global economy.

There are both benefits and problems associated with such deep integration with the global economy. On the positive side, export-oriented NIEs have been recipients of massive inflows of **foreign direct investment** spearheaded by global corporations that are seeking lower costs of production and new market opportunities (see **transnational corporations (TNCs)**). As early as the 1960s, for instance, Hong Kong and Singapore were the major destinations of offshore production for such American electronics firms as National Semiconductor and Motorola. Through these investment inflows, the NIEs benefit from **technology transfer** and managerial expertise, enhanced capital formation, foreign market access and so on. The presence of foreign firms from advanced industrialized economies in these NIEs has also stimulated domestic **entrepreneurship** and new firm growth. By the 1990s, we witness the emergence of a new generation of TNCs from these developing economies that were fast capturing market shares in major global industries.

Deep integration with the global economy, however, does come with potential risks and problems. As the NIEs are heavily dependent on major export markets in North America and, to a lesser extent, Western Europe, their domestic economies are vulnerable to unilateral protectionist policies, business cycles and economic fluctuations in these advanced industrialized economies. During the early phase of their industrialization in the 1960s and the 1970s, these export-oriented NIEs faced some significant **trade** barriers and import restraints imposed on their export goods (see **World Trade Organization/ General Agreement on Tariffs and Trade (WTO/GATT)**). The Multi-Fiber Agreement, for example, has put serious constraints on the growth of **textiles** industries in the NIEs. Under the agreement, textiles and garments exports from developing economies, in particular the NIEs, to developed countries in North America and Western Europe were subject to voluntary quota restrictions – a form of **protectionism** to prevent the complete demise of domestic textiles and garments firms in these developed countries. During the late 1980s and the 1990s, the growing liberalization of the international trade regime under the auspices of, originally, GATT and now the WTO, had opened up new windows of opportunity for the NIEs to overcome some of those trade barriers. Although non-tariff (see **tariffs**) trade barriers still exist among most developed countries, the NIEs are now enjoying much better access to foreign markets.

Another risk of deep integration for these NIEs originates from the **globalization** of finance. Reliance on exports necessarily entails some form of financial integration as well. This process of global financial integration has increased the risk of all participating economies, though developing economies and the NIEs are more vulnerable due to their weaker financial system and heavier indebtedness to foreign financial institutions. In the second half of 1997, this uneven risk of participating in the global economy became particularly apparent in the unfolding of the Asian economic crisis that brought down many of the Asian NIEs and developing economies.

While the export-oriented platform of industrialization has been credited by such international organizations as the **World Bank** and the **International Monetary Fund (IMF)**, it must be emphasized that domestic institutional capacity in these NIEs has also played a very significant role in economic development. The **developmental state**, a term often evoked to describe the relentless institutional efforts of the NIE states in spearheading economic development, has been instrumental in establishing economic development agencies and in altering market incentives in order to promote industrialization. In many ways, these NIEs have not really followed the market-liberalism mode of economic development experienced in such advanced industrialized economies as the US and the UK. Instead, their developmental states have navigated through the difficult waters of the global economy by combining both selective economic interventions and free market mechanisms. In particular, most NIE states have pursued a form of strategic industrial policy to ensure the successful development of selected "national champions" – major domestic firms – in strategic industries. By offering low-cost credits, subsidies and grants to these firms, the development state in the NIEs has intentionally altered the price signal in the market. Judging from the role of development states in the success of the NIEs, researchers in development studies have now reached some consensus on the desirability of domestic institutional capacity as a major precondition for economic development.

See also: developmental state; economic development; export-led growth; industrialization; industrialization and trade policy; late industrialization; leapfrogging; protectionism; small and medium enterprises (SMEs); technological capability; transnational corporations (TNCs); transnational corporations (TNCs) from developing economies; World Trade Organization/General Agreement on Tariffs and Trade (WTO/GATT)

Further reading

Amsden, A. (2001) *The Rise of "The Rest": Challenges to the West From Late-Industrializing Economies*, New York: Oxford University Press.

Haggard, S. (1990) *Pathways from the Periphery: The Politics of Growth in the Newly Industrializing Countries*, Ithaca NY: Cornell University Press.

Wade, R. (1990) *Governing the Market: Economic Theory and the Role of Government in East Asian Industrialization*, Princeton NJ: Princeton University Press.

Woo-Cumings, M. (ed.) (1999) *The Developmental State*, Ithaca NY: Cornell University Press.

World Bank (1993) *The East Asian Miracle*, Oxford: Oxford University Press.

HENRY WAI-CHUNG YEUNG

non-aligned movement

Non-alignment emerged out of the bi-polar politics of the **Cold War** as both a policy doctrine and a movement based on the avoidance of military alliances with either of the two superpowers, and a concomitant rejection of **conditionality** attached to **aid**. Non-alignment was not a position of neutrality, however. Its aims were not just about avoiding the entanglements of alliances with one or other of the two blocs, but about affirming the sovereignty of the newly independent nations in the face of such entanglements. While there is significant overlap between non-aligned countries and the **Group of 77 (G-77)**, at its height the non-aligned movement (NAM) represented over 100 countries and 1 billion people and it became one of the first significant platforms for poor countries to voice their own particular needs and demands in the post-World War II era.

As a doctrine, non-alignment initially developed out of the foreign policy of certain of the more politically prominent poorer nations, particularly Nehru's India, Nasser's Egypt and Tito's Yugoslavia. While the initial rhetoric of non-alignment called for global peace and **security**, there were four other long-term objectives. First, there was a desire for **economic development** within a discourse of equality, implying restructuring the global economic order. Second, countries sought cultural equality via the restructuring of the global informational order (see **globalization and culture**). Third, there was demand for the **right to self-determination**. A fourth aim was multilateralism through strong support of the **United Nations** system (see **United Nations Declaration on the Granting of Independence to Colonial Countries and Peoples, Res. 1514 (XV) 1960)**.

On this broad platform the NAM was inaugurated during a preliminary meeting of twenty non-signatory countries at the **Bandung conference (1955)**, and further consolidated at a subsequent conference in Belgrade (1961). The NAM has always been a loose structure, working through consensus and broad definitions developed at its triennial summits, rather than by putting specific policies to the vote. This loose structure has been both the major strength and major weakness of the

NAM. While it more than likely kept the movement alive through some serious challenges (such as the **debt** crisis of the 1980s) it also prevented it from taking an effective stand on issues such as the Iran-Iraq **war**.

While the NAM's initial emphasis centered on the political landscape of the Cold War and on the issue of **decolonization**, the Lusaka summit (1970) ushered in a growing focus on economic issues, such as **South-South cooperation** and calls for a new **international economic order**. The NAM largely failed in this, but has achieved some successes, primarily through its role as a lobby group within the United Nations. The formation of UNCTAD largely came out of the impetus generated by NAM at Belgrade, and Nasser's success in the 1956 Suez crisis was certainly assisted by his generating considerable support within the NAM. As these examples imply, it was in the early years of its formation that the NAM was most effective.

See also: Bandung conference (1955); Group of 77 (G-77); international economic order; South-South cooperation

Further reading

Arora, K. (1998) *Imperialism and the Non-aligned Movement*, New Delhi: Sanchar.

Singham, A. (ed.) (1977) *The Non-aligned Movement in World Politics*, Westport CT: Lawrence Hill.

SIMON REID-HENRY

non-governmental organizations (NGOs)

Non-governmental organizations (NGOs) are non-profit organizations or associations that stand independently of the state (see **state and state reform**), yet which are usually associated with some kind of political or social-developmental activity. Development NGOs form part of a larger universe of non-governmental actors, which range from small village associations to large-scale service providers and global activist networks (see **advocacy coalitions**). NGOs are active across a very wide spectrum of activities including development, **environmental movements, humanitarianism** and relief work, social welfare, micro-finance (see **micro-credit and micro-finance**) and **human rights**.

Interest in development NGOs has risen dramatically since the late 1980s, and has occurred in both developed and developing countries. NGOs in developed or industrialized countries are commonly concerned with **poverty** and **social justice** at home and abroad. In **aid**-recipient countries, or "developing" countries, NGOs old and new have been identified as potential "partners" by governments and international aid agencies (see **bilateral aid agencies; partnerships**). The subject of NGOs has grown into a major area of interest within development studies, but the research terrain has been largely dominated by donor-commissioned reports and activist case studies, leaving this potentially important and theoretically exciting field with a somewhat weak, normative literature (Clarke, 1998; Najam, 1996a). The diversity of the NGO sector and the lack of accurate, detailed data about NGOs makes generalization difficult. As Esman and Uphoff (1984:58) famously warned: "almost anything that one can say about [NGOs] is true – or false – in at least some instance, somewhere." This diversity is one of the strengths of the NGO sector, lending it a chaotic, sometimes creative character. Conceptually, a basic tension exists between the two sides of this NGO character. NGOs are both *instrumental* organizations in that they seek to get things done, but they are also *expressive* organizations, which embody a particular set of values or way of thinking about the world.

History

Despite the attention they now receive, NGOs are not a new phenomenon. Charnovitz (1997) traces the evolution of NGO roles in international affairs from "emergence" in 1775–1918 (the abolition of the slave trade, the peace movement and support for **labor rights and standards**), to the current period of NGO "empowerment" which dates from the **Earth Summit (1992) (United**

Nations Conference on Environment and Development), when NGOs became directly involved in international policy formulation alongside an increasing role as non-state actors in a wide range of service provision activities at local, national and global levels. NGOs are usually seen as belonging to the **voluntary sector** or the arena of voluntary action. This is also sometimes described in organizational terms as the "third sector" in which groups of people come together voluntarily to solve a **community**-level problem (such as repairing **irrigation** or forming a neighborhood watch security scheme). The third sector arguably predates the other two sectors of state and market.

NGOs have become important for at least three sets of reasons. First, working with NGOs has had considerable ideological attraction to bilateral (see **bilateral aid agencies**) and multilateral donors and governments during the dominance of **neo-liberalism** since the 1980s. This period has seen the adoption of privatization (see **privatization and liberalization**) policies in the form of efforts to "roll back" the state by governments in the in the North (see **decentralization; state and state reform**), and the design and imposition of **structural adjustment** policies by the **World Bank** and **International Monetary Fund (IMF)**. Second, there was by the 1990s a general disillusionment among many donors with governments' limited capacity to address problems of poverty. The search for alternative solutions brought NGOs into closer contact with the world of development agencies. NGOs, from both rich and poor countries, came to be seen by governments and development funders as effective channels for development assistance, and were then encouraged to participate in development projects and programs. NGOs were believed to be more administratively flexible; closer to the poor; highly innovative in problem solving; and more cost-effective than their corresponding state partners. Third, the recently renewed interest in **civil society** has helped to focus attention on NGOs and created a climate in which NGOs have been increased their profile and voice. In the view of NGOs as "civil society organizations," they are seen as forces that can help to balance and counter-abuses of state and market power. For example, NGOs may monitor elections to ensure

that they are conducted fairly and to encourage people to take part, or they may work in support of **fair trade** to improve commodity prices to small producers, or by campaigning against **child labor**.

Definitions

One key problem in the study of NGOs is a lack of definitional clarity. As Barrow and Jennings (2001:1) bluntly point out: "no clear definition exists of what the NGO is." The acronym "NGO" first appeared after World War II when Article 71 of the United Nations Charter provided for international non-governmental involvement in UN activities. "Non-profit," "third sector" and "voluntary" organization all tend to be used interchangeably, often without conceptual clarity or consistency. A multiplicity of specialized terms such as "intermediary NGO," "citizen organization" and "grassroots organization" further confuse the field. Najam (1996a) identified forty-nine different names for NGOs used in the literature. The lack of clarity is not just a question of semantics, but tends to inhibit comparative analysis, and of course influences resource allocation on the ground.

Most writers on NGOs begin with their own extensive definitional discussion. Clarke (1998:36) describes NGOs as "private, nonprofit organizations, with a distinctive legal character, concerned with public welfare goals," and includes philanthropic foundations, church development agencies, local membership organizations and academic think tanks but excludes many other nonprofit organizations such as hospitals, schools and quasi-governmental agencies (QUANGOs). Vakil (1997:2060) defines development NGOs as "self-governing, private, not-for-profit organizations that are geared to improving the quality of life for disadvantaged people." One influential attempt to standardize definitions for the study of the general non-profit sector was that of Salamon and Anheier (1999) who outline five essential characteristics: *formal* (institutionalized with regular meetings); *private* (separate from government even though it may receive some government support); *non-profit distributing* (any financial surplus does not accrue to owners but is plowed back into the organization); *self-governing* (able to control and manage its own affairs); and *voluntary* (some degree of voluntary participation in the organization such as a voluntary governing body) (also see **charities; voluntary sector**).

In the end, there is probably no viable "catch all" definition, and NGOs need to be differentiated along a variety of different axes. The first is the type of activities undertaken, which range from delivering credit, social services or agricultural extension advice, to campaigning on issues such as human rights, poverty or environmental concerns. The NGO sector in most countries can be split into two different groups – those that deliver services and those that undertake activist-type work such as advocacy. A tension between the two sets of motivations is often apparent within the NGO **community** or within organizations that seek to combine both approaches.

Activities

The origins of an NGO can frequently be found among a group of people wishing to provide a service to disadvantaged groups whose needs are not currently being met by state or market. This "gap-filling" motivation may form an initial driving force, as in the case of an "intermediary NGO" established in order to provide services to marginal farmers in remote, risk-prone areas unreached by official agricultural extension efforts. Alternatively, a local "community-based NGO" might be established by a group of people who want to do something for themselves, such as organizing city waste collection where public provision has broken down (see **waste management**). Service delivery work may usefully meet people's immediate needs, but raises political questions about the limits of state responsibility and **citizenship** rights. Where an NGO is externally resourced by international development funds, it also raises issues of whether such interventions are ultimately sustainable, and to whom the service has **accountability**.

The activist NGO is motivated by a vision of social, economic or political transformation. It may be engaged at the local level in trying to "empower" marginalized sections of the community, inspired by the ideas of **liberation theology** or the "small is beautiful" philosophy of the **appropriate technology** movement. It may lobby

government through political channels in order to influence upcoming policy decisions that may affect vulnerable groups (see **vulnerability**). An NGO may take a more confrontational approach in order to challenge the government, such as by campaigning against a policy, such as European agricultural subsidies, or by participating in direct action in the form of street protest, such as that witnessed at the World Trade Organization meeting in Seattle in 1999 (see **World Trade Organization/General Agreement on Tariffs and Trade (WTO/GATT)**). Najam (1999) argues that NGOs therefore can be seen as "policy entrepreneurs," which may work to oppose, complement or reform the state.

A second line of differentiation is organizational structure. Some NGOs are highly professionalized organizations with paid staff, hierarchical structures and formal bureaucratic forms of operation. Others are voluntarist in character, relying on the interest and commitment of their volunteer staff and supporters. A key distinction is between self-help, membership organizations (sometimes called "organizations *of* the poor" or community-based organizations), and the more formal NGOs set up by outsiders which exist in order to work on behalf of vulnerable groups (sometimes called "organizations *for* the poor" or "intermediary NGOs").

The values and philosophy of an NGO may vary considerably. There are NGOs that embody a transformative vision of social and economic change, while others take a more "charitable" approach to providing welfare support to disadvantaged individuals or groups. Some organizations are driven by a secular political or humanist philosophy, while others may embody religious or spiritual values. For example, Gandhian and Freirean ideologies (see **pedagogy of the oppressed**) were strong influences on the formation of many NGOs in the 1970s in South Asia and Latin America. NGOs may also be established in order to reflect the values and interests of other actors such as governments, foreign donors, business corporations or religious groups. Clarke (1998) cites the example of right-wing NGOs funded by the military in Central America, and shows how NGOs have become attractive vehicles for those of many different political persuasions (see **authoritarianism**). For liberals, the concept of the third sector helps to balance the state and the market and contributes to the spirit of active civic engagement. For conservatives, NGOs are important players within a diverse and expanding private sector, where "not-for-profit" status can be seen as adding moral authority and independence to the provision of key services. For radicals on the left, NGOs hold the promise of a new politics that centers on a range of forms of social transformation outside the traditional political parties or the attempt to capture state power (see **politics**).

Finally, NGOs can be distinguished in terms of geographical origins and reach. The distinction between Northern NGOs (NNGOs) and Southern NGOs (SNGOs) has been particularly important. NNGOs have their roots in Europe and North America and are dedicated mainly to working in the poorer countries of the South, either in development or humanitarian **emergency assistance** work. These organizations generally receive resources from public donations, from governments and from development agencies. There has been a general shift among NNGOs away from direct implementation toward working with and strengthening SNGO "partners" through **capacity building** (Lewis, 2001). SNGOs are organizations rooted within the communities in which they work, but generally have less access to resources than their Northern counterparts. The existence of transnational non-governmental organizations and the strong internationalizing tendencies of NGOs in both North and South is a sign that a straightforward distinction between NNGOs and SNGOs is no longer a clear one.

Structure and accountability

NGOs change over time and alter their structure and orientation. The four stages of "NGO generations" set out by Korten (1990) shows how NGOs move through different stages in response to their ability to learn from experience and the external opportunities that present themselves. A first generation NGO addresses people's immediate needs through providing welfare handouts and may be established as a response to a crisis. In the second generation, an NGO becomes more concerned with sustainable, developmental work aimed at building self-reliance and mobilizing local resources. The third generation brings the realization that an NGO needs to look beyond local level impact toward understanding and influencing wider polices and processes, and establishing broader institutional links locally and nationally. A fourth generation is reached when an NGO joins forces with wider social movements for change and becomes part of processes of local, national or global voluntary action. The framework is useful in that it shows how the two main NGO roles of service delivery and activism are not necessarily mutually exclusive, though a limitation of the model is that it suggests a linear progression, while in practice organizational change may take more complex, unpredictable or cyclical forms.

Like most third sector organizations, NGOs face the challenge of balancing multiple accountabilities – to users, funders, staff, supporters, local authorities and governing bodies (see **accountability**). An NGO is simultaneously accountable to *patrons* such as donors (whose concerns are usually centered upon whether funds are used for designated purposes); to *clients* such as its users in the community (who are concerned with ensuring that the NGO acts in their interests, but have no clear means of ensuring this); or the government (which may contract an NGO to carry out a particular task); and finally to *itself* (in the sense that each NGO has a vision which it seeks to actualize, and staff to whom it is responsible). NGOs frequently tend to focus on their responsibilities to their patrons (because of the threat of withdrawal of funding) far more than those to clients or to their own values (Najam, 1996b). Unbalanced accountability may lead to goal displacement, when for example an NGO moves away from an original focus on **education** work and gets involved in credit delivery when donor funds become available for this purpose even when the NGO may have no special competence in this area. Another problem is unplanned growth, where a "successful" NGO evolves into a large, hierarchical organization and takes on many of the bureaucratic problems traditionally associated with government agencies – such as being slow to respond to problems; losing touch with communities; and finding it difficult to learn from experience. Another important accountability problem is related to the unequal relationship that often exists between Northern and Southern NGOs.

Prospects

The honeymoon period between the development industry and the NGOs may now be over. Increasingly tough questions are being asked of NGOs in relation to their performance and accountability (Edwards and Hulme, 1995; Lewis and Wallace, 2000). Efforts to evaluate systematically the impact of development NGOs have generally produced mixed findings. A recent donor evaluation of NGOs in four countries showed that NGOs displayed particular strengths in maintaining a poverty focus in their work; that they could build reasonably workable **partnerships** with local community organizations; and that they were often able to provide basic **health** and **education** services effectively. But NGOs were found to be weak at social contextual analysis; their approaches to monitoring and evaluation were rarely adequate; key technical skills were lacking in their human resource base; many were more concerned with micro- than macro- level work; and the values of participation and innovation claimed in project implementation did not always live up to the claims made (Oakley, 1999). In a comparison of NGOs in South Asia, Edwards (1999) found greatly differing results. The most effective NGOs were characterized by independent thinking; clear goals; personal qualities of commitment among staff and volunteers; and close community working relationships built up gradually over time. In the context of NGO advocacy work, an assessment of NGO outcomes by Covey (1995) separates out "policy effectiveness" from "civil society" impacts, such that even if the desired policy outcome was not achieved, NGOs might still raise awareness and increase the potential community participation in public affairs.

Earlier assumptions about the comparative advantages of NGOs as development actors have therefore been challenged as certain NGO limitations have become clearer. Although many NGOs may be motivated by ambitious objectives, many lack basic management competencies. While there is evidence that some NGOs can achieve impact locally, these impacts tend to be very small-scale, leading some to argue that there is an urgent need to improve performance through "scaling up" NGO work (Edwards and Hulme, 1992). Despite the existence of some remarkable NGOs around the world, some may serve as opportunistic vehicles for individuals seeking to build political patronage or accumulate resources. The issue of performance and **capacity building** has led to a growth of interest in the management of NGOs as a specific sub-field of **development management**, and such work also draws upon the emerging field of not-for-profit management, which has an increasingly high profile in Western business schools (Lewis, 2001).

What has been the contribution of NGOs to development? There have been many positive changes in development policy and practice associated with NGOs – the growth of participatory planning techniques; the integration of **gender** concerns into development thinking; and the continuing advocacy of human rights and environmental issues. The failure of the negotiations in 1997 to secure a **Multilateral Agreement on Investment (MAI)** has been attributed in no small part to the opposition of NGOs, seen by many activists as a victory for social and environmental interests. But concerns about accountability and performance remain, and NGOs will need to address these questions if they are to prosper. A key policy challenge will the identification of appropriate forms of **public-private partnerships** (or simply **partnerships**) for NGOs to work alongside public and private sector organizations. Another important issue for the future is whether and how NGOs will be able to adapt to changing global political and economic contexts and priorities. The apparent decline in international development aid means that development NGOs that rely on this source of finance may need to seek alternative resources, either from the private sector or by moving closer to voluntarist models. The latter may be a positive trend if it brings a renewed emphasis on social and economic justice in a world increasingly dominated by corporate values. On the other hand, increasing global conflict and instability may support the future of NGOs that specialize in relief and reconstruction.

See also: accountability; advocacy coalitions; capacity building; charities; civil society; community; decentralization; environmental movements;

humanitarianism; micro-credit and micro-finance; new social movements; partnerships; people-centered development; politics; public-private partnerships; social justice; voluntary sector; women's movements

Further reading

Barrow, O. and Jennings, M. (eds) (2001) *The Charitable Impulse: NGOs and Development in East and North East Africa*, London: James Currey.

Charnovitz, S. (1997) "Two Centuries of Participation: NGOs and International Governance," *Michigan Journal of International Law* 18:2 183–286.

Clarke, G. (1998) "Nongovernmental Organizations and Politics in the Developing World," *Political Studies* 46: 36–52.

Edwards, M. (1999) "NGO Performance – What Breeds Success?" *World Development* 27:2 361–74.

Edwards, M. and Hulme, D. (eds) (1992) *Making A Difference: NGOs and Development in a Changing World*, London: Earthscan.

Edwards, M. and Hulme, D. (eds) (1995) *Beyond the Magic Bullet: NGO Performance and Accountability in the Post-Cold War World*, London: Macmillan.

Esman, M. and Uphoff, N. (1984) *Local Organizations: Intermediaries in Rural Development*, Ithaca NY: Cornell University Press.

Korten, D. (1990) *Getting to the 21st Century: Voluntary Action and the Global Agenda*, Hartford CT: Kumarian Press.

Lewis, D. and Wallace, T. (eds) (2000) *New Roles and Relevance: Development NGOs and the Challenge of Change*, Hartford CT: Kumarian Press.

Lewis, D. (2001) *The Management of Non-Governmental Development Organizations: An Introduction*, London: Routledge.

Najam, A. (1996a) "Understanding the Third Sector: Revisiting the Prince, the Merchant and the Citizen," *Nonprofit Management and Leadership* 7:2 203–19.

Najam, A. (1996b) NGO Accountability: A Conceptual Framework, *Development Policy Review* 14: 339–53.

Najam, A. (1999) "Citizen Organizations as Policy Entrepreneurs," in D. Lewis (ed.) *International Perspectives on Voluntary Action: Reshaping the Third Sector*, London: Earthscan.

Oakley, P. (1999) *The Danish NGO Impact Study: A Review of Danish NGO activities in developing countries*, Oxford: International NGO Training and Research Centre (INTRAC).

Vakil, A. (1997) "Confronting the Classification Problem: Towards a Taxonomy of NGOs," *World Development* 25:12 2057–71.

DAVID LEWIS

non-timber forest products (NTFPs)

Non-timber forest products (NTFPs) commonly refer to plant- and animal-based products such as fruit and nuts, honey, bushmeat, mushrooms, fibers, oils, resins, dyes, medicinal products, and rattans that provide an alternative to logging or timber (wood) products from trees (see **logging/ timber trade**). They are also referred to as minor forest products, non-wood forest products or (in the USA) "specialty" products. Though predominantly from closed forests, many are collected from other natural environments such as savannas, or produced with varying degrees of cultivation in farmed parklands, improved fallows, **plantation forestry** and **agroforestry** systems. NTFPs encompass a wide range of natural resources of both subsistence and economic importance. They are sometimes taken to include **fuelwood**, **ecotourism** and other environmental services.

NTFPs are commonly gathered from either communally managed or open access areas. Harvesting and primary processing of NTFPs also usually require few skills or capital inputs. Together, these factors make NTFPs important as a subsistence and income-earning activity for women and resource-poor members of society. The **Food and Agriculture Organization (FAO)** estimates that 80 percent of people in the developing world use NTFPs to meet **health** and **nutrition** needs. The so-called "hidden harvest" represented by NTFPs provides a crucial dietary supplement, particularly during seasonal hungry periods and **famine**. NTFP-based incomes can also make an essential contribution to **sustainable livelihoods**, as activities are often concentrated during the agricultural slack season. Furthermore, the continuing cultural significance of NTFPs in many societies should not be overlooked.

NTFPs are among the oldest internationally traded commodities. Interest in their development potential, however, first took off in the late 1980s when the fate of the tropical rain forests became a global concern (see **deforestation; logging/ timber trade**). Based on the "use-it-or-lose-it" approach to conservation, it was widely hoped that the sale of NTFPs could act as an economic incentive for sustainable forest management, and that NTFP **commercialization** would contribute to **rural poverty** alleviation, thereby reducing pressure on forest resources. One paper in the journal *Nature* (Peters et al., 1989) was highly influential in promoting the idea that the NTFPs in a particular forest area could be of greater value than the timber or alternative land uses. By the late 1990s, however, it was clear that NTFP commercialization would provide no easy solution to deforestation, as markets did not exist for all products; or they were inaccessible or unstable, leading to boom-and-bust scenarios. Increased trade in products might also have produced varied outcomes including overexploitation of the resource or its domestication. The very diversity of NTFPs frustrated efforts to produce any kind of generic guidelines, whether for resource inventory and management or for successful commercialization.

In the early 2000s, the research focus has shifted toward how best to support people in obtaining more secure and sustained benefits from their NTFP resources. This involves promoting recognition of their importance in national accounts, and improving the policy and legal context for their sustainable exploitation (see also **community forestry**).

See also: agroforestry; community-based natural resource management (CBNRM); community forestry; deforestation; Joint Forest Management (JFM); logging/timber trade; shifting cultivation; sustainable livelihoods

Further reading

Neumann, R. and Hirsch, E. (2000) *Commercialization of Non-Timber Forest Products: Review and Analysis of Research*, Bogor, Indonesia: Center for International Forestry Research.
Peters, C., Gentry, A. and Mendelsohn, R. (1989) "Valuation of an Amazonian Rainforest," *Nature* 339: 655–6.

KATHRIN SCHRECKENBERG

North American Free Trade Agreement (NAFTA)

The North American Free Trade Agreement (NAFTA) is a **free trade** agreement for the continent of North America. Arising from the earlier Canada-United States Free Trade Agreement (CUSFTA, 1989), NAFTA was signed in 1993 by the presidents of the USA, Canada and Mexico. Different from customs unions and other, deeper forms of **economic federalization**, e.g. common markets (such as **MERCOSUR**) or economic unions (such as the **European Union**), NAFTA's scope for the first 10–15 years is limited to the removal of the obstacles to a free movement of commodities and investment flows within the North American region. Under the free trade agreement, each member state retains its own trade barriers toward non-members' imports. At the same time, the obstacles to **labor migration** between the three countries (in particular the **migration** of Mexican subjects into the USA) are maintained as before, with the only exception of easing visa procedures for executives.

NAFTA is the first non-colonial type experience of North-South economic integration. As such, it mirrors many of the processes characteristic of dependent development. Without a truly balanced division of costs and benefits between the members and, as some say, without the reciprocity that would be needed for a more comprehensive form of regional integration in future, NAFTA is beyond comparison with the European Union (Clarkson, 2000). With per capita incomes in Mexico averaging around one eighth of levels up North, the economies of the three member states are complementary in a peculiar way: Mexico's cheap labor, Canada's resources and US capital make for a profitable combination; however, not in any equal measure for its stakeholders. Mexico's prime interest in NAFTA is to obtain free access to the consumer markets of the US and Canada and to attract investment. Canada also wants to secure access to the US market. In the USA, **transnational corporations (TNCs)** and smaller private businesses alike are the most enthusiastic supporters of the free trade agreement, profiting from the low labor cost investment opportunities south of the Rio Grande. Both Mexico's and Canada's international trade are dominated by the USA for close to 80 percent, whereas their mutual trade and investment patterns are insignificant. Coupled with the hitherto weak development of NAFTA **institutions**, US hegemony in the region will not be challenged by this regional integration scheme.

As to the immediate future of NAFTA, it may be observed that, especially in Mexico, the feeling is that NAFTA should not unavoidably evolve into a customs union. This is because analysts fear Mexico's **tariffs** on imports from non-member countries (e.g. Japan, the EU) would become molded mainly toward US business interests. Observers are still undecided whether the future may see the expansion of NAFTA toward the rest of the countries in the Western Hemisphere, thus giving way to a true Free Trade Area of the Americas.

See also: economic federalization; free trade; free trade zones (FTZs); Latin American Free Trade Agreement (LAFTA); maquiladoras; tariffs; trade

Further reading

Clarkson, S. (2000) *"Apples and Oranges:"* Prospects for the Comparative Analysis of the EU and NAFTA as Continental Systems, Florence: European University Institute (Working Paper RSC 2000/23).

Orme, W. (1996) *Understanding NAFTA: Mexico, Free Trade and the New North America*, Austin: University of Texas Press.

PAUL VAN LINDERT

nuclear energy

Nuclear energy is a method of generating electricity through a process of induced fission of uranium under controlled circumstances. Uranium–235 atoms decay naturally, by the process of alpha radiation. The process of induced fission uses the neutrons produced by this decay to split further atoms of uranium–235, which also produces great energy as heat. The heat produced is then applied to water to produce steam, which then generates electricity when it is used to drive turbines. In order for this process to work, uranium must be enriched so that it comprises at least 2–3 percent of uranium-235. (Weapons-grade uranium is composed of 90 percent or more uranium-235.) The nuclear reactor is protected against excessive heat by careful management, and by the use of radiation shields. These shields, and others, also prevent the leak of radioactive steam in the event of accident, or protect the reactor against collisions from objects outside the plant. International Atomic Energy Agency (IAEA) statistics show that in 2001, there were more than 400 nuclear power plants worldwide, or 352,400MW of installed generating capacity, which accounted for some 17 percent of global electricity production. Its importance varies nationally: in France, it provides 75 percent of electricity; in the USA there are more than 100 plants, generating 15 percent of US electricity.

Nuclear power is one of the most controversial forms of generating electricity. Proponents claim that it offers a means of producing power that is not linked to the political and environmental problems or greenhouse gas emissions of fossil fuels (see **climate change**). Critics, however, point out that the promises of the nuclear energy industry since the 1950s to provide abundant, cheap power have never been delivered, and instead the risks of severe radioactive pollution from accidents or from waste outweigh potential benefits. Public opinion has been severely affected – perhaps permanently – because of famous accidents at Three Mile Island in Pennsylvania in 1979 (where loss of cooling liquid caused part of the reactor core to melt), and in Chernobyl, Ukraine, in 1986 (where a series of explosions broke the concrete protections, releasing radioactive gases). Events such as these have encouraged perceptions of the industry as shrouded in risk, costly, and unaccountable to citizens.

Yet, nuclear power is still under consideration for two main reasons. First, there is a need to address the world's rising demand for power, especially when current oil reserves will begin to decline from approximately 2030. Second, there is increasing concern to address anthropogenic climate change and replace fossil fuels that emit greenhouse gases. Climate change scientists have estimated that a reduction in carbon dioxide emissions of 60 percent by 2050 will imply relying on fossil fuels for just 30 percent of global energy (see **energy policy**). If so, then non-greenhouse gas emitting fuels will have to increase by a factor of 15, or by 50 if nuclear power is excluded. Moreover, nuclear plants have average lives of 40–50 years. The IAEA estimates that 37 percent of nuclear plants were built before 1980; 51 percent built in the 1980s, and just 12 percent built in the 1990s, meaning that a third will come to an end before 2020, and a further half will end before 2030. Planners are asking where this current generating load will come from. Many developing countries are already committing themselves to nuclear power. In 2000, five new plants were built: two in India, one in China, and two in Japan; and thirty-three were under construction: eight in China, four in South Korea; three in Japan, two in India, one in Argentina, and the rest in central and eastern Europe.

The main incentives for nuclear power are: the rapid growth in global energy demand (see **energy policy**); a continued tendency for electricity generation to be planned centrally via grid networks; the ability for nuclear power to supply baseload electricity demand (i.e. the consistent level of demand); the relative unattractiveness of fossil fuels because of international tensions and climate change implications; and the relative lack of advance in **renewable energy** or electricity storing technologies. The inclusion of nuclear power in climate change policy (as a potential contributor to national emissions reductions targets) was disallowed in 2001, but campaigners hope it may be included later. The main barriers to further nuclear power investment include: the high economic cost; the costs (environmental and financial) of providing sufficient uranium; the hazards of

nuclear waste; public perceptions of risks; the difficulty in recruiting skilled staff (especially in developing countries); and the risk that nuclear power may enhance weapons proliferation or be targets for terrorism.

Nuclear power produces waste at various levels of radioactivity. The most dangerous, spent nuclear fuel, usually contains 3 percent fission products, 96 percent unused uranium, and 1 percent plutonium. As one example, plutonium-239 has a half-life of 24,600 years – i.e. it takes 24,600 years for half of the atoms to decay. Critics say this factor, and the geological risks and uncertainty of disposing of waste in deep vaults, are good reasons to consider nuclear power too dangerous. Proponents argue that careful management and selection of disposal sites can address these risks. The IAEA, however, estimated that global nuclear activity had produced 200,000 tons of spent fuel by 1998, and such totals will rise. Reprocessing (and re-using) spent fuel is another option, but is expensive and produces further **hazardous waste**.

See also: climate change; electrification and power-sector reform; energy policy; hazardous waste

Further reading

Grimston, M. and Beck, P. (2002) *Double or Quits? The Global Future of Civil Nuclear Energy*, London: Earthscan and Royal Institute of International Affairs.

International Atomic Energy Agency website: http://www.iaea.org/

TIM FORSYTH

nutrition

Nutrition is defined as the process by which living beings receive the **food** necessary for them to grow and be healthy. It is usually understood in terms of basic requirements of nutrients, vitamins and minerals, and overall calories, although calories consumed have to be related to calories used. The most common nutrition problems of developing countries are **malnutrition**, non-availability of clean **drinking water**, and the burden of infectious diseases (see **health**). The prevalence of protein-energy malnutrition has been high in many developing countries, resulting in diseases or conditions such as nutritional marasmus (characterized by swollen stomachs), kwashiorkor (characterized by swollen limbs), and marasmic kwashiorkor (a combination of both). Other problems may include learning disabilities, loss of mental abilities, low work capacity, and blindness (see **disability**). The **World Bank** estimated that if a country of 50 million people had the same nutritional deficiencies as South Asia, it would experience annually 20,000 deaths, 11,000 cases of mental damage and blindness, 1.3 million cases of lethargy and disability, and some 360,000 student years wasted. Three common nutritional deficiencies include lack of iron (which causes anemia), vitamin A (which is linked to blindness), and iodine (which leads to goiter and child mortality; see **infant and child mortality**). These deficiencies could waste up to 5 percent of GDP in developing countries, but could be addressed by expenditure of just 0.3 percent of GDP (World Bank, 1994:1–2).

Foods contain combinations of nutrients and other vital ingredients. Most doctors suggest that food should be consumed according to type, with bread, cereal, and rice products to be eaten 6–11 servings daily; fruit and vegetables 2–5 servings each; milk, yogurt and cheese, 2–3 servings; meat, fish, dried beans, eggs and nuts 2–3 servings; and fats, oils and sweets used only sparingly. This distribution is also called the "good food pyramid." Most vegetarians eat milk products and eggs, and as a group, these lacto-ovo-vegetarians enjoy excellent health. The advisable diet must have the proper amounts and ratios of proteins, fats and carbohydrates. Critical nutrients are essential for optimal health, including glyconutrients (supports cell-to-cell communication), phytochemicals (free radicals and anti-oxidants to support immune system), minerals, vitamins, and essential fatty acids. There are certain essential ingredients. These are fat-soluble vitamins A, D, E, and K, the other group of common water-soluble vitamins: vitamins B and C. Another nutritional group which helps to maintain homeostasis of internal body milieu, but neglected and if neglected for long shows body

changes. Mineral nutrition is also divided into two categories, macro-minerals and trace minerals. Distinction between these categories is primarily made by the concentration required in the daily diet. While macro-minerals are often required in amounts exceeding 0.5 percent of the total diet, trace minerals are often required in amounts less than 0.001 percent and are essential to optimize all physiological functions, such as reproduction, growth, immunity, and endurance. Surprisingly; however, water is the *most* important component in the whole nutritional framework. It is essential that living creatures have access to a daily supply of clean, fresh water (see **drinking water**). It is indispensable in transport of nutrients, chemical reactions and regulation of body temperature. Different individuals need different levels of nutrition: special attention may be given to pregnant or lactating mothers; infants receive most nutrition from breastmilk; menstruating women may require iron; the aged may require calcium to enhance bone strength.

There are three general approaches to addressing nutritional deficiencies: consumer education, pharmaceutical supplements, and fortification of common foodstuffs or water. A fourth possibility is regulation of the food industry (such as in requiring nutritional supplements in babymilk). Fortification may include adding iodine to salt. **Targeting** interventions is also important. Targeting may be universal (i.e. all people are included); based on medical evidence (e.g. prioritizing children with chronic diarrhea for vitamin A); or based on geographical or seasonal factors (e.g. offering iodized salt to high-altitude areas, or iron to malarious or hookworm-infected areas). Testing individuals for specific nutritional deficiencies is usually uneconomic. Nutritional supplements are sometimes offered simultaneously with **vaccination**, such as occurred with the Expanded Program on Immunization in Nepal. In South Africa, curry powder fortified with iron was offered to the Asian community. Iodized salt was made compulsory in India in 1984, although this is less efficient with rock salt as the iodine can be washed off. Other government actions can include protecting land used for foraging.

Nutritional problems in developing countries are diversifying. Obesity is now increasing, and has been attributed to over-eating, under-exercise and changing work culture, especially in Asian cities.

Sugar substitutes such as sorbitol, saccharin, and aspartame are increasingly used in many foods. Historically, the **health** (or epidemiological) transition (see **health transition**) described the tendency for poorer countries to suffer from insufficient food, and richer countries to experience ailments associated with improper or excessive food intake, such as heart disease or diabetes. Increasingly, such latter problems are occurring in developing countries. Some food companies (most notoriously, Nestlé) have attracted criticism for marketing babymilk in regions where water may be unsafe to use, and where marketing may discourage breast-feeding (see also **corporate social responsibility (CSR)**). The **World Food Programme (WFP)** of the **United Nations** has also attracted criticisms that food distributed is low in nutritional value.

See also: food; food security; health; health and poverty; health transition; malnutrition; World Food Programme (WFP)

Further reading

Brantley, C. (2002) *Feeding Families: African Realities and British Ideas of Nutrition and Development in Early Colonial Nyasaland (Malawi)*, Westport CT: Greenwood.

Caballero, B. and Popkin, B. (eds) (2002) *The Nutrition Transition: Diet and Disease in the Developing World*, New York: Academic Press.

Philips Foster, H. (1998) *The World Food Problem: Tacking Causes of Undernutrition in the Third World*, Boulder: Lynne Rienner.

Semba, R. and Bloem, M. (eds) (2001) *Nutrition and Health in Developing Countries*, Totowa NJ: Humana.

World Bank (1994) *Enriching Lives: Overcoming Vitamin and Mineral Malnutrition in Developing Countries*, Washington DC: World Bank.

DINESH VYAS

occupational health

Occupational health and safety relates to the physical, biological, chemical, mechanical, psychosocial, and organizational factors that impact directly or indirectly on human work environments. Developing countries contain 70 percent of the world's **population** and experience the majority of global work-caused, work-related ill health and accidents. 2,600 million people were estimated to be in the global workforce in 1990s and 75 percent of these were in developing countries. In 1998, there were an estimated 250 million occupational injuries each year and the **World Health Organization (WHO)** estimated 217 million cases of occupational diseases worldwide.

Occupational hazards in recent years have been particularly associated with the growth of extractive industries (see **mineral-led development**), industrialized **agriculture**, and factory **employment** resulting from **industrialization** and **foreign direct investment**. Work and **poverty** together may have a very significant adverse effect on occupational health, especially when severe heat, cold or humidity restricts the use of protective equipment, even if available. Migrants from developing countries also have poor occupational health and safety records in developed countries; for example in US agricultural and European heavy engineering sectors.

Paid work provides a major means to avoid poverty, and unpaid work provides important means of subsistence in many developing countries (see **employment**). Both types of work bring a wide range of hazards and associated risks for employees, their families and communities (see **community**). Industrialization brings new hazards or sometimes exports old hazards from industrialized nations to developing countries. Some of these hazards impact differentially on women and men, according to their susceptibility to certain pollutants, and the tasks performed. Many well recognized and understood developing country hazards flow from traditional industries such as agriculture, mining, fishing, construction, forestry and basic engineering. It is possible to remove or reduce some of these hazards by adopting relatively simple and inexpensive engineering solutions. Addressing basic ergonomic problems, for instance in key industries, would cut work-related upper limb disorders and other musculo-skeletal injuries. Rigorous prior informed consent on export of hazardous substances and technologies from industrialized to industrializing countries would also produce rapid reductions in occupational diseases and **mortality**.

Some activities, such mining in Central and Southern America, **agrochemicals** usage in Africa and Asia, and the breaking up of computers in China have proved occupationally hazardous, and have simultaneously polluted water, land and air (see **pollution**). In developing countries, multiple hazard jeopardy can apply with worker exposure, environmental exposure, and food-water-soil-air pollution. Some ages and groups may be very vulnerable: especially women and children whose work from a very early age and location can expose them to serious ergonomic and physiological risks, through threats to immune systems and organ development; and older workers in poor

health. Work organization and management control systems, for example in electronics production in developing countries, can damage the physical and psycho-social health of workers if not effectively controlled nationally and supranationally. These new industries equip or support call centers, data analysis and financial/accounting/publishing services in industrialized countries, but these may be based in India and Asia. Call centers in developing countries are not hazard and risk-free, but may be regarded as such by their workers, who will have experienced far worse working conditions elsewhere.

Effective international health and safety standards, and their independent implementation and enforcement by labor inspectors, are needed in developing countries and through the **International Labor Organization (ILO)**. Yet, critics claim these steps are impossible when some developed countries are using environmental health aspects of trade agreements as reasons to restrict or prevent imports from developing countries. Hence, developing countries are hit with hazardous work and limited, hostile markets for the goods produced. Analysts argue that good health and safety practices and standards occur when workforces are educated and informed, and are able to contribute to the monitoring, control and removal of occupational risks. However, arguments that it is cost-effective to improve occupational health and safety may fail in industrializing or de-industrializing countries when labor costs are so low. Different arguments about **fair trade**, **social justice**, and related ethical codes, may now prove most effective in raising global health and safety performance.

See also: gender and industrialization; gender division of labor; health; industrialization; International Labor Organization (ILO); labor rights and standards; pollution havens

Further reading

Castleman, B. (1999) "Global Corporate Policies and International 'Double Standards' in Occupational and Environmental Health," *International Journal of Occupational Environmental Health* 5: 61–4.

LaDou, J. (ed.) (2002) *Occupational Health in Industrializing Countries*, Philadelphia: Hanley and Belfus.

Stellman, J. (1998) *ILO Encyclopedia of Occupational Health and Safety*, Geneva: ILO. 4-volume print edition and CD-ROM.

ANDREW WATTERSON

OECD *see* Organization for Economic Cooperation and Development (OECD)

Office of the United Nations High Commissioner for Human Rights (OHCHR)

The Office of the United Nations High Commissioner for Human Rights (OHCHR), was established in 1993 to protect and promote **human rights**. It is based in Geneva, and in 2001 had more than 400 staff worldwide and an income of US$52.8 million. The OHCHR monitors human rights practices and investigates human rights abuses; advises on new human rights policies and institutions; campaigns to have all countries ratify the core human rights treaties; disseminates information on human rights; promotes human rights education (see **human rights indicators; education**) for the judiciary, the police, the military and others; and provides support to the main UN human rights bodies, including the United Nations Commission on Human Rights. OHCHR headquarters- and field-based staff also work with the **United Nations Development Programme (UNDP)**, **United Nations Children's Fund (UNICEF)**, **World Health Organization (WHO)**, the **World Bank**, the UN Security Council, UN country teams and others to integrate human rights into development policies and country programs.

See also: human rights; United Nations

CLAUDIO O. DELANG

OFFICIAL DEVELOPMENT ASSISTANCE (ODA)

see aid; bilateral aid agencies; United Nations Development Programme (UNDP); World Bank

offshore finance

Offshore finance refers to the offering of financial services in locations that are generally not lived in by the people using these services, and which offer secrecy over banking transactions. It is also highly associated with the concept of "tax havens" – or those jurisdictions offering low- or no-tax environments to **transnational corporations (TNCs)** and wealthy individuals to escape taxes onshore. Specialist offshore companies formed in tax havens offer the possibilities of nominal taxation rates on profits as low as 1–5 percent, or the option of a fixed fee of a few hundred dollars per year. Offshore finance centers (OFCs) are also tax havens but offer a range of offshore financial services including banking, fund management, captive insurance, trusts and companies and a variety of other vehicles. The main attractions of tax havens or OFCs are taxation advantages and secrecy.

Measuring the size of offshore finance is difficult because of the strict secrecy fundamental to offshore finance, and precise data are rare. Estimates suggest that over US$6 trillion, or perhaps as much as one quarter of the world's total money supply, is held offshore in over seventy tax havens and offshore finance centers. Such centers form a key part of the **globalization** of financial flows.

In some OFCs, secrecy stems from draconian bank secrecy legislation, which may treat the divulging of customers' details as a criminal act. Other OFCs, while not strictly having legal banking secrecy, create a form of bank secrecy by using many layers of offshore companies and the misuse of other artificial offshore vehicles such as trusts and charitable foundations.

However, the secrecy space created by OFCs means that they are vulnerable to abuse by criminals who seek **money laundering** of the proceeds of **drugs**, arms sales (see **arms sales and controls**) or terrorism (see **crime**). Also, secrecy results in OFCs sheltering funds fleeing from many countries, whether as **capital flight** to avoid tax or other

regulations, or as the result of **corruption** such as the skimming of a percentage of **International Monetary Fund (IMF)** loans to a country. Documented cases include funds hidden offshore by former presidents Marcos (Philippines), "Baby Doc" Duvalier, (Haiti), Mobuto (Zaire) and General Abacha (Nigeria).

OFCs are often located in small jurisdictions such as **small island developing states (SIDS)** and other microstates such as coastal or mountain enclaves. Clusters of OFCs are found on the periphery of Europe (the Channel Islands of Jersey and Guernsey, Cyprus, Malta, Monaco); near the US in and around the Caribbean (Anguilla, Bahamas, Bermuda, British Virgin Islands, Cayman Islands, Netherlands Antilles, St Lucia, Turks and Caicos Islands); Central America (Belize, Panama); the Indian Ocean (Mauritius, Seychelles); and in the Pacific (Cook Islands, Labuan, Marshall Islands, Vanuatu).

Offshore finance can form a large part of some microstate economies, contributing significantly to **gross domestic product (GDP)**, government revenues and **employment**. In extreme cases, more than 80 percent of GDP comes from offshore activities in the case of some of the largest OFCs, and up to 20 percent of the local labor force is directly employed in financial services.

Small economies, especially islands, are often constrained as a function of their smallness by diseconomies of scale; limited **natural resources**; being highly open to international trade; small labor markets; remoteness; and high transport costs. Offshore finance has often been seen as a lucrative strategy of **economic development**. Established OFCs, such as Jersey or the Cayman Islands, are seen by new entrants as successful microstate hosts of what some argue is an (environmentally) "clean," smokeless industry. However, whilst there are some benefits (**employment**; **multiplier effect**s), the costs are not minimal, and it can be argued that hosting such a powerful but footloose industry as financial TNCs may be a risky strategy. Further, the financial (and political) power of TNCs in a small economy raises questions of the danger of overreliance on one sector, and the crowding-out of other sectors such as **tourism** or **agriculture**.

OFCs are similar to **free trade zones (FTZs)** as they form part of the increasingly globalizing economy, and both may be seen as enclaves of international capital. However, the main difference is that – unlike FTZs, which may only account for a small proportion of the host economy – for many islands and small states the OFC has become the dominant economic activity.

For the global financial system, OFCs are also significant in several ways. In the **Asian crises**, damaging short-term speculative flows were facilitated by OFCs, raising questions about ineffective offshore regulation and leading to wider concerns over the stability of the global financial system. There is also an offshore (and somewhat ironic) dimension to the **debt** crisis. Many of the international banks that in the 1970s offered cheap loans to developing countries in Latin America and Africa then collected substantial flows of **capital flight** from **elites** in those same countries. This capital flight was deposited offshore in the banks' private banking branches in OFCs in the Caribbean and elsewhere. In other words, the banks were giving loans with one hand, and then taking back the funds with the other in the form of offshore private banking deposits. A report by **Oxfam** (2000) estimated that tax havens cost the developing world around US$50 billion per year as a result of tax evasion, an amount broadly equivalent to the world's total overseas **aid** programs.

From the late 1990s, there was an unprecedented confluence of international initiatives against OFCs, focusing mainly upon tax (the **Organization for Economic Cooperation and Development (OECD)** on harmful tax competition; the **European Union** on tax harmonization); and money laundering (the G7's Financial Action Task Force; the **United Nations** Programme against Money Laundering). From late 2001, OFCs were once again under pressure, especially from the US administration of President George W. Bush in the "War on Terror," by the investigation of suspected money laundering of terrorist funds through the offshore system.

See also: capital flight; crime; economic development; money laundering; multilateral development banks (MDBs)

Further reading

Hampton, M. (1996) *The Offshore Interface: Tax Havens in the Global Economy*, Basingstoke: Macmillan.

Hampton, M. and Abbott, J. (eds) (1999) *Offshore Finance Centres and Tax Havens: the Rise of Global Capital*, Basingstoke: Macmillan.

Oxfam (2000) *Tax Havens: Releasing the Hidden Billions for Poverty Eradication*, Oxfam Briefing Paper, Oxford: Oxfam GB.

Roberts, S. (1995) "Small Place, Big Money: The Cayman Islands and the International Financial System," *Economic Geography* 71:3 237–56.

MARK HAMPTON

oil and gas development

Oil and gas development refers to the development processes that occur in locations that are dominated by their production and export of oil and gas (see also **natural resources; mineral-led development**). In contrast to markets for hard minerals like copper, the oil market has been distorted by actions by governments in both developed and developing countries since the mid-twentieth century. One consequence has been to create substantial rents for low-cost oil producers like those in the Middle East. The relatively high rents of such producers were boosted dramatically in the 1970s by the efforts of the **Organization of Petroleum Exporting Countries (OPEC)** cartel to restrict global oil supply. The oil "shocks" of 1973 and 1978 each transferred 2 percent of Gross World Product from the oil-importing countries to the oil exporters. The 1978 oil shock doubled the revenue per barrel and lifted the rent component for low-cost producers above 90 percent of the oil price. In comparison, the rent on natural gas was significantly less (below 40 percent of the price) because of the higher cost of transportation to markets compared with oil. However, OPEC's ability to maintain prices virtually vanished in the late 1980s and early 1990s, and real petroleum prices declined to the levels of the early 1970s. This is partly because the sharp price increases during the 1970s encouraged new sources of petroleum production outside OPEC, an expansion of alternative energy (see **energy policy**), and energy conservation.

The scale of the positive shock from higher oil prices for oil-exporting countries depended upon the ratio of oil production to **population**. For example, the first shock generated the equivalent of an extra 11 percent of non-oil **gross domestic product (GDP)** annually for Venezuela, 16 percent for Indonesia, 23 percent for Nigeria, almost 40 percent for Trinidad and Tobago and 200 percent for Saudi Arabia. Astutely handled (see **mineral-led development**), the rents could accelerate GDP growth, as was the case in Indonesia, Malaysia and Brunei. However, most governments absorbed the rents too rapidly into the domestic economy, and per capita income dropped sharply when oil prices fell after 1982. Some countries, notably Nigeria and Venezuela, saw their per capita incomes fall back below their pre-shock level in real terms. Even Mexico, whose oil boom started relatively late, failed to learn and transform the rents into sustained higher welfare.

A significant fraction of the oil windfall revenues went into increased consumption due to expanded state subsidies and also cheaper imports that resulted from allowing the real exchange rate to strengthen sharply (see **exchange rates**). Governments might have had more success in sustaining the new levels of consumption if they saved a significant fraction of the rents abroad in a Capital Development Fund, like Kuwait, and/or made prudent domestic investments. In fact, many governments opted to "sow" the oil by developing resource-based industry (RBI), notably petrochemicals, aluminum and steel produced by **state-owned enterprises (SOEs)**. For example, Venezuela accelerated the expansion of its hydro-based metal complex at Ciudad Guyana that was intended to be a growth pole for the empty eastern region. Far from generating the planned 15 percent investment return with which to create another growth pole elsewhere, inefficiency and corruption turned Ciudad Guyana into a public sector sink for the oil revenues, with a negative real return on the US$22 billion invested. Nigeria experienced a similar outcome when it invested in steel and petrochemical complexes during the 1979–81 oil boom. Far from saving a fraction of the oil windfall,

Nigeria accumulated overseas debts exceeding US$30 billion boom that proved too onerous to service when oil prices collapsed. If the RBI plants were built as **joint venture**s with transnational corporation equity partners (see **transnational corporations (TNCs)**), as in Saudi Arabia, there were fewer problems with cost overruns and marketing, but inefficient SOE investments accounted for a sizeable fraction of the oil-exporting countries' **debt**.

Indonesia was more successful. Around one quarter of its development investment during the 1974–8 oil boom went on infrastructure. A further two fifths was allocated to prolong oil production and to diversify both foreign exchange earnings and tax revenues through liquefied natural gas (LNG) exports. Just less than one sixth went into the metal industries and a similar amount in the non-metals industries to diversify manufacturing. During the second boom, more than 40 percent of the windfall was saved abroad. Nevertheless, domestic absorption was still too high because private consumption, public consumption and investment all rose sharply. Inflation accelerated (see **inflation and its effects**) and eliminated the benefits of the 1979 devaluation. Worse, the **Dutch disease** effects (which weaken agriculture and manufacturing) were used as an excuse to extend protection of manufacturing, creating rent-seeking opportunities for those with presidential connections.

Nevertheless, sound macro-management prevented Indonesia from reaching the extremes of oil dependence seen in Nigeria and Venezuela. When oil prices fell softened in 1982 and fell in 1985, the Indonesian government made prompt adjustments to close the fiscal and current account gaps (see **fiscal and monetary policy; structural adjustment**). Indonesia also made a large devaluation in 1986 (to 60 percent of the rupiah's 1983 value), whereas Nigeria required a massive adjustment to one fifth of the naira's level by then. The Indonesian government also made prompt cuts in public spending and broadened the tax base, while drawing upon foreign loans to smooth the adjustment. Finally, a start was made on dismantling import protection for manufacturing. These reforms triggered a surge in Indonesian non-oil exports to 74 percent of total exports by 1991, with manufacturing exports tripling to 45 percent of all exports. The level of investment, investment efficiency and rate of GDP growth all recovered in the late 1980s, as Indonesia successfully adjusted and became a competitive exporter of **labor-intensive** manufactured goods.

Unfortunately, such hard-earned lessons may be lost on the emerging hydrocarbon-rich Caspian Basin countries like Azerbaijan, Kazakstan and Turkmenistan. Preliminary evidence suggests that compared with resource-poor countries in the region, oil wealth is encouraging predatory states. The governments of such states benefit from rent-seeking and **corruption** if transition reform is slow. They experience Dutch disease effects that retard job-creation in manufacturing and **agriculture** and boost income equality. Finally, the rebound in the per capita GDP from the post-Soviet economic collapse is weak.

See also: Dutch disease; environment; mineral-led development; natural resources; Organization of Petroleum Exporting Countries (OPEC); resource curse thesis

Further reading

Auty, R. (2001) "Transition Reform in the Mineral-rich Caspian Region Countries," *Resources Policy* 27:1 25–32.

Gelb, A. and Associates (1988) *Oil Windfalls: Blessing or Curse?* New York: Oxford University Press.

Ross, M. (2001) "Does Oil Hinder Democracy?" *World Politics* 53:3 325–61.

RICHARD M. AUTY

OPEC *see* Organization of Petroleum Exporting Countries (OPEC)

Organization for Economic Cooperation and Development (OECD)

The Organization for Economic Cooperation and Development (OECD) is one of the most powerful intergovernmental organizations in the world. With a membership of thirty (including the most advanced economies), its objective is to develop and harmonize policies among its members on social and economic issues, such as **tariffs**, subsidies, environmental control, and anti-trust laws. It emerged out of the Organization for European Economic Cooperation, established under the **Marshall Plan** for the reconstruction of Europe, following World War II. OECD membership is open only to countries committed to free-market enterprise and **democracy**; however, non-members are occasionally invited to subscribe to its agreements. The OECD works through specialized committees and working groups. The ultimate authority of OECD rests with its council, made up of one representative from each member country and from the European Commission. Its secretariat, located in Paris, is led by a secretary-general.

See also: international organizations and associations

JOSEPH MENSAH

Organization of Petroleum Exporting Countries (OPEC)

The Organization of Petroleum Exporting Countries (OPEC) is an international organization (see **international organizations and associations**) of oil exporting developing countries that coordinates and unifies the petroleum policies of its members. It is commonly described as a cartel of oil producers (see **cartels**). OPEC was formed in 1960 in Baghdad, Iraq, by the five founder members of Iran, Iraq, Kuwait, Saudi Arabia and Venezuela, and was registered with the **United Nations** in 1962. It now has a membership of eleven countries, with its headquarters in Vienna. The main objective of OPEC is to stabilize oil prices in international oil markets while achieving a steady income for members, yet its actions have had immense international political significance. OPEC rose to prominence in October 1973 when it declared an embargo on the shipment of oil to those countries that had supported Israel in its conflict with Egypt, and with other cutbacks in production it allowed the price of oil to rise four times between 1973 and 1974. Prices also rose temporarily higher by 150 percent in 1979 following the Iranian Revolution. These combined "oil shocks" emphasized economic recession in Europe and North America during the 1970s, and allowed the rapid generation of "petrodollars" by oil-exporting states that, in turn, helped fuel widespread lending by commercial banks that contributed to the **debt crisis** and eventually, in part, to **structural adjustment** programs. It also highlighted international **security** concerns in the Middle East, and greater attention to securing long-term energy supplies through new sources of energy (see **energy policy**), or some steps toward adopting energy-saving technologies (see also **renewable energy**), often through new government ministries (the USA created a cabinet-level Department of Energy in 1977). By 2000, the ability for OPEC to produce such major shocks to international oil markets seems to have lessened for various reasons, including divisions within its membership; an increase in global oil production from non-OPEC countries such as Russia, the UK and USA; and new pricing mechanisms that allow consumers to limit their risk. However, long-term predictions suggest that crude-oil production will remain within OPEC countries, and especially Saudi Arabia.

See also: energy policy; natural resources; oil and gas development; security

Further reading

Claes, D. (2001) *The Politics of Oil-producer Cooperation*, Boulder: Westview.
OPEC website: http://www.opec.org/

TIM FORSYTH

Orientalism

Orientalism is a word associated with the writer Edward Said (1935–2003) that refers to the romantic systems of representation that brought the "Orient" into Western learning and imagination.

Under Orientalism, the Orient (or indeed, other places or cultures considered in the same light) is defined largely according to the perceptions and expectation of the West, as a mirror image of what is inferior and alien ("Other") to the West. Orientalism is an influential concept in **post-colonialism**, and highlights the historically and politically situated manner in which knowledge about different cultures emerges and influences political debate. The concept also brought attention to the power of the nineteenth-century explorers and writers who shape narratives (see **narratives of development**). Scholars of Orientalism have argued that historic narratives portrayed the "East" as exotic and ready to be colonized, and current narratives represent Arab or Asian cultures as menacing and anti-Western.

See also: clash of civilizations; culture; narratives of development; postcolonialism

Further reading

Said, E. (1979) *Orientalism*, New York: Vintage.

TIM FORSYTH

overpopulation

Overpopulation usually refers to the belief that there are too many people living in a specific zone (defined in terms of time or space). The term may also be used for other species. The Earth's human **population** reached 6 billion in 1999; whether the world is overpopulated at that level, however, is a hotly debated question. Defining overpopulation is a complex exercise laden with controversy and resulting in characterizations full of arbitrary measures and ambiguities. Various definitions have been proposed: the point at which space and **natural resources** are inadequate to support the number of people present; when people are overcrowded and the environment begins to deteriorate; when **carrying capacity** is surpassed; when the present population cannot support itself and ensure adequate resources for future generations; when population growth surpasses the rate of agricultural production (see **Malthusian demography**).

Overpopulation is often associated with lower-income developing countries; however, it is also attributed to over-consumption of resources by wealthy countries and individuals. Population growth varies geographically, and birth rates (see **fertility**) in developing countries overall are nearly double those in developed countries. The highest population growth rates (see **population growth rate (PGR)**) often occur in regions with the lowest population densities (Sub-Saharan Africa, for example), however, and some of the countries experiencing negative rates of natural increase are among the most densely populated in the world (Japan, Germany and Italy, for example). The human population is projected to level out at approximately 9 billion people in 2050. Running out of space is not the problem; rather, quality of life and **sustainable development** are key issues.

Long-range global population projections vary dramatically depending on assumptions about several factors, including **fertility** and **mortality**. Despite lower fertility levels projected globally, and the increased mortality risks for some populations particularly associated with HIV/AIDS (see **HIV/AIDS (definition and treatment); HIV/AIDS (policy issues)**), the **United Nations** estimates that global population will increase, and then level off at nearly 9 billion people in 2050. However, this figure is contingent on couples having access to **family planning**, and that efforts to address HIV/AIDS have success. If women were to have – on average – half a child less under this scenario, the 2050 global population would be 7.4 billion. But if fertility were to remain constant at current levels, this figure could reach 12.8 billion. Average global fertility has declined from 4.5 children per woman in the early 1970s to approximately 3 in the early 2000s.

Two opposing approaches debate the concept of overpopulation. First, the *Limits to Growth* **report (1972)** perspective focuses on the factors that act to limit population growth rate. This approach began with the eighteenth-century work of Thomas Malthus (1798), who posited that critical resources – particularly food – are finite, and that human population will grow until it outstrips its resource base, at which point it will be checked by

famine, disease and conflict (see **Malthusian demography**). Malthus could not predict human beings' ability to develop technologies that have allowed population to increase beyond the carrying capacity of local areas, particularly dramatic gains in agricultural production achieved in the twentieth century. *Limits to Growth* proponents view essential resources as finite in extent, availability and recoverability. For them, certain signs indicate that the world is already overpopulated at local, regional and global scales: e.g. one sixth of humanity suffers **malnutrition** or faces famine and starvation; supplies of fresh water are declining; extinction of species and declining **biodiversity** reflect over-consumption of resources; and production of wastes and **pollution** are increasing.

The Cornucopian Perspective holds that critical resources, far from being finite and depleted, are more readily available and less expensive because of technological advances. Most importantly, population growth rates worldwide have been declining since the mid-twentieth century. Cornucopian proponents credit falling **fertility** rates in most regions of the world, although part of the slowing must be attributed to increasing **mortality** rates in some regions. Larger populations are the source of greater innovation and invention – the more people, the more ideas, the more possibilities for improving quality of life. New technologies have increased agricultural output; improving **nutrition** worldwide is seen as a matter of distribution rather than production. Medical care has increased life expectancies and decreased mortality.

See also: biodiversity; carrying capacity; environment; *Limits to Growth* report (1972); Malthusian demography; natural resources; population; sustainable development

Further reading

Brown, L., Gardner, G. and Halweil, B. (1999) *Beyond Malthus: Nineteen Dimensions of the Population Challenge*, New York: Norton.

Simon, J. (1999) *Economics Against the Grain: Population Economics, Natural Resources and Related Themes (Vol. 2)*, London: Edward Elgar.

ELLEN R. HANSEN

Oxfam

Oxfam is a non-sectarian, private British-based non-governmental organization (NGO) (see **non-governmental organizations (NGOs)**) that provides **emergency assistance** and developmental **aid** to suffering and impoverished communities (see **community**) worldwide, and campaigns on their behalf. Initially established in 1942 as the Oxford Committee for Famine Relief (formally shortened to Oxfam in 1965), its purpose was to provide essential supplies to famine-stricken populations in Greece and other war-ravaged countries in Europe. Following World War II, it expanded its remit to providing relief to those suffering from **wars**, **natural disasters** and other causes globally. The 1951 famine in Bihar, India, led to the first campaign in a developing country. In the 1960s, Oxfam began supporting community-based self-help schemes in poor areas, and in the 1970s, it began campaigning at the national and international level. By 2000, Oxfam was a confederation of eleven organizations active in more than a hundred countries. Funded from both public and private sources, its headquarters remain in Oxford, England.

See also: charities; complex emergencies; famine; humanitarianism; natural disasters; non-governmental organizations (NGOs)

EMMA SAMMAN

P

Paris 21

Paris 21 is a new international process by a global consortium of policy-makers, statisticians, and users of statistical information in support of development. It was launched in Paris in 1999, as an initiative of the **United Nations**, the **Organization for Economic Cooperation and Development (OECD)**, the **World Bank**, the **International Monetary Fund (IMF)** and the **European Union**. Paris 21 aims to build statistical capacity as the foundation for effective development policies by helping to develop well-managed statistical systems, which many developing countries lack. It also aims to help to promote a culture of evidence-based policy-making and monitoring in all countries, especially in poor countries. Paris 21's initial aim was to help countries to prepare Poverty Reduction Strategy Papers (PRSPs) (see **poverty**) and has now expanded to assist countries to prepare PRSPs as well as **Millennium Development Goals (MDGs)** reports.

See also: indicators of development; information technology; measuring development; World Summit on the Information Society (WSIS)

TAKAYOSHI KUSAGO

Paris Club

The Paris Club is an informal grouping of nineteen major creditor countries that meets approximately every six weeks, with the *ad hoc* participation of another thirteen creditor countries, to agree the rescheduling of developing country **debt** as a means of **debt relief**. It was founded in 1956 to coordinate the rescheduling of Argentina's debt, and has a small secretariat in Paris. To be eligible for rescheduling, a debtor must first have an economic program agreed with the **International Monetary Fund (IMF)**. The first principle of the club's "rules and principles" is that debtors are dealt with on a case-by-case basis, making the institution, together with the **London Club**, a creditors' cartel (see **cartels**) in which a single debtor country faces the combined negotiating power of the world's richest countries. By early 2004, the Paris Club had concluded 383 agreements covering seventy-eight debtor countries; the bulk of these agreements have been with low-income countries, especially since the beginning of the 1990s.

See also: debt; debt relief; International Monetary Fund (IMF); London Club

HOWARD WHITE

participatory budgeting

Participatory budgeting (PB) is a process and an instrument that enables the inhabitants of **municipalities** (or higher-level administrative units) to formally participate in decision-making on planning, public policies and their implementation. Through a year-round cycle of popular consultation in the elaboration of the municipal budgeting, the

community gains permanent control over the use of public resources and in this way a structural change in priorities is achieved. PB is an innovative way of strengthening direct **democracy** and stimulating good **governance**, which was pioneered and gradually refined in Brazilian cities under Worker's Party rule, most notably Porto Alegre. The PB process has effectively changed the traditional political patron-client relationships, and the low-income neighborhoods have significantly succeeded in receiving larger shares of investment funds. As budgets and accounts of separate projects are made public, the process adds to the **transparency** and **accountability** of **local government**.

See also: accountability; governance; local government; municipalities; participatory development; transparency

PAUL VAN LINDERT

participatory development

Participatory development is a bottom-up, people-centered approach aimed at developing the full potentials of people at the grassroots level (see **grassroots development**), especially the poor and marginal social groups, through their full participation in development efforts that directly affect their lives. The important role of participatory action research (see **participatory research methods**) in the process of identifying, designing, implementing and evaluating a project or program is inextricably intertwined with participatory development processes. In collaborative or participatory research processes that link theory with practice, project participants and **community** members are recognized for their capabilities and skills in producing unique and diverse knowledge of local conditions and project results (see **indigenous knowledge; local knowledge**). While participatory development started as a counterpoint to mainstream top-down development planning (e.g. **modernization theory**), it is rare since the 1980s to find a development strategy or approach which does not refer to participation or suggest that it is participatory in nature.

Participatory development movements worldwide have challenged the dominant market-oriented development approaches that were preoccupied with **aid** and **trade** and came with a string of conditionalities (see **conditionality**). They are highly critical of mainstream development agencies and workers that only consult local communities on a predetermined agenda to enlist their participation, often limited to receiving material inducements (e.g. food-for-work, wages, loans, grants), and providing information for research, or analyses that do need not necessarily lead to social transformation. They are also highly critical of the bad outcomes of "development" practices, as they advocate participatory approaches in action and research, and bottom-up planning decision-making processes at the grassroots level (see **postmodernism and post development**).

Historical origins

Participatory development advocates, especially in developing countries, began as barefoot doctors, community development activists and popular **education** advocates. Their movement was partly a reaction against how community development in rural areas was introduced in the 1950s through "participation," then understood as simply the mobilization of labor by people in the implementation of projects designed by outsiders. The increased concern for bottom-up people's participation in development processes was introduced to development studies in the 1970s by way of adult education, particularly Paolo Freire's landmark work, *Pedagogy of the Oppressed* (1970). Influenced by Freirean pedagogy that begins from "conscientization" or raising people's awareness about their local conditions, researchers working in developing-world contexts promoted the idea of participatory action research within the fields of adult education and development studies. Development education, or popular education for development goals, based on **social learning** by local community insiders and outside development workers, was seen as an important component of development processes through political organizing and raising social awareness.

Earlier experiments in participatory development in developing world during the 1970s brought some key lessons that would be re-echoed in the 1980s by proponents of participatory development from the

North, such as Robert Chambers, David Korten and Norman Uphoff. Robert Chambers, who is often credited for popularizing Participatory Rural Appraisal (PRA) (see **participatory research methods**), and the Institute of Development Studies at Sussex where Chambers was based, claim that many of the earlier PRA tools have been developed in Thailand universities. Like PRA, the Self-Esteem, Associative Strength, Resourcefulness, Action Planning, Responsibility or SARAR, is another recognized participatory methodology for working with local stakeholders in using their creative capabilities in problem-solving, planning and evaluating initiatives. SARAR was developed in the 1970s by Lyra Srinivasan in Asia and later applied by the **World Bank**, **United Nations** agencies, particularly the **United Nations Development Programme (UNDP)** and **United Nations Children's Fund (UNICEF)**, and many **non-governmental organizations (NGOs)** in their development activities. Lessons from participatory development advocates and organizations in developing countries stress the importance of popular community participation in both defining development goals and acting upon them. A desirable development path was increasingly seen as a process whereby community members come together to identify problems, mobilize local resources and seek solutions among themselves, leading to national decision-making structures based on civic freedoms and **human rights**.

The dissemination of knowledge on participatory development from academics based in developed countries, NGOs and research agencies became more routine and protuberant since the 1990s with the mainstreaming of participation and participatory development approaches by international donor agencies, particularly the World Bank. Aware of criticisms raised by participatory development advocates that conventional development practices often result in greater social **inequality**, deepening **poverty**, and power differences (see **power and discourse**), international aid agencies saw the benefits in working with NGOs advocating participatory development approaches and decentralized decision-making processes.

The World Bank's promotion of participation and participatory development approaches in its projects and programs came to full force under the so-called post-**Washington consensus** in the mid-1990s. This new consensus coincided with the Bank's interest in the non-economic, social aspects of development, matched by its internal organizational restructuring that created Social Development, Participation and Civil Society Divisions and developed increased collaboration with local NGOs. The Bank's interest in participatory development, however, started much earlier in the late 1980s and early 1990s when it commissioned its staff and hired consultants to produce a number of publications on participation, participatory development and bottom-up planning (e.g. Bhatbanagar and Williams, 1992; Cernea, 1992). The staff of the World Bank began documenting case studies based on project evaluation results showing the practical advantages of popular participation and partnership with NGOs to project efficiency and sustainability, leading to its publication of the *Participation Sourcebook* (World Bank, 1996). This book in particular intended to promote a learning mood among the Bank's staff so that they could effectively shift role from that of "external experts" to "participating stakeholders" who initiate, facilitate, and nurture participatory processes. This organizational social learning culminated in the Bank's Poverty Division's interest in conducting **participatory poverty assessment (PPA)**. Thus, the World Bank and other international agencies have begun to acknowledge that successful project and program implementation depends on the participation of people they wish to help.

Principles and benefits of participatory development

Participatory development begins from the premise that development workers need to identify and build upon strengths already present in the communities they work with. This involves learning the local realities of the people and groups who are not usually heard from or consulted. It is about trusting that local people and their organizations are capable of analyzing their own situations and planning appropriate solutions to their problems, better than an outsider would. It is about finding ways for the disempowered to develop confidence in their own voice, own abilities, and resources that could lead to their **empowerment**. The strategies of participatory development attempt to challenge social hierarchies to produce social change in the direction of equality. They also aim to empower the poor, encourage the participation of women, take local politics, conflicts and socio-cultural traditions into account and enable the achievement of sustainable gains over time. Table 7 demonstrates the differences in principles between conventional development and participatory development.

The participation or involvement of self-reliant people in development efforts provides numerous advantages. These include better decisions and management of projects due to the inclusion of local knowledge; local resource mobilization means less reliance on imported technologies, lower project expenses, and sustained by the participants beyond the project-funding period. Participatory development facilitates training and skill diffusion, and contributes to **social development** and the self-confidence of vulnerable groups such as poor

women and ethnic minorities (see **gender; indigenous people; disability**). Participatory approaches now seem capable of doing anything, from increasing project efficiency, raising social consciousness, and incorporating gender sensitivity, to getting relevant data, introducing appreciative inquiry, improving project monitoring and evaluation results, and resolving contradictions between market-oriented growth and social equity.

Some of the benefits of using participatory instead of conventional development methods are the following: (1) Participatory development approaches condition community **empowerment** and social learning by enabling a particular group (e.g. laborers, women, poor women, small farmers, etc.) or a community to analyze their conditions, giving them confidence to state and assert their priorities, present proposals, make demands and take action, leading to sustainable and effective development programs. (2) They encourage and enable the expression and exploitation of local diversity in otherwise standardized programs.

Table 7 Comparing conventional and participatory development

Issues	Conventional development	Participatory development
What approach?	Top-down approach	Bottom-up approach, grassroots
Whose knowledge counts?	Expert knowledge is privileged	Local knowledge is privileged
How is knowledge generated?	Strictly quantitative and scientific methods used; Standardization and homogeneity are preferred	Subjective experiences and qualitative research results generate bulk of knowledge; Diversity is valued
Who plans and implements?	Planned and carried out by outsiders far removed from local reality – usually members of first world countries	Planned and carried out by Community members
Relationship between development planners and beneficiaries?	Highly bureaucratic – many layers of hierarchy between development planners and beneficiaries	Facilitators and community members work together to generate knowledge and plans
Main motivator	Profit as the main motivator	Human and social advancement as the motivator
View of unpaid work?	Market forces prioritized – unpaid work/women's work ignored	Unpaid work/women s work understood as critical in maintaining the community and economy
View of power inequalities?	Enforces power inequalities, e.g. North-South, men-women, old-young, urban-rural, educated-uneducated, etc.	Challenges power inequalities by listening to, encouraging, supporting, respecting those with less power

Source: Adapted from Institute of Development Studies, Participation Group website, http://www.ids.ac.uk

(3) They promote collaborative research by identifying research priorities and initiating participatory (action) research (see **participatory research methods**) that involves a combination of methods designed to facilitate collective knowledge production that involves the affected people as co-researchers at every stage: identifying issues, gathering data, analysis of data, and use of research that result in some distinct benefit for communities or people involved. (4) They induce direct learning and updating of relevant knowledge, especially for senior professionals and officials, NGO workers, government and university staff. (5) They aid policy review and reform by changing and adapting policies through relatively timely, accurate and relevant insights.

The principles and methodologies of participatory development might be understood theoretically, but the lack of practical experience in actually promoting and implementing participatory development work remains a serious obstacle to its success. Hence, participatory development advocates attempt to continually improve on their practice, for example by increasingly recognizing the importance of gender, ethnicity (see **ethnicity/identity**) and other social axes of difference in their work. Women and ethnic minorities are often excluded from decision-making on projects, resulting in benefits to only the educated **elites**. They have addressed how gendered and racialized forms of representation affect participatory development – whose interests are being represented in any community and why this is occurring, based on the distinct experiences of community members based on class, race (see **race and racism**), household structure and other differences. Participatory development practitioners thus emphasize the importance of listening to the multiplicity of voices and heterogeneity of interests as they develop an inclusive approach to community development and deconstruct the notion of "community," suggesting its fluid and dynamic constitution and identities that are locally grounded and culturally and socially constructed.

As a more general approach, participatory development principles have influenced the growth of participatory research, participatory action research, participatory **governance**, participatory monitoring and evaluation, participatory rural appraisal (PRA), among other families of methods and tools associated with development work (see below; and **participatory research methods**).

Participatory governance

Participatory development approaches are considered critical to governance issues. Participatory governance refers to the involvement of different stakeholders, especially poor people and other marginal social groups, in decision-making processes. It is based on the "good governance" tenets of **accountability**, **transparency**, rule of **law**, and good and complete information, to guide decision-making outcomes. Participatory governance thus requires addressing not only the informational needs of the poor and other marginal social groups, but also their access to resources, decision-making powers, and political influence. As an approach to bringing about participatory development, participatory governance is mainly concerned about the empowerment of communities and **grassroots organizations** to enlarge their share of political and social power so that they could better control their lives and ensure that their needs are met, their rights respected and their priorities addressed. The use of participatory approaches in governance is critical in the success of development projects and programs, especially those related to basic human needs (see **basic needs**) and poverty reduction.

Participatory monitoring and evaluation

Participatory monitoring and evaluation (PME) is a collaborative problem-solving process that involves the collective generation and use of knowledge by stakeholders in order to assess a project, program or policy and then undertake any corrective action required through collective decision-making. The stakeholders involved in doing PME at various levels include the actual beneficiaries or end users, both women and men, of project resources and services at the community level; intermediary organizations such as NGOs, private sector agencies involved in the project, government staff, and donor agencies. Conventional monitoring is often conducted by outsiders with the assistance of local stakeholders as an ongoing activity throughout the project's lifespan while evaluation is formally done at certain times such as mid-term or near completion stage. In contrast, PME does not make a clear distinction between monitoring and evaluation, as participatory feedback mechanisms and assessment strategies are built into the project's regular activities, instead of being one-time events developed by outside experts. Traditional monitoring and evaluation is often a predetermined, linear process that tends to be extractive and responsive to management or financial accountability requirements, rather than open to the changing needs and capacities of project participants. It also tends to rely on the services of outside monitors or evaluators who are seen as more able to provide "objective" and "neutral" assessments by virtue of their distance and independence from the project. In contrast, PME utilizes a more open-ended, flexible, continuous, and iterative approach. For example, an initial self-evaluation by project stakeholders may generate preliminary findings that could be the bases of a follow-up assessment, the results of which could in turn be used to further refine the issues and generate new questions for another round of monitoring. As the process occurs, the project participants may be developing new activities, encountering new problems, or experiencing challenges posed by external forces (e.g. **natural disasters**, a slump in market prices of commodities, etc.) that may affect their perceptions of project operations. These conditions would require then new monitoring and assessment guides, especially information gathering and analysis, and subsequent action plans adapted to the changing conditions of the project and the communities involved. Simply asking community members or project beneficiaries to respond to questionnaires or conduct surveys does not qualify as PME. Rather they actively engage in designing monitoring and evaluation processes, from how to generate useful information to how to use that information for improving project results, without the help of outside experts. Outside experts or consultants may be called upon in PME only to facilitate or support the learning of stakeholders at all levels, based on their active participation in collecting and analyzing the information about their project activities, outcomes and impacts.

The use of PME approaches is often associated with **capacity building** goals. Although they take on various forms, they can involve different levels of participation, and use a variety of tools adapted from participatory rural appraisal, PME principles remain the same. They are action-oriented and emphasize the building of capacities and commitment of various stakeholders to reflect, analyze, give feedback, and take responsibility for any changes in project, program, or policy direction they recommended. Mainstream donor agencies, including the World Bank, now use PME alongside conventional monitoring and evaluation to compare and cross-check findings while aiming to promote local commitment to action.

Participatory impact assessments

Participatory impact assessments (PIAs) integrate various forms of impact assessments (e.g. environmental, economic, social, cultural) based on a consultative and qualitative method of gathering information to gain insights into the perceptions of local people regarding the outcomes and impacts of a particular development project, program or policy. These assessments are called by other names such as beneficiary assessment (BA) or participatory policy impact assessments (PPIA). Participatory forms of impact assessment are similar to PME in that both aim to make the voices and perspectives of beneficiaries and other local stakeholders heard by those managing the project, funding the program, or formulating the policies. Likewise, they also share the use of major qualitative research techniques such as participant observation, focus group discussions, semi-structured conversational interviewing, and other tools drawn from PRA.

Issues and problems in participatory development

Critics have raised several questions and issues, especially on the use of PRA, to challenge the highly optimistic claims of participatory development practitioners. One issue is on the implications of participatory development approaches on gender relations and gendered forms of participation (Guijt and Kaul, 1998; Nelson and Wright, 1995). This issue deals with the simple question of who does and who does not participate in PRA training, to the complex issue of accessibility of various kinds of knowledge, and selectivity in the type, sources, and validity of information generated by participatory development approaches. Another issue is around relations of power, social domination, accessibility, and authoritative voice in knowledge production (Cooke and Kothari, 2001). This deals with the conflation of public and private interests, the culturally specific notions of formality and informality, and the issue of what Michel Foucault called the "knowledge-power nexus" in any form of disciplinal social control. In this line of analysis, influenced by post-structuralism, the push for participation and use of participatory development approaches by international funding agencies and intermediary NGOs becomes a new form of "tyranny" or "social control" that only results in the greater manageability of the poor and other supposed beneficiaries of development initiatives (see also **politics**).

The advocacy of participatory development approaches in projects funded by international agencies has been further criticized for its depoliticization of the development agenda (see **anti-politics**), and reproduction of unequal North-South relations through ritualistic **planning** processes and co-optation of initiatives in developing societies. These criticisms are often raised in the context of how little things seem to change when so-called new orientations and principles, such as those associated with participatory development, are introduced within and by hierarchical bureaucracies and powerful **institutions** that devise behavioral rules of conduct based on technical knowledge, rational planning, routine, standardization, regularity, and predictability. As a result, the gains of participatory development approaches remain minimal. For example, the information generated from PME or PIA exercises, for example might be too descriptive, not backed by the quantitative and statistical information that often appeals more to policy-makers, and as a result, fail to serve the purpose of project or policy reform. Critics of participatory development thus seem to give more weight and importance to the influence of participatory development work within international development agencies that are more focused on market-oriented mechanisms in promoting development. While the language of participatory development has been integrated in the work of mainstream donor agencies, there is still poor acceptance or marginal treatment and ownership of participatory development principles by key decision-makers within these agencies.

See also: community; equitable development; governance; grassroots development; participatory budgeting; participatory poverty assessment (PPA); participatory research methods; people-centered development; power and discourse; social integration; social learning

Further reading

Bhatnagar, B. and Williams, A. (eds) (1992) *Participatory Development and the World Bank: Potential Directions for Change*, Washington DC: World Bank.

Cernea, M. (1992) *The Building Blocks of Participation: Testing Bottom-up Planning*, Washington DC: World Bank.

Cooke, B. and Kothari, U. (eds) (2001) *Participation: The New Tyranny?*, London: Zed.

Guijt, I. and Shah, M. (1998) *The Myth of Community: Gender Issues in Participatory Development*, London: Intermediate Technology Publications.

Institute of Development Studies Participation Research Group website: http://www.ids.ac.uk/ids/particip/index.html

Nelson, N. and Wright, S. (1995) *Power and Participatory Development: Theory and Practice*, London: Intermediate Technology Publications.

Rietbergen-McCraken, J. and Narayan, D. (1998) *Participation and Social Assessment Tools and Techniques*, Washington DC: World Bank.

World Bank (1996) *World Bank Participation Sourcebook*, Washington DC: World Bank.

LEONORA C. ANGELES

participatory poverty assessment (PPA)

Participatory poverty assessment (PPA) emerged in the 1990s within the **World Bank** and other agencies such as the **United Nations Development**

Programme (UNDP) and the United Nations Children's Fund (UNICEF) to refer to the use of field-based participatory research exercises for country-based analyses of the **poverty** situation and evaluation of poverty reduction strategies (see **participatory development; participatory research methods**). Earlier poverty assessments heavily relied on quantitative analyses of household survey data to produce national poverty profiles, as well as consumption- or income-based poverty-level lines. In turn, these analyses became the bases of national anti-poverty policies and the poverty reduction agenda of donor agencies in the late 1980s and the 1990s.

The introduction of PPA was the result of internal debates within the World Bank and other donor agencies that advocated the use of qualitative participatory research methods to complement the more conventional poverty research methods advocated by mainstream economists. PPAs emphasize the need for interdisciplinary field research methods that would capture the multidimensional and dynamic nature of poverty from the perspective of poor people themselves. This new emphasis has led to the publication of the World Bank's *Voices of the Poor* (e.g. Narayan, 2000) series that focused on the substantive findings of first-generation PPAs conducted in many developing countries. Hence, PPAs have not only broadened the conceptual agenda of poverty assessments and poverty reduction strategies, but also emphasized the right of the poor to participate in defining, analyzing and challenging the processes of poverty that directly affect them. This agenda led some writers to go beyond analyzing the "voices of the poor" and relate PPAs to participatory **governance**, or the participation of the poor in decision-making and policy setting. Hence, the first-generation PPAs were conducted within a shorter period, relying on Rapid Rural Appraisal and a variety of Participatory Rural Appraisal tools (see **participatory research methods**). However, there was not much attempt in earlier PPAs to design the research processes in a way that would enable the perspectives of the poor to influence policy-makers' attitudes and practices. In contrast, second-generation PPAs had lengthier research and consultation processes and were carefully designed to maximize policy influence by paying more attention to institutional and policy linkages. In some countries,

second-generation PPAs built on earlier arguments, and at the same time opened up spaces for the representation of poor people's perspectives in policy-setting circles.

PPAs aim in general to enrich the poverty profile by describing the experiences of poverty that statistical surveys could not capture; to understand the poor's perceptions of their access to and quality of social services; and to contribute to policy interventions by describing the impact of restrictive regulations and market constraints on the poor. Other aims are to support appropriate public policy on "social safety nets" (see **safety nets against poverty**) for vulnerable groups; and to illustrate the agency and capacity of the poor to act independently through their informal and formal **community**-based organizations.

The use of PPAs, however, has raised a number of conceptual and methodological concerns, ranging from the relationship between quantitative and qualitative information, and their respective roles in policy-setting and **governance** of poverty reduction programs. More pointed criticisms of PPAs mirror more general critiques of **participatory development** approaches when adopted by donor agencies that legitimize the technical shift to participation without challenging dominant power relations and institutional embedding of poverty.

See also: measuring development; participatory development; participatory research methods; poverty; poverty measurement

Further reading

Brock, K. and McGee, R. (2002) *Knowing Poverty: Critical Reflections on Participatory Research and Policy*, London/Sterling VA: Earthscan Publications.

Narayan, D. (ed.) (2000) *Can Anyone Hear Us?: Voices of the Poor*, New York: Oxford University Press and the World Bank.

Narayan, D. and Chambers, R. (eds) (2000) *Crying Out for Change: Voices of the Poor*, New York: Oxford University Press and the World Bank.

LEONORA C. ANGELES

participatory research methods

Participatory research methods, including participatory rural appraisal (PRA) have emerged out of a general shift in problem-solving research generally associated with development aid (see **participatory development**). Although its roots can be traced back to Paolo Freire and his 1960s activist work with the underprivileged (see **pedagogy of the oppressed**), its establishment as a body of tools and techniques dates to the late 1980s, when extractive learning and problem-solving processes in development work shifted to shared learning and problem solving.

Development **aid** and the research techniques it required emerged at the close of World War II. The dominant development paradigm in the 1950s, and 1960s was very much an evolutionary one, whereby backward societies could be assisted in modernizing themselves and subsistence economics could be converted into modern market economics. In the 1970s, as significant "development" failed for large numbers of people, social scientists began to be called in to conduct autopsies and to evaluate failed efforts. Gradually, the human factor in development emerged as important. The question, however, was how to fit long-term study of people and society into the quick-answer problem-solving requirements of development agencies and planners.

By the mid-1980s, Rapid Rural Appraisal (RRA) and Rapid Ethnographic Appraisal (REA) emerged as a set of tools to extract local people's knowledge and meet the need for quick, rapid responses to development concerns. Based on the principle of triangulation – the use of multiple researchers from various disciplines – a number of researchers from different disciplines formed a team to extract as much relevant information in as short a time as possible. This approach borrowed heavily from applied anthropology, agro-ecosystems and farming systems analysis, and geography, among other fields, and brought together a set of tools and techniques to visualize findings. The important core tools for this approach included: semi-structured interviewing, focus group discussions, mapping and modeling, matrix and preference ranking, time lines and trend analyses, as well as seasonal and historical diagramming.

By the early 1990s, dissatisfaction, particularly among **non-governmental organizations (NGOs)** working in communities (see **community**) targeted for development assistance, led to the transformation of rapid research approaches into more collaborative and participatory ones. RRA was replaced with PRA (Participatory Rural Appraisal) among NGOs and inter-governmental organizations (IGOs). Followers of Robert Chambers at the Institute of Development Studies (IDS), Sussex, among others, went a step further and encouraged the espousal of PLA – Participatory Learning and Action – for meaningful development. Unlike RRA, the main innovation of PRA and PLA (as well as PUA – Participatory Urban Appraisal – and VIPP – Visualization in Participatory Programs) was in the change of behavior and attitude of the researcher. Triangulation, first espoused in RRA, took on a new meaning. Instead of referring to multidisciplinary research teams, it came to mean a three-pronged approach combining a transformation in attitudes and behavior, a realigning of ways of communicating, and an emphasis on tools and techniques uniquely developed in each research context. With PRA/PLA the learning was no longer elicitive and extractive, but rather facilitating and shared. The objective of the research was no longer simply learning by the outside researcher in order to contribute to development plans, but rather for empowering local people so that the long-term outcome of development could be maintained by local action.

Participatory research methods address human development as problem-solving under pressure, as adaptive change. Hence, their methodological pluralism resonates well with current conditions of rapid adaptive change. Furthermore, their emphasis on facilitation – which draws out and analyzes local peoples' priorities and makes space for local diversity – is particularly well-suited to current world conditions. Where changes in local and global conditions (ecological, social and political) appear to be accelerating and increasingly unpredictable, timely feedback, prompt learning and rapid adaptive responses can be provided by participatory research methods such as PRA and PLA.

The 1990s were perhaps the heyday of the indiscriminate "participatory" research methods. As we enter the twenty-first century, many feel that the glow has begun to fade, and disillusionment has been expressed with the way in which the approach has been misused. The shortcomings and often the misappropriation of the terminology, but not the skills and tools, have begun to be questioned. The varying meanings of participation have also come under the spotlight. For example, Chambers, and the IDS school regard the key principles of PRA as **empowerment**, respect, localization, enjoyment and inclusiveness. For the **World Bank**, however, the key principles are participation, flexible approaches, teamwork, optimal ignorance and systematicization.

There are many myths about participatory research methods. They are sometimes regarded as rapid, easy, empowering, and facilitative. However, more often than not participation is adopted in word but not in practice. As a set of tools, participatory research methods require careful, focused use-planning and detailed field guides. As an approach, it is only as good as those who practice it – both the researchers/facilitators and local experts. Participation needs to be part of the entire process in order to inform the total project with which it is associated. Otherwise, it tends to raises false expectations since the local community comes to feel that its opinions and knowledge might have some weight at higher levels of authority. Finally, participatory research methods assume the existence of a coherent **community**, and hence often exclude culturally oppressed and marginalized groups.

See also: capacity building; community-based natural resource management (CBNRM); empowerment; indigenous knowledge; local knowledge; participatory development; participatory poverty assessment (PPA); social learning

Further reading

Chambers, R. (1983) *Rural Development: Putting the Last First*, London: Longman.
Chambers, R. (1992) "Rural Appraisal: Rapid, Relaxed and Participatory," *IDS Discussion Paper*, no. 311, Falmer: Institute of Development Studies.
Mikkelsen, B. (1995) "Participatory Approaches – Ranking and Scoring and Making Maps and Diagrams," pp. 117–44 in Mikkelsen, B. (ed.) *Methods for Development Work and Research: A Guide for Practitioners*, London: Sage.
Mosse, D. (1994) "Authority, Gender and Knowledge: Theoretical Reflections on the Practice of Participatory Rural Appraisal," *Development and Change* 25:3 497–525.
Pretty, J., Guijt, R., Thompson, J. and Scoones, I. (1995) *Participatory Learning and Action: A Trainer's Guide*, London: IIED.
Pottier, J. (1993) "The Role of Ethnography in Project Appraisal," pp. 13–33 in Pottier, J. (ed.) *Practicing Development: Social Science Perspectives*, London: Routledge.
Scheyvens, R. and Storey, D. (eds) (2003) *Development Fieldwork: A Rough Guide*, Thousand Oaks CA: Sage.

DAWN CHATTY

PARTICIPATORY RURAL APPRAISAL (PRA) *see* participatory development; participatory research methods

partnerships

The term "partnerships" is increasingly used in international development to refer to cooperation and collaboration between states (see **state and state reform**), **international organizations and associations**, **non-governmental organizations (NGOs)**, and businesses in the achievement of development objectives. The term has become popular following the issuing of the **Global Compact** by **United Nations** Secretary General, Kofi Annan, in 1999, in which he outlined how business may contribute to development objectives: "Thriving markets and **human security** go hand in hand; without one, we will not have the other." So-called "type-two partnerships" were also urged at the **World Summit on Sustainable Development (Johannesburg, 2002)**, as an addition to orthodox international partnerships between states. Partnerships are also mentioned in the **Millennium Development Goals**

(MDGs) as another means of achieving development objectives. Partnerships, in these general senses, are broader and more consultative than **public-private partnerships**, which generally focus upon providing public services by private companies. Partnerships in a broader sense imply consultation and collaboration between different actors for both formulating and implementing new products or services. Partnerships may be either "bi-sector" or "tri-sector" according to whether they include two or three representatives of state, market or society. They may be inspired positively by companies to create **corporate social responsibility (CSR)**, or as imaginative means of integrating commercial objectives with local requirements. They may also be inspired negatively by the desire avoid criticism, or be coerced by legislation. They may also result from the particular actions of specific business or **community** leaders.

Some examples of partnerships include the collaboration of the **United Nations Development Programme (UNDP)** with Amnesty International, the oil-company Statoil, and the Venezuelan government to provide training for judges and federal prosecutors on issues relating to international **human rights** law. In Malaysia, Coca Cola, UNDP, the Ministry of Education and local community groups train students and teachers in rural communities in information and communications technology.

For many observers, partnerships are an important and overdue contribution to harnessing private sector investment, which now overshadows state capacity in many locations. For some critics, however, partnerships represent threats to public policy because they offer chances for companies to avoid regulation, or for them to redefine the objectives of public policy for their own objectives. United Nations Environment Programme Executive Director Klaus Töpfer reputedly claimed in 2002 that type-two partnerships imply the "privatization of **sustainable development**" (see **privatization and liberalization**). Consequently, much current debate about partnerships seeks to clarify how far their instrumental impacts in advancing development objectives may be offset by their discursive effects on changing the objectives of development and the means of public debate.

See also: corporate social responsibility (CSR); Global Compact; Millennium Development Goals (MDGs); public-private partnerships; World Summit on Sustainable Development (Johannesburg, 2002)

Further reading

Nelson, J. (2002) *Building Partnerships*, New York: United Nations.
United Nations website for partnerships: http://www.undp.org/business/

TIM FORSYTH

pastoralism

Pastoralism is the breeding and rearing of certain domesticated herbivorous animals and ruminants as a primary means to provide **food**, clothing and shelter. Pastoral production involves an interaction between land, water and mineral resources, **livestock** and labor. Livestock as a capital good serves as a technology to transform otherwise unpalatable cellulose into consumable products. Pastoralism embraces both commercial livestock rearing (e.g. commercial stockrearing on the Argentinian pampas) and "traditional" pastoral nomadism which combines livestock husbandry and spatial mobility for the largely subsistence production of animal products (for example the Fulbe in West Africa or Andean montane pastoral systems). The variety of animals raised by pastoral nomads is quite small (there are six widely-distributed species: sheep, goats, camels, cattle, horses, donkeys) and is associated with seven distinctive zones (high-latitude sub-Arctic, Eurasian steppe, montane Southwest Asia, Saharan and Arabian deserts, Sub-Saharan savannas, the Andes, and Asian high-altitude plateaux). Pastoral nomadism is internally differentiated with respect to its dependence on agricultural production, forms of pasture ecology, and the animals herded. A common pastoral taxonomy distinguishes between flat/mountainous land, large/small animals and the relationship to **agriculture** (i.e. pure pastoralists versus semipastoralists). Like peasants, pastoralists exhibit significant differences in terms of household structure, **property rights**, **gender division of labor**, patterns of consumption and exchange and labor processes

(Galanty and Johnson, 1990). Pastoralism is, however, a distinctive form of ecological and cultural adaptation to specific sorts of ecosystems in which humans and animals live in a symbiotic **community** typified by a fierce independence and self-determination. Virtually all forms of pastoralism depend in some way on agricultural communities and trade with them in longstanding, culturally sanctioned sorts of ways (for example Fulani and Hausa dry-season symbiosis in northern Nigeria). Growing **commercialization**, where so-called products are exchanged for grains and manufactured goods, has the result that pastoral systems are increasingly vulnerable on the one side and subject to internal social differentiation in the other. In West Africa the proliferation of conflicts between farmers and pastoralists, and the growth of "agro-pastoralism" combining both forms of livelihood (see **livelihoods**), are manifestations of these commercial pressures. Some forms of pastoralism have been deliberately modernized – for example, group ranches among the Masaai in Kenya – but the pastoral livelihood system has proven to be robust and especially well-adapted to conditions in which rainfed or permanent agriculture are risky. New ecological research has shown how pastoralists are particularly sensitive to the non-equilibrium character of rangelands (see **environment**).

See also: agriculture; dryland agriculture; environment; livestock; Sahel

Further reading

Benke, R. Kerven, C. and Scoones, I. (eds) (1993) *Range Ecology at Disequilibrium*, London: ODI.

Galanty, J. and Johnson, D. (1990) *The World of Pastoralism: Herding Systems in Comparative Perspective*, New York: Guilford.

Sutter, J. (1982) "Commercial Strategies, Drought and Monetary Pressure," *Nomadic Peoples* 11: 26–61.

MICHAEL WATTS

PATENTS see intellectual property rights (IPRs); trade-related aspects of intellectual property rights (TRIPS)

PATRIARCHY see gender; male bias

peacekeeping

Peacekeeping is the **conflict management** technique where a neutral military force is deployed between antagonists engaged in **violence** or **war** to observe ceasefire arrangements and/or to establish demilitarized buffer zones as a necessary precondition to a negotiated peace settlement. In addition, peacekeeping operations are often involved in important post-conflict tasks such as landmine clearance (see **landmines**), refugee repatriation (see **refugees**), infrastructure (re)construction, and maintaining law and order (see **post-conflict rehabilitation; post-conflict violence**). Consequently, contemporary peacekeeping operations are increasingly integrated into holistic post-conflict development programs conducted by a combination of intergovernmental security apparatuses, **non-governmental organizations (NGOs)**, and international **aid** agencies, that aim to implement good **governance**, foster **civil society**, encourage **economic development**, **democracy**, **human rights**, the rule of **law**, and rehabilitation and reconstruction. Peacekeeping is therefore becoming an important component of a multi-dimensional development approach to states (or often so-called **weak states**) recovering from war and dislocation.

Peacekeeping developed after World War II to provide the **United Nations** with a means between diplomatic "peace-making" and military "peace-enforcement" to discharge its main Charter responsibility of maintaining international peace and security. Since the UN's first peacekeeping operation in 1948, therefore, peacekeeping has been dominated by, but not limited to, the UN, as a number of other regional organizations have also utilized peacekeeping forces (e.g. **the Economic Community of West African States (ECOWAS)** in Liberia and the **European Union** in Macedonia).

Under UN auspices, peacekeeping operations are authorized by a Security Council (SC) resolution adopted under Chapter VI of the Charter, meaning it is not legally binding on the conflicting parties, whose permission for the deployment must consequently be obtained prior to, and maintained throughout, the operation. The Secretary General bears overall responsibility for UN peacekeeping operations, while the Department of Peacekeeping

Operations (DPKO) is the operational manager. Peacekeeping forces, equipment, and finances are provided on a voluntary basis by UN member states, and peacekeepers are required to act impartially toward all antagonists and thus are only lightly armed for self-defense purposes. Currently, the DPKO's mission statement codifies the general character of peacekeeping as a pre-emptive deployment to prevent the (re)commencement of violence or cross-border spread of conflict; to maintain ceasefires as a precondition to the peaceful settlement of disputes; to assist in implementing such an agreement; and to lead conflicting state(s) in a transition to democratic governance and economic development.

Despite this apparently clear contemporary role, the history of UN peacekeeping is rather mixed. The first problem arose from the very context in which peacekeeping emerged. The veto power of the five permanent SC members meant that the USA and the Soviet Union played out their **Cold War** rivalry by vetoing any proposed UN peacekeeping operation incompatible with their own interests. For example, the Soviet Union vetoed any discussion of its 1956 invasion of Hungary, as did the USA on Vietnam throughout the 1960s. The cumulative effect of superpower veto was that from the first operation until 1989, only fifteen "first generation" peacekeeping operations were undertaken, with never more than 25,000 peacekeepers deployed worldwide. A second problem also emerged during, but has survived, the Cold War: peacekeeping may become a permanent fixture rather than a temporary intervention measure. For example, five of the UN's thirteen current operations are more than twenty-five years old.

These problems seemed insignificant, however, as post-Cold War optimism carried over into expanded possibilities for UN peacekeeping now freed of superpower veto. The UN peacekeeping **community**, exemplified in Secretary General Boutros Boutros-Ghali's 1992 *An Agenda for Peace*, sensed a new era in its operations. "Second generation" peacekeeping began with an immediate, exponential increase in the number of UN operations: in the five years from 1989 to 1994 the UN deployed eighteen new missions, a rate more than twelve times that during the Cold War.

More significant was the simultaneous expansion of traditional "level one" peacekeeping roles into what Boutros-Ghali called "peace-building." These additional "level two" tasks included the preventive deployment of peacekeepers to emerging crises, measures to stabilize and resolve internal conflicts, the provision of assistance to interim civil authorities, the protection of humanitarian operations (see **complex emergencies; conflict management; humanitarianism**), and the guarantee or denial of movement to various parties within the conflict zone. The UN's most successful example of such second-generation operations was the 1992–3 Transitional Authority in Cambodia, which undertook the administration of state functions (see **state and state reform**), the fostering of **civil society**, clearing of **landmines** and the disarming of antagonists, and eventually the supervision of elections.

This optimism soon evaporated, however, as **weak states** wracked by civil war presented multifaceted challenges which dwarfed the Cold War veto and permanence problems. First, the apparent exponential rise in intra-state ethnic violence meant the number of potential operations for an increasingly over-stretched and under-resourced UN threatened to spiral out of control. As a disastrous consequence, new operations were decided not on the necessity demanded by the conflict but by the geopolitical interests of the major powers; hence the SC's early-1990s procrastination over intervention in the disintegrating Yugoslavia, and its inability to respond to the emerging crisis in Rwanda that became **genocide** in 1994. Second, the collapse of state legitimacy meant that ethnic militias increasingly did not recognize the peacekeeping mission's "authority." Consequently, the number of UN peacekeepers killed increased dramatically: in the three years from 1993 to 1995 there were 542 peacekeeper fatalities compared with 925 for the preceding forty-five years. Third, peacekeepers were still constrained by their "self-defense only" rule of engagement that prevented, in perhaps the lowest point of peacekeeping, the defense of the UN-declared "safe havens" in Bosnia-Herzegovina in 1995 (see **ethnic cleansing**).

In combination, these problems resulted in the ultimate irony of UN peacekeeping in the troubled mid-1990s: often, peacekeepers were deployed in conflict zones where there was simply no peace to keep. Today, "third generation" peacekeeping has survived these enormously difficult trials, with the UN currently maintaining thirteen operations with just over 43,000 personnel worldwide, to provide an important component of development programs in post-conflict societies.

See also: complex emergencies; Geneva Conventions; genocide; law of armed conflict (LAC); post-conflict rehabilitation; post-conflict violence; United Nations; war

Further reading

Boutros-Ghali, B. (1992) *An Agenda for Peace*, New York: United Nations.

Chopra, J. (1999) *Peace-maintenance: The Evolution of International Political Authority*, London and New York: Routledge.

United Nations Department of Peacekeeping Operations: http://www.un.org/Depts/dpko/dpko/home.shtml

PETER MAYELL

Pearson Commission

The Pearson Commission in 1968 was one of the most important meetings for establishing international guidelines for **aid**. The Commission was conducted by former Canadian prime minister and Nobel Peace Prize winner, Lester B. Pearson, at the invitation of the new **World Bank** President, Robert McNamara, who had expressed concern at the apparent unwillingness of **bilateral aid agencies** to offer aid for fear of it being wasted on **corruption**. The Commission's aim was to review the previous twenty years of development assistance, and its official report, *Partners in Development* (1969) optimistically pointed to the apparent success of aid in inducing development, and argued that aid should be given for two reasons: moral duty to help people worse off; and enlightened self-interest. The Commission set specific aid targets that are still discussed today: total aid should amount to 1 percent of **gross national product (GNP)**, and official aid (or official development

assistance), 0.70 percent of GNP by 1975. These targets have not been met on any long-term basis, despite good performance from some countries such as Denmark, Norway and Sweden.

See also: aid; aid effectiveness and aid evaluation; bilateral aid agencies

TIM FORSYTH

peasant movements

Peasant movements are collective actions undertaken by groups of rural producers who have, or who are seeking, direct access to land (see also **peasantry; land reform; rural development**). Peasant movements are typically waged against landlords or the state (see **state and state reform**), but can also be directed against agricultural laborers. These movements are crucially concerned with the distribution of power and the means of production, and with prices and the inter-sectoral (rural-urban) **terms of trade**. More recently they have engaged the question of **globalization**, particularly around the ownership and diffusion of genetically modified crops (see **biotechnology and resistance; genetically modified organisms (GMOs)**).

The idea that peasants might take part in organized politics is comparatively new. Karl Marx was not alone in the nineteenth century in dismissing the "idiocy of rural life." Peasants, he said, were like potatoes in a sack, and no more capable of organization. This view changed in the twentieth century. Gandhi widened the anti-colonial struggle in India by campaigning successfully around issues that mattered to peasants (rents, the tax on salt, even **land reform**), and in the 1930s, the Communist Party in China was reinvented in the countryside after it was crushed in Shanghai. Ironically, while the peasantry in China was dismantled in the 1960s in favor of collective farms (see **collectivization**) and production brigades, Chairman Mao was described by Eric Wolf in the early 1970s as one of the great practitioners of "peasant war" (Wolf, 1971). During the Vietnam War, in particular, the political capacity of the peasantry was greatly celebrated.

This romanticism was tempered later in the decade. Jeffrey Paige suggested that agricultural revolts would most likely occur in deltaic areas where the distribution of land was highly uneven, and/or in regions where class and ethnic divisions strongly overlapped (Paige, 1978). In areas like the Tanjore delta in southern India, land-strapped peasants might join forces with agricultural laborers against local landlords. In other regions, the politics of the peasantry could be more conservative. There were rich, middle-income and poor peasants, as Mao had suggested. Poorer peasant households often committed members to laboring work, and in many cases were net **food** grain purchasers. Some rich peasant households leased out land to other families, and stood to gain from higher grain prices. Unity was not always easy to come by. In addition, as James Scott pointed out in the 1980s, the fact that peasantries generally were not rebellious was unsurprising. Faced with the greater force of the state, they had to resort to the "**weapons of the weak**," a phrase first used by Gandhi. Instead of peasant movements, Scott argued, we should expect to see smaller-scale acts of peasant resistance to authority, including foot-dragging, dissimulation and joke-telling (Scott, 1985).

While this is often the case, we should not discount the very significant peasant movements that emerged in the 1980s and 1990s. In Brazil, the control and distribution of land was challenged by the Movimento dos Trabalhadores Rurais Sem Tera (MST), or the landless peasants' movement. In India, meanwhile, agrarian politics shifted to questions of **urban bias** and the terms of trade. The "new agrarian politics" charged that urban India's merchants and consumers "drank the blood" of the peasantry, and enforced price twists that transferred resources to the cities. The fact that some small and marginal peasant households joined in campaigns for higher food prices forced scholars to re-evaluate rational choice models of political behavior. The language and iconography of peasant movements became a prominent area of academic enquiry. Also forcing its way on to the agenda was the question of the transnationalization of peasant movements. Jose Bove, the leader of the Confédération Paysanne in France, has been active not only in his campaigns against GM crops, Monsanto, and the **industrialization** of food

production, but also in building links to the MST and other peasant movements. These links are forged in a rolling caravan of public protests, as well as in anti-globalization demonstrations and at the **World Social Forum (WSF)** in Porto Allegre, Brazil.

See also: collectivization; globalization; land reform; peasantry; political ecology; rural development; terms of trade; weapons of the weak

Further reading

Paige, J. (1978) *Agrarian Revolution*, New York: Free Press.

Pinstrup-Andersen, P. and Schioler, E. (2000) *Seeds of Contention: World Hunger and the Global Controversy over GM Crops*, Baltimore: Johns Hopkins University Press.

Scott, J. (1985) *Weapons of the Weak: Everyday Forms of Peasant Resistance*, New Haven: Yale University Press.

Varshney, A. (1995) *Democracy, Development and the Countryside: Urban-rural Struggle in India*, Cambridge: Cambridge University Press.

Wolf, E. (1971) *Peasant Wars of the Twentieth Century*, London: Faber and Faber.

STUART CORBRIDGE

peasantry

The term "peasantry" came into use in fifteenth-century English to refer to those working on the land and living in the countryside (see **rural development**). Over time, it has generated various connotations from the authentic (see **postmodernism and postdevelopment**), to the revolutionary (see **Marxism**), to the backward (under modernization (see **modernization theory**) and, arguably, **neo-liberalism**). The term has been used or misused in various contexts, and leading to a lack of clarity about the important changes occurring to peasant people, and how they are represented.

Peasants are generally claimed to have three characteristics: access to land as a means of production; a high use of family labor; and significant or complete subsistence and self-sufficiency. Added to this, the peasantry is generally subordinate to external economic and political forces that extract surplus value (see **marginalization**). In terms of the labor process, peasants are often placed on the continuum in between proletarianization and **petty commodity production**, though analysts have questioned whether this transition is either inevitable or desirable (see **Marxism; rural development**).

In terms of development trajectories and discourses, the peasantry has been seen in various forms. Marxist theory saw the rise of modernization as a threat to peasant production (see Kautsky, 1902). **Modernization theory** characterized the peasantry as a transitional stage between tribalism and modern industrial and consumer society (see **stages of economic growth**). Structuralist, and linked Keynesian analysis, saw the peasantry as an area ripe for intervention in the struggle to achieve greater equity (albeit under the objective of achieving efficiency in the long run). Postmodernists have celebrated the peasant identity, highlighting the role of "everyday resistance" (see also **weapons of the weak**) as well as the formation of peasant-driven **new social movements** which cut across traditional axes of identity (class in particular) (see **peasant movements**). Such views are controversial. Brass (2000) for example, is dismissive of the cultural turn in peasant studies which he deems inherently conservative, reactionary, and complicit with neo-liberalism. Thinkers of this nature argue that the postmodern perspective denies the prospect of material progress for the subordinated mass of peasants who, they argue it is wrongly assumed, are content with maintaining their existing social and economic position. Postmodernism rejects universal trajectories of peasant transformation, which is welcomed by most authors, yet **actor-oriented approaches to development** discount important structural determinants such as economic class and historical political economy. Others have argued that the rise of grassroots resistance (see **grassroots activism; grassroots organizations**), such as that exemplified in the Chiapas uprising in Mexico of the early 1990s (see **Zapatistas**), represents a genuine break with the class-based resistance of the past. Instead, such movements represent the rise of an identity-based politics of local resistance

to **globalization** that may empower and emancipate the masses. The resolution of this impasse between essentially incommensurate epistemologies is hard to envisage.

The peasantry remains comparatively important in terms of livelihood generation (see **livelihoods**) and identity formation worldwide. It is difficult to be precise, but estimates of peasant numbers range from 0.5 to 1.5 billion. There can be little doubt, however, that economic liberalization associated with neo-liberalism and globalization represent a crucial transformation of peasantries. Two opposing viewpoints on the fate of the peasantry are represented by the *campesinista* (Peasantist) and *descampesinista* (De-peasantist) schools of thought, which evolved in Latin America. The former school (Stavenhagen, 1978) has argued, albeit in slightly different ways, that the peasantry is not being eliminated through the diffusion of **capitalism**, and may in fact be strengthening. This view is often associated with the views of Russian agrarian writer Chayanov (1974). In outlining the views of this group, Kay (1997:13) argues, "they view the peasantry as mainly petty commodity producers who are able to compete successfully with capitalist farmers in the market rather than viewing them as sellers of labor power and being subjected to the processes of socio-economic differentiation." *Descampesinistas* are far less optimistic, arguing that in the face of expanding capitalism, peasants will be out-competed by larger-scale capitalists and **agribusiness** and will eventually become proletarianized. This school is often associated with the ideas of Lenin. Shades in between the two extremes can be conceptualized: an important observation given the dynamism of capitalism and the variability of peasant organization across time and space. It is crucially important to acknowledge the role of local context in how global changes from **neoliberalism** occur in specific localities, rather than to assume all peasantries change in similar ways.

In Latin America, de-peasantization and de-agrarianization are simultaneously occurring. Although neo-liberal reforms have restructured economies toward specialization in non-traditional agricultural exports, agriculture's general importance is declining. In the remainder of the rapidly neo-liberalizing sector a concentration process, both in terms of access to resources (including land)

and earnings is marginalizing peasant farmers. Consequently, the peasantry is being proletarianized to varying degrees. Disguised proletarianization, where peasants become dependent on agribusiness to the extent that they effectively become employees, is occurring. Full proletarianization, where peasants are squeezed out, made landless, and join the temporary rural labor force, (or urban arrivals) is also ongoing. Perhaps the most pervasive process, however, is semi-proletarianization, where peasant farmers are forced to combine their on-farm income with other forms of livelihood generation. The transition in Chile is instructive in terms of the above processes (see Murray, 2002).

Peasant studies, then, has been shaped by broader trajectories in development thinking, but the fate of the peasantry continues to loom large in any debate – the agrarian question, to use Katusky's terminology. It is undeniable that the academy has, recently at least, avoided theorizing peasant transitions, and this is partly because the cultural turn has generated greater interest with post-productive/post-industrial themes. In the wake of globalization, the peasantry is being politically abandoned – and its demise is being wrongly interpreted as an "inevitable" outcome of globalization and neo-liberalism rather than a result of state polices (see **state and state reform**). Some critics believe this lack of attention to peasantry shows a modernist/industrialist/**urban bias** in development studies, especially when masquerading as postmodern critique. A central debate will remain then, over whether the impacts of development in terms of peasant demise and victimization are best interrogated and understood though a class-based lens (and thus informed by Marxist theory) or through new cultural approaches which privilege identity formation/preservation as resistance to globalization.

See also: agrarian reform; collectivization; intermediate classes; Marxism; petty commodity production; rural development; rural "depressor"; rural poverty; postmodernism and postdevelopment

Further reading

Brass, T. (2000) *Peasants, Populism and Postmodernism: The Return of the Agrarian Myth*, London: Frank Cass.

Bryceson, D., Kay, C. and Mooij, J. (eds) (2000) *Disappearing Peasantries?*, London: Intermediate Technology.

Chayanov, A. V. (1974) *La Organizacion de la Unidad Economica Campesina*, Buenos Aires: Nueva Vision.

Kautsky, K. (1902) *The Social Revolution*, Chicago: James Kerr.

Kay, C. (1997) "Globalisation, Peasant and Reconversion," *Bulletin of Latin American Research* 16:1 11–24.

Murray, W. (2002) "From Dependency to Reform and back again: The Chilean Peasantry in the Twentieth Century," *Journal of Peasant Studies* 29:3–4 190–227.

Stavenhagen, R. (1978) "Capitalism and Peasantry in Mexico," *Latin American Perspectives* 5:3.

WARWICK E. MURRAY

pedagogy of the oppressed

Pedagogy of the Oppressed was a book by Paolo Freire first published in 1968. Freire influenced countless social movements (see **new social movements**) with his premise that all people, including the uneducated poor, can take rein of their roles in social change. Freire contrasts two archetypes of **education**: the "banking" and liberating methods. The predominant "banking" method encourages a "culture of silence," whereby a teacher is accorded authoritarian status and "deposits" knowledge into the students, who are presumed to hold empty minds. Instead, Freire advocates a system of tackling **illiteracy** by teaching adults critical thinking skills as well as basic reading and writing. In the process, the students exchange information with the teacher and experience *conscientização* (consciousness-raising), which allows them to critically analyze the causal forces in society. Based upon actual teaching experiences, the book also forecasts the rising importance of **participatory development** models.

See also: education; participatory development; new social movements

Further reading

Freire, P. (1993) *Pedagogy of the Oppressed* [*Pedagogia dos Oprimidos*], New York: Continuum Books.

CELINA SU

pensions

Pensions are regularized payments offered to people in old age or in retirement usually offered by the state (see **state and state reform**), or by private sector companies or trust funds. The past decade has seen an upsurge of interest in pension programs as a development issue. This began with a wave of neo-liberal inspired pension reforms (see **neo-liberalism**), starting in Chile and spreading to other countries in Latin America and beyond. These reforms have replaced state or public sector pension funds with more pluralistic arrangements, including a significant private sector component. The arguments in favor of these reforms are that they promote competition (and hence efficiency), stimulate **capital markets**, and relieve the public sector of an activity it was not well suited to perform. Some of these contentions have been challenged by recent studies.

Debates about pension reform overlook the fact that most of the world's older people do not receive a pension, be it publicly or privately managed, and are unlikely to do so in the foreseeable future. However, recent research has suggested that basic old age pensions may be an affordable option for low-income countries, and may be an important source of social protection – or safety nets – for households containing older people (see **safety nets against poverty**).

See also: ageing; population; safety nets against poverty; welfare state

Further reading

Charlton, R. and McKinnon, R. (2001) *Pensions in Development*, Aldershot: Ashgate.

PETER LLOYD-SHERLOCK

people-centered development

People-centered development is an approach to development policy that overtly emphasizes realizable benefits for people, rather than advances in national macro-economic objectives, or even the disrupting of local people through **displacement** and dispossession. Conventional, large-scale modernization (see **modernization theory**) strategies and projects common during the 1950s and 1960s have often alienated many local people, through direct displacement but also because people were dwarfed by the scale of activity and/or bypassed by the resultant infrastructure, products and services. The lack of **equitable development** was also a serious concern. During the 1970s, several approaches to alternative postdevelopment (see **postmodernism and postdevelopment**) arose, "as if people mattered," to quote the subtitle of Fritz Schumacher's (1973) famous book, *Small Is Beautiful*. Planners and geographers including Walter Stöhr, Fraser Taylor, John Friedmann and Clyde Weaver were instrumental in early formulations of "bottom-up," "grassroots" (see **grassroots development**) and "agropolitan" development, and in seeking to translate them into practical policies. People-centered development is now virtually synonymous with **participatory development** and is promoted through various **participatory research methods** that involve beneficiaries centrally at all stages. They should also have a meaningful degree of control over the process rather than being marginalized by "experts."

See also: equitable development; participatory development; postmodernism and postdevelopment

DAVID SIMON

petty commodity production

Petty or simple commodity production refers to a form of household production that is fully market determined. Among household enterprises – for example Nigerian peasant farmers, highly mechanized family farms in the US Midwest or a family owned and run furniture plant in London – the domestic group possesses the means of production, provides most if not all labor, and disposes of the collective product. These are in effect "family firms" of various sorts in which the domestic unit constitutes the relations of production; it is a unit of production and consumption in which the means of production and labor are directly applied by "the family." As Harriet Friedmann (1979) puts it, such systems of production are a contradictory unit of property and labor. However, in view of the variety of circumstances in which such entities arise – late nineteenth-century India, seventeenth-century Britain, contemporary USA – the internal composition and division of labor within the household and the character of its constituent members are conditioned by the household's relation to the larger economy. In the modern period in which these small-scale systems of production have existed, persisted and often flourished, they are involved with the market in some way. They are in other words commodity producers, and their conditions and relations of production are commodified. In some settings, use values predominate and the household was reproduced largely through horizontal and vertical ties for the renewal of labor and the means of production. The market was held at arm's length. But the proliferation of markets and the effects of various colonial and postcolonial interventions have mean that forms of household production are commodity producers in which the relations between household producers are "mediated through the place each household occupies in the total nexus of relations of commodity production and exchange" (Bernstein, 1979:427). In the contemporary epoch, most household forms of production are commodity producers: they produce in some way for the market and the organization of their production is in some way shaped by it. Petty commodity producers – as distinct from household producers who are "partial" commodity producers – are fully commoditized household producers; that is to say input and outputs are determined by market prices and labor, land and credit assume fully marketized forms. Petty commodity producers (Midwestern family corn farmers) are typically more specialized and are part of more complex national and international divisions of labor (see **international division of labor**) than small-scale

commodity producers such as Nigerian peasants or south Indian tailors.

See also: capitalism; commercialization; commodification; international division of labor; peasantry

Further reading

Bernstein, H. (1979) "African Peasantries," *Journal of Peasant Studies* 6:3 420–43.
Friedmann, H. (1980) "Household Production and the National Economy," *Journal of Peasant Studies* 7:2 159–83.

MICHAEL WATTS

pharmaceuticals

Pharmaceuticals are drugs used principally in the treatment and prevention of disease but also more generally in the improvement of the quality of life. Largely – but not entirely – due to the rapid advances in **biomedicine** and biotechnology (see **biotechnology and resistance**), pharmaceuticals have since the 1970s become increasingly important components of any initiative to promote public **health**. Crucial conveyors of social as well as personal **well-being**, pharmaceuticals yield salient international development concerns with respect to their production, distribution and consumption (see **health; primary health care**).

According to the **World Health Organization (WHO)**, drugs purchases in industrialized countries represent less than 20 percent of total health spending, but up to two thirds of public and private health spending in developing countries is destined to the acquisition of pharmaceuticals. Perhaps more significantly, households in low-income countries allocate the largest portion of their health expenditure to buying medicines. Yet, despite these figures, one third of the global **population** and 50 percent of poor Africans and Asians lack access to essential medicines (see also **HIV/AIDS (policy issues)**). Essential medicines are drugs, which, if used appropriately, provide reliable treatment for critical diseases that affect the majority of the world's population.

WHO's current list of essential medicines consists of 325 drugs, including for example many of those which are used in the treatment of meningitis, **tuberculosis**, **malaria**, diabetes, heart disease and HIV/AIDS (see **HIV/AIDS (definition and treatment)**). WHO and many other important international health organizations such as **Médecins Sans Frontières (MSF)** consider improved access to essential medicines one of their top priorities.

Although a variety of factors, such as inaccurate diagnosis, inadequate prescription and poor health administration, prevent people from having access to essential medicines, prohibitive pricing tends to be singled out in debates. This is most likely due to the marked clash between pharmaceutical industry interests in industrialized countries and the public health concerns of **non-governmental organizations (NGOs)** and developing country governments. Thus the original requirement of the WTO (see **World Trade Organization/General Agreement on Tariffs and Trade (WTO/ GATT)**) that patent protection (see also **intellectual property rights (IPRs)**) – as it is enjoyed by firms in the industrialized world – be extended to pharmaceutical production in the developing world has caused sustained international controversy. Such a patent system has been upheld, critics argue, to the exclusive benefit of giant pharmaceutical companies in the industrialized world and to the detriment of public health in the developing world.

The principal argument of the pharmaceutical companies for upholding the standard twenty-year patent rights is that prospective competition with generic producers dulls the incentive for innovation. Prices would be driven so low as to impede adequate returns on research and development investment – the latter often amounting, companies assert, to several hundred million US dollars for every new drug introduced into the market.

Patent rights should be strengthened, firms maintain, precisely where there are low incentives for innovation. Ensuring such protection would spur private investment in research and development for drugs that prevent and treat neglected diseases. While it is important to note that pharmaceuticals are not the only way to combat disease, it is no less significant that an immensely

disproportionate amount of private investment is directed to research and development in drugs for global diseases – such as diabetes, heart disease and HIV/AIDS – for which strong markets exist in industrialized countries (see **health transition**). Of the six illnesses listed above, meningitis, **tuberculosis** and **malaria** occur almost exclusively in developing countries. Not only low-income and therefore low-profit expectations, but also insufficient patent protection in many developing countries, occasions a neglect of these diseases – among many others – by private pharmaceutical companies in terms of research and development spending.

The "tradeoff," however, which economist Jean Lanjouw insists exists in the implementation of a global patent system is not between corporate profits and public health. Rather, equilibrium must be reached between two goals that are indeed crucial to public health: increased access to drugs, and the maintenance of incentives for research in pharmaceutical innovation. Pharmaceutical patent implementation should proceed, Lanjouw (2003) argues, with consideration for the extent to which protection will create an incentive for firms to increase socially beneficial research and development spending. While a persuasive argument can be made for the patenting of pharmaceuticals produced for neglected diseases, it is not as clear why research and development in drugs for global diseases such as HIV/AIDS should be governed by the same incentive structure. Developing country markets constitute such a small portion of the total sales in medicines for global diseases that lifting patents would hardly affect incentives to innovation. Thus, a differentiated global patent regime – protecting drugs for neglected diseases but exposing global disease medication to competition – would otherwise produce a fairer distribution of research and development without compromising incentives.

The global HIV/AIDS pandemic highlights some of the most alarming deficiencies in the distribution of pharmaceuticals in the developing world. From South African President Mbeki's initial denial of the link between HIV and AIDS to the consistent refusal effectively to provide antiretroviral treatment for the country's estimated 4.7 million HIV-carriers, the South African government's position regarding HIV/AIDS prevention and treatment has astounded the international **community**. The unaffordability of crucial antiretrovirals has certainly played an important role in this crisis. Fortunately, generic drugs have since 2000 gradually entered the global market, thereby reducing prices significantly. At the Doha meeting of the WTO in November 2001, the Declaration on the **trade-related aspects of intellectual property rights (TRIPS)** agreement and Public Health finally recognized the rights of members to introduce compulsory licensing in their pharmaceutical industries. This was considered an important victory for big generics producers such as India and Brazil, the latter having an extremely successful HIV/AIDS treatment program that depends crucially on the provision of cheap versions of essential antiretrovirals. In August 2003, it was decided that the WTO would extend compulsory licensing rights to countries lacking adequate pharmaceutical production capacity, thus allowing them to import more affordable generic drugs.

See also: disease eradication; health; health and poverty; HIV/AIDS (policy issues); intellectual property rights (IPRs); primary health care; trade-related aspects of intellectual property rights (TRIPS); World Trade Organization/ General Agreement on Tariffs and Trade (WTO/ GATT)

Further reading

BUKO Pharma Kampagne: A critical information service about pharmaceuticals and companies in developing countries: http:// www.bukopharma.de/

Médecins Sans Frontières (2001) *Fatal Imbalance: The Crisis in Research and Development for Drugs for Neglected Diseases*, Geneva: MSF. http:// www.msf.org

Lanjouw, J. (2003) "Intellectual Property and the Availability of Pharmaceuticals in Poor Countries," in Jaffe, A., Lerner, J. and Stern, S. (eds) *Innovation Policy and the Economy, Volume 3*, Cambridge MA: MIT Press.

FELIPE KRAUSE DORNELLES

planning

"Planning" is a rational, problem-solving activity essential for human survival. Known as "town," "city," "urban," or "regional" planning, the term refers to developing courses of action, or documented plans, for the physical and social improvement of human settlements (see **housing; urban development; urbanization**). Traditionally, planning has been equated with "urbanism" or "urban design," a branch of architecture that manipulates the shape and symbolism of public space, the area between buildings. In the twentieth century, however, "planning" meaning a discipline encompassing urban design and having its own body of theory and knowledge came into general use.

As long as human beings have lived in groups, they have intentionally laid out settlements to ensure places to dwell, work, and move about. The relationship between plots of land, their uses, and the ways to interconnect them generated deliberate spatial patterns. The oldest and most popular is the "gridiron," an easily expandable network of streets crossing at right angles to each other that divides land into rectangular parcels. This form reappears throughout history, from ancient Babylon to the island of Manhattan, the colonial cities of the New World based on Spain's Law of the Indies, and many of today's walkable New Urbanist towns. Baron Haussmann's plan for Paris, designed for efficient movement of Napoleon III's troops, imposed a series of *grands boulevards* over the organic Roman walled city and a pattern of radiating, concentric circles, similar to L'Enfant's 1791 plan for Washington DC. Ebenezer Howard, in his 1902 utopian treatise, *Garden Cities for Tomorrow*, proposed new **villages** as a refuge from city squalor, formed by concentric belts of development radiating outwards from a central park. Brazil's new capital, Brasilia, by planner Lucio Costa and architect Oscar Niemeyer in the late 1950s, became the grand symbol of modern city building with its arching, cruciform plan resembling an airplane.

The modern planning profession evolved rapidly in the twentieth century with the growth of industrialized cities and increasing complexity of urban life. Patrick Geddes established the philosophical foundation when arguing that urban design without social and economic reform could not improve the urban **environment**. Planning gained a valuable association with the social sciences by relying on its methods and techniques, such as demographic surveying, statistical analysis, geographic mapping, and economic modeling. These were useful in measuring, understanding, and explaining life in the Industrial Revolution's slums beginning in the late 1800s as **urbanization** gained momentum. Planners, however, are not scientists. There are no concrete and definitive solutions to the problems they address, thus inherently involving value judgments. Instead of describing urban life, planners ask, "What should be done to improve it?" The Royal Town Planning Institute, in its "New Vision for Planning," calls planning "*value-oriented* – concerned with identifying, understanding and mediating conflicting sets of values;" and "*action-oriented* – driven by the twin activities of mediating space and making of place." Early planners strived to raise poor living conditions by imposing regulations for adequate **waste management**, clean air and **drinking water**, **housing**, safety, public transit, public health, and parks, among other quality of life or **welfare indicators**. Among the sweeping social reforms came "zoning," the chief enforcement tool to control the use of land, density of development, and building height, to protect older, residential areas, prevent incompatible land uses, and ensure adequate air and sunlight in the urban core.

Given the complexity of planning problems, planners make comprehensive plans that integrate the form and infrastructure of places with changes in their economic and social structure; provide for the efficient use of resources; consider a wide range of choices; and serve as a means for recipients to envision a better future for themselves and their descendents. Planning is thus related to **governance**, the power to enact policies establishing a framework for orderly growth and development and to implement change. In a **democracy**, the planning process is ideally deliberative, relying on the participation of all stakeholders. Because of its purpose, the problems it addresses, and methods used to resolve them, planning overlaps with the study and practice of law, public policy, and **public management**. The role of the professional planner

in the **public sector** or private sector is to advise and persuade decision-makers, recommending the best courses of action. Working in a political arena, planners may also act as facilitators in the deliberation process, advocates for a particular position, or change agents in their own right.

By the start of the twenty-first century, over half the world's **population** was living in urban areas (see **urban development**). **Globalization** through increased **telecommunications** was contributing to economic competition among urban regions. In response, planning in the Information Age incorporated specialized sub-fields in addition to physical and land use planning, including economic and **community** development (see **economic development**); redevelopment; fiscal, transportation, and environmental planning; technology and **telecommunications** development; housing; and historic preservation (see **fiscal and monetary policy; brown environmental agenda**). Since the 1960s, planners had also begun to recognize not just local but global consequences of uncontrolled growth and redevelopment of cities to meet economic objectives, at the expense of social and cultural capital (see **social capital**), cultural and ethnic diversity, **biodiversity**, and non-renewable resources. Issues of **social justice**, resulting from the widening bifurcation of **labor markets** and increasing **urban poverty** and homelessness, and environmental protection, especially from urban sprawl made possible by increasing automobile use, have come to the forefront of the profession. In the Johannesburg Declaration of the United Nations **World Summit on Sustainable Development (Johannesburg, 2002)**, planners vowed to "advance and strengthen interdependent and mutually reinforcing pillars of **sustainable development** – economic development, **social development** and environmental protection – at the local, national, regional and global levels."

See also: brown environmental agenda; fiscal and monetary policy; Habitat I and II; housing; participatory development; urban development

Further reading

Frey, H. (1999) *Designing the City: Towards A More Sustainable Urban Form*, London: Routledge.

Haughton, G. and Hunter, C. (1994) *Sustainable Cities*, London, Bristol and Pennsylvania: Jessica Kingsley.

Jacobs, J. (1961) *The Death and Life of Great American Cities*, New York: Vintage.

Mumford, L. (1961) *The City in History: Its Origins, Its Transformations, and Its Prospect*, New York: Harcourt, Brace and World.

Unwin, R. (1994) *Town Planning in Practice*, New York: Princeton Architectural Press.

JULIE A. DERCLE

plantation forestry

Plantation forestry involves the planting of large areas of fast-growing tree species. The aim is to grow high volumes of wood per area to supply an increasing demand for timber (see **logging/timber trade**) and other wood products. According to **Food and Agriculture Organization (FAO)** statistics, plantations covered almost 187 million hectares globally and supplied 22 percent of the world's industrial wood needs in 2000. Plantations occur in both temperate and tropical zones. While these monocrop plantations are usually planted on lands affected by **deforestation**, there is concern that natural forest is being converted and **biodiversity** lost. The long-term sustainability of wood production and the potential ecological impacts of exotic species are also issues. Conflicts have occurred between local communities (see **community**) and forest concession holders over community displacement and loss of forest management alternatives (see **community forestry; agroforestry; Joint Forest Management (JFM)**).

See also: biodiversity; climate change; deforestation; non-timber forest products (NTFPs); silviculture

WYNET SMITH

political ecology

Political ecology is an approach to the complex metabolism between nature and society. The expression itself emerged in the 1970s in a variety of intellectual contexts – employed by the journalist Alex Cockburn, the anthropologist Eric Wolf, and the environmental scientist Grahame Beakhurst – as a somewhat inchoate covering term for the panoply of ways in which environmental concerns were politicized in the wake of the environmentalist wave which broke in the late 1960s and early 1970s. In its academic, and specifically geographical, usage political ecology has a longer and more complex provenance – which both harkens back to human and cultural ecology and to an earlier history of relations between anthropology and geography in the 1940s and 1950s and incorporates a more recent synthetic and analytical deployment in the early 1980s associated with the work of Piers Blaikie (1985), Michael Watts (1983; 1986), and Suzanna Hecht (1985). In the 1990s, the core empirical concerns of political ecology – largely rural, agrarian and within developing countries – were expanded, and the theoretical horizons have deepened the original concerns with the dynamics of resource management and the state (see **state and state reform**), with other studies emphasizing environmental history, science studies, gender theory (see **feminist political ecology**), discourse analysis and reinvigorated **Marxism**.

Two geographical monographs – *The Political Economy of Soil Erosion* (1985) by Piers Blaikie and *Land Degradation and Society* (1987) edited by Harold Brookfield and Piers Blaikie – provided the intellectual and theoretical foundation stones for the formalization of political ecology as such. Blaikie (1985) achieved a confluence between three theoretical approaches: cultural ecology in geography, rooted in ecosystemic approaches to human behavior; ecological anthropology, grounded in cybernetics and the adaptive qualities of living systems; and the high tide of Marxist-inspired political economy, and peasant studies in particular, of the 1970s. A number of people contributed to this intersection of ideas – Richards's (1985) work on peasant science, Hecht's (1985) analysis of **rent seeking**, inflation (see **inflation and its effects**) and **deforestation** in eastern Amazonia, Grossman (1984) on subsistence in Papua New Guinea, and Watts (1983) on the simple reproduction squeeze and **drought** in Nigeria – but Blaikie pulled a number of disparate themes and ideas together, drawing in large measure on his own South Asian experiences. In rejecting the colonial model of soil erosion which framed the problem around environmental constraints, mismanagement, **over-population**, and market failure, Blaikie started from the resource manager and specifically households from whom surpluses are extracted "who then in turn are forced to extract 'surpluses' from the environment ... [leading] to degradation" (1985:124). The analytical scaffolding was provided by a number of key middle-range concepts – **marginalization**, proletarianization and incorporation – which permitted geographers to see the failure of soil conservation schemes in class or social terms, namely the power of classes affected by soil erosion in relation to state power, the class-specific perception of soil problems and solutions, and the class basis of soil erosion as a political issue. Blaikie was able to argue that **poverty** could, in a dialectical way, cause degradation – "peasants destroy their own environment in attempts to delay their own destruction" (1985:29) – and that poverty had to be understood not as a thing or a condition, but as the social relations of production, which are realms of possibility and constraint.

In this work political ecology came to mean a combination of "the concerns of ecology and a broadly defined political economy" (Blaikie and Brookfield, 1987:17), the latter understood as a concern with effects "on people, as well as on their productive activities, of on-going changes within society at local and global levels" (1987:21). This is a broad definition – an approach rather than a theory – which was adopted by the editors in the inaugural issue of the *Journal of Political Ecology* in 1995. Political ecology has three essential foci.

The first is interactive, contradictory and dialectical: society and land-based resources are mutually causal in such as way that poverty, via poor management, can induce environmental degradation which itself deepens poverty. Less a problem of poor management, inevitable natural decay or demographic growth, land degradation is seen as *social* in origin and definition. Analytically, the centerpoint of any nature-society study must be the "land manager" whose relationship to nature must be considered in a historical, political and economic context. Second, political ecology argues for regional or spatial accounts of degradation which link, through "chains of explanation," local

decision-makers to spatial variations in environmental structure (stability and resilience as traits of particular ecosystems in particular). Locality studies are, thus, subsumed within multi-layered analyses pitched at a variety of regional scales. Third, land management is framed by "external structures" which for Blaikie meant the role of the state and the core-periphery model.

If political ecology was not exactly clear what political economy implied, beyond a sort of 1970s **dependency theory**, it did provide a number of principles and mid-range concepts. The first is a refined concept of marginality in which its political, ecological and economic aspects may be mutually reinforcing: land degradation is both a result and a cause of social **marginalization**. Second, pressure of production on resources is transmitted through social relations, which impose excessive demands on the environment (i.e. surplus extraction). And third, the inadequacy of environmental data of historical depth linked to a chain of explanation analysis compels a plural approach. Rather than unicausal theories one must, in short, accept "plural perceptions, plural definitions ... and plural rationalities" (Blaikie and Brookfield, 1987:16).

Political ecology had the advantage of seeing land management and environmental degradation in terms of how political economy shapes the ability to manage resources (through forms of access and control, through forms of exclusion, and through forms of exploitation), and through the lens of cognition (one person's accumulation is another person's degradation). But in other respects political ecology was demonstrably weak: it often had an outdated notion of ecology and ecological dynamics (including an incomplete understanding of ecological agency: Zimmerer, 1994); it was often remarkably silent on the politics of political ecology; it had a somewhat voluntarist notion of human perception, and not least it did not provide a theoretically derived set of concepts to explore particular environmental outcomes or transformations. These weaknesses, coupled with the almost indeterminate and open-ended nature of political ecology, predictably produced both a deepening and a proliferation of political ecologies in the 1990s (see Peet and Watts, 1996; Bryant and Bailey, 1997). A number of studies address the question of politics, focusing especially on patterns of resistance and struggles over the environment (Peluso, 1992; Neumann, 1999), how politics as policy is discursively constructed (Fairhead and Leach, 1996; Pulido, 1996), the role of environmental history (Grove, 1995), science studies (Forsyth, 2003) and Marxist discussions of the second contradiction of **capitalism** (O"Connor, 1998). A central theme remains the dialectical relations between nature and society, despite the hugely expanded and polyglot landscape of political ecology.

See also: environment; environmental movements; feminist political ecology; gender, environment and development

Further reading

See the *Journal of Political Ecology*.

Blaikie, P. (1985) *The Political Economy of Soil Erosion in Developing Countries*, London: Longman.

Blaikie, P. and Brookfield, H. (eds) (1987) *Land Degradation and Society*, London: Methuen.

Bryant, R. and Bailey, S. (1997) *Third World Political Ecology*, London: Routledge.

Fairchild, J. and Leach, M. (1996) *Misreading the African Landscape*, Cambridge: Cambridge University Press.

Forsyth, T. (2003) *Critical Political Ecology: The Politics of Environmental Science*, London: Routledge.

Grossman, L. (1984) *Peasants, Subsistence Ecology and Development in The Highlands Of Papua New Guinea*, Princeton: Princeton University Press.

Grove, R. (1995) *Green Imperialism*, Cambridge: Cambridge University Press.

Hecht, S. (1985) "Environment, Development, and Politics," *World Development* 13: 663–84.

Neumann, R. (1999) *Imposing Wilderness*, Berkeley: University of California Press.

O'Connor, J. (1998) *Natural Causes*, New York: Guilford.

Peet, R. and Watts, M. (eds) ([1996] 2004, 2nd edn) *Liberation Ecologies*, London: Routledge.

Pulido, L. (1996) *Environmentalism and Economic Justice*, Tucson: University of Arizona Press.

Peluso, N. (1992) *Rich Forests, Poor People*, Berkeley: University of California Press.

Richards, P. (1985) *Indigenous Agricultural Revolution*, London: Hutchinson.

Watts, M. (1983) *Silent Violence: Food, Famine and Peasantry in Northern Nigeria*, Berkeley: University of California Press.

Watts, M. (1986) "Drought, Environment and Food Security," pp. 171–212 in Glantz, M. (ed.) *Drought and Hunger in Africa*, Cambridge: Cambridge University Press.

Zimmerer, K. (1994) "Integrating the New Ecology in Human Geography," *Annals of the Association of American Geographers* 84: 108–25.

MICHAEL WATTS

politics

Whether we think of politics as the art and science of government, or as the pursuit of power, it is hard to imagine development being separated from it. Interestingly, though, the modern discipline of development theory and practice has constituted politics as much as an absence as a presence since its inception in the 1950s. Despite the **Cold War** origins of development studies, modernization theorists (see **modernization theory**) liked to present "politics" as a hindrance to, or outcome of, a broader process of structural transformation (see **anti-politics**). Politics tended to throw economies off course, perhaps even in the direction of socialism, or to throw up non-democratic regimes.

This bias against politics, or against an explicit recognition of the political, was continued by many development agencies, including the **World Bank** (by statute). But politics could not be kept off the agenda. Radical theorists in the 1960s and 1970s insisted that the fundamental problems of poorer (dependent) countries were caused by an unequal distribution of economic and political power. And in the 1980s the "political" was recast as a problem for development studies by the "counter-revolution" in development theory and policy. Deepak Lal now argued that what the developing world needed most was less government (Lal, 1983). In the 1990s, the apparent failures of socialist and New Right experiments alike encouraged students of development to turn afresh to the problem (and even priority) of politics and the political. Attention was focused on the institutional bases of economic reform programs and on problems of state failure (see **state and state reform**), sometimes from a rational choice perspective. It was also focused on the "democratic deficit" that marked many poorer countries and many of the development projects that were run within them. Participation, good **governance** and democratization all became buzzwords in the new mainstream of development studies – a mainstream that was challenged to the right by talk of a "**clash of civilizations**" and regime change, and to the left by studies of **governmentality**, depoliticization and anti-developmentalism (see **postmodernism and postdevelopment**).

Arturo Escobar (1995) has convincingly argued that "development" in the modern sense of directed social and economic change was promoted by Truman as part of a Cold War discourse (see **Truman's Bold New Program (1949)**). This does not mean that all work produced on development has been written with close regard for West-East relations. Development studies is more catholic and oppositional than Escobar allows, and its organizing assumptions have not stood still over fifty years. It is significant, however, that the second article published in *Economic Development and Cultural Change* (the first journal of "development studies") was written by Morris Watnick on the "appeal of communism to the peoples of underdeveloped areas." In his view,

> the odds facing the West in the underdeveloped areas of the world today are heavily weighted against it. ... The effort to capture the imagination and loyalties of [these] populations did not begin with ... President Truman's plea for a "bold new program" of technical aid to backward areas. It began [with] the Communist International at its second world congress of 1920.
>
> (Watnick, 1952:22)

By the end of the 1950s this view was less often expressed. In *The stages of economic growth*, Walt Rostow (1960) described socialism as a "deviant case." Rostow popularized a simple version of the Harrod-Domar growth model. He suggested that poorer countries would "drive to maturity" if they

increased savings and funneled investment (including foreign **aid**) into **industrialization**. Insofar as he addressed politics, it was in the unspoken assumption that strong governments could solve the coordination problems implicit in a strategy of deferred gratification *without* resorting to socialism. This was a common view in the 1960s. Even structural-functionalist (or Parsonian) theories of modernization (see **modernization theory**) were inclined to the view that **economic development** would precede cultural change. While the construction of "modern" subjectivities remained the goal – promoting a sense of entrepreneurship and X-achievement levels where previously people had been saturated in ignorance and "tradition" – it was generally conceded that "the economy" remained the first business of state. This in turn encouraged a technocratic account of politics. The job of government was to maximize savings and industrialization, and promote a **big push** for growth. Spending on **health** and **education**, or on regional policies, would follow in the wake of this first objective, and would demand a similar degree of professionalism and objectivity on the part of policy-makers. India's second and third Five Year Plans (1956–66) exemplified this sort of thinking. They positioned the Planning Commission as an executive branch of government armed with the latest statistical techniques and input-output models. According to Ronald Inden (1995), politics was discounted in favor of the new god of **planning**, and the democratic space of public debate was filled by "wise men" who would steer the country toward a state of "development." In other countries this function might be carried out by professional soldiers, or men from the officer corps. Samuel Huntington (1957) and Samuel Finer (2002 [1962]) acknowledged the role that professional armies could play in promoting **security** and **economic growth**. The dominant assumption of this time was that **democracy** would be an *outcome* of development.

Of course, not everyone took this view, even in the 1960s. In the decade's landmark book, Barrington Moore argued that "development" was anything but a guarantor of democracy. Industrial growth in Prussia and Japan had been pushed through by strong states in the absence of **agrarian reform** programs. The survival of the Junkers (the

Prussian elite – see **elites**) and their equivalents promoted a marriage of iron and rye, and helped to pave the way for fascism. A similarly Promethean view of development was apparent in communist China, and even in India there were storm clouds on the horizon. The failure of **land reform**s in the 1950s threatened either to retard the pace of economic growth, and/or to throw the country's industrial bourgeoisie into bed with the rural elites who controlled regional Congress parties. In any case, said Moore,

> if democracy means the opportunity to play a meaningful part as a rational human being in determining one's fate in life, democracy does not yet exist in the Indian countryside. The Indian peasant has not yet acquired the material and intellectual perquisites for democratic society.
>
> (1966:408)

Moore's remarks meshed neatly with two arguments that were advanced by radical scholars of "development." In Latin America, especially, the idea that the national bourgeoisies might be strong enough to sponsor industrial development was challenged by Gunder Frank (1967) and some members of the dependency school (see **dependency theory**). Bringing politics firmly to the table, Frank charged that the development of core countries had been made possible only by the underdevelopment of peripheral countries. Members of the national bourgeoisies acted as comprador capitalists in this process, and ensured the absence of industrialization in Asia, Africa and Latin America. The only way to end this misery was to trade barbarism for socialism. Like Samir Amin (1976) in Africa, Frank spoke up for political movements that sought to "de-link" the periphery from the core countries of the capitalist world system. Far from being a deviant case, the socialism of a Cuba or China was acclaimed as the necessary and rational foundation of "real" development – a development by and for "the people" or the "lower orders" (subalterns).

Other members of the dependency school, including Cardoso and Faletto (1979), were never comfortable with Frank's logic (see **world systems theory**). They noted that significant industrial

development was being achieved in countries in East Asia. This growth had been secured after long political struggles (notably over land and fiscal policy – see **fiscal and monetary policy**) *within* countries like South Korea and Taiwan. They also disputed Frank's characterizations of unequal exchange. The South had been penalized, but mainly because the income **terms of trade** had moved against primary commodities (as Prebisch and Seers had both shown in the 1950s – see **trade**). The terms of trade would more likely be improved by pressing demands for a new **international economic order**, as happened in the 1970s, than by retreating toward "socialism in one country," or even autarky.

Where they did agree with Frank, and with Dudley Seers (1969) and many others, was in rejecting the idea that development could be measured by growth alone (not that Frank expected high **growth rate**s in the South) (see **growth versus holism**). In the 1970s and 1980s a "people-centered" definition of development (see **people-centered development**) became popular not just on the left but throughout development studies. Critiques of **trickle down** economics were now standard fare, and students of all stripes began to address the problems of women and other socially disadvantaged groups. Accounts of the "politics of development" accordingly began to widen out, and to surface at different scales. 1976 was the peak year for the expropriation of the assets of **transnational corporations (TNCs)** in the South, and this encouraged Norman Girvan and others to study corporate imperialism (see **colonialism, history of; colonialism, impacts of**) (Girvan, 1978). The coup in Chile in 1973 also brought ITT firmly into the spotlight, and with it the continuing role of the CIA in the destabilization of political life in poorer countries. Meanwhile, in Vietnam, resistance to US imperialism by men and women in the countryside encouraged some on the left to acclaim the rebellious peasant (Wolf, 1971). The peasant studies literature now grew in strength (see **peasantry**). Questions were asked about the prevalence of peasant struggles (see **peasant movements**) and whether agrarian revolts might be confined to deltaic regions (Paige, 1978). Questions were also asked about the decision-making frameworks of peasant actors, and whether these were best understood in rational choice (Popkin, 1979) or moral economy (Scott, 1977) terms. These debates were renewed in the 1980s when fresh attention was given to peasant resistance strategies (Scott, 1985), and the language and iconography of agrarian politics (see **weapons of the weak**).

It was not just the left, however, that brought politics "back" into development studies. Environmental politics and **gender** politics were now placed firmly on the agenda, and new accounts of development as "freedom" (or the building up of capabilities – see **capability approach**), and of **sustainable development**, focused attention on issues of inter-generational equity and **human rights**. **Globalization** and **fair trade** campaigns also directed attention to the needs and rights of distant strangers, and thus to development **ethics** (Corbridge, 1993).

Important as these developments have been, the biggest challenge to mainstream development theory and policy (with all its hesitancies about politics and the political) came from the New Right. The counter-revolution in development studies took shape in the 1970s in the writings of Peter Bauer (1976), Ian Little (1982), Anne Krueger (1974), and others. Following the global inflation of that decade (see **inflation and its effects**), however, and the rise of worker militancy in Western countries, the analytical and political appeal of supply-side economics, or monetarism, or public choice theory, was generalized in the 1980s. Anne Krueger now became Chief Economist of the World Bank. Many poorer countries were also now required to adopt **structural adjustment** programs to deal with the consequences of their indebtedness. Carlos Diaz-Alejandro (1984) argued that the **debt** crisis in Latin America was caused by Volcker's tight money policies in the USA. But the conviction in the **World Bank** was that domestic mismanagement was mainly to blame. Krueger argued that *dirigisme* in developing countries had promoted rent-seeking economic behavior. Politicians were also inclined to print money to buy votes, regardless of the macro-economic consequences of their actions. Politics, in short, was constituted – again – as the problem, but this time the solution was to be found in "the market(s)," not in planning. The job of politicians was to roll

back the state, which was overwhelmingly predatory. This would free people from their overbearing and self-serving masters.

Elements of this discourse continue to inform development theory and practice. Hernando de Soto (1989) famously demonstrated how difficult it was to set up a small business in Peru in the face of government over-regulation and straightforward **corruption**. And in India, there has been widespread acceptance of the argument that Indian entrepreneurs have prospered abroad rather than at home. Skepticism about the public-spirited nature of politicians is now entrenched, along with skepticism about the ability of planners to second-guess the needs and wants of ordinary people. Bureaucratic **authoritarianism** has few defenders.

But the intellectual standing of **neo-liberalism** has also been sharply criticized. Robert Bates (1988) agreed with the World Bank's (1981) argument that **food** production declines in Sub-Saharan Africa were the result mainly of entrenched systems of **urban bias**. Peasant households received below-market prices for their goods, and chose not to invest in new farming technologies. He also concurred that a **"developmental state"** would want to encourage rural grain markets and abolish food-marketing boards. But his rational choice model of politics caused him to ask why ruling politicians in the region would want to act in this way. It was all very well for the World Bank to talk about rolling back the state, but what incentive was there for an autocratic ruler to do this? And if the ruler feared a coup in an urban area, why would he challenge the politics of urban bias?

The failure of **"shock therapy"** in Russia and other parts of the ex-Soviet Union further encouraged critics of the New Right to insist upon the *politics* of market-making. The inspiration here, though, came more from Karl Polanyi (1944) than from a rational choice perspective. John Gray argued that New Right thinking was as much akin to a theocratic world-view as was extreme-left thinking: both wanted to evacuate the world of contradictions and the real work of politics. In his view, "free markets" were an impossibility (if not quite an oxymoron), but the chase after them was damaging: it promoted higher levels of **inequality** and a breakdown in social cohesion at all spatial scales, and it led to a dysfunctional hollowing out of state capacity. In Gray's view, as perhaps in Robert Kaplan's (2000) for different reasons, accounts of the rise of global terrorism could be linked directly to accounts of the "false dawn" of global laissez-faire. "The terrorist network that carried out the attacks on New York and Washington is a by-product of the weakness of the state that was actively promoted by the West during the neo-liberal period" (Gray, 2002:xv).

The World Bank's charter agreements make it difficult for the organization to come to grips with "politics" in the manner of a Gray or a Kaplan, and it continues to be charged with depoliticizing development in southern Africa (Ferguson, 1990) and elsewhere. Nevertheless, under James Wolfensohn corruption did become an object of discussion for Bank staff, and along with it questions of public service reform. And in large parts of Africa the Bank is now promising to pay attention to a body of work which is focused precisely on the question of state failure. This work includes, *inter alia*, Mamdani's (1996) work on the production of citizens and subjects in postcolonial Africa; Bayart *et al.*'s (1999) work on the criminalization of the state; and Herbst's (2000) work on state failure as a consequence both of low population densities and of the West's insistence on dealing only with (so-called) nation-states. In Herbst's view, many states in Africa have been unable to govern their territories, and have failed to achieve a monopoly over the means of **violence** (legitimate or otherwise). The "state" becomes a resource, fueled by **aid** monies, which are targeted and fought over by competing social groups. In these circumstances, the formation of functioning markets remains unlikely.

To talk about the necessity of "good governance" in this context might be a step forward, but Adrian Leftwich thinks the phrase does little justice to the seriousness of the problems facing poorer countries.

From a developmental point of view, the general but simplistic appeal for better 'governance' as a condition of development is virtuous but naive. For an independent and competent administration is not simply a product of 'institution building' or improved training, but of politics.

(Leftwich, 1993:622; See **Institutions**)

Bill Cooke and Uma Kothari (2001) have expressed similar reservations about what they call "the tyranny of participation" in modern development practice. While they welcome direct attention to the "voices of the poor," they suggest that the poor cannot be empowered entirely by themselves (see **empowerment**). John Harriss (2001) also worries that confrontations are inevitable in any meaningful pro-poor politics (over the distribution of land and resources, for example), but are ignored in accounts of participation and of human (see **human capital**) and **social capital** formation. Politics, for Harriss, needs to be more directed than this, and must have regard for the constitution not just of **civil society** but of political society.

Pervasive state failure, the globalization of terrorism, ethnic violence (Varshney, 2002), and the controversies around Huntington's talk of a clash of civilizations, have all ensured that "politics" is closer to the core of development studies than it has been previously. So too have studies of the politics of the household, the environment, and economic reform. These debates are also ensuring that the study of "politics" is sharply contested. The idea that development means "economics first, politics second" has largely had its day (though see the **Washington consensus**). But the question of how to understand politics is very properly disputed by discourse theorists, public choice theorists, rational choice theorists, Marxists, feminists, Weberians and many others besides. Only a dogmatist would expect otherwise.

See also: advocacy coalitions; anti-politics; capitalism; civil society; democracy; dependency theory; empowerment; ethics; gender; governance; governmentality; institutions; international economic order; Marxism; modernization theory; neo-liberalism; new social movements; non-aligned movement; people-centered development; power and discourse; solidarity campaigns; state and state reform; Washington consensus

Further reading

Amin, S. (1976) *Unequal Development*, New York: Monthly Review Press.

Bates, R. (1988) *Toward a Political Economy of Development*, Berkeley: University of California Press.

Bauer, P. (1976) *Dissent on Development*, Cambridge MA: Harvard University Press.

Bayart, F., Ellis, S. and Hibou, H. (1999) *The Criminalization of the State in Africa*, London: James Currey.

Cardoso, F. and Faletto, E. (1979) *Dependency and Development in Latin America*, Berkeley: University of California Press.

Cooke, B. and Kothari, U. (eds) (2001) *Participation: The New Tyranny?*, London: Zed.

Corbridge, S. (1993) "Marxisms, Modernities and Moralities: Development Praxis and the Claims of Distant Strangers," *Environment and Planning D (Society and Space)* 11: 449–72.

De Soto, H. (1989) *The Other Path: The Invisible Revolution in the Third World*, New York: Harper and Row.

Diaz-Alejandro, C. (1984) "Latin American Debt: I Don't Think We Are in Kansas any more," *Brookings Papers on Economic Activity* 2: 335–89.

Escobar, A. (1995) *Encountering Development: The Making and Unmaking of the Third World*, Princeton: Princeton University Press.

Ferguson, J. (1990) *The Anti-Politics Machine: "Development," Depoliticisation and Bureaucratic Power in Lesotho*, Cambridge: Cambridge University Press.

Finer, S. (2002 [1962]) *The Man on Horseback: The Role of the Military in Politics*, New York: Transaction.

Frank, A. G. (1967) *Capitalism and Underdevelopment in Latin America*, New York: Monthly Review Press.

Girvan, N. (1978) *Corporate Imperialism*, New York: Monthly Review Press.

Gray, J. (2001) *False Dawn: The Delusions of Global Capitalism*, London: Granta.

Harriss, J. (2001) *Depoliticizing Development: The World Bank and Social Capital*, New Delhi: LeftWord.

Herbst, J. (2000) *States and Power in Africa*, Princeton: Princeton University Press.

Huntington, S. (1957) *The Soldier and the State: The Theory and Politics of Civil-Military Relations*, New Haven: Yale University Press.

Huntington, S. (1993) "The Clash of Civilizations?" *Foreign Affairs* 72: 22–49.

Inden, R. (1995) "Embodying God: From Imperial Progresses to National Progress in India," *Economy and Society* 24: 245–78.

Kaplan, R. (2000) *The Coming Anarchy: Shattering the Dreams of the Post Cold War*, New York: Vintage.

Kreuger, A. (1974) "The Political Economy of the Rent-seeking Society," *American Economic Review* 64: 291–303.

Lal, D. (1983) *The Poverty of "Development Economics,"* London: Institute of Economic Affairs.

Leftwich, A. (1993) "Governance, Democracy and Development in the Third World," *Third World Quarterly* 14: 605–24.

Little, I. (1982) *Economic Development: Theory, Policy and International Relations*, New York: Basic Books.

Mamdani, M. (1996) *Citizen and Subject: Contemporary Africa and the Legacy of Late-colonialism*, Princeton: Princeton University Press.

Moore, B. (1966) *The Social Origins of Dictatorship and Democracy: Lord and Peasant in the Making of the Modern World*, Boston MA: Beacon Press.

Paige, J. (1978) *Agrarian Revolution*, New York: Free Press.

Polanyi, K. ([1944] 2001) *The Great Transformation: The Political and Economic Origins of Our Times*, Boston MA: Beacon Press.

Popkin, S. (1979) *The Rational Peasant: The Political Economy of Rural Society in Vietnam*, Berkeley: University of California Press.

Rostow, W. (1960) *The Stages of Economic Growth: A Non-Communist Manifesto*, London: Cambridge University Press.

Scott, J. (1977) *The Moral Economy of the Peasant: Rebellion and Subsistence in Southeast Asia*, New Haven: Yale University Press.

Scott, J. (1985) *Weapons of the Weak: Everyday Forms of Peasant Resistance*, New Haven: Yale University Press.

Seers, D. (1969) "The Meaning of Development," *International Development Review* 11: 1–14.

Varshney, A. (2002) *Ethnic Conflict and Civic Life: Hindus and Muslims in India*, New Haven: Yale University Press.

Watnick, M. (1952) "The Appeal of Communism to the Peoples of Underdeveloped Areas," *Economic Development and Cultural Change* 1: 22–36.

Wolf, E. (1971) *Peasant Wars of the Twentieth Century*, London: Faber and Faber.

World Bank (1981) *Accelerated Development in Sub-Saharan Africa: An Agenda for Action*, Oxford: Oxford University Press and the World Bank.

STUART CORBRIDGE

pollution

Pollution is the presence or introduction of substances to the **environment** that are considered harmful. It is usually discussed in relation to air, soil and water pollution, although it may also include noise pollution, and even aesthetic pollution in the case of building work. In terms of development, pollution is usually discussed as part of the **brown environmental agenda** – or the environmental problems associated with industry, **sanitation** and **urban development**. Often, developing countries are considered to have insufficient state (see **state and state reform**) or financial capacity to enforce regulations against pollution, hence encouraging high pollution rates with **industrialization** (see **pollution havens**). Pollution may also increase **mortality** and morbidity (ill health) wherever it is found (see **environment and health**).

Some economists have questioned whether pollution is a long-term phenomenon in developing economies, based on the arguments associated with the environmental **Kuznets curve** (EKC). This curve proposes an inverted U-shaped relationship between the levels of income and environmental degradation, hence arguing that pollution first rises during the initial stages of industrialization (and income generation), but then falls when income levels reach a critical level because of improvements in environmental quality. Proponents of the EKC therefore depict pollution as an unavoidable, necessary and temporary phenomenon on the road

to development. Critics, however, argue that the U-shaped relationship is largely an artifact generated by the use of cross-sectional data, and that where the relationship exists it is one manifestation of increased **inequality** – itself an adverse developmental outcome. Pollution control measures may therefore be applied only to certain locations and certain types of pollutant rather than as a benefit to all (see **brown environmental agenda**). Moreover, pollution is by no means necessary for **economic development** because technological and institutional solutions exist for avoiding it, and it may impede development. Industrializing countries may avoid high levels of pollution during **economic growth** if they can adopt environmentally-sound technologies (ESTs) at an early stage. This process is also known as **leapfrogging** because it involves passing over the period of pollution proposed in the EKC. Leapfrogging depends on achieving a successful level of **technology transfer**.

Pollution havens are also controversial. These are locations to which polluting industries are argued to relocate either because they are pushed out from developed countries where tighter environmental standards prevail, or because developing countries seek to attract polluting industries by lowering their environmental standards. Again, some have argued, controversially, that rapidly industrializing developing countries (currently such as Vietnam or China) may have a comparative advantage in attracting such polluting activities and that they should be accepted for the sake of economic efficiency. Critics suggest these arguments overlook the political economy of how **foreign direct investment** is made, and the lack of control that developing countries have in the nature of investment.

Various analysts have downplayed pollution in developing countries by claiming that environmental quality is an amenity, or a matter of aesthetics that can be compensated for by the economic growth associated with industrialization. Yet, pollution presents obvious obstacles for **human development** because they adversely affect the lives and **health** of millions of urban and rural poor in developing countries. Water pollution by human wastes is the main means of spreading **water-borne diseases** such as cholera, typhoid and diarrheal diseases that are still among the most important causes of **mortality**, especially among infants and children (see **infant and child mortality; United Nations Children's Fund (UNICEF)**). Outdoor and indoor air pollution in turn causes and aggravates various illnesses of the respiratory system, which may also affect industrial working forces (see also **gender and industrialization**). Burning animal dung for fuel has been associated with indoor air pollution, yet is not always measured in regional indications of pollution. Research in the Gambia showed that children carried on mothers' backs as they cooked in smoky huts were six times as likely to develop acute respiratory illness than other children. In Nepal and India, non-smoking women exposed to biomass smoke experienced similar death rates to male heavy smokers (World Bank, 1996:2). Air pollution levels also vary with height off the ground, meaning that children, for example, will experience different levels of exposure to taller adults. The complexity of biophysical levels of pollution, and the diversity of individuals' vulnerabilities to pollution, imply that general pollution standards are useful, but very general indicators of safe environments. Polluting companies may also manipulate the measurement of pollution: secret testing frequently reports higher levels of pollutants than tests announced in advance. Electronics companies may shift workers between different locations of factories so that gradual accumulation of lead in workers' blood levels may not show up in regular testing until later (see **occupational health**).

Fighting pollution therefore does not rely specifically upon reducing levels of emissions, but on developing holistic approaches to the political regulation of pollution, the capacity to monitor it, and on reducing people's vulnerability to forms of pollution. Reducing **vulnerability** may occur by national programs of improved health, or by addressing specific workplaces and social groups, such as factory workers or **street children**. Addressing pollution also implies increasing the transfer of ESTs, and in lobbying to ensure that some forms of localized or underemphasized pollution (such as indoor air pollution) are identified as priorities.

See also: brown environmental agenda; drinking water; environment and health; Kuznets curve; leapfrogging; occupational health; pollution havens; sanitation; sustainable development; urban poverty

Further reading

MacGranahan, G. and Murray, F. (2003) *Air Pollution and Health in Rapidly Developing Countries*, London: Earthscan.

Paavola, J. (2002) "Environment and Development: Dissecting the Connections," *Forum for Development Studies* 1: 5–32.

Stern, D. (2004) "The Rise and Fall of the Environmental Kuznets Curve," *World Development* 32:8 1419–39.

World Bank (1996) *Rural Energy and Development: Improving Energy Supplies for Two Billion People*, Washington DC: World Bank.

World Health Organization (2002) *The World Health Report 2002: Reducing Risks, Promoting Healthy Life*, Geneva: World Health Organization.

JOUNI PAAVOLA

pollution havens

Pollution havens are locations where polluting firms relocate in order to avoid stringent environmental standards. There are two versions of the pollution haven hypothesis. The first argues that increasingly strict environmental regulations reduce the competitiveness of firms and "push" them to relocate. The second suggests that developing countries "pull" firms to relocate by maintaining low environmental standards. Empirical studies have mainly analyzed changes in the **pollution** intensity of production and the allocation of **foreign direct investment**. Their results on the existence and significance of pollution havens are not decisive. Studies have found weak evidence of the above-average growth of, and foreign direct investment in, polluting industries in developing countries. Cost differentials between locations have been argued to be too small to cause clearly observable relocation. A parallel "race to bottom" – i.e. the attraction of firms to the lowest standards – phenomenon exists in the extraction of natural resources and in **occupational health** and safety.

See also: export processing zones (EPZs); foreign direct investment; maquiladoras; pollution; transnational corporations (TNCs)

JOUNI PAAVOLA

Polonoreste

The Polonoreste project was an attempt at instigating **economic development** and modernization (see **modernization theory**) in northern Brazil by a process of highway construction, and incentives for industrial and agricultural expansion. The **World Bank** lent Brazil US$445 million in 1981 to pave 1,500km of dirt tracks in the province of Rondonia, bordering Bolivia, and to create thirty-nine rural settlement centers to form development "poles" to assist in cocoa and coffee export crops. The new road allowed nearly half a million new migrants to enter the region, allegedly increasing annual **deforestation** rates of the Brazilian Amazon from 1.7 percent in 1978 to 16.1 percent in 1991, and increasing **malaria** infection and infant mortality (see **infant and child mortality**). In 1987, the World Bank's president, Barber Conable, said that Polonoreste was a "sobering example of an environmentally sound project gone wrong." In 1992 a new, Planoforo project was started to amend Polonoreste's problems by establishing new extractive reserves. But in 1995, local **indigenous people** lodged a complaint to the World Bank against Planoforo for failing to incorporate local people, or to regulate the damaging impacts of development.

See also: deforestation; displacement; indigenous people; modernization theory; transmigration; transport policy; World Bank

TIM FORSYTH

population

The dynamic relationship between population change and development has caused considerable controversy in the literature and has a long history of dispute and debate. Clearly, both population and development are interacting variables surrounded by problems of definition and uncertainty, and it is not surprising that difficulties should occur when considering the relationship between them. The model of development that followed the end of the World War II assumed developing countries should follow a developmental path similar to the advanced economies of Western Europe and North America, with associated transitions from primary **agriculture** to **industrialization** and **urbanization** (see **modernization theory**). Many observers associated this idea with the **demographic transition** that would stabilize **fertility** and **mortality**. In particular as death rates declined as a result of improved **nutrition, sanitation** and **disease eradication**, a decline in fertility was expected to follow as a shift took place from **children** valued by the family as an economic asset to the need to invest in children and ensure their quality of life. Thus the improvement in life chances represented by increased **life expectancy** would be matched by the expectation of a substantial increase in **education** and a delay in marriage and childbearing resulting in greater participation by women in **labor markets**.

Globally, the rapid growth of population is a recent phenomenon. In 1750, the world population was an estimated 0.8 billion people. In 2001, it reached 6 billion. The most rapid growth has occurred in the last fifty years, with an annual growth rate of 1.7 percent. This growth has been uneven. Many African countries, for instance, have a projected population doubling time of less than twenty-five years As the **World Bank** concludes, "Population growth would not be a problem if economic and social adjustments could be made fast enough, if technical change could be guaranteed, or if population change itself inspired technical change. But rapid population growth, if anything, makes adjustment more difficult" (*World Development Report*, 1994:165) (see **overpopulation**). Now, HIV/AIDS is having an immense impact on some populations (see **HIV/AIDS (definition and treatment); HIV/AIDS (policy issues)**). Life expectancy figures in a number of African countries have dropped by as much as ten years since the 1980s. While this has also slowed the growth of population and led to revisions in the estimates for growth in the heavily affected areas, it has added enormously to the challenges of development.

Population and carrying capacities

One of the most influential writers on population was Thomas Malthus (1766–1834), and his legacy is still strong today. **Malthusian demography**'s assertion of a law determining population growth and its relation to food production – the famous arithmetic and geometrical progression – was not accepted by many of his contemporaries, let alone later demographers. Ester Boserup (1910–99) has been one of several analysts who turned his theory on its head by arguing that far from population growth tending to exceed agricultural production, population growth was a necessary precondition for technical improvements to **agriculture**.

In general, population is a highly charged subject, or as Furedi wrote, "statements about population are intimately linked to a preoccupation with power, race and nation" (Furedi, 1997:163). The debate has tended to shift between pessimistic and optimistic predictions. The *Limits to Growth* **report (1972)** predicted Malthusian-style collapse in **economic development** and population unless steps were take to reduce world consumption. In 1984, the **World Bank** concluded that population pressure on **natural resources** would not obstruct global development. The New Right has further called for laissez-faire "market demographics," in which both the environment and the population will be controlled by unfettered entrepreneurial initiative. Meanwhile other critics point to the continuing and rapid expansion of world population and the very high costs of this expansion in many developing countries.

Some have argued that the key to understanding relationships between land, other resources, and people lies in the concept of **carrying capacity**, which specifies some recommended limit on population density or land uses. In 1984, the World Bank estimated that fourteen Sub-Saharan African countries had a scarcity of land that – with predicted population growth – were liable to **food security** risk. It also claimed that eleven further

countries had substantial areas of underused land. While this might suggest that the matter could be evened out by **migration**, it is far from likely that this will occur in the face of national or other local factors. Moreover, such close links between population density and carrying capacity have been criticized by those emphasizing the wider effects of trade, the impacts of food security and **famine**, and agricultural and **irrigation** technology. New models such as the PEDA (population, environment, development, agriculture) try to assess the effects of population on environmental factors and vice-versa, taking account of such factors as **water management**, **fuelwood** and energy provision (see **energy policy**) as well as **food**. Some models depict a vicious circle whereby the high fertility of the food-insecure population in marginal rural areas contributes to further land degradation, thus lowering agricultural production and further increasing the number of food-insecure persons (e.g. see Lutz *et al.*, 2002). Many other approaches, however, illustrate that local people may mitigate impacts of population growth on **natural resources** by the adoption of soil and water conservation methods, or local **institutions** that allow **governance** of resources (see **common pool resources; community-based natural resource management (CBNRM); environment**). For example, Tiffen and Mortimore (1994) argued, controversially, that "more people" may mean "less erosion."

Population policies

From the 1950s to the 1980s there appeared to be strong support for assumptions that **economic development** would induce a **demographic transition**. However, from the first world population conference convened by the UN in Bucharest in 1974 (see **Bucharest world population conference (1974)**) to the conference in Mexico City in 1984 and even until the **Cairo conference on population and development** in 1994, there was little to suggest that even those countries with a still high death rate and a very high birth rate were moving very far in this direction. Although death rates stabilized and life expectancy increased up to the 1980s, fertility remained high in many countries, and a number of countries had an expected doubling time for their populations of less than twenty-five years. Perhaps the most apparent factor was the diversity of experience between countries. Even so, the general tenor of most of the population predictions in the 1980s was that eventually the demographic transition would have its desired effect and population growth would stabilize. In any case, some of the more extreme policy interventions to limit growth attempted by the governments of China and India had been shown to be not very effective, quite apart from the fact that they raised **human rights** issues with regard to forced rationing of children or programs of sterilization accompanied by strong incentives to participate. One famous scheme in India promised a free transistor radio to anyone who volunteered to be sterilized.

The 1994 plan of action agreed at the Cairo conference on population and development gave particular attention to women's rights to participation in **education** and the workforce and in ownership of land and property (see **gender and property rights**). It was hoped that this rights-based approach to development (see **rights-based approaches to development**), emphasizing the status of women, would lead to a transformation of the population situation in association with the economic and **social development** of many of the poorest countries in the world.

In each decade, the population conferences have reassessed the issues of population policy and imposed a different tone on the debate. The 1974 Bucharest conference focused on how to slow down high population growth rates. The conference ten years later in Mexico City was deflected from this issue by the highly controversial issue of abortion (see **family planning**). The 1994 conference in Cairo had the great merit that it was the first to attempt to integrate population policy objectives with broader development objectives and the linkages between demographic behavior and economic and social progress. This represents a shift that has been present in development dialogs to emphasize individuals' rights and the greater effectiveness of development that involves the individual, the family and **community** in their own development, rather than imposing a top-down solution upon them. Population policy

therefore shifted away from population control programs directed toward incentives or requirements for family limitation, to greater emphases on individual choice (including **reproductive rights**) and the circumstances (such as **poverty** alleviation) where choices can be exercised freely. Many observers have claimed that this approach has had success: expanding education, especially for women, has impacted directly and indirectly on reducing high fertility. Education has also been associated with delayed marriage age, improved public health and sanitation, and reduced **child labor**.

The combined effects of the major conferences of the 1990s and the early 2000s have been more coordinated population and development policies. The Program of Action adopted in Cairo in 1994 was supplemented by the recommendations at the 1999 International Conference on Population and Development at the Special Session of the UN General Assembly (UN Population Fund, 1996 and 2000). These actions draw together proposals from the **Earth Summit (1992) (United Nations Conference on Environment and Development)** (Rio Conference) and the 1995 Beijing Conference on **gender** (see **United Nations World Conferences on Women**). The Program of Action called for completion of the demographic transition and stabilization of the population.

In the five years between the two statements, the spread of HIV/AIDS (see **HIV/AIDS (definition and treatment); HIV/AIDS (policy issues)**), particularly in Sub-Saharan Africa, led to a decline in life expectancies because of increased mortality, thus wiping out many of development gains of the earlier period. The 1998 Revision of the UN population forecast showed that for the nine African countries with an adult prevalence of HIV of more than 10 percent it was clear that ten years had been lost to the life expectancy figures at birth. Although HIV/AIDS markedly increases mortality, most of these countries have a doubling time of less that a generation, so that they will still experience considerable growth in the next twenty-five years. The population of Zimbabwe for 2015 will be 19 percent lower than it would be without the effects of HIV/AIDS, but nonetheless it will have doubled by 2028.

National population policies

National governments can use a variety of measures to try to influence and control population, but such measures may be relatively unsuccessful where they fail to protect human rights and existing cultural values (see **culture; cultural relativism**). China, for example, attempted to restrict family size by law with its "one child" policy, which also placed sanctions against families that exceeded this norm. On the pro-natalist side, in European and Asian countries where births have fallen below replacement levels, large families are encouraged through social security (see **welfare state**) or through advertising campaigns. Singapore, for example, withdrew its anti-natalist slogan of the 1960s and 1970s: "Stop at Two," and replaced it in the 1980s with "At least two. Better three. Four if you can afford it." Some demographers have described this shift in terms of a second demographic transition oriented more toward the interests of parents than children.

Studies by the Population Bulletin of the United Nations (2000) have focused on the crisis caused by below-replacement fertility and declining numbers of young to replace the active population. One of the major consequences where there is improved life expectancy is the increase in the dependency burden of the aged (see **ageing**). However, similar to concerns about the population explosion, there is a danger that rhetoric and ideology will lead to alarmist statements that do not adequately reflect reality. A statement in 1984 by President Jacques Chirac of France (while Mayor of Paris) illustrates this clearly:

> Two dangers stalk French society: social democratization and a demographic slump ... if you look at Europe and then at other continents the comparison is terrifying. In demographic terms, Europe is vanishing. Twenty years or so from now our countries will be empty and no matter what our technological strength we shall be incapable of putting it to use.

Of course, apart from its startling extremism, this statement ignores the third component of any population scenario – **migration**. **Globalization** and **international migration** allow strategies for countries with perceived under- and over-population.

For the developed world, and most countries that have achieved demographic transition, the problem of a birth rate below replacement levels has produced a crisis linked to nationalistic concepts based on assumptions of ethnic homogeneity. The reality is of course that Europe's population is declining in world terms from the 1920s, when it represented a 25 percent of the world's population, to something like 12 percent in 2000 and a projected 7 percent by 2050 (Demeny, 2003). One of the key issues from a policy point of view is the increased burden of the aged on social insurance systems where there is a declining number of employed contributors to the system (see **pensions**). The effects of globalization place a premium therefore on migration as a potential source of labor, and of children drawn from societies with a higher fertility pattern.

See also: ageing; carrying capacity; demographic transition; demographic trap; fertility; HIV/AIDS (definition and treatment); HIV/AIDS (policy issues); infant and child mortality; international migration; life expectancy; *Limits to Growth* report (1972); Malthusian demography; migration; mortality; overpopulation; population growth rate (PGR); reproductive rights

Further reading

Boserup, E. (1976) "Environment and Technology in Primitive Societies," *Population and Development Review* 2: 21–36.

Demeny, P. and McNicoll, G. (eds) (1998) *Population and Development*, London: Earthscan.

Furedi, F. (1997) *Population and Development: A Critical Introduction*, Cambridge: Polity Press.

Goldscheider, C. (1971) *Population, Modernization and Social Structure*, Boston MA: Little, Brown.

Lutz, W., Prskawetz, A. and Sanderson, W. (eds) (2002) *Population and Environment: Methods of Analysis*, New York: Population Council (published as a supplement to *Population and Development Review*, vol. 28).

Population Bulletin of the United Nations (2000) *Below Replacement Fertility*, New York: United Nations.

Population and Development Review, New York: Population Council (quarterly).

Tiffen, M. and Mortimore, M. (1994) *More People Less Erosion: Environmental Recovery in Kenya*, Chichester: Wiley.

World Bank (1994) *Population and Development: Implications for the World Bank*, *World Development Report 1994*, Washington DC: World Bank.

JOHN A. JACKSON

population growth rate (PGR)

Population growth rate (PGR) is defined as the average annual rate of change of **population** size during a specified period, and is usually expressed as a percentage. PGR is a product of the surplus, or deficit, of births over deaths and the balance of migrants entering and leaving a country. PGR may be positive or negative. For example, if a population at the beginning of a one-year period were 500,000, the birth rate (see **fertility**) was 40, the death rate (see **mortality**) was 15, the total number of migrants entering were 6,000, and the total number leaving were 7,000, then the change in the total number of people in this population would be calculated by the following formula: $(500 \times 40) - (500 \times 15) + 6,000 - 7,000$. In this example, the population grew by 11,500 people during the year. Population growth rate, expressed as a percentage, was 2.3.

See also: fertility; migration; mortality; population

WENDY SHAW

population mobility

Population mobility encompasses all forms of human movement irrespective of distance traveled and time spent away from place of usual residence. It includes all types of longer-term **migration**, both internal and international (see **international migration**), and **circular migration**, but also daily and weekly commuting and recreational movements for **tourism**. Human mobility can be conceptualized as spatial fields known as activity or action spaces that vary by social group and over time. These can be plotted to show the impact of development on the total movement of a **population** of any area. A consideration of mobility is important as it draws attention to those forms of population movement that are so often excluded from studies of migration but which can have profound implications for development, such as short-term movements to market or town that can spread diseases such as HIV/AIDS (see **HIV/AIDS (definition and treatment); HIV/AIDS (policy issues)**) and **malaria**.

See also: circular migration; migration; population

RONALD SKELDON

postcolonialism

The term "postcolonialism" is used to describe an aggregation of critical responses to the historical effects of colonialism (see **colonialism, history of; colonialism, impacts of**) and the persistence of colonial forms of power and knowledge into the present. In exposing colonial discourses and practices, postcolonialists reveal how contemporary global inequalities between rich and poor countries have been, and continue to be, shaped by colonial power relations in multiple ways. Through problematizing, deconstructing and de-centering the supposed universality of Western knowledge, postcolonial perspectives critically engage with, and resist the variety of ways in which the West produces knowledge about other people in other places.

Postcolonialism differs slightly to general debates about colonialism or **decolonization** because it focuses on the implicit and discursive elements of power, whereas the discussion of decolonization, for example, focuses mainly on the formal transfer process at the end of colonialism.

Postcolonialism, however, is a highly diverse and contested term, encompassing different critical approaches from diverse disciplines, including history, geography, cultural studies, literary criticism and, more recently, development studies. Studies variously consider the neglected stories of subaltern, marginalized figures from colonial history; the administration and structure of colonial cities; and forms of representation that circulate through films, novels and works of art from various colonial contexts. Accordingly, postcolonial studies interrogate the hegemonic understandings of space, history, subjectivities and progress that emerged out of colonial projects.

Perhaps most controversial has been the use of the term "post," fueling much debate among postcolonial theorists. For some, the term "post" merely refers to the historical period following the independence of former colonies. For others, however, this is a simplistic periodization, which implies a clear distinction between the "before" of colonialism and the "after" of independence, and conceals the colonial genealogy of contemporary international relations as well as forms of "**neocolonialism**." This emphasizes the discontinuities and obscures the continuities between a colonial past and a postcolonial present. Others suggest that the "post" implies a critical engagement "beyond" colonialism, which signifies changes in power structures but also indicates colonialism's continuing effects.

Postcolonial studies have frequently argued that mainstream development discourse has rarely acknowledged its roots in a colonial past, despite the emergence of the post-war international development industry on the relationships, perceptions and attitudes of empire. Studies demonstrate that contemporary discourses of development in "developing" countries reflect colonial influences. They further challenge Western conceptions articulated within orthodox development, and question the process by which development knowledge is produced and gains legitimacy. For example, the transitions from colonized subject to **aid** recipient, and from colonial administrator to development practitioner, can highlight the ways in which development theory and practice have been shaped and influenced by colonialism.

A discursive analysis of development began in the 1980s contemporaneously with "alternative" approaches and analyses of the language of development (see **postmodernism and postdevelopment**).

This work aims to reveal the many embedded, tenacious strands of colonial forms of knowing and representing. It is exemplified in studies showing how development ideology may valorize particular forms of Western knowledge that maintain the economic and intellectual superiority of the West, and those who focus on processes of professionalization of development knowledge and the institutionalization of development practices.

Frequently, research focuses on historical processes in which colonial rule was legitimized through the construction of various forms of distinction between colonizer and the colonized. Typically, discourses distinguished between people through "race" (see **race and racism**) and **gender**, and colonized people were defined as culturally incapable of self-government or predisposed toward wantonness and irresponsibility. Another common dichotomy is between disorganized "traditional" societies that therefore require "modernization" (see **modernization theory**). Crucially, such research has revealed that these boundaries and distinctions are still played out and reinscribed across development discourse and practice. Although "racial" and gendered assumptions tend to be subtler within development, they are no less pernicious. For example, while gender and development approaches challenge **male bias**, there are still problems with how people in developing countries, and especially women, are represented. Struggles of women are often appropriated and fitted into Western conceptual frameworks. Moreover, the tendency to construct a singular category of "women" to suggest a commonality of oppression does not distinguish between the varied histories and imbalances in power among women. It is also difficult to speak of women's agency and **empowerment** when women in some of the development literature are portrayed solely as victims of patriarchy.

Other postcolonial studies have criticized Eurocentrism (see **ethnocentrism**) evident in development theory, and especially economic modeling, which critics have considered forms of neocolonialism. Dominant approaches to development theory and practice are constructed in the West and implemented in the developing world, with Western policy-makers influencing which projects should be funded and where aid should be spent and withdrawn. Thus, the boundaries between colonizers and the colonized continue to be reinscribed in relationships between development administrators and recipients of aid. These relationships are frequently upheld by dismissing the voices of the individuals whose impoverishment and marginality they seek to address, and portraying them as victims rather than participants and directors of their own development.

One proposed response to dominant versions of development is to undertake a discursive act of decolonization, involving the recovery of lost historical voices of the marginalized and dominated. Subaltern studies has attempted to rescue these voices and has influenced debates in **participatory development**, alternative development and postdevelopment (see **postmodernism and postdevelopment**). Indeed, the role of development "experts" has been challenged by **local knowledge** and grassroots movements (see **grassroots organizations**). However, even these approaches have been criticized on the grounds that they may reinforce the centrality of Western knowledge and expertise by professionalizing and technicalizing the collection of information (see **anti-politics**).

So far, however, it has been easier to view the process of decolonization purely as the subversion of Western forms of representation, than it is to suggest what a decolonized knowledge might actually look like. This lack of critical analysis is partly because those engaged with the practice of development see themselves primarily as practitioners, and therefore presume to have little use of theory. At the same time, emphases on case studies and micro-level studies of social differentiation make each case too unique and complex to permit generalizations. Perhaps most importantly, however, has been the political imperative to distance the international aid industry from the colonial encounter so as to avoid tarnishing "humanitarian" work from the supposed exploitation of the colonial era. Postcolonial studies are still progressing, but their aims are important: to move development studies beyond its complicity with Western knowledge and power, and provide a historical context with which to evaluate the potential of future development strategies.

See also: colonialism, history of; colonialism, impacts of; culture; decolonization; ethnocentricism; marginalization; narratives of development; neocolonialism; Orientalism; power and discourse

Further reading

Crush, J. (1995) (ed.) *Power of Development*, London: Routledge.
Escobar, A. (1995) *Encountering Development: The Making and Unmaking of the Third World*, Princeton: Princeton University Press.
Kothari, U. and Minogue, M. (ed.) (2001) *Critical Perspectives in Development Theory and Practice*, Basingstoke: Macmillan.
Said, E. (1979) *Orientalism*, New York: Vintage.
Williams, P. and Chrisman, L. (eds) (1993) *Colonial Discourse and Post-colonial Theory*, London: Harvester Wheatsheaf.

UMA KOTHARI

post-conflict rehabilitation

Post-conflict rehabilitation refers to the economic, political, and infrastructural acts taken to rebuild societies and economies affected by **war**. The intellectual and institutional foundations of modern development assistance were designed to facilitate rehabilitation and recovery after World War II, particularly in Europe and Japan. The **World Bank** (initially called the International Bank for Reconstruction and Development) was founded to respond to the challenges of post-conflict rehabilitation. The **International Monetary Fund (IMF)** was formed to prevent the financial instability that many saw as having created the conditions within which fascism and political turmoil had flourished. The **Cold War** saw the expansion of the International Financial Institutions and of the **United Nations** into the developing world. In many countries, the finance provided by these organizations was designed to build the capacity of newly independent states, many of which had experienced protracted struggles against colonialism (see **colonialism, history of; colonialism, impacts of**).

The post-World War II **aid** architecture had been largely inspired by the desire to prevent, or recover from conflict. During the Cold War, however, the role of aid in **conflict management** and in post-conflict recovery was not made explicit. Conflict was political, and aid actors sought throughout the 1960s and 1970s to present themselves largely as technocrats concerned with economic policy.

In the late 1980s/early 1990s, the ending of the Cold War provided an opportunity to resolve many of the protracted, proxy conflicts in the developing world. The early 1990s saw a new framework for peace-building emerge that combined **peace-keeping** and support for **governance** and electoral processes with aid. The provision of rehabilitation assistance was seen as important to support political transition, and to provide visible signals to conflict-affected **population**s that there was hope for a return to peace and normality.

There are two key assumptions underlying assistance for post-conflict rehabilitation. The first is that the war is over. The second is that rehabilitation assistance will constitute a bridge between relief and development aid. Both assumptions have proved problematic in practice. Some countries – such as Mozambique in the 1990s – have achieved definitive political settlements to conflict. More commonly, however, **post-conflict violence** persists, and rehabilitation is attempted increasingly quickly after hostilities. Indeed, the **United Nations High Commissioner for Refugees (UNHCR)**'s approach to refugee reintegration (see **refugees**) no longer waits until a final cessation of hostilities.

During the 1990s there was a revival of the idea of the relief-development continuum, or that well managed relief would contribute to long-term development, and that well managed development would contribute to disaster prevention. Initially applied with regard to **natural disasters**, the same model was also evoked in the context of conflict-related crises. However, there remain significant problems in terms of designing aid instruments that match the seamlessness promised by most conceptual models.

These problems derive from the very different objectives of relief and development aid. The former is designed to be a short-term palliative, and is often delivered outside of state structures (see **state and state reform**) in order to avoid reinforcing existing political structures. Development aid is concerned to achieve long-term solutions, and remains premised on the existence of a strong and recognized state to legitimize and manage it. Rehabilitation assistance occupies a strange "gray zone." It has a strong resemblance to relief aid in that it is highly projectized, decentralized and often delivered through private providers (including international **non-governmental organizations (NGOs)**). However, it promises to contribute to long-term development objectives, including those of **sustainable development** and **capacity building**. While there is widespread consensus that there remain important disconnects in the instrumentation available to promote post-conflict recovery, efforts to overcome them have frequently foundered. This is largely because conventional development assistance actors cannot be fully engaged unless and until an internationally recognized, central government is in place, and there is a minimum degree of **security**.

International trust funds, United Nations transitional authorities and administrations, such as those in Cambodia, East Timor and Kosovo, have provided some important lessons in terms of how a multilateral framework can be put in place to provide an alternative basis for decision-making in the absence of state structures. The war on Iraq in 2003, which left the UK and the US governments as the occupying powers, has seen a new form of integrated, bilateral management of post-conflict rehabilitation issues, with the establishment of the Office for Reconstruction and Humanitarian Assistance, under the authority of the US Department of Defense. This may prove to be a significant innovation for the future.

See also: aid; capacity building; complex emergencies; conflict management; emergency assistance; humanitarianism; Médecins Sans Frontières (MSF); peacekeeping; post-conflict violence; Red Cross and Red Crescent; right of intervention; war

Further reading

Development Assistance Committee (2000) DAC *Guidelines on Conflict, Peace and Development Cooperation*, Paris: OECD.

Kreimer, A., Eriksson, J., Muscat, R., Arnold, M. and Scott, C. (1998) *The World Bank's Experience with Post-conflict Reconstruction*, Washington DC: IBRD.

Macrae, J. (2001) *Aiding Recovery?: The Crisis of Aid in Chronic Political Emergencies*, London and New York: Zed.

JOANNA MACRAE

post-conflict violence

Post-conflict violence refers to low-level spasmodic **violence** following a larger-scale episode of **war** that has otherwise ended. Post-conflict violence may range from latent violence suffered by civilian populations by the accidental detonation of **landmines**; the triggering of other unexploded ordnance; the health and environmental effects of wartime chemical and biological residues, and genetic defects in subsequent generations. It may also include inter-personal violence such as looting, burglary, rape, murder, assault and **torture**; to the remnants of the conflict manifest in "guerrilla" activity resisting the war victor's occupation of, or activity in, disputed territories and communities. The type and level of post-conflict violence is likely to be a function of the kind of conflict, the **conflict management** techniques applied, the nature of the ceasefire or peace agreement, and the implementation of post-war reconstruction and development strategies.

Because post-conflict violence is currently under-theorized, it is difficult to identify precisely who commits it and why. However, several possibilities are worth considering. First, there are groups who are, or at least perceive themselves to be, victims of violence perpetrated during the main conflict who believe they did not avenge that violence before hostilities ceased, and are thus driven to revenge attacks. This motivation is especially likely in cases of extreme violence such as **ethnic cleansing** and **genocide**. Alternatively, residual extreme militant groups may have a vested interest in the continuation of hostilities, perhaps for resource control in informal economies or to keep their political interests

on the post-conflict agenda. Similarly, such groups may wish to undermine the mainstream political peace process because they feel marginalized by it, or that they will lose their legitimacy if the conflict they coalesce around dissolves. A clear example of this dilemma is the "Real IRA" extremist splinter group in Northern Ireland, who just four months after the historic 1998 Good Friday peace agreement committed the worst single incident of the thirty-year "troubles" with its Omagh car bombing. Moreover, in longstanding conflicts such as in Northern Ireland – or increasingly in **weak states** torn by civil war – a whole generation has grown up knowing nothing but conflict, and the end of hostilities may represent a time of uncertainty, with little apparent prospect for alternative **employment**, **education** and re-training. The possibility for developing non-conflict-related individual and group identities might be minimal.

Therefore, post-conflict violence has the potential, in the delicate transition period from full-scale war to an enduring peace, to re-ignite the conflict. Thus, it is a major issue for **post-conflict rehabilitation** and development strategies that face the pragmatic difficulties of transforming a high-level political peace process into an actual increase in security and stability among the warring communities. As a consequence, **peace-keeping** and civilian police forces are increasingly integrated into development programs to control post-conflict violence in order to provide (relatively) safe and stable conditions amenable to rehabilitation. From a development perspective, post-conflict violence in Afghanistan and Iraq, 2002–3 onwards, will provide important insights on the implications of the phenomena for development strategies after "pre-emptive" wars.

See also: complex emergencies; conflict management; Geneva Conventions; landmines; peace-keeping; post-conflict rehabilitation; violence; war

Further reading

du Toit, P. (2001) *South Africa's Brittle Peace: The Problem of Post-settlement Violence*, Basingstoke: Macmillan.

McIlwaine, C. with Moser, C. (2000) *Urban Poor Perceptions of Violence and Exclusion in Colombia*, Washington DC: World Bank.

PETER MAYELL

postmodernism and postdevelopment

Postmodernism and postdevelment are two recent trends in development thinking that emphasize the diversity of experiences and perceptions of development agendas; and the dangers of insisting upon universalist definitions of social progress within international development. Postmodernism is the philosophical and political movement that emerged during the late twentieth century that criticized modernization (see **modernization theory**) for being ethnocentric (see **ethnocentrism**) and invasive because it denies the diversity and plurality of perspectives between individuals, cultures or societies. Postdevelopment – or anti-development criticisms – focuses on the invasive and restrictive aspects of "development" as exercized in orthodox terms of modernization, **aid** and **economic growth** because it may suppress pre- and co-existing forms of **culture** and social organization that may have diverse benefits for different societies.

Approaches to postdevelopment

Development is one of those key concepts engrained within common life, yet one which carries much controversy and potential conflict. Broadly construed, development refers to an immanent process and a set of intentions that are distinctively modern, but its meanings have been unstable, and always wrapped up with the specific historical problems it was being used to discuss. Critical and culturally informed work on development during the 1980s and thereafter turned on seeing the development project – **economic growth**, social modernization, scientific advancement, enlightened secular progress – as a form of modernity (Escobar, 1995). For what has now become the "postdevelopment" school (see Rahnema, 1997), development was moreover a *failed* modernity of catastrophic

proportions. These problems are distinctively Western and modern. Development "rehearses, in a virtually unchanged form," says Gupta (1998:36) "the chief premises of the self-representation of modernity": progress, science, reason, universal history (see **ethnocentrism; science and technology**). This self-representation of modernity by the West via the "Other" (i.e. people or things seen to be different from the mainstream – see **Orientalism**) travels in a variety of colonial and post-colonial modalities, and in so doing becomes "an inescapable feature of everyday life" (*ibid.*: 37) in the developing world. *Postdevelopment* is at once a profound rejection of conventional development as an expression of modernity, and simultaneously seeks to expose its flaws. Most commonly, post-developmentism has deployed the theoretical tools of *poststructuralism* – or debates that highlight the importance of discourse, history and power to construct meaning – to lay the groundwork for a *postmodern* alternative (see **power and discourse**).

To simplify a complex intellectual landscape, one can identify three broad genealogical threads that link postdevelopment and postmodernism. The first is a form of "new historicism" in the study of development, attempting, as Fred Cooper and Randall Packard (1997) put it in their foundational text, to locate the concept of development in: "historical conjunctures ... understood in relation to intellectual trends, shifts in global economic structures, political exigencies and institutional dynamics" (1997:29). An important early effort in this regard was the work of Arndt (1987), who in a text unencumbered by discourse or high theory, charted the shifting intellectual trends and the circulation of ideas and people from the 1950s to the neo-liberal counter-revolution three decades later. One of Arndt's insights, subsequently elaborated, was that development as a shifting set of knowledges and practices focused on the developing Other, spoke as much to the realities of the advanced capitalist states and their internal problems as to the realities of the poorest 40 percent. The link between the 1968 generation and the shift from development as growth to development as **basic needs** provision is an obvious case in point (see **growth versus holism**). None other than Richard Jolly, one of its key architects, explicitly attributed this shift to the "growing questioning of Western consumer-urban-industrial models" (cited in Arndt, 1987:108). Counter-economic discourse questioning the Holy Grail of **gross national product (GNP)** was derivative of the social crisis of the North Atlantic economies. Indian economist Deepak Lal was not far from the mark when he noted that the concern with the social, with equity and redistribution reflected the failures of the American dream and of the inability to solve the race (see **race and racism**) and **inequality** problem in the USA in particular. It is no accident that Robert McNamara – the president of the **World Bank** group from 1968 to 1981 – initially discussed US **poverty** in his first speech that concerned the concept of the poorest 40 percent. The meanings of development and its political semiotics are seen to be profoundly dialectical; ideas and people travel between North and South, and among and between sites of practice and knowledge production.

A second line of thinking explicitly engages with institutional politics, self-reflexivity and with the poststructural insight that development is a set of discursive practices and representations. Development practices can be construed as forms of what Michel Foucault (2000) called "**governmentality**," the conduct of conduct, to grasp how "the possible field of action of others" is structured, how the triad of sovereignty, discipline and government through a variety of techniques and micro-politics of power (from the map, to the national statistics, to forms of surveillance) accomplish stable rule through governable subjects (Moore, 1999). Development came to be seen as "everyday forms of state formation." Some of the path-breaking work, by Mitchell (2002), posed the business and apparatuses of development as they emerged in the post-1945 period through the **United Nations** system, foreign **aid**, and national development ministries as "regimes of truth" and as a power-knowledge nexus, but it was weak empirically, and shallow in its grasp of the development institutions themselves. A raft of new scholarship – prompted by Ferguson's (1990) excellent ethnographic account of a development project in Lesotho – has begun to explore development in a much more grounded institutional and textual way, posing hard questions about how development ideas are institutionalized and how

particular development interventions may generate conflict as much as consent; and it has begun to examine the internal dynamics and complexities of large, internally differentiated organizations (see **anti-politics; governmentality**). This tack takes the *social construction* of knowledge (by whom, which what materials, with what authority, with what effects), and the relations between knowledge and institutional practice very seriously, and in so doing can identify struggles and spaces in which important changes can be and are made.

The third thread is postmodern, and traces its lineage to the work in the 1960s of Ivan Illich (1971), and earlier to some of the populist and civic theory associated with Prudhon, the Owenite socialists and others. Associated with a number of public intellectuals and activists largely but not wholly from developing countries, it is a variegated **community** that has marched under the banner of "postdevelopment." The intellectual field which constitutes these radical critiques of development – one thinks of the work of Arturo Escobar, Gustavo Esteva, and Wolfgang Sachs and the *Post Development Reader* (Rahnema, 1997) as its compendium – is replete with the language of crisis, failure, apocalypse and renewal, and most especially of subaltern insurgencies which are purportedly the markers of new histories, social structures and political subjectivities (Corbridge, 1998). The Delhi Center for Developing Societies – to invoke one such important and visible cluster of erstwhile anti-development Jacobins – includes among its pantheon the likes of Ashis Nandy, Rajni Kothari and Shiv Visvanathan, who in their own way represent a veritable heteroglossia of alternative voices from the South, encompassing a massive swath of intellectual and political territory on which there is often precious little agreement.

Seeking diversity, opposing universality

There is perhaps questionable unity to these critiques – drawn variously from post-Marxism, ecofeminism, narrative analysis, poststructuralism, postcolonial theory (see **postcolonialism**), and postmodernism – by emphasizing their confluences around development as a flawed, in some quarters a catastrophically failed, modernist project. Much, but by no means all, of this critique draws sustenance from the idea of the third leg of modernity – the "dark side" of modernity and the Enlightenment which produced the new human sciences and the disciplines – as much as by the Marxian leg of capitalist exploitation and the Weberian (and Habermasian) leg of the colonization of the lifeworld by monetization, rationalization, calculation and bureaucratization. This tale of disenchantment carries much of the tenor, and timbre of earlier critiques of development – most vividly of the 1960s but also of the 1890s and earlier, as Michael Cowen and Robert Shenton (1996) have admirably demonstrated in *Doctrines of Development* – readily apportioning blame to the transnational behemoths (corporate and multilateral) of global **capitalism** (see **transnational corporations (TNCs)**). Running across this body of work is the notion of development as an essentially Western doctrine whose normalizing assumptions must be rejected: "it [development] is the problem not the solution" (Rist, 1997). The sacred cows – for Esteva and Prakash (1998) they are "the myth of global thinking," "the myth of the universality of **human rights**," and "the myth of the individual self" – must be substituted by what two of the postdevelopment field's key voices have called "grassroots postmodernism" (see **grassroots development**).

Arturo Ecobar's book *Encountering Development* (1995) is the most developed account of thinking about the development industry in grand post-structural terms, offering a vision of subaltern, and indigenous social movements as vehicles for other ways of doing politics (non-party, non-mass, autopoetic and self-organizing) and doing "post-development" (decentralized, **community**-based, participatory, indigenous and autonomous). Interestingly, this postdevelopment movement met up with and cross-fertilized with a largely Western academic development community energized by what was dubbed the "impasse in development" debate of the 1980s and 1990s (Booth, 1994). In effect this was a debate within the walls of Marxist development theory between its "neo" and "structural" schools over the extent to which developing-world socialism suffered from many of the trappings of industrial capitalism (and many others unique to it!), and a theory captured by economic essentialism, class reductionism, and

teleological thinking (see **Marxism**). One can argue whether this characterization of Marxist development theory is plausible or indeed an adequate account of Marxism itself in its panoply of guises. But the impasse debate spawned important new intersections between postcolonial and post-Marxist thinking, providing fertile ground on which development could be refigured by a careful reading or Ranjahit Guha or Gyatri Spivak or Edward Said (see Gupta, 1998). There is little theoretical coherence in the "impasse work" – actor-network approaches, a focus on identity politics and the cultural construction of class, a shift to "responsible politics" (Booth, 1994) – but Corbridge is right to emphasize that it, like the postdevelopment work, reinforced the need to see "the ways in which the West represents its non-Western others" (1998:95) and forces us to ask "what is development? Who says that is what it is? Who aims to direct it and for whom" (*ibid.*). Diversity became the new watchword, but this carried its own burdens (who wants a few more neo-fascist development movements in the name of letting a thousand flowers bloom?) At the same time the postcolonialists' proper emphasis on writing history differently – signaling as Stuart Hall says (1996:248) the "proliferation of histories and temporalities, the intrusion of difference and specificity into generalizing Eurocentric post-Enlightenment grand narratives" (see **narratives of development**) – in turn often mistook the word for the world, populist incantation for "new politics," and opted for a heavy dose of wishful thinking ("in the heartlands of the West," said David Slater, "modernity is in question [A]nd the fixed horizons for development and progress [are melting away]"! (1993:106).

To employ Arturo Escobar's own language in representing 1950s development economics, what sort of "world as a picture" is contained within the scopic regime of alternatives to development? On the one hand there is a certain sense of 1960s *déjà vu*. A number of accounts of globalized political economy in this work – in spite of its aversion to metanarratives and totalizing history – rests clumsily on a blunt, undifferentiated account of world capitalism, in which institutions like the World Bank have untrammeled hegemonic power, and the "Third World" appears as a monolithic, caricatured and often essentialized realm of, at worst, normalized subjects and at best hybridized, subaltern emancipatory potential. Much of the postdevelopment work does this by starting with a rather caricatured sense of the Enlightenment or modernist self-representation and then charting one of its dimensions through the nineteenth- and twentieth-century trajectory of development (see Schech and Haggis, 2000:5). For Esteva this is individualism, for Alvarez science, for Shanin progress, for Rist reason, for Kothari state rationality (see their contributions in Rahnema, 1997). For some, like Escobar (1995), this post-Enlightenment legacy congeals in a foundational moment to produce the "invention" of development in President Truman's famous inaugural address of 1949 (see **Truman's Bold New Program (1949)**). The development industry then commences, through its national accounts, data and statistical inventories and forms of **governmentality**, to produce a developing-world subject. There is something very clunky about all of these narratives. Even Gupta's (1998) sophisticated account is wide of the mark: are, as he says, the tropes of modernity in development "rehearsed unchanged"? Is the developing world past always historically "depoliticized" in development discourse? (see **anti-politics; narratives of development**).

What *is* different from the 1960s crisis of development in the postmodern critique is the degree to which the state (see **state and state reform**) as a necessary and appropriate vehicle for national aspirations, and the universalistic (and anti-imperialistic) claims for liberation are no longer axiomatic and taken for granted. Locality, culture, authenticity are the forms of identification which stand in opposition to states, and the very fictions of the nation-state and nationalism are supplanted by what Lehmann calls "multi-national populist subcultures" in search of cultural difference ["cultural difference is at the root of postdevelopment" as Escobar says]. One might say that the practical and strategic content of this vision is rooted firmly in the soil of **civil society** rather than in the state or market. But it is **civil society** of a particular sort: of **grassroots organizations**, of subaltern knowledge, of cultural economics, of hybrid autopoetic politics, of the defense of the local, of cybercultural

post-humanism. Much less is said about the civil society in its more unpleasant forms.

Criticisms of postdevelopment

One can make a number of critical observations about the intersection of postmodernism and postdevelopment. First, the Enlightenment itself has all of its contradictions, complexities and tensions *read out* of the script of postdevelopment. Second, modernity as a contradictory experience is not *read into* the shifting meanings of development. And third, there is a key difference between development as an immanent process and as a series of intentions is typically occluded. It is for this reason that *Doctrines of Development* (1996) is such an important intervention. Cowen and Shenton precisely show how in the course of the late eighteenth and nineteenth centuries an immanent conception becomes intentional development, something to be ordered to "ameliorate the disordered fruits of progress" (1996:7). Development as a state project in Europe was a response to the creative destruction of industrial capitalism. How it travels – as **trusteeship** in the colonial period, or as **structural adjustment** in our own epoch – should not obscure this ur-history which is not readily captured in a claim that developmentalism is essentialist, homogenizing and evolutionary (Gupta, 1998:33). Who would make this alloyed claim of the UNDP *Human Development Report*? Perhaps more than anything this UN agency has, through the work of Sen (1999) on capabilities and freedom (see **capability approach**), begun to radically and philosophically rethink the idea of development as economy, and in a way which surely belies Gupta's homilies (see **functionings; freedom versus choice**). Fourth is the curious, and perhaps appropriately ironic, extent to which a postmodern or poststructural sensibility is attached to claims and critiques of extraordinary totalizing power, certainty and rectitude (replete with its own essentialisms, its own magisterial claims, and its own antipathy to forms of universalistic liberal rights upon which its own position is typically predicated) – development, as Escobar (1995:10) has it, is "a historically *singular* experience." Fifth, is the extent to which the unalloyed celebration of popular energies of grassroots movements is not subject to the sort of hypercritical discourse analysis which might permit an understanding of their achievements, their political strategies, the limits of their horizons and vision. How there is a curious confluence between elements of the neo-liberal counter-revolution (the **World Bank**'s account, for example, of Africa's postcolonial modernization failure, its anti-statism and the need to harness the energies of "the people" – see **neo-liberalism**) and the uncritical celebrations (and often naive acceptance) of postdevelopment's **new social movements** and of civil society itself. How the important critique of economic reduction and class determinism (the Marxian master narrative) – and it should be added the deconstruction of the free market myopia (the Smithian master narrative) – has produced, to quote Stuart Hall, (1996:258) not alternative ways of thinking about economic questions, but instead "a massive, gigantic and eloquent disavowal."

In this sense, some of this work has curiously not engaged sufficiently with the idea of development as modernity. The creative destruction of capitalist development has, as Marshall Berman (1980) notes in *All That is Solid Melts into Air*, typically produced the experience of, and the reactions to, the solid melting into air. Modernity *contains* the tragedy of underdevelopment: development and its alternatives are dialectically organized oppositions within the history of modernity. This is not to fold the current antipathy to development simply into the grand, master narrative of modernity, but to observe that there is a danger of not learning from history, of losing touch with the roots of our own modernity, of not recognizing that modernity in any case cannot be unproblematically located in the West, and of not seeing development and its alternatives as oppositions that contain the other. It is perhaps a sign of our times that any discussion of reimagining development or development alternatives in current times begins with the word, with language and with discourse. And from there, it is a very short step to the "idea" of poverty, to the "invention" and social construction of development.

See also: anti-politics; civil society; ethnocentricism; governmentality; grassroots activism; grassroots development; modernization theory; narratives of development; Orientalism; postcolonialism; power and discourse; weapons of the weak

Further reading

Arndt, W. (1987) *Economic Development*, Chicago: University of Chicago Press.

Berman, M. (1980) *All That Is Solid Melts into Air*, New York: Vantage.

Booth, D. (ed.) (1994) *Rethinking Social Development*, London: Methuen.

Corbridge, S. (1998) "Beneath the Pavement Only Soil," *Journal of Development Studies* 24: 138–48.

Cowen, M. and Shenton, R. (1996) *Doctrines of Development*, London: Routledge.

Escobar, A. (1995) *Encountering Development: The Making and Unmaking of Development*, Princeton: Princeton University Press.

Ferguson, J. (1990) *The Anti Politics Machine*, Cambridge: Cambridge University Press.

Foucault, M. (2000) *Power*, vol. 3, New York: New Press.

Gupta, A. (1998) *Postmodern Development*, Durham NC: Duke University Press.

Hall, S. (1996) "When Was the Postcolonial?" pp. 242–60 in Chambers, I. and Curtis, L. (eds) *The Post Colonial Question*, London: Routledge.

Illich, I. (1971) *Celebration of Awareness*, London: Boyer.

Lehmann, D. (1997) "An Opportunity Lost," *Journal of Development Studies* 33:4 568–78.

Mitchell, T. (2002) *The Rule of Experts*, Berkeley: University of California Press.

Moore, D. (1999) "Subaltern Struggles and the Politics of Place," *Cultural Anthropology* 13:1 34–67.

Packard, R. and Cooper, F. (eds) (1997) *International Development and the Social Sciences*, Berkeley: University of California Press.

Prakash, M. and Esteva, G. (1998) *Grassroots Postmodernism*, London: Zed.

Rahnema, M. (ed.) (1997) *The Postdevelopment Reader*, London: Zed.

Rist, G. (1997) *The History of Development*, London: Zed.

Schech, S. and Haggis, J. (2000) *Culture and Development*, Oxford: Blackwell.

Sen, A. (1999) *Development as Freedom*, Oxford: Oxfrod University Press.

Slater, D. (1993) "The Political Meanings of Development," pp. 93–112 in Schurmann, F. (ed.) *Beyond the Impasse*, London: Zed.

MICHAEL WATTS

postsocialism

Postsocialism is a concept applied to the reforms and transformations implemented and experienced in the former socialist states (the Soviet Union, its central European satellites, China, Vietnam, Cuba, etc.) since the collapse of socialism in Eastern and Central Europe (ECE) in 1989, the end of the Soviet Union in 1991 and the consequent conclusion of the **Cold War**. In its most basic meaning, postsocialism is simply a descriptor of everything that has come after socialism, often connected to the processes of marketization (see **commercialization**) and democratization (see **democracy; civil society**). But from the latter half of the 1990s, there has been more debate concerning the validity of the concept, its relationship to "transition," its longevity, and the possibility of a postsocialist theory. Key issues within this growing debate have focused on questioning the linearity and distinctiveness of postsocialist experiences, exploring the complexities of postsocialism, and making connections to other changes elsewhere in the world.

Postsocialism is an inherently multidisciplinary concern and has engaged the interests of sociology, economics, political science, anthropology, cultural studies, management and business studies, and geography, amongst others. It is, however, not only something which is studied, but also practiced and experienced. It is constructed as much by the populations of the region as it is by academics, politicians and other actors (both within and beyond the region). Postsocialism rests on an understanding that it is still worth studying the states of the former Soviet bloc together because their common socialist histories fundamentally structure contemporary economic, political, social and cultural processes; it also therefore implies that a knowledge and understanding of actually-existing socialism is important. Postsocialism is often used interchangeably with postcommunism. Since few of the states under discussion claimed to have achieved communism, many argue that postsocialism is the most appropriate term; yet within the region itself postcommunism seems to be in more common usage, reflecting the importance of the rejection of the leading role of the Communist Party (in its various incarnations) in contemporary transformations. In the former Soviet Union, "post-Soviet" is often used as a descriptor, occasionally employed in other states to indicate the importance of the so-called "double rejection" of both socialism and external Soviet domination.

Debates over the meaning of postsocialism have been caught up in broader debates over the conceptualization of transformation in Eastern and Central Europe and the former Soviet Union. The early 1990s were epitomized by a simplistic notion of postsocialism, which saw these regions on a straightforward path from socialism to **capitalism**, a path that was seen to be linear, brief and singular; hence the literature was dominated by talk of a transition. Much early work focused on the building of markets and **democracy**, and the implementation of the so-called "four pillars" of privatization, liberalization (see **privatization and liberalization**), stabilization and internationalization, often through the construction of models of transition (see also **shock therapy**). At this time, the primary, though not exclusive, emphasis tended to be on researching formal practices, often at the institutional scale, and research questions were often validated by their contribution to elaborating the **Washington consensus** and **neo-liberalism**.

In contrast to this linear expectation of change, alternative explanations or approaches to postsocialist change developed at the same time. For example, Stark (1992) recognized the multiplicity of processes of transformation both across the region, and within different "domains." Across the region, different paces and processes of transformation indicated the (re)emergence of divisions between, for example Central Europe, the Balkans and the former Soviet states. Within countries, clear urban-rural and east-west distinctions developed, or were exacerbated, reflecting structural legacies and uneven infrastructures. At every scale, the processes of transformation were seen to be geographically uneven, constituted through a multitude of different spatial formations (historical, cultural, physical, etc.) and contributing to the remaking, further differentiation and frequent polarization of the region's geographies. Thematically, the focus of postsocialist studies was broadened from formal **institutions** of markets and democracy to include a whole range of formal and informal institutions and practices, from **labor**

markets to **nationalism**, and from **foreign direct investment** to **media**. The broadening of focus accompanied a methodological shift toward more local and often ethnographic research, and discursive studies of representation and power in postsocialism (see **power and discourse**). More attention was paid to the contradictory natures, and complexity of postsocialism. The "transition" has been messier and more prolonged than early commentators suggested, and a growing number of researchers now characterize postsocialism as fragmented and meandering, with its lived experiences structured, amongst other things, by **gender**, race (see **race and racism**), ethnicity (see **ethnicity/identity**), sexuality (see **sexualities**), age and class.

The complexity of postsocialism, in a number of important cases, is reinforced by the wars that took place since the 1990s in parts of Central Asia, the Caucasus and the Balkans. **War** is just one of the experiences which have countered the optimism of early accounts of postsocialism. Studies of postsocialism at the micro-scale have frequently indicated processes of destruction of **livelihoods**, rather than the common image of postsocialism as a period of "creative destruction" based on removing the old political and economic barriers. Another image of postsocialism leading to democratic **civil society** has also been countered by the continued existence of powerful **elites** – commonly individuals who were linked to the old communist parties – still in influence in business and local government. Postsocialism, then, has been increasingly identified with rising **unemployment** and **poverty**, **social exclusion** and emerging **health** crises. Such social crises and the widespread, but perhaps low-level, ethnic and economic conflicts which have arisen during and been exacerbated by transformation point to a wider experience of **violence** in postsocialism. In some regions, postsocialism has been characterized less by "progress" than by a reversal in development. Nevertheless, research at the local level has also pointed to the prevalence and importance of affirmative stories that show the positive construction of alternatives to mainstream market conditions.

Much postsocialist research, therefore, has sought to complicate the meaning of "transformation."

Other research, however, criticizes the whole concept of postsocialism, arguing that it embodies a triumphalist account of capitalism's victory over socialism, feeding Fukuyama's **end of history** debates. This approach may be criticized because it shifts analysis away from what is meant by socialism, and leaves orthodox notions of capitalism unchallenged. Researchers who study "transformations" argue that recognizing the plurality of postsocialisms allows us to engage in the study of comparative – or alternative – forms of capitalism. These debates echo earlier critiques of **modernization theory** because they question the linearity and unquestioned authority of capitalist progress.

In the early days of postsocialist research following 1989, there was a tendency to view processes of change as unique, largely because there were no historical precedents of social, economic and political transformation on such a large scale. At that time, the study of postsocialism was largely an extension of Sovietology, which tended to view the Soviet Union and, to a lesser extent, East Central Europe, as "special," and studied the region in isolation from developments across the social sciences and in other world regions. Since the mid-1990s however, in part as old style Sovietologists were joined in the field by researchers with different disciplinary backgrounds, studies of postsocialism have emphasized connections to broader theories of social (political, economic, cultural and spatial) change. Thus postsocialism has been connected with post-authoritarian transitions in Latin America and Asia (see **authoritarianism**), with **globalization** and economic restructuring in the developed West and with "development" and **structural adjustment**. Researchers have studied, for example, the common role of **international organizations and associations** and **transnational corporations (TNCs)** in transformations throughout the world as all were structured by the Washington consensus. There is a need to see postsocialism within the contexts of, and in parallel to, social change across the world.

The call to see postsocialism globally is also linked to a broader usage of the term to denote a change in attitude or the end of an epoch. Thus, people talk about postsocialist Cuba and China, despite their ongoing commitments to socialism in some form. Similarly, people discuss postsocialist Marxism and postsocialist Europe, for example, which suggests that changes in ECE and the former Soviet Union have impacted in these locations and on our understandings of social change more generally. This wider theorization sees postsocialism connected to the end of the bi-polar politics of the Cold War or changes to the **international economic order** founded on a new geopolitics as well as the economics of the Washington consensus. For some, the end of communism was part of the collapse of the meta-narratives of modernity; in this way postsocialism should be seen as contributing to our understandings of postmodernism, and this echoes through the growing attention to hybridity, discourse and power in postsocialist research (see **postmodernism and postdevelopment**).

Alongside the growing attention paid to change elsewhere, it is increasingly argued that to understand postsocialism, we must also understand the persistent legacies of presocialism, which echo strongly today. This argument reflects a desire to be more rigorous in the interpretation of the past, and to understand policy and practice which increasingly refers to institutions, identities and ideologies that predate socialism.

Indeed, the integration of postsocialism with presocialist analysis has prompted some critics to suggest that the term "postsocialism" be abandoned because it hides deep differences between countries usually referred to as postsocialist. Younger people in the region, for example, are increasingly unwilling to accept the term, seeing it as restrictive and backward-looking. Yet, there are still reasons for using the term. First, the legacies of socialism were not swept away overnight, and ethnographic studies demonstrate that we are only beginning to understand the deep impacts of socialism in every sphere of daily life. Second, despite differences between states, the relative conformity of ideology and policy under socialism was greater than in states we currently describe as "capitalist." Indeed, some scholars have argued that we should develop a form of postsocialist theory to parallel **postcolonialism**. Such a new theory would be expressed by postsocialist intellectuals to harness the experiences, memories, and

voices of those living the transformations in order to theorize alternatives to existing forms of socialism and capitalism (e.g. Burawoy, 2001).

See also: capitalism; Cold War; democracy; market socialism; Marxism; shock therapy; Washington consensus

Further reading

Bradshaw, M. and Stenning, A. (eds) (2003) *East Central Europe and the Former Soviet Union: The Post-Socialist States*, London: Pearson.

Burawoy, M. (2001) "Neoclassical Sociology: From the End of Communism to the End of Classes," *American Journal of Sociology* 106:4 1099–120.

Hann, C. (ed.) (2002) *Postsocialism: Ideals, Ideologies and Practices in Eurasia*, London: Routledge.

Pickles, J. and Smith, A. (eds) (1998) *Theorising Transition: The Political Economy of Post-Communist Transformation*, London: Routledge.

Sakwa, R. (1999) *Postcommunism*, Oxford: Oxford University Press.

Stark, D. (1992) "The Great Transformation? Social Change in Eastern Europe," *Contemporary Sociology* 21:3 299–304.

ALISON STENNING

poverty

Poverty is a complex, multifaceted phenomenon with a diverse range of understandings of the concept. Broadly speaking, poverty is usually referred to in three main, often overlapping, senses: material circumstances, economic conditions, and social relationships. Within each of these categories, however, there are several clusters of meaning.

Material circumstances

(1) *Need*. Poverty can be taken to refer to a lack of material goods or services; poverty consists of deprivation of things that are considered basic or essential, such as **food**, fuel, shelter, **education** or **health** care (see **basic needs**). The kinds of need which people have are disputed: the disputes relate, amongst other things, to the level of need,

how essential certain things are, whether needs are inherent in a person or socially determined. "Absolute versus relative" concepts of poverty (see **absolute versus relative poverty**) both refer, however, to a view of poverty based on need.

(2) *A pattern of deprivation.* Poverty is not only defined in terms of specific needs. People can be temporarily deprived, for example because of **natural disasters**, floods and earthquakes, without being poor. Poverty implies a constellation of deprivations, and duration – poverty is deprivation that is likely to last, and the experience of poverty is cumulative over time (see **chronic poverty**).

(3) *Limited resources.* For some, poverty is understood not in terms of need or deprivation, but of the resources that are necessary to meet needs. Homelessness or hunger can be attributed to a lack of money, rather than to a shortage of **housing** or food (see **food security**).

Economic conditions

(1) *Standard of living.* In the same way as poverty may be defined as a pattern of deprivation rather than as a set of needs, poverty may be thought of in terms of a standard of living rather than a specific limitation of resources. General standards of living are determined by the persistence of certain conditions and consumption over time (see **poverty resources**).

(2) *Inequality.* Many commentators have argued that poverty is attributable to **inequality**, but some have gone further, defining poverty in terms of inequality. Researchers for the **European Union** have argued that poverty has to be understood in terms of the relative economic capacity of a disadvantaged group. Poverty is conceptualized as a form of "economic distance" from the standard of living that is found elsewhere in society.

(3) *Economic position.* People occupy definable economic positions in relation to the structure of ownership, entitlements and **labor markets** (see **property rights; gender and property rights**).

Social relationships

(1) *Social class.* Poverty is identifiable as a social status. Arguments about the "underclass" define poverty in terms of a style and pattern of life.

(2) *Dependency.* Dependency is usually understood, in the literature on poverty, in individual terms rather than the structural terms of **dependency theory**. "The poor" may be identified with those who receive welfare benefits. The usage is unusual in academic writing: it is mainly found in the media in developed countries.

(3) *Exclusion.* Although the concept of exclusion is based on a different social paradigm from the concept of poverty, there is a strong overlap between the two. People are called "excluded" (see **social exclusion**) when they have only a limited connection with social structures, including networks of solidarity and mutual responsibility (see **social capital**), systems of social protection and the labor market. Related definitions of poverty identify poverty with the ability to participate in society. The definition of poverty adopted by the European Union states that "The poor shall be taken as to mean persons, families and groups of persons whose resources (material, cultural and social) are so limited as to exclude them from the minimum acceptable way of life in the Member State in which they live."

(4) *Lack of basic security.* The voluntary organization ATD-4th World has identified poverty strongly with a lack of "basic security," covering issues of social exclusion, lack of **human rights** and **vulnerability** to circumstances.

(5) *Lack of entitlement.* Drèze and Sen (1989), for example, argue that **famines** result not from lack of food, but from lack of entitlement to the food which is being produced (see **food security**).

Finally, poverty has also to be understood as a normative or moral concept. One of the reasons for the difficulty of defining poverty is that it is an evaluative concept: it implies not only that there is serious hardship, but also that something ought to be done about it. (This is one reason why some governments have been anxious to minimize the use of the term in policy discussions).

None of these definitions is exclusive: it is possible for a poor person to experience several of these conditions simultaneously. The scope and range of the definitions emphasize, however, the complexity and diversity of poverty. Although many researchers and writers have attempted to impose specific definitions on the concept, its widespread use means that it is associated with an extensive range of ideas and concerns. The **World Bank** (2000) asked more than 20,000 respondents in twenty-three countries about their understanding and experience of poverty. The responses were classified in ten interlocking dimensions of poverty: precarious **livelihoods**, excluded locations, physical problems (see **disability**), **gender** relations problems in social relationships, lack of **security** (see also **human security**), abuse by those in power, disempowering **institutions**, weak **community** organizations, and limitations on the capabilities (see **capability approach**) of the poor. The range of concerns stretch across most of the clusters of meaning outlined here. The fundamental flaw of any authoritative definition is that it is liable to gloss over or ignore important areas of moral concern.

Poverty in different societies

The argument is sometimes made that poverty in developed countries is unlike poverty in developing countries. "Absolute" poverty (see **absolute versus relative poverty**), which is more often associated with developing countries, refers to a minimum level of subsistence based on the essentials for survival. **Malnutrition**, lack of access to **drinking water** and ill health are paradigmatic. Relative poverty, by contrast, defines poverty in relation to social norms. Studies in developed societies have tended to focus on aspects of social exclusion, inequality, and a different set of tests of need.

There are three separable elements in these debates. The first is a contrast between minimalist and more extensive interpretations of poverty (see **absolute versus relative poverty**). Absolute poverty is often represented as minimal, but it is not necessarily so: the **United Nations**' definition of absolute poverty emphasizes the importance of access to services and education. Second, it is unclear whether needs are defined socially: most commentators agree they must be. Amartya Sen, for example, distinguishes "capabilities" from "commodities or characteristics" (see **capability approach**). "Capabilities" are the needs which everyone has; "commodities" and "characteristics" are the means through which these needs are interpreted or operationalized.

Third is the question of whether poverty is based in material circumstances or social relations. Several definitions of poverty, including those that emphasize economic distance, dependency and social exclusion, depend more on social relationships than on needs and resources. Many of the concerns expressed by people in developing countries relate to personal security (see **human security**), social exclusion and rights (see **human rights; rights-based approaches to development**). If poverty is determined by a pattern of social relationships, it is possible for the experience to be reflected in very different social contexts.

The causes of poverty

As a complex concept, poverty may be attributed to a wide range of factors. Some writers suggest that it is necessary to understand causes in order to be able to prescribe a solution. This is a fallacy: the way into a problem is not necessarily the way out of it. However, an understanding of causes can help to explain why some policies fail. Explanations about the causes of poverty are mainly important for moral reasons: they help to identify who is responsible, and so what kind of action might be taken.

Pathological explanations for poverty explain poverty in terms of the characteristics or behavior of poor people. The main categories are individual and familial explanations.

Individual explanations attribute poverty to the people who experience it: they are poor because of a bad judgment, a lack of capacity or competence, or unlucky decisions. This is one of the dominant paradigms in the USA, where poverty has often been attributed to inappropriate decisions about breeding, moral laxity or personal incompetence (see **culture of poverty**).

Familial explanations attribute poverty to genetic degeneracy, inadequate or abusive parenting and the transmission of values between generations. These propositions have consistently been refuted by longitudinal research in several countries, which has shown that the supposed patterns of transmitted deprivation do not occur.

Structural explanations attribute poverty to the structure of the society or economy in which it occurs. Poverty is represented either as the consequence of the dis-welfares produced through market economies – the casualties of competition and economic adjustment (for example, through **structural adjustment**) – or as a necessary adjunct of structural inequality.

Agency explanations attribute poverty to the failure of responsible actors, principally governments and international organizations, to alleviate it. This pattern of explanation is necessarily secondary – it does not explain why poverty occurs in the first place – but it adds an important qualification to both pathological and structural explanations, blaming the moral responsibility for poverty on inaction.

Responses to poverty

There are three main classes of response to poverty. The first is the relief of poverty, either in response to the circumstances of poor people or as part of a more general system of social protection. Social protection in developed countries is often highly individualized: resources devoted specifically to poor people may be subject to individual tests of income. Income testing is associated with a number of problems, including high administrative costs, inefficient targeting which arises from deterrence and stigmatization, and inequities stemming from the definition of over-precise boundaries. In developing countries, the **World Bank** has argued for more broadly based "indicator targeting" (see **indicators of development; poverty measurement; targeting**), focusing for example on demographic categories or geographic groups.

Second, there is the development of resources, which make it possible for poor people to meet needs. The arguments for the benefit of **economic growth** and personal income are often fundamental, but resources are not simply personal resources such as money: the establishment of a basic infrastructure of water supplies (see **water management**), **sanitation**, education, or health care also act to improve material conditions.

Third, there is prevention – putting people in the situation where the problems of poverty do not occur. **Economic development** and social protection do more than provide resources: they bring

people into a structure of relationships in which they have the ability to protect themselves.

The inter-connected nature of the problems of poverty means that responses to poverty do not have to be gauged precisely to a specific understanding of the circumstances. Alterations in economic position change material circumstances, material circumstances have implications for social relationships, and changing social relationships often lead to changes in economic position. At the same time, responses to specific problems can exacerbate others. Economic development can improve material conditions while exacerbating social inequality; economic restructuring can be associated with a loss of basic security (see **human security**); improved social protection and entitlement is associated with increasing dependency (see **poverty trap**).

See also: absolute versus relative poverty; capability approach; chronic poverty; gender and poverty; health and poverty; human security; indicators of development; inequality; inequality and poverty, world trends; marginalization; participatory poverty assessment (PPA); poverty line; poverty measurement; poverty resources; poverty trap; safety nets against poverty; social exclusion; targeting; vulnerability

Further reading

Dixon, J. and Macarov, D. (eds) (1998) *Poverty: A Persistent Global Reality*, London: Routledge.

Drèze, J. and Sen, A. (1989) *Hunger and Public Action*, Oxford: Oxford University Press.

Gordon, D. and Spicker, P. (eds) (1999) *The International Glossary on Poverty*, London: Zed.

Narayan, D., Chambers, R., Shah, M. and Petesch, P. (2000) *Voices of the Poor: Crying Out for Change*, Washington DC and Oxford: World Bank and Oxford University Press.

UNDP (United Nations Development Programme) (2000) *UNDP Poverty Report 2000: Overcoming Human Poverty*, New York: UNDP. Also at http://www.undp.org/povertyreport/

World Bank (2001) *World Development Report 2000/2001: Attacking Poverty*, Washington DC and Oxford: World Bank and Oxford University

Press. Also at http://www.worldbank.org/poverty/
wdrpoverty/report/index.htm

PAUL SPICKER

poverty line

Poverty lines refer to a threshold of income or
consumption below which people can be said to be
poor (see **poverty; poverty measurement**).
Income is the most usual measure, and poverty
lines need to be distinguished from minimum
income standards. Minimum income standards are
generally set by governments as the basis for
income support; they can be set higher or lower
than poverty lines, depending on government
priorities, and have no necessary relationship to
poverty standards. Poverty lines, by contrast,
depend on a view of the relationship between
income and need: people who have an income
below the poverty threshold are taken to be in
need.

Poverty lines have been defined in three main
ways. First, there are arbitrary lines, used to distinguish groups of people on very low incomes from
the others. The **World Bank**'s line of US$1 per
day is selected solely for convenience; even on this
very low standard, nearly 1,200 million people in
the world are poor. Second, there are lines based
on the prices of "baskets of goods," or budget
standards. This can be done through general
assessments of minimum needs, based either on a
notional minimum cost, or on the actual expenditure that is made by people living at the minimum level. In several countries the basket of goods
focuses mainly or solely on the minimum food
basket: the poverty line introduced in the USA in
the 1960s was based on an assessment of cost of
food, then assuming a ratio between the cost of
food and other household expenses. Third, standards can be drawn relative to other incomes in a
society. The **European Union** commonly measures **poverty** in terms of "economic distance,"
defining people as poor when their income is less
than 50 percent or 60 percent of the median
income. This is a measure of **inequality**: because
the median is set at 50 percent of the population, it
is logically impossible on this definition ever to

identify more than 50 percent of the **population**
as poor.

There are several weaknesses in the use of any
poverty line. Income and consumption are useful
indicators of resources, but they can be misleading:
if, for example, a child earns a minimal income
instead of entering **education**, this can give
the impression of a reduction in household
poverty. Emphasizing financial limitations may
lead to an underestimation of communal facilities,
like **health** care, transport (see **transport policy**)
and water supplies (see **drinking water**).
Equally, poverty lines mainly identify the aspects
of poverty associated with material circumstances
and economic conditions; they offer only an ill-
defined indication of the social relationships
which are central to many people's understanding
of poverty.

See also: participatory poverty assessment (PPA);
poverty; poverty measurement; targeting

Further reading

Lanjouw, J. (1997) *Demystifying Poverty Lines*,
UNDP SEPED Series on Poverty Reduction,
New York: UNDP. http://www.undp.org/
poverty/publications/pov_red/Demystifying_
Poverty_Lines.pdf

Veit-Wilson, J. (1998) *Setting Adequacy Standards:
How Governments Define Minimum Incomes*,
Bristol: Policy Press.

PAUL SPICKER

poverty measurement

Poverty is experienced in diverse ways and is
difficult to measure. Simplistic measurements, such
as defining poverty arbitrarily in terms of simple
and measurable factors like income, may avoid a
multitude of additional factors that underlie
whether individuals have access to rights, resources,
or safety nets (see **safety nets against poverty**) as
well as monetary income (for full definitions, see
poverty). Measurement has to proceed, instead,
through the construction of "indicators," or sign-
posts. Indicators, as the name suggests, point to

issues, mark out directions and help to identify trends. They should not be confused with precise measurement. The distinction in some literature between "direct" and "indirect" measures of poverty is bogus: all measures are to some extent indirect. An alternative or supplement to quantitative indices is to use participatory techniques (see **participatory poverty assessment (PPA); participatory research methods**).

Several countries, including e.g. Brazil and the Philippines, have based estimates of poverty on the assessment of research programs. The main methods of estimation are economic surveys, focusing either on income, resources or consumption, and household surveys, examining aspects of lifestyle. These approaches beg important questions as to whether the conditions they identify are equivalent to poverty. There are four main approaches to the assessment of poverty. (a) Normative approaches, which define a standard of poverty – typically, a household budget – and determine to what extent people meet that standard. (b) Comparative approaches, which define poverty in terms of the differences between the least well off and the rest of society. (c) "Subjective" approaches, which ask people whether they consider themselves poor. (d) "Consensual" approaches, which contrast general public opinion about necessities with the availability of those goods to people on low incomes. (Both "subjective" or "consensual" approaches depend on the view, widely agreed in social science, that social norms are not individual or arbitrary, but are constructed and developed socially, through contact and interchange with other people.)

Income-based measures. The most widely used indicator of poverty is probably income. Initially this is surprising, because income is a very imprecise guide to material circumstances. At the same time, income figures are often available, they lend themselves to quantification, and they are widely understood. They are also strongly associated with other issues that matter, like **nutrition** and **health**. The **World Bank**'s **poverty line** of US$372 per annum sounds exact, but it is entirely arbitrary: it is based on a dollar a day ($31 a month times 12). A poverty line of US$2 a day, another arbitrary standard, defines nearly half the world's **population** as poor.

Poverty lines refer to a threshold of income below which people can be said to be poor. This yields a head-count – a number of people who fall below the poverty threshold. The "poverty gap" is calculated from the poverty line. It refers to the distance below the poverty line which poor people fall. It measures, then, the depth of poverty, not just the numbers of poor people.

The Foster, Greer and Thornbecke (FGT) index is calculated from the poverty gap. It is calculated by taking the sum of an exponential from the poverty gap and dividing the total by the total population. The higher the exponential figure, the more weight is given to those who are furthest below the poverty line. There are several FGT indices, because a range of exponentials can be used.

The Sen index combines the head-count and the poverty gap with an indicator of inequality between poor people, the **Gini index**. Sen's argument for including inequality between poor people is that where redistribution takes place between poor people, this also needs to be taken into account. The IFAD's Integrated Poverty Index is based on the Sen Index, but it also takes into the rate of growth of the income of poor people, and a measure of the international distribution of resources.

All of these indices are vulnerable to similar objections: the dominance of income as the primary measure of poverty, and the difficulties caused by defective information. Small variations in the composition of indices can lead to significant differences in outcomes. It is important to emphasize, however, that the objective is not just to estimate the size of a problem, but the relative impact of interventions: even if the indicators are imprecise, it should be possible to make some judgment on the magnitude and direction of effects. James Foster, one of the designers of the FGT index, has consistently emphasized the importance of using a range of measures, rather than a single measure, to identify the range of problems experienced.

Composite indices. The main alternatives to income-based indicators have been composite indices, drawing on a range of social indicators to identify trends. The best-known example is probably the **United Nations Development Programme (UNDP)**'s Human Poverty Index (HPI) (see **Human Development Index (HDI)**). The HPI takes into account five basic indicators:

1   the percentage of people expected to die before age 40 (see **life expectancy**)
2   the percentage of adults who are illiterate (see **illiteracy**)
3   the percentage of people with access to health services (see **primary health care**)
4   the percentage of people with access to safe water (see **drinking water**)
5   the percentage of children under five who are malnourished (see **malnutrition**)

There are two versions of the HPI. The version given here is HPI-I, for developing countries. HPI-II, for industrialized countries, takes into account the numbers of people expected to die before age 60 rather than age 40.

Composite indices have a number of problems. The weighting of factors is often arbitrary: literacy carries equal weight to malnutrition, for example, only because there is no sensible basis on which to distinguish them. Many of the component indicators are defective: for example, ninety-seven developing countries made no return to the UNDP on what percentage of people do not have access to health care. The missing values are treated, in the calculation of the HPI, as equal to 25 percent.

The rationale for indicator research implies that indicators should be seen as pointers to general trends rather than precise measures. This has led to the practice of presenting indicators either as banks of unprocessed figures, or as indicative profiles, rather than as composites.

See also: Gender-related Development Index (GDI); human development; Human Development Index (HDI); indicators of development; measuring development; participatory poverty assessment (PPA); poverty; poverty line

Further reading

Gordon, D. and Spicker, P. (eds) (1999) *The International Glossary on Poverty*, London: Zed.
Macpherson, S. and Silburn, R. (1998) "The Meaning and Measurement of Poverty," in Dixon, J. and Macarov, D. (eds) *Poverty: A Persistent Global Reality*, London: Routledge.
United Nations Development Programme (UNDP) (1997) *Human Development Report*, Oxford: Oxford University Press.
UNDP SEPED Publication Series on Poverty Reduction, New York: UNDP. http://www.undp.org/poverty/publications/pov_red/

PAUL SPICKER

poverty resources

Poverty resources are the stocks and assets that an individual can draw upon to avoid **poverty**. "Command over resources" refers to the ability of a person to use resources for their welfare. Various approaches are used to understand command over resources. Economic analyses conventionally use three main categories. Wealth is a stock of resources. Income is an inward flow, referring to changes in the stock within a specific time period. Expenditure is an outward flow. The broad category of "command over resources" embraces all of these concepts, as well as other intangible means, including credit, status and influence, which may determine individual welfare.

Wealth is conventionally measured in terms of exchange value. The exchange value of many important commodities, such as clothing, is negligible; conversely, some items (like wedding jewellery) may have considerable exchange value that cannot effectively be realized within the culture where they occur. This means that the conventional concept of wealth has only limited relevance to personal **well-being**. The emphasis on monetary values also leads to an undervaluation of other elements of personal and social welfare. In the discussion of wealth, two further concepts have been used to supplement the focus on tradable commodities. *Human capital* refers to the skills and capacities of individuals, typically introduced through **education** and training. *Social capital* refers to the resources made available through social contact, cooperation and generalized reciprocity, typically in families but equally in neighbourhoods, communities (see **community**) and associations. Discussions of the "resources of poverty" in terms of networks of solidarity and mutual support address the same issues as discussions of social capital.

Income is much more widely used than wealth as an indicator of command over resources. Although on the face of the matter wealth seems more likely to reflect standards of living, it is difficult to identify and measure. Income is more widely used, partly because it is easier to measure, and partly because it is more directly related to patterns of consumption. Income, however, still has important limitations as an indicator of welfare. First, income reflects monetary values, which do not necessarily reflect command over resources or use value. Second, in economies that rely less on the formal mechanisms of monetary exchange, income may not truly reflect standards of living.

Consumption, though sometimes identified directly with expenditure, refers to the use of resources. Consumption is related to a person's command over resources, and it may offer a better indicator of resources over time than income. Consumption can also be difficult to measure, because some commodities (like **food**) may be exhausted, while others (like **housing**) are substantially unaffected by use. Consumption data are often used to determine the position of people in very poor economies, because of the unreliability of conventional economic indicators.

See also: capability approach; food security; indicators of development; measuring development; poverty measurement; safety nets against poverty; welfare economics; welfare state; well-being

Further reading

Dasgupta, P. (1993) *An Inquiry into Well-being and Destitution*, Oxford: Clarendon Press.
Gordon, D. and Spicker, P. (1999) (eds) *The International Glossary on Poverty*, London: Zed.

PAUL SPICKER

poverty trap

The words "poverty trap" often imply that people are "trapped in poverty," but this is not its main use in academic texts. The "poverty trap" refers to a technical problem associated with targeted benefits (see **targeting**). When benefits are focused on the poor, the effect of an improvement in income is to lead to a withdrawal of benefits or services. The effect is to exacerbate the difficulty of escaping from **poverty**. Some authors have consequently described getting out of poverty as similar to getting out of well; if a person with a low income could jump high enough, she or he would slip down again. This is sometimes represented as a disincentive effect (see **incentive structures**), but evidence on this point is unclear; there are stronger concerns about the equity of high marginal tax rates on low earners.

See also: chronic poverty; incentive structures; poverty; targeting

Further reading

Lewis, J. and Piachaud, D. (1992) "Women and Poverty in the Twentieth Century," in Glendinning, C. and Millar, J. (eds) *Women and Poverty in Britain: The 1990s*, Hemel Hempstead: Harvester Wheatsheaf.

PAUL SPICKER

POWER (ELECTRICITY) *see* electrification and power-sector reform; energy policy; renewable energy; nuclear energy

power and discourse

Dynamics of cultural or political power in development have been approached from different theoretical perspectives. The approach that focuses on development as a discourse is influenced by Michel Foucault's work on discourse and power/knowledge. It looks at development as a historically and culturally specific form of rationality that is inseparable from related regimes of practices. Discursive approaches to development have been criticized for depriving social actors of agency and providing a totalizing view of history. Building constructively on these critiques, some contributors to the debate have integrated the notion of discourse in analytical frameworks specifically aimed at understanding how power works in development.

A discursive formation is a historically rooted system of knowledge in which particular statements and practices make sense. A well-known example of this theoretical approach to the study of the phenomenon of development is Arturo Escobar's analysis of development as a historically produced discourse, which entails "specific constructions of the colonial/Third World subject in/through discourse in ways that allow the exercise of power over it" (1995:6). In discursive approaches to the study of development, some confusion is generated by a lack of specification of whether the discourse of development should be seen as singular, or if we should consider a plurality of discourses operating at the same time. Another area of debate focuses on whether discourse implies practices that are more or less imposed, or merely suggested to individuals. The confusion is partly due to variations in the definition and use of the notion of discourse in Foucault's own writings.

Foucault has defined the discursive field as the difference "between what one could say correctly at one period (under the rules of grammar and logic) and what is actually said" (Foucault, 1978:18). This definition seems to work best in grand historical reconstructions of the conditions of possibility of the phenomenon of development. It implies that all practices exist with some underlying regime of rationality that is historically rooted, and which structures knowledge, allowing certain events and patterns of agency, and rendering un-thinkable, un-sayable, and un-doable others. It also questions how social actors can act independently of discourses, which are already present and imposed on them by their culture and society. In this sense, discourse works as a structure external to individual or collective actors, and largely unacknowledged. Actors do not control or produce discourse, but instead discourse should be seen as deeply rooted systems of power that can produce reality (and as such is generally opposed to **actor-oriented approaches to development**). Foucault later went on to develop this theme in his approach to **governmentality**, which sought to express the cumulative impact of state **institutions**, discourse, and political processes that contribute to the expression of power in how states are run.

Studies inspired by this initial understanding of discourse tend to see development as an overarching structure of knowledge, which determines the ways in which development institutions and the actors involved in them are allowed to function and act. They interpret the configurations of power that shape the development field not as outcomes of the struggles of interested parties, but of the structural properties of the discourse of development. Hence, in a classic analysis of development in Lesotho, Ferguson argues that the development apparatus in Lesotho is doing what it does "behind the backs and against the wills of even the most powerful actors" (1990:18); the effects produced by development are the outcomes of "unacknowledged structures" (1990:20); and the "constellations of control" they give rise to are "all the more effective for being subjectless" (1990:19).

This type of discursive interpretation of development, however, has been criticized by authors taking a more actor-oriented perspective, who have argued that too much emphasis on external structures and discourses fails to give a cogent account of human agency; or that discourses should be seen as multivocal and stratified between different actors, rather than monolithic; and that social actors are capable of taking a discriminatory stance to discourse. Indeed, some of Foucault's later work did acknowledge the diversity, agency and pluralism in the formation of discourses.

Contributors to this debate have argued that, in the field of development, different categories of actors are stratified along axes of inequality, and so are the discourses they partake of. Consequently, the discourses of dominant individual and/or institutional actors present themselves as universal points of view, and have effects of a much greater scale than those of marginal or less powerful discourses (see Escobar, 1995; Crush, 1995). It has also been highlighted that a large number of social struggles take place at the level of bargaining and negotiation over the interpretation of discourses. Some authors have tried to identify the types of resources that actors bring to bear on policy processes to make their discourses prevail; while others have highlighted the inadequacies of Foucault's theory of power/knowledge to account for the strategic manipulation of discourses by actors differently positioned within the field of development intervention (see Rossi, 2004). Rather than undermining its usefulness, these numerous adaptations and reflections attest to the fertility of a discursive approach to the study of development.

See also: actor-oriented approaches to development; anti-politics; governmentality; narratives of development; politics

Further reading

Crush, J. (ed.) (1995) *Power of Development*, London: Routledge.

Escobar, A. (1995) *Encountering Development: The Making and Unmaking of the Third World*, Princeton: Princeton University Press.

Ferguson, J. (1990) *The Anti-Politics Machine: "Development," Depoliticization, and Bureaucratic Power in Lesotho*, Minneapolis: University of Minnesota Press.

Foucault, M. (1978) "Politics and the Study of Discourse," *Ideology and Consciousness* 3: 7–26.

Rossi, B. (2004) "Revisiting Foucauldian Approaches: Power Dynamics in Development projects," *Journal of Development Studies* 40:6 1–29.

BENEDETTA ROSSI

PREALC

PREALC (*Programa Regional del Empleo para América Latina y el Caribe*) was set up in Santiago, Chile, in 1969 by the **International Labor Organization (ILO)** as one of three regional offices as part of its World Employment Program (WEP). Other offices covered Africa and Asia. Following the ILO's development of the concept of the **urban informal sector** (UIS) in 1972, PREALC carried out a large number of important empirical studies to investigate this phenomenon, as well as providing theoretical analysis of the concept. This analysis is particularly associated with the work of Dr Víctor Tokman, the Director of PREALC from 1973 to 1988, and from 1991 to December 1993, when the ILO's operations in Latin America were reorganized and PREALC was disbanded. PREALC, by virtue of its long period of interest in informal **employment**, ensured that a large body of reliable data on the UIS in Latin America exists, unlike Africa and Asia, where there was no sustained program of empirical research.

See also: employment; entrepreneurship; International Labor Organization (ILO); micro-enterprises; urban informal sector

Further reading

ILO (1993) *PREALC: 25 Years*, Geneva: ILO.

JIM THOMAS

precautionary principle

The precautionary principle is a principle adopted at the **Earth Summit (1992) (United Nations Conference on Environment and Development)**, and forming the basis of the Community environmental policy of the **European Union**. The "principle of precautionary action" or "precautionary principle" for short is about anticipating (from the German *Vorsorge*, or foresight) and preventing environmental damage. It states that precautionary measures should be adopted when preliminary scientific evaluation indicates that there are reasonable grounds for concern that a new technology, process, activity or chemical may have potentially dangerous effects on the environment and on human, animal or plant health, even though the evidence of these negative effects is insufficient, uncertain or inconclusive compared to quantitative risk assessment. Critics have argued that the precautionary principle is being used as a protectionist measure, that it prevents innovations, and that it is redundant because risk assessment already incorporates scientific uncertainties. Its greatest challenge comes from the WTO (see **World Trade Organization/General Agreement on Tariffs and Trade (WTO/GATT)**) and other organizations such as the **World Bank** and the **International Monetary Fund (IMF)**, which are taking an increasingly important role in defining environmental policies, and which rule that countries that institute environmental protection measures that might inhibit trade can only do so on the basis of a quantitative risk assessment (see **cost-benefit analysis (CBA)**).

See also: Agenda 21; Earth Summit (1992) (United Nations Conference on Environment and Development); environment; science and technology; sustainable development

CLAUDIO O. DELANG

primary health care

Primary health care (PHC) is an approach to health care that seeks to maximize its provision to a wide range of people. It primarily entered debate about development at the 1978 International Conference on Primary Health Care at Alma-Ata, and has since been identified as the strategy for "health for all," indeed the **World Health Organization (WHO)** adopted it as its slogan. At the Alma-Ata conference, PHC was defined as a mixture of curative, preventative and promotive activities of a basic nature that involves many facets of society and the economy, besides aspects of medical care that influence health and welfare (see **health; well-being; welfare economics**). By definition, the concept of PHC is wide ranging and not purely a health activity. It comprises of numerous programs and activities. The 1978 declaration at Alma Ata integrated two main streams of activities and processes: one was the growth and extension of basic health services, and the other dealt with the development of the **community** in relation to **education**, infrastructural initiatives and resources.

Primary Health Care was designed to make basic preventative and curative care universally available at the first level of contact with the health system. With PHC, there is a commitment to equality, which means providing basic services for the whole **population** rather than high-quality specialty care for a few people. PHC therefore embodies the **basic needs** approach with the provision of essential health services with community involvement and participation. Inter-sectoral collaboration is also the key to the success of PHC initiatives, and this entails the combination of health and community development. PHC has thus emerged as the dominant approach to solving health problems only after it was realized that the existing system of health care failed to cater for the majority of the world's population. The international community has therefore espoused PHC as the major hope of solving health problems. The PHC philosophy has increasingly become health care policy especially in developing countries where the focus is on education to prevent or control health problems; promotion of adequate **nutrition** and **food** supply; **drinking water** and basic **sanitation**; maternal and child health care; **vaccination** against major diseases; prevention or treatment of common diseases and injuries and the provision of essential drugs (see **pharmaceuticals**).

PHC may not be the cheap alternative as was envisaged. It may be complex and difficult to achieve in reality, with the lack of collaboration, cooperation, coordination and involvement of all related sectors, especially in transforming or developing economies. Presently, the original Comprehensive PHC (CPHC) program that was espoused, particularly by the WHO, is considered ineffective to achieve health for all and has been replaced recently with a Selective PHC (SPHC) approach due to the problems of bottlenecks, shortage of finance and personnel. The SPHC approach reduces the scope of health services to those that are cost effective and which are required urgently. For example, in the 1980s, the **United Nations Children's Fund (UNICEF)** adopted the so-called GOBI approach (Growth monitoring and promotion – Oral rehydration therapy – Breast feeding – Immunization) as one means of SPHC. SPHC, however, does not confront the many basic health problems of communities (see **community**), and has been widely criticized for overlooking important social, political and rights-based approaches to health care (see **rights-based approaches to development; United Nations Children's Fund (UNICEF); World Health Organization (WHO)**).

See also: drinking water; gender and communicable disease; health; health and poverty; United Nations Children's Fund (UNICEF); vaccination; World Health Organization (WHO)

Further reading

Bloom, G. (1998) "Primary Health Care Meets the Market in China and Vietnam," *Health Policy* 44:3 233–52.

Koivusalo, M. and Ollila, E. (1997) *Making a Healthy World: Agencies, Actors and Policies in International Health*, London: Zed.

VADI MOODLEY

primitive accumulation

Primitive accumulation is Karl Marx's concept for the process that anticipates and subsidizes the establishment of capitalist social relations. Conceptually, this process involves the separation of producers from their means of subsistence, as the crucial step in creation of the wage-labor relation. Historically, this process takes a variety of forms. Illustrating the concept in the final section of *Capital*, Volume I, Marx refers to the classical episode of de-peasantization in England, as capitalist **agriculture** took hold, fueled by new property laws and a growing army of agricultural laborers. The world-historical significance of primitive accumulation lay in the accompanying role of merchants in bankrolling mercantilist colonial ventures, where state-sponsored (see **state and state reform**) commercial expansion nurtured a rising bourgeoisie through the exploitation of colonial labor forces. Thus, capitalist social relations emerged through a world-scale process of proletarianization. Enclosure and empire, as primitive accumulation, produce **capitalism**.

See also: capitalism; colonialism, history of; commercialization; Marxism; peasantry; slavery

Further reading

Polanyi, K. (1957) *The Great Transformation: The Political and Economic Origins of Our Times*, Boston: Beacon.

Wallerstein, I. (1974) *The Modern World System, Vol. 1: Capitalist Agriculture and the Origins of the European World-economy in the Sixteenth Century*, New York: Academic Press.

PHILIP D. MCMICHAEL

privatization and liberalization

The term "privatization" has been adopted to describe a range of different policy measures designed to reduce the role of the state in national economies (see **state and state reform**) and to enhance the scope of private ownership and the private sector. The term is closely linked to "liberalization," which has generally meant a greater deregulation of the state and **state-owned enterprises (SOEs)**, and greater involvement of the private sector. The most common use of "privatization" refers to a change in ownership of an enterprise from the state to the private sector. This can be achieved in a number of ways. First, through the sale of all, or part of the privatized enterprise equity to the public, commonly referred to as a public flotation (see also **stock markets**). Second, through the direct sale of an enterprise to an individual or group of buyers, and through forms of **joint venture** arrangements, whereby the private sector becomes involved in a state-owned enterprise. Third, management and/or workers may also raise capital and purchase a state-owned enterprise.

More generally, the process of privatization has been used to describe the transfer of control rather than ownership, from the public to the private sector. Examples of this include forms of contracting out, management contracts, leasing, franchising and concession arrangements. In these cases, it is not the ownership of assets that is transferred but the rights to use and manage these assets, often for a specified period.

Privatization is expected to contribute to a wide range of government objectives. These have generally included economic and financial related aims such as increased efficiency, improved financial performance, reduced government budgetary deficit, development of the **capital markets** and increased competition. Political objectives have also featured strongly in privatization programs around the world, such as a reduction in the size and influence of the **public sector**, and the wider distribution of asset ownership. It is possible that privatization can meet several objectives simultaneously, but it is also the case that the achievement of one objective may make the achievement of another objective more difficult. This raises the important issue for policy-makers of the potential trade-offs between objectives. For example, a much-cited trade-off is between revenue maximization and economic efficiency. The price that private investors are prepared to pay for an enterprise will be influenced by the expected future profit performance, which is likely to be affected by the degree of competition in the market. In order to generate high sales revenue from privatization, the government may need to give the purchasers a guarantee of market protection, which is likely to mean a lower efficiency performance by the privatized enterprise.

While the objectives for privatization have been varied, the theoretical reasoning for privatization has been much more narrowly based on the economic case. The theoretical argument for privatization has largely been predicated on the theory of **property rights**, so that under a competitive market environment, enterprises that are privately owned will out-perform those that are state-owned. State-owned assets have largely been viewed as the solution to so-called market failures, particularly in relation to natural monopolies. Operated as monopolies, SOEs are expected to produce socially efficient outcomes that maximize social welfare. For this to happen, politicians and bureaucrats in the state sector are assumed to act in ways that are consistent with this outcome. Whatever the level of competition, the case for privatization rests, therefore, on questioning the motives of bureaucrats and politicians, and on challenging the basis on which incentives for internal efficiency work in the state-owned sector. Public choice theory suggests that bureaucrats and politicians maximize their own utility rather than act in a society's interests, and as a result, enterprise performance under state-ownership may suffer. Property rights and principal agent theories come to similar conclusions by maintaining that the incentives to create efficient performance are lacking within state-owned structures. In contrast, it is argued that private enterprise, where property rights are more clearly identified, and monitoring and **incentive structures** operate more effectively, creates the conditions for superior performance.

Privatization has now been implemented on a worldwide scale, and has featured as a major element of the economic reform programs pursued by developing countries over the last two decades.

Privatization in developing countries has taken place in primary sector activities, manufacturing, finance, and increasingly in recent years, in infrastructure, including energy (see **energy policy**), **telecommunications** and **water management**. Although the process of privatization is continuing, the debate has switched from rationalizing privatization to assessing its impact.

Ideally, the impact of privatization ought to be assessed in terms of the objectives set for it, but where multiple objectives have been established, deciding the relative weight to be attached to each objective may not be easy, or may change over time. Similarly, objectives may be established only in broad terms that makes assessment of them difficult.

The assessment of privatization is complex, and more often than not reveals a contradictory picture. Theory has not conclusively settled the debate over which type of ownership provides superior performance. The empirical evidence is subjected to an array of methodological difficulties, and generally provides a mixed picture, making it difficult to draw too many general lessons. What the assessment literature clearly indicates, however, is that for privatization to be effective requires more than simply changing forms of ownership and control. Market **institutions**, competition and the political environment within which privatization takes place, will all influence how effectively this policy instrument will work.

See also: build-operate-transfer (BOT) projects; conditionality; decentralization; electrification and power-sector reform; neo-liberalism; new public management (NPM); postsocialism; public-private partnerships; public management; public sector; shock therapy; state and state reform

Further reading

Cook, P. and Kirkpatrick, C. (2000) *Privatization in Developing Countries*, Aldershot: Edward Elgar. Part of the International Library of Critical Writings in Economics, series editor Mark Blaug, 2 vols.

Megginson, W. and Netter, J. (2001) "From State to Market: A Summary of Empirical Studies on

Privatization," *Journal of Economic Literature* 39:2 321–89.

Shirley, M. and Walsh, P. (2000) "Public versus Private Ownership: The Current State of the Debate," *World Bank Policy Research Working Paper*, no. 2420, July.

PAUL COOK AND COLIN KIRKPATRICK

productivity

A simple definition of productivity is the amount of output produced by given amounts of inputs. It might sound a simple concept; however, productivity is an important but complex indicator of **economic growth**. Without improvements in the efficiency with which production factors and other inputs are used, high rates of economic growth are unsustainable in the long run. Technical progress is a major cause of such improvements, but not the only one. Other factors, such as economies of scale, external economies or agglomeration economies have been reported to have similar effects on productivity.

The measurement of productivity is a notoriously difficult task. It presupposes that accurate figures of output produced and inputs utilized are available. In the case of output, modern societies produce millions of different goods and services, the values of which have to be added if a single measure of output is to be constructed. Leaving aside the issue of information availability, the aggregation itself can be performed under various assumptions regarding the value of individual products or services (production cost, retail price, etc.) and the derived figures may vary considerably. Furthermore, the price or the quality of similar goods can also differ from one country to another making international comparisons of productivity levels not entirely reliable.

In the case of inputs, apart from the above problems there are some additional difficulties. The plethora of inputs utilized in the production process makes hard to attribute a specific part of the output produced to a single factor. This issue can be resolved by ignoring all the production factors apart from one and then calculating the amount of output produced per unit of the remaining factor (labor, capital, etc.). The resulting measures are named single factor productivity indices and despite their simplicity are very useful. Labor productivity, in particular, is closely associated with per capita income and thus the levels of economic **well-being**. However, by solely examining single productivity indices it is impossible to tell whether productivity rises are due to technical efficiency improvements or increases in the amounts of other factors utilized in the production process. To answer this question it is necessary to use total factor productivity (TFP) measures. The first obstacle in employing this kind of indicator is the existence of inputs for which sufficient information may not be available (**human capital**, for instance). Consequently, many analysts prefer to use the term multi-factor productivity (MFP), bearing in mind that it is almost impossible to account for all the production inputs. Nevertheless, the way in which the various factors are combined together to produce output (production function) poses the second problem. In economic theory, several different production functions have been proposed over the years, and productivity analysis depends heavily on the production function assumptions.

See also: capital intensive; economic development; economic growth; growth rate; labor-intensive

Further reading

Hulten, C., Dean, E. and Harper, M. (eds) (2001) *New Developments in Productivity Analysis*, Chicago: University of Chicago Press.

O' Mahony, M. (1999) *Britain's Productivity Performance 1950–1996: An International Perspective*, London: National Institute of Economic and Social Research (NIESR).

KONSTANTINOS A. MELACHROINOS

project appraisal

A project is an investment of resources to generate future benefits. Project appraisal is the stage where key questions are asked to decide whether a project is acceptable. Project appraisal does not take place in isolation and can be subject to significant tensions based on prevailing values, development philosophy and institutional priorities. An example of such tension is of equity versus efficiency.

Conventionally, project appraisal is to examine whether it is worth doing a project, i.e. whether the benefits in future are in excess of the sacrifice made now. **Cost-benefit analysis (CBA)** is a tool used in project appraisal process. In cost-benefit analysis, various benefits and costs are estimated and these are then translated into present values using a discount rate and then a decision criterion is applied. The net present value (NPV) criterion requires that the net benefits (i.e. discounted sum of all benefits less discounted sum of all costs) are positive. Other criteria include benefit cost ratio or internal rate of return (IRR).

An important issue in cost-benefit analysis is the choice of discount rate. Each society may discount future values differently. Choosing the discount rate is a complicated task and depends mainly on the opportunity cost of capital and time preference rate, though it can be influenced by other factors as well, such as the level of development of **capital markets**, the risk perception of the individuals in that society, political and cultural values concerning the future, and so on. Other things being the same, we would expect discount rate to be higher in a developing country where capital is scarcer than in a developed country. The issue of social time preference rate is more complicated, though all societies do exhibit some time preference when they prefer shorter queues to longer queues.

An important limitation of such an approach to project appraisal is that the decision criteria can only tell us whether the project delivers net benefits to the society but nothing about the distribution of such benefits and costs. Some analysts tried to modify this by including weights based on who receives the benefits. For example, benefits received by poor people can be weighed higher than benefits to richer individuals. However, such weights are arbitrary, and even minor changes in weights can produce quite different decisions.

In recent years, project appraisal has evolved in three different directions. In the so-called integrated project appraisal, the various social,

environmental and other concerns are integrated into project appraisal itself. For example, environmental impacts can be translated into costs or benefits using appropriate valuation methods. These are then fed into the cost-benefit analysis. Another approach is to subject projects to multi-criteria analysis, i.e. evaluate each project from a number of different perspectives, such as, social, technical, environmental, financial, and so on. The concerned experts may examine the project using relevant criteria or check-lists. Critics argue that both the integrated and multi-criteria approaches are essentially positivist and preoccupied with measurement. Another limitation of the integrated approach is that the deficiency or negative impacts of the project in relation to one criterion can be compensated for by improvement in other criteria, which raises important ethical concerns. However, project appraisal does not have to be based on quantitative methods. It is possible to take a qualitative and participatory approach, wherein the design of projects and appraisal of projects may not take place as specific events, but become a part of a process of empowering the poor. While on paper this is easy, as Chambers (1997) argues, such an approach requires a significant change in the ethos and value-systems of development professionals.

See also: aid effectiveness and aid evaluation; cost-benefit analysis (CBA); indicators of development; measuring development

Further reading

Chambers, R. (1997) *Whose Reality Counts? Putting the Last First*, London: IT Publications.
Little, I. and Mirrlees, J. (1994) "Project Appraisal and Planning – Twenty Years on," ch. 6 in Layard, R. and Glaister, S. (eds) *Cost Benefit Analysis*, Cambridge: Cambridge University Press.

P. B. ANAND

property rights

A property right refers to the ability to exclude others from one's asset property and to use, benefit from and dispose of assets in cooperation with others. Property rights may be attached to assets that are tangible (e.g. real estate) or intangible (e.g. ideas). Generally, common-property rights have higher transaction costs than private-property rights, as full account is not taken of the individual's actions on their neighbor or future generations. The greater the internalization of externalities achieved by the rights, the greater its ability to form market **institutions** and allow **economic growth**.

Property rights help society to form expectations for dealing with others. They are closely related to the concept of externalities. Externalities occur when an action of one party impinges on others without any corresponding market transaction. Because the party causing the externality does not necessarily consider all consequences, outcomes are sub-optimal for society. "Internalizing" these consequences refers to a process that enables these consequences to bear (at least in greater degree) on the party causing the externality. All that is required for internalization of externalities is the rights of use and disposal of the assets as defined by property rights. For example, a law that establishes the right of a person to their freedom necessitates a payment on the part of a firm or taxpayer sufficient to cover the cost of using that person's labor if their services are to be obtained. Thus, the cost of labor becomes internalized into the firm or taxpayer's decisions.

Assets that have no defined group of users or owners are termed "open-access" or non-property assets, and the benefit stream from the asset is available to anyone. There are three defined forms of asset ownership: private-property, common-property and state-property; where controls on the nature of asset use and disposal are assigned to individuals (or corporations), communities (see **community**) and state-agencies, respectively. With property rights defined as the ability to use, benefit from and dispose of assets, it can be seen that there are potentially multiple levels of property rights for any one asset. Rights may start with broad powers of state (see **state and state reform**) or national governments to control asset use and disposal, and end with powers of individual asset users to make investment and production decisions for asset use and disposal.

The choice of the most appropriate property right structure for a particular asset is important for ensuring that appropriate decisions are made and enforced for asset use. This is not a definitive matter; rather the optimal property right hierarchy differs, just as the specific components of each application differ. From a **new institutional economics** perspective, the central determinant for comparing property right structures is the minimization of transaction costs.

Consider now the development of property rights for a scarce asset in communities oriented to private-property. Every person has the right to use the asset. Unless each person's rights in the community are clearly restricted, this form of ownership fails to concentrate the cost associated with each person's exercise of the communal right on that person. There are, therefore, incentives to over-use the asset because some of the costs of doing so are borne by others, and the asset could be diminished too quickly (see **common pool resources**). The transaction costs of negotiating and policing curtailment of individual rights within this community will not be zero. Their size depends on the asset in question, the number and characteristics of the asset users, and the technology of asset use. Costs are increased even further because it is not possible under a common-property regime to bring the full-expected benefits and costs of future generations to bear on current users. An uneconomically large weight is given to the claim of the present generation because if a living person pays another to reduce the rate at which they use an asset, that person does not gain any monetary value for their efforts.

To internalize some of these externalities, and hence reduce transaction costs, private parcels could be allocated to smaller groups of people or individuals further down the property-right hierarchy, creating incentives to utilize resources more efficiently. A private-property right-holder will attempt to maximize the asset's present value by taking into account future time streams of benefits and costs. However, private-property regimes do not provide incentives to internalize the effects of actions on the private-property rights of others. Nevertheless, the transaction costs of negotiating over these remaining externalities is generally far less than the collective negotiations required under common-property regimes, as private-property negotiations need not include all owners, only those affected by the externality. Moreover, private-property owners have the ability to trade property to rectify externality problems. Negotiating and policing costs will be compared to costs that depend on the scale of ownership; and parcels of assets will tend to be owned in sizes that minimize the sum of these costs.

The greater the degree of internalization of externalities achieved by the property right regime, the greater its ability to support market institutions that allow **economic development**, namely voluntary exchange (or trade) and specialization of production. In many circumstances, the transaction costs of common-property regimes have a significant impact on economic growth. Access to credit is affected as the lack of individual security prevents the marketability of assets, resulting in retarded investment and slowed development of **capital markets**. In many countries, non-property or common-property rights to land tenure is one of the most influential factors stifling economic growth.

See also: common pool resources; gender and property rights; institutions; intellectual property rights (IPRs); land rights; new institutional economics

Further reading

Demsetz, H. (1967) "Toward a Theory of Property Rights," *The American Economic Review* 52:2 347–59.

Furubotn, E. and Pejovich, S. (1972) "Property Rights and Economic Theory: A Survey of Recent Literature," *Journal of Economic Literature* 10:4 1137–62.

Paul, E., Miller, F. and Paul, F. (eds) (1994) *Property Rights*, Cambridge: Cambridge University Press.

Weimer, D. (1997) *The Political Economy of Property Rights*, Cambridge: Cambridge University Press.

ELIZABETH PETERSEN

prostitution/sex work

Prostitution – or sex work – refers to the exchange of sex acts for material or monetary resources, and is a subject of concern crisscrossing the North-South divide. Prostitution is often discussed as though it has uniform properties, but it is actually diverse, with much cultural, social and historical specificity. The belief that prostitution is uniform has been supported in part by two dominant discourses in researching and activism around prostitution. The first sees prostitution as sex work, recognizing it as a form of labor and sex workers as individuals with demands and labor rights (see **labor rights and standards**). The second discourse instead defines prostitution as sexual **slavery**, and categorizes it (and all its varieties) as forced and exploitative, and the women involved as victims. It is, however, important not to polarize debate into these two positions. Not all individuals involved in sex work are willing, nor do all wish to label themselves as sex workers. Yet, simultaneously, many individuals also choose to call themselves "sex workers" in order to avoid the pejorative implication of the word "prostitute." Some critics, however, have suggested that the term, "sex work" originates from the context of Europe and North America, and contains political implications that do not always represent the situation of those working in prostitution in developing countries. Moreover, some other analysts prefer to use the term "prostituted women/men/children" instead of "prostitutes" or "sex workers" in order to acknowledge the exploitation and loss of autonomy often experienced by such people.

The different viewpoints about prostitution/sex-work may also been seen in research and policy debates about the subject. Studies adopting a sex-work perspective focus commonly on improving the rights and safety of sex workers. Research focusing on prostitution as sexual slavery generally adopts an abolitionist standpoint, and often proposes policies to punish third parties and clients as a way to eliminate prostitution. Working to empower sex-workers' rights can contribute to positive social change by establishing rights for an occupation that affects many poor women and men worldwide. Yet, seeking to regulate the clients of sex-work/prostitution is controversial. On one hand, some people have argued that it is both effective and just to educate or control clients. But on the other hand, many studies have also indicated that trying to regulate clients only worsens the working conditions of marginal sex-workers such as streetwalkers because they are forced to work under hidden and rushed conditions rather than in circumstances where they can negotiate fully. Furthermore, it is not always clear if regulating clients is effective. In Sweden, for example, research has found that policies that punish clients have resulted in few client arrests but have had an adverse effect on the sex-work market, pushing women to work from the **Internet** or other, less visible locations.

In many studies of prostitution in developing countries, the relationship between **poverty** and prostitution is assumed to be the main driving force in motivating women to enter the trade. Although poverty is indeed an important factor, this relationship should not be taken for granted, and there is a need for more research on individuals' own experiences of poverty and prostitution. For example, research in Lima, Peru, has suggested that female prostitutes sell their sexual services as a means to construct their identity as mothers and support their children. Research on child prostitutes in a shantytown outside a resort in Thailand (see **shantytowns**), indicated that children chose this "income generating activity" as a way of contributing to the family's income, and particularly to express their devotion to their parents. Pakistani young women born and living in the red-light district of Lahore are trained by their mothers to continue the century-long tradition as dancers or entertainers, which includes offering sexual services. In various parts of Latin America, poor transgender and/or transvestite individuals choose prostitution partly because their socio-economic background limits job opportunities, and they are partly constrained by their choice to change sex or cross-dress.

Despite the homogeneous portrayal of prostitutes, as the above illustrates, they are a heterogeneous group comprised of young and old women, men, children, teenagers, transvestites, and transgendered individuals, who may be heterosexual, homosexual, bisexual, childless or with children, drug addicts or runaways. They may work as dancers, escorts, and streetwalkers or in brothels, whose clients are tourists or nationals. These different elements not only warn against trying to understand prostitution as a uniform experience, but also infer that individuals' experiences of prostitution will vary greatly depending upon the type of work they do, the labor conditions, and how they perceive their own identity.

Legislation is another domain that affects sex workers. Some developed countries such as the Netherlands and Germany have legalized sex work and officially recognized it as a legitimate form of labor. More commonly, prostitution is seen as a social problem that needs a solution. China's answer to the problem is repression and reeducation aimed at pimps (the procurers of clients), clients and prostitutes. Many Latin American countries, such as Peru, Argentina, Guatemala, and Ecuador have copied European practices, and regulated prostitution by controling and registering sex workers from as early as the late nineteenth century. Such regulation was considered a measure to protect society's well-being and impede the growth of **sexually transmitted diseases (STDs)** such as gonorrhea and syphilis. Critics, however, have claimed that this approach unfairly controls the prostitute and not the client; and violates the individual's rights.

In the past decades, the relationship between prostitution and illness has once again strengthened with the spread of HIV/AIDS (see **HIV/AIDS (definition and treatment); HIV/AIDS (policy issues)**). In many societies, female prostitutes were automatically pointed to as the cause of its transmission, even when official statistics suggested causes among drug usage, or within non-commercial sex. Peer group training and prevention programs have become an accepted and relatively successful way to pass on knowledge concerning prevention. However, the majority of these programs have only targeted sex workers. Only recently are clients beginning to be included.

Regardless, globally, women and men working in prostitution are stigmatized and marginalized. This is partly because earning money from prostitution is considered unacceptable in many societies and cultures. Consequently, many prostitutes live double lives, and hide their activities in prostitution.

Other sex workers have begun to organize to fight prejudices, and the **corruption** and **violence** associated with much sex work, and consequently take action themselves to improve their working situations and demand legislation that recognizes their right to work. For example, in India, the Durbar Mahila Samahwaya Committee (DMSC) is an active organization with thousands of members that organizes annual festivals for sex workers, their friends and families. In Ecuador, the Association of Autonomous Women Workers, "22nd June," has been in existence more than twenty years. And in Cambodia, the Sex Workers Union of Toul Kork is fighting to obtain basic **human rights** for sex workers.

See also: child prostitution; HIV/AIDS (definition and treatment); HIV/AIDS (policy issues); migrant trafficking; same-sex sexualities; sex tourism; sexualities; sexually transmitted diseases (STDs)

Further reading

Alexander, P. (1997) "Feminism, Sex Workers and Human Rights," pp. 83–97 in Nagle, Jill (ed.) *Whores and Other Feminists*, New York: Routledge.

Nencel, L. (2001) *Ethnography and Prostitution in Peru*, London: Pluto.

O'Connell Davidson, J. (1998) *Prostitution, Power and Freedom*, Cambridge: Polity.

Pheterson, G. (1996) *The Prostitution Prism*, Amsterdam: Amsterdam University Press.

Prostitution Education Network: http://www.bayswan.org/penet.html

LORRAINE NENCEL

protected areas

Protected areas are those areas with restrictions on land use because of the desire to prevent damage to the environment or cultural artifacts within them. Formerly associated with national parks and a "fences and fines" management style, today the term "protected area" (PA) encompasses more holistic approaches to conservation. The World Conservation Union (IUCN), which administers an international list of protected areas (drawn up since 1962) defines a PA as "an area of land and/or sea especially dedicated to the protection of biological diversity, and of natural and associated cultural resources, and managed through legal or other effective means." IUCN subdivides these areas into six types: I strict nature reserves/wilderness areas; II national parks; III natural monuments; IV habitat/species management areas; V protected landscapes and seascapes; VI managed resource areas.

The classification reflects a gradient of supervised intervention. In categories I–III, strict protection is the rule and natural processes are paramount, with c.II and III sites integrating visitor facilities. In the managed nature reserve (c.IV), the responsible authorities intervene to conserve or restore species or habitats. Protected landscapes (c.V) are concerned primarily with conserving cultural, lived-in landscapes, with farms and other forms of land use. The increasingly important sustainable use reserve (c.VI), is an area deliberately set up to allow use of natural resources, mainly for the benefit of local people. The concept of the "biosphere reserve," pioneered by the **United Nations Education, Scientific and Cultural Organization (UNESCO)** Man and the Biosphere program of the mid-1970s reflects an ideal management approach with a zoning system for strictly protected core area(s) surrounded by buffer and transition zones.

The beneficial values of formal PAs include the retention of representative samples of natural biomes; the preservation of *in situ* **biodiversity**; the maintenance of surrounding ecosystems; as test cases for **rural development**; for scientific research and monitoring; for conservation **education**; as well as for recreation and **ecotourism**. As a result, most countries have developed systems of protected areas. Three important sectors are not, however, included in the UN list: forestry reserves and concessions (covering some 10 percent of the tropics); areas administered by foundations and private enterprise (i.e. The Nature Conservancy, USA); and **indigenous peoples**' reserves which collectively cover an area the size of Australia, and correlate strongly with areas of biological richness. Pilgrimage and natural sacred sites (such as holy mountains) may also be considered as "informal" or "traditional" protected areas.

Three international conventions cover PAs: (i) the 1971 "Ramsar Convention" on wetlands of international importance; (ii) the **World Heritage Convention (UNESCO 1972)** with some 144 exceptional natural sites; and (iii) the UNESCO International Network of Biosphere Reserves, comprising 393 reserves in mid-2001. In total, some 30,000 PAs have been created, together covering some 9.5 percent of the planet's land area, equivalent to more than the size of China and India combined. In collaboration with IUCN and UNEP (United Nations Environment Program), the World Conservation Monitoring Center (WCMC) in Cambridge, UK, administers a protected area database to provide accurate, up-to-date, digitized information on individual sites and protected area systems around the world.

See also: biodiversity; common heritage of humankind; ecotourism; environment; tourism; World Heritage Convention (UNESCO 1972)

Further reading

Child, B. (ed.) (2004) *Parks in Transition: Biodiversity, Rural Development and the Bottom Line*, London: Earthscan.
Harmon, D. and Putney, A. (eds) (2003) *The Full Value of Parks: From Economics to the Intangible*, Lanham MD: Rowman and Littlefield.

TERENCE HAY-EDIE

protectionism

Protectionism is the political and economic effort to erect barriers against international competition in goods and services within a domestic marketplace, and the act of erecting such barriers. Protectionists, called **fair trade** advocates as opposed to **free trade** advocates, often base claims for protection on national security, infant industry status (see **infant industries**) or differences in regulation or working conditions in trade-originating countries.

Protectionist barriers can take many forms, most reflected in the history of **World Trade Organization/General Agreement on Tariffs and Trade (WTO/GATT)** and **International Monetary Fund (IMF)** efforts to avoid trade and financial conflict. Thus, common tools of protectionism are high **tariffs**; quotas; product regulations unrelated to health, safety or similarly supportable standards; arbitrary government procurement policies; and dual **exchange rates** and other currency manipulations. By limiting consumer choices and raising domestic prices, protectionism demonstrates successful lobbying for the benefit of domestic producers and associated parties at the expense of domestic consumers, foreign producers and the broader economy.

See also: economic federalization; import substitution; industrialization and trade policy; infant industries; tariffs; trade; World Trade Organization/General Agreement on Tariffs and Trade (WTO/GATT)

WILLIAM B. T. MOCK

Protestant work ethic

The Protestant work ethic is a connection between religious beliefs and early forms of **capitalism**, which is seen to underpin modern Western **economic development**. The concept is most associated with the German economist and sociologist Max Weber. Weber argued that Protestant economic conduct is predicated on a need to gain assurance that the individual is among the elect, the saints already chosen (according to the Calvinist doctrine of predestination) as eventually going to heaven. Weber calls this "inner-worldly asceticism" and argues that Protestants find assurance through successful practice in the public world of mundane economic reality. Calvinism also believes that each individual has a "calling" (occupation, activity) that is partly chosen by God, and that this calling should be pursued relentlessly and fully (Weber, 1958). Hence, Calvinist entrepreneurs feel ethically bound to sustain profitability through relentless, steady and systematic activity in business. They strive for maximal returns on assets while abstaining from immediate enjoyment of the fruits of activity. Hence, capital accumulates through continuous investment and repression of feelings of solidarity toward others. Or as Weber (1978:164) said: "the Puritan conception of life . . . favored the tendency towards a bourgeois, economically rational, way of life . . . It stood by the cradle of modern 'economic man'."

See also: Christianity; culture; ethics; religion; sociology of development

Further reading

Weber, M. (1958) *The Protestant Ethic and the Spirit of Capitalism*, New York: Charles Scribner's Sons.
Weber, M. (1978) *Max Weber: Selections in Translation*, ed. W. G. Runciman. Cambridge: Cambridge University Press.

RICHARD PEET

public management

Public management refers to the way that governments manage their affairs, and particularly how they manage public services like **education** and **health** through the **public sector**. Public management may be distinguished from **development management** in two ways. First, there is an almost exclusive emphasis on government as development actor, qualified only, in recent years, by the increasing use of **non-governmental organizations (NGOs)** and the private sector to provide services to government on a contract basis (see **partnerships; public-private partnerships**). Second, unlike development management – which tends to see itself as "progressive," or critical of mainstream management practice – public management espouses value-neutrality.

Public management is generally not new in developing countries. For example, China during the pre-colonial period had an elaborate civil service system. But the main progress within public management in developing countries has mainly occurred during periods of colonial administration

and post-independence. The trend has also led to the reconsideration of a positive role for the state (see **state and state reform**) as an agency for **poverty** reduction and for facilitating **economic growth**. Colonialism (see **colonialism, history of; colonialism, impacts of**) and postcolonial periods are associated with corresponding models of public management.

In countries where colonial powers ruled directly, rather than indirectly via a local leader, public management was based on a recognizable version of the Weberian bureaucratic model. In the case of the Indian civil service, British prime minister Lloyd George referred to this as the "steel frame" of British rule. The size of the frame's interstices, as it were, depended on the interests of the colonial power. In Tanzania, for example, little investment was made in legal systems (see **law**). In neighboring Uganda, however, there was a heavy investment in education, especially with the establishment of Makerere University College.

According to McCourt and Minogue (2001), this classic colonial model of public management contained various other elements. Politics and elected politicians were kept separate from the administration and appointed administrators. Administration was seen as continuous, predictable and rule-governed. Administrators were appointed according to their qualifications, and were trained professionals. There was a functional division of labor, and a hierarchy of tasks and people. There was also an ethic of serving the public: resources belong to the organization, rather than individuals who worked in it; and public servants were expected to serve public rather than private interests.

Following independence, governments mostly preferred to flesh out the existing "frame" of administration rather than replace it. There was a massive expansion of public provision everywhere – schools, clinics and other outposts of government springing up in virgin territory – and an incursion into economic life (not seen then as qualitatively different) in the form of public enterprises and a philosophy of *dirigisme* (see **privatization and liberalization**). The tool of choice was **planning**: project planning, educational planning and so on, mirroring the ubiquitous five year plans in the economy. Given the very low base from which governments mostly began, civil servants were administering growth, with an emphasis on the recruitment and training of public servants.

When the hopes vested in the public-administration-plus-planning model were not fully realized, politicians tended to blame the arrogance and inertia of an elitist bureaucracy (see Ferguson, 1990, for a study of this in Lesotho), and some governments took steps to bring it under direct political control. For example, in socialist countries, the "cadre" system deliberately avoided the separation between elected and appointed officials in the ostensible interests of achieving developmental objectives. Certainly, the boundary between politicians and political appointees on one hand and civil servants on the other is in continual flux, with current opinion tending to support the classic public administration separation of powers by reducing the "gray area" of political appointees to a bare minimum.

Economists, for their part, influenced by "public choice" and "principal-agent" theories, tended to point to an intrinsic failure of governments to control their civil servant "agents." The number of civil servants and the cost of government did indeed rise inexorably in most countries, without a commensurate improvement in services. The ubiquitous structural adjustment debt from the 1980s onwards (see **structural adjustment; debt**) often obliged governments to switch the machinery of government into reverse gear, containing or cutting the size of government through staff retrenchment: computerized staff inventories, redundancy packages and other tools suddenly appeared.

This has been seen as representing the influence of the industrialized-country **new public management (NPM)** model, an idealized form of the actual reform experience of influential countries like New Zealand. Yet critics have also called this the "Washington model" because of its similarity to the objectives of the **Washington consensus**. NPM's positive elements, such as "empowering" managers by devolving responsibility to "executive agencies" and introducing "performance management," have been slow to spread, and have even sometimes been rescinded after introduction. (These comments may also be true of privatization (see **privatization and liberalization**), which in this context can be seen as one of the NPM elements.) Opinion is divided about whether this

sluggishness reflects simple dissemination and learning effects (any innovation needs time to spread and to bed in), or reflects an inherent inappropriateness in the NPM model.

In recent years, a positive role for the state (see **state and state reform**) has been rediscovered, with a convergence of views from at least three quarters. The first is the emphasis on primary education, especially for girls, as a "magic bullet" for improvement in **human development** indicators such as infant mortality (see **infant and child mortality**) (for example, Uganda and Kenya have adopted policies of universal primary education.) The second is the growth of the **governance** movement, emphasizing the role of legal and other **institutions** in facilitating **economic growth**. The third is the "rediscovery" of **poverty**, leading to a reassertion of the importance of key public services as mechanisms for reducing poverty.

Despite its **vulnerability** to **corruption**, capture by interest groups and sheer lumbering inefficiency, the public administration model has proved remarkably resilient. With NGOs and the private sector unable or unwilling to become largely involved in the provision of poverty-reducing public services like education and health services, and occasionally reformed by a mixture of industrialized-country private sector-derived management techniques, it seems likely to remain so.

See also: new public management (NPM); privatization and liberalization; public sector; state and state reform

Further reading

See the journal *Public Administration and Development*.

Ferguson, J. (1990) *The Anti-Politics Machine: "Development," Depoliticization and Bureaucratic Power in Lesotho*, Cambridge: Cambridge University Press.

McCourt, W. and Minogue, M. (eds) (2001) *The Internationalization of Public Management: Reinventing the Third World State*, Cheltenham: Edward Elgar.

Tendler, J. (1997) *Good Government in the Tropics*, Baltimore: Johns Hopkins University Press.

Turner, M. and Hulme, D. (1997) *Governance, Administration and Development: Making the State Work,* London: Macmillan.

World Bank (1997) *World Development Report 1997: The Changing Role of the State,* New York: Oxford University Press.

WILLIAM D. McCOURT

public sector

In capitalist democratic societies, the public sector is defined as the organizations and structures that make and implement government policies. Government policies normally consist of one or more of the following dimensions: general decision-making and its outcomes; consumption, investment and transfer of resources; and the provision or ownership of the means of production and **employment**. These public sector areas are then usually accompanied by private sector citizens and companies who undertake economic activities for their own interests, within the rules demarcated by the public sector. In a developing country context, the public/private dichotomy is challenged by the co-existence of formal legal structures with a variety of informal neo-patrimonial institutions, which may distribute goods and services and influence the governance of the **state-owned enterprises** (see **state and state reform**).

The responsibilities and objectives of the public sector frequently include **education**, **health** care, law making (see **law**); protection of the sovereignty of the state and execution of its foreign policies; the armed forces, the foreign service and visa service; national monetary circulation and valuation; **exchange rates** and interest rates: taxes (see **fiscal and monetary policy**); social welfare; and the provision of infrastructure such as transport (see **transport policy**). In addition, the public sector may comprise commodity and service production through wholly or partially publicly owned enterprises and banks. The public sector, thus, employs a considerable part of the labor force, comprising civil servants, members of the coercive powers, technical and financial staff, teachers, health staff, etc. In capitalist democratic societies, the demarcation between public and private refers to institutional differences as well as interest of preference. Institutions of politics, government and bureau populate the public sector, while market and civil society institutions (see **civil society; institutions**) inhabit the private sector.

"Public interest" is often used as a criterion for problem solving in the public sector, whereas self-interest is assumed to prevail in the private sector. It is difficult, however, to distinguish between state interest, officially stated interests and group interest, as well as the concept of private interests, which might mean both egoistic interests and merely individual interests. The demarcation regarded as social interaction – involving the concepts of exchange and authority, competition and hierarchy, laissez-faire and planning, market economy and command economy – is blurred. Fundamentally, though, public policy rests upon authority, not on exchange, and authority may be backed by governmental power and coercion (see **authoritarianism**).

Historically, the character of the public programs was interpreted as public administration, inspired by scholars like John Stuart Mill, Woodrow Wilson and Max Weber and influenced by "scientific management" in the early twentieth century as well as (later) mainstream organization theory. The public administration approach has, however, been largely overtaken by a number of new approaches. These include the **new public management (NPM)** approach and the **new institutional economics**. The new public management favors internal markets, privatization and deregulation (see **privatization and liberalization**). The public choice approach conceptualizes policy failure. Other theoretical approaches, such as public choice theory, conceptualize policy failure as the result of inadequate attention to the individual needs of participants, and the inaccurate assumption that individuals will not act in their own interests for the sake of "public" objectives.

Developing countries may have many differences from developed countries in their experience of public sectors. At the time of independence, the public sector in many developing countries accounted for a substantial part of the economy, including commodity production. In line with variations of socialism and Keynesian thinking in the mid-twentieth century, the public sector was regarded as the prime vehicle of development. During the 1980s, following the growing adoption of **neo-liberalism** and new public management, the public sector came under attack for being oversized, using societal resources inefficiently, over-regulating and distorting the economy and suffocating private initiative (see **public-private partnerships**). As a result, de-regulation, privatization and liberalization have become prevailing elements in the international development debate. Since the 1990s, discussions focused instead on the performance and public **accountability** of the public sector.

Public-sector reforms have therefore become part of the debate about the **state and state reform**. This debate includes the implementation of **governance** (including so-called "good governance"); the fight against **corruption**; **capacity building** among civil servants; and the introduction of new management and incentive systems. Much public-sector reform is driven by a growing recognition that an effective and transparent public revenue and financial management system is necessary in order to create effective governance, accountability, and to satisfy the preconditions for decreased donor dependency. **Decentralization** of government to regional and municipal levels has been high on the agenda, as a means to increase democratic legitimacy, **transparency** and efficiency in service delivery at the local level. Similarly, outsourcing of service delivery to **civil society** organizations and private companies has been encouraged (see **public-private partnerships**). Increasingly, the concept of **social capital** is also used to denote a collaborative and decentralized form of governance between the public and private sectors via informal **institutions** rather than through a centralized and distant public sector.

See also: build-operate-transfer (BOT) projects; decentralization; governance; local government; municipalities; new public management (NPM); privatization and liberalization; public-private partnerships; state and state reform

Further reading

Bratton, M. and Van der Walle, N. (2000) *Democratic Experiments in Africa: Regime Transitions in Comparative Perspective*, Cambridge: Cambridge University Press.

Chueng, A. and Scott, I. (eds) (2003) *Governance and Public Sector Reform in Asia: Paradigm Shift or Business as Usual?*, London: Routledge.

Lane, J. (1998) *The Public Sector*, London: Sage.

Rosenbloom, D., Rosenbloom, D. and Kravchuk, R. (2001) *Public Administration: Understanding Management, Politics, and Law in the Public Sector*, New York: McGraw Hill.

JØRN STØVRING AND GUNNAR OLESEN

public-private partnerships

Public-private partnerships are the collaboration of private sector companies with **public sector** bodies in order to provide infrastructure or services in accordance with public sector policy objectives. They usually are designed to attract private sector investment in order to achieve public sector policy objectives. They come in various forms, some of them involving private-profit companies, private non-profit organizations, (either in competitive or monopolistic markets), as well as public sector organizations (government and public agencies). They may be distinguished from other forms of **partnerships** or collaborations because they usually seek to provide physical infrastructure or public service previously provided by the state alone (see **state and state reform**), involving firm contractual arrangements between state and non-state actors.

The rationale for public-private partnerships usually lies in a wide range of factors, from cost reduction to the desire of governments to respond to criticisms related to the provision of public goods; low **accountability** to consumers; and exposure to political interference. These criticisms, and a perception that there was a growing need to apply private sector thinking to investment decisions behind public sector budgets, led in the late 1970s and early 1980s to the establishment of public-private partnerships as a key policy approach to those sectors traditionally considered to be inefficiently assigned by society. The transition also marked a trend toward deregulation, **decentralization** and downsizing of the public sector (see **neo-liberalism; privatization and liberalization**).

Public-private partnerships generally take two forms. The first involves the public funding of private activities. The second is related to public and private agents working together. The common link of these two types of partnership is in promoting economic activities that allow greater private sector provision of public goods, such as **waste management** or **education**.

Experience has shown that partnerships are more successful if they establish clear plans and objectives from the outset; indicate clear lines of responsibility; set achievable goals; set incentives for each partner for the successful fulfillment of objectives; and establish clear means of evaluating progress.

Much experience has suggested that public-private partnerships may successfully reduce costs in several sectors such as **technology policy**, energy (see **energy policy**), transport (see **transport policy**), **health** and education. But critics have suggested that they also include reduced participation from citizens in the policy process (see **participatory development**). In some cases, public-private partnerships might even increase the need for government administration in order to ensure public accountability. From an economic perspective this may undermine the rationale for partnerships if the cost of monitoring exceeds the marginal savings attributed to private agents. From social and political perspectives, poorly monitored partnerships may lead to loss of trust in government. Indeed, research has indicated that public-private partnerships do not necessarily reduce the overall level of government regulation in the marketplace, but instead have changed its responsibilities from being the sole provider of services to the co-provision and monitoring of services. Hence, public-private partnerships have not so far reduced government presence in the marketplace.

See also: build-operate-transfer (BOT) projects; new public management (NPM); partnerships; privatization and liberalization; public management; public sector; state and state reform

Further reading

Hart, O. (2003) "Incomplete Contracts and Public Ownership: Remarks and an Application to Public-Private Partnerships," *The Economic Journal* 113: 486 C69–76.

Rosenau, P. (ed.) (2000) *Public-private Policy Partnerships*, London: MIT Press.

OSCAR ALFRANCA

R

race and racism

"Race" is used generally as a means of classifying humans. It is believed that the word entered the English language in the fifteenth century, but despite this longevity, the term still has varying meanings in popular and academic discourse. Few social science concepts are as controversial as "race" and its related term, racism. Over the years, "race" has acquired a variety of connotations: as a sub-species of *homo sapiens* (e.g. the "Mongoloid race"); as a synonym for an entire species (e.g. the "human race"); until recently, as a group with a common cultural background (e.g. the "Jewish race"); and as a group that defines itself, or is defined by others, as having common physical characteristics such as skin pigmentation or hair color.

Despite this diverse usage, there is a growing consensus among analysts that "race" is nothing more than a social construct used to identify and describe certain physical differences among groups of people. And, as a social construct or a social myth, its social implications and cultural meanings vary according to time and place. It is now widely held that physical and biological attributes commonly used for racial categorization, such as skin color and hair texture, are arbitrary and have no objective scientific basis. The fact that differences exist among human groups is self-evident; however, any assertion of discrete categories of racially pure groups is not scientifically sustainable. Bio-logically speaking, there is only one race – the human race. The fact that any human male can copulate and procreate with any human female, regardless of race, supports this position.

Not surprisingly, some analysts (notably Robert Miles) have called for an end to the use of "race" in social discourse. Given that biological or scientific race does not exist, why do social scientists still use "race"? There is no simple answer to this. How-ever, as long as "race" continues to have con-sequences and ramifications in the real world, it would be difficult, if not counterproductive, to discard it.

One of the enduring ramifications of "race" is racism – a philosophy of racial hostility that asserts the superiority of one human group over another, based on socially constructed physical differences. Racism occurs when variations in phy-sical attributes are selectively and arbitrarily tied to a presumed superiority or inferiority of any classified group. Without racism, "race" has no social impact.

Two main forms of racism – individual and institutional racism – have been identified over the years. The former, as the name suggests, is perpe-trated by individuals without institutional backing, whereas the latter, sometimes called sys-temic racism, is imbedded in institutions. In addi-tion to these two major forms, Martin Barker has popularized the concept of "new racism," which refers to a form of racism that is usually disguised through semantic manipulations, by abandoning explicit racial concepts in favor of code words and race-neutral language. Another recent version, "democratic racism," describes the somewhat contradictory manner in which racial ideologies are simultaneously articulated with democratic principles in many Western industrialized nations. The use of free speech to disseminate racially hateful literature is a classic example.

While many analysts trace the origin of racism to Western industrial **capitalism**, there is some evidence that the phenomenon predates capitalism; indeed, *Verna* – the categorization of Hindus under the **caste** system – literally means color. Yet, the fact that the Western virus of racism eclipsed all other forms in its devastation is virtually indubitable. The historical link between racism and the enslavement and exploitation of Black Africans, under colonialism (see **colonialism, history of; colonialism, impacts of**) and **neocolonialism** is still a matter of fierce debate in the development literature (see **slavery**). While some, notably Marxist analysts, see slavery as a primarily economic system (rather than a racist issue), initiated to maximize profit, others believe that the massive enslavement of Black Africans by White Anglo-Americans had a lot more to do with racism than many would want to admit.

See also: apartheid; colonialism, history of; colonialism, impacts of; ethnicity/identity; human rights; slavery; social exclusion; sociology of development

Further reading

Barker, M. (1981) *The New Racism: Conservatives and the Ideology of the Tribe*, London: Junction Books.

Miles, R. (1989) *Racism*, London: Routledge.

JOSEPH MENSAH

rainwater harvesting

Rainwater harvesting (RWH) refers to a diverse range of technologies used to capture rainfall and make it available for human use. As rainwater is naturally free of many harmful constituents normally found in other water sources (e.g. chemical substances, heavy metals, nutrients, etc.), it is an excellent water source both for domestic and productive uses (e.g. **irrigation**). RWH has been practiced for at least 5,000 years, and it is the only source of water in many small islands such as Gibraltar, which has one of the largest RWH

systems in the world. Since the 1980s, the search for sustainable **water management** systems has led to a revival of RWH technologies both in developed and developing countries. It is expected that RWH will help to reduce the severe depletion of ground and surface water resources via **boreholes**, and help with problems associated with **drought** and **desertification**.

See also: appropriate technology; boreholes; drinking water; intermediate technology; irrigation; water management

JOSÉ ESTEBAN CASTRO

RAPID RURAL APPRAISAL *see* participatory research methods

Red Cross and Red Crescent

The Red Cross (or Red Crescent in predominantly Muslim countries) is a humanitarian organization that seeks to provide vulnerable people with assistance, especially at times of **war** and conflict (see **complex emergencies; humanitarianism**). The idea of the Red Cross originated in 1859 when the Swiss writer, Henri Dunant, came across the battle of Solferino in Italy and was shocked at the lack of attention to wounded men. Dunant organized local people to help the soldiers, and then published a book in 1862 urging the formation of national committees to give neutral assistance to wounded people without interference from warring factions. This book inspired the chairman of the Geneva Public Welfare Society, Gustave Moynier, to create a committee that eventually became known as the International Committee of the Red Cross (ICRC), and which met for the first time in 1863. The symbol of a red cross was initially inspired by the reversal of the Swiss national flag. An international conference in Geneva in 1863 proposed ten resolutions for the establishment of societies for relief to wounded soldiers that later became the future Red Cross and Red Crescent Societies. Since then, the ICRC has been closely involved in the formulation of international humanitarian law (see **international law; law of armed conflict**

(LAC)), and especially the four **Geneva Conventions** of 1949 and their two protocols of 1977.

The ICRC was the main force behind the Red Cross until the end of World War I and the formation of the **League of Nations** in 1919. At this time, a number of national Red Cross committees sought to create a new federation of National Societies that aimed to harness the potential of national Red Cross committees in reconstructing Europe, and (in the expectation of peace) to address new kinds of human suffering, such as **natural disasters**. The ICRC was reluctant to become involved in this new federation, as it feared that having representatives of national committees on the ruling committee would compromise Red Cross neutrality. The National Committees responded by creating a new League of Red Cross Societies led by Henry P. Davison, president of the American Red Cross War Committee, which was renamed in 1983 the League of Red Cross and Red Crescent Societies, and then in November 1991 to become the International Federation of Red Cross and Red Crescent Societies (IFRC). In 1928, it was agreed that the ICRC would generally be responsible for war relief, whereas the League/National Committees would generally deal with natural disasters. Today, the International Red Cross and Red Crescent Movement comprises both the ICRC and IFRC, and more than 178 member Red Cross and Red Crescent Societies worldwide.

The Red Cross movement, however, has not been without controversy. One particularly difficult question has been how far the Red Cross should maintain neutrality in the face of abuses of **human rights** (see **right of intervention**). Most controversially, this question applied to the case of the Nazi death camps in World War II. Since the end of the war, there were persistent suggestions that the ICRC knew about the existence of the death camps, but failed to speak out against them, especially at the time when allied forces could have bombed or attacked the camps. Although the ICRC apologized for "omissions and mistakes" made during the war years, it refused to give details of its activities in the death camps until 1997 when, following much public pressure, it revealed documents that confirmed the organization had known exactly what was going on for at least part

of the war. The ICRC claims that speaking out against the camps would have compromised their neutrality and would have led to the Nazis refusing Red Cross assistance to allied prisoners of war. But some outspoken critics alleged that the ICRC's silence was more likely to reflect a desire to protect relations between the Swiss government and Nazi Germany, who were collaborating in various ways at the time. The ICRC of course denies such suggestions, and the debate continues.

There have also been other controversies. In the early 1970s, the questions about World War II were supplemented by new allegations that the ICRC had remained silent about atrocities by the Nigerian government during the 1967–70 Biafran War. This controversy led, in time, to the establishment of **Médecins Sans Frontières (MSF)** and several other new humanitarian organizations that have sought to supplement or even replace the role of the ICRC within war zones. There have also been tensions between the ICRC and the IFRC, partly because of the inevitable involvement of the national Red Cross or Red Crescent societies in civil wars occurring within their own countries. The agreed different objectives of focusing on war and natural disasters became entwined and difficult to apply to the kind of crisis now known as **complex emergencies**. Since the early 1990s, the relative immunity of Red Cross workers within war zones has been threatened. Many warring factions do not recognize the terms of the Geneva Conventions, and are not prepared to treat the ICRC as neutral. Red Cross personnel have been killed. In 2003, the Red Cross headquarters was targeted in a terrorist bomb attack in Iraq.

Undoubtedly, the Red Cross (Red Crescent) provides a powerful network to provide humanitarian assistance, and insists on neutrality and independence as essential parts of being able to assist victims of conflict. Increasingly, however, critics are questioning whether this neutrality can be maintained in current forms of warfare. More importantly, critics also question how far overt neutrality may also imply an abrogation of responsibility or turning a blind eye to atrocities. These questions affect all organizations involved in **humanitarianism**. Rather than developing a consensus, different organizations are emerging to reflect different viewpoints.

See also: complex emergencies; emergency assistance; Geneva Conventions; humanitarianism; law of armed conflict (LAC); Médecins Sans Frontières (MSF); non-governmental organizations (NGOs); post-conflict rehabilitation; right of intervention; war

Further reading

Berry, N. (1997) *War and the Red Cross: The Unspoken Mission*, Basingstoke: Macmillan.
International Committee of the Red Cross website: http://www.icrc.org/
International Federation of Red Cross and Red Crescent Societies website: http://www.ifrc.org/

TIM ALLEN AND TIM FORSYTH

redistribution with growth

Redistribution and growth are two pillars of **economic development**, which were historically seen as mutually exclusive, but are increasingly considered as mutually compatible (see **growth versus holism**). In the older position, redistribution of income or resources from the well-endowed to the poorly-endowed was thought to damage **economic growth** in two ways. First, redistribution was considered inefficient, since it had to be managed by some authoritarian institution and therefore would incur some transaction costs (in Arthur Okun's terms, redistribution is like carrying water from the rich to the poor in a "leaky bucket"). Second, in the Harrod-Domar-Kaldor growth models, inequality was more conducive to growth; since growth is driven by savings in these models, and the wealthy (capital owners) were thought to be able to save more than the non-wealthy (labor), more **inequality** led to more savings and more growth.

The **Kuznets curve**, which suggested that income inequality follows an inverted-U track during income growth, also appeared to provide support for the argument that redistribution should be deferred till sufficient growth had been achieved. This conventional wisdom, placing growth and redistribution at loggerheads, began to be challenged, starting in the mid-1970s with the

publication of a research effort led by Hollis Chenery (1973), and the emerging story of the simultaneous growth and distributional successes of the East Asian "miracle" economies, especially Taiwan (see **newly industrialized economies (NIEs)**). These challenges arose from two sources. First, there was the absence of any systematic empirical relationship between growth and distribution or redistribution. Second, there were unambiguous improvements in agricultural growth with progressive land distributions or **land reform** (because small holdings are more productive than large holdings). Land distribution is a critical component of overall distribution because **agriculture** accounts for over 60 percent of **employment** in developing nations generally, and over 70 percent of employment in the least developed nations.

Therefore there are good reasons to expect that, in developing nations at least, redistribution and growth are not contrary objectives. This argument has been bolstered further when, starting in the mid-1990s, a new approach turned the conventional wisdom on its head. It is now suggested that initial inequality is detrimental to long-term growth. This happens because of political processes (rent seeking by **elites**, support for wasteful, populist programs by the poor, etc.), and the asymmetrical and low growth of **human capital**. The empirical evidence on the "high inequality to low growth" mechanism is mixed, partly as a statistical artifact of the stability of **income distributions** and fluctuations in growth spells. However, there is little doubt that egalitarian distributions of land and **education** do not damage growth prospects in any way; if anything, these redistributions improve the long-term growth potential of developing nations.

See also: economic development; economic growth; growth measurement; inequality; inequality and poverty, world trends; Kuznets curve; trickle down

Further reading

Chenery, H., Ahluwalia, M., Bell, C., Duloy, J. and Jolly, R. (1973) *Redistribution with Growth: An*

Approach to Policy, New York: Oxford University Press.

Fields, G. (2001) *Distribution and Development: A New Look at the Developing World*, Cambridge MA: MIT Press.

SANJOY CHAKRAVORTY

refugees

Refugees are people who, for reasons of threat or risk to their lives, are forced to leave their country to seek asylum in another (see **asylum seeking**). Refugees are treated as a different kind of migrants in **international law**. Their migration is non-voluntary. According to the UN Refugee Agency (**United Nations High Commissioner for Refugees (UNHCR)**), the international organization (see **international organizations and associations**) responsible for coordinating measures to protect refugees, in the first years of the twenty-first century, there were more than 20 million refugees and **internally displaced persons** in over 150 countries. Organizing support and protection for such a large number of people in different countries requires elaborate rules. The refugee system demands **humanitarianism**, but there is controversy surrounding both the aims and means of treating refugees.

Historical development

The history of the international refugee system cannot be understood without reference to the cataclysmic events that led to the collapse of three empires: the Ottoman, the Austrian-Hungarian and the Russian in the first half of the twentieth century. The collapse of these empires led to more than 20 million people becoming refugees or displaced. According to the practice of the time, they were treated as a group belonging to a nation-state, rather than as individual bearers of refugee rights. The **League of Nations** was asked to solve the problem, thus establishing the principle, now accepted, that the problem of refugees is a world problem.

The League adopted the approach of dealing with refugees group by group. The Norwegian, Professor Fridtjof Nansen, was appointed in 1921 as the League's High Commissioner for Refugees, with responsibility for Russian refugees only. It was only later that his remit was extended to other refugees such as the Armenians, the Assyrians, the Turks and the Syrians. The High Commissioner began by documenting the refugees, many of whom had become stateless (see **stateless people**). The document became known as the "Nansen Passport," and through his efforts it was eventually recognized by fifty-two countries. Nansen's solution was pragmatic: to repatriate those willing to return to their land, and to find new countries for those who decided against returning. Then, as now, states (see **state and state reform**) were only prepared to accept limited responsibility for refugees in their territory.

The world after 1950

The refugee system after World War II was grounded on a different foundation. It was based around the emerging concept of **human rights**, which were seen as individual rather than group rights. For example, Article 14:1 of the **Universal Declaration of Human Rights (1948)** stated: "Everyone has the right to seek and to enjoy in other countries asylum from persecution."

International law for refugees in the early 1950s was more comprehensive and granted more recognized rights than existed in the period of the League of Nations. The 1951 Convention for the Status of the Refugee 1951 (the 1951 Refugee Convention) stated:

A refugee is any person as a result of events occurring before 1 January 1951 and owing to well-founded fear of being persecuted for reasons of race [see **race and racism**], **religion**, nationality, membership of a particular social group or political opinion, is outside the country of his nationality and is unable or, owing to such fear, is unwilling to avail himself of the protection of that country.

To be a refugee in its technical sense, a person has, first, to cross an internationally recognized border and seek protection. This requirement excludes persons who are displaced but who are not able to seek safety in another country, or

internally displaced persons (IDPs). IDPs are those

> who have been forced to flee their homes suddenly or unexpectedly in large numbers, as a result of armed conflict, internal strife, systematic violations of human rights or natural or man-made disasters, and who are within the territory of their own country.
>
> (UN Secretary general report on IDPs, 1992)

An IDP would be entitled to seek asylum in another country if they were to cross an internationally recognized border. Under the UN definition of IDPs, a person fleeing because of "natural or man-made disasters" will not qualify for refugee status under the 1951 Refugee Convention.

The precarious position of IDPs has been long recognized, and guidelines have been issued by the UNHCR for the better treatment of such people. They are also entitled to protection under human rights and **international law** (specifically laws regulating armed conflicts – see **Geneva Conventions**) but the guidelines lack the force of law and can be ignored by governments or a rebel army. Moreover, governments themselves may abandon human rights legislation at times of emergency.

Universalizing the refugee system

The 1951 Refugee Convention was a product of Europe's experience of World War II. The terms of the Convention applied to those in Europe who became refugees before 1 January 1951. By the 1960s, the new types of refugees were non-Europeans. The principal Refugee Convention had to be amended to take account of this new development. The 1967 Protocol Relating to the Status of Refugees universalized the refugee principle, making everyone entitled to seek asylum in another country if they met the relevant conditions.

There is no world court for enforcing implementation of the Convention, and hence each signatory to the Convention must decide how it is to be implemented. Signatory states receive guidance from the Handbook on Procedures for Determining Refugee Status issued by the UNHCR, but they are not obliged to use it. Consequently, there are variations among states in how they implement the Convention, though there are basic rules that they are expected to observe when considering an application for refugee status.

Problems of application

The signatory states are only obliged to offer asylum if an applicant has a well-founded fear of persecution. The persecution must be related to the applicant's characteristics; which are listed as race, religion, nationality, membership of a particular social group, or political opinion. These terms lack precise legal definitions and are not easy to apply. Not surprisingly, there has been recourse to courts to determine their meanings (see **international law; law**). In one case, the High Court in Australia was required to decide whether black children in China constituted "a particular social group" in the context of China's one-child policy (*Chen Shi Hai v. Minister for Immigration and Multicultural Affairs (2002) 187 ALR 574* – noted in *Refugee Law: The Shifting Balance*, by Justice Ronald Sackville, June 2003). Courts have become sensitized to the political implications of their rulings on asylum applications.

The basis of refugee status is flight from the threat to life or serious harm. The burden of evidence for the applicant is therefore high, unless other considerations apply. In interpreting persecution, the applicant is required to show that the persecution and the risk to personal safety arising from it are real and capable of objective proof. Though the applicant's subjective belief of the existence of serious harm or danger is relevant, this alone is deemed insufficient proof. The applicant's subjective belief requires some confirming evidence (the objective test) that the serious risk or threat to life or safety is not imaginary. Even if the fear is well founded and the risk genuine, it still has to be shown that the applicant's government has failed or is unwilling to provide necessary protection as required under that country's **domestic law**. It is only when these conditions are met that the applicant can be deemed to have provided a satisfactory claim to protection under the Convention.

When an individual is granted refugee status, the Convention requires the refugee to obey the laws of the country of refuge. In return, the country of refuge is expected to confer certain basic rights: **employment**, non-discrimination, travel documents, social benefits and freedom of movement. Under Article 33 of the Convention, countries are prohibited from sending refugees back to where their lives will be in danger. This is known as non-refoulement. This principle is now recognized as a rule of customary international law: i.e. it is expected to be observed by all countries whether or not they are signatory to the Refugee Convention.

Current crises

The refugee **population** has remained continuously high since the 1990s and new "hotspots" are emerging due to political instability in specific regions. Hotspots' characteristics include: **war**, **genocide**, ethnic hatred (**ethnic cleansing**), expulsions, massacres, **torture**, persecution, **natural disasters** or they are failed states (see **state and state reform; weak states**). The increase in **violence** in the post-**Cold War** period caused by failed or collapsed states shows that the power to inflict harm and cruelty on the "Other" (i.e. people who are not deemed to be within mainstream **culture**) is as potent now as it ever was. In the Balkans and the African Great Lakes, events show how those consumed by hatred can destroy the fabric of their societies (see **complex emergencies; genocide**).

Sometimes refugees do not flee persecution, but to avoid the danger of being in an area of armed conflict. Conflicts may be against a government by a rebel army or insurgents. Particular problems, such as rape or the conscription of minors into a rebel army, are not covered under the Refugee Convention (see **child soldiers**). Blind spots in the legislation such as these, have led to demands for the definition of refugees to be brought up to date and related to the circumstances that produce today's refugees.

The only regional body to adopt a broad definition of refugees is the Organization of African Unity, (now the **African Union**). It recognizes any of the following factors as qualifying conditions for refugee status: "external aggression, occupation, foreign domination or events seriously disturbing public order in either part or the whole of his country of origin or nationality, is compelled to leave his place of habitual residence" (Organization of African Unity, Convention Governing the Specific Aspects of Refugee Problems in Africa, 1969, Article 2). Moreover, this article does not require the applicant to prove that the application is based on a well-founded fear of persecution.

The Latin American position set out in the 1984 Cartagena Declaration on Refugees is broader than the 1969 OAU Convention. It proposes that refugees should include: "those who have fled their country because their lives, safety or freedom have been threatened by generalized violence, foreign aggression, internal conflicts, massive violation of human rights or other circumstances which have seriously disturbed public order."

The richer industrialized countries have resisted attempts to widen the qualifying conditions. They point to hostility toward refugees and growing resentment of immigrants in their counties. They also point to the discrediting of the refugee system by people smugglers and migrant traffickers (see **migrant trafficking**).

Furthermore, many industrialized countries are critical of the open-ended nature of the refugee burden. Instead, they favor burden shedding between countries, and have introduced various measures to restrict the number of asylum seekers in their countries. An example is the use of a "safe haven," "preventative protection" or "temporary protection" scheme during the troubles in the Balkans during the 1990s. "Temporary protection" is used to avoid granting permanent settlement to a large number of refugees. Although this arrangement is not covered under the Refugee Convention, it had the agreement of UNHCR, and has led to criticisms that this could undermine the initial UNHCR mandate by placing restrictions on how refugees may escape oppression (see **United Nations High Commissioner for Refugees (UNHCR)**).

There are other restrictive measures, such as requiring the applicant to justify why a safe place was not sought in another part of the country from which the applicant was escaping. In some regions, such as the **European Union**, an applicant is denied the choice of where to seek asylum. It is a requirement for an application to be lodged in the first country of safety the applicant landed in. If the application was not made in what is considered a "safe third country," the applicant can be sent to that country. The prospect that a person may be returned to the first safe country of arrival is forcing countries to prevent asylum seekers landing in their territory in the first place. The Refugee Convention would be further undermined if the attempt by some countries to set up so-called "safe havens" near the "hotspots" succeeds.

See also: asylum seeking; citizenship; complex emergencies; displacement; humanitarianism; internally displaced persons; international law; international migration; migration; stateless people; United Nations High Commissioner for Refugees (UNHCR); war

Further reading

See *The Journal of Refugee Studies.*
Adisa, J. (1996) *The Comfort of Strangers*, Ibadan: UNHCS (Habitat)/IFRA.
Chimni, B. (ed.) (2000) *International Refugee Law: A Reader*, New Delhi: Sage.
Hatthaway, J. (1997) *Reconceiving International Refugee Law*, The Hague: Martinus Nijhoff.
Joy, D. (1992) *Refugees: Asylum in Europe*, London: Minority Rights Publications.
Soguk, N. (1999) *States and Strangers: Refugees and Displacements of Statecraft*, Minneapolis: University of Minneapolis Press.
UNHCR (2000) *The State of the World's Refugees: Fifty Years of Humanitarian Action*, Oxford: Oxford University Press.
US Committee for Refugees website: http://www.refugees.org/

PAUL OKOJIE

religion

Debates about religion and development consider the philosophical relationship of religion and development theory, and the day-to-day impacts of religion and religious organizations on development in practice. Religious belief and practice continues to influence the lives of most people living in developing countries, and is crucial to decisions that they make about their development. Despite this importance, issues of spirituality and religion have an uneasy relationship with development theory and practice, and have tended to be marginalized or ignored in academic or political debates. For instance, a survey of three major development studies journals (*World Development*, the *Journal of Development Studies* and the *Journal of Developing Areas*) between 1982 and 1998, revealed only passing reference to the topics of spirituality and religion (Ver Beek, 2002). This gap in the literature can be traced back to the modernistic belief that people will give up primitive superstitions and religious worldviews as their communities (see **community**) evolve into developed societies modeled on the West. Thus, one reason why religion has not received attention within the development debate is due to the idea dominant in **modernization theory** that secularization goes hand-in-hand with the transition to modernity and **economic development**.

Despite this attitude toward religion within international development, the relationship between **Christianity** and development has a different history. Much early development work was undertaken by Christian **missionaries** and, as such, the Christian tradition formed an important part of the link between colonialism (see **colonialism, history of; colonialism, impacts of**) and development. Poor communities often experienced "advancement" and became "civilized" with the adoption of Christianity and Western ways of thinking, at the expense of abandoning (or at least weakening) their reliance upon traditional cultural and religious systems. However, because of the tendency of much Western philosophical thought (such as from Descartes) to divorce the sacred from the secular, the practice of Christianity is largely a private affair. Social and economic life is seen as secular and scientific, and unrelated to the religious domain. Yet, this is not the case in with many religio-cultural worldviews of many people living in developing countries. Decisions, such as when to plant a field of crops or how to cure a particular illness, can be as much an occasion for ritual activity or consulting the divine, as they are for buying the best seeds or paying attention to **primary health care**. This merging of the sacred and the secular is incompatible with the vision of international development that considers that solutions to **poverty** are material and that religion and **culture** are irrelevancies.

Increasingly, however, there have been criticisms of development (see **postmodernism and postdevelopment**) as a top-down technocratic process, as well as for its **ethnocentricism**. These criticisms claim that orthodox approaches to modernization (see **modernization theory**) should also be seen as a cultural and political enterprise coming from the West. They also claim that religion and culture should be given more attention in eliminating poverty (see **power and discourse; culture**). Nevertheless, the relationship between religion and development is complex and, as a field of enquiry, is beleaguered by the fact that religion is intensely political and emotive. There are, however, a number of compelling reasons to consider the religious dimension to international development.

Religion as an aid to international development

Faith traditions already make a significant contribution toward **human development** in poor countries. From the earliest days of European colonial expansion, Christian missionaries have been involved in the provision of **education** and **health** services as well as water and **sanitation**. While this philanthropy was certainly instrumental in gathering converts, the Christian church was involved in such work long before international development emerged as a global concern. A number of the important development charities (for instance, CAFOD, Christian Aid and World Vision) continue to be rooted in Christian values. Moreover, in 1998 an organization called "World Faiths Development Dialogue" (WFDD) was set up by the president of the **World Bank**, James D. Wolfensohn, and Lord Carey, then Archbishop of Canterbury, to encourage dialog between religious traditions in the South and international development **institutions**.

Today, examples of development work can be found within all religious traditions in developing countries (for instance, the Hindu-based Ramakrishna Mission in India, the Buddhist Sarvodaya movement in Sri Lanka, or Islamic Relief, which is active in Muslim countries such as Bangladesh). Such initiatives are frequently run on a voluntary basis, are less likely to have large overheads and

normally charge little or nothing for their services (see **voluntary sector**). Moreover, in general, faith-based organizations, located in the **community**, are arguably better placed to know what the poor actually need (when compared to large international charities or development agencies) and can thus help deliver **participatory development** or **people-centered development**. They are not only aware of material needs, but also acknowledge the value of religio-cultural traditions in providing services for the poor. For example, parents in some Islamic countries are more likely to send their children to school if there is separate provision for girls and boys, and if religious values are taught alongside the mainstream curriculum (see **education**).

While a strong case can be made for supporting the development work of religious groups in the South, Western development agencies are often wary of working with such groups in case they are accused of supporting one tradition above others. There is also a concern that faith-based groups will use **aid** programs to further their own ends or to strengthen their base of followers. Some critics argue, however, that the avoidance of religious issues within development theory and practice is as much to do with how many people in developed countries view religion, rather than simply fears about colluding with religious groups.

Religion as a hindrance to international development

Religious organizations have also been criticized for allegedly being inimical to social and **economic development**. For instance, attitudes towards fatalism found in many religious traditions can be detrimental to people's social status and self-worth, and ultimately affects their chances of improving their lives economically. In Thailand for example, the Buddhist teaching about *karma* has meant that women are more likely to accept that they have an inferior status compared to that of men, which may influence them to search for ways to improve their *karma* in order to be reborn as men (see **gender**). Some critics have argued that religious beliefs have indirectly encouraged prostitution within women (see **prostitution/sex work**), by encouraging them to gain merit by providing for extended families. Furthermore, it has been reported that prostitutes claim that they do not mind dying from AIDS because they can then be reborn more quickly as men (see **HIV/ AIDS (definition and treatment); HIV/AIDS (policy issues)**). While the underlying causes of prostitution are complex, and often related to **poverty**, Buddhism may also be an important influence.

The Indian **caste** system is another example of the way in which religion contributes to social stratification over generations. People are born into a particular caste, which then dictates available opportunities as well as the way in which other members of society view them. Traditionally the only means of escaping the negative effects of the caste system was to be reborn into a higher caste in the next life, and the possibility for this depended upon one's actions and, generally, upon carrying out one's caste duty. However, in modern India, rather than rejecting religion, there is a trend toward conversion from Hinduism to another religion (usually Buddhism or Christianity) in order to enhance one's self-esteem and social status. Mass conversions of thousands of Hindus have been noted, and are a cause of serious concern to the Hindu-biased national government.

Religious **nationalism** and fundamentalism can also act as a barrier to development, where members of society outside the privileged religious group are treated as second-class citizens. For instance, religious minorities in India (particularly the Muslim **community**) feel that they suffer discrimination at the hands of the Hindu right in terms of economic policy, education and job opportunities. Similarly, with respect to women, much religious fundamentalism tends to consider that a woman's place is in the home, subservient to her husband and tending to the needs of the family. Women are denied equal access to indicators of human development such as education, health services and **employment**, and are refused their **reproductive rights**. In Catholic countries, in particular, abortion and contraception are forbidden or otherwise not easily available (see **family planning**). Thus, the relationships between **gender** and development or **gender and poverty** are also conditioned by religio-cultural factors.

More critically, women may be punished in the name of religion when their behavior is felt to fall short of standards set by a religious male elite (see **elites**). For instance, in countries such as Iran, Nigeria or Bangladesh dominant, and commonly nationalistic forms of Islam have led to the stoning of women as punishment. Despite the disadvantages posed by such regimes, however, women may often accept their second-class status. For instance, at the 1995 **United Nations World Conference on Women**, held in Beijing, it was notable that objections to aspects of the Platform for Action, around issues such as **family planning** and **fertility**, were voiced by women from religious groups, mainly Islamic and Catholic (Bayes and Tohidi, 2001). Thus, religion can act as a barrier to the implementation of the **Convention on the Elimination of All Forms of Discrimination Against Women (CEDAW)** adopted in 1979 by the General Assembly of the **United Nations**.

Religion and alternative visions of development

While some religious worldviews may hinder development, some criticisms of religion have been claimed to be covert ways of legitimizing the spread of Western models of international development (see **neocolonialism**). Similarly, the idea that religion is a help to development (and the implication that it is beneficial for development organizations to work with religious groups) has raised concerns that faith-based organizations will be manipulated into promoting Western, secular models of development. However, the extent to which religion is seen to help or hinder international development depends upon which model of development is under scrutiny. For instance, representatives of religious traditions are frequently critical of the emphasis placed upon **economic development** and the spread of consumerism at the expense of other indicators of social **well-being** (see **ethics; postmodernism and postdevelopment**). Instead, they place emphasis upon "bottom up" development that encompasses **local knowledge** and traditions where religion is recognized as important to people's quality of life. Moreover, religious voices are prominent within the Jubilee **debt relief** campaign directed at lenders such as the **World Bank** and the **International Monetary Fund (IMF)**.

Yet, many discussions of religion have also tended to romanticize culture and tradition. Within the discourse on local knowledge, for instance, religion has been drawn into the **sustainable development** debate, which some critics have claimed has essentialized **indigenous people** and **local knowledge**. In particular, the religio-cultural values and lifestyles of small-scale non-industrial communities are often considered as vulnerable and in need of protection, regardless of what those communities value for themselves.

See also: Christianity; culture; ethics; gender; Orientalism

Further reading

Bayes, J. and Tohidi, J. (eds) (2001) *Globalization, Gender, and Religion: The Politics of Women's Rights in Catholic and Muslim Contexts*, Basingstoke: Palgrave.

Ver Beek, K. (2002) "Spirituality: A Development Taboo," pp. 60–77 in Verhelst, T. and Tyndale, W. (eds) *Development and Culture*, Oxford: Oxfam.

See also the journal, *Gender and Development* 3:1 (1995) (special edition on culture) and 7:1 (1999) (special edition on religion).

EMMA TOMALIN

remittances

Remittances are the flows of wealth in cash or kind sent back by migrants to their areas of origin. They represent one of the principal flows in terms of international **trade**, having been estimated at over at around US$100 billion in 2000, larger than the amounts given to developing countries in **aid**. This amount perhaps excludes the greater part of the remittances that are sent through informal channels, by friends, or by the migrants themselves through periodic visits home, and it excludes all that are sent by internal migrants. There has been considerable debate over whether remittances are used in ways that are positive for development.

Monies may be used for consumption rather than investment, although a clear distinction between consumption and investment may be hard to sustain, with activities that are apparently consumption, such as house construction, stimulating local enterprise. Most migrants appear to use their remittances wisely, particularly for the **education** of children.

See also: circular migration; intrahousehold allocations; migration; MIRAB (migration, aid, remittances and bureaucracy)

RONALD SKELDON

renewable energy

Renewable energies are so called because they rely on renewable sources such as solar radiation, wind and water power, and the seasonal growth of biomass. Most renewable energy sources are considered clean fuels because they generate little or no toxic waste. In reality, all renewable energy technologies have some kind of environmental impact in either their manufacture or use, but in general terms they are seen to offer sustainable alternatives to fossil fuels or **nuclear energy**. Renewable energy therefore forms a key part of debates about **sustainable development**, **energy policy** and **climate change** policy in particular.

Renewable energies are usually grouped into two categories. "Large" renewable energy technologies such as hydroelectric **dams** and geothermal stations have the greatest potential to supply large totals of energy from single sites, but have been criticized for a variety of environmental and social factors. Geothermal plants may contribute to pollution of water sources, and large **dams** have been criticized for enforcing **displacement** of local people, disrupting river **livelihoods**, or for prioritizing the energy and water needs of cities above local people (see **dams; World Commission on Dams (WCD)**). "Small" technologies such as mini- (or micro-) hydropower, wind power, solar energy, hydrogen fuel, and refined biomass such as ethanol are generally considered to have fewer environmental impacts, and offer the chance of being sited within locations that are not yet supplied by grid electricity (see **electrification and** power-sector reform). In addition, biomass is considered a renewable energy, although its impacts can be varied. The crudest forms of renewable energy known to human societies are firewood and animal dung, which can produce waste that causes severe respiratory impairment when used under poor ventilation conditions commonly found in developing countries (see **brown environmental agenda**). Collection of **fuelwood** has also been blamed, sometimes controversially, for **deforestation**. The use of biomass for energy is considered renewable because it can be replaced by fresh growth, which may also sequester some or all of the carbon dioxide emitted from burning it. Controversially, some analysts have claimed that municipal solid waste may also be called "biomass" because it contains organic material, and can be used for energy production (see **energy policy**) either through incineration (or related techniques such as pyrolysis), or through non-incineration techniques such as biomethanation (see **waste management**). However, many environmentalists have opposed waste-to-energy systems based on incinerating waste because it may be energy-inefficient, and run counter to the principles of renewable energy of relying on renewable, natural, sources of regeneration.

The **United Nations** *Human Development Report 2000* shows a significant correlation (Pearson correlation coefficient of 0.83) between traditional (or non-fossil) fuel consumption, measured as a percentage of total energy use, and the rank order of **Human Development Index (HDI)**. Traditional fuels include wood, charcoal, *bagasse* (from sugarcane), animal dung, and vegetable wastes. The global average consumption of traditional or renewable fuels is 34.6 percent (standard deviation = 34.2) of total energy resources. However, the statistical relationship between the use of traditional fuels and HDI is not robust across different groupings of HDI rankings. For example, among the thirty-five poorest countries at the bottom of HDI rankings (140–74), renewable energy constitutes 78.4 percent of total energy used, but among this group, the correlation between renewable energy use and HDI rank is only 0.23. Whereas, for the ninety-four countries grouped together in mid HDI rankings (46–139), renewable energy

represents 26.2 percent of the total energy used, with a correlation coefficient of 0.59. Among the forty-five countries in the top group of HDI ranks (1–45), renewable fuel consumption represents only 3.46 percent of the total energy used, and the correlation coefficient between renewable energy use and HDI in this group is 0.37.

The analysis demonstrates the complex nature of sustainable development initiatives that focus on **technology transfer** in the energy sector. Only in the middle ranks is **human development** significantly correlated with lack of dependence on traditional fuels, but this relationship was also accompanied by a wide margin of deviation. Among poor countries, other determinants appear to be more powerful than the source of energy for improving human development. Richer countries that can afford research and development to improve the use of renewable energy have generally had little interest in doing so. Hence, the contribution of renewable energy to human development above a certain threshold remains unclear.

The biggest barrier to further investment in renewable energy technologies is the dominance of fossil-fuel markets, and the ability for large-scale power plants to feed large-scale electricity grid systems. The long-term availability of oil and coal, especially in the Middle East and Asia, indicates that the best chance for renewable energy lies in supplementing grid electricity, or in supplying niche requirements in small (mini-grid), or off-grid locations. According to **United Nations** figures, wind is the fastest growing source of renewable energy, increasing from 10 megawatts (MW) in 1980 to 14,000MW in 1999. Wind currently supplies less than 1 percent of global energy demand, and new installations of wind turbines are in developed countries such as Germany, the USA, and Spain. China, Costa Rica, and India are key developing countries that have invested in wind energy; with India planning for wind to meet 10 percent of its energy needs by 2012. The contribution of solar energy to global energy supply increased from 6.5MW in 1980 to 201.3MW in 1999. Although the cost of photovoltaic modules for capturing solar power has decreased by 50 percent in the past decade, solar panels remain associated with Japan, the USA, and Europe. The prohibitive cost of installation and maintenance has relegated the use of solar energy in developing countries to small-scale implements such as stoves, touch-lights, and radio.

Inducing investment in technologies through careful policy interventions, however, may decrease the high costs associated with renewable energy. In the UK, a significant reduction in unit costs of renewable energy technologies was achieved during the 1980s by the passing of the non-fossil fuel obligation (NFFO), which required local electricity utilities to purchase a set percentage of power from sources other than fossil fuels, and hence triggering a new wave of investment in technologies. Much of India's success in promoting renewable energy has been with the assistance of specific government agencies to address these concerns. The implementation of global **climate change** policy, and especially the **Clean Development Mechanism (CDM)** have also enhanced international interest in renewable energy investments in developing countries. The interaction of foreign investment, government policies, and new incentives from **climate change** policy imply that many old views of renewable energy as expensive and always off-grid are now being challenged, and hence making new markets for renewable energy in developing countries. The use of hydrogen cells to power public transport in Beijing is one example.

See also: climate change; electrification and power-sector reform; energy policy; fuelwood; oil and gas development; Organization of Petroleum Exporting Countries (OPEC)

Further reading

See the journal *Energy Policy*.
Flowers, L., Baring-Gould, I., Bianchi, J., Corbus, D., Droilhet, S., Elliot, D., Gevorgian, V., Jimenez, A., Lilienthal, P., Newcomb, P. and Taylor, R. (2000) *Renewables for Sustainable Village Power*, Golden, CO: National Renewable Energy Laboratory. NREL/CP-500-28595.
Interlaboratory Working Group (2000) *Scenarios for a Clean Energy Future*, Golden CO: National Renewable Energy Laboratory, NREL/TP-620-29379.

DELE OGUNSEITAN

rent seeking

Rent seeking is a term usually employed by development economists that describes monopolizing behavior in the marketplace and **corruption** (such as bribe-taking). Monopolizing behavior occurs when one or more actors attempt to control the supply of goods and services in order to create higher prices than those achievable in a free market. It is generally considered to carry high social costs because of its impacts on reducing supply of goods or demanding higher prices than necessary, or adding costs to business and political transactions. Indeed, in one of the earliest papers on rent seeking, Anne Krueger (1974) calculated that bribes constituted some 7–15 percent of business transactions in India and Turkey. Later analysts, however, have argued that rent seeking is restricted by institutional factors in the marketplace, including competition between different actors seeking monopolistic positions, and the costs of achieving monopolization such as lobbying of governments, or paying intelligent workers to conduct lobbying instead of other activities. Rent seeking is therefore increasingly explained in terms of political and social factors rather than simply by classical economics.

See also: cartels; corruption; new institutional economics

Further reading

Krueger, A. (1974) "The Political Economy of the Rent Seeking Society," *American Economic Review* 64: 291–303.

TIM FORSYTH

reproductive rights

Reproductive rights is a category of **human rights** that aims to ensure that individuals, particularly women, will have greater control over matters related to their sexuality (see **sexualities**) and reproduction. The UN-sponsored International Conference for Population and Development (ICPD) (see **Cairo conference on population**

and development) in 1994 defined it as the rights of all couples and individuals to "decide freely and responsibly the number, spacing and timing of their children and to have the information and means to do so, and the right to attain the highest standard of sexual and reproductive health." The term gained currency in the 1980s within an emerging global women's **health** movement that was comprised of activists, scholars and **non-governmental organizations (NGOs)** in both developed and developing countries. Women's health advocates highlighted some reproduction-related injustices that women experienced, regardless of which society they were in: women often have little control over who they have sexual relations with, frequently carry unwanted pregnancies, are targets of pro- and anti-natalist **population** programs, and are often victims of individual and communal acts of sexual **violence** (see **domestic violence**). As a result, women are particularly vulnerable to reproduction-related **mortality** and morbidity, especially **sexually transmitted diseases (STDs)**.

The concept of reproductive rights was thrust into the center of international debates on population and development at the ICPD in Cairo, and the UN Conference for Women, Beijing, 1995 (see **United Nations World Conferences on Women**). The reproductive rights approach emphasized women's **empowerment** rather than demographic targets as central to population **planning**. Despite disagreements among countries and women's groups regarding what was permissible freedom for individuals in sexual and reproductive matters, approximately 185 member states in each of these conferences ratified a consensus that recognized the importance of a human rights perspective in promoting reproductive health. The adoption of reproductive rights placed the onus on states (see **state and state reform**) to ensure that the freedom to exercise these rights exists; states' responsibilities include providing appropriate information about reproductive health and accessibility to safe, effective, affordable and acceptable methods of **family planning** and **health** services.

Challenges to the concept and exercise of reproductive rights (in both developing and developed countries) have been posed primarily by two forces: conservative ideologies, and economic restructuring. Religious institutions such as the Catholic church and the Islamic clergy have expressed resistance to the idea of reproductive and sexual freedoms (see **Christianity; religion**). Equally, political conservatism has significant ramifications for reproductive rights. For instance, shortly after taking office in 2000, US President George Bush Jnr passed the Global Gag Rule, which denies US funds to any organization that provides abortion services or information about abortions or lobbies for abortion, even if these are in countries where abortion is legal. A second challenge to reproductive rights comes from health sector reform. Restructuring strategies has meant withdrawal or shrinkage of services, institution of user fees, and privatization of services (see **privatization and liberalization**), all of which make the exercise of reproductive rights more elusive.

See also: family planning; gender; gender and communicable disease; health; human rights; primary health care; sexualities; sexually transmitted diseases (STDs)

Further reading

Petchesky, R. and Judd, K. (eds) (1998) *Negotiating Reproductive Rights: Women's Perspectives Across Countries and Cultures*, New York: Zed.

Sen, G. and Presser, H. (eds) (2000) *Women's Empowerment and Demographic Processes: Moving Beyond Cairo*, Oxford: Oxford University Press.

RACHEL SIMON KUMAR

resettlement

Resettlement describes the removal of human **population**s from particular regions and attempts to integrate them into new physical, social, cultural, political, and economic environments. Some forms of resettlement are relatively voluntary, as in some cases of **rural-urban migration**, trade, labor and cultural **migration**, and **transmigration** programs organized by national governments in order to stimulate **economic growth**. More commonly, however, resettlement is seen as a by-product of displacement, especially development-induced displacement.

Given the enormous number of persons displaced by development projects since the end of World War II, national governments, development agencies, **non-governmental organizations (NGOs)** and social movements have increasingly begun to emphasize the importance of resettlement policies and strategies. The **World Bank**, for example, has been actively developing resettlement and rehabilitation policies for those affected by projects they fund. The **World Commission on Dams (WCD)** and many **civil society** networks have similarly highlighted the need for comprehensive and effective resettlement strategies to deal with the issue of displacement.

The fundamental paradox that such efforts to improve resettlement strategies must contend with is that though many development projects are considered an integral part of the framework for **poverty** reduction and economic growth, their impacts often fall heaviest amongst the poor and marginalized, or the very people that such projects are meant to assist. Large-scale infrastructure projects such as **dams**, for example, may be designed to improve **irrigation**, electrification (see **electrification and power-sector reform**), flood control, and **drinking water** capacities. Yet, creating the catchment reservoir requires submerging the lands of a great many individuals, who see their homes, communities (see **community**), environments and **livelihoods** disappear. Resettlement in this instance means not only finding those affected by the project new lands, but also finding them comparable or improved sources of income and sustenance. Resettlement strategies are therefore designed ideally to maximize new opportunities for the displaced in improving their incomes and living conditions. At the least, such strategies are meant to mitigate and minimize harm to the lives and livelihoods of the displaced.

In practice, however, resettlement has often been unable to achieve these objectives. In many countries, no national resettlement policies exist to guide project planners and safeguard the displaced. In others, policies are either unsuitable or lack enforcement. Resettlement policies are designed primarily under the framework of the compensation principle, whereby evaluative tools such as **cost-benefit analysis (CBA)** are used to calculate the gains and losses felt by displaced populations. Yet, the majority of project-affected persons are marginalized groups such as landless laborers and indigenous populations with little or no legal title to property (see **land rights**). Resettlement strategies often fail to adequately compensate such groups, as they also fail to recognize the gendered nature of many development strategies, where the costs are borne disproportionately by women. Some critics argue therefore that resettlement policies must be designed in concert with more **equitable development** strategies.

See also: dams; displacement; internally displaced persons; land rights; refugees; transmigration; World Commission on Dams (WCD)

Further reading

Cernea, M. and McDowell, C. (2000) *Risks and Reconstruction: Experiences of Resettlers and Refugees*, Washington DC: World Bank.
Dwivedi, R. (2002) "Models and Methods in Development-induced Displacement," *Development and Change* 33:4 709–32.

PABLO SHILADITYA BOSE

resource curse thesis

The resource curse thesis states that countries endowed with **natural resources** may not benefit from their endowments because of an over-optimistic and lax approach to economic policy. The "curse" is often seen in comparison with resource-poor countries that, in contrast, compensate by adopting policies that are more careful, and consequently appear to grow disproportionately to resource-rich countries. Much research has suggested the curse exists: one survey of ninety-five developing countries found a negative relationship between natural-resource based exports and growth between 1970 and 1990 (Sachs and Warner, 1995). Saudi Arabia, Mexico and Venezuela are oft-cited examples in this group. Yet, there are also examples where there may be a resource "blessing" rather than curse, such as Botswana, Chile and Malaysia, where large extractive industries have accompanied **economic growth**. Some reasons for the curse include, **Dutch disease**; long-term decline in **terms of trade**; revenue volatility (especially where markets are volatile, such as in oil – see **oil and gas development**); or the crowding out of investment in other sectors because of the dominance of natural resources. Avoiding the curse may therefore depend on cultivating other industries; leaving resources unexploited; and macro-economic **fiscal and monetary policy** to avoid **inflation and its effects**.

See also: big push; Dutch disease; mineral-led development; natural resources; oil and gas development; rent seeking

Further reading

Auty, R. (2001) (ed.) *Resource Abundance and Economic Development*, Oxford: Oxford University Press.

Sachs, J. and Warner, A. (1995) "Economic Reform and the Process of Global Integration," *Brookings Papers on Economic Activity* 1: 1–118.

Stevens, P. (2003) "Resource Impact: Curse or Blessing? A Literature Survey," *Journal of Energy Literature* 9:1 3–42.

TIM FORSYTH

resource tenure

Resource tenure can be defined as all the ways that people gain legitimate access to **natural resources** for the purpose of management, extraction, use, and disposal (see also **environmental entitlements; institutions and environment; property rights; gender and property rights**). It emerged as a way of expanding on land tenure, water tenure, and tree tenure, to encompass tenure relations in multiple kinds of resources, including water (see **water management**), trees (see **deforestation**), grass, fish (see **fisheries**), **non-timber forest products (NTFPs)**, leaves, fruit (see **food**) and so on. Resource tenure is distinguished from the broader term "access" primarily through the qualification that tenure is about access that has legitimacy within a broader **community**, although legitimacy may be contested and informal.

Resource tenure is complex and multidimensional. There are typically many state laws and policies (see **state and state reform**), implemented by multiple state agencies, which are relevant to formal resource tenure. For example, departments or ministries of land, forestry, fisheries, **irrigation**, mines, and **environment**, are normally all involved in overlapping ways in resource tenure. Local, informal practices are even more complex, as they involve the accumulation of ways of doing things over many years.

One approach to thinking about this complexity is to pull apart some of the terms in the definition offered above. The idea of a "resource," for example, is not as simple as it might seem. A single item (a tree, a leaf, a ditch) can be many different resources all at once, which can be used by different people in different ways at different times of the year. The term "legitimacy" introduces questions of power and **culture** into the understanding of resource tenure. Power can be based in control of material resources such as land or trees, control of the means of **violence**, or in the more subtle ability to shape legitimacy through stories or maps. Pulling apart the term "people" shows that resource tenure is tied up with **gender**, age, class, ethnicity (see **ethnicity/identity**), and other identities. Another approach to unpacking resource tenure is to divide it into a series of distinct practices. For example, it can be understood as an effect of the negotiations that shape resource control, responsibility, and management work (Rocheleau and Edmunds, 1997). Resource tenure can also be understood as a package comprising rights of access, withdrawal, management, exclusion, and alienation.

An understanding of resource tenure is an important starting point for external interventions like **community-based natural resource management (CBNRM)**, because of how it breaks down the common assumption that rights to land-based resources are determined by land ownership. It also helps points to the way that development projects can undermine access to crucial livelihood resources (see **livelihoods**) even without physical **displacement**. This can occur if **dams**, industrial agriculture, tree plantations (see **plantation forestry**), and so on degrade resources like **fisheries** and forests. Livelihoods can also be affected if land tenure reforms or **community forestry** constrain access to resources outside of spatial boundaries defined by cadastral or community mapping.

See also: common pool resources; community-based natural resource management (CBNRM); environmental entitlements; gender, environment; gender and property rights; land reform; land rights; political ecology; property rights

Further reading

Fortmann, L. and Bruce, J. (eds) (1988) *Whose Trees? Proprietary Dimensions of Forestry*, Boulder: Westview.

Rocheleau, D. and Edmunds, D. (1997) "Women, Men and Trees: Gender, Power, Property in Forest and Agrarian Landscapes," *World Development* 25:8 407–28.

Vandergeest, P. (1999) *Resource Tenure: Readings and Resources for Researchers*, Ottawa: International Development Research Centre, Social Science CBNRM Resource Kit Volume 9. http://www.idrc.ca/cbnrm/documents/CBNRM_Toolkit/Vol9Main.htm

PETER VANDERGEEST

revolution

Revolutions are defined as a fundamental change not only of state institutions (see **state and state reform**) and the economic and social structures of a society, but equally a change in its dominant values and myths. Revolutions have often been a catalyst for development in terms of modernization (see **modernization theory**) of society.

The study of revolution has long centered on structural approaches. For example, Theda Skocpol's influential work on the revolutions in France, Russia and China led her to state that "revolutions are not made; they come." In this analysis, the major emphasis is on objective relationships and

class conflicts as the root causes for revolution, rather than on the particular autonomy and agency of specific actors (see **sociology of development**).

From the early 1980s onwards, analysts have highlighted the role of revolutionary agents (the leaders who articulate the revolutionary vision) as well as the population who responds to it. This change partly resulted from the Iranian Revolution of 1977–9, because of the role played by revolutionary Islam in making the domain of culture more politically contestable and subject to public influence.

Most revolutions of the twentieth century occurred in developing countries. Partly related to the **Cold War** world order, these revolutions tended to broadly follow the model of either Soviet or Chinese socialist thinking, which was adapted to the local conditions and particular circumstances of their societies. They usually started as popular movements with the quest for **social justice** high on the agenda (typical examples include Cuba and Nicaragua), and were often combined with the struggle for national independence from colonialism (examples include Vietnam, Angola, Mozambique, Guinea-Bissau, and Eritrea among others) (see **colonialism, history of; colonialism, impacts of**). As such, revolutions in developing countries generated a wave of hope and optimism both domestically and among an international solidarity movement. Related to the socialist ideology, successful revolutions often led to a one-party state, which at some later point in time led to economic crisis, social failure or political repression (see also **authoritarianism**). This should not make one overlook the positive legacies of revolutions in various countries, often visible in social **indicators of development** (Cuba is arguably the most successful example here).

In recent years, some theorists have questioned whether the era of revolution is over (for example, Fukuyama has asked this in his **end of history** debate). The counter-argument believes that revolutions will be part of social reality as long as social injustice and underdevelopment continue to exist (see **underdevelopment versus less developed country (LDC) versus Third World**). However, discourses about revolution, and the specific actors involved, might change. For example, some analysts have suggested that the

Palestinian uprising in the West Bank and Gaza, or the **Zapatistas** in Mexico, may count as contemporary revolutionary movements.

See also: decolonization; democracy; Marxism; peasant movements; politics; security; sociology of development

Further reading

Foran, J. (1997) *Theorizing Revolutions*, London: Routledge.

Skocpol, T. (1979) *States and Social Revolutions: A Comparative Analysis of France, Russia, and China*, Cambridge: Cambridge University Press.

Turok, B. (1980) *Revolutionary Thought in the Twentieth Century*, London: Zed.

TANJA R. MÜLLER

right of intervention

The concept of the right of intervention to stop gross violation of **human rights** and **genocide**, was developed in the 1980s by Mario Bettati, a professor of public international law in Paris. In early euphoric days of the post-**Cold War** period, governments, **non-governmental organizations (NGOs)**, and the **United Nations** used the term as a way to talk about the significance of humanitarian intervention as one of the defining characteristics of a "new world order." The right of intervention involves the use of military force to right human wrongs. The most notable advocate of the practice of military **humanitarianism** was Bernard Kouchner, one of the founders of **Médecins Sans Frontières (MSF)** who later became the head of the UN Mission in Kosovo. The interventions in Somalia (1992–3), Rwanda (1994), Bosnia (1994–5) and Liberia, Sierra Leone, Albania (1997) and Kosovo (1999) were examples of the use of military forces for protecting the civilian population of another state.

The doctrine of the right of intervention highlights the competing norms in international affairs. Since the Treaty of Westphalia in 1648, the system of sovereign states has been considered as one of the essential conditions for global order and security. A sovereign state has exclusive jurisdiction over its domestic affairs and is therefore independent from external authority. The United Nations Charter and public international law operate based on state sovereignty. Yet, the UN Charter also recognizes the need to protect human rights and promote international norms of human rights.

This contradiction is at the heart of the debate on humanitarian intervention. For some, the right of intervention undermines the principle of sovereignty and non-intervention, and transgresses the prohibition on the threats and the use of forced outlined in Article 2(4) of the UN Charter. For others, massive and systematic violations of human rights by states are crimes against humanity. Such acts constitute a breach of international human rights law and States that commit these crimes threaten international peace and **security**.

Even if the right of intervention is accepted, there is a lack of consensus on when humanitarian intervention is necessary; who are the legitimate actors; whether a United Nations Security Council (UNSC) mandate is only source legitimacy; and how to measure the success and effectiveness of the intervention. In other words, there are no clear guidelines as to how the humanitarian intervention should be conducted and what objectives should be sought. This situation runs the risks of selectivity and double standards in humanitarian intervention and of powerful states using moral arguments to disguise their strategic interests.

In the absence of clear rules of engagement and the normative ambiguities surrounding intervention, two broad approaches are being explored as possible ways forward. One approach emphasizes that the notion of sovereignty implies responsibility as well as rights; the rights of states and the rights of individuals are mutually supporting. The other approach focuses on re-establishing the credibility and legitimacy of the UN to authorize armed intervention by reforming the UNSC and the veto system.

See also: complex emergencies; ethics; human rights; humanitarianism; international law; Médecins Sans Frontières (MSF); Red Cross and Red Crescent

Further reading

International Commission on Intervention and State Sovereignty (2001) *The Responsibility to Protect: Report of the International Commission on Intervention and State Sovereignty*, Ottawa: International Development Research Centre.

Wheeler, N. (2000) *Saving Strangers: Humanitarian Intervention in International Society*, Oxford: Oxford University Press.

ROBYN LUI

right to development

The right to development approach is a rights-based perspective on development (see **rights-based approaches to development**) which suggests that all individuals are entitled to a process of economic, social, cultural and political development through which fundamental freedoms can be realized and human capabilities (see **capability approach**) might be enhanced. It is an approach that has its roots in the campaign for **human rights** that followed World War II and culminated in the **Universal Declaration of Human Rights (1948)**. The concept of human rights in this period integrated civil, political, economic, social and cultural rights, and indeed the Declaration of 1948 recognized their indivisibility. However, **Cold War** tensions led to a struggle over the definition and codification of these rights through international treaties, and in 1966 two separate covenants were adopted, one on Civil and Political Rights, and the other, the **International Covenant on Economic, Social and Cultural Rights**. Only the former was able to achieve the authority of an international treaty, and therefore the latter covenant was unable to be enforced in national legal systems.

The International Covenant on Economic, Social and Cultural Rights therefore began to be viewed as a set of guiding principles rather than as enforceable human rights, and received less attention and priority than political and civil rights. This situation was deemed unsatisfactory by many of the signatory states to the Universal Declaration of Human Rights, and a series of international conferences in the following decades debated strategies for re-integrating the two sets of rights. These discussions led to the **United Nations Declaration on the Right to Development (1986) – Res. 41/128**, which recognized development as a universal and inalienable right and as an integral part of fundamental human rights. In 1993, this approach was affirmed by a new international consensus in the **Vienna Declaration (1993)** of the Second United Nations World Conference on Human Rights.

The Declaration on the Right to Development is composed of ten articles, which affirm the indivisibility and equality of civil and political as well as economic, social and cultural rights. They also emphasize the importance of popular participation, equal opportunity of access to resources, and a fair distribution of benefits for any development plans. The articles also place a strong obligation on states (see **state and state reform**) to enact appropriate national and international development policy in order to realize these objectives.

Critics of the right to development approach and of the declaration on which it is based raise questions about the foundational basis of this right (in particular, whether development is an "inalienable right"), as well as its legitimacy and **coherence**. Others question whether this approach is enforceable under law, and how states and individuals might be monitored and evaluated as to their compliance. Yet others have suggested that economic, social and cultural rights should not be given equal status to civil and political rights.

See also: human rights; International Covenant on Economic, Social and Cultural Rights; rights-based approaches to development; United Nations Declaration on the Right to Development (1986) – Res. 41/128; Universal Declaration of Human Rights (1948); Vienna Declaration (1993)

Further reading

Sengupta, A. (2002) "On the Theory and Practice of the Right to Development," *Human Rights Quarterly* 24:4 837–89.

United Nations (1998) *The Right to Development,* New York: United Nations.

PABLO SHILADITYA BOSE

Right to Information Movement

The Right to Information Movement is part of a global campaign for **transparency**, **accountability**, and participation demanded by **civil society** organizations from governments, especially regarding decision-making and public expenditures. **Social justice** advocates, citizens' groups, **trade unions**, and **non-governmental organizations (NGOs)** have all asserted the right of communities' (see **community**) and individuals' access to knowledge and information that is important to their daily lives and long-term goals. Increasingly, private corporations have also become the targets for Right to Information advocates seeking disclosure of labor practices and their effects on workers, communities, and the environment.

Access to information for the masses has been historically difficult to achieve. Those in power are often reluctant to reveal their secrets and will invoke a variety of justifications to shield their actions. **Security** concerns and the national interest are among the most common reasons given for withholding access to information; however, even when information does become available, further constraints such as mass **illiteracy** and unfamiliarity with technical language often hamper meaningful comprehension.

Nevertheless, the concept of a Right to Information is considered fundamental by a diverse array of actors. The rise of the **new social movements** in particular has lent momentum to the struggle for open access to information. Indeed, public pressure from a diverse array of **civil society** groups has aided in the creation of freedom of information laws in many nations. In the USA, for example, the Right to Know (RTK) movement of the 1970s and 1980s, led by occupational health advocates and environmentalists, has helped to enact state and federal legislation requiring disclosure of polluting activities by various industries. An extension of this successful effort has taken shape since the late 1990s as the International Right to Know Campaign, a coalition including NGO members Amnesty International, Friends of the Earth, **Oxfam**, and Global Exchange, which focuses on industries worldwide and is pushing for the development of a "Global Chemical Right-to-Know" charter.

In India, a Right to Information Movement was launched in the early 1990s by the Mazdoor Kisan Shakti Sangathan (MKSS or Workers and Farmers Power Organization) in the North Indian state of Rajasthan as an effort to stem government **corruption** and waste. Organizing a series of public hearings, this activist NGO has fought to secure the right of ordinary people to gain access to information held by government officials, specifically information relating to expenditures. The argument made by the MKSS and similar Right to Information Movements is that citizens have a right to both know how they are governed and to participate actively in the process of auditing their representatives. The success of the MKSS led to the adoption of both state and federal legislation, including the Indian Freedom of Information Act 2002.

In 1998, the member states of the UN Economic Commission for Europe signed the Convention on Access to Information, Public Participation in Decision-Making and Access to Justice in Environmental Matters (also called the Aarhus Convention). This agreement drew upon the Rio Declaration on Environment and Development (see **Earth Summit (1992) (United Nations Conference on Environment and Development)**), urging **transparency** and public participation in **sustainable development**, yet acknowledged "citizens may need assistance in order to exercise their rights." The Aarhus Convention entered into force in 2001.

See also: information technology; Internet; local knowledge; transparency

Further reading

Foerstel, H. (1999) *Freedom of Information and the Right to Know: The Origins and Applications of the Freedom of Information Act*, Westport CT: Greenwood.

Jenkins, R. and Goetz, A.-M. (1999) "Accounts and Accountability: Theoretical Implications of the Right-to-Information Movement in India," *Third World Quarterly* 20:3 603–22.

PABLO SHILADITYA BOSE

right to self-determination

The right to self-determination holds that a "people" has the right to determine its own political status, to develop its culture, society, and economy, and to manage its own **natural resources**. It is an imprecise right, however, based on multiple views of self-determination. "External" self-determination refers to a people's right to form its own political entity, and "internal" self-determination refers to the right to have a representative government with effective participation in the political process (see **governance; politics**). While these different versions have distinct intellectual legacies (external self-determination is conventionally linked to Leninist doctrine and the colonial independence movement, whereas internal self-determination is linked to Western **human rights** and **democracy** rhetoric), they are in practice interrelated.

The right to self-determination was at first limited to colonial territories' right to external self-determination (see the **United Nations Declaration on the Granting of Independence to Colonial Countries and Peoples, Res. 1514 (XV) 1960**). The right was made secondary to territorial integrity and national unity, effectively "locking" colonial boundaries (see **decolonization**). In 1970, the right to self-determination was expanded (by the UN Declaration on Principles of International Law concerning Friendly Relations and Co-operation among States) to apply beyond colonial situations. This declaration linked self-determination's internal and external aspects by suggesting that a racial or religious group denied equal participation in the political process would be entitled to external self-determination, voiding the principle that territorial integrity or national unity should not be threatened in extreme cases.

The **Vienna Declaration (1993)** broadened this argument to include ethnic groups denied effective political participation. While representation and effective participation is usually sufficient to satisfy a people's right to self-determination, a people may have the right to external self-determination when those conditions are not met. As long as a people's human rights are respected by a government representative of its entire population, however, any claim to external self-determination is not likely to be accepted by the international **community**. In addition, the debate surrounding the break-up of Yugoslavia suggested that such a claim must be the result of a democratic process and be accompanied by a commitment to fundamental human rights.

As **international law** does not provide a clear definition of people, what groups have the right to self-determination is a political and not a legal issue. In the absence of colonial situations, to which the right to self-determination was applied in the 1960s, indigenous populations and minorities are the remaining potential peoples with the right to self-determination. Both these groups have their own specialized human rights regimes that avoid endorsing a right to external self-determination (although allowing for "non-secessionist" forms of self-determination such as regional autonomy). The recognition of such groups as peoples for purposes of the right to self-determination is thus based not only on the denial of the human right to political participation, but the international community's willingness to endorse a realignment of territorial boundaries.

See also: community; ethnicity/identity; human rights; indigenous people; nationalism; race and racism

Further reading

Cassese, A. (1995) *Self-Determination of Peoples: A Legal Reappraisal*, Cambridge: Cambridge University Press.

Musgrave, T. (2000) *Self-Determination and National Minorities*, New York: Oxford University Press.

I. NIKLAS HULTIN

rights-based approaches to development

A "rights-based" approach to development empha-sizes the recognition and enforcement of rights necessary for survival and **well-being**. Traditionally, the field of **human rights** within international development was associated with the work of humanitarian agencies engaged in the promotion of **democracy** and freedom (see **freedom versus choice**) in the developing world (see **humanitar-ianism**). In the 1990s, scholars and practitioners outside the "humanitarian world" also became increasingly interested in a "rights-based approach" to development, in which **poverty** reduction and livelihood security were strongly associated with systems of **governance** that protect and promote the interests of poor and vulnerable groups in society. At the heart of this approach is the notion that governments, donors and societies in general have a responsibility to promote and maintain a minimum standard of well-being to which all people (irre-spective of race (see **race and racism**), class, color, **gender** and other social groupings) would ideally possess a right. Morally, it is argued that states, donors and societies should recognize and enforce rights that are necessary for survival and well-being.

Ideas about rights-based approaches are reflec-tive of a wider trend in development studies, in which "good governance" has been promoted as an important means of reducing poverty and improving government performance in the devel-oping world. Profoundly influencing this body of scholarship has been the work of Amartya Sen, whose study of entitlements and **famine** (see **food security**) popularized the idea that poverty and **vulnerability** are dependent upon the assets, cap-abilities and socially-enforced entitlements that poor people have at their disposal (see **capability approach**). Reformulating the idea that good governance is essentially a matter of "getting the prices right," development agencies embraced the idea that **institutions**, such as laws, contracts, and customs, are essential for counter-balancing the historical constraints that typically privilege parti-cular groups in society. In its 2000 *World Develop-ment Report*, for instance, the **World Bank** argues that poverty reduction requires policies and programs that promote economic opportunity, **empowerment** and enhanced **security** (see also **human security; environmental security**). Along similar lines, the UK Department for Inter-national Development (DFID, 2000) has argued that "poor people have a right to expect their governments to address poverty and exclusion."

Perhaps the strongest argument in favor of a rights-based approach to development is the idea that the establishment of strong and accountable systems of governance will encourage a more equitable distribution of externally-provided resources, which can be directed toward poor and vulnerable groups. An underlying hypothesis here is that rights (to information, to vote power holders out of office, etc.) will yield strong mechanisms of **accountability**, which in turn will improve the distribution of benefits to groups that are traditionally marginalized by market and state. This conceptualization of development shows how **institutions** affect the ability of individuals and households to cope and adapt during periods of uncertainty. It also provides governments, donors and **non-governmental organizations (NGOs)** a clear mechanism to support the needs of the poor.

However, the notion that the protection of individual rights and freedoms will necessarily lead to improvements in material **well-being** is con-troversial. The substantial improvements in living standards in Taiwan and South Korea, for instance, have arguably not been contingent upon recogniz-ing individual rights and freedoms. Moreover, the idea that "Western" notions of rights and freedom should be transposed onto societies where they have little or no tradition has provoked debate about the universality of development or human rights (see **postmodernism and postdevelopment**).

Beyond these wider debates, rights-based approaches raise a number of specific concerns about the ways in which governments or other authorities define and enforce rights. First, the ability to guarantee a minimum standard of well-being entails an ability to enforce such norms. There is little experience of states acting as objec-tive arbiters in many developing countries (see **state and state reform**), particularly where states are influenced by domestic and international actors whose interests are not necessarily consistent with social redistribution. Second, and related to this, states are only one source of authority, and their capacity depends on their relations with other societal interests. Often, people's entitlements and capabilities are dependent upon highly informal structures of authority, whose underlying principles of organization may not favor social redistribution and welfare. Third, the allocation of welfare rights often creates tensions between the rights of the individual and the rights of society. For example, redistributive **land reform** in West Bengal and Taiwan confiscated the property rights of large and private landholders and redistributed land to landless rural peasants (see **peasantry**). Although these reforms are generally viewed as successful, these radical steps required the state to suspend the rights of one constituency in order to support another.

This example illustrates a fourth concern about rights-based development. Although few would doubt that poor people should have rights to social benefits such as productive land, **education**, **primary health care**, etc., the underlying principle does not sit well with the view of market **capitalism** as a system that prioritizes individual rights over social redistribution. Moreover, the systems of taxation and social redistribution, which were fundamental to **welfare state**s in North America, Western Europe and Northeast Asia, are exceedingly rare in low-income countries. Hence, blanket calls for rights concerning education, **health**, etc., are unlikely to achieve lasting reform unless they specify and create the conditions to guarantee these rights.

See also: capability approach; food security; freedom versus choice; gender and property rights; human rights; land rights; property rights; vulnerability; welfare state; well-being

Further reading

DFID (2000) *Realising Human Rights for Poor People*, DFID Strategy Paper, London: DFID.

Moser, C. and Norton, A. (2001) *To Claim our Rights: Livelihood Security, Human Rights and Sustainable Development*, London: Overseas Development Institute.

Sen, A. (1999) *Development as Freedom*, New York: Knopf.

World Bank (2000) *World Development Report 2000/1: Attacking Poverty*, Oxford: Oxford University Press.

CRAIG JOHNSON

RIO SUMMIT *see* Earth Summit (1992) (United Nations Conference on Environment and Development)

risk and insurance strategies

Risk and insurance strategies are a variety of adaptation techniques that reduce the **vulnerability** of individuals, families, or other social groups against potential **environment**al, economic, or social changes. They are a crucial means of ensuring **livelihoods** and **sustainable livelihoods**. For example, even a small income risk can mean the difference between life and death when living close to subsistence. In addition, unmitigated risk can have significant impacts on growth when it prevents farmers or enterprises from using a new technology. Risk can be separated into idiosyncratic and covariate components. In response to idiosyncratic risks, individuals in developing countries can participate in informal risk sharing networks that may be called insurance. These networks draw down assets/engage in precautionary savings, diversify income streams, change the structure of their household (e.g. by fostering out children), borrow on credit markets, or increase their **labor supply**. A variety of empirical work in economics has documented the use of these mechanisms, but often shows that insurance is incomplete. This incompleteness may be due to problems of information and enforcement. Covariate risk is traditionally the domain of government, as the source of risk will render individual strategies ineffective. Examples of this range from commodity price stabilization to **famine** relief.

See also: joint families; livelihoods; safety nets against poverty; sustainable livelihoods; vulnerability

MARKUS GOLDSTEIN

rubber

Rubber is the latex product from trees used mainly for the construction of vehicle tires. Many tropical trees produce latex, a sticky milky sap, but the rubber tree, *Hevea brasiliensis*, is the most important. Endemic to the Amazonian rain forest, it was exploited by indigenous Americans thousands of years ago. Widespread **monoculture** of rubber developed quickly after the process of vulcanization was established first by Charles Goodyear in 1839, and then adapted by Alexander Parkes in 1846. Today, it is widespread in Southeast Asia, especially Malaysia, where it occupies approximately 1.8 million hectares of plantations and smallholdings, which provide most of the world's natural rubber. Production of this renewable resource is approximately 8 million tons annually. Five to seven years elapse before trees mature. The latex is then collected by tapping in early morning, usually through a process of making sloping cuts in the tree's bark in order to allow latex to flow downwards into small vessels (sometimes coconut shells). The latex is concentrated and treated with acid to give a spongy mass of rubber which is rolled into thin sheets and wood-smoked for preservation. Rubber plantations may be owned and operated by **transnational corporations (TNCs)**, or by individual families or households who sell their latex into chains involving larger companies (see **value chains**). Rubber production may also be incorporated within programs of **agroforestry** and **sustainable livelihoods** when integrated with other forms of agricultural production.

See also: agriculture; monoculture; plantation forestry

A. M. MANNION

rural "depressor"

The "rural depressor" (or simply "depressor") was used by Daniel Thorner, a perceptive analyst of the agrarian economy of India in the 1950s, to refer to a "complex of legal, economic and social relations uniquely typical of the Indian countryside" that he thought had the effect of hindering the improvement of agricultural **productivity**. The "depressor" referred to the hierarchical structure of interests in land that has been characteristic of rural India, which has meant that a small class of landlords who performed no actual agricultural labor came to control a very substantial share of the product, mainly through the rents and the interest paid on their debts, for production and for consumption, by actual tillers of the soil. As a result of these relationships the tillers themselves were left with no surplus to invest, while the landlords had no incentive to invest: "Through the operation of this multi-faceted 'depressor,' Indian agriculture continued to be characterized by low capital intensity and antiquated methods" (Thorner, 1956:15–17). A specific instance of the "depressor" in operation comes from the observation of so-called "semi-feudal" relations of production in Eastern India, where the members of the small class of larger landowners were able to secure rents and interest payments from the cultivators, and also to make speculative trading profits by hoarding foodgrains for sale when prices are high. It was argued that such landholders had no incentive to invest in improved productivity (Bhaduri, 1983). Later scholars have developed Thorner's insight, notably by showing how in the context of an inegalitarian distribution even of generally small landholdings, it is possible for the dominant landowners to secure profits from interlinked transactions in different markets. For example, this may occur when renting out of land is tied to usurious credit and/or to a commitment to perform wage labor for the landowner on the part of the tenant (see Bharadwaj, 1985). There has been much debate amongst economists as to whether the "depressor" still obtains in rural India, following such **land reform** as has been accomplished in different parts of the country, the availability of credit at low rates of interest through the modern rural banking system, and the profitability (at least in the 1970s and 1980s) of modern agricultural technology. It is probably safe to conclude that the idea of the "depressor" still captures important structural tendencies in the Indian rural economy, and elsewhere too.

See also: agrarian reform; agriculture; intermediate classes; rural development; rural poverty

Further reading

Bhaduri, A. (1983) *The Economic Structure of Backward Agriculture*, London: Academic Press.

Bharadwaj, K. (1985) "A View on Commercialisation in Indian Agriculture and the Development of Capitalism," *Journal of Peasant Studies* 12: 7–25.

Thorner, D. (1956) *The Agrarian Prospect in India*, New Delhi: Delhi School of Economics (2nd edn Allied Publishers, 1976).

JOHN HARRISS

rural development

"Rural development" refers to development debates and policies in rural areas. The term entered the development lexicon in the 1970s, when it came to be used with reference to a distinctive set of policies and practices introduced at that time. The **World Bank** published a Sector Paper with this title in 1975, defining its subject as "a strategy designed to improve the economic and social life of a specific group of people – the rural poor," and advocating the view that the pursuit of this aim must involve the integration of more rural people into the market economy. This strategy came to be formulated in conjunction with the approach set out in the influential book **Redistribution with Growth** (Chenery et al., 1974), which was itself a result of the general disenchantment with previous approaches to development planning at national and sectoral levels. These, it was thought, had been successful in bringing about **economic growth** but not in reducing **poverty**. The new strategy was defined by its concern with equity and distributional issues, with the reduction of **inequality** in income and **employment**, and in access to public goods and services, and with the alleviation of poverty – recognized at that time as being overwhelmingly concentrated among rural people. Thus, "rural development" was conceived of as a broad and comprehensive process, aimed at poverty alleviation – rather than in terms of the goal simply of increasing agricultural production. The way in which this objective had previously dominated thinking about the rural sectors of developing countries was reflected in the "**green revolution**" that had taken off in the 1960s with the introduction of modern, higher-yielding varieties of the major cereals.

The evolution of rural development

The 1970s saw the implementation of large numbers of rural development projects and programs by different development agencies, and in some countries, every region or province had its own project sponsored by a particular donor. This was true, for example, both of Tanzania and of Nepal. Different donors' approaches differed somewhat, but most projects included infrastructural development, some production programs, credit, perhaps a marketing program (given the belief that rural development had to mean improved market integration) and work in the social sectors (see **agrarian reform; micro-credit and micro-finance**). The aim was that inputs should complement each other and that the programs would thus be "integrated." It came to be recognized by the 1980s that many of these projects, partly because of their being time-bound, had achieved little beyond the construction of infrastructure that served, primarily, the projects' own needs. Evaluations showed that they often failed, almost entirely, in regard to their own objectives; and several scholars started to ask why agencies and governments persisted with them. Robert Bates, notably, argued that the reason why governments preferred these kinds of projects to the simple alternative of ensuring that farmers received better prices, was that they made possible selective targeting of benefits by politicians to actual or potential supporters. Thus while the projects might not have been at all successful in terms of cost to (ostensible) benefit ratios, they were often "successful" in political terms (Bates 1988; see also Ferguson, 1990, for a classic study, based on fieldwork in Lesotho, of a rural development project that "failed" in regard to its economic objectives but which was very successful in extending the power of the state – see **antipolitics**). Alain de Janvry, somewhat similarly, argued with regard to Latin America that rural development projects served the function of supporting the reproduction of small-scale, "minifundia" production, in the interests of capitalist development as a whole (because the self-reproduction of the minifundistas on their tiny plots, helped to subsidize labor costs on large-scale commercial farms where the same people also worked as laborers: see de Janvry, 1981). Gavin Williams, writing with particular reference to Sub-Saharan Africa argued that, historically, state interventions in rural economies – as, for example, through settlement schemes or programs of "villagization" (see **villages**) – have been concerned with extending control over rural people and have generally been resisted by them in various ways. He concluded that the objectives of rural development "cannot be achieved by state direction of peasant producers, but only by encouraging peasant initiative based on their own experience" (1982:395).

Marxist critics, meanwhile, argued that the **commercialization** of rural economies, such as was to be encouraged by "integrated rural development projects," must often lock vulnerable rural producers into poverty, when it took place in circumstances in which ownership of critical resources, especially land, was concentrated into a few hands (see **Marxism**). It was pointed out by the Indian economist Krishna Bharadwaj (1974; see also Bharadwaj, 1985) that small producers are often "compulsively involved" in markets, if (as seems commonly to be the case) they have to market their produce at harvest time, in order to repay **debt**s and to raise further loans, even when they don't have a true surplus (above their own consumption needs) to sell. In such circumstances, it was argued, there must be a strong likelihood that the dominant parties are able to inter-link transactions in different markets (the commodity and money markets, say, or the markets for land and for labor) and so to make extraordinary profits, while small producers and laborers are left with a bare subsistence at best. The logic of "rural development" as increased market integration was thus questioned, in regard to the stated, poverty-alleviating objectives of this approach to development.

Robert Chambers, on the other hand, sought to impart a different thrust into rural development interventions, by developing a powerful normative argument for "putting the last first," and giving poor people a "voice" in the planning and

implementation of projects and programs (see Chambers, 1983; and the sequel in Chambers, 1997). Following from his inspiration, the later 1980s began to see the practice of "Rapid Rural Appraisal" and later "Participatory Rural Appraisal" as means intended to realize the "poverty first" agenda and the overcoming of the failures of rural development interventions, whether on the part of states or of **non-governmental organizations (NGOs)**. Chambers sought to broaden the definition and understanding of **rural poverty** away from income measures, and to encourage policy-makers to recognize the significance both of assets, in addition to income security, and, perhaps most vitally, of the self-respect of poor people (Chambers, 1992). His work helped also to bring about recognition of the significance of the **vulnerability** of many rural people's **livelihoods**, and his particular contribution to the deliberations of the **Brundtland Commission** on **sustainable development** (which reported in 1987 – see **Commission on Sustainable Development (CSD)**) was to underline the importance of the creation of "**sustainable livelihoods**." The methods he pioneered were intended to take account of poor people's knowledge of their own environments, as well as of their needs and interests, in place of "top-down" **planning**.

In the 1980s and early 1990s, in the context of economic **stabilization** and **structural adjustment** programs, the focus on the commercialization of rural economies was maintained, but through the price mechanism, and expenditure on rural development projects began to be reduced – though this effect did not become very strongly apparent until the 1990s. The emphasis in Sub-Saharan Africa, following the injunctions of the Berg Report (Berg, 1981), was on "getting the prices right" through freeing up markets, by – for example – eliminating the role of state marketing boards. By the end of the decade, however, adjustment policies had come under increasing attack, mainly because of their failure to take account of the needs of poor people (see **adjustment with a human face**). In 1990, the World Bank attempted what was in effect a new synthesis, bringing together a continuing insistence on the need for adjustment, with policies for poverty reduction. The *World Development Report* of 1990 proposed a two-pronged strategy, involving the pursuit on the one hand of employment-intensive growth, and on the other the provision of basic social services for poor people, together with safety nets (provision of some minimum social security) for the poorest people (see **safety nets against poverty**). This has subsequently been extended and developed, in part by the more or less explicit drawing of ideas about participation from the work of Robert Chambers (see **participatory development**). The *World Development Report* for 2000/2001 again addressed the challenge of reducing poverty and proposed a new approach built around the three key concepts of "opportunity," "security" and "**empowerment**," through participation. As the *Report* says: "The poor are the main actors in the fight against poverty. And they must be brought center-stage in designing, implementing and monitoring anti-poverty strategies" (p. 12).

Ashley and Maxwell (2001) have helpfully depicted the shifts in rural development thinking in Figure 2.

In the 1960s, the emphasis was on increasing agricultural production through state-driven "modernization" (see **modernization theory**) via the introduction of modern cereal varieties and the other inputs required for the "**green revolution**." This did not so much give way to, as be supplemented by state intervention in the name of "integrated rural development," which placed

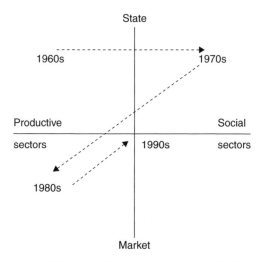

Figure 2 Rural development thinking, 1960s–90s.
Source: Ashley and Maxwell, 2001.

more emphasis on the social sectors, in the 1970s. By the 1980s the focus on stabilization and adjustment brought a shift back to production, but now based much more on market forces; and this emphasis has significantly remained in place in the approaches to poverty alleviation that have been pursued in the 1990s.

The drivers of rural development

Now, the same authors point out, the critical questions for rural development are those of whether **agriculture**, as has always been assumed, can any longer be taken as the prime driver of the development of rural economies, and second, of whether small farms in particular still have the potentials that have been ascribed to them in most thinking about rural development to date. The most influential theory about rural development, propounded by Johnston and Kilby (1975) and Mellor (1976), is based substantially on the particular development experience of Taiwan. There, successful redistributivist **land reform** in the early 1950s created an agrarian structure characterized by small but viable farms, and the government subsequently succeeded both in increasing farm incomes and in transferring resources from agriculture for investment in the non-agricultural economy. At the same time, the increasing incomes of the farmers created more demand for non-agricultural goods and services, and so a virtuous cycle of agricultural and non-agricultural growth was established. This is what Johnston and Mellor came to describe as the "food and agriculture first" strategy of development, in opposition to the mainstream of **economic development** theory up to that time, which had always emphasized the primacy of industrial development. Mellor argued that the green revolution had made possible the realization of powerful backward (for inputs) and forward (for new goods and services) growth linkages from agriculture which were transforming rural economies. Several studies did indeed seem to show that agricultural growth, provided that its benefits in terms of increased incomes were widely distributed amongst farmers, could provide a big stimulus to growth in the non-agricultural economy as well; and that it was in these circumstances that rural

labor markets were tightened, with positive effects for those, mainly poor people, depending upon labor incomes. A definitive study, for example, of the determinants of poverty reduction in India, shows that it has been based on agricultural growth (Datt and Ravallion, 1998); and other research demonstrates the further importance of growth in rural non-agriculture for poverty reduction (see Harriss, 1992 for a review).

This general theory of rural development, driven by the backward and forward linkages from food production, assumes the efficiency of small farms like those that became established, following land reform, in Taiwan. There is a good deal of empirical support for this assumption, notably in the substantial body of evidence demonstrating the "inverse relationship" between farm size and **productivity** in many countries (Berry and Cline, 1979); while research on production organization has shown that small farms often have an advantage because of the intensity of effort on the part of the family labor employed upon them, and because they do not encounter the same high costs of supervision of labor which can undermine large-scale agriculture. These costs help to explain the failure of large-scale collective or state farms of the former Soviet Union and of China (see **collectivization**) – before China moved over to the "household responsibility system" after 1979, which sought precisely to take advantage of the greater efficiency of family farming. A further reason for the comparatively higher efficiency of small farms may because of the local agronomic knowledge of farmers (certainly superior to that of central planners attempting to determine cropping plans for large areas).

Ashley and Maxwell suggest that it is possible that these arguments no longer hold. They point out that small farmers in many parts of the world are increasingly likely to be part-timers, with other sources of income, who may therefore not need to maximize their incomes from farming. They may prefer to grow low-value crops for their own needs. At the same time productive commercial agriculture, whether of **food** or non-food crops, increasingly involves commodity chains set up, for instance, by supermarket chains in the West, which impose quality and timeliness requirements, or demand levels of technical skill, that small farmers find hard to meet (see **commodification; petty commodity production**). Newer agricultural technologies, they think, seem to be capital-biased as well. In sum, small farms and farmers may no longer have the efficiency advantage that they once (often, not invariably) enjoyed. At the same time, the extraordinary global fall in agricultural commodity prices has undermined the profitability of agriculture as a business, and diversification out of agriculture has become the most dynamic source of growth in many rural economies. The old orthodoxy about how small-scale agriculture drives rural development and can stimulate the economy as a whole is no longer tenable, according to these writers.

This is probably much too stark a vision, and one that is influenced too much by a particular conjuncture in the global economy in which the prices of agricultural commodities have fallen sharply in the context of trade liberalization, but in circumstances in which major producers continue to subsidize their farmers. In many of the big developing economies there remains a strong case for land redistribution in the interests of efficiency and of securing livelihoods, as the World Bank has recognized – though, in contrast with earlier approaches to land reform, it now encourages attempts to bring about land redistribution through market mechanisms. This is still being achieved, for example, in South Africa, and in Brazil. Where **agrarian reform** is accomplished, and in the context of a more favorable international economic environment, then it is perfectly possible that the dynamics described by the old orthodoxy will still obtain.

It may well be that the market approach to land reform will not be successful, but at least the World Bank has recognized what might be described as the "rawer" issues that are involved in rural development, which concern poor people's access to resources. "Access to resources," or what Marxists refer to with their broader concept of "the social relations of production" exercise a fundamental influence on the processes of rural development, and on the options and possibilities for securing their livelihoods that rural people have. This point is also implicit, at least, in the approach that has now come to stand in the place of "integrated rural development" in the practices of leading development agencies such as the UK's Department for International Development (DFID). This is described in terms of the "**sustainable livelihoods**" framework by DFID, and it is based on a model which refers to the different "capitals" – physical, natural, human, social and financial resources – that people draw upon in securing their livelihoods. The objectives of the approach are said to be to improve the sustainability of poor people's livelihoods through *improved access to* **education**, **nutrition** and **health**; to (better managed) **natural resources** (including land, presumably); to basic and facilitating infrastructure; to financial resources; and to "a more supportive and cohesive social framework." It is recognized by the advocates of this approach that it might appear very similar to "integrated rural development," and indeed they argue that they aim to build upon the strengths of the earlier approach whilst avoiding its pitfalls. These they identify, like Chambers, with its affinities with top-down, "blueprint" **planning**, and the misleading aim of comprehensiveness. Instead, the sustainable livelihoods framework proposes to target particular core areas for intervention which are to be selected through a process of partnership with local people (see **partnerships**). Above all, perhaps, the new approach is distinguished from that of the 1970s by its emphasis upon participation and local organization (or the "social framework" referred to in the statement of objectives). Bebbington's research in the Andes on "islands of sustainability" (1997; and see also Bebbington, 1999) describes particular cases where this approach has worked – though in circumstances in which some redistribution of land was accomplished at an earlier stage. The rural development agenda has evolved, therefore, since it was first laid out in the 1970s, but around the same set of core themes.

See also: agrarian reform; agriculture; collectivization; commodification; communes, collectives and cooperatives; food; green revolution; land reform; land rights; livelihoods; Marxism; participatory research methods; petty commodity production; rural "depressor"; rural poverty; sustainable livelihoods; urban bias; villages; World Trade Organization/General Agreement on Tariffs and Trade (WTO/GATT)

Further reading

Ashley, C. and Maxwell, S. (2001) "Rethinking Rural Development," *Development Policy Review* 19:4 395–425, and other papers in this special issue.

Bates, R. (1988) "Governments and Agricultural Markets in Africa," in Bates, R. (ed.) *Toward a Political Economy of Development: A Rational Choice Perspective*, Berkeley and Los Angeles: University of California Press.

Bebbington, A. (1997) "Social Capital and Rural Intensification: Local Organisations and Islands of Sustainability in the Andes," *Geographical Journal* 163:2 189–97.

Bebbington, A. (1999) "Capitals and Capabilities: A Framework for Analyzing Peasant Viability, Rural Livelihoods and Poverty," *World Development* 27:12 2021–44.

Berg, E. (1981) *Accelerated Development in Sub-Saharan Africa: An Agenda for Action*, Washington DC: World Bank.

Berry, A. and Cline, W. (1979) *Agrarian Structure and Productivity in Developing Countries*, Baltimore: Johns Hopkins University Press.

Bharadwaj, K. (1974) *Production Conditions in Indian Agriculture*, Cambridge: Cambridge University Press.

Bharadwaj, K. (1985) "A View on Commercialisation in Indian Agriculture and the Development of Capitalism," *Journal of Peasant Studies* 12: 7–25.

Chambers, R. (1983) *Rural Development: Putting the Last First*, London: Longman.

Chambers, R. (1992) "Poverty in India: Concepts, Research and Reality," in, Harriss, B., Guhan, S. and Cassen, R. (eds) *Poverty in India: Research and Policy*, Oxford: Oxford University Press.

Chambers, R. (1997) *Whose Reality Counts? Putting the First Last*, London: IT Publications.

Chenery, H., Ahluwalia, M., Bell, C., Duloy, J. and Jolly, R. (1974) *Redistribution with Growth*, London: Oxford University Press and the World Bank.

Datt, G. and Ravallion, M. (1998) "Why Have Some Indian States Done Better than Others at Reducing Rural Poverty," *Economica* 65:257 17–38.

Ferguson, J. (1990) *The Anti-Politics Machine: Development, Depoliticisation and Bureaucratic Power in the Third World*, Cambridge: Cambridge University Press.

Harriss, J. (1992) "Does the 'Depressor' Still Work? Agrarian Structure and Development in India: Review of Evidence and Argument," *Journal of Peasant Studies* 19: 189–227.

De Janvry, A. (1981) *The Agrarian Question and Reformism in Latin America*, Baltimore: Johns Hopkins University Press.

Johnston, B. and Kilby, P. (1975) *Agriculture and Structural Transformation*, New York: Oxford University Press.

Mellor, J. (1976) *The New Economics of Growth*, Ithaca NY: Cornell University Press.

Williams, G. (1982) "Taking the Part of Peasants," in Harriss, J. (ed.) *Rural Development: Theories of Peasant Economy and Agrarian Change*, London: Hutchinson.

JOHN HARRISS

rural poverty

Rural poverty is **poverty** experienced in rural areas. According to the International Fund for Agricultural Development (IFAD), three quarters of the 1.2 billion people in the world who are reckoned to be living on less than one dollar per day live and work in rural areas. Current projections suggest that over 60 percent of such "dollar poor" people will continue to be rural dwellers in 2025, so there is no doubt that if the international commitment (made in the UN General Assembly in 2000) to reducing poverty is to be honored, rural poverty in particular must be addressed. Yet, the rural sector continues generally to be neglected, both by aid donors and by governments in poor countries (IFAD, 2001) (see **rural development**).

Poverty has conventionally been understood, and measured, in terms of income – as in the definition of "living on less than one dollar a day." The cost of a "basket" of the essential **food** and other items that are necessary to supply what are calculated to be the minimum requirements of dietary energy for a person is worked out. This gives a **poverty line**, and that proportion of the rural **population** whose incomes are not sufficient to secure the subsistence "basket" is defined as poor. It has been recognized, however, that this "income" definition of poverty is both subject to

significant error (for example, it takes little account of the availability of public goods such as **drinking water**). In a notable study, the Indian economist N. S. Jodha (1988) measured poverty trends in some Indian villages using conventional methods, and established that income poverty had increased. But he also documented the diverse ways that villagers thought and talked about their levels of living, and showed that in relation to almost all of these criteria they believed that they had got *better* off over time, rather than worse off. These criteria included such factors as the **security** and quality of their housing, the variety in their food, their access to **health** care and to **education**, and the extent of their dependence upon particular landowners, traders or moneylenders for access to land and work, markets and money. The fact that this dependence had decreased was clearly important to the village people whom Jodha studied. Reflection upon these criteria led Robert Chambers (1992) to suggest that conceptualizations of poverty should perhaps distinguish between concerns about subsistence or immediate consumption, and security in the longer run (requiring the maintenance of assets over time), and between both of these and levels of dignity or self-respect (such as may be undermined by personal dependence). In other words, poverty has a number of dimensions – including insecurity, powerlessness and low self-esteem, as well as **malnutrition**, illiteracy and low **life expectancy** – which are not necessarily at all well summed up in the simple income definition of poverty (see **basic needs; food security; human security**). Another important defining characteristic of poverty is the fact that poor people are particularly vulnerable to different kinds of shocks – whether they arise from natural hazards (see **natural disasters**) or from social factors – and that they are liable to what Chambers calls "ratchet effects" (the effects of one shock render people even less able to cope with the next).

The nature and causes of poverty do differ in different rural economies, but the rural poor in Asia (where about two thirds of them live) are generally assetless or asset-poor people depending to an important extent, or perhaps entirely, on casual wage labor. In Sub-Saharan Africa (where another quarter of them live), they are more commonly small farmers and engaged in **pastoralism** (though we should not underestimate the dependence of many poor people on casual wage labor in many parts of rural Africa). Everywhere there is a strong tendency for women to be disproportionately represented amongst the rural poor, and those in **women-headed households** are especially likely to be vulnerable (Sender, 2003). Asset **inequality**, especially inequality in land ownership (see also **gender and property rights**), lack of access to **education** and to **primary health care**, and lack of political organization, or of links with state (see **state and state reform**), market or **civil society** actors that help poor people use their assets are defining factors in accounting for rural poverty in most economies. Asset inequality underlies the economic mechanisms that lock people into poverty, and accounts for their frequent engagement in what has been described as "forced commerce" – the necessity of entering into market transactions even in circumstances in which they have no real surplus to sell (see **rural "depressor"**). These conditions account for the **vulnerability** of the **livelihoods** of many rural people to market price fluctuations, and they can lead to **famine** (when, in terms of Sen's theory of famine, their exchange entitlements suffer catastrophic decline; see **food security**).

The experience of South Asia, the region of the world that accounts for 40 percent of the rural poor, has shown that the reduction of rural poverty has been brought about by increases in average farm yields, and by public development expenditure (the former being significantly dependent upon the latter). It is likely, however, that the reduction of poverty has come to depend increasingly upon the diversification of the rural economy, and upon the tightening of rural labor markets (pushing up daily wages) such as has tended to take place when opportunities for employment outside **agriculture** have opened up.

See also: agriculture; basic needs; famine; food; food security; gender and poverty; gender and property rights; green revolution; human security; livelihoods; poverty; rural "depressor"; rural development; shifting cultivation; sustainable livelihoods; urban poverty

Further reading

Bebbington, A. (1999) "Capitals and Capabilities: A Framework for Analyzing Peasant Viability, Rural Livelihoods and Poverty," *World Development* 27:12 2021–44.

Chambers, R. (1992) "Poverty in India: Concepts, Research and Reality," in Harriss, B., Guhan, S. and Cassen, R. (eds) *Poverty in India: Research and Policy*, Oxford: Oxford University Press.

IFAD (International Fund for Agricultural Development) (2001) *Rural Poverty Report 2001: The Challenge of Ending Rural Poverty*, New York: Oxford University Press.

Jodha, N. S. (1988) "Poverty Debate in India: A Minority View," *Economic and Political Weekly* 23: 2421–8.

Sender, J. (2003) "Rural Poverty and Gender: Analytical Frameworks and Policy Proposals," in Chang, H.-J. (ed.) *Rethinking Development Economics*, London: Anthem.

JOHN HARRISS

rural-urban migration

Rural-urban migration is the **migration** of rural people to urban areas. It is generally taken to mean the decision to relocate permanently, although many other forms of **circular migration** also imply temporary migration between rural and urban areas. Rural-urban migration has occurred ever since cities became permanent features of the landscape, but generalizations about it are difficult because of the structural contexts of it and different rural and urban societies over time and space.

In the late nineteenth century, largely following an empirical study of the urban-industrial transformation in Britain, E.G. Ravenstein (1885, 1889) formulated a set of general claims about the spatial and social aspects of human mobility. Though couched as "laws of migration" they summarily claimed several regularities in rural-urban patterns of movement: (a) the majority of migrants go only a short distance; (b) migration proceeds in a series of short steps; (c) long-distance migrants, by preference, have a major center of commerce or industry as their destination; (d) each current of migration produces a reciprocal counter-current; (e) females are more migratory than males; (f) most migrants are adults; (g) large towns grow more by migration than natural increase; (h) migration increases in volume as industry and commerce develop and transportation improves; (i) the largest volume of internal migration is rural-urban migration; and (j) the major determinants of migration are economic forces.

These observations indicate that rural-urban migration became an adaptive strategy for rural people in centuries past, as their agrarian **livelihoods** were transformed, whether by internal crises as in the case of feudalism, or with the onset of **urbanization** under mercantilism and industrial **capitalism**. Ravenstein, on the other hand, did not consider the migrant's decision-making process, nor attempt to explain why some rural adults move, while others would not. For this, we can turn to another conceptual explanation, forwarded by Standing (1981), on the contextual/structural forces of peasant migration during feudal times.

Standing (1981) proposed that four conditions were necessary to make peasants in traditional communities (see **community**) become migrants: the conditions being reflected in the decay (crisis) in the traditional mode of exploitation (feudalism in Standing's example). First, migration must exist as an acceptable response to adversity or frustrated aspirations. Second, peasants come to identify their condition as neither just nor inevitable, because some reciprocal relationship between them and their feudal landlords has been violated. Third, staying and instigating a revolt is seen to have a minimal chance of success, because the peasants are not united, nor organized against oppression, **violence** or economic threats. Fourth, peasants reject customary forms of exploitation because of a growing sense of deprivation and despair that things won't get better.

This theoretical explanation distinguishes between moving and staying in times past. It can also be re-framed to explain migration among other previously immobile cohorts in rural societies. The constraining contexts of geographical situations in contemporary rural societies may differ from feudal conditions, but the conflictual relations between the powerful and powerless, the landed and landless, and crises experienced in developing-world rural societies from colonial to postcolonial times prompt similar structural responses. The newly industrializing, and modernizing, urban centers in developing countries provide the feasible destinations for the rural uprooted.

More recent research in developing countries has added further generalizations about rural-to-urban migration (see Friedmann and Wulff (1976)): (k) [a]lthough the potential migrant is always an individual, or a small family unit, the decision to migrate is frequently collective, involving members of the extended kinship group and occasionally of the rural **community** as a whole; (l) the group making the decision does so rationally on the basis of direct, personal information concerning economic and social opportunities in the target city relative to the equivalent opportunities perceived to exist in their rural origins; (m) migrants tend to come in proportionately larger numbers from densely populated areas that are in frequent contact with the destination city; (n) migrants are positively selected from their home **population**s for such characteristics as age, marital status, sex, **education** and family income. Thus, it is not the poorest but the best endowed who tend to migrate to the city. Over time, however, the degree of selectivity may very well decline; (o) migrants move in what may be called a spatially extended social field through which she or he maintains steady contact with kin, family, tribal group or home community and which, in turn, is held together by a network of reciprocal obligations; (p) migrants take various spatial pathways to their city destinations, some via step-wise movements up the urban hierarchy, others via direct "leaps" from small village (see **villages**) to distant urban center; and (q) not all moves to the city are permanent. Among the temporary forms of rural-urban migration, the following types have been singled out: reverse migration, **circular migration**, and floating (i.e. constantly moving) migration.

Both "push" factors (i.e. rural conditions) and "pull" factors (i.e. the attractions of cities) are important because both create structural contexts that influence migrants and non-migrants. However, without rural factors, migrant potential would not be generated, nor an urban destinational choice made, so the exit-calculus appears to be the primary instigator. Despite rural-urban migration being the largest specific flow among all human movements in contemporary times, considerable proportions of rural populations prefer to remain immobile, or are unwilling to permanently relocate to an urban center, or to another country (Hammer *et al.*, 1997). Rural-urban migration, therefore, is a major contributor to the rapid growth of today's cities, especially in developing countries, but there is still considerable doubt concerning when – if at all – rural areas will experience de-population.

See also: circular migration; Harris-Todaro model; migration; remittances; rural development; rural poverty; urbanization

Further reading

Friedmann, J. and Wulff, R. (1976) *The Urban Transition: Comparative Studies of Newly Industrializing Societies*, London: Edward Arnold.

Hammar, T., Tamas, K. and Faist, T. (1997) *International Migration, Immobility and Development: Multidisciplinary Perspectives*, Oxford and New York: Berg.

Ravenstein, E. G. (1885) "The Laws of Migration," *Journal of the Statistical Society* 48: 167–219.

Ravenstein, E. G. (1889) "The Laws of Migration," *Journal of the Statistical Society* 52: 241–89.

Standing, G. (1981) "Migration and Modes of Exploitation," *Journal of Peasant Studies*, 8: 173–211.

DENNIS CONWAY

S

safety nets against poverty

The concept of a "safety net" against poverty refers to the various formal and informal mechanisms that may prevent individuals or social groups falling into **poverty**. Social protection is generally concerned with the position of people who are vulnerable. **Vulnerability** depends more on the possibility of changing circumstances than it does on the experience of poverty. Social protection is more likely to offer "income smoothing," allowing the maintenance of income during periods of interruption, than the delivery of basic income to people who would not otherwise be part of the formal economy.

The **World Bank** distinguishes three main forms of social protection: labor market protection (see **labor markets**), social insurance, and social assistance. Many social protection systems are based on a principle of insurance, and cover mainly salaried employees for such circumstances as illness, disability, or old age (see **ageing; pensions**). In developing countries, the coverage of social security is often partial and focused on relatively advantaged groups, such as civil servants, and salaried workers in secure **employment**. Provision for poor people cannot generally rely on insurance, because of the difficulty of raising contributions. Where it exists, social protection for the poor tends to be state-based, tax-financed and limited in scope.

"Safety nets" are traditionally associated with social assistance provision, though the World Bank uses the term to refer more broadly to other forms of income maintenance used to manage risk (see **risk and insurance strategies**). The provision of a safety net depends on the assumption that most people will ordinarily be able to manage from alternative resources. The idea of a safety net is often associated, in consequence, with a "residual" model of welfare, where provision is seen as a last resort (see **welfare economics; welfare state**). Residual welfare is usually distinguished from "institutional" welfare, in which need and social protection are accepted as a normal part of social life. The distinction is not, however, a firm one: both residual and institutional models require some kind of safety net in order to operate effectively.

Safety nets are required principally in circumstances where goods and services may not otherwise be available, or where universal provision is not made. Several developed countries have discretionary safety nets, which work by some kind of personal claim and appraisal, but this is **labor-intensive** and depends on a manageable level of demand. The main mechanism through which safety nets operate is "selectivity," which depends on an assessment of need. Selectivity is sometimes confused with **targeting**, but the ideas are distinct. It is possible to target broadly defined groups, like old people, with no test of income; it is also possible to target poorer people through universal social policy measures, like **food** subsidies for items which are more likely to be consumed by poorer people. Selectivity depends on the distinction of eligible and non-eligible populations. The exclusion of non-eligible recipients is often associated with high administrative costs, boundary problems, and failure to reach eligible groups.

See also: food security; intrahousehold allocations; joint families; risk and insurance strategies;

pensions; poverty; targeting; welfare economics; welfare state

Further reading

Atkinson, A. (1995) *Incomes and the Welfare State*, Cambridge: Cambridge University Press. See chs 11–13.

World Bank (2001) *Social Protection Sector Strategy Paper: From Safety Net to Springboard*, Washington DC: World Bank.

PAUL SPICKER

Sahel

The Sahel, or "shore" in Arabic, is a region of Africa forming the southern edge of the Saharan desert blending seamlessly into the slightly less arid Sudano-Sahel belt to its southern edge. It passes through Senegal, the Gambia, Mauritania, Mali, Burkina Faso, Niger, northern Nigeria and Chad. Approximately 50 million people of the Sahel pursue diverse livelihood strategies including **agriculture**, **livestock** herding (see **livelihoods; pastoralism**), fishing, short and long-distance trading, and a variety of urban occupations. Ethnically and linguistically diverse, some people were organized as "headless" societies, others in hierarchically organized kingdoms, and over the centuries, several Islamic empires have risen and fallen. Farming – based on dryland (see **drylands**) grains like millet and sorghum – is almost entirely reliant on three months of summer rainfall, except along the banks of the Niger River and other natural or artificial water sources (see **irrigation; water management**). Livestock rearing is practiced throughout the Sahel region, both as an exclusive livelihood activity, as co-determinous with **agriculture** (which can be the source of conflict between herders and farmers), and in agro-pastoral livelihood systems.

There are four reasons why the Sahel has become important both materially and symbolically for international development. First, the Sahel has offered significant challenges to making a living, and even for survival. Much of the Sahel remains rural, and **economic development** has

been extremely modest. Average incomes are some of the lowest in the world. Extremes of temperature, periodic **drought**, and disease vectors frustrate traditional rainfed farming systems, and threaten herds. Their persistence, and the intensification of production as **population** densities have risen, is a testament to Sahelian adaptability and resilience (Mortimore, 1998). **Migration**, both temporary and permanent, is a key element to Sahelian livelihoods – the movement of income seekers to the West African coast is the second largest migration stream in Africa after movements around the South African mines.

Second, the Sahel offers historical lessons about the impacts of colonialism (see **colonialism, history of; colonialism, impacts of**). It was never isolated from African trade networks or from the predations of **slavery**, but colonial administration was not achieved until the turn of the twentieth century. This began sixty years of French rule (British, in Nigeria and the Gambia) that was frequently unprofitable, and based on limited dryland commodity production (particularly for cotton) and exploiting Sahelian labor for distant coastal plantations. This sixty-year period generated great resentment in the early years, and isolated resistance. France has kept strong ties, and assessment of its postcolonial legacy has been equally ambivalent (see **postcolonialism**).

Third, the Sahel came to global prominence in the 1970s as a symbol of crisis and hopelessness, and this image has endured (see also **complex emergencies; narratives of development**). Much debate about **desertification** has focused on the Sahel, although the nature of this problem and its relationship to local land use and drought is controversial. In the postcolonial era (see also **decolonization**), with newly independent nations still finding their feet and political leaders jockeying for power, a succession of dry years led to the "the quintessence of a major environmental emergency" (Raynaut, 1997) after long periods of drought and **food** shortages in the 1970s and again in the 1980s. International agencies, **non-governmental organizations (NGOs)**, and governments responded with offers of **food aid**, financial support, and some sustained development programs.

Fourth, the Sahel has become a central location for international development since this time (although **aid** flows are now declining). Efforts to instill good **governance**, profitable cooperatives, **gender** equality, better **health** care, soil conservation (see **soil erosion and soil fertility**), and the promotion of agricultural exports are legion. Political **decentralization** is the dominant theme at present. Assessments of these development efforts, and the fate of the Sahel in general, range from relatively upbeat given its status as a "late globalizer" with the potential to develop further markets and urban centers, through to pessimistic, given its rising population levels, environmental problems, and indifferent governance (Batterbury and Warren, 2001: Mortimore, 1998). Aid, modernity, and development cannot escape the Sahel's history.

See also: chronic poverty; desertification; drought; drylands; landlocked developing countries (LLDCs); migration; pastoralism

Further reading

Batterbury, S. and Warren, A. (eds) (2001) "The African Sahel 25 Years after the Great Drought," special issue of *Global Environmental Change* 11:1 1–95.

Mortimore, M. (1998) *Roots in the African Dust: Sustaining the African Drylands*, Cambridge: Cambridge University Press.

Raynaut, C. (ed.) (1997) *Societies and Nature in the Sahel*, London: Routledge.

SIMON BATTERBURY

salinization

Salinization refers to the accumulation of salts on soil surfaces often occurring under prolonged high air temperature conditions (e.g. **drylands**). Rapid surface water evaporation and the consequent proximity of groundwater to a soil surface lead to the capillary rise of water and the subsequent evaporative concentration of salts. The surface is thereby affected by the accretion of salts and the occasional development of salt crusts. Salinization has been increasingly induced through human activity, especially with the expansion of **irrigation** and the intensification of water extraction

and application, which raise groundwater levels toward soil surfaces. High salt concentrations are deleterious to most plants as a result of the degradation of soil structure (low aeration and permeability to water), the preferential subsurface water flow toward salt crystals and away from roots (water deficit stress), and the high toxicity due to the presence of large amounts of certain salts.

See also: agriculture; desertification; drylands; irrigation; soil erosion and soil fertility

SALVATORE ENGEL-DI MAURO

same-sex sexualities

Debates about same-sex sexualities focus on lesbian, gay, bisexual, transgender and intersex people (LGBTIs) in relation to development theory and practice. The topic is relevant to other debates such as **sexualities**, **human rights**, and **social exclusion**.

Development discourses have tended to ignore sexuality or include it only in relation to **population** and **family planning**, or **health** and **violence**. Development planners have historically tended to assume that sexualities in developing countries are uniformly heterosexual, and associated with risk and danger, but never pleasure or love, and development funding has been channeled accordingly. Likewise, intersex and transgender identities have been ignored. **Gender** and development approaches have emphasized the difference between a biological sex and a socially constructed gender, but in doing so have reified the "sex" category. Critics have therefore proposed that these approaches further marginalize people who feel themselves to be neither woman nor man, or whose sex does not correspond to their gender.

More generally, LGBTI people often face violence and discrimination, affecting their **education** and **livelihoods**, and rendering them vulnerable to **poverty** and **marginalization**. The numbers of LGBTIs is often grossly underestimated because due to stigma and persecution, such sexual relationships and gender identities are often kept secret. Stigmas about sexualities are being challenged by LGBTIs organizing throughout developing countries, sometimes with support from international donors. Some developing countries, such as South Africa, Brazil, Mexico, Uruguay and Croatia, have adopted legislation against discrimination on grounds of sexual orientation.

Human rights frameworks have created an entry point for LGBTI issues in relation to development. In April 2003, Brazil presented a draft resolution to the United Nations Commission on Human Rights, co-sponsored by over twenty countries, which expressed "deep concern at the occurrence of violations of human rights all over the world against persons on grounds of their sexual orientation." Although this resolution was prevented from succeeding by opposition from Muslim states and the Vatican, the presentation of this resolution in itself marks new possibilities for raising the issue of sexuality in such arenas. It also points to the use of **religion** as grounds for opposition to particular sexualities.

HIV/AIDS (see **HIV/AIDS (definition and treatment); HIV/AIDS (policy issues)**) has also created possibilities for greater recognition and access to resources for groups considered at risk, including men who have sex with men (MSM), but not lesbians, as lesbians are assumed less likely to engage in risky sexual practices. Approaches that support **empowerment** and **community** building among MSM have been recognized as most effective in promoting safer sexual behavior. Nevertheless, the association with HIV/AIDS has also led to further stigmatization and regulation.

Recognizing LGBTI issues has implications for policy regarding the family, education, health, youth and HIV/AIDS, and could result in policy changes that benefit heterosexuals also. In spite of increasing awareness of the need for such changes, development action in this area is limited by rising conservatism. For example, under President G. W. Bush, the USA has placed restrictions on US funding of organizations that promote rights to homosexuality. Once again, a Western nation channels development funding according to its assumptions of what sexualities in other countries are or should be.

See also: HIV/AIDS (definition and treatment); HIV/AIDS (policy issues); human rights; sexualities; social exclusion

Further reading

Jolly, S. (2000) "Queering Development: Exploring the Links Between Same-Sex Sexualities, Gender and Development," *Gender and Development* 8:1 78–88.

Lind, A. and Share, J. (2003) "Queering Development: Institutionalized Heterosexuality in Development Theory, Practice and Politics in Latin America," pp. 55–73 in Bhavnani, K.-K., Foran, J. and Kurian, P. (eds) *Feminist Futures: Re-imagining Women, Culture, and Development*, London: Zed.

SUSIE JOLLY

sanitation

Sanitation refers to the safe disposal of human waste and the maintenance of clean living conditions. Along with access to safe water, it is an essential yet often underestimated factor for development. Approximately half of the world's **population** lacks access to proper sanitation, with the percentage of those with access to sanitation steadily dropping. Inadequate sanitation mainly affects populations through deteriorated **health** conditions. Improper or inadequate disposal of human waste results in excreta-related illnesses and diseases, predominantly cholera and diarrhea (see **waste management**). These sicknesses produce **malnutrition**, impede healthy mental and physical development, and hinder learning abilities. In turn, these matters increase individual and state (see **state and state reform**) health care costs and create losses in labor and **productivity**.

Most often, those without access to adequate sanitation are the poorest of the population (see **marginalization; vulnerability**). Because of the rapid growth of urban areas, the poor often live in **shantytowns**. The limited economic situations of the residents do not allow for self-implementation of sewer systems. The overcrowding of their neighborhoods allows little room for such systems, even if the means were available. Lastly, settlements may be built on fragile land (that has not already been developed), and hence the installation of sewer systems is difficult.

The inability to remove waste in safe ways has tremendous consequences on health. Since no proper disposal structure exists, waste is regularly introduced to the ground. In the cases where **community** wells are available, the water becomes contaminated through the ground. Additionally, sewage infects people, homes, and **food** when it dries and becomes airborne. In general, people must pass through and be exposed to waste on a continuous basis, which compromises the health and tolerance of the population. It is argued that the lack of sanitation creates a **poverty trap** whereby individuals are often spending their limited income on acute health care resulting from excreta-related illnesses. During the period for which they are ill, individuals are unable to work, and **employment** opportunities may also be lost.

There is clearly a need to increase the provision of sanitation in rapidly urbanizing locations. However, simply transferring current solutions employed in developed countries to developing world cities may be inadequate, because there are significantly more people now facing sanitation problems in developing countries. The developed world relies heavily on ample access to water to provide adequate sanitation systems. However, the reliance on water for all sanitation services may be inappropriate given simultaneous demands for providing **drinking water**, and hence new technological solutions, often integrated with other forms of waste management may be needed.

See also: drinking water; health; primary health care; water-borne diseases; waste management; water management

Further reading

Khan, A. (1997) *The Sanitation Gap: Development's Deadly Menace*, New York: UNICEF.

World Bank (1994) "Infrastructure: Achievements, Challenges, and Opportunities," pp. 13–22 in *World Development Report 1994: Infrastructure for Development*, Washington DC: World Bank.

JANE KIM

science and technology

Scientific research and resulting technological innovations have historically been seen to be a crucial component of the development process (see also **technology policy**). Usually science and technology were seen to be controlled by the state (see **state and state reform**), and concentrated in richer countries. Passing scientific research and technologies to developing countries was also seen to be a direct means of helping developing countries. During his inaugural speech in 1949, US President Harry S. Truman (see **Truman's Bold New Program (1949)**), urged a new program "for making the benefits of our scientific advances and industrial progress available for the improvement and growth of underdeveloped areas." Such views have been reflected in the **green revolution**, where new agricultural techniques and high-yielding varieties of seeds were introduced to Asia and Africa during the 1970s following intensive scientific research, particularly from the **Consultative Group on International Agricultural Research (CGIAR)**, whose self-description states: "nourishing the future through scientific excellence." Medical assistance (see **biomedicine**) and environmental protection (see **environment; pollution**) are other topics closely related to science and technology. The cases of the **newly industrialized economies (NIEs)** of East Asia are examples where states have invested carefully in indigenous science and technology for the sake of **export-led growth** and technological competitiveness (see **developmental state**).

State-led investment in science and technology clearly remains important in shaping long-term abilities of countries to maintain highly skilled workforces, **technological capability**, and competitiveness. Many critics, however, would suggest that the international transfer of "scientific advances and industrial progress" have not proceeded as President Truman suggested. The lack of international **technology transfer** is due in part to the growing importance of private companies in science and technology, and the perceived risk to **intellectual property rights (IPRs)** and competitiveness that emerges from sharing technological progress. Successful technology transfer is generally a long-term and complex process, involving much attention to the ability to recover costs of invest-ment and in ensuring that technologies are appropriate to local needs. Furthermore, the **brain drain** of qualified technical staff away from developing countries is another factor that pre-vents the development of indigenous scientific capability.

More broadly, however, analysts are increas-ingly acknowledging that science and technology reflect social and economic contexts, and that politics affect how science is presented as authoritative knowledge (e.g. see Jasanoff *et al.*, 1995). Such views are not necessarily "anti-science" or critical of scientific organizations, but urge greater attention to the cultural and political factors reflected in science and scientific organi-zations, especially when they are involved in transferring scientific knowledge between different locations. The historic prevalence of biomedicine above **indigenous medicine** systems, for exam-ple, has been criticized for legitimizing medical practices that may be inappropriate for local needs, and which may fail to harness existing **local knowledge**. Feminist critics (e.g. Harding, 1991) have argued that much knowledge within scientific innovations and policies reflects **male bias** in various ways: the identification of pro-blems, the people included in information gath-ering, and the proposed means of implementing policies. Some critics have also argued that the green revolution (and more recently, **genetically modified organisms (GMOs)**) represented the imposition of Western-based science and tech-nologies onto diverse cultural means of produc-tion, which then marginalized those farmers (e.g. Shiva, 1992). Other examples include the criti-cism of so-called "scientific forestry," based upon **plantation forestry**, for reflecting the interests only of those who would see forests as sources of lumber (such as colonial authorities), and under-rating local forms of agriculture or forest man-agement (such as **shifting cultivation** or **community forestry**). Some analysts use the term **narratives of development** to describe examples of scientific explanations that have become seen as "received wisdom," but which are increasingly challenged by empirical work. Such analysts claim such narratives show how beliefs about causes of, or solutions to problems become

institutionalized, even when there is great uncer-tainty and controversy in possible explanations (see Forsyth, 2003).

The dissemination of scientific knowledge as "expertise" is also controversial. Historically, development "experts," such as agricultural extension workers, would tend to see their jobs as retraining local people to adopt methods that are more advanced. Such expertise may also be represented in so-called epistemic communities, which are networks of shared knowledge and objectives within scientists or development advo-cates, and are often communicated via **advocacy coalitions**. Extending epistemic communities is often portrayed as a progressive step toward increasing public understanding of science such as **climate change**, or of norms such as **human rights**. But critics have argued that epistemic communities do not always represent total inclu-sivity of all people, and may involve the commu-nication of certain beliefs that may not always be accurate or uniformly agreed upon. For example, the notion that developing countries need to receive climate-friendly technologies from devel-oped countries (such as photovoltaics) has been criticized because of the existing extent of indi-genous, and arguably, more appropriate technolo-gies in developing countries (such as biogas generators). Sometimes, the extension of "exper-tise" may also shape what is seen to be counter to the networks. Concepts such as "local knowledge" have become fashionable and representative of other themes such as **community**, **indigenous people**, and tradition, but the spatial and cultural boundaries used to define such terms may reflect the desire to oppose the more powerful network than local people's own experiences or definitions. Frequently, conflicts of expertise should not be seen as an "either/or" situation, but as the oppor-tunity to create a more inclusive integration of different kinds of expertise. Simply championing allegedly "local" knowledge for its own sake may not help address important developmental pro-blems, and may also impose outsiders' visions of what is "local" upon certain people. Yet, believing uncritically in the authority of scientific networks or epistemic communities may also overlook the inherent assumptions and political implications such **institutions** bring.

Current approaches to science and technology studies (or STS) seek to integrate themes from philosophy and sociology of science in order to show the political and cultural assumptions contained within science, and their impacts on society. Sometimes, these approaches have been stereotypically portrayed as relativistic, anti-modern, and unhelpful by some orthodox mathematicians and physicists (the so-called "Science Wars" in the 1990s typified this standoff). These criticisms, however, overlook the desire of most STS scholars to make science work better for poor people, and the need to avoid some of the insensitivities of scientific practice when applied universally and without heed to social context. The aim of a more critical approach to science and technology is to show how either is coproduced with culture and politics. Increasing the relevance of science and technology for development lies in acknowledging these social influences, and in ensuring that they are made more transparent and inclusive in the future.

See also: brain drain; Consultative Group on International Agricultural Research (CGIAR); environment; indigenous knowledge; local knowledge; narratives of development; technology policy; technology transfer

Further reading

See the journals *Science, Technology and Human Values*; *Science and Public Policy*.
Forsyth, T. (2003) *Critical Political Ecology: The Politics of Environmental Science*, London and New York: Routledge.
Gieryn, T. (1999) *Cultural Boundaries of Science: Credibility on the Line*, Chicago: University of Chicago Press.
Harding, S. (1991) *Whose Science? Whose Knowledge?*, Maidenhead: Open University Press.
International Association of Science and Technology for Development: http://www.iasted.org/
Jasanoff, S., Markle, G., Petersen, J. and Pinch, T. (eds) (1995) *Handbook of Science and Technology Studies*, Thousand Oaks CA: Sage.
Science and Development Network: http://www.scidev.net/

Shiva, V. (1992) *The Violence of the Green Revolution: Third World Agriculture, Ecology and Politics*, London: Zed.

TIM FORSYTH

sector-wide approaches (SWAps)

Sector-wide approaches (SWAps) is an approach to aid in which governments take the lead in negotiating with donors how and where **aid** money will be spent. The aim of SWAps is to ensure greater **coherence** in aid. Donors contribute to a single pool of funding to support the development of the entire sector within the framework of a locally owned strategy and approach. SWAps are being developed in countries with a high dependency on aid in sectors such as **health**, **education** and transport (see **transport policy**).

The SWAps approach was developed in the late 1990s, due to criticisms of the ineffectiveness of a multiplicity of donor projects, which create excess work for recipient governments and can lead to overlap, uneven coverage, inconsistent approaches and a lack of sustainability. Hence, the acknowledgment that pooling donor funds within the framework of a locally owned strategy and approach is more likely to achieve stated goals of more equitable service provision.

One of the main theoretical aspects of SWAps is that while they represent a partnership (see **partnerships**) between government and donors, the government is the final arbiter. If this could be achieved, it would represent a real shift in the relationship between donors and governments. In the short term, this has placed a great emphasis on strengthening the capacity of governments to develop policy, manage resources and evaluate progress toward goals (see **capacity building**).

The pooling of funds means that all donors use the same management systems; this attempts to overcome problems of inefficiency caused by separate donor projects and to increase **transparency** of both donors and government. The move away from separate projects means that donors can no longer take credit for their successes, or failures;

instead, all parties assume collective responsibility for achievements and failures within the sector.

The sector is defined in its broadest sense to include private and **non-governmental organizations (NGOs)**. It is further recognised that **civil society** has an active role to play in the design and monitoring of the SWAp. However, there are concerns that due to the emphasis on strengthening government bodies and facilities, donors and governments will dominate policy development and NGOs will be sidelined.

SWAps provide an opportunity for refocusing the work of a sector to provide services more sensitive to those in greatest need, whether by **gender**, age, social group or geographic location. The recognition of civil society's monitoring role increases the likelihood of this happening. In addition, public sector institutions can potentially be reshaped to become more gender sensitive and responsive to previously excluded groups (see **social integration**).

As SWAps are still at an early stage of implementation, there is limited evaluation of their impact. Concerns have been raised over the increased influence of donors on one hand, and the greater control by governments on the other. It is currently unclear how either of these eventualities could potentially impact on equitable service provision.

See also: aid; aid effectiveness and aid evaluation; coherence

Further reading

Cassels, A. (1997) *A Guide to Sector-wide Approaches for Health Development*, Geneva: WHO.

Foster, M. (2000) *Experience with Implementing Sector Wide Approaches: A Background Working Paper for the DFID White Paper*, London: Overseas Development Institute.

HELEN ELSEY AND SALLY THEOBALD

security

The relationship between development and security takes definition through two foci. The first is a national security focus characterized by a growing concern with underdevelopment as a threat to national security in the developing world, and a source of terrorism and other radical political movements that impact on life in the industrialized world. The second relationship, a human **well-being** focus, examines the ways in which development might address various sectoral security issues (see **environmental security; food security; job security**) to improve the quality of life for those living in the developing world. These two linkages are not mutually exclusive, but as they seek different goals, they often come into conflict with one another.

Development has been linked to state security (see **state and state reform**) at least since the **Bretton Woods** meetings, where one primary concern of the Allied powers was the prevention of economic deprivation, such as that seen in Weimar Germany, which might lead to armed conflicts. The **Cold War** perpetuated the idea of development as a means of containing security threats at the global scale. For example, modernization theorist Walter Rostow (see **modernization theory**), who also served as Richard Nixon's National Security Advisor, argued that his role in the Vietnam War was one of development theorist. From Rostow's perspective, a developed capitalist economy was less vulnerable to communist ideology, and therefore the Vietnam War served to protect places like Japan and Korea from communist expansion until their economies had developed. At the same time, development was employed as a security tool at the national scale, for example as a means of controlling rural **populations** to secure national sovereignty, such as in Tanzania's forced villagization effort of the 1960s and 1970s (see **villages**). Under villagization, the Tanzanian government sought to combine a controlled economy, modern agricultural technology, and a reworked landscape into a means ostensibly aimed at improving the quality of rural life, but most often used for control over rural residents, even at great cost to rural **livelihoods**.

Debates about development and national security are no longer dominated by Cold War modernization theory. Indeed critical development studies have highlighted the abuse of development in the name of national security. But debates about security still concern issues such as natural resource scarcity (see **natural resources**), economic scarcity and other causes of underdevelopment as threats to the state. As these issues do not easily lend themselves to military solutions, security studies have turned to other means of "containing" or "managing" these threats, means which include **economic development** and the promotion of **democracy** and transparent **governance**. Meanwhile, development practitioners and theorists have adopted security as a concept not for application to the defense of the state, but through which they can address the barriers to the improvement of the quality of life in developing countries. Even organizations such as the **World Bank** and **Organization for Economic Cooperation and Development (OECD)** have developed agendas to address conflict and post-conflict situations (see **conflict management; post-conflict rehabilitation**). In this sense, national security and development remain closely linked in the post-Cold War context, though how those links take shape, and to what end these links are forged, are still contentious points.

See also: arms sales and controls; Cold War; conflict management; environmental security; food security; human security; military and security; peacekeeping; state and state reform; war

Further reading

Duffield, M. (2001) *Global Governance and the New Wars: The Merging of Development and Security*, London: Zed.

Rotberg, R. (ed.) (2003) *State Failure and State Weakness in a Time of Terror*, Washington DC: Brookings Institution.

EDWARD R. CARR

sex ratio

A sex ratio is the relative proportion of males and females in a given population, usually expressed as the number of males per 100 females. Sex ratios are affected by gender-differentiated rates of **mortality** (including *in utero*; see **amniocentesis (sex-selection)**) and **migration**. National-level sex ratios are often used in an attempt to quantify the effects of **male bias** in mortality. It is often difficult to estimate expected sex ratios if there is no **gender** discrimination, as it is affected by sex differences in biological robustness at birth and throughout the lifecourse, and it is in turn altered by improved longevity and **population** growth. Despite these difficulties, some analysts have estimated that there were between 60 and 113 million fewer women in the world at the beginning of the twenty-first century than if there had been gender equity in survival. These estimates, however, are highly affected by the expected sex ratio and other assumptions used in the calculations.

See also: amniocentesis (sex-selection); fertility; gender; infant and child mortality; population

KAREN MOORE

sex tourism

Sex tourism is generally used to denote a variety of sexual relationships between male or female tourists and men, women and children residing in developing countries. At the one end, are short-term relationships most accurately described as a prostitute-client relationship in which a sum of money is agreed on and which takes place in a brothel or bar renowned for providing this additional service. At the other end, there are relationships of a more ambiguous nature. The borders between girl/boyfriend and sex worker are fuzzy, and for the tourist the relationship is embedded in the realm of vacation fun and romance. The duration can range from one day to the extent of the whole vacation. Monetary and material gains are undoubtedly part of the relationship, but are often perceived as gifts. In some cases, marriage is proposed or a trip to the tourist's home is another possibility. Even though many women and men earn their living from their involvement in these types of relationships, and many tourists come to their vacation destination with this type of sexual relationship in mind, this fuzziness impedes categorizing it as a purely professional relationship.

The growth of the sex tourism industry is historically inscribed in the unequal relations of power between developed and developing countries. Although **prostitution/sex work** has existed for centuries in both countries, sex tourism in Thailand

and the Philippines flourished during the USA military presence in Southeast Asia. In the Caribbean, sex tourism cannot be fully understood without historically examining the presence of European colonial powers and the institutionalization of **slavery**. Contemporaneously, the unequal relationships of power are (re)articulated in the economic differences between the tourist and the sex worker and the meanings of gender and sexuality constructed in the "exotic Other" (see **Orientalism**).

Sex tourism has generally been geared to male sex tourists. Men have been able to choose to go to sexually eroticized countries as individuals or in package tours promoting sex. In recent years, with the growth in the number of "beach boys" working in the Caribbean and West African beach resorts, women's role as paying sex tourist has become integrated into the debate. While some studies call women's participation a form of "romance tourism" as their motivations and desires may differ from men's, others claim this to be an artificial distinction glossing over women's active participation in reproducing unequal relations of power.

Sex tourism cannot be studied as an isolated phenomenon. It is embedded in the political economies of developing countries. For example, although prostitution is still formally illegal in Thailand, a large percentage of that country's **gross domestic product (GDP)** is derived from the sex industry. In an attempt to stay true to its socialist doctrine, the Cuban government tries to repress all forms of sex work. At the same time, Cuban "beauties" are used in an attempt to lure foreign currency to the island and stimulate the growth of its tourist industry. Thus, sex tourism must be seen in a framework that includes North-South relations, global and local political and economic trends, and the fluctuations in the international (sex) tourism industry.

See also: child prostitution; prostitution/sex work; slavery; tourism

Further reading

Kempadoo, K. (ed.) (1999) *Sun, Sex and Gold: Tourism and Sex Work in the Caribbean*, Lanham MD: Rowman and Littlefield.

Truong, T. D. (1990) *Sex, Money and Morality: The Political Economy of Prostitution and Tourism in South East Asia*, London: Zed.

LORRAINE NENCEL

SEX WORK *see* prostitution/sex work

sexualities

Debates about sexualities and development analyze sexual meanings, power relations, and gendered colonial legacies in such issues as **violence**, **health**, work and **human rights**. Sexuality involves desires and erotic emotions. It is expressed through socially constructed bodies, identities, practices and **institutions** across interlocking political arrangements with class, **gender**, **religion**, generational and racial-ethnic dynamics. Increasingly, analysts have acknowledged the diversity of perspectives on sexuality by referring to them as "sexualities" rather than simply "sexuality." Questions of sexualities are often discussed alongside the constructions of gender and development. Debates may also include, although not exclusively, questions of **same-sex sexualities**.

Early twentieth-century notions of sexualities relied on essentializing discourse of sexology, rooting sexuality in biology, physical attributes and hormonal activities (see **race and racism**). Such biological notions provided a racialized justification for various experiences of colonialism (see **colonialism, history of; colonialism, impacts of**). This justification institutionalized patriarchal nuclear households as the social norm in developing countries through military violence, religious indoctrination and private land enclosure. **Population** policies also reflected assumptions about sexual practice that were commonly accurate in different contexts.

While sexual violence has not been central to development, it becomes a salient public concern when, for instance, male factory supervisors commit acts of sexual violence (see **domestic violence**) against women working in **export processing zones (EPZs)**. Consequently, many women living through development face the brunt of male sexualized physical violence and emotional harassment at home, at work and during wars. Collectively these women seek ways to survive and challenge institutional violence (also see **Convention on the Elimination of All Forms of Discrimination Against Women (CEDAW); domestic law**).

Development programs have also sought to improve sexual health in developing countries (see **sexually transmitted diseases (STDs)**). The most common approach has been to provide reproductive health services to poor heterosexual married couples. Some critics, however, have argued that these approaches adopt a limited perspective, and do not address the needs or concerns of same-sex sexualities, for example. The HIV/AIDS pandemic (see **HIV/AIDS (definition and treatment); HIV/AIDS (policy issues)**) has expanded health programs to provide further attention to smaller pockets of groups who might practice "at-risk" sexual behaviors, such as gay men, sex workers and overseas contract workers. This attention has resulted in increased social regulation of these groups' sexual lives. However, in certain contexts, the new attention to questions of HIV/AIDS has helped gay men and lesbians gain assistance from the state (see **state and state reform**), and build mutually supportive networks without necessarily coming out directly about their sexualities.

Prostitution/sex work has become a prominent, yet divisive, development issue. Some feminists regard female sex workers as commodified victims of **poverty**, providing services to local and male clients from developed countries. These feminists also argue that such sex work is a form of Western domination when men receive pleasure at the expense of poor women's physical and emotional labor. Other feminists argue for a greater attention on sex workers' identities, desires, agency and their collective capability to overcome structural constraints. Yet, others have argued that prostitution/sex work should be identified and empowered as a valid livelihood strategy (see **livelihoods; sex tourism**).

Many developing-country lesbian, gay, and transgender activists have placed sexual politics on the development and human rights agenda. These activists challenge the institutionalization of heterosexuality as evident in the imprisonment, **social exclusion**, political restriction and economic **marginalization** of sexual minorities. They make visible the expressions of marginal sexual identities and sexual communities (see **community**) as well as the sexual aspects of their communal experiences locally, regionally and globally. The sexual politics in these communities have been forged and organized often under national liberation struggles (such as in South Africa) and have sought to transform the development agenda.

See also: child prostitution; gender; HIV/AIDS (policy issues); human rights; same-sex sexualities; sex tourism

Further reading

Chua, P., Bhavnani, K.-K. and Foran, J. (2000) "Women, Culture, Development: A New Paradigm for Development Studies," *Ethnic and Racial Studies* 23:5 820–41.

Fried, S. (2002) *Annotated Bibliography: Sexuality and Human Rights*, New York: International Women's Health Coalition. http://www.siyanda.org

PETER CHUA

sexually transmitted diseases (STDs)

Sexually transmitted diseases (STDs), once called venereal diseases, are caused by bacteria or viruses, and are transmitted by sexual activity with an infected person. They have placed an enormous burden of morbidity and **mortality**, particularly on developing nations, where access to treatment and care is not readily available. Northern and Western Europe have seen striking declines in the incidence of STDs, particularly gonorrhea and syphilis. However, in many developing countries, STDs remain a serious public **health** problem that contributes significantly to healthy life lost, especially among young, underprivileged women. In addition, the facilitation of HIV transmission in the presence of STDs confirms the need for political and financial commitment to prevention and treatment efforts, particularly in the developing world (see **HIV/ AIDS (definition and treatment); HIV/AIDS (policy issues)**).

STD surveillance has existed for several decades. Two methods for measuring the prevalence of STDs are commonly employed: national reporting and epidemiological surveys. Under-reporting is a serious problem in the assessment of STD prevalence. STDs are mostly asymptomatic and diagnostic tools are often not available. The stigma associated with STD infection contributes to its underestimation (see **disease, social constructions of**).

STDs can be classified both by the causative microbial agent (bacteria, protozoa or virus), as well as by the manifestation of symptoms. Bacterial and protozoal infections are mostly curative, while viral infections such as Human Papilloma Virus (HPV) or genital herpes cannot usually be cured. Symptomatically, STDs are classified into two types: ulcerative and inflammatory. Ulcerative STDs include chancroid, syphilis and genital herpes, and are characterized by the presence of ulcers. Inflammatory STDs include gonorrhea, chlamydia and trichomoniasis.

STDs share some characteristics that differentiate them from other infectious diseases. They tend to persist for long periods in an infected host, and as many are asymptomatic, they are easily spread. Individuals with large numbers of partners play a disproportionate role in STD transmission. Re-infection is a common occurrence. Young age is a major risk factor for STD acquisition, mostly because sexual partner change rates are age-dependent (see **sexualities**).

The most serious consequences of untreated STDs are in women and newborn children. Many STDs are asymptomatic in women. Additionally, women are more likely to become infected than men if exposed and, for many STDs, once infected are more susceptible to complications. Pregnant women are particularly vulnerable as mothers can often pass infection to the fetus during pregnancy, birth or breast-feeding. Active sexually transmitted infections during pregnancy may result in miscarriages, stillbirths or pre-term delivery.

There is evidence that the presence of STDs facilitates the transmission of HIV by increasing the infectivity and susceptibility to infection. However, debate exists about the contribution of STDs to the HIV pandemic, mostly because the association between STDs and HIV remains confounded by sexual behavior.

See also: epidemics; family planning; gender and communicable disease; health; HIV/AIDS (definition and treatment); HIV/AIDS (policy issues); sexualities

Further reading

Piot, P. (1994) "Sexually Transmitted Diseases in the 1990s: Global Epidemiology and Challenges for Control," *Sexually Transmitted Diseases* 21:2 7–13.

Wasserheit, J., Aral, S. and Holmes, K. (eds) (1991) *Research Issues in Human Behavior and Sexually Transmitted Diseases in the AIDS Era*, Washington DC: American Society for Microbiology.

PRERNA BANATI

shantytowns

"Shantytowns" is the name often used for urban settlements composed of low-quality **housing** that settlers have built themselves on land where they have no legal land titles, and where there is no, or poor, service provision. The term, however, is problematic because it is somewhat pejorative, and overlooks the social and political reasons that often underlie their emergence, plus the diverse ways in which settlers create **livelihoods** within shantytowns. The term is also similar to other terms such as "squatter settlement," (see **squatters**), or variously "self-help," "spontaneous," "irregular" or "informal-sector" settlements. The Brazilian word *favela* has also been used to denoted shantytowns.

Rapid and uncontrolled **urbanization** is a key cause of shantytowns. The **United Nations** estimates that by the year 2025, 5.5 billion people will live in cities (an urbanization rate of 57 percent), with 90 percent of the growth in the last fifty years having taken place in the developing world. Presently, the UNCHS (United Nations Centre for

Human Settlements) estimates that 1 billion urbanites live in slums or shantytowns, the majority of which are in developing cities. Some UNCHS figures indicate that in developing countries 30–70 percent of the urban **population** lives in irregular settlements. In Latin America, where 75 percent of people live in cities, planners estimate that 40–80 percent of urbanites live in irregular settlements. This means that 85 percent of the new housing stock built in the late 1980s and early 1990s was produced extra-legally (UNCHS, 1996). Shantytown dwellers are estimated to comprise 70 percent of Mexico City, 60 percent of Nairobi, and 25 percent of Delhi.

Shantytowns reflect a variety of development dilemmas. First, shantytowns generally reflect high levels of **rural poverty** and **rural-urban migration**, plus **poverty** affects the lives of most shantytown dwellers. While poverty is usually measured by income it is also characterized by poor access to adequate shelter, **health**, **security** and **education**. Many settlers seek livelihoods within the **urban informal sector** (see also **street-trading in urban areas**), as they may be excluded from formal **employment** opportunities in factories or elsewhere.

Initial policy approaches to shantytowns from the 1950s to the 1970s were generally repressive. National politicians found the large, sprawling and shabby settlements embarrassing for their country's public image and **tourism**, and sought to remove them forcibly. Academics and planners, however, pointed out some contradictions in this attitude. First, in many countries, housing and service provision in most shantytowns is better than in rural areas (a point apparently missed by many politicians and development "experts"). Second, standards of urban housing created by Western-educated politicians and policy-makers were - at the time - unrealistically high. In this early period, shantytowns were typified as marginal, violent cauldrons of social unrest and crime. In the 1950s and 1960s, two popular theoretical paradigms of poverty underpinned these views: the "myth of marginality" (see **marginalization**) and the "**culture of poverty**" thesis, which proposed that shantytowns largely reflected culturally-induced sites of poverty and lack of development. These theories have since been criticized for ignoring the socio-economic realities of life in the shantytowns and overlooking the importance of political intervention into the causes of poverty. But the negative stereotyping of shantytowns is still upheld by some governments and **media**.

From the late 1940s until the mid-1970s, a common response to shantytowns was to demolish them and build alternative, low-cost housing. Over time, however, it became clear that the provision of social housing was massively ineffective. In the 1980s, for example, there were shortfalls in low-income housing of 1 million units in South Africa, and 867,000 in Nigeria. The scenario in poorer countries was even more depressing.

Since the mid-1970s, however, there has been a general change in policy responses to shantytowns. This change resulted from the impacts of criticisms made by social scientists; the clear failure of so many repressive strategies; and a realization that shantytowns were to be an inevitable part of cities for the near future. Most qualitative research in shantytowns by social scientists has shown that many shantytown builders and dwellers are ambitious, hardworking and have the same values as the middle classes in their cities (see **sociology of development**). The culture of poverty argument was countered by arguments that people lived in shantytowns because of the consequences of national and international processes of **social exclusion** and spatial segregation, rather than simply because they were poor. Shantytowns were demonstrated to provide adequate shelter and **livelihoods**, including for women and **women-headed households**. New approaches prefer to look on shantytown communities (see **community**) as the rational attempts by the poor to gain a foothold in the city, a form of **human security**, and an investment in the future (Jones and Nelson, 1997). These new approaches coincided with development thinking in general that poor people be deemed capable of helping themselves and that governments' roles should be to help them in this endeavor. "Good housing should not be designed on the basis of... [outsiders'] assumptions about what the poor's needs ought to be, but should provide the flexibility by which the poor can trade off one need against another" (Gilbert and Gugler, 1992:142).

Since the 1980s, shantytown-upgrading and site and service schemes have proliferated. In the first steps agencies provide an existing shanty with roads, water-borne **sanitation**, **drinking water**, and perhaps electrification (see **electrification and power-sector reform**). In the site and service schemes agencies provide properly surveyed plots, roads, sewerage and water (the so-called "wet-core" provision) on which the urban poor were encouraged to build their own houses to minimum standard. More recently some development experts have advocated assistance in housing provision as a specific method of poverty alleviation: building houses generates employment, and income from renting rooms (Tipple in Jones and Nelson, 1999).

Since the 1990s, international agencies have also considered issues of land tenure (see ESF/ N-AERUS, 2001). Regularizing land tenure is widely thought to encourage residents to invest in upgrading housing; as well as to provide them **security** and collateral to borrow money (see **micro-credit and micro-finance**). Yet, although regularization programs are important, they are not a quick, cheap fix, which governments have often treated them as. They can only have important impacts on poverty if they are part of a larger package of public policies for improving infrastructure or service provision; urban **planning** reform; and **economic development** policies designed to maximize livelihoods. In this sense, the attention of development agencies has moved from the built environment of shantytowns themselves, to the livelihoods and opportunities for the people who live in them (ESF/N-AERUS, 2001; Fernandes, 2002).

See also: housing; land rights; livelihoods; mega-cities; micro-enterprises; planning; rural-urban migration; squatters; street children; street-trading in urban areas; urban development; urban informal sector; urbanization; women-headed households

Further reading

ESF/N-AERUS (2001) *Habitat et Modes D'Habiter*, Papers of the Workshop organized by the Network-Association of European Researchers on Urbanization in the South, Leuven and Brussels: European Science Foundation. http:// www.naerus.org

Fernandes, E. (2002) "The Influence of de Soto's The Mystery of Capital," in *Land Lines* 14:1 5–8, January. Published by the Lincoln Institute of Land Policy, http://www.lincolninst.edu/pubs/ landlines.asp

Gilbert, A. and Gugler, J. (1992) *Cities, Poverty and Development: Urbanization in the Third World*, Oxford: Oxford University Press.

Jones, S. and Nelson, N. (1999) *Urban Poverty in Africa: From Understanding to Alleviation*, London: IT Press.

UNCHS (1996) *An Urbanizing World: Global Report on Human Settlements*, Oxford: Oxford University Press.

NICI NELSON

SHELTER *see* housing; shantytowns

shifting cultivation

Shifting cultivation is a form of **agriculture** classically employed in the humid tropics by remote and migratory people. It is a system of cultivation that usually involves clearing forest or forest regrowth (commonly by the use of fire), planting crops for one or more years, and then relocating the cultivation to another piece of land, while the previously cultivated land is either abandoned or left fallow before being used again after at least one year. The use of fire is an effective means of clearing land, and the resulting ash improves soil fertility. Shifting cultivation is also known as "slash-and-burn" agriculture, although this term is sometimes considered simplistic and pejorative because it overlooks the complexity of many systems of shifting cultivation. Another term is "swidden" agriculture, based on the Old English word used to describe areas where land is cleared of vegetation and crops grown.

Precise definitions of shifting cultivation are difficult because the practice varies between different ethnic groups, and because many current forms of shifting cultivation have changed substantially in recent decades. Some early definitions of shifting cultivation distinguished between different forms of agriculture conducted by migratory and sedentary (i.e. permanently settled) farmers. The German biologist, Thomas Credner, for example, in 1935 divided shifting cultivators into two groups. The first of these were *Waldhackbauern* (forest swiddeners), such as the Karen or Khamu ethnic groups in mainland Southeast Asia who occupied land between the altitudes of 700 and 1,000 meters. The second were *Berghackbauern* (hill swiddeners), such as the Hmong or Akha in Southeast Asia, who lived above 1,000 meters. These two groups have also been generalized as "rotational" and "pioneer" cultivators (Grandstaff, 1980). The rotational groups practice a well-maintained system of fallow around permanent or semi-permanent villages (hence, the swiddens shifted). The pioneer cultivators practice a more intensive (and more exhaustive) agriculture of classically 10–20 years on the same swiddens before the whole village (see **villages**) relocated to new territory once soil had become depleted (hence, the villages shifted). Today, these classifications are considered highly idealized because – in most countries – shortage of land has made the pioneer form of cultivation almost impossible. Furthermore, the introduction of export crops such as cabbages and strawberries (often as the result of agricultural extension work), enforced **resettlement** of some shifting cultivators, and land-use restrictions in many forest areas have meant that many previously-pioneer cultivators now have become sedentarized and that fallow periods are much reduced in length. Indeed, the term "shifting cultivation" may now be questionable because much agriculture no longer "shifts."

Shifting cultivation has been widely criticized by ecologists for allegedly being a wasteful and inefficient use of resources, and contributing to **biodiversity** loss, soil erosion (see **soil erosion and soil fertility**), **deforestation** and even **climate change** (because of its use of fire). Such views are adopted, for example, by the **Consultative Group on International Agricultural Research (CGIAR)**'s "Alternatives to Slash and Burn" initiative. These views, however, have been widely criticized by a variety of agronomic, anthropological, and environmental research that has highlighted the variety of shifting cultivation

practices and the careful use of soil and **biodiversity** conservation measures by some groups (see **deforestation**). Moreover, the alleged impacts of shifting cultivation on lowland environmental problems such as water shortages or sedimentation have been challenged by research that points out the role of lowland water demand in increasing water shortages, and the long-term biophysical nature of many sedimentary or water regimes that pre-exist upland agriculture (see **watershed management; mountain development**). While shifting cultivation, or its like, still needs careful management and attention, critics suggest that its historic vilification reflects longer-term social and political resentment of remote, often migrant, farmers (who are often ethnic minorities), rather than a comprehensive understanding of their environmental impacts. Hence, managing shifting cultivation should be a political, as well as agronomic, concern, and include factors such as **citizenship** and land tenure (see **land rights**). Not acknowledging such political factors may enhance deforestation, and reduce **livelihoods** for cultivators.

See also: agriculture; agroforestry; community forestry; deforestation; environment; indigenous people; mountain development; soil erosion and soil fertility; watershed management

Further reading

Alternatives to Slash and Burn website: http://www.asb.cgiar.org/

Fox J., Dao Minh Truong, Rambo, A., Nghiem Phuong Tuyen, Le Trong Cuc and Stephen Leisz (2000) "Shifting Cultivation: A New Old Paradigm for Managing Tropical Forests," *BioScience* 50:6 521–8.

Grandstaff, T. (1980) *Shifting Cultivation in Northern Thailand: Possibilities for Development*, Tokyo: United Nations University.

TIM FORSYTH

shock therapy

"Shock therapy" – or the term, "Short, Sharp Shock" – refers to an abrupt change in economic management, widely associated with

postsocialism in Eastern and Central Europe (ECE) and the Former Soviet Union (FSU), in which it was attempted to replace planned state-socialist economies by liberal market economies. Shock therapy (also called the "big bang" approach) was originally developed in the 1980s to tackle crises of inflation (see **inflation and its effects**) in developing countries, especially Latin America. In the early 1990s, the term was adapted to refer to economic policies that essentially sought to replace centrally planned state socialism with liberal market economies.

Shock therapy was largely a reflection of the economic and political views of **neo-liberalism** generally of the 1980s. Margaret Thatcher, Helmut Kohl, and Ronald Reagan were in office, and pre-ferred economic liberalism and a minimal role for the state (see **state and state reform**). The main conceptual pillars were popular tax reductions, reduced state responsibility through the **privatization and liberalization** of state-owned enter-prises and **public sector** functions, and better economic performance. Unsurprisingly, there was little concern with the possibility of a new, speci-fically postsocialist form of **capitalism** emerging, such as "Market Leninism," and instead, the socialist experience was simply written off as a failed strategy. The focus on new policies was supported by the **World Bank** and **European Union**, and was welcomed initially with impa-tience in postsocialist countries (e.g. Poland, the Czech Republic, and East Germany) to be part of the "West."

Shock therapy consisted of three main elements: liberalization of prices and opening up the econo-my to competition; reducing subsidies to (loss-making) **state-owned enterprises (SOEs)**; and privatization of large parts of the public sector economy. Economists at the World Bank devel-oped a "liberalization index" based on the degree of privatization and liberalization and the opening up of domestic markets (de Melo *et al.*, 1996).

Despite its support at the time, shock therapies have been widely criticized. Most commonly, critics have argued that the theoretical principle of a linear progression from state socialism to apparent market **democracy** is simplistic, and avoids the difficulties in achieving this transition, and the possibilities for alternative models, or

diverse experiences of, transition (see **post-socialism**). For example, despite the intention of shock therapy to reduce the role of the state, a strong state was needed in order to follow through the reforms. Democratization was also resisted by the continuing power of **elites** before and after the collapse of socialism. The alter-native "softer" option of "gradualism" in transi-tion, with a continued role for a strong state, attracted much less attention, even though this was adopted by Hungary and most states of the Former Soviet Union (FSU). Many ECE and FSU populations experienced extreme economic depression during the 1990s. Much of the free-market modeling of economic change did not anticipate difficult market conditions.

Results of shock therapy have been mixed, partly because of the socialist legacies, poor planning, the political and economic inexperience of domestic actors, and the often unrealistic expectations of populations. Some critics now see shock therapy as useful only during initial stages of economic tran-sition, if it is followed by structural reform of the political economy (see Turnock, 1997). Com-monly, critics state that the postsocialist adapta-tion was never going to be "short," and that the avoidance of the local economic and political realities of postsocialism always meant that pro-posed policies were unnecessarily "sharp."

See also: European Bank for Reconstruction and Development (EBRD); neo-liberalism; postsocial-ism; privatization and liberalization; state-owned enterprises (SOEs)

Further reading

de Melo, M., Denizer, C. and Gelb, A. (1996) "Patterns of Transition from Plan to Market," *World Bank Economic Review* 10: 397–424.

Gros, D. and Steinherr, A. (1995) *Winds of Change: Economic Transition in Central and Eastern Europe*, Harlow: Longman.

Lavigne, M. (1999) *The Economics of Transition: From Socialist Economy to Market Economy*, Houndsmill: Palgrave.

Turnock, D. (1997) *The East European Economy in Context*, London: Routledge.

TASSILO HERRSCHEL

silviculture

Silviculture is the economic activities associated with the production of timber (see **logging/timber trade**). It refers to a diverse range of actions from preparing land for forestry, selecting trees, and harvesting lumber. In many developing countries, silviculture has led to the development of various means of harvesting forests to forms of so-called "scientific forestry," which seek to maximize timber production as a primary industry. Frequently, this may mean the use of plantations (see **plantation forestry**), and the replacement of forms of **shifting cultivation** such as the *Taungya* system of rotational harvesting adopted by some ethnic groups in Myanmar (Burma). Some critics have claimed that plantation, or "scientific" forestry has caused reductions in **biodiversity**, soil erosion (see **soil erosion and soil fertility**), and disturbance to local people who used to harvest **fuelwood**, timber, or **non-timber forest products (NTFPs)**. Furthermore, the establishment of forestry agencies within states (see **state and state reform**), especially during colonial times, accelerated the adoption of industrialized forms of silviculture. Such bureaucracies may be difficult to reform or make accessible to forms of **community forestry** that seek to increase local participation in forest management. Yet, careful silviculture can maintain diverse and valuable tree species, with high economic **productivity**, and without serious environmental impacts.

See also: community forestry; deforestation; environment; logging/timber trade; non-timber forest products (NTFPs); shifting cultivation; technology policy

Further reading

Sivaramakrishnan, K. (2002) *Modern Forests: Statemaking and Environmental Change in Colonial Eastern India*, Stanford: Stanford University Press.

MÒNICA RIVERA ESCRICH

SINGER-PREBISCH HYPOTHESIS *see* terms of trade; trade

SKILLS *see* education; illiteracy; human capital

slavery

Slavery is the enforced labor of one or more individuals for another under the threat of **violence**. Unlike other forms of abusive or exploitative working relationships, slavery implies the "ownership" of the slave by one or more owners, and the right of owners to control the life of the slave, usually also denying their **human rights**. In development debates, analysts have argued that slavery has allowed some civilizations or empires to become rich at the cost of others (see **colonialism, history of; colonialism, impacts of**). Slavery's history has also had repercussions on racism (see **race and racism**) or **social exclusion** of previously enslaved groups. Furthermore, forms of slavery still exist today.

Slavery has existed throughout most of human history, and ancient civilizations freely used slaves for **agriculture**, construction work, and menial activities. European enslavement of Africans started in the fourteenth century, often with the support of the Christian church, which saw the enrolment of slaves as an opportunity to convert them to Christianity. Slaves were also exported to provide labor in Cuba (Hispaniola). By 1540, an estimated 10,000 slaves a year were being brought from Africa to work on plantations and to exploit **natural resources**. Slaves were originally captured soldiers from tribal wars in Africa, but increasingly, raiding parties were organized. By the seventeenth and eighteenth centuries, slaves were employed in the colonies of the Americas, on tobacco, cotton, rice and sugar cane plantations. Slave markets were established in Philadelphia, Richmond, Charleston and New Orleans. The industrial revolution also enhanced demand for slaves. The invention of the cotton gin in 1793 meant that a slave could clean up to fifty times more cotton as before. Cotton was exported to Britain, where similar inventions of the spinning jenny and power loom also increased **productivity**, and hence the demand for slaves. The international cotton trade was considered dependent on the slave trade, and hence slavery and international **capitalism** were closely linked.

In Britain, trading in slaves was made illegal in 1807, and eventually the ownership and existence of slaves were banned in 1833. The government compensated slave owners and traders, including, for example, the Bishop of Exeter, who owned 665 slaves. In the USA, slavery was eventually ended by the 1861–5 Civil War. The last country in the Western Hemisphere to abolish slavery was Brazil in 1888. The international Slavery Convention in 1927 outlawed slavery worldwide.

The historic form of "chattel" slavery may now only exist through cases of threatened violence. More commonly, debt bondage (or bonded labor) may occur, where people are collateral against a loan. Another form is forced labor, where workers are tricked into accepting employment that results in slave-like conditions (see **migrant trafficking**). In some cases, this may include **prostitution/sex work** and **child prostitution**. The NGO Anti-Slavery International (see **non-governmental organizations (NGOs)**) estimates that at least 20 million people worldwide are tricked into bonded labor, and that some 700,000 people are trafficked each year. For example, Chinese and Vietnamese women are trafficked to some Pacific islands as sweatshop labor; men are trafficked from Mexico and forced to work on farms in the USA. One of the most important challenges to stopping these modern forms of slavery is to educate people in developed countries about it; to seek greater controls on the trade of goods where slave labor is suspected (see **fair trade**); and to urge international pressure on countries where slavery is suspected.

See also: child prostitution; colonialism, history of; colonialism, impacts of; human rights; migrant trafficking; prostitution/sex work; race and racism

Further reading

Anti-Slavery International website: http://www.antislavery.org/

Heuman, G. and Walvin, J. (eds) (2003) *The Slavery Reader*, London: Routledge.

Thomas, H. (1998) *The Slave Trade: The History of the Atlantic Slave Trade, 1440–1870*, Basingstoke: Macmillan.

TIM FORSYTH

small and medium enterprises (SMEs)

Small and medium enterprises (SMEs) is a classification given to small companies (as opposed to **transnational corporations (TNCs)**), which form a crucial element of a country's industrial capacity. SMEs are generally defined in relation to their **employment** size, annual sales revenue and fixed assets. While SMEs often employ less than 100 workers, it is much more difficult to define their sales and assets because these economic indicators vary by different countries. In general, we consider SMEs as local enterprises that are relatively small in their scale and scope of operations. In many developing economies, SMEs account for more than 95 percent of the total business establishments and contribute very substantially to employment, value-added and exports. Yet, they are not limited to developing countries, and SMEs constitute no less than 80 percent of the total establishments of industry in both advanced industrialized economies and developing economies.

As the backbone of most developing countries, SMEs serve very important *economic* and *social* functions. In the economic realm, SMEs often provide the starting point for many budding entrepreneurs in developing countries to engage in business activities that provide for both employment and income. In fact, many SMEs start as family businesses catering to the need of family members, friends and relatives. While this economic function of SMEs might be very important for least developed countries because there are few alternative employment avenues, SMEs can play a much more catalytic role in **economic development** through their participation in developing forward and backward linkages with large firms – domestic and foreign. In many export-oriented industrializing economies (see **export-led growth; newly industrialized economies (NIEs)**), the development of SMEs in specific industrial sectors can provide critical support to the growth and development of larger firms that depend on these SMEs for their material and service inputs. Many SMEs have also developed reciprocal and collaborative relationships with their large firm buyers. To these large firms, SMEs provide both low-cost alternatives to their outsourcing needs, and a kind of flexible "cushion" in times of unexpected economic shock that are frequent in developing countries. SMEs are thus indispensable to the development of a resilient and versatile industrial structure in an era of global time-space compression that demands higher flexibility in production and quicker turnaround time (see **flexible specialization**).

While SMEs are commonly and wrongly perceived as playing a subservient role to large firms, it must be pointed out that the strong presence of SMEs is a critical precondition for local economies to attract **foreign direct investment** and TNCs. Playing a critical role in local subcontracting networks, SMEs can offer both local product and management knowledge and "soft technology" (i.e. local technical standards and market preferences) to their large-firm customers. Successful NIEs have clearly capitalized on their local SMEs to create the favorable precondition for the development of competitive industrial **clustering**. Many of their domestic large firms have benefitted from subcontracting relationships with their local SMEs and have since developed and internationalized to become **transnational corporations (TNCs) from developing economies**.

Apart from their important economic functions, SMEs are well positioned to satisfy social needs in many developing countries. They not only provide vital avenues for entrepreneurial activities, but also form an integral part of the informal sector in many less developed countries. With the stagnation and vested political power that often plagues the formal sector in these countries, SMEs serve as an alternative avenue for people to engage in socially meaningful activities. These activities may range from manufacturing simple products in the backyard of one's house to owning a small eating-house to sell food. As a symbolic form of the moral economy, SMEs are simultaneously an economic undertaking in the Schumpeterian sense and a social platform for many families to survive the harsh daily realities in many developing countries. To many local governments, SMEs are both important sources of tax revenues and social stability.

Because of their important role in **industrialization**, we would expect SMEs to receive favorable attention in the government policies of most developing countries. Unfortunately this is not the case in reality, as most political elites in developing countries favor large firms that may be either politically connected to the ruling elite or serving specific national economic needs or shortages (e.g. **state-owned enterprises (SOEs)**). As such, the industry policies of many developing countries are targeted at large firms that have not grown out of SMEs (see **industrialization**). These large industrial firms are established as national champions to facilitate the **import substitution** industrialization strategy of such countries. Otherwise known as **infant industries**, these large firms are protected from foreign competition. SMEs, on the other hand, enjoy none of these priorities for national **economic development**. In most cases, SMEs have neither the political connections to the ruling elite nor the policy attention of most development planners. They receive little direct government subsidies/incentives or infrastructural provisions. The owners of SMEs thus rely on their entrepreneurial instincts and business networks to advance their competitive positions. In many ways, then, SMEs are much more market-driven and adaptable to different economic climates than are large firms in most developing countries.

In today's global economy, competitiveness has become key to a firm's success or failure. SMEs – whether in developing countries or advanced industrialized economies – should continue to be both nimble and flexible in their business strategies and operational practices. While they may not be able to receive much support from government's industrial and, more generally, economic policies, SMEs can remain highly competitive through their continuous learning, marketing and innovation efforts. They can be vital sources of local knowledge and market intelligence that in turn allows them to engage their larger buyers and customers. By adding significant value to global production networks, SMEs can enhance the dynamic competitive advantage of the localized clustering that is rapidly emerging in developing countries. While it might be unrealistic to expect these developing countries to concentrate their policy efforts on growing SMEs, the sustainable development of SMEs remains highly integral to the competitiveness of any economy.

See also: clustering; economic development; entrepreneurship; industrialization; infant industries; micro-enterprises; transnational corporations (TNCs); transnational corporations (TNCs) from developing economies; value chains

Further reading

Asian Productivity Organization (2002) *SMEs in Competitive Markets*, Tokyo: APO.

Chew, Y-T. and Yeung, H. W-C. (2001) "The SME Advantage: Adding Local Touch to Foreign Transnational Corporations in Singapore," *Regional Studies* 34:5 431–48.

Henderson, J., Dicken, P., Hess, M., Coe, N. and Yeung, H. W-C. (2002) "Global Production Networks and the Analysis of Economic Development," *Review of International Political Economy* 9:3 436–64.

Meyanathan, S. (ed.) (1994) *Industrial Structures and the Development of Small and Medium Enterprise Linkages: Examples from East Asia*, Washington DC: World Bank.

Perry, M. (1999) *Small Firms and Network Economies*, London: Routledge.

HENRY WAI-CHUNG YEUNG

small island developing states (SIDS)

Small island developing states (SIDS) include states such as Barbados, the Maldives, and Tahiti that have specific agendas in international development, particularly concerning the projected threats from rises in sea level resulting from **climate change**. The Association of Small Island States (AOSIS) was formed in 1990 as a negotiating group for the first meeting of the Intergovernmental Negotiating Committee for a Framework Convention on Climate Change, held in Geneva, in February 1991, with the specific purpose of representing the concerns of SIDS in climate change policy. A United Nations Global Conference on the Sustainability of Small Island Developing States was held in Bridgetown, Barbados, in 1994. This conference led to the Barbados Program of Action, which re-affirmed the principals and commitments to **sustainable development** embodied in the Rio Declaration on Environment and Development made at the **Earth Summit (1992) (United Nations Conference on Environment and Development)**. In the early 2000s, the AOSIS coalition of small island and low-lying coastal countries had forty-three members drawn from all oceans and regions of the world: Africa, the Caribbean, the Indian Ocean, the Mediterranean Sea, the Pacific Ocean and the South China Sea. Together, SIDS communities constitute about 5 percent of the global **population**.

See also: climate change; Earth Summit (1992) (United Nations Conference on Environment and Development); offshore finance; United Nations Convention on the Law of the Sea (UNCLOS)

Further reading

AOSIS website: http://www.sidsnet.org/aosis/ http://www.sidsnet.org/

DENNIS CONWAY

SMEs *see* small and medium enterprises (SMEs)

social capital

The idea of "social capital" refers to the resources of information and insurance, influence and identity that are inherent in social relationships amongst people. Although the term had been used before, from time to time, by different writers, the idea entered into discourse on development only in the mid-1990s, when it was adopted in the **World Bank**. In 1997, the idea was described in one publication put out by the Environmentally Sustainable Development Program of the Bank as "the missing link" in development; and from about that time its use expanded explosively across the social sciences and in development policy and practice. Even as this happened, however, confusion over the meaning of the term became apparent, and as two Bank researchers put it "Social capital, while not all things to all people, is many things to many people." This probably helps to account for its extraordinary success: it has proven to be a capacious idea – a "hatstand," as one writer has put it – that serves a variety of agendas.

The particular idea of social capital that took off in the 1990s was derived from the work of Robert Putnam of Harvard University – who was an influential adviser in the World Bank – first in a book entitled *Making Democracy Work: Civic Traditions in Modern Italy* (1993), and then in a series of articles that centered around the powerful metaphor of "bowling alone," concerning the supposed decline of social capital in the USA. The book, based on many years of research, presented an analysis of the functioning of regional governments in Italy which demonstrated a strong correlation between their effectiveness and something that Putnam described initially as "civic engagement," measured by an index combining data on political participation, newspaper readership and membership in voluntary associations (see **voluntary sector**). Civic engagement was shown to explain the variations across Italian regions, both in **economic growth** and in government performance, more strongly than either one explained the other. The point was, Putnam argued, that where there is a strong tradition of civic engagement, people are able to resolve their problems of collective action more easily, because of the existence of norms of reciprocity and of trust amongst them. They have more "social capital," in other words, defined by Putnam as "features of social organization, such as networks, norms and trust, that facilitate coordination and cooperation for mutual benefit." He offered a

reading of Italian history over the last millennium which showed how north central Italy had developed strong civic engagement, and hence had come to enjoy abundant social capital, and in consequence both good government and robust economic growth, in contrast with the Italian South which had no such tradition of civic engagement. The backwardness of the Italian South, its relatively low levels of economic performance and the poor quality of its governments, was the outcome of long-run historical path-dependence deriving from the early establishment there of hierarchical social structures and the weakness of horizontal associational ties between people. In spite of Putnam's pessimism about the prospects of development in the Italian South, his apparently robust demonstration of the importance of social organization in explaining different development outcomes was found powerfully persuasive – and the possible decline of social capital in the USA profoundly alarming. The task in development practice, then, or so it seemed, is "to get the social relations right" (see Woolcock, 1998). To many of Putnam's readers the key to civic engagement, and hence to the building up of social capital, lay above all in the density in a society of voluntary, "horizontal" associations, and their implications for the establishment of strong social networks. World Bank research in Tanzania then showed that, controlling for variations in household **education**, physical assets and village characteristics, people in **villages** with higher social capital, as given by a measure of the density of associational ties, enjoyed higher levels of income. The case was made. The social capital argument powerfully reinforced the idea, put forward for example in the Bank's *World Development Report* of 1997, that "strengthening **civil society**" by building local associations should be a central task for development agencies.

It has quite often happened in the history of science that the scholar responsible for the establishment of an idea has not been the one who set it up in the first place. This is true in the case of social capital. There is no doubt that it was Putnam who popularized the idea; but equally clearly, he did not "invent" it. Though earlier writers had used it, in passing, the first serious exposition of the idea of social capital was in the work of Pierre Bourdieu from around 1980. Bourdieu defined social capital, with deceptive simplicity, "by saying that it is what ordinary language calls 'connections'." What Bourdieu pointed out was how people can be understood as investing in particular social relationships, or "connections," and how these investments are fungible: membership in an exclusive club, for instance, might well be the means of establishing a person's credit worthiness, and hence her ability to raise money capital and build up a business. Particular, durable social relationships constitute, therefore, a form of capital; and it follows that this "social capital" plays a significant part in the differentiation between social classes. Those with more powerful connections are likely to accrue more of other forms of capital, too. So, for Bourdieu social capital has to be considered in the context of social power, and of the differentiation between different groups of people within a society, whereas in Putnam's use of the term it is held to be a characteristic of a society as a whole. He, in fact, took over the term from another scholar, the sociologist James Coleman, who worked, quite differently from Bourdieu, within the framework of rational choice theory. For Coleman social capital is very often the unintended consequence of the social relationships that obtain between individuals, although he did not preclude the possibility that individuals might deliberately choose to invest in particular relationships as, for example, by participating in the setting up of a parent-teacher association. Coleman's theoretical analysis lent weight, in fact, to the notion that the strength of such voluntary associations is a powerful factor in accounting for differences in all sorts of outcomes in different societies. Though he did not entirely disregard the questions about power that Bourdieu's analysis highlighted, they did not feature nearly so strongly in his conceptualization of the idea of social capital. Unsurprisingly, perhaps, it has been Coleman's conceptualization that has been more influential among the World Bank researchers who have carried forward an agenda of research on social capital, rather than Bourdieu's. (The theorization of social capital by Bourdieu and Coleman is critically discussed by Ben Fine, 2000.)

Critics have pointed to flaws in Putnam's conceptualization of social capital that are likely to affect the outcomes of the use of the idea in development practice. In the first place, Putnam, at least to begin with, ignored what has been called the "dark side" of social capital, when for example particular social groups make use of their networks and connections against the wider social interest. It has to be recognized that the social capital of one group of people can connote the **social exclusion** of others, and that social capital is not always a general "good." Latterly Putnam and his followers in the World Bank have recognized this point, by distinguishing between what they call "bonding" capital, involving close ties amongst the members of a particular social group, and "bridging" capital, involving connections between the members of different groups. "Bonding" capital on its own may well have the sorts of negative effects that are shown up in the argument about the "dark side" of social capital. An important study of ethnic conflict in India by Varshney (2002) has shown that such conflict is much less likely to occur where there is a history of connections between the members of different religious communities (see **community; religion; caste**), facilitated for instance by political parties or **trade unions**. In these cases, the "bonding" between the members of the communities is balanced by "bridging" relationships. The World Bank's *World Development Report 2000/2001* distinguished as well the category of "linking" capital, where relatively powerless people benefit from the assistance of others who are in strategic positions. An example of this, from research in several sites in the Andes, is in the way in which farmers' groups have benefitted from the assistance, for example, of university professors or well-connected **non-governmental organizations (NGOs)**, who have provided links to sources of technical innovation, capital, or markets. But it is also possible, however, that such linking is effected through patron-client relations from which poorer people may derive some benefit but at the expense of some of their freedoms.

Attempts to use the idea of social capital have commonly involved working with local organizations, and sometimes efforts to set them up. A salutary case from a development project in Eastern India has shown how such groups, in a society characterized by hierarchy and **inequality**, are easily taken over by the relatively wealthy and powerful and exploited in their own interest. The general point is that social capital has to be considered (exactly as Bourdieu argued) in the context of power differences within societies. Studies in the different circumstances of poor housing estates in the East End of London and of villages in the coalfield areas of Orissa have shown that there may be abundant social capital – strong and significant social networks – but that it is fragmented by age, sex and ethnicity (see **ethnicity/identity**). They have also shown that there are big differences between what different groups can achieve with their social capital, depending upon the other resources at their disposal (see discussion in Harriss, 2001).

The concept of social capital that has become popular in the discourse of development is distinctly apolitical. This too reflects the influence of Putnam's work – which seems to suggest that, whether in Italy or the USA, the "weak ties" between people established through ordinary socializing in clubs and sports teams, provide the foundations of effective **democracy**, rather than overtly political organizations. Yet other scholars, both of Italy and of the USA, have shown that causality probably lies in the opposite direction. Thus there is an alternative interpretation of modern Italian history, which shows that the phenomena that Putnam associates with social capital have been driven by political organization; and one of modern American history that demonstrates the causal connections between interventions by the state (see **state and state reform**), and political events, and the development of local organizing (see the discussion in Harriss, 2001). Similarly, Varshney's (2002) analysis of ethnic conflict in India suggests that the varying extent to which inter-community ties have developed in different cities depends above all upon their different political histories.

The idea of social capital has some analytical value, therefore, but it is certainly debatable as to whether it constitutes "the missing link" in development. Rather, the way in which it has been used in development practice seems to fit very well with the liberal agenda of the **Washington consensus**. It places the onus upon people, and

perhaps especially poor people, to organize themselves, and so it fits very well with the approach to development which seeks to minimize the role of the state.

See also: civil society; community; democracy; institutions; new social movements; politics; social exclusion; social integration; state and state reform; voluntary sector; Washington consensus

Further reading

Fine, B. (2000) *Social Capital Versus Social Theory: Political Economy and Social Science at the Turn of the Millennium*, London and New York: Routledge.

Harriss, J. (2001) *Depoliticizing Development: The World Bank and Social Capital*, Delhi: LeftWord, and London: Anthem (2002).

Putnam, R. (1993) *Making Democracy Work: Civic Traditions in Modern Italy*, Princeton: Princeton University Press.

Varshney, A. (2002) *Ethnic Conflict and Civic Life: Hindus and Muslims in India*, New Haven and London: Yale University Press.

Woolcock, M. (1998) "Social Capital and Economic Development: Toward a Theoretical Synthesis and Policy Framework," *Theory and Society* 27:2 151–208.

JOHN HARRISS

social contract

The social contract is a historically important concept of political philosophy referring to the ability of individuals to form associations, and therefore transform a pre-political "state of nature" into **civil society** and a political state (see **state and state reform**). Thomas Hobbes (1588–1679), John Locke (1632–1704) and Jean-Jacques Rousseau (1712–78) were the political theorists who developed this concept, in part inspired by Sophist's treaties and Plato's *Statesman*. For development studies, the concept has relevance for theorizing debates such as **governance**, **social justice**, civil society and **social capital**.

Initial debates about the social contract argued that self-preservation motivates individuals to enter into a political association, thus terminating the "state of nature." The personalities of the contracting individuals and the nature of contract(s), however, have been given various versions. Individuals agree to contract either because life in the state of nature is selfish, brutish and short (Hobbes), or because there is no universal law and impartial arbiter (Locke) or because in the absence of rights, preservation of one's life becomes obstacle to another's existence (Rousseau).

In the interest of survival, society moves from individuals to collectivity. In Hobbes's contract, individuals unconditionally surrender authority to empower a single or a group of individuals who have no reciprocal obligations. The sovereign thus conceived is the "Leviathan," or mortal god, placed above the contract. Hobbes's contract is reconcilable with despotism, as he keeps the state and government fused. Locke in his *Two Treatises of Government* (1690) mentions two contracts. By the first, some rights of law enforcement and punishment are surrendered to a contracting **community**. By the second, a contracting government is empowered to legislate. Sovereignty thus rests with the community. In Rousseau's contract, the give and take balance each other to produce positive alienation as opposed to negative alienation (as in Hobbes's contract, where contracting individuals are stripped of all rights). In surrendering to a multitude, the sovereign is thus dissolved into a public body called the "General Will," which represents common interest. The political system no doubt suffers from the antithetical pull of private wills. However, since satisfaction of private wills favor few, acting to the detriment of most, the entire body polity in the larger interest of society, ensures its negation (see **freedom versus choice**).

John Rawls has contemporarily used the social contract in his theories of justice (see **social justice**). Although accused of being ahistorical, mechanical and unrooted in geography, the social contract was an important challenge to historic belief in the divine right of monarchs to govern, and hence contributed to early ideas on **revolution**.

See also: civil society; freedom versus choice; institutions; politics; social capital; social justice

Further reading

Gildin, H. (1983) *Rousseau's Social Contract: The Design of the Argument*, London: University of Chicago Press.
Gourevitch, V. (ed.) (1997) *Rousseau: The Social Contract and Later Political Writings*, Cambridge Texts in the History of Political Thought, Cambridge: Cambridge University Press.

IPSITA CHATTERJEE

social development

In general terms, social development may be seen as putting people at the center of development (see also **people-centered development**). As such, it is concerned with eliminating **inequality** and mitigating social distress and **vulnerability** while addressing the needs, aspirations and rights of different individuals and groups of people. More specifically, however, social development has also been associated with the commitments made at the World Summit for Social Development held in Copenhagen, Denmark, in March 1995. The Copenhagen Declaration included a commitment to "a political, economic, ethical and spiritual vision for social development that is based on human dignity, **human rights**, equality, respect, peace, **democracy**, mutual responsibility and cooperation, and full respect for the various religious and ethical values and cultural backgrounds of people" (paragraph 25). This statement is further translated into ten commitments (paragraph 29) which include: eradication of absolute **poverty** by an agreed target date; supporting full **employment** as a policy objective; achieving equity and equality between men and women; protection of all human rights; attaining universal and equitable access to **education** and **primary health care**; ensuring that **structural adjustment** programs include social development goals; increasing resources allocated for social development; and strengthening the **United Nations'** role in pursuing these goals.

Five years after Copenhagen, the United Nations General Assembly (UNGAS) was convened at Geneva in June 2000 to undertake a follow-up, Social Summit+5 meeting. This meeting reaffirmed the various commitments to social development. However, neither meeting produced any specific and binding commitments on the part of **bilateral aid agencies** or **international organizations and associations** on a basis comparable to **Agenda 21** (see also **Earth Summit (1992) (United Nations Conference on Environment and Development)**).

There are several core issues in this approach to social development. As the Program of Action of Copenhagen Declaration highlights, "To promote social development requires an orientation of values, objectives and priorities towards the well-being of all and the strengthening and promotion of conducive institutions and policies" (paragraph 4). The various actions in the Program of Action are grouped under the titles of eradication of poverty, expansion of productive employment, and **social integration**. Creating an enabling environment for social development includes creating appropriate freedoms, **transparency**, and **institutions** to achieve equality in social, economic and political opportunities, and the protection of human rights. The main contribution of social development is to place poverty reduction at the core of development discussion.

The social development agenda at Copenhagen recognized that while national governments should play the main role in social development, international cooperation is crucial, sometimes coordinated by the United Nations or other multilateral organizations. The Commission of Social Development, a body of the United Nations within its Economic and Social Council (ECOSOC) is responsible for overseeing the implementation of the Copenhagen Declaration and its follow-up. The Commission has forty-six members (UN member countries).

As a concept, however, social development may be criticized on five main grounds. First, there is no universally agreed definition of social development. Proponents have claimed that a lack of formal definition allows flexibility and local determination about its meaning. Critics have said, however, that it also invites vagueness, lack of clarity and scope for confusion (see Thin, 1998).

Second, at the heart of the social development concept is a fault-line between the need to accept existing social institutions (and hence the reference to preserving institutions such as families) and the need to pursue social change. This opens up ethical dilemmas. For instance, commitment to equality versus preserving existing social institutions such as **caste** systems or racial views or cultural practices which may appear backward to other outsiders (see **cultural relativism**).

Third, the question remains that whether an essentially *anthropocentric* concept such as social development is adequate to achieve **sustainable development**, which encompasses both anthropocentric and non-anthropocentric ethical concerns. Fourth, can social development as institutional change be achieved endogenously and mainly through the agency of state while the state itself (see **state and state reform**) is an instrument of political power distribution? And fifth, the concept seems to assume that the process of creating the enabling environment and institutions is costless. Changing existing institutions and practices entails considerable costs, and even these costs will be distributed unequally. It is likely that the weakest are likely to bear the greatest proportion of such costs.

These criticisms, and the lack of binding commitments in the Copenhagen Declaration, have largely resulted in the concept of social development being discussed in general, rather than specific terms. The term is increasingly spoken of in terms of **human development**, which has been formally supported by the United Nations by the creation of the **Human Development Index (HDI)**. Furthermore, the **Millennium Development Goals (MDGs)** in 2000 have presented a new list of development objectives, which include various elements such as poverty reduction referred to in the context of social development. Nonetheless, the concept and Copenhagen meeting represent important stages in diversifying definitions of development away from **economic growth** alone, and in identifying targets for people-centered development.

See also: equitable development; human development; Millennium Development Goals

(MDGs); people-centered development; United Nations

Further reading

Thin, N. (1998) *Social Development Policies, Results and Learning: Experiences from European Agencies*, London: DFID.

P. B. ANAND

social exclusion

Social exclusion is the result of activities by which certain groups (or individuals) – because of their race (see **race and racism**), **gender**, age, or social class – are denied full participation in political, **education**, social, and economic processes associated with **economic development**. Social exclusion can also be associated with geographies, as in "spaces of exclusion." In either case, social or spatial, exclusion results from the anxieties, nervousness, or fears associated with individuals or groups who are perceived as different – "the other." Differences (real or imagined) become the basis of "distancing," which ultimately allows physical and social boundaries to be constructed and maintained. The boundaries mark the space between what is normal or mainstream and what is deviant and marginal.

Exclusion may be permanent, calculated, and deliberate, as in the case of overt racial discrimination (e.g. the **caste** system in South Asia). It may also be temporary, appealing, exciting, and an unintended consequence (e.g. when children are temporarily excluded from voting or military service because they are not old enough, or the case of adolescents "invading" an upscale indoor shopping mall).

Throughout the world, the disadvantaging of women stands out as one of the more striking forms of social exclusion (see **gender; male bias**). Even in contexts where men are away for extended periods and women make most of the household decisions, because they are not participants in the cash economy (or do not get equal pay), decision-making in and of itself confers very little status. Moreover, under conditions of fiscal crises,

occupational sex segregation, global recession, economic downsizing, or cuts in public expenditures, women are typically the first to be fired. Even women too young to be in the work force suffer when they are denied access to experiences and education. Even more interesting, in societies where women have legal rights to vote, own property, and earn an income, they are less likely to do so than men because of entrenched attitudes regarding a "woman's place." In parts of the Muslim world, female rates of participation in the labor force are among the lowest in the world, and disturbingly large gaps exist between male and female literacy rates. Being poor equals being female. In parts of South Asia, women suffer even more debilitating forms of exclusion – constrained by both their gender and caste status. Upper caste women are relegated to permanent mourning when the husband dies; in the lower caste, boys receive better **nutrition** and medical care than girls. Although some statistics suggest that women's status throughout the world has improved, there has been very limited progress in reducing gender **inequality** in most social, economic, and political contexts throughout the world, and overall women continue to be excluded from the benefits of **economic development**.

Just as exclusion is the result of discriminatory practices between groups and individuals, it can also be used to describe spaces that are off limits – spaces of exclusion (e.g. gated communities, upscale shopping malls, the whites-only areas of **apartheid** South Africa). Activities, practices, and processes associated with economic development are all highly spatialized. In other words, they play themselves out on specific spatial scales ranging from the region to the nation-state to the scale of the global geopolitical. In highly urbanized, industrialized, more developed countries, spatial exclusion is perhaps the single most powerful explanation in the creation of socio-spatial/geographical boundaries within urban areas (e.g. **ghettos**, suburbs, and gentrification). Because of its institutionalization, social exclusion is invisible in developed countries and largely goes unnoticed or criticized. In many developing countries, the geography of exclusion takes place inside cities (e.g. bidonvilles, **shantytowns**, and stranger communities) but is also markedly apparent on the larger spatial scale of the region (rural or urban) as well as the national scale (e.g. **maquiladoras** and **free trade zones (FTZs)**). Because it is based on denial of access, social exclusion is always linked to **poverty**.

See also: free trade zones (FTZs); gender; ghettos; internally displaced persons; social integration; stateless people; women-headed households

Further reading

Pierson, J. (2001) *Tackling Social Exclusion*, London: Routledge.

Sibley, D. (1995) *Spaces of Exclusion*, London: Routledge.

Sweetman, C. (ed.) (1996) *Women, Employment, and Exclusion*, Oxford: Oxfam.

RICKIE SANDERS

social integration

Social integration is a mechanism that enables parts of a social system to act together, and thus makes such systems viable. It is a cohesive force operating through complementarity and differences: it presupposes social plurality, or diversity of people and political opinions. It is relevant for debates of achieving trust in government, **governance**, **social capital**, and inclusionary **politics** and policies (also see **participatory development**).

There is no universally accepted single definition of social integration. The functionalist social theorist Talcott Parsons (1902–79) believed social integration to be a result of internalization of common values and their institutionalization within social systems. Emile Durkheim (1858–1917) attributed it to organic and mechanical solidarity. Anthony Giddens (1984) talks of individuals engaged in situations of co-presence, in time-space paths creating building blocks for integration (see **globalization; culture**).

General agreement exists, however, on two counts. First, social systems do possess a certain degree of integration, preventing their complete disintegration. Second, social systems are never completely integrated, because there will always be some gap between role expectations and performance of these roles. The total absence of integration is what Parsons described as the breakdown of normative order, or anomie, which is never completely enacted in reality.

Parsons's (1951) normative conceptualization of integration assumed a social system consisting of actors involved in multiple interactions with other actors. Each actor is a social unit located in social space, relative to other actors, which is referred to as his/her "status." The individual's performance in relation to others is called "role." A viable social system thrives on the compatibility between individual status-role bundles and that of the larger society. It is therefore imperative that, to ensure co-option, individual motivations should be complementarized with certain normative standards, or that actions should meet individual expectations referred to as ego and that the same action would stimulate expectations from others, called alter. The fulfillment of normative standards requires meeting both criteria, i.e. the satisfaction of the actor's own "need-disposition" as well as the gratification of the actor's expectations. In this process of mutuality – the integration of individual motives with the optimization of other's expectations – will standards be institutionalized and social integration be achieved. According to Parsons, levels of institutionalization may vary, with consequent implications for the stability of different social systems.

The concept of functional integration is also relevant to this approach to social integration. Functional integration is the contribution of different parts of society in complementary ways to a cohesive whole. Some social scientists argue that some sectors of society incline toward autonomy, and hence any movement toward integration creates conflict, which can only be mitigated if the system possesses sufficient insulation. Others claim that social sectors are usually unequal and create exploitative reciprocal relations. Durkheim emphasized functional integration through his idea of organic and mechanical solidarity. While investigating the moral basis of division of labor, he observed that advanced societies with a high degree of social integration had well-developed division of labor. He therefore decided to probe the link between division of labor and integration, and introduced the idea of duality in human personality, which referred to the possession of unique traits in personalities, which differentiated them from others and at the same time possessed characteristics common to others. Yet, by working in common with other people, individuals may produce a mechanical solidarity derived from a "conscience collective." This is manifested through repressive laws that subsume individuality to collectivity. Again, due to uniqueness in individuals, solidarity also develops when one seeks in others what one lacks through exchange of services made possible by division of labor. This is organic solidarity, manifested through restitutive sanctions binding contracting individuals without being generally diffused in society.

Durkheim's theories, however, have been questioned by later sociologists, who pointed out that since functional integration relied on norms of reciprocity, it too was dependent on normative integration. Similarly, Parsons stated that mechanical solidarity depended on common values and organic solidarity on norms of contract, property, etc., which too were derived from common values. Therefore, he suggested that both common values and solidarities get diffused at a higher level, thus forging a link between normative and functional integration.

A further approach to social integration refers to the manufacturing of consensus by the mass **media**, producing communicative integration. Evidence suggests, however, that communication alone is not potent enough to achieve social integration (see **information technology**).

Social integration as a concept has been evolving. Parsons's view of society was of coherence and harmony where integration was facilitated by willing actors complying with institutional norms. Marxist thinkers, on the other hand, view society as a system of exploitation where compliance was enforced by owners of the means of production, and hence **revolution** was looked upon as the mechanism for societal evolution. Integration was through exploitation and was another name for alienation. Postmodernists talk of multiple identities, numerous possibilities and choices (see **postmodernism and postdevelopment**). Overarching social structures, universal norms and codes of conduct are being overhauled in favor of diversity, conjectures and contextualities. Order itself is considered an illusion and integration is often looked upon with suspicion, accused of being hegemonizing, confused with assimilation and homogenization. A re-imagining of social integration in terms of recognition of multiple membership to identities, compositing instead of optimizing expectations, and complementarizing differences, might be useful in explaining postmodern social integration.

See also: civil society; institutions; social capital; social exclusion; sociology of development

Further reading

Giddens, A. (1984) *The Constitution of Society: Outline of the Theory of Structuration*, Cambridge: Polity.
Jones, R. (1986) *Emile Durkheim: An Introduction to Four Major Works*, California: Sage.
Mayhew, L. (1982) *Talcott Parsons: On Institutions and Social Evolution*, Chicago: University of Chicago Press.
Parsons, T. (1951) *The Social System*, London: Routledge and Kegan Paul.

IPSITA CHATTERJEE

social justice

Questions of "justice" are centrally concerned with ideas of fairness, while "social justice" emphasizes the relational aspect of fairness between individuals and groups. Debates about social justice are linked, therefore, to broad questions of **ethics**, rights, and group membership. Such discussions have, moreover, direct bearing on forms of **governance**, and how, and under what circumstances, people should be treated with equal regard, respect, and consideration. Debates among contemporary theories of social justice are concerned with the universality of principles of justice, the possibility and importance of impartiality in achieving justice, and the degree to which distribution is the central issue in evaluating social justice.

Classic discussions of social justice begin with the premise, first articulated by David Hume in *A Treatise of Human Nature* (1739), that concerns for justice arise in social situations in which there is a tension between the relative scarcity of goods and the needs and wants of people. In relationship to this classic understanding, philosophies of social justice have sought to understand the best basis for distributing the positive and negative dimensions of social life. Mainstream theories of social justice contain an egalitarian impulse, which points toward the notion of the intrinsic, equal worth of each individual. Ironically, however, mainstream theories of social justice are also concerned with justifying the conditions under which **inequality** is permissible. This irony partially reflects the difficulty in explaining the manner in which individuals are equal, how to protect or construct such equality, and how to address apparent inequalities. It also demonstrates, nonetheless, the ways in which ideas reflect the societies in which they are embedded.

In Western societies, utilitarianism has been a prevailing moral philosophy shaping ideas of social justice. This theory places value on promoting the aggregate total good (utility or pleasure) of a group. Thus, **inequality** is permissible as long as the total utility of a group increases. Two basic premises of utilitarianism are, therefore, that human **well-being** matters and that the morality of acts should be determined by their consequences. Defining "utility" remains problematic, nonetheless, as does reconciling an equal concern for all with a maximization of utility, the latter of which may lead to great material inequalities.

With the publication of *A Theory of Justice* (1971), John Rawls constructed an important alternative theory of social justice to that of utilitarianism. Rather than a teleological theory, or one concerned with ultimate, normative societal outcomes, Rawls presented a deontological theory, which begins with a just foundational order. In keeping with this, Rawls theorized an "original position," or a hypothetical social contract between people about what is just. A systematic hierarchy of principles that ensures the maintenance of the fundamental just order is embedded within this contract. In such a hierarchy, Rawls posited that the equal distribution of basic civic and political liberties takes first priority, while equality of opportunity takes the second priority. The "difference principle," which allows for forms of inequality that do not punish the worst off, takes third priority. Thus, this sense of justice begins with civil and political liberties, yet does not require an equality of outcomes; it resonates, therefore, with the precepts of liberal **democracy**.

Mainstream theories of social justice such as utilitarianism and Rawlsian social contract theory have been critiqued on numerous grounds. Communitarians argue, for example, that these theories are constructed around a liberal notion of individual self-determination. Such an assumption denies that individuals are embedded within wider communities (see **community**) that may have distinct notions of social justice. In *Spheres of Justice* (1983), Michael Walzer explores this tension between the self and community in modern society. In so doing, he also critiques a universal notion or model of justice. He suggests that particular social goods, and the value placed upon them, vary historically and geographically. Particular criteria for distribution depend, moreover, on the nature of that social good. As a result, there are multiple arenas, or spheres of justice. In suggesting that justice is multiple and particular, Walzer promotes a complex notion of equality, which posits that the distribution of one good (knowledge, for example) should not be dependent upon the distribution of another good (land, for example). In so doing, he shifts the discussion of justice away from the distribution of specific, universal goods, toward broader patterns of social domination in which possession of certain dominant social goods may distort justice within other spheres.

Feminists have also presented a multifaceted critique of mainstream theories of social justice (see **gender; women's movements**). Some have suggested that a focus on an ethics of justice applies to the public sphere, thereby excluding perspectives, experiences, and relationships developed within the private sphere. These include, for example, recognizing dependency as part of the human condition, and valuing an ethics of care and relationships. In keeping with this, certain feminists have advocated for a contextualized understanding of justice built from experience rather than abstract principles. Feminists have questioned, furthermore, the implicit goal of establishing a universal and impartial understanding of justice. Claims of impartiality have protected and masked, some feminists argue, socially constructed hierarchical relationships. Finally, certain feminists support expanding the scope of social justice beyond distribution to include such arenas as **violence** (or **domestic violence**) and cultural oppression. Justice in this regard is not only about distribution, but also about the full recognition of the circumstances of others.

See also: ethics; governance; human rights; inequality; rights-based approaches to development; social integration; well-being

Further reading

Kymlicka, W. (1990) *Contemporary Political Philosophy: An Introduction*, Oxford: Clarendon Press.

Rawls, J. (1971) *A Theory of Justice*, Cambridge MA: Harvard University Press.

Smith, D. (1994) *Geography and Social Justice*, Oxford: Cambridge University Press.

Walzer, M. (1983) *Spheres of Justice: A Defence of Pluralism and Equality*, Oxford: Basil Blackwell.

PATRICIA M. MARTIN

social learning

Social learning is a purposeful activity that refers to the process of linking knowledge (learning) to action (doing), where the knowledge of reality and of practice mutually influence each other. Knowledge or theory is based on a particular actor's prior learning and evolving experience which reflect that actor's socialization, class position, educational background and work experience. As an intellectual tradition, social learning has many disciplinary origins, antecedents and applications, ranging from developmental psychology, organizational management, **planning**, development studies, and educational studies. When applied to international development studies and development planning, social learning is understood as a conscious mode of practice based on "learning-by-doing." It assumes that the actors and learners are the same in that it is the same group of actors – be they organizations, communities (see **community**), or social movements – that learn from their own social practice.

Practice and learning are therefore seen as cumulative, iterative and continuous processes. The learning itself is manifest as a change in practical activity based on informal and shared or collective learning that is interwoven directly into social practice. Social learning processes may also involve change agents who guide or assist actors, communities, organizations, and movements in the process of changing reality. These change agents may be professionals, planners or para-professionals (e.g. trainers, facilitators, community organizers, party cadres) who bring specialized expertise or formal knowledge to enrich the learning and social practice of their client group. Together, these change agents and their clients engage in an iterative process of mutual learning, or co-learning, and action.

The intellectual roots of the social learning tradition are often traced to the philosophical instrumentalism or pragmatism of John Dewey, who popularized the term "learning-by-doing." Dewey's pragmatic epistemology or theory of knowledge presupposes the possibility of historical social progress through empirical science as a unique method of self-corrective knowing and learning from past failures and successes. This epistemological standpoint assumes that all valid knowledge comes from experience, or the interaction between human beings and their material environment, through which people come to both understand their world as well as transform it. Social knowledge could only be gained collectively, and validated only when it helps actors and organizations solve a problem. From these presuppositions, it is easy to see how Dewey's philosophy has influenced both social theory and planning theory, where history is seen as a progressive succession of plans-as-experiments that guide and organize human action and **institutions**. The simplicity and practicality of Dewey core message – "only ideas that work matter; the scientific method points the way to progress; one learns by changing reality" (Friedman,

1987:193) – has attracted many loyal disciples within and outside North America. The list of people influenced by Dewey's philosophy includes intellectuals as diverse as Mao Tse Tung, Lewis Mumford, Edgar S. Dunn Jr, Kurt Lewin, Rensis Likert, and Donald Schon.

It is, however, the influence of Dewey's social learning tradition within organizational development theory that has shaped the behaviorist approach to planning the human aspects of organizations. The then-dominant scientific management theory of Frederick Taylor (the father of Taylorism), influenced by the humanistic psychology of Carl Rogers and Abraham Maslow, gave way to a clear social learning approach in the study of group behavior and organizational change. Kurt Lewin, the social psychologist credited for the first experiments in action research, developed in the 1940s an analytical method based on social learning in the study of social interactions and group dynamics that became the basis of organizational development theory. In Lewin's theory, re-education or successful group behavioral change rests upon group members seeing and experiencing themselves as acting subjects that collectively act upon their environment. Lewin and his colleagues developed training workshops in laboratory settings to enable change agents and participants in developing their self-awareness, inter-personal skills and competence in adapting to change in organizational environments. The theory of organizational learning was further refined in the works of Chris Argyris and Donald Schon. They explored the notion of "double-loop learning," first developed in Dewey's and Lewin's writings, that entails recognition of current mismatch between an organization and its environment, and allows a major re-organization to enable the organization to adjust to its changing environment. Furthermore, they demonstrated how positive organizational characteristics such as inquiry-orientation and cooperative behavior diminish the occurrence of "games of deception" and other "dysfunctional" norms, and leads instead to a more trusting work and organizational environment. To achieve this objective, Argyris and Schon proposed similar laboratory training and other small-group interaction techniques, teaching for example the skills of "learning to learn," that were similar to those developed by Lewin and colleagues.

Development planning and international development studies have also applied social learning theory and its emphasis on studying collective behavior, in their study of development organizations, communities, and social movements. The interest in social learning has been renewed especially in light of current interests in **social capital**, **capacity building**, and participation (see **participatory development**). Recent works in organization studies and community development planning, for example, view the social capital and action competence of organizations and communities to be mutually enhanced by the social learning that accrues from the processes of community participation. Social learning is considered to be one of the key components and proven benefits of participatory development, as it makes the social, political and cultural environment more amenable to local inputs and commitments. Reflexive social learning within the context of participatory monitoring and evaluation (see **participatory research methods**) or integrated impact assessments (see **participatory poverty assessment (PPA)**) can constitute an important basis for participatory **governance**. Such integrated assessments at various levels are seen as a process of social learning involving stakeholders, researchers, scientists, policy makers and the society. Within the literature on capacity development, social learning is also seen as one of the important ingredients of organizational **capacity building**. More recently, development practitioners competent in the use of new information (and communication) technologies (ICTs) (see **information technology**) have been interested in how social learning processes could be enhanced and promoted by such new technologies. It is believed that social learning principles and processes aided by the widespread participatory use of new ICTs could help improve the quality and extent of knowledge generation, information dissemination, and public decisions made, as applied in the fields of **poverty** reduction, **humanitarianism**, **conflict management**, **gender** mainstreaming, **environment**, **climate change**, among others.

See also: capacity building; education; participatory development; social movements

Further reading

Argyris, C. and Schon, D. (1978) *Organisational Learning: A Theory of Action Perspective*, Reading MA: Addison-Wesley.

Fals-Borda, O. and Rahman, M. (eds) (1991) *Action and Knowledge: Breaking the Monopoly with Participatory Action Research*, New York: Apex.

Friedman, J. (1987) *Planning in the Public Domain: From Knowledge to Action*, Princeton: Princeton University Press.

Lewin, K. (1948) *Resolving Social Conflicts: Selected Papers on Group Dynamics*, ed. Gertrud Weiss Lewin, New York: Harper and Bros.

LEONORA C. ANGELES

SOCIAL MOVEMENTS *see* environmental movements; new social movements; peasant movements; women's movements

sociology of development

The sociology of development is concerned with understanding the ways in which people in poorer countries try to improve the quality of their lives. As such, it is an important and evolving area of investigation. Since the leaders of most poorer, or "developing" countries try to raise standards of living by **industrialization**, development sociology tends to look at the social and political effects of this economic process.

The sub-discipline has gone through a number of theoretical and substantive changes since 1949, the date of US President Harry S. Truman's speech to the **United Nations** calling for the UN to develop the "underdeveloped regions of the world," which is commonly seen as the start of the "age of development" (see **Truman's Bold New Program (1949)**). Views of classical nineteenth-century sociologists, particularly Emile Durkheim, informed the belief of neo-evolutionists in the 1950s and 1960s that societies evolved. Talcott Parsons suggested that in order for societies to move from traditional to modern, several "evolutionary universals" needed to be present. To adapt and survive, societies need the ability to acquire the sorts of cultural attributes and structures of modern societies such as a wide outlook on the world, rewards based on achievement, cities, a class system, bureaucracy and **democracy**. Modernization theorists (see **modernization theory**) drew from neo-evolutionism but were more influenced by the sociologist Max Weber in their focus on the transmission of modern attitudes and values for the success of development. Daniel Lerner saw modern techniques in communicating ideas through the mass **media** as important, and Inkeles and Smith outlined a distinct set of attitudes, such as a readiness for new experience and openness to innovation, that would "make men modern." Although modernization theory was subjected to substantial criticism in the 1970s, due to the failure of most developing countries to develop, it was revived in the 1990s to try to understand whether successes in some East Asian and former Soviet transitional economies were due to specific cultural attributes consistent with the **Protestant work ethic**, such as Confucianism. This trend revealed the continuing influence of Weber, who originally had stressed the economic importance of the work ethic.

Marxist development theory was prominent in the sociology of development in the 1970s and 1980s (see **Marxism**). Marx himself was not particularly focused upon what came to be known as developing countries, since his main interest was in the evolution of **capitalism**, which was undeveloped or nonexistent in poorer parts of the world. The main theoretical advancement, and critique of modernization theory, during this period was **dependency theory**, which drew heavily from both Luxemburg and Lenin's theories of colonialism (see **colonialism, history of; colonialism, impacts of**). The theory anticipated the withering of nation-states and the predominance of the capitalist global economy, and saw a polarization between richer and poorer areas as the inevitable outcome of the development of capitalism. Andre Gunder Frank progressed Baran's earlier notion that it is actually in the interests of capitalists to keep the developing world as an "indispensable hinterland," through a system of metropolitan and satellite areas where surplus is extracted. World metropolitan areas, for example the United States, underdevelop (or exploit and weaken) satellite areas, such as Mexico. Mexico City takes advantage of smaller cities in Mexico, which also make use of rural areas. Immanuel Wallerstein developed these ideas further in *The Modern World-System*, where he conceptualized a **world systems theory** system of capitalism, based on core (consisting of the richest countries), periphery (consisting of the poorest) and semi-periphery (the countries that were experiencing some development successes), in which wealthier areas underdeveloped poorer ones. None of these theories really addressed the issue of social class, and when they did, they saw dominant classes in developing countries as simply *comprador*, from the Portuguese "to buy," giving the impression of local groups that are bought by global interests. Dependency theorists' focus on exogenous factors of development made them vulnerable to critiques from orthodox Marxists such as Laclau, who argued that the concept of relations of production, between capitalists and workers, was being ignored. Similarly, Brenner suggested that dependency theorists' emphasis on underdevelopment neglected class struggle inside countries. Most audacious of all was Bill Warren's view that indigenous capitalist classes are emerging all over the world, and what the developing world needed was not less capitalism but more.

While there has been a tremendous influence of Marxist theories and research on the sociology of development, most of this has focused on the colonial and postcolonial state (see **post-colonialism**) rather than on class. This is because oppression was often bound up with the state and political control (see **state and state reform**). Local organizers often found it easier to mobilize opposition against foreign imperialists rather than co-nationals, although there often were links between the two. The theory of bureaucratic-**authoritarianism**, advanced by Guillermo O'Donnell in 1973, tried to explain the predominance of military rule (see **military and security**) in developing countries by linking stages of capitalist development that required wealth concentration with the rise of authoritarian regimes. This idea was later elaborated in the theory of the **developmental state**, to explain the success of the East Asian **newly industrialized**

economies **(NIEs)**, such as South Korea, Hong Kong, Taiwan, and Singapore, where a "strong state" managed relations between global business and local **elites**. Since the late 1980s, there has been a general decline in authoritarian regimes worldwide. Different explanations have been advanced to account for the emergence of democracy, some of which focus on social class.

Ruechemeyer and his colleagues suggest that democratization was resisted by landed and/or middle classes who benefitted from existing power arrangements, while working classes always struggled for democracy. Where democracies were established, they were brought about when groups who were excluded from the political process fought to be included and used democratic ideas to help them end **social exclusion**. The excluded groups' main commitment was to improve their own position rather than fight for the principle of democracy for its own sake. The transformative power of the idea and practice of democracy has been discussed in the emerging literature on the **globalization** of **human rights** discourse, which maintains that democratic transitions throughout the developing world were supported by the increasing focus in development agencies on participation (see **participatory development**), free and open elections, and genuine political competition.

The study of globalization within the sociology of development has tended to focus on economic components, and specifically on the role of **transnational corporations (TNCs)** and the **transnational capitalist class (TCC)** in the spread of capitalism worldwide. Sklair's theory of the transnational capitalist class engages with the work of Cox and Gill in international relations, both of whom were influenced by Gramsci, and observed the emergence of a global elite. Sklair elaborates earlier conceptualizations of international and global classes by dividing the class into four main factions: those associated with global corporations; globalizing bureaucrats and politicians; globalizing professionals; and globalizing merchants and media. This produces a more dynamic, if arguably overworked, notion of class in the capitalist global system. Gereffi's global commodity chains analysis moves the focus of Wallerstein's world-system away from regions to products. Understanding the way a shirt sold in the USA is produced globally tells us something about relationships between developed, transitional and developing countries, where people throughout are linked by their contribution to producing and selling a commodity. But like Wallerstein, Gereffi does not have much to say about social class.

People's sense of being connected around the world has been explored by cultural globalists who focus on the ways the transformation in the scope of the mass media, particularly television, helps to change social values. Although more people viewing global programming can be seen as a cultural process, it is also economic – being organized and driven mostly by TNCs. Global access to programs, for example soap operas and news such as CNN, is increasing rapidly. According to data from UNESCO, there were 192 million TVs in the world in 1965, 408 million in 1975, 749 million in 1985, and 1.4 billion in 1997. This represents 57 TVs per thousand people in 1965 and 240 per thousand in 1997. Even more striking is the change in geographical distribution. In 1965, only about 5 percent of the world's TV sets were in developing countries – by 1997, developing countries accounted for around 52 percent of TVs (see http://www.unesco.org for these and other relevant statistics). The total number of TV sets in developing countries has grown so rapidly in recent years that many researchers argue that a "globalizing effect" due to the mass media is taking place (see **media**).

The process of globalization transforms relations between social classes and cultures. It also has an impact on relations between women and men. Women have often been involved in the development of many of the NIEs, working in difficult conditions in factories, producing goods for export to the global marketplace. There has been a great deal of literature examining the question of whether such industrial **employment** liberates or oppresses women. While liberal feminists might argue that by valuing and recognizing women's work, they are liberated, Marxists, drawing from Engels' reasoning, emphasize that defining working women as workers rather than housewives helps to erode discrimination. Radical feminists suggest that patriarchy is common to all societies. Maria Mies, in a synthesis of Marxism and radical feminism, used the case of lace making in India to argue that labeling women making lace in their own homes as "housewives" earning extra money, rather than "workers" allows capitalists to avoid paying them fair wages and giving them basic labor rights (see **labor rights and standards**).

Many social problems, such as gender **inequality**, have rural and urban dimensions, and Long's farming system approach utilizes Giddens's structuration theory to tease out such micro/macro social relationships at the rural **community** level. This overlaps with the participatory action approach used by many practitioners to implement local development initiatives (see **participatory development**), such as **community water management** and **sanitation** systems. Sociologists of **rural development** have also always had an interest in understanding the impact of capitalist **agriculture** on peasant society (see **peasantry**). Capitalism transforms cities as well as outlying areas, and there has been massive growth in developing-world **urbanization** since the 1970s. This brings with it attendant social problems when basic services cannot keep up with a rapid influx of people from the countryside, the flourishing of the informal economic sector, and "septic fringes" that ring many cities in developing countries, where people live in squatter settlements (see **squatters; shantytowns**) characterized by extremely poor conditions.

During most of the "age of development," and up until 1991, there was an alternative to capitalist development provided by embryonic socialist experiments in many developing states, including Nicaragua, Cuba, Tanzania, Mozambique, and China, which received much critical attention from sociologists. Socialist or postsocialist leadership (see **postsocialism**) was characterized by doing one or more of the following: emphasizing central **planning**; collectivizing agriculture; imposing state control over industry and foreign trade; building a mass party; and substituting collective moral incentives for individual capitalist incentives. Most of these regimes collapsed by the end of the 1980s, and Cuba today remains closest to the aims of socialist development outlined above, though it too is opening the door to global capitalism with the development of its **tourism** economy.

By the early 1990s, there was wide agreement that the sociology of development was in a theoretical impasse. Neo-Marxist and orthodox Marxist critiques had largely canceled each other out, and the collapse of Stalinist communism signaled the end of many direct links to Marx in the literature. In the latter half of the decade, a focus on critical theory and the linguistic turn in sociology was manifested in a wide range of post- and alternative development approaches, critical of the very (Western) idea of development.

Postdevelopment theorists (see **postmodernism and postdevelopment**) direct their criticism at development itself, including both its capitalist and socialist varieties. They base their analysis on the effects of President Truman's 1949 speech, which called for a "brave new program for making the benefits of our scientific advances and industrial progress available for the involvement and growth of underdeveloped areas" (Sachs, 1992:6). From that moment onwards, they argue, people in developing countries were defined as under-developed and in need of assistance. Development became an obstacle to improving conditions of the poor and underprivileged, rather than a means to transform it. Postdevelopment is a restatement of the critique of modernization theory, but it is also a powerful interrogation of the notion that indus-trialization is necessary for developing countries. While many find the critique conceptually satisfy-ing, they are left wondering where to go next. Postdevelopment theory provides no obvious plan, other than to focus on building autonomous **grassroots development**. In many ways, the sociology of development in the early twenty-first century is revisiting storylines that have been pre-sent from the beginning: classical nineteenth-century sociologists from Tönnies to Durkheim showed an admiration for traditional society, untainted by modernity, while Marx believed in the progression of history toward a more egalitarian form of social organization. Reflexively, sociologists in their focus on postdevelopment and globalization are returning to long-standing themes critical of both modernity and tradition.

See also: capitalism; dependency theory; globali-zation; globalization and culture; Marxism; modernization theory; social exclusion; social integration; postmodernism and postdevelopment; transnational capitalist class (TCC)

Further reading

Pieterse, J. (2001) *Development Theory: Decon-structions/Reconstructions*, London: Sage.

Roberts, J. and Hite, A. (eds) (2000) *From Modernization to Globalization: Social Perspectives on International Development*, Boston MA: Blackwell.

Sachs, W. (ed.) (1992) *The Development Dictionary*, London: Zed.

Sklair, L. (ed.) (1994) *Capitalism and Development*, London: Routledge.

Sklair, L. (2002) *Globalization: Capitalism and Its Alternatives*, Oxford: Oxford University Press.

PETER T. ROBBINS

soil erosion and soil fertility

Soil erosion refers to the removal of soil by processes such as water flow or wind. Soil fertility is the capacity of soil to provide nutrients for plant growth, especially for **agriculture**. Soil erosion and its impact on soil resources, principally its effect on soil fertility, are biophysical processes of soil degradation that are probably the greatest challenge to the integrity and development potential of agro-ecosystems (see **desertification; environment**). Ninety percent of all human **food** is produced from soils varying widely in quality, nature and extent. Erosion has received widespread attention since the so-called Dust Bowl, which was the experience of intense and sometimes devastating loss of soil in the lower central plains of the USA during the 1930s. Lord Hailey in his 1939 *African Survey* described erosion as the "scourge of Africa." Soil fertility, on the other hand, is a scientific concept of the quality or health or productivity of the soil, related intimately to how a soil is used and managed. Through the selective removal of the fertile fractions of a soil – clays, silts, organic matter, which contain most of the nutrients and plant-available water capacity – soil erosion is arguably the single greatest physical threat to **food security**.

Soil erosion is the physical detachment of soil particles by wind and water and their transport to other parts of the landscape, to rivers and the sea.

Not only is the remaining soil resource reduced in its quality (on-site impacts, such as reduced soil depth, decline in nutrients, and increasing acidity) but also the eroded sediment in its deposition elsewhere can have a profound impact (off-site impacts, such as sedimentation of water bodies, damage to hydro-electric installations, and **pollution**). It should, however, be noted that erosion could be beneficial, even fundamental to the survival of societies, as in the Nile Valley. Ethiopia's loss of soil is Egypt's gain. At a field scale, farmers harvest eroded materials behind stone barriers across valleys (e.g. *nula gode* in India) to create new fields and increased production opportunities.

Soil fertility is the capacity of the soil to support crops. It encompasses soil chemical, physical and biological processes that create a soil with nutrients in available form for plant growth, the composition to provide the necessary water, air and other gases, and the micro-environment that nurtures beneficial organisms and biochemical processes.

The control of soil erosion and enhancement of soil fertility are now seen as an integral part of sustainable farming practice (see **agriculture; shifting cultivation; sustainable livelihoods**). Instead of adding **agrochemicals** for example, indigenous and adapted techniques enable farmers to sustain soil resources without external inputs. Systems such as the maize-velvetbean (*Mucuna*) **intercropping** of South America, the *zaï* pits of West Africa or **agroforestry** in general demonstrate the scientific validity of local understanding of farmers. Policies that promote both scientifically-validated and **local knowledge** are spreading. At a global level, the **United Nations Convention to Combat Desertification (UNCCD)** now recognizes such techniques, while at national levels more heterogeneous policies are being adopted to the control of soil erosion and promotion of soil fertility.

See also: agriculture; agrochemicals; desertification; environment; fertilizers; intercropping; Sahel; salinization; shifting cultivation; sustainable livelihoods

Further reading

Scoones, I. and Toulmin, C. (2000) *Policies for Soil Fertility Management in Africa*, London: DFID.
Stocking, M. (2000, 2nd edn) "Soil Erosion and Land Degradation," pp. 287–321 in O'Riordan, T. (ed.) *Environmental Science for Environmental Management*, Harlow: Pearson.

MICHAEL STOCKING

solidarity campaigns

Solidarity campaigns are coordinated and collaborative efforts by **non-governmental organizations (NGOs)**, social movements, and **grassroots organizations** to pursue broad social change strategies and promote political positions. Solidarity campaigns operate through the principle of strength through unity. When one organization advocates a particular stance or engages in a specific struggle, other, like-minded groups show solidarity by joining with them to provide support. The idea of solidarity has its roots in traditional trade union activism in which struggles for rights by workers in one field has been supported by workers in both other locations as well as in unrelated fields. The unifying bond is the notion of workers' rights, no matter what the difference in specific issues might be.

Similarly, solidarity campaigns among social movements and NGOs have often transcended both localities and particular causes. For example, many groups and organizations that have rallied together since the late 1990s under the banner of the anti-**globalization** movement are quite distinct in their motivations for challenging the spread of **neo-liberalism**. Yet, despite these differences many anti-globalization activists have managed to work together by focusing on their shared commitment to principles of **social justice**.

The broad orientation of groups engaged in solidarity campaigns, rather than the specificity of campaigns, that has led to success. Popular movements in India that oppose the construction of large **dams**, for example, have lent their support to NGOs advocating justice for the victims of the Bhopal chemical disaster and vice-versa. These

India-based anti-dam organizations (see **dams**) have also been shown solidarity by Basque anti-dam activists in Spain, environmental NGOs in Japan, and **human rights** organizations in the USA through sympathetic demonstrations, press releases, hunger strikes, and other methods. Such shows of support have sometimes extended to material assistance (as when one union local or organization donates resources to another that is on strike or engaged in a protest), but the key element of solidarity campaigns lies in the public endorsement of and alliance with the organization initiating the campaign.

Solidarity campaigns are therefore important strategic tools for social movements and NGOs in both the developing and the developed world. As with **advocacy coalitions** and other modern social movement strategies, solidarity campaigns allow participants to share resources and build relative strength by unifying in support of similar causes or against common opponents. For example, locally based social movements have found solidarity campaigns an effective way to confront foreign-based **transnational corporations (TNCs)**. While it is often difficult for **grassroots organizations** to pressure TNCs on their own, by allying with similar groups and NGOs in other countries, they are able to more effectively challenge corporations seeking to avoid the local consequences of their global reach.

See also: advocacy coalitions; environmental movements; Live Aid/Band Aid; new social movements; non-governmental organizations (NGOs); trade unions; World Social Forum (WSF)

Further reading

Khagram, S., Sikkink, K. and Riker, J. (2002) *Restructuring World Politics: Transnational Social Movements, Networks, and Norms*, Minneapolis: University of Minnesota Press.
Princen, T. and Finger, M. (1994). *Environmental NGOs in World Politics: Linking the Local and the Global*, London: Routledge.

PABLO SHILADITYA BOSE

Southern African Development Community (SADC)

The Southern African Development Community (SADC) is an organization of states (see **state and state reform**) in southern Africa to enhance mutually beneficial, self-reliant **economic growth**, broader development and **poverty** reduction. It was established by the Windhoek Treaty in 1992 to succeed the Southern African Development Co-ordination Conference (SADCC), and its secretariat in Gaborone, Botswana, has been strengthened and more centralized directorates established. Sustainable resource use and environmental protection are claimed as key principles. The ten SADCC members were joined by South Africa in 1994, followed by Mauritius, the Seychelles and Democratic Republic of Congo (DRC) by 1997. The Community thus forms a contiguous sub-regional bloc, along with two island states, and is more coherent and cohesive than the rival **Common Market for Eastern and Southern Africa (COMESA)**. A free trade zone (see **free trade zones (FTZs)**) is being implemented, while an Organ for Politics, Defense and Security targets dispute resolution and security issues. However, the involvement of Angola, Namibia and Zimbabwe in the DRC conflict since 1999, and the crisis in Zimbabwe since 2001, have hampered progress.

See also: Common Market for Eastern and Southern Africa (COMESA); economic federalization; Economic Community of West African States (ECOWAS); free trade zones (FTZs)

DAVID SIMON

South-South cooperation

South-South cooperation refers to the various initiatives among developing countries for achieving collective self-reliance in areas of mutual and shared development interest. Such initiatives gained impetus in the 1950s owing to growing consciousness in the South (or developing world) about the asymmetrical relations in economic and political power with the North (developed world) as was demonstrated by the

Bandung conference (1955). The formation of the **non-aligned movement** in 1961 and later the **Group of 77 (G-77)** in 1964 further substantiated this awareness.

International economic interdependence implies that unilateral action by states (see **state and state reform**) creates adverse impact on others. The pervasiveness of bargaining in the **governance** of international economic relations places a premium on consolidating political strength through formation of collective bargaining units such as producer associations, **cartels**, and even trading blocs in order to secure the economic interests of the South. The **Organization of Petroleum Exporting Countries (OPEC)** remarkably demonstrated the potential for such joint action by successfully pushing for higher oil prices in 1973.

The structural dependency of most Southern economies on developed countries of the North, characterized by net import of capital, concentration of exports in a few northern markets and reliance on foreign **aid** and technology, make them vulnerable to external shocks, as well demonstrated by the **debt** crisis of the 1980s. Intra-South trade is then pursued as a strategy for ameliorating such weaknesses and expanding options in the developing world for rational, self-sustaining **economic growth**. Concomitantly, various forms of regional integration have emerged to promote trade as an engine for growth in the South. Commonly these take the form of **free trade zones (FTZs)** (e.g. the **Latin American Free Trade Agreement (LAFTA)**) and common markets (e.g. **Common Market for Eastern and Southern Africa (COMESA)**). Key areas and forms of joint south action for the promotion of intra-South trade include coordinated investment in transport and communications infrastructure, agricultural research, **food** policy, energy (see **energy policy**), **science and technology**, **joint ventures** (see **transnational corporations (TNCs) from developing economies**), exchange of information and private sector development.

Despite cogent economic motives, political impetus is often a strong driving force in the establishment of trading blocs. Some potential threats to blocs include: insufficient attention to the unequal benefits of **trade** resulting from diverting trade from Northern partners; the concentration of industries in relatively more developed countries; and the different implications of loss of government revenue resulting from implementing uniform tax and tariff regimes. Further, the proliferation of overlapping regional blocs often proves counter-productive, as they generate bureaucratic bottlenecks and rent seeking opportunities that impede trade. They also stretch the limited technical capacities and resources of member countries when trying to address many responsibilities at the same time. There is consequently commonly a lack of **coherence** in policies adopted by member states.

See also: Bandung conference (1955); economic federalization; Group of 77 (G-77); non-aligned movement

Further reading

South Commission (1990) *The Challenge to the South*, Oxford: Oxford University Press

MOSES A. OSIRO

squatters

The term "squatter" generally refers to a person who lacks legal **security** over land they have built their **housing** on, and hence reference to "squatter settlements" in many developing world towns and cities (see **shantytowns**). Land tenure (see **land rights**) in these locations may vary from illegal to quasi-legal and many squatters have some right to the land they live on, even if it is informal (such as rental agreements; personal permission from indigenous owners, or through irregular payments to politicians or landowners – see **corruption**). The term "squatter" may also apply to people living on farmland or within protected land such as national parks without formal sanction from the state (see **state and state reform**) or landowners.

There is some debate about the appropriateness of the term "squatter," as it has a pejorative sense of illegality and anarchy. Indeed, squatters may include law-abiding people inclusive of both the poor and the middle class who are unable to afford the astronomical land and housing prices that often characterize cities in developing countries such as Mumbai or Shanghai. Squatters may work in the **urban informal sector**, eking out a living, but also include lower-ranking government officials, white collar workers or even, in some cases (e.g. Papua New Guinea) politicians. The term then is problematic, and care should be taken with its use. Alternative, local, terms that give a more sympathetic and accurate portrayal of relationships include *Chumchon bukberk* (pioneering community) in Thailand, *kampong* in Malaysia and Indonesia (which is a common term for **villages** irrespective of their legal status), or Traditional Housing Areas (THAs) in the Solomon Islands.

The heterogeneous nature of squatters and squatter settlements has provided a seemingly intractable challenge to policy-makers. Interest in such populations and settlements has increased since the 1960s, when it became apparent that migrants to cities (see **rural-urban migration**) had, at best, access to few resources and skills which were relevant to urban life. As a result, particularly first-generation migrants sought to build makeshift shelter in empty urban lands, both public and private. Squatter settlements are now a dominant and permanent site on the urban landscape, typically constituting between 25–50 percent of urban **populations**. Initially seen as a temporary phenomenon, both the public and private sector has failed to provide affordable and adequate shelter for squatters, even for those who are not poor (see **housing**). This failure is a legacy of imbalanced land ownership in the city leading to scarcity, but also indicates the comparative lack of economic and political power of most urban residents. Being a squatter and living in a "squatter settlement," then, is very much an inevitable manifestation of social, political and economic **marginalization** and exploitation in terms of access to **land rights**, services and urban **citizenship**. Hence, some writers have referred to squatter settlements as constituting the "popular city" and representing a powerful statement of "insurgent **citizenship**" through the occupation of space and defiance of those who would simply like them to disappear. Dealing with squatter settlements may therefore be as much about extending rights as providing housing.

See also: housing; land tenure; shantytowns; urbanization

Further reading

Hardoy, J. and Satterthwaite, D. (1989) *Squatter Citizen: Life in the Urban Third World*, London: Earthscan.

Youé, C. (2002) "Black Squatters on White Farms: Segregation and Agrarian Change in Kenya, South Africa, and Rhodesia, 1902–1963," *International History Review* 24:3 558–602.

DONOVAN STOREY

STABILIZATION *see* International Monetary Fund (IMF); structural adjustment; debt relief

stages of economic growth

"Stages of economic growth" refers to the belief, often associated with **modernization theory**, that development is an evolutionary process, which undergoes successive levels of economic **productivity**, efficiency and consumption. It is most associated with the theorist, Walt Rostow (1960), who claimed that all economies could be classified within one of five categories: the traditional society, the preconditions for take-off, the take-off, the drive to maturity, and the age of high mass-consumption.

A traditional society was defined as one with limited production functions, based on pre-Newtonian science and technology. The preconditions for take-off were initially developed during Western Europe in the late seventeenth and early eighteenth centuries as the insights of modern science were adopted in both agriculture and industry, and by the expansion of world markets. Take-off is the watershed that defines when industrial development begins, and when growth becomes a normal condition. In Britain, the first country to undergo the Industrial Revolution, the trigger for take-off in the late eighteenth century was mainly technological. More generally, however, the stimulus may also include the emergence of a political group prepared to take industrial modernization seriously. During take-off, the rate of effective investment and savings may rise from 5 percent of **gross national product (GNP)** to 10 percent or more, especially where preconditions for take-off require much initial investment in capital goods (such as claimed in Russia and Canada). The drive to maturity is when investment rises to some 20 percent of GNP, and where industry makes a transition to high levels of technological advancement, also allowing growth in production to exceed **population** growth. Industry may also shift in emphasis from coal, iron, and heavy engineering industries of the railway phase to machine tools, chemicals, and electrical equipment. Finally, the stage of high mass consumption is characterized by a shift in industry to services and consumer durables, a high level of urban population, and per capita income that easily covers basic requirements of shelter, **food** and clothing.

The stages of economic growth theory was typical of much development thinking in the mid-twentieth century, and precipitated debates about what levels of state investment were necessary to induce take off (see **state and state reform**), the emphasis of industrial policy (see **industrialization**), and the supply of capital goods. Rostow also influenced US foreign policy by acting as a security adviser to President Nixon during the Vietnam War. Yet, the theory has also been widely criticized for failing to acknowledge the historically- and spatially-specific nature of many of the supposed stages, and for simplistically proposing a blueprint model without recognizing physical or cultural differences between countries (see **narratives of development**). More importantly, perhaps, the model failed to acknowledge the international political economy reasons for the inducement or failure of **economic growth** worldwide, and assumed that investment and government policy alone might induce growth (e.g. see **dependency theory**). Most generally, many of the criticisms of **modernization theory** as a concept can also be applied to the stages of growth model, particularly in overlooking social, political or environmental factors of development. The stages of economic growth model, however, represents one of the most significant illustrations of how development policy was approached by the developed countries prior to the 1970s.

See also: big push; economic growth; industrialization; modernization theory

Further reading

Rostow, W. (1960) *The Stages of Economic Growth: A Non-Communist Manifesto*, Cambridge: Cambridge University Press.

TIM FORSYTH

state and state reform

The state may be defined as **public sector** institutions, organizations, constitutional entities and parliamentary structures that are situated in local, national, regional, and global space. This generally refers to the executive, legislative and judicial branches of government; the public service, police and armed forces; plus government enterprises and other public institutions.

The *nation-state* is the notion that there exist within countries public relationships that are sufficiently embedded to form relatively unifying processes. For instance, the question arises as to whether various nations exist as meaningful groups of people and organizations; e.g. the Democratic Republic of Congo, India, East Timor, Afghanistan, Indonesia and Russia. To answer this question requires a detailed knowledge of the extent to which regional and global forces impact on these areas, the spread of ethnic and cultural relations (see **ethnicity/identity**), and the degree to which national institutions and organizations meaningfully exist and operate. Many developing nations fail to develop as nation-states, partly due to the artificial nature of borders and the inability to resolve conflict (Alam, 2000).

Many *regional state forces* have emerged over recent decades that to some degree challenge the focus on nation-states. Primary among these are regional forms of economic, political and social integration. For instance, the West African Economic Community, the Arab Free Trade Area, the **MERCOSUR** economic community of Latin America, the Caribbean Community, and the **Association of Southeast Asian Nations (ASEAN)**, may lead to more effective regional forms of integration in the future not dissimilar to the **European Union**. Sub-national regional forces such as warlords, tribes, and **local governments** also impact on nation-states.

The existence of various *global state and private forces* also challenge the focus on certain nation-states. For instance, the power of the **United Nations**, the **World Bank**, the **International Monetary Fund (IMF)**, the World Trade Organization (see **World Trade Organization/General Agreement on Tariffs and Trade (WTO/GATT)**), the hegemonic dominance of the USA, and the operation of various global "intelligence" and "environmental" protocols, can challenge the power of weaker national structures and relationships. They illustrate the increasing importance of global state and private forms, the dominance of various superpowers, and the limitations of national legislation. For instance, under the influence of various financial crises in the 1990s (see **Asian crises**), the IMF instigated (quasi) international lender of last resort facilities in recognition of the **contagion effect**s of such crises. During the 1990s and 2000s, the WTO has sought to promote global trade in services, **intellectual property rights (IPRs)** and **agriculture**. The World Bank has sought to limit the activities of nation-states in favor of private, **community** and sub-national institutions. Financial and industrial **transnational corporations (TNCs)** have enhanced somewhat the rule of global capital while limiting the power of nation-states.

There are also various forms of national state political structures. First, there are democratic and autocratic *unitary states*: where the central authority controls most of the state decision-making arrangements. Autocratic unitary states have an institutional and organizational (formal) unity that is difficult to challenge (see **authoritarianism**). For instance, China, Burma, Cuba, and Saudi Arabia all have singular power centers engrained in politics. They have either a dominant one-party state or a reigning monarch that prevents the emergence of pluralistic institutions of power and authority. There are no effective elections or checks and balances to ensure democracy and participation. Democratic unitary states, on the other hand, have elected central governments but usually no state governments; and most nations of the world take this form. It is possible, though, even under democratic unitary state forms to have some degree of **decentralization**, as most nations have some form of local **governance**.

Many developing nations exist as *federal systems*, especially the larger nations such as India, Brazil and Russia, as well as many developed nations such as the USA and Australia. A federation is a union of states or provinces to form a united system. Under this system of government, there is a division of tasks – established by constitution – between the state and federal (plus also often local) levels of government. For instance, the federal (national) level may specialize in defense, international relations, social security and national-environmental regulations – often said to be financed by income and corporate taxation. State governments may concentrate on infrastructure, **health**, and **education** – financed by various duties and taxes (see **fiscal and monetary policy**). While the local levels undertake the maintenance of roads, walkways, building standards, and **waste management** – often financed by a levy on property.

Lastly, many underdeveloped areas are hindered by the inability to put into practice an effective state apparatus; hence the term *fragmented state*. These states nominally take a federal or (usually) unitary form, but are subject to high levels of instability, uncertainty and often conflict that make effective state maintenance and development difficult. Examples include the former Yugoslavia, the Solomon Islands, Palestine, Zimbabwe, the Congo, Zaire, Liberia, Sierra Leone and Somalia (Snyder, 2001). These fragmented states are often unable to stabilize due of the nature of colonial and postcolonial borders and institutions; lack of development and growth; the emergence of conflict and **war** between tribes and political-economic interests; warlord politics; **corruption** and fraud; diseases such as HIV/AIDS (see **HIV/AIDS (definition and treatment); HIV/AIDS (policy issues)**) and **malaria**; and **brain drain** to the advanced nations (Janicke, 1990).

State reform

During the past 20–30 years, **neo-liberalism** has influenced state reform through reducing budget deficits, privatizing public activities, giving priority to monetary policy, and freeing up labor, financial and commodity markets. This has been activated via **international organizations and associations**, nation-states, and diplomatic and military strategies. However, the financial crises of the 1990s-2000s, speculative bubble crashes, and recent research on productive public capital have led many to argue that a new post-**Washington consensus** is being developed. Such a consensus takes on board some of the neo-liberal ideas, but moderates them with reference to the need for **poverty**-relief, social and cultural capital development (see **social capital**), the significance of **education** and **health**, environmental concerns, plus decentralized governance. Indeed, Snyder has argued, for instance, that "neoliberal reform" in Mexico merely saw the "construction of new regulatory institutions at the *sub-national* level [with] different kinds of new institutions for market regulation, not in the triumph of free markets" (2001:99, emphasis added; compare with Welsch and Carrasquero, 2000).

In the emerging post-Washington consensus, reform of the state is continually necessary in order to promote innovation and new forms of state capacities. According to Amartya Sen (1999), the ability of states and other forces to expand the capabilities of citizens and institutions provides the foundation for freedom as development (see **capability approach; freedom versus choice; functionings**). How, then, can the state stimulate people's capabilities to realize their potential?

The first such area of reform is promoting *effective institutions and relationships*. Recent research has indicated that a critical co-requisite for development is the promotion of social and cultural capital, which requires people to become actively engaged in society, economy and polity through the encouragement of trust, association, and **community**. To enhance these capabilities, the state can promote the basic needs of the **population**, as well as education, mobility, health, **freedom of association** and thought, and the availability of finance for innovative community and personal projects (e.g. **micro-credit and micro-finance**).

This leads to the second area of reform, namely, the state engaging in *productive activities* that crowd-in private spending rather than unproductive ones that inhibit the private sector. Recent research has consistently supported changing the nature of state spending from transfer payments, such as **unemployment** benefits and subsidies, to productive activities such as the development of infrastructure, education, health, **telecommunications** and utilities. The state can thus promote private investment through activities that enable the development of human, infrastructure, and network capitals that provide a flow of services into the future, and provide externalities that have major social benefits through time. Such productive spending can propel both demand and **productivity** (Ghosh, 2004).

A third area of reform lies in *reducing vested interests and wastage*. Many authors have argued that state spending in developing nations often wastes the economic surplus through **corruption**, nepotism, and the dominance of vested interests (Hope, 1997). Throughout many areas of Africa, South America and Asia, the public service, political system and ancillary state activities are undertaken in an environment of favors based on tribal, family and religious sentiment, dominance of local **elites**, and low pay for public servants. Bribery, fraud and **money laundering** are common practices. Reforms that have been found to reduce such vested interests include the independent monitoring of elections, effective auditing of public accounts, open and transparent bidding for public projects, effective legal constraints on public servants, checks and balances in the political arena, and a culture of openness and honesty (see **accountability; transparency**).

The issue of vested interests is linked to the issue of *state relative autonomy* (Evans et al., 1985). If the state in developing nations works hand-in-glove with various classes and groups that lessen its independence and limit its horizons, then reform is unlikely. This is especially the case when the state supports classes that hinder progress, such as the landed gentry, exploitative moneylenders, and inefficient bureaucrats. If capitalist development is envisaged, then it is critical to promote the formation of indigenous innovative capitalists and workers. Structural conditions often lead developing nations to be stuck at the stage of agricultural and mineral exploitation and low value-added manufacturing, rather than innovative industrial and class formation.

The public service and parliament often fail due to ineffective procedures, slow committee systems, the complexity of the legal system, and inadequate skills and qualifications. The costs of red tape, operational delays, and geographical distance of officers from clients are common causes of *bureaucratic failure* (see **public management; public sector**). Ways in which these problems can be ameliorated include greater simplicity of administration, legal and administrative transparency, more effective skill development and less brain drain to the advanced nations (Turner and Hulme, 1997).

Lastly, a critical area of reform lies in the *structure of power in the global society*. Many developing states are young, inexperienced, subject to **war**, conflict, disease, **drought** and **famine**. Many are still undergoing a postcolonial process of experimentation and change. Most are caught in the low-power stakes of a peripheral nation, where the major players determine the rules of the game, and there are few prospects for improvement. Many are small and not easily benefitting from economies of scale, scope and agglomeration. In this light, reforms of the state that can benefit development are necessarily structural, long-term, and contingent. This entails promoting serious work through **international organizations and associations** as well as effective national industrial policies. The developing world requires the building of capabilities through successful access to markets, effective union with other states in the region, industrial development through successful innovative strategies, and the building of effective political-economic power in the global economy.

The state is therefore a multifarious array of **institutions**, organizations, people and capacities. Historically it has played a critical role in development, despite the recent neo-liberal trend of supporting deregulation and privatization of state functions (see **privatization and liberalization**). The post-Washington consensus posits a more positive role for the state, especially in developing people's capabilities, promoting productive public capital, and fostering progressive class relations. But various structural conditions remain that limit state reform and development. Primary among

them is the trend to corruption, the center-periphery power relations of the world economy, and the difficulty of promoting innovative change in some nations. If the emphasis is given to enhancing capabilities and enabling the population to participate in social, economic and political life, then some measure of success is likely in the long run.

See also: capability approach; civil society; corruption; decentralization; democracy; elites; governance; governmentality; politics; privatization and liberalization; public management; public sector; state-owned enterprises (SOEs)

Further reading

Alam, M. (2000) *Poverty from the Wealth of Nations: Integration and Polarization in the Global Economy Since 1760*, London: Macmillan.

Evans, P. Rueschemeyer, D. and Skocpol, T. (eds) (1985) *Bringing the State Back In*, Cambridge: Cambridge University Press.

Ghosh, B. (2004) "Development Policies for the Twenty-First Century," in O'Hara, P. (ed.) *Global Political Economy and the Wealth of Nations: Performance, Institutions, Problems and Policy*, London: Routledge.

Hope, K. (1997) *African Political Economy: Contemporary Issues in Development*, Armonk NY: Sharpe.

Janicke, M. (1990) *State Failure: The Impotence of Politics in Industrial Society*, Cambridge: Polity.

Sen, A. (1999). *Development as Freedom*, NewYork: Knopf.

Snyder, R. (2001) *Politics After Liberalism: Re-regulation in Mexico*, Cambridge: Cambridge University Press.

Turner, M. and Hulme, D. (1997) *Governance, Administration and Development: Making the State Work*, Houndmills: Palgrave.

Welsch, F. and Carrasquero, J. (2000) "Perceptions of State Reform in Latin America," *International Social Science Journal* 52:1 31–8.

PHILLIP ANTHONY O'HARA

stateless people

Stateless people are people who are discriminated against through being denied participation in, or even access to, the body politic of the state (see **state and state reform**) in which they live. Stateless people can be groups which perceive themselves as nations but who do not have their own state; **indigenous** people who are repressed on ethnic, religious, linguistic, or cultural grounds by dominant groups that control the state apparatus; or international **refugees** (or asylum seekers – see **asylum seeking**) who remain excluded from the infrastructures of their host state. Without legitimate representation in government, stateless people are denied political voice, legal recourse, and access to **health**, **education**, and other social welfare programs. In the most extreme instances, especially in **weak states**, this institutional discrimination is coupled with active physical **violence** perpetrated by the dominant group against the marginalized. All three broad types of stateless people present significant challenges for political, social (see **sociology of development**), and **economic development**.

First, nations without their own state often resort to a virulent **nationalism** to demand their **right to self-determination** to overcome the repression and underdevelopment they are subjected to. The obvious example here is the Palestinians, perhaps the world's most prominent stateless people. Enduring chronic underdevelopment, ethnic and religious discrimination, and physical violence for more than fifty years, the Palestinians have responded with a violent resistance that has perpetuated the cycle of violence, inhibited the conditions for meaningful and sustained development, and contributed to their stateless people quandary.

Second, members of indigenous groups of the so-called **Fourth World** may be full citizens of a particular state but continue to be marginalized through discriminatory state apparatuses. This exclusion is often the institutional legacy of colonialism (see **colonialism, history of; colonialism, impacts of; decolonization; postcolonialism**) that attempted to repress and/or eradicate any ethnic, religious, linguistic or other social cleavage. The prospects of long-term development for such groups, for example the Kurds in Iran, Iraq, and Turkey or the Aboriginals in Australia, continue to be problematic. This "statelessness" is a major driving force of the contemporary "new **nationalism**s" that, as the Palestinian example demonstrates, present a range of problems for development strategies.

Finally, international **refugees** seeking physical safety from war and/or disaster and freedom from political repression may become stateless people if they are unable or unwilling to be repatriated to their original state. Again, this presents significant development problems. In the short term, refugees will require immediate provision of shelter, food, and **primary health care**, which the host state may be unwilling to provide or facilitate, especially if their presence poses a danger to its own political stability. This perception of threat may hinder humanitarian assistance in refugee camps, as happened following the **genocide** in Rwanda in 1994. Beyond this, long-term refugees may produce a "second generation" born in the host state, raising the problem of **citizenship** and, by implication, rights to health, education, and other social services. Such refugee groups have the potential to become a marginalized semi-permanent group within a particular state, perpetuating the development dilemmas of all types of stateless people.

See also: asylum seeking; Fourth World; internally displaced persons; marginalization; refugees

Further reading

Guibernau, M. (1999) *Nations without States: Political Communities in a Global Age*, Cambridge: Polity Press.

PETER MAYELL

state-owned enterprises (SOEs)

State-owned enterprises (SOEs) are firms or industries that are partly or totally owned by the state (see **state and state reform**). The direct government participation in productive activities through SOEs has often been rationalized as a response to private-market imperfections or failure.

The widespread existence of increasing returns to scale, giving rise to the emergence of natural monopolies, is one of the standard economic arguments used in favor of SOEs to capture the benefits of scale economies for the public at large rather than for the owners of monopoly capital. Consequently, SOEs have been widely associated with socialist economies, although many capitalist economies also developed SOEs.

An important set of arguments for developing countries relates to **economic growth**. Where private activity is constrained by high-risk aversion, poorly developed financial markets or a paucity of information, entrepreneurial substitution has been a motive for establishing SOEs. In economies characterized by limited integration between different sectors, state investment can perform the role of ensuring that the conditions necessary for industrial growth are met. Thus, in many developing countries the need to accelerate the process of **industrialization** has led to state sector participation in sectors believed to have significant linkage effects. Even where products of these sectors can be imported at a lower cost, state-owned domestic production in these commanding heights activities may be rationalized in terms of their strategic importance. SOEs have also been established and used as an instrument for the pursuit of distributional goals, to create **employment** and to act as a counterweight against excessive concentration of private economic power.

The thrust of the criticisms against SOEs, and an explanation for their often-poor performance, has centered on the multiplicity of objectives established for their operation and the adequacy of their incentive mechanisms for internal efficiency. SOEs have suffered from the need to fulfill multiple rather than single objectives. The goal of commercial viability has often been combined with broader economic and social concerns. It has been argued that some of these objectives could more effectively be met by other economic instruments rather than SOEs. The unclear assignment of **property rights** for SOEs has led to doubts about their ability to operate with sufficient managerial incentives, and the degree of autonomy and risk-taking associated with private enterprise.

Over the last two decades, SOEs in developing economies have been subjected to a wide-range of reforms. These have included reforms without a change in state ownership to outright privatization (see **privatization and liberalization**). The reforms have generally aimed to give SOEs greater degrees of autonomy and improved **incentive structures**. Various contract and performance schemes have been introduced to establish specific targets that are within the control of management, and to institute reward systems for managers of SOEs. While examples of successfully operated state-owned enterprises (SOEs) can be found, the current consensus favors their privatization.

See also: auto industry; iron and steel; market socialism; postsocialism; privatization and liberalization; shock therapy; state and state reform

Further reading

Cook, P. and Kirkpatrick, C. (1997) "Privatisation, Public Enterprise Reform and the World Bank: Has 'Bureaucrats in Business' Got it Right?" *Journal of International Development* 9:6 887–97.

Grosh, B. (1992) *Public Enterprises in Kenya*, London: Lynn Reinner.

World Bank (1995) *Bureaucrats in Business: The Economics and Politics of Reform*, New York: World Bank/Oxford University Press.

PAUL COOK AND COLIN KIRKPATRICK

stock markets

Stock markets are where shares in companies are bought and sold. The usual model of a stock market is that adopted in most developed countries, of trading only in publicly listed companies with a high aggregate value, in a forum where trading is regulated and accountable. Less formal markets for shares also exist without such regulation, but are generally not called "stock markets." Companies sell shares in order to gain finance.

There is a growing consensus since the mid-1990s, based on a large and growing number of empirical cross-national studies, that countries with a well-developed financial system – including stock markets – tend to grow faster over subsequent

decades net of the effect of other political economic factors. Moreover, industries and firms that
rely heavily on external financing grow disproportionately faster in countries with well-
developed banks and securities markets. These
findings are especially germane for less developed
countries, since publicly listed corporations in the
developing world are relatively more reliant on
external financing to fund their new investment.
Unfortunately, this consensus and empirical confidence regarding the strong positive effect of
national financial systems on **economic growth**
breaks down when we focus on national stock
markets independent of the remainder of the
financial system.

Wealthier countries tend to have larger stock
markets, and tend to have more liquid stock
markets – meaning a high degree of trading relative
to the size of their stock market and/or economy.
Importantly, this association is independent and in
addition to the positive effect of a strong banking
system. But do these large liquid stock markets
cause economic growth? Or does the economic
growth cause the stock market development? Or
perhaps does a third political economic factor
(such as trade or **fiscal and monetary policy**)
enhance both?

To address these questions, one influential
World Bank study found that a nation's stock
market liquidity (but not necessarily size) in 1976
was strongly predictive of economic growth, capital accumulation, and **productivity** growth
seventeen years later. The primary channel for this
growth was improvements in corporate productivity. The results imply that if in 1976 Mexico's stock
market had an average level of liquidity rather
than its below-average level, per capita **gross
domestic product (GDP)** would have grown at a
0.4 percent faster rate. By 1994, this would have
accumulated into an almost 8 percent higher
average income for Mexicans.

An intuitive interpretation of these findings is
that merely "going public" and listing corporations
on a national exchange does not facilitate economic growth. Rather, those securities must be
actively traded. Liquidity enhances economic
growth because a highly liquid stock market
allows corporations to tap into savings without
locking savers into long-term ownership of the

corporation. Thus, liquid financial markets facilitate productivity improvements via critical new
investment.

Although there is considerable international
pressure for countries with national stock markets to
treat foreign investors identically to local investors,
there are numerous reasons to argue that foreign
investors' behavior creates a far more volatile stock
market. One illustration of this is foreign investors'
rational international strategy to rapidly disinvest
in one country's stock market not because of a
change in that country's economic fundamentals
but because of a greater opportunity in another
national stock market.

In sum, there is strong evidence that an active
(but not necessarily large) stock market plays an
important role, in tandem with a strong banking
system, in economic growth. There is a trade-off,
however, between the benefit of supplementing
domestic savings with foreign capital and the
increased market volatility arising from these
capital flows.

See also: capital flight; economic development;
economic growth; fiscal and monetary policy;
privatization and liberalization

Further reading

Demirgüç-Kunt, A. and Levine, R. (eds) (2001)
  *Financial Structure and Economic Growth: A
  Cross-country Comparison of Banks, Markets, and
  Development*, Cambridge MA: MIT Press.

AARON Z. PITLUCK

Stockholm 1972 world conference on environment and development

The 1972 world conference on environment and
development (WCED) at Stockholm is generally
considered the first major international meeting to
consider issues of global environmental concern. It
was, in fact, not the first international environmental meeting, but it did represent a milestone in
its attempt to take a concerted and systematic look

at the underlying causes of global environmental problems. Although it was prompted by, and mainly concerned with, the environmental issues identified by developed countries such as conservation of threatened wildlife and wilderness, it also focused on **poverty**, and the WCED put **environment** and development issues on the global political agenda. It led to the establishment of the United Nations Environment Program (UNEP) (see **United Nations**), and can be seen as the originator of a series of international environmental publications and meetings such as the Brundtland Report (see **Brundtland Commission**) and Rio **Earth Summit (1992) (United Nations Conference on Environment and Development)**. However, it was criticized at the time for its neo-Malthusian tone (see **Malthusian demography**), and there were North-South splits regarding past responsibilities and future plans. Its recommendations and principles lacked detail, and had little implementing force. None of the major problems it identified has yet been adequately dealt with.

See also: Brundtland Commission; Earth Summit (1992) (United Nations Conference on Environment and Development); environment; *Limits to Growth* report (1972)

EMMA E. MAWDSLEY

street children

Street children make **livelihoods** and sometimes live in public spaces in conditions of usual **poverty** and high **vulnerability**. Virtually all societies possess a vernacular label for street children. Reminiscent of the "urchins" of Dickensian Britain, street children are called *cabritos* (little goats) in Chile, *moustiques* (mosquitoes) in Cameroon, *saligoman* (nasty kids) in Rwanda, *omalalpayipi* (those that sleep in pipes) in South Africa, *chokora pipas* (eaters from garbage bins) in Kenya, and *raskols* in Papua New Guinea. Such labels reflect prejudice and embarrassment at society's failure to provide for its most vulnerable members, as well as hint at the threat such **children** are believed to pose by virtue of their (assumed) lifestyle. By

considering street children as out of place and control, vernacular labels support removal and detention, and by dehumanizing children they legitimate indifference, physical **violence**, sexual and psychological abuse (see **child prostitution; domestic violence**).

In order to challenge these stereotypes and to aid policy design, more technical definitions were sought. The initial attempt stressed a humanitarian approach as captured in the 1924 League of Nations Declaration on the Rights of the Child that "the orphan and the waif must be sheltered and succored." Yet, by the 1970s, it was increasingly clear that very few street children were either orphans or lacked access to shelter. Nevertheless, the sense that street children were in need of protection was retained into the 1980s. In 1983, an inter-NGO program for street children (see **non-governmental organizations (NGOs)**) suggested that street children should be defined as "pre-adults" for whom the street, in the broadest sense, was the habitual abode and source of livelihood, and who lacked adequate protection and supervision from responsible adults. This definition was adopted by UN agencies and most NGOs.

The definition, however, presented a vague starting point from which to base statistical collection. Thus, while the **United Nations Children's Fund (UNICEF)** regularly cited a figure of 100 million, and occasionally 150 million, street children worldwide, many observers regarded this to be an overestimate. In Brazil, for example, some estimates claimed as many as 30 million street children, others 7 million and some fewer than 1 million. One solution was to distinguish between children who lived and those that worked on the street. As a survey of Mexico City revealed, while there might be as many as 200,000 street-working children there were perhaps no more than 1,020 street-living children. Studies showed how street-working children, also referred to as children *on* the street, were likely to return to a secure place after work, often with their family, and were likely to attend school. By contrast, a street-living child, or child *of* the street, survived through opportunistic endeavor, including petty crime and begging, and was attributed with lower access to welfare services (see **welfare economics; welfare state**), poorer diet (see **nutrition**), greater likelihood of juvenile detention, more likely to be male, and to suffer from depression, drug use and violence (see **youth violence**). Crucially, a street-working child very rarely became a street-living child.

This kind of distinction – between street-working and street-living children – helped development agencies or governments target ameliorative strategies to specific types of street children, rather than assume they are one large group. Strategies aimed to provide street children with access to periodic medical check-ups, part-time learning opportunities and recreational facilities either on the streets or via drop-in centers or vocational training institutes. Yet, while these strategies probably improved conditions for some children, it was difficult to demonstrate significant and sustained improvement in children's lives. Moreover, it proved far easier to dedicate resources to street-working children, whose greater numbers and spatial concentration allowed economies of scale, and who require less individually tailored assistance.

Academics and practitioners recognize the tension between perfecting definitions of street children and the need to capture the diversity of experience. One argument leans toward dropping the use of the term "street children" altogether. According to this view, the concept of "child" is culturally defined and cannot be reduced to the legalistic "person under eighteen," tends to promote vulnerability by putting an implicit stress on pre-adolescence rather than capability (see **capability approach**), and ignores what happens when street children become young adults. Identification of children with the "street" is seen as empirically inaccurate, as most children occupy a variety of public and private spaces, and reasserts a range of negative meanings instead of considering the street as a positive space that can offer young people opportunities, certainly compared to abusive domestic environments.

Instead, it is argued that street children share many characteristics with other young people living in **poverty** and **social exclusion**, namely that they live in "extremely difficult circumstances," the term used to capture a range of conditions in the **United Nations Convention on the Rights of the Child (1989)**. Rather than consider street children as different, the Convention supported a view of all children as individuals with legal rights to **health**, **education**, safety, and leisure. Even advocates wonder whether folding street children into broader **rights-based approaches to development** can deliver genuine participation and services, or threaten obscurity on the development agenda.

See also: child labor; child prostitution; children; human rights; urban informal sector; United Nations Convention on the Rights of the Child (1989); urbanization; vulnerability; youth violence

Further reading

The Consortium for Street Children: http://www.streetchildren.org.uk

European Network on Street Children Worldwide: http:// www.enscw.org

The Railway Children: http:// www.railwaychildren.org.uk/

Panter-Brick, C. (2002) "Street Children, Human Rights and Public Health," *Annual Review of Anthropology* 31: 147–71.

Thomas de Benitez, S. (2003) *Green Light for Street Children's Rights*, Brussels: ENSCW.

GARETH A. JONES

street-trading in urban areas

Street-trading in urban areas is an important part of most developing countries' economic make-up and part of the **urban informal sector**. Very often it represents the only form of (self) **employment** available to poor urban dwellers. Furthermore, street-trading, or vending, generates both up- and down-stream economic activity within the environments in which it operates. Particularly within the developing economy setting, the sector is known for attracting a relatively large number of migrants and those with low levels of formal **education** (see **migration; rural-urban migration**). This helps to explain why so many participants complain of various forms of harassment by authority figures. The unequal balance of economic and political power between street-traders and those with whom they engage, not to mention their uncertain legal status, renders large numbers of them vulnerable to illicit forms of rent seeking behavior by those around them. Bribery of officialdom (see **corruption**), for example, is commonplace, especially by those without any form of licensing arrangements with the authorities. Furthermore, many street-traders find that their operational territory is continuously under threat of exploitation by other traders. As such, protection rackets are experienced even amongst those holding licenses. In this sense, the term contestable market resonates especially well when considering the jostling for space and territory one sees amongst traders on the streets.

Street-traders, particularly those operating in urban centers, make significant economic contributions to their environments. Yet, many of the harsher aspects of their working lives, such as those just raised, have struggled to reach effective levels of public debate. More commonly the literature has leaned toward lumping discussion of issues concerning urban street-traders with those relating to the urban informal sector in general. This is unhelpful to efforts required to bring about improvements to the working conditions of those concerned.

Fortunately, this situation has started to change. The setting up of several influential national and **international organizations and associations** has helped. The work of organizations such as the Indian-based Self Employed Women's Association (SEWA), representing the economic and other interests of several hundred thousand women traders in western India, is now well known beyond India. SEWA's activities, dating back to the early 1980s, have been influential in shaping international declarations such as the Bellagio Declaration of Street Vendors in 1995. The setting up of organizations such as StreetNet, in the late 1990s, has contributed to efforts designed to bring together activists, researchers and traders at both national and international levels. This must be seen as a particularly positive development. StreetNet provides a platform through which issues such as best practice and benchmarking can be shared with interested stakeholders. This organization also involves itself in different campaign activities, including those in which improved

recognition is sought for the contribution made by members of this important economic sector.

See also: entrepreneurship; micro-credit and micro-finance; micro-enterprises; rural-urban migration; shantytowns; urban informal sector

Further reading

Dabir-Alai, P. (2001) "Urban Petty Trading," in Michie, J. (ed.) *Readers' Guide to the Social Sciences*, London: Fitzroy Dearborn.

Tinker, I. (1997) *Street Foods: Urban Food and Employment in Developing Countries*, Oxford: Oxford University Press.

PARVIZ DABIR-ALAI

structural adjustment

Structural adjustment originated as a macro-economic policy of financial programming developed by Jacques J. Polak in 1957 to restore "sound finance" to national economies mired in **debt**. Debt is one mechanism by which economies expand investment and trade, and only becomes problematic under adverse conditions of repayment or further lending. Debt emerged as a significant global phenomenon in the 1980s, during the so-called "**debt crisis**," when highly indebted developing countries were compelled to submit to stringent orthodox conditions of debt repayment, termed structural adjustment loans. Austerity measures in many developing countries reversed development indices in this "lost decade."

Debt was not new to the global South. Between 1955 and 1970, several countries (including Argentina, Brazil, Chile, Ghana, Indonesia, Peru, and Turkey) had the terms of their debt rescheduled – sometimes several times – to ease the conditions of payment. And debt servicing (paying off the interest) was consuming more than two thirds of new lending in Latin America and Africa by the mid-1960s. The difference in the 1980s was that the global financial landscape had substantially altered during the previous decade, facilitating unregulated borrowing outside of the conventions of the **Bretton Woods** monetary regime

(1944–72). The rise of a global money market, fueled by expanding offshore dollar holdings from transnational corporate activity, by US deficit spending to finance the Vietnam War, and by a flood of petro-dollars following a mid-1970s spike in oil prices, encouraged the new international banks to indulge in unsecured lending to developing countries seeking development financing.

The US Federal Reserve Board triggered the debt crisis in 1980 by implementing a new monetarist policy to revalue the dollar, given its over-circulation during the 1970s global lending binge (see **fiscal and monetary policy; inflation and its effects**). Contraction of the money supply restricted credit and raised interest rates as banks competed for dwindling funds. Lending to the developing countries slowed and shorter terms were issued – hastening the day of reckoning on considerably higher-cost loans. Developing countries owed US$1 trillion debt by 1986. Even though this amount was only half the US national debt in that year, it was a significant problem because countries were devoting new loans entirely to servicing previous loans. Unlike the USA, cushioned by the dollar standard (the *de facto* international reserve currency that countries and traders preferred), developing countries were unable to continue this debt servicing. Interest rates had risen sharply, recession in developed countries reduced export revenues from developing countries, and primary export commodity prices fell 17 percent during the 1980s, leaving them with US$28 billion less in export revenues.

The **World Bank** estimated the combined average annual negative effect of these "external" shocks in 1981–2 to be 19.1 percent of **gross domestic product (GDP)** in Kenya, 14.3 percent in Tanzania, 18.9 percent in the Ivory Coast, 8.3 percent in Brazil, 29 percent in Jamaica, and over 10 percent in the Philippines. The result was that many developing countries were mired in a *debt trap*: debt was choking their economies. And in order to repay the interest (at least), states would have to drastically curtail imports and drastically raise exports.

Reducing imports of technology would jeopardize **economic growth**. Expanding exports was also problematic, as commodity prices were at their lowest since World War II and would only slide

further as world markets were flooded with more commodities. The market was not going to solve these problems alone.

The chosen course of action was debt management, via the Bretton Woods institutions, even though around 60 percent of developing-country debt was with private banks. The **International Monetary Fund (IMF)**, created in 1944 to address short-term financial imbalances, became the *de facto* global Debt manager. Debt management moved from conventional financial stabilization measures to more comprehensive structural adjustment measures, such as restructuring production priorities and government programs in a debtor country – in essence, reorganizing the economy. In combination with the World Bank, the IMF levied structural adjustment loans on indebted states to allow them to reschedule their loans and pay off their debt. Loan conditions demanded a restructuring of economic policy to ensure economic growth and regular debt service.

This regime placed responsibility for irredeemable debt on the borrowers, not the lenders. Debt was defined as a liquidity problem (shortage of foreign currency) rather than a systemic problem: as stemming from the policies of the debtor countries rather than the organization of the global financial system. This view was possible for two reasons. First, the IMF was in a position to insist that debt rescheduling (including further official loans) was possible only if individual states submitted to IMF evaluation and stabilization measures, and World Bank structural adjustment loans (see **state and state reform**). Second, despite attempts at debt strikes (by Peru, among others), debtors collectively were in a weak bargaining position, because of the differentiation among developing countries – in growth rates and size of debt.

In 1982, Mexico and Brazil became the first countries to reschedule their debt according to these new terms, which drew on the earlier Chilean example, where a military junta (1973) instituted the first experiments in monetarist policies by slashing social spending and privatizing the Chilean economy. Mexico was US$80 billion in debt; more than three quarters of this amount was owed to private banks, with US banks having almost half their capital in Mexican loans.

Debt management is fundamentally political. In Mexico, political forces were divided between a "bankers' alliance" and the "Cárdenas alliance," representing a nationalist coalition rooted in the labor and peasant classes. The outgoing president, José López Portillo, allied with the latter group, linked the huge **capital flight** from his country (US$30 billion between 1978 and 1982) to the international financial order, and recommended controls on "a group of Mexicans...led and advised and supported by the private banks who have taken more money out of the country than the empires that exploited us since the beginning of time." Portillo opposed debt management proposals by nationalizing the Mexican banking system and installing exchange controls to prevent capital flight, declaring in his outgoing speech:

> The financing plague is wreaking greater and greater havoc throughout the world. As in Medieval times, it is scourging country after country. It is transmitted by rats and its consequences are unemployment and poverty, industrial bankruptcy and speculative enrichment. The remedy of the witch doctors is to deprive the patient of food and subject him to compulsory rest. Those who protest must be purged, and those who survive bear witness to their virtue before the doctors of obsolete and prepotent dogma and of blind hegemoniacal egoism.

Portillo's conservative successor, Miguel De La Madrid, guaranteed a reversal, forcing Portillo to concede to an IMF accord initiated by the US government and the Bank of International Settlements. To effect the bailout, an international condominium formed, including the IMF (US$1.3 billion), governments of developed countries (US$2 billion), and the banks (US$5 billion in "involuntary loan"). The Mexican bailout became the model for subsequent structural adjustment programs. President De La Madrid's Mexico took an active role in undermining the possibility of a debtors' strike, and was rewarded for its refusal to participate in a regional effort to form a debtors' club in 1986.

The debt crisis began in Latin America and Africa, spreading to Eastern Europe and Asia over the next decade. As countries adopted the rules of the debt managers, restructuring their economies and reducing social protections, they reversed the post-World War II development project. Development was redefined from a nationally-organized program of economic growth to participation in the world market. In particular, the debt managers intensified export production as the first order of business, and substituted new criteria, of efficiency in the world market, as the new standard. In effect, these actions stabilized indebted economies so they could at least service, if not retire, their debt – that is, repay the interest due the banks and the multilateral financial institutions. Rescheduling bought time for debt repayment, but it also came at a heavy cost.

Structural adjustment measures include drastic reduction of public spending (especially on social programs, including **food** subsidies), currency devaluation (to inflate prices of imports and reduce export prices and thereby improve the balance of trade in the indebted country's favor), privatization of state-owned enterprises (see **privatization and liberalization; state-owned enterprises (SOEs)**), and reduction of wages to attract foreign investors and reduce export prices. Most of these measures fall hardest on the poorest and least powerful social classes – those dependent on wages and subsidies. While many businesses have prospered, **poverty** rates have climbed. Governing coalitions have crumbled as governments could no longer afford to subsidize urban social constituencies. A general erosion of living standards has swept across the countries involved.

As IMF/World Bank adjustment policies in Africa reduced food subsidies and public services, urban demonstrations and riots flared up in Tanzania, Ghana, Zambia, Morocco, Egypt, Tunisia, and Sudan. In Zambia, the price of cornmeal – a staple – rose 120 percent in 1985 following such an adjustment policy. School enrollments declined and skilled Africans migrated. Between 1980 and 1986, average per capita income declined by 10 percent, and **unemployment** almost tripled. In effect, all the "development" indicators, including **infant and child mortality**, took a downturn under the impact of adjustment policies. The greater impact on the poor, compared with higher-income groups, is borne out in an internal report of the IMF on cost increases because of adjustment in

Kenya. Relatively speaking, the poor shouldered an extra burden as the price of basic goods and services increased, from 10 percent for food to 95 percent for clothing and shoes.

The so-called "lost decade" of the 1980s meant that international development was held hostage to debt management. In the late 1980s, the **United Nations Children's Fund (UNICEF)** and the UN Commission for Africa reported that adjustment programs were largely the cause of reduced **health**, **nutrition**, and **education** levels for tens of millions of **children** in Asia, Latin America, and Africa (see **adjustment with a human face**). And in 1993, Oxfam reported that World Bank adjustment programs in Sub-Saharan Africa were largely responsible for reductions in public health spending and a 10 percent decline in primary school enrollment. Combining per capita GDP figures with changes in terms of trade and debt rescheduling, average per capita income is estimated to have fallen 15 percent in Latin America and 30 percent in Africa during the 1980s. Collectively, the debtor countries entered the 1990s with 61 percent more debt than they had held in 1982. Massive bank debt had become public debt, the repayment of which now fell on the shoulders of the governments themselves. Banks are protected from complete debt loss by governments from developed countries, whose central bankers had agreed in 1974 (with the Bank of International Settlements) to stand behind the commercial bank loans, as lenders of last resort.

Debt managers demand a shrinking of states across the developing world, through reduction in social spending and the privatization of SOEs. In rescheduling debt, governments sold off the public largesse resulting from the loan binge of the 1970s. The average number of privatizations in developing countries expanded tenfold across the decade. In the 1990s, this trend intensified, with the WTO (see **World Trade Organization/General Agreement on Tariffs and Trade (WTO/ GATT)**) developing a protocol, the General Agreement on Trade in Services (GATS), to enable the capture by foreign corporations of public services (from water, through banking to electricity). Although there is no doubt that development state **elites** had pursued excessive public financing, privatization has accomplished two radical changes: (1) reducing public capacity in developmental planning and implementation, thereby privileging private initiative; and (2) extending the reach of foreign ownership of assets in developing countries.

Structural adjustment undermines the **coherence**, and/or commercializes the sovereignty, of national economies. The mechanisms of the debt regime institutionalized the power and authority of global management within states' very organization and procedures. This was the turning point in the story of development. Throughout the Bretton Woods era, the IMF exerted considerable influence on the fiscal management of states (see **state and state reform**) by applying conditions to the loans it made to adjust short-term balance of payments. But this influence involved merely financial stabilization measures. Structural adjustment loans, by contrast, restructure economic initiatives in debtor countries and redistribute power within the state. The most widespread restructuring redistributes power from program-oriented ministries (social services, **agriculture**, education) to the central bank and to trade and finance ministries. The importance of this shift is the loss of resources to state agencies that support and regulate economic and social sectors affecting the majority of the citizenry, especially the poorer classes.

The World Bank's support for the shift from social to finance ministries was that the postcolonial development states were overbureaucratic and inefficient on the one hand, and unresponsive to their citizenry on the other. Of course, some of these observations are credible; there are many examples of authoritarian government, **corruption**, and "hollow" development financing. But the solutions proposed, and imposed, by the Bretton Woods institutions substitute growing external control of these countries in the name of financial orthodoxy, without necessarily eliminating corruption – just shifting its location within the state. This procedure not only compromises national sovereignty, but also subordinates national policy to global corporate power and its institutional supports. Despite the new emphasis on **human rights** and democratization as conditions for reform and financial assistance, the Bank remains unaccountable to the citizenry in developing countries.

Unaccountability extends to the world of finance. Structural adjustment has exposed "opened" economies to unregulated short-term capital flows. This has produced a series of market-induced financial crises (see **contagion effect**), beginning in Mexico in 1995, and spreading to East Asia in 1997 (see **Asian crises**), then to Brazil and Russia, and, at the turn of the century, Argentina. These financial crises externalize the problem of overproduction of fictitious capital via global financial markets, victimizing states low in the global currency hierarchy. They also destabilize developing economies, leading to a growing, and dangerous, dialectic of state repression of direct **democracy** initiatives (citizens taking economic matters into their own hands – such as in Argentina), as a pretext for loan rescheduling from the international financial institutions.

In sum, structural adjustment reformulated the terms of economic management, presaging the movement from the development project of the 1940s-1970s to the **globalization** project of the 1990s onwards. Political, military and business elites in developing countries certainly collaborated in this enterprise, often for the same reasons they had promoted development financing in previous decades. They are usually well placed to benefit most from infusions of foreign capital, some of which is used for patronage. Meanwhile, the debt burden is borne disproportionately by the poor. The global consequences are that **inequality** within and between states has grown exponentially.

See also: adjustment with a human face; capitalism; debt; debt crisis; debt relief; globalization; International Monetary Fund (IMF); inequality and poverty, world trends; neo-liberalism; poverty; privatization and liberalization; World Bank

Further reading

Bello, W., with Cunningham, S. and Rau, B. (1999) *Dark Victory: The United States, Structural Adjustment and Global Poverty*, London: Pluto.

George, S. (1988) *A Fate Worse than Debt: The World Financial Crisis and the Poor*, Montclair NJ: Allenheld, Osmun, and Co.

George, S. (1992) *The Debt Boomerang: How Third World Debt Harms Us All*, Boulder CO: Westview.

Helleiner, E. (1996) *States and the Reemergence of Global Finance: From Bretton Woods to the 1990s*, Ithaca NY: Cornell University Press.

McMichael, P. (2004) *Development and Social Change: A Global Perspective*, Thousand Oaks CA: Pine Forge.

Roodman, D. (2001) *Still Waiting for the Jubilee: Pragmatic Solutions for the Third World Debt Crisis*, Washington DC: Worldwatch Institute (Paper 155).

Walton, J. and Seddon, D. (1994) *Free Markets and Food Riots: The Politics of Global Adjustment*, Oxford: Blackwell.

PHILIP D. MCMICHAEL

structural violence

Structural (or "indirect") **violence** is defined by Johan Galtung (1969; 1996) as those socio-economic **institutions** and relations that oppress human beings by preventing them from realizing their potential. By broadening the definition of violence from physical or "direct" violence, Galtung and other students of peace research have sought to shift the focus away from the state (see **state and state reform**) and the military (see **military and security**) dimension of **security** toward individuals, social groups and their needs (see **human security**).

According to the "maximal" approach introduced by Galtung (1969) in his seminal work entitled "Violence, Peace and Peace Research," peace did not just mean the absence of **war**; it was also related to the establishment of conditions for **social justice**. In making this point, Galtung distinguished between personal and structural violence. Violence, for Galtung (1996:197), is all those "avoidable insults to basic human needs, and more generally to *life*, lowering the real level of needs satisfaction below what is potentially possible." Direct violence, according to Galtung, is an event; structural violence, on the other hand, is a process with ups and downs. Patterns of exploitation are likely to remain steady unless identified and addressed.

In addition to distinguishing between direct violence and structural violence, Galtung also defined "cultural violence" as those mechanisms that render acceptable both direct (as in killing, repression, or delocalization) and structural violence (exploitation, penetration or **marginalization**). Then, Galtung turned both the use of violence and the ways in which that use is legitimized by the society, into a subject of study, for students of peace research also had, until then, adopted a narrow and negative conception of peace (the absence of war) and studied conflict resolution with almost exclusive focus on the superpower relationship. Peace research, from the 1960s onwards, increasingly looked at the dynamics of economic exploitation and the economic, political and cultural dimensions of the North-South relationship.

Galtung underlined the futility of the task of trying to achieve peace without tackling the structural causes of the security of individuals, social groups and states. Distinguishing between "negative" and "positive" peace, Galtung argued that peace defined merely as the absence of armed conflict is "negative peace." Positive peace, maintained Galtung, means the absence of both direct (physical) violence, and indirect (structural and cultural) violence. Galtung emphasized that to attain positive peace, it is not enough to seek to eliminate violence; existing **institutions** and relations should be geared toward the enhancement of dialog, cooperation and solidarity among peoples, coupled with a respect for the environment. In the study of contemporary world politics, students of critical security studies have embraced Galtung's notion of structural violence to call for a comprehensive approach to security.

See also: human security; security; social justice; violence

Further reading

Galtung, J. (1969) "Violence, Peace and Peace Research," *Journal of Peace Research* 6:3 167–92.
Galtung, J. (1996) *Peace By Peaceful Means: Peace and Conflict, Development and Civilization*, London: Sage.

PINAR BILGIN

sustainable development

Sustainable development (SD) has come to mean the achievement of **economic development** at the same time as protecting **environment** and **natural resources**. The most famous definition was that achieved by the **Brundtland Commission**, in its publication *Our Common Future* (1987), as: "development that meets the needs of the present without compromising the ability of future generations to meet their own needs." But there is no unique or universal definition for SD. Part of the reason is that first, the word "development" itself lacks a unique description. Second, sustainability appears to mean different things from different perspectives. In general, SD is presently used to draw attention to the limits imposed on the extent of human economic activities by considerations of the stability of the natural environment and continuation of their crucial ecosystems' services. At the core of the concept is the question "How much economic activity or what level of material consumption by how many people can the Earth sustain?"

The concern for sustainability had found regular expressions in various forms since the 1960s. The publication of *Silent Spring* by Rachel Carson in 1962 drew wide public attention to the negative impacts of uncontroled technological development on the natural environment and especially the pesticide, DDT. This book is hailed by many as a turning point in the growth of global environmental concern. One of the earliest uses of the term "sustainable development" is found in The World Conservation Strategy prepared by the World Conservation Union (IUCN), United Nations Environment Programme (UNEP) and the World Wide Fund for Nature (WWF) (1980). However, it was the World Commission on Environment and Development (WCED) – or **Brundtland Commission** – that gave this term a global popularity, and created the most famous definition above. The IUCN, UNEP and WWF in 1991 described sustainable development as improvement in "the quality of human life while living within the **carrying capacity** of supporting ecosystems." However, the environmental concerns are facing serious challenges from the technological optimists who believe that technological solutions to all the environmental problems will be found and the continuity of **economic growth** will not be stopped. Accordingly, they argue, there is no reason for concern.

In 1992, five years after the publication of the *Our Common Future*, the **Earth Summit (1992) (United Nations Conference on Environment and Development)** created the global environmental action plan, **Agenda 21**. In order to monitor the implementation of the Earth Summit agreements, the **United Nations** established the **Commission on Sustainable Development (CSD)** in 1992, as a functional commission of the UN Economic and Social Council (ECOSOC). In this way, the CSD distinguished itself from the other organizations by being the primary forum for the review of Agenda 21. Its creation also coincided with the establishment of the World Business Council for Sustainable Development (WBCSD), an organization that represents the commitment of the business sector of the world toward SD. The global corporate sector saw in SD opportunities for investment and prospects of new markets.

In 1996, the Canada-based International Institute for Sustainable Development (IISD) developed general guidelines for the practical assessment of moves toward SD strategies through the Bellagio Principles. It identified common patterns in sustainable-development-related assessments, which serve as guidelines for the whole of the assessment process, including the choice and design of indicators, their interpretation and communication of the result. The third session of CSD in 1995 also emerged with a list of fifty-eight indicators to arrive at a broader picture of societal development. It is believed that these, and the methodology sheets developed, would enable the decision-makers to increase focus on the issue of sustainable development by ensuring the vitality of ecosystems along with sound **economic development**. Ceres principles and standard codes of conduct have also evolved toward operationalizing sustainable development, with, in 1999, the Dow Jones Sustainability Index being the first global sustainability tool of its kind to be developed. More recently, the concept of sustainable development has been further expanded in a spatial sense: the perception that sustainability in one region cannot

be achieved at the cost of causing unsustainability in another region.

However, in spite of the impressive expansion of definitions and **institutions** related to SD as described above, the concept of SD continues to suffer from an identity crisis. It has been frequently criticized from philosophical and methodological viewpoints, by many of its supporters. In the background of the complexity of the global economic system, the present ideas around SD have been seen by many as simplistic, or as a mantra that can be adopted by different actors without little significant change in practices. Different methodological approaches also underlie the diversity with which it is defined. Environmental and ecological economists, for example, employ the concept of **natural capital** to explore the impact of current development policies on ecosystems and **natural resources**. So-called "strong sustainability" considers that natural capital cannot be substituted by human made capital. "Weak sustainability" considers sustainability a "vague and general" obligation to pass on to future generations, but not a "specific one" to pass on to each constituent. Methodologies inspired by politics and social theory, however, question how far "resources" or natural capital can be defined in such known ways, and instead seek to highlight how political conflict or **governance** can influence the definition of dominant approaches to environment (see **environment**). Such analysts argue that the discussion of "sustainable development" as though it can be easily identified, and hence achievable through a variety of instrumental economic policies on behalf of an undifferentiated **population**, are too simplistic. Instead, political and social theorists seek to answer other questions, such as understanding whose agenda is most powerful in defining which environmental changes are considered to be degrading, how such definitions create political winners and losers, and who gets to participate in these debates.

See also: Agenda 21; Commission on Sustainable Development (CSD); ecodevelopment; environment; natural capital; sustainable livelihoods

Further reading

IUCN, UNEP and WWF (1980) *The World Conservation Strategy*, Gland: IUCN.

Reid, D. (1995) *Sustainable Development: An Introductory Guide*, London, Earthscan.

Scott, W. and Gough, S. (eds) (2003) *Key Issues in Sustainable Development and Learning: A Critical Review*, London: Routledge Falmer.

World Commission on Environment and Development (the Brundtland Commission) (1987) *Our Common Future*, Oxford, Oxford University Press.

JAYANTA BANDYOPADHYAY AND SHAMA PERVEEN

sustainable livelihoods

The term, "Sustainable livelihoods" (SL) refers to a framework developed in the late 1990s in order to capture for a variety of policy purposes the multiple strands that comprise people's efforts to attain and sustain an adequate living (see also **livelihoods**). While many of the ideas built upon by the SL framework were rural in origin, some antecedents explicitly refer to urban livelihoods. In the **rural development** arena, the SL framework is in direct line of descent from the entitlements theory of **famine** (see **food security; environmental entitlements**), via ideas of asset **vulnerability**, and drawing on farming systems research and participatory approaches to **rural development** (see **participatory development; participatory rural appraisal (PRA)**).

The classic definition of a livelihood that tends to underpin the SL framework derives from Chambers and Conway (1992:7), wherein a livelihood "comprises the capabilities, assets (stores, resources, claims and access) and activities required for a means of living."

The livelihoods framework regards awareness of the asset status of poor individuals or households as fundamental to an understanding of the options open to them, the strategies they adopt for survival, and their **vulnerability** to adverse trends and events. One of its basic tenets, therefore, is that **poverty** policy should be concerned with raising the asset status of the poor, or enabling existing assets that are idle or underemployed (see **underemployment**) to be used productively. The approach looks positively at what is possible rather than negatively at how desperate things are. As articulated by Moser (1998:1) it seeks "to identify what the poor have rather than what they do not have" and "[to] strengthen people's own inventive solutions, rather than substitute for, block or undermine them."

The SL framework comes in various different diagrammatic versions, although these tend to contain similar components and implied relationships between them. A feature of all variants is that they take an "all-round" or holistic view of people's livelihoods, locating people's circumstances within the social, institutional and opportunity contexts that shape those circumstances. A simplified version of the framework is given in Figure 3 below. This has five components that are widely understood to be building blocks of livelihoods work. At the center is an essentially economic relationship

Figure 3 The basic sustainable livelihoods framework.
Source: Adapted from Scoones, 1998; and Ellis 2000.

between livelihood assets, the activities in which individuals or families become engaged using their assets, and the outcomes that result from these activities in terms of improving or deteriorating welfare (see **welfare economics; welfare state**) and **well-being** of the individual or family. These economic relationships are, however, embedded in social and political relations as implied by the policy and institutional context. They are also more or less vulnerable to deterioration according to risk factors that make up the **vulnerability** context of people's livelihoods.

It can be noted that Figure 3 contains no lines or arrows denoting causalities between its elements. The reason for this is that the construction of a livelihood is a process unfolding over time, in which there are complex interdependencies between the different categories of the framework. Of course, there are subsets of this process for which causalities can be defined, for example, between assets, activities and outcomes. The spirit of the SL approach, however, states that the key factors inhibiting the improvement of livelihoods are likely to vary from one setting to another, and therefore are unlikely to be identified accurately if too many prior relationships of cause and effect are imposed *ex ante* on particular groups of the rural or urban poor.

The SL framework offers various strengths for poverty and vulnerability policies that are lacking in its forerunners. First, it permits strong recognition of the multiple and cross-sectoral character of people's livelihoods, thus moving away from former preoccupations with mainly sectoral solutions to poverty problems. Second, it connects well with vulnerability ideas that humanitarian agencies utilize in anticipating and dealing with livelihood crises (also see **complex emergencies**); indeed, contemporary vulnerability assessment methods draw heavily upon SL categories and relationships. Third, it provides an excellent foundation for making connections between micro-level circumstances and macro-level policy policies that are not just based on economic

variables like prices and **exchange rates**. Utilizing SL, micro-macro (or macro-micro) links can be pursued through the policy and institutional context of livelihoods, facilitating the identification of flaws and gaps between macro-intentions and micro-outcomes. SL provides an especially powerful approach to critical work on the Poverty Reduction Strategy Papers (PRSPs) that are the overarching policy framework governing donor-government relationships in low-income countries.

See also: community-based natural resource management (CBNRM); environmental entitlements; food security; institutions; institutions and environment; livelihoods; poverty; rural development; rural poverty; vulnerability

Further reading

Carney, D. (ed.) (1998) *Sustainable Rural Livelihoods: What Contribution Can We Make?* London: DFID.

Chambers, R. and Conway, R. (1992) "Sustainable Rural Livelihoods: Practical Concepts for the 21st Century," IDS Discussion Paper no. 296, Brighton: Institute of Development Studies.

Ellis, F. (2000) *Rural Livelihoods and Diversity in Developing Countries*, Oxford: Oxford University Press.

Ellis, F. and Freeman, H. (2004) "Rural Livelihoods and Poverty Reduction Strategies in Four African Countries," *Journal of Development Studies* 40:4 1–30.

Moser, C. (1998) "The Asset Vulnerability Framework: Reassessing Urban Poverty Reduction Strategies," *World Development* 26:1 1–19.

Scoones, I. (1998) "Sustainable Rural Livelihoods: A Framework for Analysis," IDS Working Paper no. 72, Brighton: Institute of Development Studies.

FRANK ELLIS

T

targeting

Targeting involves delivering benefits to the intended beneficiaries and excluding unwanted recipients. Targeting of social benefits based on some notion of need or entitlement is a concept that dates back to ancient Rome and beyond. One central issue is the cost in identifying beneficiaries in order to prevent leakage: this cost is hypothesized to increase exponentially with the fineness of targeting as policy moves from a universal benefit to perfect targeting. Information constraints in developing countries often prevent the income-based targeting common in developed countries, and rough correlates with income such as geographic location, social indicators (e.g. **malnutrition, gender** of the household head), or some combination are often used. Another option is self-targeting: to offer a good the wealthy would decline, such as a below market wage, but this may have high attendant stigma costs. In addition to information constraints, social policy needs to take account of the incentive effects (see **incentive structures**) of a given targeting mechanism. For example, targeting a particular region may cause a shift in **migration** patterns.

See also: aid; aid effectiveness and aid evaluation; sector-wide approaches (SWAps); welfare state

MARKUS GOLDSTEIN

tariffs

Tariffs, also known as customs duties, are those charges assessed by national governments at their borders when goods are brought into their territories. Such duties, to be distinguished from mere administrative charges, are typically calculated in relation to the value of the goods themselves, and constitute part of the goods' costs basis in the importing country's marketplace. Tariffs are a revenue source for the importing country government, a cost of doing business for the importer and, varying with the levels of the tariff, a disincentive to international **trade** generally. Tariffs may also be used as political and economic tools in influencing **economic development**, a practice that has been discouraged within the **World Trade Organization/General Agreement on Tariffs and Trade (WTO/GATT)** system.

Tariffs on imports are usually calculated based on their classification, their country of origin, and their value. They are normally based on an *ad valorem* rate, or a percentage of the value of the goods. (On occasion, the tariff will be calculated per unit, unit weight or unit volume. These are called "specific" tariffs.) Tariffs should not be confused with taxes, which are internal to the taxing country, and generally generate more income for governments. The existence of customs services may sometimes also impact on trade by delaying imports, or by providing sites of **corruption**, and hence added costs. Initially, most countries outside economic unions used their own tariff schedules, which created complexity and uncertainty in trade. From 1989, more than fifty countries adopted the Harmonized Commodity Description and Coding System for common classification purposes.

Tariffs are the simplest and most open form of **protectionism**, and the clearest in terms of economic impact. Because of this **transparency**, the GATT system has encouraged member countries to adopt tariffs for all forms of trade barriers, as a preliminary act to negotiations aimed at lowering those tariffs. From its origin in 1947, GATT negotiating rounds were mainly dedicated to reducing tariffs among the world's major trading nations.

Under the tariff binding system used in the GATT, nations agree to negotiated upper limits on their tariff rates for goods from **most favored nation (MFN) status** trading partners. Over the course of several negotiating rounds, these upper limits have been ratcheted down. Through the first six rounds of GATT negotiations, the simple average bound tariff on imports of industrial products of the major trading nations declined to approximately 5 percent. Some commentators have suggested that if average tariffs decline much more they will rapidly become "nuisance tariffs," or the level at which the costs of collecting tariffs exceed their revenue generated. By contrast, the USA average tariff rate in 1932, under the infamous Smoot-Hawley Act, was approximately 59 percent, which had fallen to roughly 25 percent by the end of World War II.

Overall, much theory and experience indicates that national economic welfare is advanced by a policy of **free trade**, which in its pure form includes adopting a policy of zero tariff rates. However, even strong free trade theorists acknowledge that some deviations from this policy may be warranted. Most analysts agree on exceptions for national **security** and **infant industries**, but there is debate about the so-called optimum tariff. According to this theory, any nation with sufficient economic power to affect its own **terms of trade** would have an optimum tariff level higher than zero, at which it could extract rents from other trading countries for allowing goods to enter its marketplace. At that optimum tariff level, the internal economic distortions caused by the tariff would be more than compensated for by the government revenues collected and the improvements

to nation's terms of trade. Despite this, the optimum tariff for any particular item is extremely difficult to identify, the rate may be very low and dynamic over time and, finally, the process is prone to political capture. For these reasons, few theorists advocate actual adoption of optimum tariffs.

Tariffs are especially important for developing countries as they encourage/discourage trade. Tariff systems often reflect colonial trade patterns, such as the British Commonwealth preferences, or regional economic dominance, such as the United States' Caribbean Basin Initiative tariff rates for most Caribbean nations. Within regional trade agreements, nations use preferential, better-than-MFN status tariff rates to promote political solidarity as well as economic development (e.g. the **North American Free Trade Agreement (NAFTA)** and the **Association of Southeast Asian Nations (ASEAN)**) and to project political influence at a distance (for example, the US free trade agreements with Israel and Jordan).

Denying MFN status to a trading partner also has important political implications. During the **Cold War**, countries of the Soviet bloc were largely outside the GATT system and therefore had relatively higher tariffs. Similarly, denial of MFN's preferential duty rates because of a country's alleged support of terrorism, weak enforcement of laws concerning **intellectual property rights (IPRs)** or **human rights** are examples of tariff linkage to non-trade issues. In such cases, countries may risk becoming both economically and politically isolated.

The gap between non-MFN tariff rates and MFN tariff rates has now widened so dramatically that it is now frequently too costly to import less-favored goods. However, at the same time, the gap between MFN tariff rates and the (typically) zero rate for selected goods from preferred developing countries is now also very small. The effect of this decline has been to weaken the value of tariff-based developing country trade preferences, like the United States Generalized System of Preferences (USGSP).

Tariffs in developed countries are now usually designed so that duties on commodities and lightly manufactured products are lower than duties on products that require higher-value input. There is also higher tariff-protection for agricultural goods from developed countries. These rates reflect the desire to promote industrial policies favoring **industrialization**, and to protect farmers. For related reasons, tariff preferences granted to developing countries tend to be for lower-value input products, with the common result of encouraging ongoing economic dependence upon production of primary commodities and light industrialization. Not surprisingly, many critics claim current tariff preferences for developing nations constitute a form of **neocolonialism**.

See also: economic federalization; industrialization; industrialization and trade policy; most favored nation (MFN) status; protectionism; trade; World Trade Organization/General Agreement on Tariffs and Trade (WTO/GATT)

Further reading

Dixit, A. (1996) *The Making of Economic Policy: A Transaction-Cost Politics Perspective*, Cambridge MA: MIT Press.

Hoda, A. (2001) *Tariff Negotiations and Renegotiations under the GATT and the WTO: Procedures and Practices*, Cambridge: Cambridge University Press.

Thomas, V. and Nash, J. (1992) *Best Practices in Trade Policy Reform*, Oxford: Oxford University Press.

WILLIAM B. T. MOCK

TAX HAVENS *see* offshore finance

technological capability

Technological capability is the ability of countries, regions or companies to assimilate or develop technology, and to put it to effective use. It is a key objective of **technology policy**, and a crucial factor in enhancing **technology transfer**. Technological capability may be achieved at national level through actions such as investing in **education** and **human capital**, especially in technological themes, universities, and industrially trained staff. Some East Asian **newly industrialized economies (NIEs)** such as South Korea and Taiwan deliberately sought to increase locally trained workforces as a means to **industrialization**. More locally, governments may provide funds for the adoption of technology, advisory centers for the use of technology, and training in technological use. Sometimes this will mean addressing the needs of investors in technology, and particularly their requirement for formal or informal systems of collecting payments for technologies (as cost-recovery for investors is one of the crucial requirements of technology transfer). Some studies have divided different countries into categories of "technology leaders" (such as the USA and Japan); "technology followers" (other **Organization for Economic Cooperation and Development (OECD)** countries), and "technology borrowers" (many poorer developing countries), although national technology policies and the emergence of **transnational corporations (TNCs) from developing economies** may change these classifications by allowing different countries to become specialized in producing technologies. More fundamentally, the regional differences in technological capability also attracts, and is influenced by, **foreign direct investment** (FDI), which accounts for approximately 60 percent of all resource flows to developing countries, yet of which some two thirds only goes to ten developing countries in Asia and Latin America. The possibilities for large-scale industrialization are therefore slim in countries (especially in Africa) that have little technological capability and little FDI. International **aid** may therefore see building technological capability in poorly endowed countries as a crucial requirement for encouraging industrialization.

See also: human capital; industrialization; leapfrogging; newly industrialized economies (NIEs); science and technology; technology policy; technology transfer

Further reading

Goldman, M. (1997) *Technology Institutions and Policies: Their Role in Developing Technological*

Capability in Industry, Washington DC: World Bank.

Lall, S. (1999) "Enhancing Technological Capabilities," pp 195–228 in UNCTAD, *World Investment Report 1999, Foreign Direct Investment and the Challenge of Development*, Geneva: UNCTAD.

TIM FORSYTH

technology policy

Technology policy aims to enhance technological innovation and diffusion among actors in both science and industry in order to enhance regional and national economic growth (see also **science and technology**). Technology is a crucial lever in fostering economic dynamism, and governments around the world seek to enhance the speed and uptake of technological learning (see **technological capability**). As a framework, technology policy combines attention to **human capital** (investment in **education**, particularly higher education, and skilled workforce development) with concern for research, business and industry development, and broader support policies such as protection for **intellectual property rights (IPRs)**, and the fostering of venture **capital markets**.

It is important to note that technology is not just "hardware" such as machinery, or new research outputs, but also includes improved ways of organizing production and knowledge. Similarly, innovation is not simply a linear stage in product development, but rather represents a continuous evolution resulting in changes to product, process (and more recently to new functions in **value chains** or even to entirely new value chains). Technology can thus also be called "know-how" for both production and generation of new knowledge, whether at the level of **human capital** and knowledge transfers, or **institutions** and organizational processes for the same. Where previously technology was conceived of as a fixed entity, i.e. a static store of knowledge that could be "transferred" (see **technology transfer**) via for example **foreign direct investment** (FDI) and **joint venture**s, currently the emphasis is more on a dynamic

understanding of knowledge flows and ongoing networks of production relations.

While some elements of science and technology policy have been around for decades, including public investment in universities and research and development (R&D), others represent newer avenues for policy-makers. Following early successes of the Silicon Valley model in the USA, there has been an increasing emphasis on enhancing linkages between the public and private sectors in research, to develop commercially-viable knowledge and products (through patents, license, and spin-off firms) whether via university-industry parks or other mechanisms.

The concept of "national innovation systems" (NIS) refers to a set of institutions such as universities, government, private firms and **partnerships**, etc. that help develop new technologies and also diffuse the same through their formal and informal relationships. The performance of a national economy then depends not only on individual research institutes and universities' research output, but crucially on how all these actors interact to generate and use new knowledge. Legal frameworks and social norms play a role in how easily knowledge is transmitted across this landscape (see **law**).

The NIS approach notwithstanding, technology policy now tends to take the region as the key unit for intervention, supplanting an earlier focus on the nation-state. While some of the Nordic countries maintain policies on "national innovation system," larger and more diversified economics in the USA and UK have for a long time taken a more territorialized approach to competitiveness. The concept of the "learning region" has gained currency of late. Here the focus is on the social relations and networks of production and learning that underpin regional competitiveness. Local production systems are advised to no longer rely solely on indigenous "tacit" or **local knowledge** and incremental change, but rather to bring in new sources of knowledge to remain competitive.

A specific element of a regional policy focus includes support for "**clustering**" (also see **industrial district model**) within the region, as well as **small and medium enterprises (SMEs)** including start-up firms in the knowledge-based innovation economy. The idea behind support for regional clusters is that knowledge-generation and sharing is enhanced among networked firms, and that public and private investment in R&D will exhibit a **multiplier effect** locally. A particularly potent form of technological diffusion is known to occur between producer and supplier firms, where feedback from customers and users is part of the transaction process spurs further innovation by firms at various levels of the value chain.

Technology policy represents a continuing challenge across developing countries where economic, and legal-political contexts vary widely. Many face legal, regulatory, financial, and other institutional hurdles such as insufficient patent protection, inflexible educational systems, and underdeveloped or non-existent venture **capital markets**. Strained public budgets in developing countries also represent a challenge to building up strong research and development systems, while private industry often too remains marginalized by restrictive public policies. Nevertheless, some countries such as South Korea, Taiwan, and Malaysia, and to a lesser extent India and Mexico, have been able to develop thriving technology-based industries, e.g. in electronics, software, **pharmaceuticals**, and automotives. These industries, which host diverse technological origins ranging from publicly-supported basic and applied research to technology transfer, and FDI knowledge spillovers to reverse engineering, have developed into world-class production centers staffed by highly-skilled engineers and technicians. Some critics note that public investment in R&D and technical education benefits only the elite group (see **elites**) of the country's workforce employed by these industries (which, further, offer few, if any, backward linkages to other sectors, thereby aggravating dualism in the economy). In response, technology policy experts increasingly emphasize the need for wide-ranging technology diffusion initiatives to cover sectors in both mature, traditional industries, and high-technology ones, while also taking care to support firms of various sizes through networking and other initiatives.

See also: foreign direct investment; human capital; industrial district model; industrialization; late industrialization; leapfrogging; public-private partnerships; science and technology; technological capability; technology transfer; value chains

Further reading

Cooke, P. and Morgan, K. (1998) *The Associational Economy: Firms, Regions and Innovation*, Oxford: Oxford University Press.

Edquist, C. and McKelvey, M. (2000) *Systems of Innovation: Growth, Competitiveness and Employment*, vols 1–2, Cheltenham: Edward Elgar.

Gertler, M. and Wolfe, D. (eds) (2002) *Innovation and Social Learning: Institutional Adaptation in an Era of Technological Change*, Basingstoke: Palgrave.

Lundvall, B. (ed.) (1992) *National Systems of Innovation: Towards a Theory of Innovation and Interactive Learning*, London: Pinter.

Morgan, K. (1997) "The Learning Region: Institutions, Innovation and Regional Renewal," *Regional Studies* 31:5 491–503.

ANNE T. KURIAKOSE

technology transfer

Technology transfer is the diffusion and inculcation of new technical equipment, practices, and development know-how from one region or company to another. Technology transfer is often called for as a prerequisite for successful **industrialization**, or the adoption of environmental policies such as **climate change** mitigation (through technologies that emit fewer greenhouse gases). Such discussions, however, often overlook the complexity of technology transfer. Successful technology transfer requires attention to commercial, competitive and managerial aspects of business development, plus building **technological capability** in different locations.

The most common oversight in discussing technology transfer is an effective understanding of what is implied by "technology." Technology is often thought of being sophisticated equipment (or "hardware"), yet it can also include the skills, know-how, and institutional support of relevant manufacturing, maintenance, or managerial resources (also called "software"). Consequently, full technology transfer can include training skills, management, and general administration to ensure the successful adoption and commercial success of new technology.

There are also debates about the word "transfer." Technology transfer implies the process of upgrading existing production and technology development processes with newer and better forms of achieving production. But these objectives may be achieved by a variety of routes. Some analysts distinguish between "vertical" and "horizontal" technology transfer, where vertical transfer refers to the point-to-point relocation of new technologies via investment often to a targeted group, and horizontal transfer describes the long-term process of embedding or upgrading technologies within local populations and economies. Vertical transfer is faster, but ownership of technology remains in the hands of investing companies. Horizontal transfer usually means sharing the right to own and manufacture technology with local producers, and is much costlier. Furthermore, "technology transfer" is never a process that commercial companies engage in overtly, but is an effect that governments or development agencies wish to create via collaboration between investors and local companies. Consequently, the actual mechanisms of technology transfer for investors include contractual arrangements such as technology leases and **joint ventures** (JVs) rather than a known and clear process called "technology transfer."

The distinction between vertical and horizontal forms of technology transfer also has important implications for government policies. Many orthodox approaches to **technology policy** have assumed that the best way to achieve technological development has been to build national expertise in technology by integrating research and development in laboratories, universities and research institutes, with national companies who then further develop, market and distribute technological products. Under this model, horizontal technology transfer is considered valuable because it allows indigenous companies to benefit from outsiders' knowledge and higher levels of technology. Some countries, such as China and Vietnam in the 1990s, have therefore adopted the strategy of

requiring outside investors to form JVs with local manufacturers, in order to create this transfer of technology. Such JVs, however, risked repelling **foreign direct investment** (FDI) by adding to its costs.

This linear model of technology development and transfer, however, is increasingly challenged by new approaches to **globalization** and **trade**. These new approaches question whether it is possible for all countries to gain international competitiveness in all technologies, and hence individual countries may gain more by allowing foreign-owned technology investment *without* requiring horizontal forms of technology transfer. The advantages of this approach are in the **multiplier effect**s of the foreign investment; the creation of a highly skilled workforce; and rapid diffusion of new (possibly environmental) technologies, rather than in attempting to achieve indigenous technological expertise. This approach has been seen in decisions to create **export processing zones (EPZs)** or **free trade zones (FTZs)** that attract foreign investment. The selection of which industries to seek either vertical or horizontal technology transfer, of course, is highly political and may vary according to different countries and different governments (see **infant industries; technology policy**).

Much debate in development studies, however, has focused on means of successful horizontal technology transfer – or practical guidelines for disseminating technology from international investment to local users. Such guidelines need to refer to the technical suitability of new technology for particular locations; the social and cultural factors underlying the purpose and use of technology (i.e. **appropriate technology**); and attention to the needs of investors, specifically in assuring technical support and cost recovery. Crucially, analysts have argued that there must be local economic demand for new technologies, and that governments should not undermine economic conditions by offering subsidies for new technologies, as withdrawal of subsidies will usually mean a collapse in market conditions. Often the responsibilities for technology transfer lie with a combination of different actors such as investing firms, **multilateral development banks (MDBs)** and agencies, local citizen groups and governments.

Failures in technology transfer are frequently the result of a lack of coordination or misplaced assumptions. In 1979, for example, the **United Nations Children's Fund (UNICEF)** located two new biomass electricity generators in Fateh-Singh-Ka-Purwa village in India. The project failed because it overestimated the supply of dung as fuel because it used national, rather than locally gathered figures. Because of this overestimation, the price of dung increased, making the biomass generators uneconomic. Similarly, in the Philippines in the 1980s, the government installed charcoal gasifiers for electricity generation as a way to enhance the pumping of irrigation water. Farmers had agreed to accept the technology because it was offered free of charge. But in practice, farmers still preferred to use rainwater because this was seen to be more reliable. The project failed because of insufficient attention to market demand and local practices. Indeed, the example indicated the need for technology to be appropriate to the needs of local users, rather than simply technically efficient in producing a desired result.

Successful technology transfer at the local scale therefore depends on the correct alignment of local technological needs; sustainable financial management; and the creation of **technological capability** – or the existence of local institutional capacity for educating people about technology, recovering costs, and incorporating (even developing) technology into industrialization. Long-term horizontal technology transfer, therefore, is a painstaking approach that may involve **partnerships** between citizens, governments and investors.

See also: appropriate technology; capacity building; climate change; foreign direct investment; joint venture; technological capability; technology policy; transnational corporations (TNCs)

Further reading

Forsyth, T. (1999) *International Investment and Climate Change: Energy Technologies for Developing Countries*, London: Earthscan and Royal Institute of International Affairs.

Heaton, G., Banks, R. and Ditz, D. (1994) *Missing Links: Technology and Environment Implications in the Industrializing World*, Washington DC: World Resource Institute.

Lall, S. (1998) "Technological Capabilities in Emerging Asia," *Oxford Development Studies* 26:2 213–43.

Lall, S. (ed.) (2001) *The Economics of Technology Transfer*, Cheltenham: Edward Elgar.

MacDonald, G. (1992) "Technology Transfer: The Climate Change Challenge," *Journal of Environment and Development* 1:1 1–39.

TIM FORSYTH

telecommunications

Telecommunications networks and services can provide an important component of the infrastructure for **economic development** and **social development**. Starting with telegraphy and voice telephone services, historically, telecommunications infrastructure and services were provided mainly by monopoly state-owned Post, Telegraph and Telephone (PTTs) administrations. With the advent of digital technologies and large increases in data communication as compared to voice traffic, the telecommunications industry has been transformed into a more competitive sector and is offering an increasingly wide variety of services. Digital technologies are transforming the telecommunications network into an infrastructure capable of carrying voice, data, graphics, video and audio signals.

Privatization and liberalization, and technological change are creating significant issues for developing countries that seek to extend telecommunications services to the majority of their citizens and business users. Shifts in policy and regulation in the industrialized countries from the 1970s onwards resulted in competitive entry in national and international telecommunications markets. Pressures to liberalize markets and to privatize telecommunications operators have come from the wealthy industrialized countries and the WTO (see **World Trade Organization/General Agreement on Tariffs and Trade (WTO/GATT)**). Developing countries increasingly are being encouraged to open their markets to foreign investors.

The extension of telecommunications networks beyond the wealthiest segments of developing country populations presents a major challenge. Potential users in rural areas of developing countries often have limited or no access to basic telephone services. However, the declining costs of telecommunications equipment and the spread of satellite and terrestrial wireless communication networks are providing a technological basis for expanding telecommunications services in developing countries. Unfortunately, despite increased investment in telecommunications in the decade of the 1990s in developing countries, for most countries a catch-up to the levels of penetration of telecommunications services is still many years away.

The constraints to the achievement of greater access in these countries are reinforced by inappropriate views of developing country market dynamics. Policy-makers and investors often assume that there is little demand for services in rural areas, despite the fact that many factors other than income levels can influence demand, including the requirements of the **public sector**. Potential telecommunications users have varied requirements for services in addition to voice telephone connections. The telecommunications infrastructure supports access to the Internet and to online services for business and government. In urban areas, investment in the telecommunications infrastructure is being used to attract investors in software development and "back office" service provision, creating new jobs for skilled personnel in some developing countries. Countries such as India have developed an international software industry that relies heavily on the telecommunications infrastructure, but investment has largely failed to bring gains for the poorer urban populations. Many developing countries are putting Universal Service Obligations in place and subsidies or development funds may be available to extend the reach of telecommunications networks. However, these initiatives may protect dominant telecommunications operators from competitive entry and result in a slow down in total investment in the telecommunications infrastructure.

Telecommunications service access is often measured by the percentage of individuals or households with access to the network, but access models are being developed to enable collective access by schools, hospital clinics, libraries and **community** centers. Evaluations of various tele-center initiatives suggest that there is a need to involve all stakeholders in decisions with respect to the services to be provided, who has access to them, and how basic maintenance and upgrading of equipment is to be funded. In many cases, policy coordination and the removal of bureaucratic barriers to action and investment are larger barriers to success than is the cost of technology.

The extension of affordable access to the telecommunications infrastructure requires the separation of supply from government departments and the creation of a regulatory institution to ensure that all potential investors and services customers are treated equitably. Competitive entry to the telecommunications supply market in some developing countries has boosted the number of mobile telecommunications subscribers and encouraged the spread of Internet access. Where users face unaffordable prices for telecommunications service, they find ways of bypassing dominant operators by using callback or voice services over the Internet. Unfortunately, these initiatives can only marginally reduce the extent of exclusion from affordable access to networks.

In 2000, the **United Nations** *Report of the High-level Panel on Information and Communication Technology* recommended that the connectivity problem should be addressed as a matter of urgency: "the overall target should be to bring connectivity to all communities by the end of 2004." The telecommunications access issue, as a subset of access to advanced information and communication technologies of all kinds, is very high on the international agenda. This is because when telecommunications access is established, the use of networks offers opportunities for local, regional and global collaboration in support of development goals. However, learning and capability building are necessary complements to investment in the telecommunications infrastructure. The focus of the debate on the "digital divide" is often on the failure of the private sector to invest sufficiently in a ubiquitous infrastructure, but such investment cannot be regarded as an end in itself. Investment is also needed in strengthening local capabilities and the knowledge base through training and **education**. This complementary investment is essential if the advantages of access to telecommunications networks are to become available to the majority of the citizens of developing countries.

The capabilities of the telecommunications infrastructure can support Internet access. An increasingly wide range of voice and data services relies on modem communication, Internetworking of local area networks, and broadband connections. The diversity of network access options is being encouraged by new generations of modems with very high digital processing capability. Developments in wireless technology, including cellular radio and rural radio systems as well as new generations of satellite technology, offer the potential for more affordable access to telecommunications services. Developments in computing and software systems are enabling the provision of new services that generate traffic for the telecommunications network, making the business case for supplying network access more attractive to investors in developing countries.

Visions of the potential of the development of electronic commerce for firms in developing countries are premised on the expectation that these countries will achieve equitable access to the telecommunications infrastructure. Similarly, electronic government initiatives using Internet platforms require an underlying telecommunications infrastructure for their success. Digital service applications can support more extensive and effective delivery of health care services and environment protection schemes. For instance, the telecommunications infrastructure can support the use of software applications such as geographical information systems to facilitate improved access to environmental information for citizens, public authorities, and businesses.

See also: information technology; Internet; measuring development; new public management (NPM); technology policy; World Summit on the Information Society (WSIS)

Further reading

Hudson, H. (1997) *Global Connections: International Telecommunications Infrastructure and Policy*, New York: John Wiley.

Melody, W. (ed.) (1997) *Telecom Reform: Principles, Policies and Regulatory Practices*, Lyngby: Technical University of Denmark.

Noam, E. (ed.) (1999) *Telecommunications in Africa (Global Communications Series)*, Oxford: Oxford University Press.

Wellenius, B. (2002) *Closing the Gap in Access to Rural Communication: Chile 1995–2002*, World Bank Discussion Paper no. 430, Washington DC: World Bank.

World Dialogue on Regulation for Network Economies: http://www.regulateonline.org/

ROBIN MANSELL

terms of trade

"Terms of trade" most commonly refers to the ratio of an index of export prices to an index of import prices (Px/Pm). This ratio is more properly known as the *net barter* terms of trade. The terms of trade are crucial for understanding economic factors behind the impact of international trade on many developing countries. Many studies in development economics have shown that (net barter) terms of trade (i.e. the ratio in prices between exported primary commodities and imported manufactured goods) will decline in the long run, meaning comparative loss of profitability for countries exporting primary goods.

In early analyses, classical economists predicted that long-run prices of agricultural products and minerals would rise in relation to those of manufactures, because limited supplies of agricultural land and mineral deposits would cause diminishing returns to increasing the labor and capital employed in those activities. In contrast, however, work after the World War II independently by Rául Prebisch and by Hans Singer showed that terms of trade for developing countries – at the time almost entirely dependent on primary products for their export earnings – had been declining since the nineteenth century (see **trade**). The

Singer-Prebisch hypothesis suggested the terms of trade had declined because of low-income elasticity of demand for primary products in developed countries' markets, and because of an inability of developing economies to shift resources out of primary production as its productivity increased. As a result, gains from increased productivity, such as generated by high-yielding varieties of seeds, would be passed on to consumers in *developed* countries in the form of lower prices, rather than as higher incomes to producers and workers in *developing* economies (see **green revolution**). While the precise formulation of the terms of trade has been widely discussed and disputed, econometric testing has generally confirmed the hypothesis. Later work by Singer on the terms of trade of manufactured exports by developing countries suggests similar productivity losses were occurring as developing countries diversified into manufactures exporting.

Variants of the terms of trade concept have been developed. The *income* terms of trade refers to the net barter terms of trade weighted by a quantity index of exports, $(Qx \cdot Px)/Pm$. The (single) *factorial* terms of trade weights export prices by an index that indicates changes in the productivity of exports $(Zx \cdot Px)/Pm$. Consequently, a fall in the net barter terms of trade may be accompanied by a rise in the total purchasing power of exports, and the relative price fall may not necessarily cancel out all productivity increases.

The terms of trade is also used in other contexts, particularly the terms of trade between **agriculture** and industry within a country. Governments in developing countries have sometimes depressed the agriculture:industry terms of trade by keeping relative agricultural prices low to provide cheap **food** for industrial workers and cheap agricultural raw materials for industry. This is a way of implicitly taxing agriculture to support industrial development.

See also: dependency theory; free trade; tariffs; trade; world systems theory

Further reading

Sapsford, D. and Chen, J-R. (eds) (1999) "The Prebisch-Singer Thesis: A Thesis for the New Millenium?" *Journal of International Development* 11:6 843–916.

Shaw, D. (2002) *Sir Hans Singer: The Life and Work of a Development Economist*, London: Palgrave. See ch. 7: "The Distribution of Gains from Trade and Investment: The Terms of Trade Controversy," pp. 49–71.

JOHN THOBURN

textiles

Textiles are fabrics made by processes such as weaving and knitting from natural and synthetic fibers including silk, wool, cotton, flax, nylon and rayon. They are classified according to materials used, as well as their structure and weave design. The garmenting (clothing) sub-sector is often analyzed along with textiles. The textile and clothing commodity chain starts with harvested fibers being spun into yarn, before being woven into textiles, including fabrics, that may then be cut and sewn into garments. Levels of value addition vary, with large profits to be made at the design, branding and retail end of the chain, often in dispersed locations around the globe. Global trade in textiles and clothing amounted to US$332 billion in 1997, according to **World Bank** figures.

As a mature and **labor-intensive** industry, textiles form an important component of the economies of many developing countries. Textiles represent a particularly important export industry for countries such as Madagascar, Nepal and Pakistan, where textiles form 30–50 percent of total merchandise exports. Developing country exports constituted 60 percent of all global textile trade in 2000, with Asia taking 51 percent of global sales. Trade disputes have been rife in the textile sector. The EU (**European Union**), for example, has brought anti-dumping cases to the WTO (see **World Trade Organization/General Agreement on Tariffs and Trade (WTO/GATT)**) against India, Pakistan, Egypt and Indonesia for products such as man-made yarn, sacks and ropes, unbleached cotton fabric and bed linen.

Developing countries also view current textile trade agreements with dismay, in part due to the differential manner in which they are applied. The

Multi-Fiber Agreement (MFA) was set up in 1974 as a temporary measure by industrialized countries fearing cheap clothing imports from developing countries. It then maintained a range of quantitative restrictions on imports imposed by countries such as Canada, the EU, Norway and the USA. The Uruguay Round Agreement on Textiles and Clothing (ATC) provides for a phased timetable for dismantling the MFA by January 2005, though implementation has been marred by the range of quotas proffered to select countries. For example while India and Pakistan possess resources such as domestic production of raw cotton and longstanding artisanal skills in textiles, other countries (such as Bangladesh and Sri Lanka) entered the garment industry propped up by bilateral quotas with the EU and USA. It is expected that MFA phase-out will benefit China and also some countries of South Asia, though much depends on whether non-tariff barriers (see **tariffs**) are once again invoked as protectionist measures by the industrialized countries, perhaps in the form of industrial standards and **labor rights and standards**.

See also: export-led growth; export processing zones (EPZs); gender and industrialization; international division of labor; labor-intensive; tariffs; trade; value chains; World Trade Organization/General Agreement on Tariffs and Trade (WTO/GATT)

Further reading

van Heerden, A., Berhouet, M. P. and Caspari, C. (2003) *Rags or Riches? Phasing-Out the Multi-Fibre Agreement*, SEED Working Paper no. 40, Geneva: ILO.

Kheir-El-Din, H. (2002) "Implementing the Agreement on Textiles and Clothing," pp. 186–94 in Hoekman, B., Mattoo, A. and English, P. (eds) *Development, Trade and the WTO: A Handbook*, Washington DC: World Bank.

ANNE T. KURIAKOSE

THIRD WORLD *see* underdevelopment versus less developed country (LDC) versus Third World

torture

Freedom from torture is included in the **Universal Declaration of Human Rights (1948)**. In the 1984 United Nations' Convention Against Torture and Other Cruel, Inhuman or Degrading Treatment or Punishment, torture is defined as:

> any act by which severe pain or suffering, whether physical or mental, is intentionally inflicted on a person for such purposes as obtaining from him or a third person information or a confession, punishing him for an act he or a third person has committed or is suspected of having committed, or intimidating or coercing him or a third person, or for any reason based on discrimination of any kind, when such pain or suffering is inflicted by or at the instigation of or with the consent or acquiescence of a public official or other person acting in an official capacity.

According to the Convention, there are no circumstances in which torture can be justified or legitimized. The Convention came into force on 26 June 1987, and by 2004 over 130 states were a party to it. Responsibility for the prevention of torture rests on states, which are obliged to report to the Committee on Torture (CAT). The CAT makes an annual report to the United Nations General Assembly for consideration (see **United Nations**).

According to the publication, *Together Against Torture* by the Coalition of International NGOs Against Torture (2001) (see **non-governmental organizations (NGOs)**), the use of torture continues in over 130 countries and is widespread in the majority of these. Many NGOs are involved in pressing for the eradication of torture through monitoring and publicizing its use, and providing information and statistics. The CAT relies heavily on input from NGOs. Independent verification of cases of torture reveals the distance between law and practice.

This distance demonstrates that it remains possible for torturers to act with impunity. The lack of enforcement of laws against torture strengthens the perpetrators and further weakens the victims. However, there have been a number of developments since the late 1990s aimed at reducing or removing impunity. The fledgling International Criminal Court has jurisdiction over cases of torture when these occur during periods of armed conflict, although the Court's jurisdiction is not yet global (see **law of armed conflict (LAC)**). Belgium allows its courts to exercise universal jurisdiction over a range of cases, including torture. The arrests of Augusto Pinochet of Chile in the UK and Hissein Habré of Chad in Senegal show that there is some willingness among states to act in cases of torture, regardless of whether their own citizens are involved.

Torture has no ideological foundation and occurs under any type of regime, from dictatorships to democracies. The effects of torture go beyond the immediate victims to the wider **community**, so that fear of torture can a means of social control and torture becomes accepted as a normal part of maintaining **security**.

See also: authoritarianism; human rights; international law; law of armed conflict (LAC); war

Further reading

Amnesty International: http://www.amnesty.org/
Dunér, B. (ed.) (1998) *An End to Torture*, London: Zed.
International Rehabilitation Council for Torture Victims: http://www.irct.org/
Peters, E. (1985) *Torture*, Oxford: Blackwell.

CLARE MILLS

tourism

Tourism is a huge global industry and important source of government revenue, contributing to **gross domestic product (GDP)** and **employment** in many developing countries. Although international tourism is the most visible form, some larger developing countries (such as India and China), or **newly industrialized economies (NIEs)** (such as Malaysia and Thailand) now have growing domestic tourism sectors. Tourism is one of the world's largest industries when measured by employment (one estimate is that one in every seventeen people in the global labor force now

works in tourism), and in terms of its rapid growth since the 1950s.

Key aspects of the international tourism industry include accommodation, restaurants, leisure facilities, heritage sites, transportation, travel agents and tour operators. Tourism to developing countries has different sub-sectors ranging from mass tourism (now with the innovation of "all-inclusive" resorts) and luxury tourism, to **ecotourism** and small-scale backpacker tourism. Mass tourism is the largest sector, often resulting in enclave development of hotel enclosures and fenced-off beaches with tourists having limited contact with local people.

In 2000, there were over 699 million international arrivals, mostly by air transport, and tourists spent $476 billion, including spending on flights (World Tourism Organization figures). The fastest growing regions measured by arrivals, such as Asia-Pacific, received an estimated 111 million international arrivals in 2000, whereas Africa saw 27 million, the Middle East 20 million and South Asia only 6 million. However, international tourism is highly sensitive to perceptions of risk and political instability in destination areas, so that for example during the 2000 Palestinian *intifada* (uprising) in Israel and the occupied territories, international tourist arrivals to Israel fell by 50 percent in the final quarter of that year.

Mass tourism originated in the long post-war boom in Europe and North America, when rising levels of disposable income and increasing leisure time resulted in growing demand for foreign holidays. New transport technologies, particularly wide-bodied jet aircraft such as the Boeing 747, led to falling real prices for long-haul leisure travel, and former luxury tourism areas in Southeast Asia, the Caribbean and Africa became mass tourism destinations. In the 1990s fuel-efficient aircraft on long-haul routes, increased competition by the airlines and the introduction of long-haul charter flights, all led to further falls in real ticket prices. This fueled further expansion of passenger numbers to an increasing number of developing countries.

Countries in Africa, Asia and elsewhere were encouraged by the **World Bank** and the **Organization for Economic Cooperation and Development (OECD)** to host international tourism which was portrayed as the "passport to development" that would generate **employment**, attract inward investment and increase prosperity. During the 1980s and 1990s under neo-liberal **structural adjustment** programs (see **neo-liberalism**), international tourism was also encouraged by the World Bank and **International Monetary Fund (IMF)** as a useful source of foreign exchange earnings to service foreign **debt**.

The demonstration effects of booming destinations such as Thailand encouraged other governments, and that country's successful "Visit Thailand Year" 1987 promotion (with accelerating visitor numbers) was widely copied by other ASEAN members (see **Association of Southeast Asian Nations (ASEAN))** in the 1990s.

Despite government enthusiasm for tourism, for many people in developing countries hosting international tourism has proved disappointing, with few apparent benefits "trickling down" to the poorest (see **trickle down**). Despite large numbers of foreign tourists, and gross economic gains from millions of holidays sold, foreign ownership of hotels, airlines and tour operators, especially by the large tourism **transnational corporations (TNCs)** has resulted in high levels of economic leakage. In some cases, leakage may be as high as 60 percent of every tourist dollar spent.

For TNCs involved in tourism, vertical integration has reduced costs and increased profits. However, for the host country foreign firms can exert a huge influence. In many developing countries tourism arguably demonstrates some of the unevenness of the distribution of **economic growth** models as noted by **dependency theory**, particularly the uneven access to political power, and the influence of TNCs based in developed countries. Mass tourism tends to require significant imports and expatriate staff. Hence, foreign-owned hotels may have limited economic linkages to the local economy.

The numbers of tourists staying in large hotels can create problems with **waste management** and **water management**, as tourist facilities demand large amounts of water for their swimming pools and golf courses. Local village supplies (see **villages**) may be affected, as seen in Goa, southern India. Another problem associated with international tourism is **sex tourism** and **prostitution/sex work** (for example in the Philippines, Sri Lanka, and Thailand). A central

issue concerns the amount of local control of tourism by the host communities (see **community**). Local **non-governmental organizations (NGOs)** have been involved in increasing local participation in Goa, and in Bali protesting over resort development that threatened temples.

For some **small island developing states (SIDS)**, particularly in the Caribbean, attracting cruise-ship tourism has become increasingly important. Large cruise liners require **capital intensive** facilities such as piers and terminals and bring millions of visitors to small islands such as the Bahamas, but despite the volume, visitor expenditure ashore is minimal. The effects of cruise ships are similar to land-based "all-inclusive" resorts having nominal linkages to the local economy.

Since the late 1980s, theorists have considered whether "sustainable tourism" is possible. On one hand, some operators have sought to develop **ecotourism** as a specifically environmentally friendly form of tourism. On the other hand, critics have suggested ecotourism might increase damage by overloading fragile destinations, portraying local people in romanticist ways (see **Orientalism**), and that a broader form of sustainable tourism needs to address mass travel to less obviously environmental locations. A further consideration, especially since the 1990s, is the impact of terrorism and war on the popularity of international travel, and how far potential downturns in tourism to specific locations might increase its perception as a risky form of development.

See also: culture; economic development; ecotourism; environment; protected areas; sex tourism

Further reading

Hampton, M. (1998) "Backpacker Tourism and Economic Development," *Annals of Tourism Research* 25:3 639–60.

Harrison, D. (ed.) (2001) *Tourism and the Less Developed World*, Wallingford: CABI.

Mowforth, M. and Munt, I. (2003) *Tourism and Sustainability*, London: Routledge.

Picard, M. (1996) *Cultural Tourism and Touristic Culture*, Singapore: Archipelago.

Scheyvens, R. (2002) *Tourism for Development*, London: Prentice Hall.

Tourism concern: NGO campaigning for ethical tourism http://www.tourismconcern.org.uk/

MARK HAMPTON

trade

The relationships between trade, **economic growth**, and development have been under discussion since the time of the classical economists several centuries ago, who believed that trade could be an "engine of growth." After World War II, a deep pessimism settled on the issue, as it seemed that developing countries faced an international environment in which their **terms of trade** would deteriorate and where they would fail to reap gains from **export-led growth** or domestic technical progress. As a result, most developing countries entered a stage of **industrialization** through **import substitution**, which in many cases gave rise to an unexpected "dependency" on developed countries for investment and technology and, except in East Asia, produced poor, long-term economic performance (see **dependency theory**). After the 1970s oil shocks, when many developing countries came to depend on multilateral agencies such as the **World Bank** and **International Monetary Fund (IMF)** for development assistance, donor-induced policies shifted toward outward-oriented development under the so-called **Washington consensus** of free market, neo-liberal views of the 1980s (see **neo-liberalism**). The debate on trade and development continues. It has become connected with discussion of the effects of openness and trade liberalization on exports, development and **poverty**, and embedded in the wider issue of the impacts of **globalization**.

Classical views on trade, growth and development

Classical economists' belief that trade could be a significant factor in increasing the rate of growth has three main strands. First, there is a dynamic productivity theory of trade. As Adam Smith argued, exporting allowed firms to expand beyond the confines of the domestic market, thus achieving greater efficiency through specialization and division of labor. By giving exporters the opportunity to achieve economies of large-scale production, it encouraged the use of machinery and new technology. A second strand in classical thinking is sometimes labeled "vent for surplus." This is an extreme case of the static reallocative gains from trade and specialization, rather than a case of faster long-term growth, but it could give rise to sustained periods of expansion. Goods or resources for which there was little domestic demand could profitably be traded for goods of greater value to domestic consumers. The vent for surplus idea could include the **employment** of underemployed labor and unused land in export production. The third element in the argument, more often associated with John Stuart Mill and connected in his writings with the people of Asia, is that trade generates important indirect benefits. These refer to the raising of the inducement to work, save and invest, by presenting people with new forms of goods that they can obtain by exporting.

The Singer-Myrdal-Prebisch view

The essentially optimistic view of the classical economists on the effects of trade on growth was seriously challenged in the 1950s. Economists were then starting to take a strong interest in the problems of developing countries, which, in the case of Africa and Asia, were in the process of obtaining independence from colonial rule (see **decolonization**). They were also starting to move away from a narrow focus on economic growth (sustained rises in per capita income) toward a wider view of development, considering income distribution and various non-economic factors. Largely working independently, Hans Singer, Gunnar Myrdal and Raúl Prebisch (S-M-P) set out a number of reasons why developing countries might lose their gains from trade.

First, was the famous doctrine – mainly associated with Singer and Prebisch – of the declining **terms of trade** for developing countries' primary commodity exports, on which they depended at the time for almost all of their foreign exchange earnings. Second, was the idea that where foreign investment has been located in developing countries, it often functioned as an enclave, an area physically but not economically located in the country concerned. For example, many mining investments used few local inputs, employed little local labor and (at that time) paid little tax to the host government. Finally, and associated more with Myrdal, was the idea that primary production might have negative effects of drawing resources into export production and away from the domestic development of manufacturing. To such negative ("backwash") effects can be added the more modern concept of the "**Dutch disease**," an idea derived originally from the economic effects of the export of North Sea gas by the Netherlands in the 1970s. This refers to a situation where a rapidly expanding primary sector such as minerals or oil, by causing a country's exchange rate to appreciate, damages the prospects for other exports by making them less profitable, and damages import-competing manufacturing and food production by encouraging cheap imports.

The S-M-P view was hugely influential in turning developing countries' policy-makers toward import-substituting **industrialization** in the 1960s and 1970s (see **import substitution**). The terms of trade hypothesis remains intact, having stood the test of time and repeated econometric testing. Singer and others have also shown the terms of trade of the **labor-intensive** manufactures now exported by many developing countries may deteriorate for similar productivity-losing reasons as those of primary products. Other strands of the S-M-P view are now less influential, and it is recognized that some primary commodities have had quite positive development effects. For instance, labor-intensive exports of tin from Malaysia and Thailand in the late nineteenth and early twentieth centuries probably were more conducive to development than most labor-intensive manufacturing exports nowadays, generating **employment**, labor skills, technological learning, a transport infrastructure, and local consumer demand. In contrast, some plantation exports may have fossilized a cheap labor policy.

The experience of import-substituting industrialization

The import substitution policies of the 1960s and 1970s initially brought rapid growth in many Latin American, Asian and African countries. However,

as easy opportunities for replacing basic consumer goods were exhausted, firms found it difficult to grow based on saturated domestic markets, and efficient import substitution in technologically complex goods was difficult to achieve. Disillusion with import substitution in practice spawned an influential line of thinking known as **dependency theory**. Relating particularly to Latin America, it traced how protection against imports of consumer durables led to domestic production for privileged **elites**. Physical controls on imports led to rent seeking as firms struggled for the lucrative right to control such imports. The need to buy inputs and raw materials from abroad, and the growing importance of foreign inward investment, gave rise to increased rather than lessened dependence on industrial countries.

However, at the time that many developing countries were fostering inefficient industries behind trade barriers, a rather different approach was adopted in East Asia. Taiwan and South Korea, following the earlier example of Japanese industrial policy, practiced a form of *export-oriented import substitution*, with industries being sheltered from competition in their domestic market with a view to eventually making them export-competitive (see **export-led growth**). In Korea in particular, for example in the motor industry, companies were allowed to sell at high profits in the protected home market only in exchange for agreeing to develop exports, which they initially were able to subsidize from home market profits until exporting became profitable.

Trade, development and the neo-liberal reaction

The international oil crises of the 1970s brought about by the **Organization of Petroleum Exporting Countries (OPEC)** sharply raised the cost to developing countries of their oil imports and pushed many into debt. These countries turned to multilateral agencies like the IMF and the **World Bank** for financial support. **Debt** problems, and a growing disillusion among economists and policy-makers with the experience of import substituting industrialization, led to major shifts in thinking on the role of trade in the 1980s. At the same time, economic policy in developed countries was turning away from traditional Keynesian economics with their stress on demand management to maintain full **employment**, and toward a concern with controling inflation (see **inflation and its effects**), privatization (see **privatization and liberalization**) of state-owned enterprises (see **state and state reform; state-owned enterprises (SOEs)**), and liberalization of **labor markets**. Associated with this move toward **neo-liberalism**, the policy agenda in developing countries came to be much influenced by market-oriented, outward-looking views advocated by the IMF and the World Bank under the so-called "Washington consensus" and imposed under loan **conditionality**. The East Asian countries' successes were portrayed either as exceptional or as examples of outward orientation, despite the fact that their export growth had been achieved from behind tariff barriers (see **tariffs**).

The multilateral agencies used stabilization and **structural adjustment** programs to impose market-oriented conditions on borrowers. Trade liberalization and large devaluations were an important part of such conditions. "Getting the prices right" was seen as the most important factor in promoting successful development. Free markets, including moves toward **free trade**, were expected to achieve this.

Trade liberalization, exports and development

Since the early 1980s, then, developing countries have been exhorted to integrate more closely with the global economy and to reduce their own trade barriers through trade liberalization. Such integration has been one of the most visible aspects of **globalization**. Subsequently, policy debates on trade and development have settled on the issue of "openness" – the state of the economy that trade liberalization is designed to achieve – and its impact on economic growth and development.

Developing countries have mostly come to trade liberalization after an extended period of import substituting industrialization. Trade liberalization is designed to reduce protection of the domestic market against imports both by moves away from quantitative measures like import quotas toward tariff-based protection, and by cuts in import tariffs. On the export side, it includes the removal or reduction of export licensing and export taxation. Import liberalization is intended to improve the economic performance of those domestic firms that can survive it. It is also argued that it can stimulate exports by removing the *anti-export bias* generated by the higher prices received by firms for goods sold in the protected domestic market. Import liberalization also stimulates exports by reducing the real exchange rate overvaluation (see **exchange rates**) associated with limiting imports by protection. Exporting leads to gains through specialization; through economies of large scale; and greater access to foreign technology.

Anti-export bias, though a strong plank in the neo-liberal case for reducing and eventually removing protection, seems not to have been a barrier to exporting manufactures in practice. Take the case of China, which has become the world's largest exporter of garments, and which has done so by attracting inward investment and by the use of efficient export processing arrangements, including import duty exemptions and drawbacks on imported fabric and other inputs. During the early 1990s when its garment exports were expanding, China was maintaining (trade-weighted) average import duties on clothing of over 80 percent and trade-weighted **tariffs** on all imports of 32 percent. Indeed, among developing countries, almost all leading exporters of manufactures, except Hong Kong, have expanded their exports while maintaining substantial protection of their domestic market against imports. In doing so, they have followed the lead of almost all the now industrialized countries, except for the UK but not excluding the USA, in protecting their home market in their early stages of industrial development while they became exporters.

In the case of countries with small domestic markets, the reason why anti-export bias is not necessarily a deterrent to exports is that producers can expand only by exporting. If such producers expand into the domestic market, it quickly becomes saturated. The domestic price falls toward the world price, thus removing the anti-export bias incentive to sell at home. And countries with large markets could follow the South Korean example and use the protected home market as a base from which to develop exports. Another, though very different, reason for the irrelevance of anti-export bias is that in developing countries, some products such as high-quality export garments may hardly be demanded in the domestic market at all.

Openness, growth and poverty

In the late 1990s and early 2000s, the development discourse has moved toward identifying development with the alleviation of **poverty**. Poverty is typically defined by organizations such as the World Bank for practical purposes as income of less than US$2 a day in terms of real purchasing power, with incomes of less than $1 a day being regarded as extreme poverty (also see **chronic poverty**). Poverty, more widely, involves a lack of entitlements to such things as health care and information, and the lack of capabilities (see **capability approach**) to turn these entitlements into states of well-being. Thus **education**, for example, by improving capabilities, works toward the reduction of poverty.

Trade liberalization can affect poverty via its influence on the rate of growth. Thus, the questions center on how openness affects growth and how growth affects poverty. Trade liberalization also can be viewed as a trade shock. It affects poor people directly through changes in prices of the goods they produce and consume, through the profits and **employment** decisions of the firms in which they work, and indirectly via its effects on government revenue and expenditure (see McCulloch *et al.*, 2001).

Although many econometric studies of developing countries have indicated that openness – in the narrow sense of low levels of tariff and non-tariff protection against imports – has a positive impact on growth, this has been strongly criticized in recent work. Rodriguez and Rodrik (2000), in a widely cited paper, argue that trade barriers are often strongly linked to other sources of bad economic performance, and that there is little evidence that low trade barriers in themselves raise **growth rate**s. On a wider definition of openness in terms of increased trade volumes, Dollar and Kraay (2001) show a positive influence on growth in developing countries, and that the incomes of the poor increase in proportion as growth proceeds. This, however, defines openness very broadly and includes export-led growth along East Asian lines.

Trade and development in the 2000s

The debate on the relation between trade, economic growth, development, and poverty reduction, is not yet resolved. Even "openness" is a concept capable of rather different interpretations. However, the Washington consensus approach to development – and its stress on free trade – has been questioned, and it is recognized that market failure is far more widespread than the "market fundamentalism" of the 1980s would have conceded. One reason is the spectacular failure of market fundamentalist policies in the former Soviet Union in the absence of market-supporting **institutions**, including the rule of law. Another, is a belated recognition that successful exporting countries like China or South Korea have developed institutions all of their own to complement their particular trade and industrial policies. Institutional development such as **property rights**, regulatory institutions, and institutions for macro-economic stability and social insurance are seen as crucial if openness to trade is to lead to development. And without appropriate "behind the border" policies, including macroeconomic stability, to complement it, increased openness to trade may be counterproductive (see Rodrik in Hoekmann *et al.*, 2002).

Nevertheless, despite the continuing controversies on trade and development, there is almost no argument to be made even for large countries like China totally to forego the gains from trade and to industrialize as closed economies. Besides the importance of exports as a driver of economic growth, there are dynamic gains to be had on the import side too, especially importing foreign technology through capital goods. Such technological gains are seen as increasingly important as economists understand better the processes of endogenous growth (see **endogenous growth theory**).

Rather than openness in itself, the issue is the speed at which countries should open their domestic markets while developing their exports. In some cases where the domestic industrial structure has been well developed under import substitution, import liberalization may be a way of driving domestic firms into exporting. South Africa appears to be such a case, but the costs of such

shock therapy in terms of employment and poverty have been high (Roberts and Thoburn, 2003). For low-income countries in the 2000s trying to increase exports of manufactures, the rules of the game are rather different from those faced by East Asia thirty years previously. WTO members are under pressure to reduce their trade barriers, as has been the case in China for example since it joined the WTO in 2001 (see **World Trade Organization/General Agreement on Tariffs and Trade (WTO/GATT)**). WTO rules such as those on **trade-related aspects of intellectual property rights (TRIPS)** limit the freedom of action to impose trade-related rules like export proportions or local content requirements on **foreign direct investment**. New exporters also face a fallacy of composition problem. They benefit individually by expanding their exports, but if many similar countries also expand their exports of classic labor-intensive goods like garments, shoes or toys, there is a risk of their prices falling in the world market. Thus, the terms of trade of developing countries decline once again. Such export expansions also risk import restrictions being imposed on them if they appear to "disrupt" Western markets. And even entering into export production in labor-intensive goods is not easy. Such exports are usually organized in international **value chains**, where leading firms – in the case of garments and shoes, often retailers or brand owners in Western countries – control the terms of entry and the functions exporters are allowed to perform.

See also: colonialism, history of; dependency theory; economic growth; export-led growth; export processing zones (EPZs); free trade; free trade zones (FTZs); globalization; import substitution; industrialization and trade policy; most favored nation (MFN) status; tariffs; terms of trade; value chains; world systems theory; World Trade Organization/General Agreement on Tariffs and Trade (WTO/GATT)

Further reading

Dollar, D., and Kraay, A. (2001) *Trade, Growth and Poverty*, Washington DC: World Bank Policy Working Paper 2615. http://econ.worldbank.org/files/2207_wps2615.pdf

Hoekman, B., Mattoo, A. and English, P. (eds) (2002) *Development, Trade and the WTO: a Handbook*, Washington DC: World Bank.

McCulloch, N., Winters, L. and Cirera, X. (2001) *Trade Liberalization and Poverty; A Handbook*, London: Department for International Development and Centre for Economic Policy Research.

Oxfam (2002) *Rigged Rules and Double Standards: Trade, Globalisation, and the Fight Against Poverty*, London: Oxfam. http://www.maketrade-fair.org

Roberts, S. and Thoburn, J. (2003) "Adjusting to Trade Liberalisation: The Case of Firms in the South African Textile Sector," *Journal of African Economies* 12:1 74–103.

Rodriguez, F. and Rodrik, D. (1999) "Trade Policy and Economic Growth: A Skeptic's Guide to the Cross-national Evidence," Cambridge MA: National Bureau of Economic Research, Working Paper 7081. www.nber.org/papers/w7081

Rodrik, D. (1999), *The New Global Economy and Developing Countries: Making Openness Work*, Washington DC: Overseas Development Council.

Thoburn, J. (1977) *Primary Commodity Exports and Economic Development*, London: Wiley.

UNCTAD (2002) *Trade and Development Report, 2002*, New York and Geneva: UNCTAD.

JOHN THOBURN

trade-related aspects of intellectual property rights (TRIPS)

Trade-related aspects of intellectual property rights (TRIPS) are the procedures for protecting **intellectual property rights (IPRs)** (IPRs) when undertaking international trade. The TRIPS Agreement forms part of the 1994 Uruguay Round agreements of the WTO (see **World Trade Organization/General Agreement on Tariffs and Trade (WTO/GATT)**), and requires each WTO member to provide procedures within its national regime to ensure their enforcement. Members are also required to give both national treatment (i.e. no discrimination against foreigners) and **most favored nation (MFN) status** treatment (i.e. no discrimination between foreign nationals) in protecting IPRs. Non-compliance is addressed through the WTO dispute settlement system.

The TRIPS preamble acknowledges the "developmental and technological objectives" of IPR protection. The agreement provides that such protection should contribute to the "transfer and dissemination of technology" (Art. 7) (see **technology transfer**), and obliges developed countries to provide incentives to enterprises and **institutions** in their territories to promote technological transfer to developing countries (Art. 66). The effects of these provisions remain to be seen.

TRIPS incorporates substantive provisions from certain multilateral conventions administered by the **World Intellectual Property Organization (WIPO)**, while imposing further obligations. A new obligation of particular contention is the Article 27 requirement that patents be available for inventions (both products and processes) in "all fields of technology." In the area of public health, there are justified concerns that obligatory patent legislation for **pharmaceuticals** will impede access to life-saving medicines by poor people, especially in developing countries (CIPR, 2002). On this matter, the WTO Ministerial Declaration in Doha (2002) clarifies that TRIPS should be interpreted and implemented in a manner supportive of members' right to protect public health and "promote access to medicines for all" (Art. 4). The Doha Declaration also exempted developing countries from pharmaceutical product protection until 2016 (Art. 7), instead of 2006 as for other obligations. Developing countries still need to provide such patents by 2005, if they have not already done so.

TRIPS Article 27 also requires new plant varieties be protected by patents or a *sui generis* system. Such IPRs, particularly patents, have the potential to interfere with farm-level experimentation and ongoing practices by farmers in replanting, exchanging or selling seeds from their crops (see **genetically modified organisms (GMOs)**). Although further empirical evidence is needed, they have been said to threaten farmers' rights, **biodiversity** and even **food security** in developing countries.

While some are keen to de-link IPRs from trade, those seeking solutions within TRIPS emphasize the right of each member state to adopt measures necessary to protect public health and **nutrition**, and "to promote the public interest in sectors of vital importance to their socio-economic and technological development" (Art. 8). The potential exceptions to exclusive IPR are also stressed – for example, enabling access in developing countries to copyrighted educational materials through concepts of "fair use" or "fair dealing." Of particular relevance in the context of access to patented medicines are the potentials for compulsory-licensing or "government use" (Art. 31). However, since developing countries and LDCs often lack the infrastructure for pharmaceutical manufacture, much hinges on TRIPS interpretation or reforms to facilitate imports of generics from other countries (CIPR, 2002). Meanwhile, TRIPS does not restrict members' legislative freedom to allow parallel imports of pharmaceuticals into their country.

See also: intellectual property rights (IPRs); most favored nation (MFN) status; pharmaceuticals; technology transfer; World Intellectual Property Organization (WIPO); World Trade Organization/ General Agreement on Tariffs and Trade (WTO/ GATT)

Further reading

CIPR (Commission on Intellectual Property Rights) (2002) *Integrating Intellectual Property Rights and Development Policy*, London: CIPR.

Watal, J. (2001) *Intellectual Property Rights in the WTO and Developing Countries*, London: Kluwer Law International.

TZEN WONG

trade unions

Trade unions can be characterized as organizations that represent workers in their struggle for the improvement of wages and working conditions (see **labor rights and standards**). Trade unions emerged in Europe at the end of the nineteenth century in Europe and at the beginning of the twentieth century in most developing countries. The main role of trade unions is to represent their members' interests and channel their demands into collective bargaining or political action. Although trade unions primarily represent their membership, their intention to represent all working people has often led to questions about which workers trade unions should represent and the question, particularly in developing countries, whether in fact trade unions only represent workers in the formal economy, which may limit their role as legitimate representatives of the whole working population.

Trade union action takes place through collective bargaining about wages and working conditions with employers and sometimes the state. The strike is a crucial tool for trade unions to put pressure on employers and governments during collective bargaining. Trade unions also play a significant political role, although their formal role is restricted to representing their members at the workplace. In some cases, particularly in Europe, trade unions participate in national-level bargaining with governments and employers' organizations. During the 1970s, 1980s and later, labor movements demanded democratization in countries such as South Korea, Brazil and South Africa, linking workers' demands to political change (see **democracy; politics**). With this in mind, one can say that trade unions have significantly broadened their scope and purposes, becoming more similar to social movements (see **new social movements**) and **non-governmental organizations (NGOs)**.

Globalization and the intensification of foreign investment have resulted first in a crisis and gradually in a redefinition of the role of trade unions. As trade unions and collective bargaining systems are organized on a national basis, global economic integration has often reduced the effectiveness of trade union action, as mobile international capital can take advantage of variations in labor standards and wages. In addition, governments have tended to adjust labor legislation in order to attract **foreign direct investment**. The growth of the **urban informal sector** in developing countries also means that the traditional constituency of trade unions, workers with full-time contracts in the formal sector, has eroded and that trade unions have to broaden the demands they represent and increase their attractiveness for unemployed workers, workers in the informal sector, women and ethnic minorities. Trade union responses to

the challenges of globalization also vary, with some trade unions improving service provision to workers in order to attract more members, and others establishing links with NGOs and social movements, often combined with a strategy to internationalize trade union and labor rights campaigns.

See also: casualization of work; foreign direct investment; International Labor Organization (ILO); labor markets; labor rights and standards; solidarity campaigns

Further reading

Jose, A. (ed.) (2002) *Organized Labour in the 21st Century*, Geneva: International Institute for Labour Studies.

Harrod, J. and O'Brien, R. (eds) (2002) *Global Unions? Theory and Strategies of Organized Labour in the Global Political Economy*, London: Routledge.

MARIEKE RIETHOF

TRANSITIONAL ECONOMIES *see* market socialism; postsocialism; shock therapy

transmigration

Transmigration (or *Transmigrasi*) was a major program of state-sponsored (see **state and state reform**) **resettlement** of poor families from the densely populated central Indonesian islands of Java, Bali and Lombok to the larger and less populated territories of Sumatra, Kalimantan and Irian Jaya in the outer islands of Indonesia. Although forms of it existed before, the official Transmigration scheme started in 1969, and – supported by the **World Bank** – reached its peak between 1979 and 1984, with a total **migration** of 1,860,930 individuals for that five-year period. The Indonesian President Sukarno in the 1960s described Transmigration as "a matter of life and death for the Indonesian people" because it aimed to displace very high rates of **population** growth in some areas, and induce **economic growth** in the outer islands. In 1985, some agricultural areas in

Java had population densities of more than 1,000 people per square kilometer compared with similar figures of 69 for Sumatra, 14 for Kalimantan and 3 for Irian Jaya. Critics, however, claimed that Transmigration could in no way offset the large population inequalities, and that it was partly inspired by a desire to create national unity within the vast territory of Indonesia by placing Javanese people in outer islands. Transmigration was also blamed for accelerating **deforestation**, and for displacing local peoples. It is now generally seen as a case of insensitive top-down state planning associated with modernization (see **modernization theory**).

See also: displacement; migration; modernization theory; resettlement

TIM FORSYTH

transnational capitalist class (TCC)

The concept of the transnational capitalist class (TCC) refers to an international elite of business entrepreneurs (see **elites**) that also represent a willing alliance between capitalists in both rich and poor countries. The concept is controversial. The concept of class, let alone TCC, is commonly seen as deeply problematic for the analysis of developing world societies (see **sociology of development**). Most conceptual and/or empirical studies of the capitalist class focus on indigenous petty or small-scale capitalists, on the one hand, or the incursions of foreign capital on the other. The idea that indigenous capitalists from developing countries could possibly be allied with capitalists from the rich industrialized countries on any but the most dependent terms is of very recent origin.

The idea of an international bourgeoisie has been part of Marxist and neo-Marxist theory for some time (see **Marxism**), and capitalists from developing countries in this theoretical tradition have been conceptualized largely as part of a comprador class. The concept of the TCC parallels the radical critique of capitalist **globalization**, and though its roots are certainly Marx-inspired it

distances itself from the neo-Marxist dependency tradition. While the international bourgeoisie tends to be conceptualized in state-centrist terms and to focus mainly on business leaders, the TCC is global in scope and, for some researchers, includes groups in addition to business leaders who also directly serve the interests of global **capitalism**. The concept is anticipated by several authors, notably in Robert Cox's thesis on the emergence of a global class structure and in the work of Stephen Gill on the Trilateral Commission, where he identifies a "developing transnational capitalist class fraction."

The TCC class plays a central role in Sklair's theory of the capitalist global system, where it is the characteristic institutional form of political transnational practices in the global capitalist system (paralleling the role of **transnational corporations (TNCs)** in the economic sphere and consumerism in the culture-ideology sphere). In this formulation the TCC is analytically divided into four main fractions: those who own and control the major transnational corporations and their local affiliates (the corporate fraction); globalizing bureaucrats and politicians (the state fraction) (see **state and state reform**); globalizing professionals (the technical fraction); and merchants and **media** (the consumerist fraction).

As Sklair and Robbins have demonstrated in their research on major TNCs domiciled in developing countries, based on a longitudinal analysis of the *Fortune* Global 500, well over one hundred corporations from developing countries have appeared in lists of the world's biggest companies by revenues (see **transnational corporations (TNCs) from developing economies**). These range from state-owned oil (see **oil and gas development**) and energy (see **energy policy**) conglomerates to banks, **telecommunications** and electronics corporations from China to Brazil, from South Korea to Mexico, from India to Venezuela. These corporations and their affiliates provide many local and some global members of the TCC.

While most theory and research on class continues to be state-centrist, focusing largely on classes within specific countries, the growing influence of globalization in the study of development appears to be encouraging more scholars to work in the global as well as the local context. In such an environment, increased interest in concepts like the transnational capitalist class is to be expected.

See also: capitalism; elites; globalization; intermediate classes; Marxism; sociology of development; transnational corporations (TNCs); transnational corporations (TNCs) from developing economies

Further reading

Carroll, W. and Carson, C. (2002) "The Network of Global Corporations and Elite Policy Groups: A Structure for Transnational Capitalist Class Formation," *Global Networks* 3:1 29–58.

Sklair, L. (2001) *The Transnational Capitalist Class*, Oxford: Blackwell.

Sklair, L. and Robbins, P. (2002) "Global Capitalism and Major Corporations from the Third World," *Third World Quarterly* 23:1 81–100.

LESLIE SKLAIR

transnational corporations (TNCs)

A transnational corporation (TNC) is a business that has its headquarters in one country and various operations in one or more other countries. The terms "multinational corporation," "international corporation," and "multinational enterprise" are often used interchangeably with TNC or may be given more specific definitions specifying the types of operations involved. Classically, TNCs were generally considered to be companies with headquarters in developed countries, although the **newly industrialized economies (NIEs)** and some oil producing states are now home to TNCs (see **transnational corporations (TNCs) from developing economies**). TNCs do most of their business with other developed countries, but about 20 percent of TNC activity is with the developing world and it is here that their impact is most felt.

Transnationals during the capitalist era may be traced to trading companies in the sixteenth century that brought goods back to Europe from various colonial areas. The industrial revolution increased the need for raw materials, and early TNCs were involved in **agriculture, mineral-led development** and shipping. A desire to convert resource areas into new markets for manufactured goods generated a further expansion of TNCs. The saturation of the home market increased an interest in overseas sales. The internationalization of one company often drove its competitors to internationalize also in order to maintain market share.

The development of instantaneous telecommunications and the significant reduction in transportation costs due to containerization made the international expansion of production possible, and in the last half of the twentieth century TNCs became increasingly associated with overseas manufacturing operations. As manufacturers internationalized, so too did companies providing a wide range of financial, legal, accounting, advertising and management services. Developing countries with well-educated populations were able to obtain back-office businesses related to data entry activities. **Tourism** is the other major industry that is dominated by TNCs and by alliances of such companies, such as the airline group Star Alliance.

Many TNCs are now involved more in the organizing and coordinating of production rather than the actual production itself. Figures for the current number of TNCs range from 37,000 to 50,000. While companies such as Ford, McDonalds and IBM quickly come to mind, the majority of TNCs are small and employ less than 250 people. Small TNCs often use specialized niche marketing, flexibility and ingenuity to outperform the larger well-known companies. TNCs often work through affiliated companies of which there are an estimated 200,000. Collectively the TNCs hold about 40 percent of all private-sector assets and produce about a third of all of the goods produced for market economies. TNCs control about 75 percent of all world trade in commodities, manufactured goods and services. About one third of all activities are intra-firm movements. Globally, TNCs employ about 4 percent of the workforce and in developing countries, about 12 percent (UNRISD, 1995; UNCTAD, 1999).

Most TNCs begin as exporting firms. If they are successful, they open sales units overseas. Increased access to regional markets may be obtained by moving production facilities to other countries. TNCs may begin sourcing their finished products from a number of different countries. The ultimate TNC views the world as both global production site and market, and organizes its operations in such a way as to maximize its global profits.

There are many reasons why a company might decide to become international in scope. Companies want to maximize profits, and this requires either reducing costs or increasing revenues. The evasion of **trade unions**, and access to large numbers of low-paid workers is often given as a main reason for the transfer of operations to the developing world. A circuit board designer in India may earn as little as 10 percent of the income of a person with the same job in California.

The traditional economic reasons for location, such as access to raw materials or semi-processed goods, are still important for some companies. Lower costs for land acquisition may also be a factor. Avoidance of government regulations, including working standards and environmental controls, may also attract some firms (see **pollution havens**). The ability to avoid various income taxes is another possible consideration. Vertically integrated TNCs (where production, distribution and marketing are all owned by one company) can adjust product prices to transfer profits to the country with the lowest tax rates.

On the revenue side, establishing operations in a developing country may provide access to local or regional markets with the avoidance of trade barriers such as **tariffs** and quotas. Countries such as Mexico, Brazil, India and China contain large untapped markets for a wide range of goods, and being the first company in the area creates an early monopoly position and an economic advantage over competitors.

As the countries of the developing world gained their independence, they saw **industrialization** as the road to prosperity but they lacked the factors of production. TNCs were attractive to these countries because they could provide the necessary requirements for development. The TNC would provide capital for the construction of factories, it would bring with it the technology required to enter the modern world. It would provide jobs for both skilled and unskilled workers, provide opportunities for the development of managerial

skills, and would relieve the pressures from **rural-urban migration**. The TNC would also increase tax revenues and personal savings, providing investment money for the construction of infrastructure. The TNC also provides access to markets, thus increasing exports and assisting in the paying down of debts. The TNC might also encourage industries and bring previously unavailable goods into local markets.

Clearly, advantages existed for both the TNC and the host nation, and a symbiotic relationship seemed possible. In reality, what was best for the TNC might not be what was best for national development. In the 1970s, it became common to describe TNCs as exploitive giants who could be socially disruptive and hurt local industries. However, many observers maintain that TNCs are not intrinsically harmful or beneficial. Today, TNCs still carry a lot of negative baggage with them. In part, this is due to the way the early TNCs operated, and in part it is based on fear of what they could do if they wanted.

One of the main problems with TNCs is that they often do not deliver what they seem to promise. TNCs are prepared to bring in capital but they are also interested in protecting their investments. They are attracted to countries with stable governments; where they can develop trust and acceptance; where start-up costs will be minimized (such as by the availability of existing infrastructure); and where they will be able to access local suppliers and labor. In these areas they are prepared to provide **foreign direct investment** (FDI). If the risk is felt to be higher, the TNC will opt for franchise operations, **joint venture**s or partnerships where their financial commitment is limited (see **build-operate-transfer (BOT) projects**). Some countries cannot attract TNCs at all. Among the developing countries receiving FDI, five received 55 percent of the total while the forty-eight least developed countries received less than 1 percent (UNCTAD, 1999). This figure does not measure other kinds of arrangements, for example where locally owned firms are contracted to produce products. Such arrangements may be more important than FDI in both the total development picture and the degree of TNC influence in it.

Critics also claim there is usually a very small **technology transfer** to the host country, and it is often specific to the TNC's operations. Technology is often a step behind the leading edge, although a few countries with well-educated workers have moved into research and development operations. This may provide opportunities for local industries to capture markets from TNCs, as happened with the South Korean shipbuilding industry.

Some TNCs will want unskilled labor that they can train for specific jobs while others will want skilled laborers, but managerial skills are limited to the operation of local factories, at best, as business decisions are made elsewhere. **Capital intensive** operations create few jobs.

TNCs are often associated with sweatshops and poor working conditions, but in many places, although wages are low by developed world standards they are higher than what local employers pay. Many TNCs have given in to consumer pressure in the developed world markets to ensure working conditions in developed world factories are acceptable. TNCs have a reputation for hiring young, single, females, based on a **gender** stereotype that they are more dexterous, accurate and less likely to protest even when paid lower wages (see **gender and industrialization**). This has not always proved to be true. In some cases, TNCs have disrupted local societies and cultures. Young women who go to work in factories leave the village (see **villages**) and often are not welcome when they want to return because of the changes in lifestyle that they have adopted, and because they are beyond the customary age of marriage.

TNCs do not seem to be a basis for indigenous **industrialization**. The manufacturing process may produce little in the way of value-added, as most of the profit is in the retail end, attached to the use of a brand name. Industrialization is limited to a very small area. Most factories are in port cities or in **export processing zones (EPZs)** where revenues for the host government are limited by agreements that allow profits to be repatriated to the home country. TNCs that sell into the local market may put locally owned industries out of business. However, the use of local suppliers may improve the quality of the products being made locally.

Industrialization is further complicated because too many developing countries are attempting to produce the same goods, making it impossible for them to trade with their neighbors and creating a surplus on the world market. Indeed, in some cases the global demand for products such as **iron and steel** or **textiles** is decreasing.

It is often argued that TNCs are footloose in nature (i.e. not linked to any specific geographical location) and hence may close down, leaving a large unemployed industrial workforce (see **unemployment**). If the TNC relies on local suppliers and has developed a specialized, skilled workforce, it will develop a considerable amount of inertia. As companies become more global in their ownership and management, they become less loyal to a home country and more loyal to their shareholders. This makes them less likely to close down profitable operations in a developing country just because overall business has declined. Similarly, the common contention that all TNCs are environmental polluters does not necessarily match their diverse nature, or evidence that shows that many **state-owned enterprises (SOEs)** or locally owned industries are far dirtier then TNCs.

It is also claimed that TNCs have a one-sided power relationship with developing countries. However, as the number of TNCs increases, those developing countries that can attract companies have more choice as to which ones they will invite in, and as their economies mature, they have a better ability to negotiate terms for the entrance of a TNC.

It is often argued that largely because of the operation of TNCs, a set of global consumptive preferences has developed in **food**, clothing and entertainment activities. This has created a global landscape of shops, restaurants and service stations. It seems that Western culture has invaded nearly every part of the world (see **globalization and culture**). Conversely, only certain locations can attract TNC production facilities; therefore, TNCs have also had the effect of increasing the differences between places, especially where income levels are concerned. This has happened both between nations and within nations. Whether for better or worse, TNCs are major agents of change in the developing world. The growing field of **corporate social responsibility (CSR)** is now an attempt to ensure such impacts are positive.

See also: build-operate-transfer (BOT) projects; capitalism; corporate social responsibility (CSR);

economic development; Fordism versus Toyota-ism; foreign direct investment; industrialization; joint venture; technology transfer; transnational capitalist class (TCC); transnational corporations (TNCs) from developing economies

Further reading

Doz, Y. and Hamel, G. (1998) *Alliance Advantage*, Boston MA: HBS Press.

Dunning, J. (ed.) (1997) *Governments, Globalization and International Business*, Oxford: Oxford University Press.

Swann, G., Prevezer, M. and Stuart, D. (eds) (1998) *The Dynamics of Industrial Clustering*, Oxford: Oxford University Press.

UNCTAD (1999) *World Investment Report*, New York: United Nations.

UNDP (1998) *Globalization and Liberalization*, New York: United Nations.

UNRISD (1995) *State of Disarray*, Geneva: United Nations.

WILLIAM R. HORNE

transnational corporations (TNCs) from developing economies

Transnational corporations (TNCs) refer to business firms that own and control at least one operation outside their countries of origin. The existence of TNCs from developing economies can be dated back to the late nineteenth century. Their proliferation and internationalization, however, mirror the recent **economic development** of their economies of origin. As their home economies develop over time, these business firms can no longer find sufficient domestic markets to sustain their corporate growth and development. Their expansion into foreign countries is therefore an inevitable outcome of pursing a market-seeking strategy.

Not all TNCs from developing economies emerge from this market-seeking strategy. The pull factor can sometimes be significant enough to attract business firms from developing economies to invest abroad. Very often, access to foreign technology and proprietary knowledge serves as a critical pull factor. For example, high-tech firms from such **newly industrialized economies (NIEs)** as Taiwan and South Korea have invested heavily in the USA and some European countries in order to develop technological capabilities (see **technological capability**) of their home economies and to get better access to host market and product intelligence. This **globalization** strategy of TNCs from developing economies has been known as strategic asset-seeking, in that technology and market know-how are conceived as key strategic assets in global competition.

Still, many TNCs from developing economies are in either natural resource-seeking industries (e.g. mining, oil and plantations – see **natural resources; mineral-led development; oil and gas development; plantation forestry**) or service-oriented industries (e.g. property development, hotel, retailing and trading). The internationalization of resource-seeking TNCs from developing economies can be explained by the geographical location of these natural resources. Service-oriented TNCs from developing economies, on the other hand, are often driven by such considerations as market opportunities and social networks. Both groups of TNCs often invest in nearby developing economies within the same home region, due to similar cultural and historical conditions and levels of economic development. Consequently, Latin American TNCs often tend to operate mostly within Latin America and East Asian firms within Asia.

TNCs from developing economies pose as both collaborators and competitors to global corporations from advanced industrialized economies. Indeed, many firms from developing economies internationalize to become TNCs primarily because they serve as subcontractors and/or suppliers in the global production networks orchestrated by large global corporations. As these global corporations are penetrating into emerging markets, they demand their suppliers and subcontractors to follow them to the host economies. Moreover, some TNCs from developing economies are facing increasing cost pressures as the income and wages in their home economies rise over time. Since lower cost of production is their major competitive advantage against global corporations, these TNCs do relocate their production facilities to nearby developing economies to reduce cost pressures. The internationalization of TNCs from the Asian NIEs into China since the 1980s is a good example of such a cost-driven form of **foreign direct investment**.

See also: auto industry; economic development; Fordism versus Toyotaism; foreign direct investment; iron and steel; joint venture; newly industrialized economies (NIEs); small and medium enterprises (SMEs); transnational corporations (TNCs)

Further reading

Mathews, J. (2002) *Dragon Multinational: A New Model for Global Growth*, Oxford: Oxford University Press.

Yeung, H. Wai-chung (ed.) (1999) *The Globalisation of Business Firms from Emerging Economies*, 2 vols, Cheltenham: Edward Elgar.

Yeung, H. Wai-chung (2002) *Entrepreneurship and the Internationalisation of Asian Firms: An Institutional Perspective*, Cheltenham: Edward Elgar.

HENRY WAI-CHUNG YEUNG

transparency

Transparency is the degree to which information about a particular fact, activity or policy is made available to an interested party. It is a term used in many fields, including **corruption**, disarmament and arms control, **economic development**, environmental protection, financial markets, **governance**, **international organizations and associations**, political economy, regulation, and **trade**. Official transparency can be defined as a measure of the degree to which the policies, actions and functions of governments or intergovernmental organizations (IGOs) are open to public scrutiny and meaningful review. Thus, open meeting acts, freedom of information acts, and publication of judicial opinions and draft regulations are all acts of official transparency. If all information has a cost of acquisition, then policies of official transparency lower the public's acquisition costs for official information.

Transparency has many forms. What is common is that each provides the government or IGO with a duty to disclose information to those in a position to value it. Within the **World Trade Organization/General Agreement on Tariffs and Trade (WTO/GATT)**, one example is the emphasis on urging signatories to convert all their non-tariff barriers into equivalent **tariffs**, which are clearer in their economic impact and are more easily negotiated down. Verification procedures in arms control treaties abound with transparency provisions, which also serve as confidence-building measures because of the atmosphere of openness transparency fosters. WTO/GATT open bidding requirements in government procurement are transparency obligations.

Policies of official transparency provide substantial development benefits. There is an inverse relationship between **corruption** and transparency, documented by the NGO Transparency International's *Global Corruption Report* (see **non-governmental organizations (NGOs)**). Without transparency, official discretion is unbounded and officials are able to exact rents from parties needing government favor or permission. Likewise, strong evidence has accumulated that transparency in law and governance contributes to the development of the rule of law and of political **accountability**. Such issues have implications for **media**, **politics**, **domestic law** and **freedom of association**.

Empirical evidence, as from the **Asian crises** of the 1990s, demonstrates that international investment patterns are closely related to lack of information and transparency. In the absence of strong information, both **foreign direct investment** and foreign portfolio investment tend to follow herd-like patterns, as investors seek safety and derive secondary information from the investment patterns of others. This results in suboptimal allocation of investment resources, and in rapid collective reaction when additional (especially negative) market information becomes available. The consequences for regional development are well documented.

See also: accountability; corporate social responsibility (CSR); governance; politics; Right to Information Movement; state and state reform

Further reading

Cross, C., Clark, C. and Bekker, S. (1995) *Coming Clean: Creating Transparency in Development Funding in South Africa*, Durban: Indicator Press.

Mock, W. (2000) "An Interdisciplinary Introduction to Legal Transparency: A Tool for Rational Development," *Dickinson Journal of International Law* 18:2 293–304.

Transperancy International: http://www.transperancy.org

WILLIAM B. T. MOCK

transport policy

Transport is an integral cause and effect of development. It is also characterized by an immense variation of types, costs, and impacts within different transport systems. Much discussion of development projects focus on high-impact, high-cost forms of transport that can revolutionize access to remote areas, or improve congestion in cities – such as building airports, roads and railways. But many chronically poor people are dependent on walking, bicycles, or animal-drawn means of transport. Upgrading traditional transport, however, is impeded by the difficulty of recovering the costs of investment in poor areas, and by the shortage of state funds (see **state and state reform**). A further problem is the inheritance of colonial transport systems that may not serve current needs. Linking transport development to **poverty** alleviation also depends on increasing access to transport, which may require attention to social and economic factors as well as the construction of infrastructure.

Much debate about transport considers the purpose and proposed users of different options. Much large-scale transport construction in developing countries was conducted during colonialism (see **colonialism, history of; colonialism, impacts of**), and frequently aimed to enhance the export of agricultural or mineral products, or to achieve military **security**. For example, railway networks in Latin America and Africa were initially built to connect agricultural or mineral production regions with seaports. Settlements grew up around the "lines of rail," but they also contributed to **urbanization** in the ports, and did not integrate regions in the hinterland. This problem was addressed to some extent in China after the **revolution** in 1949, when the state deliberately built railway lines connecting regions within the national interior, rather than from the interior to the coast. In Africa, railway gauges frequently differed between previously French- and British-occupied countries as a strategy to deter potential invasion. Since independence, these different gauges make cross-national transport and **trade** difficult without new investment. In India, there were four main gauges used and fifty-two breaks of gauge between different networks (although occasionally different gauges reflected the need for smaller wheelbases in mountainous areas). Also, much colonial transport infrastructure was of a cheap quality, which has required further investment for maintenance. A newer dilemma includes the construction of airports for **tourism** development rather than for local users. In some locations such as Tahiti in the South Pacific, the construction of airports large enough for Boeing 747s has been criticized for prioritizing outsiders' interests before local residents, and for creating further pressure on transport systems in the island. Construction of airports or major roads also creates environmental disruptions.

Other aspects of transport **planning** have been controversial, especially when they reflect the desire of the state to introduce rapid modernization (see **modernization theory**) to remote regions and peoples. Brazil, for example, attracted controversy when – following the construction of its new capital city, Brasilia from the 1920s in the center of the country – it completed a highway to the Amazonian town of Belem in 1964. Between 1960 and 1970, the population living on the highway rose from 100,000 to 2 million, the number of settlements grew from 10 to 120; and the number of side roads increased from none to 2,300km. A further Transamazonia highway was started in the 1970s from Recife on the Brazilian northeastern coast to Peru, where a 20km zone on either side of the road was divided into 100ha lots for **agriculture**. These roads were criticized for enhancing **deforestation**; bringing socially damaging change to **indigenous peoples**; and for encouraging side roads that reflected the geometry of the agricultural plots, rather than actual terrain (see also **Polonoreste**). In Guatemala, the Atlantic Highway has been called an example of poor planning because it added little additional value to a pre-existing railway on this route, and because the road was poorly maintained after construction (Hilling, 1996:176). State-led transport planning may also increase access. In India, the government in 1943 authorized that all states would assess their own road requirements, and that no village would be more than 3.2km from a road. This has still to be achieved in some remote or hilly regions. Sometimes lack of state funding creates further problems. In 1994, the **United Nations** estimated that US$12 billion spent on maintaining road systems in Africa during the 1980s would have saved later repair work of US$45 billion (Vasconcellos, 2001:232).

Much transport expansion since World War II, however, has been dominated by the private sector, and by the purchase of private transport, rather than reliance on public transport. In the 1990s, much transport policy, and **World Bank** involvement in transport infrastructure, sought to champion private-sector investment and expanding the role of competitive markets in transport services. Private ownership of transport such as cars has been both a status symbol and an indicator of high levels of consumption. But the rapid growth of car and motorcycle ownership has also increased traffic accidents, with greater risks for non-car owners (pedestrians) in low-income countries. Statistics show that in the USA (in 1995) and Australia (1990) fatalities arising from traffic accidents were 13 and 18 percent for pedestrians, and 79 and 65 percent for people in four-wheeled vehicles. But in Delhi (in 1994) and Nairobi (1977–94), pedestrians accounted for 42 and 65 percent, and four-wheeled occupants 12 and 30 percent (Vasconcellos, 2001:199). Public transport has, in many cities, been underfunded and bureaucratic. Advertising from car manufacturers has also tended to represent public transport as socially undesirable. In many cities, "intermediate" means of transport have evolved using minibuses and auto rickshaws owned by cooperatives or individuals: these include the "bemos" of Indonesia; the "si-lors" and "tuk tuks" of Thailand; the "jeepneys" of the Philippines; the

"porpuestos" of Venezuala; and the "bakassi" of Sudan.

Access to transport systems is one of the key indicators of their contribution to development. Mobility is the measurement of the number of trips made each day by individuals, and evidence suggests this rises with income. Evidence, however, indicates that women often carry a heavier burden than men in terms of time and effort spent on transport, and have less power to influence the evolution or purpose of transport systems (Fernando and Porter, 2002). In India, for example, cultural factors may place restrictions on how, and with whom, women may travel. In eastern and northern Uganda, for example, women may travel by bicycle, but in central Uganda, men dominate bicycle travel. Household allocations of duties may also influence who has to undertake which tasks of transport. Access to transport also affects access to **health** care, **education**, and **labor markets**. A further concern about transport development is its impact on **environment** and **pollution**. Some **municipalities**, such as in Brazil and India, have ensured that public buses used compressed natural gas rather than diesel oil. Hydrogen cells have also been introduced in buses in Beijing. Unrestricted gasoline or diesel use adds pollutants such as carbon dioxide (CO_2), carbon monoxide (CO), sulfur dioxide (SO_2) and nitrogen oxides (NO, NO_2) into the atmosphere, thus making transport relevant to both local environmental policy and **climate change**.

Policy analysts suggest that transport planning needs to be made more integrated and inclusive: **gender** has to be considered; as must the needs of the disabled (see **disability**); and all road users should be consulted. Planners should not just build highways, but sidewalks (pavements), with well-marked intersections and crossings. Vasconcellos (2001:244) proposes that transport development should include the four principles of **accountability**; social progressiveness (i.e. advancement of social objectives); equity (consideration of safety and potential disadvantages); and environmental sustainability. But history has shown that transport systems follow trends of **economic development**, and the requirements of those who pay for them. Seeking inclusive transport policy may be similar to other developmental objectives of participatory governance and **transparency** in other aspects of planning.

See also: auto industry; disability; energy policy; planning; public-private partnerships; urban development

Further reading

Fernando, P. and Porter, G. (eds) (2002) *Balancing the Load: Women, Gender and Transport*, London: Zed.

Hilling, D. (1996) *Transport and Developing Countries*, London: Routledge.

Vasconcellos, E. (2001) *Urban Transport, Environment and Equity: The Case for Developing Countries*, London: Earthscan.

Whitelegg, J. and Haq, G. (eds) (2003) *The Earthscan Reader on World Transport Policy and Practice*, London: Earthscan.

World Bank (1996) *Sustainable Transport: Priorities for Policy Reform*, Washington DC: World Bank.

TIM FORSYTH AND JEFF TURNER

trickle down

"Trickle down" refers to the notion that markets autonomously engender redistribution of benefits of **economic growth** from the rich to the poor. Its merit derives from the supposed efficiency of market-based allocation and distribution mechanisms, and it was a key assumption of **modernization theory**, or the **stages of economic growth** model. Growing income disparities in developing countries in 1970s raised pessimism about the assumption that the trickle down effects of economic growth are a sufficient condition for alleviating **poverty** in these countries, and that instead a variety of barriers exist for wealth to trickle down to poorer people. Poverty reduction demands purposive and holistic interventions to countervail the processes that perpetuate deprivation; this constitutes the test for trickle down theory. Hence, development cooperation has shifted from pursuit of economic growth *per se* to promotion of **economic development**, and hence to more inclusive forms of **social development** and

human development (see **growth versus holism**). There is renewed emphasis on **participatory development**, **aidtargeting** and **redistribution with growth** policies. At the micro level, social indicators have been incorporated in cost-benefit analyses (see **cost-benefit analysis (CBA)**) of **aid** supported projects in order to ensure they instill equitable distribution of benefits.

See also: modernization theory; poverty; redistribution with growth; social exclusion; stages of economic growth

MOSES A. OSIRO

triple bottom line

The triple bottom line is a new approach to financial accounting that aims to reflect environmental and social aspects of a firm or country's performance as well as the financial "bottom line" of profit and loss. In effect, this means developing criteria for assessing performance in social and environmental terms and then publishing these alongside financial results. In principle, the triple bottom line is an innovative way to start measuring and evaluating different companies' or countries' **economic growth** in a more holistic, comparative and transferable manner (see **corporate social responsibility (CSR); growth versus holism**). In practice, however, there is still great controversy about how environmentally- or socially-responsible actions can be evaluated in neutral or comparable terms, and concerning who should set such yardsticks.

See also: corporate social responsibility (CSR); growth versus holism; participatory budgeting

Further reading

MacGillivray, A. and Zadek, S. (1995) *Accounting for Change*, London: New Economics Foundation.

Norman, W. and MacDonald, C. (2003) "Getting to the Bottom of 'Triple Bottom Line'," *Business Ethics Quarterly* 14:2 243–62.

TIM FORSYTH

Truman's Bold New Program (1949)

President Harry S. Truman declared his "Bold New Program" for the developing world in his inauguration speech of 20 January 1949. The program was part of a wider strategic doctrine that set out to establish the USA's post-World War II ambitions. Some writers, such as Wolfgang Sachs, have claimed that it represented the birth of development theory and practice. In his address Truman declared:

> We must embark on a bold new program for making the benefits of our scientific advances and industrial progress available for the improvement and growth of underdeveloped areas. The old imperialism – exploitation for foreign profit – has no place in our plans. What we envisage is a program of development based on the concepts of democratic fair dealing.

Truman's reference to the "underdeveloped world" (see **underdevelopment versus less developed country (LDC) versus Third World**) was most significant at the time in establishing a distinction between rich and poor countries based on levels of income. Subsequently the Bold New Program has been criticized as creating binary categorizations in the post-war period and establishing a strategic dependency of the developing world on Western **aid** and "expertise." Others, though, place a lesser emphasis on Truman's influence on contemporary development praxis.

See also: dependency theory; modernization theory; underdevelopment versus less developed country (LDC) versus Third World

DONOVAN STOREY

trusteeship

The concept of trusteeship refers to the act of taking responsibility for world development (see Cowen and Shenton, 1996). Trusteeship is explained as being at the heart of nineteenth-century development thought and later under colonialism (see **colonialism, history of; colonialism, impacts of**) and **postcolonialism**. It provided the bridge between disorderly immanent development, and intentional orderly development in times of chaotic change, especially that wrought by unbridled **capitalism**. Through trusteeship, which came to be principally guided by the state (see **state and state reform**), development was entrusted to actors who saw themselves as developed and who believed they could act to determine the process of development for others deemed less-developed. Thus, trusteeship established essentially positivist conservative doctrines that were counterpoints to progress and change in indigenous societies. It may be argued that trusteeship as a principle and practice did not end with formal colonialism, and still plays an important part in contemporary forms of development policy and thought.

See also: colonialism, history of; colonialism, impacts of; power and discourse

Further reading

Cowen, M. and Shenton, R. (1996) *Doctrines of Development*, London: Routledge.

DONOVAN STOREY

tuberculosis

Tuberculosis (TB) is a significant public **health** problem and one of the leading global causes of adult **mortality**. It is estimated that one third of the world's population (approximately 2,200 million people) are infected with *Mycobacterium tuberculosis*, the bacterium that causes TB. However, each infected individual only has a 10 percent lifetime risk of developing the disease (if they are not HIV infected). The presence of HIV/AIDS infection is a strong risk factor for the progression of latent TB infection to active disease (see **HIV/AIDS (definition and treatment)**). Over 10 million people are estimated to be co-infected with TB and HIV. This has contributed to the number of TB cases doubling or even trebling in some African countries over the past decade.

TB disproportionately affects the poor. In 2001, 98 percent of the 2 million annual TB deaths and

95 percent of the 8.4 million new TB cases occurred in developing countries. Within countries, there is also evidence that the prevalence of TB is higher among the poor, and other vulnerable groups, such as minority ethnic groups and homeless people.

The **World Health Organization (WHO)**'s recommended treatment strategy for detection and cure of TB is Directly Observed Treatment Short Course (DOTS), which has been promoted on a global scale since 1993. DOTS combines five elements: political commitment; microscopy services; drug supplies; surveillance and monitoring systems; and use of highly efficacious regimes with direct observation of treatment. Once patients with infectious TB have been identified using microscopy services, health and **community** workers, trained volunteers, and in some cases family members, directly observe patients swallowing the full course of the correct dosage of anti-TB medicines. Direct observation is intended to enhance compliance with a long and difficult treatment process that involves taking many drugs, which often have side effects, over a 6–8 month period.

Key challenges in TB control involve increasing case detection (the number of people diagnosed with TB) and improving treatment outcomes (increasing the number of people who successfully complete TB treatment and are cured of TB). Ensuring quality health services and diagnostic procedures is therefore critical to improving TB control. This needs to be coupled with a consideration of the different barriers patients may face in accessing and adhering to TB treatment, including financial and opportunity costs and the stigma associated with TB. Difficulties in negotiating these barriers may be particularly acute for some groups, such as poor women in developing countries. Thus, **poverty** is perpetuated and development hindered. Strategies under discussion to improve case detection and treatment outcomes include incentive schemes to encourage people suffering from TB to access diagnosis and treatment services, and **partnerships** between the public sector and private and traditional providers.

See also: health; disease eradication; disease, social constructions of; HIV/AIDS (definition and treatment); HIV/AIDS (policy issues)

Further reading

Nair, D., George, A. and Chacko, K. (1997) "Tuberculosis in Bombay: New Insights from Poor Urban Patients," *Health Policy and Planning* 12:1 77–85.

World Health Organisation (2002) *The Global Plan to Stop Tuberculosis*, Stop TB Partnership, Geneva: WHO.

SALLY THEOBALD, RACHEL TOLHURST AND
BERTEL S. SQUIRE

U

UNCLOS *see* United Nations Convention on the Law of the Sea (UNCLOS)

underdevelopment versus less developed country (LDC) versus Third World

The terms "underdeveloped," "LDC" (less developed country), and "Third World," and others, have all been used to describe nations with middle or low national incomes, or which experience classic problems of "development." All of these terms, however, are controversial because they tend to reflect a specific paradigm of development thinking, or a historically specific socio-economic observation of development. Critics have therefore argued that scholars and practitioners of development studies need to be aware of the impacts of using language that has connotations about how other countries and people are seen and classified. Indeed, the choice of words with which we describe people and countries affected by development practice is inherently political.

The term most commonly used at present is "developing world." This term defines **poverty** by class and **vulnerability** regardless of geographic location. It recognizes that development occurs in both wealthy and poor countries (and hence the similar term, "developing countries," overlooks the fact that poor people may live in wealthy countries and vice-versa). "Developing world" is associated with both market-based and international solutions to development, such as

structural adjustment programs and market deregulation.

A number of other terms are also used. The two terms "less developed countries" (LDCs) or "undeveloped countries" have been criticized for reflecting historic views that development is a linear process which will result in an eventual convergence of all countries. These terms are associated with **modernization theory**, or the optimistic belief that investment in **industrialization** and rationalization of markets and social services will eventually result in high-mass consumption and better standards of living. Current development thinking highlights that not all modernization and industrialization strategies lead to these successful outcomes, and that many countries or people remain locked in conditions of poverty because of reasons of political economy. Moreover, arguments from alternative/ postdevelopment (see **postmodernism and postdevelopment**) have suggested that there are many developmental problems in countries with high levels of modernization, and hence it is not always possible to distinguish clearly between countries that are "more" or "less" developed; or those that are "undeveloped."

A term with distinctly different connotations is "underdevelopment." This term reflects the view that participation within the international economy through international **trade** further impoverishes poorer nations because of inherent biases within the international economy. Underdevelopment is used therefore both as a verb and an adjective. This term is associated with **dependency theory**.

Terms that reflect socio-economic/historical observations on middle- or low-income countries are also used. The term "Third World" has changed meaning dramatically since it was first coined in the 1950s. Initially, the "Third World" had three layers of meaning. The first distinguished poor countries as a new international voting bloc with independent interests to Western and socialist countries. Second, it acknowledged that the poor were roughly one third of the world's **population**. And finally, the term, in its French origin, had connotations of the **peasantry**; the third level of pre-French Revolution society. From its origin as a positive term, the Third World has become a derogative term and is now rarely used: indeed, it suggests blanket generalizations about levels of development that are not borne out by cross-national comparisons, or at the scale of individuals or social groups within countries. A variation, the "Two-Thirds World," highlights the increasing number of the world's population living in poverty.

A further growing concept to describe rich/poor or developed/developing world is "North-South." This term reflects the general geographic divide between wealthy and poor countries. With a few exceptions, the majority of the world's poor reside in the Southern Hemisphere, while the majority of the world's wealthy live in the Northern Hemisphere. A variation, the "Global South," is used to indicate all poor people in all countries, who experience **marginalization**, and who may be targeted by development assistance. This latter term acknowledges both the growing diversity in the definition of poverty – from wealth alone to consideration of other factors such as political representation or opportunities – and the appreciation that poverty and developmental needs occur within rich countries too (see **Fourth World**).

Another term to describe the global socio-economic reality is "real/unreal worlds." The "real world" is experienced by the majority of the world's population and is characterized by low income, poor health, shorter **life expectancy** and lack of political freedom. The "unreal world" is experienced by a minority of the world's population and is characterized by over-consumption, longer life expectancy and high income. This term implies that long-term survival or **sustainable development** may involve wealthy countries

changing their lifestyles to more closely resemble that experienced by the majority of the world's population. A similar term to describe this alternative view is "maldevelopment," which highlights the negative effects of **economic growth** and modernization (see **modernization theory**), and may be applied to a variety of rich and poor countries.

The purpose of these controversies over definitions is to be aware of the implications of using classifications that do not acknowledge their implications of how and to whom development is targeted. New discussions will doubtlessly highlight potential problems with existing nomenclature. But remaining critical of how we define development practice is an important way to ensure that it remains relevant.

See also: economic development; Introduction; participatory development; sociology of development

MATTHEW CLARKE

underemployment

Underemployment refers to the condition where workers are employed at less than their full capacity. In many developing countries, most workers do not have access to **unemployment** benefits if they lose their jobs. Some who work for large national or international firms may be covered by benefit schemes, but they form a very small percentage of the labor force. For this reason, the majority cannot afford the luxury of being unemployed and have to have jobs of some kind. The result is that statistics on unemployment for most developing countries remain relatively low even in the depths of major economic recessions (e.g. around 10 percent or less of the work force). In reality, a major feature of the labor markets in most developing countries is not unemployment, but *under*employment.

Underemployment is defined to have two components. First, there is direct underemployment, which is when a worker would like to work more hours than she or he is currently working, but cannot find the extra work. The second component is indirect underemployment (or inadequate employment) and is defined to cover situations in which (a) a worker works long hours, but earns very low pay; or (b) there is an inadequate utilization or mismatch of the occupational skills of the worker, leading to a poor use of **human capital**. Indirect underemployment characterizes the situation of many workers in the **urban informal sector** (UIS), where long hours are worked to obtain a very low pay. For example, during the process of **structural adjustment**, large numbers of workers in **public sector** enterprises were dismissed as these enterprises were prepared for privatization (see **privatization and liberalization**). In many cases, the only option for these workers was to make work for themselves in the UIS, often in activities that did not utilize their professional skills: for example, lawyers working as taxi drivers in Latin American countries.

While both kinds of underemployment may be caused by a lack of effective demand and tackled by general policies to increase aggregate demand (see **fiscal and monetary policy**), underemployment caused by the mismatching of skills with available jobs may need special remedial policies, such as retraining (see **education; skills**).

The definition of underemployment is quite general, so it can exist in developed as well as developing countries. However, the scale of the problem tends to be very different. For example, while about 7 percent of full-time workers in the UK in 2002 were directly underemployed, the rate was about 17 percent in the Philippines in 2001.

See also: employment; International Labor Organization (ILO); labor supply; micro-enterprises; unemployment; urban informal sector; welfare state

Further reading

Dooley, D. and Prause, J. (2004) *The Social Cost of Underemployment*, Cambridge: Cambridge University Press.

Stofferahn, C. (2000) "Underemployment: Social Fact or Socially Constructed Reality?," *Rural Sociology* 65:2 311–30.

JIM THOMAS

UNDP *see* United Nations Development Programme (UNDP)

unemployment

Unemployment refers to the situation where workers who are willing and able to work are unable to find gainful **employment**. It is measured as the percentage of labor force out of work. Institutional and structural factors, as well as the lack of aggregate demand, are the primary causes of unemployment.

Analysis of unemployment and policy prescriptions to reduce it is often carried out in terms of factors affecting the "natural" rate of unemployment and those that determine the deviation of the actual rate from the "natural" rate. The "natural" rate is understood as the average rate of unemployment around which the economy fluctuates or toward which the economy gravitates in the long run. In its classical formulation, or the Kaleckian conceptualization, as the Non-accelerating Inflation Rate of Unemployment (NAIRU), there is a general agreement on the factors affecting it. It is determined by institutional and structural factors. These, in turn, are analyzed under the categories of frictional unemployment, structural unemployment and unemployment due to wage rigidity.

Workers have preferences and abilities, while jobs have their attributes. Unemployment resulting from the time it takes workers to search for work is known as frictional unemployment. Lack of information about job vacancies and impediments to geographical mobility create frictions in **labor markets**. The age and sex composition of workers are also important determinants of frictional unemployment. While women tend to enter and exit the labor force more frequently than men, young workers frequently change jobs (see **child labor; gender and industrialization**). Each such instance is accompanied by a period of frictional unemployment. Hence, the larger the proportion of women and young people in the labor force, the higher frictional unemployment tends to be. Measures that aid the flow of information on available jobs can reduce frictional unemployment. In the specific case of women and young people, policies that enable them to sustain a job (measures such as provision of affordable child care) can also reduce frictional unemployment. Some economists argue that unemployment insurance and benefits, by reducing the cost of unemployment to jobseekers, lower the search effort and hence increase frictional unemployment.

Changing technology renders some skills redundant and increases demand for others. This, in turn, creates unemployment, which has both inter-sectoral and regional dimensions, and is referred to as structural or sectoral unemployment. Policies like the provision of educational facilities, re-training and those that facilitate geographical mobility are usually prescribed to tackle structural unemployment.

Wages are too "high" or rigid when they are above the market clearing levels attainable in a competitive situation. The supply of labor at these "high" wages exceeds the number of jobs employers are willing to offer and is also referred to as "wait unemployment" as firms have to ration the jobs among workers. The presence of minimum wage laws, **trade unions** and the practice of paying "efficiency" wages are cited as the more obvious instances of interference with market forces (demand and supply) causing wage rigidity. While the proponents of minimum wage laws argue that they are necessary to increase the income of the working poor, their critics point out that they prevent the poor from getting jobs and hence job experience and hence ultimately prevent them from getting jobs in the future. Collective bargaining by trade unions is another factor that is said to result in unemployment because unions bargain for higher wages and allow firms to decide the level of employment. The theory of "efficiency" wages argues that firms pay "higher" wages (leading to unemployment) as this improves the overall work effort and the average quality of the workforce. By reducing labor turnover, it also leads to a fall in the expenditure associated with hiring and training of workers, and there are obvious gains to be made by firms following this practice. Thus, government interference and the extent of monopoly in factor and product markets also influence the "natural" rate of unemployment.

Classical macroeconomics and its New Classical variant argue that policies that affect aggregate demand in the economy (see **fiscal and monetary policy**) are ineffective in tackling unemployment. Only under uncertainty, which leads to informational inadequacies, can demand management affect unemployment by influencing output. But this is possible only in the short run, as in the long run economic agents recognize and adjust for incorrect information. The theory of rational expectations negates the latter possibility also. It argues that as rational agents do not repeat mistakes, if demand management policies are used to affect employment, they will start expecting it and adjust their behavior accordingly, thus negating any possibility of reduction in unemployment below the "natural" rate. Keynesian macroeconomists argue that there is room for demand management policies to tackle unemployment, but there has been a long-standing controversy on this subject.

Despite differences, there is a general agreement that under circumstances where informational inadequacies lead to non-market clearing outcomes, policies of demand management have a role to play in reducing unemployment. Economists recognize that demand management policies of the government may influence the "natural" rate itself. For example, by increasing employment temporarily, such policies increase the employability of workers by providing them enhanced work experience. This reduces frictional unemployment and brings down the "natural" rate itself.

See also: computable general equilibrium (CGE) models; economic development; employment; fiscal and monetary policy; labor markets; labor rights and standards; trade unions; underemployment

Further reading

Barro, R. and Grossman, H. (1971) "A General Disequilibrium Model of Income and Unemployment," *American Economic Review* 61: 82–93.

Friedman, M. (1977) "Inflation and Unemployment," *Journal of Political Economy* 85: 451–72.

Hall, R. (1979) "A Theory of the Natural Rate of Unemployment and the Duration of

Unemployment," *Journal of Monetary Economics* 5: 153–69.

Keynes, J. M. (1936) *The General Theory of Employment, Interest and Money*, London: Macmillan.

AJAY RANJAN SINGH

UNESCO *see* United Nations Education, Scientific and Cultural Organization (UNESCO)

UNHCR *see* United Nations High Commissioner for Refugees (UNHCR)

UNICEF *see* United Nations Children's Fund (UNICEF)

United Nations

The United Nations (UN) is the world's premier inter-governmental organization, and has been closely involved with both formulating and implementing international development since the organization's founding in 1945. The chief objective of the UN has been to form a system of international negotiation that may prevent future world wars and promote global development. More expansively, however, it is also a move toward a system of global negotiation and adjudication through the key arenas of conventions and agreements (which different states may or may not choose to ratify); the Security Council (which produces binding commitments on members); and the UN General Assembly (which produces resolutions that are not binding). The UN makes it clear that it is not a "world government" and that all initiatives are with the backing of its member states. But in recent years, some governments – particularly that of the USA – have challenged this statement, and instead have sought to portray the UN as an unnecessary constraint on individual states. The UN has also been criticized for other reasons, including ineffectiveness, wasting resources, and for failing to represent adequately the interests of developing countries; charges that the

UN acknowledges or addresses to varying degrees (see also **Food and Agriculture Organization (FAO); International Labor Organization (ILO); Office of the United Nations High Commissioner for Human Rights (OHCHR); United Nations High Commissioner for Refugees (UNHCR); United Nations Children's Fund (UNICEF); United Nations Development Programme (UNDP); World Food Programme (WFP))**.

The UN's history lies in international attempts to avoid **war**. The chief precursor of the UN was the **League of Nations**, which was established in 1919 after World War I, but which became ineffective during the approach to World War II (e.g. see **world economic conference (London, 1933)**). Discussions for a replacement organization took place during World War II. The term "United Nations" was first used by US President Roosevelt in 1942 to refer to the Allied forces, and in 1944, representatives of China, the Soviet Union, the UK and USA drew up plans for a new organization. The UN was finally established on 24 October 1945 by representatives of fifty countries who signed the United Nations Charter at the United Nations Conference on International Organization in San Francisco (they were later joined by Poland, making it fifty-one countries). The Charter outlined four purposes for the UN: to maintain international peace and **security**; to develop friendly relations among nations; to cooperate in solving international problems and in promoting respect for **human rights**; and to be a center for harmonizing the actions of nations. When states become members of the UN they agree to accept this Charter. In 2002, all 191 formally recognized nation-states were members of the UN.

The different UN bodies

The UN has six main organs.

General Assembly (UNGAS): This is the largest negotiating chamber of the UN, where all UN member states are represented and have a vote each. Discussions focus on key issues such as international peace and **security**, admitting new members, and the UN budget, and matters here are decided by a two-thirds majority of votes. Other matters are decided by majority votes. In recent years, a special effort has been made to reach decisions through consensus rather than by taking a formal vote. UNGAS is the closest to a "parliament of nations" within the UN, and its recommendations are an important indication of world opinion. Resolutions, however, are not legally binding on member states, and hence critics suggest that the greater accession of developing countries to the UN in recent years has meant that richer countries have less influence in shaping resolutions, and hence they are less likely to respect UNGAS resolutions. Moreover, UNGAS controls the budgets for UN specialized agencies administered under the Economic and Social Council, including the specialized agencies most involved with development (e.g. the **United Nations Development Programme (UNDP)**). This control of funding has been claimed to restrict UN development activities because the major donors are reluctant to allocate funds to agencies that they cannot effectively control.

Security Council: This has prime responsibility for maintaining international peace, and is usually associated with decisions affecting the most serious international negotiations. There are fifteen Council members. Five of these – China, France, the Russian Federation, the UK and USA – are permanent members, and essentially represent the victors of World War II. The other ten are elected by UNGAS for two-year terms. Except for procedural issues, decisions cannot be agreed if any permanent member presents a veto. On famous occasions – such as the decision to oust Iraqi forces from Kuwait in 1990 – the Security Council has effectively supported military action by calling on member states to use "all necessary means" to resolve a problem. Critics claim that Security Council membership is too restrictive, and should now reflect other powerful countries that contribute to UN activities (such as Germany, Japan, the Netherlands, Norway and Sweden), or a greater representation of developing countries. Another option is to reduce the number of permanent members.

Economic and Social Council (ECOSOC): This coordinates the economic and social work of the UN, and contributes most immediately to topics in international development. The Council has fifty-four members, elected by UNGAS for three-year terms. This body has the overall authority for programs such as the **United Nations Development Programme (UNDP)** or regional offices (see below). Critics suggest this dependency on UNGAS has resulted in shortage of funding.

Trusteeship Council: This was originally established to supervise the administration of eleven Trust Territories that eventually became self-governed. The last to become so was Palau in the South Pacific (see **small island developing states (SIDS)**). The Trusteeship Council is now composed only of the five permanent members of the Security Council, and may only meet when circumstances dictate. Some observers have suggested that the Trusteeship Council may be used again for countries undergoing post-war changes in leadership.

International Court of Justice (ICJ): This decides disputes between countries, and consists of fifteen judges elected jointly by the General Assembly and the Security Council. The use of the court is voluntary, but if states choose to use it, they are bound by its decisions. The ICJ is based in The Hague.

Secretariat: This carries out the administrative work of the UN, and is headed by the Secretary General, who provides the most visual figurehead for the UN. Duty stations include UN Headquarters in New York, as well as UN offices in Geneva, Vienna, Nairobi and other locations.

In addition to these six bodies, the UN System includes the **International Monetary Fund (IMF)** and **World Bank**; and twelve other independent organizations known as "specialized agencies" are linked to the UN through cooperative agreements. These agencies, among them the **World Health Organization (WHO)** and the **International Labor Organization (ILO)**, are autonomous bodies created by intergovernmental agreement.

UN activities

The UN works to produce treaties on a variety of topics of **international law**; it may sponsor military interventions for **peacekeeping**; and provide advice, research and assistance through its diverse bodies of the UN system.

Disarmament and peacekeeping: The UN has been involved in a variety of treaties linked to disarmament, such as the Nuclear Non-Proliferation Treaty (1968), the Comprehensive Nuclear-Test-Ban Treaty (1996) and treaties establishing nuclear-free zones. Other treaties include the prohibition of the development, production and stockpiling of chemical weapons (1992) or the Ottawa convention outlawing **landmines** (1997). The Vienna-based International Atomic Energy Agency works against the proliferation of nuclear weapons. The Organization for the Prohibition of Chemical Weapons in The Hague similarly restricts chemical weapons.

The UN has worked to defuse various crises that threatened international peace (including the 1962 Cuban Missile Crisis, and the 1973 Arab-Israeli War); and has worked to produce a series of internationally agreed limitations on the activities of terrorists after the attacks on the USA of 11 September 2001. Peacekeeping activities involve a variety of actions, including bringing hostile parties to agreement through diplomatic means, often using the Security Council or the International Court of Justice. The UN supervises elections in zones associated with historic conflict, such as in Namibia (1989), Cambodia (1992–3), or East Timor (1999). Member states may also contribute to military forces – the so-called "Blue Helmets" – that may observe a ceasefire, establish buffer zones during negotiations and clear landmines. For example, the UN acted as peacekeeper on the ceasefire line between India and Pakistan in Jammu and Kashmir in 1949, in Cyprus since 1964, or in Croatia (1992–5). Between 1948 and 2004, there have been fifty-four UN peacekeeping missions, involving contributions from some 123 countries.

Human Rights: The UN (through UNGAS) published the **Universal Declaration of Human Rights (1948)**. The Declaration laid the groundwork for more than eighty further conventions and declarations on human rights, including the **International Covenant on Economic, Social and Cultural Rights** (1966) and the **Convention on the Elimination of All Forms of Discrimination Against Women (CEDAW)** (1979). Others include the **United Nations Convention on the Rights of the Child (1989)**, or other acts concerning **torture**, **refugees**, and

genocide (see **right to development**). The UN Commission on Human Rights (see **Office of the United Nations High Commissioner for Human Rights (OHCHR)**), an intergovernmental body, holds public meetings to review the human rights performance of states, to adopt new standards and to promote human rights around the world.

International Law: The UN Charter urges the UN to develop international law, and it has achieved more than 500 conventions, treaties and standards. States that ratify conventions are legally bound by them. The International Law Commission and UN Commission on International Trade Law prepare laws for discussion, although specific laws are administered by relevant UN bodies. For example, the UN Environment Programme administers international environmental agreements. After the apparent violations of humanitarian law in the former Yugoslavia, the UN in 1993 also adopted means to end impunity for persons accused of war crimes. In 1994, the Council set up a further tribunal to hear cases involving accusations of genocide in Rwanda. In 1998, governments agreed to establish an International Criminal Court, operable from 2002.

Humanitarian Assistance: The UN system supplies **food**, shelter, and medicines for humanitarian crises (see **complex emergencies; humanitarianism**). The UN Office for the Coordination of Humanitarian Affairs raises funds. The UN coordinates its response to humanitarian crises through a committee of all the key humanitarian bodies, chaired by the UN Emergency Relief Coordinator. Members include the **United Nations Children's Fund (UNICEF)**, **United Nations Development Programme (UNDP)**, the **World Food Programme (WFP)** and the UN Refugee Agency (**United Nations High Commissioner for Refugees (UNHCR)**).

Shaping Development Agendas: The UN coordinated the adoption of the **Millennium Development Goals (MDGs)** in 2000 as key priorities in international development concerning the reduction of **poverty**, lack of **education**, **gender** disparities, etc., and addressing HIV/AIDS policy (see **HIV/AIDS (policy issues)**). Programmes and funds under the UN System work under the authority of UNGAS and ECOSOC to carry out the UN's economic and social mandate. One of the main UN achievements during its early years was to establish a system of comparable national accounting, calculating **gross national product (GNP)** and **gross domestic product (GDP)** per country.

Criticisms of the UN

The UN has undoubtedly achieved significant steps in mitigating military conflict, assisting development, and providing forums for international discussion. But to many observers it is also an organization that reduces its potential impact by being overly bureaucratic, wasteful of money, and overly dominated by powerful rich nations. Perhaps most importantly, the opposition of the US administration under President George W. Bush has portrayed the UN as an ineffective and unnecessary delay on actions wished by specific states, particularly concerning the US desire in 2003 to invade Iraq to overthrow Saddam Hussein without waiting for full UN Security Council approval. Some observers have proposed the US policy in this respect was a deliberate attempt to undermine the UN's global authority, and to prevent its ability to constrain individual states in the future. Similar statements have been made by the US unilateral withdrawal (under George W. Bush) from the UN Framework Convention on Climate Change (and its Kyoto Protocol) in 2001 (see **climate change**). In 2002, President Bush also cut off US$34 million in funding from the UN Population Fund, claiming that it supported forced abortions and sterilizations in China. The impact of such acts on the UN is still unclear: on the one hand, UN procedures were undoubtedly bypassed by the US-UK invasion of Iraq in 2003. But on the other hand, the unexpected length of military operations in Iraq forced the USA to reconsider the UN as a potential peacekeeper, thus showing its continued value to the USA.

The UN has also been constrained by its funding arrangements. The UN relies on formally assessed contributions from member states (according to an assessment of what they can pay), and voluntary contributions. Yet, many states (including the USA) have refused to pay their full assessment, partly to encourage reform of the UN. Some reform was achieved in the 1999 Helms-Biden legislation,

which established benchmarks for international organizations (see **international organizations and associations**). In 2003, the USA's arrears to the UN were over US$1.3 billion, of which only some US$600 million has been agreed to be repaid. The history of the UNDP was also affected by the preference of the USA to provide money to the World Bank and IMF largely because donors have greater control over how such funds were spent.

Many critics also like to point out how the UN has become associated with high salaries and lavish facilities in developing countries, which are claimed to clash with the poverty it is trying to fight. The UN adopts a quota system for employment based on nationality, which makes critics fear that UN professionals are not always appointed on grounds of merit. UN bureaucracies remain difficult to reform. The United Nations Environment Programme (UNEP), for example, was established in Nairobi in 1972, but has remained physically distant from other UN agencies, and the establishment of the **Commission on Sustainable Development (CSD)** in 1992 (see **Earth Summit (1992) (United Nations Conference on Environment and Development)**) has been claimed either to undermine or overlap with UNEP. The funding restrictions of ECOSOC have also been claimed to weaken the activities of some UN programs. Other critics have claimed that the initial UN organizations established during the mid-twentieth century to enhance **industrialization** and modernization (see **modernization theory**) (such as UN Conference on Trade and Development, UN Industrial Development Organization and WTO) (see **World Trade Organization/General Agreement on Tariffs and Trade (WTO/GATT)**) may hold greater power than those created to address social and environmental problems (such as UNEP or the United Nations Women's Fund, UNIFEM). Other criticisms refer to the apparent diversity and occasional opposition of different programs within different agencies (e.g. see **United Nations Children's Fund (UNICEF); World Health Organization (WHO)**).

Proponents of the UN claim such criticisms are inevitable for an organization this size and with these ambitions. For all its faults, contradictions and weaknesses, the UN system has achieved many things – not least a limiting of conflict during the

The UNITED NATIONS system

UNITED NATIONS

PRINCIPAL ORGANS OF THE UNITED NATIONS

| INTERNATIONAL COURT OF JUSTICE | SECURITY COUNCIL | GENERAL ASSEMBLY | ECONOMIC AND SOCIAL COUNCIL | TRUSTEESHIP COUNCIL | SECRETARIAT |

Military Staff Committee
Standing Committee and ad hoc bodies
International Criminal Tribunal for the Former Yugoslavia
International Criminal Tribunal for Rwanda
UN Monitoring, Verification and Inspection Commission (Iraq)
United Nations Compensation Commission
Peacekeeping Operations and Missions

Main committees
Other sessional committees
Standing committees
and ad hoc bodies
Other subsidiary organs

PROGRAMMES AND FUNDS

UNCTAD
United Nations Conference on Trade and Development

ITC
International Trade Centre (UNCTAD/WTO)

UNDCP
United Nations Drug Control Programme

UNEP
United Nations Environment Programme

UNHSP
United Nations Human Settlements Programme (UN-Habitat)

UNDP
United Nations Development Programme

UNIFEM
United Nations Development Fund for Women

UNV
United Nations Volunteers

UNFPA
United Nations Population Fund

UNHCR
Office of the United Nations High Commissioner for Refugees

UNICEF
United Nations Children's Fund

WFP
World Food Programme

UNRWA**
United Nations Relief and Works Agency for Palestine Refugees in the Near East

UNAIDS
Joint United Nations Programme on HIV/AIDS

OTHER UN ENTITIES

OHCHR
Office of the United Nations High Commissioner for Human Rights

UNOPS
United Nations Office for Project Services

UNU
United Nations University

UNSSC
United Nations System Staff College

RESEARCH AND TRAINING INSTITUTES

INSTRAW
International Research and Training Institute for the Advancement of Women

UNICRI
United Nations Interregional Crime and Justice Research Institute

UNITAR
United Nations Institute for Training and Research

UNRISD
United Nations Research Institute for Social Development

UNIDIR**
United Nations Institute for Disarmament Research

FUNCTIONAL COMMISSIONS

Commission for Social Development
Commission on Human Rights
Commission on Narcotic Drugs
Commission on Crime Prevention and Criminal Justice
Commission on Science and Technology for Development
Commission on Sustainable Development
Commission on the Status of Women
Commission on Population and Development
Statistical Commission

REGIONAL COMMISSIONS

Economic Commission for Africa (ECA)
Economic Commission for Europe (ECE)
Economic Commission for Latin America and the Caribbean (ECLAC)
Economic and Social Commission for Asia and the Pacific (ESCAP)
Economic and Social Commission for Western Asia (ESCWA)

United Nations Forum on Forests

Sessional and Standing Committees
Expert, ad hoc and related bodies

RELATED ORGANIZATIONS

IAEA
International Atomic Energy Agency

WTO (trade)
World Trade Organization

WTO (tourism)
World Tourism Organization

CTBTO Prep.com
PrepCom for the Nuclear-Test-Ban-Treaty Organization

OPCW
Organization for the Prohibition of Chemical Weapons

SPECIALIZED AGENCIES*

ILO
International Labour Organization

FAO
Food and Agriculture Organization of the United Nations

UNESCO
United Nations Educational, Scientific and Cultural Organization

WHO
World Health Organization

WORLD BANK GROUP
IBRD International Bank for Reconstruction and Development
IDA International Development Association
IFC International Finance Corporation
MIGA Multilateral Investment Guarantee Agency
ICSID International Centre for Settlement of Investment Disputes

IMF
International Monetary Fund

ICAO
International Civil Aviation Organization

IMO
International Maritime Organization

ITU
International Telecommunication Union

UPU
Universal Postal Union

WMO
World Meteorological Organization

WIPO
World Intellectual Property Organization

IFAD
International Fund for Agricultural Development

UNIDO
United Nations Industrial Development Organization

SECRETARIAT

OSG Office of the Secretary-General
OIOS Office of Internal Oversight Services
OLA Office of Legal Affairs
DPA Department of Political Affairs
DDA Department for Disarmament Affairs
DPKO Department of Peacekeeping Operations
OCHA Office for the Coordination of Humanitarian Affairs
DESA Department of Economic and Social Affairs
DGACM Department of General Assembly and Conference Management
DPI Department of Public Information
DM Department of Management
OIP Office of the Iraq Programme
UNSECOORD Office of the United Nations Security Coordinator
OHRLLS Office of the High Representative for the Least Developed Countries, Landlocked Developing Countries and Small Island Developing States
ODC Office on Drugs and Crime
UNOG UN Office at Geneva
UNOV UN Office at Vienna
UNON UN Office at Nairobi

* Autonomous organizations working with the United Nations and each other through the coordinating machinery of the Economic and Social Council.
** Report only to the General Assembly.

Published by the United Nations
Department of Public Information
DPI/2299 - February 2003

Figure 4 The United Nations system

Cold War. The best defense of it is perhaps that it is the only such organization. Any reform of the UN will need to ensure that the key benefits and capacities of this ambitious organization are not lost in attempts to reduce its current inefficiencies.

Figure 4 illustrates the UN system.

See also: Convention on the Elimination of All Forms of Discrimination Against Women (CEDAW); Earth Summit (1992) (United Nations Conference on Environment and Development); Food and Agriculture Organization (FAO); governance; International Labor Organization (ILO); international law; International Monetary Fund (IMF); United Nations Children's Fund (UNICEF); United Nations Development Programme (UNDP); United Nations High Commissioner for Refugees (UNHCR); World Bank; World Food Programme (WFP); World Health Organization (WHO); World Trade Organization/General Agreement on Tariffs and Trade (WTO/GATT)

Further reading

Ryan, S. (2000) *The United Nations and International Politics*, Basingstoke: Macmillan.

Schlesinger, S. (2003) *Act of Creation: The Untold Story of the Founding of the United Nations*, Boulder: Westview.

Singer, H. (2001) *International Development Cooperation: Selected Essays by H. W. Singer on Aid and the United Nations System*, ed. D. Shaw, Basingstoke: Palgrave.

United Nations website: http://www.un.org/

TIM FORSYTH

United Nations Agenda for Development

The United Nations Agenda for Development is an agreement by the international **community** on the central issue of development adopted by the General Assembly of the UN in 1995, after a process of consultation that begun with the General Assembly resolution 47/181 of 22 December 1992.

The Agenda addresses not only the traditional components of development such as **economic growth; trade**; finance; **science and technology; poverty** eradication; **employment** and **human capital** development; but also places new emphasis on the role of **democracy; human rights**; participatory approaches (see **participatory development**); **governance**; and the **empowerment** of women.

The Agenda has three objectives: strengthen international cooperation for development by implementing all international agreements and commitments; enhance the role, capacity, effectiveness and efficiency of the **United Nations** system in development; and promote development based on an integrated approach (i.e. that peace, **economic development** and **social development**, environmental protection and **democracy** are interdependent and mutually reinforcing).

See also: United Nations; United Nations Declaration on the Right to Development (1986) – Res. 41/128

MAFALDA DUARTE

United Nations Children's Fund (UNICEF)

The United Nations Children's Fund (UNICEF) was created in 1946 as part of the post-World War II attempt to provide **food**, clothing and **primary health care** to **children**, and became a permanent part of the **United Nations** in 1953. Its main objectives have been to protect children, especially those at risk from **war** and **chronic poverty**, especially as defined within the 1959 United Nations Declaration on the Rights of the Child, and then the **United Nations Convention on the Rights of the Child (1989)**, which established a framework for **human rights** for children.

Some notable landmarks in UNICEF's history include the 1979 International Year of the Child, which promoted events to highlight children's rights; the 1981 Breastfeeding Code (see **nutrition; infant and child mortality**); and the publication of the landmark report, *Adjustment with a Human Face* (1987) criticizing **structural adjustment** for its impacts on vulnerable groups such as children. UNICEF has been notable for its use of well-known actors and pop stars to act as "goodwill ambassadors," starting with Danny Kaye in 1954. UNICEF has a joint status as a non-governmental organization (see **non-governmental organizations (NGOs)**) and international organization (see **international organizations and associations**), and hence has used this status to attract funding from a variety of sources. UNICEF won the Nobel Peace Prize in 1965.

Much of UNICEF's growth and achievements since 1980 reflected the work of its director, Jim Grant (1980–95), who launched in 1982 what was called the Child Survival Revolution, focusing on GOBI (Growth monitoring and promotion – Oral rehydration therapy – Breast feeding – Immunization), which aimed to provide selective health care. But critics argued that this approach downgraded the initial recommendations for primary health care discussed at the 1979 Alma Ata conference, and undermined the broader social basis for comprehensive care acknowledged by the **World Health Organization (WHO)**. Some also claimed that ready-made oral rehydration packages were too expensive for poor people, and that more effort should have gone into teaching the use of inexpensive family-prepared fluids (Werner, 2001). Most controversially, some critics suggest that the UNICEF's emphasis on rapid **vaccination** campaigns may have been associated with the spread of HIV/AIDS, notably in Africa (see **HIV/AIDS (policy issues)**).

In 1987, UNICEF announced the Bamako Initiative, which aimed to strengthen primary health care by financing it through selling **pharmaceuticals**, and hence providing basic health equipment, medicines, and support in Sub-Saharan Africa. The Initiative was criticized, however, for allegedly encouraging a dependency on imported pharmaceuticals, for overlooking the lack of local capacity in targeted zones, and for failing to consult the WHO before it was announced. The Bamako Initiative also seemed to match **World Bank** objectives of developing management systems that assumed a diminished role of the state (see **state and state reform**) (Koivusalo and Ollila, 1997:53).

Since the 1990 World Summit for Children, UNICEF stressed GOBI-FFF (i.e. GOBI plus **Family planning** – Female literacy – and Food supplementation), in order to widen its priorities from specific elements of health care to considerations of female literacy and rights too. Toward the end of the 1990s, UNICEF became the UN partner agency for governments in implementing the **United Nations Convention on the Rights of the Child (1989)**. This has shifted the agency toward a more rights-based approach to development (see **rights-based approaches to development**).

See also: children; infant and child mortality; maternal mortality; nutrition; primary health care; United Nations; vaccination; World Health Organization (WHO)

Further reading

Koivusalo, M. and Ollila, E. (1997) *Making a Healthy World: Agencies, Actors and Policies in International Health*, London: Zed.

UNICEF website: http://www.unicef.org/

Werner, D. (2001) "Elusive Promise: Whatever Happened to 'Health for All'?" *New Internationalist* 331 (Jan–Feb 2001). http://www.newint.org/

TIM ALLEN AND TIM FORSYTH

United Nations Convention on the Law of the Sea (UNCLOS)

The United Nations Convention on the Law of the Sea, 1982 (UNCLOS) is the international framework for governing conflicts between ownership of resources in international seaways. The first UN Conference on the Law of the Sea (1958) adopted four international treaties concerning territorial waters, the high seas, and the continental shelf. In 1968, a UN General Assembly committee endorsed the principle that the natural resources of the ocean floor beyond the limits of national jurisdiction – a 200 nautical mile exclusive economic zone (EEZ) – be treated as the "**common heritage**

of humankind" not subject to appropriation by any state. These principles were reiterated in UNCLOS 1982, an integrated convention that entered into force in 1994. Key provisions stipulate that coastal states exercise sovereignty over their territorial sea up to twelve nautical miles (but foreign vessels be allowed "innocent passage" through those waters); they must prevent maritime **pollution**; and that land-locked states have a right of access to the sea. Innovative proposals have also been made for a comprehensive UN multilateral tax for the high seas, payable to the International Sea-Bed authority based in Jamaica.

See also: common heritage of humankind; international law

TERENCE HAY-EDIE

United Nations Convention on the Rights of the Child (1989)

The United Nations Convention on the Rights of the Child (1989) lays down fifty-four articles and two optional protocols that define the fundamental **human rights** of **children**. It has been hailed as the UN convention most readily and universally adopted in the history of the organization. The overarching principle of the Convention is that state parties should at all time give precedence to "the best interests of the child." By 2003, only two states (see **state and state reform**), the USA and Somalia, have so far not ratified the Convention. The Convention has proven far less effective in influencing the course of justice in member states' courts than in raising awareness about social issues in developing countries. The Geneva-based UN committee on the rights of the child reviews every five years, ratifying countries' progress in implementation. Reviews may turn out embarrassing for governments of developing countries facing rising incidence of **child labor, child soldiers, street children** or **child prostitution**. International **non-governmental organizations (NGOs)** have particularly welcomed the Convention as a benchmark for their policies.

The Convention has attracted a variety of controversies, both on the interpretation of articles and on underlying presuppositions. Some NGOs and child advocates have, for instance, invoked Article 12 on children's right to express their views in support of the claim that the deliberations leading up to **International Labor Organization (ILO)**-Convention 182 on the worst forms of child labor (1999) should have included spokespersons of working children. Working children's definition of their best interests would have involved recognition of work as a source of pride and dignity and a concern for improving working conditions rather than a call for immediate abolition of the worst forms of child labor. The best interests principle has also more generally triggered debates around street children, child soldiers and child prostitution, and questioned images of these children as mere victims.

The universal moral values implied in the Convention have also been the object of controversy. These values would posit the Western experience of childhood as a superior model, and treat diversity as an anomaly or deficiency. Assumptions that children are socially incompetent, economically useless and mainly driven by self-interest would cast a negative light on the often-precious mechanisms of survival of developing-world children (Boyden, 1990). Their economic roles would unduly be seen as a "lack" of protection, their social competence as a "lack" of motherly care, and their devotion to the family and care for siblings as a "lack" of protection and opportunities (Nieuwenhuys, 1998). A growing consensus among both child advocates and researchers recognizes children's agency, and seeks to uncover the social and historical processes in which the integrity of diverse childhood experiences is shaped.

See also: child labor; child prostitution; children; human rights; street children; United Nations

Further reading

Boyden, J. (1990) " 'Childhood and the Policy Makers': A Comparative Perspective on the Globalization of Childhood," pp. 186–215 in

James, A. and Prout, A. (eds) *Constructing and Reconstructing Childhood: Contemporary Issues in the Study of Childhood*, London: Falmer Press.

Nieuwenhuys, O. (1998) "Global Childhood and the Politics of Contempt," *Alternatives* 23:3 267–90.

OLGA NIEUWENHUYS

United Nations Convention to Combat Desertification (UNCCD)

The United Nations Convention to Combat Desertification (UNCCD) was adopted in Paris in 1994, but its roots are in the **Earth Summit (1992) (United Nations Conference on Environment and Development)**, the 1977 UN Plan of Action to Combat Desertification, and the **drought**s in **Sahel** and other developing regions. The convention defines **desertification** as "land degradation in arid, semi-arid and dry sub-humid areas resulting from various factors, including climatic variations and human activities." UNCCD seeks to combat desertification by prevention and reduction of land degradation, rehabilitation of degraded land, and reclamation of desertified land. It requires affected countries to prepare national and regional action programs specifying planned roles, strategies and actions in combating desertification. It also provides financial assistance for developing countries for implementing these programs. Critics have deemed UNCCD ineffective, and have pointed to the controversies concerning the nature and cause of desertification. But the increased attention to **climate change** and development has also raised the profile of the UNCCD, and by 2004, it was ratified by 191 countries.

See also: desertification; drought; dryland agriculture; drylands; pastoralism; Sahel

JOUNI PAAVOLA

United Nations Declaration on the Granting of Independence to Colonial Countries and Peoples, Res. 1514 (XV) 1960

This **United Nations** declaration, passed in 1960, rejected colonialism (see **colonialism, history of; colonialism, impacts of**) as a violation of fundamental **human rights** and of the United Nations Charter, and called for steps to grant self-determination to all non-self-governing peoples and territories. It was considered an important stage in defining the **right to self-determination**, although it fell short of allowing any disruption of a country's national unity or territorial integrity. The declaration defined the right to self-determination broadly as the right to pursue development freely through economic, cultural, or social means, and to receive political independence. The declaration did not, however, clarify what constitutes a people for purposes of this right, nor the extent to which the right to self-determination was applicable beyond postcolonial contexts.

See also: human rights; indigenous people; nationalism; right to self-determination; United Nations

I. NIKLAS HULTIN

United Nations Declaration on the Right to Development (1986) – Res. 41/128

The United Nations Declaration on the **Right to Development** in 1986 (also known as the UN General Assembly Declaration on the Rights of Development, Resolution 41/128) gave explicit language to define the link between **human rights** and development as already proposed in the **Universal Declaration of Human Rights (1948)**. The 1986 Declaration defined as "an inalienable human right (see **human rights**) by virtue of which every human person and all peoples are entitled to participate in, contribute to, and enjoy economic, social, cultural and political development, in which all human rights and fundamental freedoms can be fully realized."

The Declaration binds both individual states (see **state and state reform**) and the international **community**. It includes full sovereignty over **natural resources**, self-determination, popular participation in development, equality of opportunity, and the creation of favorable conditions for the enjoyment of other civil, political, economic, social and cultural rights.

An open-ended Working Group and an independent expert on the Right to Development are in charge of implementation. The High Commissioner for Human Rights is also responsible for promoting and protecting the realization of the Declaration.

See also: human rights; right to development; United Nations; Universal Declaration of Human Rights (1948)

MATTEO SCARAMELLA

United Nations Development Programme (UNDP)

The United Nations Development Programme (UNDP) is the specialized agency of the **United Nations** most concerned with international development. It has field offices in 166 countries, and is largely engaged in **capacity building** for the themes of democratic **governance; poverty** reduction; crisis prevention and recovery (see **complex emergencies**); energy (see **energy policy**) and **environment; information technology**; and addressing HIV/AIDS (see **HIV/AIDS (definition and treatment); HIV/AIDS (policy issues)**). The UNDP publishes the influential annual *Human Development Report*, highlighting the concept of **human development**, which includes **life expectancy** and **education** as well as income per capita.

The organization now known as UNDP was established officially in 1966, but its origins lie in a variety of organizations and initiatives concerning overseas **aid** during the early years of the UN. The first decision to provide funds specifically for developing countries was taken at the UN General Assembly's third session in 1948, which also authorized the first UN multidisciplinary mission (to Haiti) in the same year. In 1949, following US President Harry S. Truman's inaugural address (see **Truman's Bold New Program (1949)**), the USA provided more money for overseas assistance, which led to the establishment of the UN Extended Programme of Technical Assistance (EPTA), administered under the Technical Assistance Board (TAB), with initial offices in Pakistan and Libya, followed quickly by Ghana, India and the Philippines. It soon became clear, however, that donors preferred to fund the activities of the International Bank for Reconstruction and Development (**World Bank**) because the voting rights for this organization allowed donors greater ability to say how funds were spent, whereas EPTA was controlled through the Economic and Social Council of the UN. Indeed, EPTA's resources for developing countries were US$20 million, compared with nearly US$20 billion allocated to Europe by the **Marshall Plan**, World Bank, and **International Monetary Fund (IMF)**. The UN responded to this problem in 1958 by creating the so-called UN Fund for Economic Development, run by the former Marshall Plan director, Paul Hoffman, and his deputy, the economist W. Arthur Lewis (see **dual economy**). This fund, however, did not attract much more funding, and critics suggested its acronym ("UNFED") was unfortunately accurate, partly inspiring its renaming as the Special UN Fund for Economic Development (SUNFED) (see Raffer and Singer, 1996). Following the so-called "Kennedy compromise" of the new US president in 1960, SUNFED became acknowledged as the source for technical assistance and **food aid**, whereas the newly created International Development Association (IDA) became the main provider of so-called soft financial aid, and was located in the World Bank (although critics suggested that IDA still issued technical assistance). Following much debate about their dual roles, TAB and SUNFED were formally merged in 1966 under the new name of UNDP.

Today, some observers have claimed the impacts of this history have been seen in the willingness of UNDP to engage in positive criticism of the World Bank, specifically concerning approaches to "good governance," the advancement of human development as an indicator of development (see **indicators of development**), and the need to consider local **capacity building** and capabilities (see **capability approach**) in development rather than **structural adjustment** alone. Similarly, the 1993 *Human Development Report* also criticized the **Organization for Economic Cooperation and Development (OECD)** Development Assistance Committee (DAC) for failing sufficiently to support primary **education**, and for allegedly blurring the lines between human development (with its specific attention to **health** and education capacity), with **humanitarianism** (Singer and Raffer, 1996:184). UNDP was instrumental in setting the **Millennium Development Goals (MDGs)**, seeking a variety of wide-reaching objectives for development in **health**, education, **environment**, and **rights-based approaches to development**.

See also: human development; Millennium Development Goals (MDGs); United Nations; World Bank

Further reading

Raffer, K. and Singer, H. (1996) *The Foreign Aid Business: Economic Assistance and Development Cooperation*, Cheltenham: Edward Elgar.

Russett, B. (no date) "United Nations Development Programme," New Haven: University of Yale United Nations Studies Program. http://www.yale.edu/unsy/UNDPhist.htm

UNDP (annual publication)*Human Development Report*, Oxford and New York: Oxford University Press for UNDP.

UNDP website: http://www.undp.org/

TIM ALLEN AND TIM FORSYTH

United Nations Education, Scientific and Cultural Organization (UNESCO)

The United Nations Education, Scientific and Cultural Organization (UNESCO) is the **United Nations** specialized agency responsible for encouraging collaboration between nations concerning education, science, culture, and communication. Its original charter was signed on 16 November 1945, and it came into effect in 1946. UNESCO's constitution stated: "Since wars begin in the minds of men, it is in the minds of men that the defenses of peace must be constructed...the peace must therefore be founded, if it is not to fail, upon the intellectual and moral solidarity of mankind." UNESCO's purpose was defined as:

> to contribute to peace and security by promoting collaboration among nations through **education**, science and **culture** in order to further universal respect for justice, for the rule of **law** and for the **human rights** and fundamental freedoms which are affirmed for the peoples of the world, without distinction of race, sex, language or **religion**, by the Charter of the United Nations.
>
> (See **science and technology; race and racism**)

Some precursors to UNESCO were the International Committee of Intellectual Co-operation (CICI) (based in Geneva, 1922–46), with its executing agency, the International Institute of Intellectual Co-operation (IICI) (based in Paris, 1925–46). UNESCO also overlapped with the International Bureau of Education (based in Geneva, 1925–68), although since 1969 this bureau has been part of the UNESCO secretariat.

UNESCO has operated programs from some sixty field offices worldwide, and has promoted projects to enhance local literary, cultural history, and teacher-training skills. It is currently actively involved in seeking to achieve the **Millennium Development Goals (MDGs)**, particularly, to achieve universal primary education in all countries by 2015; eliminate **gender** disparity in primary and secondary education; and help countries implement a national strategy for **sustainable development**. It is the lead agency for the UN Literacy Decade, starting in 2003. UNESCO also oversees the **World Heritage Convention (UNESCO 1972)**, which protects sites of outstanding physical or cultural value such as Halong Bay in Vietnam, or Angkor in Cambodia. Some other notable activities by UNESCO include the Nubia Campaign between 1960 and 1980 in

Egypt, to relocate the Great Temple of Abu Simbel and prevent it being flooded by the Aswan Dam. UNESCO also coordinated the 1990 World Conference on Education for All in Jomtiem, Thailand, which sought to provide basic education for all children, youths and adults, and which led to the World Education Forum meeting in Dakar, Senegal in 2000, which committed governments to providing basic primary education. Since 1971 UNESCO has also overseen the Man and Biosphere program, which encourages interdisciplinary research, demonstrations and training in managing **natural resources**, and has been an important influence on sustainable development debates. The organization has also published histories of Africa and other regions, and in 1975 established the United Nations University in Tokyo. UNESCO also founded the Organization of Asia-Pacific News Agencies (OANA), an association of news agencies from the Asia-Pacific region in 1961 (see **media**).

UNESCO's greatest controversy occurred during the late 1970s and early 1980s, when some developed countries alleged UNESCO was actively engaged in allowing communist and developing countries to attack the West. UNESCO developed a plan called the New International Information Order, as a source of information about developing countries. At a time when **Cold War** rhetoric was at its highest, including the withdrawal of the USA from the 1980 Moscow Olympics, and of the Soviet Union from the 1984 Los Angeles Olympics, the USA and other countries alleged that UNESCO was supporting anti-West propaganda. The USA withdrew in protest from UNESCO in 1984, followed by the UK in 1985, resulting in a severe reduction in the organization's budget and activities. The UK rejoined in 1997, and the USA in 2003.

See also: education; media; Millennium Development Goals (MDGs); science and technology; United Nations; World Heritage Convention (UNESCO 1972)

Further reading

Cattaneo, M. and Trifoni, J. (2003) *World Heritage Sites of UNESCO*, Rome: White Star Editions.
UNESCO website: http://www.unesco.org/

TIM FORSYTH

United Nations High Commissioner for Refugees (UNHCR)

The Office of the United Nations High Commissioner for Refugees (UNHCR) – or more simply, the UN Refugee Agency – was established in 1950 under the UN General Assembly with an international mandate to protect **refugees** and resolve international crises involving refugees. The organization is a successor to the UN Relief and Rehabilitation Agency and International Refugee Organization formed after World War II. UNHCR was initially given a three-year mandate to resettle 1.2 million European refugees, but its mandate has been extended every five years. It has since become the world's largest humanitarian organization, and has been involved in more than 120 countries, earning the Nobel Peace Prize in 1954 and 1981.

UNHCR has been involved in various recent **complex emergencies**, including assisting some 1.8 million refugees in the Balkans in the 1990s; relocating 60,000 refugees in Guinea (West Africa) during **war** between groups in Sierra Leone and Liberia in 2000–1; and working to repatriate refugees to Eritrea from Sudan in 2001. UNHCR has worked in **partnerships** with various organizations including the International Committee of the Red Cross (see **Red Cross and Red Crescent**), **Office of the United Nations High Commissioner for Human Rights (OHCHR)**, and the International Organization for Migration.

Despite its widespread activities, UNHCR has attracted criticisms, notably for not adequately fulfilling its mandate to protect refugees. Some have argued that its capacities to do this have been eroded by its expansion in the 1990s into a humanitarian relief organization, the policy of promoting "preventive protection" of refugees within their own country, and the establishment of "safe havens" where refugees may go for protection. This latter strategy, adopted during the directorship of Sadako Ogata (1991–2000), has been proposed as a means to provide assistance to refugees before they cross international boundaries, and partly reflects the growing unwillingness of many countries in the post-**Cold War** period to accept refugees. In turn, this has also meant an increased attention to **internally displaced persons**. According to critics, "the agency's involvement in vaguely defined humanitarian activities ... has diluted its role as the main international actor responsible for promoting asylum" (McNamara and Goodwin-Gill, 1999:2) (see **asylum seeking**). Refugees are technically defined as individuals who have crossed international boundaries to seek protection. Hence, critics argue, actions by the UNHCR to prevent refugees crossing boundaries may undermine its original mandate to protect refugees.

Such problems of preventive protection were experienced most seriously when, in 1993, the UN declared a safe haven around Srebrenica in Bosnia-Herzegovina to protect local Muslim populations. The UN commander told the Muslims: "I will never abandon you." In 1995, however, the Bosnian Serb army besieged the enclave, and the UN peacekeeping soldiers from the Netherlands – numbering just some hundreds – were unable to resist them, leading to the massacre of an estimated 7,000 Muslims. In 2003, an inquiry held the Dutch government responsible for the disaster, although it was clear that neighboring UN forces refused air strikes to support the Dutch, and that the number of peacekeepers allowed for this operation were too few. There are other examples. For example, the UN safe haven established in 1991 to protect the Kurds in northern Iraq following the 1991 Gulf War was also criticized for providing insufficient policing. The most controversial critics have questioned whether the UNHCR is now more concerned with controlling international flows of refugees than with protecting refugees.

See also: asylum seeking; complex emergencies; displacement; humanitarianism; internally displaced persons; refugees; United Nations

Further reading

McNamara, D. and Goodwin-Gill, G. (1999) *UNHCR and International Refugee Protection*, Working Paper no. 2, Refugee Studies Program, Queen Elizabeth House, Oxford: Queen Elizabeth House.

Steiner, N., Gibney, M. and Loescher, G. (2003) *Problems of Protection: The UNHCR, Refugees, and Human Rights*, London: Routledge.
UNHCR website: http://www.unhcr.org

TIM ALLEN AND TIM FORSYTH

United Nations World Conferences on Women

Five world conferences on women have been convened by the **United Nations** since its inception in 1945, each with the objective of establishing rights and opportunities for women in development (see **gender**). Early in its history, UN efforts on behalf of women addressed issues of legal and civil rights, and the global collection of data on women. In the last three decades, five conferences have taken up a range of women's issues, including peace; health; environment, **refugees**; political participation; and **population** control, among many others. These conferences derived from a decision by the UN declaring 1975 International Women's Year, which evolved into the UN Decade for Women 1976–85. The initiative of "Women in Development" (see **women in development (WID) versus gender and development (GAD)**) provided the impetus for addressing the interlocking elements of equality, **education**, **employment** and **empowerment** – all given different weight throughout the Decade. Three conferences, held in Mexico in 1975, Copenhagen in 1980, and Nairobi in 1985, set the agenda for the Decade, monitored progress and assessed results. Two later conferences, in Beijing in 1995 and New York in 2000, continued the work of the earlier meetings. Conference attendance ranged from 133 official delegations and 4,000 NGO (see **non-governmental organizations (NGOs)**) Forum participants in Mexico 1975, to 189 government representatives and 30,000 NGO Forum participants in Beijing 1995 (http://www.un.org/womenwatch). Each conference produced one or more major documents detailing women's condition, and included suggestions and plans for the alleviation of women's problems. The conferences brought together women's concerns across local, regional and international scales; they showed the links between global policies and the microlevel, and how they are gendered.

Most conference attendees were government officials or delegates who represented the concerns of their respective states as they related to the issues presented. International agencies and NGOs who advise the UN had limited rights to speak. In response to this, running parallel to the official meetings of the UN General Assembly were NGO Forums organized to bring together independent feminist groups and individuals. Although less formal than the official conferences, the NGO Forums have played a significant role in global **women's movements**, and created a surge in the number of women participating in international feminist networks. In the twenty years that passed between the Mexico and Beijing conferences, NGO numbers have increased dramatically and NGOs have come to have a direct influence on proceedings. The conferences have also introduced women to formal UN processes through their inclusion in participant delegations.

UN Conferences on Women serve as important symbols that legitimize women's concerns for national leaders. State officials are forced to address women's issues and take sides on conference declarations that speak plainly about women's **inequality**, **marginalization** and **poverty**. One responsibility of conference attendance is to submit sex-disaggregated data on many basic indicators, which serve to confront planners with the results of their own policies (see **Gender Empowerment Measure (GEM); Gender-related Development Index (GDI)**). New organizations have been created for continued research and writing on women.

At the beginning of the UN Decade for Women, dominant understandings of feminism were "Western" despite evidence of feminist organizations and histories in other parts of the world. During the Decade, regional feminist groups that address local concerns emerged and criticized Western feminists' narrow understandings of non-Western women's experiences (see also **feminism and ecology; gender, environment and development**). Although highly contentious, these confrontations succeeded in expanding

hegemonic meanings of feminism, creating dialog and demonstrating that cross-cultural exchange and agreement is possible. However, some activists continue to fear dilution and co-optation of radical and grassroots activism through international conference participation. UN Conferences on Women have also been criticized for using women to represent a North-South unity that flies in the face of the "disunity necessary for **globalization**" (Spivak, 1995). Feminists continue to interrogate conference themes, questions, concepts and approaches.

Mexico 1975

The first UN Conference on Women coincided with International Women's Year 1975, and led to the proclaiming of the UN Decade for Women 1976–85 five months later by the UN General Assembly. Mexico 1975 is seen as the beginning of global dialog on gender equality. The conference was initially called by the General Assembly to highlight the need for goals, strategies and plans for women's advancement. Three key objectives were set by the General Assembly: (1) full gender equity and the end of gendered discrimination; (2) integration and full participation of women in development; and (3) an increase in women's contribution to world peace. The conference resulted in an item known as the World Plan of Action, which set minimum targets to be met by 1980. The document focused on: equal access for women to **education**, **employment**, political participation, **health** care services, **housing**, **nutrition** and **family planning**.

At the conference differences emerged between participants. Broadly speaking, women of the Eastern bloc had peace concerns, while Western women were concerned with equality, and women of the South were most interested in development. Women from the developing world took offence at the patronizing attitudes of women from the developed world. In the end, the three issues of equality, peace, and development became general goals for the three conferences that took place over the course of the Decade. The Mexico conference has been criticized for creating a comprehensive list of issues without simultaneously embracing a framework for analyzing the causes of women's problems. Feminists also noticed that compared to other UN conferences, the Mexico conference was underfunded and underprepared.

Copenhagen 1980

The Mid-Decade Conference in Copenhagen 1980 met to assess the progress made under the 1975 World Plan of Action. Delegates again took up concerns with women's equal access to education, employment and health care services. There was increased awareness that women's rights under the law did not match women's ability to exercise these rights. Suggestions for women's participation in **economic development** were rapidly accepted. Governments embraced the efficiency approach, which calls for the inclusion of women as the under-utilized half of the population in development efforts. Based on an acceptance that women must be integrated into all areas of development, the UN General Assembly called for a world survey on women and development. A Program of Action was adopted that called for national measures to ensure women's control of property, and their rights to inheritance and children (see **gender and property rights**). The Program of Action also urged an end to the stereotyping of women.

Political tensions between participants from developed and developing countries continued to surface in Copenhagen. While all sides did engage with women in development and feminism, they struggled over the basic issue of defining women's issues. Small groups of women from the South, like DAWN (Development Alternatives for Women in a New Era), came to the conference prepared to define development for women, mobilize women and debate the global implications of feminism.

Nairobi 1985

The World Conference to Review and Appraise the Achievements of the UN Decade for Women: Equality, Development and Peace in Nairobi 1985 (aka the End of the Decade Conference) faced the disturbing fact that data revealed only a small minority of women had benefitted during the UN Decade for Women. The situation of women in the developing world showed minimal change. The

objectives stated in the Program for Action from the Copenhagen conference had not been met. Thus, participants strove to find new ways to meet the Decade's three goals of development, peace and equality. They emerged with a document known as Forward-Looking Strategies. In it, governments declared that all issues are women's issues; therefore, women's participation in decision-making in all areas is recognized as both a right and a necessity. Within each individual government's ability, primary measures for women's national equality (constitutional/legal participation, social participation and political participation – see **participatory development**) were to be activated. Governments were encouraged to devolve responsibility for women's issues to all institutions and programs. The UN itself was requested to establish a focus on women's issues in all sectors of its work. In addition to topics of previous concern, Nairobi conference delegates focused on immediate concerns about **debt crisis** in the developing world, **famine** in Africa, the plight of **refugees** and migrants, and **environment**.

Previous geographic divisions became unified under the three themes as participants acknowledged their inseparability, e.g. there can be no development without peace and no peace without equality. Another positive change was a more diverse women's presence in the NGO Forum, including the visibility of lesbian concerns (see **same-sex sexualities**). For some, however, the conference and its predecessors remained stuck in a mistaken fundamental principle that economic development will bring about gender equality.

Beijing 1995

The Beijing 1995 conference opened amidst unprecedented media attention, in part due to huge attendance, complaints about the great distance (more than 50km) between the NGO Forum site and the site of the UN conference, and criticisms of China's **human rights** record. Delegates renewed their global commitment to women's **empowerment** and unanimously adopted the Beijing Declaration and Platform for Action. The Platform for Action covered critical areas of concern, many of which had been covered before (e.g. health and poverty), but also drew attention to such issues as the girl child, conservative backlash, **domestic violence**, and **media**. Broadly speaking, women's rights were equated with human rights, thus gender equality is a concern of all and a benefit to all. The idea behind the Platform for Action was that governments would consider the holistic, gendered aspects of all their plans. The importance of women making decisions at all levels emerged and was linked to topics such as environment, macroeconomic policy, **population** and development. A shift of focus from "women" to "gender" also occurred (see **women in development (WID) versus gender and development (GAD)**). In contrast to "women," the term "gender" takes into consideration male/female social relations and social structures. Beijing 1995 recognized that basic structures of **inequality** had not yet been changed.

The Platform for Action acknowledged the connection between politics and economy. Gendered differences in economic power, **property rights** and poverty are shown as inextricably linked, making the argument that changes in social and economic structures are necessary. As occurred earlier in Nairobi, current affairs also entered the agenda of conference participants: the effects of **structural adjustment**, the failure of socialism (see **postsocialism**), HIV/AIDS (see **HIV/AIDS (definition and treatment); HIV/AIDS (policy issues)**) and the reduction of social program budgets came up as new topics. Geographic divides over issues were acknowledged but did not prove as divisive as at earlier meetings.

Beijing plus 5

Beijing plus 5 is the informal name given to a special session of the UN General Assembly entitled "Women 2000: Gender Equality, Development and Peace for the Twenty-First Century" that was held at the UN headquarters in New York in June 2000. Not, officially speaking, an International Conference on Women, more than 10,000 NGO representatives and UN delegates met to assess progress made according to the 1995 Beijing Declaration and Platform for Action. Attendees also made further suggestions for implementation of the Platform for Action, resulting in the adoption of a Political

Declaration, and a Critical Areas of Concern document. The document Critical Areas of Concern included many previously noted topics such as poverty, environment, **conflict management** and empowerment, but also addressed communications and **information technology**, **ageing**, and roles of men and boys in achieving gender equality. It also reiterated commitments to eliminate harmful, gender-biased practices such as honor killings, forced marriages and **female genital mutilation**. Governments were requested to abandon gender discriminatory legislation by 2005 and to provide greater access to treatment for women and girls with HIV/AIDS.

See also: Cairo conference on population and development; Convention on the Elimination of All Forms of Discrimination Against Women (CEDAW); gender; gender and property rights; power and discourse; United Nations; women in development (WID) versus gender and development (GAD); women's movements

Further reading

Chen, M. (1995) "Engendering World Conferences: The International Women's Movement and the United Nations," *Third World Quarterly* 16:3 477–94.

Pietilä, H. and Vickers, J. (1996) *Making Women Matter: the Role of the United Nations*, London: Zed.

Sen, G. and Grown, C. (1985) *Development, Crises and Alternative Visions: Third World Women's Perspectives*, Bangalore: DAWN Secretariat.

Spivak, G. (1995) "'Woman' as Theatre: United Nations Conference on Women, Beijing 1995," *Radical Philosophy: A Journal of Socialist and Feminist Philosophy*, 75: 2–4.

Stienstra, D. (1994) *Women's Movements and International Organisations*, New York: St Martin's Press.

Tinker, I. (1990) *Persistent Inequalities: Women and World Development*. New York: Oxford University Press.

United Nations WomenWatch: http://www. un.org/womenwatch

KATHLEEN O'REILLY

Universal Declaration of Human Rights (1948)

The Universal Declaration of Human Rights (UDHR) was adopted by the **United Nations** General Assembly in 1948. The UDHR declares the inherent dignity and inalienable rights of all humans, articulates shared universal values, underlines states' responsibilities to individuals, and affirms the individual as a subject of **international law**. The rights delineated in the UDHR include civil and political rights as well as social and economic ones. The UDHR emphasizes that these rights are applicable to all persons without any discrimination based on personal status or the status of the territory to which a person belongs. Although a declaration, and thus not formally binding, it is considered to be part of customary international law or expressive of peremptory norms of international society. It remains the foundation of much contemporary discussion of **human rights**, including persistent debates on their universality or the existence of a hierarchy of rights.

See also: human rights; international law; United Nations Declaration on the Right to Development (1986) – Res. 41/128

I. NIKLAS HULTIN

urban agriculture

Urban agriculture (UA) comprises the production of **food**/non-food crops, from plants and trees, as well as animal husbandry (**livestock**, fowl, **fisheries**, and so forth), within cities and around their peripheries. At the heart of UA's potential are problems associated with where it should be practiced. UA is typically practiced on-plot (residential land) or off-plot (public land). Depending on the specific activities, on-plot UA is often controversial and may offend nearby residents when farmers engage in livestock or poultry production because it creates smells, noises, and possibilities of health risk (see **health; pollution**). Legality issues surrounding off-plot practice vary considerably, often depending on the strictness of urban land use policies of particular urban and national governments (see **law**).

While UA is practiced all over the world in various forms, debates within international development have mainly focused on its role in the **urban informal sector** of many developing countries. Informal sectors of many developing countries have grown and diversified as a direct result of increases in **urban poverty**. Consequently, a distinction should be made between UA that aims to supplement household **food security** and/or increase economic opportunity; and community gardening, which is more commonly practiced within advanced capitalist societies. While there have been modest success stories of implementing UA in distressed urban communities (see **community**) within Canada and the USA, for the most part this has remained a leisurely/recreational activity.

UA has the potential to contribute to increasing quality of life through improvements in economic, social and environmental **well-being** of cities in developing countries. The main barriers to UA are a lack of financial resources from many poor households, plus inadequate institutional frameworks; limited access to agricultural inputs (i.e. land, water, seeds, tools); a lack of technical knowledge; and a lack of organization capacity (see **capacity building**). Some of these issues have been overcome through the creation of UA cooperatives that through pooled resources and knowledge have become especially productive (see **communes, collectives and cooperatives**). Cuba has received the most international attention concerning UA and cooperatives, because of the innovative and industrious approaches initiated after support from the Soviet Union ceased with the demise of that entity at the end of the 1980s.

Despite UA's potential to increase the quality of life for those involved, it is problematic to see it as equally beneficial for all people involved. "Urban farmers" should not be lumped together without considering divisions of **gender**, class, etc. Ironically, research has shown that UA is not the most important source of urban food, and that poor people are not always the main beneficiaries of UA production (see **food security**).

The future of UA production depends largely on both urban governmental structures recognizing the potential benefits inherent to UA (see **local government; municipalities**). However, as it is mostly a **grassroots development** activity, as such its recognition and implementation will also largely depend on how far UA is seen to increase quality of life for participants.

See also: agriculture; community-based natural resource management (CBNRM); grassroots development; livestock; urban informal sector; urban poverty

Further reading

Guyer, J. (1987) *Feeding African Cities: Studies in Regional Social History*, Manchester: Manchester University Press.
Smit, J., Ratta, A. and Nasr, J. (1996) *Urban Agriculture: Food, Jobs, and Sustainable Cities*, New York: UNDP.

NIK HEYNEN

urban bias

Urban bias (UB) refers to a tendency to prioritize urban areas and people in development plans and assistance. UB involves, first, an *allocation*, to persons or organizations located in towns, of shares of resources so large as to be inefficient and inequitable, or second, a *disposition* among the powerful to allocate resources in such a way (Lipton, 1977: 44–66). The *UB hypothesis* is that UB – modest or absent in nineteenth-century development in Europe and North America, which indeed now feature rural bias – has since about 1950 pervaded most developing countries for most resources (e.g. **health**, **education**, savings, public expenditures, and access to income, as mediated among other things by farm – non-farm terms of trade). UB, it is argued, has led to large, dysfunctional disparities between rural and urban incomes, prospects and welfare. UB-induced under-allocation of resources to rural areas not only redistributes from poor to less-poor (and usually from less-unequal to more unequal areas), but also harms efficiency. For example, clinics and teachers are least available in worse educated and less-healthy places, where they are

most needed and often would be most productive. Pressure to enrich urban **elites** also induces over-allocation of even the reduced rural resources to larger farmers, because they are more likely to sell output to, and to save or spend in, towns. Such allocation is also inefficient. Large farmers face higher costs in supervising and finding workers, and hence usually generate less **employment** and output per hectare than do small farmers. Due to its rural-urban and inter-urban misallocations, it is argued, UB cuts developing countries' **gross national product (GNP)**, and increases their **poverty** with a given level or growth of GNP.

How pervasive is the allocative form of UB? Proving UB requires demonstrating the widespread existence, inefficiency and inequity of substantially worse rural than urban *outcomes*. Since market response – rural people moving toward better lives, urban capital moving toward better returns – would normally slash inefficient disparities of outcome eventually, the persistence of such disparities strongly suggests *relative* rural powerlessness and diffuseness, so urban power generates exogenous intervention to maintain the disparities. However, these usually vary between, say, health and education. Though "only the vector sum of all state interventions…will clinch whether [overall UB] exists or not" (or has changed) at state level (Varshney, 1993:19), the same country and time interventions in rural-urban **terms of trade** might well be urban-biased, in health neutral, and in education rural-biased. Furthermore, not only the state (see **state and state reform**) can make interventions (by fixing markets, or by giving this or that group or region special advantages within an otherwise unfixed market). Powerful non-state groups can also intervene (for example, colluding industrialists, landlords, teachers, unionized workers), and can change rural-urban allocations through non-market action. Hence final proof of *overall* UB or its absence or change is elusive: all one can do is, honestly and reputably, seek the best evidence of rural-urban allocations for many particular countries, subsectors and times, and seek general conclusions about their scale, trends, causes and effects.

Thus Bates (1981) and Varshney (1993) showed how,

> to extract resources for the treasury, city and industry, African states set prices that hurt the

countryside [and by] distributing state largesse . . . divide up the countryside into supporters that benefit from state action and opponents. . . . [Rural] collective action is difficult because the agricultural sector is very large [and] dispersed, [so the] free-rider problem impedes collective action.

(Varshney, 1993:14–15)

Anne Krueger and her colleagues, in a series of works in the mid-1990s, disaggregated such pro-urban price distortion, showing that it was greatest in Africa, and that it usually relied more on industrial protection and exchange-rate manipulation (see **exchange rates**) than on marketing boards or other direct squeezes on farm prices. Lipton (1977) showed that rural-urban gaps in welfare and earnings in developing countries, most strikingly in Africa, exceeded earlier or current gaps in now-developed countries (there is now much more and stronger evidence: Eastwood and Lipton, 2000). Lipton also linked these larger gaps to developing countries' much higher excesses of farm over non-farm output-per-worker, and attributed the excesses partly to low ratios of farm to non-farm capital and investment. These findings were despite demonstrably higher ratios of extra output to extra capital in farming than in the rest of the economy.

Both Bates and Lipton have linked allocative to dispositional UB, and situated the latter in ideology. Bates located state action to repress farm prices in Africa (while steering resources to food-surplus farmers) in the dependence of governments on surplus-seeking bureaucracies, and particularly of socialist governments on urban labor and hence on net food consumers. Lipton (1977: ch. 4) traced dispositional UB to a variety of sources. These included, paradoxically, colonial and Gandhian versions of pastoral idealization of the rural; classical political economy (see **Marxism**); to neo-classical economics (which is surprisingly under-used as a critique of UB); and – despite Kautsky's prescient analysis – to Leninist extraction theory, the subsequent Soviet **industrialization** debate, and their impact on non-communist postcolonial elites (see **decolonization;postcolonialism;postsocialism**).

Immediately following the work of Bates and Lipton, many questioned the pervasiveness of urban bias across developing countries and sectors.

Of course particular examples of alleged UB are always contestable, but general questioning of the UB hypothesis has become rarer in recent years. There is now growing evidence of large and generally non-decreasing rural-urban outcome disparities in many developing countries (indeed, some, such as China and Tanzania, were wrongly hypothesized in 1977 by Lipton to show low UB). However, there are major challenges to UB theorizing (compare Moore and Harriss, 1984, with Varshney, 1993). Why don't workers move to towns, and capital to **villages**, until disparities associated with UB are eliminated? (**Rural-urban migration** is often overstated by official data, and in the form of "rural skill drain" can actually sharpen rural-urban disparities.) Relatedly, does UB make sense in a world of rural industry, **urban agriculture**, and increasingly many households with both urban and rural incomes and interests? Doesn't the reduction in many developing countries in state action, and in price distortion, imply a decline in allocative UB? In Varshney (1993), Lipton argues that the evidence of non-decreasing urban-rural disparity, combined with clearly falling state anti-farm price intervention, suggests worsening *non-price* UB, such as in the location of schools, clinics, roads, and other public expenditures. But, there are alternative explanations. For example, might persistent rural-urban income gaps be increasingly attributable to a creeping internationalization of UB, in the form of policies that glut world agricultural markets and undermine farm prices, while slashing the real value and share of **aid** to **agriculture**, even more than to dispositional UB in the South? (see **neo-liberalism; structural adjustment; World Trade Organization/General Agreement on Tariffs and Trade (WTO/GATT)**). Such issues are still discussed (see further reading).

See also: rural development; rural poverty; rural-urban migration; urbanization

Further reading

Bates, R. (1981) *Markets and States in Tropical Africa*, Berkeley: University of California Press.

Eastwood, R. and Lipton, M. (2000) *Rural-urban Dimensions of Inequality Change*, Working Paper 200, Helsinki: United Nations University (World Institute for Development Economics Research).

Harriss, J. and Moore, M. (eds) (1984) *Development and the Rural-urban Divide*, London: Frank Cass (also published as *Journal of Development Studies* 20:3 (1984).

Lipton, M. (1977) *Why Poor People Stay Poor: Urban Bias and World Development*, London: Temple Smith, and Cambridge MA: Harvard University Press; 2nd edn 1988, Aldershot: Avebury.

Varshney, A. (ed.) (1993) *Beyond Urban Bias*, London: Frank Cass (also published as *Journal of Development Studies* 29:4 (1993).

MICHAEL LIPTON

urban development

Urban development comprises the list of social, economic, political, cultural, and physical issues that relate to **housing**, **poverty**, **public management** and **governance**, and **health** dilemmas in urban areas. **Urbanization** is a widespread and urgent phenomenon in the developing world. **United Nations** figures show that between 1970 and 2002, the number of cities with more than 1 million inhabitants grew from 163 to 350. In 1995, 15 percent of the world's population lived in **mega-cities** of more than 5 million population; 21 percent in large cities of between 1 and 5 million; and 64 percent in small and medium cities of less than 1 million. By 2015, eighteen of the world's twenty-one largest cities of more than 10 million people will be in the developing world. By 2030, an estimated 60 percent of the world's population will be urban, with the majority of that growth occurring in developing nations. In 2000, average urban populations were 34 percent in Sub Saharan Africa, 40 percent in Asia, and more than 70 percent in Latin America (see **urbanization** for more statistics).

Urban development problems include the tremendous growth of unserviced **shantytowns** (see also **ghettos**) and areas inhabited by **squatters**

where millions of urban residents lack adequate access to **drinking water** and **sanitation**, and decent housing. Cities also experience **pollution** and transport problems (see **transport policy; brown environmental agenda**). Indeed, in many locations such as Shanghai, Jakarta, or Rio de Janeiro, cities exhibit dual characteristics of flamboyance and abject poverty. **Inequality** is generally greater in urban than in rural areas. Much historic urban **planning** has been characterized by top-down mentalities, which have not included the poor. In many localities, financially weak **local governments** are unable to perform functions, so that households and informal **institutions** are becoming the main providers of infrastructure, housing and social services.

Much policy debate has questioned how far urban development problems are related to changes or failures in **rural development**. European experience, for example, has linked urban growth to changes in land tenure and rural economies that made it difficult for farm laborers to achieve **livelihoods**. But analysts in developing countries believe that not all **rural-urban migration** is caused by failed rural economies, or the enclosure of rural land into private ownership. Much movement between urban and rural locations is **circular migration**, or the short-term seeking of employment in order to send back **remittances** to families in rural locations. Furthermore, rural-urban migration is partly prompted by the hope of improving incomes, rather than by the absence of incomes in rural zones. It is more accurate to say that both urban and rural areas experience changes simultaneously, and are becoming increasingly linked, than to say that the urban sector is growing because of the failure of the rural sector.

Another question is how far urbanization or the growth of urban development problems lead to **urban bias**, or the prioritization of urban agendas in all development policy? Urban bias may result from the deliberate choice of policy-makers to place urban items of more value in planning than rural development, or by the tendency for policy-makers to come from urban middle classes, and hence not appreciate rural development problems. Such trends reflect a growing "urbanism" in development thinking, and the emphasis upon cities as the norm.

There is much evidence linking urbanization to **urban poverty**, and sometimes to **globalization** – or the increasing integration of cities into global markets. But research also indicates that the urban poor can adopt practices that enhance urban livelihoods, and hence that addressing urban poverty should consider such responses (Rakodi with Lloyd-Jones, 2002). Much research on shantytowns, for example, has pointed to the ingenuity and adaptability of settlers to achieve livelihoods despite the lack of formal **land rights**, or the provision of formal housing. The **urban informal sector**, including **street-trading in urban areas**, offers means of achieving livelihoods through trade when formal **employment** is lacking, but can also be where the urban poor are most concentrated. Research on architecture and on planning are now emerging as new arenas of politics and development, by reflecting the diversity of urban settlers, the diverse purposes for which buildings can be used, and the decisions of local governments to promote poor people's interests through building design.

A further arena of change lies in the provision of services within cities. The availability of labor and emerging **community**-based organizations (CBOs) (see **community**) in urban areas offer new means for poor people to collaborate with **municipalities**. For example, the NGO Exnora (see **nongovernmental organizations (NGOs)**), based in Chennai, India, has developed means by which urban poor people may be employed as residential waste collectors in richer neighborhoods of the city in ways that provide income for poor people, a high level of service provision, and a model for incorporating poor people in **public-private partnerships** (see **waste management**). This model has been replicated in many other cities and in other countries. **Urban agriculture** is also growing as a source of **food**, and as a means of reducing reliance on trade within cities.

Different paradigms, concepts, and theories are used to explain urban development problems and to provide the most viable solutions. New urbanism (see Tagliaventi, 2002), for example, subscribes to historicism and is geared toward the creation of "livable sustainable communities" by providing housing, work places, shops, entertainment, schools, parks, and civic facilities essential to the daily lives of the residents, all within easy walking distance of each other. On the other hand, there is the notion of "glocalization" (see Czarniawska, 2002), which aims to represent the interconnected processes of globalization and localization. This concept is gaining importance as a means of cultivating relationships between various urban development stakeholders at different spatial levels. Achieving sustainable urban development, defined by the United Nations as meeting the growing needs of the present without compromising the ability of future generations to meet their own needs, is the common crosscutting theme.

The most critical urban development challenge is perhaps that of management and **governance**. Urban management refers to the political and administrative structures of cities and the major challenges that they face to provide social and physical infrastructure and services. This includes managing urban economic resources, particularly land and the assets of the built environment, creating employment, and attracting investment in order to improve the quality and quantity of goods and services available. The traditional view associates urban management primarily with municipal and central government. This is a largely supply-driven model, whereby the state and its agencies have the statutory responsibilities of management. The provision of services and their maintenance are, therefore, viewed as rights that citizens expect, partly because of taxes they pay and partly because of the political legitimacy that they give both to the state and local authorities. There are indeed **local government** statutes or decrees in both developed and developing countries that define local responsibilities and also articulate center-local relationships.

The liberalization of policy, planning controls, and globalization processes are changing the roles and relationships between those stakeholders involved in the development and management of cities. The result is that cities, and the planning of cities, are becoming increasingly fragmented, while inequality and environmental problems are intensifying. A more recent view of urban management, thus, articulates a broader governance view that focuses on the role civic society plays and expands the range of stakeholders to include private sector agencies, NGOs, CBOs, and a variety of interest groups. Within this broader perspective, urban development and management is more participative, broader in outlook, more transparent, and less bureaucratic (see **decentralization**). The urban **livelihoods** approach seeks to empower urban settlers to reduce poverty by increasing their asset base via various means, and with attention to five types of "capital:" human, social, financial, physical and natural. In turn, this may mean increasing **micro-credit and micro-finance**; allowing greater local control over housing and basic infrastructure; and building means for citizens to influence their engagement with market forces.

Overall, the importance and centrality of cities is internationally recognized through the 1996 Habitat II Agenda (see **Habitat I and II**) and the Istanbul Declaration on Human Settlements. These statements include a commitment to: empower people with the responsibility for the promotion, creation, and development of socially sustainable human settlements; enhance social cohesion in cities; produce policy-relevant knowledge on urban management, particularly on social, economic, and political urban governance; and support innovative initiatives in the field of city professional **education**.

See also: brown environmental agenda; ghettos; Habitat I and II; housing; municipalities; planning; public management; public-private partnerships; rural-urban migration; shantytowns; squatters; street children; street-trading in urban areas; urban agriculture; urban bias; urban informal sector; urbanization; urban poverty

Further reading

Czarniawska-Joerges, B. (2002) *A Tale of Three Cities: Or the Glocalization of City Management*, Oxford: Oxford University Press.

Rakodi, C. with Lloyd-Jones, T. (2002) *Urban Livelihoods: A People-centred Approach to Reducing Poverty*, London: Earthscan.

Satterthwaite, D. (ed.) (1999) *The Earthscan Reader in Sustainable Cities*, London: Earthscan.

Tagliaventi, G. (ed.) (2002) *New Urbanism*, Florence: Alinea.

United Nations (2001) *Cities in a Globalizing World: Global Report on Human Settlements*, Virginia: Earthscan.

DOUG FEREMENGA

URBAN ENVIRONMENT *see* brown environmental agenda

urban informal sector

The urban informal sector (UIS) refers to a variety of **employment** and commercial activities in cities that are generally small, unregulated, and commonly controlled within families, and which use **labor-intensive** indigenous technologies and skills acquired outside formal schooling (see also **entrepreneurship; micro-enterprises**). The UIS may be compared with the so-called formal sector of employment, which generally tends to be **capital intensive**, dominated by overseas capital, corporate ownership, large scale of operation, and often imported technology, formally acquired skills and protected markets. A key difference between the formal and informal sectors is that the informal sector has relatively few barriers of entry for poor people, especially migrants to urban areas.

In 1969, the **International Labor Organization (ILO)** launched its World Employment Program (WEP), which included research on urban employment. Initially, the ILO analyzed labor forces in terms of those who were employed and unemployed. However, some early studies of **labor markets** in developing countries found that the number of unemployed did not correspond to the difference between the total labor force and the number employed. The ILO therefore developed the concept of the UIS as a means of describing the missing members of the labor force, first discussing the term in its 1972 report on Kenya.

By the mid-1970s, while the ILO continued to struggle with the problem of defining the UIS and measuring its size, a number of economists associated with the **World Bank** attempted to provide a theoretical model of the UIS (see Fields,

1975). The theory adapted a common job-search model for labor markets in developed countries. It assumed that there was a formal sector that paid a higher wage than the given, fixed wage available in rural employment, but with a fixed number of jobs available. There was an informal sector that was competitive, but which paid a lower wage than the formal sector. Rural migrants to urban areas could choose to be unemployed and search full-time for a formal sector job, or work in the informal sector and search part-time for a formal sector job. The second choice generated some earnings, but reduced the probability of finding a formal sector job as compared with being unemployed and searching full-time. Given the expected wage in the formal sector and the wages in the informal sector and the rural area, the flow of migrants and the size of the informal sector adjusted to give an equilibrium solution.

However, as Fields later admitted (in Turnham *et al.*, 1990), this comparative static analysis failed to take account of the dynamics of the UIS, as many of those involved in the UIS were not trying to move into the formal sector and, in some cases, actually moved from the formal sector into the UIS. While further attempts have been made to model the UIS, it is fair to say that a satisfactory dynamic economic model of its behavior has still to be developed.

In the 1978 the journal *World Development* devoted its September/October issue to an examination of the UIS, and presented views of social scientists other than economists. Sociologists who contributed took the view that the dichotomy between the formal and informal sectors proposed by economists was false and that informal sector activities were a form of **petty commodity production** taking place in a spectrum of activities involving international **capitalism** (see Moser, 1978). The great majority of economists completely ignored this view and little if any discussion resulted from the special issue. While sociologists and Marxists continue to present this view of the UIS, economists, who have tended to dominate aggregate work on the UIS, continue to use a dichotomous approach to the subject.

Although the ILO failed to provide a completely satisfactory formal definition of the UIS, a working definition was developed that enabled the size of the UIS to be measured. Those included are (i) own-account workers (i.e. self-employed), but excluding professionals, such as doctors, lawyers, etc.; and (ii) those working in small enterprises that do not have formal characteristics, such as corporate ownership or the use of capital intensive imported modern technology. In practice, there is usually insufficient information available about small enterprises to distinguish between formal and informal firms, so all enterprises below a certain size (usually five or ten people) are included in the UIS. This has the effect of biasing upward the estimated size of the UIS, but the effect is found to be small in those cases where information is available to make the adjustment. Some early studies included domestic servants in the definition of the UIS, but these are now tabulated separately, because they are wage earners employed by the formal sector.

Using these definitions, the ILO *World Labour Report 2000* estimated the size of the UIS (as a percentage of total urban employment), suggesting that in seventeen African countries the average was 52 percent. For twelve Asian countries, the average was 33 percent, while for twenty Latin American and Caribbean countries the average was 42 percent. Individual country studies suggest the UIS is an important source of employment for both men and women, with men tending to be found in small-scale manufacturing and women in marketing and home working, such as producing **food** for sale and garment making. The UIS is also characterized by a high level of **child labor** and as an easy point of entry into the labor market for migrants (see **labor markets**). For countries where data are available over time, the evidence is that employment in the UIS tends to increase on the downturn of the economic cycle, as workers are forced out of the formal sector.

While the UIS is clearly important as a source of urban employment, in many UIS occupations, individuals work very long hours for very low earnings and are classified as being underemployed (see **underemployment**) by the ILO. As a result, the UIS makes a relatively small contribution to total urban income generation, which is dominated by the profits and earnings in the formal and **public sector**s.

An alternative view of the UIS has linked it to legal status, so that formal = legal and informal = illegal. However, this view is a gross over-simplification, as research carried out by **PREALC** has shown (see Tokman, 1992). Rather than a sharp dichotomy between legal formal enterprises and illegal informal ones, in reality there is a spectrum from completely legal to completely illegal (see **crime**). Some large enterprises, usually **transnational corporations (TNCs)**, are completely legal and some informal (usually home workers) are completely illegal, but the rest are distributed along the spectrum between the two extremes. The position chosen on the spectrum seems to be a rational decision, based on an analysis of the costs and benefits of legality. Thus, if the first step to becoming legal is a one-off cost, such as obtaining a permit and this does not cost very much, the enterprise is likely to get a permit. However, when the costs of legality are ongoing and high, such as paying workers the minimum wage or making insurance contributions (see **risk and insurance strategies**) on their behalf, the enterprise may not comply with the law, as the benefits are not seen to be sufficient to justify the extra costs.

In the early 1970s, at the beginning of the ILO's work on the UIS, one of the pioneers, Professor Hans Singer, noted "an informal enterprise is like a giraffe; it's hard to describe but you know one when you see one," and many who have studied the subject since have agreed. While it is difficult to define precisely and is heterogeneous in nature, the concept of the UIS has played a useful role in focusing on an important range of economic activities in most developing countries. However, there have been some important changes since the ILO formulated the concept of the UIS. At that time, employment conditions were markedly different between the formal and informal sectors, particularly in developed countries. Then the typical formal sector worker was a male, semi-skilled, industrial worker who enjoyed considerable fringe benefits (such as a pension and social security payments provided by an employer) and belonged to a strong trade union. In recent years, as a result of the competition that has come through **globalization**, the typical formal sector worker is more likely to be a worker on a short-term contract or working part-time (possibly a woman), in the service sector and probably not belonging to a trade union (see

casualization of work). Given these changes in the formal sector, the 1970s formal sector model has lost its relevance as an ideal toward which developing countries might aim. As a result, the ILO's concept of the **decent work deficit** represents a recent attempt to analyze the problems of the UIS and possible policies to deal with these problems.

See also: casualization of work; decent work deficit; employment; entrepreneurship; International Labor Organization (ILO); labor markets; labor migration; labor rights and standards; micro-enterprises; PREALC; street-trading in urban areas

Further reading

Bangasser, P. (2000) *The ILO and the Informal Sector: An Institutional History*, Geneva: International Labor Office, Employment Paper 2000/9.

Fields, G. (1975) "Rural-urban Migration, Urban Unemployment and Underemployment, and Job-search Activity in LDCs," *Journal of Development Economics* 2: 165–87.

ILO (1972) *Employment, Incomes and Equality: A Strategy for Increasing Productive Employment in Kenya*, Geneva: International Labor Office.

Moser, C. (1978) "Informal Sector or Petty Commodity Production: Dualism or Dependence in Urban Development," *World Development* 6: 1041–64.

Thomas, J. (1995) *Surviving in the City: The Urban Informal Sector in Latin America*, London: Pluto.

Tokman, V. (ed.) (1992) *Beyond Regulation: The Informal Economy in Latin America*, London: Lynne Rienner.

Turnham, D., Salomé, B. and Schwarz, A. (eds) (1990) *The Informal Sector Revisited*, Paris: OECD Development Centre.

JIM THOMAS

urban poverty

Urban poverty denotes both **poverty** in urban areas and specific types of poverty. Throughout the 1980s and 1990s, urban poverty became an increasingly important issue in developing countries, as levels of **urbanization** and international recession grew. It is commonly estimated that around half the populations of the poorest cities in developing countries live in poverty, although this is both difficult to measure or generalize. The key characteristics of urban poverty include inadequate income and an unstable asset base, inadequate shelter (see **housing**) and provision of public infrastructure and basic services (see **sanitation**), as well as insufficient protection from or access to the law, and a lack of voice and powerlessness (see **empowerment**).

While many such characteristics of deprivation also apply to **rural poverty** and poverty in general, there are some specific dimensions linked with processes of urbanization. These relate to a broader conceptualization of poverty that identifies disadvantage as multi-dimensional and multi-faceted. Although rural and urban poverty are interconnected, there are higher levels of **commodification** in cities, meaning that urban dwellers have to earn an income, and to buy all their goods and services. Urban poverty is also highly dependent on individuals' positions in the labor market. Invariably there is insufficient regular **employment** available, with the informal economy (see **urban informal sector**) absorbing the bulk of workers, and this often provides only meager incomes. Both income poverty and **vulnerability** are especially marked in cities where people have to buy **food**, water and pay for shelter as well as other services such as electricity (which are often free or absent in the countryside) (see **drinking water; electrification and power-sector reform**). Indeed, the urban poor often pay more for services than middle and upper income groups. The urban poor are consequently more vulnerable to the vagaries of market conditions than those in the countryside (see vulnerability). The urban poor may also have a smaller asset base than rural dwellers, with fewer common goods such as **livestock** or land that can be stored to guard against future shocks (such as **unemployment** or illness). In turn, urban poverty is more likely to be experienced by individuals rather than by collective groups.

Another key characteristic of urban poverty relates to environmental hazards; urban dwellers are more exposed to industrial **pollution** from factories concentrated in cities, as well as vehicular

and water pollution (see **brown environmental agenda**). The urban poor invariably reside in settlements with poor **sanitation** and waste disposal facilities (see **waste management**). These can undermine health status and erode the most valuable asset of the urban poor – their labor – thus deepening poverty and vulnerability.

The final specific set of characteristics associated with urban poverty is social fragmentation. Linked with how urban poverty may be experienced in an individualized way, inter-household mechanisms of trust and collaboration (often referred to as **social capital**) may be weaker for the urban poor than rural dwellers. Although urban households usually maintain strong ties with those in the countryside, it may be more difficult for them to develop coping mechanisms and an asset base, especially if they are migrants (see **rural-urban migration**). High levels of social diversity exacerbate this trend. For instance, there is often greater household diversity in cities, especially manifested in higher proportions of **women-headed households**. In some cases, these households live in greater levels of income poverty, although these types of households are often better off in other ways. Finally, levels of **crime** and **violence** are usually higher in cities, often increasing vulnerability.

Although rural poverty remains more widespread than urban poverty throughout developing countries in terms of **poverty line** indicators, the latter has grown at a faster rate in the last few decades. While increasing urban poverty has been linked with rising levels of urbanization, macroeconomic reforms have also contributed to this. **Structural adjustment** programs (SAPs) have led to increases in poverty in general and urban poverty in particular. Although there is still some debate as to the exact causal relationship between SAPs and poverty, it is now widely accepted that SAPs have not led to poverty reduction, and in most cases led to widespread deterioration in the resources and opportunities available to poor people (see **marginalization**).

SAPs have had extensive impacts on the urban poor, partly because they were intended to remove some **urban bias** in development programs, especially through removing anti-agricultural price distortions. The spread of urban poverty was associated with increases in food prices, especially of basic foodstuffs, coupled with a reduction or elimination in food subsidies (see **food**). In turn, user charges on urban services were introduced or increased, public expenditure was reduced, real wages declined, and many industrial and public sector workers lost their jobs (see **public sector**).

The combination of these forces led to the emergence of the "new poor" or the "chronic poor" (see **chronic poverty**), referring to those who experienced poverty for the first time as a direct result of SAPs. This group is distinguished from the "structural poor" who have always lived in poverty regardless of the vagaries in the economy. Moreover, research conducted by the **United Nations Children's Fund (UNICEF)** and others has indicated that the adverse effects of SAPs have been borne more by women than by men (see **gender and poverty**). This outcome is the result of more women working in the public sector than men, and because **gender** roles prescribed that women had primary responsibility for developing time-consuming coping strategies to deal with increasing poverty.

While SAPs are now being replaced by various forms of **debt relief** as part of the **Heavily Indebted Poor Countries (HIPC) initiative**, placing poverty at the center of the debate, some have argued that urban poverty is slipping in priority within international development debates. This is most forcibly illustrated by the relative absence of discussion of urban poverty in the **World Bank**'s *World Development Report 2000/2001* on "Attacking Poverty."

See also: gender and poverty; Habitat I and II; housing; intrahousehold allocations; microenterprises; poverty; rural poverty; shantytowns; squatters; street-trading in urban areas; structural adjustment; urban development; urban informal sector; urbanization; vulnerability; women-headed households

Further reading

Environment and Urbanization (1995) 7:1 "Urban Poverty: Characteristics, Causes and Consequences" (special issue).

IDS Bulletin (1997) 28:2 "Urban Poverty: A New Research Agenda" (special issue).

Moser, C. (1998) "The Asset Vulnerability Framework: Reassessing Urban Poverty Reduction Strategies," *World Development* 26:1 1–19.

CATHY McILWAINE

urbanization

Urbanization is the growth of urban areas and their populations. The growth of urban regions has been one of the most striking demographic and geographic trends of the nineteenth and twentieth centuries. According to **United Nations** estimates, in 1800, only 3 percent of the world **population** was urban. By 1900, this had risen to approximately 10 percent, and by 2000, this was 47 percent (of which 76 percent was in developed countries, 40 percent in developing countries). By 2030, the total world urban population will be an estimated 60 percent, mostly in the developing world. The **World Bank** (2002) estimates that Sub-Saharan Africa has an urban population of 34 percent; Asia is 40 percent urban; and Latin America, Europe and North America are more than 70 percent urban. Yet growth rates vary: Africa's rate of urbanization is an average 4 percent per year (although it can be as high as 8 percent in some locations); Asia 2.4 percent, Latin America 1.7 percent; Oceania 1.2 percent; North America 1.0 percent; and just 0.3 percent for Europe. One crucial impact of this phenomenal growth is the emergence of large cities. In 2000, there were 411 cities worldwide of more than one million residents, and that some of these will be so-called **mega-cities**, which have more than 10 million residents (although some estimates use 5 million). The United Nations estimates that in 2015, eighteen of the world's twenty-one mega-cities of more than 10 million people will be in the developing world. Asia will have by far the greatest proportion with ten. Asia is the region with the fastest overall absolute growth in urban areas: by 2015, the urban population of Asia will be larger than the urban population of all the other regions of the world combined.

Urbanization raises a number of important problems, but also some benefits for developing countries. It is important to note that urbanization is simply the growth of cities and their populations. Questions of **urban development**, or urban **livelihoods**, are affected by urbanization, but are not always directly related to urban growth rates. Similarly, the concept of "urbanism" – or the growing consideration of urban issues in society – is often associated with urbanization, but not necessarily caused by it. Measuring urbanization also reflects the difficulty of identifying what is an urban area. Some countries use a lower limit of just 200 people to define a settlement as urban, while others employ a figure of 50,000. The term "peri-urban" describes regions on the division between urban and rural zones.

The causes of urbanization are complex, and reflect changes in both urban and rural sectors, and in local and global economies. Urbanization is undoubtedly related to growing populations in rural areas, and **rural–urban migration**, but is commonly swamped by natural increase from existing urban populations (although some countries, notably Indonesia and Brazil, have experienced declines in urban **fertility** since the 1980s). In developed countries, urbanization was generally associated with a vertical shift in the labor force from **agriculture** to industry during **industrialization**. But in many developing countries, the trends in urbanization have changed over time. Much initial urbanization was linked to **employment** in export-oriented industries such as jute, cotton and **textiles** (as in Kolkata), coffee (Sao Paulo), cocoa (Accra) and mutton or cereals (Buenos Aires). But much later rural-urban migration has been associated with the movement of rural peasants to the **urban informal sector**, which is not directly linked to formal industrialization or **employment** within factories. Much rural-urban migration is not necessarily permanent, and may include **circular migration**, or the increasing sharing of income earning between urban- and rural-based activities by different family or household members. Continuous short-term visits to urban areas may precede permanent relocation. Urbanization is also linked to the extension of transport infrastructure (see **transport policy**), and the removal of restrictions on **migration**.

Another topic of concern is whether urbanization may proceed too quickly or at the expense of the rest of a country. The concept of "over-urbanization" has been discussed in the past to describe a situation where urban **unemployment** may result from too many people arriving in a city. This concept has been discredited in recent years because much industrial growth in developing countries since World War II has sought to employ labor at decreased rates because of the increase of **capital intensive** production techniques, and because tertiary (or services-related) employment has grown rapidly. Consequently, analysts have suggested that there are diverse factors underlying changes in employment in cities, rather than urbanization alone. Indeed, much research into **urban poverty** has indicated that the urban poor work in the urban informal sector, and hence seeking ways to diversify opportunities for these workers may be the most effective means of **poverty** alleviation in cities. That said, the implications of urbanization for human **security** are far-reaching. Challenges faced by cities with deteriorating **environment**al and social conditions are substantial (see **brown environmental agenda**). The environmental and social changes linked to urbanization create particular attention to human **vulnerability**, especially for social groups without formal means of employment or political representation, such as **street children**. **Shantytowns** – or fast-built settlements with poorly defined **land rights** – may develop for migrants.

Similarly, the concept of "urban primacy" has been used to describe cities that are unusually large and which dominate, or even act as parasites on, national economies (for example, Bangkok is some forty times larger than Thailand's second largest city). Such primary cities develop because of the focus of transport networks, especially for exports, on these cities, which may be located at the mouths of large rivers, or be the only large seaport in a country. In some ways, these large cities have acted as "engines of growth" by creating large markets (see **big push**), and providing arenas where business is conducted in ways that attract international investment. But they are also usually associated with congestion, and real-estate markets that contrast greatly with provincial towns. They may also absorb scarce state resources (see **state and state reform**), and encourage mentalities among residents and government workers that place the cities at higher priorities than other provinces and encourage anti-urban feelings in rural populations.

Some countries have sought to address high rates of urbanization by intervening in other sectors or provinces. For example, China's township and rural enterprises program has advanced rural industrialization as a way to address rapid city growth and urban unemployment. Satellite new towns have been built around Shanghai to diversify urban growth. This technique has also been used in Venezuela around Caracas (in the Tuy Valley), and by the construction of Korangi and North Karachi in Pakistan. Brasilia (Brazil) and Abuja (Nigeria) are examples of new capital cities built in national interiors away from existing megacities. The Indonesian **Transmigration** program is perhaps the largest example of state-sponsored **resettlement** of urban dwellers to rural provinces. The **Habitat I and II** conferences in 1976 and 1996 helped define international agendas for addressing development problems related in part to urbanization.

Urbanization, of course, is a demographic phenomenon, and reflects other demographic changes. Recent research on the impacts of HIV/AIDS (see **HIV/AIDS (definition and treatment); HIV/AIDS (policy issues)**) has suggested that urban levels of HIV infection are four to ten times those of rural areas (see Dyson, 2003), and indeed that infectious diseases are positively associated with population density. Higher levels of urbanization seem to facilitate the spread of HIV. Moreover, evidence suggests that urban settlers with HIV/AIDS prefer to leave cities in order to return to home villages, and that families who have lost one or more parents because of HIV/AIDS may also return to home villages. Consequently, for countries seriously affected by HIV/AIDS, projections of future urbanization may need to be revised downward to take account of this.

See also: rural-urban migration; shantytowns; street-trading in urban areas; urban bias; urban development; urban informal sector; urban poverty

Further reading

Dyson, T. (2003) "HIV/AIDS and Urbanization," *Population and Development Review* 29:3 427–42.

Gilber, A. and Gugler, J. (1994, 2nd edn) *Cities, Poverty, and Development: Urbanization in the Third World*, Oxford: Oxford University Press.

Jones, G. W. and Visaria, P. (eds) (1997) *Urbanization in Large Developing Countries: China, Indonesia, Brazil and India*, Oxford: Clarendon Press.

United Nations Human Settlements Program (2001) *The State of the World's Cities Report 2001*, Nairobi: UNCHS.

World Bank (2002) *World Development Indicators 2002*, Washington DC: World Bank.

MESBAH-US-SALEHEEN

V

vaccination

Vaccination, whereby antigens are given in an effort to produce immunization against that same disease when encountered in the future, is a relatively cheap and easy **health** intervention with tremendously successful results. It is not only effective in virtually eliminating the possibility of contracting a disease for an individual, it also serves as a public good whereby transmission of infection is significantly lowered for the rest of the **population**. It is considered one of the most cost-effective health interventions available.

The **World Health Organization (WHO)** makes available a vaccine package, the Expanded Program on Immunization (EPI), which includes vaccines for six illnesses: bacillus Calmette-Guréin, oral poliovirus, diphtheria, tetanus, pertussis and measles. The entire cost of a full EPI immunization is estimated to be US$17 per child. Today, approximately 75 percent of **children** in the world receive these vaccines, which can account for more than three million saved lives. However, a further estimated three millions deaths and eighty-three million illnesses, most of which are in developing countries, could be prevented through more thorough vaccination efforts. Further, the 75 percent rate of EPI vaccine coverage is falling and the rates are still glaringly low for newer vaccines which still have patents (see **intellectual property rights (IPRs)**) on them.

Additionally, research and development for vaccines for diseases that are predominately found in developing countries is sparse. In particular, research on **tuberculosis**, **malaria**, and the HIV/AIDS strains (see **HIV/AIDS (definition and treatment); HIV/AIDS (policy issues)**) that are prevalent in developing countries is staggeringly low. Of the US$56 billion spent on health research in the world, only 10 percent of it is devoted to research and development for these diseases. And of that, just over 10 percent is spent on preventative care. The remainder is allocated to developing pharmaceutical treatments (see **pharmaceuticals**) that are prohibitively costly for most of the world's population.

In 1999, the Global Alliance for Vaccines and Immunization (GAVI) was formed in an effort to improve vaccination rates and in particular, to improve coverage for those in developing countries in order to reduce the disparity between vaccination rates in developed and developing countries. GAVI was formed as a collaboration between WHO, the **United Nations Children's Fund (UNICEF)**, the **World Bank**, the Bill and Melinda Gates Foundation, the Rockefeller Foundation, national governments of both developing countries and donor countries, industry and the research **community**. GAVI works to effect changes through funding, improved health infrastructures, higher rates of immunization, and new and innovative approaches to health care. Finally, it is important to remember that in today' economy, development of such vaccines becomes a true global public good (see **global public goods**).

See also: disease eradication; health; primary health care

Further reading

Mehrotra, S. and Jolly, R. (eds) (1997) *Development with a Human Face: Experiences in Social Achievement and Economic Growth*, Oxford: Clarendon Press.

JANE KIM

value chains

Value chains refer to the different stages at which value is added to a product, or when the product changes economic value. Stages may include the production, marketing and distribution of a product from the raw materials to the final consumer good, including its eventual disposal. The concept derives originally from the work by Michael Porter on competitiveness (e.g. Porter 1985). Much recent debate has considered international value chains as a set of national and international input-output relations that can influence which countries – or economic actors – can derive which proportion of value from the production of specific goods. If value chains are entirely controlled by developed countries or **transnational corporations (TNCs)**, comparatively little benefit may accrue to producers and other economic actors in developing countries. But value chains may boost local development if they allow value to remain with diverse economic actors in developing countries. Value chains are therefore helpful in understanding **globalization** and competitiveness, and in making globalization work better for the poor.

In recent decades, developing countries' success at exporting has depended on being able to gain access to international value chains. In such chains, dominant firms, usually from North America, Europe or Japan, determine whether (and on what conditions) new producing countries and their firms can participate, and where and how the products will be sold. International value chains characterize not only manufacturing but also agricultural activities such as export horticulture.

Increasingly, however, economic actors at particular stages of the chain are able to exercise power over the activities of other agents in the chain. These powers include the power to enforce barriers to entry. They also include the power to impose and enforce labor and environmental standards, and to influence the possibilities for producers to upgrade their functions within a chain. Such power relations also influence the distribution of profits (*rents*) along the chain, and are best understood in terms of **governance**. Kaplinsky and Morris (2001:30–2) distinguish three types of governance: *legislative* governance (setting standards), *judicial* governance (monitoring performance), and *executive* governance (supply chain management). Governance can also be exercised by actors outside the chain, such as bodies monitoring conformance to ISO (International Organization for Standardization) standards and **non-governmental organizations (NGOs)** monitoring labor standards (see **labor rights and standards**).

In some cases (e.g. the motor industry), powerful producing firms may determine the worldwide pattern of production and trade in final products and components. These are known as *producer-driven* value chains.

Another type of governance occurs in what Gereffi (1999) has popularized as *buyer-driven* value chains, of which clothing is a prime example. In this case, final buyers in the North America, Europe or Japan, usually without garment or fabric factories of their own, organize production on a worldwide basis. Such buyers include department stores; specialty stores selling their own branded products (e.g. *The Gap*); firms producing branded goods for sales by others (e.g. *Liz Claiborne*); supermarkets; discount stores; and in the case of Japan, the major *sogashosha* trading companies. Sometimes the organization of production is direct, but often it is done through intermediaries based in **newly industrialized economies (NIEs)** such as Hong Kong. Such intermediaries include manufacturing companies that invest directly in producing companies, and some specialized trading companies. Some Western clothing manufacturers also outsource their production. In buyer-driven chains, design and marketing are key activities leading to the generation of rent.

In clothing, buyers' decisions where to source are conditioned by a search for the lowest cost for an acceptable quality in relation to a search for short lead times. An important additional influence are trade agreements, including the Multifiber Agreement (MFA) (due to be phased out by 2005), which limits exports of garments and **textiles** by particular countries to the USA and **European Union**. The MFA has led buyers to seek out countries with unrestricted exports. This in turn has led to a much more dispersed pattern of international production than, for example in footwear, where a few major producing countries such as China and Brazil are particularly important.

Entering an international value chain as a new exporter can have significant implications for development and **poverty** alleviation in the producing country. For example, Vietnam rapidly developed its exports to Europe and Japan of garments and textiles, footwear and seafood since the early 1990s, and promises to become an important exporter to the USA under a bilateral trade agreement signed in 2000. During the 1990s, retrenched textile workers were among the losers from entry into the garment and textiles value chain as **employment** fell while output and exports rose. A driving force in these changes was investment in labor-saving machinery to meet international standards of quality. On the other hand, the rapidly expanding garment industry drew into employment additional workers, mainly young women including internal migrants from low-income provinces, thus reducing the incidence of poverty (see also **gender and industrialization**). In export horticulture in Africa, meeting the strict standards of British supermarkets sourcing fresh vegetables has led to some shifts in production toward large farms and away from smallholders, with complex poverty impacts.

See also: clustering; globalization; industrialization; industrial standards; small and medium enterprises (SMEs); trade; transnational corporations (TNCs)

Further reading

Dolan, C. and Humphrey, J. (2001) "Governance and Trade in Fresh Vegetables: The Impact of UK Supermarkets on the African Horticultural Industry," in Morrissey, O. and Filatotchev, I.

(eds) *Globalization and Trade: Implications for Exports from Marginalized Economies*, London: Frank Cass.

Gereffi, G. (1999) "International Trade and Industrial Upgrading in the Apparel Commodity Chain," *Journal of International Economics* 48:1 37–70.

Gereffi, G., Humphrey, J., Kaplinsky, R. and Sturgeon, T. (2001) "Globalization, Value Chains and Development," in Gereffi, G. and Kaplinsky, R. (eds) "The Value of Value Chains: Spreading the Gains from Globalization," *Institute of Development Studies Bulletin* 32:3 1–9 (special issue).

Kaplinsky, R. and Morris, M. (2001) A *Handbook of Value Chain Research*, http://www.ids.ac.uk/ids/global/pdfs/VchNov01.pdf

Nadvi, K. and Thoburn, J. (2004) "Vietnam in the Global Garment and Textile Value Chain: Impacts on Firms and Workers," *Journal of International Development*, 16:1 111–23.

Porter, M. (1985) *Competitive Advantage: Creating and Sustaining Superior Performance*, New York: Free Press.

JOHN THOBURN

Vienna Declaration (1993)

The Vienna Declaration and Program of Action of 1993 was the culmination of the World Conference on **human rights**. It covers existing social, economic, cultural, civil and political rights, but also highlights certain priority areas and contemporary concerns. Notably, it asserts that "all human rights are universal, indivisible and interdependent and interrelated" and that "**democracy**, development and respect for human rights and fundamental freedoms are interdependent and mutually reinforcing." In terms of acknowledging contemporary concerns, the Declaration identified sexual harassment, trafficking in humans (see **migrant trafficking; slavery**), **ethnic cleansing** and human rights abuses in **war**, migrant workers (see **migration**), people with **disability**, and **indigenous people**s. The Declaration is also committed to increased coordination within the **United Nations** system, establishing the **Office** of the United Nations High Commissioner for Human Rights (OHCHR). The Declaration represents a post-**Cold War** reaffirmation of international human rights, and one that is also broader and more inclusive than the **Universal Declaration of Human Rights (1948)**.

See also: human rights; rights-based approaches to development; Office of the United Nations High Commissioner for Human Rights (OHCHR); United Nations; Universal Declaration of Human Rights (1948)

EDWARD NEWMAN

villages

Villages are the principal units of settlement in most, though not all, rural societies. Their geographical character is diverse, varying from tightly concentrated, nucleated settlements to ones that are highly dispersed. Their size, too, varies a lot, and there are different conventions in different countries about the distinction between a "village" and a "town." The latter is usually taken to have a number of service functions in regard to the surrounding rural area in which there are a number of villages or mobile populations. Villages are usually associated with particular tracts of agricultural land or of other resources, and in many cases there is some kind of collective village ownership or control over these resources.

The extent to which villages are also administrative units of the state (see **state and state reform**), as well, varies from society to society, though across much of Asia they had administrative functions even before the colonial period. They were then taken as the basic unit of colonial administration, for example by the British in India and Sri Lanka, and by the Dutch in Indonesia. In all these countries, the post of village headman became an important one, and there were prolonged battles – not finally resolved until well after the end of the colonial empires – over the hereditary or merit base of appointment to these positions. In many instances, the holding of the post of headman supplied the base for constructing considerable local power on the part of particular individuals. The Indian village

was regarded by colonial administrators as a kind of "little republic" which enjoyed a good deal of autonomy and practiced a significant measure of self-government. This autonomous, "republican" character was certainly over-stated, both because villages were also parts of wider social and economic systems and because most of their "citizens," in class- and status-divided societies, had no "voice" at all in the **governance** of village affairs. Historians and anthropologists have argued subsequently that the "little republic" idea was a myth. But it has been a powerful myth, in India and elsewhere, and it has continued to exercise influence in the practices of development. Not infrequently, the idea of the "traditional village" (in Sri Lanka, for example, that of the *purana gama*) has been deployed as a powerful rhetorical device by politicians in the construction of myths of the nation. For Gandhi, most notably, there was a whole alternative approach to development, based on more or less self-sufficient, and largely self-governing, village communities (see **community**). These ideas, though they were rejected as the basis for India's national development, have spilled over into development planning very generally (not just in India), when it has too often been assumed that villages constitute "communities" in a normative sense, and that village society is characterized by reciprocity and solidarity. This assumption has often proven unjustified, and, as the eminent Indian anthropologist M. N. Srinivas is reported as having once said, it should be recognized that villages are often much more "back-to-back" than "face-to-face" societies. This is because of the common existence of conflict between social groups and classes in village society. It is not unusual to find that village societies are divided between different factions, headed by particular "big men" who command the loyalties of some others through patronage, and who compete with each other for positions of power and authority – such as "village headman" or, in the context of formally democratic politics, for elected office as members or chairmen of local councils or state assemblies. Such local leaders have often come to be crucial intermediaries in the politics of postcolonial states (see **postcolonialism**), delivering the votes of their dependents to leaders at higher political levels, in the context of a pervasive structure of patron-client relations throughout the political system. Their power may also help to account for the ways in which different markets, such as that for labor, are fragmented on village lines (see **labor markets**).

Villages have, however, very often been taken as the basic units for efforts at "community development," or more recently for exercises in "participation." Such efforts have commonly foundered either because assumptions about the potential for collective action in village society prove to be unfounded, or because the extent to which these interventions are taken over by powerful individuals, who are pursuing their own economic and political interests, not collective interests, is not recognized. David Mosse has shown, for instance (1994), how village-based participatory research exercises can easily become arenas in which powerful people are able to represent their own as collective knowledge or interests (see **participatory development**). Collective, "community" oriented action certainly does occur in villages across the world, but it should not be assumed always to exist, or to exist outside the context of the state. Robert Wade found in a study of the local management of water in a large-scale irrigation system in southern India (1988) that there are villages in which there exist self-organized water management councils that employ and pay staff to oversee water distribution and the protection of cultivation (see **institutions and environment**). But such local bodies do not exist everywhere within the same quite small region, and it appears from his analysis that it is only in very particular physical and social circumstances that such local, village-based collective action occurs.

Villages have frequently been taken as the principal sites for research into development problems by economists and other social scientists (e.g. see Hart, 1986; Lanjouw and Stern, 1998; and by an anthropologist, Harriss, 1982). In such countries as India, China and Indonesia there are traditions of "village studies" conducted by both official research agencies and by independent researchers. Such research can contribute considerably to understanding of development processes, though ideally in combination with larger-scale survey methods (as discussed in Bardhan, 1989), and they must certainly not neglect the significance of relationships outside the village boundary.

See also: collectivization; communes, collectives and cooperatives; community; grassroots development; land reform; peasantry; rural development

Further reading

Bardhan, P. (ed.) (1989) *Conversations Between Economists and Anthropologists*, Delhi: Oxford University Press.

Harriss, J. (1982) *Capitalism and Peasant Farming: Agrarian Structure and Ideology in Northern Tamil Nadu*, Bombay: Oxford University Press.

Hart, G. (1986) *Power Labor and Livelihoods*, Berkeley: University of California Press.

Lanjouw, P. and Stern, N. (eds) (1998) *Economic Development in Palanpur over Five Decades*, Oxford: Oxford University Press.

Mosse, D. (1994) "Authority, Gender and Knowledge: Theoretical Reflections on the Practice of Participatory Rural Appraisal," *Development and Change* 25:3 497–525.

Wade, R. (1988) *Village Republics*, Cambridge: Cambridge University Press.

JOHN HARRISS

violence

Violence is commonly thought of in overt or sudden terms, such as in **war**, or in **domestic violence**. But in the social sciences and development studies, violence has also been used to describe social systems based on tacit or chronic coercion such as **slavery**, or – according to some feminist writers – **male bias** and patriarchy. The study of violence should therefore consider the long-term and structural causes of oppression, rather than simply the flashpoints when they occur. Similarly, some have questioned whether the process of development, or a movement toward greater liberty for all, inevitably comprises some elements of violence.

Some initial approaches to political science and anthropology assumed the human condition to be close to violence, and hence progress could be measured by how far violence was avoided. The British philosopher Thomas Hobbes, in *Leviathan* (1651) famously wrote, "the life of man, solitary, poor, nasty, brutish, and short." The anthropologist

Lewis Henry Morgan, in his foundational *Ancient Society* (1877) argued that human societies progressed through three stages: savagery (where life depended on wild plants with no agriculture or animal domestication); barbarism (with initial agriculture); and civilization (starting with the art of writing). The necessity of human violence and the teleology of this transition have since been criticized as simplistic (see **social contract**), but notions of entrenched violence continue. Marxist analysis has proposed that human society represents a formalized system of **marginalization** and expropriation of the proletariat by the bourgeoisie. Feminists have suggested that suppression of women may be analyzed in similar terms (e.g. Kapadia, 2001). For Bates (2001), "development" as a process implies the reorganization of violence, rather than its extinction: coercion serves purposes in maintaining social orders that benefit powerful groups, and especially in securing the conditions for profitable investment. Such approaches to social oppression have also considered confrontation – including occasional violence – as an inevitable or likely outcome. Structural social theorists such as Jürgen Habermas, have predicted **revolution**, or (less violently) **new social movements**, as predictable and necessary responses to oppressive social systems (see also **social integration**). Consequently, social movements may be forms of social confrontation or limited violence that lead on to better, and more representative politics.

Prolonged coercion, however, may spill over into overt and sudden violence. Vandana Shiva (1991), for example, argued that inter-ethnic violence in India's Punjab during the 1980s should be explained as the result of successive suppression of society and local means of **agriculture** by the **green revolution** since the 1970s. Such views, however, have been considered to underplay the benefits brought by the green revolution. Prolonged patriarchy is reflected in domestic violence against women. Johan Galtung's concept of **structural violence** describes contexts where organizational or cultural factors impede the ability of individuals to reach fulfillment. Peter Uvin (1998) argued, controversially, that development **aid** and assistance in Rwanda during the 1980s and 1990s so contributed to **inequality** and structural violence that it made the eventual bloodshed in 1994 between Hutus and Tutsis more violent. In developed countries, too, violent events such as shootings in schools or rising gun crime have caused fears of a "culture of violence," with some possible causes including alienation of youth (see **youth violence**), and the influence of violent films, video games or pop music.

Many observers have questioned whether violence is increasing, in physical, structural, or socially embedded terms. This question is difficult to answer, as it depends on definitions of violence or **crime**, plus changes in state capacity (see **state and state reform**) for controlling confrontation (such as by policing), and the changing arenas for social criticism under **globalization** (see **globalization and culture**). Some commentators have feared a global rise in terrorism, although some may argue – controversially – that the US War on Terror is itself an imposed system of rules upon so-called "rogue states." Yet, despite these debates, it is important not to lose sight of the alienating and shocking nature of much violence – at the scale of individuals as well as internationally. Much international development is organized on the optimistic notion that violence can be lessened, or refocused as political commentary and criticism. Criticizing oppressive political systems, and increasing means for open political debate, may be ways to turn violence from a negative to a positive force (McIlwaine, 1999).

See also: complex emergencies; crime; domestic violence; genocide; post-conflict violence; slavery; revolution; structural violence; war; youth violence

Further reading

Bates, R. (2001) *Prosperity and Violence: The Political Economy of Development*, New York: Norton.

Kapadia, K. (ed.) (2001) *The Violence of Development: The Politics of Identity, Gender and Social Inequalities in India*, Delhi: Kali for Women.

McIllwaine, C. (1999) "Geography and Development: Crime and Violence as Development Issues," *Progress in Human Geography* 23:3 453–63.

Shiva, V. (1991) *The Violence of the Green Revolution: Third World Agriculture, Ecology and Politics*, London: Zed.

Uvin, P. (1998) *Aiding Violence: The Development Enterprise in Rwanda*, Bloomfield CT: Kumarian.

TIM FORSYTH

voluntary sector

The voluntary sector refers to a grouping of organizations that are defined by being neither public- nor private-sector organizations. It consists of **charities**, **non-governmental organizations (NGOs)**, not-for-profit organizations and voluntary associations. Although the sector is defined through its difference from public bodies, and from private companies, there is clearly some blurring of boundaries through such bodies as inter-state organizations and private company charitable trusts. The voluntary sector also forms part of **civil society**, although there is current debate around the differences between the two and how they include or exclude particular categorizations.

The voluntary sector is a disparate group of organizations. It ranges from organizations that are often used as a method of delivering contracted government services to service users, to campaigning organizations that contest environmental plans to life saving groups. The voluntary sector does not include membership organizations and tends not to include **grassroots organizations**, although the boundaries are far from rigid, and seem to fit a continuum of the in-between spaces unoccupied by private or public sectors.

Traditionally, the voluntary sector has been rarely considered in state planning (see **state and state reform**); however, this is rapidly changing and the sector is becoming more and more involved with consultation, tendering and delivery of services (see **public-private partnerships; neo-liberalism; new public management (NPM)**). Tendering, however, has meant voluntary sector organizations being in competition with private sector companies, and this has led to complaints of changing the object of the voluntary sector, with NGOs having to become more competitive and learn how to operate managerially as private companies, as well as the loss of longitudinal connection to working within communities (see **community**). Indeed, it is often the case that the only difference between private and voluntary organizations is the end-point of their profits. Consequently, certain large actors in the voluntary sector can provide the contacts and management structure that allows them to compete in the tendering process offered by states for public-service provision (see **state and state reform**). These services are then channeled through a narrow range of actors in the sector and consequently may not include community or **grassroots organizations**. Often the voluntary sector can make strong inroads into government powers within a state in which they are seen as the most powerful actors.

The increased delivery of government contracts and state-sponsored objectives has led to criticisms of unaccountability (see **accountability**). The failure of the voluntary sector to make a substantial difference in development has led to increased pressure on making *trust* a documentable process (see **transparency**). If the voluntary sector can have either self-, or government-imposed, regulation then it can begin to work with state organizations and so win tenders and deliver services that would otherwise have gone to the private sector. This is also a method of increasing public trust in the voluntary sector, which, although traditionally has received a high level of support from members of the public, has seen this level fall through continued requests for funds for an ever-increasing amount of emergency and development work, and a surprisingly low level of documented "success."

The voluntary sector's ability to work with local communities is also controversial. Usually, this work involves a democratic process of involving and debating with citizens, which represents a level of **participatory development** with grassroots organizations and **new social movements**. Yet, the difficulty of distinguishing between the various actors within the voluntary sector and civil society may result in the hiding of important divisions within civil society itself, and sometimes representatives that are skilled enough to engage with government may not be representative of the people many groups are hoping to support. As Nelson (2002:388) argues,

if these [development] NGOs fail to forge coalitions with the emerging social movements, they will continue to be the targets of such attacks from the populist left and will be increasingly identified as an elite [see **elites**], professional wing of the NGO movement, with limited claim to mass political support and legitimacy.

Nevertheless, the diversity of the voluntary sector shows that many organizations have managed to offer a counterpoint to neo-liberal governments concerned with increasing private finance initiatives, and it remains a contested and lively arena for development issues to be piloted. Often the voluntary sector has managed to innovate and energize difficult development issues, and usually through keeping longitudinal connections with local people. The success of the Voluntary Health Association in India in affecting state policy, for example, is partially due to sophisticated use of **media** and government discourse, but also because it retains strong links with local health workers on the ground across the country (Edwards and Hulme, 2002).

The voluntary sector, as a key player in civil society, has the potential, although not necessarily the cohesion, to make a sizable impact toward development goals. Future work needs to clarify the relationship between the voluntary sector and grassroots movements (see **grassroots activism; grassroots development**) in order to ensure that the voluntary sector can be more representative of people at the local level.

See also: accountability; charities; civil society; non-governmental organizations (NGOs)

Further reading

Burnell, P. (1991) *Charity, Politics and the Third World*, Hertfordshire: Harvester Wheatsheaf.

Edwards, M. and Hulme, D. (2002) "Scaling Up the Development Impact of NGOs: Concepts and Experience," in Edwards, M. and Fowler, A. (eds) *The Earthscan Reader on NGO Management*, London: Earthscan.

Mercer, C. (2002) "NGOs, Civil Society and Democratization: A Critical Review of the Literature," *Progress in Development Studies* 2:1 5–22.

Nelson, P. (2002) "New Agendas and New Patterns of International NGO political Action,"

Voluntas: International Journal of Voluntary and Non-profit Organizations 13:4 377–92.

DAVID LAND

vulnerability

Vulnerability is an important characteristic of social groups, individuals and of natural systems. It exists when it is questionable whether an ecosystem, or marginalized social groups, can cope with change. The vulnerability of groups or individuals depends on their capacity to respond to external stresses, which may come from environmental variability and change, or from social upheaval and change. The term has become prominent in debates concerning global environmental change; social coping with **natural disasters**; **food security**; the impacts of economic **globalization**; uneven development; and financial crises (see **Asian crises; shock therapy**).

Vulnerability does not exist in isolation from the wider political economy of resource use. It is made up of a number of components including exposure and sensitivity to hazard or external stresses and the capacity to adapt. In this context hazard is the probability of occurrence of an extreme event whose influence extends over a particular area with particular characteristics. These characteristics to which social groups are vulnerable include magnitude, frequency, duration and real extent of the hazard. Sensitivity is extent to which a human or natural system can absorb the impacts without suffering long-term harm or some significant change. This concept of sensitivity, closely related to resilience, can be observed in physical, ecological, and social systems. Adaptive capacity is the ability of a system to evolve in order to accommodate environmental hazards or policy change, and to expand the range of variability over which it can cope.

There are generic features of social vulnerability to all hazards and types of stress. These are the resources available to cope with exposure, the distribution across the landscape and between socio-economic groups, and the **institutions** that mediate resource use and **coping strategies** (see **environmental entitlements; institutions and** environment; sustainable livelihoods). If institutions fail to plan for hazards or for changing social conditions and risks, social vulnerability can be exacerbated. A key issue in the analysis of vulnerability is its social differentiation. Virtually all types of natural hazard and all social and political upheaval have vastly different impacts on different groups in society. For many natural hazards, the vulnerability of human **populations** is based on where they reside, their use of **natural resources**, and the resources they can draw upon to cope (see **poverty resources; safety nets against poverty**). But analysis shows that the poor and marginalized have been most at risk from natural hazards. Poorer households tend to live in riskier areas in urban settlements, putting them at risk from flooding, disease and other chronic stresses. Thus the normative implications of this concept are that focusing on the means of reducing vulnerability may redirect social welfare provision and resource allocation to a wider set of priorities and root causes of fragile or marginalized **livelihoods**.

See also: capability approach; environment; food security; institutions and environment; livelihoods; marginalization; natural disasters; poverty; risk and insurance strategies; safety nets against poverty

Further reading

Adger, W., Kelly, P. and Ninh, N. (eds) (2001) *Living with Environmental Change: Social Vulnerability, Adaptation and Resilience in Vietnam*, London: Routledge.

Moser, C. (1998) "The Asset Vulnerability Framework: Reassessing Urban Poverty Reduction Strategies," *World Development* 26: 1–19.

W. NEIL ADGER

W

war

War generally refers to a state of armed conflict, usually involving armies, and most often between nation-states (see **state and state reform**). A variety of other definitions may be used, however, referring to the use of diplomacy, propaganda, economic pressure and other means of hostility. Moreover, the common definition of war ignores situations in which political **violence** is widespread and even endemic without quite meriting the name of war. Similarly, one state can exist in a condition of declared war against another state but this does not necessarily mean that actual armed conflict will occur between them.

War certainly involves conflict and force. Predominantly, the assumption is that regular government forces have been involved on at least one side in a process of open armed conflict; that both sides are centrally organized; and have some continuity of objectives between clashes. Many "wars" last only days or months, while other lower-intensity conflicts can continue for decades. Armed conflicts have been running since the late 1970s in Afghanistan, and since the 1980s in Somalia, Sri Lanka and Sudan. "Media wars" (those with high coverage from the **media**, such as the US-Vietnamese conflict, and Gulf Wars I and II) usually command greater attention in world affairs, and consequently it can be a source of surprise to many people in developed countries to learn that other conflicts have been continuing for years. Also, not all wars are between nation-states but can be confined to one region or province of a country (e.g. Aceh in Indonesia). They may not all involve a massive commitment to the kind of technological supremacy that characterized US interventions such as in Afghanistan (2002) and Iraq (2003). Wars may also involve irregular, or non-formally recognized rebels or guerilla groups, rather than formal armies. Thus, in many cases, it is not always clear when a war, as opposed to a smaller-scale conflict, has really begun or when it will really end.

War impacts on development objectives and policies in diverse ways. **Poverty** can cause war but war can also cause poverty. Issues of causality are not always clear-cut and can be multifaceted. Some critics have claimed that many explanations of war in Africa adopt simplistic notions of age-old "tribal" hatreds, rather than acknowledge the diverse causes of conflict, including the role of international political economy, and the influence of colonialism (see **colonialism, history of; colonialism, impacts of**). Furthermore, solutions to conflict also need to be wide-ranging and multifaceted. The close connections between war and **debt** (where countries with a heavy burden of debt also often carry a heavy burden of **violence**) are now receiving increasing scrutiny and attention in development theory and practice.

Researching war is often difficult because – as the saying goes – truth is the first casualty of war. There tends to be little reliable information about the scale of death (especially civilian casualties) and suffering caused by war. It is also difficult to calculate the number of people that have been displaced internally within their own countries by war (see **displacement; internally displaced persons; refugees**). It is also unclear if some research conducted by organizations such as the **World Bank** may give sufficient attention to the role of their own policies of economic adjustment in contributing to war (see **neo-liberalism; structural adjustment**). World Bank reports have typically focused on wars within or between states and over the authority of statehood, but there is a growing recognition within the Bank of the widespread use of violence in many societies.

War, of course, impacts on many other serious problems of development. In recent years, some of the world's worst **famines** (Cambodia, Ethiopia, Somalia, Mozambique and Sudan) have been caused or exacerbated by war (and sometimes famine, or food shortages, have been used as weapons of war). Warfare in some countries has ceased to be the means but has become an end in itself, by presenting an effective means of continual resistance, or by allowing the continued existence in power of **elites**. It is sometimes unclear how many "wars" are actually in existence at any one time. But it is clear that the overwhelming majority of countries in conditions of conflict are in the developing world.

Since 1945, there has been the general expectation and claim that "development" would, by corollary, automatically bring peace. This has not, however, been the case in the first sixty years of post-war global development and if anything "war" seems more widespread than in the late 1940s when the **United Nations** was established. According to the **United Nations Development Programme (UNDP)**, conflicts between countries in the 1990s killed some 220,000 people (a two-thirds decrease since the 1980s) but it has been noted that "civil conflicts" are more damaging today than ever. In the 1990s, some 3.6 million people died in wars within states and the number of **refugees** and **internally displaced persons** rose by some 50 percent. The end of the **Cold War** was heralded by some observers as the beginning of a new period of global peace and stability. But many wars have continued or grown since the beginning of the 1990s, and sometimes the transitions caused by the end of the Cold War have contributed to their causes (analysts have pointed to conflicts in Somalia and Chechnya as examples). The continued commitment of the world's wealthiest economies to spending massive amounts of monetary resources on military defense, intelligence and **security**, indicates the growing importance of war (see **arms sales and controls**). In 2002–3, the USA increased defense spending by 16 percent. Some critics have suggested such trends point to the failure of the United Nations to fulfill its stated objectives of promoting demilitarization and disarmament.

See also: arms sales and controls; complex emergencies; displacement; famine; humanitarianism; landmines; military and security; politics; post-conflict violence; refugees; security; torture; violence

Further reading

Collier, P. and Bannon, I. (2003) *Breaking the Conflict Trap: Civil War and Development Policy*, Washington DC: World Bank.

Livingston, S. (1996) "Suffering in Silence: Media Coverage of War and Famine in the Sudan," pp. 68–89 in Rotberg, R. and Weiss, T. (eds) *From Massacres to Genocide: The Media, Public Policy and Humanitarian Crises*, Washington DC: Brookings Institution.

Power, M. (2002) "Patrimonialism and Petro-Diamond Capitalism: Peace, (Geo)politics and the Economics of War in Angola," *Review of African Political Economy* 90: 6–22.

Sen, A. (1991) *War and Famines: On Divisions and Incentives*, London: Suntory-Toyota International Centre for Economics and Related Disciplines (DEP; no. 33).

Smith, D. (1994) *War, Peace and Third World Development*, Oslo: International Peace Research Institute.

MARCUS POWER

Washington consensus

The "Washington consensus" is a controversial but popular term to summarize the predominantly neoliberal policy recommendations (see **neo-liberalism**) made by dominant development institutions since the 1980s. The term was first coined by economist

John Williamson in 1989. Williamson was referring to ten general policy recommendations which he felt were common to the **World Bank**, **International Monetary Fund (IMF)**, key **aid** donors, the US Congress and Administration in the late 1980s and early 1990s, and which would dominate development policy for the foreseeable future. These were (1) Fiscal discipline; (2) Redirection of public expenditure; (3) Tax reform; (4) Financial liberalization; (5) Adopting a single, competitive exchange rate (see **exchange rates**); (6) **trade** liberalization; (7) Eliminating barriers to **foreign direct investment**; (8) Privatization (see **privatization and liberalization**) of **state-owned enterprises (SOEs)**; (9) Deregulating market entry and competition; and (10) Ensuring secure **property rights**. These recommendations were representative of neo-liberalism. While the list created a popular simplification for understanding mainstream institutional development thinking at the time, the ten policies were by no means universally shared or supported. Critical events in the 1990s, such as the Mexican and **Asian crises**, as well as changes in the leadership of key institutions, acted to divide thinking on these reforms, their pace and where the emphasis should lie. It may be argued, however, that some of these policies continue to elicit widespread institutional support.

See also: fiscal and monetary policy; International Monetary Fund (IMF); neo-liberalism; privatization and liberalization; structural adjustment; World Bank

DONOVAN STOREY

waste management

Waste management (WM) – the task of collecting and disposing of wastes from individuals, families and businesses – is an important amenity essential for quality of life. WM includes a number of aspects – understanding the waste generation process; (primary) collection of wastes; transporting (or secondary collection of) such wastes to disposal sites; and treatment and disposing of wastes in an appropriate manner. WM was originally a part of environmental engineering. It has evolved into

a profession in its own right with educational qualifications and professional bodies (for example, the Chartered Institute of Waste Management or the International Solid Waste Association). Earlier approaches to waste management suggested a hierarchy of waste disposal options. A more recent view is that of Integrated Waste Management – where the various types of wastes and the disposal options are not considered as a hierarchy but inter-related and a part of multiple and holistic approaches to deal with a complex problem (McDougal and White, 2001).

Waste is any material that is unwanted or discarded by its owners or users. Wastes can be categorized based on the type of waste, sources and disposal options. Organic wastes include food leftovers, plant and vegetable matter and garden waste. These are mostly *biodegradable*, i.e. they can be broken down and consumed by microorganisms in soil and made harmless. Some organic wastes (newspapers, cardboard and packaging materials) may not be biodegradable. Our waste also includes many other "inorganic" items that are not biodegradable.

Wealth and waste: In general, there is a relationship between wealth and waste generated: the higher the per capita **gross domestic product (GDP)**, the greater is the amount of waste generated per person. Data from Asia suggest that the quantity of waste generated per person per day varies from 0.46kg in India; to 0.5kg Nepal and Bangladesh; 0.52kg in the Philippines; 0.76kg in Indonesia; 1.10kg in Thailand; about1.5 kg in Japan and the Republic of Korea and up to 5kg in Hong Kong (World Bank, 1999). Unlike in the case of other environmental indicators, the **Kuznets curve** for municipal waste generation does not seem to have a turning point (see World Bank, 1992:11). Within a given city too, monthly income and amount of waste generated per capita are correlated (Anand, 1999).

Waste collection: Primary collection remains one of the weakest links in WM in the developing countries. A majority of households live in rural areas where there is hardly any waste collection system. Even in cities in such countries, the areas where the poor live tend to have limited waste collection. Waste picking is a survival strategy adapted by some among the poor in such cities. Usually, they tend to come from socially marginalized communities (see **community**) with little or no **education**. Providing secure **livelihoods** for them remains a challenge.

Waste disposal: There are five main methods of waste disposal. (1) The most popular "method" is simply to dump the wastes at a far-away enough place. This is symptomatic of an attitude of "out of sight is out of mind." However, nature can degrade only the biodegradable materials and those too up to a certain limit. Inorganic wastes remain in the environment for very long periods and can pose serious **health** and environmental consequences (see **brown environmental agenda; pollution**). (2) In the controlled *landfill* method, wastes are deposited between layers of soil and maintained there for a certain period. Then another layer of waste is deposited and covered by a layer of soil, and so on. This method is used to fill low-lying lands, and once the land reaches a certain height, other sites will need to be found. Using land – a non-renewable resource – to dispose of wastes is considered unsustainable. Also, burying non-biodegradable items is not exactly disposing of them. Landfills can generate gas and liquid wastes (*leachate*) and thus cause air and water **pollution** for a long time. (3) Another disposal option is of incineration or burning wastes in special incinerators – but this uses up valuable energy and there are serious arguments about the resultant air pollution and generation of toxins known as dioxins. For some wastes such as clinical wastes, incineration may be necessary. In the case of other wastes, incineration alone has given way to "waste to energy" approaches where the wastes are either burnt to produce electricity and hot water (via technologies such as pyrolysis), or organic wastes are subjected to biomethanation, or the extraction of methane using bacteria without burning waste. Some other technologies shred waste to produce "refuse derived fuel" (RDF). (4) Exporting wastes to other countries is another option. However, it is a messy business with potential negative publicity and the transport costs can be significant. (5) In the sustainable waste management approach, the emphasis is to reduce waste generation in the first place, i.e. to re-use and recycle where possible. Milk bottles and beverage bottles are often washed and re-used; in other cases, bottles (or cans) once used are crushed (or melted) and re-cycled as raw

material to produce other glass bottles (or cans). In yet other cases, certain materials in waste are reclaimed as raw materials to produce other materials.

Role of non-governmental organizations in WM: The key to sustainable waste management lies in being able to segregate wastes such that all organic matter can be used to produce compost; much inorganic matter is reused or recycled. However, it is expensive to segregate items once they end up in the bin. Source segregation, i.e. segregation of wastes at the point of origin, requires changing attitudes and habits related to waste generation and storage. This requires motivation, **education** and examples. Some NGOs (see **non-governmental organizations (NGOs)**) across the world have successfully promoted campaigns to change behavior patterns. A well-known example is of Exnora in southern India. In this case, households in a neighborhood formed associations (called Civic Exnoras) to collect waste and so keep the streets clean. The households contribute monthly subscriptions that are used to pay wages to the waste collection workers. Successful Civic Exnoras are those that utilize the economies of scope to provide various other services at the local level, where the management team is seen to work collectively (Anand, 2003). Others (for example, in the Netherlands and Germany) favor carrots (deposit refund systems) and sticks (taxes and regulations) to change behavior.

See also: Basel Convention on hazardous waste; brown environmental agenda; hazardous waste; livelihoods; pollution; renewable energy; urban development; urbanization

Further reading

Anand, P. B. (1999) "Waste Management in Madras Revisited," *Environment and Urbanization* 11:2 161–76.

Anand, P. B. (2003) "From Conflict to Co-operation: Some Design Issues for Local Collective Action Institutions in Cities," *Journal of International Development* 15:2 231–44.

McDougal, F. and White, P. (2001) *Integrated Solid Waste Management: A Life Cycle Inventory*, Oxford: Blackwell Science.

World Bank (1999) *What a Waste: Solid Waste Management in Asia*, Washington DC: World Bank.

P. B. ANAND

water management

Water management refers to the processes of controlling, developing, and allocating freshwater, releasing wastewater back into the environment, protecting human lives and assets against water risks, and preserving water resources. It is a highly complex enterprise, which requires a holistic approach to deal with the environmental, socio-economic, technical, political, legal-institutional, cultural, ethical, and transgenerational aspects characterizing human interactions with water.

Achieving efficient water management is a top political and developmental priority. For instance, the **United Nations** estimates that maintaining global **food security** will demand an increase of 15 to 20 percent in water withdrawals until the year 2025, while tackling dryland agricultural problems (see **dryland agriculture**) would require a reduction of at least 10 percent in water extractions during the same period. It will be difficult to achieve these goals, simultaneously given that water use in **agriculture** accounts for 70 percent of total water withdrawals. Also, high **population** growth and rapid **urbanization** are exacerbating the competition for available freshwater: it is estimated that by the year 2020 over two thirds of the world's population will be living in **mega-cities**, most of which will be located in water-stressed regions of Asia, Africa and Latin America.

One of the key problems of water management is allocation. It is estimated that there is enough freshwater to satisfy the needs of every human being in total. But there are sharp inequalities in the distribution of, or access to water both between and within countries. On one hand, researchers in **environmental** security have suggested that the number of conflicts over water will continue to rise: fewer than ten countries control about 60 percent of the world's freshwater, while about 300 river and lake basins and a large number of underground aquifers are shared by two or more countries. Other analysts suggest that threats of conflict are overstated, and that there needs to be a greater awareness of diverse, and trade-based sources of water. The concept of "virtual water," for example, refers to the ability of a country to reduce its water demand by importing goods (such as grain) that have already used water, and hence reduce the country's total water requirements (Allan, 2001). Similarly, discussions of **desertification** as a function of water shortages have been questioned by analysts who claim the focus should be on long-term causes of **drought** and local socio-economic strategies of adaptation, rather than simply on increasing overall supplies of water (see **desertification; Sahel**).

Until the 1970s, water management encompassed mainly those activities needed for making water available for domestic, industrial, or agricultural purposes, and to protect humans from water disasters, such as floods. This situation was underscored by a perception of water as an almost infinite resource, with little regard for its socio-economic and environmental values, or for the transgenerational consequences of current water management decisions and practices. This stage was characterized by a supply-driven approach, where the development of water resources through large-scale infrastructure works (e.g. **dams**) dominated the field. Over time, however, the need for a more holistic approach to water management was recognized, largely because of increasing competition for water resources, overpumping and depletion of aquifers and the mounting **pollution** of water bodies.

Thus, since the 1980s, and particularly following the **Brundtland Commission**, water management has been extended to include water demand management and the environmental protection of water resources. The United Nations Conference on Water and the Environment (held in Dublin in January 1992 as a preparation meeting for the **Earth Summit (1992) (United Nations Conference on Environment and Development)**) produced a new framework known as the "Dublin Principles." The principles asserted the social and economic values of water, and called for an integrated water management framework, promoting **community** participation, institution and **capacity building**, and the enhancement of women's role in water management. These principles were later incorporated in Chapter 18 of **Agenda 21**, which came to constitute the baseline for **sustainable development** policies.

Because of these initiatives, there has been a shift from traditional supply-driven water management to a more balanced approach of integrating demand and supply. This Integrated Water Management model envisages the holistic management of inland surface and underground waters (aquifers, rivers, lakes, etc.) and coastal zones, in order to account for the ecological and development needs of both marine and freshwater environments. This broad program has introduced a diverse range of policy prescriptions, including economic instruments for water demand management (e.g. **tariffs**); greater monitoring of water use (e.g. metering); enhancing efficiency (reducing water wastage and leakage, or reusing water); and enhancing water awareness and water-wise practices among users. Part of this process has seen greater attention to the financial and political governance of water, such as by creating water markets to boost intra- and intersectoral efficiency in water use; or by promoting a more active role of the private sector *vis-à-vis* the state through privatization (see **privatization and liberalization**) and **public-private partnerships**. Greater stakeholder participation may be encouraged through **community**-based organizations, **water user associations (WUAs)**, and non-governmental organizations (NGOs).

Despite the significant progress achieved by the adoption of this holistic approach, the legal and institutional framework required for its full implementation has not yet been accomplished. To a certain extent, it has been given institutional sanction for the first time in the European Water Framework Directive that came into force in 2000. In practice, however, most countries, even in the developed world, still lack an adequate legal and institutional framework for integrated water management, while socio-technical and economic constraints continue to hamper much basic water management activities in many countries. For instance, adequate treatment of wastewater is almost unknown in developing countries, where only an estimated 5 percent of wastewater is treated before releasing it back into the environment.

These issues are being currently addressed by a number of *ad hoc* organizations, notably by the World Commission on Water for the Twenty-first Century, which explore ways for designing and implementing politically-acceptable local water management schemes, in order to give effect to the principles and policies agreed at the global level.

See also: boreholes; dams; development management; drinking water; drought; drylands; environment; irrigation; rainwater harvesting; Sahel; water-borne diseases; watershed management; World Commission on Dams (WCD)

Further reading

See the journals *Water International*, *Natural Resources Forum*, and *Water Resources Research*.

Allan, T. (2001) *The Middle East Water Problem: Hydraulics and the Global Economy*, London: Taurus.

European Union (2000) "Directive of the European Parliament and of the Council 2000/60/EC Establishing a Framework for Community Action in the Field of Water Policy," 23 October, Luxembourg: EU.

Winpenny, J. (1996) *Managing Water Resources*, London: Overseas Development Administration.

JOSÉ ESTEBAN CASTRO

water user associations (WUAs)

Water user associations (WUAs) usually refers to organizations promoted since the late 1970s to achieve sustainable **water management** systems in **irrigation** agriculture. It also applies more generally to organizations representing water users sharing the same water resources (e.g. river-basin management boards). WUAs are specific responses to current debates about water management, rather than the long-standing tradition of farmer-managed irrigation systems (e.g. in China, Mexico, Spain, and Thailand). WUAs acknowledge the need to include stakeholder participation within long-term technical interventions in water management (e.g. water-efficient irrigation technologies), and bureaucratic reforms about water (e.g. **decentralization** of irrigation management from the state (see **state and state reform**) to local people). This reflects the increased concern with the role of local organizations and other institutions of **civil society** in the processes of environmental **governance** and **sustainable development**.

See also: community-based natural resource management (CBNRM); irrigation; water management; watershed management

JOSÉ ESTEBAN CASTRO

water-borne diseases

A water-borne disease is the generic name given to infections that depend in part upon water for their transmission or for their prevention. Diseases occur when people ingest water that contains pathogens. Some analysts, however, have argued that attention needs to be placed on water-related infections in general, which may include three other transmission routes for water-related diseases. First, the water-washed route refers to infections of the intestinal tract (e.g. cholera, dysentery and other diarrheal diseases); of the skin or eyes (e.g. fungal infections and trachoma); or of infections carried by lice or mites (e.g. epidemic typhus and relapsing fever). Intestinal diseases can be reduced by adequate levels of **sanitation** and hygiene derived mainly from the use of increased quantities of water, irrespective of the water quality. Second, the water-based transmission is produced by pathogens that spend a part of their life cycle in intermediate aquatic hosts (e.g. schistosomiasis), and then are ingested with water or penetrate the body through the skin. Third, the insect-vector transmission route is caused by insects that either breed in water or bite near water (such as **malaria**, yellow fever, and dengue).

Water-related infections are amongst the main causes of **mortality** in the developing world, affecting about 900 million people and accounting for the deaths of about 2 million children each year (see **infant and child mortality**). They include cholera, malaria, typhoid, dengue, infectious hepatitis, diarrheal diseases and dysenteries. In addition, developed countries have also been increasingly affected by water-related diseases such as cryptosporidiosis (an infection caused by the ingestion of oocysts of the parasite *Cryptosporidium parvum*), which is derived from the intensification of economic activities such as industrial farming and the consequent contamination of water resources. There is a wide range of factors underscoring the resilience of these diseases, among which it is worth stressing the chronic infrastructure deficits in the sectors of health and essential services such as **drinking water** supply and sanitation in most developing countries (see **health**).

Despite the important efforts promoted by the International Water Decade (1981–90), since the 1980s there has been a re-emergence of once-eradicated water-related diseases. This situation has been blamed on the increasing levels of **inequality** and **poverty** in large areas of the developing world, particularly in rapidly growing urban and peri-urban areas, together with the development of drug resistant insect vectors and the global warming associated with **climate change**. Furthermore, many of the diseases are practically very difficult to control. The oocysts of *Cryptosporidium parvum*, for example, are very difficult remove via traditional water treatment methods as they are four to six micrometers in diameter, and they are resistant to chlorine and other drugs used for disinfection. There is no known cure for the disease, which has prompted a major revision of health-related **water management** in developed countries.

All water-borne diseases can also be transmitted by other means that allow the ingestion of materials infected with human or animal excreta. There is only one disease, Guinea worm or dracunculiasis, which is exclusively water-borne, hence transmitted only by ingesting infected water. This disease, which is also water-based because the parasite responsible (*Dracunculus medinensis*) spends part of its life cycle as a larvae in an intermediate aquatic host (the micro-crustacean Cyclops), could be completely eradicated by providing safe drinking water to the **population** in the affected areas, especially in Sudan, Sub-Saharan African countries, and Yemen. The struggle against this disease has been one of the success stories of the International Water Decade, as shown by the massive decline in its global incidence from an estimated figure of several million people in the 1970s to less than 90,000 cases by 1999. The **World Health Organization (WHO)** expects that during the next two decades the transmission of this disease could be completely eradicated through the introduction of safe drinking water systems supported by increased **community** awareness and surveillance in endemic areas.

However, some water-related diseases such as dengue, which had been eradicated from many countries in the early twentieth century, have become widespread since the 1980s. Since the early 1990s, health experts have reported unusual high levels of dengue in many regions of the world, ranging from Southeast Asia and the Western Pacific to Latin America. According to estimations, 2.5 billion people are at risk in 100 countries, which in 1993 prompted the WHO to give top priority to the prevention and control of this infection. Dengue is a water-related viral disease transmitted mainly by the female of the mosquito *Aedes aegypti*, which can also transmit yellow fever. Although some progress has been made, there is still no effective vaccine against dengue.

Although a complete eradication of the transmission of infectious diseases is unfeasible, especially in developing countries, a significant reduction can be achieved by improving the provision of safe water and sanitation, and enhancing **health** services through **capacity building**, training, and applied research. The effective involvement of the communities at risk is also essential, given the need for prevention (e.g. through enhanced domestic cleanliness), early detection, and monitoring.

See also: brown environmental agenda; disease, social constructions of; drinking water; health; health and poverty; malaria; pollution; primary health care; sanitation; urban development; vaccination

Further reading

See the *Bulletin of the World Health Organization* for up-to-date information and articles on water-related infections.

Bourne, P. (ed.) (1984) *Water and Sanitation: Economic and Sociological Perspectives*, Orlando FL: Academic Press.
World Health Organization (2000, revised edn) *Report on Infectious Diseases: Removing Obstacles to Healthy Development*, Geneva: WHO.

JOSÉ ESTEBAN CASTRO

watershed management

Watersheds are areas of land where water – both on and below the surface – drains in one direction, and hence provides water supplies to other regions. They are commonly identified in upland (or mountainous) areas, where rainfall is often concentrated. Much environmental policy concerning watersheds assumes that people living in watersheds are bound by the same physical system, and that the purpose of watershed management is to ensure reliable outward flows of water to other regions. In turn, these assumptions have often led to strict policies regulating land use in watershed areas, and frequently featuring forestry as a means of protecting water supplies. These assumptions, however, are the source of much debate, and critics have suggested they overlook the diversity of water users both in uplands and lowlands; overstate the influence of some forms of upland **agriculture** on watershed services; and make a variety of mistakes about the influence of forestry on watersheds.

Calder (1999) lists six "myths" (or narratives – see **narratives of development**) of watershed management that are commonly discussed in developing countries, and yet which have been questioned, or even rejected by hydrological research (see also Hamilton, 1988; Bruijnzeel, 1990). The first is that forests increase rainfall. This view exists because of the association of forests with concentrations of rainfall. But research indicates that forests only "make" rainfall in limited locations, such as at high altitudes in so-called cloud forests, and that diverse climatic and orographic (topography-induced) causes of rainfall are more important. As a result, removing or planting forests may not necessarily affect total rainfall. Some global climate models have even predicted that removing the entire Amazon forest would decrease rainfall locally by only about 0.5mm per day (although this is no argument for such destruction) (see Calder, 1999:23). Hence, forests only have limited effects on rainfall, although their influence cannot be totally dismissed.

The second "myth" is that forests increase run-off. Here the evidence is clearer: most trees use more water (through evapotranspiration) than shorter vegetation, and hence reforestation is more likely to *decrease* total water availability. The third belief is that forests regulate dry-season water flows, by facilitating precipitation in cloud forests, or by maintaining deeper soil profiles that hold water during dry seasons. Evidence suggests that impacts of forests are site-specific, but that afforestation need not necessarily increase dry-season flows. The fourth statement is that forests reduce erosion: research shows that erosion occurs both under forests and under agricultural land, and that test-plot data showing higher rates on agricultural land tends to underestimate gully erosion, which is more prevalent under trees. Moreover, some **plantation forestry** (e.g. teak) may actually enhance erosion rates. Plus, if grasslands replace forests, erosion rates drop markedly. The fifth belief is that forests reduce floods: evidence suggests that forests can influence (reduce) flood magnitude within small basins, but for wider regional assessments there is no scientific evidence of **deforestation** causing floods, despite anecdotal reports. The sixth statement is that forests improve water quality: this is generally confirmed by research (although **agrochemicals** may still cause **pollution**).

The implication of these arguments is not to support deforestation, nor to suggest that deforestation is without impacts, but to show that reforestation, or plantation forestry especially, may not address problems of water shortages or watershed degradation, and that other processes (such as increasing water demand in lowlands) may cause water shortages. Such arguments were also made in relation to so-called "Himalayan environmental degradation," which is the belief that upland **population** growth may cause deforestation and slope failure, leading to floods and sedimentation in lowlands. Critics argued this macro-model of causality overlooked the influence of rainfall on lowland flooding, or the ability of upland communities to manage land-use impacts. Furthermore,

the sheer variety and uncertainty of physical measurements of soil and water flows from watershed zones allow different actors to interpret or present data in ways that support their own political objectives (see discussions in **mountain development; narratives of development**).

Some political analysts have argued that much orthodox watershed management is dominated by lowland desires to guarantee water supplies and to control upland areas, especially if ethnic minorities who live there are considered a **security** threat. Such views may also influence policies concerning **shifting cultivation**, including the resettlement of villages from scheduled watershed areas. This has happened in Thailand since the 1960s, where some critics have suggested sites chosen for resettlement have in part reflected zones of historic insurgency rather than areas of clearly defined hydrological properties. In 1998, China introduced a logging ban ostensibly to reduce lowland flooding despite the controversies discussed above. Other countries – such as South Africa or New Zealand – have avoided this approach, and instead have adopted alternative means of controlling floods, thus indicating that the political cultures of watershed agencies or governments may influence the selection of watershed policy. Some analysts have argued that watershed management should be done on a decentralized and participatory manner, which aim to maximize both upland **livelihoods** and lowland water supplies. In such cases, providing **land rights** or **citizenship** to upland farmers may be considered as steps to ensure sustainable agriculture, rather than an initial emphasis on reforestation.

See also: deforestation; indigenous people; mountain development; narratives of development; plantation forestry; shifting cultivation; silviculture; soil erosion and soil fertility; water management

Further reading

Bonell, M. and Bruijnzeel, S. (eds) (2004) *Forests, Water and People in the Humid Tropics: Past, Present and Future Hydrological Research for Integrated Land and Water Management.* Cambridge: Cambridge University Press.

Calder, I. (1999) *The Blue Revolution: Land Use and Integrated Water Resources*, London: Earthscan.

Farrington, J., Turton, C. and James, A. (1999) *Watershed Development and Rural Livelihoods in India*, Delhi and Oxford: Oxford University Press.

Hamilton, L. (1988) "Forestry and Watershed Management," pp. 99–131 in Ives, J. and Pitt, D. (eds) *Deforestation: Social Dynamics in Watershed and Mountain Ecosystems*, London and New York: Routledge.

Oikos and IIRR (International Institute of Rural Reconstruction) (2000) *Social and Institutional Issues in Watershed Management in India*, New Delhi: Oikos, and Silang, Philippines: IIRR.

TIM FORSYTH

weak states

The term "weak state" refers to a state (see **state and state reform**) that has a tenuous hold over society, lacks legitimacy, and therefore has insufficient capacity to implement policy and draw competing forces into its institutional fold. The term was popularized by Joel Migdal in his 1988 book, *Strong Societies and Weak States*. In order to answer why so many states were not playing the developmental role expected of them after independence, Migdal examined the relationship of states to societies, and especially the problems some states had in imposing their will upon societies. His proposition was that weak states and strong societies prevailed in developing countries. State strength and capacity though may alter over time, and be issue-dependent. For example, **land reform** and taxation (see **fiscal and monetary policy**) are often extremely difficult issues for many states, but they may be more able to reform domestic economic policy in line with **aid** donor expectations.

Weak states may seek to compromise policy in order to elicit support, but this in turn affects their ability to lead development and maintain independence. A weak state's power is thus relational to various non-state actors and organizations in society. For example, in Melanesian states it is

almost impossible for the state to override the indigenous rights of traditional landowners over land (see **indigenous people**), especially chiefs, and compromise is always necessary. In effect, a "politics of survival and accommodation" wins out over a "politics of change." In conclusion, Migdal did not envision strong states emerging in the developing world "without severe social dislocations [or] additional conducive conditions."

In the 1990s, Migdal tempered his initial distinction between states and societies and focused on questions of how some states survive, as well as further examining the dynamics between states and societies. Part of this work also involved a deconstruction of the "state" and "society" rather than seeing them as discrete parts. In thinking about how weak states survive today, Migdal gives preference to three factors: international support (e.g. through aid and **international law**); successful interactions with their citizens (through patron-client relations); and their ability to create meaning for their citizens (e.g. through efforts at inclusive **citizenship**). Survivalist states may also be adept at garnering legal and even emotional support from society – despite their failures. For example, despite its widespread "failure" to address inequality and meet the needs of many of its citizens, the Philippines continues to maintain itself as a functioning **democracy** and even compels millions to defend it against non-state actors, as witnessed in several coup attempts from the late 1980s. Likewise, the Fijian state, despite being wracked by ethnic and political divisions, is still seen as preferable to traditional or military leaders, even when they represent the majority culture.

Migdal's concepts have become somewhat influential in the political analysis of states in developing countries (see **politics**). It has inspired research and writing on the development and functioning of states and societies from Melanesia to Africa on topics as wide-ranging as political **violence** and repression; divided plural states; **globalization**; the geographical limitations of states; economic crises; **complex emergencies** and so on. Critics have pointed to the overarching desire to protect or promote the state as preeminent in terms of social control and order, and the omission of state analysis which examines its role in representing and perpetuating exploitative social relations under **capitalism**. Nevertheless, the term remains a useful entry point for analysis of the role between states and societies in a range of contexts.

See also: citizenship; civil society; democracy; politics; postsocialism; state and state reform

Further reading

Migdal, J. (1988) *Strong Societies and Weak States: State-society Relations and State Capabilities in the Third World*, Princeton: Princeton University Press.

DONOVAN STOREY

weapons of the weak

The term, "weapons of the weak" refers to the diverse means of political activism available to poor and marginalized communities in developing countries. The concept comes from the 1985 book of the same name by James C. Scott. In the book, Scott argued that the rarity of open revolt among subordinate groups did not necessarily support Gramsci's theory of engineered consent and compliance with the ideological hegemony of **elites**. Rather, it reflected the dangers that accompanied such confrontations. Based on fourteen months of anthropological fieldwork in Sedaka village, Malaysia, Scott explored ordinary, everyday forms of resistance amongst the poor. He drew attention to foot dragging, petty theft, gossip, mockery and other "backstage" or covert acts, in the symbolic, material and ideological struggles waged within the village (see **villages**). The poorer villagers were all too aware of their exploitation, and they acted to defend their interests as best they could within the narrow opportunities open to them. Scott's ideas have been applied to other subaltern groups, such as slaves and women, and represent a critical intervention in debates around Marxism, consciousness and hegemony.

See also: environmental movements; grassroots activism; marginalization; Marxism; peasant movements; peasantry; political ecology; villages

Further reading

Scott, J. (1985) *Weapons of the Weak: Everyday Forms of Peasant Resistance*, New Haven: Yale University Press.

EMMA E. MAWDSLEY

WEDO *see* Women's Environment and Development Organization (WEDO)

welfare economics

The basic objective of welfare economics is to evaluate alternative states of the economy and determine whether economic, social, environmental or political interventions have improved or worsened the welfare of individuals and society. This objective has long been associated with economics, although the means of defining and measuring welfare is controversial, and often implies that the basis of welfare economics largely rests upon value judgments, which may vary according to the analyst's/policy-maker's own philosophic paradigm. Most welfare economists therefore seek to make as few value judgments as possible, and to make their basis for doing so explicit.

Welfare economics' overall objective is to maximize social welfare. It has three smaller objectives: to define social welfare and its criteria; identify factors that prohibit optimal levels of social welfare; and establish policies to maximize social welfare. Early approaches to welfare economics sought to measure and accurately compare welfare levels using cardinal (or zoned) maps, for different social groups and time scales. These approaches tended to result in policy interventions that saw redistribution of income or resources as a key solution. In the early 1900s, however, measuring welfare cardinally was not considered practical or necessary when ordinal (i.e. ranked) measures could be undertaken. This position soon became the entrenched position within the economic literature and became known as new welfare economics. The shift from cardinal to ordinal measures also resulted in a reduced emphasis on policy interventions to increase social welfare through redistribution, and an emphasis instead on measures to increase welfare in absolute terms.

Two important assumptions of new welfare economics are the Pareto Criteria and rationality. The Pareto Criteria exists when it is no loner possible to make one person better off without making another person worse off. Such improvements, however, are difficult to locate. The Pareto Compensation case was developed to overcome this difficulty. A Pareto Compensation exists if the winners of a policy change can compensate the loser for their loss and still be better off themselves.

The second major assumption of modern welfare economics is rationality, in which individuals' decisions result in optimal social outcomes. However, individuals operating selfishly do not guarantee optimal social outcomes. Choices are not made within a framework of stable, pre-existing, limitless cognitive capacity, certainty, and full knowledge of the choices faced by others. Actual choices are made with consideration of others, altruism and non-welfarism.

Important applications of welfare economics include **cost-benefit analysis (CBA)**, welfare measurement (see **welfare indicators**), economic **planning**, optimal growth, and optimal taxation and mechanism design. Welfare economics is also closely linked to health and environmental economics. Welfare economics also considers various other issues such as liberty, freedom (see **freedom versus choice**), **social justice**, equity, efficiency, intergenerational equity, and **poverty**.

See also: anti-politics; cost-benefit analysis (CBA); indicators of development; welfare indicators; welfare state; well-being

Further reading

Arrow, K., Sen, A. and Suzumara, K. (2002) *Handbook of Social Choice and Welfare Economics*, vols 1 and 2, Amsterdam: North Holland.

Boadway, R. and Bruce, N. (1984) *Welfare Economics*, Oxford: Blackwell.

MATTHEW CLARKE AND SARDAR M. N. ISLAM

welfare indicators

Welfare indicators are statistical measurements intended to assist policy-makers in gauging quality of life. Traditional measures of **economic development** provide a unidimensional view of development. They focus on absolute levels and rates of change in variables such as **gross national product (GNP)**, purchasing power and consumption, growth of labor force employed in industry, etc. Decades of **United Nations** and **World Bank** initiatives revealed that bottom line economic measures are only one aspect of economic development. If done properly, the process should also bring with it broader changes in overall **well-being**. Critics have claimed, however, that income **inequality** has worsened, and that there has been insufficient progress in addressing **infant and child mortality**, **malnutrition**, low levels of **life expectancy**, inadequate **food security**, etc. Welfare indicators shift attention away from these "bottom line statistical measures" and provide a multidimensional perspective that emphasizes social conditions and the overall sustainability of the development process. Many would argue that the level of economic development is captured more reliably with welfare indicators that provide a sense of who gets what, e.g. access to **health** care, provision of **basic needs**, **sanitation**, and life expectancy.

The earliest effort to monitor the quality of life, or overall welfare of the world's population, was the **Human Development Index (HDI)**. The HDI was developed by the United Nations Development Programme and is updated annually. It is based on the assumption that at all levels of development the three essential outcomes for people are a long and healthy life; the acquisition of knowledge needed to communicate and participate in the life of a **community**; and access to resources needed for a decent standard of living. Accordingly, the three variables of life expectancy, **education**, and personal income are relevant. The HDI is calculated so that the country with the best combined score on all three indicators has a perfect index score of 1.0, while the country that ranks worst in the world on all three indicators has an index score of 0. Interestingly, the HDI is not strongly correlated with per capita **gross domestic** product (GDP). This inconsistency between per capita income rates and HDI levels is further evidence of the need to supplement economic measures with human and social dimensions.

Other attempts to assess overall welfare or the quality of life have included variables such as the status of women. Data show that not only is poverty on the rise in many lesser developed countries, women in particular are worse off today than they were a decade ago. Therefore, in addition to the HDI, the UN now computes the **Gender-related Development Index (GDI)**. A further index is the Human Poverty Index (HPI). It focuses on people who lack human essentials – longevity, knowledge, and a decent human life.

The Core Welfare Indicators Questionnaire (CWIQ) is the most recent attempt to gauge welfare and quality of life. It was developed through a collaborative effort between the World Bank and **United Nations Children's Fund (UNICEF)**. The CWIQ was developed for use in the countries of Sub-Saharan Africa (SSA). The countries of SSA are among the poorest in the world and have benefitted least from initiatives designed to improve social and economic conditions. Data from the CWIQ are designed to show precisely who is, and who is not benefitting from development efforts. According to the Bank, the goal of the CWIQ is to provide key social indicators for different population subgroups within and across countries. It collects data on indicators of household well-being and indicators of access, usage, and satisfaction with community and other basic services. By the early 2000s, it had only been employed in Kenya and Ghana.

See also: Human Development Index (HDI); Gender-related Development Index (GDI); Gender Empowerment Measure (GEM); indicators of development; measuring development; welfare economics; well-being

Further reading

UNDP (United Nations Development Programme) (2001) *Human Development Report*, Oxford: Oxford University Press. http://hdr.undp.org/reports/global/2001/en/

World Bank (2001) *World Development Report, 2002*, Washington DC: World Bank. http://econ.worldbank.org/wdr/

World Bank (2003) *African Development Indicators 2003: Drawn from the World Bank Africa Database (2003)*, Washington DC: World Bank.

RICKIE SANDERS

welfare state

A welfare state is a political institution (see **institutions**) characterized by legal obligations to provide citizens with **safety nets against poverty**, thus translating the entitlements so created into **citizenship** rights. The rationale for welfare state lies in the need for state interventions in the market (see **state and state reform**) to compensate for failures of free markets to autonomously engender equitable distribution of incomes and equality of opportunity. Welfare state policies commonly are designed to promote private investment, regulate industrial relations and enforce **labor rights and standards**, stabilize business cycles (through income smoothing measures) and mitigate processes and structures that generate deprivation through, for example income redistribution measures. Poor economic **governance** and **structural adjustment**s that limit the revenue generating capacity of the state hamper the effectiveness of welfare state policies in developing countries. Consequently, donor interventions in **capacity building**, in governance and in **public management** have been introduced to ameliorate such weaknesses.

See also: pensions; public management; public sector; safety nets against poverty; welfare economics; welfare indicators

MOSES A. OSIRO

well-being

The concept of well-being refers to how well a person lives. It is used for various sorts of evaluation of a person's situation, but is more appropriately used for those evaluations that focus on the quality of the person's "being."

Conceptions of well-being include the following. First, well-being can be conceived as pleasure or satisfaction. This utilitarian conception is used rhetorically in economics, and empirically investigated in "subjective well-being" research in psychology and sociology. Its normative weight is limited by the many factors which mold felt satisfactions (see **functionings**), and by perverse pleasures (such as pleasure in others' suffering). Second, well-being has been seen as preference fulfillment (i.e. the achievement of pre-set objectives). This conception faces some of the same objections as the first. Third, well-being can be seen as free choice: choice is assumed to fulfill preferences, or to be all that matters (see **freedom versus choice**). Fourth, well-being can be conceived as opulence; material wealth is assumed to be the key to choice, preference fulfillment and/or satisfaction. Fifth, well-being may be seen as the attainment of certain values which can be specified independently of the individual concerned (e.g. good **health**, physical and mental). There are many such ("objective list") theories of well-being, which very largely overlap. The broad stream of "quality-of-life research" investigates these "objective" aspects of well-being. Sixth, well-being may be seen as the possession of a favorable range of valued opportunities. This conception comes from Sen's **capability approach**, and has influenced the conception of **human development** adopted in the 1990s in much of the **United Nations** system and elsewhere.

In general, economists have used the first four of these conceptions, with in practice especial attention to monetary income and wealth. The last two conceptions are influenced by the philosophical tradition of Aristotle, which views human well-being as not just a single type of sensation or action but as the fulfillment of a deep and various nature, central to which is that people are reasoning social actors. Conceptions of well-being as happiness or pleasure are called hedonic, in contrast to eudemonic conceptions of well-being as a more complex and reflective fulfillment.

Well-being is thus a vague concept, that can span various aspects of life and is subject to normative debate, rather than a sharply and consensually defined single object. Given the concept's close links to normative definitions of development, the vagueness is not surprising. However, much utilitarian philosophy and utilitarian-influenced economic analysis has tended to identify well-being in terms of the single entity of "utility," commonly seen as a sort of "mental money." In this sense, well-being was reduced to well-feeling, typically seen as pleasure. Well-feeling was widely assumed to be one-dimensional, and a component of it ("welfare," sometimes called "material welfare") was assumed to be separable, derived from economic goods and services, and of central importance (see **welfare economics**). Income became treated as the key measure of well-being in this economic approach and in conventional development economics.

Much research indicates that the dimensions and main sources of well-being are both different and broader than those traditionally stressed in economics. For example, many studies in low-income countries show that poor people's lists of priorities include both material and non-material aspects (e.g. Narayan, 2000). In more affluent countries, non-market sources of well-being (e.g. family, friends, health, recreation) appear considerably more important for satisfaction than are market sources, and amongst the market sources, experiences during work time or **unemployment** can determine satisfaction more than do levels of income or consumption (e.g. Ackerman et al., 1997; Easterlin, 2002). This thriving research field on what are valued aspects of life takes us far beyond the equation of development with **economic growth** alone.

See also: capability approach; ethics; freedom versus choice; functionings; growth versus holism; measuring development; welfare economics; welfare indicators

Further reading

Ackerman, F., Kiron, D., Goodwin, N., Harris, J. and Gallagher, K. (eds) (1997) *Human Well-Being and Economic Goals*, Washington DC: Island Press.

Easterlin, R. (ed.) (2002) *Happiness in Economics*, Cheltenham: Edward Elgar.

Narayan, D., Narayan-Parker, D. and Walton, M. (eds) (2000) *Voices of the Poor*, 3 vols, New York: Oxford University Press and http://www.worldbank.org/poverty/voices/reports.htm

DES GASPER

white revolution (milk)

The term white revolution refers to the rapid expansion of milk production in India since the early 1970s. The term was modeled on the **green revolution**, which involved the introduction of new agricultural technologies to developing countries.

India's milk production has more than tripled since the early 1970s, to over 80 million tons in 2002–3, making it the world's largest producer of milk (see **Food and Agriculture Organization (FAO)** publications). The five largest milk producing states, Uttar Pradesh, Punjab, Rajasthan, Maharashtra and Madhya Pradesh, account for over 50 percent of this production. Producers are mainly small or medium farmers who own one or two cows or buffaloes, which are fed largely on crop residues. India's milk processing capacity also rapidly expanded over this period.

An important contribution to the white revolution was made by Operation Flood (OF) (1970–96), the government dairy development program implemented by the National Dairy Development Board, and supported by the European Economic Commission (EEC), the World Food Program and the **World Bank** (WB). Funding for OF was primarily generated through the commercial selling of **food aid** from the **European Union**.

OF aimed to provide a reliable market for existing producers (linking rural producers with urban markets), to provide for milk processing, and to enable access to inputs. The organizational structure was a three-tier system (at the village, district and state levels) of farmer-owned cooperatives inspired by a successful cooperative in Anand.

In the late 1990s OF had over 6 million active cooperative members in over 55,000 village-level cooperatives. In 1996, WB funding for OF was phased out, with the explanation that the private sector might be more competitive than the cooperative sector.

There are conflicting views on how much credit for the white revolution can be given to OF, partly because of the low proportion of total milk production originating from the program's cooperatives: 6.3 percent in 1996–7 according to the World Bank. It is also controversial whether the poorest farmers and women have disproportionately benefitted from the program.

Skeptics of the term white revolution hold that average milk yields and per capita milk consumption in India still lie substantially below those in developed countries. Environmental **pollution** has also been raised as a concern, in particular the pollution of water supplies by untreated dairy plant effluent and the large emission of methane by cattle, implicated in global **climate change**.

Indian dairy production was until 1991 sheltered by the government's **import substitution** policies. Fears have been voiced that since then the lowering of import **tariffs** and the elimination of quantitative restrictions on imports to comply with WTO rules (see **World Trade Organization/General Agreement on Tariffs and Trade (WTO/GATT)**) have started to undermine local producers. There are signs of increasing imports of (in some cases subsidized) milk products from, among others, the European Union, the USA, and Australia. Exports of milk products from India remain negligible, partly because of problems in complying with sanitary standards.

See also: food; green revolution; livestock; rural development

Further reading

See the journal *Economic and Political Weekly*, http://www.epw.org.in/
World Bank (1998) *India: The Dairy Revolution. The Impact of Dairy Development in India and the World Bank's Contribution*, Washington DC: World Bank.

ULLI HUBER

WHO *see* World Health Organization (WHO)

women in development (WID) versus gender and development (GAD)

The debate about women in development (WID) versus gender and development (GAD) refers to differing approaches to incorporating women and **gender** roles in development policy over time. Crudely speaking, WID tends to focus on women as a group in their own right, whereas GAD nominally gives priority to gender relations. Although WID and GAD are often presented as dichotomous approaches, the fact that GAD evolved out of WID makes for a number of similarities between them, particularly insofar as "gender work" is still primarily concerned with women (see **gender**).

The term "WID" dates to the early 1970s and is usually attributed to the Women's Committtee of the Washington DC Chapter of the Society for International Development. Concern with the "predicament" of women in developing regions at this time was fueled by feminist critiques of "gender-blindness" in the design and execution of development projects. This "blindness" led to women being "overlooked," sidelined, and even harmed by interventions. These concerns were adopted when the WID approach was formally adopted by the United States Agency for International Development (USAID) during the 1970s. This approach saw women as an untapped force in **economic growth**, and sought to include women more in forms of **economic development**. WID entered its heyday during the United Nations Decade for Women (1975–85) (see **United Nations World Conferences on Women**). The call to integrate women in development provoked the formation of so-called "national machineries" to fulfill this objective in more than 100 countries. These steps were complemented by larger-scale initiatives such as the establishment of women's representatives, bureaus, and programs in regional and **international organizations and associations** including the **European Union**, **World Bank**, **United Nations** and **International Labor Organization (ILO)**.

While different types of WID policy emerged during the 1970s and 1980s, three common factors stand out. First, WID comprised a focus on women as an analytical and operational category. Second, it created separate organizational structures for women. Third, it developed female-specific policies and projects. At one level, these contributions signaled a major breakthrough for women: never before had resources been apportioned to women's development in this way, nor had so many women infiltrated the ranks of the international development system. At another level, however, there were also issues of concern. One concern was to question how far women can be seen as a single identifiable interest group, rather than socially differentiated on grounds of class, ethnicity (see **ethnicity/identity**), age and so on (see **sociology of development**). Concerns also emerged around the notion that it was women's *exclusion* from the development process which was the problem, and not the *process* itself. WID seemingly assumed that women would benefit by being "slotted in" to existing (male-biased) development structures (see **male bias**) presupposed that the problem of "women's development" was a "logistical problem," rather than something requiring a "fundamental reassessment of gender relations and ideology" (Parpart and Marchand, 1995). In short, while WID undoubtedly led to greater visibility of women in the development process, its tendency to opt for "add-on" solutions implied treatment of the symptoms, rather than the sources, of **gender inequality**.

GAD, in contrast, evolved during the 1980s and advocated a different set of strategies. GAD is by no means a singular entity and is open to a complex variety of subjective interpretations. But one of its basic premises is that gender is a dynamic social construct, and that meaningful and sustainable change can only occur by directing interventions to gender relations, which clearly involves men as well as women. The adoption of GAD makes gender, rather than women, the centerpiece of interventions.

GAD approaches call for the transformation of policy agendas from a gender perspective through the process of "mainstreaming." Mainstreaming entails reworking structures of decision-making and institutional cultures in order to incorporate concerns about gender in a central and organic manner, rather than peripherally, sporadically and mechanically. Indeed, the shift from WID to GAD has been claimed to bring a sharper realization of the entrenchment of gender inequalities in development organizations themselves, including themes such as staffing, promotion, access to parental leave and support, and inter-personal relations between colleagues. Developing so-called gender competence may be achieved through gender training, building gender networks in organizations, or by devising **accountability** measures for good gender practices. In practice, however, the principles of GAD interventions do not always match up to their rhetoric.

Despite the successes of GAD, some critics have claimed that the recent adoption of gender concerns within development thinking indicates "a high degree of co-option of politicized feminist objectives rather than their success in transforming the development agenda" (Pearson, 2000). To some extent this is reflected in the fact that despite several years of WID *and* GAD interventions, women's situations have often changed little, if not deteriorated, in many countries. Another criticism is that GAD has bypassed men. One of the most pressing issues in the future is for GAD initiatives to pay more than lip service to gender relations and to make dedicated efforts to engage men in gender and development planning from the policy level to the grassroots.

Another suggestion for improving GAD is to move away from the idea that gender is *the* major axis of social differentiation to making greater attempts to understand how gender differentiation links with other divisions and identities (see **ethnicity/identity**). This move could enhance the appreciation of power relations in poor societies, and help to better target prorities for development and **social justice**.

See also: ethnicity/identity; gender; male bias; women's movements; United Nations World Conferences on Women; women-headed households

Further reading

Chant, S. and Gutmann, M. (2000) *Mainstreaming Men into Gender and Development: Debates, Reflections and Experiences*, Oxford: Oxfam.

El-Bushra, J. (2000) "Rethinking Gender and Development Practice for the Twenty-first Century," pp. 53–62 in Sweetman, C. (ed.) *Gender in the 21st Century*, Oxford: Oxfam.

Parpart, J. and Marchand, M. (1995) "Exploding the Canon: An Introduction and Conclusion," pp. 1–22 in Marchand, M. and Parpart, J. (eds) *Feminism/Postmodernism/Development*, London: Routledge.

Pearson, R. (2000) "Rethinking Gender Matters in Development," pp. 383–402 in Allen, T. and Thomas, A. (eds) *Poverty and Development: Into the Twenty-first Century*, Milton Keynes: Open University Press.

SYLVIA CHANT

women-headed households

Women- (or female-) headed households are commonly defined as dwelling and/or consumption units in which the senior woman lacks a co-resident legal or common-law spouse. This classification may also extend to include the physical presence of another adult male such as a father, brother or grown-up son.

Women-headed households are a heterogeneous group. They can be headed by single, separated, divorced or widowed women. The first three statuses may also apply to *de facto* (as opposed to *de jure*) female heads whose male partners contribute money but are not co-resident as a result of **labor migration**. *De facto* and *de jure* female-headed households range from women living alone, to units consisting of mothers and children, to extended arrangements where female heads share their homes with relatives, friends or workmates (Chant, 1997).

The routes by which women enter female household headship, and the proportions of households headed by women, vary widely. It is difficult to generalize across regions, but levels of female household headship are usually low in areas where considerable importance is attached to formal marriage, such as Asia, the Middle East and North Africa. In such areas, the majority of women enter this state through widowhood, although desertion by men has become more common in parts of India and Bangladesh as rates of international male labor migration have risen. Both national and international **migration** play an important role in giving rise to women-headed households in Sub-Saharan Africa and Latin America, although in the latter, non-marriage and separation are also significant. In the Caribbean, where ties among women, children and female kin have historically been stronger than conjugal bonds, out-of-wedlock birth is the principal pathway to female household headship. Here proportions of households headed by women are the highest in the world (Folbre, 1991).

Despite regional differences, households headed by women are generally acknowledged to have increased in most parts of the South in the last few decades, and are presently around 20 percent of households worldwide. This said, it is difficult to establish precise trends because census bureaus in many developing societies have only recently begun to register **gender** breakdowns of household headship, and have often been inconsistent in their use of terminology and definitional criteria.

Specific reasons for increases in female household headship vary in accordance with the particular histories of individual countries, although some factors are generally significant. Some of the most important factors are the growth in capitalist development and "modernization" (see **modernization theory**) since World War II, which have undermined traditional economic and kinship structures. In most cases, traditional kinship structures were patriarchal and gave women limited access to income and resources in their own right (see **gender**). Another factor has been the growing demand for waged female labor brought about by the growth in **foreign direct investment**, and the spread of factories operated by **transnational corporations (TNCs)**, especially those specializing in the assembly of garments, electronics and other light industrial goods (see **gender and industrialization**). The trend toward female waged employment has been exacerbated by declining **employment** opportunities for men, especially at the lower end of the occupational hierarchy. The inability to fulfill social expectations to be family breadwinners also appears to make men in some countries less likely to marry, and is also associated with rising rates of conjugal breakdown.

Another important factor in the trend toward women-head households is **poverty**, often linked with neo-liberal (see **neo-liberalism**) economic restructuring (via **structural adjustment** policies), which has placed greater strain on family relationships, as well as diminishing the prospects for women's (re)incorporation in the households of parents and male relatives following widowhood, divorce or abandonment.

Demographic factors associated with rising female household headship include increased geographical mobility and gender-selective **migration**, such as in parts of Sub-Saharan Africa where men predominate in **rural-urban migration**, leaving women heading households in the countryside. Declining **fertility** is another demographic trend with implications for rising rates of female headship. It lessens the childcare burdens of lone mothers, thereby increasing their ability to take-up paid work. A declining number of **children** may also diminish the chances of older women being taken into children's households in the future.

Also important in accounting for increases in female household headship are women's growing sexual and reproductive freedom, access to divorce, and rights to the custody of children (see **reproductive rights**).

There have always been women-headed households. But their growing numbers raise a number of challenges to the orthodox household ideal in many societies of a patriarchal nuclear unit consisting of a married couple and their children. For example, the growth in female household headship is often tied to the notion of a worldwide "feminization of **poverty**" with the idea that women-headed units are prone to be disproportionately concentrated among low-income groups, and to suffer greater extremes of poverty than their male-headed counterparts. In turn, material privation is assumed to prejudice the life chances of children, alongside the psychological problems purportedly emanating from "father absence," lack of maternal attention, and limited parental discipline. Poverty and intergenerational disadvantages clearly do apply to some women-headed households in developing countries. But these patterns are also found in other types of household unit. Furthermore, research increasingly shows that conventional stereotypes about female household headship are crude, overly generalized and lacking in substantiation. In particular, feminist analysts have suggested that there is insufficient empirical evidence and too many weaknesses in existing data and methodologies to warrant unilaterally negative conclusions. (For example, the methods of scrutinizing **intrahousehold allocations,** or tracking family influences on child and youth development, have been criticized for being insufficiently researched). Indeed, in some instances, female household headship can prove to be personally empowering for women, and materially and psychologically beneficial to their offspring (especially where conjugal unions were conflictive) (see **empowerment**).

These discussions raise important questions about the place of women-headed households in social policy. Should female-headed units be treated as simply one variant of a range of contemporary household forms? If so, should they be entitled to benefit from policy interventions that target women and families in general? Or should they be targeted as a "residual group" in need of special assistance? (see Buvinic and Gupta, 1997).

See also: children; employment; empowerment; gender; gender and industrialization; intrahousehold allocations; labor migration; livelihoods; poverty; women in development (WID) versus gender and development (GAD)

Further reading

Buvinic, M. and Gupta, G. R. (1997) "Female-headed Households and Female-maintained Families: Are they Worth Targeting to Reduce Poverty in Developing Countries?," *Economic Development and Cultural Change* 45:2 259–80.

Chant, S. (1997) *Women-headed Households: Diversity and Dynamics in the Developing World*, Basingstoke: Macmillan.

Folbre, N. (1991) "Women on Their Own: Global Patterns of Female Headship," pp. 69–126 in Gallin, R. and Ferguson, A. (eds) *The Women and International Development Annual Volume 2*, Boulder: Westview.

SYLVIA CHANT

Women's Environment and Development Organization (WEDO)

The Women's Environment and Development Organization (WEDO) is a transnational advocacy network devoted to bringing women's and **gender** issues into sustainable development policy, **governance**, and economic/**social justice**. Founded in 1990 by former USA congresswoman Bella Abzug and feminist activist Mim Kelber, WEDO is directed by an international board of activists. It was first noteworthy for sponsoring the **World Women's Congress for a Healthy Planet (1991)**, which formulated Women's Action **Agenda 21** as input into the **Earth Summit (1992) (United Nations Conference on Environment and Development)**. Since then, WEDO's Women's Caucus has been a central participant and negotiator in key UN conferences, including the **Cairo conference on population and development**, 1994; the Copenhagen World Conference on **social development** 1995; the Beijing UN World Conference on Women, 1995; and the **World Summit on Sustainable Development (Johannesburg, 2002)**. At that time, it updated the Women's Action Agenda for a Healthy Planet for 2015.

See also: environment; feminism and ecology; feminist political ecology; gender; gender, environment and development; United Nations World Conferences on Women; World Women's Congress for a Healthy Planet (191)

DONNA D. RUBINOFF

women's movements

Women's movements (as distinct from organizations) are extremely varied, differing according to social factors such as region, class, ethnicity (see **ethnicity/identity**), nationality, generation, and **religion** and in terms of what they consider to be their priorities. These movements involve a social or political phenomenon of some significance in support of women's interests or claims which would transform social relations in order to enhance women's position (Molyneux, 1998) (see also **new social movements**). They may be affiliated to or independent of more formal organizations such as political parties, their members might operate a "double militancy" through membership or participation in other political structures, and they have different relationships with the state (see **state and state reform**) (Beckwith, 2000). In many societies, the social and economic division of labor and the role of women in reproduction have led them to organize separately from men. Western feminists have tended to assume that women organizing together are inherently feminist, while women from developing countries tend to be wary of this label. Women are not a unitary group and **gender** is not the sole basis of the struggle for the equal rights of women (Waylen, 1994; Basu, 1995).

At the global level, the development of women's movements has been bound up with international systems of **governance**. Through their activism in the **League of Nations** after World War I, women achieved international conventions on issues such as the rights of married women and **employment** standards. A model of cooperation developed between **non-governmental organizations (NGOs)** and international NGOs, enabling issues which concerned women to be placed on the international agenda. When they found obstacles at the national level it was possible for women to take their grievances to **international organizations and associations** (Pietilä, 2002).

During the UN Decade for Women (1976–85) (see **United Nations World Conferences on Women**) and the subsequent series of conferences, the dominance of Western feminists was thoroughly debated. While Western feminists focused on prioritizing women's autonomous organizing for what they saw as the specific, universal interests of women, women's movements in the South emphasized social and economic issues such as poverty, access to land, **fuelwood, drinking water**, safe environments. There was a conflict between the universalist claims of Western feminism and the more **community**-based concerns of women in developing countries (Basu, 1995).

By the 1985 Nairobi conference on women, there were many women's organizations active on community issues, which had developed through local struggles but which were beginning to make significant global and trans-national connections. At successive UN conferences, notably Vienna, 1993 and Beijing, 1995, women's organizations pressed for a redefinition of **human rights** in order to make space for the recognition of abuses committed by non-state actors within the private domain, such as rape and **domestic violence**.

The processes of democratization (see **democracy; civil society**) made an impact on women's movements. Evidence from mobilizations against Latin American military governments shows that women's movements which had supported human rights or pressed for social justice lost ground under civilian rule, finding it difficult to gain influence in formal democratic **institutions**. Women in Central and Eastern Europe found that liberalization and democratization (see **shock therapy**) meant fewer numbers of women in elected positions, the rolling back of abortion rights, reduced access to child care and the opening up of exploitative labor market positions in the service sector, particularly the sex industry (see **prostitution/sex work**). Where the "woman question" had previously been incorporated in the state (see **state and state reform**), issues and spaces began to emerge for an autonomous women's movement (Waylen, 1994).

Research into the conditions for the emergence of women's movements suggests that they depend on social factors, the form taken by the family, the political structure, relations between women, and the wider characteristics of **civil society**.

Other women's mobilizations have focused on resistance to issues that threaten their lives, providing inspiration to global movements. Through their leadership of these mobilizations, women gained knowledge of the political process and frequently empowered themselves. Examples would be mobilizations against or in favor of religious or nationalist fundamentalism (Basu, 1995), the peace movement, and environmental activism such as the **Chipko movement** in 1970s India where women hugged trees to prevent logging (see **logging/timber trade**), or the Kenyan Green Belt movement (see **feminist political ecology; feminism and ecology**).

See also: civil society; feminism and ecology; feminist political ecology; gender; new social movements; United Nations World Conferences on Women

Further reading

Basu, A. (1995) *The Challenge of Local Feminisms*, Boulder CO: Westview.

Beckwith, K. (2000) "'Beyond Compare?' Women's Movements in Comparative Perspective," *European Journal of Political Research* 37:4 431–68.

Molyneux, M. (1998) "Analysing Women's Movements," in Jackson, C. and Pearson, R. (eds) *Feminist Visions of Development*, London: Routledge.

Pietilä, H. (2002) *Engendering the Global Agenda: The Story of Women and the United Nations*, New York: United Nations Non-Governmental Liaison Service (NGLS).

Waylen, G. (1994) "Women and Democratization: Conceptualizing Gender Relations in Transition Politics," *World Politics* 46: 327–54.

CATHERINE LLOYD

World Bank

The World Bank is the world's largest development bank, providing loans, policy advice, technical assistance and knowledge-sharing services to low and middle income countries to reduce **poverty**. It is also one of the most controversial and criticized actors in international development. It is composed of five closely associated institutions: the International Bank for Reconstruction and Development (IBRD, established 1945); the International Development Association (IDA, established 1960); the International Finance Corporation (IFC, established 1956); the Multilateral Investment Guarantee Agency (MIGA, established 1988); and the International Center for Settlement of Investment Disputes (ICSID, established 1966). The "World Bank" is the name that has become used for the IBRD and IDA together, which are organizations provide low-interest loans, interest-free credit, and grants to developing countries.

A controversial institution of global proportion, the World Bank (or then, the IBRD) was originally designed in the mid-1940s, along with its "twin," the **International Monetary Fund (IMF)**, to reduce the danger of worldwide financial crises, restore foreign **trade**, and supply reconstruction capital to war-torn countries at the end of World War II (see **Bretton Woods; Marshall Plan**). In July 1944, delegates from forty-four countries approved the bold plan to finance the World Bank and IMF at the international conference in **Bretton Woods**, New Hampshire. Scripted by the UK's John Maynard Keynes and the US's Harry Dexter White, the plan also assured a central role for elite Northern countries in the **governance** of the post-war global economy. It is reported that the initial organization called the IBRD only had the word "development" added at the conference largely at the suggestions of the Indian delegation, who shared the same railway carriage as Keynes on the way to the meeting. Despite the apparent need for a supra-national governance body, and even with the support of the capital-rich countries, the World Bank remained a minor international actor for its first twenty-five years. It was not until the late 1960s, when ex-US Secretary of Defense Robert McNamara was appointed Bank President, that the Bank become a globally significant institution (see **institutions**), producing a political economy of development that has since become dominant and a global discourse that has become common sense around the world. By the early twenty-first century, few national economic plans for developing or transitional countries are approved without the consent of the World Bank, and few international protests occur without the World Bank being an important focus of the protestors' ire (see **World Social Forum (WSF)**). The World Bank has redefined the meaning of development and reframed the terrain of North-South relations, making it an enormously influential, as well as contentious, global institution.

Based in Washington DC, headed by a succession of prominent Wall Street figures, and kept on a short leash by the US Treasury and State Department, the World Bank started off by making very conservative loans to only a few countries at a time. Although quite normal for the post-war era, it may seem unusual today that none of these loans went toward "improving" the condition of the rural poor, or for "poverty alleviation." In the beginning, the World Bank typically lent to transport and power sectors (see **transport policy; electrification and power-sector reform; energy policy**), which were considered to be the bottlenecks to industrial **economic growth** for developing countries. Most contracts to build and equip these large infrastructural projects were directed to firms based in Western Europe and the USA; the Bank's attractive low-interest loans were distributed in the currencies of Western Europe and the USA, and their banks facilitated and profited from the transactions. Furthermore, most Bank loans in the early years did not go to the capital-poor countries with the highest rates of poverty, but to middle- and high-income countries. In 1951, for example, the largest of the Bank borrowers included Australia, India, Italy, France, the UK, and Japan. Of the loans that did go to capital-poor countries, many were distributed to countries such as France, the UK, and Belgium, for development projects in their present and former colonies, such as Gabon, Algeria, the Congo, Northern and Southern Rhodesia, Nigeria, and Kenya. In the beginning, Wall Street considered it too risky to lend to newly independent nations directly, except in small doses, and as such, the World Bank's role was merely to re-ignite the post-war global economy without undermining the basic structure of the colonial relationship between North and South (see **colonialism, history of; colonialism, impacts of**).

This domination by richer countries' interests was partly the result of the voting rights established for donors to the IBRD and IDA. Under IBRD and IDA rules, donors gained influence with the amount of money donated, and hence unsurprisingly, the IBRD and IDA attracted more money than the co-existing United Nations bodies such as the UN Extended Programme of Technical Assistance (EPTA, established 1948) or Special UN Fund for Economic Development (SUNFED, established 1958). EPTA and SUNFED were later to become the **United Nations Development Programme (UNDP)**, and were governed under the UN Economic and Social Council, which gave more voting rights to recipient rather than donor countries. Some say the IDA was created also to

deal with the US holdings of inconvertible currencies which were accrued after the US Public Law 480 (1954) allowed US agricultural surpluses to be sold overseas as a form of **aid** in return for domestic currencies (Raffer and Singer, 1996:54).

Only during the Bank's McNamara era (1968–80) did the World Bank become an independent global entity that generated its own development agenda and its own impact on the global economy. As the former US Secretary of Defense who ran the ignominious war in Indochina, and previously the president of Ford Motor Company, McNamara always thought big. In his first days in office, he was astonished that the World Bank's annual budget was so small (less than US$1 billion as compared to his US$70 billion dollar military budget), and that very little of it was invested in what he called the "the bottom 40 percent" of the world's **population**, those living in "absolute poverty." In his first public speech as Bank president, he shocked his conservative colleagues when he dismissed the one economic indicator that marked the Bank's success in its development mission, rising gross national products (see **gross national product (GNP)**). McNamara openly described the Bank's record as dismal for having ignored this large population of impoverished people, about whom the Bank had very little knowledge. He noted that since 1960 in the developing world:

> The average annual growth thus far has been 4.8 percent. ... And yet ... you know and I know that these cheerful statistics are cosmetics, which conceal a far less cheerful picture. ... [M]uch of the growth is concentrated in the industrial areas, while the peasant remains stuck in his immemorial poverty, living on the bare margin of subsistence.
>
> (McNamara, 1997)

Within his first few weeks in office, McNamara demanded that his loan officers drum up new projects that focused on improving the lives of the poorest, especially those "who live on the soil," to help them "rise out of the pit of poverty." He was not just a development dreamer, but a realist who had just lost the hearts and minds of millions of peasants in the US war in Indochina. In his new job, he saw an opportunity to challenge the "red" (anti-colonial) revolutions sweeping the world with the "**green revolution**" based on large capital investments used to import agro-industrial inputs from the North for **rural development**. By putting the Bank's full weight behind the high-yield variety seed technologies for use in **agriculture**, McNamara hoped to win over peasants and governments alike to the World Bank's technocratic and **capital intensive** solutions amidst radical political demands for equitable land redistribution and democratization of access to **natural resources**.

In transforming the World Bank, McNamara took three bold steps. First, he asked his treasurer to create a new vehicle for raising capital that would bypass the limits of the US Treasury and the US bond market, and instead help stimulate a global bond market in which the Bank could liberally float large bonds in multiple currencies. These World Bank bonds attracted **Organization of Petroleum Exporting Countries (OPEC)** dollars as well as capital from Japanese and Western European investors looking to invest outside of the economically depressed US economy. Five months into his tenure, McNamara borrowed more funds on capital markets than in any calendar year of the Bank's history. Second, he transformed the organizational **culture** at World Bank headquarters: He wanted the whole enterprise to be motivated and justified through an incentive system that rewarded loan officers for their ability to conjure large and ambitious loan projects and sell them to cash-strapped borrowers. In short time, he enlarged the Bank's staff by 120 percent, and in his first five-year term, the Bank financed more projects (760 versus 708) and loaned more money (US$13.4 billion versus US$10.7 billion) than it had during the previous twenty-two years combined. The Bank began to lend large amounts of capital to a growing number of countries, which led to its increased influence in economic decision-making across regions. Third, he established a worldwide system for training professionals and for conducting research on the themes that the Bank aggressively promoted. This network of agricultural research institutes, development centers, and university programs, has supplied the Bank and governments with like-minded professionals trained

and equipped with data and resources to support new World Bank initiatives in different local political settings. By cultivating "champions" locally and instituting new knowledge-producing techniques, the World Bank became the world's authority and expert on development and on the "developing world," with professionals trained in Bank-style development economics and assessment tools.

In its tremendous growth spurt of the 1970s, the World Bank touched so many lives and **institutions** of the South *and* North, with an impact on the ways in which states managed societies (see **state and state reform**) and the ways in which Northern capital invested in the South. But in this effort to lend broadly and intensively, the Bank was spread very thin across developing countries, and it financed a number of highly contentious projects over which it had only limited oversight or control. During and following the McNamara era, the Bank built large **dams**, highways, power plants, and mining projects that devastated environments and pushed out millions of people from their homes and away from the ecological conditions on which their livelihoods depended (see **displacement**). The most egregious projects – and those that reached global notoriety – were in Indonesia, forcibly resettling millions of ethnic minorities and destroying wetlands and forests (see **transmigration**), and in the Amazonian rainforest, pushing indigenous forest dwellers out while pulling colonizers in to log, cattle ranch, and farm (see **Polonoreste; transport policy**).

By the mid-1980s, when the Bank threw its full weight behind a highly controversial mega-dam project in the Narmada Valley of western India, protests within India triggered a transnational advocacy coalition (or network – see **advocacy coalitions**) that mobilized activist campaigns in the capital cities of the Bank's largest Northern supporters (see **environmental movements; dams**). This anti-dam campaign gained great momentum from parallel campaigns protesting mega-projects in other borrowing countries. Combining tactics of hunger strikes, mass mobilizations, and high-profile public hearings in Washington DC and elsewhere, an inchoate anti-Bank activist network tarnished the image of the World Bank and called into question publicly, for the first time in history, its legitimacy and its development framework. The more that Bank leaders stubbornly dismissed the allegations, the more widespread became the disdain for the Bank's way of doing business.

By the early 1980s, another problem with the Bank's style of large-scale capitalist development financing surfaced. For many of the Bank's clients, years of borrowing for capital intensive projects, and the costly environmental and social clean-ups that many projects required, led to the accumulation of hefty debts. Ideally, governments could have repaid their development loans from revenues generated from the commodities produced from their investments in transportation, hydroelectric dams, power plants, and export-oriented agriculture; but the world-market prices of many of the goods produced with Bank financing had plummeted. Many key commodities that the Bank assiduously promoted for production across developing countries were being replaced by commodities produced in developed countries, such as corn syrup for sugar, glass fiber for copper, soy oils for tropical oils, and synthetic alternatives to **rubber**, cotton, jute, and timber (McMichael, 2000). By 1986, developing-world **debt** had risen to US$1 trillion and many countries were using Bank and IMF loans and precious export earnings for the sole purpose of servicing their ballooning debts. Consequently, the World Bank had a *net inflow* of capital from its borrowers, receiving far more from its borrowers than it was lending (see **debt crisis**).

In spite of the fact that development investment had backfired and had left borrowers' economies in crisis, the World Bank's power worldwide actually grew. Developed countries responded to the debt crisis, which also greatly threatened the banking industry in developed countries, by further empowering the Bank and IMF to become the global arbiter of developing countries' foreign debts. With renewed vigor, the Bank imposed a series of structural demands upon its borrowers to produce even more for export rather than for domestic needs, to reduce trade barriers and **tariffs** for imports from developed countries, and to open up key public sectors to international competition (i.e. **telecommunications**, energy (see **energy policy**) and mining, insurance, banking, transport, **health**). The ensuing era of "**structural adjustment**" was supposed to have been a short-lived "shock" (see **shock therapy**) that would help countries to ride out a short period of economic restructuring, after which liberalized trade relations between developed and developing countries would kick in. Instead, shock therapy became repetitive cycles of large debt-servicing loans and additional conditionalities (see **conditionality**) that only further destabilized borrowers. By the late 1980s, the **United Nations Children's Fund (UNICEF)** reported that World Bank structural adjustment programs were responsible for the "reduced health, nutritional, and educational levels for tens of millions of children in Asia, Latin America, and Africa" (McMichael, 2000) (see **adjustment with a human face**).

Even as the World Bank became an institution of global proportion, widespread protest campaigns challenged its legitimacy. When the World Bank celebrated its 50th anniversary in 1994, it was met with a worldwide campaign dedicated to closing it down, calls that also resonated amongst conservative power brokers in Washington DC and on Wall Street. The "Fifty Years is Enough" campaign represented dozens of different organizations and protest groups. Since then, this campaign has transformed itself into a loose-knit transnational movement with representatives worldwide battling with the Bank over policies and projects, while also challenging its sibling global organizations and trade agreements such as the WTO (see **World Trade Organization/General Agreement on Tariffs and Trade (WTO/GATT)**), the IMF, and **North American Free Trade Agreement (NAFTA)**. Because World Bank loan conditionalities have since become a common mechanism used to transform (e.g. mostly liberalize) the economic and social institutions of its borrowers, landless peoples and fisherfolk movements, indebted farmers networks, and mass-based organizations have joined the anti-Bank movement in order to stop Bank-instigated privatization policies (see **privatization and liberalization**) unfolding in their countries, with their harsh effects on wages, land reform, and the pricing and access to **drinking water**, electrification (see **electrification and power-sector reform**), **housing**, **education**, and health services (see **peasant movements**).

World Bank supporters argue that the Bank's failures are the result of the Bank becoming too big and ambitious, stretching its original development mission far beyond financing "brick and mortar" projects (Pincus and Winters, 2002). With its nose into so many aspects of running a country, from HIV/AIDS pharmaceutical pricing plans (see **pharmaceuticals; HIV/AIDS (definition and treatment); HIV/AIDS (policy issues)**)to currency devaluation mechanisms (see **Asian crises; fiscal and monetary policy; inflation and its effects**), the Bank can no longer claim to be a distant and objective facilitator of the project of development. This proximity to national power and political decision-making has made the World Bank extremely vulnerable to a wide array of grievances from different sectors of society. In sum, in its phenomenal rise to global power, the World Bank has become vulnerable to opposition from multiple sectors of societies all over the world.

At the turn of the new millennium, the World Bank has responded to its critics by expanding its leadership role in a number of new development domains: environmentally **sustainable development**, good governance, greater **accountability** and **transparency**, and the financing of and new **partnerships** with "**civil society**." Yet, the reputation of the World Bank remains stained and its new endeavors highly scrutinized. One reason is that the Bank has yet to reconcile its own highly inequitable power structure. When the Bank started, five countries controlled more than half of the total vote within the Bank's voting structure, with the USA alone holding nearly 30 percent of the total vote. Six decades later, and after extolling the virtues of accountability and client-based ownership of development, the Bank's voting power structure has hardly changed: The "Big Five" countries (the US, UK, Germany, France, and Japan) still control approximately 38 percent of the vote, while 46 African countries have together only 5 percent of the vote and typically only have two representatives on the Bank's 24-member board of Executive Directors.

Second, the Bank's asymmetric voting structure reflects proportionately the dollar amount of contracts that countries' firms receive from Bank loans (e.g. dam construction, turbines, computers,

consultancies). When the Bank first opened for business, it was a common "truth" amongst the leadership from developed countries that developing countries could develop only through **technology transfer**, capital, goods, and expertise from the North. Indeed, in the first few decades, most of the money loaned to developing countries purchased goods and services from the North, 60 percent of which came from just the Big Five countries. Yet, after sixty years of World Bank-style development, developing countries still purchase a lion's share of the goods and services for World Bank projects from developed countries, with more than 50 percent of foreign procurement dollars from Bank loans going directly to firms in the USA, UK, Japan, Germany, and France. How should we define and assess World Bank-led development if it has not led to the capacity of its borrowers to supply its own – or its neighbors' – materials for economic growth? That so many development dollars continue to flow into the countries that control the majority voting bloc at the Bank raises fundamental questions about the Bank's project of development and its relationship to maintaining inequitable North-South economic relations. As its toughest critics ask: Does World Bank development serve the rich rather than the poor, the North better than the South? Can the development project be reformed under the leadership of the World Bank?

By contrast, reformers have called for the World Bank to retreat from its "mission creep" and get back to its roots of a lean and smart development bank. They argue that the expert-led World Bank still has a **comparative advantage** over highly politicized state agencies for making tough decisions about economic **planning** and development. But since the Bank is not supposed to interfere with member countries' internal political affairs, according to its original Charter (Article III, Section viii of the IDA Articles of Agreement), it is handcuffed when negotiating national policies without discussing important political reforms. These observers insist that the Bank should be given *more* power over national policy-making. Meanwhile, others ask: Whom exactly does the World Bank represent? Until the World Bank reconciles its sixty-year record of serving its Northern voting bloc better than its borrowers – especially the world's majority poor **population** – the World Bank may never overcome public questioning of its legitimacy and purpose.

See also: adjustment with a human face; antipolitics; conditionality; debt; debt crisis; debt relief; International Monetary Fund (IMF); governance; neo-liberalism; shock therapy; structural adjustment; trade; United Nations Development Programme (UNDP); Washington consensus

Further reading

Bretton Woods Project: A critical information service on the World Bank and IMF: http://www.brettonwoodsproject.org/

Escobar, A. (1994) *Encountering Development: The Making and Unmaking of the Third World*, Princeton: Princeton University Press.

Ferguson, J. (1990) *The Anti-Politics Machine: Development, Depoliticization, Bureaucratic Power in Lesotho*, Minneapolis: University of Minnesota Press.

George, S. and Fabrizio S. (1994) *Faith and Credit: The World Bank's Secular Empire*, London and New York: Penguin.

Goldman, M. (2004) *Imperial Nature: The World Bank and the Making of "Green" Neoliberalism*, New Haven: Yale University Press.

IFI watchnet: A critical information service on international financial institution such as the World Bank: http://www.ifiwatchnet.org

Kapur, D., Lewis, J. and Webb, R. (eds) (1997) *The World Bank: Its First Half Century*, 2 vols, Washington DC: Brookings Institution.

McMichael, P. (2000, 2nd edn) *Development and Social Change: A Global Perspective*, Thousand Oaks CA: Pine Forge Press.

McNamara, Robert (1997) "To the Board of Governors, Washington, D.C., September 30, 1968," in McNamara, *The McNamara Years at the World Bank* (Baltimore: Johns Hopkins University Press, 1981:3–5), p. 217 in Kapur, D., Lewis, J. and Webb, R. (eds) *op. cit.*

Pincus, J. and Winters, J. (2002) *Reinventing the World Bank*, Ithaca NY: Cornell University Press.

Raffer, K. and Singer, H. (1996) *The Foreign Aid Business: Economic Assistance and Development Cooperation*, Cheltenham: Edward Elgar.

Rich, B. (1994) *Mortgaging the Earth: The World Bank, Environmental Impoverishment and the Crisis of Development*, London: Earthscan.

MICHAEL GOLDMAN

World Commission on Dams (WCD)

The World Commission on Dams (WCD) was an international body overseeing debates about the construction and use of large dam projects (see **dams**). The WCD was created in April 1997 with support from the **World Bank**, the International Union for the Conservation of Nature (World Conservation Union) and a large number of **non-governmental organizations (NGOs)**. The WCD carried out its work under the direction of a number of Commissioners drawn from several of the constituencies involved in its creation. This influential group comprised activists, donor groups, educationalists, environmentalists, NGO representatives (see **non-governmental organizations (NGOs)**) and several academics from diverse fields of interest. The Commissioners came from countries as far afield as Australia, Brazil, India, South Africa, Sweden and the United States.

The Commission's remit was to assess the extent to which large dams (those with a minimum height of 15 meters, measured from their foundation) contributed to development efforts worldwide. The WCD promoted a framework under which dams' role in harnessing water and energy resources (see **energy policy**) could be assessed. This framework enabled the Commission to work in establishing internationally acceptable criteria for the planning, design, construction, and the eventual decommissioning, of large dams. Given the complex economic, environmental and social issues encountered in the construction of large dams, the Commission ensured that its key decision-making functions were driven by the need to accommodate a wide range of interests and opinion. As such, an emphasis on participatory decision-making was regarded as an essential aspect of this project (see **participatory development**).

In November 2000, the WCD published its report *Dams and Development: A New Framework for Decision-making*. As planned, the publication of this document coincided with the Commission's own disbandment. It is difficult for an organization such as the WCD to continuously avoid controversy, and some NGOs have argued that the WCD was too uncritical about large dams. It is important to note, however, that the WCD was established to represent diverse groups, and judgments about its contribution need to acknowledge the diverse opinions about dams. In this overall sense, the work of the WCD has been positive to the debate on the need for large dams. Indeed, since February 2001, the United Nations Environment Programme (UNEP), under its Dams and Development Project, has been continuing the work initiated by the WCD.

See also: dams; energy policy; environment; water management; World Bank

Further reading

Dubash, N., Dupar, M., Kothari, S. and Lissu, T. (2001) *A Watershed in Global Governance: An Independent Assessment of the World Commission on Dams*, Washington DC: World Resources Institute.

World Commission on Dams (2000) *Dams and Development: A New Framework for Decision-making. The Report of the World Commission on Dams*, London: Earthscan.

PARVIZ DABIR-ALAI

world economic conference (London, 1933)

The world monetary and economic conference – or "London Conference of 1933" – was an attempt at addressing the world depression of the 1930s by currency stabilization, regulating international **debt,** and other economic agreements. It was one of the first significant attempts at international economic coordination (see **international economic order**). The meeting, however, failed to reach agreement largely because President Roosevelt of the USA refused to commit his country to any joint exchange rate policy (see **exchange rates**) with Britain and France. Furthermore, the USA was also suspicious that France and Britain might default on war debts from World War I (France and Britain had agreed to cancel German reparations in June 1932, which was conditional on US cancellation of their war debts). The USA was also suspected the British of expanding **trade** within its own empire and Commonwealth, hence cutting out the USA. Germany too, worried other participants by indicating that it inclined to autarky. Because of these failures, customs and currency restrictions became more stringent. The later **Bretton Woods** agreement of 1944 sought to avoid these impasses, and instead create the structures of global economic **governance**.

See also: Bretton Woods; international economic order; trade

TIM FORSYTH

World Food Programme (WFP)

The World Food Programme (WFP) was established in 1963 as the **United Nations** chief distributor of food in locations of **famine, complex emergencies**, and **refugees**. It differs from the United Nations **Food and Agriculture Organization (FAO)** because it aims to feed hungry poor people, whereas FAO sets up norms for world **agriculture** and offers technical expertise. Both WFP and FAO are based in Rome. Initially established on a three-year basis, the WFP was confirmed on a continuing basis by the FAO and United Nations General Assembly in 1965 "for as long as multilateral **food** is found feasible and desirable." The 1974 World Food Conference in Rome later recommended a reconstitution of the WFP in accordance with the creation of the International Fund for Agricultural Development (IFAD) and the FAO Committee on World Food Security. In 2002 alone, WFP fed 72 million people in eighty-two countries. It now has thirty-five member states. The typical food ration (where no other food is available) is calculated at 2,100 kilocalories per person per day, or 15kg per person per month. However, some recent criticisms have concerned whether the rations – comprising typically cereals, pulses, vegetable oil, salt, sugar, and bread – have sufficient **nutrition** for affected individuals, and whether they were initially inspired more by the food surpluses of donor countries than the needs of recipients. A further concern has been that WFP food rations have been sold in local markets, thus questioning whether food is reaching the right people.

See also: complex emergencies; emergency assistance; famine; food; food security; humanitarianism; nutrition; refugees; United Nations; war

TIM FORSYTH

World Health Organization (WHO)

The World Health Organization (WHO) is the **United Nations** specialized agency for health. It was established in 1948, bringing together a number of pre-existing health organizations. WHO's objective, as set out in its Constitution, is the attainment by all peoples of the highest possible level of health. Health is defined by the WHO Constitution in extremely broad terms as a state of "complete physical, mental and social **well-being**" and not merely the absence of disease or infirmity. This definition has led to controversies concerning whether health care should be comprehensive or selective. Indeed, in the 1980s and 1990s, the **United Nations Children's Fund (UNICEF)** adopted a selective approach to **primary health care** that focused on key variables such as growth monitoring, breastfeeding, and immunization, which some critics claimed overlooked the broad remit of health provision identified by the WHO.

The WHO performs a number of tasks. It cooperates with member countries to strengthen their health services and to train health workers. It coordinates biomedical research; informs on the

incidence of internationally important diseases and on the spread of **epidemics**. It was instrumental in **disease eradication**, such as smallpox, which was eventually eradicated in 1978. It publishes information on the effects of environmental **pollution**; sets global standards for vaccines and antibiotics; and takes a role in public campaigns, for example to discourage tobacco and alcohol consumption. The WHO secretariat, based in Geneva, is staffed by some 3,500 health and other experts and support staff.

The WHO, however, operates under various constraints and criticisms. The WHO is registered only as an international organization (see **international organizations and associations**), and therefore has fewer opportunities to raise money than UNICEF, which is jointly registered as a non-governmental organization (see **non-governmental organizations (NGOs)**) and international organization. Some critics have suggested that funding constraints on the WHO have allowed donors to influence the creation of special programs based in the WHO's headquarters in Geneva rather than integrated into national programs in developing countries because special programs are easier for donors to control. Critics also allege, "instead of working in a coordinated way towards a set of centrally agreed goals, the organization has become an umbrella within which its independent programmes compete for funds" (Godlee, 1995:179).

Some critics also believe that the WHO's success at eradicating smallpox has led to a continued desire to eradicate other diseases, even where the potential circumstances and benefits of eradication are less clear (see **disease eradication**). Eradicating **malaria**, for example, is much more difficult than smallpox because of the possibility for migrant people and animals to act as reservoirs, and the growing resistance of mosquitoes to anti-malarial **pharmaceuticals**. Hence, critics suggest, there should be less effort in research for a "magic bullet" to solve malaria, but instead more attention to **primary health care**, reducing social **vulnerability**, and **capacity building** such as promoting environmental health and standards setting in affected regions. The WHO has also been criticized for being slow to counter HIV/AIDS (see **HIV/AIDS (definition and treatment); HIV/ AIDS (policy issues)**), or failing to place sufficient pressure on pharmaceuticals companies to secure cheap drugs.

There has been praise, however, for WHO's programmes (headquartered in Burkina Faso) to control diarrheal diseases – which emphasizes prevention – and onchocerciasis (River Blindness) – which involves the spraying of blackfly breeding grounds. The WHO also took a dominant role in recommending travel restrictions during the epidemic (see **epidemics**) of SARS (Severe Acute Respiratory Syndrome) in 2002–3, which observers claimed showed the value of having an organization such as the WHO.

See also: disease eradication; epidemics; health; HIV/AIDS (definition and treatment); HIV/AIDS (policy issues); primary health care; United Nations; United Nations Children's Fund (UNICEF); vaccination

Further reading

Godlee, F. (1995) "WHO's Special Programmes: Undermining from Above," *British Medical Journal* 310: 178–82.
WHO website: http://www.who.int/

CLAUDIO O. DELANG

World Heritage Convention (UNESCO 1972)

The World Heritage Convention is the name given to the 1972 **United Nations Education, Scientific and Cultural Organization (UNESCO)** Convention concerning the Protection of the World Cultural and Natural Heritage. This convention built upon the Charter of Venice (1964), and recognized sites of "outstanding universal value" for the collective memory of humanity. Based on the twin concepts of "authenticity" and "integrity," the ten nomination criteria (six cultural, four natural) refer to unique archaeological, monumental, aesthetic, geological, and biological values of sites. Famous campaigns have helped relocate the Egyptian temple of Abu Simbel; introduce tougher environmental protection

measures for the Galapagos Islands; and mobilize international support to restrict looting and support locally beneficial tourism around Angkor Wat in Cambodia. Prior to submission to the intergovernmental World Heritage Committee, nominations are evaluated by the International Council of Monuments and Sites (ICOMOS), for cultural and mixed properties; and by the World Conservation Union (IUCN), for natural sites. State parties (see **state and state reform**) must submit regular monitoring reports, and a fund exists for sites in danger. In 2004, 788 sites were inscribed on the list.

See also: common heritage of humankind; cultural heritage; culture; ecotourism; protected areas; United Nations Education, Scientific and Cultural Organization (UNESCO)

TERENCE HAY-EDIE

World Intellectual Property Organization (WIPO)

The World Intellectual Property Organization (WIPO) is a **United Nations** specialized agency mandated to promote the protection of intellectual property (IP) throughout the world by harmonizing national legislation toward common objectives (see **intellectual property rights (IPRs)**). The organization administers more than twenty IP-related treaties, and serves as a forum for negotiating new treaties. Existing international treaties include the Berne Convention for the Protection of Literary and Artistic Works (originally adopted in 1886), and the Paris Convention for the Protection of Industrial Property (1883). These set minimum protection standards for IPRs while procuring "reciprocal recognition" of rights among signatory states. WIPO also facilitates patent applications in multiple countries simultaneously through the Patent Cooperation Treaty (PCT) – indeed, the bulk of the agency's funding comes from patent application fees under this treaty. WIPO plays a key role in providing technical assistance to developing countries on legal reforms and training to implement their obligations under the **trade-related aspects of intellectual property rights (TRIPS)**

Agreement administered by the WTO (see **World Trade Organization/General Agreement on Tariffs and Trade (WTO/GATT)**).

See also: intellectual property rights (IPRs); trade-related aspects of intellectual property rights (TRIPS); World Trade Organization/General Agreement on Tariffs and Trade (WTO/GATT)

TZEN WONG

World Social Forum (WSF)

The World Social Forum (WSF) is an international arena where **non-governmental organizations (NGOs)**, **trade unions**, and other **civil society** organizations coalesce to promote alternatives to the global expansion of **neo-liberalism**. Initiated in Porto Alegre, Brazil, in 2001, the WSF annually brings together several tens of thousands of citizens from over a hundred countries. Forum attendees are committed to the development of "a society centered on the human person" (WSF Charter of Principles). Participants come together around the slogan "Another World Is Possible," and engage in reflective thinking, action building, and inter-linking that is international in scope. They advocate an "alter-globalization" that focuses on **people-centered development** and **social justice**.

The WSF evolved as a counterweight to the World Economic Forum (WEF), and the two occur simultaneously. Established in 1971, the WEF plays a key role in charting the global, neo-liberal economic agenda. Its members include chief executives of the largest **transnational corporations (TNCs)**, as well as influential political leaders, and academics worldwide. The WEF's exclusive annual sessions were conducted in Davos, Switzerland, until 2002.

The World Social Forum (WSF) is, effectively, the progeny of an international movement that became manifest as massive protests accompanied the 1998 **Multilateral Agreement on Investment (MAI)** in Europe, the demonstrations against the WTO meeting in Seattle in 1999 (see **World Trade Organization/General Agreement on Tariffs and Trade (WTO/GATT)**) as well as **International Monetary Fund (IMF)** and **World Bank** sessions in Washington DC, at the turn of the century. Critics highlight that these international financial institutions dictate the global economic order while evading democratic control. Whereas some WSF attendees believe that reforming the **Bretton Woods** institutions and their sister entities is essential, others contend that only a fundamental systemic change would suffice. Participants do not adhere to a universal political manifesto.

See also: civil society; globalization; non-governmental organizations (NGOs); solidarity campaigns

MARLÈNE ELIAS

World Summit on Sustainable Development (Johannesburg, 2002)

The World Summit on Sustainable Development (WSSD) was held to discuss new initiatives on **environment** and development ten years after the **Earth Summit (1992) (United Nations Conference on Environment and Development)** in Rio, and thirty years since the **Stockholm 1972 world conference on environment and development**. More than 50,000 people attended. The summit produced both advances and setbacks. Critics claimed the summit should have produced new conventions with binding commitments, or advanced existing conventions such as on **climate change**. The summit organizers, however, pointed out that these other conventions now had meeting schedules of their own, and that the chief purpose of WSSD was to initiate discussion on new topics. Some topics discussed included an agreement to restore global fish stocks by 2015, and allowing more fish to remain as **food** in producing communities. The **European Union** (EU) announced its "Water for Life" initiative, aiming to halve the proportion of people without access to **sanitation** by 2015. Further agreements included reducing **biodiversity** loss, protecting marine environments, and the Partnership for Principle 10, which urged greater right to information (see **Right to Information Movement**). The **United Nations** also discussed new "type-two partnerships," involving strategic alliances between states(see **state and state reform**) and non-state actors such as large **non-governmental organizations (NGOs)** and businesses, as a means of implementing policy. Proponents claimed **partnerships** were effective means of enhancing state capacity and **corporate social responsibility (CSR)**. Critics claimed partnerships empowered both **globalization** and environmental damage resulting from business. The WSSD produced a Johannesburg Plan of Implementation, which stated that local people should benefit from exploitation of **natural resources** by **transnational corporations (TNCs)**, and that UN conventions are not subservient to WTO decisions (see **World Trade Organization/General Agreement on Tariffs and Trade (WTO/GATT)**). WSSD, however, did not specify targets for **renewable energy**, nor provide firm action on trade-related aspects of development such as reducing agricultural subsidies in the EU or USA, or the patenting of **pharmaceuticals** for HIV/AIDS (see **HIV/AIDS (definition and treatment); HIV/AIDS (policy issues)**). Despite obvious failings, many agree that WSSD provided some long-overdue attention to questions poverty-related aspects of environment.

See also: capacity building; Earth Summit (1992) (United Nations Conference on Environment and Development); environment; fisheries; Millennium Development Goals (MDGs); partnerships; pharmaceuticals; sanitation; sustainable development; water management

Further reading

Middleton, N. and O'Keefe, P. (2003) *Rio Plus Ten: Politics, Poverty and the Environment*, London: Pluto.

TIM FORSYTH

World Summit on the Information Society (WSIS)

The World Summit on the Information Society (WSIS) is a two-phase international conference sponsored by the **United Nations** and administered by the International Telecommunications Union (ITU). Part one of WSIS, held in December 2003 in Geneva, and part two, November 2005 in Tunis, intend to establish Information and Communication Technology (ICT) policy statements and a plan of action at both international and state (see **state and state reform**) levels.

Struggles over ICT policy involve key actors including: the ITU (190 member states and approximately 650 mostly corporate non-governmental members); other UN related bodies including the ICT Task Force; a range of private entities; and **civil society** bodies, many represented by Communication Rights in the Information Society (CRIS). Key policy conflicts at the WSIS include: the conceptualization of access to ICTs and communication as a human right (see **human rights**); commercial versus social/political emphasis of ICT policy; **intellectual property rights (IPRs)**; and **governance**, surveillance, and **security** issues.

See also: information technology; Internet; media; Paris 21; telecommunications

DONNA D. RUBINOFF

world systems theory

World systems theory emerged in the 1960s as a radical critique of **modernization theory**, which had been the norm for international development policy since the end of World War II. Usually associated with W. W. Rostow and the Harvard social scientists Samuel Huntington and Talcott Parsons, modernization theory posited a sequence of stages from "traditional" to "modern" that it was believed all societies must separately and independently pass through on the path to development (see **stages of economic growth**). Since **economic development** was seen as a product of endogenous socio-political maturity, it was believed that contact and coordination with "modern" countries strengthened the developing world's ability to push off the weight of tradition and "take off." In a variety of ways, this model was the basis for development policies as different as Keynesian corporatism, neo-classical monetarism, **import substitution**,

industrialization, communist stage theory, and direct colonialism (see **colonialism, history of; colonialism, impacts of**).

World systems theory, usually associated with Immanuel Wallerstein, Andre Gunder Frank and the Latin American dependency school of economic history (see **dependency theory**), arose during the anti-colonial movement of the 1960s in response to the "neo-imperialist" and Euro-normative assumptions that were believed to underpin modernization theory. Rejecting the national focus that blamed the colonized for their own **poverty** and "traditionalism," it took, as its unit of analysis, the world system, which was blamed for creating and continuing to maintain global **inequality** and economic dependence in the former colonial world.

In his pioneering 1966 essay "The Development of Underdevelopment," Frank argued that modernization theory was based on an idealized and possibly unrepeatable version of the development of North Atlantic **capitalism** that ignored 500 years of accumulation and pillage. "Underdevelopment," wrote Frank, "is not original or traditional and neither the past nor the present of the underdeveloped countries resembles in any important respect the past of the now developed countries." Using the word "underdeveloped" to suggest an active impoverishment of the "Third World" by the "First World," rather than either blocked or absent development (see **underdevelopment versus less developed country (LDC) versus Third World**), he argued that modernization theory "fails to explain the structure and development of the capitalist system as a whole and to account for its simultaneous generation of underdevelopment in some of its parts and economic development in others" (p. 17).

In the decade and a half after Frank's article, world systems theorists drew on the insights of radical developing world intellectuals and political leaders, such as J. C. Mariategui, Amilcar Cabral, Eric Williams, C. L. R. James, and Ernesto ("Che") Guevara to debate the origins and nature of the world system. During this period, two principal theoretical perspectives emerged. The first, associated with Frank and Wallerstein, was influenced by Adam Smith and Rosa Luxemburg and came to be called the "dependency" or "circulationist"

approach. This referred to its focus on trade, unequal exchange, a coercive global division of labor, and the systematic transfer of value from the "dependent" geographic regions of "the periphery" to the European "core." Guyanese political martyr Walter Rodney provided a particularly interesting version of this in his 1972 classic *How Europe Underdeveloped Africa*, connecting the enrichment of Europe to the impoverishment of Africa through mass removal of labor power during the slave trade (see **slavery**).

The other perspective, often called "modes of production," is associated with Samir Amin, Eric Wolf and Ernest Mandel, and draws on Lenin and Trotsky's theories of imperialism and "combined and uneven development." Capitalism, argued these writers, is a system that was born and developed, not through quantitative growth and imperial transfer of wealth from periphery to core, but because of an historical transformation in the mode of mobilizing social labor that yielded a connected set of changes in the structure of society and the state (see **state and state reform**). The capitalist system, argued these writers, is driven by internal "laws of motion" that dictate a progressive accumulation of capital through revolutionizing production in its "core" as well as physical expansion to a "periphery." In this view imperialism, dependency, and traditionalism in the developing world are historical and contingent features of the combined and uneven growth of the capitalist world system, not its cause.

The development policies that generated from world systems theory in the 1960s and 1970s were ambitious programs combining older nationally based **import substitution** projects with anti-imperialism, **revolution**, and "de-linking," the term for pursuing markets and economic relations that were not dominated by North Atlantic or Japanese capitalism. In its heyday, "dependency" and world systems theory informed **United Nations** economists, international bankers, university lecturers, revolutionaries, and "non-aligned" heads of state (see **non-aligned movement**), as well as mass audiences who read journalist Eduardo Galleano's book *Open Veins of Latin America* (1973) and saw the films of Tomas Gutierrez-Alea, Gilo Ponte-Corvo, Glauber Rocha, Miguel Littin, and Osmene Sembene.

The 1980s were tough on *dependistas*, de-linkers, and world systems theorists. The "oil shock" of the 1970s (see **Organization of Petroleum Exporting Countries (OPEC)**), the global recession of 1982–3, the rise of **structural adjustment** policies, and the disintegration of the USSR put the alternative and autarkic visions of **economic development** favored by world systems theorists into doubt. Around the world import substitution projects and other protected or state-owned forms of development collapsed or were privatized as economic reform governments broke national strikes, floated currencies, dismantled public services and oversaw the largest devalorization of capital since World War II.

These vast changes in the world economy led to the emergence of new ways of theorizing the world system, such as the **new international division of labor** (NIDL) and **globalization**. Embracing the inevitability of the international capitalist market, the new approaches presented the autarky and anti-imperialism of the 1960s and 1970s as idealistic and mistaken. The world system came to be viewed as a juggernaut of technical innovation, socio-political change, and exogenous modernity that could be harnessed through radically open markets, economic privatization (see **privatization and liberalization**), **export-led growth**, and coordination with advanced industrial economies and international financial institutions. A dramatic example of these changes was the 1994 election of Fernando Henrique Cardoso as president of Brazil. An internationally known world systems theorist of the 1960s and 1970s, Cardoso had retreated from his dependency perspective and served as Brazil's pro-free-market finance minister during the early 1990s.

See also: capitalism; dependency theory; Economic Commission for Latin America and the Caribbean (ECLAC); international division of labor; revolution; terms of trade; trade

Further reading

Frank, A. G. (1966) "The Development of Underdevelopment" *Monthly Review* 18:4 17–31.

Brenner, R. (1977) "The Origins of Capitalist Development: A Critique of Neo-Smithian Marxism," *New Left Review* 104: 25–92.

Wallerstein, I. (1974) *The Modern World System*, New York: Academic Press.

Wolf, E. (1982) *Europe and the People Without History*, Berkeley: University of California Press.

ANTHONY MARCUS

World Trade Organization/General Agreement on Tariffs and Trade (WTO/GATT)

The World Trade Organization (WTO) and General Agreement on Tariffs and Trade (GATT) system regulates international **trade** in goods and services using a system of objectives and rules laid out in articles of agreements among member governments. Established on 1 January 1995, the WTO is a more formal, institutionalized version of GATT, signed by twenty-three governments in 1947. As an organization, the WTO consists of a Director General, a Deputy Director General, and a secretariat (or bureaucracy) housed in Geneva, Switzerland. The WTO is headed by a Ministerial Conference meeting at least every two years. Below this is the General Council, normally made up of trade ambassadors and heads of delegations, meeting several times a year in Geneva. The General Council also meets as the Trade Policy Review Body (TPRB) and the Dispute Settlement Body (DSB). The WTO has procedures for resolving trade issues under the Dispute Settlement Understanding – countries bring disputes to the WTO if they think their rights under agreements are being infringed, and judgments are made by specially-appointed independent experts. Numerous specialized committees, working groups and working parties deal with individual agreements and other areas, such as the **environment**, development, membership application and regional trade agreements. Three other working groups deal with the relationship between trade and investment, the interaction between trade and competition policy, and **transparency** in government procurement. The existing councils and committees examine the area of electronic commerce. The WTO Secretariat, based in Geneva, has a staff of 550, mostly lawyers, and is headed by a Director General and a Deputy Director General. Like the **International Monetary Fund (IMF)** and the **World Bank**, the WTO also exists as a broader institution, in this case consisting of trade representatives sent from member countries to meetings organized at a number of levels, and thousands of specialists, consultants and lobbyists. The 145 members of the WTO, as of 2003, accounted for 97 percent of world trade. Twenty-five other countries are negotiating membership. Two thirds of the members of the WTO are "developing nations" although the descriptions "developed" and "developing" are self-designations; although for some agreements, the WTO also uses the **United Nations** classification of Least Developed Countries (comprising approximately forty-eight countries, of which around thirty are WTO members). Developing countries, and especially the Least Developed Countries, are granted longer time periods for implementing agreements and commitments. Decisions are made by the entire membership, typically by consensus. Indeed, votes by the entire membership never happen. Should they do so, the system is one country, one vote, unlike the IMF and World Bank where votes are weighted by economic size. A majority decision is possible, but has never been used, and was rare under the GATT. WTO agreements have to be subsequently ratified by member states. The WTO operates within a conception of international economic relations that, while changing in emphasis over time, has consistently advocated the "liberalization of trade" – that is, the freeing of international movements of commodities and (recently) services from governmental restraint. Freeing trade from **tariffs** and other governmental restrictions, and thereby allowing competition and markets to function more freely at the international level, is said to lead to more rapid **economic growth** that benefits everyone. While GATT was relatively uncontroversial, the WTO lies at the center of controversy over **globalization**. Indeed protests against the WTO ministerial meeting in Seattle in 1999 have come to symbolize the entire debate over the future course that globalization might take.

Since GATT lacked an organizational structure, the Interim Commission for the International Trade Organization within the United Nations served as an administrative body regulating the agreement. This provisional GATT secretariat coordinated eight rounds of multilateral trade negotiations among an increasing number of countries over a half-century, essentially lowering **tariffs** on traded goods. The last round of negotiations, the Uruguay Round, lasting from 1986 to 1994, signified a new phase in world trading history within a new era of neo-liberal globalization. The Round produced a particularly large number of new trade agreements on textiles, **agriculture**, export subsidies and dumping, together with two agreements with significant effects on the **environment**, **food** and **health** security, the Agreements on Technical Barriers to Trade, and the Agreement on Sanitary and Photo-Sanitary Measures. The Uruguay round also established the WTO as enforcing organization (Dunkley, 2000).

Additionally, three trade agreements covering entirely new areas emerged from the Uruguay Round: GATS, TRIPS (see **trade-related aspects of intellectual property rights (TRIPS)**) and TRIMs:

1   The General Agreement on Trade in Services (GATS) extended internationally-agreed rules and commitments, comparable with those of the GATT dealing with physical commodities, into the rapidly growing area of the international exchange of services, equivalent in value to about one quarter of the international trade in goods.

2   The Agreement on TRIPS addresses: the applicability of basic GATT principles, together with those of already-existing international agreements, to the provision of **intellectual property rights (IPRs)**; enforcement measures for those rights; and multilateral dispute settlement procedures.

3   The Agreement on Trade Related Aspects of Investment Measures (TRIMs) deals with investment issues thought to restrict and distort trade.

The agreement finalizing the Uruguay round was signed in the Moroccan city of Marrakesh in 1994 and was, for the most part, routinely approved by the legislatures of member countries. The

Uruguay Round vastly expanded the coverage of international trade agreements and greatly increased the power of the global institution responsible for regulating what were now movements of goods, services, ideas and capital. Under the WTO, ministerial meetings have subsequently been held at Singapore in 1996, Geneva, 1998, Seattle, 1999, Doha (Qatar) 2001, and Cancun in 2003.

The basic power of GATT and the WTO resides in GATT Article I, the General **most favored nation (MFN) status** clause, saying that any advantage, privilege or immunity granted by any member country to another shall be immediately and unconditionally accorded to all other member countries. That is, lower **tariffs** granted to a favored nation are automatically extended to all members of GATT/WTO, but are not necessarily granted to non-members, unless negotiated separately through bilateral agreements. By joining GATT/WTO a country can gain far freer access to global markets for its exports, with the WTO ensuring that the full range of access rights is granted and exercised. This places the WTO at the center of power in the regulation of the global economy, in a position different in emphasis (in that trade is the focus), but at least equal in importance, to that occupied by the IMF or the World Bank.

The WTO is an institution formed through the interactions of governments under certain conditions. Governments meet at the WTO through their trade ministers, representatives, and delegates under specific circumstances – to discuss trade issues, often with declared immediate objectives in mind, to reduce trade barriers, settle trade-related problems – and with an overall purpose, to increase the volume of trade, increase production and raise incomes. However, critics charge that dialog centers on **free trade** within an overall neo-liberal conception of economic growth, justified through the universalistic belief that trade benefits everyone, mainly as consumers. Critics say that the WTO acts in the interest of **transnational corporations (TNCs)** in creating a global economic space freed from governmental regulations that might otherwise restrict the movement of capital. Furthermore, the WTO itself, as an organization, is active in the formation, promotion and protection of the free trade component of an overall neo-liberal ideology. It promotes the extension of its own powers of regulation into vast new areas, like intellectual property rights (IPRs), that are governed in the most undemocratic of ways – within closed rooms, where an already committed expertise rationalizes foregone conclusions. For critics, trade is a discourse that has to be opened to broader, more democratic debate, where social movements represented by highly informed **non-governmental organizations (NGOs)** are active participants, and alternative conceptions like **fair trade**, under which workers get a living wage and environments are actively protected, contend with equal force.

See also: economic development; fair trade; free trade; globalization; industrialization and trade policy; intellectual property rights (IPRs); international economic order; most favored nation (MFN) status; neo-liberalism; protectionism; tariffs; terms of trade; trade; trade-related aspects of intellectual property rights (TRIPS)

Further reading

Dunkley, G. (2000) *The Free Trade Adventure*, London: Zed.

Global Exchange (1999) *A Citizen's Guide to the World Trade Organization*, San Francisco: Global Exchange.

Peet, R. (2003) *Unholy Trinity: The IMF, World Bank and WTO*, London: Zed.

Wallach, L. and Sforza, M. (1999) *Whose Trade Organization? Corporate Globalization and the Erosion of Democracy*, Washington DC: Public Citizen Foundation.

RICHARD PEET

World Women's Congress for a Healthy Planet (1991)

World Women's Congress for a Healthy Planet (1991) was organized by the **Women's Environment and Development Organization (WEDO)** and provided input into the **Earth Summit (1992) (United Nations Conference on Environment and Development)**. Convened in Miami in 1991, the World Women's Congress brought together 1,500 participants from eighty-three countries to formulate and approve the Women's Action Agenda 21 (WAA 21) as input into **Agenda 21**, which was one of the key outputs from the Earth Summit. WAA 21 proposed gender equality in the operation of the Earth Summit and within Agenda 21, attention to women's resources and needs, and set out a vision for **sustainable development** and peace from the perspective of the women who participated in the Congress. Of note, WAA 21 moved beyond issues of **biodiversity** and environmental ethics to incorporate the environmental and social impacts of militarism, global **trade** and **debt**, land tenure, and reproductive health (see **gender and communicable disease; reproductive rights; sexually transmitted diseases (STDs)**). Since 1991, the WAA 21 has been updated for 2002 and 2015.

See also: Agenda 21; Earth Summit (1992) (United Nations Conference on Environment and Development); feminism and ecology; United Nations World Conferences on Women; Women's Environment and Development Organization (WEDO)

DONNA D. RUBINOFF

World Women's Planet (1992)

The World Women's Planet (WWP), known originally as *Planeta FEMEA*, was the women's tent at the **Earth Summit (1992) (United**

Nations Conference on Environment and Development) in Rio. Organized by the Brazilian women's delegation, WPP served as a central meeting place for the conference women's and **gender** advocates and organizations. Within this space, participants negotiated women's and gender issues in **Agenda 21**, and coordinated its Population and Environment section. In this vein, they broadened the document's emphasis on **population** growth as a cause of environmental degradation to include industrial and military pollutants, toxic waste, over-consumption by the industrialized countries, and international **trade** and economic systems that encourage exploitation of people and nature. Since 1992, *Planeta FEMEA* has re-emerged at the **World Social Forum (WSF)** in Porto Alegre, Brazil in 2001 and inspired the All Women's Voices Tent at the **World Summit on Sustainable Development (Johannesburg, 2002)**.

See also: Earth Summit (1992) (United Nations Conference on Environment and Development); environment; feminism and ecology; feminist political ecology; gender, environment and development; Women's Environment and Development Organization (WEDO)

DONNA D. RUBINOFF

Y

youth violence

Violence perpetrated by young people is one of the most visible manifestations of **violence** in a global context of generally rising levels of violence. Youth homicide rates have been increasing steadily throughout the developing world since the beginning of the 1980s, to such an extent that in contemporary Latin America, for example, homicide now constitutes the leading cause of death among 10–29 year-olds. Just as for violence in general, the developmental consequences of youth violence are varied. They include causing death and injury, infrastructural destruction, reducing economic **productivity**, and undermining the social fabric, among others. In many ways, though, the developmental consequences of youth violence are arguably magnified because they involve youth. Over 1.5 billion of the 1.8 billion young people projected to be in the world in 2010 will live in developing countries, where it is estimated that they will constitute 30 percent of the **population**. Youth therefore represent a large proportion of the potential **human capital** and **social capital** of developing societies, and youth violence poses a severe threat not only to generational development, but for the progress of developing societies as a whole.

It is important to view youth violence in context. Although youth violence arguably constitutes a particularly critical specific manifestation of violence, many forms of youth violence are intimately connected to other forms of violence, and moreover cannot be understood in isolation from wider social processes. For example, the phenomenon of **child soldiers** can only be properly understood within the wider context of the dislocation of **war**, while numerous studies have connected juvenile delinquency with the lack of opportunities in contexts of high **unemployment**. Youth violence is, moreover, a highly multidimensional phenomenon, as is well illustrated by its manifestation in the form of youth gangs. Although a feature of many developing societies, youth gangs vary tremendously in their forms, functions, and consequences, both between and within regions of the world. In contemporary Latin America, for example, youth gangs have become the most visible face of violence. Most acts of criminal violence in the region involve youth, and in particular young males, who make up the overwhelming bulk of youth gang membership. The extent, nature, and consequence of their violence, however, depends very much on context-specific factors, including the nature of the state (see **state and state reform**), levels of unemployment, economic opportunities, histories of war, and migratory patterns (see **migration**).

See also: child soldiers; children; street children; structural violence; violence

Further reading

Krug, E., Dahlberg, L., Mercy, J., Zwi, A. and Lozano, R. (eds) (2002) *World Report on Violence and Health*, Geneva: World Health Organization, ch. 2.

Rodgers, D. (1999) *Youth Gangs and Violence in Latin America and the Caribbean: A Literature Survey*, Latin America and Caribbean Region Sustainable Development Working Paper no. 4 (Urban Peace Program Series), Washington DC: World Bank.

DENNIS RODGERS

Z

Zapatistas

Zapatistas was the name given to members of the peasant revolutionary army led by Emiliano Zapata against the dictatorship of General Porfirio Díaz during the Mexican **revolution** (1910–17). The name was later adopted by the Zapatista National Liberation Army (EZLN), a peasant indigenous movement in the Mexican state of Chiapas that rose up in arms against the federal government on 1 January 1994 (see **peasant movements**). The rebellion was timed to start on the same day as the instigation of the **North American Free Trade Agreement (NAFTA)** was being celebrated by the USA and Canada, thus symbolizing the Zapatistas' opposition to **capitalism**, **globalization**, and **neo-liberalism**. The Zapatistas acquired worldwide publicity thanks to their charismatic spokesperson, Sub-Commander Marcos. The movement has succeeded in exposing the situation of **social exclusion** and **inequality** affecting the indigenous population in Mexico, which lives in conditions of extreme **rural poverty** and is still deprived of the most basic **citizenship** rights.

See also: globalization; North American Free Trade Agreement (NAFTA); peasant movements; revolution

JOSÉ ESTEBAN CASTRO

Index

Note: Page numbers in **bold** refer to main subject entries. Bold page numbers after a person's name indicate entries written by this person.